CW01183135

SUNDERLAND AFC: THE ABSOLUTE RECORD
THE PLAYERS
JAMES FARRELL

# SUNDERLAND AFC: THE ABSOLUTE RECORD

# THE PLAYERS

## WRITTEN BY ROB MASON

Dedicated to: Leo Mason, the author's grandson, born just as this volume went to print.

**A TWOCAN PUBLICATION**

**ISBN: 978-1-915571-25-0**



**PICTURE CREDITS:**

Action Images, Alan Gibson, Alan Hewson, Ian Horrocks, Brian Leng, Rob Mason, Press Association, Frank Reid, Paul Days & Ryehill Football, Sunderland AFC.

# Foreword

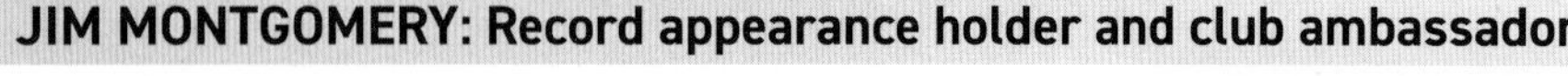

**JIM MONTGOMERY: Record appearance holder and club ambassador**

**When I was born in 1943, the club had been going for 64 years. Now we are not far off the 150th anniversary. Like anyone from Wearside I was brought up with stories of the greats. Just a few years before I was born Raich Carter, Bobby Gurney and co had helped the club to win all three of the trophies they could go for - league title, FA Cup and Charity Shield - in the space of a year.**

Further back in the early history of SAFC Charlie Buchan was the biggest name when the League was won and the cup final reached in the same year just before the First World War. Going back even further the club's first great goalkeeper Ted Doig won four league title medals. Whenever anyone - including today's players - walk through the main entrance of the Stadium of Light they have a reminder of Ted Doig and the rest of 'The Team of All The Talents' on the wonderful oil painting from the 1890s that dominates the entrance hall.

Up to the end of the 2021-22 season, when Sunderland won at Wembley to win promotion, a grand total of 1,124 players had played a competitive game for Sunderland. Club historian Rob Mason has written a detailed profile of each and every one of those players whether they played hundreds of times or just came on as a substitute once. I've known Rob for many years, was delighted to once ring him to invite him to become an Honorary Member of the Former Players' Association and have never known anyone who knows as much about the club's history.

I am incredibly proud to have played 627 competitive games and right from my debut in 1961, when Brian Clough scored a hat-trick, to the modern day I've played alongside and seen hundreds of players. We always welcome a former player to each home game onto our table in corporate hospitality and frequently these returning players speak so warmly about their time at the club and the passion of the supporters.

Football clubs would be nothing without fans. If anyone had any doubt as to how loyal and passionate Sunderland's supporters are, the way they have stuck with the club in such vast numbers in the really tough recent seasons illustrates that the fans are as good as the greatest of players.

I played with many great players at Sunderland, Charlie Hurley and Dave Watson to name just two, but I could fill the page with a list of them. I don't need to do that because on the pages that follow you will discover detailed biographies of every player right back to club founder James Allan.

Too many players such as Jimmy Davison, Norman Clarke, Ritchie Pitt, Peter Stronach and Kieron Brady for instance saw their careers cut far too short through injury. Others - most famously Jimmy Thorpe - lost their lives too early and some were killed in action during the World Wars. Every one of them is paid tribute to and remembered in this book which is indeed The Absolute Record of every single player who has been fortunate enough to play for this great club.

# Introduction

**I've been putting off writing this book for years. Many people have asked me to do this, not least the dear departed former secretary of the Sunderland Former Players' Association Winston Young. Although, including Christmas annuals, around 50 of the 60 plus books I have written are on Sunderland I've previously not produced an A to Z of every player to play for The Lads. I was put off mainly by the daunting task of researching and writing about so many players. Boy have Sunderland had a lot. Before 2022-23 kicked off with newcomers such as Dan Ballard and Aji Alese beginning the list for updates, Sunderland have had 1,124 male players who have played a competitive game for the club in a national or international competition.**

In contrast, to the same date Manchester United have had 947 for example and 983 have played a competitive match for Aston Villa. With the welcome and rapid rise of the women's game in the modern era there is an opportunity for someone to produce a companion volume on female footballers, one of whom (Jill Scott) I was delighted to include at the second Sunderland Hall of Fame awards evening which was featured in The Absolute Record Volume One.

The second reason it has taken me so long to produce this book is that there was already the excellent, 'All The Lads' written by Garth Dykes and Doug Lamming and published in 1999 and 2000. To the best of my knowledge neither Garth or Doug were Sunderland supporters which makes their achievement all the more admirable. I only ever spoke to Garth and Doug on the phone. They asked me to provide them with colourful anecdotes on players which I happily did. In the acknowledgement to, 'All The Lads' they kindly wrote, "Rob Mason, a man devoted to Sunderland AFC has proved an invaluable source of assistance, supplying much additional detail and wry observations, as well as giving up his time most generously to the book",

I extend similar thanks to Messrs Dykes and Lamming, but there would be little point to 'The Absolute Record, The Players' if I did not think I could improve upon 'All The Lads.' In no way is this intended as a slight on 'All The Lads' which is an excellent book that I have used so extensively over the years that my working copy is covered with notes indexing the programmes, magazines or books in which I have interviewed the player concerned or written the contact details of one or more of their descendants. As over two decades have passed since the publication of 'All The Lads' a large amount of extra or corrected information has come to light, often through the research of my colleague Mike Gibson and sometimes through interviews I have done with the players or their descendants, many of whom unearth not just footballing mementoes but sometimes personal documentation.

Additionally, with over 330 players having made a first-team debut since 'All The Lads' was published, between a quarter and a third of the club's players have come onto the scene since Dykes and Lamming's landmark work. In the early stages of writing this book I agreed with the publisher that there was only any point in providing this volume if we were going to do it thoroughly and that is what I have tried hard to do.

Every effort has been made to make this book as accurate as possible. For whatever errors remain I hope you as the reader will remember that even Jim Baxter occasionally misplaced a pass and the search for perfection goes on. Indeed as the motto Consectatio Excellentiae on the club badge states, 'In Pursuit of Excellence.' Of course, rather like when you occasionally hear news of the latest discovery of antiquities from ancient Egypt, football historians always live in hope of future discoveries that tell us more about the (relatively) ancient past.

As always, thank you for buying this book. I hope that you enjoy it, find out things you did not know and learn about some of the players from before you started going as well as the ones you have seen play.

**Rob Mason**

August 2022

## ACKNOWLEDGEMENTS

**Without doubt my biggest thanks for help with this book go to Mike Gibson. Along with Barry Jackson and myself, Mike also worked on Volume One of SUNDERLAND: THE ABSOLUTE RECORD (2020), both editions of Sunderland, the Complete Record (2005 & 2012) and also produced his own work, All the Dates (2009). Since before the turn of the century Mike has been the most amazing help to me, generously allowing me access to his lifetime's work of his database of Sunderland players. As well as detailing heights, weights, dates of birth and death etc this often also includes notes that offer golden nuggets of information, many of which have been used in this book. One of many such examples of this is the tragic personal tale of James Leslie, the scorer of the first goal at Roker Park in 1898.**

Mike has also undertaken the gargantuan task of carefully reading everything I have written in this volume. His feedback has resulted in numerous errors being corrected and has also seen many extra pieces of information added. To say Mike's contribution has been invaluable would be a massive understatement and I am extremely grateful to him for the immense effort he has put in to helping this project come to fruition. It should also be noted that many of the difficult to obtain pictures of players from long ago have been provided by Mike. Like me, Mike's aim has always been simply to share information with Sunderland supporters and through such sharing gradually add to what we know about the entire history of the club and its personalities without worrying about who gets the credit for unveiling any information. Working together is always the best way of doing the best job possible and thanks to Mike this book is definitely much better than it would have been without his assistance. It must be made clear that any errors that remain in this book are entirely my responsibility.

Andrew Smithson, Barry Jackson and Niall McSweeney are long-standing expert friends who each possess a vast knowledge of the club and I am very grateful to each of them for their comments and feedback on the drafts of this book. Scott Ainsley at SAFC has also been a great asset when it comes to establishing the heights and weights of modern era players.

There are many other people to thank too, starting with Newcastle United's official club historian Paul Joannou. As Volume One of the Absolute Record made clear, inspiration for the Absolute Record came from Paul's magnificent double volume 'Ultimate Record of Newcastle United'. With the huge overlap of all things red and white and black and white, as historians of SAFC and NUFC, Paul and I regularly help each other. For instance it was Paul who established the details of Norman Clarke's appearance for Greenwells at St James' Park as well as providing a photo of Matthew Scott. Sadly, Lance Hardy, the author of the superb, 'Stokoe, Sunderland & 73' is no longer with us. Lance was a dear friend of mine and we worked on three books together. Other than Sunderland, Lance's other footballing love was Worksop Town and so in the early stages of this book it was Lance who sourced Gary Bennett's appearance record for Worksop.

My former counterparts at Norwich City and Aston Villa, Peter Rogers and Rob Bishop are always fonts of knowledge on their clubs when I contact them as is Mark Andrews of the Arsenal website thearsenalhistory.com

Other people to be particularly helpful with specific requests include my good friend Jim Brown, club historian at Coventry City, Ian Watts the club historian at Stockport County, Bill Gilby at Raith Rovers, Patrick Conway for Grimsby Town, Mark Wilbraham of Rochdale and Phil McMenemy regarding queries concerning players who appeared for Barrow FC. Dave Robinson, Registration secretary for the Northern League is to be thanked for his assistance with the record of Chris Black.

A particularly big thank you is due to Paul Briggs of twocan for the support he has shown to both volumes of 'The Absolute Record' project. Paul designed and published both books having taken on the mammoth task of the two biggest books either of us have ever worked on. My wife Barbara has long since got used to me burning way past the midnight oil and not having time to do as much as I might to help her in the garden! She for one is delighted this book is now finished and I have to thank her for having substantially more than 50% of our combined patience.

Last but very far from least I want to thank all of the players who I rang up to personally check sometimes obscure details of their careers, often from long ago. I should also thank many of their wives who often are the record keepers of the family. Every player I contacted was delighted to hear I was working on this book and keen to have their facts correctly recorded. In particular I want to thank 1973 FA Cup heroes Dennis Tueart and Ritchie Pitt who each have kindly signed 50 copies of the book so that the first 100 people to pre-order this volume could receive their book autographed by a club legend. The pride of all the players I contact in having played for Sunderland is always obvious. This is never more true than my first and greatest footballing hero Jim Montgomery who has kindly provided the Foreword.

My sincere thanks to all.

# Preface

**Unless like me you are a self-confessed 'football anorak' you can skip this bit! If on the other hand the minutiae of the facts and figures that follow are something that fascinate you hopefully the explanatory notes in this section will make things clear.**

## LIST OF TEAMS

In listing the clubs of a player (L) means the player was on loan. Where a loan became a 'permanent' move without the player turning out for another club in between the loan is not indicated. For example in the profile of Darren Byfield his long list of clubs includes moves to Rotherham United and Oldham Athletic. In both cases these loans became 'permanent' moves so the loans are not listed. The same player does have an (L) signifying a loan spell for four of his other loans that did not materialise into transfers.

It has been my policy to list senior teams players were attached to. School and boys clubs have been mentioned in the text where relevant. With regard to the summer of 1967 when Sunderland's squad moved lock, stock and barrel to Vancouver to play twelve games representing the city of Vancouver as Vancouver Royal Canadians I have referred to this, where relevant, in the text rather than listing VRC as another club. In the same summer numerous other sides such as Stoke and Wolves took on similar cities as part of a fledgling North American Soccer League.

Frequently, amongst lists of clubs played for you will see in brackets (WW1 Guest) or (WW2 Guest). This indicates that during either World War One or Two a player was able to play as what was called a 'Guest' player for other clubs. Often the club a player represented as a 'Guest' was a team near to where he was stationed during war-time.

## HEIGHTS AND WEIGHTS

Weights particularly can vary, for example 1912-13 title-winning goalkeeper Joe Butler is recorded as 12st in 'All The Lads' and 11st 4lbs in 'Absolute Record Volume One.' Clearly in many cases the weight of a player varies, sometimes as he develops from young player to mature man. Weights provided are ones recorded mainly in the middle of their careers, but are intended only as a guide. The same applies for heights as youngsters mature or in some cases small players may wish to add an inch or two to their stature. Two examples are Ernie Taylor and Milton Nunez.

## BIRTHS AND DEATHS

Variants in birthplaces, dates of birth and dates of death compared to what has previously been published (including sometimes in 'Absolute Record Volume One', published in 2020), are almost always due to extensive and meticulous research done by Mike Gibson. For instance it had long been thought that John Auld, the first captain of 'The Team of All The Talents' of the 1890s had been born in Lugar in Ayrshire but it is now believed that in fact he was born in Kilmarnock. Similarly Johnny Campbell was previously believed to have been born in Renton although it has now been discovered that his birthplace was actually Edinburgh.

When you see Q1, Q2, Q3 or Q4 as a date of birth or death, Q stands for quarter. Sometimes a date is not known precisely, but research has found that their birth or death was registered in one of the four quarters of the year, so for example a player whose death is listed in a particular year as Q2 will mean the death was registered in the second quarter of the year, that is: April, May or June.

Trying to note the county of each player's birthplace has been a major problem. Players born in Sunderland for instance are given as born in County Durham if born before the creation of Tyne and Wear in 1974, but as born in Tyne and Wear since then. Similar changes have occurred in many other areas. To give one example, William Ellis' birthplace is given as Willenhall in Staffordshire as he was born in 1895. Willenhall is now part of the Metropolitan Borough of Walsall in the West Midlands rather than Staffordshire. It may well be that if you have specific knowledge of an area and realise I have given the incorrect county for the relevant year, if this has occurred please accept my apology.

## TEAM NAMES

I have attempted to refer to teams as they were called at the time. For example until 1929 Sheffield Wednesday were officially known just as Wednesday. Until 1968 Hartlepool United were Hartlepools United when both the s and United were dropped with United being restored to the name in 1977.

Many other clubs including Arsenal, Birmingham, Stoke and Orient to name just a few have had name changes over the decades so if you see a team named differently to how they are now, for instance Swansea City being referred to as Swansea Town, this is why.

## MISSING PLAYERS

As well as the hundreds of players you will find in this book who are not in 'All The Lads' there are two players who feature in 'All The Lads', but are not included here. This is because in the first occasion the player appears to have not existed - at least not under the name given. His 'ghost' biography is below:

**LOGAN, D**

**POSITION:** Outside-left

**DEBUT:** v Redcar, A, 24/10/1885

**LAST MATCH:** v Redcar, A, 24/10/1885

**TEAMS:** Sunderland

**SAFC TOTALS:** 1 appearance / 0 goals

Listed as playing at outside-left on his only official appearance in the club's second-ever English (FA) Cup tie, but details of his background are unknown. However, this mystery may have been because perhaps D Logan did not exist, at least not as someone who played for Sunderland. Research from Mike Gibson says, "There has always been some doubt over the team that played for Sunderland v Redcar on 24 October 1885 as the Sunderland Echo only gave a proposed side (22 October) and the only published line-up available after the game is in the York Herald on 26 October.

The difference is at right-back there was a player named English (could be the same as Ingliss who the Echo noted on 22 October would be a reserve for Kirtley in goal) and D Logan at outside-left compared with D Monaghan in the Echo of 22 October. It is possible that D. Logan was in fact G Monaghan as in an Echo of 14 December 1887 it is stated that Monaghan first assisted SAFC v Cathedral in a 9-0 win. This game was played the week before the Redcar game.

This could indicate he was brought down from Scotland a week ahead of the cup tie to strengthen the Sunderland team. He later joined regularly in summer 1887." While it is impossible to be certain it is the opinion of the author and Absolute Record Volume

One co-author Mike Gibson that the name D Logan was simply used to disguise the fact that it was Monaghan who was playing. Monaghan seems to have been mired in controversy. He was at the centre of a major controversy with Middlesbrough as discussed in his entry in the M section.

The second player to appear in 'All The Lads' but to have been discarded here is A. Naisbett who was previously thought to have played at West Bromwich Albion on 28 October 1899. In 2022 most reporters at matches upload their own copy immediately onto websites or social media. Others simply email their reports to their publications. There is no longer any need - as still happened until recent years - for some reporters to be on the phone dictating copy to be instantly typed and immediately published, as happened with the old Football Echo reports for example.

The emergence of 'Naisbett' appears to have been something as simple as a match report being misunderstood during telegraphed match reports with the name (Bill) Raisbeck being mistaken or perhaps Naisbett did exist and was intended to play but did not. The Sunderland Echo of the time clearly lists the teams in its match report.

Joe Butler

SUNDERLAND v. WEST BROMWICH ALBION.

VICTORY OF THE ALBION.

These teams met at West Bromwich on Saturday in a League engagement. It was their first during the present season. The return meeting is fixed for March 3rd. The teams and officials were as follows:—

SUNDERLAND: Goal, Doig; backs, McCombie and McNeill; half-backs, Raisbeck, McAllister, and Jackson; forwards, Crawford, Leslie, Hogg, Fulton, and McLatchie.

WEST BROMWICH ALBION: Goal, Reader; backs, Adams and Williams; half-backs, Dunn, Jones, and Banks; forwards, Paddock, Perry, Simmons, Walker, and Garfield.

Referee—Mr F. Bye (Sheffield).

Linesmen—Messrs A. Pennington and W. H. Taylor.

**The first ever picture of Sunderland in red and white stripes, 24 September 1887**

## LENGTH OF BIOGRAPHIES

As you would expect club legends command more space although if a particular player does not get quite as much space as you might have imagined please consider that this is probably due to the demands of the design of the book - although every effort has been made to properly recognise the contributions of players.

What might surprise you is that some players who did not necessarily have long or great careers at Sunderland have longer entries than might be expected or warranted as a result of their time on Wearside. Good examples of this are, Jack Dowsey, George Goddard, Mick Harford, Tom Morrison and John Morrison. Where this is the case it is usually because their overall career deserved a full explanation or simply because I felt their tale was one worth telling.

In the writing of the biographies I have utilised obituaries I have written for the official club website safc.com and also drawn on a series called 'Forgotten Men' which I produced for Sunderland's match programme in 2020-21, a season affected by the Covid 19 pandemic meaning that the articles were only seen by those people who subscribed to the programme.

Mick Harford

# A

## AGBOOLA, Reuben Omojola Folasanje

**POSITION:** Left-back

**BIRTHPLACE:** Islington

**DATE OF BIRTH:** 30/05/1962

**HEIGHT:** 5' 9" **WEIGHT:** 11st 0lbs

**SIGNED FROM:** Southampton, 09/01/1985

**DEBUT:** v Southampton A, 29/01/1985*

**LAST MATCH:** v Blackburn Rovers, H, 07/09/1991

**MOVED TO:** Swansea City, 09/11/1991

**TEAMS:** Cheshunt, Southampton, Sunderland, Charlton Athletic (L), Port Vale (L), Swansea City, Woking, Gosport Borough

**INTERNATIONAL:** Nigeria

**SAFC TOTALS:** 156+14 appearances / 0 goals

***Agboola's initial appearance had come in an abandoned game with Liverpool on 12/01/1985**

**Reuben Agboola became a cult hero in his time at Sunderland and the club's first international with an African country. London born, Reuben had a Nigerian father and qualified for Nigeria who he represented twice while on Sunderland's books.**

Having started his senior career with Southampton, after over 100 games for the Saints, Agboola was signed by Len Ashurst. Apparently there had been no love lost between Reuben and his Southampton manager Lawrie McMenemy so he was less than thrilled when McMenemy replaced Ashurst in the summer ahead of his first full season on Wearside. Although he started McMenemy's first three league games, he featured in just 18 of the 85 league games McMenemy managed.

Immediately restored to the starting line-up following McMenemy's departure the following season, he missed just eight league games as Sunderland won the third division under Denis Smith. Reuben remained a regular over the next two seasons, playing in both Play-Offs with Newcastle and the 1990 final with Swindon.

## AGNEW, David George (Dave)

**POSITION:** Goalkeeper

**BIRTHPLACE:** Belfast

**DATE OF BIRTH:** 31/03/1925 - 14/09/1966

**HEIGHT:** 5' 11½" **WEIGHT:** 12st 4lbs

**SIGNED FROM:** Belfast Crusaders, 11/01/1950

**DEBUT:** v Aston Villa, H, 30/08/1950

**LAST MATCH:** v Aston Villa, H, 30/08/1950

**MOVED TO:** Blyth Spartans, 10/07/1953

**TEAMS:** Belfast Crusaders, Sunderland, Blyth Spartans

**SAFC TOTALS:** 1 appearance / 0 goals

**Northern Ireland amateur international goalkeeper Dave Agnew made just one first-team appearance for Sunderland.**

Agnew was criticised for Villa's opening goal scored by Wales international Ivor Powell moments before half time and while he was blameless for the late goals that saw Villa come back to draw having been 3-1 down with 12 minutes to go, he never got another day in the limelight. Unluckily Agnew suffered a multiple fracture of his left arm playing for Sunderland Reserves against West Stanley in October 1951. He did not play again until his first game for Blyth Spartans. In this game he suffered a triple fracture of his left wrist in September 1953.

## AGNEW, Liam John

**POSITION:** Midfield

**BIRTHPLACE:** Sunderland

**DATE OF BIRTH:** 11/04/1995

**HEIGHT:** 5' 10" **WEIGHT:** 11st 4 lbs

**SIGNED FROM:** Youth product, 01/07/2011

**DEBUT:** v Fulham, A, 03/02/2015

**LAST MATCH:** v Fulham, A, 03/02/2015

**MOVED TO:** Boston United, 02/09/2016

**TEAMS:** Sunderland, Boston United, Harrogate Town, Boston United (L), York City (L), Blyth Spartans (to May 2022)

**SAFC TOTALS:** 0+1 appearance / 0 goals

**After his debut at Craven Cottage Liam was understandably buzzing about making his first appearance for his home down club and looking to the future. Sadly there were to be no more first-team games for the crisp-passing midfielder who joined the ranks of home-grown local lads who must have left the club believing they deserved more of a chance to show what they could do.**

Having worked his way through the Sunderland youth system, Liam's appearance from the 87th minute in an FA Cup win at Fulham proved to be his solitary opportunity. He had been on the bench for eleven consecutive Premier League games the previous season and was an unused Premier League sub a further four times in the season when he did appear in the cup.

Having been loaned to Boston, Liam eventually threw in his lot with the National League North club after being released at the end of the 2015-16 season, going on to captain the club, and later played as a late sub for Harrogate Town in their successful National League North Play-Off final against Brackley Town in 2018.

## AGNEW, Stephen Mark (Steve)

**POSITION:** Midfield

**BIRTHPLACE:** Shipley

**DATE OF BIRTH:** 09/11/1965

**HEIGHT:** 5' 8" **WEIGHT:** 11st 0lbs

**SIGNED FROM:** Leicester City, 11/01/1995

**DEBUT:** v Oldham Athletic, A, 14/01/1995

**LAST MATCH:** v Bury, A, 23/09/1997

**MOVED TO:** York City, 01/07/1998

**TEAMS:** Barnsley, Blackburn Rovers, Portsmouth (L), Leicester City, Sunderland, York City, Gateshead

**SAFC TOTALS:** 62+8 appearances / 10 goals

**Steve Agnew was a creative midfield player and a hard worker for his side. He had regularly done well against Sunderland, but Steve's stint at Sunderland was characterized by injury problems. Signed by Mick Buxton for £250,000, Agnew had only been at the club a few weeks when Peter Reid took over.**

Agnew played 29 times as Endsleigh Division One was won in his first full season.He then played in Sunderland's first nine Premier League games, netting a winner against Coventry. However, after the return fixture at Coventry on New Year's Day Agnew did not play another league game until the following season when he played in three of the opening four league games. He ended his Sunderland sojourn in a Coca Cola (League) Cup tie at Bury the following month.

Once Blackburn's record signing at £700,000 he only played four times for Rovers, after over 200 in all competitions for his first club Barnsley. He later won promotion as a teammate of Simon Grayson at Leicester City in 1993-94, making 36 league appearances but missing the play-offs through injury.

Following his time on Wearside, Agnew played a total of 85+5 games for York City, scoring five times, before finishing his playing days with Gateshead. He later went into coaching, becoming caretaker manager at Middlesbrough and Sheffield Wednesday as well as assisting Steve Bruce at Newcastle.

## AGNEW, William Barbour (Bill)

**POSITION:** Full-back

**BIRTHPLACE:** Kilmarnock

**DATE OF BIRTH:** 30/12/1880 - 19/08/1936

**HEIGHT:** 5' 9" **WEIGHT:** 12st 0lb

**SIGNED FROM:** Kilmarnock, 05/05/1908

**DEBUT:** v Manchester City, A, 01/09/1908

**LAST MATCH:** v Bristol City, H, 01/01/1910

**MOVED TO:** Falkirk, 29/09/1910

**TEAMS:** Afton Lads (New Cumnock), Kilmarnock, Newcastle United, Middlesbrough, Kilmarnock, Sunderland, Falkirk, Third Lanark, East Stirlingshire

**INTERNATIONAL:** Scotland

**SAFC TOTALS:** 28 appearances / 0 goals

**The first man to play for Sunderland as well as Newcastle (44 appearances) and Middlesbrough (73 appearances), Bill Agnew was a full-back who won three Scottish caps and twice represented the Scottish League whilst in his second spell with Kilmarnock, who he left to return to north-east England with Sunderland.**

Scotland conceded just one goal in the three games Agnew played for his country, against Ireland in March 1907, Wales in March 1908 and Ireland later the same month. Future Sunderland teammate Charlie Thomson (then of Hearts, but who would debut for Sunderland on the same day as Agnew) was a scorer on Agnew's international debut.

Named after an elder brother who had died at the age of just six weeks in the year before the footballer was born, Bill Agnew gave good service to Sunderland, but an injury suffered against Notts County a week earlier cost him his place on the famous day in 1908 when Sunderland travelled to his old club Newcastle and won 9-1. Prior to signing for East Stirlingshire in September 1913, he had a month working as trainer to Third Lanark Juniors.

## AINSLEY, George Edward

**POSITION:** Inside-right

**BIRTHPLACE:** South Shields

**DATE OF BIRTH:** 15/4/1915 - February 1985

**HEIGHT:** 5' 11" **WEIGHT:** 12st 11lbs

**SIGNED FROM:** South Shields St Andrews Juniors, 17/10/1931

**DEBUT:** v Chelsea, A, 06/05/1933

**LAST MATCH:** v Manchester City, H, 11/04/1934

**MOVED TO:** Bolton Wanderers, 17/08/1936

**TEAMS:** South Shields St Andrews Juniors, Sunderland, Bolton Wanderers, Leeds United, Birmingham (WW2 Guest), Blackpool, Bradford City, Crewe Alexandra, Huddersfield Town, Liverpool, Manchester United, Southport and Sunderland, Bradford City, Highland Park

**SAFC TOTALS:** 4 appearances / 0 goals

**Local lad George Ainsley only played a handful of games for Sunderland before going on to coach the national teams of Bermuda, Ghana, Pakistan and Israel as well as coaching in India, the USA and South Africa. He also coached at Cambridge University and managed Workington in the Football League in the mid-1960s, taking them to their highest position of fifth in Division Three in 1965-66.**

During World War Two, Ainsley served in the RAF and represented numerous teams as a 'Guest' player, appearing for Sunderland against Gateshead on Boxing Day 1942. With Leeds either side of the war he totalled 33 goals in 97 games, while with Bolton, he made seven top-flight appearances without scoring in the first half of 1936-37 between his spells at Roker Park and Elland Road.

As a boy, he had played for Co Durham Schools and South Shields St. Andrews Juniors before coming to Sunderland for whom he first appeared on Boxing Day 1931 against Gateshead reserves, by which time he had already scored 35 times that season for his team in South Shields. Ainsley was also known as a talented impersonator of show business people, politicians - and no doubt, football managers. At the age of 47 he put his boots back on as player/manager of Highland Park in Johannesburg in South Africa where he had been a member of the FA touring party with Johnny Mapson in 1939.

## AISTON, Samuel James

**POSITION:** Winger

**BIRTHPLACE:** Fenham, Newcastle

**DATE OF BIRTH:** 25/11/1976

**HEIGHT:** 6' 2" **WEIGHT:** 13st 4lbs

**SIGNED FROM:** Newcastle United, 01/07/1994

**DEBUT:** v Ipswich, A, 02/09/95

**LAST MATCH:** v Grimsby Town, H, 07/11/1998

**MOVED TO:** Shrewsbury Town, 04/07/2000

**TEAMS:** Newcastle United, Sunderland, Chester (L), Stoke City (L), Shrewsbury Town, Tranmere Rovers, Northampton Town, Burton Albion (L), Wrexham, Stafford Rangers, Hednesford Town, Gainsborough Trinity

**SAFC TOTALS:** 5+19 appearances / 0 goals

**Having played at youth level for Newcastle, Sam Aiston was a wiry winger who came into the team as a teenager as Peter Reid took his side to the Endsleigh Division One title in 1995-96.**

Aiston played in 14 league games that term, ten of those as a sub and with ten of those appearances before Christmas. He came off the bench in Sunderland's first Premier League game and came back into the reckoning around the turn of the year before being loaned to Chester where he played alongside Peter Reid's brother Shaun and for Reid's old Everton teammate Kevin Ratcliffe. Sam started the final 14 games of the season as Chester qualified for the fourth tier Play-Offs where he started both games against Swansea.

Returning to Sunderland, Aiston featured in three of the opening four games of the following 1997-98 campaign, but in October of that year suffered a serious knee ligaments injury in a reserve game at West Brom. After just over a year out, he returned in a Worthington (League) Cup tie with Grimsby, but a league outing against the same side eleven days later proved to be his last in a Sunderland shirt.

In later life Sam became a Primary School teacher after a long career where the highlight was almost 200 appearances for Shrewsbury who paid Sunderland a reported £50,000 for him after a successful loan.

# A

## AITKEN, George Gilbert Miller

**POSITION:** Centre-half / half-back

**BIRTHPLACE:** Lochgelly

**DATE OF BIRTH:** 28/5/1925 - 22/1/2003

**HEIGHT:** 5' 10" **WEIGHT:** 13st 8lb

**SIGNED FROM:** Third Lanark, 23/11/1951

**DEBUT:** v Fulham, H, 24/11/1951

**LAST MATCH:** v Fulham, A, 03/09/1958

**MOVED TO:** Gateshead, 05/03/1959

**TEAMS:** Lochore St. Andrew's, Lochgelly Albert, East Fife, Third Lanark, Sunderland, Gateshead

**INTERNATIONAL:** Scotland

**SAFC TOTALS:** 267 appearances / 3 goals

**George Aitken was a member of the 'Bank of England Team' of the fifties. Signed for £19,500 in 1951 he gave good value, always being a regular in the team at half-back throughout the decade and playing in the FA Cup semi-finals of 1955 and 1956.**

An uncompromising competitor, Aitken was capped three times by Scotland while with Sunderland, twice late in 1952 and once in the spring of 1954. He had earlier won five caps with East Fife, thereby making him that club's most capped player, a record that still stood in 2022.

George had been part of a famed half-back line with East Fife, winning the Scottish League Cup in 1947-48 after beating Falkirk in a replay at Hampden. Managed by the future Rangers manager Scott Symon, two years later Aitken played against Rangers in front of over 118,000 at Hampden as the Glasgow giants defeated East Fife in the Scottish Cup final. Following his retirement after playing for Gateshead when they dropped out of the Football League Aitken was employed as a car dealer on Wearside.

## ALLAN, Adam McIlroy

**POSITION:** Centre-half

**BIRTHPLACE:** Newarthill, Motherwell

**DATE OF BIRTH:** 12/9/1904 - 12/8/1967

**HEIGHT:** 6' 0" **WEIGHT:** 12st 6lbs

**SIGNED FROM:** Falkirk, 08/04/1927

**DEBUT:** v Portsmouth, H, 27/08/1927

**LAST MATCH:** v Everton, A, 03/05/1930

**MOVED TO:** Reading, 25/07/1930

**TEAMS:** Regent Star (Glasgow), Falkirk, Sunderland, Reading, Queen of the South, Bo'ness

**SAFC TOTALS:** 65 appearances / 0 goals

**Adam Allan arrived at Sunderland for the sizeable fee of £5,000 in a double deal with new Scottish international Robert Thomson, with Adam valued at £1,200 according to a report in 1930.**

Falkirk had done the double deal as they required funds for ground reconstruction. Similarly, when Adam left Sunderland he did so in a double deal involving James Oakley and a fee of £2,500. Renowned for his heading, Allan appeared in the opening ten games of his first season of 1927-28 and 20 in all. He played 30 times in his second term and 15 in his third, the last appearance coming on the final day of the season.

## ALLAN, James

**POSITION:** Forward

**BIRTHPLACE:** Newton, Ayrshire

**DATE OF BIRTH:** 09/10/1857 - 18/10/1911

**INITIATED THE BEGINNING OF THE CLUB:** 10/1879

**DEBUT:** v Redcar, A, 08/11/1884

**LAST MATCH:** v Morpeth Harriers, A, 22/10/1887

**TEAMS:** Sunderland

**SAFC TOTALS:** 3 appearances / 0 goals*

**James Allan has a place of unique importance in the history of the club. He was the person who introduced association football to Wearside. Having played soccer in his native Scotland, James brought a round ball to Sunderland to introduce locals to the sport in 1879.**

He spent around a year encouraging his fellow teachers to develop their interest in the game before the announcement of the creation of the Northumberland & Durham Cup along with the invitation to enter the competition, propelled Allan and his associates to formally announce they had formed the football club they had been developing under Allan's tuition.

As a player Allan also wrote himself into the record books by scoring an amazing twelve times in a 23-0 win over Castletown in 1884.

***Note that - as with other players of his era - Allan's appearance and goals statistics listed here relate only to League and FA Cup games (in Allan's case just the FA Cup). In his day, friendlies and challenge matches were frequently played, but are not included in statistical records of competitive games. He had played in Sunderland's first known game against Ferryhill in 1880 and scored twice in the second known game against Ovingham.**

Sadly, Allan's association with Sunderland ended horribly. Following a controversial cup tie with Middlesbrough, Allan left to form a rival club called Sunderland Albion and had hopes of usurping his earlier club. Albion thrived for a while, but ultimately were short-lived, becoming defunct in 1892.

As the founder of the club, James Allan was inducted into the Sunderland AFC Hall of Fame at the inaugural dinner in 2019, the award being received by his Great Great Grandson Brendan O'Donnell.

## ALLAN, Robert Sloan

**POSITION:** Goalkeeper
**BIRTHPLACE:** Cronberry, Ayrshire
**DATE OF BIRTH:** 16/05/1879 - Date of death not known
**HEIGHT:** 6' 0½" **WEIGHT:** 12st 6lbs
**SIGNED FROM:** Cronberry Eglington, 29/08/1907
**DEBUT:** v Aston Villa, A, 09/09/1907
**LAST MATCH:** v Bristol City, H, 25/12/1907
**MOVED TO:** Returned to his old job as a miner in May 1908
**TEAMS:** Cronberry Eglington, Sunderland, Hearts
**SAFC TOTALS:** 11 appearances / 0 goals

**Born to Irish parents in Scotland, Allan's surname appears in some records as Allen. Oddly the other goalkeeper called Allen (Thomas) was also born in the 1800s and also debuted at Aston Villa.**

R S Allan began with ten consecutive top flight appearances. After conceding nine goals in his last two away games - albeit with a home clean sheet in between - he was left out. He was brought back a few weeks later for a Christmas Day meeting with Bristol City, but after being beaten three times (in a draw) he was not called upon again.

He left Sunderland in May 1908 and returned to his original job as a miner in Auchinleck. Ten weeks later he was in a group of miners rescued from an underground fire at Highouse Colliery in Ayrshire on 22 July 1908.

Before coming to Sunderland he had been secretary of the Cronberry Eglington club as well as playing for them while working as an ironstone miner. Prior to his move to Sunderland he is known to have played in practice matches for Sunderland using the name Wilson.

## ALLAN, Thomas

**POSITION:** Goalkeeper
**BIRTHPLACE:** Camlachie, Glasgow
**DATE OF BIRTH:** 04/07/1883 – 25/05/1963
**HEIGHT:** 5' 8½" **WEIGHT:** 12st 0lb
**SIGNED FROM:** Hearts, 25/04/1908
**DEBUT:** v Aston Villa, A, 09/09/1907
**LAST MATCH:** v Blackburn Rovers, H, 11/02/1911
**MOVED TO:** Hearts, 01/05/1911
**TEAMS:** Wellwood Star, Rutherglen Glencairn, Hearts, Sunderland, Hearts, Motherwell
**SAFC TOTALS:** 26 appearances / 0 goals

**Only 5' 8½", but a well-respected goalkeeper known for his bravery, Tom Allan's only spell in England was with Sunderland who he played for in between two spells with Hearts.**

Having won four junior caps with Scotland, he gained one senior representative honour, playing for the Scottish League as they beat the Irish League 3-0 in October 1911.

At Motherwell he missed only two games in his first season of 1914-15, but made just three other appearances for the club as his career was curtailed by World War One.

As with his fellow goalkeeper R.S. Allan, Tom Allan was often referred to as Allen. Indeed his birth certificate and census records list him as Allen, but he was most commonly known as Allan before and after his football career when he worked as a bricklayer.

## ALLAN, William Michael (Willie)

**POSITION:** Half-back
**BIRTHPLACE:** Sunderland
**DATE OF BIRTH:** 11/09/1853 - 08/02/1929
**DEBUT:** v Redcar, A, 08/11/1884
**LAST MATCH:** v Redcar, A, 08/11/1884
**TEAMS:** Sunderland
**SAFC TOTALS:** 1 appearance / 0 goals

**Allan's claim to fame is that he played in Sunderland's first FA Cup tie. He played at centre-half in a 1-0 win at Redcar long before the beginning of the Football League.**

Like other players of that era Allan's other games were in friendly or challenge matches and therefore not included in official records of appearances in competitive games in national or international competitions. He is known to have played at left-back at the start of the 1881-82 campaign. By trade he was a joiner.

## ALLARDYCE, Samuel

**POSITION:** Centre-half
**BIRTHPLACE:** Dudley
**DATE OF BIRTH:** 19/10/1954
**HEIGHT:** 6' 2" **WEIGHT:** 14st 0lb
**SIGNED FROM:** Bolton Wanderers, 01/07/1980
**DEBUT:** v Everton, H, 16/08/1980
**LAST MATCH:** v Liverpool, A, 02/05/1981
**MOVED TO:** Millwall, 17/09/1981
**TEAMS:** Dudley Town, Bolton Wanderers, Sunderland, Millwall, Tampa Bay Rowdies, Coventry City, Huddersfield Town, Bolton Wanderers, Preston North End, WBA, Limerick, Preston North End
**SAFC TOTALS:** 26+1 appearances / 2 goals

**Big Sam Allardyce had scored against Sunderland both home and away for Bolton in Sunderland's promotion season of 1975-76, his goal at Burnden Park being a stunning long distance header.**

Allardyce had come through the ranks at Bolton, winning the Lancashire Youth Cup in 1971 for a club where over two spells he eventually totalled 226+5 games and 24 goals - an April 1978 screamer against Orient rivalling his header against the Rokermen as the best of his career.

After being promoted under Ken Knighton in 1980, Sunderland brought in Allardyce who was a colossus at centre-half. Sunderland topped the embryonic top-flight table after two games at which point Sam scored his first goal for Sunderland at home to Lawrie McMenemy's Southampton although defeat to the Saints began a decline that meant the season degenerated into a relegation battle.

Having played regularly until December, Allardyce was ruled out until April, returning in what proved to be Ken Knighton's last match as manager. Allardyce went on to be a manager himself, an extensive career seeing him do superbly at Sunderland only to leave the club for an ill-fated brief spell as England manager in 2016.

As a player, Sam won promotion to the top flight with Bolton in 1978 and from the bottom tier with Preston in 1987 when he was named in the PFA Fourth Division Team of the Year. As a manager, he won the League of Ireland First Division with Limerick in 1992, the Third Division with Notts County in 1998 and promotion to the Premier League via the Play-Offs with Bolton in 2001 and West Ham in 2012. However, he established his managerial reputation by taking Bolton into European football and then becoming renowned for his ability to take over struggling teams and keep them in the top-flight. Eventually, he was relegated with West Brom in 2021 after one of his most glorious escapes had come with Sunderland in 2016 when his January acquisitions of Jan Kirchhoff, Wahbi Khazri and Lamine Kone transformed the side.

# A

## ALLEN, Thomas

**POSITION:** Goalkeeper

**BIRTHPLACE:** Moxley, Wednesbury

**DATE OF BIRTH:** 01/05/1897 - 10/05/1968

**HEIGHT:** 5' 11" **WEIGHT:** 11st 4lbs

**SIGNED FROM:** Wolverhampton Wanderers, 13/05/1919

**DEBUT:** v Aston Villa, 06/09/1919

**LAST MATCH:** v Burnley, A, 20/03/1920

**MOVED TO:** Southampton, 01/06/1920

**TEAMS:** Bilston United, Old Park Works, Hickman's Institute FC, Wolverhampton Wanderers, Sunderland, Southampton, Coventry City, Accrington Stanley, Northampton Town, Kidderminster Harriers, Cradley Heath

**SAFC TOTALS:** 20 appearances / 0 goals

**Tommy Allen came to Sunderland early in a long career that was delayed by the Great War. Although he played only 19 league games (plus one in the FA Cup) for the Lads - all of them in the 1919-20 campaign - he went on to top 500 league games.**

Clearly he was one who got away as apparently he was missed off the club's retained list by accident. Signing for Southampton, he was ever-present as they became Division Three South champions in 1921-22 when he conceded a meagre 21 goals in 42 games.

Allen spent eight years with the Saints before he signed for his old Southampton teammate James McIntyre at Coventry City for whom he played 154 league games plus nine times in the FA Cup.

## ALMOND, Patrick Joseph

**POSITION:** Centre-back

**BIRTHPLACE:** Ashington, Northumberland

**DATE OF BIRTH:** 13/12/2002

**HEIGHT:** 6' 0" **WEIGHT:** 14st 1lbs

**SIGNED FROM:** Trainee, 01/07/2019

**DEBUT:** v Manchester United U21s, H, 13/10/2021

**LAST MATCH:** v Manchester United U21s, H, 13/10/2021

**MOVED TO:** Released, 25/05/2022

**TEAMS:** Sunderland, Blyth Spartans

**SAFC TOTALS:** 1 appearance / 0 goals

**Named on the bench for Football League Trophy matches against Fleetwood and Lincoln (the latter the semi-final) in 2020-21, the physically imposing Almond debuted in the same competition the following season having worked his way through the academy he joined as a 12-year-old.**

In January 2022, he joined Blyth Spartans on loan before being released at the end of the season after which he was badly hurt in a car crash.

## ALNWICK, Benjamin Robert

**POSITION:** Goalkeeper

**BIRTHPLACE:** Prudhoe

**DATE OF BIRTH:** 01/01/1987

**HEIGHT:** 6' 2" **WEIGHT:** 13st 12lbs

**SIGNED FROM:** Youth product, 01/07/2001

**DEBUT:** v Leicester City, H, 23/04/2005

**LAST MATCH:** v Preston North End, 14/10/2006

**MOVED TO:** Tottenham Hotspur, 02/01/2007

**TEAMS:** Sunderland, Tottenham Hotspur, Luton Town (L), Leicester City (L), Carlisle United (L), Norwich City (L), Leeds United (L), Doncaster Rovers (L), Leyton Orient (L), Barnsley, Charlton Athletic, Leyton Orient, Peterborough United, Bolton Wanderers (to 2020)

**INTERNATIONAL:** England Under 21

**SAFC TOTALS:** 22 appearances / 0 goals

**The son of a kick-boxing champion and brother of fellow goalkeeper Jak Alnwick (who was a youth teamer at Sunderland before starting his senior career with Newcastle, where one of his appearances was against Sunderland during the record breaking red and white 'six in a row' run), Ben was thrown in at the deep end at Sunderland.**

He debuted in the game where promotion was clinched against Leicester City in 2005. Following injury to Thomas Myhre initially Michael Ingham deputised but after a couple of unconvincing displays manager Mick McCarthy turned to 17-year-old Ben.

Picking the ball out of the net after only five minutes was not a great start, although the rookie keeper was not at fault for the goal and rose to the occasion with a couple of terrific saves, one from David Connolly who would be top scorer as Sunderland won promotion again two years later.

Alnwick made five Premier League appearances the following season. He made eleven early season appearances as the second tier was won for the second time in three seasons in 2006/07. He was then transferred to Spurs in a deal that saw Marton Fulop move in the opposite direction. Alnwick went on to make ten or fewer league appearances for ten clubs, mainly on loan, before topping 80 games with both Peterborough United and Bolton Wanderers.

## ALONSO, Mendoza Marcos

**POSITION:** Left-back

**BIRTHPLACE:** Madrid

**DATE OF BIRTH:** 28/12/1990

**HEIGHT:** 6' 2" **WEIGHT:** 13st 5lbs

**SIGNED FROM:** Loaned from Fiorentina, 01/01/2014

**DEBUT:** v Manchester United, H, 07/01/2014

**LAST MATCH:** v West Bromwich Albion, H, 07/05/2014

**MOVED TO:** Returned to Fiorentina, 12/05/2014

**TEAMS:** Real Madrid, Bolton Wanderers, Fiorentina, Sunderland (L), Chelsea (to 2020)

**INTERNATIONAL:** Spain

**SAFC TOTALS:** 19+1 appearances / 0 goals

**An excellent attacking left-back who maintained his popularity after leaving Sunderland with regular positive red and white comments on social media, Alonso was the son and grandson of Spain internationals, his grandfather Marcos Alonso Imaz having been part of the Real Madrid side who won the first five European Cups. The Sunderland defender's father, also Marcos, played for Racing Santander, Atletico Madrid, Barcelona and Logrones.**

A finalist in the League (Capital One) Cup for Sunderland in 2014, Alsono had been one of only two players to score in the still successful semi-final penalty shoot-out at Manchester United. Two years after playing for Sunderland on loan from Fiorentina with whom he totalled 85 games, scoring five times, he was transferred to Chelsea for a reported £24m. Although he did not play in the 2021 Champions League final as Chelsea beat Manchester City, Alonso had played in home and away wins over Atletico Madrid as well as that season's FA Cup final, lost to Leicester.

At Chelsea Marcos also won the Premier League in 2017, the FA Cup a year later (playing against Manchester United in the final) and the Europa League in 2019 (when he was an unused sub as Arsenal were defeated in the final). In 2017-18 he was chosen as a member of the PFA Premier League team of the year.

## **ALTIDORE,** Josmer Volmy **(Jozy)**

**POSITION:** Forward

**BIRTHPLACE:** Livingston, New Jersey

**DATE OF BIRTH:** 06/11/1989

**HEIGHT:** 6' 1" **WEIGHT:** 12st 6lbs

**SIGNED FROM:** AZ Alkmaar, 09/07/2013

**DEBUT:** v Fulham, H, 17/08/2013

**LAST MATCH:** v Hull City, H, 26/12/2014

**MOVED TO:** Toronto FC, 16/01/2015

**TEAMS:** New York Metrostars/Red Bulls, Villareal, Xerex (L), Hull City (L), Bursaspor (L), AZ Alkmaar, Sunderland, Toronto FC, New England Revolution (to June 2022)

**INTERNATIONAL:** USA

**SAFC TOTALS:** 29+23 appearances / 3 goals

**Jozy Altidore became the first player to score an international hat-trick while on Sunderland's books. The USA striker did this on 14 August 2013 in a 4-3 friendly win over Bosnia.**

Sent off against Sunderland while with Hull, he arrived on Wearside for a reported fee of £9m during the era of Paolo Di Canio and Director of Football Roberto De Fanti. His transfer to Toronto in a swap deal for goal machine Jermain Defoe was rightly seen as a tremendous piece of business by De Fanti's successor Lee Congerton. Nonetheless, as of the end of June 2022, Altidore had 42 international goals to his name from 115 appearances.

Having impressed at the IMG Soccer Academy Jozy joined the New York Metrostars who became New York Red Bulls. Debuting on 23 August 2006 as a sub in a defeat to D.C. United, he was still only 16 when he attracted headlines for a 25-yard winner against Columbus Crew. By the summer of 2008 Altidore moved to Europe becoming the first MLS star to attract a $10m fee when he moved to Villareal for whom he debuted as a sub against Deportivo La Coruna on 1 November 2008, soon becoming the first American to score in La Liga. That strike against Athletic Bilbao proved to be his only league goal for Villareal who loaned him to Xerex of Spain, Hull City and Bursaspor of Turkey. Jozy scored just once for Hull and Bursaspor in 28 and 12 league games respectively (plus a League (Carling) Cup goal against Southend for Hull) but did not make a league appearance for Xerex.

Success returned after AZ of the Netherlands became his new club in July 2011. Scoring as a sub in a win over PSV Eindhoven got him off to a good start which he followed up with two goals on his full debut against NEC Nijmegen. 22 goals in his first season were bettered with 31 - including three hat-tricks - in his second campaign at which point Sunderland stepped in.

He was not a success. There was always the feeling that given his physique Altidore should be putting himself about a bit more. Unlike some who followed him, there never appeared to be a lack of commitment from the player, but equally, he rarely appeared to be bang at it. As he came off the bench in what proved to be a famous win at Chelsea in 2014, Lee Cattermole could be heard screaming at Jozy letting him know what was wanted. Altidore went on to win what proved to be the match-winning penalty, but there remained the feeling that if he had Cattermole's drive he would have been a much better player.

Having gone to Toronto the goals started to come for him once again, starting with two on debut at Vancouver Whitecaps who were then managed by ex-SAFC man Carl Robinson. It set the tone for the success Altidore had with Toronto where he scored 79 goals in 173 games before transferring to New England Revolution in February 2022.

## **ALVAREZ,** Ricardo Gabriel **(Ricky)**

**POSITION:** Midfield / Forward

**BIRTHPLACE:** Buenos Aires

**DATE OF BIRTH:** 12/04/1988

**HEIGHT:** 6' 2" **WEIGHT:** 13st 3lbs

**SIGNED FROM:** Internationale, 01/09/2014

**DEBUT:** v Spurs, H, 13/09/2014

**LAST MATCH:** v Aston Villa, H, 14/03/2015

**MOVED TO:** Sampdoria, 04/01/2016

**TEAMS:** Boca Juniors, Velez Sarsfield, Internazionale, Sunderland, Sampdoria, Atlas, Velez Sarsfield

**INTERNATIONAL:** Argentina

**SAFC TOTALS:** 8+9 appearances / 1 goal

**Ricky Alvarez's time on Wearside was mired in controversy. Alvarez was part of the Argentina squad who lost to Germany in the 2014 tournament. In the tournament he came off the bench to replace Lionel Messi in a 3-2 win over Nigeria. With only three subs able to be named per match, this was the only game where Alvarez made the matchday squad. He played for Argentina nine times, his only goal being in a friendly against Slovenia shortly before the 2014 World Cup.**

At this time, Alvarez was playing in Italy with Inter where he played for Claudio Ranieri. Two months after being part of the Argentina squad in the 2014 FIFA World Cup, Alvarez came to Sunderland in a move that became entangled in dispute between Sunderland and Inter. This apparently concerned an issue over whether the Wearsiders were contractually obliged to convert an initial loan into a transfer for the player who had been injured while with the English club.

Arguments became very complicated and related as to whether previous injuries to the player had been fully disclosed. Almost five years after Alvarez first came to Sunderland a FIFA tribunal ruled against Sunderland in the dispute. Although he started fewer than ten games for Sunderland and totalled fewer than 20 appearances, the total cost of Alvarez to the club may well have been higher than the club's record transfer outlay.

Alvarez had come through the youth system of Boca Juniors having previously been associated with Caballito Juniors and Club Parque, but it wasn't until he joined Velez Sarsfield that he experienced first-team football, tasting early success as Velez won the 2009 Clausura.

On 5 July 2011, he moved to Inter, linking up with Sulley Muntari and debuting in a Milan derby in the Italian Supercup - in Beijing! There would be 73 Serie A games for Alvarez at Inter, and eleven goals. Following his stint at Sunderland he scored four times in 46 games for Sampdoria, 15 games without scoring for Atlas in Mexico and finally three more goals in 21 games back at Velez Sarsfield before retiring in 2021.

## **ALVES, Frederik** Ibsen

**POSITION:** Centre-back

**BIRTHPLACE:** Hvidovre, Denmark

**DATE OF BIRTH:** 08/11/1999

**HEIGHT:** 6' 2" **WEIGHT:** 12st 4lbs

**SIGNED FROM:** West Ham United, 13/08/2001, on loan

**DEBUT:** v Blackpool, A, 24/08/2021

**LAST MATCH:** v Sheffield Wednesday, H, 30/12/2021

**MOVED TO:** West Ham United, 14/01/2022, end of loan

**TEAMS:** Herfølge, Hvidovre, Coritiba, Silkeborg, West Ham United, Sunderland (L), Brondby

**INTERNATIONAL:** Denmark Under 21

**SAFC TOTALS:** 7+3 appearances / 0 goals

**Having arrived on a season-long loan from West Ham in 2021,Alves returned to his parent club half way through the campaign having failed to make a serious impression. By the end of the month he had left West Ham on a permanent transfer to Brondby. The Hammers had brought him in from Danish football a year earlier, but his English experience before coming to Wearside was restricted to a dozen games at Under 21 level.**

An elegant, ball playing defender of Brazilian, as well as Danish, parentage he began playing in Denmark, but at 15 moved to his mother's country in South America where he played for Coritiba. In September 2018 he made his senior debut for Silkeborg and played 18 times in a promotion season, making an international debut in March 2019 at Under 20 level against Romania. He added 21+1 games in the Danish Superliga as Silkeborg struggled unsuccessfully against relegation, but his performances earned a move to West Ham for around £1m. Having played twice for Denmark at the European Under 21 championships in 2021 when his country reached the quarter-finals, he came back to West Ham before coming to Sunderland. His only two league appearances for Sunderland were as a substitute.

## ANDERSON, George Albert

**POSITION:** Goalkeeper

**BIRTHPLACE:** Haydon Bridge

**DATE OF BIRTH:** 06/06/1887 - 28/05/1956

**HEIGHT:** 5' 10" **WEIGHT:** 12st 0lbs

**SIGNED FROM:** Mickley Colliery, 02/05/1911

**DEBUT:** v Middlesbrough, A, 30/12/1911

**LAST MATCH:** v Spurs, H, 28/09/1912

**MOVED TO:** Aberdeen, 26/05/1914

**TEAMS:** Haydon Bridge, Mickley Colliery, Sunderland, Aberdeen

**SAFC TOTALS:** 10 appearances / 0 goals

**George Anderson played ten pre-World War One games for Sunderland, but went on to become a director of Aberdeen and manager of Dundee where he also became a director.**

Joining Aberdeen just before the Great War, Anderson played 213 games for the Dons. Indeed the Northumbrian became synonymous with the area as he also kept wicket for Aberdeenshire CCC, ran an ice-cream and confectionery business, became a councillor, and during World War Two became caretaker manager of the football club in place of Dave Halliday, Sunderland's record seasonal goalscorer.

In addition to also serving Aberdeen as a director, he managed Dundee for 329 games between the summers of 1944 and 1954. No-one else has ever managed Dundee for as many games. Anderson steered them to the Scottish League Cup in 1951-52 and 1952-53. He also took Dundee to a Scottish Cup final and runners-up spot in the league.

However, he was affected by ill-health that caused him to miss the 1952 League Cup final. Eventually, this caused him to step down from the manager's role, although he continued as a Dundee director and was subsequently inducted into the Dundee Hall of Fame.

## ANDERSON, Russell

**POSITION:** Centre-back

**BIRTHPLACE:** Aberdeen

**DATE OF BIRTH:** 25/10/1978

**HEIGHT:** 5' 11" **WEIGHT:** 11st 10lbs

**SIGNED FROM:** Aberdeen, 27/06/2007

**DEBUT:** v Wigan Athletic, A, 16/8/2007

**LAST MATCH:** v Luton Town, A, 28/08/2007

**MOVED TO:** Derby County, 25/10/2010

**TEAMS:** Aberdeen, Sunderland, Plymouth Argyle (L), Burnley (L), Derby County, Aberdeen

**INTERNATIONAL:** Scotland

**SAFC TOTALS:** 1+1 appearances / 0 goals

**Sunderland was the first of several short stops in England for Aberdeen stalwart Anderson, but he bookended his career with his hometown team making more appearances in his second shorter spell with Aberdeen than his entire English sojourn.**

After a reported £1m move there was just one substitute appearance in the league for Sunderland v Wigan where he conceded a penalty. His only other competitive game was in a League Cup start against Luton where he suffered injury to his ankle ligaments.

After loans from Sunderland to Plymouth Argyle (14/0) and Burnley (4/0) - where he suffered a cruciate ligament injury - Russell did relatively well at Derby (34/1), but it was after re-joining Aberdeen when he enjoyed success, captaining the club to triumph in the Scottish League Cup final in 2014. Russell was capped eleven times between 2002 and 2008. His son Jevan went on to play for Burton Albion while after his own playing career ended, Russell became a financial advisor in Aberdeen having gained a Diploma in Financial Planning whilst still playing.

## ANDERSON, Stanley

**POSITION:** Wing-half

**BIRTHPLACE:** Horden

**DATE OF BIRTH:** 27/02/1934 - 10/06/2018

**HEIGHT:** 5' 9" **WEIGHT:** 11st 12lbs

**SIGNED FROM:** Horden C.W. 01/06/1949

**DEBUT:** v Portsmouth, H, 04/10/1952

**LAST MATCH:** v Cardiff City, H, 28/09/1963

**MOVED TO:** Newcastle United, 06/11/1963

**TEAMS:** Horden C.W., Sunderland, Newcastle United, Middlesbrough

**INTERNATIONAL:** England

**SAFC TOTALS:** 447 appearances / 35 goals

**The only Sunderland player capped by England during the 1960s, Anderson had been part of the 1962 World Cup squad. One of the most loved players in the club's history, Stan's career also saw him become the only man to play alongside both Johnny Mapson and Jim Montgomery, the club's two FA Cup winning goalkeepers of 1937 and 1973.**

An apprentice plumber to the age of 21, Stan bucked the trend of the fifties 'Bank of England' team by being the homegrown youngster who became a regular, but he was never out of place amongst the imported big-names. A class act at wing-half, Anderson became Sunderland's record outfield appearance maker and remains the second highest having only been overtaken by Len Ashurst. Including 'keepers Jim Montgomery and Ted Doig, Anderson is fourth overall in the list of highest appearance makers.

His 1963 move to Newcastle was against his initial wishes, but manager Alan Brown wanted to replace the legendary figure with Martin Harvey. Anderson's stature was highlighted by the terrific reception he received when returning with the Magpies for his own Testimonial. The following season he captained Newcastle to their own promotion and went on to become the only man to skipper the north-east's big three when he became captain of Middlesbrough. There were 84 appearances and 14 goals for the Tynesiders with 22 games and two goals added on Teesside.

At Boro he moved into management, succeeding Sunderland legend Raich Carter. He went on to manage AEK Athens, QPR, Doncaster Rovers and Bolton Wanderers, working with Peter Reid at Burnden Park. He also coached Panathinaikos and scouted for Manchester City and Newcastle United.

For England he won four Under 23 caps - being sent off against Bulgaria in Sofia in May 1957 and played at 'B' level in 1957 having been reserve against Scotland at Roker Park in March 1954. His Under 23 debut came as a ninth minute sub in a 6-0 win over Scotland in Glasgow on an occasion when on the evening before he had played in goal for England Under 23s in a practice match against Rangers at Ibrox after England keeper Reg Matthews had missed his train. Anderson's goalkeeping only had to last 25 minutes as heavy rain caused an abandonment.

In April 1962, Stan won full caps - one of which is on display at the Stadium of Light - against Austria at Wembley and Scotland at Hampden, performances which secured his spot in the squad for the summer World Cup in Chile. In the same month as his dismissal for England Under 23s, Stan was fined six months' worth of benefit qualifications for receiving illegal payments at Sunderland. This was refunded four years later due to the apparent illegality of the Football League's ruling. His biography 'Captain of the North' was published in 2010.

## ANDREWS, Arthur

**POSITION:** Left-half

**BIRTHPLACE:** Lintzford, Rowlands Gill, Co. Durham

**DATE OF BIRTH:** 12/01/1901 - 03/05/1971

**HEIGHT:** 5' 9" **WEIGHT:** 12st 0 lbs

**SIGNED FROM:** Durham City, 20/11/1922

**DEBUT:** v Everton, A, 09/12/1922

**LAST MATCH:** v Manchester United, H, 04/04/1931

**MOVED TO:** Blyth Spartans, 28/08/1931

**TEAMS:** Lambton Star, Durham City, Sunderland, Blyth Spartans, Spennymoor United

**SAFC TOTALS:** 245 appearances / 2 goals

**A stalwart of the team of the twenties who finished in the top three of the top-flight in four seasons out of five in the middle of the decade, Andrews was part of the redoubtable half-back line that also featured Charlie Parker and penalty expert Billy Clunas.**

Had it not been for Clunas perhaps Andrews might have scored more than twice in almost 250 games for the Lads. He had scored from the spot in one of 13 League appearances for Durham City, a strike against Accrington Stanley shortly before moving down river to Sunderland.

Durham had been in the North Eastern League when Andrews joined them as an amateur in May 1920. His league debut came against Rochdale in March 1922 during Durham's first season as a Football League club. At Sunderland he was a model of consistency, making between 28 and 41 appearances in a sequence of seven successive seasons during the 1920s.

After retiring from football he became a policeman and spent many years as Greenkeeper at Grindon Mill bowling club. He also played bowls for Durham County in the fifties having represented the county at golf three decades earlier. His sons Arthur and John were both on Sunderland's books in the late 1930s, but did not make the first team.

## ANGELERI, Marcos Alberto

**POSITION:** Defender

**BIRTHPLACE:** La Plata, Buenos Aires

**DATE OF BIRTH:** 07/04/1983

**HEIGHT:** 5' 11" **WEIGHT:** 11st 9lbs

**SIGNED FROM:** Estudiantes, 24/07/2010

**DEBUT:** v Manchester United, A, 26/12/2010

**LAST MATCH:** v Notts County, H, 08/01/2011

**MOVED TO:** Estudiantes, 20/07/2012

**TEAMS:** Estudiantes, Sunderland, Estudiantes, Malaga, San Lorenzo, Nacional, Argentinos Juniors

**INTERNATIONAL:** Argentina

**SAFC TOTALS:** 1+2 appearances / 0 goals

**Having cost a reported £1.5m, Angeleri's solitary start came in a dismal home FA Cup defeat to a Notts County side who were two divisions lower than Premier League Sunderland. Angeleri joined Sunderland in the summer of 2010 during a pre-season training camp in Portugal where he first appeared in a friendly with Hull City.**

An Argentina international with four caps, Angeleri had won the Primera Division Apertura in 2006 and the Copa Libertadores three years later (although he did not appear in either leg of the final for Alex Sabella's Estudiantes). He did play for San Lorenzo (the team Sunderland signed Claudio Marangoni from in 1979) as they beat Boca Juniors to win the Argentine Super Cup in 2015.

Troubled by knee injuries in his time in England, Angeleri - who had been named in the top ten of voting for South American Footballer of the Year in 2008 - left Sunderland after two years to re-join Estudiantes where 23 league appearances took his total for the club to 207. He returned to Europe to play 61 times for Malaga before spells of 48, 13 and seven league games back in Argentina and Uruguay with San Lorenzo, Nacional and Argentinos Juniors.

## ANGELL, Brett Ashley Mark

**POSITION:** Centre-forward

**BIRTHPLACE:** Marlborough

**DATE OF BIRTH:** 20/08/1968

**HEIGHT:** 6' 1" **WEIGHT:** 12st 0lbs

**SIGNED FROM:** Everton, 22/03/1995

**DEBUT:** v Barnsley, A, 24/03/1995

**LAST MATCH:** v Norwich City, A, 19/08/1995

**MOVED TO:** Stockport County, 22/11/1996

**TEAMS:** Portsmouth, Cheltenham Town, Derby County, Stockport County, Southend United, Everton, Sunderland, Sheffield United (L), WBA (L), Stockport County, Notts County (L), Preston NE(L), Walsall, Rushden & Diamonds, Port Vale, QPR

**SAFC TOTALS:** 11 appearances / 1 goal

**Having been a forward with a penchant for scoring against Sunderland, Brett Angell had a torrid time after being signed by Mick Buxton for a reported £600,000. He wasn't helped by Buxton being sacked one game after signing him with Peter Reid quickly deciding Angell wasn't for him, and at one point apparently having him train with the youth team.**

Brett's debut saw him appear to score, only for the goal to be disallowed as referee David Allison ruled he hadn't got a touch and the ball had gone in directly from a throw-in. Perhaps if that goal had been given, confidence might have blossomed, but instead it plummeted as his only goal for the Lads came in a League Cup tie against Preston. This followed a similarly barren spell at Everton - where he had hit the bar on his full debut - and only netted once in 21 games in all competitions.

However, in a long career, Angell did score 202 goals in 546 games, won promotion with Southend, Stockport, Preston and Walsall and was inducted into the Stockport Hall of Fame. He also won a Player of the Year award with Southend. Having worked as a reserve and youth team coach at Portsmouth in 2005-06, from 2014-2019 he resurfaced in football as manager of Hawkes Bay United in New Zealand.

## ANICHEBE, Victor Chineedu

**POSITION:** Forward

**BIRTHPLACE:** Lagos, Nigeria

**DATE OF BIRTH:** 23/04/1988

**HEIGHT:** 6' 3" **WEIGHT:** 13st 8lb

**SIGNED:** As free agent, 02/9/2016 (had been released by WBA, 30/06/2016)

**DEBUT:** v Crystal Palace, H, 24/09/2016

**LAST MATCH:** v Swansea City, H, 13/05/2017

**MOVED TO:** Beijing Enterprises, 01/07/2017 (one day after his Sunderland contract expired)

**TEAMS:** Everton, WBA, Sunderland, Beijing Enterprises

**INTERNATIONAL:** Nigeria

**SAFC TOTALS:** 15+4 appearances / 3 goals

**Victor Anichebe grew up on Merseyside where he moved to as a one-year-old. Beginning with Everton, he played for the Toffees reserves when he was just 15 years of age, playing alongside another future Sunderland forward in James Vaughan.**

Future Sunderland manager David Moyes gave 17-year-old Anichebe a debut in the FA Cup against Chelsea in January 2006. That season he was Everton Reserves Player of the Year with the club's Young Player of the Year award following a season later.

A powerfully built target-man whose game was based on trying to hold the ball up, Victor went on to win an Olympic silver medal in 2006, coming on as a substitute in the final as his team lost 1-0 to an Argentina side that included Lionel Messi.

A red card challenge from Kevin Nolan in a game at Newcastle United caused the Evertonian to suffer long-term cartilage and knee damage which apparently eventually led to a six-figure out of court settlement by Newcastle United in March 2011. Anichebe did return to action after a year out, but left Everton for WBA after 27 goals in 168 appearances - 94 of those games being as substitute.

West Brom paid a reported £5m for Anichebe, but there were just nine goals in 63 games, 32 of those as sub - one of those goals coming in an FA Cup tie with Gateshead. He did not score at all in 14 appearances in his last season with Albion while at Sunderland three goals shared over his fourth and fifth appearances were the only times he found the back of the net.

Anichebe's cousin Iffy Onoura played for nine clubs including Huddersfield Town and Sheffield United between 1989 and 2004.

## ANNAN, Walter Archibald (Archie)

**POSITION:** Right-back

**BIRTHPLACE:** Wilsontown, Lanarkshire

**DATE OF BIRTH:** 23/03/1877 - 23/01/1949

**HEIGHT:** 5' 9" **WEIGHT:** 11st 10lbs

**SIGNED FROM:** Edinburgh St. Bernards, 25/04/1902

**DEBUT:** v Notts County, H, 04/04/1903

**LAST MATCH:** v Notts County, H, 04/04/1903

**MOVED TO:** Sheffield United, 16/01/1904

**TEAMS:** West Calder, Edinburgh St. Bernards, Sunderland, Sheffield United, Bristol City, Burslem Port Vale, Mid Rhondda (player-manager)

**SAFC TOTALS:** 1 appearance / 0 goals

**Archie Annan's solitary Sunderland appearance came when he stood in for Andy McCombie late in the season as the Lads won 2-1 as they sought to defend their league title - which they eventually missed out on, finishing a point behind champions (Sheffield) Wednesday.**

The following January, Annan moved to the other side of Sheffield, debuting that month at Everton, the first of 27 league appearances for United. At Bramall Lane he understudied England international Harry Thickitt who was evidently impressed with Archie who he signed once he took over as manager of Bristol City. It was with the Robins that Annan excelled, playing in the FA Cup final of 1909 and being ever-present in his first two seasons of 1905-06 and 1906-07 as Bristol City won the second division and then finished as runners-up in the top-flight. Although Archie picked up a runners-up medal having lost the cup final to Manchester United, he proudly wore his cup medal on a chain around his neck for the rest of his life.

Following a spell with Burslem Port Vale, Annan became player/manager of Mid Rhondda in the Southern League before returning to Bristol City as a coach and scout, subsequently becoming a police officer in the city where he also played local cricket. One of 13 children, he was a life-time tee-totaller and had worked as a coal pit roadman in his early years as a footballer in Scotland.

## ARCA, Julio Andres

**POSITION:** Midfield / left-back

**BIRTHPLACE:** Quilmes, Argentina

**DATE OF BIRTH:** 31/01/1981

**HEIGHT:** 5' 9" **WEIGHT:** 11st 13lbs

**SIGNED FROM:** Argentinos Juniors, 25/07/2000

**DEBUT:** v West Ham United, H, 05/09/2000

**LAST MATCH:** v Portsmouth, A, 22/04/2006

**MOVED TO:** Middlesbrough, 26/07/2006

**TEAMS:** Argentinos Juniors, Middlesbrough, Willow Pond, South Shields

**INTERNATIONAL:** Argentina Under 21

**SAFC TOTALS:** 165+12 appearances / 23 goals

**A cult-hero at Sunderland, Arca was just a teenager when he moved from the other side of the world to come to Wearside for a fee of £3.5m. A debut goal helped to get him off to a good start and he further endeared himself to the crowd through a mixture of excellent ability and outstanding attitude.**

Arca adapted to English football quickly and went on to deliver some exquisite moments. The most memorable was a stunning goal at Bradford City where he took the ball three-quarters of the length of the pitch before chipping the Bantams' 6' 6" keeper.

In coming to Sunderland Peter Reid succeeded in having Julio qualified to play without a work permit due to the discovery of Arca having Italian grandparents and subsequently the obtaining of an Italian passport. Later, in the summer of 2005, a pre-season tour of Canada and the USA necessitated a cross-border crossing where Sunderland's late Press Officer Louise Wanless and I drummed into Julio that he was Italian as we went through border control between Vancouver and Seattle. "Oh what part of Italy are you from?" the border guard asked of Julio. "Buenos Aires" replied Arca as Louise and I tried not to hold our heads in our hands. "Gee that's great. Next please" said the geographically challenged immigration official.

Later, Arca gave excellent service to Middlesbrough - notably declining to celebrate when scoring against Sunderland. Julio played slightly more games in total for Boro than Sunderland, but there were more starts for the Black Cats, his Boro figures being 155+30 with nine goals. After seeing his career restricted by injury, he later made a come-back in Sunday football with the Willow Pond pub in Sunderland before signing for South Shields with whom he enjoyed terrific success, culminating in a 2017 FA Vase triumph against Cleethorpes Town at Wembley. In 2015, while still living in Sunderland, he became a part-time coach to Sunderland's Under 14s. One of the genuinely nicest lads to play for Sunderland, Julio was also one of the very best of the modern era.

## ARCHBOLD, Robert

**POSITION:** Full-back
**BIRTHPLACE:** Eastwood, Renfrewshire
**DATE OF BIRTH:** 06/10/1868 - 18/11/1943
**SIGNED FROM:** Glasgow Thistle, 1888
**DEBUT:** v Elswick Rangers, H, 27/10/1888
**LAST MATCH:** v Elswick Rangers, H, 27/10/1888
**TEAMS:** Glasgow Thistle, Sunderland
**SAFC TOTALS:** 1 appearance / 0 goals

**Robert Archbold's only competitive game for the Lads came in a 5-3 FA Cup win in the days before Sunderland joined the Football League.**

He is also known to have played in a friendly the following week in a 5-1 victory over Long Eaton Rangers when apparently he played on the left flank having played as a right-back in the cup-tie. During the 1888-89 season he appeared in Sunderland's reserve team. Like many of his time, Robert was a shipyard plater before, during and after his football career. Outside of football he became the Master of the Williamson Lodge of Freemasons in Sunderland.

## ARDLEY, George Henry

**POSITION:** Right-half
**BIRTHPLACE:** Langley Park
**DATE OF BIRTH:** 19/09/1897 - 03/07/1927
**HEIGHT:** 5' 8½" **WEIGHT:** 10st 9lbs
**SIGNED FROM:** Langley Park 13/5/1920 after appearing on trial
**DEBUT:** v Liverpool, H, 01/05/1920
**LAST MATCH:** v Liverpool, H, 01/05/1920
**MOVED TO:** Shildon FC, 04/05/1921
**TEAMS:** Langley Park, Sunderland, Shildon FC
**SAFC TOTALS:** 1 appearance / 0 goals

**George Ardley was 22 when he played his only first-team game for Sunderland as an amateur in the last home game of the first Football League season after the Great War during which Ardley served in the Royal Garrison Artillery.**

Sadly, he was to pass away in the year of his 30th birthday. He had two seasons at Sunderland, the second as a professional, but spent the rest of his playing days in local non-league football.

## ARMSTRONG, Gordon Ian

**POSITION:** Midfield
**BIRTHPLACE:** Newcastle
**DATE OF BIRTH:** 15/07/1967
**HEIGHT:** 6' 0" **WEIGHT:** 12st 11lb
**SIGNED FROM:** St. Montague Juniors, 01/01/1983
**DEBUT:** v West Bromwich Albion, A, 24/04/1985
**LAST MATCH:** v Preston North End, A, 15/08/1995
**MOVED TO:** Bury, 12/07/1996
**TEAMS:** Sunderland, Bristol City (L), Northampton Town (L), Bury, Burnley, Accrington Stanley, Radcliffe Borough
**SAFC TOTALS:** 393+23 appearances / 61 goals

**An underrated player whose consistency and commitment contributed to him becoming the seventh highest appearance maker in the club's history (to 2022). Never a winger as such, Armstrong predominantly played on the left of the midfield where his height was often a telling factor in an area of the pitch not noted for aerial combat, goal kicks often being aimed for him to head on.**

Twice the club's Young Player of the Year, Gordon's ability in the air was never better seen than in the FA Cup quarter-final replay with Chelsea in 1992. His last minute winner was one of the finest headers ever seen at Roker Park. Meeting Brian Atkinson's corner at the Roker End near the edge of the box, Armstrong thundered his header home in the most memorable moment of Sunderland's surge to the final. Goals were a regular ingredient of Gordon's game. During that cup final season he hit double figures in the league alone. One of those was a screamer from 30 yards at Swindon, although it is a goal often overlooked in lists of great goals as it came in a 5-3 defeat.

Two seasons earlier, in 1989-90 - when he also played at Wembley in the Play-Off final - not only was Armstrong ever-present in 46 league games, he made a record 59 appearances in all competitions.

Towards the end of his time at Sunderland, Gordon went on loan to Bristol City (6/0) and Northampton Town (4/1) while after leaving the Lads he scored four times in 69 league games for Bury and four in 93+20 appearances for Burnley where he was signed by Stan Ternent who he had played for at Bury.

Armstrong captained the Clarets for much of his time at Turf Moor before extending his career with Accrington Stanley in their first Conference season. After a year there Gordon joined Radcliffe Borough only to break his arm on the first day of the season in 2004 and move on to Stalybridge Celtic the following October as assistant manager to Peter Wragg.

Gordon's younger brother Chris made almost 250 league appearances, mainly for Sheffield United, while Gordon's son James later played for Sunderland at Under 18 and Under 23 level. After his playing days Gordon worked with Rochdale and scouted for Leeds United before becoming an agent. He was involved in more than one attempt to take over the club which he continues to hold dear to his heart.

## ARMSTRONG, Keith Thomas

**POSITION:** Winger

**BIRTHPLACE:** Corbridge, Northumberland

**DATE OF BIRTH:** 11/10/1957

**HEIGHT:** 5' 8" **WEIGHT:** 11st 5lbs

**SIGNED FROM:** School, 01/07/1974

**DEBUT:** v Cardiff City, H, 04/10/1977

**LAST MATCH:** v Notts County, H, 15/04/1978

**MOVED TO:** Oulu Palloseura, 01/03/1979 after being released from contract, 01/03/1979

**TEAMS:** Sunderland, Newport County (L), Scunthorpe United (L), Workington, Newcastle United, Oulu Palloseura (L), Bulova, Oulun Palloseura, Workington, Koparit, Oulun Palloseura, FC Kuusysi, Kokkolan Palloveikot, Kemin Palloseura, Vasa IFK, TP-Seinajoki, IFK Mariehamm, Rovaniemen Palloseura

**SAFC TOTALS:** 7+4 appearances / 0 goals

**Later a three time league title winner in Finland with Oulun Palloseura in1979 and 1980 followed by Kuusysi in 1984, Keith Armstrong was given an opportunity at Sunderland by Jimmy Adamson. After an autumn debut, he enjoyed a run of ten consecutive appearances - including as sub - in the spring. Although he was named as an unused sub the week after his final appearance, he didn't play again despite the team losing just once in his last nine games, and winning Keith's final three.**

In October 1980, he scored in the European Cup at Anfield - although his Finnish club Oulun Palloseura were beaten 10-1 by Bob Paisley's Liverpool. The previous year he had a short spell back in the north east of England with Newcastle United although he did not make a league or cup appearance for the Magpies.

A big name in Finnish football he went on to manage Rovaniemen Palloseura, T-Seinajoki, FC Haka on two occasions, HJK and Ilves. Manager of the Year in Finland in 2000 in the middle year of winning three successive titles with FC Haka (who he had earlier taken to promotion), Armstrong also succeeded in winning promotion with TP-Seinajoki.

He later won back to back titles with HJK in 2002 and 2003, completing the double of league and cup in the latter of those years. In 2006, he won a second Manager of the Year award after finishing second with HJK.

Having become a TV pundit, he lost his job as manager of Ilves Tampere due to missing a match in order to present Premier League coverage on TV. He subsequently returned to management with FC Haka and has scouted for the Finnish national team.

## ARNOTT, Kevin William

**POSITION:** Midfielder

**BIRTHPLACE:** Bensham, Gateshead

**DATE OF BIRTH:** 28/09/1958

**HEIGHT:** 5' 10" **WEIGHT:** 11st 2lbs

**SIGNED FROM:** Newcastle juniors, 14/12/1974

**DEBUT:** v Wrexham, A, 12/01/1977

**LAST MATCH:** v Middlesbrough, H, 03/04/1982

**MOVED TO:** Sheffield United, 22/05/1982

**TEAMS:** Newcastle Juniors, Sunderland, Blackburn Rovers (L), Sheffield United, Blackburn Rovers (L), Rotherham United (L), Vasalund, Chesterfield, Gateshead, Nykarbley, Hebburn, Jarrow Roofing, Boldon C.A.

**SAFC TOTALS:** 149+3 appearances / 18 goals

**'Ossie' Arnott was a supremely talented footballer. A class act on the ball, he had a deft touch, could thread a pass through the eye of a needle and had a penchant for a spectacular goal. With all due respect to the clubs he went on to play for, it remains a mystery as to why Arnott's post Sunderland CV doesn't include the top teams in the land.**

Kevin came into the team as one of 'Charlie's Angels' - discoveries of legendary scout Charlie Ferguson - who came into the team to give a fillip to Jimmy Adamson's goal-shy strugglers early in 1977.

Goals against Middlesbrough, a sensational floated strike against Newcastle and Manchester United in his first few home games (that also saw him be integral in 6-1 and 6-0 wins over West Ham and West Brom) earmarked Arnott as a special talent.

Having come through the youth system with another of Charlie's Angels in Gary Rowell, 'Ossie' provided much of the supply from which Rowell took over from Len Shackleton as Sunderland's record post-war scorer (a record since taken by Kevin Phillips). This was never better seen than in the February '79 4-1 win at Newcastle. The following season he was the star player - scoring in every round - as Sunderland won the prestigious Daily Express 5-a-side tournament and more importantly opened the scoring on the night promotion was won against West Ham United.

Bobby Saxton took him on loan to Blackburn Rovers in November 1981 where he made 17 consecutive appearances, scoring twice. The following season he returned to Ewood Park for a second loan, this time scoring once in 11+1 games, but this was after he had left Sunderland. Arnott had signed for Ian Porterfield at Sheffield United. Playing alongside Mick Henderson and John MacPhail, Arnott debuted for the Blades at Portsmouth on the opening day of the 1982-83 season, but only played seven league games plus six cup games in his first season. However, he was ever-present in his second term as United were promoted from the third tier, Arnott eventually totalling 151+2 games and scoring 15 goals.

Having also had a (9/2) loan with Rotherham United in 1983 Arnott swapped Sheffield for Stockholm in 1987 when he joined Vasalunds from where he reprised his 1979 Daily Express form when loaned to play indoor football in Dallas. After 30 games and three goals in Sweden, Kevin returned to England with Chesterfield, initially on loan.

There were four goals in 71 league games for the Spireites before a knee injury ended his professional career after which he played for Gateshead, back in Scandinavia with Nykarleby IK of Finland and finally back in north east England local football where he became player-coach of Jarrow Roofing. After retiring Kevin worked in the family building firm and for a company that supplied car parts to Nissan.

## ARTHUR, Joseph Arthur (Joe)

**POSITION:** Winger

**BIRTHPLACE:** South Shields

**DATE OF BIRTH:** 11/07/1891 - 22/04/1975

**HEIGHT:** 5' 8" **WEIGHT:** 11st 0lbs

**SIGNED FROM:** South Shields Parkside, 30/05/1910

**DEBUT:** v Bury, A, 14/04/1911

**LAST MATCH:** v Bolton Wanderers, A, 09/03/1912

**MOVED TO:** South Shields, 11/08/1912

**TEAMS:** South Shields Parkside, Sunderland, South Shields, Preston Colliery (WW1 Guest), Southport Central

**SAFC TOTALS:** 2 appearances / 0 goals

**Left winger Joe Arthur made only two appearances, almost a year apart. Sunderland failed to score in either game, but Arthur had a near impossible task of competing for a place with England international Arthur Bridgett.**

In later life Joe worked as a ship rivetter and during World War One served in the 15th Battalion of the Durham Light Infantry.

## ASHURST, Jack (Jackie)

**POSITION:** Defender

**BIRTHPLACE:** Coatbridge

**DATE OF BIRTH:** 12/10/1954

**HEIGHT:** 6' 0" **WEIGHT:** 11st 0lbs

**SIGNED FROM:** Renton Juniors, 01/07/1969

**DEBUT:** v Atalanta, A, 02/06/1972

**LAST MATCH:** v Burnley, A, 22/09/1979

**MOVED TO:** Blackpool, 19/10/1979

**TEAMS:** Renton Juniors, Sunderland, Blackpool, Carlisle United, Leeds United, Doncaster Rovers, Bridlington Town (L) Rochdale, Frickley Athletic

**SAFC TOTALS:** 152+14 appearances / 4 goals

**A defender who played in half the league games of the 1975-76 Division Two title-winning season having also played in the third and fourth rounds as the FA Cup was won in 1973, a contribution that led to him having a share in a Freedom of the City award bestowed in 2022.**

Able to play at centre-back, right-back or as a holding midfield player, Ashurst was a solid and steady performer who was eventually sold for Blackpool's record fee of £110,000 shortly after his old Roker coach Stan Ternent had taken over from Bob Stokoe at Bloomfield Road. Ashurst went on to make over 600 league appearances, including almost 200 for Carlisle (where he was signed by Stokoe), and eleven short of 100 and 150 for Leeds and Doncaster respectively.

After his days in football were over Jackie worked for a dry food packaging company and later as a stores administrator at an electrical shop in Knaresborough.

## ASHURST, Leonard (Len)

**POSITION:** Left-back

**BIRTHPLACE:** Fazackerley, Liverpool

**DATE OF BIRTH:** 10/03/1939

**HEIGHT:** 5' 9½" **WEIGHT:** 11st 4lbs

**SIGNED FROM:** Prescott Cables, 27/12/1957

**DEBUT:** v Ipswich Town, H, 20/09/1958

**LAST MATCH:** v Coventry City, A, 24/03/1970

**MOVED TO:** Hartlepool United as player/manager, 08/03/1971

**TEAMS:** Liverpool (amateur), Wolves (amateur), Prescott Cables, Sunderland, Hartlepool United

**SAFC TOTALS:** 452+6 appearances / 4 goals

**'Lennie the Lion' was a tough tackling left-back who went on to become Sunderland's record outfield appearance record holder and later returned as manager. Ever-present in the first ever promotion season of 1963-64, Len scored one of his rare goals that term with a thunderbolt of a shot against Newcastle.**

An English Schools Trophy winner with Liverpool boys,Ashurst was capped seven times by England at youth level. A week after playing at Spurs in an FA Cup quarter-final replay in 1961, he returned to White Hart Lane to be the full-back partner of future World Cup winner George Cohen as England beat West Germany 4-1, at Under 23 level. Bobby Moore was another teammate on that occasion. Len first appeared at Roker Park for England in a youth international against Hungary on 25 October 1956.

To his great disappointment he was released by his home town team Liverpool and joined Sunderland after his England youth coach George Curtis of SAFC saw him at Wolves who Len had joined after leaving Anfield. A plan was hatched to engineer his release from Wolves who he told he was homesick and wanted to continue his apprenticeship as a printer. Consequently he briefly signed for Merseyside club Prescot Cables before coming to the north east.

Just under two years after his England appearance at Roker he made his Sunderland debut on 20 September 1958 against Ipswich in the same game as his 1964 promotion winning teammates Cec Irwin and Jim McNab. Len remained an important part of the first team scene until 1970. A model of consistency, in his first nine seasons he made a minimum of 30 appearances and in the first six years of the sixties that minimum was 40, with 50 games being topped in 1961-62 and 1962-63.

Moving down the A19, Ashurst bridged the move into management as player-manager of Hartlepool United, adding 51+4 appearances and two goals to his Sunderland tally. Later he managed Gillingham, Sheffield Wednesday, Newport County and Cardiff City who he took to promotion in 1983 before taking over at Sunderland in 1984.

Incredibly after winning the Welsh Cup with Newport, he took the little Welsh club to the quarter-finals of the European Cup winners' Cup in March 1981, narrowly going out 2-3 on aggregate. At Sunderland Ashurst led the Lads to their first ever League (Milk) Cup final in 1985, but was unable to stop the team being relegated along with Norwich who defeated his side at Wembley and was sacked at the end of the season.

Ashurst went on to manage in the Middle East. He coached the national teams of Kuwait and Qatar as well as club side Al-Wakrah in Qatar before returning to the UK in 1989 to take over Cardiff City for a second spell. In 1991 he travelled to Malaysia to manage Pahang before finishing his managerial career in 1993 at Weymouth. He was proudly accepted into the elite group of managers acknowledged by the League Managers' Association for managing in 1000 games and accepted the award from Arsene Wenger at the Stadium of Light.

In total, Ashurst had over half a century in the game. He went on to work with the Premier League in establishing Academy football and spending many years as a Match Delegate, assessing refereeing in the Premier League. In the week of his 70th birthday, Len released his self-penned autobiography, 'Left Back in Time'. He also had testimonials at Sunderland, Cardiff and Newport. He was inducted into the Sunderland Hall of Fame at its inaugural dinner in 2019.

## ASORO, Joel Joshghene

**POSITION:** Striker

**BIRTHPLACE:** Osterhaninge, Sweden

**DATE OF BIRTH:** 27/04/1999

**HEIGHT:** 5' 8" **WEIGHT:** 11st 0lbs

**SIGNED FROM:** IF Brommapojkarna, 26/05/2015

**DEBUT:** v Middlesbrough, H, 21/08/2016

**LAST MATCH:** v Wolves, H, 06/05/2018

**MOVED TO:** Swansea City, 14/07/2018

**TEAMS:** IFK Haninge, IF Brommapojkarna, Sunderland, Swansea City, FC Groningen (L), Genoa (L), Djurgardens IF

**SAFC TOTALS:** 14+19 appearances / 3 goals

**A speed merchant who came to Wearside from Sweden as a 16-year old, Asoro always appeared full of self-belief and moved on following Sunderland's second successive relegation in 2018.**

A fee reportedly in the region of £1m took him to Swansea where he failed to score in 4+14 outings after which the Welsh club loaned him to FC Groningen for whom he scored twice as they won 2-1 at Vitesse Arnhem in his fourth match.

There would be only one more goal in his 15 Eredivisie games and after one more game for Swansea in the League (Carabao) Cup, he was loaned out again, this time to Genoa, but he did not make an appearance for the Italian club and in February 2021 returned to his home city of Stockholm with Djurgardens where to June 2022 he had seven goals in 14+22 games.

## ATKINS, Ian Leslie

**POSITION:** Defender / Midfielder

**BIRTHPLACE:** Sheldon, Birmingham

**DATE OF BIRTH:** 16/01/1957

**HEIGHT:** 6' 0" **WEIGHT:** 12st 3lbs

**SIGNED FROM:** Shrewsbury Town, 27/07/1982

**DEBUT:** v Aston Villa, A, 28/08/1982

**LAST MATCH:** v Leicester City, A, 12/05/1984

**MOVED TO:** Everton, 03/11/1984

**TEAMS:** Shrewsbury Town Sunderland, Everton, Ipswich Town, Birmingham City, Colchester United (player/manager)

**SAFC TOTALS:** 86+1 appearances / 6 goals

**Ian Atkins was a top class player with the only pity of his time at Roker Park being that he didn't stay longer - albeit he later returned as assistant manager from July 1993 to July 1994 (working alongside his old Ipswich teammate Terry Butcher) and again later as European scout from July 2007 to June 2012.**

Having scored 19 goals in his last season as a centre-forward with his first club Shrewsbury, Ian moved to Sunderland with striker Alan Brown going in the opposite direction as a make-weight along with a fee of £30,000.
The deal proved to be a bargain secured by manager Alan Durban who had given Atkins his league debut at Shrewsbury. Atkins was an instant success at Sunderland. Used in midfield or defence on Wearside, he looked a class act and soon became captain.

A childhood Aston Villa fan, Birmingham-born Atkins debuted in a stunning 3-1 win at Villa Park in their first game after becoming European champions. During his two seasons at Sunderland Atkins played regularly, always maintaining a high standard. His quality was such that in the summer of '84 Everton paid £60,000 to add him to their squad that went on to win the league title and European Cup Winners' Cup. Such was the competition for places he didn't debut until Boxing Day - back at Roker Park, just one of eight league and cup appearances he made that term, one of these being as a substitute in a Cup Winners' Cup game with Fortuna Sittard.

Searching for regular football he moved on from Goodison Park after a year, moving to Ipswich Town where he went on to equal his SAFC total of 77 league appearances. In total Atkins went on to make 591 league appearances, the first 279 having been with the Shrews. In an extensive career, Atkins went on to manage Colchester, Cambridge, Doncaster, Northampton, Chester, Carlisle, Oxford, Bristol Rovers and Torquay United.

After ending his managerial career with Torquay, Sunderland, Villa and Wolves were amongst the clubs he assisted, mainly in international recruitment. As of the beginning of 2021, Atkins was working as a European / South American Recruitment Consultant as well as being involved in coach education and media work.

## ATKINSON, Brian

**POSITION:** Midfielder

**BIRTHPLACE:** Darlington

**DATE OF BIRTH:** 19/01/1971

**HEIGHT:** 5' 10" **WEIGHT:** 12st 0lbs

**SIGNED FROM:** School, 01/07/1987

**DEBUT:** v Plymouth Argyle, H, 04/04/1989

**LAST MATCH:** v Crystal Palace, H, 03/12/1995

**MOVED TO:** Darlington, 08/08/1996

**TEAMS:** Sunderland, Carlisle United (L), Darlington, Newton Aycliffe (player and then later ass. manager)

**INTERNATIONAL:** England Under 21

**SAFC TOTALS:** 142+27 appearances / 6 goals

**Brian Atkinson was a good passer of the ball who won representative honours and played in the 1992 FA Cup final and the Play-Off final two years earlier. As well as winning promotion following Play-Off final opponents Swindon's punishment, Brian also featured briefly in the 1995-96 winning campaign, albeit his seventh appearance of that season proved to be his last for the club.**

Always a quality footballer, he won six England caps at Under 21 level. Four of these came in the 1991 Toulon tournament when he started three games including the final as England beat France. The following year he played every minute of Sunderland's run to the FA Cup final, scoring two of his seven goals for the club in the cup run.

He went on to top 200 appearances for his home town Darlington who he later managed in addition to holding assistant manager roles at Newton Aycliffe and Spennymoor. In November 2021 Brian returned to Newton Aycliffe as manager.

## AULD, John Robertson (Johnny)

**POSITION:** Defender

**BIRTHPLACE:** Kilmarnock, Ayrshire

**DATE OF BIRTH:** 07/01/1862 - 29/04/1932

**HEIGHT:** 5' 10½" **WEIGHT:** 12st 7lbs

**SIGNED FROM:** Third Lanark, 28/05/1889

**DEBUT:** v Blackburn Rovers, A, 18/01/1890

**LAST MATCH:** v Small Heath, 09/02/1895*

**MOVED TO:** Newcastle United, 14/10/1896

**TEAMS:** Kilmarnock 2nd XI, Lugar Boswell, Third Lanark, Queen's Park, Third Lanark, Sunderland, Newcastle United

**SAFC TOTALS:** 115 appearances / 7 goals

***The Small Heath game on 09/02/1895 was Auld's last official competitive game, but he also played v Hearts (A) 27/04/1895 in the unofficial World Championship game. This is not included in his totals above.**

**The first captain of 'The Team of All The Talents' Johnny Auld was a centre-half who was in his prime when he came to Sunderland in May 1899, having excelled north of the border where he had won the Scottish Cup with Queen's Park.**

Auld played in the FA Cup for Sunderland before they joined the Football League. He then played in the club's first ever league game and skippered the side for their first two seasons as a League club, captaining the team to the title in the second of those seasons.

He remained a regular player winning two more title medals and scoring in the 1895 game against Hearts that saw Sunderland declared world champions. On 14 October 1896, as a veteran, Auld became the first player to be transferred from Sunderland to Newcastle United after both clubs entered top level football.

He played 15 times for Newcastle, scoring three goals. He went on to become a director of Newcastle and later came to his old club Sunderland's rescue.

During World War One when Sunderland were suffering serious financial problems Auld acted as a financial guarantor for the club. He also paid for the funeral of his old 'Talents' teammate Johnny Campbell who had fallen on hard times.

Johnny Auld was inducted into the Sunderland AFC Hall of Fame at the inaugural dinner in 2019, the award collected by his grandson Robin Auld, then in his 90s and a former chairman of Ashbrooke Rugby Club.

## ATKINSON, Paul

**POSITION:** Winger

**BIRTHPLACE:** Chester-le-Street

**DATE OF BIRTH:** 19/01/1966

**HEIGHT:** 5' 10" **WEIGHT:** 10st 2lbs

**SIGNED FROM:** Pelton Boys, 01/05/1981

**DEBUT:** v Norwich City, H, 27/08/1983

**LAST MATCH:** v Notts County, H, 19/03/1988

**MOVED TO:** Port Vale, 14/06/1988

**TEAMS:** Pelton BC., Sunderland, Port Vale, Stafford Rangers (L), Hartlepool United (L), Gateshead, Eppleton CW., Esh Winning, Evenwood Town, South Shields, Crook Town

**SAFC TOTALS:** 60+16 appearances / 7 goals

**Winger Atkinson was just three weeks beyond his 17th birthday when he spectacularly scored against Wolves making him the second youngest player (Behind John Lathan) to score a top flight goal for Sunderland at Roker Park. A player with pace to burn, 'Atky' was making only his fourth appearance when he first found the back of the net having been given an opportunity by Alan Durban.**

Four of his seven goals came in November 1987, braces in a 7-0 win over Southend and 2-0 FA Cup victory over Darlington. Capped 18 times by England at junior levels Paul's potential was never fully realised as his career was cruelly cut short after joining Port Vale for whom he scored twice on his debut. Paul played just three more games for Vale, scoring once more. He was loaned to Stafford Rangers and Hartlepool United. Debuting for Pools in a fourth division game with Burnley on 20 March 1990, he scored once in 11 games for Hartlepool, six of those coming as a sub. Having broken his ankle six times in his career Paul went on to finish his playing days in local non-league football before finding employment as a contract manager for a company associated with utilities companies.

# B

## BA, El-Hadji

**POSITION:** Midfielder
**BIRTHPLACE:** Paris, France
**DATE OF BIRTH:** 05/03/1993
**HEIGHT:** 6' 0" **WEIGHT:** 11st 0lbs
**SIGNED FROM:** Le Havre, 10/07/2013
**DEBUT:** v Carlisle United, H, 05/01/2014
**LAST MATCH:** v Swansea City, H, 11/05/2014
**MOVED TO:** Charlton Athletic, 29/06/2015
**TEAMS:** Aulnay, Le Havre, Sunderland, SC Bastia (L), Charlton Athletic, Stabaek, Sochaux, Lens, Guincamp, Apollon Limassol (to July 2022)
**INTERNATIONAL:** France Under 20 / Mauritania
**SAFC TOTALS:** 1+2 appearances / 1 goal

**A teammate of Riyad Mahrez at Le Havre, rumour had it that Sunderland's scouting network led by Roberto De Fanti had spotted Ba rather than the man who would go on to win the Premier League with both Leicester City and Manchester City.**

Just a teenager when he came to Wearside, Ba made a goalscoring debut when he came off the bench in an FA Cup tie with Carlisle. Prior to that, Ba had been an unused sub in five Premier League games and would be for another four before finally getting the last 19 minutes of the last game of the season, after a dramatic escape from relegation had been achieved by Gus Poyet. He had succeeded Paolo Di Canio shortly after Ba had arrived in England.

Subsequently loaned to Bastia - for whom he debuted at PSG - Ba later played Championship football for Charlton where twelve of his 25 appearances were as sub. He also played in three League (Capital One) Cup games for the Addicks before joining Norwegian outfit Stabaek. He made eleven appearances before returning to French football, initially with Sochaux and Lens, where he scored his first goal since his strike for Sunderland against Carlisle, with a late equaliser in a French League Cup tie in August 2018 only for his side to lose on penalties. In July 2022 he signed for Apollon Limassol in Cyprus having made a full international debut for Mauritania against Sudan the previous month.

## BABB, Philip Andrew (Phil)

**POSITION:** Defender
**BIRTHPLACE:** Lambeth, London
**DATE OF BIRTH:** 30/11/1970
**HEIGHT:** 6' 0" **WEIGHT:** 11st 0lbs
**SIGNED FROM:** Sporting Lisbon, 28/05/2002
**DEBUT:** v Blackburn Rovers, A, 17/08/2002
**LAST MATCH:** v Crystal Palace, H, 17/05/2004
**MOVED TO:** Retired, 31/05/2004
**TEAMS:** Millwall, Bradford City, Coventry City, Liverpool, Tranmere Rovers (L), Sporting Lisbon, Sunderland
**INTERNATIONAL:** Republic of Ireland
**SAFC TOTALS:** 60 appearances / 0 goals

**Possessing the pedigree to have impressed in four games at the 1994 FIFA World Cup, winning the League Cup the following year after a big money move to Liverpool and having done the double with Sporting Lisbon in 2001-02, Babb's move to Sunderland that summer was met with disappointment rather than delight after his signing was teased with a silhouette on the club website.**

Only one goal was conceded in his first three Premiership games as a central defender for Sunderland, but ultimately Babb became part of a team relegated with a dismal 19 points. Having started the opening 26 games under Peter Reid and Howard Wilkinson, he found himself an unused sub in Wilkinson's last three league games and remained there under Wilko's successor Mick McCarthy, before dropping out of the picture altogether.

The former Republic of Ireland manager called upon Babb for the opening game of his first full season, but it was not until around Christmas that Babb was able to play regularly. He went on to help the side to the semi-finals of the Play-Offs and FA Cup before retiring after a penalty-shoot out Play-Off loss to Crystal Palace in which he showed the character to step up and score, having never scored (at the right end) in his time at the club.

He went on to manage Hayes and Yeading United in the Conference South from May 2013 until February 2015. From 2006 he had led a group of former Sunderland players investing in Golf Punk magazine, as well as working as a TV pundit.

## BACH, Philip (Phil)

**POSITION:** Right-back
**BIRTHPLACE:** Mount Flint, Bitterley, Shropshire
**DATE OF BIRTH:** 29/09/1872 - 30/12/1937
**HEIGHT:** 5' 10½" **WEIGHT:** 12st 0lbs
**SIGNED FROM:** Reading, 18/05/1897
**DEBUT:** v Sheffield Wednesday, A, 04/09/1897
**LAST MATCH:** v Stoke, A, 25/03/1899
**MOVED TO:** Bristol City, 05/07/1900
**TEAMS:** Middlesbrough Swifts, Reading, Sunderland, Bristol City, Cheltenham Town
**INTERNATIONAL:** England
**SAFC TOTALS:** 47 appearances / 0 goals

**The second player to be capped by England while with Sunderland, full-back Bach later became a member of the FA party that toured Germany in 1899, but his only cap came at Roker Park in February of that year when he played against Ireland in what remains England's record home win of 13-2.**

13-2 was also the score on Bach's first appearance for the FA in Germany the following November in Berlin. That was the first of four games he played in six days on that tour, the FA team following up by beating Germany 10-2 the next day at the same venue, before beating Austria 8-0 and then the Germans again, this time by 7-0 - an incredible aggregate of 51 goals to six in his five representative games, although his appearances for the FA were after he had swapped Wearside for Teesside.
At Sunderland he played in two thirds of the games as Sunderland were runners-up in the top-flight in his first season of 1897-98 and remained a regular in the year of his international recognition.

At Middlesbrough, Phil became a director of the club in February 1911 following a scandal which centred around Boro's attempt to bribe Sunderland. Five months later, Bach took over as chairman. It was a position he held until 1925 and then again between 1931 and 1935. Middlesbrough FC was something of a family concern. In 1892, Phil's brother Frank was a director. Another brother, Thomas, captained the club while a further brother, Richard, was groundsman and trainer.

From 1925 until his death in 1937, Phil Bach also served as an FA Councillor, joining both the Football League Management Committee and International Select Committee in 1929. His status as a senior soccer administrator was further enhanced by him also becoming President of the North-Eastern League and vice-President of the North Riding FA. When he passed away, the famous FA Secretary Stanley (later Sir Stanley) Rous attended his funeral.

Outside of football, Phil Bach was also a hotelier, firstly in Cheltenham and later in Middlesbrough.

## BAINBRIDGE, Jack McKenzie

**POSITION:** Defender

**BIRTHPLACE:** Southport

**DATE OF BIRTH:** 21/05/1998

**HEIGHT:** 6' 1" **WEIGHT:** 12st 8lbs

**SIGNED FROM:** Free Agent, 11/07/2018 after being released from Swansea City, 30/06/2018

**DEBUT:** v Morecambe, A, 13/11/2018

**LAST MATCH:** v Gillingham, A, 19/11/2019

**MOVED TO:** Released, 23/06/2020

**TEAMS:** Southport, Everton, Swansea City, Sunderland, Southport (to June 2022)

**SAFC TOTALS:** 2+1 appearances / 0 goals

**Youngster Bainbridge made two starts in the Football League Trophy which was sponsored as the Leasing.com Trophy when he participated in Sunderland colours. He also appeared as an extra-time substitute as Sunderland lost an FA Cup replay at Gillingham.**

For Everton, he played at Under 23 level playing against the first teams of Bolton, Cheltenham and Blackpool in the Football League Trophy in the first half of the 2016-17 campaign.

Initially with his local club Southport from the age of ten, Jack progressed through the youth system at Everton and continued his development with Swansea before coming to Sunderland. Following his release by the Black Cats, Bainbridge trained alone for a couple of months during the Covid 19 lockdown of 2020 before returning to his home town club, signing on 31 August 2020.

## BAKER, Joseph Henry (Joe)

**POSITION:** Striker

**BIRTHPLACE:** Woolton, Liverpool

**DATE OF BIRTH:** 17/07/1940 - 06/10/2003

**HEIGHT:** 5' 8" **WEIGHT:** 11st 12lbs

**SIGNED FROM:** Nottingham Forest, 30/06/1969

**DEBUT:** v Coventry City, A, 09/08/1969

**LAST MATCH:** v Orient, H, 11/01/1971

**MOVED TO:** Hibs, 14/01/1971

**TEAMS:** Coltness United, Hibs, Armadale Thistle (L), Torino, Arsenal, Nottingham Forest, Sunderland, Hibs, Raith Rovers

**INTERNATIONAL:** England

**SAFC TOTALS:** 43+1 appearances / 12 goals

**Joe Baker was a classic goalscorer, but way past his best by the time he came to Sunderland, although he did show glimpses of his greatness, notably with a hat-trick against Charlton Athletic.**

An England international with three goals from his eight caps, Baker was born on Merseyside, but moved to his mother's country of Scotland when he was only six weeks and considered himself Scottish. He did actually play for Scotland schoolboys before becoming the first player to play for England while with a club outside the Football League (Hibs) since the Football League came into being.

He came to prominence with Hibs, scoring four times in a cup quarter-final with Edinburgh rivals Hearts in 1958 and nine in another cup game against Peebles Rovers. Having set a Hibs season record of 42 goals in just 33 games in 1959-60 (part of his Hibs total of 159 goals) he moved to Torino (where he partnered Denis Law) for the then astronomical £75,000 in 1961.

Shortly after scoring a Turin derby winner against Juventus, Joe was seriously injured in a car crash after which he moved to England in 1962 for Arsenal's record fee of £70,000. 100 goals in 156 games for the Gunners made him a contender for England's 1966 World Cup squad, but having been named in the long list of 40 players in April of that year, he did not make the squad although he was asked to remain on standby. Baker's final cap had been won in January 1966 in his home city of Liverpool (at Goodison). He had scored in his two previous internationals, including one in a win over Spain in Madrid. He had also scored for England Under 23s against France at Roker Park in 1959.

Baker moved to Nottingham Forest in 1966, helping them to finish as runners-up in the top-flight in his first season with their challenge hampered by his late season injury. After 41 goals in 118 league games for Forest, Joe joined Sunderland for £30,000, but could only score twice in 24 league games as the club's second relegation came about in 1969-70. Two goals on the opening day of the following season were soon followed by a Roker Park hat-trick against Charlton that gave him five goals in his first four games of the season. Three goals in his final two league games gave Baker ten in 16 league appearances before his departure was hastened by the arrival of record signing Dave Watson who had been brought in as a centre-forward.

Leaving Wearside for a second spell at Hibs, Baker finished his playing days with Raith Rovers and totalled 301 league goals in 507 games. He later managed Fauldhouse United and Albion Rovers and gave his last ever interview to me for the SAFC club magazine 'Legion of Light.'

Joe's brother Gerry was born in New York and was a USA international while listing Manchester City, Hibs and Ipswich amongst his clubs - and going one better than his brother by once scoring ten goals in a Scottish Cup tie. A biography on the Baker brothers published in 2013 was entitled, 'The Fabulous Baker Boys: The Greatest Strikers Scotland Never Had'.

## BALDWIN, Jack

**POSITION:** Centre-back

**BIRTHPLACE:** Barking, London

**DATE OF BIRTH:** 30/06/1993

**HEIGHT:** 6' 1" **WEIGHT:** 11st 0lbs

**SIGNED FROM:** Peterborough United, 28/07/2018

**DEBUT:** v Luton Town, A, 11/08/2018

**LAST MATCH:** v Burnley, A, 28/08/2019

**MOVED TO:** Bristol Rovers, 20/07/2020 following release from SAFC, 17/06/2020

**TEAMS:** Faversham Town, Hartlepool United, Peterborough United, Sunderland, Salford City (L), Bristol Rovers, Ross County (to June 2022)

**SAFC TOTALS:** 42 appearances / 3 goals

**Jack Baldwin initially impressed with his whole-hearted displays after joining Sunderland following their demise into a second spell in the third tier. Brought in by Jack Ross - like Baldwin a former Hartlepool player - Baldwin played regularly for much of the season, but was left out after shouldering much of the blame for a 5-4 home defeat by Coventry City in April 2019.**

He didn't play in the league for Sunderland again, signing off having been part of a side who won away to Premier League Burnley in the League (Capital One) Cup the following August, on the first occasion Sunderland beat a team two divisions higher than themselves.

Baldwin made his league debut a week before Christmas in 2011 for Hartlepool in a home defeat to Colchester. He made 78+7 appearances for Pools scoring six times, impressing enough to earn a £500,000 move to Peterborough where he played 113+5 games with five goals before coming to Sunderland. After leaving Sunderland - following a 13+4/1 loan to Salford, Baldwin had 42+7 games with Bristol Rovers (scoring twice) before a move north to Ross County where he played alongside Jake Vokins. Jack's goal against Celtic on the tenth anniversary of his Hartlepool debut was his second goal from 13+1 appearances.

# B

## BALL, Kevin Anthony

**POSITION:** Defender/ Midfield

**BIRTHPLACE:** Hastings, East Sussex

**DATE OF BIRTH:** 12/11/1964

**HEIGHT:** 5' 9" **WEIGHT:** 12st 0lbs

**SIGNED FROM:** Portsmouth, 11/07/1990

**DEBUT:** v Spurs, H, 28/08/1990

**LAST MATCH:** v Watford, A, 27/11/1999

**MOVED TO:** Fulham, 09/12/1999

**TEAMS:** Hastings, Coventry City, Hastings, Portsmouth, Sunderland, Fulham, Burnley

**SAFC TOTALS:** 375+13 appearances / 27 goals

**Kevin Ball's impact at Sunderland goes beyond his own performances and statistics. Kevin earned his respect, from supporters, managers and most importantly his fellow players. As captain, 'Bally' could be guaranteed to get the maximum out of the players in his side. That wasn't down to aggression - not that anyone of sane mind would pick a fight with Kevin - but the fact that he led by example.**

If anyone wasn't pulling their weight, they would be left in no doubt about the responsibilities that came with their privileges as players. Taking over from Paul Bracewell after the 1992 FA Cup final, Bally moved from his previous centre-back position into a holding midfield role and did enough to warrant the claim that he was Sunderland's player of the 1990s. Player of the Year in 1990-91, he collected the Supporters' Association award four times.

Bally was the epitome of the player who gives 100%. There was no such thing as a 50-50 ball in Bally's mind. It was always his, perhaps it came with the name? A model of consistency, Kevin was never a player that you had to apply the term 'on his day' to. You knew what you were going to get and that was never less than everything.

In the exciting seasons that accompanied the opening of the Stadium of Light, it was the other 'SuperKev' who took the headlines along with Niall Quinn, but the person who let them and others play was Bally, dominating the centre of the park and clearing the stage for the front line virtuosos.

The 1999 'Division One' medal which came with 91 goals and 105 points was very different to the one Kevin won three years earlier when Sunderland were still at Roker Park. On that occasion, Sunderland had 22 points fewer as they took the title, but were still four clear of their nearest challengers as in a very different side, Kevin controlled matters on and off the pitch.

The chant 'Ooh Bally Bally' automatically accompanied a Kevin Ball tackle, like a calling card for the recipient. It has long been known that on Wearside, a tackle can be appreciated as much as a goal and Kevin Ball was a master of the art. Renowned as a hard-tackler, Kevin was a better footballer than many gave him credit for. He went on to twice take over as caretaker manager, did a superb job as Under 18s coach and became club ambassador until leaving that role in 2022.

## BARDSLEY, Philip Anthony (Phil)

**POSITION:** Full-back

**BIRTHPLACE:** Eccles, Greater Manchester

**DATE OF BIRTH:** 28/06/1985

**HEIGHT:** 5' 10" **WEIGHT:** 12 st 6lbs

**SIGNED FROM:** Manchester United, 22/01/2008

**DEBUT:** v Birmingham City, H, 29/01/2008

**LAST MATCH:** v Swansea City, H, 11/05/2014

**MOVED TO:** Stoke City, 22/05/2014

**TEAMS:** Manchester United, Royal Antwerp (L), Burnley (L), Rangers (L), Aston Villa (L), Sheffield United (L), Sunderland, Stoke City, Burnley (to June 2022)

**INTERNATIONAL:** Scotland

**SAFC TOTALS:** 176+24 appearances / 11 goals

**Hard tackling full-back Bardsley was a throwback in the modern era. Always dependably determined, 'Bardo' was a solid and consistent performer who scored some notable goals from distance, including one in the 2014 League (Capital-One) Cup semi-final second leg back at his old club Manchester United.**

Prior to that Bardsley had outlasted head coach Paolo Di Canio who had banished him from the first-team squad after Phil had been photographed surrounded by banknotes in a casino.

Qualifying as his father was born in Glasgow, Phil won all 13 of his Scotland caps while with Sunderland, the second of them alongside clubmate Craig Gordon. Debuting against Spain at Hampden in October 2010, his final cap came in 2014 against Poland in Warsaw three days after playing at Wembley for Sunderland against Manchester City.

A lover of rhyming slang. 'Mixed Grill,' as Phil called himself, started at Manchester United as an eight-year-old after playing for a side called the Charlestown Lads Club. Debuting for United in a December 2003 League Cup defeat to WBA, he went on to play 18 times for the Old Trafford giants, eight of those in the Premier League. During this time, he also gained the experience of 48 further games through a series of loans before being transferred to Sunderland for whom he played exactly 200 times, more than double the most he played for anyone else.

Big mates with Lee Cattermole at Sunderland, the pair shared an aggressive and totally committed approach when on the pitch. Decidedly old school, Bardo was an excellent full-back.

## BARNES, Peter Simon

**POSITION:** Winger

**BIRTHPLACE:** Manchester

**DATE OF BIRTH:** 10/06/1957

**HEIGHT:** 5' 10" **WEIGHT:** 11st 0lbs

**SIGNED FROM:** Bolton Wanderers, 15/02/1989

**DEBUT:** v Swindon Town, A, 18/02/1989

**LAST MATCH:** v Swindon Town, A, 18/02/1989

**MOVED TO:** Released, 23/03/1989, after one month trial

**TEAMS:** Manchester City, WBA, Leeds United, Real Betis, Leeds United, Manchester United (L), Coventry City, Manchester United, Ballymena United (L), Manchester City, Bolton Wanderers (L), Port Vale (L), Wimbledon (L), Hull City, SC Farense, Bolton Wanderers, Sunderland, Stockport Co. (L), Footscray Jugoslav United Soccer Team, Bury, Drogheda United, Tampa Bay Rowdies, Stafford Rangers, Northwich Victoria, Wrexham, Radcliffe Borough, Mossley, Hamrun Spartans, SC Farense, Cliftonville.

**INTERNATIONAL:** England

**SAFC TOTALS:** 1 appearance / 0 goals

**The scorer of Manchester City's 'other' goal in the 1976 League Cup final (along with Dennis Tueart's famed bicycle-kick), Peter Barnes played just once for Sunderland - in a 4-1 defeat at Swindon when he was replaced by Tony Cullen after an hour - although he did play at the Stadium of Light in May 2017 for Manchester City Former Players' Association against their Sunderland counterparts.**

Capped 22 times by England, his club career saw him play in Spain, Portugal, Australia, the Republic of Ireland, USA, Malta and Northern Ireland. His father Ken played over 250 games for Manchester City and over 100 for Wrexham.

Four days younger than Gary Rowell, Barnes was PFA Young Player of the Year in 1976. When sold to WBA for £748,000 in 1979, it remained the Baggies record purchase for 18 years until another man with Sunderland connections - Kevin Kilbane - became Albion's first £1m player. Barnes' later move from WBA to Leeds for £930,000 in 1981 was West Brom's record sale at the time.

For England, he debuted against Italy at Wembley in 1977, scored against Wales at Cardiff on his fourth appearance and against Hungary at Wembley in his sixth game. He later marked his 12th and 13th caps with goals in a win over Scotland at Wembley and Bulgaria in Sofia. The last of his caps came in a May 1982 Wembley win over the Netherlands.

After a playing career that increasingly saw very short spells at clubs - including Sunderland - Barnes later dabbled in management with Gibraltar and Runcorn as well as working as a TV pundit in Malaysia.

## BARRIE, Alexander (Alex)

**POSITION:** Centre-half

**BIRTHPLACE:** Camlachie, Glasgow

**DATE OF BIRTH:** 19/08/1878 - 01/10/1918

**SIGNED FROM:** St Bernards, 06/05/1902

**DEBUT:** v Stoke, A, 08/11/1902

**LAST MATCH:** v Everton, A, 30/03/1907

**MOVED TO:** Rangers, 03/06/1907

**TEAMS:** Parkhead Juniors, Edinburgh St. Bernards, Sunderland, Rangers, Kilmarnock, Abercorn

**INTERNATIONAL:** Scotland Juniors

**SAFC TOTALS:** 71 appearances / 2 goals

**Alex Barrie was one of the Sunderland players who lost their lives in the First World War. He spent five seasons on Wearside, his best year being in 1905-06 when he played 27 games. After a season with Rangers during which he appeared 14 times (scoring in a win over Hearts at Ibrox) Alex (sometimes referred to as Alec) played 112 times for Kilmarnock until moving to Abercorn on 12 September 1912.**

During the Great War, he joined the Highland Light Infantry, becoming a corporal. Just five weeks before the end of the war, Barrie was killed in action at the Battle of the Canal du Nord. He was buried at the Flesquieres Hill British Cemetery. 100 years to the day after his death, Barrie's great great nephew Robert Lee travelled from London to lay a wreath in his honour at the remembrance plaque situated by the Fans' statue at the Stadium of Light.

Alex Barrie scored his only league goal for Sunderland in his second game at Grimsby and made his third appearance at Newcastle. Over the next four seasons he played between ten and 23 league games for Sunderland.

After his playing days came to an end, Barrie worked as a bricklayer before joining the armed forces at the age of 36. The tenth of eleven children, Barrie lost his father when he was only 12, Barrie senior being found drowned in the Clyde with a verdict of suicide recorded.

## BARTLEY, John (Jack)

**POSITION:** Left-half

**BIRTHPLACE:** Houghton-le-Spring

**DATE OF BIRTH:** 15/05/1909 - 10/10/1929

**HEIGHT:** 5' 8½" **WEIGHT:** 11st 6lbs

**SIGNED FROM:** Chester-le-Street, 16/09/1926

**DEBUT:** v Blackburn Rovers, A, 01/01/1927

**LAST MATCH:** v Leeds United, H, 05/10/1929

**TEAMS:** Bank Head Albion, Chester-le-Street, Sunderland

**SAFC TOTALS:** 19 appearances / 1 goal

**Jack Bartley's story is one of the saddest in SAFC's history. Just five days after the 20-year-old's most recent appearance in Division One alongside Davie Halliday, Ernie England and Jock McDougall, those three greats would be amongst the pall bearers at Jack's funeral. The day after playing against Leeds at Roker Park Bartley complained of a sore throat and by the Thursday he had died, of Laryngeal Diptheria.**

Three days before his final game, young Jack had impressed so much in a game against Everton that eerily on the day of his death Sunderland received a bid for him from the Toffees.

Joining the trio of teammate pall-bearers at Bartley's funeral was Sir Walter Raine who had become chairman of the club that week. He was accompanied by former chairman F W Taylor and Colonel Prior, a future chairman of Sunderland. Manager Johnny Cochrane also attended, as did a host of other past and present players including Bobby Gurney, Patsy Gallacher, Bill Murray (a future manager), Albert McInroy, Billy Hogg and Charlie Parker, the latter the player-coach of Carlisle United at the time. Newcastle United, Middlesbrough, Hartlepools United, The Durham FA, North Eastern League and Houghton & District League were also represented at the funeral which passed from the family home in Bowlby Street in Houghton to Mautland Square. The funeral procession was reportedly fully half-a-mile long as hundreds of mourners lined the route.

Jack had previously played for St Michael's School, the representative side of the Lambton and Hetton Schools League and Durham County. He had worked at Houghton Colliery before signing for Sunderland the day after impressing in a trial match on 15 September 1926. Generations later, his relation Sue married Sunderland star of the 1960s, Colin Suggett.

## BASSILA, Christian Armel

**POSITION:** Midfielder

**BIRTHPLACE:** Paris

**DATE OF BIRTH:** 05/10/1977

**HEIGHT:** 6' 4" **WEIGHT:** 13st 1lb

**SIGNED FROM:** Strasbourg, 24/08/2005

**DEBUT:** v Chelsea, A, 10/09/2005

**LAST MATCH:** v Spurs, A, 12/02/2006

**MOVED TO:** Larissa, 31/07/2006

**TEAMS:** INF Clairefontaine, Lyon, Rennes, West Ham United (L), Strasbourg, Espanyol (L), Sunderland, Athlitiki Enosi Larissa, Energie Cottbus, Guingamp

**INTERNATIONAL:** France Under 21

**SAFC TOTALS:** 13+1 appearances / 0 goals

**A physically powerful midfielder, Bassila always appeared very studious when seen bespectacled off the pitch. On it, Christian was a player who looked like he was going to be great, but often didn't seem to be as commanding as envisaged and his time at Sunderland was ultimately short-lived as he struggled with niggling injuries. Relegated at the end of his first season, he took a contract option to allow him to depart without a fee to SAFC.**

Coming from French football, ultimately, he didn't cope with the English game despite his attributes. He had previously played just three league games during a season-long loan to West Ham from Rennes. After leaving Wearside, he went into Cypriot football with AEL and played in Germany before returning home to France with Guingamp, a second division side he captained from centre-back in the 2009 Coupe de France final as they beat Rennes.

In 2015, Christian moved into coaching, working with the younger teams of Olympique Lyonnais before becoming director of youth at INF Clairefontaine (the French national football centre) in 2019.

## BATTH, Daniel Tanveer (Danny)

**POSITION:** Centre-half

**BIRTHPLACE:** Brierley Hill, West Midlands

**DATE OF BIRTH:** 21/09/1990

**HEIGHT:** 6' 3" **WEIGHT:** 13st 3lbs

**SIGNED FROM:** Stoke City, 18/01/2002

**DEBUT:** v Portsmouth, H, 22/01/2022

**LAST MATCH:**

**MOVED TO:**

**TEAMS:** Wolverhampton Wanderers, Colchester United (L), Sheffield United (L), Sheffield Wednesday (L), Middlesbrough (L), Stoke City, Sunderland (to January 2022)

**SAFC TOTALS:** 11+1 appearances / 1 goal (to June 2022)

## BATTH, (Danny) (Continued)

**A powerful and committed centre-half, Batth made an impressive debut having been brought in to help deal with the team's previous inability to deal with powerful aggressive forwards. A promotion winner from League One with Sheffield Wednesday in 2012 and Wolves in 2014, when he was named in the League One and PFA Teams of the Season. He had been Young Player of the Year at Wolves in 2009-10 and went on to gain promotion from the Championship with the Molineux club in 2018.**

With Wolves he totalled 204+8 appearances, scoring 14 goals. During his time with Wanderers, he had a series of loans playing a further 87+4 times spread across four clubs, over half of those coming with Sheffield Wednesday where he scored two of his three loan goals. In January 2019 Stoke paid a reported £3m for Danny who played exactly 100 league games for the Potters, including six as sub, in addition to seven further cup games and a total of six goals.

## BAXTER, James Curran (Jim)

**POSITION:** Half-back

**BIRTHPLACE:** Hill of Beath, Fife

**DATE OF BIRTH:** 29/09/1939 - 14/04/2001

**HEIGHT:** 5' 10½" **WEIGHT:** 11st 4lbs

**SIGNED FROM:** Rangers, 25/05/1965

**DEBUT:** v Leeds United, A, 21/08/1965

**LAST MATCH:** v Chelsea, A, 02/12/1967

**MOVED TO:** Nottingham Forest, 15/12/1967

**TEAMS:** Raith Rovers, Rangers, Sunderland, Nottingham Forest, Rangers

**INTERNATIONAL:** Scotland

**SAFC TOTALS:** 98 appearances / 12 goals

**One of the most naturally talented footballers ever to play for Sunderland, in the eyes of many, Jim Baxter remains the best player ever produced by Scotland. Supremely skilful, 'Slim Jim' described his own left-foot as 'the claw'. He would tell teammates to shout 'Feet' or 'Space' to him and he would ensure that the ball was delivered as required.**

Chosen to represent the Rest of the World against England in the FA's Centenary game at Wembley in 1963, earlier that year he had scored both goals as Scotland beat England 2-1 at the national stadium. Four years later at the same stadium, Baxter produced his most famous performance when inspiring Scotland to inflict England's first defeat since becoming world champions the previous year. At the time, Baxter was on Sunderland's books, but despite two goals on his home debut and numerous eye-catching displays, Baxter's time on Wearside was characterised as much by alcohol as artistry.

Sadly, his fondness for drink saw the player increasingly known as Bacardi Jim rather than Slim Jim. Tales of his drinking climaxed during the summer of 1967 when Sunderland played throughout the summer in North America under the guise of Vancouver Royal Canadians.

Signed by former Rangers player and Scotland manager Ian McColl for a club record £72,500, for all his incredible attributes, undoubtedly, Baxter was a disruptive influence at Sunderland with a clique gathering around Jim in conflict with those who saw their leader as Charlie Hurley. Baxter's career was over by the age of 31. He needed two liver transplants by the age of 55 and passed away, aged 61, of pancreatic cancer.

Ten of his 34 caps were won while with Sunderland who sold him to Nottingham Forest in December 1967 in the first

£100,000 transfer Sunderland were involved in. Sunderland had asked for under £100,000, but Forest were keen to join what they saw as 'the £100,000 club' - such was the magical appeal of Baxter - who Forest gave a free transfer to after 49 appearances.

Jim had first appeared at Roker Park in October 1961, playing against the army for the Black Watch as he did his national service. Earlier that year, he had played in the first ever European Cup Winners' Cup final. While Rangers lost on that occasion to Fiorentina, with Baxter as their king-pin they did win nine trophies between 1961 and 64.

## BEACH, Henry Cyril

**POSITION:** Inside-right

**BIRTHPLACE:** Hounslow, Middlesex

**DATE OF BIRTH:** 23/06/1908 - 14/01/1994

**HEIGHT:** 5' 9" **WEIGHT:** 11st 0lbs

**SIGNED FROM:** Charlton Athletic, 14/09/1932

**DEBUT:** v Blackburn Rovers, A, 01/10/1932

**LAST MATCH:** v Sheffield Wednesday, A, 15/10/1932

**MOVED TO:** Temporarily retired in Summer 1933

**TEAMS:** Hounslow Town, Charlton Athletic, Sunderland, Peterborough United, Haysco FC

**SAFC TOTALS:** 3 appearances / 0 goals

**Cyril Beach played in three consecutive top-flight games in October 1932. Having previously scored five times in 31 games for Charlton, Beach made a Sunderland debut described as 'brilliant' by the North Mail newspaper who reported he was 'largely responsible' for Sunderland's first away win of the season, Beach creating two of Patsy Gallacher's hat-trick.**

A week later, Beach hit the bar in a goalless draw with Leeds on his only home appearance, but after playing in a defeat at Sheffield Wednesday he never played again - perhaps not unconnected with the match also seeing the debut of another inside-forward and arguably the finest footballer to ever play for the Lads: Raich Carter. Beach played a handful of games for Peterborough in non-league in 1935 and later became a film studio technician.

## BEAGRIE, Peter Sydney

**POSITION:** Winger

**BIRTHPLACE:** Middlesbrough

**DATE OF BIRTH:** 28/11/1965

**HEIGHT:** 5' 9" **WEIGHT:** 10st 8lbs

**SIGNED FROM:** Everton, 26/09/1991, on loan

**DEBUT:** v Middlesbrough, A, 29/09/1991

**LAST MATCH:** v Bristol Rovers, H, 26/10/1991

**MOVED TO:** Everton, 26/10/1991, end of loan

**TEAMS:** Hartlepool United, Guisborough, Middlesbrough, Sheffield United, Stoke City, Everton, Sunderland (L), Manchester City, Bradford City, Everton (L), Wigan Athletic (L), Scunthorpe United, Grimsby Town

**INTERNATIONAL:** England B

**SAFC TOTALS:** 5 appearances / 1 goal

**Famed for his somersault celebration long before Kenwyne Jones marked his Sunderland goals in such style, Peter Beagrie had just one opportunity to demonstrate his celebratory acrobatics in Sunderland colours, scoring in a 4-2 home win over Brighton.**

He impressed during a brief loan spell from Everton, but just five of an impressive career total of 780 games were for the Lads. Always a goal threat, Beagrie also topped a century of career goals, 90 of his 103 coming in the league.

Beagrie had a brief stint in coaching with his last club Grimsby, but moved into media work only to be reportedly dismissed by Sky Sports in 2017 after a court case where he was found guilty of assaulting his girlfriend.

## BECTON, Thomas (Tom)

**POSITION:** Inside-forward

**BIRTHPLACE:** Preston, Lancashire

**DATE OF BIRTH:** 02/01/1878 - 08/11/1957

**HEIGHT:** 5' 7" **WEIGHT:** 11st 4lbs

**SIGNED FROM:** New Brighton Tower, 08/05/1899

**DEBUT:** v Burnley, H, 16/09/1899

**LAST MATCH:** v Wolves, H, 01/01/1900

**MOVED TO:** Kettering Town, 13/08/1900

**TEAMS:** Preston North End, New Brighton Tower, Sunderland, Kettering, Bristol Rovers, Kettering, Oswaldthistle Rovers, Colne, Rossendale United, Leyland

**SAFC TOTALS:** 15 appearances / 6 goals

**The brother of England international Frank Becton and Martin Becton, who also played league football, Tommy had a year at Sunderland where he made a scoring debut with the winner in a 2-1 home win over Burnley.**

However despite a good scoring record - his last goal coming in a 4-2 win away to Newcastle just before Christmas - Tommy's time with SAFC was soon over with the Lancastrian spending the rest of his career in the Southern League and local football in his home county. Prior to becoming a professional footballer Tom worked as a cotton weaver.

## BEDFORD, Henry (Harry)

**POSITION:** Inside-right

**BIRTHPLACE:** Calow, Derbyshire

**DATE OF BIRTH:** 15/10/1899 - 24/06/1976

**HEIGHT:** 5' 9" **WEIGHT:** 12st 4lbs

**SIGNED FROM:** Newcastle United, 13/01/1932

**DEBUT:** v Everton, H, 16/01/1932

**LAST MATCH:** v Sheffield Wednesday, A, 23/04/1932

**MOVED TO:** Bradford Park Avenue, 12/05/1932

**TEAMS:** Grassmoor Ivanhoe, Nottingham Forest, Blackpool, Derby County, Newcastle United, Sunderland, Bradford, Chesterfield, Heanor Town

**INTERNATIONAL:** England

**SAFC TOTALS:** 7 appearances / 2 goals

**Harry Bedford may be forgotten at Sunderland, but he certainly wouldn't be elsewhere. An England international, he played only seven times for the Lads in the thirties.**

His two goals for Sunderland disguise the fact that he was a prolific scorer elsewhere scoring 308 goals in 486 league games, a figure that included ten hat-tricks. He also scored four times in three league games and nabbed another four-goal haul when representing the Football League against the Irish League in 1924.

Sunderland actually signed him from Newcastle for whom he had scored 18 times in 32 games. For Derby County Bedford was top scorer for five years in a row. A 1925 move to the Baseball Ground saw Derby pay Blackpool twice the £1,500 the Seasiders had invested in Harry four and a half years earlier. Bedford blasted 118 goals in 180 games for Blackpool. Starting as he meant to go on with seven in his first ten appearances, he became the country's leading goalscorer in consecutive seasons between 1922 and '24 with 32 second division goals in each of those campaigns.

Blackpool signed Bedford after he had devastated their defence while playing for Nottingham Forest, who he had joined as an amateur having started with his Boy Scouts side Bonds Main before progressing into local league football with Grassmoor Ivanhoe in the Chesterfield area. During World War One he

turned out twice for Nottingham Forest and once for Huddersfield before becoming a professional with Forest in 1919, scoring eight goals in 14 games before Blackpool moved in for him.

During his time with Blackpool, Bedford was capped by England in a 4-2 win over Sweden in Stockholm in May 1923. Almost a year and a half later, Harry's second and final cap saw him score in a 3-1 win over Ireland at Goodison Park when he had Sunderland's Warney Cresswell as a teammate, and scored after receiving a pass from future Sunderland forward Bob Kelly.

By the time Bedford came to Sunderland, he was 32 and past his best. His first two games in January 1932 came in defeats at the ground where he had scored for England and then back at his old haunt of Bloomfield Road in Blackpool. Home fans were not disappointed though as Harry marked his Roker Park debut by opening the scoring in a 5-1 beating of Portsmouth. However, there would be just one more goal for Sunderland, that coming in his seventh and final game at Sheffield Wednesday in the penultimate game of the season.

Come the end of the season, Harry was allowed to move on. A year in the second division with Bradford Park Avenue preceded a 1933 transfer to home town Chesterfield where frustratingly the Spireites finished runners-up in Division Three North (to Barnsley who were captained by Sunderland old boy George Henderson) when only the champions went up.

Heanor Town became Bedford's last club as a player, Harry doubling up as trainer. From October 1937 until the following May, he returned to the north-east as trainer at Newcastle before becoming part-time masseur at Derbyshire County Cricket Club when he took over the Vulcan Arms and later the Grapes Inn pubs in Derby. Rarely one to keep out of the news, in 1939 Bedford ended up in court after a dispute with a bookmaker over the outcome of a darts match.

Almost a decade after the end of the war, Bedford re-surfaced in the football world as manager of Belper Town in January 1954 and then had a year in charge of Heanor Town beginning in March 1955. Bedford passed away in Derby in June 1976 and 30 years later was inducted into Blackpool FC's Hall of Fame.

## BEE, Francis Eric (Frank)

**POSITION:** Inside-forward

**BIRTHPLACE:** Nottingham

**DATE OF BIRTH:** 23/01/1927 - 26/07/2010

**HEIGHT:** 5' 11" **WEIGHT:** 10st 9lbs

**SIGNED FROM:** Nottingham Forest, 01/06/1947

**DEBUT:** v Blackburn Rovers, A, 31/01/1948

**LAST MATCH:** v Preston North End, H, 13/03/1948

**MOVED TO:** Blackburn Rovers, 28/02/1949

**TEAMS:** Nottingham Boys Brigade, Nottingham Forest, Sunderland, Blackburn Rovers, Peterborough United, Boston United, Ilkeston Town

**SAFC TOTALS:** 5 appearances / 1 goal

**Hopes Frank Bee might have had of making it at Sunderland were not helped by the debut of Len Shackleton in the next match after his own debut.**

Bee was dropped for Shack's debut, but played alongside the 'Clown Prince of Soccer' in the next four games, each making their home debut together against Huddersfield - when both scored in a 2-0 win.

In fact, both Bee and Shackleton had already played - and both scored - at Roker Park in a 5-1 friendly win over Barnsley a fortnight earlier, a game played on a free weekend as Sunderland were out of the FA Cup. Bee also stung in his competitive home debut against Huddersfield. In only the second minute he collided with Bob Hesford - the father of future Sunderland keeper Iain Hesford - who was stretchered off and taken to Monkwearmouth Hospital with a fractured ankle. Getting on the scoresheet against stand-in keeper Jimmy Glazzard, along with Shack, Bee earned great write-ups in the press, but played his final game for Sunderland just three weeks later, signing off in the same game as 1937 cup final scorer Eddie Burbanks.

Sunderland finished one place above Bee's debut opponents Blackburn who were relegated and took Bee to Ewood Park the following season where he made four second division appearances, all in March, although they were to prove his only Rovers appearances.

## BEESLEY, Colin

**POSITION:** Winger

**BIRTHPLACE:** Stockton, Co Durham

**DATE OF BIRTH:** 06/10/1951

**HEIGHT:** 5' 6" **WEIGHT:** 9st 12lbs

**SIGNED FROM:** Youth product, 01/07/1966, Professional, January 1969

**DEBUT:** v Stoke City, H, 01/03/1969

**LAST MATCH:** v Southampton, A, 08/03/1969

**MOVED TO:** Released, 31/05/1972

**TEAMS:** Sunderland, Ipswich Town, Stockton, Scarborough, Corby Town, Crook

**SAFC TOTALS:** 0+3 appearances / 0 goals

**Nicknamed Scobie after the famous jockey Scobie Breasley, Colin Beesley played in all nine games as the FA Youth Cup was won in 1969, getting a goal in the 6-0 second-leg win over WBA in the final.**

By this time Beesley's first-team career was over. His performances earlier in the run had seen him make a trio of appearances within a week between the quarter and semi-finals of the Youth Cup. When he left, Beesley became the first player to depart the club having seen all of his first-team experience consist solely of substitute appearances.

Under Bobby Robson, Colin spent a month in pre-season with Ipswich in 1972, lodging with Eric Gates, but never played a competitive game. Having lived the dream of playing in the top -flight for his local team, in 2022 Colin was still an enthusiastic season card holder at the Stadium of Light as well as an active member of the Former Players' Association. In 2008, Colin managed Norton & Stockton Ancients in over 40s football.

## BELFITT, Roderick Michael (Rod)

**POSITION:** Forward

**BIRTHPLACE:** Bournemouth

**DATE OF BIRTH:** 30/10/1945

**HEIGHT:** 5' 11½" **WEIGHT:** 11st 11lbs

**SIGNED FROM:** Everton, 23/10/1973

**DEBUT:** v Crystal Palace, 27/10/1973

**LAST MATCH:** v Aston Villa, A, 26/04/1975

**MOVED TO:** Huddersfield Town, 10/05/1975

**TEAMS:** Retford Town, Leeds United, Ipswich Town, Everton, Sunderland, Fulham (L), Huddersfield Town, Worksop Town, Frickley Athletic, Bentley Victoria.

**SAFC TOTALS:** 39+6 appearances / 4 goals

**Signed by Bob Stokoe shortly after the 1973 FA Cup triumph, although Belfitt had a decent pedigree his acquisition was viewed by many supporters as not being of the quality of the rest of the cup team and he struggled for popularity at Roker.**

Apparently bought as a forward, he struggled for goals and having arrived soon after the injury that ended Ritchie Pitt's playing days, found himself increasingly asked to play in defence. Just over a year after his arrival on Wearside, Rod was allowed to go on loan to Fulham before leaving at the end of his second season when signing for his old Leeds teammate Bobby Collins at Huddersfield.

Huddersfield had been the venue of Belfitt's senior debut with his first professional club Leeds with whom he went on to score a hat-trick in a 1967 Inter-Cities Fairs Cup semi-final first leg against Kilmarnock, and play in the 1967 and 1968 finals as well the 1968 League Cup final. As Leeds won the league in 1968-69, he scored against Sunderland at Elland Road. Following his football career Rod became a draughtsman and later a financial advisor.

## BELL, Edward (Ted)

**POSITION:** Right-back

**BIRTHPLACE:** Burnopfield, Co Durham

**DATE OF BIRTH:** 23/12/1881 - 05/12/1946

**HEIGHT:** 5' 10" **WEIGHT:** 11st 0lbs

**SIGNED FROM:** Bishop Auckland, 01/03/1905

**DEBUT:** v Everton, H, 18/11/1905

**LAST MATCH:** v Bolton Wanderers, H, 30/11/1907

**MOVED TO:** Spennymoor United, 27/09/1908

**TEAMS:** Hobson Wanderers, West Stanley, Bishop Auckland, Seaham White Star, Sunderland, Spennymoor United, South Shields Adelaide

**SAFC TOTALS:** 23 appearances / 0 goals

**Other than for his time at Sunderland, Ted Bell spent his playing career in local non-league football, combining his sport with his profession as a school teacher - like Charlie Buchan and Sam Aiston for instance, carrying on the tradition of the people who originally set up the club as Sunderland and District Teachers' Association Football Club. Bell was an accomplished musician and pianoforte tutor.**

As captain of Sunderland reserves - or Sunderland 'A' as they were known at the time, Bell lifted the Durham Senior Cup and Northumberland League Cup in 1905-06 in his second season with the club. All but two of his first-team appearances came in 1905-06 with a single appearance coming in each of the following two campaigns.

## BELL, John Cuthbert (Paddy)

**POSITION:** Goalkeeper

**BIRTHPLACE:** Seaham Colliery, Co Durham

**DATE OF BIRTH:** 17/10/1905 - 03/05/1980

**HEIGHT:** 6' 0" **WEIGHT:** 12st 7lbs

**SIGNED FROM:** Seaham Colliery, 04/09/1924, amateur, Professional, 28/11/1924

**DEBUT:** v Leeds United H 26/03/1927

**LAST MATCH:** v Grimsby Town, H, 08/11/1930

**MOVED TO:** Walsall, 27/11/1930

**TEAMS:** Ryhope Colliery, Seaham Colliery, Sunderland, Walsall, Accrington Stanley, Bradford Park Avenue, Seaham Colliery

**SAFC TOTALS:** 40 appearances / 0 goals

**Having established a reputation in local football, Paddy Bell came into the Sunderland side for the last eight games of the 1926-27 season helping the Lads to finish third on the last occasion the title went to Tyneside.**

Although he was unlucky to be injured on his debut when he had to go off after 50 minutes (although Leeds were still beaten 6-2), Bell was an able deputy for Albert McInroy, the only keeper (to 2022) to win an England cap while with Sunderland. Paddy had another sequence of seven successive games in the autumn of 1927 and eleven in a row almost exactly two years later. He was also an accomplished wicket keeper for Seaham Harbour cricket club and after retiring from playing football served as secretary for Seaham Colliery Welfare FC. Born John Cuthbert Lloyd and brought up by his grandparents John & Mary Bell, he used his mother's maiden name of Bell throughout his football career.

## BELL, Richard (Dick)

**POSITION:** Winger

**BIRTHPLACE:** East Greenock

**DATE OF BIRTH:** 04/09/1915 - 23/11/1962

**HEIGHT:** 5' 10" **WEIGHT:** 10st 0lbs

**SIGNED FROM:** Port Glasgow Athletic, 08/06/1935

**DEBUT:** v Leeds United, A, 24/04/1937

**LAST MATCH:** v Leeds United, A, 24/04/1937

**MOVED TO:** West Ham United, 08/07/1937

**TEAMS:** Port Glasgow Athletic, Sunderland, West Ham United, Clapham (WW2 Guest), Southend United (WW2 Guest)

**SAFC TOTALS:** 1 appearances / 0 goals

**Dick Bell made two Football League appearances, one for Sunderland and one for West Ham for whom he scored. His opportunity for Sunderland came on the left wing on the Saturday before the 1937 FA Cup final.**

For West Ham, Bell played in his best position of inside-left and scored against WBA at the Boleyn Ground in April 1939. Whatever hopes 'Brindle' (as he was nicknamed) had of carving out a top class career crashed with the outbreak of World War Two during which he joined the Essex Regiment Territorials and later the Royal Artillery while continuing his football as a Guest player with a couple of southern clubs. Bell was a distant relation of Sunderland manager Johnny Cochrane, being his first cousin once removed.

## BELLION, David

**POSITION:** Forward

**BIRTHPLACE:** Paris, France

**DATE OF BIRTH:** 27/11/1982

**HEIGHT:** 6' 0" **WEIGHT:** 11st 9lbs

**SIGNED FROM:** Cannes, 03/07/2001

**DEBUT:** v Fulham, A, 22/08/2001

**LAST MATCH:** v Newcastle United, H, 26/04/2003

**MOVED TO:** Manchester United, 01/07/2003

**TEAMS:** Cannes, Sunderland, Manchester United, West Ham United (L), Nice, Bordeaux, Nice (L), Red Star (Paris)

**INTERNATIONAL:** France U21

**SAFC TOTALS:** 8+16 appearances / 1 goal

**A live-wire speed-merchant, French forward Bellion regularly thrilled supporters of the reserve team in games played at New Ferens Park the home of Durham City. First-team followers saw relatively little of Bellion's potential, although he did score the winner in Peter Reid's last home game as manager - against Aston Villa in 2002.**

Following relegation in 2003, Sunderland's big names were shipped out in something of a fire-sale and more than one departing player cast envious glances in Bellion's direction as he was snapped up by Manchester United.

The Red Devils thought they had captured him on a free, but astute work by chairman Bob Murray ensured that Sunderland received a settlement reported to be over £2m.

After returning to France he went on to win five pieces of silverware, including the Ligue 1 title with Bordeaux in 2008-09, scoring four goals, including a brace against Le Havre. After retiring from playing, Bellion became the creative director at Red Star in his home city of Paris.

## BEN HAIM, Tal

**POSITION:** Defender

**BIRTHPLACE:** Rishon Le Tsiyon, Israel

**DATE OF BIRTH:** 31/03/1982

**HEIGHT:** 5' 11" **WEIGHT:** 11st 9lbs

**SIGNED FROM:** Manchester City, on loan, 01/02/2009

**DEBUT:** v Arsenal, A, 21/02/2009

**LAST MATCH:** v West Ham United, A, 04/04/2009

**MOVED TO:** Manchester City, end of loan, 25/05/2009

**TEAMS:** Maccabi Tel Aviv, Bolton Wanderers, Chelsea, Manchester City, Sunderland (L), Portsmouth, West Ham United (L), QPR, Toronto (L), Standard Liege, Charlton Athletic, Maccabi Tel Aviv, Beitar Jerusalem (to Jan 2021)

**INTERNATIONAL:** Israel

**SAFC TOTALS:** 5 appearances / 0 goals

**Capped 96 times by Israel, Tal Ben Haim had an extensive career in English football and was brought in to Sunderland on loan by Ricky Sbragia who had previously coached him at Bolton Wanderers. Appearing at right back and in central defence, Ben Haim was an unused sub three times in addition to his five appearances, with the only victory coming on one of the occasions he was left on the bench - a 1-0 home win over Hull.**

Ben Haim captained Bolton in European competition, made his Chelsea debut at Wembley in the Community Shield and moved to Manchester City for £5m, debuting in the UEFA Cup at Barnsley against EB/Streymur of the Faroe Islands. Although publicly critical of manager Avram Grant at Chelsea, he later played for his fellow Israeli again at both Portsmouth and West Ham United. After returning to his first club Maccabi Tel Aviv, he was sent off in a Champions League match against his old side Chelsea.

Between 2000 and 2002, Ben Haim served in the Israeli Defence Force and in 2003 won the Israel Premier League.

## BENDTNER, Nicklas

**POSITION:** Forward

**BIRTHPLACE:** Copenhagen, Denmark

**DATE OF BIRTH:** 16/01/1988

**HEIGHT:** 6' 3" **WEIGHT:** 13st 0lbs

**SIGNED FROM:** Arsenal, on loan, 31/08/2011

**DEBUT:** v Chelsea, H, 10/09/2011

**LAST MATCH:** v Fulham, A, 06/05/2012

**MOVED TO:** Arsenal, end of loan, 14/05/2012

**TEAMS:** Tarnby Boldklub, Kjobenhavns Boldklub, Arsenal, Birmingham City (L) Sunderland (L), Juventus (L), VfL Wolfsburg, Nottingham Forest, Rosenborg, Copenhagen, Tarnby FF (to Jan 2021)

**INTERNATIONAL:** Denmark

**SAFC TOTALS:** 27+3 appearances / 8 goals

**Confidence is a big quality in footballers, particularly so for forwards (and goalkeepers). Bendtner was never lacking in confidence. He was always full of self-belief, at times perhaps too much. Reportedly four years after his time at Sunderland, a Danish newspaper bought him a square foot of land in Scotland to enable him to really have the title Lord, Nicklas having long since been nicknamed Lord Bendtner in his homeland.**

Shortly before he came to Wearside, he had fathered a child with Baroness Caroline Luel-Brockdorff. With a later girlfriend, model Philline Roepstorff, he signed up to do a reality TV show on Danish television called 'Bendtner and Philline' exploring the glitzy life-style of a couple dubbed the Beckhams of Denmark.

On the other hand in 2018 he was sentenced to 50 days in jail for assaulting a taxi driver. He had also been in trouble while with Sunderland, at one point issuing a public apology after being arrested and bailed accused of damaging cars on an evening out in Newcastle with Lee Cattermole shortly after a couple of unsavoury incidents while on international duty. Prior to joining Sunderland, he had had problems with his own car, writing off his Aston Martin while walking away with nothing more than a few bruises. It was an incident that appeared to add to his sense of invincibility.

He was however, a player for the big occasion - not least when keeping his composure to score with a penalty in a 1-1 draw at Newcastle followed by the winner against Liverpool at the SoL a week later. Those goals were part of eight he scored in a season-long loan that made him top-scorer in 2011-12 in a campaign where Martin O'Neill took over from Steve Bruce who had brought him in.

At international level, he scored on his Denmark debut at the age of 18 and went on to score 30 international goals in 81 games including one against Cameroon at the 2010 FIFA World Cup finals. However, it was his brace against Portugal at Euro 2012 which attracted more attention. This was due to him celebrating the second by revealing a bookmakers logo on his underwear - an offence which led to a UEFA imposed ban and a fine of 100,000 Euros, albeit the betting company paid the fine - Bendtner again walking away feeling invincible.

Notably on the occasion of Sunderland's pre-season friendly at FC Midtjylland in Denmark in 2013, I was given a tour of the home team's training ground. On the wall of the main corridor was a poster of the Danish national team with Lord Bendtner's picture defaced. Evidently, he was not as universally loved as perhaps he hoped.

## BENNETT, Gary Ernest

**POSITION:** Defender

**BIRTHPLACE:** Manchester, Lancashire

**DATE OF BIRTH:** 04/12/1961

**HEIGHT:** 6' 1" **WEIGHT:** 12st 11lbs

**SIGNED FROM:** Cardiff City, 18/07/1984

**DEBUT:** v Southampton, H, 25/8/1984

**LAST MATCH:** v Luton Town, H, 15/04/1995

**MOVED TO:** Carlisle United, 15/11/1995

**TEAMS:** Ashton United, Manchester City, Cardiff City, Sunderland, Carlisle United, Scarborough, Darlington, Worksop Town, Durham City, Hebburn Town

**SAFC TOTALS:** 434+9 appearances / 25 goals

**Fifth on the all-time list of appearance makers, 'Benno' was brought to the club by the record outfield appearance maker Len Ashurst who had been Gary's manager at Cardiff. Bennett had made his name at Cardiff having begun with his home town team Manchester City.**

## BENNETT, Gary (Continued)

Famously scoring against England's Peter Shilton within two minutes on his debut, Benno had a penchant for scoring as well as stopping goals. Headed goals against Gillingham and Manchester City on days Sunderland were relegated in 1987 and 1991 illustrated that Gary would always fight to the last, such as when he scored an exquisite last-minute winner against Manchester United in 1990.

In some respects that goal, which saw him lift the ball over Britain's costliest defender Gary Pallister before curling it beyond keeper Les Sealey, typified Bennett. An orthodox defender would not have been up-field in open play, but Benno was never in danger of being orthodox!

Big, powerful, aggressive and determined, he became an inspirational captain and was Player of the Year in 1986-87 and 1993-94 - no other player has been Player of the Year in years so far apart, a testament to Gary's service.

Gary never played without giving it his all and he did not suffer fools gladly, most famously his sorting out of Coventry's David Speedie, when the pair of them ended up in the Clock Stand paddock in a League Cup quarter-final in 1990, passing into legend.

After sterling service to Sunderland Bennett played alongside future Sunderland man Rory Delap - and briefly his old Sunderland colleague Brian Atkinson - at Carlisle. Gary scored five times in 26 games, all but two of them in defence, but couldn't stop the newly-promoted Cumbrians from slipping back into the bottom tier of the Football League.

Re-joining his old Carlisle manager Mick Wadsworth at Scarborough in that fourth tier, Gary was ever-present in 1996-97 as he helped his club to a mid-table berth, playing alongside Sunderland old boys John Kay and Stephen Brodie. The following season Bennett missed just four games as Scarborough qualified for the Play-Offs.

Bennett's 1985 League (Milk) Cup final teammate Dave Hodgson then persuaded Gary to join Darlington where he debuted alongside another Roker old boy in Dariusz Kubicki at Rotherham in October 1998. At Feethams, Benno also played with a host of players with Sunderland connections: Marco Gabbiadini, Brian Atkinson and ex Roker reserves Steve Gaughan, David Preece, Paul Heckingbottom and Phil Brumwell as well as Craig Liddle who would go on to coach Sunderland Under 18s.

Gary's first season with the Quakers also brought a goal in an FA Cup draw with his first club Manchester City, followed by a final appearance back at Maine Road where Darlo only lost in extra-time. After one more season with Darlington, Gary played briefly for Worksop Town in 2001 before a short return to Scarborough.

For Worksop, Benno played a couple of games away to Burton and Bournemouth, the latter an FA Cup game in which Worksop also fielded Chris Waddle as a sub. In total Gary played in 604 Football League matches.

Benno went on to manage Darlington, serve as chairman of the Sunderland Former Players' Association and for many years summarise SAFC games on local radio. Moreover, as one of the first black footballers to play for Sunderland he did more than anyone to combat racism on Wearside.

Having become a hero on the pitch, for many years Gary gave the same sort of commitment he showed as a player to his work to fight against racism in football. He was awarded an MBE for his work against racism in the New Year's Honours in 2022.

At Manchester City and Cardiff City, Gary was joined on the books by his brother Dave who went on to score for Coventry as they won the FA Cup final in 1987.

## BENT, Darren Ashley

**POSITION:** Forward

**BIRTHPLACE:** Tooting, London

**DATE OF BIRTH:** 06/02/1984

**HEIGHT:** 5' 11" **WEIGHT:** 1 st 7lbs

**SIGNED FROM:** Tottenham Hotspur, 05/08/2009

**DEBUT:** v Bolton Wanderers, A,15/08/2009

**LAST MATCH:** v Newcastle United, 16/01/2011

**MOVED TO:** Aston Villa, 18/01/2011

**TEAMS:** Godmanchester Rovers, Ipswich Town, Charlton Athletic, Tottenham Hotspur, Sunderland, Aston Villa, Fulham (L), Brighton & HA (L), Derby County, Burton Albion.

**INTERNATIONAL:** England

**SAFC TOTALS:** 63 appearances / 36 goals

**Bent arrived for a fee of £10m that including add-ons of £6.5m, remained Sunderland's record to 2022, although Didier Ndong was later often reported incorrectly to be the record purchase having cost £13.5m.**

Darren's arrival at Sunderland was in large part down to the persuasiveness of Steve Bruce. I sat behind Bruce and Chief Executive Margaret Byrne on the coach from Peterborough to a local airport and then from Newcastle airport back to the Academy of Light after a pre-season friendly at Posh as Bruce and Byrne negotiated with Bent's agent, the deal being concluded the following day.

For the first year, Bent proceeded to make his big money purchase look like a bargain as it seemed everything he hit went in - even with the aid of a beach-ball! Debuting along with Fraizer Campbell and new midfield duo Lorik Cana and Lee Cattermole in Bruce's first game at Bolton, Bent bagged the only goal of the game and followed that up with a goal that opened the scoring (in a defeat) on his home debut against Chelsea who had finished third the previous term.

Bent proceeded to score regularly, a hat-trick in the return match with Bolton in March making him the scorer of Sunderland's first top-flight hat-trick at the SoL (Arsenal's Freddie Ljungberg in May 2003 had scored the only previous top-flight hat-trick). Ever-present in his first season, his 24 Premier League goals made him the top-flight's third top scorer behind Didier Drogba and Wayne Rooney who spear-headed the attacks of the top two Chelsea and Manchester United. Bent scored exactly 50% of 13th-placed Sunderland's goals and added another against Premier League opposition in the FA Cup.

Like Phillips, Bent had the talent to be in the right place at the right time. Oddly, so many of his goals were not well-struck, but they regularly found the target. Darren's form got him back into the England team for his first start in over three years. Capped against Brazil in Doha in November 2009, he started again against Japan at the end of the season in Graz. Early the following season, Bent became the first player to score for England while with Sunderland since Len Shackleton, doing so as a sub against Switzerland in Basle. Bent was the first since Charlie Buchan (v France in Paris in 1923) to score for England overseas.

By the time he scored twice at Anfield to earn a point at the end of September, Darren had five goals in the opening six games of his second season and was on course to reach SuperKev-like status at Sunderland, but shortly afterwards things turned sour.

Early in the January transfer window, a week after playing at Aston Villa he was strangely subdued in a home derby with Newcastle before the bombshell dropped that he wanted a move. He quickly moved to Aston Villa for more than double the club's previous record sale (£8m for Kenwyne Jones). An initial £18m meant Sunderland more than got their money back on the player although his relatively poor form for Villa meant Sunderland probably didn't get all of the additional £6m from additional causes. In three and a half seasons with Villa he never reached double figures in terms of league goals for the club who loaned him out three times.

Bent's last act at the Stadium of Light was a cruel one, the 216th and final goal of his career - one of only two for his final club Burton Albion - relegated Sunderland to League One in April 2018.

North East Football Writers' Association Footballer of the Year and Sunderland Player of the Year in 2009-10, Bent had been Ipswich's Young Player of the Year in 2002-03 and Charlton's Player of the Year in 2005-06 (when he scored twice at Sunderland on the opening day of the season). He was on the losing Spurs side in the 2009 League (Carling) Cup final having won his only senior winner's medal in the same competition the previous season with Tottenham as an unused sub.

## BERRY, Stephen Andrew (Steve)

**POSITION:** Midfield

**BIRTHPLACE:** Gosport, Hampshire

**DATE OF BIRTH:** 04/04/1963

**HEIGHT:** 5' 7" **WEIGHT:** 11st 6lbs

**SIGNED FROM:** Portsmouth, 05/07/1984

**DEBUT:** v Southampton, H, 25/08/1984

**LAST MATCH:** v Grimsby Town, A, 17/09/1985

**MOVED TO:** Newport County, 12/12/1985

**TEAMS:** Gosport Borough, Portsmouth, Aldershot (L), Sunderland, Newport County, Swindon Town, Aldershot, Northampton Town, Maidstone United, Stevenage Borough, Kettering Town (player/manager), Rushden & Diamonds, Stevenage Borough, Bedford Town, Cogenhoe United

**SAFC TOTALS:** 43+4 appearances / 2 goals

**Steve 'Chuck' Berry was a regular for SAFC in his only full season of 1984-85 when they were relegated from the top flight, but reached the League (Milk) Cup final. Berry played in all ten cup games including the Wembley final, but was never a popular player despite his unceasing effort.**

Never the easiest on the eye, Berry did a lot of unsung running and covering for the team, but in the eyes of supporters at least, the free-transfer signing lacked the necessary quality despite

scoring in two of his first four first division appearances at Roker Park. Having been signed by Len Ashurst, he was soon discarded by new manager Lawrie McMenemy for whom he only started one game, had one as sub and was once an unused sub a month after what proved to be his final appearance.

Following his playing days, Berry became head of a recruitment company in Paris.

## BERTRAM, Ernest Edward Alfred (Ernie)

**POSITION:** Left-half

**BIRTHPLACE:** Dissington, Northumberland

**DATE OF BIRTH:** 30/06/1881 - 03/11/1942

**SIGNED FROM:** South Shields, 21/08/1903

**DEBUT:** v Small Heath, A, 05/03/1904

**LAST MATCH:** v Small Heath, A, 05/03/1904

**MOVED TO:** Released, 31/05/1906

**TEAMS:** South Shields, Sunderland, Darlington, South Shields Adelaide

**SAFC TOTALS:** 1 appearances / 0 goal

**In three years at Sunderland, Bertram got just one competitive first-team opportunity. That came in a 2-1 defeat at Small Heath who later became Birmingham City. His chance came as two of the three half-backs were rested ahead of the Durham Senior Cup final.**

Small Heath were battling against relegation and Bertram could have punished them, only to hit an early chance over the bar on a pitch described at the time as being 'little more than a quagmire.'

Although Bertram did not get a further outing in a series of end of season friendlies, a fortnight before his only competitive first-team game, he did play in a 6-3 friendly win over at Feethams over Darlington who he later played for between 1907-09. Whilst playing football, he worked as a merchant's clerk and became an electrical supplies salesman after retiring from the game.

## BERTSCHIN, Keith Edwin

**POSITION:** Centre-forward

**BIRTHPLACE:** Enfield, London

**DATE OF BIRTH:** 25/08/1956

**HEIGHT:** 6' 1" **WEIGHT:** 11st 8lbs

**SIGNED FROM:** Stoke City, 25/03/1987

**DEBUT:** v Portsmouth, A, 28/03/1987

**LAST MATCH:** v Rotherham United, A, 07/05/1988

**MOVED TO:** Walsall, 28/07/1988

**TEAMS:** Barnet, Ipswich Town, Birmingham City, Norwich City, Jacksonville Tea Men (L), Stoke City, Sunderland, Walsall, Chester City, Aldershot, Solihull Borough, Evesham United, Barry Town, Worcester City, Hednesford Town, Tamworth, Stafford Rangers.

**INTERNATIONAL:** England Under 21

**SAFC TOTALS:** 30+13 appearances / 10 goals

**The scorer of Sunderland's first ever third division goal and also the last of that 1987-88 season, Keith Bertschin was a striker who scored regularly against Sunderland before coming to the club. Bertschin had scored in the Play-Off second-leg against Gillingham the previous season, but had been unable to keep Sunderland up.**

But for an injury sustained at Fulham early in the opening third tier campaign, Keith may have enjoyed a more successful time on Wearside. Manager Denis Smith had signed Marco Gabbiadini to partner Bertschin, but by the time Keith was fit again, Gabbiadini - who had scored his first goals for the club in that game at Fulham - had established an outstanding partnership with Eric Gates and Bertschin found himself as the back-up striker.

A promotion winner with Birmingham City and Norwich City as well as Sunderland, Bertschin was Stoke City's Player of the Year in 1986 and topped over 100 league goals in a career which stretched from the mid-1970s to the early 1990s and continued to 1998 as he carried on his playing days with a host of non-league clubs.

As a coach, he worked alongside Steve Bruce at Birmingham, Wigan, Sunderland and Hull, being in charge of the reserve team while with Bruce at the Stadium of Light. He also coached Solihull Moors, taking the club's ladies team as well as well as their men's side.

## BEST, Robert (Bobby)

**POSITION:** Winger / Centre-forward

**BIRTHPLACE:** Mickley, Northumberland

**DATE OF BIRTH:** 12/09/1891 - 08/06/1947

**HEIGHT:** 5' 5" **WEIGHT:** 10st 7lbs

**SIGNED FROM:** Mickley Colliery Welfare, 26/08/1911

**DEBUT:** v Aston Villa, A, 07/10/1911

**LAST MATCH:** v Manchester City, H, 14/01/1922

**MOVED TO:** Wolves, 08/09/1922

**TEAMS:** Mickley C.W. Sunderland, Sunderland Rovers (WW1 Guest), Wolves, Durham City, Hartlepools United, West Stanley

**SAFC TOTALS:** 97 appearances / 24 goals

**The scorer of a Christmas Day hat-trick in a 5-2 win away to Newcastle United in 1914, one of his goals on a frosty surface at St James' saw him leave three Magpies floundering in his wake before finding the back of the net.**

Best had scored twice in a 6-0 win at Spurs a week earlier and was certainly good value for the £20 Sunderland had paid Mickley CW for the player who hailed from the same place as Bob Stokoe and started to show his value straight away with a debut goal in a win at Villa.

At times Bobby struggled to get into the team, standing in for right-winger Jackie Mordue just three times during the near-double 1912-13 season, while in 1914-15, even eight goals in nine games could not earn a regular place.

Although not counted in his official totals, Best played more than anyone in the Victory League that got football going again after the Great War, scoring eight times in those 25 games in addition to his Football League and English (FA) Cup record above. A goal came on his first Football League appearance after the war, but it would be one of just five in 45 post war FL appearances.

With Wolves, Bobby debuted in a second division game at Manchester United in September 1922, but failed to score in 23 games for the Molineux men. Following a spell with Durham City as they finished bottom of Division Three North he joined Hartlepools United in June 1924, debuting at home to Rochdale at the end of August, the first of 76 appearances during which he scored nine goals before returning to Wearside to work for the local authority.

His younger brother Jerry kept goal over 200 times for Coventry as well as playing for Halifax Town, Rotherham United, Worksop Town and Newark Town. Bobby also had a cousin, also called Jerry Best, who was a goalkeeper for Leeds, Newcastle (3 appearances), Darlington, Clapton Orient and Hull City before going to play in the USA with teams such as Providence Clamdiggers and New Bedford Whalers.

Bobby was a miner before becoming a player and served in the Durham Light Infantry and then a munitions factory during the Great War. Following his retirement from football, Best was employed by Sunderland Corporation. Troubled by bronchitis during his playing days, this was the cause of his early death.

## BETT, Frederick (Freddie)

**POSITION:** Inside-right

**BIRTHPLACE:** Scunthorpe, Lincolnshire

**DATE OF BIRTH:** 05/12/1920 - 14/04/2005

**HEIGHT:** 5' 7" **WEIGHT:** 10st 8lbs

**SIGNED FROM:** Scunthorpe & Lindsey United, 02/12/1937 as an amateur (signed professional forms three day later on his 17th birthday)

**DEBUT:** v Liverpool, A, 12/03/1938

**LAST MATCH:** v Liverpool, A, 22/04/1939

**MOVED TO:** Coventry City, 17/05/1946

**TEAMS:** Scunthorpe & Lindsey United, Sunderland, Lincoln City (WW1 Guest), Nottingham Forest (WW1 Guest), Chester (WW1 Guest), Coventry City, Lincoln City, Spalding United, Holbeach United, Bourne Town.

**SAFC TOTALS:** 3 appearances / 0 goals

**Anfield was the setting for two of Bett's three first-team appearances, a 1-1 draw on the latter occasion being a marked improvement on the 4-0 reverse on his debut. In between he played at Roker Park in a 2-2 draw with Bolton.**

In 1945-46, Fred scored in both legs of the Division Three North cup final for Chester against Rotherham United before signing for Coventry where his debut goal at Burnley was the first of four goals in five games as he totalled eleven in 27 games. He went on to score twice in 14 games for Lincoln. During World War Two he served in the Royal Northumberland Fusiliers stationed at Chester.

## BINGHAM, William Laurie (Billy)

**POSITION:** Winger

**BIRTHPLACE:** Belfast

**DATE OF BIRTH:** 05/08/1931 - 09/06/2022

**HEIGHT:** 5' 7½" **WEIGHT:** 10st 2lbs

**SIGNED FROM:** Glentoran, 18/10/1950

**DEBUT:** v Stoke City, H, 02/12/1950

**LAST MATCH:** v Burnley, H, 22/02/1958

**MOVED TO:** Luton Town, 24/07/1958

**TEAMS:** Glentoran, Sunderland, Luton Town, Everton, Port Vale

**INTERNATIONAL:** Northern Ireland

**SAFC TOTALS:** 227 appearances / 47 goals

**A huge figure in post-war football, as well as being my mam's favourite player at Roker Park in the fifties, Billy Bingham won the first 33 of his 56 Northern Ireland caps while with Sunderland, the last five of them at the 1958 FIFA World Cup finals as the Irish reached the quarter-finals.**

He was the first Sunderland player to appear at the finals of the World Cup and at the time it made him Sunderland's most capped international. Bingham netted four goals for his country while with the Lads - the first of them against his Sunderland teammate Willie Fraser who was in goal for Scotland at Hampden in November 1954.

The 1958 World Cup was not the end of Bingham's relationship with the World Cup. In 1982 and 86, he managed Northern Ireland to the finals, in 1982 famously defeating host nation Spain as the Irish topped their group.

A nippy right-winger who could slip past his man and supply his centre-forward, Bingham played in the semi-final of the FA Cup for Sunderland in 1955 and 1956, also scoring ten times in 35 league games in the first of those two campaigns as the Bank of England team also finished fourth in the top-flight.

Over eight seasons from 1950-51 to 1957-58, before his World Cup adventure, Billy was a stalwart at Sunderland.

The 1958 World Cup was held in Sweden, but it wasn't the first time the Swedes had witnessed how good a player Billy was. In May 1953, he had scored one of his best ever goals in a friendly for Sunderland in a 5-3 friendly win away to Malmo, the side who would contest the 1979 European Cup final against Brian Clough's Nottingham Forest.

In May 1957, Bingham was fined six months benefit qualifications as a punishment for being one of 14 players to have received illegal payments from the club. This was refunded to Bingham in 1962, due to what was deemed the illegality of the Football League's decision.

In 1963, he won a league title medal having scored the opening goal of the season for Everton, one of five he scored in 23 appearances. A leg break two seasons later caused his retirement after which Bingham embarked on an extensive managerial career. Beginning at Southport in the fourth division he then took charge of Plymouth Argyle with much of that time seeing him also manage Northern Ireland and his country's Under 23 team. He went on to manage Linfield, the national side of Greece, Everton, PAOK Salonika and Mansfield Town before returning to manage Northern Ireland again, this time from February 1980 to November 1993, a year in which he became non-executive director of Blackpool, a role he retained until 1997. He was awarded the MBE in 1983. His biography, simply entitled 'Billy' was published in 1986.

## **BIRCHAM,** Walter **Clive**

**POSITION:** Winger

**BIRTHPLACE:** Philadelphia, Co Durham

**DATE OF BIRTH:** 07/09/1939 - 06/06/2020

**HEIGHT:** 5' 6" **WEIGHT:** 10st 0lbs

**SIGNED FROM:** Shiney Row Swift, 21/09/1956 as a professional after being a part-time apprentice since August 1954.

**DEBUT:** v Lincoln City, A, 23/08/1958

**LAST MATCH:** v Middlesbrough, A, 10/10/1959

**MOVED TO:** Hartlepools United, 05/02/1960

**TEAMS:** Shiney Row Swift, Sunderland, Hartlepools United, Boston United, Boston FC, Skegness, South Shields

**SAFC TOTALS:** 28 appearances / 2 goals

**Clive set up Sunderland's first-ever goal outside of the top division on his debut as a teenager at Lincoln in August 1958. He then marked his home debut against Fulham with a goal.**

Like the famous Preston and England winger Tom Finney, Bircham was a plumber. This meant he was only a part-time player because he was serving his time in his trade where there was more money to be made than in football, during the age of the maximum wage. Consequently, manager Alan Brown eventually left Bircham out of the side after he had played in the opening 18 games of the season.

Clive later returned to the side to total 26 appearances that year, adding another goal in a home win over Bristol Rovers. There would be just two more games the following season, the last in a draw at Middlesbrough in October 1959.

Four months later, Clive was transferred to Hartlepools United for whom he went on to play 114 games, scoring 17 goals. He was good enough to play at a higher level, but in the days of national service, Bircham could avoid having to do time in the army due to his job as an essential worker as a plumber for the National Coal Board. Had he moved further afield, he would have had to give up that job and go into the forces.

Clive's sporting interests extended to being a successful racehorse owner and playing cricket for Philadelphia and Langley Park while he always continued to be a regular at Sunderland matches. He never regretted his decision to focus on his plumbing rather than finding leaks in opposition defences. Clive Bircham Heating Services became a very successful business in Sunderland.

Older brother Barney played for Sunderland during World War Two as well as representing Grimsby, Chesterfield, Colchester, Gateshead and Hull City.

## **BJORKLUND, Joachim** Thomas

**POSITION:** Centre-back

**BIRTHPLACE:** Vaxjo, Sweden

**DATE OF BIRTH:** 12/02/1971

**HEIGHT:** 6' 0" **WEIGHT:** 12st 6lbs

**SIGNED FROM:** Venezia, 28/01/2002

**DEBUT:** v Manchester United, A, 02/02/2002

**LAST MATCH:** v Crystal Palace, H, 17/05/2004

**MOVED TO:** Wolves, 05/08/2004 following release by SAFC, 31/05/2004

**TEAMS:** Osters, IFK Gothenburg, Vicenza, Rangers, Valencia, Venezia, Sunderland, Wolves

**INTERNATIONAL:** Sweden

**SAFC TOTALS:** 55+10 appearances / 0 goals

**Joachim Bjorklund had played in Italy, Spain and Scotland as well as his native Sweden before coming to Sunderland. He had 78 caps, all won before coming to Wearside. He had won the Copa Del Rey, Spanish Supercup and Intertoto Cup with Valencia who he also reached two UEFA Cup finals with.**

He also had three Swedish Allsvenskan titles to his name in successive seasons with Gothenburg as well as having won the SPL and Scottish League Cup with Rangers. He duly demonstrated the class and composure to be expected from a player of his pedigree in his three seasons at Sunderland although he was in a team that struggled despite his contribution.

Joachim's father Karl-Gunnar was a Sweden international who went on to have an extensive managerial and coaching career in Scandinavia while his son Kalle (who was born in Valencia during Joachim's time there) won caps for Sweden at youth level and played for Stockholm-based Hammerby where Joachim became assistant manager in 2018. Joachim is also the nephew of Tommy Svensson who managed Sweden from 1991 to 1997. During this time, Joachim was part of the Sweden squad that reached the semi-final of the FIFA World Cup, playing in a narrow defeat to Brazil at the Los Angeles Rose Bowl.

## **BLACK, Alan** Douglas

**POSITION:** Full-back

**BIRTHPLACE:** Tradeston, Glasgow

**DATE OF BIRTH:** 04/06/1943

**HEIGHT:** 6' 0" **WEIGHT:** 12st 0lbs

**SIGNED FROM:** Dumbarton, 14/09/1964

**DEBUT:** v Manchester United, H, 24/02/1965

**LAST MATCH:** v Liverpool, A, 12/02/1966

**MOVED TO:** Norwich City, 06/09/1966

**TEAMS:** Drumchapel Amateurs, Dumbarton, Sunderland, Norwich City, Dumbarton

**SAFC TOTALS:** 4+2 appearances / 0 goals

**Like Geoff Butler, Alan Black was a sixties full-back who barely played at Sunderland before becoming successful with Norwich. Thrown into the deep-end on his Sunderland debut in front of over 51,000 at Roker Park, he helped achieve a clean sheet as a Manchester United team including George Best, Bobby Charlton and Denis Law were beaten 1-0.**

Three days later, he kept his place in a 1-0 defeat at Fulham before the evergreen Len Ashurst returned to fitness after which he waited until December for a further opportunity. Finally just under a year after his debut, his final assignment was no easier, coming off the bench after an hour against champions-elect Liverpool at Anfield where two goals in the five minutes after he came on included Roger Hunt (who would play in that year's FIFA World Cup final) completing his hat-trick.

As Hunt won the World Cup, Black moved to Norwich where he stayed until 1974 when he returned to Dumbarton who he had left to join Sunderland. At Carrow Road, Black played over 200 times including 20 as the Canaries won the second division title in 1971-72 when he shared duties in the number three shirt with Sunderland old boy Butler. Prior to coming to Sunderland, where he signed after three weeks of a month-long trial, he had turned down the offer of a move to top-flight Blackpool in order to finish an apprenticeship in engineering. Later inducted into the Norwich Hall of Fame, in 2011 he was still working as a taxi driver in West Dunbartonshire.

## BLACK, Christopher David (Chris)

**POSITION:** Midfielder

**BIRTHPLACE:** Cramlington, Northumberland

**DATE OF BIRTH:** 07/09/1982

**HEIGHT:** 6' 0" **WEIGHT:** 12st 0lbs

**SIGNED FROM:** Trainee, 01/07/1999

**DEBUT:** v Aston Villa, A, 03/05/2003

**LAST MATCH:** v Crewe Alexandra, A, 22/11/2003

**MOVED TO:** Doncaster Rovers, 25/03/2004

**TEAMS:** Sunderland, Doncaster Rovers, Bedlington Terriers

**SAFC TOTALS:** 2+1 appearances / 0 goals

**The mysterious case of Chris Black saw the homegrown player given his chance by Mick McCarthy in the final two games of the dismal relegation season of 2002-03. Without pulling up any trees, Black showed youthful energy and willingness.**

The following season he made a single autumn substitute appearance before joining Doncaster on a free transfer where after a debut at Oxford a couple of days after signing, he disappeared apparently to sort out personal problems. Before signing permanently for Sunderland, he played regularly for the club at Under 17 level whilst still at school. In 2006-07 he briefly re-surfaced in the Northern League with Bedlington Terriers.

## BLACK, John Ross

**POSITION:** Inside-forward

**BIRTHPLACE:** Denny, Stirlingshire

**DATE OF BIRTH:** 26/05/1900 - 14/12/1993

**HEIGHT:** 5' 8" **WEIGHT:** 11st 0lbs

**SIGNED FROM:** Denny Hibernian, 25/04/1921

**DEBUT:** v Birmingham, A, 01/10/1921

**LAST MATCH:** v Arsenal, H, 08/10/1921

**MOVED TO:** Nelson, 23/08/1922

**TEAMS:** Gordon Highlanders, Denny Hibs, Sunderland, Nelson, Accrington Stanley, Chesterfield, Luton Town, Bristol Rovers

**INTERNATIONAL:** Scotland Junior

**SAFC TOTALS:** 2 appearances / 0 goals

**John Black had been an amateur before coming to Sunderland in April 1921, subsequently becoming a professional on the penultimate day of August. He had the toughest of tasks on his debut, being asked to stand in for Charlie Buchan. Buchan was back for Black's second game when Buchan's early goal proved the winner, but Black didn't do enough to warrant another appearance.**

He went on to enjoy a good career nonetheless, playing for Nelson in the Third Division North, debuting against Southport in September 1922 and scoring his first goal to defeat Tranmere the following month. He ended the campaign with five goals in 23 games as Nelson won their league. Having dropped out of Nelson's second division side in September, Black returned to Third Division North the following February when joining Accrington Stanley for whom he scored five goals in 14 league games before being transferred to Chesterfield for £25 in the close-season of 1925.

After playing 19 times in his first season, a broken leg at the start of 1925-26 resulted in him only managing two more games for the club, but he did much better at his next team Luton where he played almost 100 times prior to making one short of half a century for his final club Bristol Rovers, before he retired in 1932. His brother Adam is Leicester's record appearance maker having played 528 league games for the Foxes, 39 of them in the second division title-winning season of 1924-25. A full-back, he was ever-present in a quarter of his 16 seasons at Leicester.

## BOE, James

**POSITION:** Goalkeeper

**BIRTHPLACE:** Gateshead, Co Durham

**DATE OF BIRTH:** 05/01/1891 - 1973

**HEIGHT:** 6' 0" **WEIGHT:** 11st 7lbs

**SIGNED FROM:** Rodsley FC, 01/05/1914

**DEBUT:** v Everton, A, 21/11/1914

**LAST MATCH:** v Everton, A, 21/11/1914

**MOVED TO:** Contract not renewed, 30/04/1915

**TEAMS:** Rodsley, Sunderland, Southport Central

**SAFC TOTALS:** 1 appearance / 0 goals

**Goalkeeper James Boe conceded seven goals on his only first-team appearance. He was not held culpable by the press, but nonetheless he never got another game - although oddly in Sunderland's very next match he was called upon as a linesman.**

On a frosty pitch, Everton's finishing was clinical. The Toffees were 5-0 up by the 32nd minute with Bobby Parker completing his hat-trick in the second half. Sunderland started the second half with nine players although Charlie Buchan and George Phillip did manage to return, Buchan bagging Sunderland's consolation. There was no consolation for Boe who had started on Sunderland's books as an amateur after joining from a Gateshead amateur side. During World War One he served with the army and after retiring from football became a slinger in a foundry.

## BOLDER, Robert John (Bob)

**POSITION:** Goalkeeper

**BIRTHPLACE:** Dover, Kent

**DATE OF BIRTH:** 02/10/1958

**HEIGHT:** 6' 1" **WEIGHT:** 14st 8lb

**SIGNED FROM:** Liverpool, 16/10/1985 after loan starting on 21/9/1985

**DEBUT:** v Shrewsbury Town, A, 21/09/1985

**LAST MATCH:** v Carlisle United, H, 08/02/1986

**MOVED TO:** Charlton Athletic, 11/08/1986

**TEAMS:** Dover Town, Sheffield Wednesday, Liverpool, Sunderland, Luton Town (L), Charlton Athletic, Dagenham & Redbridge

**SAFC TOTALS:** 29 appearances / 0 goals

**Initially signed on loan from Liverpool on the same day Alan Kennedy left Anfield for Roker, Bolder had cost the Merseysiders £125,000 in 1983 after making his name with over 200 games for Sheffield Wednesday.**

Unable to dislodge Bruce Grobbelaar from the number one shirt at Liverpool, he was on the bench for Liverpool 21 times, but never got a game. One of those times as a named sub saw him win a European Cup winner's medal in 1984 on the occasion Grobbelaar demonstrated his famous 'wobbly legs' in a penalty shoot-out against Roma.

In contrast, his 29 games at Sunderland were all consecutive appearances before he went on loan to Luton with goalkeeper Andy Dibble coming on loan in the opposite direction. Bolder had made his name with 196 league games for Sheffield Wednesday for whom he was signed by Len Ashurst. After leaving Sunderland, Bolder went on to play almost 300 times for Charlton.

## BOLLANDS, John Frederick (Johnny)

**POSITION:** Goalkeeper

**BIRTHPLACE:** Middlesbrough, Yorkshire

**DATE OF BIRTH:** 11/07/1935

**HEIGHT:** 5' 10" **WEIGHT:** 11st 2lbs

**SIGNED FROM:** Oldham Athletic, 16/03/1956

**DEBUT:** v Birmingham City, H, 18/04/1956

**LAST MATCH:** v Ipswich Town, A, 19/09/1959

**MOVED TO:** Bolton Wanderers, 25/02/1960

**TEAMS:** South Bank, Oldham Athletic, Sunderland, Bolton Wanderers, Oldham Athletic

**INTERNATIONAL:** England Under 23

**SAFC TOTALS:** 63 appearances / 0 goals

**Johnny Bollands was a spectacular goalkeeper who inspired the young Jim Montgomery. Indeed, on the night the Montgomery Suite was named at the Stadium of Light Bollands was invited along as a special guest.**

Bollands played for Sunderland in five seasons being number one in 1956-57 when he made 40 appearances in total, the only season in which he reached double figures. Starting and ending his senior career with Oldham Athletic, he was given his league debut with the Latics by future Sunderland manager George Hardwick. After retiring from the game, Johnny took over his father's job at Teesport Docks and also worked as a long distance lorry driver.

## BOLTON, Arthur Frederick

**POSITION:** Centre-forward

**BIRTHPLACE:** Hexham, Northumberland

**DATE OF BIRTH:** 21/11/1912 - 22/04/2001

**HEIGHT:** 5' 10" **WEIGHT:** 11st 10lbs

**SIGNED FROM:** Ashington, 21/11/1938

**DEBUT:** v Charlton Athletic, A, 26/11/1938

**LAST MATCH:** v Huddersfield Town, H, 29/04/1939

**MOVED TO:** Ashington, 30/08/1946

**TEAMS:** North Shields, Ashington, Sunderland, Stockton (WW2 Guest), Ashington

**SAFC TOTALS:** 8 appearances / 1 goal

**Five days after signing from North Eastern League football, Bolton was thrust into top-flight action in place of Bobby Gurney at Charlton. It was the first of six successive games in which his big moment came when his third-minute left-footer opened the scoring against Liverpool.**

Unfortunately, that ended up being in a 3-2 defeat. Late in the season he was brought back for the return at Anfield and made his final appearance the following week.

Bolton had actually been on Sunderland's books briefly as an amateur around 1935 without making an appearance at first-team or reserve level. Before signing as a professional, he worked as a salesman for a gas company in Whitley Bay. After 'Guesting' for Stockton in 1939-40, he served in the RAF during World War Two.

## BOLTON, Joseph (Joe)

**POSITION:** Left-back

**BIRTHPLACE:** Birtley, Co Durham

**DATE OF BIRTH:** 02/02/1955

**HEIGHT:** 5' 11½" **WEIGHT:** 11st 12lbs

**SIGNED FROM:** School, 01/06/1970
Professional from 02/02/1972

**DEBUT:** v Watford, H, 17/04/1972

**LAST MATCH:** v Liverpool, A, 02/05/1981

**MOVED TO:** Middlesbrough, 14/07/1981

**TEAMS:** Sunderland, Middlesbrough, Sheffield United Matlock Town

**SAFC TOTALS:** 315+10 appearances / 12 goals

**Joe Bolton became a real cult hero and in an exceptionally rare interview contributed to my Sunderland Cult Heroes book published in 2008.**
**Joe came into the team as a 17-year-old with manager Alan Brown - a man renowned for giving young players a chance - keeping him in the team for the last four games of the season.**

Bolton began the following cup-winning season in the team playing the opening two league games and then coming back for what would be Brown's final two matches in the autumn. By the end of the season, the youngster had played 14 times and scored his first goal in his first match under Bob Stokoe. However, having played in the FA Cup third round and replay with Notts County he had seen experienced new signing Ron Guthrie come in to take over the left-back slot.

While his role in the cup final was to look after Bobby Kerr's and Billy Hughes' teeth, it wasn't long before Bolton was getting his own teeth into any wingers with the misfortune to be up against him. In the days of just a single sub, he came off the bench in the opening game of the 1973-74 campaign and played 37 times in all competitions, all but four of those as starts. Two of his appearances came in the European Cup Winners' Cup against Sporting Lisbon.

After continuing to contest the number three shirt with Guthrie in 1974-75, Joe established himself as first choice in the second division title-winning season of 1975-76 and was ever-present in the top flight the following season. Joe was involved in two promotion-winning seasons as he played in just over half the games in 1979-80 which proved to be his penultimate one at the club.

Following the appointment of Alan Durban as manager in the summer of 1981, the new boss wanted Joe to have a 'trial period' of 12 games before offering him a new contract. Having played every game of the previous season bar three missed due to suspension, and having topped over 300 games for the club, Joe rejected the need for a trial and left. With Middlesbrough and Newcastle keen to sign him, he plumped for Boro ahead of the Magpies, purely because the Teessiders were in the top division and Newcastle were not.

He went on to play 59 league games for Boro before over 100 for Sheffield United, signing for Ian Porterfield and linking up with Roker old boys Kevin Arnott and Micky Henderson.

Long-established as one of the game's hardest men, Bolton was offered the chance to continue his career by another legendary tough-nut, Norman Hunter, who was managing the Blades' near-neighbours Rotherham, but a knee injury meant that Joe's playing days were over at the age of 31. He did play four games as player-manager of Matlock Town before becoming a long-distance lorry driver. One of the most down to earth players Sunderland have ever had, the chant 'Joe, Joe, Joe Bolton!' still makes the supporters who saw Joe wince at the thought of being tackled by him.

## BOLTON, Lyall (Laurie)

**POSITION:** Wing-half

**BIRTHPLACE:** Gateshead, Co Durham

**DATE OF BIRTH:** 11/06/1932 - 08/08/2018

**HEIGHT:** 6' 1" **WEIGHT:** 12st 3lbs

**SIGNED FROM:** Reyrolles Juniors, 11/08/1950

**DEBUT:** v Preston North End, H, 21/03/1956

**LAST MATCH:** v Portsmouth, H, 27/10/1956

**MOVED TO:** Chelmsford City, July 1957

**TEAMS:** Newcastle United, Reyrolles, Sunderland, Chelmsford City

**SAFC TOTALS:** 3 appearances / 0 goals

**In addition to his three league appearances, Bolton also got games in some prestige friendlies, such as one at Norwich to inaugurate Carrow Road's floodlights.**

Bolton had been on the books for almost six years when, at the age of 23, he made his debut four days after the Lads had lost in the FA Cup semi-final for the second consecutive year. It came in a 2-2 home draw with Preston that dropped Bill Murray's team from fifth to seventh in the top flight. Coming in for Stan Anderson, Bolton lined up against the great Tom Finney and alongside the likes of Len Shackleton, Billy Elliott and Charlie 'Cannonball' Fleming, the latter scoring in all three of the games 'Laurie' appeared in.

Bolton did well enough to get another game a fortnight later at Manchester City, this time as left-half rather than right-half in a 4-2 defeat. Seven months later, he was called upon for a final time in a 3-3 draw at home to Portsmouth before moving on to Chelmsford City in July 1957. His early connection with Newcastle United was as a junior player.

# B

## BONE, John

**POSITION:** Centre-half
**BIRTHPLACE:** Wingate, Co Durham
**DATE OF BIRTH:** 19/12/1930 - 08/05/2002
**HEIGHT:** 6' 1" **WEIGHT:** 11st 10lbs
**SIGNED FROM:** Wingate Colliery Welfare, 12/05/1951
**DEBUT:** v Leicester City, A, 13/11/1954
**LAST MATCH:** v Sheffield Wednesday, A, 06/10/1956
**MOVED TO:** Cambridge City, 03/07/1958
**TEAMS:** Hartlepools United, Wingate Colliery Welfare, Sunderland, Cambridge City, King's Lynn
**SAFC TOTALS:** 11 appearances / 0 goals

**Bone started out at Hartlepools United as an amateur before playing for Wingate Colliery Welfare. Having caught the eye in local football, John came to Sunderland and played across three seasons from 1954-55 to '56-57 playing twice in each of his first and last campaigns and seven in the middle one, all in the league.**

His best run came in the spring of 1956 when he played in the home games against Spurs and Manchester United either side of defeats at Manchester City and Charlton.

At Cambridge City, Bone's most notable game was a 1959 friendly to inaugurate Cambridge's floodlights when he played against a West Ham team that included a young Bobby Moore.

## BONTHRON, Robert Pollock (Bob)

**POSITION:** Right-back
**BIRTHPLACE:** Burntisland, Fife
**DATE OF BIRTH:** 14/07/1880 - 19/02/1947
**HEIGHT:** 5' 9½" **WEIGHT:** 12st 4lbs
**SIGNED FROM:** Manchester United, 02/05/1907
**DEBUT:** v Manchester City, H, 02/09/1907
**LAST MATCH:** v Preston North End, 18/01/1908
**MOVED TO:** Northampton Town, 06/05/1908
**TEAMS:** Raith Athletic, Raith Rovers, Dundee, Manchester United, Sunderland, Northampton Town, Birmingham, Leith Athletic
**SAFC TOTALS:** 23 appearances / 1 goal

**Bonthron came into English football when leaving Dundee for Manchester United in May 1903, debuting against Bristol City in a second division match the following September.**

He made 134 appearances for United scoring three goals, one of them a penalty against Leicester in April 1904. A promotion winner with United in 1905-06, during that season a group of Bradford City supporters were prosecuted after attacking him following his role in a home defeat for the Bantams. Having been promoted, Bonthron played for United against Sunderland at Roker Park in October 1906 and although Sunderland won that match 4-1, he must have made a positive impression as Sunderland signed him at the end of that season.

Making his debut on the opening day of 1907-08 against his former local rivals Manchester City, Bonthron scored the winner in his next match against Notts County and kept his place at right-back until Christmas Day, playing his final match for the club the following month. He went on to add to his success with Manchester United by helping Northampton to win the Southern League in 1909 and after his football days were over became a coal trimmer back in his home town of Burntisland on the Firth of Forth.

## BORINI, Fabio

**POSITION:** Forward
**BIRTHPLACE:** Bentivoglio, Italy
**DATE OF BIRTH:** 29/03/1991
**HEIGHT:** 5' 11' **WEIGHT:** 11st 8lbs
**SIGNED FROM:** Liverpool, 02/09/2013, on loan
Re-signed, 31/08/2015
**DEBUT:** v Arsenal, H, 14/09/2013
**LAST MATCH:** v Chelsea, A, 21/05/2017
**MOVED TO:** Liverpool, 12/05/2014, end of loan
and AC Milan, 30/06/2017, on loan
followed by 'permanent' move, 30/06/2018
**TEAMS:** Bologna, Chelsea, Swansea City (L), Liverpool, Sunderland (L), Liverpool, Sunderland, AC Milan, Hellas Verona, Fatih Karagumruk (to 2021)
**INTERNATIONAL:** Italy
**SAFC TOTALS:** 73+20 appearances / 17 goals

**Borini's well-taken Wembley goal put Sunderland ahead in the 2014 League (Capital One) Cup final again at Manchester City. The Italian had a penchant for important goals, many of them spectacular. Highlights included a screamer against Newcastle at the Stadium of Light in October 2013 and a coolly taken penalty to open the scoring as another victory was achieved in the return at St James'. All of his goals came with the player's customary goal celebration of one hand knife-like in his mouth as the other arm was raised.**

Fabio originally came to Sunderland on loan in 2013-14 making a total of 40 appearances in all competitions, including games as sub, scoring ten times, a record that saw him crowned 'Young Player of the Year'. After being back at Liverpool for a season, Sporting Director Lee Congerton (who had worked with him at Chelsea) secured his signature in 2015, although Head Coach Dick Advocaat was not initially over-enamoured with his acquisition. Borini actually scored more goals during his year's loan than he did after signing for the club. He netted seven over two seasons and 53 total appearances after being bought, with his third season spent out on loan.

Borini believed he should always be at a top club challenging for honours and didn't really relish throwing in his lot with a team who might struggle. Indeed, he was reported to have rejected a £14m bid from Sunderland immediately after his season on loan. When he did return a year later it was for an undisclosed fee, but believed to be some £4 to £6m lower than the earlier offer. Nonetheless, Fabio still had his fabulous moments and remained a popular player, terrific goals at home to Crystal Palace and Chelsea being amongst his high points.

Having returned to Italy with Milan, he scored his first goal in a Europa League qualifying game, but waited eight months for a goal in Serie A, finally netting in a win at Spal in February 2018. Converted from a forward to often being used as a wing -back with Milan, he would only score four Serie A goals in 51 appearances (21 of these as sub). One of these came against Hellas Verona who he moved to in January 2020 and scored a debut Serie A goal back at his first club Bologna. The following month he cancelled out a Cristiano Ronaldo goal as Verona came from behind to beat Juventus, but there would be just one more goal for the club in the year he spent with them before a January 2021 move to Fatih Karagumruk in Turkey.

At the other end of his career, Borini was only 18 when Carlo Ancelotti gave him a debut for Chelsea. The following season the goals flowed during a loan spell at Swansea under Brendan Rodgers who he had worked with at Chelsea and who later signed him for Liverpool. Following his Swansea loan however, it was initially back to Italy where after a controversial issue surrounding the apparent signing of a pre-contract with Parma, he moved to Roma.

Nine goals in his year (24 games) in the Italian capital included one in the Rome derby against Lazio and two in a win over Inter, as well as inevitably the only goal of a meeting with Parma. That was enough to persuade Rodgers to invest over £10m in Fabio as his first signing having taken over at Anfield. Although he scored on his home debut in a Europa League win over Belarus outfit Gomel, as would later happen at Milan, he would wait eight months for a league goal. It was worth the wait however as when the goal finally arrived it did so in a 6-0 win at Newcastle - on a day when Jordan Henderson scored twice.

Captain of Italy at the 2010 UEFA European Under 19 championship, Borini won one full cap in a 2012 friendly with the USA. Other than arguably his season with Roma and his brief loan with Swansea, Borini's best times came with Sunderland. He didn't really cut it at Anfield or the San Siro and if he'd been prepared to devote himself to Sunderland, he could have developed into a major figure. As it was, up to 2022 he remains the only player to score for Sunderland in a major (excluding the Football League Trophy for lower league clubs) cup final for Sunderland since Ian Porterfield.

## **BOULD,** Stephen Andrew **(Steve)**

**POSITION:** Centre-half

**BIRTHPLACE:** Stoke, Staffordshire

**DATE OF BIRTH:** 16/11/1962

**HEIGHT:** 6' 4" **WEIGHT:** 14st 2lbs

**SIGNED FROM:** Arsenal, 03/07/1999

**DEBUT:** v Chelsea, A, 07/08/1999

**LAST MATCH:** v Manchester City, A, 23/08/2000

**MOVED TO:** Retired due to injury, 26/09/2000

**TEAMS:** Stoke City, Torquay United (L), Arsenal, Sunderland

**INTERNATIONAL:** England B

**SAFC TOTALS:** 21+2 appearances / 0 goals

**Steve Bould only played for Sunderland briefly, but succeeded in making a major impact. Brought in by Peter Reid to add experience and know-how to the defence, the veteran met the highest expectations, being composed, commanding and instilling those qualities into his teammates.**

Captaining the side, Bould played regularly until January in his first season, helping newly-promoted Sunderland to fifth in the FA Carling Premiership when he dropped out of the side through injury.

Unfortunately, Bould only managed one more game that term, as a sub a couple of months later. The following season saw Steve play only once - in the second game of the season at Manchester City - before injury forced his retirement. It was to be his final game and his 500th league game with exactly 400 of them being in the top flight.

A veteran at Sunderland, Bould had been a stalwart of 375 games with Arsenal with whom he won two league titles before the creation of the Premiership and one after it came into being. In 1994, he also won the European Cup Winners' Cup, helping the Gunners to their classic 1-0 scoreline in the final when he was part of their famed back four alongside Tony Adams with Lee Dixon and Nigel Winterburn at full-back.

## **BOWYER, Ian**

**POSITION:** Midfielder

**BIRTHPLACE:** Ellesmere Port, Cheshire

**DATE OF BIRTH:** 16/11/1962

**HEIGHT:** 5' 11" **WEIGHT:** 11st 3lbs

**SIGNED FROM:** Nottingham Forest, 13/01/1981

**DEBUT:** v Manchester United, H, 28/01/1981

**LAST MATCH:** v Brighton & HA, A, 05/12/1981

**MOVED TO:** Nottingham Forest, 07/01/1982

**TEAMS:** Manchester City, Leyton Orient, Nottingham Forest, Sunderland, Nottingham Forest, Hereford United

**INTERNATIONAL:** England B

**SAFC TOTALS:** 16 appearances / 1 goal

**Ian Bowyer had a silverware-laden career, but had a disastrous time at Sunderland where the club off-loaded him for under a fifth of what they had paid under a year earlier.**

A European Cup Winners' Cup winner with Manchester City in 1970 and two-time European Cup winner with Nottingham Forest in 1979 and 1980, he also won the league title with Forest in 1978, the League Cup with them in 1978 and was an unused sub as they retained the trophy a year later. In 1980, he also played as Forest beat Barcelona in the European Super Cup.

After beginning with Manchester City, Bowyer spent a couple of years with Orient, making his last league appearance for the club against Sunderland five days before the 1973 FA Cup final. In each of his two spells with Forest, either side of his spell at Sunderland, Bowyer made over 200 league appearances as a model of midfield consistency and took Brian Clough's team to their first European Cup final by scoring the winner in the semi-final second leg away to FC Koln.

Brought to Sunderland by Ken Knighton for a reported £250,000, Bowyer played seven games before being injured. He came back a couple of games later, but missed the end of the season under caretaker manager Mick Docherty. He returned to the team 15 games into the new season, again against Manchester United who he had debuted against, this time being part of a 5-1 home defeat. After just seven games of his second season Bowyer bowed out, becoming one of a long list of players who did well elsewhere, but not at Sunderland and was sold back to Forest for £45,000.

He went on to manage Hereford United between 1987 and 1990, winning the Welsh Cup in 1990. He later coached at Cheltenham, became assistant to his old Forest teammate Peter Shilton at Plymouth and went on to be assistant manager at Rotherham, coach at Birmingham, Manchester City, Forest and then be assistant boss at MK Dons and Rushden & Diamonds.

Ian gave his son Gary a league debut at Hereford and also worked with him at Forest and Rotherham before Gary became a manager in his own right, managing Blackburn, Blackpool, Bradford City, Salford City and Dundee to June 2022.

## **BOYLE, Peter**

**POSITION:** Left-back

**BIRTHPLACE:** Carlingford, County Louth

**DATE OF BIRTH:** 26/04/1876 - 24/06/1939

**SIGNED FROM:** Albion Rovers, 05/11/1896

**DEBUT:** v Blackburn Rovers, H, 19/12/1896

**LAST MATCH:** v Bury, H, 29/10/1898

**MOVED TO:** Sheffield United, 01/12/1898

**TEAMS:** Coatbridge, Albion Rovers, Sunderland, Sheffield United, Motherwell, Clapton Orient, Wigan Town, Chorley, Eccles Borough, York City

**INTERNATIONAL:** Ireland

**SAFC TOTALS:** 33 appearances / 0 goals

**Peter Boyle was an Irish international who played in three FA Cup finals, winning two of them. He came to Sunderland way back in 1896 and played in the era as Sunderland survived the relegation Test Matches in the last hurrah of the famed, but aging, 'Team of All The Talents' in 1897.**

The following year, Boyle played in 23 of Sunderland's 30 league games as they finished runners-up to Sheffield United, the team where he would go on to enjoy enormous success. This would be the final season at the Newcastle Road ground. He would go on to make one further appearance, appearing in the fifth league game at Roker Park on the day of the ground's first hat-trick, as Hugh Wilson scored all three in a 3-0 win over Bury on 29 October 1898.

The following December, a £175 fee - a considerable sum in those days, especially for a full-back - took Peter to Sheffield United for whom he made his debut against Sunderland. Things were looking good for the Blades at the time. A 2-0 victory over the Wearsiders maintained their unbeaten home record and lifted them to fourth in the table. As the season progressed, the side fell away in the league as they focussed on the cup. Boyle missed just one game to the end of the season, coming back to Roker Park on the last day of the campaign, losing 1-0 as United escaped relegation by one place.

As Peter returned to Roker, he may have brought his FA Cup winner's medal with him to show his old teammates. A fortnight earlier, Boyle had played in the final as Sheffield United thrashed Derby at Crystal Palace. Peter had played in all ten games as the Blades took the trophy. Four of those, including one that was abandoned at half-time due to crowd trouble, was in an epic semi-final against Liverpool who were managed by former Sunderland boss Tom Watson.

Boyle's first full season at Bramall Lane saw him miss just six games as the Blades finished as runners-up to Aston Villa in the league, notably scoring the first senior goal of his career in a home win against Wolves in October. He was a runner-up in the cup the following term (1900-01) playing in the final and the final replay as Southern League Tottenham Hotspur took the trophy.

Sheffield United's halcyon period in the FA Cup (or English Cup as it was known) continued the following season when Boyle won another winner's medal. He played in all nine games including the final and another final replay as this time, Southampton were beaten in the final. The initial drawn final saw Alf Common score United's goal. He was with Sheffield United between two spells with Sunderland prior to becoming the world's first £1,000 player when he was transferred to Middlesbrough. While Boyle was winning the cup with Sheffield United, Sunderland were winning the league.

Boyle had another two seasons as a regular at Bramall Lane, once (at Bury in January 1903) even taking over in goal when the famed 20-stone goalkeeper Bill 'Fatty' Foulke was injured.

Leaving Sheffield in May 1904 following a dispute over a Benefit Match, he joined Motherwell for a season before having two years with Clapton Orient. He then moved to Wigan Town in August 1907 by which time he was 30. He had only four months with Wigan before joining Chorley for just one month before finally signing for Eccles Borough.

Boyle began his playing days in junior football in the Coatbridge area of Glasgow and had played for Gaelic Club in his native Ireland before joining Albion Rovers who he left to join SAFC.

## BOYLE, Peter (Continued)

During his time with Sheffield United, Boyle was capped five times by Ireland including a meeting with England in Belfast in March 1902 when he was up against Sunderland's Billy Hogg. Almost exactly two years later in the same city his Blades teammate Alf Common scored twice on Boyle's third appearance against England, all of which were lost.

From July to December 1912, Peter Boyle re-surfaced as player/manager of York City in the Midland League. His influence at Sheffield United carried on to the 1925 FA Cup final when his son Tommy played for Sheffield United alongside Ernest Milton, brother of Sunderland's 1913 title winner Albert Milton who was killed in action during World War One. Tommy Boyle also played for Manchester United, Macclesfield Town, Northampton Town and Scarborough where he finished as player/manager in 1936. Around 1930, Peter Boyle was working at a pit at Brodsworth, near Doncaster.

## BRACEWELL, Paul William

**POSITION:** Midfield

**BIRTHPLACE:** Heswall, Merseyside

**DATE OF BIRTH:** 16/11/1962

**HEIGHT:** 5' 8" **WEIGHT:** 10st 9 lbs

**SIGNED FROM:** Stoke City, 29/06/1983, Everton, 29/09/1989 and Newcastle United, 23/05/1995

**DEBUT:** v Norwich City, A, 27/08/1983

**LAST MATCH:** v Bury, A, 23/09/1997

**MOVED TO:** Everton, 15/05/1984, Newcastle United, 12/06/1992 and Fulham, 09/10/1997

**TEAMS:** Stoke City, Sunderland, Everton, Sunderland, Newcastle United, Sunderland, Fulham

**INTERNATIONAL:** England

**SAFC TOTALS:** 268+2 appearances / 6 goals

**1992 FA Cup final skipper, Paul Bracewell had four spells at Sunderland (as of 2022). At the club three times as a player, the last also as assistant manager alongside his old Everton midfield teammate Peter Reid, 'Brace' became Development coach in 2013. He went on to coach the first-team under Dick Advocaat prior to becoming assistant manager for the second time on 22 October 2015 under Sam Allardyce. He retained the role until 17 June 2017 having had a couple of days in July 2016 when alongside Robbie Stockdale he served as joint caretaker manager for a friendly with Rotherham.**

Bracewell was first brought to Wearside by Alan Durban who had nurtured him at Stoke City. As neat and tidy a player as any team could want, Brace's talent was knitting play together many years before possession football became the name of the game for many. Bracewell was a master of keeping the ball and keeping it moving. His passes were mainly simple, invariably measured and perfectly weighted while his reading of the game would always ensure he was available to receive the ball.

Paul's first season at Sunderland saw him miss only four games, but following the sacking of his mentor Durban, he was especially keen to move on, and joined Everton. In his first season at Goodison, Bracewell was a key member of the team as the Toffees won the league title (playing 37 of the 42 games) and European Cup Winners' Cup, (8 out of 9 games including the final). He also played in all seven games as his club reached the FA Cup final. He played in the Wembley defeat. It was one of four FA Cup finals Brace played in, but he never managed a winner's medal.

Also a losing finalist with Everton in 1986 and 89, in 1992, he captained Sunderland as they lost 2-0 to Liverpool in the last match of his second spell at the club.

In total, Paul made 140+3 appearances for Everton. It was a tally that would have been far higher, but for an ankle injury sustained in a challenge with future Sunderland striker Billy Whitehurst at Newcastle on New Year's Day 1986. In 1985, Bracewell had won what proved to be his only three full England caps. In April 1986, England manager Bobby Robson named Brace as one of his six standby players for that summer's FIFA World Cup and there can be little doubt that. but for his injury, Paul would have played at that tournament.

On 23 August 1989, he returned to Sunderland on loan, making that transfer 'permanent' on 28 September, signing for his old Stoke City skipper Denis Smith. Although not quite as mobile as in his first spell, Brace had lost none of his quality and was able to play regularly until, after captaining Sunderland at Wembley, he reportedly turned down a one-year contract, to join the Kevin Keegan revolution at Newcastle who offered him a longer deal.

Rarely a scorer at Sunderland, he struck with a fierce volley against Southend United five minutes into his debut as he kick-started Keegan's campaign that led to Newcastle winning the second-tier title. It was one of three goals he scored in 73 league games for the Magpies before the arrival of his old Everton midfield partner Peter Reid as manager at Roker Park saw Brace bounce back. Returning on 23 May 1995 as player/assistant manager, Paul was the metronome in the centre of Reid's team as he missed just eight of the 46 games in helping steer Sunderland to promotion as champions.

After being the only ever-present in Sunderland's first-ever Premiership season, early the following term he re-joined Keegan who by now was manager of Fulham. Brace moved to Craven Cottage as player/assistant manager having reportedly turned down the manager's position at his first club Stoke. He retired as a player in 1999 after 62 league appearances for the Cottagers and went on to manage Fulham from May 1999 until March 2000. In October of that year, he accepted the manager's job at Halifax where he stayed until the following August. In 2003, Paul began coaching at Walsall, having a spell as the Saddlers caretaker manager in February 2004.

He went on to work for the FA coaching 16 to 20-year-olds and also set up his own Complete Football Academy in Gosforth in 2007. A player of high quality, 228 of his 587 league appearances were made with Sunderland, far more than he made for any other club. Having captained Sunderland in an FA Cup final and served the club extensively after his playing days were over, Paul Bracewell has to go down as an important figure in Sunderland's post-war history.

## BRADSHAW, Thomas Dickinson (Tom)

**POSITION:** Winger

**BIRTHPLACE:** Stalmine, Lancs

**DATE OF BIRTH:** 15/03/1876 - 04/10/1953

**HEIGHT:** 5' 9" **WEIGHT:** 11st 6lbs

**SIGNED FROM:** Blackpool, 18/05/1897

**DEBUT:** v (Sheffield) Wednesday, A, 04/09/1897

**LAST MATCH:** v Blackburn Rovers, A, 25/12/1897

**MOVED TO:** Nottingham Forest, 18/01/1898

**TEAMS:** Lostock Hall, Preston North End, Blackpool, Sunderland, Nottingham Forest, Leicester Fosse, New Brighton Tower, Reading, Swindon Town, Preston North End, Southport Central, Earlstown, Accrington Stanley, Wellingborough, Leicester Fosse, Rossendale United, Glossop NE

**SAFC TOTALS:** 14 appearances / 2 goals

**One of five debutants on the opening day of the last season at the Newcastle Road Ground, Bradshaw's lifetime ranged from being assistant cricket coach at the famous Harrow School around 1907, being convicted for wife-beating in 1908 and in 1913, assisting former England international Edgar Chadwick as coach of the national football team of the Netherlands, for a 4-2 defeat to Belgium on the day after Sunderland's first English (FA) Cup final appearance.**

Before coming to Sunderland, Bradshaw had been on the books of Preston North End, but debuted for Blackpool in their opening season of league football against Newton Heath (who became Manchester United), going on to score against Newcastle United later in the term.

Debuting for Sunderland on the opening day of 1897-98, he played in 14 of the first 15 games, making his final appearance on Christmas Day in a season where Sunderland became runners-up. Later that season, he was reserve for Forest in the English (FA) Cup final against Derby who he had scored against earlier in the season on Wearside - kept out of the cup final side by former Newcastle East End and West End player Tom McInnes.

In addition to a much travelled football career, Bradshaw also became a professional cricketer for Preston Cricket Club and after retiring worked as a salesman.

## **BRADY,** Alexander **(Alec)**

**POSITION:** Inside-forward

**BIRTHPLACE:** Cathcart, Glasgow

**DATE OF BIRTH:** 09/02/1870 - 19/10/1913

**HEIGHT:** 5' 5½" **WEIGHT:** 11st 6lbs

**SIGNED FROM:** Renton, 01/08/1888 and Burnley, 08/02/1889

**DEBUT:** v Elswick Rangers, 27/10/1888

**LAST MATCH:** v Elswick Rangers, 27/10/1888

**MOVED TO:** Gainsborough Trinity, 10/11/1888 and Everton, 15/08/1889

**TEAMS:** Dundee Harp, Renton, Sunderland, Gainsborough Trinity, Burnley, Sunderland, Everton, Broxburn (L), Celtic, (Sheffield) Wednesday, Clydebank, Renton

**SAFC TOTALS:** 1 appearances / 0 goals

**An FA Cup second qualifying round game was Brady's only appearance for Sunderland in an official national competitive game, but like others of his era, he also appeared in the bread and butter games of the time which were friendlies or challenge matches played throughout the year. Notably he scored twice in a 7-2 victory over Corinthians on 9 February 1889, the day after he commenced his second spell with the club.**

Brady had more success at Everton scoring a total of 20 times in 36 games including a hat-trick in a record 11-2 FA Cup win over Derby on 18/01/1890 and twice in an 8-0 win over Stoke on his debut on 02/11/1889. He played in Sunderland's first two league games against Everton in 1890-91 - when Everton were champions with Brady missing just one game - before moving on to Celtic at the end of that season.

Described as, 'A wee barrel of a man', the Glaswegian left Merseyside for Celtic on 10/08/1891 debuting in a 3-1 defeat at Hearts five days later. Also known variously as Alick and as Bradie rather than Brady, he proved to be part of Celtic's first-ever major senior trophy-winning team as they won the Scottish Cup, the former Sunderland man scoring twice in a 5-3 win over Rangers during the cup run. They were two of six goals he scored in five games in the Scottish Cup along with four in ten league games in addition to winning the Glasgow Charity Cup - beating Rangers in the final - and the Glasgow Cup, when he scored in a 7-1 final victory over Clyde.

On 03/09/1892, Brady returned to England signing for 'Wednesday' where he played in their first-ever Football League game and scored as they beat Sunderland in the first league meeting of the clubs on 29/10/1892 in Sheffield. He also scored for Wednesday against Sunderland in March 1895, and the following season played in every cup game as Wednesday won the (FA) Cup for the first time. The successful cup run included knocking Sunderland out along the way as his wing partnership alongside the famed 'Olive Grove Flyer' - England international Fred Spikesley - brought Wednesday's first success. This added to his CV of being in Everton's first title win and Celtic's first Scottish Cup triumph. He finished with 39 goals in 178 games for Wednesday, ending against Stoke in January 1899.

During his time with Gainsborough, Brady worked in an engine works, while when he was with Burnley, he supplemented his income by working as a window cleaner and after his playing days, was employed as a ship's caulker in Glasgow. In September 1888, he was suspended for two months for signing forms for both Everton and Burnley. Brady's brother Joseph, played for Renton, Newcastle East End, Sheffield United and St Bernards between 1888 and 1894.

## **BRADY, Kieron** John Paul

**POSITION:** Winger

**BIRTHPLACE:** Coatbridge, Glasgow

**DATE OF BIRTH:** 17/09/1971

**HEIGHT:** 5' 9" **WEIGHT:** 11st 13lbs

**SIGNED FROM:** Youth Team, 01/07/1988

**DEBUT:** v Plymouth Argyle, H, 18/11/1989

**LAST MATCH:** v Charlton Athletic, H, 11/04/1992

**MOVED TO:** Released, 13/05/1993

**TEAMS:** Sunderland, Doncaster Rovers (L)

**INTERNATIONAL:** Scotland Under 16s, Republic of Ireland Under 21s

**SAFC TOTALS:** 18+22 appearances / 7 goals

**One of the most naturally talented players to grace the Sunderland shirt, sadly Kieron's playing days were far too short-lived due to a rare vascular condition that meant Kieron's career as a footballer crashed when he was only 22. On talent alone he had the potential to be a major star.**

Brady's performance against West Ham at Roker Park in 1990 was one that signalled Sunderland had a potential superstar on their hands - something those who had watched him coming through the ranks already knew. Brady slalomed through the Hammers defence at will, scoring with a stunning bicycle kick in the same game.

Years later, Brady re-invented himself as a deep-thinking and highly articulate advocate for the dispossessed and downtrodden, campaigning for asylum seekers and championing LGBT rights. Additionally, he regularly impressed as an insightful and searingly honest pundit covering Sunderland on local radio.

## **BRAMBLE, Titus** Malachi

**POSITION:** Centre-back

**BIRTHPLACE:** Ipswich, Suffolk

**DATE OF BIRTH:** 31/07/1981

**HEIGHT:** 6' 3" **WEIGHT:** 16st 1lb

**SIGNED FROM:** Wigan Athletic, 23/07/2010

**DEBUT:** v Birmingham City, H, 14/08/2010

**LAST MATCH:** v Manchester United, H, 30/03/2013

**MOVED TO:** Contract not renewed, 30/06/2013

**TEAMS:** Ipswich Town, Colchester United (L), Newcastle United, Wigan Athletic, Sunderland, Stowmarket Town

**INTERNATIONAL:** England Under 21

**SAFC TOTALS:** 46+5 appearances / 1 goal

**The heaviest player to play for Sunderland (to 2022), Titus weighed in at over 16 stone in 2013. He is also the only player to score for and against Sunderland both deliberately and accidentally. Before signing for Sunderland he had scored against the Lads for his home town Ipswich and put through his own goal while playing for Wigan. After coming to the club Bramble scored for his own team against Stoke, but netted own goals in games with both Everton and Manchester United.**

At his best, a dominant powerful central-defender, Bramble made his name with Ipswich, doing so well that Sir Bobby Robson splashed out £6m to take him to Newcastle in 2002 when he was only 21. As in his later stint at Sunderland, Titus offered a mixture of being commanding and calamitous, occasional lapses in concentration preventing him going to the top level, something indicated by ten England Under 21 caps, but never seriously coming into the reckoning as a full international.

After 157 appearances for Newcastle, he was allowed to leave on a free transfer and joined Wigan Athletic in 2007 returning to Newcastle to score against his old club in November 2008 in a season where he was named both Player of the Year and Player's Player of the Year for the Latics.

A fee reported to be in the region of £1m brought him back to the north east when his former Wigan boss Steve Bruce signed him for Sunderland. After 24 games in his first season, eight in his second and 17 in his third, Titus was released. During his middle season on Wearside, he was suspended from 29/09/2011 to 09/11/2011 while police allegedly investigated a sexual assault and drug possession charge from which the player was exonerated. After leaving Sunderland, he went on to appear in a friendly for West Ham against Cork and for Ipswich against Barnet, but could not earn a new contract as a player, instead becoming coach of the Tractor Boys Under 11s. He retained that role while becoming player-coach of Stowmarket Town in the Eastern Counties Football League in 2014.

One of Bramble's brothers, Tesfaye, played for numerous lower league clubs, mainly at Southend United and also represented Montserrat, but reportedly, spent time in prison having been convicted of rape in 2011.

## **BRAND, Ralph** Laidlaw

**POSITION:** Forward

**BIRTHPLACE:** Edinburgh, Lothian

**DATE OF BIRTH:** 08/12/1936

**HEIGHT:** 5' 7" **WEIGHT:** 10st 0lbs

**SIGNED FROM:** Manchester City, 11/08/1967

**DEBUT:** v Leeds United, A, 19/08/1967

**LAST MATCH:** v West Ham United, A, 19/10/1968

**MOVED TO:** Raith Rovers, 20/08/1969

**TEAMS:** Carrickknowe School, Slateford Athletic, Rangers, Broxburn Athletic, Rangers, Manchester City, Sunderland, Raith Rovers, Hamilton Academical

**INTERNATIONAL:** Scotland

**SAFC TOTALS:** 32 appearances / 7 goals

**Ralph Brand was a much decorated player who became one of Jim Baxter's clique at Roker Park under Ian McColl. A scorer on his home debut against Fulham, he scored three goals in his first five games, but rarely was able to produce his best football for Sunderland - and certainly not on his final appearance as the club record defeat of 8-0 was equalled at West Ham United.**

A deep thinker on the game, Brand was finely balanced and deceptively good in the air given his modest height. He came to prominence in one of the first televised schoolboy internationals, playing for Scotland against England at Wembley in 1952 when the Scotsman newspaper invited his parents to their offices to watch the game as, like most people, they did not own a television.

Brand scored five goals in his first three full internationals and finished with eight goals from as many caps, while for the Scottish League, he netted eight times in only five appearances. At club level, Ralph became the only man (as of 2022) to score in three successive Scottish Cup finals from 1962 to '64, including both the original match and replay as Celtic were beaten in 1963. As a teammate of Baxter, he also played in both legs of the 1961 European Cup Winners' Cup final for Rangers against Fiorentina. He also won four league titles while at Ibrox as well as four League Cup winners medals, his 206 goals for Rangers making him the club's third highest post-war scorer, as of 2022.

Brand enjoyed success in England too, winning Division Two at Manchester City as a teammate of Sunderland's 1964 promotion hero Johnny Crossan in 1966. Following his retirement, Brand managed Darlington and Albion Rovers before coaching Dunfermline Athletic and subsequently running a shop in Edinburgh as well as working as a taxi driver.

## **BREBNER, Ronald Gilchrist (Ronnie)**

**POSITION:** Goalkeeper

**BIRTHPLACE:** Darlington, Co Durham

**DATE OF BIRTH:** 23/09/1881 - 11/11/1914

**HEIGHT:** 5' 11" **WEIGHT:** 11st 7lbs

**SIGNED FROM:** Elgin City, 04/05/1905

**DEBUT:** v (Sheffield) Wednesday, H, 02/12/1905

**LAST MATCH:** v Notts County, 27/12/1905

**MOVED TO:** Rangers, 05/02/1906

**TEAMS:** Darlington Trinity, Edinburgh University, Elgin City, Sunderland, Rangers, Chelsea, Corinthians, London Caledonians, Stockton Nomads, Leicester Fosse.

**INTERNATIONAL:** England amateur & Great Britain

**SAFC TOTALS:** 2 appearances / 0 goals

**A gold medallist at the 1912 Olympics, Dr. Ronald Brebner played as an amateur, signing for Sunderland after impressing, despite letting in five goals in a friendly with Elgin City in April 1905. While in the north east, Brebner worked as a dental surgeon. As an amateur, he was able to also play for Corinthians and London Caledonians while he was in the capital working at his dental practice in London's West End.**

His two games for SAFC in 1905 saw him keep a clean sheet on his debut, but be beaten four times on his second outing. The following year, he made a single appearance for Chelsea in October and would return to Stamford Bridge in 1913-14 to make 17 Division One appearances.

1907 saw Ronnie play his first international game for the England amateur team, playing as Ireland were beaten 6-1 at White Hart Lane. His 23rd and final appearance would also be against Ireland in Belfast in October 1912. The previous February he had played against Wales at Bishop Auckland. At one point he also played in a trial North v South game for the full England team, but did not win a full England cap.

In 1908, around the time he played for Stockton (for whom he once saved three penalties in one game), Ronnie joined the Durham Light Infantry as a 2nd Lieutenant. During the same year, he was an unused reserve for Great Britain who won gold at the London Olympics. January 1911 saw his home town Darlington call upon him for an English (FA) Cup game where the non-league Quakers were away to first division Sheffield United. Brebner had a blinder as Darlington produced a 1-0 giant-killing that resulted in 500 Darlington supporters chairing him off the Bramall Lane pitch at full-time.

In 1912 in Stockholm at the Olympics, Brebner was first choice and played in all three games, keeping clean sheets against Hungary and Finland - saving a penalty at 0-0 against Hungary - before helping GB to a 4-2 final victory over Denmark.

Tragically, in the year after he won his gold medal, he was badly injured in his 18th and final second division game for Leicester Fosse at Lincoln City on Boxing Day 1913. Ronnie never recovered from the complications that arose from the injury and he passed away in London the following November, aged only 33. He is buried in Darlington West cemetery where he shares a grave with his father, a gunmaker who also died young. At the age of 38, his horse and cart overturned when negotiating a ford at Neasham.

## **BRECONRIDGE, John** Nisbet

**POSITION:** Forward

**BIRTHPLACE:** Mauchline, Ayrshire

**DATE OF BIRTH:** 05/10/1865 - 22/04/1925

**SIGNED FROM:** North Sands Rovers, August 1888

**DEBUT:** v Elswick Rangers, H, 27/10/1888

**LAST MATCH:** v Newcastle East End, 17/11/1888

**MOVED TO:** Not resigned, 30/04/1891

**TEAMS:** Mauchline, North Sands Rovers, Sunderland

**SAFC TOTALS:** 2 appearances / 3 goals

**John, whose official surname was Breckenridge, was one of a number of Scottish players who joined Sunderland in August 1888 to replace those who had defected to the newly-formed Sunderland Albion. Prior to moving to Wearside to work in the William Pickersgill & Co Ltd shipyards, he had played for his home club, Mauchline, and representative games for Ayrshire County.**

The scorer of Sunderland's first-ever hat-trick in either the FA Cup or Football League, Breconridge's feat came on 27 October 1888 at the old Newcastle Road ground in a FA Cup second qualifying round game against Elswick Rangers. Sometimes recorded as Brackenridge, the totals above only cover competitive official games, but he also appeared in friendlies for Sunderland - most notably scoring twice in the first 15 minutes of a 12-0 win over Druids on Boxing Day 1888.

Immediately after retiring from playing, John refereed in the Northern Alliance League. During and after his playing career, he was a lofts-man in the shipyards and sadly died aged 59 in a tramcar on his way to work.

## **BREEN, Gary** Patrick

**POSITION:** Centre-back

**BIRTHPLACE:** Hendon, London

**DATE OF BIRTH:** 12/12/1973

**HEIGHT:** 6' 3" **WEIGHT:** 13st 3lbs

**SIGNED FROM:** West Ham United, 04/08/2003
Had left WHU, 10/06/2003

**DEBUT:** v Millwall, H, 16/08/2003

**LAST MATCH:** v Aston Villa, A, 07/05/2006

**MOVED TO:** Wolves, 20/07/2006

**TEAMS:** Charlton Athletic, Maidstone United, Gillingham, Peterborough United, Birmingham City, Coventry City, West Ham United, Sunderland, Wolverhampton Wanderers, Barnet

**INTERNATIONAL:** Republic of Ireland

**SAFC TOTALS:** 113+2 appearances / 7 goals

**Brought in by his former international manager Mick McCarthy, Gary Breen arrived just after Sunderland had been miserably relegated in 2003. Appointed captain, Breen was the building block on which Sunderland were rebuilt and won promotion two years later having been Play-Off and FA Cup semi-finalists in his first year.**

Always wary of people, a consequence of his experiences with the press in Ireland, nonetheless, Gary was an excellent captain, off the pitch as well as on it. His role in changing a losing mentality to a winning one should not be underestimated, although he would never allow anyone to become too optimistic either, 'being under no illusions' becoming not much short of a catch-phrase for him in discussions.

Defeat on Breen's debut was the final one of the record 17 successive losses suffered in 2003. He was influential in the next four games being won, notching his first goal to open the scoring in a 4-0 victory at Bradford. But for fate conspiring to bring defeat to Millwall (his debut opponents) late in his first season, Gary would have joined the select band to have skippered Sunderland in an FA Cup final. He did however captain the club to promotion in his second term.

While his team was out of its depth in Breen's third and last campaign as relegation with a record low 15 points was suffered, Gary was always up for the fight, playing in all but three of the games. He was not one of the players in a hard-working team who lacked quality. Gary impressed so much for McCarthy's Ireland at the 2002 FIFA World Cup (in which he scored against Saudi Arabia) that both Barcelona and Inter Milan expressed interest in him, the Italians so much that they tried to sign Breen only for him to fail a medical.

Early years had seen Breen begin with Charlton, but make his debut after joining Maidstone who were then a league club. Progressing up the footballing ladder with Gillingham, Peterborough and Birmingham brought him into the Premier League in 1997 with Coventry where he would experience relegation after the fourth of his five seasons with the Sky Blues.

Having missed out on a move to Inter after the 2002 World Cup, he joined West Ham only to suffer relegation in a season where only 14 of his 18 appearances came in the league before he was reunited with McCarthy on Wearside. It was McCarthy who he joined again after leaving Sunderland, this time at Wolves where he was again made captain. As he reached the veteran stage, Gary joined Barnet as player/coach in December 2008, becoming assistant manager at the end of the season. In 2013, he returned to the Stadium of Light as coach of Peterborough United and expressed a wish to one day return as manager of Sunderland AFC.

## BRIDCUTT, Liam Robert

**POSITION:** Midfield

**BIRTHPLACE:** Reading, Berkshire

**DATE OF BIRTH:** 08/05/1989

**HEIGHT:** 5' 9" **WEIGHT:** 11st 7lbs

**SIGNED FROM:** Brighton & Hove Albion, 31/01/2014

**DEBUT:** v Newcastle United, A, 01/02/2014

**LAST MATCH:** v Leicester City, H, 16/02/2015

**MOVED TO:** Leeds United, 16/8/2016 following loan from 26/11/2015

**TEAMS:** Chelsea, Yeovil Town (L), Watford (L), Stockport County (L), Brighton & Hove Albion, Sunderland, Leeds United, Nottingham Forest, Bolton Wanderers (L), Lincoln City

**INTERNATIONAL:** Scotland

**SAFC TOTALS:** 25+11 appearances / 0 goals

**Signed by his former Brighton boss Gus Poyet, Bridcutt was thrust into the heat of a derby at Newcastle for his debut and significantly impressed as Sunderland won 3-0. This remained the high point of his short time at Sunderland as he never reached the hoped-for standards Poyet had witnessed on the south coast.**

To Poyet's credit, although he had brought in Bridcutt from his old club, he recognised that Liam did not offer as much to the side as Lee Cattermole could in the same position.

Sadly for Bridcutt, he wasn't helped by being cup-tied when he arrived at Sunderland when the club had already reached the Capital One (League) Cup final. He had previously come on as a sub for the final six minutes of Brighton's defeat at home to Newport County.

Qualifying for Scotland through a grandfather, he was capped against Serbia eleven months before joining Sunderland. In 2016, he won a second cap against Denmark while still technically a Sunderland player, although he was on loan to Leeds who he would subsequently sign for.

Twice Player of the Year at Brighton, in 2021 he was part of the Lincoln City side that beat Sunderland in the League One Play-Off semi-final.

## BRIDGE, Wayne Michael

**POSITION:** Left-back

**BIRTHPLACE:** Southampton, Hampshire

**DATE OF BIRTH:** 05/08/1980

**HEIGHT:** 5' 11" **WEIGHT:** 12st 13lbs

**SIGNED FROM:** Manchester City, 31/01/2012, on loan

**DEBUT:** v Norwich City, H, 01/02/2012

**LAST MATCH:** v Manchester United, A, 13/05/2012

**MOVED TO:** Manchester City, 14/05/2012, end of loan

**TEAMS:** Southampton, Chelsea, Fulham (L), Manchester City, West Ham United (L), Sunderland (L), Brighton & HA (L), Reading

**INTERNATIONAL:** England

**SAFC TOTALS:** 5+5 appearances / 0 goals

**Brought in on loan by Martin O'Neill shortly after he became manager, Bridge's most notable appearances were in the FA Cup quarter-final and replay with David Moyes' Everton. In addition to his ten games, he was also named as an unused sub on a further eight occasions, itself an indication that despite his extensive international experience, he couldn't hold down a regular first-team place. The eleventh of his 36 England caps was won at the Stadium of Light against Turkey in 2003.**

Player of the Year in 2000-01 at his hometown club Southampton, Bridge had certainly held a regular place with the Saints, at one point making 113 consecutive appearances. After playing in the 2003 FA Cup final, a big money £7m move took him to Chelsea with fellow England international Graeme le Saux moving the opposite way in part-exchange. A Premier League winner in his second season at Stamford Bridge, although an injury at Newcastle curtailed his season in February, the following term he was loaned to near-neighbours Fulham, but returned to the Blues to win both domestic cups in 2007. He also played in the following season's League (Carling) Cup final against Spurs, but gave away a penalty as Chelsea were beaten.

In January 2009, an undisclosed fee reported to be in the region of £10m took Wayne to Manchester City after almost 150 games for Chelsea. At City, he only managed 58 appearances with his loan to Sunderland being one of three, City farmed him out on.

Some of the player's career was overshadowed by a spat with his Chelsea and England teammate John Terry regarding a personal matter concerning Bridge's girlfriend. In the summer of 2014, after announcing his retirement because of a knee injury, he married pop singer Frankie Sandford of The Saturdays who had appeared at the Stadium of Light the previous month. His celebrity life-style then saw him appear in the 2016 series of the TV show 'I'm a Celebrity - Get Me Out of Here', but he did not last any longer there than he had at Sunderland.

## BRIDGES, Michael

**POSITION:** Forward

**BIRTHPLACE:** North Shields, Tyne and Wear

**DATE OF BIRTH:** 05/08/1980

**HEIGHT:** 6' 1" **WEIGHT:** 11st 2lbs

**SIGNED FROM:** Monkseaton, 22/02/1995 and Bolton Wanderers, 24/12/2004, following loan

**DEBUT:** v Port Vale, H, 10/02/1996

**LAST MATCH:** v Crewe Alexandra, A, 12/03/2005

**MOVED TO:** Leeds United, 23/07/1999 and Bristol City, 25/07/2005

**TEAMS:** Newcastle United, Berwick Rangers, Sunderland, Leeds United, Newcastle United (L), Bolton Wanderers, Sunderland, Bristol City, Carlisle United, Sydney (L), Carlisle United (L), MK Dons, Newcastle Jets, Lambton Jaffas

**INTERNATIONAL:** England Under 21

**SAFC TOTALS:** 46+67 appearances / 23 goals

**There is always the wish that the club's youth system will produce a star forward. That is exactly what happened with Michael Bridges - or 'Stick-man' as the skinny youngster was nicknamed. Unfortunately as Bridges came into his own, his way to the first-team was blocked by the presence of Sunderland's record post-war goalscorer Kevin Phillips.**

Michael actually debuted over a season before SuperKev arrived. Given the Man of the Match champagne on his debut - even though he only came off the bench for the last 28 minutes - he was too young to drink it. Always brilliant at evading defences, no Southend players - or anyone else - seemed to see Michael score his first goal soon afterwards in heavy fog at Roots Hall, but plenty saw Bridges score his first home goals soon afterwards. Sent on with quarter of an hour left as Sunderland trailed at home to Huddersfield, manager Peter Reid gave the youngster the instruction of getting a goal. The Stick-man promptly scored twice against former Sunderland keeper Tony Norman to give Sunderland a ninth successive league win, the best run since 1892.

## BRIDGES, Michael (Continued)

Sixty two of Bridges 98 league appearances were as substitute. Much more than a goalscorer, Stick-man could have been renamed Silk-man such was the smoothness of his play. He was a real class act with an astute football brain, seeing passes and angles as top players do. But for injury, he appeared to be a certainty to be capped at full level by England.

Following an apparent contract dispute, a fee of £5m made him Sunderland's record sale as he signed for Leeds United. Bridges quickly looked like a bargain as he scored a hat-trick on his second appearance against Southampton and ended his first season with 19 Premiership goals. This made Michael the top-flight's fourth top scorer - as Sunderland's Phillips led the way with 30. The Leeds man's goals helped Leeds to qualify for the Champions League having finished third, but an injury in a Champions League game with Besiktas led to years of problems from a player who had his best years taken away from him.

In what became a very well-travelled career that would eventually see extensive experience in Australia, Bridges briefly returned to Sunderland to feature in the 2004-05 promotion season, but little of the electric pace from a standing start was still there.

In December 2020, Bridges was reported to have applied for a coaching role in the academy at Sunderland. As one of the club's finest ever products - who once scored five times in a 10-0 Under 18 win over Chesterfield at the Charlie Hurley Centre - Michael could certainly lead by example.

## BRIDGETT, George Arthur

**POSITION:** Winger

**BIRTHPLACE:** Forsbrook, Staffordshire

**DATE OF BIRTH:** 11/10/1882 - 26/07/1954

**HEIGHT:** 5' 8½" **WEIGHT:** 11st 8lbs

**SIGNED FROM:** Stoke FC, 15/01/1903

**DEBUT:** v Sheffield United, H, 17/01/1903

**LAST MATCH:** v Manchester City, A, 30/03/1912

**MOVED TO:** South Shields, 27/07/1912 as player/manager

**TEAMS:** Burslem Park FC, Trentham FC, Stoke FC , Sunderland, South Shields (player/manager), North Shields, Port Vale, Sandbach Ramblers

**INTERNATIONAL:** England

**SAFC TOTALS:** 348 appearances / 116 goals

**Only Dave Watson won more caps for England while with Sunderland than the eleven won by left-winger Bridgett. Maintaining an excellent goalscoring record for a wide-man, Arthur scored three times in those eleven appearances, including in 6-1 and 11-1 wins over Austria in Vienna in England's first overseas tour. England won 10 and drew one of his eleven games, scoring 56 times and conceding just eight. He also twice represented the Football League.**

A religious man who refused to play on Christmas Day or Good Friday, Lay Preacher Arthur was a member of the Brotherhood Movement and gave a sermon at the club's annual service on 'the ethics of good sportsmanship'. Bridgett came to love Sunderland so much he Christened a son born while he was at the club as Samuel Francis Charles so he had the initials SFC. Samuel told me himself that this was in tribute to Sunderland, not Stoke.

Bridgett came to Wearside after just seven league games with Stoke who he had played for as an amateur. Noted as an accurate crosser of the ball, he went on to become a legendary figure at Sunderland, captaining the club in 1907-08 having top-scored in the previous two seasons, incredibly with 25 goals in 1906-07, regardless of spending almost the whole campaign on the wing. Two of the goals Bridgett scored came on 5 December 1908 in the legendary 9-1 win at Newcastle.

He left Sunderland in the summer of 1912 to become player-manager of South Shields who tried, but failed, to gain election to the Football League at the end of his first season, as Sunderland won the league and reached the FA Cup final. During World War One, he scored for Port Vale in a 5-2 win over Manchester United in his only war-time game for the Potteries club, but later returned to sign for them as a 41-year-old in 1923, some eleven years after his previous league game. Showing he was still a class player, Bridgett scored after only 90 seconds for the only goal of a game against Clapton Orient and went on to net five times in 17 games before leaving at the end of the season.

Bridgett stayed in football and had FA Cup success in the 1920s - in the women's FA Cup! One of his brothers, Len, was the manager and coach of the Stoke Ladies team in 1921. Four of Arthur's nieces - Len's daughters - played for Stoke Ladies. Len organised the first English Ladies FA Challenge Cup and even provided the trophy which up to the 1990s at least, was still in the possession of the Bridgett family, Stoke having won the competition.

Another of Arthur's brothers, Edwin, played for Whitburn and South Shields before World War One while the pair also ran a fish business with Arthur also keeping a poultry firm in Whitburn during his time with Sunderland.

## BROADHEAD, Nathan

**POSITION:** Forward

**BIRTHPLACE:** Bangor, Gwynedd

**DATE OF BIRTH:** 05/04/1998

**HEIGHT:** 5' 10" **WEIGHT:** 11st 7lbs

**SIGNED FROM:** Everton, 16/08/2021, on loan

**DEBUT:** v Burton Albion, A, 17/08/2021

**LAST MATCH:** Wycombe Wanderers, N, 21/05/2022

**MOVED TO:** Returned to Everton, 25/05/2022, end of loan

**TEAMS:** Everton, Burton Albion (L), Sunderland (L), Wigan Athletic (L) (to August 2022)

**INTERNATIONAL:** Wales Under 21

**SAFC TOTALS:** 20+7 appearances / 13 goals

**Taken on a season-long loan from Everton, Nathan had made his senior debut for the Toffees as a late sub away to Cypriot team Apollon Limassol in the Europa League in December 2017. In April 2021 he made a Premier League debut as a late sub at Brighton and was on the bench for Everton in their opening game of the 2021-22 season before switching to Sunderland after those two appearances for the Goodison club.**

He debuted for the Wearsiders in the familiar surroundings of Burton Albion having previously been loaned to the Brewers in 2019-20. Nathan netted three times for them in a total of 15+7 appearances in a hamstring injury interrupted season eventually curtailed by Covid.

With Everton as a young player, he won the Dallas Cup and Milk Cup before being Toffees Under 18s and Under 23 Player of the Year. He had joined Everton after a trial with Wrexham and a six-week spell at Liverpool's academy. As an Under 11, Broadhead also took part in the British Under 11 gymnastics championships.

With Wales he scored a winner against England in his home town of Bangor in an Under 19s UEFA European Championship qualifying game in 2016, going on to score a hat-trick against Luxembourg three days later. Capped 18 times at Under 23 level, Nathan was brought into the national side's training camp ahead of the delayed 2020 Euros.

He did exceptionally well at Sunderland and scored his sixth goal in as many games in a League (Carabao) Cup quarter-final at Arsenal only to pull his hamstring in his last match to the end of 2021, but returned to play a significant role in helping the club to win promotion. Called up for the full Wales squad at the end of the season he had to withdraw through injury.

## BROADIS, Ivan Arthur (Ivor)

**POSITION:** Inside-forward

**BIRTHPLACE:** Poplar, London

**DATE OF BIRTH:** 18/12/1922 - 12/04/2019

**HEIGHT:** 5' 9" **WEIGHT:** 11st 0lbs

**SIGNED FROM:** Carlisle United, 31/01/1949

**DEBUT:** v Arsenal, A, 05/02/1949

**LAST MATCH:** v Aston Villa, H, 05/09/1951

**MOVED TO:** Manchester City, 05/10/1951

**TEAMS:** Northfleet, Spurs (Amateur), Millwall (Amateur), Carlisle United, Sunderland, Manchester City, Newcastle United, Carlisle United, Queen of the South

**INTERNATIONAL:** England

**SAFC TOTALS:** 84 appearances / 27 goals

**The death of Ivor Broadis, at the age of 96 years and 115 days, brought to a close the life of Sunderland and England's oldest living player. Broadis was one of the finest footballers to wear the red and white stripes. Measure that by the fact that greats including Bill Shankly, Alex Ferguson, Tom Finney, Jackie Milburn, Mike Summerbee and Trevor Ford have been amongst those to praise him to the skies.**

Broadis was the first man to score twice in a World Cup game for England. He once netted a hat-trick as Sunderland beat Manchester United 5-3 at Old Trafford and as the youngest ever person to manage in the Football League, he did the most sensible thing possible as player-manager of Carlisle - and transferred himself to 'Bank of England Club' Sunderland.

Broadis scored 156 goals in 505 career league games in England and Scotland. A Londoner, in 1940 the Broadis' home was destroyed in a bombing raid. Fortunately, the family survived. Ivor joined the RAF, flying over 500 hours during the war, serving as a flight lieutenant navigator on RAF Wellingtons and Lancaster bombers.

Posted to RAF Crosby-on-Eden after the war, Ivor was offered the player/manager position at Carlisle United. He scored 55 goals in 94 games in two and a half seasons before selling himself to Sunderland in January 1949.

Broadis' first full season on Wearside saw Sunderland go as close as they have to a post-war league title. Only a late season home loss to relegation bound Manchester City cost a seventh championship. Ivor missed just one match. Injury restricted him to just 20 appearances in 1950-51, but there were ten goals including two hat-tricks.

Broadis was sold to Manchester City for £7,000 more than the £18,000 that had been paid for him. A month after leaving Sunderland, Ivor made his England debut. He would score eight goals in 14 internationals. The last three of his caps came in the 1954 World Cup during which his brace against Belgium in Switzerland made him the first man to score more than once in a World Cup finals game for England.

After a dozen goals in 79 games for City, a return to the north east came in the shape of a move to Newcastle. He would play 51 times for Newcastle, scoring 18 times before returning to Carlisle as player/coach and finally finishing his playing days with Queen of the South.

In a subsequent 45-year career as a journalist, he probably made the occasional mistake, as all writers do. Hopefully none were so bad as the league official who, when he was first registered as a young player mis-read his real name Ivan as Ivor! The name stuck with him for ever. That may have been a terrible mistake, but Ivor's engine kept running for almost a century.

Made a Freeman of Carlisle, Broadis was a giant of the game from a bygone era, but one who was able to tell the tale of Sunderland's 1950 title near miss, the 1954 World Cup and those 500 hours of World War Two flying time.

## BRODIE, Stephen Eric

**POSITION:** Forward

**BIRTHPLACE:** Sunderland, Co Durham

**DATE OF BIRTH:** 14/01/1973

**HEIGHT:** 5' 10" **WEIGHT:** 11st 0lbs

**SIGNED FROM:** Southmoor School, 01/07/1989

**DEBUT:** v Notts County, A, 28/8/1993

**LAST MATCH:** v WBA, H, 07/05/1995

**MOVED TO:** Scarborough, 10/02/1997
after two month loan

**TEAMS:** Sunderland, Doncaster Rovers (L), Scarborough, Swansea City, Chester City, Nuneaton Borough (L), Forest Green Rovers (L), Droylsden (L), Leigh RMI (L), Droylsden, Witton Albion

**SAFC TOTALS:** 1+11 appearances / 0 goals

**Stephen Brodie was a nippy home-produced striker who was given a debut by Terry Butcher, but had to wait seven months for another opportunity by which time Mick Buxton was in charge. All of his appearances over the 1993-94 and 1994-95 seasons were off the bench apart from his last one where Peter Reid gave him a start after safety had been assured.**

Brodie was allowed to go on loan to Doncaster and Scarborough with a trial at Northampton in between where he played a couple of times for the Cobblers reserves. Scoring in three of his first six games for Scarborough helped his move to the Seaside become 'permanent' as he became part of an ex-SAFC contingent that included Gary Bennett and John Kay.

Reaching double figures in the goal charts in all of his four full seasons with the club, Stephen returned to the Football League with Swansea after his last two seasons at Scarborough had been at Conference level. However, after just two goals in half

a season he was on the move again, returning to the Conference with Chester for whom he only played four times before joining Nuneaton where one of his early goals was back at Scarborough.

A brief return to Chester preceded brief loans to Forest Green and Leigh Genesis, all in the Conference with a last goal once again back at Scarborough before playing out his career in the Northern Premier League. On a personal note Stephen was the only player to play a league game for Sunderland who I taught in my teaching days. I taught him everything he knows about English Literature ...but not football.

## BROWN, Alan

**POSITION:** Forward

**BIRTHPLACE:** Easington, Co Durham

**DATE OF BIRTH:** 22/05/1959

**HEIGHT:** 5' 11½" **WEIGHT:** 12st 11lbs

**SIGNED FROM:** Youth product, 01/01/1975
Professional, July 1976

**DEBUT:** v Norwich City, H, 18/12/1976

**LAST MATCH:** v Notts County, H, 27/02/1982

**MOVED TO:** Shrewsbury Town, 27/07/1982
part of deal to bring Ian Atkins to Sunderland

**TEAMS:** Sunderland, Newcastle United (L), Shrewsbury Town, Doncaster Rovers

**SAFC TOTALS:** 99+28 appearances / 25 goals

**Known as the Easington Express, Brown was a speed merchant who scored prolifically while coming through the ranks, but then struggled for goals at first-team level where his early games saw him be unlucky time after time, not least when hitting the underside of the bar at Anfield. Given a debut in Jimmy Adamson's second game in charge Brown played in eleven out of the next twelve league games before dropping out of the picture still waiting for his first senior goal.**

Given six opportunities the following (1977-78) season, he waited until his second appearance of his third season before finding the back of the net. When his first goal did come it was on his 20th appearance - the longest any Sunderland forward had ever played before getting on the scoresheet. Jon Stead and Danny Graham have both since surpassed that number.

Having finally scored against Fulham at Roker Park, Brown showed exactly how fast he was by storming alongside the Main Stand side exhilarated to have finally netted. It was one of the most memorable goal celebrations. The Roker End strike was the first of a quarter-century of goals Alan scored. The final day of the same season saw the sixth of these bring victory at Wrexham on a day when Sunderland waited for results elsewhere hoping to have secured promotion only to have just missed out.

As promotion was won the following year under Ken Knighton, Alan scored 13 times, nine of them in the league including a hat-trick at home to Oldham.

## BROWN, Alan (Continued)

Two of his four in the League Cup came in a 2-2 draw at Newcastle on a night where after a draw, he scored the decisive penalty as Sunderland won their first-ever penalty shoot-out. Back in the top-flight he played regularly in 1980-81, one of his five goals earning a draw at Old Trafford.

The appointment of Alan Durban as manager saw Brown on the side-lines, his only goal in eight appearances for the Welsh manager coming on his last appearance before he was used as a make-weight in a move to Shrewsbury as Durban moved for his former player Ian Atkins. A hat-trick against Reading was the highlight of his time with the Shrews where after a couple of years he signed for Doncaster who were managed by Billy Bremner who had been Leeds United's captain against Sunderland at Wembley in 1973.

Later a prison officer, Alan Brown's son Chris later also played for Sunderland. Neither were any relation to former manager Alan Brown.

## BROWN, Arthur Samuel

**POSITION:** Centre-forward

**BIRTHPLACE:** Gainsborough, Lincolnshire

**DATE OF BIRTH:** 06/04/1885 - 27/06/1944

**HEIGHT:** 5' 9" **WEIGHT:** 11st 12lbs

**SIGNED FROM:** Sheffield United, 22/06/1908

**DEBUT:** v Manchester City, A, 01/09/1908

**LAST MATCH:** v (Sheffield) Wednesday, A, 30/04/1910

**MOVED TO:** Fulham, 19/10/1910

**TEAMS:** Gainsborough Church Lads Brigade, Gainsborough Trinity, Sheffield United, Sunderland, Fulham, Middlesbrough

**INTERNATIONAL:** England

**SAFC TOTALS:** 55 appearances / 23 goals

**Signed for £1,600, at the time it was a world record transfer fee for the player who four years earlier had become England's second youngest ever international at the age of 18 (behind Clement Mitchell who had played in 1880). In February 1906, Brown had scored on his second - and what proved to be last - England appearance against Ireland in Belfast.**

Brown attracted interest from Sunderland after scoring four times against them in a 5-3 defeat at Bramall Lane in the season before he signed, four of 95 goals he scored in 178 games for the Blades, 22 of them coming in 1904-05 when he was the division's top scorer. The Sheffield club had paid £350 for him in 1902 after he sprang to prominence with two goals in three second division games for Gainsborough Trinity.

While Arthur did well for Sunderland, he was suspended by the club for refusing to move to Wearside as he chose to stay in Gainsborough due to the ill health of his wife Floris who he had married in the December before his transfer to Sunderland. It was as a result of this unwillingness to move to Wearside that he was allowed to move to Fulham after just over two seasons. In the first of those campaigns he scored 20 goals. He was the only forward not to score in the record 9-1 win at Newcastle though he did score at St James' that season in the cup, having scored the winner at his old club Sheffield United in an earlier round.

At Fulham he scored just nine times in 41 league games before returning to the north east with Middlesbrough where the £400 Boro paid for him brought just four league appearance, but no goals. By trade Brown was a Master Builders Merchant and monumental mason.

## BROWN, Christopher Alan (Chris)

**POSITION:** Forward

**BIRTHPLACE:** Doncaster, South Yorkshire

**DATE OF BIRTH:** 11/12/1984

**HEIGHT:** 6' 4" **WEIGHT:** 13st 7lbs

**SIGNED FROM:** Trainee, 01/02/1999
Professional, 09/08/2002

**DEBUT:** v Crewe Alexandra, A, 21/09/2004

**LAST MATCH:** v Leicester City, A, 01/01/2007

**MOVED TO:** Norwich City, 11/01/2007

**TEAMS:** Sunderland, Doncaster Rovers (L), Hull City (L), Norwich City, Preston North End, Doncaster Rovers, Blackburn Rovers, Bury

**INTERNATIONAL:** England Youth

**SAFC TOTALS:** 34+35 appearances / 11 goals

**The son of former Sunderland striker Alan Brown, Chris made his league debut on loan from Sunderland to Doncaster where he had been born, his father having ended his career there. Chris made a scoring debut and netted six times in his first eight games for Rovers.**

Having earned a Division Three championship medal in his year's loan, he returned to Sunderland to score twice on his debut in a League (Carling) Cup tie at Crewe. However, despite breaking his duck at the first time of asking, he did not score until his eleventh league appearance, bringing unwelcome comparisons with his dad's start. By the end of the season he had seven goals from a total of 40 appearances as he emulated his first season at Doncaster by winning a medal, this time in the Championship.

After a single Premiership outing as a sub at Anfield, Chris joined Hull on loan, scoring once in 13 Championship outings before returning to Wearside and scoring the winner against Fulham in what was the last home game of the season - and the only home win. He went on to score the first goal of Roy Keane's reign at Derby and netted two more as he won a third medal in his first four years as Keane's SAFC won the Championship. However, he had left the club mid-way through the season, sold to Norwich following his reported involvement in a sex-tape scandal. Three years earlier Brown had received a police caution along with two youth team colleagues for firing paint-balls from a car.

Sent off on his first start for Norwich, he scored just once in 18 league appearances for the Canaries who had invested £325,000 in him, but he went on to have a long career scoring a total of 69 goals in 258+128 appearances in all competitions. From 2020, he became the co-host of the 'Undr the Cosh' podcast with his former PNE teammate Jon Parkin.

## BROWN, Cyril

**POSITION:** Centre-forward

**BIRTHPLACE:** Ashington, Northumberland

**DATE OF BIRTH:** 25/05/1918 - 15/04/1990

**HEIGHT:** 5' 9" **WEIGHT:** 11st 0lbs

**SIGNED FROM:** Brentford, 20/04/1945

**DEBUT:** v Grimsby Town, A, 05/01/1946

**LAST MATCH:** v Birmingham City, A, 13/02/1946

**MOVED TO:** Notts County 09/08/1946

**TEAMS:** Glentoran, Darlington, Felixstowe, Brentford, Hartlepools United (WW2 Guest), Sunderland, Notts County, Boston United, Rochdale, Peterborough United

**SAFC TOTALS:** 6 appearances / 5 goals

**Cyril Brown was at Sunderland in 1945-46 when his superb record of five goals in six games all came in the FA Cup in the only season where FA Cup games were played over two legs. During the same season he also played 23 games in League North scoring a more modest four goals. Those games however, are not considered first-team games in official records, League North being a competition played before the Football League resumed the following season.**

A native of Ashington, Cyril worked as a miner in his home town during World War Two, but had begun his football career at Felixstowe before signing for Brentford in January 1939. Although he didn't play for the Bees before the war, he made a single appearance for them in 1940-41. Playing for Hartlepools as a war-time 'Guest', Brown began with a debut hat-trick against Bradford City two days before Christmas in 1944 and went on to score 14 times in as many games. This brought him to Sunderland's attention, not least as two of his goals were scored against Sunderland in February 1945.

It was a case of 'Nice One Cyril' as he made an instant impact with the opening goal in a 3-0 debut win at Newcastle on 2 April 1945 in League North, the first of five goals in nine games that season as he played as a 'Guest' player while still registered with Brentford.

Following his time on Wearside, Cyril had a year on the fringes at Notts County, spent a season as a teammate of my uncle Harry Dagg at Boston United and then had three seasons at Rochdale before signing for Sunderland's all-time record scorer Bobby Gurney at Peterborough in 1951.

## BROWN, Harold Archer (Archie)

**POSITION:** Centre-forward
**BIRTHPLACE:** Escomb, Co Durham
**DATE OF BIRTH:** 16/09/1897 - 17/04/1958
**HEIGHT:** 5' 11" **WEIGHT:** 12st 0lbs
**SIGNED FROM:** Shildon, 20/01/1922
**DEBUT:** v Manchester United, H, 21/01/1922
**LAST MATCH:** v Middlesbrough, A, 25/02/1922
**MOVED TO:** Leadgate Park, 09/09/1922
**TEAMS:** Stanley United, Shildon, Sunderland, Leadgate Park, Chilton Colliery, Shildon, QPR, Shildon, Darlington, Spennymoor, Witton Park Institute
**SAFC TOTALS:** 6 appearances / 1 goal

**Having come out of local football after scoring a record 61 goals in a North Eastern League season, 'Archie' Brown had a tremendous debut on a really heavy pitch creating an equaliser and scoring the winner against bottom of the table Manchester United. Selected for the next five games he didn't score again as just one point was taken and was quickly discarded.**

He had been in such demand that Birmingham had been fined for an illegal approach for him while he was at Stanley United. After leaving Sunderland, Brown was banned from taking part in any football between 10/02/1923 and 04/03/1924 for failing to reply to letters from the FA.

He did later come back to prominence in 1924-25 in the Southern League with QPR, making his debut in a goalless draw at Newport in August 1924. However, after just three goals and two wins in 13 Southern League games, he returned to local football back in the north east playing as a left-back rather than as a forward. After retiring he became a caretaker and grave-digger as Escomb Cemetery near Bishop Auckland. Archie's brother George played for Hartlepools Utd and Halifax Town from 1933-1937.

## BROWN, John Reid (Jock)

**POSITION:** Centre-forward
**BIRTHPLACE:** Baillieston, Glasgow
**DATE OF BIRTH:** 25/08/1878 - 02/08/1959
**HEIGHT:** 5' 8" **WEIGHT:** 12st 0lbs
**SIGNED FROM:** Dalziel Rovers, 20/05/1897
**DEBUT:** v (Sheffield) Wednesday, A, 04/09/1897
**LAST MATCH:** v Bolton Wanderers, A, 21/01/1899
**MOVED TO:** Portsmouth, 15/05/1899
**TEAMS:** Dalziel Rovers, Sunderland, Portsmouth, Middlesbrough, Luton Town, Kettering Town
**INTERNATIONAL:** Scotland Junior
**SAFC TOTALS:** 34 appearances / 9 goals

**Jock Brown scored in Sunderland's last ever game at the old Newcastle Road ground against Nottingham Forest. He had joined Portsmouth in 1899 helping them to second place in their first-ever season in the Southern League before returning to the north east after a year to join Boro for whom he scored five goals in 21 second division games, plus another five in nine FA Cup games (including qualifying games) in 1900-01.**

After a single year on Teesside, Jock joined Luton Town and a year later moved on to Kettering. After his playing days were over, he became a steelworker and then a gardener. Before coming to Sunderland he had played in the final of the Lanarkshire Junior Football Association Cup for Dalziel Rovers in both 1896 and 1897, helping them to beat Calderbank Volunteers after earlier losing to Mossend Brigade.

## BROWN, Norman Liddle

**POSITION:** Winger
**BIRTHPLACE:** Willington Quay, Northumberland
**DATE OF BIRTH:** 30/01/1885 - Q3 1976
**HEIGHT:** 5' 7" **WEIGHT:** 10st 8lbs
**SIGNED FROM:** Willington Athletic, 15/11/1904
**DEBUT:** v Everton, A, 19/11/1904
**LAST MATCH:** v (Sheffield) Wednesday, A, 13/04/1907
**MOVED TO:** Brentford, 18/07/1907
**TEAMS:** Willington Athletic, Sunderland, Brentford, Luton Town, Southend United, Millwall Athletic, Newcastle City, North Shields, Blackpool
**SAFC TOTALS:** 28 appearances / 2 goals

**Two days after signing from Willington Quay, Norman Brown was thrust into a first division game at Everton where he replaced the suspended Billy Hogg as Sunderland won to end the Merseysiders 100% home record, L R Roose keeping goal for the Toffees. The victory was the only one in the five games Brown played in during his first season.**

He had a better record the following year, the Lads winning seven of Brown's 13 games with him scoring against Notts County in the league and Gainsborough Trinity in the cup. His third season saw him have two sequences of five successive games.

At Millwall, he made his home debut in only the fifth game played at the Den, a Southern League fixture with Leyton, later turning out against Spurs in the English (FA) Cup. There were a total of 22 games and four goals for the Lions. In his final season of 1913-14 in Division Two of the Football League with Blackpool, he played at centre-forward. After scoring on his first two appearances, he didn't score in any of his other eleven games, losing his place to Joe Lane who had been signed for £400 from Sunderland.

## BROWN, Thomas

**POSITION:** Inside-right
**BIRTHPLACE:** Sunderland, Co Durham
**DATE OF BIRTH:** Unknown
**HEIGHT:** 5' 9½" **WEIGHT:** 12st 0lbs
**SIGNED FROM:** Royal Rovers, 02/05/1907
**DEBUT:** v Manchester City, H, 02/09/1907
**LAST MATCH:** v Manchester City, H, 02/09/1907
**MOVED TO:** St Mirren, 07/05/1908
**TEAMS:** Sunderland Royal Rovers, Sunderland, St. Mirren, Hamilton Academical (L)
**SAFC TOTALS:** 1 appearance / 0 goals

**A former corporal in the Boer War whilst on the books of Sunderland Royal Rovers, Brown caught the attention of the town's top team who signed him for the 1907-08 season.**

## BROWN, Thomas (Continued)

Billy Hogg was injured in Sunderland's first practice match of the season giving Brown the opportunity to play in his place. After 60 minutes of the game all was going well having scored a brace to put the Whites 3-0 up against the Stripes. However, towards the end of the game, Tom was stretchered off with a chest injury that required a few days recuperation in hospital. Five days after leaving hospital he was one of five debutants on the opening day, his appearance in a 5-2 home defeat by Manchester City at least gave him the consolation of being involved in a goal as the legendary George Holley poached a goal on a rebound from Brown's shot.

Unable to break back into the first-team, Tom crossed the border to play in Scottish football. After a few months at St Mirren though he was reported for drunkenness as well as complaints about his behaviour at the Paisley Theatre and warned by the Directors about his 'moral character'.

In June 1910, Woolwich Arsenal enquired about Brown and St Mirren replied that their asking price for the player was £150 and no more was heard from the Gunners. Around Christmas time that year, he signed on loan for Hamilton Academical, his last known club.

## BROWN, Wesley Michael (Wes)

**POSITION:** Defender

**BIRTHPLACE:** Longsight, Manchester

**DATE OF BIRTH:** 13/10/1979

**HEIGHT:** 6' 1" **WEIGHT:** 13 st 8lbs

**SIGNED FROM:** Manchester United, 07/07/2011

**DEBUT:** v Liverpool, A, 13/08/2011

**LAST MATCH:** v Bournemouth, H, 23/01/2016

**MOVED TO:** Contract not renewed, 30/06/2016

**TEAMS:** Fletcher Moss Rangers, Manchester United, Sunderland, Blackburn Rovers, Kerala Blasters

**INTERNATIONAL:** England

**SAFC TOTALS:** 83+4 appearances / 1 goal

**After a silverware-laden 362 appearances for Manchester United, Brown came to Sunderland around the same time as his long-standing Old Trafford teammate John O'Shea. Given the stature of the pair, either or both of them could have swaggered around the Academy of Light with a touch of arrogance. This was never the case as Wes and John were as good off the pitch as they were on it.**

Debuting for Manchester United at Leeds in May 1998, Wes went on to be a key player in some of the club's best years under Sir Alex Ferguson. Playing in 13 seasons with a high of 52 appearances in 2007-08 when he won the Champions League, Premier League and Community Shield, Brown won 16 trophies with the club, including five Premier League titles and the Champions League twice.

He added another cup final appearance in Sunderland colours, playing in the 2014 League (Capital One) Cup final against Manchester City having helped the Lads defeat his old club from the other side of Manchester at the semi-final stage.

Almost three months after leaving Sunderland, Brown signed a short-term deal with Blackburn Rovers for whom he played six times before finishing his career in the lucrative Indian Premier League with Kerala Blasters in 2017-18, where he played for Rene Meulensteen who had been one of his coaches at Manchester United.

For England, Wes debuted as a 19-year-old, being substituted by Sunderland's Michael Gray who was also debuting alongside Kevin Phillips in Hungary in 1999. It was the first of 23 caps won by Wes.

Brothers Reece and Clive were also footballers, Reece reaching Under 20 level for England, while Clive played non-league after coming through the youth system at Manchester City.

## BROWNING, Tyias Charles

**POSITION:** Defender

**BIRTHPLACE:** Liverpool, Merseyside

**DATE OF BIRTH:** 27/05/1994

**HEIGHT:** 5' 11" **WEIGHT:** 12st 0lbs

**SIGNED FROM:** Everton, 08/07/2017, on loan

**DEBUT:** v Derby County, H, 04/08/2017

**LAST MATCH:** v Aston Villa, A, 06/03/2018

**MOVED TO:** Everton, 07/05/2018, end of loan

**TEAMS:** Everton, Wigan Athletic (L), Preston North End (L), Sunderland (L), Guangzhou Evergrande (to June 2022)

**INTERNATIONAL:** England Under 21 / China

**SAFC TOTALS:** 28+1 appearances / 0 goals

**Browning was highly rated when he came on loan to Sunderland from Everton for what proved to be the season where Sunderland slipped straight through the trapdoor of the Championship with immediate relegation straight after dropping out of the Premier League. Like many others in that team, he struggled.**

Early on in his Sunderland career, Browning gave the ball away cheaply very late on for former Sunderland forward Daryl Murphy to score the only goal of the game for Nottingham Forest. It seemed to typify that although he might look reasonably solid throughout the game, supporters always had the worry that the player had a mistake in him.

Tyias had come through the Everton youth system, joining one of his home city's clubs as a ten-year-old and going on to captain the Toffees Under 21 team, being the club's Player of the Year at that level in 2013-14. In September of 2014, he was thrown in at the deep end as a 72nd-minute substitute in a derby with Liverpool at Anfield and next time out being used as a sub against Manchester United at Old Trafford. In total he went on to play nine games for the Toffees including one in a home Europa League defeat to Krasnodar of Russia after Everton had already secured progression and fielded a much changed team.

He went on to play Champions League football - in the Asian Champions League. In February 2019, Browning moved to Guangzhou Evergrande in the Chinese Super League, debuting for them against Japanese outfit Sanfrecce Hiroshima in the continental competition. Eligible to play for China due to having a Chinese grandfather and becoming a naturalized Chinese citizen in September 2019, the former Sunderland man was called up by China in September 2020 and debuted against Guam in May 2021. He took the Chinese name Jiang Guangtai.

## BUCHAN, Charles Murray (Charlie)

**POSITION:** Forward

**BIRTHPLACE:** Plumstead, London

**DATE OF BIRTH:** 22/09/1891 - 25/06/1960

**HEIGHT:** 6' 1" **WEIGHT:** 12st 8lbs

**SIGNED FROM:** Leyton, 21/03/1911

**DEBUT:** v Tottenham Hotspur, A, 01/04/1911

**LAST MATCH:** v Burnley, H, 02/05/1925

**MOVED TO:** Arsenal, 02/07/1925

**TEAMS:** Woolwich Polytechnic, Plumstead St Nicholas, Plumstead FC, Elder Tree FC, Woolwich Arsenal, Northfleet, Leyton, Sunderland, Guards Depot, Chelsea (WW1 Guest), Birmingham FC (WW1 Guest), Huddersfield Town (WW1 Guest), Leeds City (WW1 Guest), Arsenal

**INTERNATIONAL:** England

**SAFC TOTALS:** 411 appearances / 223 goals

**The all-time top league goalscorer in Sunderland's history, volume one of the Absolute Record detailed the extra-goal belatedly credited to Buchan, taking his league tally to 210.**

Regardless of his goalscoring prowess - only Bobby Gurney has scored more in all competitions - Buchan was more than simply being a phenomenal goalscorer. During World War One, Charlie won the Military Medal for bravery. After he retired from playing in 1928, he moved into journalism. Buchan went on to co-found the Football Writers' Association and instigate the Footballer of the Year Award.

His magazine, Charles Buchan's Football Monthly became the world's top selling football magazine. Branching out in publishing he also set up Melody Maker and Disc magazines, held parties, that on one occasion, John Lennon attended and at one point even briefly employed a young Cliff Richard as his office boy. At the beginning of his time as a Sunderland player, Buchan also doubled up as a teacher at Cowan Terrace School which was near Park Lane.

## BUCHAN, Charlie (Continued)

Following his playing days, Buchan became a renowned broadcaster in the early days of sports coverage on the BBC, covering England games and summarising on weekly broadcasts which went out at 7.25 on a Saturday evening.

Buchan had been an outstanding and inspirational footballer who was England's centre-forward in the first ever international at Wembley. He won only six caps, a tally that would have been far higher, but for World War One. Having been named as reserve for England in March 1912 against Scotland at Hampden, Charlie took ten minutes of his debut in February 1913 to score against Ireland in Belfast - an occasion when for the only time Sunderland had three players in the England team. That cap came during Sunderland's finest season when Buchan scored 30 times as he top-scored as Sunderland won the league and reached the cup final. It was one of seven occasions Buchan was Sunderland's top scorer - scoring a minimum of 20 goals in each of those seasons.

The scorer of Sunderland's last goal before football ceased due to the Great War, and also of the first goal after it, all of Buchan's other international appearances came in the 1920s. The first of these saw him score after seven minutes against Wales at Highbury which would become his home ground after an unusual move from Sunderland.

A reserve for England against Ireland at Roker Park in October 1920, he went on to captain England as a Sunderland player in two of his next appearances, scoring in the second of those against France in Paris. Having Scottish parents, London-born Buchan could have been a Scottish international, Scotland having asked him to play for them in 1912.

The first man to score five goals in a league match for Sunderland - against Liverpool in 1912 - it had been the act of scoring five goals in a game in a rare game up-front for Woolwich Polytechnic (where he was mainly a left-back) that resulted in Charlie being converted to a forward. Plumstead St Nicholas, Plumstead and Elder Tree all benefited from having Buchan in their football teams before he signed as an amateur with Woolwich Arsenal while he also turned out for Northfleet FC.

In May 1910, he signed for Leyton from where he attracted Sunderland's attention. His return to the capital 14 years later came in unusual circumstances. The Gunners refused to pay Sunderland's asking price of £4,000 for a player who by then was almost 34. Instead they agreed to pay £2,000 plus £100 for every goal he scored in his first season. He cost them more than the asking price by netting 21 times!

Buchan had two brothers who played professionally, John and Tom. The latter was on Sunderland's books in 1910 without playing for the first-team, but he managed over 100 games for Bolton and 60 split between Blackpool and Tranmere Rovers.

Charlie Buchan's award for being inducted into the National Football Museum Hall of Fame sits proudly in the foyer of the Stadium of Light. Buchan was one of the most important figures in the game before and after the First World War. He was inducted into the Sunderland Hall of Fame at its inaugural dinner in 2019 when the award was collected by his granddaughter Frances Klepp, who in 2010, had republished his autobiography, 'A Lifetime in Football' originally released in 1955.

## BUCHANAN, David

**POSITION:** Forward
**BIRTHPLACE:** Newcastle, Northumberland
**DATE OF BIRTH:** 23/06/1962
**HEIGHT:** 5' 9" **WEIGHT:** 11st 7lbs
**SIGNED FROM:** Blyth Spartans, 20/08/1986
**DEBUT:** v Huddersfield Town, A, 23/08/1986
**LAST MATCH:** v Bury, H, 12/09/1987
**MOVED TO:** Released, 01/05/1988
**TEAMS:** Leicester City, Northampton Town, Peterborough United, Blyth Spartans, Sunderland, York City (L), Blyth Spartans, Newcastle Blue Star, Bedlington, Whitley Bay
**INTERNATIONAL:** England Youth and England semi-pro
**SAFC TOTALS:** 29+9 appearances / 11 goals

**Leicester City's youngest-ever player when he debuted on the same day as Gary Lineker, Buchanan was just 16 years and 192 days when he made his entrance in league football on New Year's Day 1979, and marked the occasion with a goal against Oldham.**

Following spells with a couple of clubs in the lower leagues, Dave dropped out of the Football League altogether, but was given a route back by Lawrie McMenemy after he had won a couple of caps at semi-pro level in 1986.

Given the first 19 league games of McMenemy's second season in 1986-87, Buchanan scored five times in that spell, including a brace in a 4-2 away win at Plymouth. Ending the campaign with eight league goals from 24+9 games, he was joint top league scorer alongside Mark Proctor, half of whose tally were penalties. Buchanan also scored three times in two League (Littlewoods) Cup appearances that season, but did not play in the crucial Play-Off matches against Gillingham that saw Sunderland relegated to the third division for the first time.

David played one game for Sunderland in the third division under Denis Smith before going on loan to York who he had scored those League Cup goals against the season before. He later spent some time in Norwegian football and the north-east non-league circuit, but having come into the game as a 16-year-old, by the age of 28 he had retired and took up a career in leisure management.

## BUCKLE, Harold Redmond (Harry)

**POSITION:** Winger
**BIRTHPLACE:** Belfast
**DATE OF BIRTH:** 06/03/1882 - 02/01/1965
**HEIGHT:** 5' 10" **WEIGHT:** 11st 10lbs
**SIGNED FROM:** Cliftonville, 15/10/1902
**DEBUT:** v Stoke, A, 08/11/1902
**LAST MATCH:** v Middlesbrough, H, 01/01/1906
**MOVED TO:** Portsmouth, 08/05/1906
**TEAMS:** Cliftonville Casuals, Cliftonville Olympic, Cliftonville, Sunderland, Portsmouth, Bristol Rovers, Coventry City, Belfast Celtic, Glenavon, Belfast United, Fordsons
**INTERNATIONAL:** Ireland
**SAFC TOTALS:** 46 appearances / 14 goals

**Harry Buckle scored in two derbies with Newcastle as well as working on the building of The Titanic! After debuting for Cliftonville in 1901, in August 1902 Harry won his first cap for Ireland, playing against Scotland in a game to raise funds for the victims of the Ibrox Disaster, which had killed 25 people.**

Two months later, he signed for reigning champions Sunderland who he debuted for at Stoke the following month. Debuting in the same game was Alex Barrie who was killed in World War One. Playing as an amateur, it was Buckle's only game for Sunderland that season, but he established himself after coming into the side again a week short of a year after his debut, this time at West Brom.

By December he was a hero. Having scored in three successive games, Buckle got a couple and had a hand in the other in a 3-1 win away to Newcastle on Boxing Day. It was a day when the referee missed his train and a reserve official took charge, but Buckle had most definitely arrived and ended the season with nine goals from 21 games.

Harry started the first five and last five games the following season, but only played four times in between, as he contested the left-wing berth with future England international Arthur Bridgett. An appearance for Ireland against England in March 1904 led to Harry's recall at Roker Park. Buckle always had a goal in him and duly netted his fourth of the season in the penultimate fixture as a 3-1 win away to Newcastle threatened to derail the Magpies first ever title win. Buckle played in another derby victory over Newcastle on the opening day of the following 1905-06 season, but after the arrival of Belfast-born boss Bob Kyle, Harry's game was up come New Year's Day.

Although Harry left Sunderland to join Portsmouth in May 1906, it appears Sunderland never left him. "Every Saturday when Sports Report came on, he would tell everyone to be quiet because he wanted to hear the Sunderland result" reported his grandson Roy who for many years ran a Sunderland themed bar called 'The Weigh House' in Cork. "He was never too bothered about the results of the other teams he played for, but he had to hear the Sunderland result."

In his solitary season on the south coast, Buckle helped Pompey to runners-up spot in the Southern League before switching to Bristol Rovers who were also a Southern League side. One of four new forwards signed by 'The Gas', Buckle and his future Coventry teammate Ike Turner both scored on their debuts as Rovers slaughtered New Brompton (later Gillingham) 9-1 on the opening day of the season.

An opening-day crowd of 4,000 almost tripled to 11,000 for a 3-0 win over Brentford three days later, but Buckle's Bristol could not keep it up and eventually finished sixth. Harry did well enough personally though to earn a third and final international appearance, becoming the second Rovers player to be capped when selected for a 1-0 win over Wales at Aberdare in April 1908, shortly before moving to Coventry.

In the process of stepping up from the Birmingham and District League to the Southern League in the summer of 1908, Buckle was a major signing for them. Harry - who had played in a Representative XI for the Southern League the previous season - would miss only one of the 43 league and cup games, top-scoring from the wing with 16 goals, some of them his trademark 'pile-drivers.'

Although at 5' 10" he was tall for a winger - especially in those pre-World War One days - Harry was notorious for not wanting to head the ball, always preferring to bring it down. However, he was decent with his feet and notched what is considered City's first hat-trick in senior football in a 5-3 win over Portsmouth on 13 April 1909.

The star name in the side as a full international with top-flight experience, and still in his prime at 27, Buckle was asked to become Coventry's player/manager for the 1909-10 campaign. Having finished 20th of 21 teams in their first Southern League campaign, Harry lifted the club to eighth place second time around, again finishing as top scorer. His 17 goals from 38 league games were added to by one more in the FA Cup.

Buckle's Southern League City sensationally managed wins over two first division sides in a glorious cup run, winning away to Preston North End and knocking out Nottingham Forest at home. City reached the quarter-final against Everton (who had beaten Sunderland in the previous round). Harry played in all but two of the 42 league and cup games in his third season at Coventry, scoring ten goals including the club's second Southern League hat-trick in a 5-1 win over Southend the week before Christmas in 1910, soon followed by the winner in a big cup tie away to top flight 'Wednesday'. As Coventry finished tenth, he signed off with his 44th goal in his 126th match as Norwich City were beaten 3-1 at Highfield Road on the last day of the season in 1911.

It was after his experience at Coventry that Harry left England behind to return home to Belfast. Joining Belfast Celtic in 1911, he had three years there, gaining representative honours as part of an Irish League XI in 1912 and 1913. Having returned to Belfast, Harry also got a job in the Harland and Wolff shipyard, which was unusual for a Catholic at the time. Nonetheless, he worked there for several years as his football career continued with Glenavon at the outbreak of the Great War and later Belfast United where he reprised his Coventry role as player/manager.

Life wasn't easy as a Catholic. Reportedly at one point he suffered a face injury after a bolt was thrown at him while on another occasion he was tossed into the river. There was worse as his grandson Roy remembered, "He came back to Belfast and worked in the shipyards on the Titanic. My grandfather was a Roman Catholic and was friendly with a foreman who was a Protestant. The foreman came out to him one day and said, 'Harry, go home. They're going to do in a Catholic.' Later that day they reportedly drowned two Catholics and Harry never went back. He went to live in Cork and stayed there until he died.

In Cork he got a job with the Ford Motor Company in a managerial and secretarial capacity. He also played for their works team Fordsons who later became Cork FC. By now very definitely a veteran, but still a player with a touch of class, Buckle played in two FAI Cup finals for Fordsons, both played on St Patrick's Day. In 1924, he appeared against Athlone Town and two years later lifted the cup days after his 44th birthday after helping to beat Shamrock Rovers when he was again player/manager. He still kept playing for one more season, scoring once in 1926-27 to add to the seven league goals he had scored for Fordsons in the previous couple of seasons.

## BUCKLEY, Michael John (Mick)

**POSITION:** Midfielder

**BIRTHPLACE:** Salford, Greater Manchester

**DATE OF BIRTH:** 04/11/1953 - 07/10/2013

**HEIGHT:** 5' 6" **WEIGHT:** 10st 7lbs

**SIGNED FROM:** Everton, 31/08/1978

**DEBUT:** v Preston North End, H, 02/09/1978

**LAST MATCH:** v Norwich City, A, 16/04/1983

**MOVED TO:** Hartlepool United, 25/08/1983

**TEAMS:** Everton, Sunderland, Hartlepool United, Carlisle United, Middlesbrough

**INTERNATIONAL:** England Under 23

**SAFC TOTALS:** 130+5 appearances / 8 goals

**Mick Buckley's face stared out from the cover of the Everton programme on the night Sunderland were controversially relegated at Goodison Park in 1977. He came to the club a year later and became an important member of the side, being an industrious midfielder who could pass well, often looking for an incisive penetrating ball while his tackling could be ferocious.**

Small and well-balanced, Mick's natural ability was amply illustrated when he was part of the five-a-side team that won the prestigious Daily Express tournament at Wembley Arena in 1979. During that same season, Mick played 30 times as promotion was won and two years later one of his occasional goals came on the last day of the season against Manchester City to guarantee Sunderland's survival.

At his first club Everton, Buckley had blossomed under fifties Sunderland winger Billy Bingham, starting 33 times in 1974-75 when the Toffees finished three points off the top of the top-flight. In May 1972, he had scored the winning goal for England against West Germany in the final of the UEFA European U18 Championship in Spain. At Under 23 level, he played against Portugal in Lisbon in November 1974 and Czechoslovakia the following October in Trnava. Teammates in those Under 23 games included Alan Kennedy and Tony Towers who both later came to Sunderland.

Between his time at Everton (where he scored 12 goals in 158 games) and Sunderland, Buckley played for QPR on a pre-season tour of Germany at a time when Everton were trying to sign Dave Clement and Buckley was being touted as a potential makeweight in the deal along with Neil Robinson, only for QPR manager Frank Sibley to be replaced by Alec Stock and the proposed move break down.

After leaving Sunderland, Buckley briefly played as a non-contract player for Hartlepool before signing for Bob Stokoe at Carlisle prior to a season-long return to the north east with Boro in 1984-85. Following his retirement, Mick ran a pub in South Shields, later moving back to the north west as a publican in Whitefield where he sometimes put up Sunderland supporters when the Lads were in the area. He also worked as a driver for Norweb and as a courier.

Mick passed away when only 59, former Sunderland player Joe Hinnigan joining numerous old Everton colleagues at his funeral. Buckley had become a self-confessed alcoholic who had lost his home and his marriage. The Everton Former Players' Foundation tracked him down and sent him to the Sporting Chance clinic. One of four brothers (Gary played for Manchester City) Mick had grown up in Salford, idolised Manchester United and captained Manchester schoolboys as well as representing Lancashire. Despite his beloved United - and Man City - wanting to sign him, 'Buck' followed the advice of his father and joined Everton having also attracted the interest of Liverpool and Burnley.

## BUCKLEY, William Edward (Will)

**POSITION:** Winger

**BIRTHPLACE:** Oldham, Greater Manchester

**DATE OF BIRTH:** 21/11/1989

**HEIGHT:** 6' 0" **WEIGHT:** 12st 12lbs

**SIGNED FROM:** Brighton & HA, 14/08/2014

**DEBUT:** v WBA, A, 16/08/2014

**LAST MATCH:** v Arsenal, A, 20/05/2015

**MOVED TO:** Bolton Wanderers, 01/07/2017

**TEAMS:** Oldham Athletic, Rochdale, Watford, Brighton & Hove Albion, Sunderland, Leeds United (L), Birmingham City (L), Sheffield Wednesday (L), Bolton Wanderers

**SAFC TOTALS:** 10+14 appearances / 0 goals

**Head coach Gus Poyet was very keen to bring Buckley from their previous club Brighton for an undisclosed fee reported to be in the range of £2.5m. A lanky and gangly winger, Buckley never really looked the part in the top-flight for Sunderland and was never popular with the crowd, but he did have one stellar moment. During the six-in-a-row run over Newcastle United in December 2014, it was Buckley's cushioned last-minute pass that teed up Adam Johnson to score the only goal of the game at St James'.**

Buckley never reached double figures in starts at Sunderland, all of his appearances coming in the first of his three seasons at the club, the last two of which brought a trio of loans.

Released by Oldham without making a first-team appearance, Buckley began with Rochdale, debuting in February 2008 and going on to play at Wembley for the club as a sub in the 2008 League Two Play-Off final which was lost to Stockport County.

Following a move to Watford, a good season in 2010-11 led to a club record £1m move to fellow Championship outfit Brighton for whom he scored the winner in their first win at their new stadium. It was one of 19 he notched in 109 games for the Seagulls. In total, 112 of his 306 league appearances were as a substitute. As of June 2022, he was without a club after making the last of his grand total of 232+115 league and cup games (44 goals) for Bolton in January 2020.

## BURBANKS, William Edwin (Eddie)

**POSITION:** Winger

**BIRTHPLACE:** Bentley, South Yorkshire

**DATE OF BIRTH:** 01/04/1913 - 26/07/1983

**HEIGHT:** 5' 7" **WEIGHT:** 10st 4lbs

**SIGNED FROM:** Denaby Colliery, 13/02/1935

**DEBUT:** v Portsmouth, H, 27/04/1935

**LAST MATCH:** v Preston North End, H, 13/03/1948

**MOVED TO:** Hull City, 15/06/1948

**TEAMS:** Thorne Town, Denaby Colliery, Sunderland, Blackpool (WW2 Guest), Chesterfield (WW2 Guest), Doncaster Rovers (WW2 Guest), Manchester United (WW2 Guest), Leeds United (WW2 Guest), Hull City, Leeds United

**SAFC TOTALS:** 155 appearances / 29 goals

**One of only four men to score in an FA Cup final for Sunderland, Eddie's goal made the score 3-1 against Preston North End in Sunderland's first-ever game at Wembley in 1937. Just as Charlie Buchan scored Sunderland's last league goal before World War One and the first after it, Burbanks did the same either side of World War Two.**

However, his goal at Arsenal in September 1939 was expunged from official records as were all appearances and goals from the season which was abandoned after just three games. Post-war, his penalty against Derby (who included Raich Carter) in the first post-war league game in August 1946 came after the 1945-46 season when the FA Cup had been played along with a League North tournament in which Burbanks also scored in the opening game.

A clerk in the electrical department of Doncaster Corporation before becoming a professional footballer, Eddie cost Sunderland £750 when signing the player who did magnificently in later taking over from all-time great Jimmy Connor. Though right-footed, Burbanks became a regular on the left wing.

A goalscoring debut in the last home game of 1934-35 season preceded a season on the sidelines as Connor was ever-present as the league title was won the following year. It was in the cup-winning campaign of 1936-37 that Burbanks began to establish himself. After a run of games in the autumn - when he scored in the Charity Shield win over Arsenal at Roker Park - Eddie came in for Connor after the latter broke his leg in the FA Cup fourth round.

Burbanks ended the campaign with a cup final goal, shooting home twelve minutes from time to give Sunderland a 3-1 lead they never relinquished. A noted deliverer of corners, it had been a Burbanks flag kick which resulted in Bobby Gurney scoring Sunderland's first.

Burbanks' final game for Sunderland would be against cup final opponents Preston before he signed for his fellow cup final scorer and skipper Raich Carter at Hull City, where he went on to win the Division Three North title in his first full season of 1948-49. Last stop for Eddie was with Leeds United where he became United's oldest-ever player when he captained the side three weeks after his 41st birthday in the final game of his career, back at Hull City on 24 April 1954. Burbanks had only played once since September, but was made captain for his send off by his former Hull manager and Sunderland captain - Raich Carter.

Eddie's goal in the 1937 FA Cup final wasn't his only cup final goal. Six years to the day after his Wembley goal for Sunderland, he scored at Bloomfield Road for Blackpool against Sheffield Wednesday in the first leg of the League North Cup final, also playing in the second leg as he collected another winner's medal.

During the war, appropriately enough, the winger served in the RAF, Burbanks seeing service in India. Following his retirement Eddie lived in Hull and ran a confectionery shop.

## BURGE, Lee Stephen

**POSITION:** Goalkeeper

**BIRTHPLACE:** Hereford

**DATE OF BIRTH:** 09/01/1993

**HEIGHT:** 6' 2" **WEIGHT:** 12st 11lbs

**SIGNED FROM:** Coventry City, 03/07/2019

**DEBUT:** v Accrington Stanley, A, 13/08/2019

**LAST MATCH:** Arsenal, A, 21/12/2021

**MOVED TO:** Released, 25/05/2022 Northampton Town from 01/07/2022

**TEAMS:** Coventry City, Nuneaton Borough (L), Sunderland, Northampton Town (to July 2022)

**SAFC TOTALS:** 66 appearances / 0 goals

**Burge began the 2020-21 season by conceding just one goal in his first seven games. That came from a third-minute penalty he conceded himself in the opening league game against Bristol Rovers. Going into a subsequent match against Portsmouth, Burge had to hold out for just over an hour to join Ted Doig and Jim Montgomery in going 600 minutes of league football without conceding a league goal.**

Although he was beaten just seven minutes into that game with Pompey, to be mentioned in the same breath as those legends is high praise indeed. Burge hadn't had to be exceptional, but he was generally solid enough behind a mean defence that did a good job of protecting him. Later the same season, he became the first Sunderland goalie to save two penalties in the same game when he did so against Doncaster Rovers.

At this point, Lee was in his second season at Sunderland. His first campaign had seen him mainly the number two to Scotland international Jon McLaughlin. Burge came from Coventry where his 160 games in all competitions included playing at the Stadium of Light in the Sky Blues freak 5-4 victory in April 2019. His debut for Coventry had come after former Sunderland reserve Joe Murphy left the club with Lee's second start seeing him sent off for retaliation in an FA Cup defeat to non-league Worcester City. In 2016-17 he played 40 league games as Coventry won promotion from League Two and in the same season helped his side to Wembley success in the Football League (Checkatrade) Trophy final alongside his future Sunderland teammate Jordan Willis and against another future Wearside colleague in Oxford's Chris Maguire.

Later the same season he was blamed for a goal conceded in the first leg of the Play-Off semi-final at Lincoln due to his poor clearance, but he redeemed himself with a penalty save in the second leg, although he was criticised for not coming off his line as the Imps netted the decisive goal of the two-legged tie. Nonetheless, his 18 league clean sheets that season was the best since Thomas Sorensen's 24 in 1998-99, with Burge's run of 544 minutes without conceding in September and October 2020 being the seventh longest run without conceding a league goal in the club's history. Moreover, Lee's achievement in saving four of six penalties equalled the club record held by Robert Ward in 1906-07 and Chris Turner in 1984-85.

## BURLEY, George Elder

**POSITION:** Right-back

**BIRTHPLACE:** Cumnock, East Ayrshire

**DATE OF BIRTH:** 03/06/1956

**HEIGHT:** 5' 9½" **WEIGHT:** 11st 0lbs

**SIGNED FROM:** Ipswich Town, 25/09/1985

**DEBUT:** v Huddersfield Town, H, 28/09/1985

**LAST MATCH:** v Scunthorpe United, A, 05/12/1987

**MOVED TO:** Gillingham, 08/07/1988

**TEAMS:** Ipswich Town, Sunderland, Gillingham, Motherwell, Ayr United, Falkirk, Motherwell, Colchester United

**INTERNATIONAL:** Scotland

**SAFC TOTALS:** 66 appearances / 2 goals

**A top class cultured right-back, in none of Burley's 628 career league games could he have faced a more talented opponent than on his debut. Bobby Robson gave him a debut at Old Trafford in 1973 when he was up against George Best.**

The first 394 of those league games were with Ipswich for whom he also played in the 1978 FA Cup final as they beat Arsenal, although he did not feature in their 1981 UEFA Cup final triumph. Capped eleven times by Scotland, all of his appearances came between May 1979 and the same month three years later.

Burley was 29 when Lawrie McMenemy made him one of the experienced players he brought to Roker Park. Coming into the side after McMenemy's well-documented losing start, Burley began with a win and made 27 consecutive league appearances. George's second season saw him match his tally of 27 league games, but he had dropped out of the first-team picture as the season ended in relegation to the third division for the first time.

Burley never played for Sunderland in the third tier, new manager Denis Smith's more robust signing John Kay being ever-present as the division was won. Burley scored in a 7-1 win over Rotherham in the Football League (Sherpa Van) Trophy, but his only other appearance in his third campaign proved to be his last - being part of an FA Cup defeat at Scunthorpe.

Probably the player who was most reluctant to do an interview in my time writing for the club, Burley became well-travelled in the latter stage of his career and went on to have an extensive career as a manager, becoming manager of Scotland and Premier League Manager of the Year in 2000-01 having taken Ipswich to fifth in the table a year after guiding the Tractor Boys to promotion via the Play-Offs. A decade before his Manager of the Year achievement he took Ayr United to the inaugural final of the Scottish Challenge Cup - the Scots equivalent of the Football League Trophy - which they lost to Dundee. Colchester United, Derby County, Hearts, Southampton, Crystal Palace and Cypriot club Apollon Limassol also featured on Burley's managerial CV which totalled exactly 700 games.

## BURLINSON, W

**POSITION:** Half-back

**DEBUT:** v Redcar, A, 08/11/1884

**LAST MATCH:** v Redcar, A, 08/11/1884

**TEAMS:** Sunderland

**SAFC TOTALS:** 1 appearance / 0 goal

**This player remains a mystery, partly as contemporary newspapers report his surname as both Burlinson and Burlison. Although known to have played five times in 1884-85 in a variety of positions, Burlinson's only appearance to count in official records (as the other games were friendlies) was in Sunderland's first-ever English (FA) Cup tie which was lost 3-1.**

He is thought to have commenced his Sunderland career around 1882. During the early 1880s, there were at various times, J Birlison, T Birlison, W Birlison, W Burlison, W T Birlison, W J Burlison, W Burlinson, reported as playing for Sunderland. An 1882 report states that brothers Birlison played for Sunderland second team against Elswick Leather Works (18/02/1882). James Allan's wife was Priscilla Burlison and she had a brother two years older than her called William. It is quite possible that he, William John Burlison, was the person who played against Redcar in the FA Cup tie in November 1884.

## BUTCHER, Terence Ian (Terry)

**POSITION:** Centre-back

**BIRTHPLACE:** Singapore

**DATE OF BIRTH:** 28/12/1958

**HEIGHT:** 6' 4" **WEIGHT:** 14st 0lbs

**SIGNED FROM:** 14/07/1992, on trial which was made 'permanent', 28/08/1992

**DEBUT:** v Swindon,A, 15/08/1992

**LAST MATCH:** (as player) v Notts County, A, 08/05/1993

**MOVED TO:** Sacked as Manager, 26/11/1993

**TEAMS:** Ipswich Town, Rangers, Coventry City, Sheffield Wednesday, Sunderland, Clydebank

**INTERNATIONAL:** England

**SAFC TOTALS:** 41+1 appearances / 1 goal

**One of England's greatest centre-backs, Terry Butcher won 77 caps, seven of them as captain and played at the FIFA World Cups of 1982, 1986 and 1990. However, he did not have the greatest of times at Sunderland where he served as a veteran player/manager having earlier served Coventry City in the same capacity.**

Born in the British Military Hospital in Singapore where his father was a Naval Officer, Butcher became a legendary figure at Ipswich Town, winning the UEFA Cup in 1981, being Player of the Year in 1985 and 1986 and scoring 16 times in 271 league appearances, before financial demands saw Ipswich keen to sell him following relegation in 1986.

A fee of £725,000 (an Ipswich record) took him to Ibrox where he went on to play 127 SPL games for Rangers, winning three league titles and the League Cup twice. On 15 November 1990 he returned to England as player/manager of Coventry City, but only played six times, a figure that caused consternation at Coventry who were paying him as a player as well as a manager only for Terry to rarely select himself. Dismissed in January 1992, he re-surfaced at Sunderland as a player only the following summer having kept fit by training with Sheffield Wednesday where his old international teammate Trevor Francis was manager and allowed him to play for the Owls reserves.

Coming to Sunderland, Butcher always seemed the likely successor to manager Malcolm Crosby and so it proved with his appointment as player/manager on 1 February 1993. He had formed a determined central-defensive pairing with Kevin Ball and endeared himself to the crowd by acting as cheerleader to the Fulwell End whenever a win was achieved.

After leaving SAFC, Butcher played three games for Clydebank in November 1993. He produced two autobiographies, the first, 'Both Sides of the Border' in 1987, with the second in 2005 simply called, 'Butcher: My Autobiography.' Butcher has been inducted into the Halls of Fame of both Ipswich and Rangers as well as the Scottish Football Hall of Fame.

## BUTLER, Geoffrey (Geoff)

**POSITION:** Full-back

**BIRTHPLACE:** Middlesbrough

**DATE OF BIRTH:** 26/09/1946

**HEIGHT:** 5' 8" **WEIGHT:** 11st 3lbs

**SIGNED FROM:** Chelsea, 11/01/1968

**DEBUT:** v Burnley, H, 20/01/1968

**LAST MATCH:** v Manchester City, H, 21/09/1968

**MOVED TO:** Norwich City, 30/10/1968

**TEAMS:** Middlesbrough, Chelsea, Sunderland, Norwich City, Baltimore Comets Iona, AFC Bournemouth, Peterborough United, Trowbridge Town, Salisbury City

**SAFC TOTALS:** 3+2 appearances / 0 goals

**Left-back Butler cost Sunderland the then sizeable fee of £65,000 in 1968 and was a Wembley finalist in 1973 - albeit in the League Cup final for Norwich where he played most of his career. Sunderland cut their losses on the player selling him for £40,000 less than they had paid just ten months before his departure.**

After making his name with his hometown Middlesbrough, Butler had made a mere nine league appearances for Chelsea who had spent £57,000 on him before making a profit by selling him to Sunderland after just four months at Stamford Bridge. Signed by Ian McColl who was dismissed shortly after Geoff's debut, he found himself surplus to requirements as his debut under McColl remained his solitary league start for the club, returning manager Alan Brown using him only twice as a sub.

Evidently, he had impressed in his other two games under McColl as his pair of FA Cup appearances were against Norwich who signed him later in the year. It was at Carrow Road where he had his best years, being part of their second division promotion side of 1972 as well as playing against Spurs in the League Cup final the following year. In total, he played 378 times in the Football League as well as having a stint in the USA.

He later managed Salisbury City, beginning as player/manager in February 1983, but left the club in apparently contentious circumstances in 2001, having become the longest-serving manager in the league having also been commercial manager and managing director.

Oddly, former South Africa national team coach Jeff Butler - a person whose death in 2017 led to FIFA president Gianni Infantino sending condolences to Danny Jordaan the president of the South African FA - had been exposed as a fraud having been found to have passed off Geoff Butler's career in England as his own!

## BUTLER, Joseph Henry (Joe)

**POSITION:** Goalkeeper

**BIRTHPLACE:** Dawley Bank, Shropshire

**DATE OF BIRTH:** 10/01/1879 - 30/11/1939

**HEIGHT:** 5' 9" **WEIGHT:** 11st 4lbs

**SIGNED FROM:** Glossop North End 04/10/1912

**DEBUT:** v Chelsea, A, 05/10/1912

**LAST MATCH:** v WBA, A, 28/03/1914

**MOVED TO:** Lincoln City, 29/05/1914

**TEAMS:** Stockport County, Clapton Orient, Stockport County, Glossop North End, Sunderland, Lincoln City, Rochdale (WW1 Guest), Stockport County (WW1 Guest), Liverpool (WW1 Guest), Glossop (WW1 Guest), Macclesfield (WW1 Guest)

**SAFC TOTALS:** 79 appearances / 0 goal

**Joe Butler is one of a long line of great Sunderland goalkeepers and was a major influence in the club's greatest-ever season of 1912-13 when they won the league and reached the cup final. It didn't look like being a good season until Butler arrived along with defender Charlie Gladwin. The pair transformed Sunderland's season, defeat in Butler's debut leaving them second bottom after seven games.**

Butler would not miss a game for the rest of the season and indeed, all 79 of his games for the club were consecutive appearances. During this time, he kept 27 clean sheets, a ratio of 34.18%, while the 84 goals he conceded in total is the best ratio of any Sunderland goalkeeper to play at least 50 times in the top flight. Mart Poom and Jon McLaughlin are the only keepers to better his ratio in all first-team games, but played at a lower level.

Prior to joining Sunderland, Butler had spent four years with Glossop who were a second division side with whom he made 152 consecutive appearances and helped them to the English (FA) Cup quarter-finals in 1908-09 when they lost 1-0 in a replay to eventual finalists Bristol City. He also gave great service to Stockport County, his three spells with the club spanning more than two decades while with Macclesfield he played after the Great War.

Measuring only 5' 9" Butler was a miner whose father was unknown. His mother's twin sister had a son called Cecil Blakemore who was an inside-forward with numerous teams including Crystal Palace, Bristol City, Brentford, Norwich and Swindon during the 1920s and 1930s.

## BUTLER, Paul John

**POSITION:** Defender

**BIRTHPLACE:** Moston, Manchester

**DATE OF BIRTH:** 02/11/1972

**HEIGHT:** 6' 2" **WEIGHT:** 13st 0lbs

**SIGNED FROM:** Bury, 10/07/1998

**DEBUT:** v QPR, H, 08/08/1998

**LAST MATCH:** v Bristol Rovers, 31/10/2000

**MOVED TO:** Wolves, 31/01/2001

**TEAMS:** Bradford City, Rochdale, Bury, Sunderland, Wolves, Leeds United, MK Dons, Chester City

**INTERNATIONAL:** Republic of Ireland

**SAFC TOTALS:** 93+2 appearances / 4 goals

**Paul Butler was a proper stopper centre-half. He arrived for the record breaking 1998-99 promotion-winning season in which he missed only two games and made a major difference. Along with the introduction of new keeper Thomas Sorensen, Butler was a significant factor as Sunderland conceded only 28 goals in 46 games - a third fewer than the previous season when they just missed out on promotion - and won Nationwide Division One by a country mile.**

By February of the following season, his form in the Premier League - where until the latter's injury he learned from veteran Steve Bould - earned Paul what would be his only full international appearance with the Republic of Ireland against the Czech Republic where he was one of three Sunderland players, along with Niall Quinn and Kevin Kilbane. However, he was replaced at half-time after giant forward Jan Koller (who once interested Peter Reid) had scored twice against him.

Butler also played at 'B' level for Ireland and enjoyed an extensive career that ended just three games short of 600 league appearances during which he won promotion with Bury and Wolves as well as on Wearside. After retiring from football he got into trouble after reportedly assaulting a guest at a golf club event in Cheshire which resulted in him being sentenced to 120 hours community service.

## BUTLER, Thomas Anthony (Tommy)

**POSITION:** Midfielder

**BIRTHPLACE:** Ballymun, Dublin

**DATE OF BIRTH:** 25/04/1981

**HEIGHT:** 5' 8" **WEIGHT:** 10st 7lbs

**SIGNED FROM:** Trainee, 20/09/1997
Professional, 25/06/1998

**DEBUT:** v Walsall, H, 14/09/1999

**LAST MATCH:** v Nottingham Forest, 10/01/2004

**MOVED TO:** Dunfermline, 10/09/2004

**TEAMS:** Belvedere, Sunderland, Darlington (L), Dunfermline, Hartlepool United, Swansea City, Alnwick Town, Newcastle Blue Star, Wear United, Ryhope CA

**INTERNATIONAL:** Republic of Ireland

**SAFC TOTALS:** 17+19 appearances / 0 goals

**Tommy Butler was tipped to become a superstar when a youngster, initially struggled with the level of expectation, but later went on to play well over 100 games for Swansea City as well as winning two full caps for the Republic of Ireland.**

Having been his country's Player of the Year at Under 15 level, Butler broke into the Sunderland side under Peter Reid during 1999-2000. Although never really establishing himself as a first-team player he made his international debut against Finland in Helsinki at the start of the 2002-03 campaign, when he was joined on the international stage by club mates Jason McAteer and Kevin Kilbane, a second cap following two months later as a sub against Switzerland in Dublin.

By the time of what proved to be his final appearance for Sunderland, Tommy was approaching his 23rd birthday. He remained an easy on the eye footballer, but he was not holding down a first-team place let alone dominating games as some had expected he would be able to do. Whether true or not is open to conjecture, but the rumour was that the player had fallen out of love with the game and wanted to give up. Ultimately, this appeared to cause a problem with the club who were reported to have considered legal action against the player for breach of contract with the matter apparently later settled before a planned tribunal.

It was after signing for Swansea in 2006 that Tommy started to show what a good player he could be, finally becoming a regular and playing 50 times as they won promotion to the Championship in 2008 as League One winners. In 2015, Tommy began to try his hand in management with Newcastle United women's team.

## BYFIELD, Darren Asherton

**POSITION:** Forward

**BIRTHPLACE:** Sutton Coldfield, West Midlands

**DATE OF BIRTH:** 29/09/1976

**HEIGHT:** 5' 11" **WEIGHT:** 12st 0lbs

**SIGNED FROM:** Rotherham United, 06/02/2004

**DEBUT:** v Watford, A, 07/02/2004

**LAST MATCH:** v Burnley, A, 09/05/2004

**MOVED TO:** Gillingham, 21/07/2004

**TEAMS:** Aston Villa, Preston North End (L), Northampton Town (L), Cambridge United (L), Blackpool (L), Walsall, Rotherham United, Sunderland, Gillingham, Millwall, Doncaster Rovers, Oldham Athletic, Walsall, Solihull Moors, AFC Telford United, Tamworth, Solihull Moors, Redditch United

**INTERNATIONAL:** Jamaica

**SAFC TOTALS:** 8+9 appearances / 5 goals

**Byfield was a speedy striker who didn't quite have the quality to be top level, but was a decent asset, largely due to his pace. Having started in the Premier League with Aston Villa, for whom he also appeared in the UEFA Cup, the first two of four loans from Villa were with David Moyes' Preston and Ian Atkins' Northampton.**

After a total of ten appearances for Villa, mostly as substitute, Byfield moved to nearby Walsall where in 2001 he came off the bench in extra-time to score the winning goal with a 20-yarder against Reading in the Second Division Play-Off final at the Millennium Stadium. Up front with Byfield was former Sunderland striker Don Goodman while another Roker old boy Brett Angell was also on the bench against a Reading side captained by future Sunderland manager Phil Parkinson.

The previous season, Byfield had contributed to Northampton winning promotion from the Third Division during a brief loan, but those promotions would be his only successes. During his Rotherham days, Darren emulated Craig Russell by scoring four goals in a 6-0 win over Millwall, but it was another home-grown Sunderland forward in Michael Proctor who moved to the Millers in exchange for him.

At Sunderland, he came into the side in the spring of the 2003-04 season and featured in 17 of the last 18 league games, at one point scoring in four games out of five, as Sunderland ended up missing out on promotion via the Play-Offs in which he didn't play. Byfield also missed out on the FA Cup semi-final having been cup-tied as he had played against former club Northampton earlier in the competition for Rotherham.

Moving on at the end of the season, he later played at Wembley in a Play-Off defeat to Hull during his time with Bristol City where he played for Gary Johnson, the father of future Sunderland boss Lee Johnson.

Capped six times by Jamaica with whom he played at the 2003 CONCACAF Gold Cup, Darren completed his playing days with Redditch United where he served as player/manager. He also managed Stratford Town, Walsall Wood and Alvechurch. From June 2008 to November 2009 he was married to pop singer Jamelia.

## BYRNE, Chris Thomas

**POSITION:** Midfielder

**BIRTHPLACE:** Hulme, Manchester

**DATE OF BIRTH:** 09/02/1975

**HEIGHT:** 5' 9" **WEIGHT:** 10st 2lbs

**SIGNED FROM:** Macclesfield Town, 02/06/1997

**DEBUT:** v Sheffield United, A, 10/08/1997

**LAST MATCH:** v Stockport County, A, 01/11/1997

**MOVED TO:** Stockport County, 21/11/1997

**TEAMS:** Crewe Alexandra, Flixton, Droylsden, Macclesfield Town, Sunderland, Stockport County, Macclesfield Town.

**SAFC TOTALS:** 5+5 appearances / 0 goals

**The curious case of Chris Byrne is a striking example of someone doing something that seems unbelievable. A talented footballer with the world at his feet after joining SAFC, and being in the starting line-up as he made his home (and full) debut in the opening league game at the Stadium of Light in 1997, the Mancunian effectively threw it all away due to problems in his personal life.**

Swiftly sold by Sunderland to Stockport who that season finished eighth in Nationwide Division One, it was during Byrne's second spell with Macclesfield that he reportedly, ended up in intensive care after being shot in the leg in a gangland-style shooting in St George's Street in his home town of Hulme where he had been left to bleed to death.

This happened in 2007. Ten years earlier, he had missed a Sunderland Coca-Cola (League) Cup game with Bury having been arrested for allegedly hiding a murder suspect in a hotel as police investigated a fatal machete attack on a 41-year-old man in Old Trafford. Two years later, Byrne was convicted of committing a burglary in a chemists in Urmston, being sentenced to 240 hours of community service having been arrested following a struggle with a police officer. He had also been sought by police following burglaries at two plumbers in Burnley and Chorley.

Former Manchester United star Sammy McIlroy and his Macclesfield assistant Gil Prescott (who later succeeded former Sunderland forward Peter Davenport as Macclesfield manager) first spotted Byrne playing semi-professional football at Droylsden and signed him on non-contract forms in January 1997. Byrne scored a hat-trick in the first half-hour of his Macclesfield debut against Kidsgrove Athletic in the Staffordshire Senior Cup, but it was another hat-trick four months later that propelled him into the club's folklore when his goals in an away win at Kettering secured Macc's promotion to the Football League.

Never able to settle away from the north-west, Byrne's return to his home area with Stockport was ruined by two cruciate ligament injuries that seriously hindered any attempt he might have made to stay out of trouble and focus on his football. Released by County manager Andy Kilner in 2001, Byrne went back to Macclesfield under Prescott who were still a league club. He finished his football career at Macclesfield in 2003.

## BYRNE, John Frederick

**POSITION:** Forward

**BIRTHPLACE:** Wythenshawe, Manchester

**DATE OF BIRTH:** 01/02/1961

**HEIGHT:** 6' 0" **WEIGHT:** 12st 4lbs

**SIGNED FROM:** Brighton & Hove Albion, 23/10/1991

**DEBUT:** v Bristol Rovers, H, 26/10/1991

**LAST MATCH:** v Watford, A, 29/09/1992

**MOVED TO:** Millwall, 26/10/1992

**TEAMS:** York City, QPR, Le Havre, Brighton & Hove Albion, Sunderland, Millwall, Brighton & Hove Albion (L), Crawley Town, Shoreham, Whitehawk

**INTERNATIONAL:** Republic of Ireland

**SAFC TOTALS:** 43 appearances / 15 goals

**John Byrne scored in every round as he steered Sunderland to the FA Cup final of 1992, only to miss a good chance at 0-0 in the Wembley showpiece - a miss that decades later, he admitted still haunted him every day. Nonetheless without Byrne Sunderland may well not have been in the final against Liverpool.**

A skilful and inventive footballer, Byrne deserved to win much more in his career than just the Fourth Division League title with his first club York City in 1984. Under Denis Smith, who later brought him to Sunderland, 'Budgie' top scored with 28 goals as the Minstermen topped a century of points with a squad that included John MacPhail, Ricky Sbragia, Malcolm Crosby, Viv Busby, Roger Jones and Alan Hay who all later came to Sunderland as players, managers or coaches.

After making his name with York, Byrne moved on to QPR who he had impressed against in the League Cup and who he later played for in the 1986 League Cup final against Oxford United.

At international level he won 23 caps for the Republic of Ireland, but none came at Euro 88 or Italia 90 although he made the squads for both tournaments. Later finishing his career in non-league, he briefly had a spell as joint manager of Shoreham in the Sussex County League before becoming a musculoskeletal podiatrist, treating Brighton & Hove Albion players as well as working for the NHS.

# C

For 'Cabral' see Adilson Tavares Varela in the letter T section.

## CALDWELL, Steven (Steve)

**POSITION:** Centre-back

**BIRTHPLACE:** Stirling, Stirlingshire

**DATE OF BIRTH:** 12/09/1980

**HEIGHT:** 6' 2" **WEIGHT:** 13st 13lbs

**SIGNED FROM:** Newcastle United, 27/06/2004

**DEBUT:** v Crewe Alexandra, H, 10/08/2004

**LAST MATCH:** v Preston North End, H, 30/12/2006

**MOVED TO:** Burnley, 31/01/2007

**TEAMS:** North Broomage, Hearts, Newcastle United, Blackpool (L), Bradford City (L), Leeds United (L), Sunderland, Burnley, Wigan Athletic, Birmingham City, Toronto

**INTERNATIONAL:** Scotland

**SAFC TOTALS:** 80+1 appearances / 5 goals

**Steve Caldwell headed the goal that beat Leicester to clinch promotion in 2004-05, a season in which Caldwell made just over half of his total Sunderland appearances. At Newcastle, he had made his full Premier League debut against Sunderland in November 2000, although in total, this was his fourth outing for the Magpies.**

Steve came from a footballing family. The son of Tom Caldwell, who had played for East Stirlingshire and was a Scotland Junior international, and the older brother of Gary who was capped by Scotland and managed Wigan as well as listing the Latics as one of the clubs he played for (most notably Celtic). Prior to joining Newcastle, Steve had a trial for Blackburn Rovers. After 37 appearances for Newcastle (including 13 as sub) and several loans, he was released and swapped Tyneside for Wearside.

An honest and whole-hearted player and natural leader, Steve eventually succeeded Gary Breen as captain at Sunderland, a role he also carried out at international level with Scotland's Under 21s and 'B' team. He also won 12 full caps.

Steve's three seasons at Sunderland were certainly eventful as he played in two promotion campaigns with a relegation in between. While a major figure in the 2005 promotion, in 2006-07 he played just eleven times after being appointed skipper, the last before the turn of the year as Roy Keane replaced him.

Signed on a free, Caldwell was transferred to Burnley in January 2007 for a reported fee of £200,000 rising to a potential £400,000. Former Sunderland assistant manager Steve Cotterill was his gaffer at Turf Moor and handed him the captaincy. Caldwell won promotion with Burnley in 2009, playing at Wembley in the Play-Off final as the Clarets beat a Sheffield United team that included Matt Kilgallon and Greg Halford.

After 119 games, in 2010 he moved to Wigan where he became teammates with his brother Gary. The pair had been together at Newcastle, but Gary had never played for the first-team. They had played alongside each other for Scotland and did so for the first time in club football against Arsenal in January 2011. Following a season with Wigan, Steve switched to Birmingham who while in the Championship enabled Steve to play European football for the first time since his days with Newcastle, the Blues having qualified for the Europa League as League Cup winners in their relegation season.

Becoming skipper at St Andrews, Steve went on to play for Lee Clark when the former Sunderland and Newcastle man succeeded Chris Hughton at the start of Steve's second season which would be his last in English football. In 2013 Caldwell went to Canada, the initial loan move to Toronto resulting in him making the transfer permanent as he played until 2015, again becoming captain before taking up a corporate role with the club and becoming a pundit on Canadian TV.

## CAMP, Lee Michael John

**POSITION:** Goalkeeper

**BIRTHPLACE:** Derby, Derbyshire

**DATE OF BIRTH:** 22/08/1984

**HEIGHT:** 6' 1" **WEIGHT:** 11st 11lbs

**SIGNED FROM:** Cardiff City, 31/01/2018, on loan

**DEBUT:** v Ipswich Town, H, 03/02/2018

**LAST MATCH:** v Reading, A, 14/04/2018

**MOVED TO:** Cardiff City, 07/05/2018, end of loan

**TEAMS:** Derby County, Burton Albion, QPR (L), Norwich City (L), QPR, Nottingham Forest, Norwich City, WBA, AFC Bournemouth, Rotherham United, Cardiff City, Sunderland, Birmingham City, Coventry City, Swindon Town, Clitheroe, Wrexham (to June 2022)

**INTERNATIONAL:** England Under 21 / Northern Ireland

**SAFC TOTALS:** 11+1 appearances / 0 goals

**Sunderland's tradition of truly great goalkeepers was sorely put to the test in 2017-18 when after a decade in the top-flight, the club slid straight through the Championship and were relegated to League One in bottom place. The decision to allow Vito Mannone to leave as well as Jordan Pickford appeared to be a monumental error. Replacements Jason Steele and Robbin Ruiter did so badly that by January a third keeper was recruited in the shape of Lee Camp.**

It can't have been easy for the experienced goalkeeper to come into a side bereft of confidence, but he endured a torrid time and failed to keep a single clean sheet as Sunderland struggled, with him ending the season on the bench. In the eyes of many supporters, he was the poorest of the three keepers that season,

but had the goalkeeper's security blanket of waving his arms around and appearing to blame everyone else whenever a goal was conceded. If nothing else, it was at least a ploy to protect some self-confidence and that alone showed some mental toughness that in his time at Sunderland, Steele at least seemed to lack.

Thankfully, Lee didn't always do as badly as he did at Sunderland. He was Rotherham's Player of the Season in 2015-16 and had won Nottingham Forest's award in 2009-10 when he also was named in the PFA Championship Team of the Year. During that season, Lee won the December Championship Player of the Month award in a campaign where at one point he was unbeaten in over ten hours of football. The following year he captained Forest and was runner-up as their Player of the Year as he maintained a commendable level of consistency. He was also Young Player of the Year at Derby County in 2002-03. The year before his Millers award he had played in nine league games as AFC Bournemouth won the Championship while early in his career he had helped QPR to promotion from the third tier when playing a dozen games on loan from Derby.

The Rams loaned him out several times, his first senior games coming in the Conference with Burton for whom he let in seven goals on his second home appearance. A league debut followed in April for Derby in a 3-2 defeat at Walsall where he came on as a sub against the Saddlers who included future Sunderland player Carl Robinson.

At international level, Camp played in the first ever match at the new Wembley in March 2007, but was beaten after only 25 seconds as Giampaolo Pazzini went on to score a hat-trick in a game which also featured Nedum Onuoha, Kieran Richardson, Anton Ferdinand and Justin Hoyte who all played for Sunderland at some point. That was one of five Under 21 caps Camp won for England after which he gave his allegiance to Northern Ireland who he qualified for via a grandfather. He won nine full caps beginning with an appearance against Serbia four years and a day after his Wembley England appearance.

## CAMPBELL, Fraizer Lee

**POSITION:** Striker

**BIRTHPLACE:** Huddersfield, Yorkshire

**DATE OF BIRTH:** 13/09/1987

**HEIGHT:** 5' 11" **WEIGHT:** 12st 10lbs

**SIGNED FROM:** Manchester United, 11/07/2009

**DEBUT:** v Bolton Wanderers, A, 15/08/2009

**LAST MATCH:** v Bolton Wanderers, H, 15/01/2013

**MOVED TO:** Cardiff City, 21/01/2013

**TEAMS:** Huddersfield Town, Stile Common FC, Manchester United, Royal Antwerp (L), Hull City (L), Spurs (L), Sunderland, Cardiff City, Crystal Palace, Hull City, Huddersfield Town (to June 2022)

**INTERNATIONAL:** England

**SAFC TOTALS:** 36+36 appearances / 10 goals

**"Can we have him back please?" came the plaintive cry of a Tigers supporter after Campbell bagged four goals against his old club for Sunderland in a pre-season friendly in Portugal in July 2010.**

At his best, Campbell was a live-wire. He had been brought in by Steve Bruce to add strength to an attacking department where the first choice front two were Darren Bent and Kenwyne Jones. He played regularly in his first season, but often as a sub or in a game where he was subbed. While there were three cup goals, he had to wait over six months for his first Premier League goal and then scored in three games out of four.

Looking sharp at the start of his second season, Fraizer saw his world crash when he damaged his cruciate ligaments in the month after that four-goal haul against Hull. Seven months later, he suffered a re-occurrence in training and didn't manage a come-back for 16 months after the initial injury. Returning with a goal in a cup-tie with Middlesbrough, Campbell came back with a bang. Three days later, his return to Premier League action saw him score a screamer against Norwich.

This earned him his only call up to the senior England squad under the caretaker leadership of Stuart Pearce who had previously selected him for all 14 of his England Under 21 caps. On the same night his daughter was born, Fraizer came on for the last ten minutes of a 3-2 Wembley defeat by the Netherlands - England scoring twice and conceding once in the minutes Campbell was on the pitch. Campbell came on for Danny Welbeck who had been at Sunderland the previous season. The same game had earlier seen another substitution involving a pair of players with Sunderland connections when Stewart Downing replaced Adam Johnson.

Following the excitement of returning from long-term injury with goals and an England cap, the toll of coming back from the injury showed as Fraizer didn't score again until December. That goal back at his former club Manchester United proved to be his last for the Lads as he was transferred the following month, his final 14 appearances all being as a sub.

Debuting for Cardiff with the winner after coming off the bench at Leeds he marked his home debut with a brace to beat Bristol City and had five goals in his first five games after another winning brace at Wolves. In total, he scored 16 times for the Bluebirds in 52 appearances before a summer 2014 move to Crystal Palace. 27 of his 50 games for the Eagles were as sub, but there were just eight goals in three years. The only Premier League goal of his last two seasons with the club came back at Hull where he finally returned to in the summer of 2017. Eighteen goals and 77 appearances later, he signed for home town Huddersfield where he had been part of the Terriers Centre of Excellence before joining Manchester Utd as a ten-year-old.

He had debuted for the Old Trafford club in a Premier League derby away to Manchester City in August 2007. It was his only Premier League appearance for United who allowed him to go on a trio of loans - including a hugely successful one to Hull - before selling him to Sunderland. At his best, Fraizer possessed the 'X-Factor' - a programme his younger brother Ashford took part in as a member of boy band 'The Risk' in 2011.

## CAMPBELL, John Middleton (Johnny)

**POSITION:** Forward

**BIRTHPLACE:** Edinburgh, Midlothian

**DATE OF BIRTH:** 19/02/1869 - 08/06/1906

**HEIGHT:** 5' 9" **WEIGHT:** 12st 3lbs

**SIGNED FROM:** Renton, 22/06/1889

**DEBUT:** v Blackburn Rovers, A, 18/01/1890

**LAST MATCH:** v Newton Heath, 26/04/1897

**MOVED TO:** Newcastle United, 11/05/1897

**TEAMS:** Renton Union, Renton, Sunderland, Newcastle United

**SAFC TOTALS:** 215 appearances / 154 goals

**One of the greatest names in Sunderland's history, Johnny Campbell was the main goal threat in the great 'Team of All The Talents' who won the league in three seasons out of four and became world champions in the 1890s. What's more, in each of the seasons when Sunderland were league champions in 1892, 1893 and 1895, Campbell was the country's top scorer.**

No player to have topped 200 games for Sunderland can get near to Johnny's goals to games ratio, while of those to have played over 50 times, only Dave Halliday and Brian Clough can improve upon it. In total, Campbell's tally of 154 goals in 215 games breaks down to 136 goals in 186 league games, 18 in 25 (FA) cup ties and none in four Test Matches as Victorian era play-offs were known. Campbell's strike rate of 0.716 would have been even higher, but for a final season where he bagged just four goals in 35 appearances having previously bagged 150 goals in 180 games. That final relatively barren season came under the managership of his step brother Robert Campbell.

The pair may have been half-brothers. Johnny was born John Middleton and added the name Campbell after being adopted, with the belief being that John may have been the illegitimate child of Robert's father.

As well as being Sunderland's leading marksman in three title-winning seasons, Campbell was also part of the side who were proclaimed world champions in 1895. At this time, England and Scotland were far and away the most advanced football playing nations and Sunderland's triumph over Hearts came on the first occasion the reigning league champions of each country met with such an accolade at stake. However, the cup winners of the two countries had previously played for the title with Campbell also a world champion in 1888 when he played for Renton who beat English cup holders WBA after playing - but surprisingly not scoring - in the Scottish Cup final as Cambuslang were thrashed 6-1 at Hampden. In the history of these 'World Championship' games Campbell was the only man to be on the winning side for a Scottish and an English team.

While with Renton, Campbell played for a Scottish XI against a touring Canadian side on 19 September 1888 helping his side to a 4-0 win four days before the Canadians came to Wearside to inflict a 3-0 defeat on Sunderland. However, Campbell's appearance was in a game not regarded as a full international and he remained uncapped, not helped by the fact that after joining Sunderland the following summer his great years in England came at a time when the Scots looked to only select players who were playing in Scotland.

Understood to be Sunderland's first professional player, Campbell came to Wearside before Sunderland joined the Football League. He played numerous times in friendly games before what is considered his official debut. This came on his first competitive appearance, in an English (FA) Cup tie against Blackburn Rovers who went on to win the trophy having been taken to extra-time by Sunderland. That performance helped Sunderland's application to join the league and when they did so the following season, Campbell marked the occasion by scoring in the first three games.

Top-scoring in that first season with 18 goals having played in all but one of the 22 fixtures, he registered Sunderland's first ever league hat-tricks both home and away, scoring four at Bolton and three at home to Villa in addition to another hat-trick in the cup at home to Nottingham Forest. They were three of five goals he scored in as many cup games, one of which was the club's first as a league club and was the winner against Everton who were league champions that season. However, it was the goal that got away which caused controversy. In the semi-final against Notts County Sunderland drew, but in the days before goal nets, had a 'goal' from Campbell disallowed as it was ruled to have not gone through the goal. This incident played a significant role in nets being introduced - evidently debates about technology in football not being the preserve of the 21st century. Had that 'goal' been given, Sunderland may well have reached a final and may even have gone on to win the trophy. Notts lost in the final to Blackburn Rovers who Campbell had scored three times against that term.

Campbell scored four in a 6-1 home win over Blackburn the following season as he netted (nets had been introduced!) 31 in 24 appearances as he fired Sunderland to the title. Goal machine Johnny added another six goals in five games as the cup semi-final was reached again.

The following season, Johnny scored in the first eleven games, getting 17 goals in that spell, beginning with an opening-day hat-trick. Again totalling 31 league goals as Sunderland retained the title, he added three more in three cup games.

In comparison, 18 goals in 25 games as Sunderland were runners-up in 1893-94 was a modest return - although in fact still tremendous. Ever-present with 30 games in 1894-95, he was again the top scorer with 20 in addition to a couple in the cup. Although contemporary reports are conflicting, Campbell is also understood to have scored two of Sunderland's five goals as they beat Hearts to become world champions. There were another 16 goals in total the following season before Johnny's final campaign under his step brother.

Able to give as good as he got in an age of robust play, Campbell was thick set and powerful, but his time on Wearside was up and at the age of 28 he was allowed to move on to second division Newcastle in a joint deal with John Harvie, another former Renton player. Debuting with a goal for the Magpies against Woolwich Arsenal on 4 September 1897 Campbell added 12 goals in 29 games to his red and white total helping United to their first-ever promotion in his one full season after the top flight was extended following Newcastle's complaints about a contrived result that cost them a promotion place in the Test Matches.

Johnny played in Newcastle's first two top-flight matches. but was then sacked by the club for breaking club rules in becoming manager of a pub called The Darnell on Barrack Road. He went on to run pubs at Alnwick Castle and the Turf Hotel on Wearside.

Astonishingly, Campbell's career came to an end before he was 30 years old and yet to 2022, only Jimmy Greaves, Steve Bloomer and Thierry Henry could claim to have been the top-flight's top scorer more often than Campbell.

Aged only 37, Johnny died suddenly in 1906. He had fallen on such hard times that his old Sunderland skipper John Auld, by now a director of Newcastle United, paid for his funeral.

## CAMPBELL, William Gibson (Billy)

**POSITION:** Right-winger

**BIRTHPLACE:** Belfast, Co Antrim

**DATE OF BIRTH:** 02/07/1944

**HEIGHT:** 5' 6½" **WEIGHT:** 9st 10lbs

**SIGNED FROM:** Distillery, 09/09/1964

**DEBUT:** v Sheffield United, A, 21/11/1964

**LAST MATCH:** v Fulham, A, 19/03/1966

**MOVED TO:** Dundee, 31/05/1966

**TEAMS:** Distillery, Sunderland, Dundee, Motherwell, Linfield, Hamilton Academical, Lossiemouth

**INTERNATIONAL:** Northern Ireland

**SAFC TOTALS:** 5 appearances / 0 goals

## CAMPBELL, Billy (Continued)

**Billy Campbell was a winger who played in a European Cup tie against Benfica (who had played in the last three finals) on one wing while Tom Finney was on the other and in international football while George Best was on the opposite flank.**

Signed while Sunderland were managerless following promotion in 1964, Campbell debuted in George Hardwick's first match in charge. In for just a single game, Bill was then overlooked until the last two fixtures of the season.

With the introduction of substitutes in Campbell's second season, he was named on the bench in four early-season games including being named 12th man in the second game subs were allowed. He did get two more games, but Sunderland failed to score in away defeats at Everton and Fulham.

Growing up on the Shankill Road, Billy was only 16 when he debuted for Distillery (once the club of Sunderland managers Bob Kyle and Martin O'Neill) on 29 April 1961. Becoming a regular at Grosvenor Park in 1962-63, he scored twice in a 4-2 win over Belfast rivals Linfield as Distillery won the Northern Irish league for the first time since 1906.

Qualifying for the European Cup, Campbell had the distinction of playing on one wing while the legendary Tom Finney was on the other, having come out of retirement at the age of 41 to play against Benfica. The Irish side earned a 3-3 first leg draw in Belfast before being beaten 5-0 at the original Stadium of Light. After that experience, Campbell ended the season by scoring the winner against Glentoran in the final of the County Antrim Shield, one of 15 goals he scored in a campaign that brought his first Under 23 cap against Wales. Wales were also the opposition when a second cap at that level came in February 1965 in a 2-2 draw at Ninian Park while he was on Sunderland's books.

After being transferred to Dundee, he went on to enjoy such success that the fans dubbed him 'King Billy.' In 1967, he helped the Taysiders reach the League Cup final, but missed the final as his side were beaten 5-3 by Celtic. The following year, he played in the Fairs Cup semi-final against Leeds who fielded eight of the side who would face Sunderland at Wembley five years later.

After over 100 games for Dundee, Campbell made a further 110 appearances for Motherwell before becoming player/manager of Linfield in March 1974. He led them to the Irish League championship in 1974-75 before resigning in October 1975. Returning to Scotland, Billy signed for Hamilton, making the first of three appearances on Boxing Day against Morton. Campbell completed his playing days with Lossiemouth in the Highlands before re-joining Motherwell as assistant manager to Willie McLean.

At full international level, he was called up by former Sunderland winger Billy Bingham for a debut at Windsor Park in a 1-0 win over Scotland. The following month he played alongside Sunderland's John Parke and Martin Harvey in a 2-0 defeat against England at Wembley, but his most famous game came in a 4-1 win over Turkey (four days after Sunderland lost 8-0 at West Ham) in October 1968 when he scored and starred so much that the Turks were said to have mistook him for Best who had a comparatively quiet night.

Sadly, within days of that performance Billy dislocated a hip playing against Hearts for Dundee. It robbed him of his pace and he was never considered to have reached the same standard again. He did however, win three more caps against the USSR, Scotland and Wales the following season. Campbell was also capped three times by Northern Ireland at amateur level in 1964 and '65 while he was with Sunderland, scoring on the last of those appearances against Scotland in February 1964.

## CANA, Lorik Agim

**POSITION:** Midfield
**BIRTHPLACE:** Pristina, Kosovo
**DATE OF BIRTH:** 27/07/1983
**HEIGHT:** 6' 1" **WEIGHT:** 12st 1lb
**SIGNED FROM:** Olympique de Marseille, 24/07/2009
**DEBUT:** v Bolton Wanderers, A, 15/08/2009
**LAST MATCH:** v Wolves, A, 09/05/2010
**MOVED TO:** Galatasaray, 08/07/2010
**TEAMS:** Dardania Lausanne, Paris St Germain, Olympique de Marseille, Sunderland, Galatasaray, Lazio, Nantes
**INTERNATIONAL:** Albania
**SAFC TOTALS:** 33+2 appearances / 0 goals

**Lorik Cana had real presence. Brought in by Steve Bruce to provide a new midfield axis with Lee Cattermole, after drawing at Manchester United and beating Liverpool, the Lads were seventh after nine Premier League games before injury to Cattermole disrupted the partnership.**

Often used as a centre-back elsewhere, particularly at international level, Lorik only occasionally operated in that role for Sunderland. Never one to take prisoners, Cana was never far away from a card with eleven yellows and a red in his 35 games in England.

He had established himself as a genuine leader as captain, but shocked the club when returning for his second season to announce that he wanted to be away. Whether he had been tapped up by Galatasaray is impossible to say, but Lorik's departure was certainly a disappointment. A deep thinking person with a love for discovering local history, sadly his history on Wearside was too short-lived.

Fiercely proud of being from Albania, he won a record 92 caps - 41 of those as captain. One of the two red cards (there were 26 yellows) he received in international football came in his country's first-ever match at the Euro finals - against Switzerland in 2016, but he also played in their surprise victory over Romania at that tournament.

In January 2015, he became Honorary Ambassador for Kosovo and Albanian FA Ambassador in October 2017, as well as a United Nations Ambassador against Poverty.

His senior journey had begun in April 2003 with a debut for PSG against Nantes where he would end his career. Cana's first full season saw him play in the Coupe de France final as Chateauroux were beaten 1-0 at the Stade de France, while he was a regular as PSG finished runners-up to Lyon. Qualification for the Champions League saw Lorik play against Chelsea (who included future SAFC man Wayne Bridge) but the following season he moved on to Olympique de Marseille for whom he made a goalscoring debut against his old team. However, the boot was on the other foot at the end of the season as he played in a French cup final defeat to his former club.

Continuing to play at a high level in France, he helped Lyon to runners-up spot in Ligue 1 in 2006-07 and reached the cup final again a year later when as captain of Marseille he scored in a penalty shoot-out as his side lost out to Sochaux-Montbeliard. Third in 2007-08, during that season he played in a Champions League win against Liverpool at Anfield.

Following Lorik's stint at Sunderland, he was troubled by injuries at his next two clubs, but did play in the 2013 Coppa Italia final as Lazio beat rivals Roma. Lorik's middle name of Agim was after his father, a Yugoslav international who played for Pristina, Dinamo Zagreb, Genclerbirligi, Samsunspor and Lausanne between 1975 and 1990.

## CARMICHAEL, Robert Walker (Bob)

**POSITION:** Inside-right
**BIRTHPLACE:** Baillieston, Glasgow, Lanarkshire
**DATE OF BIRTH:** 24/10/1883 - 08/05/1953
**HEIGHT:** 5' 9" **WEIGHT:** 11st 0lbs
**SIGNED FROM:** Shettleston, 04/01/1907
**DEBUT:** v Bury, H, 20/04/1907
**LAST MATCH:** v Bury, H, 20/04/1907
**MOVED TO:** St Mirren, 25/05/1908
**TEAMS:** Shettleston, Sunderland, St. Mirren, Oldham Athletic, Third Lanark, Clyde, Shelbourne, Dumbarton
**SAFC TOTALS:** 1 appearances / 0 goals

**Bob Carmichael's solitary game for Sunderland came in a late season 5-3 home loss to Bury, a match that secured the Shakers safety and resulted in relegation for Derby County and Stoke. In a game played in torrential rain Carmichael failed to impress, the Newcastle Daily Chronicle pulling no punches in reporting, "It was apparent early on that reserve-team man Carmichael who came from Scotland early in the season was no use to league football. He was a passenger throughout the game".**

Two days before his turn of year signing from Glasgow club Shettleston, Carmichael had been listed as Carr when playing in a trial game against Sunderland's A team.

He went on to score three goals in 16 games for St Mirren, once in five outings for Oldham and eleven times for each of Third Lanark and Clyde in 39 and 35 games respectively.

After World War One, he played six league games for Dumbarton, scoring twice. During World War Two, he became assistant coach at Rangers in July 1943 until after the war and as well as scouting for the Ibrox club, he then remained in the game as groundsman at Partick Thistle until his death at the age of 69.

## CARNEY, Jacob Andrew

**POSITION:** Goalkeeper

**BIRTHPLACE:** Rotherham, South Yorkshire

**DATE OF BIRTH:** 21/04/2001

**HEIGHT:** 6' 0½" **WEIGHT:** 12st 13lbs

**SIGNED FROM:** Manchester United, 02/07/2021

**DEBUT:** Manchester United Under 21s, H, 13/10/2021

**LAST MATCH:**

**MOVED TO:**

**TEAMS:** Manchester United, Stocksbridge (L), Brighouse Town (L), Portadown (L), Sunderland

**SAFC TOTALS:** 1 appearance / 0 goals (to June 2022)

**A debutant against the Under 21s of his former club in the Football League Trophy, Carney was loaned out three times by Manchester United, winning a Player of the Month award at Portadown where he made 27 appearances and earned rave reviews.**

Burnley and Brighton were reported to have been keen on Jacob when he came to Sunderland after eleven years in the academy at Manchester United.

## CARR, Henry (Harry)

**POSITION:** Centre-forward

**BIRTHPLACE:** Southbank, Middlesbrough, Yorkshire

**DATE OF BIRTH:** 08/12/1886 - 17/11/1963

**HEIGHT:** 5' 8" **WEIGHT:** 12st 0lb

**SIGNED FROM:** South Bank, 06/10/1910

**DEBUT:** v Blackburn Rovers, A, 08/10/1910

**LAST MATCH:** v Blackburn Rovers, A, 08/10/1910

**MOVED TO:** Middlesbrough, 14/11/1910

**TEAMS:** South Bank, Sunderland, Middlesbrough, South Bank, Hartlepools United, South Bank, Hartlepools United, South Bank

**INTERNATIONAL:** England amateur

**SAFC TOTALS:** 1 appearances / 0 goals

**Harry Carr had four brothers who like him, all played for Middlesbrough. One of these was Jack Carr who was twice capped by England, the first of those at Ayresome Park in 1905. Harry also played for England, but at amateur level, scoring twice against Ireland in 1910 during one of several spells with Teesside club South Bank.**

It was eight goals scored in three early season games for South Bank early in 1910-11 that led to Harry's opportunity at Sunderland, and again Ireland had an influence as Carr stood in for George Holley who was on duty for the Football League against their Irish counterparts. By all accounts, Harry put in an industrious performance, but clearly didn't make enough of an impression to feature again as top-of-the-table Sunderland edged a 1-0 win over joint bottom of the league Blackburn.

Although he never got another chance for Sunderland, Harry did play three further top flight games in the same season, scoring three goals for Boro. A debut goal against Oldham in February 1911 came in a defeat and two days later there was little consolation in scoring twice as Spurs romped to a 6-2 win. Nonetheless, he probably deserved more than just one more game which came in a defeat at Liverpool the following month.

After a short spell back at South Bank, Harry joined Hartlepools, debuting against Wallsend Park Villa in the North Eastern League on Christmas Day 1911. It was one of four games he played for the club where he scored once.

Harry went on to score the winner in the 1913 FA Amateur Cup final as South Bank beat Oxford City at Bishop Auckland after a 1-1 draw at Reading's Elm Park. Nicknamed 'Pep' on Teesside, Harry went on to become trainer of South Bank after his playing days were over.

## CARTER, Darren Anthony

**POSITION:** Midfielder

**BIRTHPLACE:** Solihull, West Midlands

**DATE OF BIRTH:** 18/12/1983

**HEIGHT:** 6' 1" **WEIGHT:** 12st 6lbs

**SIGNED FROM:** Birmingham City, 16/09/1994, on loan

**DEBUT:** v Preston North End, H, 18/09/2004

**LAST MATCH:** v West Ham United, H, 04/12/2004

**MOVED TO:** Birmingham City, 06/12/2004, end of loan

**TEAMS:** Birmingham City, Sunderland (L), WBA, Preston North End, Millwall (L), Cheltenham Town, Northampton Town, Forest Green Rovers, Solihull Moors

**INTERNATIONAL:** England Under 20

**SAFC TOTALS:** 8+2 appearances / 1 goal

**Darren Carter was brought in on loan by Mick McCarthy and contributed to a successful promotion campaign, not least with a debut goal in a home win. It wasn't the first time he had scored for the home side at the Stadium of Light. He had scored for England Under 20s against Italy. It was one of eleven caps he won at that level, three of which came at the 2003 FIFA World Youth Championships in the UAE when a team including Matt Kilgallon and Michael Chopra were eliminated without scoring a goal.**

As a teammate of Stern John, Darren scored the decisive penalty to take Birmingham into the Premier League in 2002 with victory over Norwich City at the Millennium Stadium. Having made 85 Premier League appearances early in his career for Birmingham and West Brom, Darren played extensively in the championship, but played in the National League for his last six seasons with his last two clubs, being named in the National League team of the Season with his home town Solihull Moors in 2018-19. In November 2021, he was announced as the interim manager of Birmingham City women's team.

## CARTER, Horatio Stratton (Raich)

**POSITION:** Inside-forward

**BIRTHPLACE:** Hendon, Sunderland, Co Durham

**DATE OF BIRTH:** 21/12/1913 - 09/10/1994

**HEIGHT:** 5' 8" **WEIGHT:** 10st 6lbs

**SIGNED FROM:** Sunderland Forge, 01/11/1930

**DEBUT:** v Sheffield Wednesday, A, 15/10/1932

**LAST MATCH:** v Wolves, A, 06/05/1939

**MOVED TO:** Derby County, 21/12/1945

**TEAMS:** Sunderland Forge, Sunderland, Esh Winning (L), Hartlepools United (WW2 Guest), Notts County (WW2 Guest), Huddersfield Town (WW2 Guest), Cardiff City (WW2 Guest), York City (WW2 Guest), Nottingham Forest (WW2 Guest), Derby County, Hull City, Cork Athletic

**INTERNATIONAL:** England

**SAFC TOTALS:** 278 appearances / 128 goals

**Arguably the finest footballer ever to play for Sunderland, Raich Carter himself would be very likely to agree, "My dad always thought he was the best player no matter who he was playing for" noted his son, also called Raich Carter, when Horatio Stratton Carter was inducted into the Sunderland AFC Hall of Fame at its inaugural dinner in 2019.**

Carter had justifiable cause to hold more than a touch of arrogance. Raich would be more likely to be included in an all-time England XI than any other player ever to wear the red and white stripes. The only player to win the FA Cup either side of World War Two, Carter captained Sunderland when they won the trophy for the first time in 1937, scoring the decisive second goal as the final was won 3-1. A year earlier he had scored 31 goals from inside-right as the league title was won and in between those trophies scored the winner against Arsenal as the Charity Shield was also added to Sunderland's haul of silverware.

It has been claimed that Carter was the great great great nephew of Captain James Cook, the celebrated adventurer who 'discovered' Australia, but research from Mike Gibson (one of the co-authors of Volume One of Sunderland: The Absolute Record) shows there is no family heritage link with Margaret Cook, Captain Cook's sister who is the only person who had family that had offspring.

Carter's own international travels would have been far greater had many of his best years not been lost to the war. First capped as a 20-year-old against Scotland at Wembley in 1934, he made his last international appearance in 1947 away to Switzerland. At the time this was the second longest span for an England player. The first six of his 13 official caps came while he was still with Sunderland, as were two of his seven goals. In addition to this, Carter played in 17 war-time games while still with his hometown club. He also played four times for the Football League and later, while playing as a veteran in Cork, represented the League of Ireland against the Football League.

## CARTER, Raich (Continued)

Carter was a supremely talented schemer with the vision to see what was possible and the ability to make it happen. He would dictate games with distinction. Possessing the ability to shoot powerfully with either foot, this was combined with a body swerve that could leave defenders facing the wrong way while his first touch was that of a master.

His dad Robert died in 1928 before Raich signed for Sunderland. Carter senior was also from Hendon and played for Burslem Port Vale, Stockport County, Fulham and Southampton before the First World War. Raich himself was rejected by Leicester City in December 1930 on the grounds of being too small. Eighteen when he debuted for Sunderland, Carter quickly became a regular in the side and from his second season onwards always reached double figures in the goals charts, hitting 61 across the glorious seasons of 1935-36 and 1936-37.

In addition to the figures above, Carter scored three more goals in the three league games of the 1939-40 season before that campaign was declared null and void with the outbreak of World War Two. He then went on to add another 58 goals in 78 war-time appearances including scoring in both legs of the 1942 League War Cup final with Wolves. Carter's very last (unofficial) game for Sunderland came on 15 December 1945 against Manchester United at Manchester City's Maine Road.

Six days later, he signed for Derby County on his 32nd birthday, Sunderland having turned down his suggestion that he was offered a ten-year contract. Carter had played for Derby during the war as a 'Guest' while stationed at an RAF pilot rehabilitation centre in Loughborough. His first wife Gertrude had also moved from Sunderland to Spondon near Derby 18 months before they married in Spondon on the Monday before Carter captained Sunderland to the cup in 1937, centre-forward Bobby Gurney being his best man.

Having won the FA Cup in 1946 with Derby where he had formed a fabulous partnership with the great Irish inside-forward Peter Doherty, a quirk of the fixture list brought Raich back to Roker for his league debut for his new club as Derby lost 3-2. That was the first of 63 league appearances he made for Derby during which he scored 34 goals. At the end of March 1948, Raich moved to Hull as player/assistant manager to Major Frank Buckley. Within a month, he was player/manager and took the Tigers to the Division Three North title and quarter-final of the FA Cup as well as bringing in his fellow 1937 FA Cup final scorer Eddie Burbanks and future Sunderland player Don Revie. The FWA Footballer of the Year Award only began in 1947-48. Carter was runner-up in its second season while with Hull, but would surely have won the award more than once had it existed when he was at his peak.

Like Revie, Carter later managed Leeds United. Taking over in May 1953, he took them to promotion to the top flight three years later. Three months before moving to Elland Road, Carter agreed a lucrative short-term contract with Cork Athletic, winning the FAI Cup and the Munster Cup. In February 1960, he became manager of Mansfield, but suffered relegation three months later. By January 1963, Raich was back in the north east when he took over as Middlesbrough manager, remaining there until February 1966 when he was sacked.

On top of such a fantastic footballing career, Carter also played cricket for Durham and three first-class matches for Derbyshire, his two-footed ability as a footballer (he was best with his left) being further illustrated by the fact he was a right-handed batsman, but a left arm bowler.

When Hull City welcomed Sunderland to open their new stadium in 2003, the clubs competed for the Raich Carter Trophy. Carter's major footballing medals are on display in Sunderland City Centre Museum & Winter Gardens while near his birthplace a Sports Centre bears his name near a mural of Carter on the side of the Blue House pub, situated near Sunderland's first ground, the Blue House Field.

From 1952, Raich Carter's Soccer Stars magazine was in circulation. Its name changed in 1955, but it lives on into the 2020s, having been incorporated into the well-respected World Soccer magazine in 1970. His autobiography 'Footballer's Progress' was published in 1950 with a further biography, 'Raich Carter: The Story of One of England's Greatest Footballers' produced in 2003.

In later life, Raich ran the sports department of a shop in Hull where he has a road named after him. From 1969, he was also a member of the Pools Panel which decided on the results of postponed games for the football pools. Carter also has the unique distinction of being the only Sunderland footballer cast in wax at Madame Tussauds, an accolade he received in 1937 as Sunderland's cup-winning captain.

## CARTER, Timothy Douglas

**POSITION:** Goalkeeper

**BIRTHPLACE:** Bristol

**DATE OF BIRTH:** 05/10/1967 - 19/06/2008

**HEIGHT:** 6' 1" **WEIGHT:** 12st 0lbs

**SIGNED FROM:** Bristol Rovers, 24/12/1987

**DEBUT:** v Bristol City, H, 23/04/1988

**LAST MATCH:** v Peterborough United, A, 07/11/1992

**MOVED TO:** Hartlepool United, 24/07/1993

**TEAMS:** Bristol Rovers, Newport County (L), Sunderland, Carlisle United (L), Bristol City (L), Birmingham City (L), Hartlepool United, Millwall, Blackpool, Oxford United, Millwall, Halifax Town

**INTERNATIONAL:** England Youth

**SAFC TOTALS:** 50 appearances / 0 goals

**Tim Carter's first senior appearance for Sunderland came at Wembley in a goalless draw (and penalty shoot-out defeat) in the Football League (Mercantile Credit) Centenary tournament on 16 April 1988. With that game being just 20 minutes each way, his actual debut came a week later at home to his hometown team Bristol City. Carter had come from the blue half of Bristol, debuting for Rovers as an 18-year-old.**

In April 1985, Carter won three England Youth caps at a tournament in Cannes playing in 2-1 and 3-1 defeats to the USSR and the Netherlands either side of a 2-2 draw with Italy. After 47 league games for the Gas, Tim came to Sunderland. In four of his six seasons at Roker Park, he played two or fewer league games, but in the 1989-90 promotion season, he played 26 times while there were 16 appearances in his last campaign of 1992-93.

During his time on Wearside, Tim went on three loans before calling time on his spell as a number two at Sunderland. He went on to become first choice at Millwall before ending his playing days at Halifax where in the Shaymen's first season back in the Football League he kept goal ten times, being substituted in the last of his career tally of exactly 200 league games in a goalless draw at home to Rochdale in April 1999.

The following year, Tim returned to Sunderland as academy goalkeeping coach, stepping up to first-team coach in 2003. He held that role until July 2007 when he resumed his duties with the academy after Roy Keane brought in his old Manchester Utd colleague Raimond van der Gouw to coach the senior keepers.

Having worked with Estonia's best-ever goalkeeper Mart Poom at Sunderland, Tim had become the part-time goalkeeping coach for Estonia, often joking that whenever he went to Tallinn he was accommodated at a top hotel in the Presidential Suite, loving the fact that this made it the President Carter Suite. Ever since first arriving at Sunderland as a young lad with the broadest of Bristol accents, Tim had always seemed a likeable lad with a sense of humour - often claiming in his later years that bending to put his socks on counted as his warm up.

Very sadly in the summer of 2008 at the age of just 40, Tim was found dead in the Stretford area of Manchester. With injuries consistent with hanging and having left handwritten notes for his family, a verdict of suicide was recorded. Apparently a major factor in Tim's death was his struggle to accept the disability of his son Jensen who had been born with cerebral palsy in 2003. Five months after Tim's death, County Durham and Darlington Foundation Trust were reported to have admitted liability for 'negligent delay' in the child's delivery. A seven figure settlement was agreed in the High Court in London to help the boy to be cared for throughout his life. Evidently, whatever the highs and lows of the game of football, the tragic death of Tim Carter and the struggles of his son and the wider family put football into perspective.

## CARTERON, Patrice

**POSITION:** Right-back

**BIRTHPLACE:** St Brieuc, France

**DATE OF BIRTH:** 30/07/1970

**HEIGHT:** 6' 0" **WEIGHT:** 12st 2lbs

**SIGNED FROM:** St. Etienne, 08/03/2001, on loan

**DEBUT:** v Chelsea, A,17/03/2001

**LAST MATCH:** v Everton, A, 19/05/2001

**MOVED TO:** St. Etienne, 21/05/2001, end of loan

**TEAMS:** St Brieuc, Laval, Rennes, Olympique Lyonnais, St Etienne, Sunderland, AS Cannes

**SAFC TOTALS:** 8 appearances / 1 goal

**An elegant long-striding full-back, Patrice Carteron made a striking impression in his brief stay at Sunderland with a spectacular goal at the Stadium of Light to earn a derby draw with Newcastle in April 2001. The French full-back gained his reward for a lung-bursting run to overlap and get on the end of a Don Hutchison through ball to score at the North Stand. It was one of eight of the last nine games of the season that Patrice played in as Peter Reid's Sunderland finished seventh in the Premier League.**

## CARTERON, Patrice (Continued)

Carteron's cameo in English football was a brief period away from an extensive playing career in France where his highlights included winning the Intertoto Cup with Lyon in 1997 and Ligue 2 with Saint-Etienne in 2004.

However, after his playing days, Patrice broadened his horizons and coached and managed extensively in Africa and the USA. After managing Cannes and Dijon, winning promotion to Ligue 1 with the latter in 2012, he became head coach of Mali, leading them to third place in the African Cup of Nations. He went on to win an African Champions League trophy and two Congolese titles with TP Mazembe, managed Wadi Degla in Egypt, Riyadh club Al-Nassr in Saudi, Phoenix Rising in Florida, Egyptian club Al-Ahly who he took to the final of the African Champions League and Moroccan club Raja Casablanca with whom he won the African Super Cup. He went on to win the same trophy after a return to Egypt with Zamalek, also taking the Egyptian Super Cup. In 2020, he returned to Saudi with Al Taawoun in January 2021 only to return to manage Zamalek two months later.

## CASE, Norman

**POSITION:** Centre-forward

**BIRTHPLACE:** Prescot, Liverpool, Lancashire

**DATE OF BIRTH:** 01/09/1925 - 23/01/1973

**HEIGHT:** 5' 8"

**SIGNED FROM:** Ards, Northern Ireland, 30/09/1949

**DEBUT:** v Stoke City, H, 26/12/1949

**LAST MATCH:** v Aston Villa ,H, 30/08/1950

**MOVED TO:** Watford, 16/12/1950

**TEAMS:** Sheffield United, Leyton Orient, Rochdale, Ards, Sunderland, Watford, Yeovil Town (L), Rochdale, Hamilton Academical, Cheltenham Town, Canterbury City

**INTERNATIONAL:** Northern Irish League

**SAFC TOTALS:** 4 appearances / 2 goals

**Having failed to get a game with any of his three previous league clubs, Norman Case marked his Football League debut with two goals as Len Shackleton scored the other in a 3-0 Boxing Day win over Stoke in 1949. It kept him his place in the return at Stoke 24 hours later, but he was unable to stay in the team once Dicky Davis was fit again, hardly surprisingly as Davis was the first division's top scorer that season.**

There were just two more appearances for Norman, one towards the end of the season and one early the next, before he moved on to Watford where he scored four times in ten games. Moving to Rochdale in February 1952, Norman played twice for the Spotland club without scoring.

He fared better with 23 goals in a productive loan spell with Yeovil and in his native Northern Ireland, once scoring five goals in a game for Ards against Coleraine. Norman also netted on his one appearance for the Northern Irish League, albeit a consolation goal in an 8-1 loss to their Scottish counterparts before 62,000 at Ibrox in September 1949, shortly before he signed for Sunderland.

During World War Two, he had been discharged from the Royal Navy after 18 months service due to pulmonary tuberculosis. Following his retirement from football he worked in his wife's family business as a carpenter.

## CATTERMOLE, Lee Barry

**POSITION:** Midfielder

**BIRTHPLACE:** Stockton, Co Durham

**DATE OF BIRTH:** 21/03/1988

**HEIGHT:** 5' 10" **WEIGHT:** 12st 8lbs

**SIGNED FROM:** Wigan Athletic, 12/08/2009

**DEBUT:** v Bolton Wanderers, A, 15/08/2009

**LAST MATCH:** v Charlton Athletic, N, 26/05/2019

**MOVED TO:** Mutually cancelled contract, 01/07/2019

**TEAMS:** Middlesbrough, Wigan Athletic, Sunderland, VVV Venlo

**INTERNATIONAL:** England Under 21

**SAFC TOTALS:** 242+19 appearances / 10 goals

**At Sunderland for a decade in an era when long-service largely seemed a thing of the past, as of June 2022, Lee Cattermole's tally of 144 teammates at the club was the most by any player ever. Seven red cards also made Cattermole the record holder for the most dismissals in a Sunderland shirt, like the teammate fact, an indicator of the age in which he played.**

Occasionally guilty of the 'Clattermole' label he was given, Lee was a much better footballer than many gave him credit for. He wouldn't have captained England Under 21s or played in the Premier League for so long if that wasn't the case.

Always highly committed, Lee captained the side, but even when he relinquished the arm band, he was still effectively a leader on the pitch, driving people on and demanding that 100% was given. On days when his radar was working well, his ability to spread the play by pinging passes forward could also be an effective weapon.

A really deep thinker on the game, Lee felt his game really developed under Gus Poyet who restored Cattermole as his first choice holding midfielder ahead of Liam Bridcutt who he had bought from their old club Brighton, evidently with the intention of Bridcutt taking over from 'Catts' as the lynch-pin.

Troubled by injuries and suspensions, only in his penultimate season at Sunderland did Cattermole manage as many as 30 league starts, although there were only two campaigns where he began fewer than half the league fixtures. To his credit, he played many times when he was nowhere near fit, but regularly made himself available to try and help the team. Rarely a scorer, he registered a goal only three times before his final season when in the third tier he found the net seven times, becoming the sixth player in the club's history to score in three different divisions. However, that season it was his penalty that was saved to settle the shoot-out at Wembley in the Checkatrade Trophy final with Portsmouth.

The son of former Middlesbrough reserve player Barry Cattermole, Lee began with Boro, becoming their youngest-ever captain at the age of 18 years and 47 days. He had debuted in a Tyne-Tees derby as a 17-year-old and took the Man of the Match award. He played for Boro in the 2006 UEFA Cup final, but was disappointed to only come on as sub for the last five minutes as Boro were beaten 4-0 by Seville in Eindhoven.

A £3.5m transfer fee took him to Wigan in July 2008, but despite signing a three-year contract after one season Wigan almost doubled their money as his ex-Latics boss Steve Bruce invested £6m to enable Lee to follow him to Sunderland. It proved excellent value for money as Cattermole gave Sunderland such long service and captained the side from 2010 to 2013 until Paolo Di Canio preferred John O'Shea.

Leaving Sunderland in 2019 after his final match was a third appearance for the club at Wembley - in the 2019 Play-Off final v Charlton - Cattermole completed his playing days with a season in the Netherlands with Eredivisie club VVV Venlo. He then took his coaching badges and began his coaching career working with youngsters back at his first club Middlesbrough while still referring to Sunderland as 'Us' while making his debut as a pundit on Sky TV when commenting on Sunderland's win at Ipswich in January 2021.

## CELUSTKA, Ondrej

**POSITION:** Right-back

**BIRTHPLACE:** Zlin, Czechoslovakia

**DATE OF BIRTH:** 18/06/1989

**HEIGHT:** 6' 1" **WEIGHT:** 12st 8lbs

**SIGNED FROM:** Trabzonspor, 12/08/2013, on loan

**DEBUT:** v Fulham, H, 17/08/2013

**LAST MATCH:** v Swansea City, A, 11/05/2014

**MOVED TO:** Trabzonspor, 12/05/2014, end of loan

**TEAMS:** Tescoma Zlin, Slavia Prague, Palermo (L), Trabzonspor, Sunderland (L), FC Nurnburg, Antalyaspor, Sparta Prague (to June 2022)

**INTERNATIONAL:** Czech Republic

**SAFC TOTALS:** 20+7 appearances / 0 goals

**An unused sub for Sunderland in the 2014 Capital One Cup final, Celustka didn't score for Sunderland, but during his loan spell with the club took just three minutes of his international debut in November 2013 to score against Canada. He became a regular international with the Czech Republic starring for them at the delayed Euro 2020 tournament in 2021.**

He broke into senior football in the 2007-08 season in the Czech Republic with Tescoma (later Fastav) Zlin before a brief taste of Serie A in Italy when he came off the bench for the last twelve minutes of a home win for Sicilian side Palermo, getting onto the pitch just in time to celebrate with Fabrizio Miccoli as he completed his hat-trick.

The following summer he signed for Slavia Prague with whom a highlight came on his return to Italy as he scored the only goal of the game as Inter were beaten in a Champions League match at the San Siro. That was one of six Champions League appearances Celustka made that season followed by two Europa League games.

2012 brought a switch to the Turkish Super Lig with Trabzonspor with whom he debuted in a 1-1 draw at Kardemir in August, the first of 19 appearances in his first season before he was loaned to Sunderland.

Released by Trabzonspor at the end of his loan in England, Celustka moved to Germany, a free transfer taking him to Bundesliga 2 outfit FC Nurnberg. Ondrej spent a season there returning to Turkey with Antalyaspor with whom he was sent off on his return to Trabzonspor just before Christmas in 2015.

Antalyaspor provided the longest spell of Celustka's career. In five years Celustka played in 142 league games, all but four of them as starts. He also continued to play for the Czech Republic. He appeared in a 5-0 defeat to England at Wembley in March 2019, but claimed an assist for the opening goal (scored by Jakub Brabec) the following October at his former club Slavia in what was England's first defeat in a major tournament qualifying game for a decade.

In August 2020, Celustka joined Sparta Prague, debuting that month at FC Brno. He again tasted European football at the San Siro, but this time on the losing side in a Europa League game with Milan while his second European appearance for Sparta saw him sent off at Lille.

## CHALMERS, James (Jamie)

**POSITION:** Outside-left

**BIRTHPLACE:** Old Luce, Wigtownshire

**DATE OF BIRTH:** 03/12/1877 - 12/07/1915

**HEIGHT:** 5' 10" **WEIGHT:** 12st 0lbs

**SIGNED FROM:** Greenock Morton, 04/05/1897

**DEBUT:** v (Sheffield) Wednesday, A, 04/09/1897

**LAST MATCH:** v Bolton Wanderers, H, 24/09/1898

**MOVED TO:** Preston North End, 13/10/1898

**TEAMS:** Beith, Greenock Morton, Sunderland, Preston North End, Notts County, Beith, Partick Thistle, Watford, Tottenham Hotspur, Swindon Town, Norwich City, Beith, Bristol Rovers, Clyde

**SAFC TOTALS:** 27 appearances / 5 goals

**Chalmers was 37 when he lost his life, killed in action at Gallipoli during World War One. In a career that took in a dozen clubs, his claim to fame at Sunderland had been in scoring the last ever league goal on the old Newcastle Road ground prior to the club's move to Roker Park.**

Wigtownshire-born, Chalmers had played for Beith and Morton before crossing the border and joining Sunderland. He played regularly throughout 1897-98, scoring five goals, two of them in the final match at Sunderland's home for a dozen years and where they had lifted three league titles. Those goals against Forest helped Sunderland to runners-up position as the club's time at Newcastle Road came to an end.

Early the following season, Chalmers was on the move after appearing in the first-ever league game at Roker Park. He had caught Sunderland's eyes with eight goals in 18 games for Morton. Afterwards, he scored twice each for Preston and Notts County in ten and 25 games. He continued to regularly be on the move. Southern League Spurs were the first club he spent more than one season at, debuting in a defeat at Northampton in January 1903. Chalmers' only Southern League goal for Spurs came against Brighton in October of the same year having scored his first goal in the London League against QPR the previous March.

He played much more regularly in two years at Swindon for whom he scored 13 times in 62 games between 1904 and 1906. He then had 14 games over two years with Norwich and a final English appearance in one game for Bristol Rovers for whom he scored before he finished his playing days back in Scotland.

During the Great War, Chalmers served as a private (number 8266) in the 4th Battalion Royal Scots Fusiliers, having enlisted at Kilmarnock in August 1914 as part of the South Scottish Brigade, Lowland Division. In May 1915, as part of what by now was the 155th Brigade, 52nd (Lowland) Division, Chalmers sailed from Liverpool going via Mudros to Gallipoli where the battalion disembarked on June 7th.

James Chalmers' death is recorded as 12 July 1915, just over a month after landing and three months into the Gallipoli campaign which by this point had become a war of attrition. Carlyon's splendid history of the Gallipoli disaster notes that the 155th Brigade saw its first real action on the day of Chalmers' death, 12 July 1915, attacking a height called Achi Baba in fierce heat and wearing full traditional British combat gear. 'Chaos' and 'a scene from hell' is how the writer describes it with huge losses in an attack on the Turkish support trenches. Many of Chalmers' battalion fell here.

## CHAMBERLAIN, Alec Francis Roy

**POSITION:** Goalkeeper

**BIRTHPLACE:** March, Cambridgeshire

**DATE OF BIRTH:** 20/06/1964

**HEIGHT:** 6' 2" **WEIGHT:** 13st 1lb

**SIGNED FROM:** Luton Town, 01/07/1993

**DEBUT:** v Derby County, A, 14/08/1993

**LAST MATCH:** v Tranmere Rovers, A, 05/05/1996

**MOVED TO:** Watford, 05/07/1996

**TEAMS:** Ramsey Town, Ipswich Town, Colchester United, Everton, Tranmere Rovers (L), Luton Town, Chelsea (L), Sunderland, Liverpool (L) Watford

**SAFC TOTALS:** 107+1 appearances / 0 goals

**The first goalkeeper to come on as a sub in the league for Sunderland - replacing Tony Norman against Southend in October 1994 - Alec Chamberlain collected a couple of medals while with Sunderland. One was a 1995-96 Championship medal and the other was a 1995 League Cup winner's medal won as an unused sub for Liverpool while on loan from the Black Cats.**

Chamberlain didn't get a game for the Anfield club, but was on the bench as Bolton were beaten at Wembley on a day when each side included a pair of players with Sunderland connections: Alan Stubbs, Jason McAteer, Phil Babb and Stig Inge Bjornebye - the latter at one point coming very close to signing for the club.

Alec was a very calm and composed goalkeeper who rarely made a spectacular save, largely because his positional sense was outstanding. He was doing well as Sunderland moved towards the Endsleigh Division One title when Peter Reid made the surprising move of dropping him to bring in Shay Given. The young Irish keeper was exceptional, but when he got injured, Chamberlain came back in for the final six games of the season and only conceded in the last game at Tranmere after the title had already been secured.

## CHAMBERS, Brian Mark

**POSITION:** Midfielder

**BIRTHPLACE:** Newcastle, Northumberland

**DATE OF BIRTH:** 31/10/1949

**HEIGHT:** 5' 10" **WEIGHT:** 10st 12lbs

**SIGNED FROM:** Newcastle United Youths, 01/07/1965

**DEBUT:** v Luton Town, A, 31/10/1970

**LAST MATCH:** v Nottingham Forest, A, 24/04/1973

**MOVED TO:** Arsenal, 10/05/1973

**TEAMS:** Newcastle United, Sunderland, Arsenal, Luton Town, Bournemouth, Halifax Town, Poole Town, Salisbury City, Dorchester Town, Swanage, Poole Town

**INTERNATIONAL:** England schoolboy

**SAFC TOTALS:** 57+14 appearances / 7 goals

**Brian Chambers suffered the disappointment of not quite making it into Sunderland's cup-final 12 in 1973. Named in the Wembley programme as the single substitute allowed in those days, Chambers had been on the bench in the semi-final, but while he had played 17 times that season, he hadn't featured in the two games before the final.**

Five days after the cup final the elegant midfield schemer signed for Arsenal. Ironically, after being an unused sub against them in the cup semi-final, Chambers played for the Gunners against Wolves in the third place play-off which was held over to the start of the following season. By this time, he had appeared as a sub for Arsenal in a couple of friendlies in Norway and went on to play against Rangers in front of 65,000 at Ibrox in pre-season, but when the real stuff came around he got only two games in the league and one in each of the cups - his debut coming as a sub in his hometown of Newcastle in September 1973.

## CHAMBERS, Brian (Continued)

Moving to Luton after a season at Highbury, Brian played 76 league games for the Hatters followed by 59 for Millwall and 42 for Bournemouth before finishing his league career by playing in ten of the last eleven games of the 1980-81 season in Division Four with Halifax Town, the last at home to Aldershot three days short of eight years since the 1973 cup final. In total, Chambers made 251 Football League appearances, scoring 31 times.

The first 63 of those came for Sunderland. An unused sub in the first game after the club were relegated in 1970, Brian's bow came on his 21st birthday as a sub at the end of October where he did well enough to earn a first start in the next game. After 20 league appearances in his opening campaign, Brian's best season was the next - 1971-72, where all but one of his 26 league games were starts and two of this three goals came in a 3-0 home win over Charlton in January 1972.

After his Football League days were over, Brian extended his career in non-league football in the south of the country, including spells as player/manager of Swanage and Poole. He settled in Bournemouth and became a financial advisor.

Although he missed out on Wembley glory with Sunderland, he did win a trophy at the club, playing in both legs of the FA Youth Cup final in 1967 against Birmingham City after scoring a key goal in the two-legged semi-final with Scunthorpe. In 2021, he agreed to accept the Freedom of the City of Sunderland as part of a group of players to feature in the cup run, in his case as an unused sub in both of the famous games with Manchester City as well as the semi-final.

## CHAPMAN, Lee Roy

**POSITION:** Forward

**BIRTHPLACE:** Lincoln, Lincolnshire

**DATE OF BIRTH:** 05/12/1959

**HEIGHT:** 6' 1½" **WEIGHT:** 13st 5lbs

**SIGNED FROM:** Arsenal, 28/12/1983

**DEBUT:** v Luton Town, H, 31/12/1983

**LAST MATCH:** v Leicester City, A, 12/05/1984

**MOVED TO:** Sheffield Wednesday, 12/07/1984

**TEAMS:** Stafford Rangers, Stoke City, Plymouth Argyle (L), Arsenal, Sunderland, Sheffield Wednesday, Niort, Nottingham Forest, Leeds United, Portsmouth, West Ham United, Southend Utd (L). Ipswich Town, Leeds United (L), Swansea City, Stromsgodset IF

**INTERNATIONAL:** England 'B'

**SAFC TOTALS:** 16+1 appearances / 4 goals

**Signed by Alan Durban who had nurtured him at Stoke City, Lee Chapman was a centre-forward who had a disappointing time at Sunderland. He played for just half a season before being sold for half the £200,000 paid for him. He scored just four times for the Lads, but one of his goals came in a key game on the last day of the 1983-84 season. On that occasion, Lee opened the scoring in a win at Leicester in a match that at the start of play Sunderland had to get a result to be sure of survival.**

Having seen his mentor Durban sacked during his short time at the club, Chapman swiftly moved on. A tall blond leader of the line, Chapman had the physical attributes to do well, but rarely looked the part, although totalling 202 goals in 575 league appearances, evidently he was a quality forward. Those figures include four goals from 15 games in brief spells in French and Norwegian football with his best spells coming in Yorkshire with Leeds United and Sheffield Wednesday.

It was the Owls he moved to from Sunderland. He was an instant hit at Hillsborough under Howard Wilkinson. The opening one of 19 league and cup goals in his first season came at Newcastle on his second appearance while inevitably another came against Sunderland who were relegated as Chapman helped Wednesday to a healthy eighth place. Thirteen goals came in his second season in South Yorkshire before successive seasons where he topped 20 goals.

Reunited with Wilkinson at Leeds, he played the last 21 games of the 1989-90 season, his 12 goals helping them to win Division Two on goal difference. In Lee's first full season at Elland Road he was the top scorer in the country with 31 goals in all competitions, 21 of those in the league as Leeds finished fourth. A year later, he top-scored for Leeds with 20 goals (16) league as Wilko's Whites became league champions in the last year before the beginning of the FA Premier League.

He went on to score Leeds' first goals in the Premiership, netting both in a 2-1 win over Wimbledon on the opening day of the season. Playing up front with Eric Cantona, both were soon on the scoresheet together in a European Cup tie with VfB Stuttgart.

Chapman's time at Leeds was not his first success under a manager with Sunderland connections. He moved to Leeds from Brian Clough's Nottingham Forest with whom he played in the 1989 League Cup final as they beat Luton (for whom Mick Harford scored).

In the same season, Chapman scored twice at Wembley himself as Forest beat an Everton team that included Paul Bracewell in the Full Members' Cup final. Chapman also played for Forest back at his old home ground of Hillsborough on the horrendous day of the disaster in an FA Cup semi-final with Liverpool.

Surprisingly, given the fulfilment of his potential after leaving Roker, Chapman never won a full cap. A solitary cap at 'B' level against Iceland at Watford in 1991 - where he was substituted by future Sunderland forward Brian Deane and Brian Clough's Sunderland-born son Nigel scored the only goal - was the closest he came.

Chapman also won a single Under 21 cap. Ten years before his 'B' team recognition fewer than 6,000 attended a game with the Republic of Ireland at Anfield where his teammates included Iain Hesford, Mark Proctor and David Hodgson who all played for Sunderland at some point.

Famously, Lee married actress Lesley Ash with whom in 2011 he was reported to have threatened to sue the News of the World due to a phone-hacking scandal. The pair later opened wine bars in Leeds and London.

Chapman's father Roy had an extensive career with Aston Villa, Lincoln City, Mansfield Town and Port Vale amongst the teams he played for. Chapman senior also managed Lincoln City, Stockport County and Stafford Rangers, taking the latter to several pieces of silverware including the FA Trophy in 1972 and 1979.

## CHILTON, Frederick

**POSITION:** Full-back

**BIRTHPLACE:** Washington, Co Durham

**DATE OF BIRTH:** 10/07/1935

**HEIGHT:** 5' 9" **WEIGHT:** 12st 2lbs

**SIGNED FROM:** Usworth Colliery, 12/05/1953

**DEBUT:** v Wolves, A, 12/09/1956

**LAST MATCH:** v Burnley, A, 12/10/1957

**MOVED TO:** North Shields, 01/05/1959

**TEAMS:** Usworth CW, Sunderland, North Shields

**INTERNATIONAL:** England Police

**SAFC TOTALS:** 3 appearances / 0 goals

**Fred Chilton was regularly flown home by Sunderland from Germany, where he was on National Service, to play for the reserves. Before he joined Sunderland, Wolves had shown interest in Fred who went on to make his debut at Molineux.**

As he was still on National Service, Chilton had to make his own way from Catterick (where he was in the Seventh Royal Tank Regiment) to Manchester and then on to Wolverhampton where he met up with the team. He duly lined up against future Sunderland winger Harry Hooper as his direct opponent in a Wolves team that also included England skipper Billy Wright.

All of Chilton's league appearances were away from home, the others at West Brom and in a heavy defeat at Burnley in what was Charlie Hurley's second game - but he did play at Roker Park in a cup final before signing for Sunderland. Playing for Usworth, who walloped Wardley 7-1, it was shortly after that match that Fred was first asked to come to Sunderland.

After his third and last league appearances Chilton also appeared in a friendly at Norwich watched by Carrow Road's biggest gate of the season as Sunderland inaugurated the Canaries floodlighting system.

A reserve for most of his time, he later played alongside former Newcastle star Frank Brennan at North Shields where Fred stayed for two years. Chilton went on to join the police, working in Hollycarrside in Ryhope before becoming part of the plain clothes CID in Seaham and subsequently the Regional Crime Squad, working from Berwick to Hull looking at major incidents including murders. His appearance for England Police came in a win over the RAF at Manchester City. In later life, he lived in Houghton and enjoyed making carved walking sticks.

## CHIMBONDA, Pascal

**POSITION:** Defender

**BIRTHPLACE:** Les Abymes, Guadeloupe

**DATE OF BIRTH:** 21/02/1979

**HEIGHT:** 5' 11" **WEIGHT:** 11st 7lbs

**SIGNED FROM:** Tottenham Hotspur, 26/07/2008

**DEBUT:** v Liverpool, H, 16/08/2008

**LAST MATCH:** v Blackburn Rovers, H, 24/01/2009

**MOVED TO:** Spurs, 26/01/2009

**TEAMS:** Le Havre, Bastia, Wigan Athletic, Spurs, Sunderland, Blackburn Rovers, QPR, Doncaster Rovers, Market Drayton Town, Carlisle Utd, Colwyn Bay, Arles-Avignon, Washington, Ashton Town

**INTERNATIONAL:** Guadeloupe and France

**SAFC TOTALS:** 16 appearances / 0 goals

**Born in the Caribbean, Chimbonda played three times for Guadeloupe in 2003 qualifying games for the Gold Cup and made another three appearances nine years later in qualification games for the Caribbean Cup. In between he was part of the France squad at the 2006 FIFA World Cup alongside another future Sunderland player in Louis Saha.**

Chimbonda never played as France reached the final, which they lost to Italy on penalties. Then with Wigan Athletic, Pascal's only senior appearance for France had been in the final three minutes of a World Cup warm-up match against Denmark shortly before the tournament. International recognition by France followed his inclusion in the 2005-06 PFA Premier League Team of the Year.

Chimbonda was one of a trio of new signings from Spurs (along with Steed Malbranque and Teemu Tainio) to debut for Sunderland on the opening day of the 2008-09 season. Used at right-back, Pascal was an athletic and physically imposing footballer, but never reached the heights expected on Wearside. Missing from the line-up in the next game back at his old club Tottenham, Chimbonda played in the following seven league games, but after that, never managed more than two in a row. By January, he had played his last game for the club, the man who signed him, Roy Keane, by this time having been replaced by Ricky Sbragia.

Two days after his last appearance for Sunderland, Chimbonda made a swift return to Spurs. The undisclosed fee was understood to have been close to the price paid for him the previous summer which was reportedly around the £3m mark. Pascal was to play just five times in his second spell with Spurs though the handful of appearances took him to over 100 for the club, his final game for Tottenham being back at Sunderland in a 1-1 draw less than two months after his departure from the Stadium of Light.

After seven months back in London, he was on the move again, this time to Blackburn for whom he soon scored the winner in a local derby with Burnley. A year and a half after leaving Spurs he returned to London for a six-month stint at QPR where he made only three appearances as sub. He then had spells with Doncaster (16 games) and Carlisle (28 games) sandwiched either side of a brief period with Northern Premier League Division One South outfit Market Drayton Town.

Returning to France in October 2014, he played four Ligue 2 games with Arles-Avignon. Three years later, he popped up back on Wearside, signing for Northern League Washington FC. Still not finished with football a year later at the age of 39, he signed for Ashton Town of North West Counties League Division One North - the 10th tier of English football. It was a far cry from being part of the squad with the 2006 World Cup finalists or playing in the League Cup final which he had done in 2006 and 2008.

In the first of those, Pascal played alongside Graham Kavanagh for Wigan in Cardiff against a Manchester United team who included Wes Brown, John O'Shea, Louis Saha and sub Kieran Richardson who all had spells at Sunderland. While he picked up a loser's medal, in Cardiff in 2008 he was a Wembley winner for Spurs against Chelsea when he had no fewer than five SAFC connections amongst his team's matchday squad: Malbranque, Tainio, Alan Hutton, Younes Kaboul and Darren Bent with Wayne Bridge the red and white connection amongst the opposition.

## CHISHOLM, Gordon William

**POSITION:** Defender/ Midfielder

**BIRTHPLACE:** Glasgow, Lanarkshire

**DATE OF BIRTH:** 08/04/1960

**HEIGHT:** 6' 1" **WEIGHT:** 12st 0lbs

**SIGNED FROM:** Possilpark YMCA, 01/09/1976, Professional, April 1978

**DEBUT:** v Sheffield United, A, 12/08/1978

**LAST MATCH:** v Grimsby Town, A ,17/09/1985

**MOVED TO:** Hibernian, 20/09/1985

**TEAMS:** Sunderland, Hibs, Dundee, Partick Thistle

**SAFC TOTALS:** 226+9 appearances / 16 goals

**David Corner took the blame for the concession of the only goal of the 1985 League (Milk) Cup final against Norwich, but the actual goal was deflected in by Gordon Chisholm, albeit Chis was blameless for a shot that deflected off him.**

Having come to Wearside as a youngster, Gordon debuted in an Anglo-Scottish Cup game and went on to play well over 200 times including 13 league appearances in the 1979-80 promotion season in a campaign in which he also scored in Sunderland's first penalty shoot-out as Newcastle were beaten in the League Cup.

156 of Gordon's 197 league appearances for Sunderland came in the top flight, but after the relegation that accompanied the 1985 Wembley loss, he played just once more in the second tier before being transferred to Hibernian.

Debuting spectacularly with a goal in a League Cup semi-final win against Rangers enabled him to achieve the distinction of playing in the England and Scottish League Cup finals in the same calendar year, but he was on the losing side again, going down 3-0 to Alex Ferguson's Aberdeen for whom future SAFC caretaker manager Eric Black scored twice, ex-Roker man Iain Munro being one of Gordon's teammates at Hampden.

At Dundee - where he signed for future Sunderland reserve team coach Jocky Scott - 'Chis' became only the second man to captain the club to two trophies, after Alfie Boyd who led the Dee to back-to-back League Cups in the early fifties. Gordon lifted the B&Q Centenary Cup in November 1990 and the First Division Trophy the following season in 1992.

Debuting for Dundee in a 2-0 win at Motherwell in September 1987, he tightened a previously porous defence, but later in the season damaged a disc in his back and missed the end of the season as the side fell away and missed out on a European place. Fit again for the start of the following campaign, Gordon registered his first goal for the club on the opening day of the season, the first of 16 he scored in 175 appearances.

Relegated in 1990, after promotion two years later, Gordon moved to Partick Thistle following the dismissal of Iain Munro as manager with Chis soon joining the coaching staff at Thistle, retiring as a player at the end of the end of his first season at Firhill. He went on to coach at Clydebank and be assistant manager of Ross County, Airdrie, Falkirk and Dundee United where he became manager in March 2005.

Succeeding Ian McCall, he won the SPL manager of the month award in his first month in charge. The first man to manage both Dundee clubs, Chisholm took United to the Scottish Cup final. They qualified for Europe despite losing the final 1-0 to Celtic, but lost a qualifying game to MYPA of Finland and by January 2006, he was sacked.

Re-uniting with McCall at Queen of the South, when McCall left to take over at Partick in the summer of 2007, Gordon again took over from him. Chis brought unprecedented success to the Dumfries club, taking them into Europe after reaching the 2008 Scottish Cup final where they pushed a Rangers side, including Carlos Cuellar, narrowly losing 3-2. The UEFA Cup journey however was short-lived, losing both legs of their qualifying round to FC Nordsjaelland of Norway.

In March 2010 he returned to Dundee, taking over from Jocky Scott as manager, but after just seven months the club went into administration. After almost a year and a half out of football, during which he worked as an estate agent, Chis returned to the game as assistant manager of East Fife in March 2012 becoming caretaker manager from August to October that year before taking his career full circle when he returned to Sunderland as International Development coach on 13 November 2012.

## CHISHOLM, Kenneth MacTaggart

**POSITION:** Inside-left

**BIRTHPLACE:** Glasgow, Lanarkshire

**DATE OF BIRTH:** 12/04/1925 - 30/04/1990

**HEIGHT:** 5' 11" **WEIGHT:** 12st 7lbs

**SIGNED FROM:** Cardiff City, 30/12/1953

**DEBUT:** v Aston Villa H, 01/01/1954

**LAST MATCH:** v Birmingham City, H, 18/04/1956

**MOVED TO:** Workington, 01/06/1956

**TEAMS:** Queen's Park, Manchester City (WW2 Guest), Bradford Park Avenue (WW2 Guest), Leicester City (WW2 Guest), Chelsea (WW2 Guest), Portsmouth (WW2 Guest), Bradford (WW2 Guest), Partick Thistle, Leeds United, Leicester City, Coventry City, Cardiff City, Sunderland, Workington, Glentoran, Spennymoor, Los Angeles Kickers

**INTERNATIONAL:** Scotland Victory international

**SAFC TOTALS:** 86 appearances / 38 goals

## CHISHOLM, Ken (Continued)

**Whether 'Soccer's Happy Wanderer' ended up playing in Los Angeles four years after reputedly dancing with Marilyn Monroe on Sunderland's 1955 tour of the USA is open to conjecture. Certainly during that trip, 'Chis' regularly visited a New York restaurant near Broadway on Tuesday mornings which Monroe frequented for lunch while working at the nearby Lee Strasberg's Actors' Studio.**

Chisholm had first been to the United States during World War Two when he trained as an RAF pilot, becoming an officer in bomber command. After starting his football career in his native Scotland, and playing for several clubs as a 'Guest' player during the war, he became a professional with Partick Thistle and did well enough to earn an £8,000 move to Leeds in Division Two.

Debuting in a home defeat to Fulham, Ken never missed a game until Leeds cashed in on him with a £10,000 sale to Leicester after he scored ten times in 23 games in the 1948-49 season. In the second half of that campaign, he added another six goals including one in the FA Cup semi-final against Portsmouth at Highbury. Future Sunderland centre-forward Don Revie got the Foxes other two goals in that victory in a season where only a last game of the season draw helped his club to avoid relegation from the second division. In the Wembley final, Chisholm played in a defeat to Wolves.

Ken was on the move again the following season, his value having risen to £16,500 after 13 goals in 26 games, but his new team Coventry were another second division club. A player who counter-balanced his renowned love of the good life by being a hard trainer, he kept the goals coming with 35 goals in 71 appearances. This led to another move to Cardiff in March 1952 where after 33 goals in 62 games, during which he helped the Bluebirds to promotion to the top-flight, he became one of the Bank of England Club Sunderland's signings, this time a fee of £15,000 changing hands.

Joining Len Shackleton on the scoresheet in a home win over Villa signalled that Chisholm would maintain his form at Roker. In his first full season, Ken top-scored with 22 goals as Sunderland reached the semi-final of the cup and finished fourth in the top-flight. His haul included a hat-trick of headers in a thrilling 4-3 win over Manchester United on a day when another of his headers came back off the underside of the bar. The following season Chisholm didn't play so regularly, playing only three games after January and ending the campaign with nine goals from 26 appearances.

By now into his thirties, he started to slip down the footballing ladder with a £6,000 move to Workington and in April 1957 was banned from the Football League for life for receiving illegal payments. This ban was lifted when a court case ruled the Football League did not have the right to ban players in such a manner. From January 1958 he had a six month spell as player/manager of Glentoran before his move to Los Angeles where his career was ended with a broken leg. Whether Marilyn Monroe came to tend to him is not recorded.

## CHOPRA, Rocky Michael

**POSITION:** Striker

**BIRTHPLACE:** Newcastle, Tyne & Wear

**DATE OF BIRTH:** 23/12/1983

**HEIGHT:** 5' 9" **WEIGHT:** 11st 8lbs

**SIGNED FROM:** Cardiff City, 13/07/2007

**DEBUT:** v Spurs, H, 11/08/2007

**LAST MATCH:** v Newcastle United, 01/02/2009

**MOVED TO:** Cardiff City, 04/07/2009

**TEAMS:** Newcastle United, Watford (L), Nottingham Forest (L), Barnsley (L), Cardiff City, Sunderland, Ipswich Town, Blackpool, Kerala Blasters, Alloa Athletic, Kerala Blasters, West Allotment Celtic

**INTERNATIONAL:** England Under 21

**SAFC TOTALS:** 24+18 appearances / 8 goals

**Scoring a last-minute winner against Spurs after coming off the bench to debut in the first game after promotion in 2007, former Newcastle striker Michael Chopra was an instant hero. While he went on to notch the occasional away goal, he had to wait until the penultimate home fixture of the season to score another in front of home fans, though when it came, it was a key strike in an important 3-2 win over Middlesbrough.**

He added two more when Boro returned early the following season, but when he left the club after his £5m transfer, his goals tally at the SoL had not equalled the goals he had scored there before joining Sunderland.

Infamously, his only Premier League goal for his first club Newcastle had come on a day when Sunderland keeper Kelvin Davis lost concentration allowing Chopra to net just 15 seconds after coming off the bench. The goal was an equaliser and sparked a collapse that spawned the Tyneside taunt, '4-1 and even Chopra scored.' Later the same calendar year, he scored twice in a 2-1 win for Cardiff, while in November 2002, he scored two in England colours in an Under 21 international lost 3-5 to Italy.

The defining moment for Chopra in a Sunderland shirt came back at his first home St James'. It was February 2009 when he found himself with a glorious chance to score for Sunderland. Like most strikers Chopra would rarely pass when he could shoot himself, but on this occasion he elected to pass to Kenwyne Jones. It wasn't a good pass and the chance was lost. Many people felt Chopra just didn't want to be a boyhood Magpie who scored for Sunderland at St James'. Michael himself later pointed out that in the reverse fixture, he had hit the bar and was eager to score. However, he never played for Sunderland again.

Shipped back to Cardiff on loan, that move eventually became a full transfer. In total, 56 of his 105 Football or Premier League goals came for the Bluebirds where he was Player of the Year in 2006-07. In the same season, Michael was selected for the PFA Championship Team of the Year, an accolade he achieved again three seasons later.

Having been the first player of Indian parentage (his father) to score in the Premier League (with that derby goal against Sunderland) in the latter part of his career, Chopra had two spells playing in the Indian Premier League.

Never far from a headline, Michael marked his debut for Newcastle by failing from the penalty spot in a League Cup shoot-out the day after Bonfire night in 2002. Next time out, he appeared as a late sub at Barcelona in a Champions League defeat. His first goal came later in the season after joining Watford on loan when he burst onto the scene with four goals in an astonishing 7-4 win at Burnley.

A couple of years later, he included two hat-tricks in a 17-goal season on loan to Barnsley. He bettered that with 22 for Cardiff in the season before Sunderland signed him and got within one of that tally when back with the Bluebirds in 2009-10 when his total included one in the Play-Off final lost to a Blackpool side that included David Vaughan. On the other hand, Chopra endured some horridly barren runs such as in 2013-14 when he failed to score at all in 20 games for Blackpool.

Following his career, Chopra worked as a football agent based in Amsterdam. He also suffered from a gambling addiction which saw him admitted to the highly-regarded Sporting Chance clinic. He was also reported to have been found guilty of 'suspicious betting activity' having been charged by the British Horseracing Authority who subsequently gave him a ten-year ban. In 2020, he was apparently part of a consortium involving his former teammate Alan Shearer who were attempting to buy Newcastle United. In June 2022 he signed for West Allotment Celtic of the Northern League.

## CIRKIN, Dennis

**POSITION:** Left-back

**BIRTHPLACE:** Dublin, Republic of Ireland

**DATE OF BIRTH:** 06/04/2002

**HEIGHT:** 5' 11" **WEIGHT:** 12st 4lbs

**SIGNED FROM:** Tottenham Hotspur, 11/08/2021

**DEBUT:** v MK Dons, A, 14/08/2021

**LAST MATCH:**

**MOVED TO:**

**TEAMS:** Ridgeway Rovers, Tottenham Hotspur, Sunderland

**INTERNATIONAL:** England Under 20

**SAFC TOTALS:** 37+4 appearances / 0 goals (to June 2022)

**Born in Ireland to Latvian parents, Cirkin moved to England when he was three. A fluent Russian speaker, Dennis started out his football journey in Sunday League football in Wanstead, before joining David Beckham's old team Ridgeway Rovers prior to joining Spurs at Under 10 level.**

With Tottenham, he frequently played in age groups above his own as he came through the ranks operating in a wide variety of positions before settling at left-back. He played in the first ever game at the Tottenham Hotspur Stadium when it staged an Under 18s fixture with Southampton as a test event. Named on the bench by Jose Mourinho for FA Cup games with Middlesbrough and Southampton as well as a Premier League game with Everton, he never actually got a competitive outing for Tottenham.

Capped by England at Under 16 and 17 level, Cirkin's Under 20 debut came as a sub against Romania at St George's Park on 6 September 2021 shortly after his move to Sunderland where he won promotion in his first season.

## CISSE, Djibril Aruun

**POSITION:** Striker

**BIRTHPLACE:** Arles, France

**DATE OF BIRTH:** 12/08/1981

**HEIGHT:** 6' 0" **WEIGHT:** 13st 0lbs

**SIGNED FROM:** Olympique de Marseille, 21/08/2008, on loan

**DEBUT:** v Spurs, A, 23/08/2008

**LAST MATCH:** v Portsmouth, A, 18/05/2009

**MOVED TO:** Olympique de Marseille, 25/05/2009, end of loan

**TEAMS:** Auxerre, Liverpool, OL Marseille, Sunderland (L), Panathinaikos, Lazio, QPR, Al Gharafa (L), Rubin Krasnodar, Bastia, St Pierroise, Yverdon Sport, AC Vicenza 1902

**INTERNATIONAL:** France

**SAFC TOTALS:** 32+6 appearances / 11 goals

**'Sunderland's number nine' - as the chant went - was a great character and an excellent striker. Coming off the bench to score the winner on his debut at Tottenham illustrated that the man who had won the Champions League three years earlier with Liverpool was a class act.**

Djibril certainly liked the big occasion. Having insisted he would score in the derby, he duly scored the 'other' goal on a day best remembered for Kieran Richardson's rocket as Newcastle were beaten in October 2008. It was Cisse's first home strike. He went on to also score in the return fixture which was drawn 1-1 as he finished joint-top league scorer on ten with Kenwyne Jones, adding another in the FA Cup for good measure.

A flamboyant figure with the hairstyles, tattoos and flash cars to match, Cisse was at Sunderland for just one season before returning to his parent club Marseille for whom he had scored twice in the French Cup final a year before coming to Sunderland. Former Sunderland loan striker Anthony le Tallec also scored in that game for Sochaux who won on penalties. Cisse converted his spot-kick on that occasion (as did his teammate Lorik Cana) as he had for Liverpool when they won the Champions League in a shoot-out after the Reds famously came back from 3-0 down against AC Milan in 2005. Djibril went on to score twice in the UEFA Super Cup final as he claimed the Man of the Match award after coming off the bench as CSKA Moscow were beaten 3-1. The following year he scored in the FA Cup final as Liverpool beat West Ham on penalties.

Three years earlier, Cisse had scored in the final of the Coupe de France, equalising as his Auxerre side went on to beat Paris St Germain with future Sunderland man Benjani part of the winning side, while future Spurs boss Mauricio Pochettino was Djibril's direct opponent. Cisse's collection of cup triumphs continued when he played in the 2010 Greek Cup final as Panathinaikos beat Aris to complete the league and cup double.

There was also an international cup win on the Cisse CV as he helped France to win the Confederations Cup in 2003, partnering Thierry Henry up front as Cameroon were beaten at the same Stade de France ground he had won his domestic cup on with Auxerre the same year. Cisse scored nine goals in 41 internationals, one of his caps coming at the 2010 FIFA World Cup against host nation South Africa who included future SAFC man Steven Pienaar. Ten years earlier, Cisse had been a World Championship winner at Under 19 level.

Djibril came from a footballing family. His father Mangue captained the Ivory Coast team while a cousin, Oliver Kapo, listed Juventus and Celtic as well as Birmingham and Wigan amongst the nine clubs he played for. In 2021, Djibril was still playing, but found the time to star on the French TV series 'The Masked Singer' belting out pop songs as an addition to the increasing DJ work he was undertaking as his career came towards an end.

## CLACK, Charles Edward (Ted)

**POSITION:** Winger

**BIRTHPLACE:** Highworth, Wiltshire

**DATE OF BIRTH:** 04/06/1896 - 11/04/1984

**HEIGHT:** 5' 9½" **WEIGHT:** 10st 3lbs

**SIGNED FROM:** Pontypridd, 19/05/1921

**DEBUT:** v Cardiff City, A, 03/12/1921

**LAST MATCH:** v Preston North End, A, 24/03/1923

**MOVED TO:** Bristol City, 18/05/1923

**TEAMS:** Highworth Town, Pontypridd, Sunderland, Bristol City, Nuneaton, Hinckley Town, Holywell Amateur

**SAFC TOTALS:** 9 appearances / 0 goals

**Ted Clack lived until he was almost 90, but was fortunate to not lose his life in the First World War before playing for Sunderland in the early 1920s. He was wounded three times and received the Military Medal for bravery at Ypres in 1917. He had also served at Gallipoli in 1915.**

Despite those wounds, which included one to each leg, Clack came to Sunderland after winning the Welsh Cup with Pontypridd in 1921. Before the war, he had won the Swindon and District Junior Cup as a teenager in 1913 when he was with his home club of Highworth Town.

At Sunderland he added further medals, helping the club to the Shipowners' Cup and the Durham Senior Cup but at first-team level he was never on the winning side, drawing three and losing the other six of his games. Given what he went through in the service of his country in both World Wars, a few dodgy results should have been the least of his worries. Other than at Sunderland, two outings for Bristol City in the second division was his only other experience of professional football.

During World War Two, Ted became a Staff Sergeant serving in France where he was part of the Dunkirk evacuation before he was sunk by a torpedo en-route to North Africa and spent nine hours in the Mediterranean four days before Christmas in 1942.

After being discharged from the forces in July 1943, he went on to spend almost two decades working for Sketchleys dry cleaners as a store-keeper and took an active interest in his local football clubs until well into his sixties.

## Clark, Benjamin

**POSITION:** Centre-back / Midfielder

**BIRTHPLACE:** Shotley Bridge, Co Durham

**DATE OF BIRTH:** 24/01/1983

**HEIGHT:** 6' 1" **WEIGHT:** 13st 11lbs

**SIGNED FROM:** Manchester United, 01/07/1999

**DEBUT:** v Luton Town, A, 26/09/2000

**LAST MATCH:** v Crewe Alexandra, A, 21/09/2004

**MOVED TO:** Hartlepool United, 22/10/2004

**TEAMS:** Manchester United, Sunderland, Hartlepool United, Gateshead, South Shields

**INTERNATIONAL:** England Under 20

**SAFC TOTALS:** 9+5 appearances / 0 goals

**Ben Clark was so highly thought of, Sunderland were understood to have paid £175,000 to bring the untried youth player back to the north east from Manchester United. Clark had made 38 appearances for England at Under 15 to Under 17 level and went on to play as high as Under 20 level.**

Comfortable on the ball, he was probably best at centre-back, but could play anywhere in defence or as a holding midfield player. Having debuted in a second leg League (Worthington) Cup tie where Sunderland began with a 3-0 lead, he was first on the bench for a FA Carling Premiership game at Leicester five months later, but waited almost another two years for a taste of league football as a sub at home to Southampton, but that 26 minute cameo was to be his only appearance at the top level.

A promotion winner with Hartlepool in 2006-07 as they went up from League Two - a year after being relegated with them - Ben played 185 times for the club before becoming captain of Conference outfit Gateshead who he captained and went on to manage in the first four months of 2019.

## CLARK, Henry (Harry)

**POSITION:** Inside-left
**BIRTHPLACE:** Grangetown, Sunderland
**DATE OF BIRTH:** 11/09/1934 - 26/12/2016
**HEIGHT:** 5' 7" **WEIGHT:** 10st 4lbs
**SIGNED FROM:** St Benet's, 01/06/1956
**DEBUT:** v Chelsea, A, 23/03/1957
**LAST MATCH:** v Portsmouth, A, 01/05/1957
**MOVED TO:** Blyth Spartans, 01/06/1958
**TEAMS:** St Benets FC, Sunderland, Blyth Spartans
**INTERNATIONAL:** RAF & Combined Services
**SAFC TOTALS:** 6 appearances / 0 goals

**Harry Clark had the tough job of being an inside-left trying to get a game while Len Shackleton was at the club. Having worked with 'the Clown Prince of Soccer', he went on to work with real life comics such as Benny Hill after giving up football to go to Art School in Backhouse Park, in doing so, turning down interest from Aberdeen.**

Harry did continue to play for a while with Blyth, but was then approached to go into television after gaining his degree. Between 1966 and 1989 the shows he worked on as a set-designer included those starring Benny Hill, Des O'Connor, Mike & Bernie Winters, Max Bygraves and Jim Davidson to mention just a few.

In 1975, by which time Harry was in his forties, he made the briefest of 'comebacks' when scoring a couple in a match between the Design Department and Construction Departments at Thames Television while at TV parties, he was known to be the life and soul of such events,

Before his football career, Harry served with the RAF in Singapore although most of that time appears to have been spent playing football across Asia! It was on 6 June 1955 that J Hall of SAFC wrote to Clark at his RAF base in Singapore inviting him to come to Roker Park when he returned home as Squadron Leader C Martindale had strongly recommended him.

To mark his 80th birthday in 2014, Harry's family and friends produced a private book entitled, 'Harry Clark: This is Your Life.' It's a publication that shows what a rich and varied life Harry led.

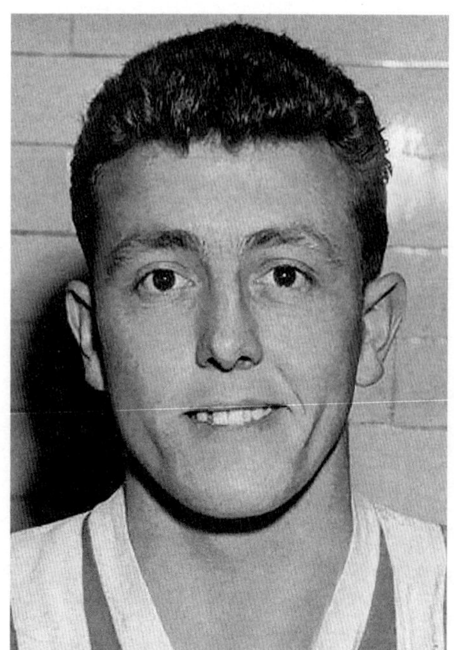

## CLARK, James McNicoll Cameron (Jimmy)

**POSITION:** Centre-half
**BIRTHPLACE:** Cathcart, Glasgow
**DATE OF BIRTH:** 11/12/1913 - Date of death unknown
**SIGNED FROM:** Clydebank Juniors, 12/06/1933
**DEBUT:** v Derby County, A, 02/02/1935
**LAST MATCH:** v Manchester United, H, 21/04/1937
**MOVED TO:** Plymouth Argyle, 20/10/1937
**TEAMS:** Clydebank Juniors, Sunderland, Plymouth Argyle
**SAFC TOTALS:** 50 appearances / 0 goals

**Twenty eight of Clark's half century of Sunderland appearances came in 1935-36 as the league title was won. All but five of these were made by early January when an injury forced him off after only a quarter of a 1-0 win at Manchester City. He returned to play 18 times the following term including one match in what was a triumphant cup run, but was allowed to move on to Plymouth early the following season.**

Debuting for Argyle at Tottenham, he played six successive games, but after injury, appeared just once more that term. The following season he was able to play regularly managing 30 league games and one FA Cup appearance - back at Roker Park where Sunderland won 3-0.

World War Two brought a premature close to Clark's career. He joined the Guards before becoming a bomber pilot with the US Air Detachment and subsequently the Canadian and South African Air Force, serving in the Far East. After the war he settled in South Africa managing Cape Town City, Southern Suburbs and Durban City. His maternal grandfather Niven McNicoll is reputed to have played for Sunderland Albion in 1889.

## CLARK, Lee Robert

**POSITION:** Midfield
**BIRTHPLACE:** Wallsend, Northumberland
**DATE OF BIRTH:** 27/10/1972
**HEIGHT:** 5' 8" **WEIGHT:** 11st 7lbs
**SIGNED FROM:** Newcastle United, 02/06/1997
**DEBUT:** v Sheffield United, H, 10/8/1997
**LAST MATCH:** v Birmingham City, H, 09/05/1999
**MOVED TO:** Fulham, 07/07/1999
**TEAMS:** Wallsend Boys Club, Newcastle United, Sunderland, Fulham, Newcastle United
**INTERNATIONAL:** England Under 21
**SAFC TOTALS:** 83+2 appearances / 16 goals

**Lee Clark was a talented craftsman of a midfielder. Never the quickest, he was nonetheless constantly on the move, always available for a pass and when in possession, delivered his own passes with care and precision. He also had a decent shot on him, best witnessed with two howitzers which won a game at Stoke just a couple of months after his debut.**

Although devoted to his hometown team Newcastle, he had been persuaded by Peter Reid to become Sunderland's record signing, the reported fee of £2.5m almost doubling the previous record paid for Niall Quinn. Clark's loyalties - subconsciously perhaps - were on show on the day he signed as he chose to turn up in a suit of very fine black and white stripes. Nonetheless, Lee never ever failed to give 100% on the pitch for Sunderland. Like Lee Cattermole in a later era, he was a lad from the region besotted with football and gave it all he had.

In his two seasons at Sunderland, Clark was named in the PFA Division One Team of the Year on both occasions despite missing three months of the second of those seasons after breaking his leg on the opening day of the campaign. Unfortunately, after playing a key role as the schemer in the record breaking 105 point season of 1998-99 'Clarkie' never got to play in the Premiership for Sunderland. A couple of weeks after Sunderland's final league match Lee went to Wembley as a supporter to see Newcastle in the FA Cup final. Just as Peter Reid had talked Lee into signing for Sunderland some Newcastle supporters talked Clark into briefly wearing a t-shirt bearing the derogatory message SMB. Inevitably the player was photographed in it and sadly his time at the club was up, Sunderland making a profit on the player when selling him to Fulham, then managed by Paul Bracewell.

A decent and honest lad, Clark later confessed that he felt his biggest mistake was in signing for the rivals of Newcastle and admitted he would have found it difficult to play against the Magpies for the red and whites. Had he done so, he may have faced a similar dilemma Michael Chopra was later accused of (See Chopra section).

Clark had been attached to Newcastle United since joining their Centre of Excellence as a ten-year old. He had been the Magpies Player of the Year when they won promotion and the First Division in 1992-93 as United's only ever-present.

At Fulham he completed a hat-trick of second tier titles in 2001 and captained the Cottagers who he played 178 times for. At the age of 32, he returned to Newcastle adding a further 25 appearances to take his grand total for his first club to 265 (64 of which were as sub). In June 2006, he became first-team coach at St James' until November 2007 when he accepted a post as assistant manager of Norwich City. He stayed at Carrow Road until December 2008 when he was appointed manager of Huddersfield Town. In an age of short-lived managerial appointments he was in charge of the Terriers until February 2012 taking them on a record 43 match unbeaten run during that spell.

Four months after leaving the Yorkshire club, Clark became manager of Birmingham City until October 2014 when he took over as Blackpool boss. Leaving the Seasiders in May 2015, he waited until the following February for his next opportunity which came at Kilmarnock where he was in post for a year until he returned to England with Bury where he remained for eight months. There was then a return to the north east as manager of Blyth Spartans where he was in charge from June 2019 until March 2020, later taking over as Director of Football at Blue Star.

At international level, Clark came close to a full cap, being an unused sub for Glenn Hoddle's England at the Tournoi de France in the summer of 1997 against Italy, France and Brazil. All of his eleven Under 21 caps came under the management of Lawrie McMenemy for whom he debuted away to Czechoslovakia in May 1992 with the last coming 18 months later away to the Netherlands.

## CLARK, William (Willie)

**POSITION:** Outside-right

**BIRTHPLACE:** Whifflet, Lanarkshire

**DATE OF BIRTH:** 25/03/1881 - 17/03/1937

**HEIGHT:** 5' 7" **WEIGHT:** 11st 0lbs

**SIGNED FROM:** Bristol Rovers 02/05/1908

**DEBUT:** v Manchester City, A, 01/09/1908

**LAST MATCH:** v Bradford City, H, 23/04/1910

**MOVED TO:** Bristol City, 18/10/1910

**TEAMS:** Cambuslang Hibernian, Port Glasgow Athletic, Bristol Rovers Sunderland, Bristol City, Leicester Fosse

**INTERNATIONAL:** Anglo-Scots v Home Scots trial match 1908

**SAFC TOTALS:** 44 appearances / 4 goals

**Winger Willie Clark hailed from a similar area of Glasgow to where Billy Hughes came from several decades later. Having been an iron turner before becoming a professional footballer, Clark commenced with 35 goals for Port Glasgow which drew the attention of Bristol Rovers with whom he won the Southern League in his first season of 1904-05.**

Over four years and 133 Southern League games, Willie equalled his tally of goals from Scotland and came to Sunderland in the summer of 1908. After starting the first five games of the next season, an injury following an excellent personal performance in a defeat at Villa ruled him out until March when he returned with a first goal against his future club Leicester Fosse. Willie's second year at Sunderland included a run of 31 consecutive appearances until he missed the last match of the campaign after which he went back to Bristol - this time to City in exchange for John Cowell. However, after one season, he was on the move again, joining Leicester where he made just six appearances, his only goal coming in a November defeat at Hull. Sometimes known as Billy, he returned to Bristol to become a publican in the Clifton area of Bristol where he passed away a few days before his 56th birthday.

## CLARKE, Clive Richard Luke

**POSITION:** Left-back

**BIRTHPLACE:** Dublin

**DATE OF BIRTH:** 14/01/1980

**HEIGHT:** 5' 11" **WEIGHT:** 12st 3lbs

**SIGNED FROM:** West Ham United, 08/08/2006

**DEBUT:** v Birmingham City, H, 09/08/2006

**LAST MATCH:** v Stoke City, A, 17/10/2006

**MOVED TO:** Contract terminated, 05/02/2008

**TEAMS:** Stoke City, West Ham United, Sunderland, Coventry City (L), Leicester City (L)

**INTERNATIONAL:** Republic of Ireland

**SAFC TOTALS:** 2+2 appearances / 0 goals

**Sunderland lost a League (Carling) Cup tie at Luton on the night news came through that Clive Clarke had suffered a heart attack while playing on loan for Leicester at Nottingham Forest. The Forest-Foxes cup-tie was duly abandoned at half-time with Clarke subsequently fitted with a pace-maker and advised to retire on medical grounds, something he did five months later.**

Clarke had been signed by Niall Quinn in his brief spell as manager at the Stadium of Light. He had given a decisive penalty away on his debut as a sub and was then injured on his full debut three days later. Once Roy Keane took over as manager, Clarke had another couple of games, but was quickly sent out on loan to Coventry where he made a dozen appearances.

Evidently not in Keane's plans, Clarke was sent out on loan again at the start of the following season with the game where he suffered a cardiac arrest only his second for Leicester. It is worth noting that when Leicester's cup match with Forest was replayed, the Foxes sportingly allowed Forest to score the first goal as they had led when the original match was abandoned - but won the tie 3-2.

Clive Clarke had been in English football since 1996 when he came to Stoke as a trainee from Newton Schoolboys in County Wicklow. A Football League (Auto Windscreens) Trophy winner in Millennium Year and Second Division Play-Off winner two years later, he totalled 264 appearances for Stoke and had won two full caps for the Republic of Ireland in 2004 before joining West Ham in the summer of 2005. Substituted in all three of the games he played for the Hammers, his move to Sunderland was meant to be a fresh start. That fresh start ended up being to become a football agent after his heart attack brought his career to a close.

## CLARKE, Jack Raymond

**POSITION:** Winger

**BIRTHPLACE:** York, Yorkshire

**DATE OF BIRTH:** 23/11/2000

**HEIGHT:** 5' 11" **WEIGHT:** 11st 6lbs

**SIGNED FROM:** Tottenham Hotspur, 26/01/2022, on loan and Tottenham Hotspur, 09/07/2022

**DEBUT:** v Bolton Wanderers, A, 29/01/2022

**LAST MATCH:**

**MOVED TO:**

**TEAMS:** Leeds United, Tottenham Hotspur, Leeds United (L), QPR (L), Stoke City (L), Sunderland (L), Tottenham Hotspur, Sunderland

**INTERNATIONAL:** England Under 20

**SAFC TOTALS:** 11+9 appearances / 1 goal (to June 2022)

**Former Sunderland full back Ian Harte acted as agent for Jack Clarke who played alongside Niall Huggins at Leeds and Danny Batth during a loan to Stoke City. Clarke burst onto the scene with Leeds to the extent that in July 2019, Spurs paid a reported fee of around £10m for his signature. It seemed a good deal for Leeds as they immediately took the player back on loan, although he only added three further appearances to his total for the club which was extended to 7+21 games in which he scored twice. Two of those substitute appearances came in unsuccessful 2019 Championship Play-Offs with Derby.**

In January 2020 Jack played against Leeds on debut having gone on loan to QPR for who he made six sub appearances in the Championship and got one start in the FA Cup. 2020-21 saw Spurs find three substitute appearances for their investment, the first a month before he left his teens and all in cup ties.

This was followed by another loan, this time to Stoke City where he got half a dozen starts along with eight appearances off the bench. Prior to coming to Sunderland Jack got a third European appearance for Tottenham and three games in the Football League (Papa John's) Trophy for his club's Under 21s, scoring in the last of these at League One Oxford. For Sunderland his best game was in the second leg of the successful Play-Off semi-final at Sheffield Wednesday before he signed off with a substitute's appearance as Wycombe were beaten at Wembley in May 2022. However, Sunderland signed him on a permanent deal later that summer. At international level, Jack debuted at Under 20 level in September 2019 against Netherlands Under 20s and four days later scored the winner on his second appearance.

## CLARKE, Jeffrey Derrick

**POSITION:** Centre-half

**BIRTHPLACE:** Hemsworth, Yorkshire

**DATE OF BIRTH:** 18/01/1954

**HEIGHT:** 6' 0½" **WEIGHT:** 13st 8lbs

**SIGNED FROM:** Manchester City, 19/06/1975

**DEBUT:** v Middlesbrough, A, 02/08/1975

**LAST MATCH:** v Southampton, A, 08/05/1982

**MOVED TO:** Newcastle United, 14/07/1982

**TEAMS:** Manchester City Sunderland, Newcastle United, Brighton & HA (L), Ankaragucu, Whitley Bay, Winlaton West End

**INTERNATIONAL:** England schools

**SAFC TOTALS:** 215+3 appearances / 6 goals

**Jeff Clarke came in part exchange for the great Dave Watson and the finest accolade that could be paid to Clarke was that despite Sunderland losing their most capped England international in Watson, the defence was still strong with Clarke as his replacement. A colossus at the heart of the back four, Clarke was strong, good in the air, but much more than simply a stopper centre-half. He was a talented footballer and particularly when paired with Shaun Elliott, formed a superb central defensive partnership.**

From his debut at Middlesbrough in the Anglo-Scottish Cup Jeff made 40 consecutive appearances before he was injured and missed the run in as the Division two title was claimed in his first season. Similar misfortune befell him a year later when after playing in the first 33 games, he was injured in February and did not play again as Sunderland were narrowly and dramatically relegated.

Jeff did not play again until December after which he appeared in every game but one to the end of the season The following season was a similar tale as after missing just three of the first 42 games, he was restricted to a single substitute appearance from the final seven fixtures, but it was the next campaign of 1979-80 for which he is best remembered. As Sunderland won promotion, Clarke was stretchered off in the penultimate game at Cardiff, missing the glory night as promotion was clinched in front of a capacity crowd against West Ham. He had missed just two league games and an Anglo-Scottish Cup tie.

## CLARKE, Jeff (Continued)

Ruled out of the entire first season back in the top-flight, Jeff returned on the opening day of 1981-82, missed just one game up to the beginning of February and then featured just three more times before being given a free transfer at the age of 28 and switching to Newcastle.

Any doubts about welcoming a former Sunderland stalwart were soon dispelled at St James' as Jeff's quality shone through. Unbelievably unlucky, having missed the climax of both promotions seasons he was part of at Sunderland, the same happened to Clarke at Newcastle. After being United's joint top appearance maker in his first season, missing just three of 46 games, in his second year as Newcastle were promoted, under Sunderland's 1973 FA Cup-winning coach Arthur Cox, injury restricted Jeff to just 14 appearances.

In total he played 134 times for the Tynesiders. He also had a loan at Brighton and the delights of a spell in Turkey and north-east non-league football. In November 1988, he became Football in the Community Officer at NUFC, remaining in that role until June 1993 when he became reserve team coach until 1997.

Having qualified as a physiotherapist, gaining his degree from Salford University Jeff became physio to Nissan FC and coached at Middlesbrough before returning to Sunderland as youth team physio from 1998 to 2002. In 2003, Jeff moved to Leeds United as physio for a year before taking up the same role at Dundee United where he was still employed in 2021, by this time looking after the club's younger players.

Between 2001 and 2016, Jeff's son Jamie played for Mansfield Town, Rochdale, Boston United, Grimsby Town, York City, Gainsborough Trinity, Guiseley, Arbroath and Montrose.

## CLARKE, Norman Samson

**POSITION:** Outside-left

**BIRTHPLACE:** Ballyloughan, Northern Ireland

**DATE OF BIRTH:** 01/04/1942

**HEIGHT:** 5' 11" **WEIGHT:** 11st 4lbs

**SIGNED FROM:** Ballymena United, 14/02/1962

**DEBUT:** v Middlesbrough, H, 18/08/1962

**LAST MATCH:** v Portsmouth, A, 14/11/1962

**MOVED TO:** Retired, 29/04/1965

**TEAMS:** Ballymena United, Sunderland, Ballymena United, Gateshead, Sunderland Greenwells

**INTERNATIONAL:** Northern Ireland Under 21, Great Britain

**SAFC TOTALS:** 5 appearances / 0 goals

**Norman Clarke had a testimonial at Sunderland despite only playing five games and only being at the club for three years. The man with the middle name of Sunderland's future mascot had come to Sunderland with a big reputation as a raw diamond having played for Northern Ireland Under 23s, the Irish League and his country's amateur side as well as being capped at youth level. He had also played for the Great Britain Olympic Trial team against a Caribbean XI at Ipswich, setting up two goals in the opening quarter of an hour as GB won 7-2.**

Northampton Town tried to sign Norman after that performance, but he was under contract to Ballymena United (with whom he won the Ulster Cup) and had begun an Arts degree in Ancient History, French and Psychology at Queen's University having gained 3 'A' Levels. He was also approached by Arsenal and Falkirk who had seen him play at Hampden in an amateur international. Amongst his other suitors was Jackie Milburn of Linfield. Norman did not sign for the legend of Tyneside, but did play alongside him for the Irish League against the Scottish League at Windsor Park in September 1960.

Before coming to Sunderland, only the reluctance of his mother to a move stopped Norman signing for Wolves where he had trained and impressed. However, when called up for Northern Ireland's first-ever Under 23 international along with Sunderland's Martin Harvey and Jimmy O'Neill, manager Alan Brown flew to Belfast with them and signed Norman who had been dubbed 'the new Burbanks' after Sunderland's 1937 cup-final scorer Eddie.

Sunderland won all four of Norman's league appearances, all of which came at Roker Park in the opening half-dozen fixtures of the 1962-63 season. A couple of months later he played in a League Cup, his only away game being a draw at Portsmouth. Just 20 at the time of his first-team adventure, Norman damaged his cruciate ligaments playing for the reserves against Middlesbrough in late March, just three days before his 23rd birthday. It was an injury that ended his career.

Forced to retire, Norman began working for Plessey Telecommunications in July 1965 and then took up a teacher training place in Belfast in September 1966 - the month of his Testimonial at Roker Park. Bobby Charlton, Jim Baxter, Johnny Crossan and Mike Summerbee were amongst the stars to turn out for Norman who re-joined Ballymena the following month and played his first game in two and a half years against Portadown. After two and a half years, he became Ballymena's manager only to resign after a month having decided to concentrate on playing.

Following a few games for Gateshead, in n 1969, he returned to Sunderland to work at Plesseys having given up on plans to teach, but in 1975 became player/manager of Sunderland Greenwells who he took to the Northern Alliance Cup final against Carlisle City at St James' Park in April of 1976 when Norman played, only for his team to lose 4-0.

Two years later, Norman moved to London and began to scout for Liverpool, vetting their future opponents. In 1997, he self-published his autobiography 'Ballymena Boy.'

## CLARKE-SALTER, Jake Liam

**POSITION:** Centre-back

**BIRTHPLACE:** Carshalton, London

**DATE OF BIRTH:** 22/09/1997

**HEIGHT:** 6' 1" **WEIGHT:** 11st 0lbs

**SIGNED FROM:** Chelsea, 08/01/2018, on loan

**DEBUT:** v Cardiff City, A, 13/01/2018

**LAST MATCH:** v Burton Albion, H, 21/04/2018

**MOVED TO:** Chelsea, 07/05/2018, end of loan

**TEAMS:** Chelsea, Sutton United, Chelsea, Bristol Rovers, Sunderland (L), Vitesse Arnhem (L), Birmingham City (L), QPR (to July 2022)

**INTERNATIONAL:** England Under 20

**SAFC TOTALS:** 8+3 appearances / 0 goals

**A FIFA Under 20 World Cup winner with England in 2017, Clarke-Salter had won the FA Youth Cup with Chelsea in the three previous seasons. He also won the UEFA Youth League while with Chelsea who he captained. A debutant for the Blues in April 2016 in a win at Aston Villa, he went on loan to Bristol Rovers to gain experience, playing a dozen games for the Gas in League One.**

Stepping up to the Championship when coming to Sunderland on loan in the January 2018 transfer window, after a League (Carabao) Cup appearance for his parent club, he struggled in a team that were unsuccessfully trying to avoid relegation. Sent off in successive appearances against Middlesbrough and Preston, his home debut against Hull was Jake's only appearance on a winning side while at Sunderland.

A goal on debut to his next loan club Vitesse Arnhem was his only goal in 28 games for the Netherlands club after which he was loaned out again, this time to Birmingham who he re-joined in a second loan in October 2020 after spending 2019-20 at St Andrew's. In the summer of 2022 he signed a four-year deal at QPR.

## CLOUGH, Brian Howard

**POSITION:** Centre-forward

**BIRTHPLACE:** Middlesbrough

**DATE OF BIRTH:** 21/03/1935 - 20/09/2004

**HEIGHT:** 5' 10½" **WEIGHT:** 11st 1lbs

**SIGNED FROM:** Middlesbrough, 14/07/1961

**DEBUT:** v Walsall, A, 19/08/1961

**LAST MATCH:** v Aston Villa, H, 09/09/1964

**MOVED TO:** Retired and became youth coach, 14/11/1964

**TEAMS:** Great Broughton, South Bank, Billingham Synthonia, Middlesbrough, Sunderland

**INTERNATIONAL:** England

**SAFC TOTALS:** 74 appearances / 63 goals

**Renowned as one of the most successful and charismatic managers the game has known, Brian Clough twice came close to managing Sunderland. He was interviewed by both Keith Collings and Sir Tom Cowie, but neither felt able to appoint a man who would demand so much control.**

Given the phenomenal success he had in taking Nottingham Forest from Division Two to two European Cups - in the days when you had to actually win the league to qualify for the European Cup - and Derby County from the second division to a European Cup semi-final, it remains a regret for supporters that Cloughie never got the chance to lead Sunderland. In total, Clough the manager won 16 trophies.

He did lead the line as a centre-forward and did so in remarkable style. Setting a post-war goalscoring record of 34 goals in his first season, he had 28 goals in as many games up to the fateful day on Boxing Day 1962 when his and Sunderland's world crashed when he tore his medial and cruciate ligaments in a challenge with Bury keeper Chris Harker. The cruciate knee injury ended Brian's career. Two seasons later, he attempted a come-back after showing tremendous determination to return, but after three games and one more goal realised that the game was up and it was time to retire from playing.

He was a huge miss to Sunderland who in the season he was injured missed out on promotion on goal average. Had Clough continued Sunderland would have been near certainties to win the promotion that came a year later.

Having begun with his hometown club Middlesbrough, Clough totalled 251 league goals in only 274 appearances, at one point scoring at least 40 goals in four successive seasons for the Teessiders. No player in the history of English football to have scored 200 or more league goals - not Dixie Dean, Jimmy Greaves, Arthur Rowley or anyone else - can match Clough's goals to games ratio of 0.916.

All Brian's international caps came while he was with Middlesbrough. October 1959 saw him play against Wales in Cardiff and against the previous year's FIFA World Cup finalists Sweden at Wembley. Clough had scored on his one appearance at 'B' Level in a February 1957 win over Scotland where he played alongside Stan Anderson and Harry Hooper. Later the same month, he debuted for England Under 23s against Scotland at Ibrox. In May of that year he scored in a 2-1 Under 23 defeat away to Bulgaria (alongside Anderson) and netted in another 2-1 loss away to Wales the following April when he played alongside Jimmy Greaves.

Brian began his post-playing career with Sunderland youth team, nurturing talents such as Colin Todd and John O'Hare who would later enjoy success with him elsewhere. Having helped Sunderland to the semi-finals of the FA Youth Cup in 1965, Clough was appointed manager of Hartlepools United in October 1965 on the recommendation of Len Shackleton - after Pools had been turned down by Alvan Williams.

The first trophy of Brian's managerial career came with Hartlepools - the Durham Senior Cup with Gateshead beaten 10-0 on aggregate in the final. Swiftly snapped up by Derby County, he won Division Two in 1969, the Watney Cup in 1971 and the league title a year later. As Sunderland won the FA Cup in 1973, the Rams reached the semi-final of the European Cup, Clough forever remaining adamant that his side lost to Juventus and some alleged skull-duggery involving the referee.

In 1972, Clough had resigned and decided to take over at Coventry only to quickly change his mind. However, in November 1973, he became manager of Brighton until the end of the season when he infamously took charge of Leeds United. In an era characterised in the book and film 'The Damned United', Clough challenged the culture created at Elland Road by another Middlesbrough-born former Sunderland centre-forward Don Revie. After just 44 days Clough was sacked, but his greatest managerial days were still to come.

In January 1975, he became manager of Nottingham Forest. Remaining in that position until May 1993, he was made Manager of the Year in 1978 and awarded an OBE in 1991 as he took silverware galore to the banks of the Trent. He was given the Freedom of Nottingham in 1993.

A host of biographies exist on Clough, who appointed former Roker Park office junior and later, assistant secretary Malcolm Bramley as his secretary at Derby. The main A52 road between Derby and Nottingham is now named Brian Clough Way while there are statues to Brian in Middlesbrough, Derby and Nottingham.

Clough's Sunderland-born son Nigel went on to play for England as well has having his own managerial career (being boss of Burton when they relegated Sunderland to League One in 2018) while Brian's brother Des played for Stockton in the later 1950s.

## CLUNAS, William McLean (Billy)

**POSITION:** Right-half

**BIRTHPLACE:** Johnstone, Renfrewshire

**DATE OF BIRTH:** 29/04/1899 - 01/09/1967

**HEIGHT:** 5' 9½" **WEIGHT:** 12st 5lbs

**SIGNED FROM:** St Mirren, 29/11/1923

**DEBUT:** v Huddersfield Town, H, 01/12/1923

**LAST MATCH:** v Grimsby Town, H, 08/11/1930

**MOVED TO:** Greenock Morton, 24/08/1931

**TEAMS:** Kilbarchan, St Mirren, Sunderland, Greenock Morton, Inverness Thistle

**INTERNATIONAL:** Scotland

**SAFC TOTALS:** 271 appearances / 44 goals

**Billy Clunas scored more penalties for Sunderland than anyone in history. 30 of his goals came from the spot with only Gary Rowell and Tony Towers bettering Billy's 91% success rate (of players to take at least ten penalties). Not surprisingly known as 'The Penalty King', Clunas twice scored two spot-kicks in one game: at Leeds in December 1928 and at home to Manchester City the following February.**

Ten of his successful penalties came in 1928-29, the season Dave Halliday set the club record of goals per season with 43. He could have topped a half century if Clunas had not been on spot-kicks. With two other goals that season, Clunas set his own record of most goals in a season by someone who was not a forward. It took until 1987-88 for this to be exceeded; by another penalty expert John MacPhail.

Other than his prowess from the penalty spot, Clunas was renowned as an accurate passer of the ball and a fine tackler. Capped for the first time in the first international to be held at Wembley in April 1924 when he faced clubmate Charlie Buchan in a 1-1 draw, Clunas scored as he won his second and final cap in a 3-0 win over Wales in Cardiff in October 1925. The goal made him the second Sunderland player - after Charlie Thomson - to score for Scotland.

Returning to his native Scotland after almost a decade on Wearside, Clunas is known to have missed a fourth penalty when Celtic's John Falconer denied him in the 86th minute of a 3-3 draw with Greenock Morton in September 1931, a month after leaving Roker Park. In September 1934, he became player/coach of Inverness Thistle before becoming secretary of his hometown team Johnstone (not St Johnstone) in June 1938.

## COADY, Michael Liam

**POSITION:** Defender

**BIRTHPLACE:** Dipton, Co Durham

**DATE OF BIRTH:** 01/10/1958

**HEIGHT:** 5' 11" **WEIGHT:** 10st 3lbs

**SIGNED FROM:** Durham Schools, 01/02/1975

**DEBUT:** v Leeds United, A, 09/04/1977

**LAST MATCH:** v Preston North End, A, 16/02/1980

**MOVED TO:** Carlisle United, 07/07/1980

**TEAMS:** Sunderland, Carlisle United, Sydney Olympic, Wolves, Sydney Olympic, Barrow

**SAFC TOTALS:** 4+2 appearances / 0 goals

**Shortly after an impressive debut at Elland Road, Mick Coady suffered a broken leg and was ruled out for twelve months. Making his comeback in September 1978, he played in three successive games, but then waited until February 1980 for his one remaining opportunity, as a sub.**

## COADY, Michael (Continued)

After being released, he signed for Martin Harvey's Carlisle United, debuting on the opening day of the 1980-81 season in a Division Three game with Sheffield United. He went on to play in every game but one in a season where Bob Stokoe succeeded Harvey in September. However, having finally managed to play regularly, there were just eight appearances for Mick in his second season at Brunton Park. He then went to Australia to play for Sydney Olympic for almost three years until a return to the UK with Wolves. As with his time with Carlisle, Sheffield United provided the opposition on his debut for Tommy Docherty's side in January 1985. There would be just six more games that season, including the last three as Wolves finished bottom of Division Two.

The Molineux men were relegated again in Coady's second season, but after just eight appearances he returned to Australia in March 1986 with Sydney Olympic, although within six months he was back in the UK on trial with Lincoln City before going back Down Under until 1990.

In 2003, Mick's 14-year old son Seb scored the winning goal in the final of the Under-15 Nike Premier Cup at the newly-opened Academy of Light playing for Middlesbrough against West Ham.

## COATES NION, Sebastian

**POSITION:** Centre-back

**BIRTHPLACE:** Montevideo

**DATE OF BIRTH:** 07/10/1990

**HEIGHT:** 6' 5" **WEIGHT:** 13st 5lbs

**SIGNED FROM:** Liverpool, 01/09/2014, on loan then, 01/07/2015, on permanent basis

**DEBUT:** v Stoke City, H, 23/09/2014

**LAST MATCH:** v Arsenal, A, 09/01/2016

**MOVED TO:** Sporting Lisbon, 28/01/2016, on loan then, 02/02/2017, on permanent basis

**TEAMS:** Nacional, Liverpool, Sunderland, Sporting Lisbon

**INTERNATIONAL:** Uruguay

**SAFC TOTALS:** 29+3 appearances / 0 goals

**Sebastian Coates was a South American international, but had British heritage, his Great Grandparents having emigrated from Scotland to Uruguay. Originally at Sunderland on loan from Liverpool, he subsequently signed for the Lads, but was often viewed by many to be slow and cumbersome. His record makes a mockery of such criticism.**

He played at the 2018 FIFA World Cup in a 3-0 win for Uruguay over the hosts Russia and came on as a late sub as England were beaten in the 2014 tournament. He also played in every minute of Uruguay's games at the 2012 London Olympics a year after winning the Copa America when he was named the competition's Best Young Player.

At club level, Coates won the championship in Uruguay in 2009 and 2011 with Nacional and won three Portuguese league titles with Sporting to 2021, being their Player of the Year in 2020 and named in the Primeira Liga Team of the Year in 2020-21 before heading off to the Copa America.

## COGLIN, Stephen (Steve)

**POSITION:** Winger

**BIRTHPLACE:** Bilston, Staffs

**DATE OF BIRTH:** 14/10/1899 - Q4 1965

**HEIGHT:** 5' 7" **WEIGHT:** 10st 4lbs

**SIGNED FROM:** Willenhall, 07/05/1924

**DEBUT:** v Liverpool, A, 25/10/1924

**LAST MATCH:** v WBA, H, 15/01/1927

**MOVED TO:** Grimsby Town, 15/02/1927

**TEAMS:** Moxley White Star, Darlaston, Lichfield City, Wednesbury, Willenhall, Sunderland, Grimsby Town, Notts County, Worcester City, Hereford United, Cannock Town, Bromsgrove Rovers, Archdales FC, Hallow

**SAFC TOTALS:** 20 appearances / 9 goals

**For a player who spent much of his career in West Midlands non-league football, Steve Coglin did remarkably well at Sunderland averaging almost a goal per two games from the wing. After a couple of outings in 1924-25, he started the following season in the side, but quickly dropped out despite scoring in two of the first three games having been criticised in the press for being too small and weak. He got just three more games that season scoring once more before his best and last season of 1926-27.**

The highlight of his six goals in 12 games that term was joining goal-machine Dave Halliday in scoring a hat-trick in a 7-1 thrashing of Burnley after also scoring in the two previous games. He joined Halliday on the scoresheet again when Halliday got another hat-trick later in the season against WBA, but despite his efforts, Coglin was deemed surplus to requirements and moved on to Grimsby mid-way through the season. He went on to help the Mariners to promotion two years later scoring 39 times in 118 games before adding three more in 13 games for Notts County in 1931-32.

Coglin played under that surname despite having been born Stephen Cocklin. During the Great War he joined the 5th Battalion Notts & Derby Regiment in 1917 at the age of 18. After his playing days, he coached Worcester City from August 1938 to July 1956 having scored 42 times in 12 games for them as a player. He died in the city aged 66.

## COLBACK, Jack Raymond

**POSITION:** Midfielder

**BIRTHPLACE:** Killingworth, North Tyneside

**DATE OF BIRTH:** 24/10/1989

**HEIGHT:** 5' 9" **WEIGHT:** 11st 5lbs

**SIGNED FROM:** Trainee, 01/07/2008

**DEBUT:** v Wolves, A, 09/05/2010

**LAST MATCH:** v Swansea City, 11/05/2014

**MOVED TO:** Newcastle United, 09/06/2014

**TEAMS:** Sunderland, Ipswich Town (L), Newcastle United, Nottingham Forest

**INTERNATIONAL:** England Under 20

**SAFC TOTALS:** 109+27 appearances / 5 goals

**Jack Colback fell from favour with Sunderland supporters when becoming the first player of the 21st century to move from Sunderland to Newcastle. He did so on a free transfer having come to the end of his contract shortly after playing at Wembley in the 2014 League (Capital One) Cup final.**

Having come through the ranks at Sunderland since he was ten, Colback had done well for Sunderland, but left after being offered a contract that was apparently significantly inferior to many of his teammates regardless of having appeared in all but eleven Premier League games in his last three seasons at the club.

Comfortable on the ball and good at retaining possession, Jack had come through the ranks in an excellent Under 18 team alongside Jordan Henderson and Martyn Waghorn as they won their league and reached the semi-final of the FA Youth Cup. He went on to captain the Under 21s to the Totesportcasino.com Reserve League Cup and Durham Challenge Cup.

Colback's first-team career at Sunderland did not get off to a good start. Over-eager, he was sent off for two cautions at Wolves, although he had only come off the bench for the final 14 minutes of the last day of the 2009-10 season. He had made his first senior appearance in August 2009 at WBA while on loan to Ipswich.

Within a couple of months of moving to Newcastle, Colback was selected for a full England squad only to have to withdraw through injury. At Sunderland he had been capped once at Under 20 level coming on for the last eleven minutes of a win over Italy at QPR in 2009.

A regular in his first three seasons at St James' he won a Championship medal in his third term after being relegated a year earlier. After 102 appearances in his first three years on Tyneside there were none in the last three as he became a marginalised figure spending two lengthy loans at Nottingham Forest before signing for Forest in August 2020 following his release by the Magpies.

## COLE, Andrew Alexander (Andy)

**POSITION:** Striker

**BIRTHPLACE:** Lenton, Nottingham

**DATE OF BIRTH:** 15/10/1971

**HEIGHT:** 5' 10" **WEIGHT:** 12st 11lbs

**SIGNED FROM:** Portsmouth, 23/08/2007

**DEBUT:** v Everton, A, 24/11/2007

**LAST MATCH:** v Spurs, A, 19/01/2008

**MOVED TO:** Nottingham Forest, 07/07/2008

**TEAMS:** Arsenal, Fulham (L), Bristol City, Newcastle United, Manchester United, Blackburn Rovers, Fulham, Manchester City, Portsmouth, Birmingham City (L), Sunderland, Burnley (L), Nottingham Forest

**INTERNATIONAL:** England

**SAFC TOTALS:** 3+5 appearances / 0 goals

**A prolific scorer with the Uniteds of Newcastle and Manchester, Andy Cole's only goal for Sunderland came at Hetton in the Durham Challenge Cup against Norton & Stockton Ancients. Lured to Wearside as a veteran by his ex-Old Trafford teammate Roy Keane, Cole should have come to Sunderland long before Cole went to Newcastle.**

Sunderland scout Freddie Anderson had recommended him to manager Denis Smith when Cole was a youngster about to be let go by Arsenal. However, Smith got sacked and duly signed Cole three days after becoming manager of Bristol City!

Cole cost the Robins a record £500,000, a fee they made a handsome profit on when selling him to Newcastle for a club record £1.75m a year to the day after signing him. He had scored 20 goals in 41 league games for the Ashton Gate club. He had previously netted three in 13 on loan to Fulham after a solitary league opportunity for the Gunners in December 1990. Coming to St James' in March 1993, he hit the ground running with 13 goals before the end of the season as Kevin Keegan's side won the Championship and promotion.

After a rapid-fire 68 goals in 84 games in just 22 months in the north east, he had more than tripled his value as he was transferred to Manchester United for a fee of £6m plus Keith Gillespie. At Newcastle, Andy had been the Premier League's top scorer in 1993-94 when he was also the PFA Young player of the Year. The goals simply kept flowing with 121 in 275 games for Manchester United. Newcastle were on the receiving end of nine, more than he scored against any club for the Red Devils while in February 1995, he became the first player to score five in a Premier League game (against Ipswich).

A treble winner in 1998-99 when he played in the Champions League final against Bayern Munich as well as winning the Premier League and FA Cup, Cole collected four other Premier League medals, another FA Cup winner's medal and an Inter-continental Club Cup winner's medal while with Manchester United. Andy added a League (Worthington) Cup winner's medal with Blackburn in 2002, scoring in the final against Spurs.

Despite having reached his 30th birthday, Manchester United managed to sell him for more than they had paid, an £8m fee taking him to Blackburn Rovers in December 2001. After 27 goals in 87 league games, he returned to London with Fulham where his tally was 12 in 31. Next stop was back to Manchester, but with City where he scored nine in 22 as his career began to wind down. There were just three goals in 18 league games at Portsmouth and one in five on loan to Birmingham.

Coming to Sunderland, he debuted as a sub in a 7-1 defeat at Everton and things did not get that much better as he struggled and was loaned to Burnley where the goal touch returned with six in 13. Finishing his career with his hometown club Nottingham Forest, he retired in November 2008 after not finding the net in his ten games.

At international level, Andy's only goal in 15 caps won between March 1995 and October 2001 came deep into injury time as he won his 13th cap in Albania.

His son Devante played for England up to Under 19 level and in 2021 was playing for Barnsley, one of ten clubs he had played for to that point. Dad Andy coached MK Dons, at Huddersfield for Lee Clark and at Southend. He also releaseda record called Outstanding and regardless of tales that circulated saying he wanted to be known as Andrew rather than Andy told me 'Andy's OK with me' when asked about it while at Sunderland.

In 2017, Andy underwent a kidney transplant and subsequently raised much money for Kidney Research UK

## COLEMAN, John George (Tim)

**POSITION:** Inside-forward

**BIRTHPLACE:** Kettering, Northamptonshire

**DATE OF BIRTH:** 26/10/1881 - 20/11/1940

**HEIGHT:** 5' 6" **WEIGHT:** 11st 3lbs

**SIGNED FROM:** Everton, 02/05/1910

**DEBUT:** v Newcastle United, H, 01/09/1910

**LAST MATCH:** v Preston North End, H, 15/04/1911

**MOVED TO:** Fulham, 18/06/1911

**TEAMS:** Kettering Town, Northampton Town, Arsenal, Everton, Sunderland, Fulham, Nottingham Forest, Ebbw Vale, Tunbridge Wells Rangers, Maidstone

**INTERNATIONAL:** England

**SAFC TOTALS:** 33 appearances / 20 goals

**Tim Coleman was one of the great stars of pre-World War One football and a man who fought with distinction on the pitch, in the war - where he won the Military Medal for extreme valour in combat - and for the rights of footballers as he was particularly active in the early days of players trying to form a union.**

Physically small and slight, he was a giant of the game and a giant of a personality. Known for being fleet of foot, Coleman was renowned for his passing and shooting - including his ability to shoot from the lip - as apparently he could talk as well as play for England

He was reported as killed in action during the Great War, but thankfully, the trio of reports recording his death on 29 December 1915 were proved wrong 48 hours later, Tim lived until November 1940 when he died after falling off a ladder while working as a window cleaner.

Coleman saw extensive action on the Western Front, one of his comrades being Tommy Barber who had a leg shattered, just three years after scoring the winner in the FA Cup final of 1913 for Villa against Sunderland. As the Football League came in for intense criticism for continuing in 1914-15, the FA offered to form a 'Footballers' Battalion' as part of the Middlesex Regiment. Made up of players and supporters, Tim Coleman was one of the first to join.

Coleman had commenced his career in his home town of Kettering. Having continued to make his name with Northampton, he joined Woolwich Arsenal in 1902, debuting against Preston in September of that year and going on to score 79 goals in 172 league games. Transferred to Everton for a £700 fee in 1908, Tim contributed 30 goals in 71 games. The Toffees had kept

tabs on Tim since he scored a brilliant individual goal against them in their first-ever league meeting with (Woolwich) Arsenal in 1904 and they'd had ample opportunity to watch him play for England against Ireland at Goodison Park the previous year. That England cap won at Everton was Coleman's solitary full international and saw him in direct competition with the Irish left-half, English McConnell of Sunderland.

A year earlier Tim had been 'Reserve' against Wales in Cardiff and Scotland at Hampden. Tim also played for The Football League on three occasions. Coleman's last season at Everton had seen him, ever the principled maverick, become the only Everton player to insist on supporting the first attempts to form a players' union - the forerunner to the PFA. It caused him enormous problems, but as on the pitch or the battlefield, ever the rebel, he refused to give in.

At Sunderland, he scored the winner on his debut against Newcastle and ended his one campaign at Roker as top scorer with 20 goals from 33 games. That was a more than decent record from an inside, rather than centre, forward, especially when you consider his clever play created many more. During his time at Sunderland, Coleman lived at 38 Roker Baths Road and as well as his wife and children had three boarders: fellow Sunderland players Billy Cringan, Harry Read and David Main.

He was then re-united with his old Arsenal manager Andy Kelso at Fulham for whom he scored 45 goals in 94 league games before bagging 14 goals in 37 appearances for Nottingham Forest during 1914-15.

Larger than life, Tim was a renowned joker. At Arsenal his party trick was to impersonate the Gunners skipper and he had absolutely zero respect for authority. Due in court in Nottingham in February 1915 for being drunk and disorderly while a Forest player, he failed to turn up, subsequently having a warrant issued for his arrest. Co-incidentally, it was a referee from Nottingham, a Mr Adams, who took charge of his last game for Sunderland when, legend has it, Coleman played the first half of a game for Sunderland wearing a false moustache. Removing it at half-time drew the ire of the referee who thought Sunderland were bringing on a substitute (it would be another half century before subs were allowed). Tim had the last laugh, the 'tache-less' Tim opened the scoring after the break with a 30-yarder to steer Sunderland to victory. Typically Tim Coleman was not called Tim at all. He was Christened John George, became known as 'Tiddy' and eventually was universally called 'Tim.'

Thirty-eight when the Great War ended, he played for Ebbw Vale and then showed he had not lost his ability by scoring 39 goals in 37 games for Tunbridge Wells Rangers. Moving into management, he took charge of Maidstone United reserves (for whom his son Arthur was top scorer) in 1921-22 before moving briefly to Switzerland and then - after being passed over for a job as coach at Bournemouth - Holland where he led SC Enschede (forerunners of Twente) to the Dutch league title in 1926.

No superstar pay in Coleman's day, when his football career came to an end, he returned to London where he worked as a labourer until his death. A biography of Tim Coleman by George Myerson called 'Fighting for Football' was published in 2009.

# C

## COLEMAN, Keith

**POSITION:** Left-back
**BIRTHPLACE:** Washington, Co Durham
**DATE OF BIRTH:** 24/05/1951
**HEIGHT:** 5' 9" **WEIGHT:** 11st 0lbs
**SIGNED FROM:** Washington, 01/06/1966
**DEBUT:** v Swindon Town, H, 11/09/1971
**LAST MATCH:** v Preston North End, H, 16/12/1972
**MOVED TO:** West Ham United, 20/05/1973
**TEAMS:** Sunderland, Arsenal (L), West Ham United, KV Mechelen, Darlington
**SAFC TOTALS:** 54+1 appearances / 2 goals

**Keith Coleman played in all nine games as he captained Sunderland to FA Youth Cup triumph in 1969. After becoming a first-team regular in 1971-72 when he played in 37 games, in 1972-73 he had played in 15 of the 17 matches leading up to the appointment of Bob Stokoe.**

Whereas previous manager Alan Brown favoured youth, Stokoe looked for experience, so after playing in the first three games under the new boss, Keith was side-lined. Coleman never played for Sunderland again, although he was an unused sub in the FA Cup fourth-round replay at Reading. Within days of that tie, Keith had been loaned to Arsenal, but he dislocated his shoulder on his debut for the reserves (alongside fellow loanee Ritchie Pitt and against Ray Wilkins) for the Gunners against Chelsea on 10 February 1973. It was his only appearance for the Gunners.

Sold to West Ham for £20,000 15 days after Sunderland won the FA Cup, Keith debuted in a League Cup tie at home to Liverpool at the beginning of October and came into the league line up the following weekend going on to play in the remaining 30 games of the season. The following campaign he appeared in over two thirds of the Hammers' league games and a third-round FA Cup win at Southampton, but missed out on the rest of the cup run as for the second time in three seasons he was at the cup winning club without being involved in the glory.

He did however, get to play in a senior final a year later, but was on the losing side at the Heysel Stadium in Belgium where West Ham went down 4-2 to Anderlecht. He had played in the last six games of the cup run, coming on as a sub for his old Sunderland teammate Mick McGiven in a third round match at FC Den Haag. In total Coleman started 111 games for West Ham as well as coming on as a sub six times.

A year after playing in his European final in Belgium, Keith went to that country to play for KV Mechelen. Two years later, he returned to the north east to play 25 games in the 1979-80 season for Darlington under Billy Elliott his old Sunderland coach who he had played for when Billy was caretaker/manager between Brown and Stokoe.

Coleman went on to scout for Sheffield Wednesday before settling in Cyprus where he remained understandably disappointed about how his time at Sunderland came to an end. Invited to become one of the 1973 squad to receive the Freedom of the City of Sunderland in 2021, Keith politely declined.

## COLLIN, George

**POSITION:** Left-back
**BIRTHPLACE:** Oxhill, Co Durham
**DATE OF BIRTH:** 13/09/1905 - 01/02/1989
**HEIGHT:** 5' 9" **WEIGHT:** 11st 9lbs
**SIGNED FROM:** Derby County, 18/06/1936
**DEBUT:** v Sheffield Wednesday, A, 29/08/1936
**LAST MATCH:** v Liverpool, 17/04/1937
**MOVED TO:** Port Vale, 23/06/1938
**TEAMS:** West Stanley, West Ham United, Arsenal, West Stanley, Bournemouth & Boscombe Athletic, West Stanley, Derby County, Sunderland, Port Vale, Burton Town
**SAFC TOTALS:** 33 appearances / 0 goals

**Having been on West Ham's books as an amateur, Collin signed as a professional for Arsenal in 1923, but never got a game for either the Hammers or the Gunners. Released by Arsenal, he returned home to the north east to spend 1924-25 with West Stanley before returning south with Bournemouth whose boss was Leslie Knighton who had been Collin's manager at Arsenal.**

After two years with Bournemouth, Collin returned to West Stanley having seen his spell on the south coast ruined by a broken leg which at one point looked like being sufficient to curtail his career, but after only four months, he got another chance in the league with Derby County who took him for £500. The left-back did so well for Derby that in the summer of 1936 reigning league champions Sunderland thought he was good enough to strengthen their squad.

At Derby he had made 334 first-team appearances and matured into a consistent left-back. Debuting for Sunderland on the opening day of the 1936-37 season, Collin did not miss a game until mid-January. Sunderland would go on to win the FA Cup in 1937, but after being injured in the first game of that run - a 3-2 victory at Southampton - Collin would not feature in the rest of what became a glorious cup-run. He did go on to make another seven league appearances during the season, but none of these were consecutive.

Collin would spend one more season at Sunderland without adding to his first-team appearances before moving on to Port Vale, but he did leave Sunderland with a medal. While he missed out on the cup final, he did win the Charity Shield while with Sunderland, playing in a 2-1 win over cup-holders Arsenal at Roker Park in October 1936. A month later he took over in goal after only 12 minutes when Johnny Mapson was injured in a defeat at Charlton, a result that cost league leaders Sunderland their place at the top of the table.

After a season of struggle in Division Three South with Port Vale, Collin became manager of Burton Town in August 1939, but with World War Two about to begin, there were more battles than football ones to concern the new manager who stayed in the area as an inspector in a textile factory and died in Derby in February 1989.

Not as famous a singer as England winger Colin Grainger who appeared on the same bill as the Beatles, nonetheless George Collin once recorded a gramophone record.

## COLLINS, Danny

**POSITION:** Defender
**BIRTHPLACE:** Chester
**DATE OF BIRTH:** 06/08/1980
**HEIGHT:** 6' 2" **WEIGHT:** 12st 10lbs
**SIGNED FROM:** Chester City, 11/10/2004
**DEBUT:** v Rotherham United, A, 25/10/2004
**LAST MATCH:** v Blackburn Rovers, H, 22/08/2009
**MOVED TO:** Stoke City, 01/09/2009
**TEAMS:** Mold Alexandra, Buckley Town, Chester City, Vauxhall Motors (L), Sunderland, Stoke City, Ipswich Town (L), West Ham United (L), Nottingham Forest, Rotherham United, Grimsby Town
**INTERNATIONAL:** Wales, England C (semi-professional) and also Wales Minor Counties at cricket
**SAFC TOTALS:** 146+17 appearances / 3 goals

**Danny Collins first played at the Stadium of Light seven weeks before he joined Sunderland. Having thus far spent his career in non-league, Collins had just come into the league with Chester where he had played in every game but the last one as they won the Conference in 2004. He had played in Chester's first dozen games back in the Football League - scoring the winner against Macclesfield in his club's first win back in the league.**

Having stepped up to Sunderland, he played 14 times as the Championship was won in his first season. Just over a year after playing in the Conference, Danny found himself in the Premier League. He played regularly in the second half of the season, being one of a nucleus of players who gave their all in extremely difficult circumstances as the team went down with a record low number of points. His character showed again as he was a regular starter as the team bounced back by winning the league straight away.

Collins won Player of the Year awards in the next two seasons, taking the Supporters' Association award in 2007-08 and both that and the official club award the season after. A determined competitor who read the game well, showed quality on the ball and was effective at centre-back or left-back, Danny became a very popular figure with the crowd, but was allowed to move to Stoke for a reported £2.75m (rising to £3.5m) in the summer of 2009, a massive profit on the £140,000 he had cost.

After 50 Premier League appearances in his first two seasons with the Potters, Collins went on loan to Ipswich and Nottingham Forest in the Championship before signing for Forest in 2012 where he took over the captaincy in the first of his three seasons at the City Ground.

Moving to Rotherham United in the summer of 2015, Danny scored against Forest in only his second game for the Millers. It was one of two goals he claimed in 26 games in his season there before completing his playing days with three seasons in League Two with Grimsby, topping a century of games with the Mariners.

Having started modestly, Collins had played 147 Premier League games, 97 of them with Sunderland. He also established a notable international record. A full international with Wales for whom he won a dozen caps, the first seven of them were won with Sunderland, his debut coming against Hungary in February 2005.

Not quite Willie Watson, but Collins also played international cricket having once represented Wales Minor Counties against Italy. Danny was a left-arm spinner and decent batsman in the Liverpool ECB Premier League with Northop Hall, whose star player was Mushtaq Ahmed who played 55 Tests for Pakistan. Collins played 33 times for Northop Hall, taking 23 wickets and scoring 344 runs. As well as playing cricket against Italy, Collins played football against the Italian Olympic side in a 'C' international for England. That game in February 2004 was a 4-1 defeat at Shrewsbury, his England 'C' (non-league XI) debut having come in a goalless draw away to the Netherlands in March 2003. During his time with England C, Danny's roommate was future Sunderland manager Lee Johnson.

Always helpful and approachable to the media, Danny began to forge his own media career after retiring from playing. In 2021 he was summarising Sunderland games on the club's own stream and co-presenting SAFC's official 'Unfiltered' podcast.

## COLLINS, John Douglas

**POSITION:** Midfielder

**BIRTHPLACE:** Newton, South Yorkshire

**DATE OF BIRTH:** 28/08/1945

**HEIGHT:** 5' 8" **WEIGHT:** 9st 9lbs

**SIGNED FROM:** Plymouth Argyle, 09/03/1977

**DEBUT:** v Aston Villa, A, 23/03/1977

**LAST MATCH:** v Brighton & Hove Albion, H, 01/10/1977

**MOVED TO:** Tulsa Roughnecks, 12/02/1978

**TEAMS:** Pinxton Miners' Welfare, Rotherham United, Grimsby Town, Burnley, Plymouth Argyle, Sunderland, Tulsa Roughnecks, Rochdale

**SAFC TOTALS:** 5+2 appearances / 0 goals

**Into his thirties by the time he came to Roker Park, Doug Collins had played for manager Jimmy Adamson at Burnley. He got just a handful of games for Sunderland where supporters were increasingly disturbed by Adamson bringing in Burnley old boys on and off the pitch. For Sunderland, Collins was slow and never really got the chance to find his best form.**

During the season he came to Sunderland, Doug had played regularly in Division Two for Plymouth where one of his teammates was Micky Horswill, the pair being on the scoresheet together in a win at Blackpool. Collins had only been with Argyle for a few months having previously spent eight years at Turf Moor. One of exactly 200 games he started for the Clarets was at Roker Park in Bob Stokoe's first match as Sunderland manager in 1972. Collins also came of the Burnley bench 17 times and scored 19 times for the club.

Doug had come to Burnley's attention after impressing against them in a League Cup tie in 1968 for Grimsby for whom he played over 100 times. Influential in Burnley's promotion winning team in the year Sunderland won the cup, Collins went on to help the Clarets win that season's Charity Shield, taking part as Division Two champions as Sunderland declined the invitation to take part.

Following his stint at Sunderland, Collins went to the USA with Tulsa, but within a few months was back in England as coach at Derby County before taking over as player/manager of Rochdale in January 1979 only to be replaced by Bob Stokoe when sacked eleven months later. Emigrating to Australia, Collins briefly coached Sydney Olympic before taking over a McDonald's franchise and becoming very involved with his church.

## COLLINS, Neill William

**POSITION:** Centre-back

**BIRTHPLACE:** Irvine, North Ayrshire

**DATE OF BIRTH:** 02/09/1983

**HEIGHT:** 6' 3" **WEIGHT:** 12st 6lbs

**SIGNED FROM:** Dumbarton, 13/08/2004

**DEBUT:** v Reading, A, 31/08/2004

**LAST MATCH:** v Cardiff City, H, 31/10/2006

**MOVED TO:** Wolves, 05/01/2007

**TEAMS:** Queens Park, Dumbarton, Sunderland, Hartlepool United (L), Sheffield United (L), Wolves, Preston North End, Leeds United, Sheffield United, Port Vale (L), Tampa Bay Rowdies

**INTERNATIONAL:** Scotland 'B'

**SAFC TOTALS:** 20+4 appearances / 2 goals

**A promotion winner with Sunderland, Wolves and Leeds United, Neill Collins was a centre-back who was confident on the ball, even if occasionally a little too confident. He came to Sunderland from Scottish football shortly before his 21st birthday and played in eleven league games as the Championship was won in his first season under Mick McCarthy.**

In July of 2005, he won four Under 21 caps beginning with a 3-2 win in Belarus after first being an unused sub against Italy the previous March. Restricted to a couple of FA Cup appearances in the Premiership relegation season of 2005-06 when he was named as an unused sub just once in the league (at Everton), he spent most of the season on loan at Hartlepool and Sheffield United appearing 25 times for Martin Scott's Hartlepool and twice for Neil Warnock's Blades.

Back at Sunderland in 2006-07, Neill made eight more appearances, scoring the last goal of Niall Quinn's brief reign as manager before he was re-united with McCarthy at Wolves. Initially going to Molineux on loan from 2 November until 1 January, the move was then made permanent, the reported fee of £150,000 being a six-fold increase on what Collins had cost when coming from Dumbarton who he had captained.

Sunderland had taken him on following unsuccessful trials with Charlton, Rangers, Hibs, Falkirk and Dundee United. Collins had come to Dumbarton from Queens Park having begun as a youth player with Kilmarnock.

Wolves were to provide Collins with the best years of his career, 84 of his 97 games for the club coming in the championship including 23 as they won promotion, although again he never got an opportunity to play at the top level. It was while he was with Wolves that Neill was capped by Scotland at 'B' level, coming on as a sub against the Republic of Ireland B at Airdrieonians in November 2007.

A loan to Preston quickly became permanent although a couple of months after signing a long-term contract he was on the move again following a change of manager, this time joining future Sunderland manager Simon Grayson at Leeds, again initially on loan. Collins played in nine late-season games as Leeds United won promotion from League One and after 21 appearances for them back in the Championship was transferred again, this time to Sheffield United.

Relegated that year with the Blades, Neill went on to spend another five years in League One at Bramall Lane, eventually totalling over 200 games for the club from where he had a loan to Port Vale in his penultimate campaign. Moving to America in 2016 with Tampa Bay Rowdies, he played 67 games for them before taking over as their head coach in 2018.

## COLQUHOUN, John Mark

**POSITION:** Forward

**BIRTHPLACE:** Stirling

**DATE OF BIRTH:** 14/07/1963

**HEIGHT:** 5' 7" **WEIGHT:** 10st 0lbs

**SIGNED FROM:** Millwall, 09/07/1992

**DEBUT:** v Swindon Town, A, 15/08/1992

**LAST MATCH:** v Portsmouth, H, 01/05/1993

**MOVED TO:** Hearts, 26/ 07/1993

**TEAMS:** Grangemount, Stirling Albion, Celtic, Hearts, Millwall, Sunderland, Hearts, St Johnstone

**INTERNATIONAL:** Scotland

**SAFC TOTALS:** 15+8 appearances / 0 goals

**John Colquhoun was a cultured winger - off as well as on the pitch. Enthused by politics he was involved in the players' union and while a Celtic player, stood on a picket line at a Lanarkshire colliery during the 1984-85 miners' strike. A right-winger on the pitch, but a left-winger off it. He is also a lover of literature and particularly John Steinbeck.**

After his retirement, John became rector of the University of Edinburgh as well as a member of Sportscotland, the nation's agency for sport. Colquhoun also worked as a pundit and journalist - notably for Scotland on Sunday - before becoming a football agent.

# C

## COLQUHOUN, John (Continued)

Colquhoun began with SAFC - that's Stirling Albion FC, where he combined playing with working as a painter and decorator as well as finding employment on building sites. A fee of £50,000 took him to Celtic as a 20-year-old in November 1983 with his Hoops debut coming at his future club Hearts on 17 December. His father - also John - had been a Celtic player from 1957-59, but did not play first-team football until a transfer to Oldham for whom he scored in the Latics record win over Southport in 1962. He also played for Scunthorpe United.

At Parkhead, Colquhoun junior understudied Davie Provan, but managed to play 37 times for the club scoring four goals. A £60,000 move to Hearts in the summer of 1985 resulted in him making a scoring debut - against Celtic. For much of that 1985-86 season it looked as if the Tynecastle club were going to win the league. Topping the table from Christmas - Colquhoun scoring both as they won at Rangers between Christmas and New Year - his side missed out at the death. Defeat on the final day at Dundee as Celtic stuffed St Mirren 5-0 cost Colquhoun's side the title by three goals on goal difference. John had been their only ever-present. There was to be more disappointment a week later as he played in the cup final, lost to Aberdeen. Colquhoun had netted the winner in the semi-final v Dundee United at Hampden.

Ten years later, he would score in another cup final for Hearts against Rangers - and hit the bar - but it was in a 5-1 defeat where he had bigger things to worry about as his father was dying and unable to be at the Hampden showpiece.

Leaving Hearts for Millwall in 1991 on the first two of the three occasions he scored for the Lions, John was joined on the scoresheet by Alex Rae and then Mick McCarthy, the latter becoming his manager in March 1992 following the departure of Bruce Rioch. Colquhoun's home debut was against Sunderland, but he missed the Roker return. Roker Park became John's home ground after a single season in London. Despite his pace, Colquhoun never scored in his season at Sunderland, although had a linesman been more eagle-eyed perhaps, he would have had one at home to West Ham with a shot that appeared to cross the line at the Fulwell End only for play to be waved on.

Returning to Hearts at the end of the season - as part of the deal that brought Derek Ferguson to Wearside - John added over 100 more appearances taking his total for the club where he was inducted into their Hall of Fame to 345 league games. Finally, he added six appearances for St Johnstone in 1997. At international level, Colquhoun was capped twice, in away draws with Saudi Arabia and Malta in 1988 while he was with Hearts.

## COMMON, Alfred

**POSITION:** Inside-right

**BIRTHPLACE:** Millfield, Sunderland

**DATE OF BIRTH:** 25/05/1880 - 03/04/1946

**HEIGHT:** 5' 8" **WEIGHT:** 13st 0lbs

**SIGNED FROM:** South Hylton Juniors, 01/08/1900 and Sheffield United, 31/05/1904

**DEBUT:** v Wolverhampton Wanderers, A, 15/09/1900

**LAST MATCH:** v Wolverhampton Wanderers, H, 08/02/1905

**MOVED TO:** Sheffield United, 28/10/1901 and Middlesbrough, 16/02/1905

**TEAMS:** Hylton FC, Jarrow, South Hylton, Sunderland, Sheffield United, Sunderland, Middlesbrough, Arsenal, Preston North End

**INTERNATIONAL:** England

**SAFC TOTALS:** 40 appearances / 13 goals

**Not many footballers become spoken about in the House of Commons, but Alf Common's move from Sunderland to Middlesbrough in 1905 for the world's first £1,000 transfer fee caused consternation in Parliament as MPs pondered what the game had come to.**

Coming into the Sunderland side from local football in 1900, Alf played in 14 of the 34 games as the Lads were runners-up in the top-flight in his first season. Scoring twice against Sheffield United on the opening day of the next campaign evidently created an impression as after playing in the next three fixtures of what was a title-winning season for Sunderland, Alf was bought by the Blades. Compensation for missing out on a league medal came in the shape of a FA Cup medal. Common played in all nine games as the trophy was won, his three goals including the winner against Newcastle and one in the final against Southampton, United eventually winning in a replay.

After two more seasons at Bramall Lane, Common re-signed for Sunderland. Claiming he wanted to return to Wearside due to business interests he came in a double deal of £520 that included the transfer of goalkeeper AE 'Tal' Lewis. Back at Roker, Alf marked his first home game with a brace in a 5-0 win over Notts County and scored his last league goal at Middlesbrough in January. That all-action display in which he also hit the bar clearly created an impression in the corridors of power at Ayresome Park. The result left Boro second from bottom and Sunderland third from top, but a month later Common was persuaded to swap a title chase for a relegation battle as Sunderland accepted that historical fee of £1,000. The fee was actually bigger than that as the deal included Sunderland coming to Boro for a friendly the following weekend - filling a free cup weekend as both clubs were already eliminated. The agreement saw Sunderland pay their own expenses and Boro keep all the gate receipts from a 14,000 crowd. Common played, but did not score as Sunderland won 2-1.

There was however, an instant dividend for Boro as a competitive debut penalty from Alf gave them their first away win in two years. Both wins came at Sheffield United - Common having scored against Middlesbrough in their previous victory at Bramall Lane. Goals in three further home wins helped keep Boro up in 1905.

Top scoring with 24 goals in his first full season on Teesside, he netted in both games against Sunderland and notched a couple of hat-tricks. Partnering the legendary Steve Bloomer, both scored in a defeat at Roker in 1907 as Alf continued to score regularly until the last of his seasons at Boro when one of his five goals came in a home win over Sunderland. Finally totalling 65 goals in 178 Boro games, Common left for Arsenal in 1910.

Starting the first 22 games of his opening season with the Gunners he was injured on his return to Sunderland, ending the campaign with six goals from 32 games. Alf did better in his second year, being far and away Arsenal's top gun with 17 goals having played in all but one game. Things did not go so well in the following 1912-13 season when after failing to score in a dozen games he was transferred to Preston in December, finishing his career with 18 months at Deepdale.

As so many players once did, Alf's post-playing career saw him become a publican. He ran the Cleaver Hotel in Darlington before taking over the Alma Hotel in nearby Cockerton. In 1936 his application to be the FA's coach in Durham Secondary Schools was unsuccessful. The FA had recognised him as a player, England capping him three times while he was with Sheffield United and once during his time on Teesside. He scored twice, both goals coming in a 3-1 win over Ireland in Belfast in 1904.

## CONNELLY, Lee John

**POSITION:** Striker

**BIRTHPLACE:** Glasgow

**DATE OF BIRTH:** 18/10/1999

**HEIGHT:** 5' 10" **WEIGHT:** 10st 0lbs

**SIGNED FROM:** Queens Park, 01/07/2016

**DEBUT:** v Carlisle United, A, 09/10/2018

**LAST MATCH:** v Gillingham, A, 19/11/2019

**MOVED TO:** Queen of the South, 30/06/2021

**TEAMS:** Queens Park, Sunderland, South Shields (L), Alloa Athletic (L), Queen of the South (to June 2022)

**INTERNATIONAL:** Scotland Under 17

**SAFC TOTALS:** 0+5 appearances / 0 goals

**Livewire Lee Connelly was a prolific scorer in his first pre-season as a youth player at Sunderland, his non-stop never-say-die running forcing many a mistake he was swift to pounce on. Capped by Scotland at Under 15, 16 and 17 level, he worked under the guidance of Ricky Sbragia at international level.**

2018-19 saw him play in three Football (Checkatrade) League Trophy games and be an unused sub in the final league game of the campaign at Southend. After a spell on loan to South Shields, he returned to Sunderland to make another FLT (Leasing.com) appearance before coming off the bench for the last seven minutes of extra-time in an FA Cup defeat at Gillingham.

Subsequently joining Alloa Athletic on loan in January 2020, Lee scored his first senior goal in a 2-0 win over Inverness Caledonian Thistle and re-joined Alloa for a second loan in 2020-21 bringing his total for the Wasps to 10+11/ 2. The second of his goals came against Queen of the South who he signed for in June 2021 under the management of Allan 'Magic' Johnston.

## **CONNER,** John

**POSITION:** Centre-forward

**BIRTHPLACE:** Renfrew, Glasgow

**DATE OF BIRTH:** 27/12/1892 - 30/12/1973

**HEIGHT:** 5' 8½" **WEIGHT:** 10st 7lbs

**SIGNED FROM:** Perth Violet, 13/05/1912

**DEBUT:** v Blackburn Rovers, H, 18/09/1912

**LAST MATCH:** v Burnley, A, 11/03/1914

**MOVED TO:** Distillery, 14/05/1914

**TEAMS:** Central Half Holiday, Perth Violet, Sunderland, Distillery, Crystal Palace, Newport County, Bristol City, Millwall, Chatham, Yeovil and Petters United, Southend United, Yeovil and Petters United

**INTERNATIONAL:** Scotland Junior

**SAFC TOTALS:** 9 appearances / 5 goals

**John Conner led the line in a couple of early season games in 1912-13 when after a slow start the team went on to win the league and reach the cup final. He came to the fore in the following campaign with a brace in a home win against Middlesbrough followed by goals in three successive rounds of the cup. Despite five goals in seven games that term though, his services were not retained.**

He was to experience success with Crystal Palace after the Great War when he was top scorer with 29 goals when ever-present in the side that convincingly won Division Three in 1920-21 - nine of those goals coming in the final five games. During the same season, he also scored the winner in the London Challenge Cup final against Clapton Orient. After 37 goals in 61 league games for Palace he also had a decent scoring record at Newport where he netted 26 goals in 85 league appearances.

Sometimes known as Jack, he scored three times in 16 games for Bristol City and made his final two league appearances with Millwall in November 1925 only for the Lions to fail to score in either home game in a season where they finished third in Division Three South. He finished his career with Yeovil & Petters United in the late 1920s before returning to his native Scotland.

## **CONNOLLY, David** James

**POSITION:** Striker

**BIRTHPLACE:** Willesden, London

**DATE OF BIRTH:** 06/06/1977

**HEIGHT:** 5' 9" **WEIGHT:** 11st 0lbs

**SIGNED FROM:** Wigan Athletic, 31/08/2006

**DEBUT:** v Derby County, A, 09/09/2006

**LAST MATCH:** v Wigan Athletic, H, 05/01/2008

**MOVED TO:** Contract not renewed, 31/05/2009

**TEAMS:** Watford, Feyenoord, Wolves (L), Excelsior (L), Wimbledon, West Ham United, Leicester City, Wigan Athletic, Sunderland, Southampton, Portsmouth, Oxford United (L), AFC Wimbledon

**INTERNATIONAL:** Republic of Ireland

**SAFC TOTALS:** 32+10 appearances / 13 goals

**One of the half a dozen deadline-day arrivals as Roy Keane swept into the club, Keane's old Republic of Ireland teammate was a well-travelled striker who had the kind of guts Keane respected. This was never better illustrated than in the last home game of the promotion season under Keane.**

Needing to beat Burnley in front of a packed stadium and live on TV, Connolly had no hesitation in stepping up for a second crucial penalty despite having an earlier spot-kick saved.

Once he hit the back of the net there were no wild celebrations of relief. Instead, Connolly just rushed to get the ball to re-start play as Sunderland searched for the winner which they duly got in sensational style courtesy of Carlos Edwards. The action typified Connolly's professionalism which saw him top score as the Coca-Cola Championship was won, his 13 goals including the final goal of the season in a 5-0 win at Luton that clinched the title.

Connolly had also had a penalty saved at the 2002 FIFA World Cup, Spain's Iker Casillas denying the Republic of Ireland striker in a second round shoot-out after Connolly came off the bench for his only appearance at the finals. The previous World Cup had seen him sent off against Belgium as the Irish lost in a play-off place for the finals. More positively, he had netted an international hat-trick against Liechtenstein in a qualifying game for that tournament. In total, Connolly scored nine times for Ireland in 41 appearances. He also scored for Ireland against Sunderland at the Stadium of Light in Niall Quinn's Benefit game in 2002.

At club level, he totalled 178 league goals in 460 games and 193 goals in 510 appearances overall. Winning the Championship on Wearside was the highlight of his club career with a Football League (Johnstone's Paint) Trophy medal in 2010 his only other senior medal - although he only played the last five minutes of Southampton's 4-1 Wembley win over Carlisle United.

The Saints and Wimbledon were the only two clubs he played over 60 games for with his total never reaching as many as 70 anywhere. With West Ham he played in the 2004 Play-Off final lost to Sunderland's conquerors Crystal Palace at the Millennium Stadium while with Wolves, David once scored four times in a match against Bristol City. Early in his career he experienced continental football with Excelsior in the Netherlands.

Connolly could have come to Sunderland much earlier. Reportedly, it was Connolly Sunderland's scouts were at Watford to watch when Kevin Phillips subsequently came to the fore. SuperKev became a legend at Sunderland, but in his own time, David Connolly also enjoyed success.

## **CONNOR,** James **(Jimmy)**

**POSITION:** Winger

**BIRTHPLACE:** Renfrew, Renfrewshire

**DATE OF BIRTH:** 01/06/1909 - 08/05/1980

**HEIGHT:** 5' 7½" **WEIGHT:** 10st 5lbs

**SIGNED FROM:** St Mirren, 05/05/1930

**DEBUT:** v Manchester City, H, 30/08/1930

**LAST MATCH:** v Blackburn Rovers, A, 16/02/1939

**MOVED TO:** Retired, 17/04/1939

**TEAMS:** Paisley Carlisle, Glasgow Perthshire, St Mirren, Sunderland

**INTERNATIONAL:** Scotland

**SAFC TOTALS:** 283 appearances / 62 goals

**The great old Sunderland historian and Supporters' Association stalwart Billy Simmons always used to say Jimmy Connor was his favourite player of the thirties team he watched as a boy. That is some accolade given Raich Carter and Bobby Gurney were amongst the stars in that side.**

Connor was a flying winger with an adhesive touch on his left foot. Always keen to cut inside and shoot, he was a regular taker as well as maker of goals. One of two ever-presents in the title-winning season of 1935-36, Jimmy was on the scoresheet in a 7-2 win at Birmingham on the day the league was won.

He had been a regular throughout the thirties, playing between 35 and 47 games in six successive seasons from his arrival in 1930. Injury prevented Jimmy from adding a cup medal the year after his league one. After scoring in the fourth round at Luton, Connor's cruciate ligament was damaged in the replay in which he also netted. After missing a season and a half, Connor attempted a come-back in a late season game before returning in the autumn. He managed a run of six games, soon followed by another run of five appearances, but was then injured in February 1939, once again in a cup-tie, this time at Blackburn. It was to be his final first-team appearance, something that became a certainty when he again damaged cruciate ligaments in an attempted come-back game for the reserves in April of that year.

He had made his name with 17 goals in 99 league games for St Mirren after playing local and junior football. The first of his four full caps arrived a fortnight after leaving St Mirren for Sunderland. Not quite 21, he had not yet debuted for his new club when he lined up against France in Paris, when goals late in each half from Newcastle's Hughie Gallagher gave the Scots a 2-0 victory. In September 1931, his home international debut saw him play in a 3-1 win over Ireland at Ibrox.

On 14 April 1934, Sunderland beat Middlesbrough 2-0, but had to do so without Connor or Raich Carter who were on opposite sides at Wembley. It was Carter's international debut and he had the happier day as Scotland were beaten 3-0. The following October, on the occasion of Connor's last cap, he was joined at inside-left by clubmate Patsy Gallacher who opened the scoring in a 2-1 defeat against Ireland in Belfast.

When his career was over, Jimmy ran a newsagents in Marley Potts in Sunderland and also had a shop near the Grange pub on Newcastle Road. His sons Jimmy and Gil (Gilbert) played, Gil for Tow Law and Willington and Jimmy for Ryhope CW, Stanley United, Darlington and Bishop Auckland. In September 1959 Jimmy junior played at Roker Park as part of a Wearside League XI that were beaten 5-1 by Sunderland's youth team.

## COOK, Jordan Alan

**POSITION:** Midfielder / forward
**BIRTHPLACE:** Sunderland
**DATE OF BIRTH:** 20/03/1990
**HEIGHT:** 5' 9" **WEIGHT:** 12st 8lbs
**SIGNED FROM:** Trainee, 30/07/2007
**DEBUT:** v Manchester United, 26/12/2010
**LAST MATCH:** v West Ham United, A, 22/05/2011
**MOVED TO:** Contract not renewed, 30/06/2012
**TEAMS:** Sunderland, Darlington (L), Walsall (L), Carlisle United (L), Charlton Athletic, Yeovil Town (L), Walsall, Luton Town, Grimsby Town, Gateshead, Hartlepool United (to June 2022)
**SAFC TOTALS:** 0+3 appearances / 0 goals

**Although he produced a marvellous bit of skill within moments of entering the fray as a sub on his Premier League debut at Old Trafford, Jordan Cook only got another couple of appearances off the bench and a total of 30 minutes actual playing time having been at the club since he was seven - just three of those minutes coming at the Stadium of Light in a home defeat by Chelsea.**

Prior to his Sunderland debut, Jordan had played five times in League Two on loan to Darlington where he suffered a serious setback with a cruciate knee ligament injury. Between his second and third appearances for Sunderland, an eight game spell in League One with Walsall produced a first career goal against Brentford. His last season as a contracted Sunderland player saw Cook go on loan to Carlisle, scoring four times in 14 League One games, over half of which were as sub.

Released by Sunderland, Jordan made the big move to London with Charlton in the Championship, but there were to be only two league starts amongst his total of 14 appearances for the Addicks who loaned him to Yeovil (one sub appearance) before he signed for Walsall in 2014. 83 appearances for the Saddlers included one at Wembley in the 2015 Johnstone's Paint (Football League) Trophy final lost to Steve Cotterill's Bristol City and a goal on his final appearance in a League One Play-Off semi-final loss to Barnsley. The following season Jordan was in Play-Off action again, this time in League Two encounter against Blackpool for his new club Luton. While that Play-Off was again unsuccessful, he did play in ten League Two games for the Hatters in the first half of the following 2017-18 campaign as Luton went on to promotion.

Cook later had a two year spell with Grimsby where he was a teammate of Danny Collins before dropping into non-league on a return to the north east with Gateshead and Hartlepool.

## COOKE, Frederick Robert

**POSITION:** Forward
**BIRTHPLACE:** Kirkby-in-Ashfield, Nottinghamshire
**DATE OF BIRTH:** 05/07/1896 - 22/09/1976
**HEIGHT:** 5' 10" **WEIGHT:** 12st 6lbs
**SIGNED FROM:** East Kirkby, 25/08/1919
**DEBUT:** v Bradford Park Avenue, H, 24/04/1920
**LAST MATCH:** v Oldham Athletic, H, 09/04/1921
**MOVED TO:** Swindon Town, 11/05/1921
**TEAMS:** East Kirkby, Sunderland, Swindon Town, Accrington Stanley, Bangor City
**SAFC TOTALS:** 12 appearances / 5 goals

**Fred Cooke enjoyed a decent return of five goals from a dozen appearances, seven of which came at inside-left with the other five at centre-forward. As with so many instances of Sunderland players in the distant past, Cooke was an example of the old saying that if a player was needed, the club only had to send someone to whistle down a coal mine. Before his footballing career took off, Fred had been a pony driver below ground.**

It was the legendary Charlie Buchan he was in harness with on his debut, the pair setting each other up to score within three minutes of each other in a 2-0 victory. Cooke enjoyed a sequence of nine successive appearances at the turn of the year in 1920-21 when a highlight was scoring the winner against Manchester City while the final game of his Sunderland days saw him score with a penalty.

The summer of 1921 saw Fred move to Swindon Town. He scored 15 times in 33 Division Three South games over two seasons with the Robins before a move to Accrington Stanley where he scored one goal for every five of his 25 appearances. Finally, a £40 fee secured his services for Bangor City in October 1924. He stayed in Bangor after his playing days becoming a golf club steward.

## COOKE, John

**POSITION:** Forward / winger
**BIRTHPLACE:** Salford, Greater Manchester
**DATE OF BIRTH:** 25/04/1962
**HEIGHT:** 5' 8" **WEIGHT:** 11st 0lbs
**SIGNED FROM:** Manchester United, 07/12/1978
**DEBUT:** v Bristol Rovers, H, 24/11/1979
**LAST MATCH:** v Ipswich Town, H, 11/05/1985
**MOVED TO:** Sheffield Wednesday, 12/06/1985
**TEAMS:** Sunderland, Carlisle United (L), Sheffield Wednesday, Carlisle United, Stockport County, Chesterfield, Gateshead, Spennymoor
**INTERNATIONAL:** England Under 20
**SAFC TOTALS:** 48+15 appearances / 5 goals

**Nicknamed 'The Black Box' behind the scenes at the club as he always survived the crash as new managers brought in their own staff while kit-man Cooke remained, John was finally made redundant in 2020. A consequence was the departure of his son Jay Turner-Cooke who had been playing for the Under 18s, but left shortly afterwards to subsequently sign for Newcastle United.**

John Cooke had been at the club as kit-man for quarter of a century, his cheeky banter always being an integral part of keeping up spirits. In the last home game of the curtailed season before John's time at the club came to an end, it was notable that it was 'Cookie' that Kyle Lafferty ran to, to celebrate with after scoring against Gillingham.

'Sixth man' when Sunderland won the Daily Express five-a-side championships at Wembley Arena in 1979, John made his first-team debut that season, his first goal on the second of his four appearances that term securing a 1-0 win, in a season where Sunderland were promoted a point clear of missing out.

It was a notable contribution, but over the next five seasons John never managed to score more than once per season. During his last season as well as playing in a handful of games as the team were relegated, he played in a League (Milk) Cup quarter-final win at Watford as the Lads eventually made it to the final.

In 1981 Cooke won three caps at Under 20 level, scoring on his debut in the FIFA World Youth Championship quarter-final as Egypt were beaten in Australia. Having come on as a sub in that match, he started the semi-final where England lost 2-1 to Qatar in Sydney. He got a third cap as Romania won the third-place game in Adelaide.

After leaving Sunderland, Cooke's best years came with Carlisle for whom he played over 100 times while he also topped over half a century of league appearances for each of Stockport and Chesterfield. In May 2022, a testimonial was staged for John at South Shields.

## COOKE, Terence John (Terry)

**POSITION:** Winger
**BIRTHPLACE:** Marston Green, Birmingham
**DATE OF BIRTH:** 05/08/1976
**HEIGHT:** 5' 7" **WEIGHT:** 9st 9lbs
**SIGNED FROM:** Manchester United, 29/01/1996, on loan
**DEBUT:** v Tranmere Rovers, H, 30/01/1996
**LAST MATCH:** v Luton Town, H, 24/02/1996
**MOVED TO:** Manchester United, 25/02/1996, end of loan
**TEAMS:** Manchester United, Sunderland (L), Birmingham City (L), Wrexham (L), Manchester City, Wigan Athletic (L), Sheffield Wednesday (L), Grimsby Town, Sheffield Wednesday, Colorado Rapids, North Queensland Fury, Gabala
**INTERNATIONAL:** England Under 21
**SAFC TOTALS:** 6 appearances / 0 goals

**Shortly after his month-long loan at Sunderland, Terry Cooke won one of his four England Under 21 caps at Roker Park against Croatia in April 1996, playing alongside future Sunderland keeper Kelvin Davis who came on as a sub. That international was a final warm-up game for the following month's Toulon Tournament in which Terry played against Belgium, Angola and Portugal - being sent off in a 3-1 defeat to the Portuguese. He had earlier also been capped at Under 16 and 18 level.**

With Sunderland, he made six successive appearances during a promotion season, three draws and a defeat preceding back to back 1-0 wins. Four and a half months before coming to play for Peter Reid on Wearside, Cooke had made his Premiership debut for Manchester United against Bolton at Old Trafford.

He had since played seven times for the Red Devils including a UEFA Cup tie against Rotor Voldograd of Russia on a night when keeper Peter Schmeichel had scored a last-minute equaliser. Cooke had also scored for United, joining Andy Cole on the scoresheet, but in a 3-1 League (Coca-Cola) Cup win at York which was not enough to wipe out a 3-0 first-leg deficit in which Terry had played in the Old Trafford shock - as had future Sunderland man Darren Williams for the Minstermen.

Following his return from Sunderland, Cooke would play just once more for United in a League (Coca-Cola) Cup loss at Leicester the following November. In a long and well-travelled career, Manchester City became the only English team he played more than 25 league games for, the first 17 of his 37 for City coming on the fourth and last of his loans from United - his performances persuading City to pay their neighbours £1m for his signature.

In 2005, he moved to America where he played over 100 times in four years with Colorado Rapids. Terry then spent a year playing in Australia before finally moving to Gabala, a club in Azerbaijan where he played for former England centre-back Tony Adams.

## COOPER, Colin Terence

**POSITION:** Centre-back

**BIRTHPLACE:** Sedgefield, Co Durham

**DATE OF BIRTH:** 28/02/1967

**HEIGHT:** 5' 11" **WEIGHT:** 11st 11lbs

**SIGNED FROM:** Middlesbrough, 12/03/2004, on loan

**DEBUT:** v Reading, A, 20/03/2004

**LAST MATCH:** v Derby County, H, 27/03/2004

**MOVED TO:** Middlesbrough, 06/04/2004, end of loan

**TEAMS:** Middlesbrough, Millwall, Nottingham Forest, Middlesbrough, Sunderland (L)

**INTERNATIONAL:** England

**SAFC TOTALS:** 0+3 appearances / 0 goals

**A boyhood Sunderland supporter who came on loan as a veteran and saw his three appearances as a substitute total a meagre 20 minutes. Brought in by Mick McCarthy who he had played alongside at Millwall, Colin had started with Middlesbrough for whom he played over 200 times in his first spell with the club during which the Teessiders struggled with liquidation.**

A £300,000 fee took him to Millwall in the summer of 1991 with the Lions making a massive profit when they collected £1.7m from Forest for him two years later after 87 games for the Londoners. Having been selected for the PFA Division One Team of the Year in his last year with Millwall, he achieved the same accolade in the first and last of his five seasons with Forest (having played in the Premier League in the middle three). Colin won his two England caps while with Forest for whom he played 180 times in the league scoring 20 times, mainly through his ability to get on the end of set-pieces. England conceded three goals on each of his appearances, a 3-3 draw with Sweden at Leeds and a 3-1 Wembley defeat to Brazil, both in June 1995.

Colin also won eight Under 21 caps, being a member of the team who were runners-up at the 1988 Toulon Tournament.

Three years after his full England caps, a by now much more affluent Middlesbrough paid £2.5m to bring back their club hero who took his final tally of appearances for the club to 422. Following his retirement as a player in 2006, Colin became reserve team manager at Boro, becoming first-team coach after six months and later taking over from Sunderland's 1992 FA Cup final manager Malcolm Crosby as assistant manager in June 2009. The following October, he very briefly became caretaker manager after the departure of Gareth Southgate.

After leaving to become assistant manager of Bradford City, Colin also became caretaker manager of the Bantams before being replaced by future Sunderland boss Phil Parkinson. From May 2013 to October 2014 he managed Hartlepool United where he became League Two manager of the month in October 2013.

Always a hugely respected figure in football, Colin set up the Finlay Cooper Fund following the tragic death of his son.

## COOPER, Kevin Lee

**POSITION:** Winger

**BIRTHPLACE:** Derby

**DATE OF BIRTH:** 08/02/1975

**HEIGHT:** 5' 8" **WEIGHT:** 10st 4lbs

**SIGNED FROM:** Wolverhampton Wanderers, 07/01/2004, on loan

**DEBUT:** v Millwall, A, 17/01/2004

**LAST MATCH:** v Millwall, A, 17/01/2004

**MOVED TO:** Wolverhampton Wanderers, 18/03/2004, end of loan

**TEAMS:** Derby County, Stockport County, Wimbledon, Wolves, Sunderland (L), Norwich (L), Cardiff City, Yeovil Town (L), Walsall (L), Tranmere Rovers (L), Chesterfield, Newport County, Neath, University of Glamorgan

**SAFC TOTALS:** 0+1 appearances / 0 goals

**Kevin Cooper came to Wearside as an experienced winger, but made just one 13-minute cameo appearance in red and white, coming off the bench just once from the five times he was named as a sub. He had debuted for his hometown team Derby as a sub at Watford in May 1995 and had since played well over 150 games for Stockport and over 40 for Wimbledon who paid £800,000 for his signature and sold him to Wolves a year later, his former Stockport manager Dave Jones investing £1m in him.**

Debuting for the Molineux club at Burnley in March 2002, Kevin helped them to that season's Division One Play-Off scoring the only goal of the semi-final second leg v Norwich, although it was to no avail as the Canaries won on aggregate. Scoring in his first two appearances of his first full season with Wolves got him off to a good start as again Wolves reached the Play-Offs, Kevin appearing in the semi-final, but not the victorious final as Wolves were promoted with a squad that included Alex Rae, Paul Butler and Joleon Lescott who all had spells at Sunderland.

Cooper was to appear just once in the Premiership as a sub before coming on loan to Sunderland in January. While his Wearside loan brought no more football, afterwards he quickly went to Norwich for whom he played at the Stadium of Light later in the season and helped them to win the Championship as Sunderland finished third. He was to play for Dave Jones a third time, at Cardiff before drifting down the divisions and into non-league playing in the Conference South with Newport and the Welsh Premier League with Neath.

After finishing playing, Cooper's career took him to Malaysia and Switzerland as manager of One Malaysia Cardiff City and subsequently Servette and FC Wil. In between his stint in the far east and continental Europe, he returned to Cardiff City to coach the Bluebirds Under 21s while from January to April in 2017, he returned to the north east as assistant manager to his mentor Dave Jones at Hartlepool. Two years later, Kevin returned to Malaysia as Head Coach at ATM FA. In 2021, his son Oli made his senior debut playing in the FA Cup against Stevenage for Swansea City.

## CORNER, David Edward

**POSITION:** Defender

**BIRTHPLACE:** Sunderland

**DATE OF BIRTH:** 15/05/1966

**HEIGHT:** 6' 2" **WEIGHT:** 12st 13lbs

**SIGNED FROM:** School, 01/07/1982

**DEBUT:** v Nottingham Forest, A, 01/09/1984

**LAST MATCH:** v Rotherham United, H, 24/11/1987

**MOVED TO:** Leyton Orient, 19/07/1988

**TEAMS:** Sunderland, Cardiff City (L), Peterborough United (L), Leyton Orient, Darlington, Gateshead

**INTERNATIONAL:** England Under 20

**SAFC TOTALS:** 42+3 appearances / 3 goals

**Forever blighted by being blamed for the 1985 League (Milk) Cup final defeat when he tried to shepherd the ball out for a goal kick only to be robbed as Norwich went on to score the only goal of the game, such blame was harsh on a lad of 18 playing only his fifth match.**

David had done well in a league win at Norwich the week before and played his part in a quarter-final win at Watford. He had however, had a torrid time on debut early in the season when he was subbed as Peter Davenport (who would play for Sunderland in their next cup final in 1992) completed a hat-trick for Brian Clough's Nottingham Forest.

Corner was highly-rated enough to be selected for England at the FIFA World Youth Championships in Russia in the summer after his Wembley woe. He played against Paraguay, China and Mexico as England were eliminated with Michael Thomas (who would score against Sunderland for Liverpool in the 1992 FA Cup final) one of his teammates. David scored in his first cup appearance after the League (Milk) Cup final, netting his first senior goal in an FA Cup win over Newport County. After a dozen appearances in that second season, Corner played 22 times in 1986-87 including appearing in both legs of the ill-fated relegation Play-Off with Gillingham.

## CORNER, David (Continued)

In addition to 33 league games for Sunderland, Corner managed another 34 elsewhere, the final 15 with Darlington after he led them back into the Football League as Conference champions in 1990. Those appearances were enough to earn David a Division Four winner's medal in 1991 under his old Roker teammate and player/manager Frank Gray, along with ex-Roker goalkeeper Mark Prudhoe. After a knee injury forced him out of professional football, David went on to play over 100 times for Gateshead before becoming an insurance agent and then a policeman. His experiences were later turned into a successful one-man stage monologue written by Jeff Brown and called 'Cornered.'

## CORNFORTH, John Michael

**POSITION:** Midfielder

**BIRTHPLACE:** Whitley Bay, Northumberland

**DATE OF BIRTH:** 07/10/1967

**HEIGHT:** 6' 1" **WEIGHT:** 11st 5lbs

**SIGNED FROM:** Whitley Bay Youths, 01/07/1984

**DEBUT:** v Ipswich Town, H, 11/05/1985

**LAST MATCH:** v Aston Villa, H, 23/03/1991

**MOVED TO:** Swansea City, 02/08/1991

**TEAMS:** Whitley Bay, Sunderland, Doncaster Rovers (L), Shrewsbury Town (L), Lincoln City (L), Swansea City, Birmingham City, Wycombe Wanderers, Peterborough United (L), Cardiff City, Scunthorpe United, Exeter City

**INTERNATIONAL:** Wales

**SAFC TOTALS:** 23+15 appearances / 2 goals

**A debutant on a day when Sunderland had already had relegation from the top-flight confirmed, when Cornforth got his second league game for Sunderland the club had dropped two divisions. By the time he finished at the club, Sunderland had climbed back to the top flight only to be relegated again. Both goals John scored came in the same game, a 4-2 win over York in the 1987-88 third division promotion season when he appeared in a dozen league games.**

Qualifying for Wales through his paternal grandmother, Cornforth won full caps in defeats to Bulgaria and Georgia in 1995 whilst on the books of Swansea City. As a teammate of Colin Pascoe, he had scored in a penalty shoot-out at Wembley as the Swans beat Huddersfield in the Autoglass Trophy (Football League Trophy) final. Of his many clubs, the Swans were the only one Cornforth played as many as 50 league games for, with 149 for the Welsh club.

Moving into management, he took charge of Exeter City, Newport County, Torquay United and Witheridge as well as coaching Crediton United and in South Korea. He also worked abroad when he went to Kuwait in 2011, but as a tanker driver rather than in football. By February 2013, he was back in the north east as coach at Horden CW then later assistant manager at Blyth Spartans. In 2021, he was living in Sunderland, in Ryhope. Sunderland's 2008 FA Youth Cup semi-final side included his nephew Joe Cornforth.

## COTON, Anthony Philip (Tony)

**POSITION:** Goalkeeper

**BIRTHPLACE:** Tamworth, Staffordshire

**DATE OF BIRTH:** 19/05/1961

**HEIGHT:** 6' 2" **WEIGHT:** 13st 7lbs

**SIGNED FROM:** Manchester United, 12/07/1996

**DEBUT:** v Leicester City, H, 17/08/1996

**LAST MATCH:** v Southampton, A, 19/10/1996

**MOVED TO:** Manchester United, 21/09/1998, as goalkeeper coach

**TEAMS:** Tamworth, Mile Oak Rovers, Birmingham City, Hereford United (L), Watford, Manchester City, Manchester United, Sunderland

**INTERNATIONAL:** England B

**SAFC TOTALS:** 12 appearances / 0 goals

**Tony Coton saved a penalty 54 seconds into his league debut for Birmingham, denying Sunderland's John Hawley - two days after Christmas in 1980. Twenty years later, he could claim some responsibility for Thomas Sorensen's derby penalty save against Alan Shearer as he had advised Sunderland to sign the Dane.**

In between, Coton had become Player of the Year with Birmingham, won the same award three times in six seasons at Watford and twice in five and half years with Manchester City. At City, he played alongside and for Peter Reid who went on to sign him for Sunderland from Manchester United, where Tony had been back-up to Peter Schmeichel. At Watford, Coton had become only the second player to be inducted into the club's Hall of Fame.

Brought to Sunderland when attempts to sign Shay Given failed, Coton kept a clean sheet on debut in Sunderland's first-ever Premier League game. He had not played a first-team game for over two years, but it was one of six he kept in eleven full appearances with Coton only being beaten by a penalty when playing a blinder at Derby. Unfortunately, his 12th game (and 501st league game in total) would be Tony's last as his leg was broken in five places at Southampton.

While he had already stepped down from the goalkeeper coach role he had accepted on joining Sunderland in order to focus on his own game, following his injury, Tony took over as reserve team coach, leading his side to their league title, but subsequently left Sunderland after a dispute regarding insurance payments, with the club settling out of court.

Returning to Old Trafford, he was Sir Alex Ferguson's goalkeeping coach from 1998 to 2008. After subsequent spells scouting for Wigan, Bolton and Aston Villa - where he worked for Steve Bruce - Coton came back to Sunderland on 11 June 2018 as Head of Recruitment until 17/07/2020.

At international level, Coton's only cap was as a sub for David Seaman in an April 1992 'B' international against France at QPR, a game in which his future Sunderland teammate Paul Stewart also played.

## COVERDALE, William Robert (Bobby)

**POSITION:** Wing-half / outside-left

**BIRTHPLACE:** West Hartlepool

**DATE OF BIRTH:** 16/01/1892 - 07/01/1959

**HEIGHT:** 5' 8" **WEIGHT:** 11st 4lbs

**SIGNED FROM:** Rutherglen, 28/08/1912

**DEBUT:** v Blackburn Rovers, A, 17/10/1914

**LAST MATCH:** v Middlesbrough, A, 06/11/1920

**MOVED TO:** Hull City, 09/05/1921

**TEAMS:** Rutherglen, Sunderland, Hull City, Grimsby Town, Bridlington Town

**INTERNATIONAL:** Scotland Junior

**SAFC TOTALS:** 22 appearances / 1 goal

**Having signed for SAFC as a 20-year-old at the start of the club's greatest-ever season, Coverdale could not get into the team as the league was won and cup final reached. Indeed he waited until October 1914 to get a first-team debut. By this time allied forces had been on the continent for over two months, but at home, league football continued with Bobby appearing at outside-left as Sunderland lost at Blackburn Rovers.**

By the following February as Germany mounted a naval blockade of Britain, Bobby was just breaking through in the world of football, playing at left-half in a 5-4 win at Oldham and a 1-0 home win over Manchester United. There would be one more appearance that season, on the wing in a win at WBA.

There were more battles to fight for Coverdale who joined the Durham Light Infantry. Having played as a 'Guest' for Hull, he returned to the red and whites in April 1918 playing in a Durham Senior Cup replay with South Shields soon followed by Victory League wins over Hartlepools and Durham City before being part of the side who thrashed Crook Town 8-0 in the DSC final at Darlington's Feethams.

When the Football League resumed in 1919-20, Coverdale was called upon in the seventh game of the season against Everton and went on to play nine times that year as Sunderland finished fifth. There would be eight more appearances early the following season, the last at Middlesbrough.

At the end of the season he moved on to Hull City where he stayed for three years before playing for Grimsby Town and Bridlington Town. Once capped as a junior international with Scotland, it was later discovered that he was ineligible, being born in West Hartlepool, although before joining Sunderland he had played for Rutherglen Glencairn.

## COWAN, James Clews (Jimmy)

**POSITION:** Goalkeeper

**BIRTHPLACE:** Paisley, Renfrewshire

**DATE OF BIRTH:** 16/06/1926 - 20/06/1968

**HEIGHT:** 5' 11" **WEIGHT:** 12st 8lbs

**SIGNED FROM:** Morton, 11/06/1953

**DEBUT:** v Charlton Athletic, A, 19/08/1953

**LAST MATCH:** v Liverpool, A, 03/04/1954

**MOVED TO:** Third Lanark, 20/11/1955

**TEAMS:** St Mirren, Morton, Sunderland, Third Lanark

**INTERNATIONAL:** Scotland

**SAFC TOTALS:** 29 appearances / 0 goals

**Capped 25 times by Scotland, Jimmy Cowan was a renowned goalkeeper by the time he signed for Sunderland, but confided in Johnny Mapson that he was playing with a bad knee injury. That may have contributed to a costly time in goal for Sunderland as he conceded five on his debut and another five in his second home match, not keeping a clean sheet until his 18th game and letting in four on his final appearance.**

His caps had come between 1948 and 1952 when with Morton, Cowan managing eight shut-outs at international level. Prior to that, Cowan had played for a British Forces touring team in Europe in late 1946. He had played in a 3-1 win for Scotland over England at Wembley in April 1949 and was also beaten just once as England won in front of over 133,000 at Hampden the following April, a game which clinched England's place at their first FIFA World Cup in 1950.

One of Cowan's teammates that day was future Sunderland manager Ian McColl on one of five occasions the pair played together for Scotland. In 1951, he lined up alongside Charlie Fleming and against Trevor Ford for the Rest of Great Britain against Wales in a Wales FA 75th anniversary match.

Cowan came up against McColl twice at Hampden, in the 1948 Scottish Cup final where Jimmy was beaten once in the drawn first game and the replay defeat to Rangers watched by phenomenal crowds of 129,176 and 133,750. They were two of over 150 games Cowan played for Morton after never making a league appearance for his first team St Mirren. With Third Lanark, he made six league appearances in the season after leaving Sunderland.

Jimmy Cowan was inducted into the Scottish Football Hall of Fame in 2007. His son Ronnie was elected to the House of Commons in 2015 as the SNP MP for Inverclyde.

## COWAN, Walter Gowans (Wattie)

**POSITION:** Inside-right

**BIRTHPLACE:** Dalziel, Lanarkshire

**DATE OF BIRTH:** 20/01/1874 - 14/10/1960

**HEIGHT:** 5' 8½" **WEIGHT:** 10st 12lbs

**SIGNED FROM:** Motherwell, 13/05/1895

**DEBUT:** v Blackburn Rovers, H, 07/09/1895

**LAST MATCH:** v Notts County, H, 19/04/1897

**MOVED TO:** Motherwell, 03/05/1897

**TEAMS:** Motherwell, Sunderland, Motherwell

**SAFC TOTALS:** 19 appearances / 7 goals

**Known as 'Wattie' or 'William the Silent' from his time with Motherwell, Cowan spent two seasons with Sunderland, arriving when 'The Team of All The Talents' were reigning league and world champions. Scoring the winner on his debut got Wattie off to a fine start and though he had to work hard for a first-team place, he did well with five goals in nine outings in his first season, all of his strikes coming in home wins.**

His second campaign was not so successful, though his two goals were both winners in away games at Blackburn and Stoke. Having finished second from bottom, Sunderland took part in Victorian era Play-Offs known as Test Matches. His last two matches were in such fixtures against Notts County before he returned to Motherwell where after his football career he became an iron plater.

## COWELL, John William Richardson (Jack)

**POSITION:** Centre-forward

**BIRTHPLACE:** Blyth, Northumberland

**DATE OF BIRTH:** 09/06/1887 - 19/07/1937

**HEIGHT:** 5' 8" **WEIGHT:** 11st 0lbs

**SIGNED FROM:** Bristol City, 18/10/1910

**DEBUT:** v Manchester City, A, 22/10/1910

**LAST MATCH:** v Woolwich Arsenal, H, 28/01/1911

**MOVED TO:** Distillery, 06/05/1911

**TEAMS:** Springwell, Rowlands Gill, Spen Black & White, Castleford Town, Selby Mizpah, Rotherham Town, Bristol City, Sunderland, Distillery, Belfast Celtic, Durham City

**INTERNATIONAL:** England B

**SAFC TOTALS:** 14 appearances / 6 goals

**It was a case of 'have boots, will travel' for former coal miner putter Jack Cowell. He usually spent no more than a season with most of his clubs, including Sunderland. Those boots certainly had goals in them, notably at Selby where 23 goals in only eleven games earned him a step up to Midland League Rotherham Town in 1907. He spent two years at that club, who later merged with Rotherham County to become Rotherham United, before moving to Bristol City just after they had played in the 1909 FA Cup final.**

Cowell made a swift start with the Robins scoring a hat-trick in a 4-1 home win over Middlesbrough in his first month and later in the season scoring all four goals as Nottingham Forest were thrashed 4-0 at Ashton Gate. A total of 20 goals in 37 league games saw him return to his native north east with Sunderland in a swap deal for winger Willie Clark.

He made a bright start with two goals within the space of three minutes - the second described in match reports as 'a dazzler' - in a three-all draw at Manchester City on debut. That promise earned him seven more successive starts, but he only got on the scoresheet again in a home win over his old club Bristol City. He did better with three goals in a six game run in the side later in the season, but left to go to manager Bob Kyle's old club Distillery. He stayed in Northern Ireland when moving to Belfast Celtic in November 1914, before serving in the North Irish Horse Regiment during World War One. After the war he returned to the north east to play for Durham City.

## COXFORD, John (Jack)

**POSITION:** Left-half

**BIRTHPLACE:** Seaton Hirst, Northumberland

**DATE OF BIRTH:** 25/07/1904 - 29/05/1978

**HEIGHT:** 5' 9" **WEIGHT:** 12st 6lbs

**SIGNED FROM:** Stakeford United, 07/05/1924

**DEBUT:** v Blackburn Rovers, A, 18/04/1925

**LAST MATCH:** v Arsenal, A, 20/11/1926

**MOVED TO:** Birmingham, 28/04/1927

**TEAMS:** North Seaton Colliery, Stakeford United, Sunderland, Birmingham, Bournemouth & Boscombe Athletic, Poole Town, Northfleet United

**SAFC TOTALS:** 10 appearances / 0 goals

**Jack Coxford stood in for Arthur Andrews in one late-season game in 1924-25 as a 20-year-old and had his best term the following season when he made seven first division appearances. These included the first three games of the campaign which were won 3-1, 6-2 and 5-2 as new signing Dave Halliday went goal crazy. Halliday was again on the mark on both of Coxford's final back-to-back games in November 1926 as Liverpool and Arsenal were beaten.**

# C

## COXFORD, Jack (Continued)

Moving to Birmingham, like Sunderland a top-flight side, he debuted at Blackburn - as he had with Sunderland - and played eight times in his first season, the Blues using him at centre-half. After seven appearances the following year - the last against Newcastle - he was on the move again, going south where he remained after 134 games for Bournemouth and two for Poole Town. Finishing his playing days as captain of Northfleet, he coached the club who were known as Tottenham's nursery side and there he coached Bill Nicholson, Vic Buckingham and Ted Ditchburn amongst others.

After working as an aircraft sheet metal worker during World War Two, Coxford became a trainer at Tottenham Hotspur in 1946, becoming assistant trainer to Cecil Poynton in the fifties. Having played with Sunderland in the twenties, Coxford was still with Spurs when they toured the USA and Canada in 1969 having been part of Bill Nicholson's set-up in their glorious double year of 1961, when they came to Roker Park in the FA Cup quarter-final, although primarily in his time at White Hart Lane he worked with the reserve team.

## CRADDOCK, Jody Darryl

**POSITION:** Centre-back

**BIRTHPLACE:** Redditch, Worcestershire

**DATE OF BIRTH:** 25/07/1975

**HEIGHT:** 6' 0" **WEIGHT:** 12st 0lbs

**SIGNED FROM:** Cambridge United, 30/07/1997

**DEBUT:** v Bury, H, 16/09/1997

**LAST MATCH:** v Arsenal, H, 11/05/2003

**MOVED TO:** Wolverhampton Wanderers, 31/07/2003

**TEAMS:** Christchurch, Cambridge United, Woking (L), Sunderland, Sheffield United (L), Wolves, Stoke City (L)

**SAFC TOTALS:** 158+10 appearances / 2 goals

**Jody Craddock was a deservedly popular player. He gave great service after signing on the day the Stadium of Light staged its first-ever game. After excelling for his former Sunderland manager Mick McCarthy at Wolves, he staged a testimonial against Sunderland at Molineux.**

Tragically Jody and his wife Shelley lost a son, Jake, to cot death in August 2002. Somehow, Jody managed to continue and develop his career. He had begun his Football League career with Cambridge United who having plucked him from Dorset based Christchurch, handed Jody a senior debut against Stockport County a fortnight before Christmas in 1993. Quickly a regular for the Us Craddock was an ever-present for them in 1995-96 before being selected for the PFA Division Three team of the season the following year after which he jumped two divisions when signing for Sunderland.

Brought into Peter Reid's team after a calamitous team performance at Reading in the autumn, Jody barely missed a game for the rest of the season in which he played at Wembley in the unsuccessful Play-Off final with Charlton. During the next promotion-winning campaign Craddock was in the matchday squad for exactly half the games, but only played six times, remaining an unused sub for most of a glorious season. The following year, he found himself out on loan at Sheffield United under the managership of Adrian Heath who had just left Sunderland to take over at Bramall Lane. Returning to Sunderland, Craddock got back into the team and went on to start the final 15 Premiership games of the season, remaining a regular for the rest of his time at the club.

Mick McCarthy intended to build his team around Craddock and his new signing Gary Breen as the former Republic of Ireland manager began his first full season after relegation in 2003. Devastated when learning Craddock was to be sold as Sunderland played a pre-season match at Hearts, McCarthy was to be re-united with Craddock when he took over at Molineux himself three years later. Promoted to the Premier League in 2009, he scored against Sunderland at the Stadium of Light in Sunderland's last home game of 2010-11, helping Wolves to a crucial result that helped keep them up. It was his only goal at the Stadium of Light - his two for Sunderland coming at Bolton on the day Kevin Philips scored his 100th and at Arsenal with the final goal of the Peter Reid era.

237 of Craddock's career total of 577 games came for Wolves who he captained. Almost 2,000 Sunderland supporters were in the crowd of 9,000 that watched Craddock's testimonial in May 2014 with all proceeds going to Birmingham Children's Hospital where the Craddock's son Toby was being treated for leukaemia.

Outside of football, Jody is an accomplished artist. His work was first featured in the SAFC magazine 'Legion of Light' and he went on to stage numerous exhibitions and during 2017-18 designed the covers for all 25 issues of the Wolves programme.

## CRAGGS, John James (Jack)

**POSITION:** Winger

**BIRTHPLACE:** Trimdon Grange, Co Durham

**DATE OF BIRTH:** 18/02/1881 - 23/05/1950

**SIGNED FROM:** Trimdon Grange, 01/03/1900 and Reading, 01/05/1903

**DEBUT:** v Everton, H, 16/11/1901

**LAST MATCH:** v Nottingham Forest, A, 15/10/1904

**MOVED TO:** Reading, 06/05/1902 and Nottingham Forest, 16/11/1904

**TEAMS:** Trimdon Grange, Sunderland, Reading, Sunderland, Nottingham Forest, Sutton Town, Houghton Rovers, West Stanley

**SAFC TOTALS:** 43 appearances / 15 goals

**John Craggs was born as John Owens, but later changed his name. He had two spells with Sunderland. Mainly a reserve or 'A' team player in his first spell when he played six times as the league title was won in 1901-02, he contributed goals in a couple of home wins.**

After a season with Reading who he helped to become runners-up in the Southern League, Craggs returned to his native north east and played in every game of the 1903-04 season finishing joint top scorer with centre-forward Billy Hogg, although Craggs was on the right-wing, one of his goals coming in a cup-tie at Manchester City.

Despite this success, Craggs played just twice more, moving to Nottingham Forest a month after impressing in a victory there when he got a chance on the left flank as Arthur Bridgett was away playing in an inter-league match.

After a couple of seasons in Nottingham, John dropped into the non-league game. By 1911, Jack had returned to his former profession of coal miner in Trimdon and later served with the Royal Northumberland Fusiliers in World War One. Jack's son, also called John, played several games for Newcastle United reserves in 1928-29 and had trials with Clapton Orient, Hartlepools United and Brentford in the early 1930s.

## CRAIG, Robert (Bobby)

**POSITION:** Left-back

**BIRTHPLACE:** Consett

**DATE OF BIRTH:** 16/06/1928 - 10/02/2016

**HEIGHT:** 5' 9" **WEIGHT:** 10st 8lbs

**SIGNED FROM:** Leadgate Juniors, 01/11/1945

**DEBUT:** v WBA, H, 24/09/1949

**LAST MATCH:** v WBA, H, 24/09/1949

**MOVED TO:** Headington United, 09/08/1951

**TEAMS:** Leadgate Juniors, Sunderland, Headington United, Bedford Town

**SAFC TOTALS:** 1 appearance / 0 goals

**As a 17-year-old, Bobby Craig chose to sign for Sunderland, but could have been a sprinter having clocked 10.2 seconds for the 100 yards. He played just once, in a 2-1 win over West Bromwich Albion watched by a 50,000 plus crowd against an Albion attack that included three England internationals.**

Although that win over the Baggies remained his only senior first team game, three days later he was one of three members of that side who enjoyed another 2-1 win, this time at Gateshead in the Durham Senior Professional Cup along with Johnny Mapson and Bert Davis. Moving on to Headington (who became Oxford United) he signed for pre-war Sunderland player Harry Thompson. Bobby became a loyal servant of Headington, helping them to win the Southern League on goal average in 1952-53 before finishing his career as captain of Bedford Town. After his retirement from football, Craig ran a carpentry business and passed away in Wantage Community Hospital at the age of 88.

## CRAWFORD, James Adam

**POSITION:** Winger

**BIRTHPLACE:** Leith, Edinburgh

**DATE OF BIRTH:** 03/02/1875 - 02/01/1949

**HEIGHT:** 5' 6" **WEIGHT:** 11st 0lbs

**SIGNED FROM:** Reading, 06/05/1898 and Middlesbrough, 1903 (specific date not known)

**DEBUT:** v Preston North End, A, 03/09/1898

**LAST MATCH:** v Notts County, A, 07/04/1900

**MOVED TO:** Derby County, 11/05/1900

**TEAMS:** Rangers, Abercorn, Reading, Sunderland, Derby County, Middlesbrough, Sunderland

**SAFC TOTALS:** 57 appearances / 5 goals

**James Crawford played in the first-ever game at Roker Park having debuted the week before in the opening game of the season at Preston. He went on to miss just two games all season and started the first 15 of 1899-1900 as Sunderland stayed in the upper reaches of the table, eventually finishing third.**

He went on to play over 40 times in 18 months at Derby County before signing for Middlesbrough. Debuting against Gainsborough Trinity in December 1901, he made 22 successive appearances as Boro won promotion, but got just four games for them in Division One. Although he re-joined Sunderland, Crawford was unable to add to his tally of first-team appearances. After retiring, he became a publican in Middlesbrough and also became the father-in-law of Andrew Wilson who numbered Middlesbrough and Chelsea amongst his clubs as well being an international for Scotland.

## CRESSWELL, Frank

**POSITION:** Inside-left

**BIRTHPLACE:** South Shields, Co Durham

**DATE OF BIRTH:** 05/09/1908 - 02/12/1979

**HEIGHT:** 5' 7½" **WEIGHT:** 11st 2lbs

**SIGNED FROM:** Westoe Central, 07/11/1925

**DEBUT:** v Huddersfield Town, A, 14/09/1926

**LAST MATCH:** v Burnley, A, 25/08/1928

**MOVED TO:** WBA, 10/06/1929

**TEAMS:** Tyne Dock, Westoe Central, Sunderland, WBA, Connah's Quay Nomads, Chester City, Notts County, Chester City

**INTERNATIONAL:** England Schools

**SAFC TOTALS:** 13 appearances / 1 goal

**Former England schoolboys captain Frank Cresswell joined his more famous brother Warney in the Sunderland line-up, thus becoming only the second pair of brothers to play for Sunderland in a league game, after the Shaw brothers in April 1906. The Cresswell brothers only played together three times as Warney left in the February of Frank's breakthrough season in which the younger brother made five appearances.**

Frank's only goal came in the first of seven games he played in 1927-28, against Huddersfield who he debuted against, but after one more appearance in 1928-29, he was transferred to West Bromwich Albion for £975 in the summer of 1929. Playing alongside former Sunderland boys player Tommy Glidden (who would captain Albion's 1931 FA Cup-winning side when they became the last second division team to win the FA Cup before Sunderland in 1973) Frank scored six times in 31 games, two of these in a 7-3 Black Country derby win over Wolves.

Despite doing well at the Hawthorns, after one season he dropped down to non-league Connah's Quay Nomads and subsequently Chester who he helped climb into the Football League a year later, after a season where he scored 27 goals.

A complicated transfer system at the time meant he was technically still registered with West Brom until Chester entered the Football League. Other than six months with Notts County from January 1934 (scoring four in 16 games) Frank stayed with Chester until forced to retire through a broken kneecap in 1937 having scored 57 times in 168 Division Three North games. In 1933, he had won the Welsh Cup with them, beating Wrexham in the final and two years later lost at the same stage to Tranmere Rovers.

After a failed attempt at a come-back with Chester in May 1938, he became chief scout to his brother Warney at Northampton Town until the outbreak of World War Two before working in insurance following his retirement from the game.

## CRESSWELL, Warneford (Warney)

**POSITION:** Right-back

**BIRTHPLACE:** South Shields, Co Durham

**DATE OF BIRTH:** 05/11/1897 - 20/10/1973

**HEIGHT:** 5' 9" **WEIGHT:** 10st 13lbs

**SIGNED FROM:** South Shields, 03/03/1922

**DEBUT:** v Sheffield United, H, 04/03/1922

**LAST MATCH:** v Leicester City, H, 29/01/1927

**MOVED TO:** Everton, 03/02/1927

**TEAMS:** South Shields, North Shields Athletic, Greenock Morton (WW1 Guest), Hearts (WW1 Guest), Hibs (WW1 Guest), Spurs (WW1 Guest), South Shields, Sunderland, Everton

**SAFC TOTALS:** 190 appearances / 0 goals

**Warney Cresswell would be a contender for a place in an all-time Sunderland XI. A regular in the 1920s team that finished in the top three in four years out of five, he won five of his seven England caps with Sunderland before going on to claim two league titles, the FA Cup and the Division Two title with Everton, in addition to representing the Football League five times.**

It took a world record transfer fee of £5,500 to prise him from second division South Shields in 1922, a fee even more amazing given it was for a full-back rather than a forward. Shortly before his sale to Sunderland, South Shields had rejected an even bigger bid of £6,000 from reigning league champions Burnley only for the club to relent and sell the player when he voiced his opinion about being denied the opportunity to step into the top flight.

When he left Sunderland five years later, it was for a fee quoted as £7,000, although the Athletic News reported it was actually £4,750. Whatever the sale fee, Sunderland undoubtedly got their money's worth from a player renowned as, 'The Prince of full-backs'. Appointed club captain in January 1924, the relatively lightweight Cresswell was adept at jockeying wingers into positions where they were hemmed in and lost the ball or had to turn back.

Renowned for his positional sense, ability to read the game and his passing, in many respects Cresswell was ahead of his time, not least as he excelled in an era when changes to the offside law resulted in enormous amounts of goals being scored. Indeed, in Warney's first full season at Everton in 1927-28, he was a teammate of Dixie Dean when he registered English football's all-time record of 60 league goals in a season.

Warney's fourth international cap had come in a win over Ireland at Goodison Park in 1924 and having made that venue his home ground in February 1927, won the league title with the Toffees in 1928, won the Charity Shield the following year, but then suffered relegation in the tightest of tables in 1930. Moving from his normal right-back berth to left-back, he was ever-present as his club bounced straight back by winning the second division title and reached the FA Cup semi-final. He then missed only two games as the comeback was completed as the top-flight title was won again in 1932.

Although he missed the famous cup games with Sunderland in 1935, Warney stayed with Everton until his retirement in May 1936, his 306th and last game for Everton coming at Bolton in September 1935.

At the other end of his career, Cresswell played for three clubs in the Scottish League during World War One as league football there continued once it had ceased south of the border. He also played as a 'Guest' for Tottenham Hotspur before becoming a gunner in the Royal Field Artillery only to become a prisoner of war.

Just three years before the outbreak of World War Two he became player/manager of Port Vale on 13 May 1936. Leaving on 14 April of the following year, within four days he took over as manager of Northampton (appointing brother Frank as chief scout) Two years later, his contract was terminated shortly after football ceased due to World War Two. He then became a sergeant/instructor with the FA and army.

After the war, in 1947 he was unsuccessfully interviewed for the manager's job at Newcastle United after which he managed Dartford, but returned to Wearside to manage the Sheet Anchor Inn in Dundas Street near Roker Park. He then went back to Merseyside as a cinema manager, but passed away in South Shields. Having won his first England cap when still with Shields, he remains the only player to win a cap with the club for whom he played 104 times.

His son Corbett played for Carlisle United, Horden CW and Bishop Auckland, winning the FA Amateur Cup three years in a row with Bishops in the fifties. Great granddaughter, swimmer Kate Haywood was BBC Young Sports Personality of the Year in 2003, was a medallist in the 2002 and 2010 Commonwealth Games and took part in the 2008 Olympics.

# C

## CRINIGAN, William (Billy)

**POSITION:** Half-back

**BIRTHPLACE:** Muirkirk, Ayrshire

**DATE OF BIRTH:** 15/05/1890 - 12/05/1958

**HEIGHT:** 5' 9" **WEIGHT:** 11st 1lbs

**SIGNED FROM:** Douglas Water Thistle, 10/06/1910

**DEBUT:** v Spurs, H, 26/11/1910

**LAST MATCH:** v Wednesday, H, 13/03/1915

**MOVED TO:** Celtic, 18/09/1917

**TEAMS:** Douglas Water Thistle, Sunderland, Wishaw Thistle (L), Ayr Utd (L), Celtic, Third Lanark, Motherwell, Inverness Thistle, Bathgate

**SAFC TOTALS:** 82 appearances / 3 goals

**Sunderland were the only non-Scottish club Billy Cringan played for, but with the Football League suspended from 1915 due to World War One, his time on Wearside was curtailed with him moving to Celtic after a loan spell which was his third from the Roker Park club. For Sunderland he played in all the half-back positions, but despite ending the 1913-14 season by scoring in two of the three games he played at centre-forward, Cringan returned to left-half the following season after George Phillip was signed.**

Known as Willie at Celtic where he played as a centre-half, Cringan combined playing for the club with working as a miner during the war and was twice arrested for alleged 'desertion' when playing in Celtic games. He debuted in an Old Firm derby at Ibrox as he helped his new team keep a clean sheet in a Charity Cup tie on 12 May 1917. Cringan won league titles with Celtic in 1917, 1919 and 1922 and the Scottish Cup in 1923.

Having captained the club to the last two of those honours, his acceptance of the captaincy from 1921 ultimately led to his demise. As skipper, he represented his teammates in asking the directors to discuss a proposed bonus system and was speedily transferred to Third Lanark after 214 appearances which brought nine goals. He also fell foul of the directors at Third Lanark for refusing to play at right-half in a cup-tie at Hearts. Internationally, he won five caps and represented the Scottish League four times. He captained Scotland on his debut against Wales in 1920. The Scots were unbeaten in his five games, two of which were against England.

Following his retirement in 1925, Cringan coached in Belgium, became the Scottish Quoits champion in 1926 and took over the Star Inn pub in Bathgate. His brother Jimmy had an unsuccessful trial at Sunderland in August 1920, however, played over 250 games for Birmingham including the 1931 FA Cup semi-final against Sunderland. Another brother Robert played for Ayr United while former Hearts, Carlisle and Scotland player Peter Nellies was Billy's brother-in-law. The pair played alongside each other for the Scottish League.

## CROSSAN, John Andrew (Johnny)

**POSITION:** Inside-left

**BIRTHPLACE:** Londonderry, County Londonderry

**DATE OF BIRTH:** 29/11/1938

**HEIGHT:** 5' 8" **WEIGHT:** 11st 2lbs

**SIGNED FROM:** Standard Liege, 20/10/1962

**DEBUT:** v Grimsby Town, H, 03/11/1962

**LAST MATCH:** v Arsenal, H, 16/01/1965

**MOVED TO:** Manchester City, 22/01/1965

**TEAMS:** Derry City, Coleraine, Sparta Rotterdam, Standard Liege, Sunderland, Manchester City, Middlesbrough, Tongren, Foyle Harps

**INTERNATIONAL:** Northern Ireland

**SAFC TOTALS:** 99 appearances / 48 goals

**Top scorer in Sunderland's first-ever promotion season in 1963-64, Johnny Crossan was the favourite player of many due to the quality of his play, will to win and of course, his goals. Crossan appeared to glide across the turf, his close control a nightmare for defenders he frequently ran at. Ever-present in all 49 games in the promotion campaign, Crossan's 27 goals included two in the FA Cup quarter-final away to holders Manchester Utd.**

Two seasons after being promoted with Sunderland, Crossan captained Manchester City to promotion, scoring 16 in all competitions that term. He later returned to the north-east when costing Middlesbrough their record transfer fee of £32,500 in 1967, although illness and injury restricted him on Teesside.

Exactly half of Johnny's 24 caps and ten goals for Northern Ireland were registered during his two years and three months as a Sunderland player, one of those goals coming against England at Wembley. He might have come to Sunderland much sooner. Having been described as 'Ireland's Jimmy Greaves' when still a teenager, Sunderland tried to buy him from Derry City. Because he was an amateur, Derry could not receive a fee for him so they proposed to Johnny that if they accepted Sunderland's offer, reportedly of between £6,000 and £10,000, they would split it with him if he signed as pro.

It did not end well as a dispute allegedly saw Crossan demand a bigger portion of the deal. Dropped from the Derry team, he moved to Coleraine at the end of the season when his agreement with Derry was at an end. Coleraine were managed by the brother of the great Peter Doherty (Raich Carter's fellow inside-forward in the great Derby team of the immediate post-war years). At the time, Peter Doherty was managing Bristol City and when the brothers arranged the transfer of the talented youngster, Derry duly reported themselves and the player to the authorities. Consequently, Crossan was given a worldwide life ban from the game!

Crossan's appeal was backed by PFA chairman Jimmy Hill and it transpired that Crossan's ban applied only to the British Isles, so in August 1959, he duly moved to Sparta Rotterdam. Ironically, while with Sparta he was allowed to make his Northern Ireland debut against England at Wembley. He was also able to play for Sparta, not only against Rangers at Ibrox in a European tie, but then also against Rangers at Arsenal's Highbury in a replay after the tie finished level on aggregate.

In 1961, he signed for Belgian champions Standard Liege and after helping knock out Rangers, played against the great Real Madrid side of the era in a European Cup semi-final in 1962. It was at the end of that season that Sunderland chairman and England selector Syd Collings had a chance meeting with Irish FA president Harry Cavan at an England friendly in Peru (ahead of that year's FIFA World Cup in Chile). Over a drink, Collings persuaded Cavan to help lift the ban with the assistance of the promise of Sunderland coming to play a friendly at Linfield. Come 20 October that year on the day Crossan's ban was lifted a fee of £27,500 brought him to Sunderland.

Johnny later returned to Belgium, where he had business interests, from 1970-75 with Tongren. He went on to manage Sligo Rovers and became a BBC radio summariser in Ireland.

Still running a sports-shop in Derry at the age of 80, 'Jobby' Crossan was still playing five-a side football into his seventies. He was some player. His brother Eddie of Blackburn Rovers was also capped by Northern Ireland. A biography, 'The Man They Couldn't Ban' was published in 2020.

## CROSSLEY, Charles Arthur (Charlie)

**POSITION:** Inside-forward

**BIRTHPLACE:** Willenhall, Staffordshire

**DATE OF BIRTH:** 17/12/1891 - 29/04/1965

**HEIGHT:** 5' 8" **WEIGHT:** 12st 0lbs

**SIGNED FROM:** Walsall, 12/02/1914

**DEBUT:** v Spurs, H, 14/03/1914

**LAST MATCH:** v Preston North End, A, 03/04/1920

**MOVED TO:** Everton, 22/04/1920

**TEAMS:** Short Heath United, Willenhall Swifts, Siemens Institute, Willenhall Swifts, Hednesford Town, Walsall, Sunderland, Spurs (WW1 Guest), Clapton Orient (WW1 Guest), Huddersfield Town (WW1 Guest), Everton, West Ham United, Swindon Town, Ebbw Vale

**INTERNATIONAL:** England triallist in North v England

**SAFC TOTALS:** 46 appearances / 17 goals

**A debutant scorer in a home win over Spurs, Charlie Crossley also scored in his second game at Roker Park as Everton were thrashed. In the following 1914-15 campaign, he managed six goals in 14 games before his career stalled due to the cessation of the league because of World War One.**

A 'Guest' for a trio of clubs during the war, when he served in the Royal Navy as a stoker on a submarine, he also scored

twice in his one Victory League game for Sunderland and had his best season when the Football League resumed in 1919-20, netting nine in 24.

Those performances saw Crossley come into the England reckoning. On 25 February 1920, he made up the left flank for the North alongside his Roker teammate Harry Martin. Playing at St James' Park, Charlie scored, but with another Sunderland player, Charlie Buchan, scoring twice for England, Crossley's side lost 5-3.

Shortly afterwards he signed for Everton and became an instant hit. Top scorer with 18 goals in his opening season at Goodison, his tally included two in a home cup win against Newcastle who he also scored his first Everton goal against. Things did not go so swimmingly in his second season when after just three goals in 15 games he moved on to second division West Ham. There was just one goal from 16 games as the Hammers won promotion. He appeared in the first cup tie of the season at Hull, but after that did not feature in their cup side as the Hammers reached the first final at Wembley, the 'White Horse final.'

After a single season in London, Crossley moved to Swindon Town for a couple of years, scoring 14 goals in 44 games before taking over as player/manager of Ebbw Vale from September 1925. After retiring from football, he became a general shopkeeper in Walsall.

## CUELLAR JIMENEZ, Carlos Javier

**POSITION:** Centre-back

**BIRTHPLACE:** Madrid

**DATE OF BIRTH:** 23/08/1981

**HEIGHT:** 5' 8" **WEIGHT:** 12st 0lbs

**SIGNED FROM:** Aston Villa, 02/07/2012

**DEBUT:** v Arsenal, H, 18/08/2012

**LAST MATCH:** v Spurs, A, 07/04/2014

**MOVED TO:** Contract not renewed, 30/06/2014

**TEAMS:** Inter Argibay, Santa Ana, Pegaso, San Federico (L), Numancia, Calahorra (L), Osasuna, Rangers, Aston Villa, Sunderland, Norwich City, Almeria, M Petah Tikva, Ironi Kiryat Shmona, Beitar Jerusalem, Bnei Yehuda

**SAFC TOTALS:** 33 appearances / 1 goal

**Carlos Cuellar was a cool customer on and off the pitch. As a centre-back, he was composed and capable. Off the pitch, he was relaxed, never far away from a smile and while the rest of the squad showed up for training in the obligatory footballer sports cars or Range Rovers, Carlos would turn up in his mini, emblazoned with his squad number of 24 on the doors. In 2015 he became a vegan to help extend his career.**

Brought to Sunderland on a free transfer by his ex-Aston Villa manager Martin O'Neill, he debuted by helping his new side earn a goalless draw at Arsenal. A regular in his first season on Wearside, Cuellar only appeared five times in his second term.

Released in the summer of 2014, on 20 August 2014 Carlos became a Canary with Norwich in the Championship, but played just ten times before returning to his home country Spain for a season. Subsequently, he ended his career with a quartet of clubs in Israel where he won the Israel State Cup in 2019 as Bnei Yehuda of Tel Aviv defeated Maccabi Netanya on penalties.

Cuellar's senior career extended for 18 years, commencing with a senior debut for CD Numancia at Xerex CD in the Spanish second division in September 2001. In 2005, he was an unused substitute in the Copa Del Rey final for Osasuna who lost to Real Betis, but also helped the club qualify for Europe via their league position.

His sole Ibrox season of 2007-08 saw him reach the UEFA Cup final under Dick Advocaat. While that was lost to Zenit St Petersburg, he also played in two other finals, beating Hearts in the League Cup final and Gordon Chisholm's Queen of the South in the Scottish Cup. It was also an outstanding campaign on a personal level as he was named the Scottish Premier League and Scottish Football Writers Player of the Year after playing a club record 65 times in his season with Rangers.

Rangers cashed in accepting an £8m bid from Aston Villa. As at Rangers, Carlos made his debut in the UEFA Cup. Often used as a right-back as well as a centre-back at Villa, 94 of his 120 appearances over four seasons were in the Premier League. Under Martin O'Neill, Cuellar played alongside Stewart Downing in the 2010 League (Carling) Cup final lost to a Manchester United side that featured Jonny Evans and also Darron Gibson off the bench.

After retiring in the summer of 2019, the following October he returned to Rangers to play in a Legends game against Liverpool and in 2020 was living in Pamplona and undertaking his coaching badges.

## CUGGY, Francis (Frank)

**POSITION:** Right-half

**BIRTHPLACE:** Longbenton, Walker, Northumberland

**DATE OF BIRTH:** 16/06/1889 - 27/03/1965

**HEIGHT:** 5' 9" **WEIGHT:** 11st 4lbs

**SIGNED FROM:** Willington Athletic, 24/03/1909

**DEBUT:** v Aston Villa, A, 12/02/1910

**LAST MATCH:** v Chelsea, A, 12/03/1921

**MOVED TO:** Wallsend, 30/05/1921

**TEAMS:** Willington Athletic, Sunderland, South Shields (WW1), Wallsend

**INTERNATIONAL:** England

**SAFC TOTALS:** 187 appearances / 4 goals

**In terms of professional football, Frank Cuggy was effectively a one-club man, his stint for South Shields during the First World War being while he was paid a retainer by inactive Sunderland on the understanding he would re-join them after the war.**

On the only occasion Sunderland had three players in the England side, Cuggy was one of them. This was in February 1913. Right-half Cuggy was part of the famed 'Roker Triangle' with right-winger Jackie Mordue and inside-right Charlie Buchan. All three were selected for a game with Ireland in Belfast. (Cuggy's father John was Irish). It was also Buchan's debut, but despite him scoring England lost 2-1 in a game in which there were seven debutants, with Mordue winning just his second cap. It was the first time England had ever lost to Ireland.

Without their triangle, Sunderland won at Middlesbrough that weekend to go top of the table, Boro were also without two players in the England team. Exactly a year later, Cuggy played at Middlesbrough in winning his second cap, but again in a defeat to Ireland. On this occasion he was joined in the international side by his teammate Harry Martin. The pair had recently played for the North against England at Roker Park with another Sunderland player, George Holley, scoring in a 4-3 win for England. Cuggy's representative honours also included three appearances for the Football League.

During the glorious 1912-13 season the league game missed while on international duty was one of six Cuggy was absent for while he was one of ten players to play all nine games in the cup. Known to be a determined attacking wing-half with good ball control, he was evidently a top-class player.

Cuggy played regularly in the first post-war season, but after just three appearances in the second, left to become player/manager of Wallsend in the North Eastern League for the 1921-22 season. On 2 November 1923, he sailed from Southampton to Vigo in Spain where he became coach of the newly-formed Celta Vigo (following the merger of two teams). Cuggy coached there for five years helping his team to win the regional Galician Championship in their first three seasons during which they twice reached the semi-final of the Copa Del Rey.

Returning to England, Cuggy worked in the shipyards and was known to be a paid up member of the United Society of Boilermakers and Iron Shipbuilders from 16 September 1914 until 19 May 1927. When World War Two began in 1939, he was working as a store labourer in a Wallsend bakery and was buried in Wallsend when he died aged 75.

## CULLEN, Anthony (Tony)

**POSITION:** Winger

**BIRTHPLACE:** Felling, Co Durham

**DATE OF BIRTH:** 30/09/1969

**HEIGHT:** 5' 6" **WEIGHT:** 11st 7lbs

**SIGNED FROM:** Free agent, 12/09/1988

**DEBUT:** v Walsall, H, 11/02/1989

**LAST MATCH:** v Cambridge United, A, 12/10/1991

**MOVED TO:** Swansea City, 01/08/1992, on trial

**TEAMS:** Newcastle United, Sunderland, Carlisle United (L), Rotherham United (L), Bury (L), Swansea City, Doncaster Rovers, Gateshead, Jarrow Roofing, Tow Law Town, Seaham Red Star

**SAFC TOTALS:** 12+23 appearances / 1 goal

**Right-winger Tony Cullen had come through the youth system at Newcastle United and after joining Sunderland, featured in seven games in the spring of 1989 before starting the first couple of matches in the 1989-90 promotion season. During that campaign Cullen made the teamsheet in the opening 22 games either starting, coming off the bench or at least being an unused sub.**

Over Christmas he went on loan to Carlisle, scoring in a 3-1 debut win over Stockport and playing in a Boxing Day defeat at Burnley, playing in an unfamiliar left-wing role in his two fourth division games for the Cumbrians. Returning to Roker, Tony made another half-dozen appearances in the promotion season, including one as a sub in a draw at Newcastle, but he was out of the side by the time the Play-Offs came around.

Once promoted to the top-flight, Cullen came off the bench in the opening two games and would make one more sub appearance as well as getting starts at home to Liverpool and Manchester City. In between his pair of starts, Tony got his only goal in a 6-1 League (Rumbelows) Cup win at Bristol City. He also played in the same competition the following season, but that would be one of just two appearances in his last year of 1991-92.

Evidently Cullen's days were numbered as the calendar year had seen him go out on a trio of loans which brought seven league appearances and a goal. Upon leaving Sunderland, he signed for former Roker coach Frank Burrows at Swansea in October 1992 after a trial period. He would go on to score three times in 27 league appearances for the Jacks before further trial spells with Doncaster and York in 1993 without adding to his league tally before dropping into non-league.

## CUMMINS, Stanley

**POSITION:** Winger

**BIRTHPLACE:** Sedgefield, Co Durham

**DATE OF BIRTH:** 06/12/1958

**HEIGHT:** 5' 6" **WEIGHT:** 9st 1lb

**SIGNED FROM:** Middlesbrough, 13/11/1979 and as free agent, 30/10/1984, from Crystal Palace

**DEBUT:** v Notts County, H, 17/11/1979

**LAST MATCH:** v Aston Villa, H, 04/05/1985

**MOVED TO:** Crystal Palace, 18/07/1983 and Minnesota Strikers, 30/08/1985

**TEAMS:** Middlesbrough, Minnesota Kicks (L), Sunderland, Seattle Sounders (L), Crystal Palace, Sunderland, Minnesota Strikers, Kansas City Comets

**SAFC TOTALS:** 159+6 appearances / 32 goals

**Stan Cummins was just 20 when he became Sunderland's record signing when bought for £300,000, although this was well below the £1m tag Jack Charlton had labelled him with on Teesside. Had little Stan cost that higher fee, at his best he would have still looked good value. With a low centre of gravity, close control, a dash of speed and eye for goal, Cummins was terrific in his first spell at the club.**

Highlights included a great goal on the night promotion was won against West Ham in 1980, in a season when he also scored on his debut, bagged four goals in a match against Burnley and netted home and away to Newcastle. The following year when he was Player of the Year, Stan scored the last-day winner at Liverpool in a game Sunderland went into thinking they might have to win to stay up.

Signed by Ken Knighton, Cummins later came under the charge of Alan Durban whose book 'Give Us Tomorrow Now' claims that Cummins was not always the easiest player to handle.

After four seasons at Roker, Cummins controversially left on a free transfer, joining Crystal Palace - who were a division lower than Sunderland - after exercising his right to move when the new contract Sunderland offered him was no better than his existing deal. Rather like Marco Gabbiadini not long after, Cummins' time at Palace was short-lived as 15 months after leaving he was back at Roker, this time signed by Len Ashurst.

However, having played for Palace in the League (Milk) Cup, including two games against Sunderland, he was cup-tied as the

Lads reached the final. Combined with niggling injuries Stan's second stint was restricted to 18 games in which he didn't score. He had scored eight times in 33+1 games for Palace.

At international level, future Sunderland youth supremo Jim Morrow did not select Cummins after an England boys trial, believing him to be too small for a Wembley game with Germany that Stan ended up watching having gone on a school trip. As a 17-year-old, Cummins was given his league debut for Boro by Jack Charlton for a match with Ipswich in November 1976. It was one of just 44 league games Stan played for his first club (9 goals).

For a player who is so well remembered in English football, it is strange to think Cummins left the English game when he was just 26. Before signing for Sunderland he had spent the summer of 1977 in the USA with Minnesota Kicks and in 1981 left Sunderland for Seattle Sounders in a similar arrangement. Leaving Sunderland for the final time in 1985, Stan spent three years with Minnesota Strikers (123 games/41 goals) before finishing his playing days with Kansas City Comets in 1988-89 (48 games/6 goals).

Having excelled in the Sunderland team who won the Daily Express Five-a-side Trophy at Wembley Arena in fine style in the month he joined the club, and also helped Sunderland win a Six-a-side tournament in 1985 (a fund raising event for the Bradford City fire Disaster Fund), it was perhaps no surprise that Cummins went to the USA to play for Minnesota in the Major Indoor Soccer League. He enjoyed considerable success there, winning the MISL Eastern Division in 1988.

Although he spent much of his time after retirement living in the USA, during his spells back in England, Cummins coached Norton & Stockton Ancients, Shotton and Willington as well as managing Ferryhill Athletic.

## CUNNING, Robert Robertson Innes (Bobby)

**POSITION:** Winger

**BIRTHPLACE:** Dunfermline, Fife

**DATE OF BIRTH:** 12/02/1930 - 24/01/1983

**HEIGHT:** 5' 7" **WEIGHT:** 10 st 7lbs

**SIGNED FROM:** Port Glasgow, 14/06/1950

**DEBUT:** v Middlesbrough, A, 14/10/1950

**LAST MATCH:** v Arsenal, A, 11/11/1950

**MOVED TO:** Hamilton Academical, 25/10/1951

**TEAMS:** Dunoon, Port Glasgow, Sunderland, Hamilton Academical, Glasgow Rangers

**SAFC TOTALS:** 4 appearances / 0 goals

**Bobby Cunning's arrival on the Sunderland scene was twice delayed, once as he waited to be demobbed from the RAF and having joined, his potential first-team bow was held up when he fractured his collar bone in a reserve game with Workington late in August 1950. When it came, Cunning's spell in the limelight was short-lived. His four appearances came in the space of five games spread over less than a month.**

His only home appearance was also the home debut of Trevor Ford who crashed in a hat-trick as Sheffield Wednesday were beaten 5-1, but seven days later, a defeat by the same scoreline at Arsenal proved to be Bobby's valedictory outing.

Moving to Hamilton, Bobby came into his own with regular football as he scored 16 times in helping Academical to promotion to the top-flight in 1953. Although his club were immediately relegated, Cunning impressed at the higher level. Having done so well at Hamilton a £2,500 move to Rangers on 7 September 1954 looked to have re-opened the door to the big-time for Bobby, but he managed only three more games for Rangers than he did for Sunderland.

Two of these were in the Glasgow Cup including his debut against Clyde and the final which was lost to Partick Thistle. By March 1955, his first-team adventure at Ibrox was over, problems with his vision contributing to a premature end to his career. Having been a grocer while with Hamilton he returned to that trade, but passed away before the age of 53. His brother John (known as Ian) played for the British Army Cadet Force during Bobby's season with Rangers.

## CUNNINGHAM, Kenneth Edward (Kenny)

**POSITION:** Centre-back

**BIRTHPLACE:** Dublin, Republic of Ireland

**DATE OF BIRTH:** 28/06/1971

**HEIGHT:** 5' 11" **WEIGHT:** 12st 7lbs

**SIGNED FROM:** Birmingham City, 19/07/2006

**DEBUT:** v Coventry City, A, 06/08/2006

**LAST MATCH:** v Barnsley, H, 21/10/2006

**MOVED TO:** Contract not renewed, 30/06/2007

**TEAMS:** Home Farm, Tolka Rovers, Millwall, Wimbledon, Birmingham City, Sunderland

**INTERNATIONAL:** Republic of Ireland

**SAFC TOTALS:** 12 appearances / 0 goals

**The best known of Niall Quinn's signings in his brief spell as manager, 72 times capped Republic of Ireland international Kenny Cunningham did not do well at Sunderland. His short back-pass cost a goal in a 3-2 home defeat to Plymouth in his third game as the first three matches of the new 'Drumaville' era were lost.**

He played the opening eleven games of the season, but only one afterwards as his old international colleague Roy Keane restructured the side. Reluctant to do an interview, once he did speak, Kenny was an intelligent and thoughtful person, but clearly Sunderland did not see the best of a player who was a veteran when he came to the club.

At the other end of the scale, Cunningham had been 18 when he came into English football with Millwall. Debuting in March 1990, Kenny made five appearances having forced his way into the side at right-back, but was powerless to prevent the Lions finishing bottom of the top flight.

Playing alongside Mick McCarthy and Alex Rae, Cunningham appeared in exactly half of Millwall's league fixtures in his first full season as they qualified for the Play-Offs. Initially getting games at full-back, in the latter stages he played regularly at centre-back. However, once McCarthy took over as manager, Kenny played most of his 145 games for the club at right-back.

From November 1994 to the summer of 2002, he became part of a Wimbledon team in transition. Under the management of Joe Kinnear, Cunningham's time with the Dons came while they were tenants of Crystal Palace at Selhurst Park. After over 300 games he moved to Birmingham City where he signed for Steve Bruce.

It was at St Andrews where he played his best football being the club's Player of the Year in his first season as they consolidated after promotion. Kenny remained a regular for the club for four years until their relegation when he was notably outspoken in his criticism of the club before joining Sunderland who had gone down with them.

At international level, he played for his old Millwall boss McCarthy, appeared twice at the 2002 FIFA World Cup, captained his country and partnered future Sunderland skipper Gary Breen in central defence.

## CUNNINGTON, Shaun Gary

**POSITION:** Midfielder

**BIRTHPLACE:** Bourne, Lincs

**DATE OF BIRTH:** 04/01/1966

**HEIGHT:** 5' 9" **WEIGHT:** 11st 0lbs

**SIGNED FROM:** Grimsby Town, 17/07/1992

**DEBUT:** v Swindon Town, A, 15/08/1992

**LAST MATCH:** v Middlesbrough, H, 21/03/1995

**MOVED TO:** WBA, 11/08/1995

**TEAMS:** Bourne Town, Wrexham, Grimsby Town, Sunderland, WBA, Notts County, Kidderminster Harriers, Evesham United

**SAFC TOTALS:** 59+6 appearances / 9 goal

**Manager Malcolm Crosby invested most of the money made from the run to the 1992 FA Cup final on midfielder Cunnington. He had a decent first season, scoring the winner in his first home league game against Tranmere and finishing as second top scorer to Don Goodman with eight goals from his 37 appearances. It was a season of struggle in which Sunderland survived relegation to the third division only thanks to results elsewhere on the final day.**

The following season, Shaun again scored in a victorious first home league game, but endured a miserable injury hit season, playing only 13 times. His third and last campaign was even more of a disappointment as he managed just eight games, five of those as a sub. At this point he signed for his old Grimsby manager Alan Buckley at West Bromwich Albion, Sunderland recouping slightly more than a third of the £650,000 they were reported to have paid for the midfielder.

At the Hawthorns, Cunnington was one of 14 ex-Grimsby personnel at the Baggies in 1995-96. Injured on his debut against Charlton on the first day of the season, he ended up making ten appearances in total in his opening year, but missed both games against Sunderland. The next season was no better. Cunnington came on as a sub in Albion's first five games, but made just one further substitute appearance before signing for Sam Allardyce at Notts County in March 1997.

After ending that season with eight appearances for the 'other' Magpies, who finished bottom of the third tier, Cunnington was able to start just three games and make twice that number of appearances off the bench as Notts won their league in his one full season at the club.

Despite Shaun's injury record, his ability meant there were still clubs willing to take a chance on him and in August 1998 he signed for Conference club Kidderminster Harriers before finally playing for Evesham United. After retiring as a player Cunnington moved into the restaurant business (Rossini's in Droitwich) and stayed in football becoming caretaker-manager at Kidderminster Harriers in November 2004. He went on to manager Alvechurch, Willenhall Town, Halesowen Town and Evesham United between 2006 and 2013.

By this time he was 47 and had over three decades in the game having made his first appearance for Bourne Town reserves when he was only 15. His league debut had been made as a 16-year-old for Wrexham against Bristol Rovers a week before Christmas in 1982. Undoubtedly, Shaun's early years were his best. In six years with Wrexham he played more than 250 times including the Welsh Cup finals of 1983 and 1986. After losing to Swansea on the first occasion, he picked up a winner's medal by beating Kidderminster Harriers and went on to play four times in the following season's European Cup Winners' Cup.

In recent years, Shaun has been a Senior Recruitment Consultant, been the proprietor of his own SGC Associated Ltd Recruitment business and from 2009 to date in 2021, the Catering Sales Manager for Booker Wholesale Foods Ltd in Worcestershire.

## CURRAN, Edward (Terry)

**POSITION:** Forward

**BIRTHPLACE:** Kinsley, West Yorkshire

**DATE OF BIRTH:** 20/03/1955

**HEIGHT:** 5' 10" **WEIGHT:** 12st 4lbs

**SIGNED FROM:** Free agent, 10/11/1986

**DEBUT:** v Grimsby Town, A, 15/11/1986

**LAST MATCH:** v Hull City, A, 03/03/1987

**MOVED TO:** Dismissed, 15/04/1987

**TEAMS:** Doncaster Rovers, Nottingham Forest, Bury (L), Derby County, Southampton, Sheffield Wednesday, Atvidaberg (L), Sheffield United, Everton, Huddersfield Town, Panionios, Hull City, Sunderland, Grantham Town, Grimsby Town, Chesterfield, Goole Town

**SAFC TOTALS:** 9 appearances / 1 goal

**The fact that Terry named his 2012 autobiography 'Regrets of a Football Maverick' tells its own tale. At his best, Curran was an exceptionally exciting player I saw regularly when living in Sheffield as Wednesday were promoted from the third division in 1979-80.**

When he came to Sunderland six years later, I hoped for similar, but sadly Terry is remembered at Sunderland for being dismissed the day after flashing a V sign at supporters who barracked him at a reserve match against Manchester City at Roker Park on 14 April 1987.

Curran was not the only departure that week. The day after he was sacked, manager Lawrie McMenemy did his infamous midnight flit. Curran had played for McMenemy at Southampton.

The previous weekend, Sunderland had lost dismally at home to Sheffield United and the reserve game with City was lost 3-2. It was Curran's tenth reserve team game of a season in which one of his two second-team goals came in a home win over Newcastle, but as he was substituted against City, he responded to catcalls from the Main Stand and made his offensive gesture.

In contrast to his time at Sunderland, Terry's time with the blue half of Sheffield made him a cult hero. Nicknamed TC, he was as popular at Hillsborough as that other great TC, Tony Currie had been at Bramall Lane. Curran even recorded a single of the Owls fans anthem 'Singing the Blues', while when he was sent off in a game at Oldham in September 1980 it sparked a riot of Wednesday followers that resulted in FA closing the terraces at Hillsborough for the next four games.

Terry had debuted for Wednesday at Watford in March 1979 just two weeks after playing in the League Cup final for McMenemy's Southampton who lost to Curran's old club Nottingham Forest at Wembley. Curran had dropped two divisions to come to Sheffield where his flair and flamboyance instantly endeared him to the crowd as he teamed up with Ian Porterfield and Chris Turner in Jack Charlton's side. For a while he also played alongside future Sunderland man Rodger Wylde, another fabulously popular flair player at Hillsborough.

In his first full season, Curran scored 24 goals in 45 games as Wednesday won promotion. His hero status was heightened by goals in both derbies with the Blades, one in a 4-0 Boxing Day home game watched by a third division crowd of over 49,000 with the other a screamer to earn a draw at Bramall Lane. Rarely far from the headlines, after falling out with Big Jack, Curran crossed the city to sign for Ian Porterfield at Sheffield United, rubbing salt into his former fans wounds when the fee was settled by tribunal with the Blades getting a steal.

It was not just at Sunderland that red and white didn't really suit him. Although he scored twice in his second home game for United, there was just one more in his 44 games in his one season there. Although the Blades were in the third tier, Curran's quality was always above that and a return to the top flight with Everton followed, initially on loan.

A teammate of Peter Reid and Paul Bracewell at Goodison (but never in the same team as Ian Atkins) he appeared eight times as Everton won the league title in 1984-85. He also appeared four times in their run to lifting the European Cup Winners' Cup.

In an eventful career that also saw him win promotion with Clough's Nottingham Forest, switch from there to their rivals Derby County and have spells in Sweden and Greece, Curran also managed Goole Town and Mossley. He coached numerous South Yorkshire clubs and worked at Rotherham United's Centre of Excellence.

Later the manager of a hotel in West Yorkshire, Curran bought a transport café on the A1, later making his fortune by selling the site to a developer. For many years he was known to always be the first to apply whenever the job as manager of Sheffield Wednesday became vacant. Definitely a football maverick, albeit one whose time at Roker was short-lived.

Whilst a youngster at Doncaster Rovers, he kept being called Terry as this was his elder brother's name; this moniker stuck and so he was known as Terry throughout his career. In July 2022, he became manager of the newly-formed Doncaster City FC for their inaugural season.

## **CURRAN,** Patrick Joseph **(Pat)**

**POSITION:** Inside-right

**BIRTHPLACE:** Sunderland, Co Durham

**DATE OF BIRTH:** 13/11/1917 - 17/12/2003

**HEIGHT:** 5' 8½" **WEIGHT:** 10st 3lbs

**SIGNED FROM:** Sunderland St Joseph's, 25/01/1936 as an amateur. Pro, 07/10/1936

**DEBUT:** v Birmingham, A, 26/02/1938

**LAST MATCH:** v Birmingham, A, 26/02/1938

**MOVED TO:** Ipswich Town, 11/10/1938

**TEAMS:** Sunderland, Ipswich Town, Watford, South Shields (WW2 Guest), Bradford City

**SAFC TOTALS:** 1 appearance / 0 goals

**Pat Curran played once for Sunderland and nine times for Ipswich shortly before World War Two. His son Barry Curran later became Mayor of Sunderland. Born in Sunderland Street in the East End of the town in November 1917, Pat played in a 2-2 draw at Birmingham in February 1938.**

Curran was one of four reserve-team forwards to feature in the five man forward line as players with knocks were evidently kept back for the following week's FA Cup quarter-final at Tottenham - a game that provided the biggest ever attendance at White Hart Lane (75,038) and which Sunderland won.

A reserve for the rest of his time at Roker Park, Pat once featured in a second string side sprinkled with internationals who won 9-1 at Walker Celtic. The son of a father from Sligo who played for Sunderland Royal Rovers, Curran left Sunderland to sign for Ipswich Town in October 1938 for a fee of £750.

Nine months later, Ipswich sold him on to Watford, recouping £300. During the war he played as a 'Guest' for South Shields and after the war he played five times and scored once (against Southport) for Bradford City. There he played alongside his old Sunderland colleague Matt Middleton under the managership of John Milburn, brother of Jackie and uncle to the Charlton brothers.

## **CURTIS,** John **(Jack)**

**POSITION:** Winger

**BIRTHPLACE:** South Bank, North Yorkshire

**DATE OF BIRTH:** 13/12/1888 - 08/03/1955

**HEIGHT:** 5' 6" **WEIGHT:** 11st 0lbs

**SIGNED FROM:** South Bank, 03/12/1906

**DEBUT:** v Wednesday, H, 08/12/1906

**LAST MATCH:** v Wednesday, H, 08/12/1906

**MOVED TO:** South Bank, 01/09/1907

**TEAMS:** Eston United, South Bank St Peter's, Sunderland, South Bank, Shildon, Gainsborough Trinity, Spurs, Fulham, Brentford, Stockport County, Brentford (WW1 Guest), Middlesbrough, Shildon

**INTERNATIONAL:** England trial

**SAFC TOTALS:** 1 appearance / 0 goals

**Jack Curtis got just one game for Sunderland who were his first senior club, but he went on to play 89 times for Spurs, one of which was Spurs' first-ever game in the top flight on 1 September 1909. It came at Roker Park when he missed a great chance in the opening minute. He went on to score in their first-ever top-flight win later that month and opened the scoring and hit the post as Sunderland were thrashed 5-1 on their first league visit to White Hart Lane in March 1910.**

Curtis was doing so well as a regular in the Spurs line-up that the previous January he was selected to play in an England trial match at Anfield. A tricky winger, he was not helped by the international trial match being played on an icy surface, but continued to impress at Spurs, even scoring their first-ever league goal against (Woolwich) Arsenal.

Later in the calendar year, he played in the London FA Charity Cup final against Fulham at Stamford Bridge. Fulham would become his next club. He played alongside former Sunderland forward Tim Coleman in the first two games of 1913-14, but they would be Curtis' only appearances for the club.

He moved on to Brentford, scoring once in 16 games in 1914-15 in the Southern League second division before returning to the Football League with Stockport where he got one goal in 15 second division games in 1914-15, the last season before the Football League stopped because of the great War.

During the war he served as a driver in the Royal Garrison Artillery and Tanks Corps and finished his career with five first division appearances for Middlesbrough in 1919-20. Two of his brothers-in-law played professionally: George Clawley listing Spurs amongst five clubs he appeared for between 1893 and 1914 while Bert Gilboy played for Huddersfield and Preston amongst others between 1911 and 1921.

## **CURRY,** Mitchell

**POSITION:** Centre-forward

**BIRTHPLACE:** Washington, Tyne & Wear

**DATE OF BIRTH:** 14/07/1999

**HEIGHT:** 5' 10" **WEIGHT:** 11st 5lbs

**SIGNED FROM:** Unattached, 16/09/2020

**DEBUT:** v AFC Wimbledon, H, 15/12/2020

**LAST MATCH:** v AFC Wimbledon, H, 15/12/2020

**MOVED TO:** Inter Miami CF, 01/06/2021

**TEAMS:** Middlesbrough, Harrogate Town, Inverness CT (L), Gateshead (L), Sunderland, Miami CF, Fort Lauderdale CF (L)

**SAFC TOTALS:** 0+1 appearances / 0 goals

**Having been released by Middlesbrough on 30 June 2020, Mitchell was a free agent when signing for Sunderland two and a half months later. Three years almost to the day before he joined Sunderland, Curry had played against Accrington Stanley in the Football League Trophy for Boro Under 21s.**

The following month he joined Harrogate Town on loan scoring once in five games for a club where former Sunderland midfielder Paul Thirlwell was assistant manager.

At the start of the next season, Mitchell went on loan to Inverness Caledonian Thistle in the Scottish Championship. Debuting in a League Cup tie at Peterhead in July 2019. He got a first goal in a League Challenge Cup win over Alloa, soon followed by a league goal against Morton. They would be his only goals in 15 appearances (of which six were starts) before returning to Boro after six months and immediately being loaned out to Gateshead, for whom he scored once in four games.

A quick player who likes to run the channels, having signed for Sunderland he made a quick impression with a debut goal for the Under 21s at Burnley. Curry came to the boil in the autumn when six goals in four Under 21 games resulted in him making a first-team debut as a 75th minute substitute just a day after scoring twice against Norwich City in an Under 21 fixture. He did not play for Sunderland again and the following summer joined David Beckham's Inter Miami from where he was loaned to Fort Lauderdale CF.

# D

## DA SILVA BARRIOS, Paulo César

**POSITION:** Defender

**BIRTHPLACE:** Asuncion, Paraguay

**DATE OF BIRTH:** 01/02/1980

**HEIGHT:** 5' 11" **WEIGHT:** 11st 13lbs

**SIGNED FROM:** Toluca, Mexico, 13/07/2009

**DEBUT:** v Norwich City, A, 24/08/2009

**LAST MATCH:** v Notts County, H, 08/01/2011

**MOVED TO:** Real Zaragoza, 31/01/2011

**TEAMS:** Atlantida, Presidente Hayes, Sport Columbia, Cerro Porteno, Perugia, Lanus, Venezia, Cosenza, Libertad, Toluca, Sunderland, Real Zaragoza, Pachuca, Toluca, Libertad, 12 de Octubre

**INTERNATIONAL:** Paraguay

**SAFC TOTALS:** 19+5 appearances / 0 goals

**Capped 150 times by Paraguay who he played for at the 2006 and 2010 FIFA World Cups, Da Silva was a clever defender. Not one to dive into a challenge, he was adept at jockeying forwards and shepherding them into less dangerous areas. This was never better seen than when he marked Lionel Messi who he excelled against more than once at international level and in club football in Spain.**

Paolo first came onto the international scene when he played for his country's Under 17 team in 1994 when he was only 14. Always destined to be a star for Paraguay, who he went on to captain, Paolo played at the FIFA World Youth Championships of 1997 and 1999. At the 2006 World Cup, he only played as a very late sub against a Trinidad & Tobago team that included a quartet of players who played for Sunderland. In 2010 however, he started every game as Paraguay won their group and went on to reach the quarter-finals, claiming the assist for Cristian Riveros to score against Slovakia.

Da Silva played at the top level in Paraguay, Italy, Argentina, Mexico, England and Spain and won the league title in Paraguay in 2002 and 2003 with Libertad, and Mexico in 2005 and 2008 with Toluca, as well as winning the Mexico Super Cup in 2006. Two years later, he was named as the best player in the first division in Mexican football.

At Sunderland, he played 21 times in his first season, but made only three further appearances in his second term. A year after he left Sunderland, I had a chance encounter with Paolo in a hotel in La Paz in Bolivia ahead of a World Cup qualifying game. Leaving his teammates to come and talk to me, he was eager to know about everything that was going on at Sunderland, illustrating that even if you are from Paraguay rather than Pallion once you've been at Sunderland it can never leave you.

## DAJUKU, Leon

**POSITION:** Right-winger

**BIRTHPLACE:** Waiblingen, Germany

**DATE OF BIRTH:** 12/04/2001

**HEIGHT:** 5' 11" **WEIGHT:** 11st 4lbs

**SIGNED FROM:** Union Berlin, 31/07/2021, on loan signed, 25/05/2022

**DEBUT:** v Wigan Athletic, A, 21/09/2021

**LAST MATCH:**

**MOVED TO:**

**TEAMS:** Spvgg Rommelshausenm Stuttgart, Bayern Munich, Union Berlin, Sunderland

**INTERNATIONAL:** Germany Under 19

**SAFC TOTALS:** 19+8 appearances / 4 goals

**A deadline-day acquisition on a season-long loan from Union Berlin who he had just joined from Bayern Munich, Dajuku made his Bundesliga debut as a 17-year-old for Stuttgart at Borussia Mönchengladbach in December 2018 and signed for Bayern Munich the following October after one more appearance.**

He twice came off the bench in the Bundesliga for Bayern in 2019-20 in a season where they won the Champions League and the domestic double. For Dajaku - who arrived at Sunderland on the same day as his former Bayern teammate Thorben Hoffman - on a personal level, success with Bayern was more about winning the third tier of German football in Bayern's II team where he scored seven goals in 43 games.

2020-21 saw Leon spend much of the campaign on loan to Union Berlin who loaned him to SAFC after completing his transfer. Dajaku has three goals to his name in six games for Germany Under 19s having also been capped at Under 17 and 18 level. His transfer to Sunderland was completed in the summer of 2022.

## DALE, Fred Hetherington

**POSITION:** Half-back

**BIRTHPLACE:** Monkwearmouth

**DATE OF BIRTH:** 14/9/1864 - 30/07/1927

**HEIGHT:** 5' 6" **WEIGHT:** 10st 7lbs

**SIGNED FROM:** Monkwearmouth Workmen's Hall, 01/04/1884

**DEBUT:** v Redcar, A, 24/10/1885

**LAST MATCH:** v Middlesbrough, H, 03/12/1887

**MOVED TO:** Retired from playing, 1888

**TEAMS:** Monkwearmouth Workmen's Hall, Sunderland

**SAFC TOTALS:** 6 appearances / 0 goals

**Fred Dale became Sunderland's caretaker-manager, captained the club and his image is well known from the fixture card from 1887-88 pictured on the back cover of Volume One of the Absolute Record. His six appearances listed here cover just FA Cup games. He appeared in SAFC's pre-league days and played most of his football in the days of regular friendlies and challenge matches, his first-ever appearance coming against Wearmouth in April 1885.**

Dale played in Sunderland's second and third FA Cup (then known as the English Cup) ties. These were lost as the first one had been, but then he played in every round as Sunderland beat Morpeth Harriers (after a replay was ordered) and Newcastle West End. Dale then played in a draw with Middlesbrough and in a winning replay, Sunderland were disqualified after Boro won an appeal that Sunderland had fielded three players claimed to be professionals. Born in Dame Dorothy Street in Monkwearmouth, Fred had been captain of Monkwearmouth Workman's Hall Club before captaining Sunderland in 1887-88 and 1888-89.

On 15 October 1904, it was announced that Dale would take temporary charge of Sunderland as manager Alex Mackie was suspended from 4 November 1904 until 31 May 1905. The Lads won seven, drew two and lost six of the 15 games Dale supervised, his highlights including home and away 3-1 wins over Newcastle United.

In between his spells as a Sunderland player and caretaker boss, Fred became a member of the Durham FA, refereed in the Northern Alliance League in 1892-93 and worked as a Foreman Plater and Yardsman at Sunderland shipyard. After finally leaving SAFC, Dale continued to recommend local players to the club after Bob Kyle became manager.

## DALTON, James Joseph

**POSITION:** Defender

**BIRTHPLACE:** Easky, Co Sligo

**DATE OF BIRTH:** 18/10/1885 - 22/02/1941

**HEIGHT:** 5' 11½" **WEIGHT:** 13st 0lbs

**SIGNED FROM:** Canada Tourists, 26/09/1891

**DEBUT:** v Wednesday, A, 02/09/1893

**LAST MATCH:** v Blackburn Rovers, A, 21/10/1893

**MOVED TO:** Nelson, 01/08/1894

**TEAMS:** Clitheroe Olympics, Clitheroe Town, Low Moor, Pawtucket Free Wanderers, Sunderland, Nelson

**INTERNATIONAL:** Canadian Tourists

**SAFC TOTALS:** 3 appearances / 0 goals

**Given that James Dalton listed Rhode Island (USA) side Pawtucket Free Wanderers amongst his clubs in the 1800s is indicative of his well-travelled free spirit, or at least it was until he appeared to end up in jail!**

Born in Ireland, Dalton soon moved to England and began playing football in Lancashire before emigrating to America when in his late teens. He became a naturalized US citizen after working in a paper mill in Fall River Massachusetts and joined Pawtucket after a spell working in Chicago. He was one of nine players from US clubs who joined ten Canadians as part of the Canadian Tourists team who came to the UK in 1891.

Dalton played over 20 times on this tour, scoring his only goal against the Highland Light Infantry in December. Evidently he impressed against Sunderland on the fourth game of the tour in September with locals also having the chance to see him when he played against Sunderland Albion ten weeks later. He also played against England, twice against Wales and also against Scotland who included future Sunderland player Andrew McCreadie, then of Rangers.

At Sunderland, Dalton debuted in the centre-half position he regularly occupied with the Canadian tourists, but operated at right-back in his two subsequent league appearances. After leaving Sunderland he signed for Lancashire League club Nelson, but was released after a month when arrested for being drunk and disorderly. A mechanic by trade, he was listed as a prisoner in Cheetham Prison in Manchester in the 1901 census. He died in Chicago but is buried in Gary, Indiana.

## DANIEL, Peter William

**POSITION:** Midfield

**BIRTHPLACE:** Hull, East Yorkshire

**DATE OF BIRTH:** 12/12/1955

**HEIGHT:** 5' 9" **WEIGHT:** 11st 4lbs

**SIGNED FROM:** Minnesota Kicks, 16/08/1984

**DEBUT:** v Tottenham Hotspur, H, 04/09/1984

**LAST MATCH:** v Hull City, H, 12/10/1985

**MOVED TO:** Lincoln City, 26/11/1985

**TEAMS:** Hull City, Wolves, Minnesota Kicks, Sunderland, Lincoln City, Burnley, North Ferriby United

**INTERNATIONAL:** England U23

**SAFC TOTALS:** 45+1 appearances / 0 goals

**Brought back from American soccer by Len Ashurst, Peter Daniel was a solid midfielder who could win the ball and knew how to use it. He played in all but one of the ten games of the run to the League (Milk) Cup final in his first season, but after playing throughout the campaign, missed much of the run in as the team were relegated. The following season under Lawrie McMenemy his time was short-lived, finishing with a game against his hometown team Hull.**

While Daniel played in a losing League Cup final for Sunderland, he had won the trophy five years earlier, setting up the winning goal for Wolves who beat Brian Clough's Nottingham Forest whose Wembley teamsheet included a quartet of players with SAFC connections: Martin O'Neill, Frank Gray, Ian Bowyer and John O'Hare. Wolves had paid £182,000 (ten times what he later cost Sunderland) to buy Peter from Hull. He made 48 appearances in his opening season at Molineux, becoming Wanderers' penalty taker as they reached the FA Cup semi-final.

Daniel stayed with Wolves until 1984, scoring 16 goals in his 194 appearances during a spell when he endured relegation counter-balanced by instant promotion before his brief spell in the USA. He also played over 100 times for his first club Hull during which time he made his international debut for England Under 21s against Scotland in April 1977 at Bramall Lane, his teammates including Peter Reid, Keith Bertschin and Peter Barnes. Daniel went on to play in six of the next eight Under 21 internationals including an 8-1 win over Finland at his club ground of Boothferry Park

After leaving Sunderland, Peter played for Lincoln, becoming player/manager 16 months later, only to be unable to stop the Imps becoming the first club to suffer automatic relegation from the Football League in 1987 after a calamitous collapse. Resigning from that post, he returned to action as a player with Burnley and had the swan song of another Wembley appearance as a teammate of Leighton James in the Associate Members Cup final, losing to his old club Wolves.

Daniel went on to have an extensive career managing in non-league with North Ferriby United, Pontefract Collieries, Winterton Rangers, Denaby United, Goole, Ossett Town and Brigg Town, having two spells with Pontefract and Winterton, winning promotion, a league title and cup in his first spell with Winterton in the Northern Counties East League.

## DANIEL, William Raymond

**POSITION:** Centre-half

**BIRTHPLACE:** Swansea, Glamorgan

**DATE OF BIRTH:** 02/11/1928 - 06/11/1997

**HEIGHT:** 5' 11½" **WEIGHT:** 12st 5lbs

**SIGNED FROM:** Arsenal, 17/06/1953

**DEBUT:** v Charlton Athletic, A,19/08/1953

**LAST MATCH:** v Leeds United, H, 22/04/1957

**MOVED TO:** Cardiff City, 16/10/1957

**TEAMS:** Swansea Town, Arsenal, Sunderland, Cardiff City, Swansea Town, Hereford United

**INTERNATIONAL:** Wales

**SAFC TOTALS:** 153 appearances / 7 goals

**Ray 'Bebe' Daniel had just won the league title with Arsenal when he left the Gunners to become one of the 'Bank of England Club's' big signings. Unfortunately, he was one of those players drawn to the club during the days of the maximum wage, helped by the inducement of illegal payments.**

When Sunderland were punished for this in April 1957, Daniel was one of the people suspended 'Sine Die' (meaning suspended with no end to the suspension). This ban was actually lifted within a month when a court ruled the Football League had no right to issue such a suspension. Instead, Daniel and 13 other players were fined 22 days wages and had two years of benefit qualifications withdrawn, although this was refunded in 1962 when that punishment was ruled illegal.

1957 was not a good year for the Wales international who lost his international place and with it the opportunity to play at the 1958 FIFA World Cup. Daniel's debut at international level had taken place at Roker Park in 1950 against England while he was with Arsenal. Nine of his 21 caps would be won while with Sunderland, the first against England at Cardiff in 1953 and the last in 1957 against Czechoslovakia in Prague.

People often think of Charlie Hurley as the first ball-playing centre-half at Sunderland, but Ray Daniel was also very composed and confident in possession. He had a deft touch and while stories of Len Shackleton's party-piece of flicking a coin from one foot to the other and then flicking it into his breast pocket are legendary, Daniel used to do the same - but would sometimes juggle it there via his thigh and shoulder!

After working his way to Highbury via Swansea Schools, Plasmarl Youth Club and Swansea Town, where he played as an amateur, Ray joined Arsenal after the war. It was a war in which his brother Bobby, who was also an Arsenal player, was killed in a 1943 RAF sortie. At Arsenal, Ray first played in a junior friendly against Cheltenham as a 17-year-old amateur on 14 September 1946. After completing his National Service between 1947 and 1949, a full debut followed on the final day of the 1948-49 season against Charlton who he would also make his Sunderland debut against four years later.

Including reserve games and friendlies, Daniel played a total of 239 times in Arsenal's colours, exactly 100 of these being competitive first-team outings. An FA Cup finalist against Newcastle in 1952, when he played the full game with a broken arm in a plaster-cast, Ray missed only one match as the Gunners took the title in 1953, but shortly after playing against Rapid Vienna in Bruges on a celebratory end of season tour, a record fee for a defender of £27,500 brought him to Wearside, where he linked up with his friend and international colleague Trevor Ford.

On just his seventh appearance for Sunderland, Ray was part of the side that decimated his old team 7-1. He became a class act at the heart of the Roker defence for four seasons, playing in the FA Cup semi-finals of 1955 and 56 and captaining the side. His winner in the fifth-round replay against Sheffield United in 1956 was a rare goal until he started taking penalties the following season, one of his spot-kicks coming in an 8-1 win over Charlton.

After leaving the north east, Daniel returned to South Wales, initially with Cardiff, but after just six league appearances was soon back to his home town of Swansea. He then became player-manager of non-league Hereford United in the summer of 1960, spending seven years with the club for whom, as a veteran, he managed 317 appearances. At Sunderland, Ray had occasionally been used as a centre-forward and he often chose to play there when picking the team, scoring 66 goals for Hereford in the process.

Upon his retirement from the game, Daniel became a publican in Swansea. Subsequently, he became regional manager for Courvoisier brandy and later a sub-postmaster in Cockett in the Swansea suburbs. His Sunderland-born daughter Karen became a journalist with the Daily Mirror.

## DAVENPORT, Calum Raymond Paul

**POSITION:** Centre-back

**BIRTHPLACE:** Bedford

**DATE OF BIRTH:** 01/01/1983

**HEIGHT:** 6' 4" **WEIGHT:** 14st 1lb

**SIGNED FROM:** West Ham United, 02/02/2009, on loan

**DEBUT:** v Manchester City, A, 22/03/2009

**LAST MATCH:** v Chelsea, H, 24/05/2009

**MOVED TO:** West Ham United, 25/05/2009, end of loan

**TEAMS:** Coventry City, Spurs, West Ham United (L), Southampton (L), Norwich City (L), West Ham United, Watford (L), Sunderland (L), Wootton Blue Cross, Elstow Abbey

**INTERNATIONAL:** England Under 21

**SAFC TOTALS:** 7+1 appearances / 0 goals

**Calum Davenport was an athletic, long-striding centre-back who came to Sunderland on loan under the management of Ricky Sbragia as relegation was fought. His most notable contribution came in his penultimate match at Portsmouth when his buccaneering run and right-wing cross led to a goal for Kenwyne Jones.**

Davenport had been an unused sub for five consecutive games before he got an opportunity as sub only to have to miss the next fixture as it was against his parent club West Ham. Subsequently, he started the final seven games of the season. Only one was won, but nonetheless, Sunderland escaped the drop.

Davenport returned to West Ham that summer only for his career to be turned upside down when he was involved in a stabbing incident which led to his contract at West Ham being ended the following March without him having played since his return from Wearside. Trial periods at Nottingham Forest and Simon Grayson's Leeds followed, but when nothing materialised, the player re-surfaced in the United Counties League with Wootton Blue Cross.

## DAVENPORT, Calum (Continued)

The stabbing incident occurred at the home Calum shared with his mother in Bedfordshire. He reportedly received emergency surgery after being stabbed in the legs. The assailants included the boyfriend of Davenport's sister with the attacker duly jailed for the incident. The complicated case saw Davenport also charged with assault on his sister in October 2009. He was cleared of those charges the following summer. In March 2015 he was also apparently arrested following an alleged assault in the dressing rooms after playing for Elstow Abbey against Cranfield United.

It was all a far cry from the early part of a promising career that after apparently being expelled from school saw Davenport go on to win eight Under 21 caps for England having already gained representative honours at Under 19 and 20 level. He had debuted alongside Anton Ferdinand, Justin Hoyte, Jon Stead, Darren Bent and Stewart Downing for England Under 21s in a 2-0 win over Austria in September 2004 and went on to add Matt Kilgallon, Kieran Richardson and Lee Camp to the Sunderland connections he had at international level.

Davenport's league debut came for Coventry in their last Premiership match before relegation in 2001. He became the Sky Blues Young Player of the Year in 2002-03 and Player of the Year in 2003-04 preceding a £1.3m move to Spurs that summer. Although he only played 20 times for Tottenham, who loaned him out three times, it cost the first of those loan clubs - West Ham - £3m to buy him in January 2007. A year later he was loaned to Watford only for that spell to be ruined by a serious neck injury. His next, and effectively, last stop in senior football then came at Sunderland.

As he recovered from the horrific fall from Premier League player to assaults and arrests, Davenport turned to religion, attending St Matthias Church in Plymouth and duly becoming baptised. In 2019, he was coaching eight to ten year olds at the Sir John Hunt Community Sports College in Whitleigh near Plymouth.

## DAVENPORT, Peter

**POSITION:** Forward
**BIRTHPLACE:** Birkenhead, Cheshire
**DATE OF BIRTH:** 24/03/1961
**HEIGHT:** 5' 11" **WEIGHT:** 11st 3lbs
**SIGNED FROM:** Middlesbrough, 17/07/1990
**DEBUT:** v Norwich City, A, 25/08/1990
**LAST MATCH:** v Notts County, A, 08/05/1993
**MOVED TO:** Released on free transfer, 13/05/1993
**TEAMS:** Everton, Cammell Laird, Nottingham Forest, Manchester United, Middlesbrough, Sunderland, Airdrieonians, Stockport County, Southport, Macclesfield Town, St Helens Town (L). Congleton Town, Bangor City
**INTERNATIONAL:** England
**SAFC TOTALS:** 89+31 appearances / 18 goals

**Peter Davenport was a classy forward, an England international who Manchester United once splashed out a big fee of £570,000 for in 1986. He came to Wearside from Teesside for £300,000 in the summer of 1990, manager Denis Smith's idea being that Davenport's guile would slot in as a direct replacement for the ageing and released Eric Gates as a foil for Marco Gabbiadini.**

It was a fair assessment by the gaffer, but 'Dav' was never able to produce the same sort of almost telepathic understanding with his partner that was seen in the 'G-Force,' even though both found the scoresheet on Peter's debut.

Sunderland were relegated in his first season, Davenport scoring seven times having played in almost exactly two-thirds of the fixtures. It was to be Peter's best goals return in his three seasons at the club, Gabbiadini having been sold early in his second. That second season saw Marco's replacement Don Goodman partnered with John Byrne as the first choice front two, but Goodman was cup-tied as Malcolm Crosby's Sunderland reached the FA Cup final. This allowed Davenport to regularly partner Byrne, contributing to the cup run with a couple of goals including one in the dramatic quarter-final replay with Chelsea at Roker. Although sometimes used out wide, Peter largely stayed in the league side. He found goals hard to come by, but did score at Roker against both Newcastle and his old club Boro. It was a similar story in his last campaign with just four league goals including a penalty in 34 league games, 14 of which were as sub, and so it came as no surprise when he was released.

Three months later, he moved into Scottish football and later returned to his native north-west of England to study sports science at Manchester University. Spells as assistant and caretaker manager of Southport preceded managerial appointments with Macclesfield Town, Bangor City, Colwyn Bay and back at Southport. From May to August 2010 he was assistant manager at Bradford Park Avenue.

It had been Brian Clough who had spotted Peter's potential. Cloughie took the former Everton amateur to Forest from Birkenhead club Cammell Laird in exchange for a set of kits. Davenport scored 54 goals in 118 league games for Clough, including a hat-trick against Sunderland on David Corner's debut in 1984. He had also claimed the match-ball at Ipswich on only his fifth league appearance, on a day when his teammates included Frank Gray, Ian Bowyer and Mark Proctor - Ian Wallace also being a teammate at Forest.

Two months after his hat-trick against Sunderland, he made his debut for England B against New Zealand. Later the same season, he came off the bench for the last 17 minutes of a 2-1 win for England over the Republic of Ireland at Wembley. Playing against John Byrne and Mick McCarthy and alongside Terry Butcher and Chris Waddle, it was to be Davenport's solitary full cap although he was selected for a summer tour to Mexico and the USA only to have to withdraw through injury.

At Manchester United he scored 26 times in 106 games, all of which came in domestic competitions. Moving from Manchester to Middlesbrough in November 1988 for £700,000 he scored just seven times in 59 league games (the first a winner against Manchester United) before moving up the A19. Despite playing for Brian Clough and (Sir) Alex Ferguson, Davenport's only cup final appearance came under Malcolm Crosby at Sunderland where his teammates nicknamed tee-totaller Davenport 'Ceefax' as he always was in possession of the latest football information.

## DAVIS, Herbert (Bert)

**POSITION:** Right-winger
**BIRTHPLACE:** Bradford, Yorkshire
**DATE OF BIRTH:** 11/08/1906 - 17/07/1981
**HEIGHT:** 5' 4" **WEIGHT:** 10st 0lbs
**SIGNED FROM:** Bradford Park Avenue, 25/04/1932
**DEBUT:** v Manchester City, H, 27/08/1932
**LAST MATCH:** v Derby County, A, 09/09/1936
**MOVED TO:** Leicester City, 11/12/1936
**TEAMS:** Guiseley, Bradford PA, Sunderland, Leicester City, Crystal Palace, Bradford PA, Huddersfield Town (WW2 Guest), York City (WW2 Guest)
**SAFC TOTALS:** 162 appearances / 40 goals

**Along with John Harvie and Reuben Smith, Bert Davis is the joint smallest player to play for Sunderland - although Milton Nunez may have been smaller although officially recorded as being an inch taller than Bert's 5 '4". Davis might have been little, but he was fierce, being sent off twice at a time when Sunderland had previously only suffered 15 dismissals in 45 years of league football.**

An outside-right who came to prominence after leaving his job as a Mill Hand to help hometown club Bradford Park Avenue score over 100 goals in romping away with the Division Three North title in 1927/28, Bert came to Sunderland four years later after totalling 46 goals in 172 league games for Avenue.

An ever-present in his second and third seasons at Roker Park, Bert played 25 times as the league title was won in his third campaign of 1935-36 when for the third season in a row, he reached double-figures in goals from the wing. At Leicester he played only nine times in 1936-37 as he compensated for missing out on Sunderland's FA Cup triumph that season by helping the Foxes to promotion before moving on to Crystal Palace where he played 29 times, scoring five goals. After the war Bert scouted for Bradford City.

## DAVIS, Kelvin Geoffrey

**POSITION:** Goalkeeper

**BIRTHPLACE:** Bedford

**DATE OF BIRTH:** 29/09/1976

**HEIGHT:** 6' 1" **WEIGHT:** 11st 4lbs

**SIGNED FROM:** Ipswich Town, 14/06/2005

**DEBUT:** v Charlton Athletic, H, 13/08/2005

**LAST MATCH:** v Aston Villa, A, 07/05/2006

**MOVED TO:** Southampton, 21/07/2006

**TEAMS:** Luton Town, Torquay Utd (L), Hartlepool United (L), Wimbledon, Ipswich Town, Sunderland , Southampton

**INTERNATIONAL:** England Under 21

**SAFC TOTALS:** 35 appearances / 0 goals

**Eleven minutes into his debut Kelvin Davis came out and clearly got his angles all wrong as he gave Charlton's Darren Bent far too much of the goal to aim at. For the most part he did not get any better, being responsible for a collection of calamities, not least when he apparently failed to see another future Sunderland forward in Michael Chopra when he scored a few seconds after coming off the Newcastle bench to turn a derby Sunderland had worked hard to lead in.**

And yet Kelvin commands respect for two main reasons. Firstly, he had the occasional blinder, such as keeping a clean sheet at title-chasing Manchester United on the night Sunderland's relegation was mathematically confirmed in 2006. Secondly, when he was taken out of the first team, the easiest thing in the world for Kelvin would have been to quietly sit on the bench and pick up his money, but he was determined to earn it by quickly getting his place back, facing the music and never doing anything less than his best.

In more recent years Sunderland supporters have seen some players who lacked Kelvin's character in that respect and he deserves to be recognised for it. In addition to character, Davis' strength was his agility. He could make stunning spectacular saves, never better seen than in a pre-season friendly at AZ in the Netherlands ahead of his league debut for Sunderland.

After leaving the Stadium of Light he gave great service to Southampton. Having joined them in 2006, he was still there in 2021 as assistant manager. In a decade as a player he made 271 league appearances and captained the team for three years. He had a testimonial with the Saints in 2016. Prior to coming to Sunderland, he had spent eight years with Luton where he came through the youth system, had loans with Torquay and Hartlepool and had four years with Wimbledon and two with Ipswich.

He won Player of the Year awards with Ipswich and Southampton and was included in the PFA Divisional Team of the Year twice in the Championship and twice in League One. At international level, one of his three Under 21 caps came at Roker Park in a 1996 meeting with Croatia. Thirty three of his career total of 53 Premier League appearances in an overall total of 687 games were made with Sunderland.

## DAVIS, Richard Daniel (Dicky)

**POSITION:** Centre-forward

**BIRTHPLACE:** Birmingham, Warwickshire

**DATE OF BIRTH:** 22/01/1922 - 11/08/1999

**HEIGHT:** 5' 9½" **WEIGHT:** 13st 0lbs

**SIGNED FROM:** Morris Jacobs, 24/02/1939

**DEBUT:** v Leeds United, A, 07/12/1946

**LAST MATCH:** v Middlesbrough, H, 28/11/1953

**MOVED TO:** Darlington, 25/05/1954

**TEAMS:** Aston, Morris Jacobs, Sunderland, Aldershot (WW2 Guest), Aston Villa (WW2 Guest) Brentford (WW2 Guest), Darlington

**INTERNATIONAL:** England schoolboys

**SAFC TOTALS:** 154 appearances / 80 goals

**Dicky Davis was top scorer in the top-flight with 25 league goals in 34 league games in 1959-50 when Sunderland came close to winning the league, but that was not enough to keep him in the team as the 'Bank of England Club' splashed out a record fee to sign Trevor Ford as centre-forward the following October.**

Having played alongside Len Shackleton for England schoolboys, Davis signed for Sunderland from Birmingham youth outfit Morris Jacobs before World War Two, but had to wait until after the war for his debut. After an almost eight-year wait for his Sunderland debut, Dicky did play in eight different seasons for the Lads before moving to Darlington where he added 32 more goals in 93 league games.

He later returned to Roker Park as manager of the Black Cat Club in the late sixties having gone into the drinks trade after his retirement from football. He retired from working life in 1983 having latterly been a salesman for Allied Breweries.

## DAVISON, Arnold (Arnie)

**POSITION:** Forward

**BIRTHPLACE:** Monkwearmouth, Co Durham

**DATE OF BIRTH:** 17/02/1864 - 31/08/1910

**HEIGHT:** 5' 8" **WEIGHT:** 10st 2lbs

**SIGNED FROM:** Monkwearmouth Workmen's Hall, 01/04/1884

**DEBUT:** v Newcastle West End, A, 13/11/1886

**LAST MATCH:** v Newcastle East End, H, 17/11/1888

**MOVED TO:** Retired from playing, 1890

**TEAMS:** Monkwearmouth Workmen's Hall, Sunderland

**SAFC TOTALS:** 7 appearances / 2 goals

**Arnie Davison was the first player to score for Sunderland in red and white stripes, doing so on the first day such a strip was worn on 24 September 1887 against Darlington St Augustine's. Having been educated at Gainford School, Davison joined Sunderland as a 20-year-old from Monkwearmouth Workmen's Hall Club.**

Before turning to soccer, Arnie had been an aspiring rugby player with Humbledon while working as a shipbuilder's clerk. His seven appearances in official records all came in English (FA) Cup ties, but he played many more times in the age of regular friendlies and challenge matches before he became one of the local players to be sidelined as the increasingly affluent club turned to higher quality Scottish players.

Davison was certainly not affluent. He suffered from a spinal disease, became wheelchair bound and lived in Sunderland workhouse from 1899 to his death in 1910 at the age of just 46.

## DAVISON, James Hawkins (Jimmy)

**POSITION:** Winger

**BIRTHPLACE:** Hendon, Sunderland

**DATE OF BIRTH:** 01/11/1942 - 01/02/1987

**HEIGHT:** 5' 11" **WEIGHT:** 11st 7lbs

**SIGNED FROM:** Sunderland schools, 01/07/1958

**DEBUT:** v Scunthorpe United, A, 21/11/1959

**LAST MATCH:** v Chelsea, H, 18/05/1963

**MOVED TO:** Bolton Wanderers, 02/11/1963

**TEAMS:** Sunderland, Bolton Wanderers, Queen of the South, South Shields

**SAFC TOTALS:** 72 appearances / 11 goals

**Jimmy Davison was even younger than Arnie Davison when he passed away due to a heart attack when he was still living in his birthplace of Cairo Street in Hendon. He had come into the side in the month of his 17th birthday, at the time becoming SAFC's second ever-youngest player.**

He did well enough to keep his place for the next three games and ended that first season with nine appearances. He stayed on the fringe of the first team for the next two seasons and had his best, but last, campaign in 1962-63 when he started 41 games in all competitions and scored all but one of his ten goals for the club.

Two of those goals came in a 6-2 win over Grimsby two days after his 20th birthday. In the same game, Brian Clough netted a hat-trick, but the injury that effectively ended Clough's career came the following month. But for that, Davison would almost certainly have been revered as a promotion winner at Sunderland. Instead, he beat his teammates into the top flight with a transfer to Bolton, debuting against Liverpool in November 1963. However, as Sunderland were promoted at the end of that season, Bolton went down, Davison having played in exactly half of their league games before moving on to Queen of the South.

## DAYKIN, Thomas (Tom)

**POSITION:** Half-back

**BIRTHPLACE:** Shildon, Co Durham

**DATE OF BIRTH:** 30/07/1882 - 20/07/1960

**HEIGHT:** 5' 8" **WEIGHT:** 11st 7lbs

**SIGNED FROM:** Shildon Athletic, 23/03/1905

**DEBUT:** v Manchester City, A, 01/04/1905

**LAST MATCH:** v Newcastle United, A. 05/12/1908

**MOVED TO:** Birmingham, 11/12/1908

**TEAMS:** Eldon Albion, Bishop Auckland, Eldon Albion, Hobson Wanderers, Shildon Athletic, Sunderland, Birmingham, Spennymoor, South Shields

**SAFC TOTALS:** 48 appearances / 0 goals

**Talk about going out with a bang - Daykin's last game for Sunderland was in the legendary 9-1 win at Newcastle! A versatile player at Roker, he moved on to Birmingham a week after that victory and almost doubled his Sunderland games total with the Blues. A fortnight after playing in the north-east derby Daykin debuted for Birmingham in a home second division defeat to Glossop.**

Having never scored for Sunderland he got the first goal of his career against Spurs the following March. It would be his only goal for the club for whom he made his final appearance against Barnsley in January 1912 before he returned to the north east.

Daykin initially came to Sunderland's attention by playing against Sunderland 'A' for Eldon Albion in the final of the Durham Senior Cup in 1903. Although he lost that game, he gained a winner's medal with Sunderland three years later against Hebburn Argyle.

## DE BOCK, Laurence Henry Cristine (Laurens)

**POSITION:** Left-back

**BIRTHPLACE:** Dendermonde, Belgium

**DATE OF BIRTH:** 07/11/1992

**HEIGHT:** 5' 10" **WEIGHT:** 11st 11lbs

**SIGNED FROM:** Leeds United, 02/09/2019, on loan

**DEBUT:** v Sheffield United, A, 25/09/2019

**LAST MATCH:** v Bolton Wanderers, H, 26/12/2019

**MOVED TO:** Leeds United, 31/12/2019, end of loan

**TEAMS:** HO Kalken, Standaard Weteren, Lokeren, Club Brugge, Leeds United, Oostende (L), Sunderland (L), ADO Den Haag (L), Zulte Waregem (to 2022)

**INTERNATIONAL:** Belgium Under 21

**SAFC TOTALS:** 8+2 appearances / 0 goals

**Laurens De Bock signally failed to impress during a loan period in what proved to be the season where Sunderland finished in their lowest-ever league position. Seemingly lacking in confidence, De Bock appeared hesitant and yet evidently was a player of some quality. At international level, he represented Belgium 55 times at various levels from Under 16 to Under 21 and during the 2014-15 season was twice called up to the senior squad, although as of 2022 was yet to make a full debut.**

He twice won the Belgian Cup, playing in the 2012 final for Lokeren as they defeated Kortrijk, and three years later helping Club Brugge to beat Anderlecht. A year later, he played as Brugge beat Standard Liege to lift the Belgian Supercup in a season when his club also won the Belgian league title.

Such success at club and international level did not go unnoticed and in January 2018 he was signed by Leeds who failed to win any of the seven Championship games he played in his first season, conceding four goals in each of his first two home games. Leeds shipped him out on a series of loans, with the last of those at Zulte Waregem becoming a permanent transfer in 2022.

## DEANE, Brian Christopher

**POSITION:** Centre-forward

**BIRTHPLACE:** Leeds, West Yorkshire

**DATE OF BIRTH:** 07/02/1968

**HEIGHT:** 6' 3" **WEIGHT:** 14st 2lbs

**SIGNED FROM:** Leeds United, 24/03/2005

**DEBUT:** v Reading, H, 09/04/2005

**LAST MATCH:** v West Ham United, A, 29/04/2005

**MOVED TO:** Released, 10/05/2005

**TEAMS:** Doncaster Rovers, Sheffield United, Leeds United, Sheffield United, Benfica, Middlesbrough, Leicester City, West Ham United, Leeds United, Sunderland, Perth Glory, Sheffield United

**INTERNATIONAL:** England

**SAFC TOTALS:** 0+4 appearances / 0 goals

**Famously the scorer of the first-ever Premier League goal for Sheffield United v Manchester United on 5 August 1992, Brian Deane became Sunderland's oldest debutant at the age of 37 and 58 days. He was also the scorer of the first competitive goal at Leicester City's new ground in 2002. He won three England caps in 1991 and 1992 under Graham Taylor and also played in three 'B' internationals.**

Although he never scored for Sunderland while with the club, he did score for Sunderland at Roker in September 1989, putting through his own goal when playing for Sheffield United.

Brian began his extensive career with Doncaster, joining Rovers in December 1985, moving to Sheffield United two and a half years later after scoring 13 times in 65+10 appearances in all competitions. It was to be the first of three spells with the Blades where he would end his playing career with a total of 121 goals in 269+3 games for the club. He first left Bramall Lane in the summer of 1993, costing his hometown team Leeds £2.9m at the end of the Premiership's first season.

Replacing Lee Chapman, his eleven goals helped Leeds to fifth place in his first season. Following four years at Elland Road he returned to Sheffield United for £1.5m after a total of 45 goals in 179+22 games. This time the move back to South Yorkshire was short-lived as six months later a fee of £1m took Deane to Graeme Souness' Benfica. By now, Brian was much sought after and regularly on the move. After just 17 games and seven goals in Portugal, Middlesbrough invested £3m. There were 19 goals in 79+16 outings for the Teessiders before a switch to Leicester where he was signed by his former Sheffield United manager Dave Bassett.

At the start of his first full season with the Foxes, Deane netted both goals in the opening game at what was then called the Walkers Stadium. He had just under two years at Leicester, scoring 19 times in 48+8 games before a move to West Ham where 20 of his 32 games were as a sub as he netted seven goals.

At the age of 35 he returned to Leeds for a second spell in 2004, scoring seven times in 24+9 games before coming to Sunderland who became the only club he failed to score for. Although Brian only made four substitute appearances, he did so in helping Mick McCarthy's team get over the line as promotion was won, the last two of his games being against old clubs Leicester and West Ham as first promotion and then the Coca-Cola Championship were won.

As Sunderland went up, Deane went Down Under with Perth Glory where he scored once in seven games before a final brief spell back at Sheffield United. The last game of a lengthy career came at Bramall Lane in April 2006 by which time he was 38.

Six years later Brian resurfaced as manager of Norwegian side Sarpsborg 08 FF. He later coached at Leeds and in 2019 became 50% owner of Kosovo Superleague club Ferizaj.

## DEATH, William George (Billy)

**POSITION:** Winger

**BIRTHPLACE:** Rotherham, West Riding, Yorkshire

**DATE OF BIRTH:** 13/11/1900- 03/07/1984

**HEIGHT:** 5' 9½" **WEIGHT:** 11st 7lbs

**SIGNED FROM:** Mansfield Town, 24/03/1924

**DEBUT:** v Burnley, A, 29/09/1924

**LAST MATCH:** v Middlesbrough A 05/05/1928

**MOVED TO:** Exeter City, 14/09/1928

**TEAMS:** Broome Athletic, Rotherham Town, Notts County, Mansfield Town, Sunderland, Exeter City, Gillingham, Mansfield Town, Grantham, Sutton Town, City Transport FC (Nottingham)

**SAFC TOTALS:** 56 appearances / 14 goals

**Billy Death's only first-team goal in the last of his four seasons at Sunderland in 1927-28 came on his final appearance and helped to condemn Middlesbrough to relegation while helping Sunderland to stay up. He also scored in two derbies with Newcastle.**

The previous January he had scored seven times in an 11-0 reserve-team win over Walker Celtic, including a four-minute hat-trick. It must have been some half-time team talk as the game was goalless at the break.

In his first two seasons at Roker, Billy played in just under half the games, but that reduced to under a quarter of the fixtures in each of his latter two seasons meaning it was no surprise that he moved on, particularly as a change of manager accompanied the end of his last campaign.

After retiring from the professional game, he became a bus driver but did not hang up his boots as he regularly turned out for Nottingham City Transport FC.

## DEFOE, Jermain Colin

**POSITION:** Striker

**BIRTHPLACE:** Beckton, London

**DATE OF BIRTH:** 07/10/1982

**HEIGHT:** 5' 7" **WEIGHT:** 10st 4lbs

**SIGNED FROM:** Toronto, 16/01/2015 and as a free agent, 31/01/2022

**DEBUT:** v Spurs, A, 17/01/2015

**LAST MATCH:** v Lincoln City A 19/03/2022

**MOVED TO:** AFC Bournemouth, 01/07/2017 Retired, 24/03/2022

**TEAMS:** Senrab FC, Charlton Athletic, West Ham United, AFC Bournemouth (L), Spurs, Portsmouth, Toronto, Sunderland (L), AFC Bournemouth, Rangers, Sunderland

**INTERNATIONAL:** England

**SAFC TOTALS:** 88+12 appearances / 37 goals

**Jermain Defoe was a class act, a clinical goalscorer who developed a wonderful relationship with young supporter Bradley Lowery and scored a goal fit to win any game let alone a crucial derby.**

At the time of his 300th career goal, Jermain picked the screamer that won a derby at the Stadium of Light in April 2015 as the best of his career. Defoe always says he just smashed Steven Fletcher's knock-down as he was too tired to do anything else, but any tiredness was made light of as he sprinted away in tears of joy.

Sometimes scorers of great goals are not great goalscorers, but Defoe definitely was. Playing in a struggling team, he scored 15 Premier League goals in back-to-back seasons - adding a League Cup hat-trick for good measure. Neither was he just a fox in the box. He worked for the team, looking to link-up play when he could and when necessary - such as on the night a goalless draw at Arsenal secured safety from relegation - could be found even covering full-backs such was his commitment to the cause.

Defoe did not stay at the top of his game for so long by chance. He was a model professional who looked after mind and body, even turning vegan to prolong his career. When he left English football to play for Rangers, Jermain was eighth on the all-time list of Premier League scorers. The fact he was just one behind Robbie Fowler might have tempted him to stay in England. Like Peter Davenport, Defoe had an encyclopaedic knowledge of his goals and kept a list of Premier League scorers and their totals on a note on his bathroom mirror to study whenever he shaved or cleaned his teeth. This was to use it as a motivation to know how many goals he needed to rise up the list.

Another list he entered was to join the select list of players to score for England while on Sunderland's books, becoming just the third man (after Len Shackleton and Darren Bent) to do so since World War Two. Defoe scored in a FIFA World Cup qualifier against Lithuania in March 2017.

In that Wembley international he was accompanied by Sunderland fan Bradley Lowery who suffered from terminal childhood cancer and who had formed a deep bond with Defoe who took him to his heart. Jermain won 57 full caps becoming the oldest player to score 20 times for England, being 34 years and 170 days old when he netted on the first of his two appearances as a Sunderland player

Player of the Year at Sunderland in 2015-16, he had cost West Ham over £1m to buy him from Charlton in 1999. Loaned to AFC Bournemouth the following year, he shot to prominence by scoring in a record ten successive league games. After returning to West Ham, he subsequently moved to Spurs for an initial £6m in 2004. Four years later, Tottenham shelled out £15m to buy him back from Portsmouth. In February 2014, he moved to Canada with Toronto, but the following January came to Sunderland in perhaps the best exchange deal SAFC ever negotiated with Jozy Altidore going in the opposite direction.

Rather like Niall Quinn Defoe enjoyed some of his best years late in his career on Wearside before returning to AFC Bournemouth on a lucrative contract when Sunderland were relegated in 2017. After 18 months with the Cherries. Defoe signed an 18-month loan-deal with Rangers, winning his first league title with the Gers in 2021.

In November 2021 following the departure of manager Steven Gerrard to Aston Villa, Defoe took temporary charge at Ibrox along with fellow coaches Brian Gilmour, David McCallum and Colin Stewart. On the evening of transfer deadline in January 2022 he returned to Sunderland where he became the club's oldest player but retired after less than two months without scoring in his second spell.

In 2018 he received the OBE. for services to his own Foundation which he had set up five years earlier. Jermain Defoe: The biography was published in 2010, when his career still had over a decade to run.

## DELAP, Rory John

**POSITION:** Midfield

**BIRTHPLACE:** Sutton Coldfield, West Midlands

**DATE OF BIRTH:** 06/07/1976

**HEIGHT:** 6' 3" **WEIGHT:** 13st 0lbs

**SIGNED FROM:** Southampton, 31/01/2006

**DEBUT:** v Birmingham City, A, 25/02/2006

**LAST MATCH:** v Derby County, A, 09/09/2006

**MOVED TO:** Stoke City, 09/01/2007, after loan spell from 11/10/2006

**TEAMS:** Carlisle United, Derby County, Southampton, Sunderland, Stoke City, Barnsley (L), Burton Albion

**INTERNATIONAL:** Republic of Ireland

**SAFC TOTALS:** 12+1 appearances / 1 goal

**Schoolboy javelin champion Rory Delap's prowess with a devastating long-throw is something that was never revealed in his time at Sunderland. Only after he moved to Stoke after playing in Roy Keane's first match as manager did the Republic of Ireland international become renowned for his low trajectory long throws which became synonymous with Stoke under the management of Tony Pulis.**

Having initially been loaned to the Potters by SAFC. he was allowed to make his home debut against Sunderland only to suffer a broken leg. Thankfully, Rory recovered and went on to play over 200 games for Stoke including the 2011 FA Cup final as one of six Stoke players who also played for Sunderland, losing 1-0 to Manchester City who had three SAFC connections (Thomas Sorensen, Marc Wilson, Kenwyne Jones, Dean Whitehead and unused sub Danny Collins as well as Delap for Stoke and Joleon Lescott, Adam Johnson and unused sub Shay Given for City.) Delap's son Liam made a Premier League debut for Manchester City in September 2020.

Rory began his career in Carlisle, winning promotion in 1995 and the Football League Trophy two years later, playing in the Wembley final against Colchester United. He went on to have four Premier League seasons with Derby, being the Rams top scorer with eight goals in 1999-00.

## DELAP, Rory

(Continued)

In 2001 Southampton paid a club record £4m for Delap who turned out over 150 times for the Saints, being a regular in the first four of his five seasons until Southampton were relegated. Injury cost him a place in the 2003 FA Cup final.

After retiring from playing, Rory coached at Derby and Stoke, having a brief spell as caretaker-manager at Stoke. For the Republic of Ireland, Delap won eleven caps, eight of those as a substitute.

## DEMPSTER, James Barclay (Jimmy)

**POSITION:** Goalkeeper
**BIRTHPLACE:** Newarthill, Lanarkshire
**DATE OF BIRTH:** 30/01/1896 - 20/03/1957
**HEIGHT:** 5' 9" **WEIGHT:** 11st 7lbs
**SIGNED FROM:** Newarthill Thistle, 03/03/1920
**DEBUT:** v Blackburn Rovers, H, 05/04/1920
**LAST MATCH:** v Liverpool, A, 11/01/1922
**MOVED TO:** Airdrieonians, 02/06/1922
**TEAMS:** Newarthill Thistle, Sunderland, Airdrieonians, St Johnstone, Dundee United, Bo'Ness, Bathgate, Bo'Ness, Obuasi
**SAFC TOTALS:** 43 appearances / 0 goals

**Sometimes keepers score last-minute equalisers when desperately sent forward for a corner, but few if any, score winners as Jimmy Dempster once did - and in a cup final!**

However, the former Sunderland keeper was playing at outside-left in Ghana for Obuasi against Kumasi in the Tennant Cup final on 10 August 1935. Dempster had just arrived in West Africa as a shaft master for a gold mining company, a position he stayed in until 1946. He later continued in mining - but for coal after returning to Scotland. During World War One he had served in the Highland Light Infantry and the Machine Gun Corps.

At Sunderland, Dempster started with three clean sheets in the final five fixtures of 1919-20. He did even better in his first full season, playing in the last 26 games (keeping nine clean sheets), but in his third and last campaign of 1921-22, he played only a dozen games suffering an ignominious end when conceding five on his final appearance in a cup replay at Liverpool, albeit the men from Anfield were that season's league champions. Jimmy had conceded just three goals in three other games against Liverpool that season.

After leaving Roker Park he made 15 league appearances for Airdrieonians in a season and a half before moving on to St Johnstone in January 1924, helping the Perth outfit to the Scottish Second Division title making 13 appearances. During his first full campaign of 1924-25 he was ever-present, but overworked as mid-table St Johnstone conceded more goals than anyone but bottom of the league Third Lanark. During this season he played in St Johnstone's final match at the Recreation Ground and their first at Muirton Park. Starting the following season with eleven appearances, there appears to have been a fall-out as having been transfer-listed in January 1926, he did not play again until moving to Dundee United on 3 February 1927, but he was unable to stop them finishing bottom of the first division.

While Dundee United went down, Dempster stayed up, transferring to Division Two champions Bo'Ness on 12 May only to suffer relegation again at the first time of asking having played 24 of their 38 games. After no further appearances in 1928-29, he moved to second division Bathgate on Boxing Day, playing eight times for the West Lothian side in the season they resigned from the Scottish League. Come Christmas Eve, he returned to Bo'Ness making 18 appearances in Division Two before retiring - until his resurfacing as a cup-winning winger in Ghana!

## DENAYER, Jason Gregory Marianne

**POSITION:** Centre-back
**BIRTHPLACE:** Jette, Brussels
**DATE OF BIRTH:** 28/06/1995
**HEIGHT:** 6' 0½" **WEIGHT:** 11st 0lbs
**SIGNED FROM:** Manchester City, 31/08/2016, on loan
**DEBUT:** v Everton, H, 12/09/2016
**LAST MATCH:** v Swansea City ,H, 13/05/2017
**MOVED TO:** Manchester City, 22/05/2017, end of loan
**TEAMS:** FC Ganshoren, Anderlecht, JMG Academy, Manchester City, Celtic (L), Galatasaray (L), Sunderland (L), Galatasaray (L), Olympique Lyonnais (to 2022)
**INTERNATIONAL:** Belgium
**SAFC TOTALS:** 25+2 appearances / 0 goals

**Denayer was highly rated when he came on loan to relegation-doomed Sunderland and went on to fulfil his potential elsewhere. In his almost season-long loan at Sunderland, he was part of a team that had considerably more talent, but considerably less character and fight than the previous relegation side of 2005-06. Injuries did not help Denayer at Sunderland. Nor did manager David Moyes' tendency to sometimes ask Jason to play in midfield rather than in his best position of centre-back.**

It was at Lyon that Denayer really shone. Appointed captain and having scored in a derby victory over St Etienne in his first season in France, he went on to help Lyon knock Manchester City out of the Champions League in 2020.

Before going to Man City, where he worked under Patrick Vieira in the academy, Denayer had never played as a defender in eleven-a-side football. A senior debut came during his first loan which was to Celtic where he made a scoring debut, gained Champions League experience, won the SPL and League Cup, played alongside Virgil van Dijk and was voted Scotland PFA Young Player of the Year as well as Celtic's Young player of the Year.

Next stop was another loan, this time to Gatatasaray who he would re-join on a second loan after his spell with Sunderland. The Turkish giants also provided Champions League football and another trophy, Jason producing the assist for the winner as rivals Fenerbahce were beaten in the Turkish Cup final in his first spell while a Super-Lig title was added in 2017-18. In September 2020, Denayer marked his 20th full international with a first goal in a 2-0 win away to Denmark and went on to play at the following summer's delayed Euro 2020 tournament.

## DEVINE, Joseph Cassidy (Joe)

**POSITION:** Inside-left
**BIRTHPLACE:** Dalziel, Motherwell, Lanarkshire
**DATE OF BIRTH:** 09/08/1905 - 09/05/1980
**HEIGHT:** 5' 8½" **WEIGHT:** 10st 7lbs
**SIGNED FROM:** Newcastle United, 31/01/1931
**DEBUT:** v Blackburn Rovers, H, 04/02/1931
**LAST MATCH:** v Leicester City, A, 22/04/1933
**MOVED TO:** QPR, 26/05/1933
**TEAMS:** Bathgate, Burnley, Newcastle United, Sunderland, QPR, Birmingham, Chesterfield
**SAFC TOTALS:** 77 appearances / 7 goals

**Noted for his adhesive ball control, Joe Devine moved to Burnley for a £250 fee in 1925 after impressing with Bathgate despite them finishing fifth from bottom in the Scottish Second Division.**

29 goals in 121 games for Burnley, where he operated in either inside-forward position or at centre-forward, drew the attention of Newcastle United who paid £5,575 for his signature in January 1930.

A goal on his home debut in a 3-5 defeat to Sheffield United was small consolation as his new team propped up the table, but next time out he was instrumental in a 3-0 derby win over Sunderland that provided the turning point in United's season. Dovetailing with Magpie legend Hughie Gallacher, Devine finished as second top scorer with eight goals from 16 games. These included a last-day winner against West Ham. Without that goal, Newcastle would have been relegated.

Despite his heroics, by the following February Joe was on the move to Sunderland for the very specific fee of £2,599. He got off to a great start as Sunderland led 7-0 at half-time on his debut, Joe being one of the scorers in an eventual 8-2 win. Although he added another late-season goal in a win over West Ham, Sunderland were not in the sort of trouble Newcastle had been and finished mid-table. Unfortunately, there would be no improvement in his first full season as Sunderland remained locked in mid-table, one of Joe's five goals being a mere consolation in a 1-4 home defeat to his old club Newcastle.

After playing in just over half the games in his third season - another one in mid-table - Sunderland recouped most of their outlay on Devine, selling him to QPR for £2,500 in May 1933. Immediately appointed captain by the Division Three South club, he debuted in a home win over Brighton at the start of the season and went on to score ten times in 65 games in all competitions before returning to the top flight after 18 months, this time to Birmingham for £2,000.

As at QPR, Joe was made skipper at St Andrew's, debuting against Stoke in the first game of 1935. In his first full season with the Blues, his only goal came in an early-season draw with champions Arsenal while he was part of the home side who lost 7-2 to Sunderland on the day the Lads secured the title in 1936.

After two goals in 56 appearances, Joe joined Chesterfield in May 1937 going on to become their coach straight after World War Two. He went on to coach in Iceland with Valur in 1948 as well as scouting for Bristol City, refereeing in the Highland League back home in Scotland and running the Peacock Pub in Cutthorpe near Chesterfield.

His uncle was Joe Cassidy, a Scotland international who was the hero of Celtic's 1923 cup-winning campaign and also played for Cardiff, Clyde, Dundee, Ballymena, Morton and Dundalk in addition to loans to six clubs while with Celtic.

## DI GIUSEPPE, Marcus (Bica)

**POSITION:** Centre-forward

**BIRTHPLACE:** Sao Paulo, Brazil

**DATE OF BIRTH:** 12/03/1972

**HEIGHT:** 6' 2" **WEIGHT:** 12st 7lbs

**SIGNED FROM:** Callao (Peru), 17/09/1999, initially on trial

**DEBUT:** v Walsall, A, 21/09/1999

**LAST MATCH:** v Walsall, A, 21/09/1999

**MOVED TO:** 01/10/1999, released after trial

**TEAMS:** Pequeninos do Jockey, Sao Paolo, Botafogo, Sporting Crystal, Salzburg, Deportivo Municipal, Paniliakos, Sport Boys Callao, Sunderland, Walsall, Portuguesa Santista, Universitario, Danubio, Deportivo Wanka, Estudiantes de Medicina, Coronel Bolognesi

**SAFC TOTALS:** 0+1 appearances / 0 goals

**Known as 'Bica' although he had Marcos (albeit spelled incorrectly) on the back of his shirt in his one appearance for Sunderland, the club's first Brazilian played only played 45 minutes, coming on as a half-time sub in a 5-0 League Cup away win at Walsall.**

He did manage to net in his one reserve game against Manchester United. Sunderland had given him a chance after he had been out of football for six months after apparently testing positive for cocaine, but he did not last long. Nonetheless, the opponents in his one first-team game saw fit to throw the Brazilian a lifeline, but after one late substitute appearance in a local derby win away to Kevin Kilbane's West Brom, he was released.

'Bica' had begun with Pequeninos do Jockey when he was seven-years-old, spending seven years with the club playing at U9, U11, U13, and U15 levels, before four years with Sao Paolo where he played U17 and U19 football prior to joining Botafogo in 1993-94. From there, he left Brazil to go to Sporting Cristal in Peru, scoring once in five games as they won their league title for the third successive season in 1995-96. That summer, he made a first move to Europe signing for Austria Salzburg who later became Red Bull Salzburg. After three goals in 18 league games in Austria, Marcos moved to Greece where he played for newly-promoted Paniliakos in 1997-98. As with Salzburg, he scored three goals, this time in 15 games as his team finished in mid-table.

With Sport Boys Callao back in Peru there were six goals in ten games before Peter Reid added him to the range of overseas players he took a look at. After his spell in England, Bica returned to Peru in 2000 with Club Universitario de Deportes. Seven goals in eight games there led to a move to Uruguay with Danubio in the capital Montevideo, but after only three games he went back to Peru with Deportivo Wanka where he played 14 times without scoring. Subsequent spells with Estudiantes de Medicina and Coronel Bolognesi completed his playing days by 2005, eleven goals in 24 matches for his last club following none in five for de Medicina. After retiring from his well-travelled career, Marcus became a football agent.

## DIAKITE, Modibo

**POSITION:** Centre-back

**BIRTHPLACE:** Bourg-la-Reine, France

**DATE OF BIRTH:** 02/03/1987

**HEIGHT:** 6' 4" **WEIGHT:** 13st 12lbs

**SIGNED FROM:** Lazio, 01/07/2013

**DEBUT:** v Southampton, A, 24/08/2013

**LAST MATCH:** v Kidderminster Harriers, H, 25/01/2014

**MOVED TO:** Left by mutual consent, 01/09/2014

**TEAMS:** Sampdoria, Pescara, Lazio, Sunderland, Fiorentina (L), Deportivo la Coruna, Cagliari, Frosinone, Sampdoria, Ternana, Bari, Ternana (to June 2022)

**SAFC TOTALS:** 8 appearances / 0 goals

**One of the influx of players brought in by Director of Football Roberto De Fanti, Modibo Diakite (whose surname was actually listed as Diakhite on his passport) only played a handful of times. His best game was undoubtedly in the only league victory he was part of, his performance helping achieve a clean sheet in a 1-0 win at Everton. He also played in an FA Cup win over Kidderminster after which he was loaned to Fiorentina for the rest of the season.**

Although born in France, Modibo grew up in Italy and began in youth football in Genoa with Sampdoria. A debut came at the age of 19 in a Serie B goalless draw for Pescara at Mantova after which he moved to Rome with Lazio. Udinese provided the opposition for his Serie A debut in April 2008 and also his first goal eight months later. Over seven years, he had made just 65 league appearances, (scoring once more) prior to his short-lived move to Sunderland. A teammate of future Sunderland skipper Lorik Cana at Lazio, Diakite did not play in either of the Italian Cup finals Lazio won in his time there (although he was an unused sub against Sampdoria in 2009) but did play as they won the Italian Supercup in 2009.

Following his few months on loan from Sunderland in Florence with Fiorentina, Spain became Diakite's next stop with a season at La Coruna - where his side conceded eight to Real Madrid on Diakite's debut - after which he returned to Italy. He continued to make regular moves without playing a great deal, 18 appearances for Frosinone in 2015-16 being his best total to 2021. At Sunderland, he told a story that his foot had been run over by a tractor when he was a boy. No-one was ever sure if this was true, but sometimes when he passed the ball, people began to wonder.

## DIAMOND, Jack Tyler

**POSITION:** Winger

**BIRTHPLACE:** Gateshead, Tyne & Wear

**DATE OF BIRTH:** 12/01/2000

**HEIGHT:** 5' 8" **WEIGHT:** 10st 7lbs

**SIGNED FROM:** Sunderland Youths, 01/07/2017

**DEBUT:** v Carlisle United, H, 09/10/2018

**LAST MATCH:**

**MOVED TO:**

**TEAMS:** Sunderland, Spennymoor Utd (L), Harrogate Town (L), Lincoln City (L)

**INTERNATIONAL:** Republic of Ireland

**SAFC TOTALS:** 21+22 appearances / 2 goals (to June 2022)

**By the age of 21, Jack Diamond had played at Wembley twice, coming off the bench as Sunderland won the Football League (Papa John's) Trophy in March 2021, just seven and a half months after scoring while on loan to Harrogate Town as they won the National League Play-Off final against Notts County when Jack received the Man of the Match award.**

Jack had scored in three of the last four regular National League games for Harrogate before the 2019-20 season was curtailed due to the Covid 19 pandemic, those goals being his first league goals of a season in which he played 32 games in total for the Yorkshire club where ex Sunderland midfielder Paul Thirlwell was assistant manager with veteran former Sunderland striker Jon Stead up front. Diamond had also been on loan to Harrogate for six months the previous season having had just under six weeks on loan to Spennymoor United in the spring of 2019.

Joining Sunderland as a 13-year-old, at 16 he made three Football League Trophy appearances in 2017 for Sunderland Under 21s while Sunderland were in the Championship. The following season his trio of games in the same competition were at first-team level, Sunderland having sunk into League One. The first of those was at home to Carlisle with the same fixture in the same competition two years later providing his first goal for Sunderland. A league debut followed two weeks later at Swindon with a first league goal coming in a 4-0 rout of Lincoln at Sincil Bank a couple of months later.

As Phil Parkinson was succeeded by Lee Johnson in the SAFC hot-seat, Diamond began to be called upon more frequently, his pace, youthful energy and ability to carry the ball forward and to stretch defences being an asset, one clearly witnessed at Wembley where he became the only player to have played in every game of the successful cup-run. Loaned to Harrogate again in 2021-22 he was their joint top-scorer with 14 goals.

## DIBBLE, Andrew Gerald (Andy)

**POSITION:** Goalkeeper

**BIRTHPLACE:** Cwmbran, Monmouthshire

**DATE OF BIRTH:** 08/05/1965

**HEIGHT:** 6' 0½" **WEIGHT:** 13st 7lbs

**SIGNED FROM:** Luton Town, 20/02/1986, on loan

**DEBUT:** v Huddersfield Town, A, 01/03/1986

**LAST MATCH:** v Stoke City, H, 03/05/1986

**MOVED TO:** Luton Town, 05/05/1986, end of loan

**TEAMS:** Cardiff City, Luton Town, Sunderland (L), Huddersfield Town (L), Manchester City, Aberdeen (L), Middlesbrough (L), Bolton Wanderers (L), WBA (L), Oldham Athletic (L), Sheffield United (L), Rangers (L), Sheffield United, Luton Town, Middlesbrough, Altrincham, Barry Town, Hartlepool United, Carlisle United (L), Stockport County, Wrexham, Accrington Stanley

**INTERNATIONAL:** Wales

**SAFC TOTALS:** 12 appearances / 0 goals

**'Officer' Dibble proved to genuinely be 'Top-Cat' at Sunderland. Brought in for a dozen late season games of Lawrie McMenemy's first season, Andy was only 20 as he became one of a quartet of goalkeepers used that term. Dibble excelled and made himself a hero with clean sheets in the last two games which Sunderland needed to win to avoid what could have been an ignominious first relegation to the third tier.**

They were the only back-to-back league clean sheets of the season. Indeed, only two league clean sheets had been achieved all season until 'Officer's' arrival, but this pair were part of four he kept in the last six games.

Dibble was at Sunderland on loan from Luton Town where Bob Bolder went in a reciprocal move. Dibble had been given a league debut on his 17th birthday by Len Ashurst as he played for Cardiff against Crystal Palace. It was one of 62 league appearances Andy made for the Bluebirds. In a career of close to 400 English and Scottish League games, only at Manchester City did he top 100 games, at ten of his clubs making fewer appearances than his dozen at Sunderland. However, for much of his decade at City, Andy was reserve to Tony Coton and went on loan to five clubs during his time there.

Dibble's greatest day came a couple of years after his stint at Sunderland. In 1988 he was named Man of the Match as his Luton side - which included Mick Harford - defeated Arsenal 3-2 in the League Cup final at Wembley where he saved a penalty from Nigel Winterburn. Andy went on to win the FAW Premier Cup with Wrexham in 2003 and 2004 while in 1996-97, he made seven SPL appearances as back up to Andy Goram as Rangers won the Scottish League with Ally McCoist one of their most prominent men.

With his final club Accrington Stanley, 'Officer Dibble' progressed onto the coaching staff going on to work as goalkeeper coach at Coventry - where he worked alongside Adrian Heath - Peterborough, Rotherham - where he became caretaker/manager - and from January 2017 back at his first club Cardiff.

Internationally, he won three full caps, the last in February 1989 as Wales drew 3-3 in Tel Aviv against Israel. Andy's son Christian played for Bury and Barnsley as well as in non-league football.

## DICHIO, Daniele Salvatore Ernest (Danny)

**POSITION:** Centre-forward

**BIRTHPLACE:** Hammersmith, London

**DATE OF BIRTH:** 19/10/1974

**HEIGHT:** 6' 2" **WEIGHT:** 11st 0lbs

**SIGNED FROM:** Sampdoria, 26/01/1998

**DEBUT:** v Norwich City, A, 28/01/1998

**LAST MATCH:** v Leeds United, H, 31/03/2001

**MOVED TO:** WBA, 04/12/2001

**TEAMS:** QPR, Welling United (L), Barnet (L), Sampdoria, Lecce (L), Sunderland, WBA, Derby County (L), Millwall. Preston North End, Toronto

**INTERNATIONAL:** England Under 21

**SAFC TOTALS:** 35+62 appearances / 18 goals

**Like Mickey Bridges struggling to dislodge Kevin Phillips, Dichio had the difficulty of trying to replace Niall Quinn. Dichio was decent in the air and quite mobile for a big man, but compared to the brilliant Quinn, was always doomed to be in Niall's shadow. From his four seasons at Sunderland, only when Quinn was injured in the 1998-99, did Danny start more than two league games. He made a strong contribution to that promotion campaign with ten goals from 16 starts, plus 20 appearances off the bench.**

That promotion season might not have been necessary had Dichio stepped up to take a penalty in the previous season's Play-Off final shoot-out. Instead as a forward who had come on as sub, he watched left-back Mickey Gray fail from the spot after a lung-bursting 120 minutes.

Being a deputy was nothing new for Dichio at Sunderland. At QPR he had under-studied Les Ferdinand, while at Sampdoria he had sometimes been back-up to 1990 FIFA World Cup winner Jurgen Klinsmann and Italy international Vincenzo Montella. Dichio only started two games for Sampdoria who loaned him to Lecce where Dichio played six league and cup games scoring his only Serie A goal against Brescia in November 1997.

Known as 'Mellow D' due to his part-time disc-jockeying, Londoner Dichio had an Italian father but his time playing in Italy came to an end when Peter Reid brought him to Sunderland. Dichio had been a youngster impressing in the junior ranks when Reid played for QPR as a veteran. Reid had tried to sign Dichio when he went to Sampdoria and wasted no time in bringing him back when the move did not work out.

At QPR Danny had scored 23 times in 66+22 appearances. Two of those goals came on his first two appearances, the second at Newcastle. His first full-season at Loftus Road saw him Rangers top scorer in the Premiership with ten goals - including an early autumn purple patch of six in four games - from just 22 starts (plus 8 as sub) - and that in a struggling team that went down.

Having been loaned to Welling United and Barnet while with QPR, during his time at Sunderland Danny was loaned to WBA in August 2001. The initial loan was curtailed by a broken foot, but he returned to the Hawthorns the following November before making that move permanent. Nine goals in his first season helped the Baggies to promotion and with it an additional £100,000 to Sunderland as part of his transfer deal, taking the full fee to £1.25m representing a profit to Sunderland of half a million.

Back in the Premiership, he was Albion's joint-top scorer, but this was with just five goals, one of which was against Sunderland who were the only team to finish beneath West Brom. In 2004, he scored twice against Sunderland, this time in a league game for Millwall. Later in the season he played against Sunderland in an FA Cup semi-final although he missed the final due to suspension. Danny had joined the Lions after a loan spell from WBA who had also loaned him to Derby.

Dichio's final stop in England was with Preston North End for whom he scored his first goal against Sunderland. In 2007, he moved to Canada to join the newly-formed Toronto FC, going into the history books as their first-ever scorer with a goal against Chicago Fire on 12 May 2007 - in the same game becoming their first-ever player to be sent off. After retirement, he stayed in Toronto, mainly working with their academy while also becoming a pundit on Canadian TV.

In a long and well-travelled career, he played more games for Sunderland than any of his other clubs. As well as playing for England schoolboys, Dichio won one cap at Under 21 level, coming on as a sub in a 2-2 draw with Norway in Stavanger in October 1995.

## DICKMAN, Jonjo

**POSITION:** Midfield

**BIRTHPLACE:** Hexham, Northumberland

**DATE OF BIRTH:** 22/09/1981

**HEIGHT:** 5' 11" **WEIGHT:** 11st 12lbs

**SIGNED FROM:** Sunderland Youths, 01/07/1998

**DEBUT:** v Manchester City, A, 21/04/2003

**LAST MATCH:** v Manchester City, A, 21/04/2003

**MOVED TO:** Darlington, 01/03/2005

**TEAMS:** Sunderland, York City (L), Darlington, Consett

**SAFC TOTALS:** 1 appearance / 0 goals

**Perhaps the least known of the Dickman brothers and yet the only one to play a first-team game for Sunderland. Jonjo came on as a half-time sub at Manchester City in a game where Sunderland lost 3-0 after trailing 2-0 when he was introduced. Although he was at the club for seven years coming through the ranks this was Jonjo's solitary first-team appearance.**

Almost a year after his game at City Jonjo played twice on loan for York in a goalless draw at Oxford and a heavy defeat at Kidderminster Harriers. Eleven months on from that he signed for former Sunderland forward David Hodgson at Darlington. Playing alongside Craig Russell, Neil Wainwright, Mark Convery and Clark Keltie, who all had Sunderland connections, Dickman played eight late-season games as the Quakers just missed out on a Play-Off place on goal difference. In total he went on to play 46 league games for Darlington, scoring three times.

Jonjo's brothers Elliott and Lewis became very influential figures behind the scenes with Sunderland's young players. Having seen his own career which brought England youth honours stymied by injury, Elliott became a highly respected coach at the club for many years running the Under 18 and Under 23 teams amongst many varied responsibilities. A third brother Lewis coached at the club and returned as Academy manager in February 2021.

## DILLON, John

**POSITION:** Winger

**BIRTHPLACE:** Coatbridge, Lanarkshire

**DATE OF BIRTH:** 09/11/1942 - 11/08/2019

**HEIGHT:** 5' 8" **WEIGHT:** 11st 4lbs

**SIGNED FROM:** Bellshill Athletic, 01/07/1958

**DEBUT:** v Middlesbrough, A, 24/09/1960

**LAST MATCH:** v Leyton Orient, H, 14/10/1961

**MOVED TO:** Brighton & Hove Albion, 29/06/1962

**TEAMS:** Bellshill Athletic, Sunderland, Brighton & HA, Crewe Alexandra, Albion Rovers, Queen of the South, Stranraer, Hamilton Academical, Ashfield, New Blackburn Athletic

**SAFC TOTALS:** 23 appearances / 1 goal

**Coming from the same part of Glasgow as Billy Hughes, John Dillon was red and white to the core. He was so proud of having played for Sunderland that right up to his death at the age of 76, he would regularly travel down to Wearside from Glasgow to spend the weekend staying at the sea-front, have a drink with some old mates and come to the match. He also made it to Wembley in 2014 to see the League (Capital One) Cup final against Manchester City.**

John came so close to his own moment of cup glory. He started and so nearly finished a move that came close to putting Sunderland 2-1 up late on in the famed FA Cup quarter-final with Spurs in 1961. Sunderland's scorer in that drawn game was Willie McPheat, a fellow Scot who was born and died in the same years as John. For many years Willie suffered from dementia and resided in a Glasgow nursing home. Dillon loyally visited him every Friday afternoon for years, taking two buses across Glasgow to do so, and to reminisce about their times in red and white. Even when Willie reached the stage where John doubted he was taking any of his talk in, John kept going - just like he did on the pitch.

All but the last of Dillon's games for Sunderland came in that 1960-61 season, his goal coming in a 4-1 home win over Portsmouth. He went on to score three times in 21 games for Brighton and once in five outings with Crewe before going back to Scotland with Albion Rovers where he became inducted into their Hall of Fame, once scoring four goals in a game against Airdrieonians. He also played in a friendly against Celtic's Lisbon Lions in their first game after returning to these shores as the first British team to win the European Cup. At the tail end of his playing days, Dillon played for a couple of non-league sides in West Lothian before becoming a school janitor.

## DIOUF, El-Hadji Ousseynou

**POSITION:** Forward

**BIRTHPLACE:** Dakar, Senegal

**DATE OF BIRTH:** 15/01/1981

**HEIGHT:** 5' 11" **WEIGHT:** 13st 0lbs

**SIGNED FROM:** Bolton Wanderers, 28/07/2008

**DEBUT:** v Liverpool, H, 16/08/2008

**LAST MATCH:** v Aston Villa, H, 17/01/2009

**MOVED TO:** Blackburn Rovers, 30/01/2009

**TEAMS:** Sochaux, Rennes, Lens, Liverpool, Bolton Wanderers, Sunderland, Blackburn Rovers, Rangers (L), Doncaster Rovers, Leeds United, Sabah FA

**INTERNATIONAL:** Senegal

**SAFC TOTALS:** 13+3 appearances / 0 goals

**Diouf was a colourful character and a flair player whose most notable contribution in his brief time at Sunderland was winning the free-kick from which Kieran Richardson scored his famous goal against Newcastle in October 2008.**

Brought in by Roy Keane, (who he had played against as Liverpool beat Man United in the 2003 League Cup final) Diouf was a high-profile player who had starred at the 2002 FIFA World Cup Keane had walked away from. The Senegal striker had been named in that year's FIFA World Cup all-star team and had been African Footballer of the Year for the second successive season at that point when he was also named as the BBC African Footballer of the Year. The same calendar year also saw El-Hadji reach the final of the African Cup of Nations, although he missed a penalty in the shoot-out of the final against Cameroon.

He could be a tough individual to get the best out of. Throughout his career, Diouf had a number of disciplinary issues both for club and country, combined with a series of incidents involving spitting and driving offences. Some of his best football was played under Sam Allardyce at Bolton, a club for whom he scored their first goal in Europe and his last goal against Sunderland. It was Allardyce who later took him off Sunderland's hands when Big Sam signed him for Blackburn.

El-Hadji had joined Bolton from Liverpool who in 2002 paid a reported £10m at the time of his World Cup exploits as he helped Senegal to the quarter-final. He scored twice on his home debut at Anfield, but soon found himself on the bench and utilised on the right-wing rather than through the middle.

Later, during his stint at Blackburn, Diouf moved on loan to Rangers, helping them to win the SPL. He also came off the bench for the last three minutes of extra-time in the League Cup final where he managed to get a caution within a minute as Rangers beat Celtic on a day where he was one of four men on the Gers teamsheet with Sunderland connections along with Kyle Lafferty, Alan Hutton and David Healy. Ki Sung-Yueng and Anthony Stokes were amongst the Celtic subs.

Although El-Hadji came close to another reunion with Allardyce, who by now was with West Ham, his next stop was at Doncaster Rovers where he spent half a season before joining Leeds where he spent a couple of years before finishing his playing career in Malaysia with Sabah FA where, as was often the case, controversy followed him to the end. Prior to coming into British football he had a season each in France with Sochaux and Rennes from 1998 to 2000 before two seasons with Lens where he scored 18 goals in 54 league games, qualifying for the Champions League in his second season as Lens were runners-up to Lyon.

Diouf's older brother Dame played for over ten clubs in Germany, mainly at lower levels with a spell in the Bundesliga with Hannover at the time of his brother's World Cup exploits. After his own football career, El-Hadji became a Goodwill Ambassador for sport and ran his own sports newspaper in his home city of Dakar. In 2004, El-Hadji Diouf was one of 125 living players named by Pele as the best in the world as part of FIFA's centenary celebrations.

## DITCHBURN, John Hurst (Jock)

**POSITION:** Centre-half

**BIRTHPLACE:** Hunslet, West Riding of Yorkshire

**DATE OF BIRTH:** 14/03/1897 - January 1992

**HEIGHT:** 5' 10" **WEIGHT:** 12st 0lbs

**SIGNED FROM:** Blantyre Victoria, 17/08/1923

**DEBUT:** v Sheffield United, A, 26/01/1924

**LAST MATCH:** v Bury, H, 14/10/1925

**MOVED TO:** Exeter City, 08/05/1926

**TEAMS:** Blantyre Thistle, Cambuslang, Blantyre Victoria, Sunderland, Exeter City, Exeter Loco, Exeter City

**SAFC TOTALS:** 6 appearances / 0 goals

**Born near Leeds, Ditchburn was known as Jock due to his Scottish heritage and the fact that he had been brought up north of the border from the age of three. Sunderland were unbeaten in the four games he played in his debut season as they finished third in the top-flight. There was defeat in his one game of the following season at Tottenham Hotspur, but he was on the winning side in his third and last campaign on his final appearance as Bury were beaten at Roker Park.**

Having moved to Exeter, Jock got to play regularly. He had two spells with the Grecians who re-signed him from East Devon League side Exeter Loco after letting him go in 1928. After eventually totalling 91 games, he retired in 1934 having a Benefit match when the Magpies of Notts County came to St James Park. He went on to work on the Exeter ground-staff and worked in railway maintenance.

# D

## DJILOBODJI, El Hadji Papy Mison

**POSITION:** Centre-back

**BIRTHPLACE:** Kaolack, Senegal

**DATE OF BIRTH:** 01/12/1988

**HEIGHT:** 6' 4" **WEIGHT:** 12st 12lbs

**SIGNED FROM:** Chelsea, 05/08/2016

**DEBUT:** v Middlesbrough, H, 21/08/2016

**LAST MATCH:** v Carlisle United, A, 22/08/2017

**MOVED TO:** Contract terminated, 12/09/2018

**TEAMS:** ASC Saloum, Senart-Moissy, Nantes, Chelsea, Werder Bremen (L), Sunderland, Dijon (L), Guincamp, Gazisehir Gaziantep FK (to June 2022)

**INTERNATIONAL:** Senegal

**SAFC TOTALS:** 23+1 appearances / 0 goals

**David Moyes invested a reported £8m in Djilobodji whose value had more than doubled since Chelsea bought him from Nantes. His solitary appearance for Chelsea had come at Walsall in the League Cup when he was used as a substitute in added time. The Stamford Bridge club had loaned him to Werder Bremen where he played 14 times in the Bundesliga as well as a couple of German cup games. Djilobodji scored twice in Germany, one of his goals being the winner against Eintracht Frankfurt on his last appearance.**

At Sunderland, all but one of his appearances came in his first season. He was sent off against Hull and later received a four-match suspension after being charged with violent conduct by the FA following a match with West Brom in January which proved to be his last game of the season.

After playing in a League Cup tie at the start of the following season, Djilobodji went on loan to Dijon in Ligue 1 where he played 31 times, scoring at Strasbourg and being sent off against Metz. The following season, he returned to Sunderland having failed to find a new club. Not being up to the required level of fitness, he was reportedly sacked.

He resurfaced as a sub for Guincamp the following January at Paris Saint-Germain who scored the last three of their goals in a 9-0 win during his 17 minutes on the pitch. Papy then scored the winner on his full debut in a cup game at Nancy before being sent off on his home debut in a defeat to Reims. This violent offence cost him a six-match ban after which he played just twice more before leaving the club.

Moving to Turkey with Gazisehir in the summer of 2019, he began with a 5-0 defeat at Fenerbahce, but scored six goals in 33 games in his first season and continued to perform better there than at any time since his time with Nantes. Over seven seasons there he had played 186 times helping the club to promotion in 2013 before joining Chelsea two years later shortly after playing for Senegal at the African Cup of Nations.

## DOBSON, George David

**POSITION:** Midfielder

**BIRTHPLACE:** Harold Wood, Romford, London

**DATE OF BIRTH:** 15/11/1997

**HEIGHT:** 6' 1" **WEIGHT:** 11st 7lbs

**SIGNED FROM:** Walsall, 25/07/2019

**DEBUT:** v Oxford United, H, 03/08/2019

**LAST MATCH:** v AFC Wimbledon, H, 15/12/2020

**MOVED TO:** Charlton Athletic, 01/07/2021

**TEAMS:** Arsenal, West Ham United, Walsall (L), Sparta Rotterdam, Walsall, Sunderland, AFC Wimbledon (L), Charlton Athletic

**INTERNATIONAL:** Wales

**SAFC TOTALS:** 38+9 appearances / 2 goals

**Signed by Jack Ross, midfielder Dobson lacked nothing in energy, commitment or attitude, but did not live up to expectations in terms of the quality required. Rarely a scorer throughout his career, George did net a well-taken goal in a Carabao (League) Cup win at Burnley as Sunderland beat a team two divisions above them for the first time and he also netted in an 8-1 win over Aston Villa Under 21s in the Papa John's (English Football League) trophy which Sunderland went on to win.**

Long before that Wembley triumph however, George had left to go on loan to AFC Wimbledon (22+2/1), his final Sunderland appearance before that having been against the Dons just before Christmas.

From the ages of eight until 17 he had been part of the Arsenal Academy, joining West Ham upon his release and at this point being converted from a centre-back into a midfielder. He never played for either of the big London clubs and made his debut on loan to Walsall who he later signed for after a spell in the Eredivisie with Sparta Rotterdam.

He played five times with Sparta, starting with a debut against Lee Cattermole's future club VVV Venlo in August 2017. 34 days later he made his last first-team appearance, against AZ Alkmaar and three months after that was back on home soil with the Saddlers having also played half a dozen times for Sparta's Development team Jong Sparta. In July 2021, he signed for Charlton and was part of the Addicks team who won at Sunderland in October of that year.

## DOCHERTY, Michael (Mick)

**POSITION:** Defender/Midfielder

**BIRTHPLACE:** Preston, Lancashire

**DATE OF BIRTH:** 29/10/1950

**HEIGHT:** 5' 6" **WEIGHT:** 9st 8lbs

**SIGNED FROM:** Manchester City, 31/12/1976

**DEBUT:** v Coventry City, H, 03/01/1977

**LAST MATCH:** v Wrexham, A, 05/05/1979

**MOVED TO:** Retired, 18/09/1979

**TEAMS:** Burnley, Manchester City, Sunderland

**INTERNATIONAL:** England Youth

**SAFC TOTALS:** 79+1 appearances / 7 goals

**Although he had only been at the club for three and a half years Sunderland staged a testimonial for Mick Docherty in the week before the crucial last game of the 1979-80 promotion season. QPR - then managed by Docherty's dad Tommy - provided the testimonial opposition at Roker Park.**

Mick's career had been cut short by a knee injury sustained in a pre-season friendly at Lucerne in Switzerland in July 1979. In January 1980, he had joined the coaching staff and come the closing stages of the following season would become caretaker/manager overseeing a famous final-day win against Liverpool at Anfield. He remained at the club as first-team coach for another two seasons under Alan Durban.

An England youth international, Docherty junior had captained Burnley's 1968 FA Youth Cup winning side. A first-team debut for the Clarets followed the following December against Stoke, but he really came to prominence at Turf Moor after future Sunderland manager Jimmy Adamson took over the team as Adamson switched Mick from midfield to right-back. He went on to help Burnley to promotion in 1972-73 as Sunderland won the FA Cup. However, Mick tore his knee ligaments at Huddersfield just before promotion was sealed and there was worse to follow as on his first division debut at Sheffield United where he suffered a cruciate ligament injury. There would be just one more league appearance over the next two seasons - coincidentally back at Bramall Lane.

Thankfully by 1975-76, 'Doc' had recovered to play 27 games taking his Burnley tally to 168+6, but he lost his place after one match following the sacking of Adamson who later brought him to Sunderland. In between, he briefly played for Manchester City. Debuting against Manchester United at Old Trafford in May 1976, his eleventh and final appearance came the following September away to Juventus alongside Dave Watson and Dennis Tueart in the UEFA Cup.

Mick arrived at Roker with Sunderland rock-bottom, his debut being the seventh game in a sequence of ten where the team failed to score, let alone win. A couple of games later, youngsters Shaun Elliott and Kevin Arnott debuted, joining with fellow youngster Gary Rowell as the team was transformed, but that transformation was also down to the introduction of the experienced Mick who missed just one league game to the end of a season in which ultimately Sunderland were relegated in controversial circumstances involving Coventry who Docherty had debuted against. In Mick's second full season, promotion was missed by a whisker behind Stoke despite Docherty scoring the winner in a crucial late-season win over the Potters at the Victoria Ground.

Having qualified as a coach while still a teenager, Docherty was well equipped to adapt after injury ended his playing days. After leaving Sunderland, he managed Hartlepool between June and December 1983 before coaching Wolves and Blackpool prior to a return to Turf Moor in January 1989 as assistant manager to Frank Casper. 18 months later, he moved to Hull to become assistant to Stan Ternent, but when the pair left the Tigers after half a season, Docherty returned to the north west as coach of Rochdale where he soon became manager, remaining in charge at Spotland for 18 months.

The summer of 1988 brought a reunion both with Ternent and Burnley where this time he stayed for six years. Next stop was Gillingham in 2005 where he assisted his former Burnley colleague Ronnie Jepson, but by 2008, Mick was once again at Burnley, this time in a role greeting corporate guests. Four days after the 40th anniversary of captaining the Clarets to the FA Youth Cup he left the club again, once again linking up with Ternent and Jepson, this time at Huddersfield, but yet again the wheel went full circle when he finally returned to Burnley as a coach at their Centre of Excellence as well as coaching at Burnley college.

## DODDS, Leslie

**POSITION:** Goalkeeper

**BIRTHPLACE:** Newcastle, Northumberland

**DATE OF BIRTH:** 12/10/1936

**HEIGHT:** 5' 9" **WEIGHT:** 13st 0lbs

**SIGNED FROM:** Newburn, 25/08/1952

**DEBUT:** v WBA, H, 21/08/1954

**LAST MATCH:** v Manchester United, A, 03/12/1955

**MOVED TO:** Released, 01/05/1960

**TEAMS:** Newburn, Sunderland, Stamfordham

**INTERNATIONAL:** England Schools

**SAFC TOTALS:** 6 appearances / 0 goals

**Capped four times by England at Schools level, Leslie Dodds was a goalkeeping link between the 1937 and 1973 FA Cup-winning goalkeepers Johnny Mapson and Jim Montgomery, the former being a veteran when Leslie signed with the latter being a youngster at the club when Dodds departed.**

During the 'Bank of England' era when he was at the club, Dodds did well to get half a dozen league appearances, one of which was away to Manchester United where he faced Duncan Edwards who had been a teammate when they played together for England boys. Dodds also played against Raich Carter and John Charles in his very first game for Sunderland in a friendly with Leeds in which Carter played as a 'Guest' for the Elland Road outfit.

Leslie's league debut against West Brom on the opening day of the 1954-55 season came when Scotland international Willie Fraser could not get leave from the Forces. Dodds was beaten twice, but Sunderland won in front of just under 57,000. He was to play four times that season and twice the next. After leaving Sunderland, a month's trial at Bristol City was ruined by a back injury that kept him in bed for three weeks. Following six months recuperation, Dodds signed for Stamfordham with whom he won their league and the Northumberland Minor Cup, but after snapping his Achilles tendon playing five-a-side his career came to a premature end.

He went on to work for an engineering firm on Team Valley before spending 22 years working in the Housing Department at Sunderland Council. A resident of Cleadon, Leslie continued to support the lads, even becoming a season ticket holder in the Roy Keane era.

## DOIG, John Edward (Teddy)

**POSITION:** Goalkeeper

**BIRTHPLACE:** Letham, Forfarshire

**DATE OF BIRTH:** 29/10/1866 - 07/11/1919

**HEIGHT:** 5' 9½" **WEIGHT:** 12st 2lbs

**SIGNED FROM:** Arbroath, 17/09/1890

**DEBUT:** v WBA, A 20/09/1890

**LAST MATCH:** v Manchester City, A, 02/04/1904

**MOVED TO:** Liverpool, 12/08/1904

**TEAMS:** Arbroath, Blackburn Rovers, Arbroath, Sunderland, Liverpool, St Helens Recreationals

**INTERNATIONAL:** Scotland

**SAFC TOTALS:** 457 appearances / 0 goals

**Inducted into the Sunderland Hall of Fame in 2020, Teddy Doig is one of the greatest names in the club's history. One of only two men (with Jamie Millar) to win four top-flight league titles with Sunderland, he remains third on the all-time appearances list which he led for over six decades until Jim Montgomery and Len Ashurst came along.**

Doig remains the holder of the player with most top-flight appearances for the club with 417 games at that level. Having played at a time when friendly games were played throughout the season and were usually as fiercely contested as league games, a claim is even made by Doig's grandson Eric that Teddy (or Ned as he is often referred to, especially outside of Wearside) actually topped Montgomery's total of 627 competitive appearances. Certainly Doig is known to have played in a minimum of 216 such friendly games taking his Sunderland total to 763 games - although of course, Monty also played in many friendly fixtures. www.doigsden.co.uk is a website which owes much to Eric Doig's determination to pay homage to his grandfather.

Teddy Doig played in Sunderland's first-ever league victory - only for the points to be deducted as Doig had not been correctly registered. Nonetheless, over the next 14 years, Doig earned the team plenty of points, keeping 147 clean sheets (in competitive games) along the way. He is the goalkeeper on the famous Thomas MM Hemy painting that dominates the entrance hall of the Stadium of Light, albeit at the time of that 1895 painting, goalkeepers wore the same colour shirt as the rest of the team.

Part of Doig's kit was always a cap, regardless of the weather. Prematurely bald and apparently very sensitive of this, legend has it that Doig would retrieve his cap before the ball if it came off. In Doig's day, he became so famous that on one occasion a postcard was delivered to the club from Paris. The address consisted of a drawing of a goalpost with a dog and the letter 'i' positioned above the dog. The only word on the address was England.

Ever-present in the league for six seasons at Sunderland, Doig twice managed 100 or more consecutive appearances (September 1890 to January 1894 and April 1896 to April 1899).

Doig had started with Arbroath debuting against Dundee Harp in February 1886 and going on to win two caps with the Red Lichties, a feat still unequalled in 2022. As a boy, he began playing as a winger for St Helena, a local club, but soon found his destiny as a goalkeeper after reputedly making his own goal constructed from wooden beams obtained from a shipyard. To this he tied a ball on a rope to the crossbar so he could practise punching the ball.

Before coming to Sunderland, Doig had signed for Blackburn Rovers, playing a single game for them in a 9-1 Football League win over Notts County on 16 November 1899. Upon leaving Wearside, he signed for his old Sunderland manager Tom Watson at Liverpool, going on to help the Anfield club to promotion in 1905 as the club's only ever-present.

He then went on to play eight games early in the 1905-06 season as Liverpool went on to win their first league title. When well into his forties, Doig went on to play regularly for St Helens Recreationals, his final known game being against Manchester United reserves on 30 April 1910. Doig died four years after Tom Watson, both are buried in Anfield cemetery, roughly a penalty area's distance apart.

For much of his time with Sunderland, Scotland had a policy of not picking players with English clubs. However, he did play in numerous trial matches between 'Home' Scots and Anglo Scots, sometimes accompanied by clubmates Hugh Wilson, Jimmy Hannah and Johnny Campbell. During his time with Sunderland Doig was capped against England in 1896, 1899 and 1903, being joined by Alex McCombie and James Watson on the last of those occasions.

Doig was also on Sunderland's books on the day of the first Ibrox disaster on 5 April 1902 when 25 people died. While that international was played to its conclusion, the game was subsequently declared null and void. When that international was restaged at Aston Villa the following month, Doig was unable to play due to a rare injury. Known as 'The Prince of Goalkeepers', Teddy Doig was a King rather than a prince at Sunderland.

## DONALDSON, Alexander Pollock

**POSITION:** Right-winger
**BIRTHPLACE:** Barrhead, Glasgow
**DATE OF BIRTH:** 04/12/1890 - 01/01/1972
**HEIGHT:** 5' 7½" **WEIGHT:** 10st 0lbs
**SIGNED FROM:** Bolton Wanderers, 18/03/1922
**DEBUT:** v Preston North End, A 01/04/1922
**LAST MATCH:** v Middlesbrough, A, 18/04/1923
**MOVED TO:** Manchester City, 17/05/1923
**TEAMS:** Ripley Athletic, Sheffield United, Bolton Wanderers, Leicester Fosse (WW1 Guest), Arthurlie (WW1 Guest), Port Vale (WW1 Guest), Sunderland, Manchester City, Crystal Palace, Chorley, Ashton National, Chorley
**INTERNATIONAL:** Scotland
**SAFC TOTALS:** 45 appearances / 1 goal

**Alex Donaldson won six caps for Scotland and another three in war-time games during World War One. The last of his caps came a few days before his transfer to Sunderland in March 1922. Eight years earlier he had been due to play in an international trial at Sunderland between England and the North. Born in Renfrewshire, Donaldson had lived in the midlands of England since his teens and had been subject to an England call-up before he revealed he was Scottish.**

Having played in non-league and had eight months with Sheffield United without getting a game, Donaldson had made his Football League debut for Bolton Wanderers in September 1912. His teammates included Tommy Barber who would score the only goal of that season's cup-final against Sunderland having moved to Aston Villa. Later in the same campaign, Donaldson would be in the Trotters' team on the day Sunderland mathematically clinched the league title.

Despite losing several seasons to the Great War, Donaldson managed 146 games for Bolton, the last in January 1922, two months before a £2,000 transfer to Sunderland.

On only his fourth appearance for the Lads, Donaldson assisted four first half goals in a 6-2 win over his old club. The following 1922-23 season would be Alex's only full season on Wearside. He made 35 league appearances as Sunderland finished runners-up to Liverpool, his only goal being a winner against Arsenal.

Moving to Manchester City in May 1923, Donaldson made just seven appearances in his one injury-hit season at Maine Road. Following a failed trial at Crystal Palace, Alex played out what had been an excellent, but war-interrupted, career with Chorley and Ashton United. At the beginning of World War Two, he worked as a Capstan Lathe Hand in Leicester. In the 1950s, he was the licensee of The Gardeners Arms in Bolton.

## DOSSENA, Andrea

**POSITION:** Left-back
**BIRTHPLACE:** Lodi, Italy
**DATE OF BIRTH:** 11/09/1981
**HEIGHT:** 5' 11" **WEIGHT:** 12st 11lbs
**SIGNED FROM:** Napoli, 02/09/2013
**DEBUT:** v Newcastle United, H, 27/10/2013
**LAST MATCH:** v Liverpool, A, 26/03/2014
**MOVED TO:** Released from contract, 30/04/2014
**TEAMS:** Verona, Treviso, Udinese, Liverpool, Napoli, Palermo (L), Sunderland, Leyton Orient, Chiasso, Piacenza
**INTERNATIONAL:** Italy
**SAFC TOTALS:** 10+1 appearances / 0 goals

**Sunderland certainly did not see the best of Andrea Dossena who arrived at the club just before his 32nd birthday and was sent off on his second appearance, against Hull. He came to Sunderland during the reign of Paolo Di Canio and Roberto De Fanti, but suffered as new signings so often do when the people who brought him in departed. By the turn of the year, he had played his penultimate game under new head coach Gus Poyet, but in late March, the former Liverpool player was brought out of the cold for a valedictory appearance at Anfield.**

Sunderland had been the opponents for Dossena's Premier League debut in August 2008 as Liverpool won 1-0 at the Stadium of Light. Three days earlier, Andrea had made his Liverpool bow in the Champions League at Standard Liege. Although he had cost £7m, he only played 31 times for Liverpool of which 13 were Premier League starts, but his two goals were in big games against Real Madrid in the Champions League and Manchester United in the Premier League.

Dossena's career path had seen Andrea relegated in his second season as a professional with Verona. He was relegated again with Treviso, but progressed with Udinese where he did well enough to make an international debut in October 2017 against South Africa, going on to win nine of his ten caps after joining Liverpool. Having moved to Napoli in January 2010, he returned to Anfield in the Champions League only to be responsible for a defensive lapse when his back-pass led to a goal for Steven Gerrard. In 2012, he played for the final five minutes as Napoli defeated Juventus in the Coppa Italia final, but after three years at Napoli he moved to Palermo on loan in January 2013, but could not stop the Sicilian club from being relegated.

Leyton Orient became the fourth club he was relegated with. Joining the O's six months after being released by Sunderland, he made 15 appearances for the London club. In 2015-16 Andrea made 19 appearances for Swiss second-tier team Chiasso followed by six the following term back in Italy with Piacenza in Serie C. In 2019, he moved into management in Serie D with Crema and took over at Ravenna in Serie D in July 2021, moving on to Renate in Serie C in June 2022. Notably, while teammates turned up for training at Sunderland in their affluent footballer cars, Dossena often arrived via bicycle.

## DOUGALL, Thomas (Tommy)

**POSITION:** Winger
**BIRTHPLACE:** Wishaw, Lanarkshire
**DATE OF BIRTH:** 17/05/1921 - 16/01/1997
**HEIGHT:** 5' 7" **WEIGHT:** 10st 12lbs
**SIGNED FROM:** Brentford, 10/11/1948
**DEBUT:** v Chelsea, H, 04/12/1948
**LAST MATCH:** v Bolton Wanderers, A, 18/12/1948
**MOVED TO:** Yeovil Town, 28/07/1950
**TEAMS:** Morris Motors, Coventry City, Guildford City, Brentford, Sunderland, Yeovil Town, Tonbridge, Dover
**SAFC TOTALS:** 3 appearances / 0 goals

**Tommy Dougall was called upon for three consecutive games on the right-wing during Len Duns' absence in December 1948. He had previously played two league games for Brentford and these appearances would be his only five in the Football League having not got a game at Coventry other than in war-time.**

He had played for Coventry in war-time football whilst on leave from the Royal Navy, debuting in an 8-0 Christmas Day win over West Brom in 1943 and playing once more that season. His first goal came two days before the following Christmas at home to Wolves, the first of seven goals in 19 games that term.

In 1945-46 before the Football League resumed in 1946-47, he made a solitary appearance at Charlton in September. After retiring from playing, Tommy moved into management with Hillingdon Borough and later Kingstonian from April 1967 to October 1970. His younger brother, Gordon, also followed him into management with Atherstone and Bedworth United (1964-1972).

His father Jimmy was also an outside-right who started out at Motherwell and was inducted into the Coventry City Hall of Fame having played 238 games between 1919 and 1926 when he was sold to Reading only to be forced into retirement after just twelve games for his new club.

## DOWNING, Stewart

**POSITION:** Winger
**BIRTHPLACE:** Middlesbrough
**DATE OF BIRTH:** 22/07/1984
**HEIGHT:** 5' 10" **WEIGHT:** 10st 4lbs
**SIGNED FROM:** Middlesbrough, 29/10/2003, on loan
**DEBUT:** v West Bromwich Albion, A, 01/11/2003
**LAST MATCH:** v Coventry City, A, 08/12/2003
**MOVED TO:** Middlesbrough, 11/12/2003, recalled from loan
**TEAMS:** Marton, Middlesbrough, Sunderland (L), Aston Villa, Liverpool, West Ham United, Middlesbrough, Blackburn Rovers
**INTERNATIONAL:** England
**SAFC TOTALS:** 7 appearances / 3 goals

**Stewart Downing was a revelation when he arrived as a teenager on loan from Middlesbrough, his debut display at the Hawthorns instantly showing that he had the pace and ability to tear teams apart despite that game finishing goalless. He went on to score in half of his other six games, including a penalty, only for rave reviews to lead to his recall to Teesside. Over the years, a return to Sunderland was often mooted, but never materialised.**

Later in the season of his Sunderland loan, Stewart would be an unused sub as a Boro team, including Bolo Zenden, won the League Cup final against Sam Allardyce's Bolton. Two years later, he played in the UEFA Cup final, alongside sub Lee Cattermole, as Boro lost to Seville.

Downing scored 17 goals in 157+24 games for his hometown team where he was twice Player of the Year. After Boro were relegated, Stewart became Martin O'Neill's first signing for Aston Villa. Having cost the midlands club £12m, he increased his value to £20m by the time he was transferred to Liverpool two years later when the reigning Villa Player of the Year.

There had been nine goals in 61+2 games for Villa, but at Liverpool Stewart struggled with just three goals from 53+12 appearances, his debut being against Sunderland at Anfield in August 2011. He did score in the penalty shoot-out as Liverpool beat Cardiff in the final of the 2012 League Cup in which he was named 'Man of the Match' when he was a teammate of Jordan Henderson. Later the same season, he played in the FA Cup final as Liverpool lost to Chelsea.

Downing went on to play for West Ham United (66+3/7), Middlesbrough again (126+27/9) winning promotion in 2017, before joining Blackburn Rovers under Boro legend Tony Mowbray who had been WBA manager on the day Downing debuted for Sunderland.

For England, Downing won 35 full caps, debuting as a 20-year-old against the Netherlands at Villa Park in February 2005 with his last cap coming in November 2014 as Scotland were beaten at Celtic Park. He never scored for England at full level, but did make three appearances as a sub at the 2006 FIFA World Cup finals in Germany and was a squad member - without playing - at Euro 2012.

## DOWSEY, John (Jack)

**POSITION:** Inside-right
**BIRTHPLACE:** Hunwick, Co Durham
**DATE OF BIRTH:** 11/04/1905 - 27/10/1942
**HEIGHT:** 5' 9" **WEIGHT:** 10st 8lbs
**SIGNED FROM:** Carlisle United, 20/11/1927
**DEBUT:** v Bury, H, 11/02/1928
**LAST MATCH:** v Birmingham, H, 29/09/1928
**MOVED TO:** Notts County, 15/02/1929
**TEAMS:** Hunwick Villa, Willington, Newcastle United, West Ham United, Carlisle United, Sunderland, Notts County, Northampton Town, Nuneaton Town
**SAFC TOTALS:** 11 appearances / 1 goal

**Jack Dowsey met a sorry end, reportedly found hanging in the stable of the Red Lion Pub he was assistant manager of in Costock, Nottinghamshire when he was just 37. Having caught the eye in local soccer (where his brother Joe captained Willington), Newcastle United signed Jack as an amateur in March 1924, making him a professional three months later.**

He played three times for the Magpies, debuting against Spurs at St James' in November 1925 and holding his place for the next two games at Cardiff and West Brom. Mainly employed as a reserve on Tyneside, he scored 54 times in two seasons as he helped Newcastle to win the North Eastern League before he was sold to West Ham United for £250 in May 1926.

The Hammers gave Jack a single game on the right-wing in the third game of the season at (Sheffield) Wednesday, but retained his registration when allowing him to link up with Carlisle United the following August. Dowsey played for the Cumbrians in their last season before being admitted to the Football League. Their first-team played in the North Eastern League he had excelled in with Newcastle and he evidently impressed against Sunderland (who romped away with the NEL title that season) as they signed him in November. The fee of £125 had to be paid to West Ham as they held his league registration form.

Jack got off to a good start with Sunderland, getting good write ups in the local press for his debut and scoring in his second game as Portsmouth were beaten 5-3 at Fratton Park. However, it would be his only goal in nine games that season and there would be just two more appearances the following season, coincidentally against the same clubs he played his first two games against.

By February he was sold, moving to Notts County in a £500 double deal with Ike McGorian. With his second set of Magpies, Dowsey played 103 league games, helping them to the Division Three South title in 1931. In November of that year he moved on to Northampton for whom he made 95 appearances, by now playing at wing-half. He stayed there until the summer of 1934 when he made his final football move to Nuneaton where he played as a centre-half in the Birmingham & District League.

## DOYLE, Callum Craig

**POSITION:** Centre-back
**BIRTHPLACE:** Manchester
**DATE OF BIRTH:** 03/10/2003
**HEIGHT:** 6' 0" **WEIGHT:** 13st 3lbs
**SIGNED FROM:** Manchester City, 16/07/2021, on loan
**DEBUT:** v Wigan Athletic, H, 07/08/2021
**LAST MATCH:** v Wycombe Wanderers, N, 21/05/2022
**MOVED TO:** Manchester City, 25/05/2022, end of loan
**TEAMS:** Manchester City, Sunderland (L), Coventry City (L) (to June 2022)
**INTERNATIONAL:** England Under 19
**SAFC TOTALS:** 34+10 appearances / 1 goal

**Just 17 when he arrived on loan from Manchester City, Doyle debuted on the opening day of the 2021-22 campaign and quickly established himself as a calm and composed central defender. Already an England Under 18, a first Under 19 cap arrived early into his time at Sunderland when he played in a 2-0 win over Italy at St George's Park on 2 September 2021, a second appearance following four days later against Germany at the same venue.**

Doyle's first move away from his home city came after he had made 12 appearances for Manchester City Under 23s as they took the PL2 title in a season in which Doyle also played 14 games for the Under 18s as well as playing against Lincoln and Tranmere in the Papa John's Trophy which was won by SAFC. At Sunderland he played regularly, particularly in the first part of the season and signed off with substitute appearances in all three games as promotion was won via the Play-Offs in 2022. During the summer he joined Coventry on loan.

## DOYLE, Stephen Charles (Steve)

**POSITION:** Midfielder
**BIRTHPLACE:** Port Talbot, Glamorgan
**DATE OF BIRTH:** 02/06/1958
**HEIGHT:** 5' 9" **WEIGHT:** 11st 9lbs
**SIGNED FROM:** Huddersfield Town, 15/09/1986
**DEBUT:** v Ipswich Town, A, 20/09/1986
**LAST MATCH:** v West Bromwich Albion, A, 06/05/1989
**MOVED TO:** Hull City, 11/08/1989
**TEAMS:** Preston North End, Huddersfield Town, Sunderland, Hull City, Rochdale, Chorley
**INTERNATIONAL:** Wales Under 21
**SAFC TOTALS:** 114+1 appearances / 2 goals

**Never a popular player with supporters frustrated by his limitations, nonetheless, Steve Doyle was remarkably consistent in his three seasons at the club, making 36, 37 and 42 appearances. Doyle caught Lawrie McMenemy's eye playing against Sunderland on the opening day of the 1986-87 season for Huddersfield and after four more games for the Terriers was sold by future Sunderland manager Mick Buxton for £60,000.**

Doyle came into a struggling side that slipped into the third division for the first time, but played his part in ensuring immediate promotion and was a sub at Wembley in the 1988 League Centenary tournament against Wigan (a shortened unofficial game not included in official appearances). Promotion with Sunderland was one of three promotions Doyle won from the third tier, also going up with Preston in 1978 and Huddersfield in 1983 (briefly playing alongside former Sunderland winger Roy Greenwood).

Including one sub appearance, Steve played exactly 100 league games for Sunderland, almost 200 for Preston - where he had been the club's youngest-ever debutant, over 150 for Huddersfield, almost 50 for Hull and over 100 for Rochdale - where he played alongside Peter Reid's brother Shaun, before being released by Mick Docherty - in a career total of 626 league appearances.

He might have been a Newcastle player, having gone on trial with fellow PNE release John Anderson in 1982 only for the Magpies to take the Irishman, but not the Welshman. Doyle won two caps for his country at Under 21 level, one as an overage player and without winning a full cap was called up for a senior international squad in February 1987 for a game with Russia in Swansea while with Sunderland. He went on to become player/coach at Chorley eventually managing the club between January and April 1987. He had moved to Chorley as assistant to Dave Sutton, his old Huddersfield and Rochdale teammate.

## DUNCAN, Cameron

**BIRTHPLACE:** Shotts, Lanarkshire

**DATE OF BIRTH:** 04/08/1965 - 02/05/2017

**HEIGHT:** 6' 1" **WEIGHT:** 11st 0lbs

**SIGNED FROM:** Fir Park Boys Club, 15/12/1983

**DEBUT:** v Grimsby Town, A, 22/03/1986

**LAST MATCH:** v York City, A, 03/09/1986

**MOVED TO:** Motherwell, 20/05/1987, following release from SAFC

**TEAMS:** Fir Park Boys Club, Sunderland, Motherwell, Partick Thistle, Ayr United, Albion Rovers

**INTERNATIONAL:** Scotland Youth

**SAFC TOTALS:** 3 appearances / 0 goals

**Cameron Duncan saved a penalty on his only league appearance for Sunderland, but was only given two further games in the League Cup the following season.**

Cammy came to Sunderland after impressing on trial in a youth game at Sheffield United in November 1983, but returned to Scotland with Motherwell for whom he played 69 games in total, His quality persuaded Partick Thistle to pay a club record £60,000 for Duncan's signature on 20 October 1989.

He went on to make 56 appearances for the Jags before enjoying a six-year spell with Ayr United where he signed for his old Roker teammate George Burley and played in 148 league games after joining in an exchange deal for Sammy Johnston in March 1991. Duncan completed his career with ten more games for Albion Rovers, the last at Cowdenbeath in February 1997. Cameron passed away from cancer at the age of 51.

## DUNLOP, William (Billy)

**POSITION:** Right-half

**BIRTHPLACE:** Annbank, Ayrshire

**DATE OF BIRTH:** 16/08/1869 - 25/05/1960

**HEIGHT:** 5' 6½" **WEIGHT:** 11st 6lbs

**SIGNED FROM:** Annbank, 06/01/1893

**DEBUT:** v Wednesday, H, 28/01/1893

**LAST MATCH:** v Burnley, H, 10/12/1898

**MOVED TO:** Rangers, 30/06/1899

**TEAMS:** Annbank, Sunderland, Rangers, Partick Thistle, Annbank

**SAFC TOTALS:** 148 appearances / 6 goals

**A league title-winner with Sunderland in 1892-93 and 1894-95, Dunlop played in the last match at Newcastle Road, the first season at Roker Park and was the uncle of the legendary Jamie Millar.**

A coal-miner before becoming a professional footballer, Dunlop played five games as he helped Sunderland to retain the league title in 1893. Two years later, he played in 18 of the 30 league fixtures as 'The Team of All The Talents' won the title again with Dunlop in the side as SAFC were proclaimed world champions after a challenge match with Scottish champions Hearts.

In 1899, he returned to Scotland with Rangers, making six league appearances in a season with the Ibrox club before signing for Partick Thistle on 4 June 1900. Billy debuted for the Jags in a friendly away to Rangers who he had just left. Just nine days later on 25 August 1900 he played the last of his three games for Thistle at St Mirren. He then returned to Annback both in terms of playing and going back to mining.

Often known as Wullie in Scotland, Dunlop's brother Walter played for Annbank, Sheffield United and Darwen, although he never made a league appearance for the Blades.

## DUNN, Barry

**POSITION:** Winger

**BIRTHPLACE:** Sunderland, Co Durham

**DATE OF BIRTH:** 15/02/1952

**HEIGHT:** 5' 8½" **WEIGHT:** 10st 5lbs

**SIGNED FROM:** Blue Star, 27/09/1979

**DEBUT:** v Preston North End, H, 29/09/1979

**LAST MATCH:** v Norwich City, A, 22/11/1980

**MOVED TO:** Preston North End, 03/10/1981

**TEAMS:** Silksworth CW, Bishop Auckland, Tow Law, Gretna, Koksijdes Blue Star, Sunderland, Preston North End, Darlington, Gretna, Humbledon Plains Farm

**SAFC TOTALS:** 18+7 appearances / 2 goals

**Barry Dunn was a wiry winger similar in style to Andy Welsh who came to Wearside a quarter of a century later. All but three of Barry's appearances came in the 1979-80 season as he helped Sunderland to win promotion to the top flight contributing a couple of goals that earned vital away points. Having come out of the Wearside League to sign for Sunderland Dunn had done well to be so successful in Division Two and got three top-flight appearances, two as sub and all away from home.**

Not only had Barry come from non-league football, but did so as a mature player of 27 rather than as a youngster. He had played in Belgium and was still registered with Koksijdes when Sunderland signed him. Reportedly £5,000 of the £8,000 fee went to the Belgian club with the rest destined for Blue Star who he had scored for at Wembley in the FA Vase final in 1978.

On leaving Roker Park, Barry was bought by Tommy Docherty at Preston. Debuting at Bristol City in October 1981 he played eight successive games scoring in the last of them at Wimbledon when he was a teammate of future Sunderland midfielder Steve Doyle. These would be Dunn's only league appearances for the Deepdale outfit who cancelled his contract the following March.

The following summer Barry signed for Darlington where Billy Elliott and George Herd were in charge. Barry scored in both of his first two games and netted a brace against Northampton shortly before his 16th and final league appearance arrived between Christmas and the New Year. He also got to play in the League (Milk) Cup against Peterborough who he could have signed for as a 21-year old only for the proposed move to collapse. Some six years after his time with the Quakers, Barry resurfaced playing locally for Humbledon and Plains Farm.

After retiring, Barry returned to the game working for the Press Association from 2001 being a familiar figure in the press rooms and players' tunnels at both Sunderland and Newcastle. In December 2020, his son Davis Keillor-Dunn played against Sunderland in the Football League Trophy for Oldham. Keillor-Dunn had also played for Ross County, Falkirk (on loan) and Wrexham.

## DUNNE, Cieran James

**POSITION:** Midfielder/left-back

**BIRTHPLACE:** Falkirk, Stirlingshire

**DATE OF BIRTH:** 08/02/2000

**HEIGHT:** 5' 10½" **WEIGHT:** 10st 10lbs

**SIGNED FROM:** Falkirk, 23/08/2019

**DEBUT:** v Fleetwood Town, A, 10/11/2020

**LAST MATCH:** v Oldham Athletic, H, 01/12/2021

**MOVED TO:** Released, 25/05/2022

**TEAMS:** Hutchison Vale, Forth Valley Football Academy, Falkirk, Sunderland, Cove Rangers (to August 2022)

**SAFC TOTALS:** 1+1 appearances / 0 goals

**Dunne's debut was short lived as he had to go off with a dislocated shoulder four minutes after coming on as a sub on a night where he was one of six debutants.**

He had come to prominence with Falkirk for whom he debuted at home to St Mirren in October 2017 as a sub and was given a first start at Queen of the South a week later. Cieran's five appearances for the Bairns included two as sub and all came in consecutive games before he joined Sunderland. He had an unsuccessful trial with Doncaster Rovers and as of mid-July 2022 was seeking a new club.

## DUNNE, James Gerard (Jimmy)

**POSITION:** Defender

**BIRTHPLACE:** Drogheda

**DATE OF BIRTH:** 19/10/1997

**HEIGHT:** 6' 0" **WEIGHT:** 11st 11lbs

**SIGNED FROM:** Burnley, 09/01/2019, on loan

**DEBUT:** v Scunthorpe United, A, 19/01/2019

**LAST MATCH:** v Portsmouth, H, 11/05/2019

**MOVED TO:** Burnley, 31/05/2019, end of loan

**TEAMS:** St Kevin's Boys, Manchester United, Burnley, Barrow (L), Accrington Stanley (L), Hearts (L), Sunderland (L), Fleetwood Town (L), QPR (to July 2022)

**INTERNATIONAL:** Republic of Ireland Under 21

**SAFC TOTALS:** 13+1 appearances / 1 goal

**Young defender Jimmy Dunne gave his all during a loan spell with Sunderland for whom he was twice an unused sub at Wembley, the second time in the 2019 League One Play-Off final after making his final appearance for the club in the semi-final first leg against Portsmouth. Sunderland were one of five loans he was sent on by Burnley for whom he scored on his Premier League debut at Leicester in September 2020.**

As a nine-year-old, Dunne became associated with Manchester United's academy, moving to Burnley at the age of 18. Loaned to National League Barrow, he was sent off on his fourth appearance at Solihull Moors in August 2017, but got a couple of goals in 21 games where his progress was such that mid-way through that season he stepped up to League Two where he helped Accrington Stanley to the League Two title, making 20 appearances, albeit he was sent off on the last of these.

With Hearts, one of his two goals came away to Rangers whilst he played against Celtic in front of over 60,000 at Murrayfield in a Scottish League Cup semi-final. Three months later, Jimmy was wearing the red and white of Sunderland, soon scoring in a 1-1 draw at Oxford. After a final loan at Fleetwood, he was transferred to QPR in July 2021.

Capped at Under 21 level by the Republic of Ireland for the first time against Iceland in March 2018, as of July 2022, he awaited a full cap although he had been selected for senior squads.

## DUNS, Leonard (Len)

**POSITION:** Outside-right

**BIRTHPLACE:** Newcastle, Northumberland

**DATE OF BIRTH:** 28/09/1916 - 20/04/1989

**HEIGHT:** 5' 8" **WEIGHT:** 11st 8lbs

**SIGNED FROM:** Newcastle West End, 04/09/1933

**DEBUT:** v Portsmouth, A, 02/11/1935

**LAST MATCH:** v Preston North End, H, 22/03/1952

**MOVED TO:** Retired, 31/05/1952

**TEAMS:** West End Albion, Newcastle West End, Sunderland, Aldershot (WW2 Guest), Bristol City (WW2 Guest), Brentford (WW2 Guest), Reading, (WW2 Guest), Newcastle United (WW2 Guest), Notts County (WW2 Guest), WBA (WW2 Guest), Lovells Athletic (WW2 Guest), Wrexham (WW2 Guest), Shrewsbury Town (WW2 Guest)

**SAFC TOTALS:** 245 appearances / 54 goal

**Sunderland's right winger in the 1937 FA Cup final, Len Duns' shirt and medal from that match are on permanent display at the Stadium of Light courtesy of supporter Peter Coates. Duns was an outstanding servant to Sunderland where he was one of the generation of players whose total of appearances would have been far greater, but for losing six years when he would have been at his peak due to World War Two. He amassed over 100 league appearances on each side of the war during which he served with the Royal Artillery.**

Duns was just 20 when the cup was won with only Bobby Gurney scoring more than his five goals in the cup run. That 1936-37 campaign was by far Len's best for goalscoring as he also contributed 16 in the league, a tally that included two in a remarkable 5-5 draw at Middlesbrough.

Len came to Sunderland early in the month of his 17th birthday and debuted shortly after turning 19. This was during the title winning term of 1935-36 when he played 17 times in the league, two of his five goals coming on his home debut against Preston who would be both his Wembley opponents the following season and also on his final game almost 17 years later.

The winger appeared in a further 30 war-time games for Sunderland including the three league games in the abandoned 1939-40 season. During the war, he also 'Guested' for numerous clubs including Newcastle United for whom he scored eight times in 20 games beginning with a debut at Hartlepools United on 21 October 1939. A Tynesider, he had been rejected by Newcastle as a boy. Len was also a keen cricketer scoring 1884 runs as an opening batsman for Benwell Hill CC who he had a long association with, only broken for a short spell when he was the professional at Dawdon CW. He captained Benwell in 1954 and 1955 and ran a fruit and veg shop in Blandford Street in Sunderland.

## DYCE, Tyrese

**POSITION:** Left-back/Left-midfield

**BIRTHPLACE:** Birmingham, West Midlands

**DATE OF BIRTH:** 19/04/2001

**HEIGHT:** 5' 11" **WEIGHT:** 13st 1lb

**SIGNED FROM:** Released by WBA, 01/07/2021

**DEBUT:** v Manchester United Under 21s, H, 13/10/2021

**LAST MATCH:** v Oldham Athletic, H, 01/12/2021

**MOVED TO:** Released, 25/05/2022

**TEAMS:** West Bromwich Albion, Sunderland, Spennymoor (L)

**INTERNATIONAL:** England Under 19

**SAFC TOTALS:** 1+1 appearances / 1 goal

**A scorer on his first-team debut against Manchester United Under 21s in the Football League (Papa John's) Trophy, Dyce came from WBA where he came through the academy system and captained the Baggies under 18s.**

Released by Albion, he played as a triallist for Sunderland in the Premier League 2 Play-Off semi-final victory at the end of the 2020-21 season before joining the Lads in the summer, but only ever playing in the Football League Trophy.

## EDEN, William (Billy)

**POSITION:** Right-winger

**BIRTHPLACE:** Stockton

**DATE OF BIRTH:** 01/07/1905 - November 1993

**HEIGHT:** 5' 7" **WEIGHT:** 10st 4lbs

**SIGNED FROM:** Darlington, 10/10/1929

**DEBUT:** v Newcastle United, H, 19/10/1929

**LAST MATCH:** v Liverpool, A, 26/03/1932

**MOVED TO:** Darlington, 24/11/1932

**TEAMS:** Loftus Albion, Darlington, Sunderland, Darlington, Tranmere Rovers, New Brighton (WW2 Guest), Crewe Alexandra (WW2 Guest)

**SAFC TOTALS:** 71 appearances / 21 goals

**At his best, winger Eden led full-backs a merry dance, appropriately enough, as Billy was a member of a dance band during the early thirties. He effectively cost Sunderland £900 as they recouped £500 of the £1400 they had paid Darlington for him when he was re-sold to the Quakers three years after coming to Roker Park.**

Eleven goals in 30 games for the Feethams club attracted Sunderland's attention with the Wearsiders thrusting him immediately into the deep end with a debut in a narrow derby victory. Billy kept his place for another three games in the autumn before Eden blossomed in the spring as he played the final 14 games, notching six league goals including four in a three-game purple-patch.

Billy's first full season was his best, his ten goals in 30 league games including two in a 5-0 hammering of Newcastle. He also scored before St James Park's record crowd - St James Exeter that is, as his second cup goal of the season took Sunderland through to the semi-final in which he played against Birmingham. However, in his third term, Eden lost his place to Jimmy Temple although he did go out with a bang, scoring the equaliser as Sunderland came from behind to defeat Liverpool at Anfield.

Following his second spell at Darlington, Billy moved to Merseyside in March 1935 with Tranmere with whom he won Division Three North in 1937-38, by this stage of his career appearing on the left-wing as well as the right. Following his retirement, Billy did what so many of his contemporaries did and became a publican.

## EDGAR, Daniel (Dan)

**POSITION:** Left-half

**BIRTHPLACE:** Jarrow

**DATE OF BIRTH:** 03/04/1910 - 23/03/1991

**HEIGHT:** 5' 9½" **WEIGHT:** 11st 5lbs

**SIGNED FROM:** Jarrow St Bedes, 05/06/1930 and Walsall, 05/05/1931

**DEBUT:** v Bolton Wanderers, H, 19/03/1932

**LAST MATCH:** v Blackburn Rovers, A, 20/10/1934

**MOVED TO:** Walsall, 27/11/1930 and Nottingham Forest, 05/06/1935

**TEAMS:** Jarrow St Bede's, Sunderland, Walsall, Sunderland, Nottingham Forest

**SAFC TOTALS:** 46 appearances / 0 goals

**Edgar did not debut until his second spell with Sunderland having gained some experience with nine league appearances with Walsall between his two stints at Roker Park. His first run of games for Sunderland saw five victories in seven appearances in the spring of 1932, finishing with a win at Newcastle.**

Despite missing a big chunk of the middle of the following season through injury, it was Edgar's best campaign as he played a total of 37 times including an appearance before the club's record official attendance of 75,118 for a cup quarter-final replay with Derby.

At Nottingham Forest, he played 104 games over three seasons with a best of 43 games in 1936-37. The last of his Forest appearances came against Southampton in March 1938 after which a cartilage injury ended his career just before his 28th birthday. The only goal of Dan's career came in a home win for Forest over Swansea Town in October 1937. After retiring from football Edgar worked as a general labourer having been employed in the shipyards before becoming a footballer.

## EDGAR, James

**POSITION:** Outside-right

**BIRTHPLACE:** Birtley, Co Durham

**DATE OF BIRTH:** 16/10/1880 - 31/08/1967

**HEIGHT:** 5' 6" **WEIGHT:** 10st 0lbs

**SIGNED FROM:** Birtley 08/12/1905

**DEBUT:** v Bolton Wanderers, A, 17/02/1906

**LAST MATCH:** v Manchester City, A, 21/04/1906

**MOVED TO:** Released, 01/05/1906

**TEAMS:** Birtley, Sunderland, Birtley, Hebburn Argyle, Birtley

**SAFC TOTALS:** 2 appearances / 0 goals

**James Edgar was in his mid-twenties when his performances in the Northern Alliance prompted Sunderland to sit up and take notice. After playing for Sunderland 'A' in a trial game Edgar was signed up and given opportunities in a couple of away games at Bolton and Manchester City.**

As a winger, the games largely passed him by as the two heaviest league defeats of the season (6-2 and 5-1) were suffered and he was duly released at the end of the season. Edgar returned to local football and worked as a colliery blacksmith outside the game.

## EDWARDS, Akenhaton Carlos

**POSITION:** Right-winger

**BIRTHPLACE:** Patna, Trinidad

**DATE OF BIRTH:** 24/10/1978

**HEIGHT:** 5' 11" **WEIGHT:** 11st 2lbs

**SIGNED FROM:** Luton Town, 03/01/2007

**DEBUT:** v Preston North End, A, 06/01/2007

**LAST MATCH:** v Norwich City, A, 24/08/2009

**MOVED TO:** Ipswich Town, 01/09/2009

**TEAMS:** Patna United, Queen's Park CC (Trinidad), Defence Force, Wrexham, Luton Town, Sunderland, Wolves (L), Ipswich Town, Millwall, MA Pau All Stars, Central FC, Woodbridge Town, Bury Town (to June 2022)

**INTERNATIONAL:** Trinidad & Tobago

**SAFC TOTALS:** 37+19 appearances / 5 goals

**Magnificent in the 2006-07 promotion season when he arrived in January, Carlos was a quality winger who had the added bonus of possessing a venomous shot. His late winner on the night promotion was all but mathematically sealed against Burnley was the best goal in the opening decade at the Stadium of Light and arguably the best goal seen there in its opening quarter of a century.**

That spectacular strike against the Clarets was one of a series of screamers Edwards scored that season, others at Southampton and Birmingham also being tremendous. All of Edwards' five goals for Sunderland came in the 15 games he played as part of the promotion push. In only one of those 15 games did he taste defeat as his arrival corresponded with a surge in form that saw Sunderland sweep to the title.

In the Premier League, Carlos did not have such a good time. He was called upon only 13 times in 2007-08 and the following year found 16 of his 22 Premier League appearances were off the bench in a season where he was also loaned to Wolves. In his final season - and under his third manager at the club in Steve Bruce - Edwards was an unused sub in the first two games, was played out of position in a big League (Carling) Cup win at Norwich and was then allowed to move on.

His time at Sunderland was short-lived, but his impact in helping the Lads to promotion was stunning and was duly recognised by his inclusion in the PFA Championship Team of the Year. Edwards was also twice included in PFA Team of the Year selections with Wrexham where he was the club's Player of the Year in 2002-03.

Before coming to Sunderland he had won promotion from the fourth tier with Wrexham in 2003, a season in which he won the middle one of three Welsh Cups with the club with whom he went on to win the Football League Trophy in 2004-05. In that final, Wrexham defeated Southend United at the Millennium Stadium in Cardiff.

After leaving Sunderland, Carlos became Player of the Year at Ipswich Town in 2011-12 in a season where he played alongside Grant Leadbitter, Daryl Murphy, Michael Chopra; who was the club's top-scorer, and Tommy Smith who came to Sunderland in 2020, but did not play.

Internationally, Edwards won 92 caps for Trinidad & Tobago scoring four times, three of his goals coming while on Sunderland's books - one of these being in a World Cup qualifying game against Costa Rica at the Dwight Yorke Stadium. Three of his appearances came at the 2006 FIFA World Cup finals in Germany where he played the full games against Sweden, England and Paraguay.

Always a dedicated professional, in 2021 Edwards was still playing in the Isthmian League for Bury Town.

## EJARIA, Oviemuno Dominic Okpanachi (Ovie)

**POSITION:** Midfielder

**BIRTHPLACE:** Southwark, London

**DATE OF BIRTH:** 18/11/1997

**HEIGHT:** 6' 1" **WEIGHT:** 11st 11lbs

**SIGNED FROM:** Liverpool, 31/01/2018, on loan

**DEBUT:** v Ipswich Town, H, 03/02/2018

**LAST MATCH:** v Wolverhampton Wanderers, H, 06/05/2018

**MOVED TO:** Liverpool, 07/05/2018, end of loan

**TEAMS:** Arsenal, Liverpool, Sunderland (L), Rangers, Reading (to June 2022)

**INTERNATIONAL:** England Under 21

**SAFC TOTALS:** 9+2 appearances / 1 goal

**As might be expected of a loanee from Liverpool with England youth honours, Ovie Ejaria was a player with evident ability, but he came into a Sunderland side which was struggling badly and was not able to significantly affect games. He did sign off with a goal on the final day of the season, but it was a day when the pressure was off as already crowned champions Wolves lost to already relegated Sunderland.**

The previous summer, Ejaria had been part of the England squad that won the FIFA Under 20 World Cup. He appeared in two of the seven games, coming on as a sub in the opening match v Argentina and playing against host nation South Korea. At Sunderland, he played alongside another loanee, Jake Clarke-Salter, who had also been part of that triumphant England team. Ejaria is also eligible to be selected by Nigeria.

As a boy, Londoner Ejaria spent nine years as part of the Arsenal academy before switching to Liverpool for whom he made his first-team bow in a League Cup game at Derby on 20 September 2016. In total, Ovie played eight times for Liverpool including two substitute Premier League appearances, all of which were made before coming to Wearside.

Following his loan at Sunderland, a second loan took him under the wing of Steven Gerrard at Rangers for whom he played 28 times. He scored twice including a Europa League goal in Russia against FC Ufa on a dramatic night as Rangers edged a crucial game despite having only nine men. A third loan took Ejaria to Reading who he eventually signed for in the summer of 2020 for a reported £3.5m

## EL KARKOURI, Talal

**POSITION:** Defender

**BIRTHPLACE:** Casablanca, Morocco

**DATE OF BIRTH:** 08/07/1976

**HEIGHT:** 6' 2" **WEIGHT:** 12st 10lbs

**SIGNED FROM:** Paris St Germain, 31/01/2003, on loan

**DEBUT:** v Tottenham Hotspur, A, 08/02/2003

**LAST MATCH:** v WBA, H, 19/04/2003

**MOVED TO:** Paris St Germain, 12//05/2003, end of loan

**TEAMS:** Raja Casablanca, Ittihad Tanger (L), Servette, Paris St Germain, Aris Salonika (L), Sunderland (L), Charlton Athletic, Al Gharafa (L), Qatar CC, Umm - Salal

**INTERNATIONAL:** Morocco

**SAFC TOTALS:** 8+1 appearances / 0 goals

**Brought in by Howard Wilkinson, Morocco international El Karkouri operated as a holding midfielder on his debut at Tottenham, but was swiftly moved into the back four as Wilkinson attempted to shore up a porous defence. All of Talal's appearances came in consecutive games, but he was powerless to prevent the scenario where not a single point was garnered in his time at the club.**

Despite the terrible run Sunderland were on while he was at the club, El Karkouri was no mug. The following season he won the Coupe de France playing in the final for PSG alongside Lorik Cana as Chateauroux were beaten in the final. In that campaign, Talal also played in the final of the African Cup of Nations as his country narrowly lost to Tunisia when he was a teammate of Marouane Chamakh who later came close to joining Sunderland when Steve Bruce was manager.

El Karkouri played 53 times for Morocco scoring six goals. After kicking-off his career in his home country he played in Switzerland before gaining Champions League and UEFA Cup experience as well as winning the French Cup with PSG with whom he also had a loan in Greek football as well as in England with Sunderland. Although his SAFC career was brief, he later spent three seasons in London with Charlton who paid £1m for him when they were in the Premier League. Talal went on to complete his playing days with three clubs in lucrative Qatar. At Charlton he made a total of 77+10 appearances, scoring eight goals.

## ELLIOT, Isaac Edmondson

**POSITION:** Full-back

**BIRTHPLACE:** Greystoke, Penrith, Cumberland

**DATE OF BIRTH:** 19/09/1862 - 30/03/1949

**SIGNED:** 1883

**DEBUT:** v Redcar, A, 08/11/1884

**LAST MATCH:** v Newcastle West End, A, 13/11/1886

**MOVED:** 1887

**TEAMS:** Sunderland

**INTERNATIONAL:** England Under 21

**SAFC TOTALS:** 2 appearances / 0 goals

**Hardly surprisingly, given the origins of the club as Sunderland and District Teachers' Association, Isaac Elliott was a schoolmaster whilst playing for Sunderland.**

Although the 'And District Teachers' Association' part of the club's name had long since been dropped when he appeared in the two early English Cup (Later known as the FA Cup) ties listed, his debut being in Sunderland's first-ever game in the competition. Elliott also played for Sunderland in friendly and challenge matches, but only his two English Cup games count as official appearances.

## ELLIOTT, David (Dave)

**POSITION:** Left-half

**BIRTHPLACE:** Tantobie, Co Durham

**DATE OF BIRTH:** 10/02/1945

**HEIGHT:** 5' 9" **WEIGHT:** 11st 10lbs

**SIGNED FROM:** Gateshead, 01/07/1961

**DEBUT:** v Derby County, H, 22/02/1964

**LAST MATCH:** v Aston Villa, A, 27/12/1966

**MOVED TO:** Newcastle United, 29/12/1966

**TEAMS:** Wallsend Corinthians, Gateshead, Sunderland, Newcastle United, Southend United, Newport County, Bangor City, Newport County, Caernarfon Town

**SAFC TOTALS:** 35+1 appearances / 0 goals

**Dave Elliott was still a teenager when he came into the side in the latter stages of the first-ever promotion season of 1963-64. Injury to Jimmy McNab enabled Elliott to come into a very settled side for eight successive appearances which included a derby at St James' and all three games of the epic FA Cup quarter-final with holders Manchester United.**

Never one to let the team down, nonetheless Elliott remained on the fringes of the side, only reaching double-figures in terms of games in one of his four first-team seasons. That was in 1965-66 when he played 14 times.

He moved to Newcastle between Christmas and New Year in 1966, debuting for the Magpies at Spurs just four days after his final game in red and white. Elliott did well at Newcastle, stiffening their midfield as he helped the Tynesiders to avoid relegation and go on to qualify for Europe whereupon he played in their first-ever European match against Feyenoord. That was one of 86+4 games he played for the St James' Park outfit for whom he scored four times as he kept the midfield ticking over in the manner to be expected of a player who gave up being a motor mechanic to become a footballer.

From January 1971 to April 1975, Dave threw in his lot with Southend United clocking up 194 games for the Shrimpers before becoming player/manager of Newport County, a post he held for 15 months. He stayed in Wales to have spells as player/manager of Bangor City and Caernarfon Town,

## ELLIOTT, Dave (Continued)

but in between returned to Newport to play and coach for his old Sunderland teammate Len Ashurst.

He also returned to Bangor for a second spell, this time simply managing the club from February 1981 to October 1984 in addition to linking up with Ashurst again as a coach at Cardiff City. As boss of Bangor, he led them as the first club from North Wales to play at Wembley as they met Northwich Victoria in the 1984 FA Trophy final, but as happened to his pal Len Ashurst with Sunderland a year later, Elliott's side lost the final in a season where they were also relegated, albeit they did not lose at Wembley, but in a replay at Stoke. Bangor numbered Spennymoor and Gateshead amongst the victims of their cup run.

Elliott opened a sports shop in Bangor called Dave Elliott Sports and remained in Wales after his retirement, daughter Louise becoming a BBC Wales TV and radio presenter.

Dave came from a sporting family; unusually both his parents played football (John had trials at Arsenal until injury cut short his prospects and Alice played for Lintz); his uncles George and Joe Hickman played for WBA and Aston Villa respectively in the 1920s. George also played cricket for Warwickshire and Durham.

## ELLIOTT, Robert James (Robbie)

**POSITION:** Defender

**BIRTHPLACE:** Gosforth, Northumberland

**DATE OF BIRTH:** 25/12/1973

**HEIGHT:** 5' 10" **WEIGHT:** 10st 12lbs

**SIGNED FROM:** Newcastle United, 05/08/2006

**DEBUT:** v Southend United, A, 19/08/2006

**LAST MATCH:** v Stoke City, A, 17/10/2006

**MOVED TO:** Leeds United, 02/01/2007

**TEAMS:** Wallsend Boys Club, Newcastle United, Bolton Wanderers, Newcastle United, Sunderland, Leeds United, Hartlepool United

**INTERNATIONAL:** England Under 21

**SAFC TOTALS:** 8 appearances / 0 goals

**Briefly at Sunderland in the period where Roy Keane took over from Niall Quinn, Elliott's debut came in a dismal defeat at Southend better remembered for an impressive first appearance by the former Barcelona B midfielder Arnau. Shortly afterwards, Elliott played in the first three games under Keane and after being dropped, quickly returned for what proved to be his final appearance at Stoke.**

On that occasion, his tackle resulted in a broken leg for Rory Delap who was on loan to the Potters from Sunderland. Robbie did later sit on the bench three times as an unused sub, but having initially joined Sunderland on a one-month contract, which had extended to the middle of the season, he swiftly moved on to Leeds.

Elliott had endured more than his fair share of his own injury problems. At his first professional club, Newcastle United, he had come back from a cruciate ligament injury as well as recovering from shin splints, while at Bolton he had broken a leg on his home debut and went on to be troubled by hernia and groin injuries. However, he did play a total of 85+18 times for the Trotters scoring seven times. He helped the club to win promotion to the Premier League in 2001 when he came on as a sub as Sam Allardyce's Bolton convincingly defeated David Moyes' Preston at the Millennium Stadium. A talented footballer, assured on the ball, Elliott played both at left-back and in midfield for Newcastle for whom he made a total of 165+23 appearances across two spells, scoring 12 times.

Following his brief spell on Wearside, Elliott had 6+2 games in half a season with Leeds United who finished bottom of the Championship as Roy Keane's Sunderland won it. Robbie then returned to the north east with Hartlepool where he spent the 2007-08 season in League One, playing 15+1 games before retiring. That summer he returned to St James' Park as Fitness and Conditioning coach, a role he fulfilled for a year before becoming a freelance fitness coach on both sides of the Atlantic working with the US national team following the completion of a sports science degree. In 2012, he established his own Robbie Elliott Foundation.

Elliott won two England caps at Under 21 level during 1995-96, the second of these at Middlesbrough's Riverside Stadium against Austria.

## ELLIOTT, Shaun

**POSITION:** Centre-back

**BIRTHPLACE:** Haydon Bridge, Northumberland

**DATE OF BIRTH:** 26/01/1957

**HEIGHT:** 6' 0" **WEIGHT:** 11st 6lbs

**SIGNED FROM:** Haydon Bridge, 01/07/1974

**DEBUT:** v Wrexham, A, 12/01/1977

**LAST MATCH:** v Stoke City, H, 03/05/1986

**MOVED TO:** Norwich City, 22/08/1986

**TEAMS:** Haydon Bridge, Sunderland, Seattle Sounders (L), Norwich City, Blackpool, Colchester United, Albany Capitals (L), Gateshead, Bishop Auckland, Whitley Bay, Durham City

**INTERNATIONAL:** England B

**SAFC TOTALS:** 363+5 appearances / 11 goals

**Shaun Elliott also played in midfield, but always saw himself as a centre-back and quite rightly, because while he was such a good player he was decent in midfield, he was undoubtedly best at centre-back. This was especially the case when he was paired with Jeff Clarke who he had a partnership with that was as good as the celebrated attacking partnerships of the likes of Gates and Gabbiadini or Quinn and Phillips.**

Having played briefly for Newcastle United as a youth team centre-forward, Shaun soon came to Sunderland as a defender. His arrival in the first-team saw him debut in the same game as fellow youngster Kevin Arnott. Combining with Gary Rowell, who had already broken into the team, the trio were dubbed, 'Charlie's Angels' with reference to a popular TV programme of the day and Sunderland's chief scout Charlie Ferguson. Elliott, Arnott and Rowell were highly influential in transforming the performances of manager Jimmy Adamson's struggling team in 1976-77, although in the final analysis Sunderland were controversially relegated.

Shaun established himself in the side to the extent that when Sunderland returned to the top flight, he missed just a single game, as he had the year before when promotion was missed by a whisker. Elliott's consistency carried on as he played in 38 of the 42 league games as Sunderland stayed up in 1980-81 and he missed just six games the following season. Half of these were the first three fixtures as his summer spell in the USA with Seattle overlapped the English season. He scored four goals in 21 games for the Sounders.

In all, Elliott played 159 times in the top flight across five seasons until Sunderland were relegated again in 1984-85. During the same season he played seven times in the run to the League (Milk) Cup final only for him to miss the final where he would have been captain due to suspension. After one more season at Sunderland, he was moved on by Lawrie McMenemy, signing for the 1985 League Cup final conquerors Norwich.

Having been largely injury free during his time at Sunderland Elliott struggled with niggling injuries at Carrow Road, playing just 39 games across two seasons, scoring twice. In August 1988, he moved on to Blackpool in Division Three where as a teammate of Barry Siddall, he returned to regular football playing a total of 48 times in his first season as the Tangerines narrowly avoided relegation. He stayed at Bloomfield Road until December 1990 when he moved to Colchester, by which time he had been relegated with the Seasiders for whom he totalled 79+1 games without scoring, his final appearance coming at Cardiff in March 1990.

Signed for Colchester by Ian Atkins for £7,000, Elliott debuted for the U's at Merthyr Tydfil in the Conference which he helped Colchester to win in his first full season after being runner-up in the season he arrived. As with his time with Seattle, Shaun spent one of his summers as a Colchester player in the USA, making 13 appearances for Albany Capitals in the summer of 1991. He returned to the north east with Bishop Auckland after 56 starts plus ten games as sub for Colchester for whom he found the back of the net once. In March 1995, he moved on to Whitley Bay before finally spending the following season with Durham City.

In the early 2000s, Shaun returned to Norwich to work as a car salesman and while he remained in East Anglia, Elliott remained a staunch supporter of Sunderland. At international level he deserved a full cap, but had to make do with three caps at 'B' level. His international debut came at Roker Park against Spain in March of the 1980 promotion season when Alan Kennedy was amongst his teammates. The following October he played in England's next 'B' international against the USA at Old Trafford when Peter Barnes was a teammate, while his final cap came in the return with Spain in Granada in March 1981. In October 1980, Shaun's younger brother Scott signed for Sunderland on associate schoolboy terms, but unfortunately did not progress as Shaun had.

## ELLIOTT, Stephen William

**POSITION:** Forward

**BIRTHPLACE:** Dublin, Ireland

**DATE OF BIRTH:** 06/01/1984

**HEIGHT:** 5' 8" **WEIGHT:** 11st 8lbs

**SIGNED FROM:** Manchester City, 01/06/2004

**DEBUT:** v Coventry City, A, 07/08/2004

**LAST MATCH:** v Colchester United, A, 21/04/2007

**MOVED TO:** Wolverhampton Wanderers, 19/07/2007

**TEAMS:** Belvedere, Stella Maris, Manchester City, Sunderland, Wolves, Preston North End, Norwich City (L), Hearts, Coventry City, Carlisle United, Shelbourne, Drogheda United, Morpeth Town

**INTERNATIONAL:** Republic of Ireland

**SAFC TOTALS:** 59+29 appearances / 23 goals

**Known as 'Sleeves' due to the frequency with which he would shout 'Sleeves up', Stephen made his name at Sunderland where he won two promotions and burst onto the international scene. After two substitute appearances in the Premiership for Manchester City, where he was a teammate of Claudio Reyna, Elliott was brought to Sunderland by former Republic of Ireland manager Mick McCarthy.**

The gaffer had been impressed by him at international junior levels, indeed Elliott had scored a hat-trick on his full Under 21 debut against Poland in August 2003. Sleeves came within one goal of top scorer Marcus Stewart as promotion was won in his first season, 15 of his 16 goals coming in the league.

Restricted to 11+4 Premiership appearances as relegation with a record low points followed, Elliott's two goals were both crackers against the Uniteds of Manchester and Newcastle. He did not play many more games the following season as promotion was won again, this time often being used on the right of midfield, scoring five goals as a second championship medal was collected.

Before getting the chance to return to the top flight following his second promotion with Sunderland, Stephen signed for McCarthy again, this time at Wolves. There would be just over a year at Molineux before he moved on to Preston North End after 19+13 appearances in which he scored five times as Wolves missed out on the Play-Offs on goal difference.

At Deepdale, once again he was frequently used as an impact sub, 24 of his 53 games seeing him come off the bench, with seven goals scored. During his time at Preston, Sleeves was loaned to Norwich where he scored twice in 4+6 games as he helped the Canaries to the League One title. More success came Stephen's way after an August 2010 move to Hearts which reunited him with Kevin Kyle.

A first goal came in a derby win over Hibs on his first start while in his second season he enjoyed another victory over Hibs, this time to the tune of 5-1 in the Scottish Cup final. He also tasted Europa League football with the Edinburgh club. In two years in Scottish football, Sleeves scored eleven times in 47+18 appearances.

In 2012-13, he had a season with Coventry before a year with Carlisle, his statistics being four goals in 14+11 games for the Sky Blues and one goal in 5+13 appearances for the Cumbrians. In 2016, he went to play in Ireland, briefly with Shelbourne and subsequently Drogheda only to suffer relegation after scoring twice in 19 games. Finally, he came back to the north east of England in November 2017 playing the rest of that season in the Northern League with Morpeth Town, scoring five times in 21 games.

For Ireland, his full international debut against Croatia came three months after his Sunderland debut by which time he had scored eight goals for his new club. He went on to win all nine of his international caps while with Sunderland.

Articulate and forthright in his opinions, Sleeves only ever wanted the best for Sunderland who became the club he felt closest to after scoring more goals and playing more games for the Lads than any of his other clubs. From 2020, he began contributing a weekly column in the Sunderland Echo.

## ELLIOTT, William Henry (Billy)

**POSITION:** Left-wing, left-half, left-back

**BIRTHPLACE:** Bradford, West Riding of Yorkshire

**DATE OF BIRTH:** 20/03/1925 - 21/01/2008

**HEIGHT:** 5' 7" **WEIGHT:** 10st 7lbs

**SIGNED FROM:** Burnley, 23/06/1953

**DEBUT:** v Charlton Athletic, A, 19/08/1953

**LAST MATCH:** v Cardiff City, H, 13/12/1958

**MOVED TO:** Wisbech Town, 03/07/1959

**TEAMS:** Bradford Park Avenue, Huddersfield Town (WW2 Guest), Burnley, Sunderland, Wisbech Town

**INTERNATIONAL:** England

**SAFC TOTALS:** 212 appearances / 26 goals

**Bought for £26,000 during the 'Bank of England Club' days, Billy Elliott became a Sunderland stalwart. An England international, tough-nut Elliott gradually moved from left-wing to left-half and finally left-back as he aged, but he always remained a fierce competitor. Twice an FA Cup semi-finalist with Sunderland as a player, he was the trainer when the cup was won in 1973 having been caretaker-manager earlier in the season. Six years later he came close to leading the team to promotion when he had 26 games as caretaker manager, a spell that included the day of Gary Rowell's hat-trick in a 4-1 win at Newcastle United.**

As a player, Billy came into the sport early, debuting as an amateur during World War Two as a 15-year-old for Bradford Park Avenue against Rotherham. In peace time, he played 176 league games for Bradford Park Avenue (where he was a teammate of Len Shackleton who he would reunite with at Sunderland) scoring 21 times, but suffered relegation to Division Three North in 1949-50 having played alongside former Sunderland forward George Ainsley for the two previous seasons. Most notably, Billy had written himself into Park Avenue folklore with the goal that knocked that year's league champions Arsenal out of the FA Cup at Highbury in 1948.

In August 1951, Burnley signed him in a £25,000 deal that saw Terry Lyons go in part exchange. Elliott won all five of his England caps whilst with the Clarets, his international debut coming in a 1-1 draw with Italy in front of 93,000 in Florence in May 1952, England's goal coming from ex-Sunderland inside-forward Ivor Broadis. It was a match where at half-time, watches from a Swiss manufacturer were parachuted onto the pitch as gifts for the players and officials. Who says marketing is only a modern day preserve of the game?

On the same tour he won his second cap against Austria in the famous game where Nat Lofthouse was dubbed 'The Lion of Vienna', Billy having a hand in the opening goal. Elliott scored three times in his five games from the wing, including two on his final appearance in a 5-0 Wembley win over Belgium in November 1952, but despite that record was never picked again, although he did represent the Football League five times.

With Burnley, he debuted at Middlesbrough on 1 September 1951. In two seasons at Turf Moor Billy played 40 and 42 games in league and cup, scoring six and ten goals in those campaigns. Never one to take prisoners, Elliott became the only Burnley player sent off in the first 19 years after the war. Future hard-men Joe Bolton and Kevin Ball might be impressed to learn that Elliott's crime for his dismissal was 'a look of intent.'

What perhaps helped lead to his move to Sunderland was Elliott's best-ever game in a Burnley shirt which came in a 5-1 win over Sunderland when the goals came from future Sunderland manager Jimmy Adamson and four from future Roker forward Bill Holden.

Once at Sunderland, Billy played 38, 47, 36, 38 and 44 appearances until only nine in his final 1958-59 campaign which was Sunderland's first outside the top-flight. In April 1957, he had been one of 14 players banned indefinitely for receiving illegal payments in the age of the maximum wage. Billy began the run to the first of this FA Cup semi-finals for Sunderland in 1955 with the third-round winner against his old club Burnley.

# E

## ELLIOTT, Billy (Continued)

In his post playing days, Elliott travelled widely. From October 1961 to 1963 he worked as the coach of the Libyan national team. He then scouted for Sheffield Wednesday before coaching the US Forces in Germany from 1964 until '66. In July of that year as England won the FIFA World Cup, Elliott took over as manager of Royal Daring FC in Belgium. After 18 months in that job he returned to Sunderland as coach to Alan Brown. When Brown was sacked four and a half years later, Billy became caretaker-manager, significantly being responsible for moving Dave Watson from centre-forward to centre-half.

Leaving Sunderland the month after the FA Cup was won in 1973, Billy went on to manage cup winners himself with Brann in Norway in 1976, having taken his team to runners-up position in their league the year before. After again taking Brann to second spot in 1978, the lure of Sunderland brought him back to Roker Park for a third time, going on to take Sunderland so close to promotion, finishing fourth despite being just two points behind champions Crystal Palace. Passed over for the manager's job despite support from Bill Shankly, Elliott took over at Darlington where he was assisted by Jimmy Shoulder.

He stayed with the Quakers until the end of the 1982-83 season retiring at the age of 58 after Darlington finished eighth from bottom in Division Four. In his retirement, Billy lived in a flat overlooking Roker Pier. He had a heart attack at the Stadium of Light in 1999, but fought back from that just as he consistently fought back from any setbacks throughout his long career.

## ELLIS, William Thomas (Billy)

**POSITION:** Outside-left

**BIRTHPLACE:** Willenhall, Staffordshire

**DATE OF BIRTH:** 05/11/1893 - 18/11/1939

**HEIGHT:** 5' 8½" **WEIGHT:** 11st 4lbs

**SIGNED FROM:** Hickman's Steelworks, 01/03/1919

**DEBUT:** v Middlesbrough, A, 06/03/1920

**LAST MATCH:** v Tottenham Hotspur, A, 22/10/1927

**MOVED TO:** Birmingham, 24/11/1927

**TEAMS:** Highfield Villa, Willenhall Swifts, Bilston Juniors, Hickman's Steelworks FC, Sunderland, Birmingham, Lincoln City, York City, Blyth Spartans

**INTERNATIONAL:** Football League

**SAFC TOTALS:** 202 appearances / 32 goals

**Billy Ellis was Sunderland's left-winger for much of the 1920s in a spell where the Lads finished in the top three in four years out of five between 1922-23 and 1926-27. It came as a surprise when he moved nearer to his home area when signing for Birmingham especially as he had had an off-day when the Blues were beaten at Roker Park a couple of months before his transfer.**

Debuting for Birmingham at Portsmouth just a week after his last match for Sunderland, Ellis went on to score four times in 23 games in his first campaign at St Andrews. Although he scored in the first two games of 1927-28, his only full season with Birmingham was a disappointment. After helping his side to win 4-3 at his old stomping ground of Roker Park in late September, Ellis dropped out of the side after another couple of games. Come the summer, he moved on to Lincoln City, scoring a dozen goals in the 33 games he played for the Imps over 16 months before signing for York City in November 1930.

Playing at centre-forward for the Minstermen, Ellis opened the scoring on his debut in a Division Three North win over Nelson. He then played in the next game at Wigan Borough, missed the following fixture back at his old club Lincoln and then played in the next game at New Brighton before quickly calling time on his ever-so brief time at the club and signing for Blyth Spartans.

After retiring from football, Ellis worked for the unemployment assistance board, while when World War Two began, Billy became a volunteer air raid warden only to pass away in Sunderland in the month of his 46th birthday. Billy's son, also called Billy, played for Sunderland reserves, but mainly played for Dorking where he worked as a teacher.

## ELLISON, Raymond

**POSITION:** Full-back

**BIRTHPLACE:** Newcastle, Northumberland

**DATE OF BIRTH:** 31/12/1950

**HEIGHT:** 5' 7" **WEIGHT:** 11st 6lbs

**SIGNED FROM:** Newcastle United, 28/02/1973

**DEBUT:** v Oxford United, H, 03/03/1973

**LAST MATCH:** v Luton Town, A, 10/03/1973

**MOVED TO:** Torquay United, 01/07/1974

**TEAMS:** Newcastle United, Sunderland, Torquay United, Workington, Gateshead, Tow Law Town, Whitley Bay

**SAFC TOTALS:** 2 appearances / 0 goals

**Less heralded than the other two Newcastle reserves signed shortly after Bob Stokoe took over - Ron Guthrie and David Young - Ray Ellison's two appearances saw him play in both full-back berths, on the second occasion standing in for Dick Malone against Luton seven days before 'SuperDick' returned against the same opposition in the FA Cup quarter-final. Ray remained as a reserve for another season before joining Torquay.**

He had made just seven appearances in total for Newcastle who he joined as a junior in July 1966 becoming a professional in October 1968 and debuting against Derby three years later, by which time he was almost 21. All of his appearances for the Magpies - including a Texaco Cup game - came in October 1971 meaning that at the time of his SAFC debut, Ellison had not played a senior game for 16 months.

At Torquay, he played 11+5 league appearances as a teammate of future Sunderland assistant manager Lew Chatterley who was player/coach at Plainmoor. His penultimate away game was at Workington who he duly joined that summer. Ellison enjoyed 64 league games for Workington, scoring the first two goals of his career in 1975-76 when Workington propped up the entire Football League.

During that term, former Sunderland man Brian Heslop was a teammate while in his second season of 1976-77 he would be joined by ex-SAFC men Malcolm Moore and Paddy Lowrey, but although Ellison scored the winner on the opening day of the season with a penalty, the Reds finished bottom of the pile again and were voted out of the league. Ellison's final league game had come against Doncaster at the end of January with the player joining Gateshead the following month.

He subsequently played for Tow Law Town before becoming player/coach of Whitley Bay in June 1980 and managing Alnwick Town in 1983-84. After his playing days were over, Ellison worked as a taxi driver before becoming a meat wholesaler.

## ELLISON, Samuel Walter

**POSITION:** Outside-right

**BIRTHPLACE:** Leadgate, Co Durham

**DATE OF BIRTH:** 27/08/1923 - Dec 1994

**HEIGHT:** 5' 9" **WEIGHT:** 11st 3lbs

**SIGNED FROM:** Middlesbrough Crusaders, 01/01/1944

**DEBUT:** v Blackpool, A, 18/01/1947

**LAST MATCH:** v Portsmouth, H, 08/02/1947

**MOVED TO:** Consett, 26/07/1947

**TEAMS:** Middlesbrough Crusaders, Sunderland, Consett, Reading, Brighton & Hove Albion

**INTERNATIONAL:** England

**SAFC TOTALS:** 3 appearances / 0 goals

**Having attracted interest due to his performances in local football, Ellison came to Sunderland as a 20-year-old and got his first opportunity on the last day of the 1943-44 war-time League North competition at Middlesbrough. The following season he played once at Bradford City in October while in 1945-46 he appeared eleven times in the same competition, mostly on the left-wing and scored the first two of his four goals in a 4-2 home win over Manchester United.**

That season saw the return of the FA Cup, but it was not until the following January that he made his official debut in peace-time football. Having waited so long for the opportunity, Ellison's moment in the limelight came and went in the space of three games, albeit Sunderland won two and drew the other.

Unable to dislodge 1937 cup-winning wingers Len Duns and Eddie Burbanks, Ellison had been singled out for praise on his debut as Sunderland won 5-0 at Blackpool in a week when manager Bill Murray had been scouring the north west looking for a new right-winger.

Released by Sunderland at the end of the season, he returned to local football for a couple of years before moving to Third Division South Reading in 1949-50, playing four games as they finished in mid-table.

Ellison, who worked as a Plate Mill stocktaker at the start of World War Two, died in the Isle of Wight when he was 71.

## ELMOHAMADY ABDEL-FATTAH, Ahmed Eissa

**POSITION:** Midfielder / right-back

**BIRTHPLACE:** El-Mahalla El-Kubra , Egypt

**DATE OF BIRTH:** 09/09/1987

**HEIGHT:** 5' 11" **WEIGHT:** 12st 10lbs

**SIGNED FROM:** ENPPI, 01/07/2010

**DEBUT:** v Birmingham City, H, 14/08/2010

**LAST MATCH:** v Wigan Athletic, A, 19/01/2013

**MOVED TO:** Hull City, 27/06/2013

**TEAMS:** Ghazi El-Mahalla, ENPPI, Sunderland, Hull City, Aston Villa

**INTERNATIONAL:** Egypt

**SAFC TOTALS:** 35+26 appearances / 1 goal

**A long-striding and athletic player with the ability to whip across swinging centres from the right flank, Ahmed Elmohamady was brought in by Steve Bruce who later signed him for both Hull and Aston Villa. In the summer of 2022 he became a club ambassador for Villa.**

At Sunderland, 'Elmo' initially came on a short trial a year before actually signing. When he did arrive, it was originally on a season-long loan with a loan fee reportedly of half a million pounds with the transfer made 'permanent' on 9 June 2011 after he had started 27 games and appeared eleven times as a substitute in his first year. However, once the transfer was completed, the player appeared much less frequently.

In 2011-12, he started just seven Premier League fixtures and none whatsoever in 2012-13 when he spent all but a couple of weeks in mid-January on loan at Hull under Bruce where he won promotion from the Championship.

Having been named the Tigers Player of the Year during his season on loan from Sunderland, he went on to play in the FA Cup final in his first season after completing his full transfer to the club. His Wembley teammates included David Meyler, sub Paul McShane and unused sub Steve Harper, all of whom had spells at SAFC.

Ahmed had won the domestic cup in Egypt in 2005 with ENPPI who beat Ittihad Alexandria in the final. In 2016, he had more joy with Hull winning the Championship Play-Off final by beating Sheffield Wednesday at Wembley.

After 198+20 games and twelve goals for Hull, Elmohamady once again linked up with Steve Bruce, this time at Villa where he went on to make 101+28 appearances (4 goals), winning the Championship Play-Offs against Derby in 2019 and playing in the final of the League (Carabao) Cup a year later, losing to Manchester City. Sunderland academy product Conor Hourihane was a teammate on both occasions while another Sunderland product, Martyn Waghorn was part of the defeated Rams side.

At international level, Ahmed made his full debut for Egypt against Ivory Coast in August 2007, played in the African Cup of Nations the following year as Egypt lifted the trophy and won 19 of his 92 caps while with Sunderland, scoring the first two of his six goals while with the Wearsiders.

## EMBLETON, Elliott John

**POSITION:** Midfield

**BIRTHPLACE:** Durham, Co Durham

**DATE OF BIRTH:** 02/04/1999

**HEIGHT:** 5' 9" **WEIGHT:** 11st 0lbs

**SIGNED FROM:** 01/07/2016

**DEBUT:** v Wolverhampton Wanderers, A, 09/12/2017

**LAST MATCH:**

**MOVED TO:**

**TEAMS:** Sunderland, Grimsby Town (L), Blackpool (L) (to June 2022)

**INTERNATIONAL:** England Under 20

**SAFC TOTALS:** 40+28 appearances / 9 goals

**A naturally talented midfielder, adept at travelling with the ball and with a terrific passing range, sweeping diagonals with either foot being a speciality, Embleton had to wait a long time for a run in Sunderland's side.**

Niggling injuries and sometimes the reluctance of managers to give young players a chance meant that from being an unused sub six times in the Premier League campaign of 2016-17, he waited until December 2017 for a very brief debut after which he would make only a single league start for Sunderland by the end of 2019-20 regardless of being capped 36 times by England at various levels from Under 17 to Under 20.

In 2017, he won the Toulon Tournament with his international Under 20 team when he scored in the penalty shoot-out as Ivory Coast were defeated in the final after he had scored against Scotland at the semi-final stage.

During 2018-19, he performed well alongside Danny Collins in an impressive loan period with Grimsby Town, scoring four times from his 30 games which included a solitary appearance as a sub. At the start of 2021, Embleton joined Blackpool on loan after appearing in a dozen games over the previous three months with Sunderland. He helped the Tangerines to promotion as Sunderland missed out, playing in the Play-Off final against Sunderland's semi-final conquerors Lincoln City, having scored a brilliant goal in Blackpool's semi-final with Oxford United. More importantly he opened the scoring in Sunderland's 2022 Play-off final win over Wycombe with a blistering shot after bursting from the half-way line.

## ENGLAND, Ernest (Ernie)

**POSITION:** Left-back

**BIRTHPLACE:** Shirebrook, Nottinghamshire

**DATE OF BIRTH:** 03/02/1901 - 22/02/1982

**HEIGHT:** 5' 8" **WEIGHT:** 11st 8lbs

**SIGNED FROM:** Shirebrook, 20/12/1919

**DEBUT:** v Manchester City, A, 27/12/1919

**LAST MATCH:** v Nottingham Forest, H, 15/02/1930

**MOVED TO:** West Ham United, 29/10/1930

**TEAMS:** Shirebrook, Sunderland, West Ham United, Mansfield Town, Notts County, Frickley Colliery

**INTERNATIONAL:** England schoolboy & international triallist

**SAFC TOTALS:** 352 appearances / 0 goals

**A fixture at left-back throughout the 1920s. Having come into the team less than a fortnight before the roaring twenties arrived, from 1920-21 to 1926-27, he played in 257 of the 294 league fixtures - going on to add 40 out of 42 in 1928-29 having been ever-present in 1922-23 and missing just one fixture in 1926-27. Although he never won a full cap, Ernie played in England trial games in 1926-27 and 1927-28.**

Despite playing at left-back, England was right-footed. He was a tough, uncompromising defender from the era when clearing your lines was the priority rather than the auxiliary attacking role full-backs are expected to also offer in the modern era. After signing off his long and distinguished career at the start of the thirties in an FA Cup tie against his local club Nottingham Forest, Ernie eventually ended up on the opposite bank of the Trent at Notts County. He joined the Magpies as assistant trainer in May 1937 as his old club Sunderland lifted the FA Cup, staying with the Meadow Lane club until the summer of 1944.

He had left Wearside in the autumn of 1930, a £500 fee taking him to West Ham where he debuted in a 5-5 draw with Aston Villa, but only played four more times before moving to Mansfield just as they joined the Football League in 1931. His swan-song with the Stags saw England make 137 appearances as captain for the club where he finally scored his first goal (a penalty after more than 360 games) and then became assistant trainer in August 1936 to former Sunderland colleague Jack Poole after spending the 1935-36 season captaining Frickley Colliery.

Nicknamed 'Mac' at Mansfield, perhaps because he had spent so much time at Sunderland, perceived to be nearer to Scotland than it is, he also turned his hand to cricket in his years at Field Mill, playing for Langwith Loco.

## ENTWISTLE, Wayne Peter

**POSITION:** Centre-forward

**BIRTHPLACE:** Bury

**DATE OF BIRTH:** 06/08/1958

**HEIGHT:** 5' 11" **WEIGHT:** 11st 8lbs

**SIGNED FROM:** Bury, 04/11/1977

**DEBUT:** v Charlton Athletic, A, 03/12/1977

**LAST MATCH:** v Oldham Athletic, A, 01/09/1979

**MOVED TO:** Leeds United, 05/10/1979

**TEAMS:** Bury, Sunderland, Leeds United, Blackpool, Crewe Alexandra, Wimbledon, Grays Athletic, Carlisle United, Bolton Wanderers, Burnley (L), Stockport County, Wigan Athletic, Altrincham, Hartlepool United, Bacup Borough, Radcliffe Borough, Curzon Ashton

**INTERNATIONAL:** England Youth

**SAFC TOTALS:** 53+2 appearances / 16 goals

**The scorer of the 'other' goal on the day Gary Rowell netted his famous hat-trick at Newcastle in 1979, Entwistle had scored his own hat-trick three months earlier. That came in a 5-0 rout of Bristol Rovers that completed a purple patch of six goals in five games.**

# E

## ENTWISTLE, Wayne (Continued)

A scorer on his debut, Entwistle had a decent goals to games ratio, but realised his limitations and played to his strengths. Despite not being particularly big for a centre-forward, he used his physicality and as his long list of clubs indicates was always in demand. He left Sunderland to sign for Leeds where he reunited with Jimmy Adamson who had signed him for Sunderland. At Elland Road, he debuted alongside a trio of veterans from the 1973 FA Cup final in Trevor Cherry, Paul Madeley and Eddie Gray and ended his first season with two goals from 7+4 top-flight appearances.

He did not play for Leeds the following season, leaving for Blackpool as Adamson was replaced by Allan Clarke. It was a two division drop from first to third with the Seasiders who were relegated to the bottom tier in Wayne's first year. Debuting alongside Iain Hesford, Jackie Ashurst and Ricky Sbragia, Entwistle scored on his subsequent home debut, but other than a cup goal against Fleetwood, did not net again until two late season strikes, ending his time with the Tangerines with eight goals from 29+6 appearances.

A brief eleven-game goalless stint with Crewe from March 1982 preceded a summer move to Wimbledon where he spent the 1982-83 campaign scoring three times in nine games as the Wombles won Division Four. There was then a brief interlude with Grays Athletic before a return to Bury, where 32 goals came in 83 league games led to a 1985 move to Division Two Carlisle. At Brunton Park he signed for Bob Stokoe and reunited with Jackie Ashurst as well as teaming up with John Cooke, John Halpin and Pop Robson.

Although he scored in his first two home games, his Carlisle career would be curtailed by October, those goals being his only ones in 8+1 games. Dropping a division to Bolton, Wayne debuted alongside Sam Allardyce, but would not score in 6+3 games before being loaned to Burnley where three goals came in eight games before an October 1986 move to Stockport County. There he netted eight in 49 league games before two substitute appearances in a third spell with Bury, six goals in 29 league games for Wigan and finally after a short stint with Altrincham, a final burst in the Football League with two games for Hartlepool before spending the twilight years of his career in non-league.

After retiring, Wayne's world saw him run Wayne Entwistle Farm Fresh Foods dealing in meat wholesaling. He also worked in construction, being employed on Tyne Tunnel 2 and became an enthusiastic long-distance cyclist.

## ERIKSSON, Jan Jonas Jakob

**POSITION:** Centre-back

**BIRTHPLACE:** Sundsvall, Sweden

**DATE OF BIRTH:** 24/08/1967

**HEIGHT:** 6' 0" **WEIGHT:** 13st 3lbs

**SIGNED FROM:** Helsingborgs, 07/01/1997

**DEBUT:** v Aston Villa, A, 01/02/1997

**LAST MATCH:** v Aston Villa, A, 01/02/1997

**MOVED TO:** Tampa Bay Mutiny, 23/01/1998

**TEAMS:** GIF Sundsvall, IFK Sundsvall, AIK Stockholm, Norkopping, Kaiserslautern, AIK Stockholm (L), Servette, Helsingborgs, Sunderland, Tampa Bay Mutiny

**INTERNATIONAL:** Sweden

**SAFC TOTALS:** 1 appearance / 0 goals

**Eriksson was a top Sweden international brought in by Peter Reid, but discarded after one game when the manager assessed that 'his legs had gone.' Some felt Reid's judgement was harsh, but the fact that afterwards the player saw his career out in the more sedate setting of soccer in the USA indicates that Reid was probably right. On his solitary appearance for Sunderland Eriksson deflected the only goal of the game into his own net and also picked up a caution as Sunderland headed towards a relegation.**

The Swede had a solid pedigree. He had scored from a Stefan Schwarz corner against England at Euro 92 when his teammates also included Joachim Bjorklund. It was one of two goals the defender scored in the tournament, half of his tally of goals from 35 internationals. He was selected for the 1990 and 1994 FIFA World Cups, but did not play at Italia 90 and had to withdraw because of injury four years later.

At club level, after beginning in Sweden, Eriksson's experience took in spells in Germany (where he was a Bundesliga runner -up with Kaiserslautern in 1993-94) and Switzerland before coming to England where he had once been on trial at Newcastle prior to Euro 92. Jan did get to play at Roker Park, appearing in the stadium's Farewell game against Liverpool when he played in front of Chris Woods who had been the England keeper he had scored against at the Euro's. Eriksson even got a goal for Sunderland in a pre-season friendly at Portadown in July 1997, but although he was an unused sub in nine Premier League games, that disappointing debut at Villa Park proved to be his only competitive appearance for the club.

Eriksson's father Jan-Ake Eriksson and younger brother Patrik Eriksson-Ohlsson played in Sweden, Patrik winning the league title, the Allsvenskan, with Djurgardens.

## ERSKINE, William Charles (Billy)

**POSITION:** Outside-right

**BIRTHPLACE:** Monkwearmouth, Co Durham

**DATE OF BIRTH:** 14/06/1865 - 31/05/1935

**SIGNED FROM:** Monkwearmouth Workmen's Hall Club, 1885

**DEBUT:** v Redcar, A, 24/10/1885

**LAST MATCH:** v Newcastle West End, A, 13/11/1886

**MOVED TO:** Retired, 1888, to be a full-time teacher

**TEAMS:** Monkwearmouth Workmen's Hall, Sunderland

**INTERNATIONAL:** England schoolboy and international triallist

**SAFC TOTALS:** 2 appearances / 0 goals

**Continuing in the earliest traditions of the club, William Erskine was a pupil teacher at Moor Board School before playing football and continued teaching after playing for Sunderland.**

In addition to the frequent friendlies played in the days before the Football League was established, he played in Sunderland's second and third English (FA) Cup ties.

## ETUHU, Dickson Paul

**POSITION:** Midfielder

**BIRTHPLACE:** Kano, Nigeria

**DATE OF BIRTH:** 08/06/1982

**HEIGHT:** 6' 2" **WEIGHT:** 13st 4lbs

**SIGNED FROM:** Norwich City, 17/07/2007

**DEBUT:** v Tottenham Hotspur, H, 11/08/2007

**LAST MATCH:** v Portsmouth, A, 23/02/2008

**MOVED TO:** Fulham, 29/08/2008

**TEAMS:** Manchester City, Preston North End, Norwich City, Sunderland, Fulham, Blackburn Rovers, AIK Stockholm, IFK Rossjoholm

**INTERNATIONAL:** Nigeria

**SAFC TOTALS:** 19+2 appearances / 1 goal

**Dickson Etuhu was found guilty of match fixing by a court in Sweden in 2019, although the outcome of the trial was subject to appeal. Etuhu received a five-year ban from football as his punishment having been accused of offering to fix a 2017 match between IFK Gothenburg and AIK. Along with former IFK Rossjoholm player Alban Jusufi, he was alleged to have offered AIK goalkeeper Kyriakos Stamatopoulos £160,000 to underperform.**

The goalkeeper reported the matter and the game was postponed. Etuhu moved to IFK Rossjoholm from AIK soon afterwards. Etuhu was fined and placed on probation by the authorities as his lawyers prepared to take the case to the Supreme Court.

Etuhu had been in his prime when he joined Sunderland from Norwich for a reported £1.5m during the reign of Roy Keane. Etuhu did not have Keane's quality in midfield - who could? - but he did bring a physical presence and went straight into the side, appearing in all but two games up to the turn of the year, all but two of those in the starting line-up. However, once the January transfer window opened and the squad was strengthened, Dickson fell out of favour, playing only twice more despite scoring in one of those games.

Internationally, Etuhu made 33 appearances for Nigeria, helping them to third place in the African Cup of Nations in 2010. Later that year he played in all three of Nigeria's games at the FIFA World Cup in South Africa, including one against Lionel Messi's Argentina.

At that time, Dickson was with Fulham who he had joined from Sunderland and with whom he played in the same year's Europa League final which was lost to Atletico Madrid. After 99+28 appearances (and six goals) for the Cottagers, he moved on to Blackburn Rovers where he played 20+4 times with one goal before his ill-starred switch to Sweden.

Like his younger brother Kelvin (who also listed Carlisle United in a lengthy career CV), Etuhu began with Manchester City. Debuting against Birmingham City in September 2001, he played 12+1 times before David Moyes paid £300,000 to take him to Preston in January 2002. Deepdale was where Etuhu had the longest spell of his career, making exactly 100 league starts in a North End total of 112+37 appearances with 18 goals. A loan to Norwich became a permanent deal to the Carrow Road club where after 64+6 games and 7 goals he moved to Sunderland.

## EVANS, Corry

**POSITION:** Midfielder

**BIRTHPLACE:** Belfast

**DATE OF BIRTH:** 30/07/1990

**HEIGHT:** 5' 11" **WEIGHT:** 12st 9lbs

**SIGNED FROM:** Blackburn Rovers, 31/07/2021

**DEBUT:** v Wigan Athletic, 07/08/2021

**LAST MATCH:**

**MOVED TO:**

**TEAMS:** Greenisland Boys, Manchester United, Carlisle United (L), Hull City, Blackburn Rovers, Sunderland

**SAFC TOTALS:** 32+8 appearances / 2 goals (to June 2022)

**The brother of Jonny Evans who had two long and successful loans at Sunderland, Corry joined in the summer of 2021. Like his older brother, Corry started with Manchester United.**

A regular under Ole Gunnar Solskjaer in United's reserves, he was named as a sub in the Premier League on 24 May 2009 against Hull who he later played for.

It was the nearest he got to playing for Manchester United. After a loan to Carlisle where his only appearance - and league debut - came at Bristol Rovers on 30 October 2010, he initially joined the Tigers on loan before being transferred. A goal on his debut was one of six in 81+16 games before a 2013 move to Blackburn, where he made 188+31 appearances, scored five times and won promotion from League One.

For Northern Ireland, he debuted in 2009, played at Euro 2016 and won his 68th cap against Lithuania in November 2021. Able to play in midfield or at centre-back, Evans was appointed team captain upon signing for Sunderland and led by example as he guided the team to promotion in 2022.

## EVANS, John (Jack)

**POSITION:** Inside-left

**BIRTHPLACE:** Hetton-le-Hole, Co Durham

**DATE OF BIRTH:** 21/10/1932 - February 2009

**HEIGHT:** 5' 9½" **WEIGHT:** 11st 3lbs

**SIGNED FROM:** Norwich City, 13/08/1954

**DEBUT:** v Portsmouth, A, 11/09/1954

**LAST MATCH:** v Portsmouth, A, 11/09/1954

**MOVED TO:** Chesterfield, 30/04/1956

**TEAMS:** Hetton Juniors, Norwich City, Sunderland, Chesterfield, Boston United, South Shields, North Shields

**SAFC TOTALS:** 1 appearance / 0 goals

**Although he spent almost a decade in professional football from joining Norwich when he turned 17 in October 1949 until leaving Chesterfield at the end of the 1955-56 season, Jack Evans' appearance in a 2-2 draw at Fratton Park a month into his two-season spell at Sunderland proved to be the solitary league appearance of his career.**

Contemporary match reports argued the speed of thought of the game was too much for him and although an inside-forward schemer, he did his best work in harrying and chasing. Jack finished his playing career back in the north east with both Shields' clubs, scoring five in his second trial game with 'North' under the watchful eye of manager and former Sunderland player Ken Walshaw.

## EVANS, Jonathan Grant (Jonny)

**POSITION:** Centre-back

**BIRTHPLACE:** Belfast, Northern Ireland

**DATE OF BIRTH:** 03/01/1988

**HEIGHT:** 6' 2" **WEIGHT:** 12st 2lbs

**SIGNED FROM:** Manchester United, 04/01/2007 and 04/01/2008, both times on loan

**DEBUT:** v Preston North End, A, 06/01/2007

**LAST MATCH:** v Arsenal, H, 11/05/2008

**MOVED TO:** Manchester United, 08/05/2007 and 12/05/2008, end of loans

**TEAMS:** Manchester United, Royal Antwerp (L), Sunderland (L), WBA, Leicester City (to June 2022)

**INTERNATIONAL:** Northern Ireland

**SAFC TOTALS:** 35 appearances / 1 goal

**Still a teenager when he first came to Sunderland, and just a day after his 20th birthday when he arrived for a second spell on loan from Manchester United, Evans had a cool and composed head on young shoulders. The club would have loved to have kept him, but he went back to success at Old Trafford, but oh how United must have regretted not keeping him for the duration of his career.**

Roy Keane spotted the potential of partnering the cultured Evans with the colossal Nyron Nosworthy. Their combination provided the platform for the 2006-07 Coca-Cola Championship winning season in which Sunderland went from tenth to top between Evans' debut and his first league defeat.

A post-match chat between Keane and Sir Alex Ferguson after a heavy home Boxing Day loss to Manchester United the following season led to Evans coming back to Sunderland for a second spell. This time at a higher level, his arrival came when Sunderland were in the bottom three with his influence helping guide the Lads to safety. Although his two stints were only for half a season each, it was enough to secure Jonny the Young Player of the Year award in both terms.

Evans had joined Manchester United as a trainee on 1 July 2004, becoming a professional the following April. In between his loans on Wearside, he made his United debut in a home League Cup defeat to Coventry in September 2007, but then enjoyed a big European Cup win over Dynamo Kiev on his second appearance followed by a tough draw at Roma in the same competition. His Premier League debut came on his second loan at Sunderland with his bow in that competition for his parent club coming at Chelsea the following September.

Evans eventually tallied 198 games for United with seven goals along the way, (one of these against Sunderland in the 2014 Capital One Cup semi-final) before he was sold to WBA for £8m in August 2015. Having won his first silverware with Sunderland, he left Old Trafford having added the Club World Cup in 2008, the League Cup in 2009 and 2010, the Community Shield in 2010 and 2011 and a trio of Premier League titles from 2009, 2011 and 2013.

In three seasons at the Hawthorns, Evans became the Baggies Players' Player of the Year in his first year and went on to captain the club for whom he played 93+3 games, scoring five times before moving to Leicester City who activated a clause in his contract upon West Brom's relegation. He added to his silverware with the Foxes, winning the FA Cup in 2021.

For Northern Ireland, Johnny debuted in a sensational 3-2 European Qualifying win over Spain in 2006 shortly before his first loan to Sunderland and ahead of his Red Devils debut. Future Sunderland man David Healy scored a hat-trick on Evans international debut when he was also a teammate of Kyle Lafferty. Evans went on to become a vital member of his national side, playing at all four of their games at Euro 2016 and in 2021 was approaching his 100th cap. Many of his caps were won alongside his brother Corry.

# F

## FAIRLEY, Thomas (Tom)

**POSITION:** Goalkeeper

**BIRTHPLACE:** Philadelphia, Co Durham

**DATE OF BIRTH:** 12/10/1932 – 16/04/2017

**HEIGHT:** 5' 10" **WEIGHT:** 12st 0lbs

**SIGNED FROM:** Bankhead Juniors, 11/10/1951

**DEBUT:** v Stoke City, A, 28/03/1953

**LAST MATCH:** v Bolton Wanderers, A, 03/04/1953

**MOVED TO:** Carlisle United, 30/04/1956

**TEAMS:** Newbottle, Houghton Athletic Juniors, Shiney Row, St Oswalds, Bankhead Juniors, Sunderland, Carlisle United, Hartlepools United, Cambridge City, South Shields, North Shields, Annfield Plain

**SAFC TOTALS:** 2 appearances / 0 goals

**Like so many players of his era and before, Tom Fairley earned his chance at Roker Park after impressing scouts in local football. He was 20 when his big chance came. With number one Harry Threadgold injured, veteran pre-war cup winner Johnny Mapson came in for what proved to be his final appearance before Fairley was given an opportunity in a floodlit friendly against Racing Club de Paris.**

He impressed with a clean sheet in front of a near 30,000 crowd causing manager Bill Murray to give him a league debut two days later at Stoke only to have to pick the ball out of his net after only seven minutes. Despite conceding three goals in defeat, Fairley was perceived to have done well in an injury hit side and held his place for the next match at Bolton. However, this was to be a tougher afternoon as Sunderland slumped to a heaviest defeat of the season, 5-0, with one of Nat Lofthouse's hat-trick coming when the England centre-forward outjumped the keeper for a cross.

Fairley stayed at Sunderland for another three seasons without getting another competitive game, but at least he did not ask to be dropped as his predecessor at Carlisle, Keith Mitton, had done after a 4-0 derby defeat at Workington. Signed at the end of that 1955-56 campaign, Fairley debuted for the Cumbrians on the opening day of 1956-57 in a Division Three North 2-2 draw at home to Oldham where Ivor Broadis was one of Carlisle's scorers. Despite mid-table Carlisle having such a leaky defence they conceded almost two goals a game Fairley missed just one of their 50 league and cup games in his first season. However, despite starting the first two matches of the following season he would play just seven times that term and four in 1958-59 before moving on to Hartlepools where he played no first-team football at all in his season before playing for Cambridge City and subsequently seeing out his playing days back in north east local football.

## FALL, William

**POSITION:** Left-half

**BIRTHPLACE:** Tyne Dock, Northumberland

**DATE OF BIRTH:** 26/10/1900 - 15/08/1965

**HEIGHT:** 5' 9" **WEIGHT:** 11st 7lbs

**SIGNED FROM:** Tyne Dock, 09/08/1923

**DEBUT:** v Preston North End, H, 03/09/1924

**LAST MATCH:** v West Ham United, H, 25/04/1925

**MOVED TO:** Contract not renewed, 02/05/1925

**TEAMS:** Tyne Dock, Sunderland, West Stanley

**SAFC TOTALS:** 4 appearances / 0 goals

**Will Fall sounds like a look ahead to the days when footballers dived as soon as someone looked at them, but he played in an era when even if you were hurt the last thing you wanted to do was to look as if you had been.**

Fall came out of local football and was given an opportunity soon after becoming a professional after a year at the club as an amateur. He stood in for the injured Arthur Andrews for the second, third and fourth games of 1924-25, being on the winning side in his two home games. His final appearance protected his unbeaten Roker Park record when he appeared in the penultimate home game, but he had not done enough to be placed on the retained list and returned to local football and his job as a locomotive fireman.

## FARQUHAR, William Inkster (Billy)

**POSITION:** Inside-forward / centre-forward / half-back

**BIRTHPLACE:** Fordyce, Banffshire

**DATE OF BIRTH:** 03/09/1877 - 23/09/1916

**HEIGHT:** 5' 7" **WEIGHT:** 10st 10lbs

**SIGNED FROM:** Elgin City, 25/01/1899

**DEBUT:** v Wednesday, A, 18/02/1899

**LAST MATCH:** v Manchester City, A, 27/04/1907

**MOVED TO:** Contract not renewed, 31/05/1907

**TEAMS:** Elgin Caledonian, Elgin City, Sunderland

**SAFC TOTALS:** 198 appearances / 16 goals

**Billy Farquhar played almost 200 games for Sunderland, but came close to playing none. He had his bags packed and was intending to sign for Rangers only for manager Alex Mackie to nip in at the last minute and get him to sign for Sunderland in his home of Elgin.**

He got off to a good start with goals in his first three home games and played for the Lads for nine seasons. During his first three and a half years he managed between 10 and 18 league games, but in the next four appeared in between 31 and 35 league matches. Farquhar captained the team in 1905-06 during which he was awarded a benefit game. In his final year of 1906-07 Farquhar played in only the last two games of the season, mirroring his start with a goal on his final home appearance.

A versatile player, he operated at his preferred, and thought to be strongest, position of half-back in the 1901-02 title-winning season. After retiring from football, Billy continued his original profession of dental mechanic in Sunderland working for the surgeon James Lishman and continued in that role after joining the army. His death at an early age from tuberculosis at his father's home in Elgin followed a spell in Stanhope Sanatorium.

## FEENAN, John Joseph

**POSITION:** Right-back

**BIRTHPLACE:** Newry, Co Down

**DATE OF BIRTH:** 01/07/1914 - October 1994

**HEIGHT:** 5' 10½" **WEIGHT:** 11st 4lbs

**SIGNED FROM:** Belfast Celtic, 21/08/1936

**DEBUT:** v Brentford, H, 19/09/1936

**LAST MATCH:** v Wolverhampton Wanderers, A, 06/05/1939

**MOVED TO:** Shelbourne, 23/12/1939

**TEAMS:** Newry Town, Belfast Celtic, Sunderland, Shelbourne, Bray Unknowns

**INTERNATIONAL:** Republic of Ireland

**SAFC TOTALS:** 29 appearances / 0 goals

**John Feenan cost Sunderland £1750 when he came to the reigning league champions in the summer of 1936. He got five games in his first campaign, but all were in the league with none in the FA Cup as the cup was brought to Wearside.**

Although not part of the cup side, in the month that Sunderland won the trophy in 1937, Feenan became the first Sunderland player to win caps with the Republic of Ireland, playing away to Switzerland and France. It would be another two decades before Charlie Hurley became Sunderland's second Republic of Ireland cap.

Feenan did make what was his only cup appearance the following season in his most productive campaign of 16 games, but only managed half that number in 1938-39. Feenan did not feature in the three games of the abandoned 1939-40 season and had returned to Ireland before war-time football got under way.

He played for Shelbourne in the 1939-40 and '40-41 seasons and Bray Unknowns in 1941-42 before returning to Shelbourne as manager from 1942 to 1946. At the beginning of World War Two, he was known to have been an aircraft worker in Gloucester, the city where he died in 1994.

## FEENEY, Morgan

**POSITION:** Defender

**BIRTHPLACE:** Bootle, Merseyside

**DATE OF BIRTH:** 08/02/1999

**HEIGHT:** 6' 3" **WEIGHT:** 12st 2lbs

**SIGNED FROM:** Everton, 21/08/2020

**DEBUT:** v Aston Villa U21s, H, 08/09/2020

**LAST MATCH:** v Aston Villa U21s, H, 08/09/2020

**MOVED TO:** Carlisle United, 20/01/2021

**TEAMS:** Everton, Tranmere Rovers (L), Sunderland, Carlisle United (to June 2022)

**INTERNATIONAL:** England Under 19

**SAFC TOTALS:** 1 appearance / 1 goal

**Morgan Feeney was terribly unlucky at Sunderland. Coming from Everton where he had been a very highly thought of youngster, he scored on his only first-team appearance, but was then injured and released from his short-term contract shortly after a new regime came into the club.**

Feeney's first-team appearance had come in the Football League (Papa John's) Trophy which Sunderland went on to win. The game against Aston Villa's Under 21 team saw Sunderland score eight goals for the first time in over 60 years.

He had made his Everton debut in the Europa League in November 2017 coming off the bench in a 5-1 Goodison defeat to Atalanta, but fared better on his second outing, helping the Toffees to a 3-0 victory at Apollon Limassol on his first start. They would be Morgan's only first-team appearances for the club he had been at since he was seven, but he did captain Everton Under 21s to a Premier League Under 21 cup final win over Newcastle in 2019. Prior to joining Everton at such a young age, he had been associated with Liverpool.

A league debut arrived at Bolton on loan to Tranmere in February 2020, but it would be his only appearance in an injury hit spell with Rovers. His injury woes continued when he broke his foot in training before he could make his debut, who he still had not played for by the end of his first season at the club.

## FERDINAND, Anton Julian

**POSITION:** Centre-back

**BIRTHPLACE:** Peckham, London

**DATE OF BIRTH:** 18/02/1985

**HEIGHT:** 6' 2" **WEIGHT:** 12st 11lbs

**SIGNED FROM:** West Ham United, 27/08/2008

**DEBUT:** v Wigan Athletic, A, 13/09/2008

**LAST MATCH:** v Swansea City, A, 27/08/2011

**MOVED TO:** QPR, 31/08/2011

**TEAMS:** West Ham United, Sunderland, QPR, Bursaspor (L), Antalyaspor, Reading, Southend United, St Mirren

**INTERNATIONAL:** England Under 21

**SAFC TOTALS:** 81+10 appearances / 0 goals

**Anton Ferdinand never scored for Sunderland, but his celebratory Michael Jackson style 'moonwalk' looked like it had been well rehearsed when Anton found the back of the net in a thrilling game with Spurs only to have his moonwalk cut short when the goal was disallowed.**

Ferdinand was from a famous footballing family. Brother Rio was a top star with England, Leeds and Manchester United having begun his career with West Ham. Cousin Les also played for England and numbered Newcastle, Spurs, QPR and West Ham amongst his clubs, while another cousin, Kane, played for Southend United and Peterborough United amongst others.

Anton started as a nine-year-old with West Ham, making his debut at the age of 18 at Preston on the opening day of the 2003-04 season. He quickly made a strong impression and at the end of his second campaign had another date with destiny v Preston (who included Dickson Etuhu) as he helped the Hammers to beat them in the Play-Off final to secure promotion to the Premier League. That game took place at the Millennium Stadium at Cardiff where twelve months later Anton failed with the decisive penalty in a shoot-out which settled the FA Cup final against Liverpool, for whom Djibril Cisse had scored.

Anton joined Sunderland for a reported fee of £8m, arriving in the same week as George McCartney returned from West Ham. Ferdinand's first season proved to be his best as he started every Premier League game bar four after joining. In the next two seasons he started just over half the league games as well as being no stranger to coming on from the bench, but early in his fourth term with the club he was sold by Steve Bruce.

Returning to his home environment of the capital with QPR, Ferdinand's sixth game with Rangers saw him embroiled in controversy after he alleged Chelsea captain John Terry had racially abused him. Terry was later acquitted at Westminster Magistrates' Court, but subsequently banned and fined by the FA as well as being stripped of the England captaincy. In November 2020, Anton presented a BBC TV programme entitled 'Football, Racism and Me' in which he reflected on the incident.

After two years at Loftus Road during which time he made 46+3 appearances, Ferdinand left QPR from whom he had spent the second half of his last season on loan in Turkey with Bursaspor, where he debuted against Galatasaray and played a further six games as they qualified for the Europa League. Having done well in Turkey, he then signed for Antalyaspor, but played only three games, ending his time in the country as he had begun it with a 1-1 draw against Galatasaray.

A proposed move to play in Thailand then collapsed leading to a return to England with Reading, but in two years he played just 24+2 games, all but two of those coming in his second season where he ended his spell by playing back at his former club QPR. Next stop was Southend United where his goal against Coventry in December 2016 was his first since he had scored for West Ham against Fulham almost nine years earlier. Anton started 68 games and had another three as sub for Southend, scoring twice in his two years before going north to join St Mirren in September 2018. He made a good start as alongside future Sunderland goalkeeping coach Craig Samson he helped St Mirren to hold Celtic to a goalless draw on his debut. It was the first of 18 SPL appearances for Ferdinand who signed off with a last-minute appearance as a substitute in a Play-Off against Dundee United which The Buddies won on penalties.

At international level, Anton played for England at Under 21 level having also represented his country's Under 18s and Under 20s. He debuted for the Under 21s at Middlesbrough in August 2004 when his teammates included Justin Hoyte, Matt Kilgallon, Darren Bent, Jon Stead and Stewart Downing. Three years later in the UEFA European Under 21 championships he played once, in a semi-final against hosts the Netherlands. The match went to a lengthy penalty shoot-out in which Ferdinand scored and missed as England lost 13-12 on what was his 17th and final appearance.

## FERGUSON, Derek

**POSITION:** Midfielder

**BIRTHPLACE:** Glasgow

**DATE OF BIRTH:** 31/07/1967

**HEIGHT:** 5' 8" **WEIGHT:** 10st 11lbs

**SIGNED FROM:** Hearts, 26/07/1993

**DEBUT:** v Derby County, A, 14/08/1993

**LAST MATCH:** v Sheffield United, H, 01/04/1995

**MOVED TO:** Falkirk, 04/09/1995

**TEAMS:** Roystar Boys Club, Burnbank Boys Club, Gartcosh United, Rangers, Dundee (L), Hearts, Sunderland, Falkirk, Dunfermline Athletic, Portadown, Partick Thistle, Adelaide Force, Ross County, Clydebank, Alloa Athletic, Hamilton Academical

**INTERNATIONAL:** Scotland

**SAFC TOTALS:** 75 appearances / 1 goal

**Derek Ferguson was a technically gifted midfielder capable of incisive passing combined with an edge to his game that meant he was good without the ball too. Nonetheless, he will always be best remembered at Sunderland for a car accident before his debut when he crashed, injuring several of Sunderland's new signings.**

In a summer when the club had invested more than at any time in its history, Derek's debut on the opening day of the season saw Sunderland's heaviest-ever first-day defeat (5-0) in the aftermath of manager Terry Butcher's pre-season plans being decimated by the accident. Ferguson himself was very candid about the crash in his autobiography 'Big Brother', published in 2006, indeed the book even begins with the crash.

Derek's brother Barry played 45 times for Scotland and 288 league games for Rangers as well as doing a tour of English 'B's playing for Blackburn, Birmingham and Blackpool, also having a spell as caretaker-manager of the Tangerines. He also managed Clyde (where he finished his playing days) and Kelty Hearts as well as playing on loan for Fleetwood. Derek's son Lewis won Under 21 honours for Scotland and after starting with Hamilton, played over 100 games for Aberdeen for whom he scored the winning goal of the 2018 League Cup semi-final against his dad's old club Rangers at Hampden. He went on to play in the final, lost to Celtic.

Derek won two full caps for Scotland, as well as winning honours at 'B' and Under 21 level. He was only 20 when he won his first full cap in a friendly in Malta in March 1988. Two months later, he figured in a Rous Cup draw with Columbia, but was never able to add to his full cap collection. At this time he was in the first of two spells at Rangers where he had first been seen as a 15-year-old in a 1983 testimonial for Tom Forsyth.

## FERGUSON, Derek (Continued)

Derek was only 24 days beyond his 16th birthday when he became Rangers youngest-ever player on his competitive debut against Queen of the South in August 1983. By the time he was named Man of the Match in the 1986 League Cup final Fergie was seen as a star in the making. As Celtic were beaten in that final, Ferguson's teammates included a quartet with Sunderland connections in Chris Woods, Jimmy Nicholl, Ally McCoist and skipper Terry Butcher - who later signed him for Sunderland.

Ferguson played in the final as Rangers retained that trophy against Aberdeen, but not seeing eye-to-eye with manager Graeme Souness, Fergie faded from the Ibrox picture and after a 1989-90 loan to Dundee, moved on to Hearts in the summer of 1990 as the Jambos splashed out a club record £750,000 for his signature. At Tynecastle, the team revolved around him in his three seasons in Edinburgh before he moved to Sunderland with John Colquhoun going the opposite way in part-exchange after he had scored six goals in 14+7 games.

At Sunderland, Derek started all but five of the 46 league games in his first season, holding his place as Mick Buxton replaced Butcher, but Sunderland spent much of the campaign much lower than their final position of 12th with no promotion charge ever looking likely. The only goal of his time at Roker came in that campaign in an FA Cup tie with Carlisle.

In his second season he started half the games, the last one being Peter Reid's first match and also the final one of Ferguson's time in red and white. Sold to Falkirk, he spent three years there before a succession of moves which included short stints in Ireland and Australia.

Moving into management he was player/manager at Clydebank, coached at Albion Rovers and managed Stranraer and junior club Glenafton Athletic before moving into media work with BBC Scotland.

## FERGUSON, Matthew

**POSITION:** Right-half

**BIRTHPLACE:** Bellshill, Glasgow

**DATE OF BIRTH:** 06/10/1875 - 12/06/1902

**HEIGHT:** 5' 7½" **WEIGHT:** 11st 4lbs

**SIGNED FROM:** Mossend Brigade, 04/05/1896

**DEBUT:** v Bury, H, 01/09/1896

**LAST MATCH:** v Bury, H, 16/04/1902

**MOVED TO:** Falkirk, 04/09/1995

**TEAMS:** Bellshill Hawthorn, Wishaw Thistle, Mossend Brigade, Sunderland

**INTERNATIONAL:** Scotland Junior

**SAFC TOTALS:** 181 appearances / 4 goals

**Matthew was captain of reigning league champions Sunderland when he died of pleuropneumonia at the age of 26. He had played in 29 of the 34 games in the league season just ended, missing the last two. Ferguson had been remarkably consistent in his six seasons at Sunderland, playing between 25 and 30 league games in each of those campaigns.**

In the first of those in 1896-97 his 30 league appearances made him ever-present at the tail end of the 'Team of All The Talents' era when instead of chasing silverware, Sunderland chased survival. This meant contesting the Play-Offs of the time, then known as Test Matches and involving teams at the bottom. Ferguson played in all four of those as well as both cup-ties making him the only outfield player to play every game of the season.

In his next two seasons he played in the final match at Newcastle Road and the first at Roker Park. It was a time of improvement as the next great team after 'The Talents' took shape. Third in 1900, Ferguson became skipper in 1900 leading his team to runners-up spot in 1901 before triumphing with the title in 1902. Tragically, Matthew did not survive the summer to go on and help his team defend their tag as Champions.

A half-back who scored two of his four goals for the club from penalties, he famously once played the entire game in goal in a friendly against Tottenham Hotspur on the second day of the twentieth century.

## FERGUSON, Robert Gibson (Bob)

**POSITION:** Right-half

**BIRTHPLACE:** Blythswood, Glasgow

**DATE OF BIRTH:** 05/01/1902 - April 1946

**HEIGHT:** 5' 9½" **WEIGHT:** 11st 0lbs

**SIGNED FROM:** Battlefield Juniors, 16/08/1921

**DEBUT:** v Liverpool, A, 11/01/1922

**LAST MATCH:** v Huddersfield Town, A, 06/12/1924

**MOVED TO:** Middlesbrough, 30/01/1925

**TEAMS:** Battlefield Juniors, Sunderland, Middlesbrough, Crystal Palace, Barrow, Northwich Victoria

**SAFC TOTALS:** 36 appearances / 1 goal

**Bob chose to sign for Sunderland after a successful trial in a pre-season practice game a week after Falkirk had offered him a position. At Sunderland from the 1921-22 to 1924-25 seasons, Ferguson featured once in his first season and twice in his last, but in between made 15 and 18 appearances respectively.**

A debutant in a heavy 5-0 FA Cup replay defeat at Liverpool when he played in his preferred position of centre-half, he operated at right-half in one short of a third of the league fixtures the following year as he helped Sunderland to runners-up spot. A year later, he stood in at both right-half and left-half with a couple of matches at centre-half as Sunderland finished third.

Having been close to success at Sunderland, Ferguson went on to twice win the second division championship later in the twenties with Middlesbrough where he played at centre-half. He played 31 times as promotion was won in 1926-27, the season when George Camsell scored his record breaking 59 goals. Boro went straight back down with Bob playing in the final match when Boro were relegated on the final day after losing at home to Sunderland, who thus escaped. However, Boro were immediately promoted again, this time Ferguson appearing 19 times. By now struggling to hold his place on Teesside, he was increasingly utilised at right-back from 1929-30 and after playing the opening three games of 1930-31 at left-back, signed off his Boro career having scored twice in 159 games.

After unsuccessful trials at third tier clubs Crystal Palace and Barrow in September and October 1932, he became player/manager of Northwich Victoria in July 1933 before emigrating to South Africa in the February of 1937 to take up a coaching position. He died in the Transvaal at the age of 44. A Glaswegian, son of a police superintendent, Ferguson had begun with Battlefield Juniors who were connected with Queen's Park.

## FINLAY, John

**POSITION:** Inside-right

**BIRTHPLACE:** Wrekenton, Co. Durham

**DATE OF BIRTH:** 16/02/1919 - 05/03/1985

**SIGNED FROM:** Ouston United, 09/05/1938

**DEBUT:** v Charlton Athletic, A, 11/09/1946

**LAST MATCH:** v Charlton Athletic, A, 11/09/1946

**MOVED TO:** Released, 1947

**TEAMS:** Ouston United, Grimsby Town, Sunderland, Carlisle United (WW2 Guest), Hartlepools Utd (WW2 Guest)

**SAFC TOTALS:** 1 appearance / 0 goals

**Signed 24 hours after being released as an amateur by Grimsby Town in 1938, Finlay had an eight-year wait for his only first-team game which came in a dismal 5-0 defeat at Charlton when he was one of a trio of debutants alongside Bill Walsh and Tommy Reynolds, both of whom went on top a century of appearances.**

In 1939-40, he made four appearances as a 'Guest' player for Carlisle United and one for Hartlepools United before joining the army in 1940, rising to the rank of corporal and serving in India. After his time with Sunderland, Finlay played for the Durham Police team while a family connection with football was through his father who was a trainer at East Fife.

## FINNEY, Thomas (Tom)

**POSITION:** Winger

**BIRTHPLACE:** Belfast, Northern Ireland

**DATE OF BIRTH:** 06/11/1952

**HEIGHT:** 5' 10" **WEIGHT:** 11st 8lbs

**SIGNED FROM:** Luton Town, 29/06/1974

**DEBUT:** v Newcastle United, H, 03/08/1974

**LAST MATCH:** v Crystal Palace, H, 06/03/1976

**MOVED TO:** Cambridge United, 20/08/1976

**TEAMS:** Distillery, Crusaders, Luton Town, Sunderland, Cambridge United, Brentford, Cambridge United, Cambridge City, Ely City, March Town, Histon Town

**INTERNATIONAL:** Northern Ireland

**SAFC TOTALS:** 15+9 appearances / 1 goal

**Tom Finney had caught Bob Stokoe's eye at Roker Park on his sixth appearance in English football. The young Irish winger had burst onto the scene with five goals in his first four starts before playing against Sunderland, but in a season where Luton went on to win promotion, he had faded from the scene and not scored again. After making 13+1 league appearances, he was not involved as Luton lost to Sunderland in the last game of the season, but that gave Stokoe the chance to sound out the signing of a player who arrived at Roker the following month.**

Debuting as a substitute in a Texaco Cup game against Newcastle, Finney was regularly named as sub in his first season, but waited until January for a full debut in the FA Cup against Chesterfield, followed by his only league start of his first season against Manchester United. As a 15-year-old, Finney had had trials at Manchester United along with Sammy McIlroy, but had to decline the opportunity of a second trial at the club having just taken a job with a gas company.

Before featuring at the start of his second season, he made a scoring debut for Northern Ireland against Norway in Oslo in September 1974. The first seven of his 14 caps were won with Sunderland, his other international goal, a winner against Wales, also coming while he was on Sunderland's books. Along with Martin O'Neill and Jimmy Nicholl, he was part of Billy Bingham's Northern Ireland squad at the 1982 FIFA World Cup in Spain, but did not play. By that time, Tom was with Cambridge United who he left Sunderland to join in the summer of 1976 after helping the Lads win the Division Two championship, when he scored once in eight mid-season appearances.

With new signing Roy Greenwood cup-tied, Finney also got to play in every FA Cup tie as Sunderland reached the quarter-finals, that tie being his final appearance.

Promotion to the top-flight signalled the end of Tom's time at Sunderland at which point he moved to Ron Atkinson's Cambridge, reuniting with their assistant manager Paddy Sowden who had been the man who persuaded him to leave Ireland and sign for Luton Town.

At Cambridge Finney excelled, winning back-to-back promotions from Division Four to Two in 1977 and 1978 and going on to be inducted into the club's Hall of Fame. In total, he played 332 league games for the club (61 goals) in two spells separated by a short stint of 24 games and three goals at Brentford in 1984. Continuing his career in non-league, he finished his playing days with Histon Town who he managed from 1993 to 1995. Having spent his career as a winger unlocking defences, following his retirement from football Finney moved into security.

## FLANAGAN, Thomas Michael (Tom)

**POSITION:** Defender

**BIRTHPLACE:** Hammersmith, London

**DATE OF BIRTH:** 21/10/1991

**HEIGHT:** 6' 2" **WEIGHT:** 12st 0lbs

**SIGNED FROM:** Burton Albion, 28/06/2018

**DEBUT:** v Stoke City Under 21s, H, 04/09/2018

**LAST MATCH:** v Portsmouth, H, 22/01/2022

**MOVED TO:** Shrewsbury Town, 31/01/2022

**TEAMS:** MK Dons, Kettering Town, Gillingham (L), Barnet (L), Stevenage (L), Plymouth Argyle (L), Burton Albion, Sunderland, Shrewsbury Town (to June 2022)

**INTERNATIONAL:** Northern Ireland

**SAFC TOTALS:** 108+7 appearances / 5 goals

**Having just returned from injury a few days earlier, Tom Flanagan limped out of Sunderland's 2021 Football League Trophy (Papa John's) final victory, moments before half-time. It was his third Wembley appearance for Sunderland. Able to play across the back-four, Flanagan played in 42 games in his first season including all three in the unsuccessful Play-Offs as well as the Football League Trophy (Checkatrade) final which was lost to Portsmouth on penalties.**

On the international scene, Tom won one Under 21 cap in 2012 and was called into the senior squad for the first time in 2016, winning his first full cap in June 2017 against New Zealand, playing alongside Conor McLaughlin and Kyle Lafferty, who he would go on to play alongside at Sunderland, as well as ex-SAFC loanee Jonny Evans. Sunderland reserve Sam Brotherton was on the bench for the Kiwis. Having joined Sunderland, Flanagan went on to win further international honours, beginning with caps in wins over Luxembourg and the Czech Republic in the autumn of 2019.

At club level, Flanagan debuted for MK Dons as a sub in a heavy defeat to Carlisle on 13 February 2010. A loan to Conference Premier Kettering Town preceded his full Football League debut a year and two days after his initial game as a sub, this time at home to Leyton Orient. Following 45 appearances for MK Dons, who also loaned him out to a quartet of league clubs, Tom moved on to Burton helping them to promotion from League One on his first season of 2015-16. There were to be 82 appearances in three seasons with the Brewers, but he was not involved in the game where Burton sealed Sunderland's relegation in 2018. He left Sunderland on the final day of the January 2022 transfer window to sign for Steve Cotterill's Shrewsbury Town and returned to score at the Stadium of Light later that season but graciously did not celebrate the goal.

## FLEMING, Charles (Charlie)

**POSITION:** Inside-forward / centre-forward

**BIRTHPLACE:** Blairhall, Fife

**DATE OF BIRTH:** 12/07/1927 - 14/08/1997

**HEIGHT:** 5' 11" **WEIGHT:** 11st 10lbs

**SIGNED FROM:** East Fife, 04/01/1955

**DEBUT:** v Blackpool, A, 05/02/1955

**LAST MATCH:** v Everton, H, 18/01/1958

**MOVED TO:** Bath City, 14/07/1958

**TEAMS:** Blairhall Colliery, East Fife, Sunderland, Bath City, Toronto City (L), Trowbridge Town

**INTERNATIONAL:** Scotland

**SAFC TOTALS:** 122 appearances / 71 goals

**'Cannonball' Fleming's nickname does not need much working out. He blasted home goals and lots of them. His strike rate of 0.582 goals per game puts him above Kevin Phillips and Charlie Buchan in sixth place on the best strike rate list behind only Dave Halliday, Brian Clough, Johnny Campbell, Trevor Ford and Bobby Gurney.**

In Fleming's two full seasons at Roker he scored 32 and 27 goals. It was a surprise when he left for Bath City just as he turned 31, but in his second season there, struck 44 times as they won the Southern League. He had been familiar with silverware in his native Scotland with East Fife. Charlie scored in the League Cup finals of 1949-50 and 1953-54 as Dunfermline and Partick Thistle were beaten, the latter including future Sunderland man Andy Kerr. Fleming also played against future Sunderland manager Ian McColl in the Scottish Cup final of 1950 as his Fife side went down to Rangers. Earlier that season Charlie had scored what many reckon to be East Fife's best-ever goal. It settled a League Cup semi-final with Rangers at Hampden when his long weaving run and shot made the tie 5-4 late in extra-time.

# F

## FLEMING, Charlie (Continued)

Having been named as a reserve for two Scottish League Select XI matches in 1948, Cannonball waited until 1953 to be capped by Scotland. Despite netting twice in a 3-1 win over Northern Ireland, it was to be his only full cap. Two years earlier he had scored against Wales for a Rest of Great Britain Select XI. In that game, in honour of the 75th anniversary of the Welsh FA, Charlie was a teammate of future Sunderland goalkeeper Jimmy Cowan, who was beaten by current SAFC centre-forward Trevor Ford.

Fleming had joined East Fife in June 1947, scoring twice on his debut against Stenhousemuir on 7 April 1948. After 175 goals in 244 games for East Fife, Charlie's transfer to Sunderland saw Tommy Wright and a cash adjustment of £7,000 go to East Fife in one of the most successful deals ever pulled off in the 'Bank of England Club' era.

Also known as 'Legs,' Fleming finished his playing days as player/manager of Trowbridge Town after a six-year spell as player/manager at Bath City where he plundered 216 goals in 300 games, before coaching around the world. In 1970, he went to Sydney, Australia to coach Hakoah FC until October 1971 after which he coached in the USA and Canada - where he had briefly played in 1964 - before returning to the UK to find employment with the National Coal Board.

## FLETCHER, Ashley Michael

**POSITION:** Centre-forward

**BIRTHPLACE:** Keighley, West Yorkshire

**DATE OF BIRTH:** 02/10/1995

**HEIGHT:** 6' 3" **WEIGHT:** 12st 4lbs

**SIGNED FROM:** Middlesbrough, 31/01/2018, on loan

**DEBUT:** v Ipswich Town,H, 03/02/2018

**LAST MATCH:** v Wolves, H, 06/05/2018

**MOVED TO:** Middlesbrough, 07/05/2018, end of loan

**TEAMS:** Bolton Wanderers, Manchester United, Barnsley (L), West Ham United, Middlesbrough, Sunderland (L), Watford, New York Red Bulls (L), Wigan Athletic (L) (to August 2022)

**INTERNATIONAL:** England Under 20

**SAFC TOTALS:** 15+1 appearances / 2 goals

**A young striker on loan in a struggling team, Ashley had a tough time at Sunderland. Good enough to have been signed as a professional by Manchester United when he was still in his teens, Fletcher gained experience with a loan to Barnsley where he was brought in by future Sunderland boss Lee Johnson. Although Johnson left before the final, Fletcher went on to play and score at Wembley in the Football League Trophy final. In that game, the Tykes were captained by former Sunderland reserve Conor Hourihane and had Josh Scowen and Lewin Nyatanga on their bench while opponents Oxford United included Chris Maguire.**

Fletcher's Wembley goal was one of eight he scored in 16+11 games for Barnsley, but there would be no breakthrough at Manchester United before a summer 2016 move to West Ham United. Debuting in the Europa League as a late sub against NK Domzale of Slovenia, his first goal for the Hammers was satisfyingly back at Old Trafford in a League Cup quarter-final, albeit in a heavy defeat. Despite that being Ashley's only goal for the London club in 3+17 appearances, his performances and potential persuaded Middlesbrough to pay £6.7m to bring him to Teesside after a year with West Ham.

Although he featured in 20 games in his first half a season, Boro loaned him to Sunderland in the first transfer window after he was bought. Goals in wins over Derby and Wolves on his last appearance were scant reward for his effort and persistence as he played through a spell where he seemed bereft of confidence, but refused to hide, revealing later that he had worked with psychologist Martin Perry to help him cope.

Returning to Boro, Fletcher progressed with nine goals the following season subsequently rising to 13 in the next campaign eventually totalling 28 goals in 70+38 games before a free transfer move to Watford. After two goals in 3+3 games he went on loan to New York Red Bulls in March 2022.

At international level, a debut goal came in November 2015 away to France while his home debut against Canada at Doncaster saw him line up alongside Sunderland's Rees Greenwood.

## FLETCHER, Steven Kenneth

**POSITION:** Centre-forward

**BIRTHPLACE:** Shrewsbury, Shropshire

**DATE OF BIRTH:** 26/03/1987

**HEIGHT:** 6' 1" **WEIGHT:** 12st 12lbs

**SIGNED FROM:** Wolverhampton Wanderers, 24/08/2012

**DEBUT:** v Morecambe, H, 28/08/2012

**LAST MATCH:** v Arsenal, A, 09/01/2016

**MOVED TO:** Contract not renewed, 30/06/2016

**TEAMS:** Hibs, Burnley, Wolverhampton Wanderers, Sunderland, Olympique de Marseille (L), Sheffield Wednesday, Stoke City, Dundee United (to July 2022)

**INTERNATIONAL:** Scotland

**SAFC TOTALS:** 83+25 appearances / 23 goals

**The only player to score two international hat-tricks whilst on Sunderland's books, Steven Fletcher did so against footballing minnows Gibraltar, both hat-tricks coming in 2015. Those goals took his Scotland tally as a Sunderland player to seven making him Sunderland's top scorer for Scotland and only the fifth player to score more than one hat-trick for Scotland.**

Born in England, Fletcher was brought up in his mother's country Scotland from the age of ten and began his football career with Hibs, debuting for them as a substitute in April 2004 against Kilmarnock, scoring twice against the same club three years later in the League Cup final. That cup-winning campaign saw Steven become the Scottish Football Writers' Young Player of the Year, an award he won again the following season.

Following 52 goals in 136+53 appearances, a fee of £3m secured his signature for Burnley who paid a club record fee in June 2009. On a personal level Fletcher did well, top-scoring for the Clarets with a dozen goals including eight in the Premier League as he won the Players' Player of the Year award, but it was not enough to stop Burnley being relegated.

Having adapted well to English football, Fletcher's value had doubled to £6.5m after one year at Turf Moor as former Sunderland boss Mick McCarthy matched this club's record fee to secure him for Wolves.

Fletcher spent two years at Molineux scoring ten and 12 Premier League goals and 24 in all competitions in 45+23 games, but after again being part of a relegated team, asked for a transfer. Once again his transfer value had massively increased as Martin O'Neill invested £12m to sign him for Sunderland. After debuting in the League Cup, Fletcher arrowed home two goals at Swansea on his Premier League debut for the club and proceeded to score in each of his next three games as he was named Premier League Player of the Month.

Steven stayed at Sunderland for four seasons, spending part of his last term on loan at Marseille. He also scored in a couple of derbies with Newcastle and played at Wembley in the 2014 League (Capital One) final, missing a late chance to equalise against Manchester City. During his loan in France, he also played in a cup final, being a teammate of future Sunderland defender Javier Manquillo as Marseille were beaten 4-2 by Paris Saint-Germain in the 2016 Coupe de France.

Released after four seasons at Sunderland, Fletcher's next stop was at Sheffield Wednesday. Having helped the Owls reach the Play-Offs in his first season, Steven scored in the semi-final against Huddersfield. As at Sunderland, Steven would stay in Sheffield for four years, scoring 38 goals in exactly 100 starts, plus another 36 games as a sub. In the summer of 2020, Fletcher decided to sport red and white stripes again, this time as a Stoke City player.

He scored 12 goals in 47+35 games before signing for former Sunderland manager Jack Ross at Dundee United in July 2022.

## FLO, Tore Andre

**POSITION:** Centre-forward

**BIRTHPLACE:** Stryn, Norway

**DATE OF BIRTH:** 15/06/1973

**HEIGHT:** 6' 4" **WEIGHT:** 13st 8lbs

**SIGNED FROM:** Rangers, 30/08/2002

**DEBUT:** v Manchester United, H, 31/08/2002

**LAST MATCH:** v Mansfield Town, A, 13/08/2003

**MOVED TO:** Siena, 22/08/2003

**TEAMS:** Sogndal, Tromso, SK Brann, Chelsea, Rangers, Sunderland, Siena, Valerenga, Leeds United, MK Dons, Sogndal

**INTERNATIONAL:** Norway

**SAFC TOTALS:** 26+7 appearances / 6 goals

**Flo was a record signing who proved that spending big money does not always equate to success. Flo was such a flop that the joke was that the club shop had run out of the letter P as supporters added that letter to the record signing's name they had had printed on the back of their shirts. Sunderland Echo reporter Graeme Anderson renamed him Tore Andre Four as that was the mark he gave Flo out of ten in so many of his reports.**

Yet, Flo was a player of some calibre, but he was not a good fit at Sunderland. Like Lilian Laslandes, he had the nigh on impossible task of trying to replace Niall Quinn. Flo though, was a different kind of player. While tall he was not good in the air and preferred the ball to his feet. Also, he did not appear to be the kind of player you wanted in a battle. Rather like Jeremain Lens in later years, he arrived having been used to being in a team that dominated and served a stream of chances up for him. There had been five pieces of silverware in his three seasons at Chelsea and two in the second of his two years with Rangers.

At Sunderland, a debut goal at home to Manchester United maintained his excellent record of scoring in his first game, something he made a habit of throughout his well-travelled career. Despite getting off to a good start, Flo struggled. Even when he did well, he could be unhelpful. After perhaps what was the best of his goals in a draw at Charlton, Sunderland's Press Officer had to use all of her persuasive powers to push him into being willing to do an interview. In eleven of the 23 league games he started, Flo was replaced while two of his meagre tally of six goals came in a 7-0 League Cup win against Cambridge which was the sort of scenario he thrived in, i.e. when his team was dominating and he could accept the chances.

An overall career tally of 192 goals in 545 games spread across Norway, England, Scotland and Italy combined with 23 goals in 76 internationals indicates the ability Sunderland paid to sign was there, but mere glimpses were seen in Flo's time on Wearside.

At Chelsea, he appeared as a late sub in three winning cup finals: against Middlesbrough in the League Cup and Real Madrid in the European Super Cup in 1998 and as Aston Villa were beaten in the FA Cup two years later, playing alongside Gus Poyet on two of those occasions, the future Sunderland head coach scoring the winner against Madrid. In 1998, he started the European Cup Winners' Cup final, Gianfranco Zola scoring the only goal of the game against VfB Stuttgart moments after replacing Flo. He also picked up a winner's accolade as an unused sub in the 2000 Charity Shield as Manchester United were beaten after having Roy Keane sent off.

A hat-trick against Spurs and three goals in a Champions League tie against Barcelona were amongst the Norwegian's highlights for the Stamford Bridge club. Having paid £300,000 to bring him from Norwegian football, the Blues made a handsome profit when selling him for £12m to Rangers in November 2000, the fee being the biggest for any Scottish club and the most ever for a Norwegian.

A debut goal in a 5-1 win over Celtic was the first of 13 in 22 in his first season and 22 in 42 in his second. Playing under the captaincy of Derek Ferguson's brother Barry, Flo opened the scoring in the 2002 Scottish League Cup final as Ayr United were beaten 4-0. Later the same season Ferguson scored as with Flo an unused sub, the Norwegian picked up another winners medal as Martin O'Neill's Celtic were beaten in the Scottish Cup final.

After leaving Sunderland on a free transfer, he joined newly-promoted Siena in Serie A before returning to Norway and then playing for his old Chelsea teammates Dennis Wise and Poyet at Leeds. Eight months after announcing his retirement in March 2008, he made a comeback with MK Dons and after retiring again at the end of the season, resurfaced two years later back at his first club Sogndal who had just been promoted.

At international level, Flo debuted against England in Oslo in 1995 (alongside one-time Sunderland triallist Stig-Inge Bjornebye) and scored as Brazil were beaten at the 1998 FIFA World Cup. His brother Jostein and cousin Havard were also full internationals while two other brothers, a nephew and the nephew of one of his brothers all played in the Norwegian top-flight.

In 2012, he returned to Chelsea behind the scenes and as of 2021, Flo was in a role as loan player technical coach.

## FOGARTY, Ambrose Gerald (Amby)

**POSITION:** Inside-left

**BIRTHPLACE:** Dublin, Ireland

**DATE OF BIRTH:** 11/09/1933 - 03/01/2016

**HEIGHT:** 5' 7" **WEIGHT:** 10st 4lbs

**SIGNED FROM:** Glentoran, 26/10/1957

**DEBUT:** v Birmingham City, A, 09/11/1957

**LAST MATCH:** v Hartlepools United, 13/11/1963

**MOVED TO:** Hartlepools United, 13/11/1963

**TEAMS:** Home Farm, Bohemians, Glentoran, Sunderland, Hartlepools United, Cork Hibernian, Cork Celtic

**INTERNATIONAL:** Republic of Ireland

**SAFC TOTALS:** 174 appearances / 44 goals

**Amby Fogarty was a talented footballer who was also a feisty battler. A craftsman of an inside-forward, but for the riches Sunderland possessed in George Herd and Johnny Crossan, Fogarty would have stayed in the team for longer. Although he scored in one of the three games he played early in the first-ever promotion season of 1963-64, this was in the days of no substitutes and with Sunderland having a very settled side he moved on.**

Fogarty had come into the side mid-way through the first-ever relegation season in 1957 and was in the side on the dreaded day when demotion was confirmed at Portsmouth. He barely played in his first full season, but returned with both goals in a win at Sheffield United in September 1959 to begin a run of seven goals in as many games. Amby ended the season with a dozen goals to his name and hit ten the following year, his tally including one in Sunderland's first-ever League Cup tie (at Brentford). As the team went close to promotion in 1961-62, he was averaging a goal every three games until injury curtailed his campaign a year to the day before the Boxing Day injury that did for Brian Clough. The pair were big pals, Amby being Best Man when Clough wed.

Amby was a teammate of Charlie Hurley in all ten of the internationals Fogarty played while with Sunderland, scoring in three of those games. After signing for Bobby Gurney at Hartlepools - where his £10,000 fee stood as a record for over two decades - he became the first man capped with the club when he played against Spain in March 1964. By this time he had played 15 games in Division Four having not missed a match since he signed. Fogarty's creativity had helped local lad Terry Francis score a hat-trick on Amby's home debut with Fogarty scoring himself on his second appearance at the Victoria Ground. Pools though finished in the re-election zone, but he improved the team so, that in his first full season they finished above the re-election zone for the first time in the sixties.

Reunited with Clough when the latter began his managerial career at Pools, Fogarty began to play at half-back rather than inside-forward. After 144 games and 25 goals (including friendlies) Amby was released from his contract in March 1967 to enable him to move to Cork Hibernian as player/coach. 7,000 attended a benefit game against Sunderland.

He went on to manage Cork Celtic, Drumcondra, Galway United and Athlone Town, with whom he qualified for the UEFA Cup, before finishing with Galway Rovers. At the other end of his career, Amby had played in the Irish Cup final of 1956 against Distillery for Glentoran for whom he scored 28 goals in 98 appearances before Sunderland paid just over £3,000 for him.

## FOGGON, Alan

**POSITION:** Outside-left

**BIRTHPLACE:** West Pelton, Co Durham

**DATE OF BIRTH:** 23/02/1950

**HEIGHT:** 5' 9" **WEIGHT:** 13st 3lbs

**SIGNED FROM:** Manchester United, 23/09/1976

**DEBUT:** v West Ham United, A, 25/09/1976

**LAST MATCH:** v Norwich City, H, 18/12/1976

**MOVED TO:** Southend United, 27/05/1977

**TEAMS:** West Stanley, Newcastle United, Cardiff City, Middlesbrough, Rochester Lancers, Hartford Bi-Centennials, Manchester United, Sunderland, Southend United, Hartlepool United (L), Consett, Whitley Bay

**INTERNATIONAL:** England Youth

**SAFC TOTALS:** 9+1 appearances / 0 goals

## FOGGON, Alan (Continued)

**A player for all of the north-east's three biggest clubs, Foggon was a success on Tyneside and Teesside, but way past his best in his brief stint on Wearside. And yet, Alan was only 26 when he came to Sunderland and 28 when he walked away from the professional game.**

Sunderland were newly-promoted, but struggling when he came into the team just as Bob Stokoe's reign was coming to an end. Three of his ten games for Sunderland were against Manchester United who he had started the season with - two of the three games he played for the Red Devils being against his former clubs Newcastle and Boro.

He had debuted for Newcastle as a 17-year-old at Arsenal in February 1968, going on to play for England in the group phase of a UEFA Youth tournament in France two months later when he appeared in draws with Bulgaria and the USSR either side of a narrow win over the Netherlands. Alan went on to play 69+11 games for the Magpies, scoring 16 goals, one of which came in the 1969 Inter-Cities Fairs Cup final. Unlike most wingers who are typically light-weight, Foggon topped 13 stones despite his modest height, but when in full flow, the schoolboy sprint champion could take some stopping. This was certainly the case when he joined Middlesbrough in October 1972 after little over a year with Cardiff where his only goal in 17 league games came against Brighton a month before he was transferred.

There was no shortage of goals once he got to Middlesbrough. A goal on his first start against Oxford United was the first of 49 from 124+12 games. 19 of these came in his first full season as Boro swept to the Division Two title under Jack Charlton, Foggon scoring in both games against Sunderland. He was top scorer again the following year with 16 of his 18 goals coming in the top-flight where he missed just one game. By this time, it was a case of Foggon the Tees rather than the Tyne, but his time at Boro came to an end in April 1976 when after a difficult spell, which included being suspended by the club for missing training, he decided to ply his trade in the USA where he scored four goals in 19 games with Hartford after failing to score in seven outings with Rochester.

After his return to England with Manchester United and subsequently Sunderland, Foggon rapidly slid down the football ladder. After signing for Southend for whom he played 22 league games in 1977-78 as the Shrimpers went on to win promotion from Division Four, he was loaned to Hartlepool. His second goal for Hartlepool and last senior strike of his career, brought derby victory at Darlington, but after 18 games in which he was unable to prevent Hartlepool finishing in the re-election zone, he dropped into local football and went on to work in the pub trade in Spennymoor before managing a security company in Newcastle.

Foggon was capped by England at youth level, debuting in a goalless draw with Bulgaria.

## FORD, Peter Norman

**POSITION:** Full-back

**BIRTHPLACE:** Tradeston , Glasgow

**DATE OF BIRTH:** 30/10/1865 - 19/02/1939

**HEIGHT:** 5' 6½" **WEIGHT:** 9st 7lbs

**SIGNED FROM:** Manchester South End, 15/09/1887

**DEBUT:** v Newcastle West End, H, 05/11/1887

**LAST MATCH:** v Newcastle East End, H, 17/11/1888

**MOVED TO:** Not re-signed, 30/04/1891

**TEAMS:** Roseburn, Manchester South End, Sunderland

**SAFC TOTALS:** 4 appearances / 0 goals

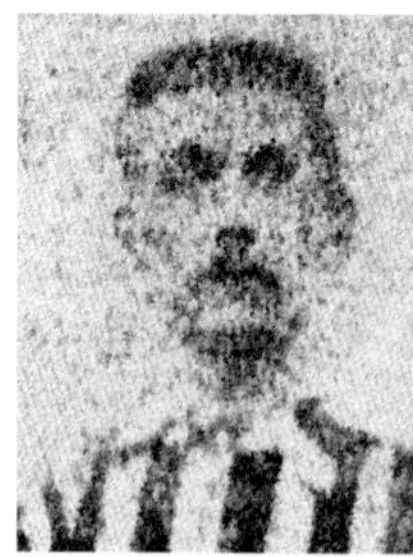

**A full-back who was with Sunderland from 1887 until their first league season in 1890-91. Ford never managed a league appearance, but as well as numerous friendlies, appeared in a quartet of English (FA) Cup games, three in his first season and one in his second. In his latter years at Sunderland, he played for the 'A' team, effectively the reserves. He then became a referee, operating in the Northern Alliance in 1892-93.**

Known as 'Little Peter', he had worked as a clerk in an iron foundry while living in Glasgow where he played for the Maryhill-based Roseburn Club before playing in Manchester. While he was at Sunderland, Ford was employed as a shipyard clerk and continued in this role after finishing with football. Having started playing bowls for the Roker Park Club in the 1890s, he was still active in that sport in the 1920s.

## FORD, Tony

**POSITION:** Outside-right

**BIRTHPLACE:** Grimsby, Lincolnshire

**DATE OF BIRTH:** 14/05/1959

**HEIGHT:** 5' 9" **WEIGHT:** 12st 8lbs

**SIGNED FROM:** Grimsby Town, 27/03/1986, on loan

**DEBUT:** v Bradford City, H, 29/03/1986

**LAST MATCH:** v Stoke City, H, 03/05/1986

**MOVED TO:** Grimsby Town, 05/05/1986, end of loan

**TEAMS:** Grimsby Town, Sunderland (L), Stoke City, WBA, Grimsby Town, Bradford City (L), Scunthorpe United, Barrow, Mansfield Town, Rochdale

**SAFC TOTALS:** 8+1 appearances / 1 goal

**Tony Ford played nine times for Sunderland as a loan player during a dismal 1985-86 season, but they were part of his staggering career total of 1,080 games which made him the first outfield player to reach 1,000 appearances. 931 of those games were in the Football League, again, a record for an outfield player. A winger for much of his career, including his spell at Sunderland, Tony retreated to right-back in his latter years.**

Awarded the MBE for his Services to Football, Ford's career was not one of glory. In between becoming Grimsby's youngest-ever player when he debuted away to Walsall in October 1975 at the age of 16 and 164 days, he finally signed off after playing for Rochdale against Torquay United in November 2001 when he was 42. In all that time, he won a trio of Player of the Year awards with his hometown and first club Grimsby, the Division Three title with the Mariners in 1980 and the Football League Group Cup two years later.

Other than that, the only tangible recognition for his supreme efforts were a couple of England B caps won in the space of three days in May 1989 when he was a teammate of future Sunderland man Paul Stewart. Ford came on as a sub for Paul Gascoigne in a win away to Iceland followed by a start away to Norway. Watched by crowds of only 775 and 1,500, they were as low key as most of Tony's career.

Sunderland represented Ford's first foray away from his home town Grimsby. Brought in by Lawrie McMenemy, Tony made a scoring debut as a sub and went on to start every game to the end of the season helping Sunderland to battle away from relegation. After over 400 games for Grimsby, he moved on that summer, but to Stoke, the opposition on his final Sunderland performance. Three years later, the Potters made a tidy profit, the reported £145,000 secured from WBA being £110,000 more than he had cost.

He returned to Grimsby for another three seasons before (following a brief loan to Bradford City) a switch to their arch-rivals Scunthorpe where he signed for his old Grimsby junior teammate Dave Moore. Continuing to give good service, Tony had two seasons at Scunthorpe before the arrival of Mick Buxton as manager signalled the end of Tony's time with the Iron. Still not finished, he briefly dropped into non-league with Barrow before enjoying another six seasons split evenly between Mansfield and Rochdale where he continued to play as well as assisting future Sunderland assistant manager Steve Parkin at both Mansfield and Rochdale. Fans at his final club recognised his age, chanting: 'He's big, he's bad, he's older than me Dad, Tony Ford, Tony Ford. He's nearly 43 he's got an MBE, Tony Ford, Tony Ford.'

He went on to have further spells as assistant manager at Barnsley and back at Rochdale, eventually leaving the game in December 2006.

## FORD, Trevor

**POSITION:** Centre-forward

**BIRTHPLACE:** Swansea, Glamorganshire

**DATE OF BIRTH:** 01/10/1923 - 29/05/2003

**HEIGHT:** 5' 11" **WEIGHT:** 13st 4lbs

**SIGNED FROM:** Aston Villa, 27/10/1950

**DEBUT:** v Chelsea, A, 28/10/1950

**LAST MATCH:** v Liverpool, H, 14/11/1953

**MOVED TO:** Cardiff City, 28/11/1953

**TEAMS:** Tower United, Swansea Town, Clapton Orient (WW2 Guest), Aston Villa, Sunderland, Cardiff City, PSV Eindhoven, Newport County, Romford, Gloucester City (Guest)

**SAFC TOTALS:** 117 appearances / 70 goals

**One of the finest centre-forwards ever to pull on a red and white striped shirt. Trevor Ford played as if his life depended on it. If you ever wanted to see a striker 'Get stuck in!', Ford was your man. Famously on his home debut against Sheffield Wednesday he scored a hat-trick, broke a defender's jaw and smashed a goal-post. Under a fortnight later, Trevor scored twice on his second appearance at Roker Park after signing for Sunderland. Those goals were for Wales against England, but continued to excite supporters of the 'Bank of England Club' who had seen Ford signed for a British record fee of £29,500.**

Ford was worth every penny. His goals ratio for Sunderland of 0.598 games per goal has only ever been bettered by Dave Halliday, Brian Clough and Johnny Campbell. Having scored 17 in his first season after arriving in late October, Ford plundered 22 goals in each of the following two campaigns and nine in 12 games in 1953-54, before being sold to Cardiff for £500 more than he had cost. He won the Welsh Cup with the Bluebirds in 1956, beating former club Swansea in the final. Tough as teak, Trevor dished out stick and dealt with what came his way without complaint, often playing on once injured in the pre-substitute era.

Infamously, he did not get on with 'The Clown Prince of Soccer' Len Shackleton. While Shack was the genius, Ford was the grafter. Although initial reports of their partnership spoke of

how well they played together, that relationship soon faltered with each critical of the other in their autobiographies. Shack's was not the only autobiography to upset Ford. He successfully sued England goalkeeper Gil Merrick who had complained of Ford's physical approach to goalkeepers. Ford pointed out, he had never been cautioned or sent off for his playing style.

It was also the age of the maximum wage as well as no subs. In addition to being supplied with a job as manager of a garage by way of bolstering his wages, Britain's record signing was also one of the 14 Sunderland players suspended indefinitely having been found guilty of receiving illegal payments from the club, albeit this was over three years after he had left. Due to his ban from British football, Ford moved to PSV Eindhoven where he signed for future Sunderland manager George Hardwick. After scoring 21 in 53 games he was able to return to the UK, but by the time he joined Newport County he was 37.

Capped 38 times by Wales, Trevor scored 23 times, at the time a record for his country. Twelve of those goals came in 13 appearances while with Sunderland. He also played international cricket at schoolboy level and famously was on the field as 12th man for Glamorgan on the day West Indian legend Gary Sobers smashed six sixes from one over.

After his footballing days were over, Ford returned to the motor trade he had been employed in while playing for Sunderland, at various points working on Wearside and in South Wales. In 1993, he briefly returned to the game as a non-executive director at Cardiff City. His autobiography 'I Lead the Attack' was published in 1957, while in 2016 a further authorised biography was released. Ironically, for someone who turned down the chance to play for Arsenal before coming to Sunderland during World War Two Ford served as an anti-aircraft gunner in the Royal Artillery.

## FOREMAN, John Joseph

**POSITION:** Winger

**BIRTHPLACE:** Tanfield Lea, Co Durham

**DATE OF BIRTH:** 06/10/1913 - 17/10/1964

**HEIGHT:** 5' 9" **WEIGHT:** 11st 4lbs

**SIGNED FROM:** Crook Town, 06/05/1933

**DEBUT:** v Manchester City, H, 11/04/1934

**LAST MATCH:** v Middlesbrough, H, 14/04/1934

**MOVED TO:** West Ham United, 20/09/1934

**TEAMS:** Tanfield Lea, West Stanley, Crook Town, Sunderland, West Ham United, Bury, Swansea Town, Workington (L), Hartlepools United, Crewe Alexandra (WW2 Guest)

**SAFC TOTALS:** 2 appearances / 0 goals

**Having come out of local football to play for Sunderland as a 20-year-old, John Foreman's career as a first-teamer at Roker Park spanned just three days before he moved to West Ham for whom he scored seven in 51 games, before one goal in four games for Bury prior to signing for Swansea Town in December 1937.**

Although Swansea retained his Football League registration, Foreman moved to non-league Workington in the summer of 1938, joining Hartlepools in 1939 after the Welsh club released him. Debuting for Hartlepools against Barrow on 26 August 1939, he played in the three games of the abandoned 1939-40 season before playing three times as a 'Guest' later that season for Crewe. In 1946, he returned to Hartlepool to make a one-off appearance. After retiring from football, John worked for Rolls Royce in Crewe until his death in October 1964.

## FORSTER, Derek

**POSITION:** Goalkeeper

**BIRTHPLACE:** Walker, Newcastle, Northumberland

**DATE OF BIRTH:** 19/02/1949

**HEIGHT:** 5' 9" **WEIGHT:** 11st 2lbs

**SIGNED FROM:** School, 01/07/1964

**DEBUT:** v Leicester City, H, 22/08/1964

**LAST MATCH:** v Bristol City, A, 15/04/1972

**MOVED TO:** Charlton Athletic, 01/07/1973

**TEAMS:** Sunderland, Charlton Athletic, Brighton & HA, Consett, Evenwood, Blyth Spartans, North Shields

**INTERNATIONAL:** England schoolboys

**SAFC TOTALS:** 19 appearances / 0 goals

**At the age of 15 years and 185 days, Derek Forster became the youngest-ever top-flight player when he debuted on the opening day of the season after SAFC's first-ever promotion in 1964. With Jim Montgomery injured and manager Alan Brown departed, the side was selected by the directors who chose the England schoolboy international in preference to reserve team keeper Derek Kirby, even though Forster had spent part of the pre-season on a fortnight's family holiday in Blackpool!**

Forster was beaten three times - but so was Leicester's England goalkeeper Gordon Banks at the other end. Derek kept his place for defeats at West Brom and Chelsea, but after picking the ball out of net ten times in those three games, was taken out of the firing line with Sandy McLaughlan signed in Monty's absence.

Derek did not play again until the summer of 1967 when he featured in the first five games as Sunderland represented Vancouver Royal Canadians in North America. These games are not included in Derek's total of 19 matches for Sunderland.

In January 1968, with Monty indisposed, Forster got his first league game for two and a half years. As with his debut it came against Leicester at home. Later in the season there were two more opportunities, at Anfield where he was beaten twice and against Wolves at home where he kept his first clean sheet. Unfortunately for Forster, Monty's consistency meant there was just one more appearance for him in the next three seasons before 1971-72 provided the opportunity he had waited for.

Three runs in the side brought a dozen games with a best sequence of five in a row, but after not appearing at all in the cup-winning season of 1972-73, by which time Trevor Swinburne had taken over as second choice keeper, Forster moved on.

During the period 1964-65 to 1968-69, Derek played in all 36 games Sunderland played in the FA Youth Cup, earning winners' medals in 1967 and 1969, saving a penalty in the 1966 final and helping the Lads to the semi-final in 1965.

Joining Charlton, Derek started the first seven games of the season, conceding four at home to York on the opening day, but only played twice more before Brian Clough stepped in to sign him for Brighton. Clough had still been at Sunderland when Derek debuted.

Brighton had only conceded nine goals in as many games when Forster came in for his first game only to concede six at Walsall. He played just twice more before leaving in 1976. Subsequently, Derek enjoyed a 30-year career working with Sunderland city's Leisure department, but retired after losing his left eye to cancer in 2007.

As a boy, he had been centre-forward with Newcastle Schools' Under 11s until one day the goalkeeper did not turn up, Forster took over and is so often the case with goalkeepers, he then remained in that position. He was capped five times by England at Schoolboy level numbering Colin Todd, Colin Suggett, Joe Royle and Trevor Brooking amongst his teammates.

## FORSTER, Henry (Harry)

**POSITION:** Full-back

**BIRTHPLACE:** Consett, Co Durham

**DATE OF BIRTH:** 10/03/1884 - date of death unknown

**HEIGHT:** 5' 7½" **WEIGHT:** 11st 6lbs

**SIGNED FROM:** Annfield Plain, 18/04/1905

**DEBUT:** v Sheffield United, A, 09/02/1907

**LAST MATCH:** v Wednesday, A, 26/12/1911

**MOVED TO:** West Ham United, 07/06/1912

**TEAMS:** West Stanley, Annfield Plain, Sunderland, West Ham United

**SAFC TOTALS:** 110 appearances / 0 goals

**Harry Forster's Sunderland career started and ended in Sheffield, his debut at Bramall Lane resulting in a modest 3-2 defeat compared to a record 8-0 reverse on his final appearance at Hillsborough on a day when Sunderland trailed 7-0 at half-time. It was an ignominious end for a player who topped a century of appearances playing in both full-back berths as well as both wing-half positions, a testimony to his ability to play with either foot.**

In February 1912, he was suspended by the club but made his peace with the directors three days later and was allowed to resume training. He did not play again though and after six years service, in which his best season was 1908-09 when he played 38 times, he moved on to West Ham.

He debuted for the Irons on the opening day of the 1912-13 campaign in a 4-0 Southern League win at Exeter, going on to play 25 times, mainly at left-back, as they finished third. He also played four games in the English (FA Cup). Three of these were against WBA before his side were hammered 5-0 by Aston Villa who Sunderland would meet in that season's final. In his second season in London, Harry played the first 15 games of the season, his final one for the club coming in a home defeat to Southend United on 6 December 1913.

He was still involved with football at the beginning of World War Two coaching Blackhall Mill FC. His son was killed during that war while a Great Great grandson played for Warwickshire Under 15s.

## FOSTER, John Samuel (Jack)

**POSITION:** Centre-forward

**BIRTHPLACE:** Parkgate, Yorkshire

**DATE OF BIRTH:** 19/11/1877 - 05/02/1946

**HEIGHT:** 5' 7" **WEIGHT:** 11st 8lbs

**SIGNED FROM:** Watford, 06/12/1907

**DEBUT:** v Birmingham, A, 07/12/1907

**LAST MATCH:** v Middlesbrough, A, 15/02/1908

**MOVED TO:** West Ham United, 01/05/1908

**TEAMS:** Rotherham Church Institute, Thornhill United, Blackpool, Rotherham Town, Stockport County, Watford, Sunderland, West Ham United, Southampton, Huddersfield Town, Castleford Town, Morley

**SAFC TOTALS:** 8 appearances / 3 goals

**A club record fee of £800 was invested in Jack Foster, but it proved unsuccessful as after only a handful of games he returned to the south on doctor's advice. The Yorkshireman had made a good start with a debut goal in an away win and later scored twice in a big New Year's Day win at home to Woolwich Arsenal, but nonetheless, his move was a costly and ineffective one.**

Twelve goals in 13 Southern League games early in the season had persuaded Sunderland to splash out on Foster who had come to prominence with Blackpool in 1901-02 when one of his six goals in 28 Division Two games (making him joint top scorer) came in the first-ever league meeting with Blackpool's local rivals Preston North End.

Having left Sunderland for Southern League West Ham, Foster scored in his first two games and included a hat-trick against Portsmouth in his total of nine goals in 15 games, but by March he moved even further south, signing for Southampton in exchange for Frank Costello. His time with the Saints was also short-lived as after just two months that featured one goal from six appearances, he returned north just 12 months after - as the club's record signing - he had left on the understanding that he needed to live in the south for health reasons.

Signing for Huddersfield, Jack was their top scorer with 25 goals in 1909-10 in the club's final season in the Midland League before being admitted to the Football League. As Huddersfield stepped up, he left the club to play in non-league whilst working as a chimney sweep, the same profession as his father and how he made his living before playing football (perhaps a surprising occupation given the reasons for his departure from Wearside), but returned to Huddersfield in 1912 as trainer.

He went on to become their assistant manager under the great Herbert Chapman who led The Terriers to three successive league titles in the early twenties. In August 1926, Foster became assistant manager to Newcastle United legend Colin Veitch at Bradford City, becoming caretaker-manager of the Bantams for the final four months of the 1927-28 season as they finished sixth in Division Three North, having been relegated the previous year.

In 1929, he returned to Huddersfield to manage their second team and a decade later, he was still in the game scouting for Portsmouth and then Birmingham just before World War Two. Jack returned to Yorkshire during WW2 after his health suffered during bombing raids in the midlands and passed away in Huddersfield in February 1946.

## FOSTER, John Thomas (Jackie)

**POSITION:** Outside-right

**BIRTHPLACE:** Southwick, Co Durham

**DATE OF BIRTH:** 21/03/1903 - date of death unknown

**HEIGHT:** 5' 6½" **WEIGHT:** 10st 2lbs

**SIGNED FROM:** Murton CW, 01/09/1920

**DEBUT:** v Huddersfield Town, A, 25/09/1920

**LAST MATCH:** v Preston North End, A, 30/04/1921

**MOVED TO:** Ashington, 11/06/1921

**TEAMS:** Murton CW, Sunderland, Ashington, Halifax Town, Grimsby Town, Bristol City, Brentford, Barrow, Colwyn Bay United, Ashford

**SAFC TOTALS:** 6 appearances / 0 goals

**Jackie Foster had to wait until he had completed his Boilermaker's apprenticeship in Scotland before he joined Sunderland as a 17-year-old. All of his appearances came in the 1920-21 season when he was on the winning side just once, on his home debut against Huddersfield a week after debuting away to the same side.**

He also played cricket for Sunderland CC while on Sunderland's books, but after his solitary season at Roker Park moved on to join Ashington in time for the Colliers first season as a Football League club in Division Three North.

After two seasons at Portland Park, in which Ashington had to apply for re-election after their second term, Foster moved on to Halifax Town. Debuting for the Shaymen at home to Grimsby on 8 September 1923, he held his place for the rest of the season, one of his two league goals being a Christmas Day winner against Hartlepools United. He also scored in an FA Cup run that ended with a three-game epic against Manchester City which was eventually settled at Old Trafford. The second of Foster's two seasons with Halifax saw him take his total for the club to 82 games and three goals before he enjoyed successive promotions with Grimsby Town in 1925-26 and Bristol City in 1926-27 without playing sufficient games to earn a medal.

It was third time lucky as he did get a Division Three South medal with Brentford in 1933 in the final season of a four-year 141 game spell with the Bees where his brother James was a reserve. He then spent three years with Barrow in Division Three North. After having a trial with Ashford in October 1937 he returned to Brentford - who were by now in the top flight - as part of the ground staff. After World War Two, he worked on the continent with Royal Verviers Club of Belgium. His brother Tom married one of Sandy McAllister's daughters.

## FOTHERINGHAM, Alexander

**POSITION:** Full-back

**BIRTHPLACE:** Inverness, Invernesshire

**DATE OF BIRTH:** 03/10/1870 - 12/07/1925

**SIGNED FROM:** Inverness Caledonians, 28/03/1899

**DEBUT:** v Bury, A, 31/03/1899

**LAST MATCH:** v Bury, A, 31/03/1899

**MOVED TO:** Inverness Caledonians, 04/04/1899

**TEAMS:** Inverness Caledonians, Sunderland, Inverness Caledonians

**SAFC TOTALS:** 1 appearance / 0 goals

**Fotheringham's one game in his brief trial came in a 2-1 win at Bury in which Bill Pallister also played his only first-team game. Fotheringham swiftly returned to Inverness and his picture framing business which he continued after his football career.**

Four years before playing for Sunderland, Alex turned down an offer to join Small Heath (who became Birmingham City) and a year after playing for Sunderland he returned south for a trial with Nottingham Forest, but did not play a competitive game for them. Contemporary reports likened his style of play to the famous former Sunderland and Glasgow Rangers full-back Donald Gow. Alex's sportsmanlike spirit led to him refereeing many important fixtures in the Inverness area after retiring from playing the game.

## FRASER, John Watson

**POSITION:** Outside-right

**BIRTHPLACE:** Belfast, Northern Ireland

**DATE OF BIRTH:** 15/09/1938 - 13/03/2011

**HEIGHT:** 5' 7½" **WEIGHT:** 11st 9lbs

**SIGNED FROM:** Glentoran, 27/02/1959

**DEBUT:** v Huddersfield Town, H, 28/02/1959

**LAST MATCH:** v Bristol City, H, 14/11/1959

**MOVED TO:** Portsmouth, 12/05/1960

**TEAMS:** Dundela, Distillery, Notts County, Distillery, Glentoran, Sunderland, Portsmouth, Margate, Watford, Durban, Westview Apollon, Germiston Callies, Corinthians

**INTERNATIONAL:** Northern Ireland 'B'

**SAFC TOTALS:** 22 appearances / 1 goal

**One of several players scouted in Northern Ireland in the late fifties, Fraser had previously come to England as a 16-year-old with Notts County, but had returned home after a month due to homesickness. Having become an apprentice fitter in the shipyards after leaving school he progressed in Irish football until signed by Alan Brown.**

Thrust straight into a league match a day after signing, Fraser played in ten of the last 12 games in Sunderland's first season outside the top flight and the first nine of the following campaign, making his final appearance in November 1959, the same month as he played against France in winning a 'B' cap for his country.

Moving to Portsmouth, he played once in 1960-61 before dropping into the Southern League with Margate where, while working as a welder with an engineering firm, he won the Kent Senior Shield. He scored 20 goals in 47 games in his one season, the highlights being a goal in an FA Cup first round win over Bournemouth & Boscombe Athletic after he had scored two and made three in the final qualifying round against Guildford. Fraser's form earned him another chance in the Football League with Watford where he scored three times in 24 appearances before he moved to South Africa in 1964.

He won the South African Bowl in his time with Durban between 1964 and 1966 before playing for three other South African clubs, finishing at Corinthians in 1969. Having assisted the South African national team as a coach in the late sixties, Fraser returned to Durban as manager between 1971 to 74 and had a footballing swansong with Berea FC in 1977. He remained in South Africa until 2004 before returning to Ireland.

## FRASER, William Alexander Noel (Willie)

**POSITION:** Goalkeeper

**BIRTHPLACE:** Melbourne, Australia

**DATE OF BIRTH:** 24/02/1929 - 07/03/1996

**HEIGHT:** 6' 0" **WEIGHT:** 11st 13lbs

**SIGNED FROM:** Airdrieonians, 16/03/1954

**DEBUT:** v Tottenham Hotspur, A, 20/03/1954

**LAST MATCH:** v Sheffield Wednesday, A, 19/09/1958

**MOVED TO:** Nottingham Forest, 26/12/1958

**TEAMS:** Cowie FC, Stirling Juniors, Third Lanark, Airdrieonians, Sunderland, Nottingham Forest, North Shields

**INTERNATIONAL:** Scotland

**SAFC TOTALS:** 143 appearances / 0 goals

**Willie Fraser won both of his Scotland caps while with Sunderland. Debuting with a clean sheet against Wales in October 1954 seven months after coming to Wearside, the following month at Hampden he was beaten by clubmate Billy Bingham of Northern Ireland.**

Though born in Australia, Fraser's parents were from Stirling and Inverness and having returned to Scotland when he was five, Willie had been brought up there. Starting just after World War Two, he made 63 league appearances for Third Lanark and 103 for Airdrieonians, one of the most famous seeing him keep a clean sheet against a dominant Celtic in November 1952.

There was another clean sheet on Willie's debut for Sunderland in a 3-0 win at Spurs having joined the 'Bank of England Club' for a fee of £7,000. Quickly establishing himself as number one keeper ahead of fellow Scotland international Jim Cowan, Fraser played a total of 45 games in each of his first two full seasons before missing almost all of 1956-57 when the reason for his absence in the closing stages was down to him becoming one of the 14 players to be indefinitely suspended having been found guilty of receiving illegal payments. When the suspension was lifted Willie returned to play regularly in the relegation season of 1957-58, but after conceding eleven goals in the last two of eight games he played in the second division, Fraser moved on to Nottingham Forest for £2,000 less than Sunderland had paid for him.

His time there was short-lived as in his two games for Forest he conceded even more than in his final two games for Sunderland: a 7-1 debut loss at home to Birmingham City being followed by a 5-1 thrashing at Luton the following month. He quickly returned to the north east with North Shields.

After his retirement from football, Willie worked at Northern Autoport as a car salesman and later sales director. Having been a part-time market gardener with his father during the formative years of his football career, he subsequently set up a florists business in Cupar in Fife. During his National Service with the army, he served with the Royal Electrical and Mechanical Engineers, playing for the Army against a Scotland XI in March 1953 whilst still with Airdrieonians.

## FREDGAARD, Carsten

**POSITION:** Midfield

**BIRTHPLACE:** Blovstrod, Denmark

**DATE OF BIRTH:** 20/05/1976

**HEIGHT:** 6' 0" **WEIGHT:** 12st 4lbs

**SIGNED FROM:** Lyngby, 19/04/1999

**DEBUT:** v Chelsea, A, 07/08/1999

**LAST MATCH:** v Luton Town, H, 19/09/2000

**MOVED TO:** FC Copenhagen, 14/05/2001

**TEAMS:** Lyngby, Sunderland, WBA (L), Bolton Wanderers (L), FC Copenhagen, Farum, Randers, Akademisk Boldklub, Hillerup IK, FC Graesrodderne

**INTERNATIONAL:** Denmark

**SAFC TOTALS:** 3+2 appearances / 2 goals

**There was much excitement when Sunderland spent a reported £1.8m on Fredgaard. Promotion had just been secured and the signing of a player nicknamed Lightning and who had just been a Player of the Year runner-up in his home country augured well for squad strengthening. This was especially the case as he won what proved to be his only full cap in the month he debuted for Sunderland. Carsten had scored 16 goals in 33 games in his last season in Denmark, taking his tally for Lyngby to 33 goals in 120 games.**

Fredgaard though was doomed to disappointment at Sunderland despite scoring twice on his second start in a 5-0 League (Worthington) Cup win at Walsall. He had debuted as a sub on the opening day of the season in a big defeat at Chelsea, but this would prove to be his only Premier League appearance for Sunderland although he was named as sub a further three times.

Soon nicknamed Chocolate Fireguard in Sunderland, as that was how much use he was perceived to be, by February he was sent out on loan to West Brom where he played five times, debuting against Crewe Alexandra only to have his loan cut short after breaking a rib. At the start of his second season, Fredgaard was given an outing for Sunderland as a sub in a League Cup tie with Luton, but that proved to be his final appearance for the club who loaned him out to Sam Allardyce's Bolton for three months over the winter. Four of his five appearances for the Trotters were off the bench, his only start once again featuring Crewe.

At the end of the season, Fredgaard returned to Danish football, Sunderland being due 50% of the fee when he left Copenhagen with whom he was on the fringes as they won the Superliga in 2002-03. In 2006, he won the Danish Cup playing against Esbjerg in the final when he was named Man of the Match. Following his retirement, Carsten worked in TV in Denmark a program scheduler.

# F

## FULLARTON, William Graham McMaster

**POSITION:** Centre-half

**BIRTHPLACE:** Ardrossan, Ayrshire

**DATE OF BIRTH:** 19/07/1876 - 20/08/1940

**HEIGHT:** 6' 1" **WEIGHT:** 13st 0lbs

**SIGNED FROM:** Queen's Park, 10/12/1903

**DEBUT:** v Notts County, A, 12/12/1903

**LAST MATCH:** v Arsenal, A, 21/10/1905

**MOVED TO:** Nottingham Forest, 26/10/1905

**TEAMS:** Vale of Leven, Queen's Park, Sunderland, Nottingham Forest, Plymouth Argyle

**SAFC TOTALS:** 33 appearances / 1 goal

**William Fullarton followed the well-trodden path from Ayrshire to Wearside coming to the club after a season with Queen's Park who had finished eighth out of ten clubs in his one season there. Arriving mid-way through the 1903-04 campaign, Fullarton played just twice, but in his first full campaign played regularly until missing the final seven fixtures. His one goal had come in his 25th and penultimate appearance of the season in a victory at Stoke.**

Returning the following autumn he had five games under new manager Bob Kyle before a very sizeable fee - especially for a defender - took him to Nottingham Forest. As at Sunderland, he debuted away to Notts County, his game for Forest on 4 November 1905 being a local derby of course. Just over a month later, he played against Sunderland in the sixth of his 21 games for Forest who he left at the end of the season after they were relegated on goal-average behind Middlesbrough, despite Fullarton playing in a late-season victory back at Roker Park.

Forest were not best pleased with Fullarton's decision to depart so soon after costing them £500 and they refused to release his playing registration when he left to go to Plymouth Argyle as manager. Turning 30 in the month he moved into management, he wanted to be player/manager, but was unable to. It was a brave move to go to Southern League Plymouth who were in serious financial straits, but evidently he saw it as an opportunity. He started with a 4-0 defeat in the 'Docklands derby' at Portsmouth, but won his first two home games.

In the circumstances finishing 15th out of 20 teams was commendable, but his services were dispensed with at the end of the season as Argyle decided to do without a manager as a cost-cutting exercise.

No doubt disillusioned with football, he emigrated to New Zealand in May 1907 shortly after his last game at Brentford. Fullarton's brother David had been at Sunderland in November 1905 without playing for the first-team. David signed for Plymouth during his brother's reign and made a total of 42 appearances. Following William's departure, David moved to New Brompton (who became Gillingham) where he spent three seasons. William remained in New Zealand, passing away in Otago on the South Island, aged 64.

## FULOP, Marton

**POSITION:** Goalkeeper

**BIRTHPLACE:** Budapest, Hungary

**DATE OF BIRTH:** 03/05/1983 - 12/11/2015

**HEIGHT:** 6' 5" **WEIGHT:** 14st 7lbs

**SIGNED FROM:** Tottenham Hotspur, 23/11/2006

**DEBUT:** v Luton Town, H, 09/12/2006

**LAST MATCH:** v Chelsea, A, 16/01/2010

**MOVED TO:** Ipswich Town, 05/08/2010

**TEAMS:** MTK Hungaria, BKV Elore (L), Bodajk (L), Spurs, Chesterfield (L), Coventry City (L), Sunderland, Leicester City (L), Stoke City (L), Manchester City (L), Ipswich Town, WBA, Asteras Tripolis

**INTERNATIONAL:** Hungary

**SAFC TOTALS:** 49+1 apps / 0 goals

**Marton Fulop came to Sunderland after impressing on what was his third loan from Spurs - Ben Alnwick going to Tottenham as part of the same deal. Given that he was from Hungary, his nickname within the squad of 'Never' related to his surname and his appetite. A popular member of the squad who always had a smile, tragically Marton passed away of cancer at the age of just 32 - the same as his squad number at Sunderland.**

Like his father Ferenc, Marton was a full international. He played 24 times for Hungary, debuting against France in Metz in 2005. Ferenc was a member of Hungary's squad at the 1978 FIFA World Cup finals. He did not actually play at the tournament, but three years later, did play in a game with stars such as Pele and Bobby Moore in the film 'Escape to Victory!' He later became technical director of the Hungary national side.

Having debuted for Sunderland against Luton Town, Marton spent most of the 2006-07 season as back-up to Darren Ward before he was brought back for the final game of the season in the reverse fixture at Luton on the day the Championship title was secured. The summer signing of Craig Gordon for a British record fee for a keeper only toughened Fulop's task, his solitary game for Sunderland the following season (though he played while out on loan) coming again on the last day of the season, against Arsenal. Injury to Gordon the following season led to Fulop's finest campaign as he played 30 times, all but four of those in the Premier League.

Although both Leicester and Stoke made bids for Marton after successful loans from Sunderland, it was Championship outfit Ipswich he eventually moved to, signing for Roy Keane who had bought him for Sunderland. After 38 games in his one season at Portman Road, Fulop returned to the Premier League with West Brom, but played only three times before moving to Greece where he joined his final club Asteras Tripolis in 2012. 28 games there took his club total to 232.

## FULTON, William

**POSITION:** Inside-left

**BIRTHPLACE:** Alva, Stirlingshire

**DATE OF BIRTH:** 18/11/1876 - 30/10/1957

**HEIGHT:** 5' 8" **WEIGHT:** 11st 6lbs

**SIGNED FROM:** Preston North End, 06/05/1898

**DEBUT:** v Stoke, H, 26/11/1898

**LAST MATCH:** v Newcastle United, H, 28/04/1900

**MOVED TO:** Bristol City, 10/05/1900

**TEAMS:** Alva Albion, Preston North End, Sunderland, Bristol City, Derby County, Alloa Athletic

**SAFC TOTALS:** 31 appearances / 7 goals

**Arriving at Sunderland during the first year at Roker Park, Fulton established himself in the side towards the end of the season, but in his second campaign only managed to mirror his first year's record of 13 league appearances and two goals.**

No doubt his most satisfying goal would be the only one of the game on 20 January 1900 that defeated his former club Preston where he had failed to make a league appearance. He fared better in the English (FA) Cup, scoring three times in five games, the first of those against Bristol City probably helping towards his move there at the end of his second term on Wearside.

Combining his football with working as a joiner whilst at Bristol, he helped City to finish runners-up to Southampton in the Southern League where he scored once for every three of his 24 appearances in his season before moving to Derby County. Injuries sadly curtailed his time with Derby and after a year, he moved back to Scotland with Alloa Athletic. After retiring from football, he followed a well-trodden path of becoming a licensee. His brother Robert was a player in the 1890s for Alva Albion Rovers and King's Park.

# G

## GABBIADINI, Marco

**POSITION:** Striker

**BIRTHPLACE:** Nottingham, Nottinghamshire

**DATE OF BIRTH:** 20/01/1968

**HEIGHT:** 5' 10" **WEIGHT:** 11st 2lbs

**SIGNED FROM:** York City, 22/09/1987

**DEBUT:** v Chester, H, 26/09/1987

**LAST MATCH:** v Grimsby Town, H, 21/09/1991

**MOVED TO:** Crystal Palace, 26/09/1991

**TEAMS:** Poppleton Juniors, York City, Sunderland, Crystal Palace, Derby County, Birmingham City (L), Oxford United (L), Panionios, Stoke City (L), York City, Darlington, Northampton Town, Hartlepool United

**INTERNATIONAL:** England B

**SAFC TOTALS:** 183+2 appearances / 87 goals

**One of those rare players such as Raich, Julio and Shack where only one name is needed, Marco was the hero of his generation. An exciting striker, full of pace, power and determination, he followed the managerial leadership of Denis Smith and Co from York City where he was sold to Sunderland by Bobby Saxton. Marco soon became the darling of the crowd. After hitting the post on his debut, he scored twice in each of his next three games and never looked back.**

Quickly forming an almost telepathic understanding with ex-England veteran Eric Gates, the pair became known as the 'G-Force.' 22 goals in Gabbiadini's first season were followed by 23 the following year and 26 in his third, the last of these being his most famous strike to seal the 1990 Play-Off victory at Newcastle. Having jettisoned the Lads from the third tier to the first in three seasons Marco found goals harder to come by, but was still top-scorer with nine in 30+1 league games in the top-flight. Unfortunately, by then his partner Gates had moved on and Marco did himself early in 1991-92 after a sensational six-minute hat-trick against Charlton on his penultimate appearance.

He smashed Sunderland's record sale when moving to Crystal Palace for £1.8m in 1991, but after seven goals - one a winner at Liverpool - in 22 games, swiftly moved on to Derby where he spent his mid-twenties, winning promotion as runners-up to Sunderland in 1996. Marco made more appearances (227) for the Rams than he did for the Black Cats, but it was at Sunderland that he scored most goals - 87 to 68.

While he had substantial periods of 82 and 120 games late in his career with Darlington and Northampton, undoubtedly Sunderland and Derby were the places where he was at his peak. In the year between Derby and Darlington he had a short spell of eleven games and four goals in Greece with Panionios, 2+6 games without scoring for Stoke and a short loan back at his first club York. Finally, at Hartlepool a fine career came to an end as a result of a knee injury, Marco's final outing against Plymouth in November 2003 coming shortly before Hartlepool played at the Stadium of Light in the FA Cup. Nonetheless, Marco did claim a Stadium of Light hat trick - in Jimmy McNab's Testimonial in 1999.

Gabbiadini had been on the scene since debuting as a 17-year-old sub for York at home to Bolton in March 1985. In November 1986, he became the youngest player to net a hat-trick for the Minstermen, doing so against Darlington in the Freight Rover Trophy. In a remarkably long career for a forward, Gabbiadini scored 276 times in 791 games. Capped twice by England at Under 20 level against Bulgaria and the USA in the 1989 Toulon tournament, the following year he played for England B against Czechoslovakia at Roker Park.

In 2022 Marco was still a regular pundit on BBC Local Radio's Total Sport, a role he had covered SAFC on since 2009. A successful hotelier in York for many years, Marco also ran a successful sports management company.

## GABBIADINI, Ricardo

**POSITION:** Striker

**BIRTHPLACE:** Newport, Monmouthshire

**DATE OF BIRTH:** 11/03/1970

**HEIGHT:** 6' 0" **WEIGHT:** 13st 0lbs

**SIGNED FROM:** York City, 01/06/1988

**DEBUT:** v Leeds United, A, 14/10/1989

**LAST MATCH:** v Leeds United, A, 14/10/1989

**MOVED TO:** Released from contract, 26/02/1991

**TEAMS:** York City, Sunderland, Blackpool (L), Grimsby Town (L), Brighton & HA (L), Crewe Alexandra (L), Hartlepool United, Scarborough, Carlisle United, Frickley Athletic, Sligo Rovers, Gainsborough Trinity, Goole Town, Denaby United, Ossett Town, Bradford Park Avenue, Harrogate Town, Pontefract Collieries

**SAFC TOTALS:** 0+1 appearance / 0 goals

**The brother of Marco - other than in pre-season friendlies and the 2011 Northern Masters Six-a-Side tournament - the nearest the Gabbiadinis got to playing alongside each other for Sunderland was on Ricardo's solitary first-team appearance when he came on as a sub for his brother at Elland Road. While Marco was a huge goalscoring hero on Wearside, Ricardo's first-team career lasted for just 32 minutes against Howard Wilkinson's Leeds.**

Ricardo's brief opportunity came in the week after he had returned from a loan spell at Blackpool where he had scored three times in five Third Division games. His elevation to the first-team squad was further enhanced by a late brace of goals in a friendly on the day he returned from Blackpool. The game, to celebrate Peterlee Newtown's new floodlights, saw the unique occurrence of four Gabbiadini goals as both brothers found the net in a 4-3 win. This brief spell in the first-team limelight was the highlight of Ricardo's Sunderland career and he was subsequently loaned out a further three times before coming to the end of his contract.

Signed by Hartlepool in March 1991, he debuted at Walsall the following month, but would only start two league games for Pools where he made a total of 10+13 appearances returning five goals. He did play for Pools against Marco in the League Cup in October 1991, Marco scoring for Crystal Palace on that occasion.

Ricardo then had a 3+4 game stint at Scarborough in 1992, scoring against Cardiff, before joining Carlisle. Cardiff were on the receiving end again as one of his five goals for the Cumbrians came at Ninian Park. It was a good spell for Ricardo for whom 21 of his 27 appearances came as starts in 1992-93. After this he dropped into non-league football, also having a successful stint in Ireland. With Sligo Rovers in 1993-94 he won promotion from the League of Ireland First Division as well as the First Division Shield and the FAI Cup, being part of a famous side that defeated Derry City in the final.

Like his older brother, he moved into the family trade as a hotelier in York.

## GALBRAITH, Thomas (Tom)

**POSITION:** Outside-right

**BIRTHPLACE:** Bonhill, West Dumbartonshire

**DATE OF BIRTH:** 15/01/1875 - date of death unknown

**HEIGHT:** 5' 8" **WEIGHT:** 11st 0lbs

**SIGNED FROM:** Vale of Leven, 12/01/1898

**DEBUT:** v Bolton Wanderers, H, 22/02/1898

**LAST MATCH:** v Everton, A, 11/04/1898

**MOVED TO:** Leicester Fosse, 06/08/1898

**TEAMS:** Renton, Vale of Leven, Sunderland, Leicester Fosse, Vale of Leven

**SAFC TOTALS:** 2 appearances / 0 goals

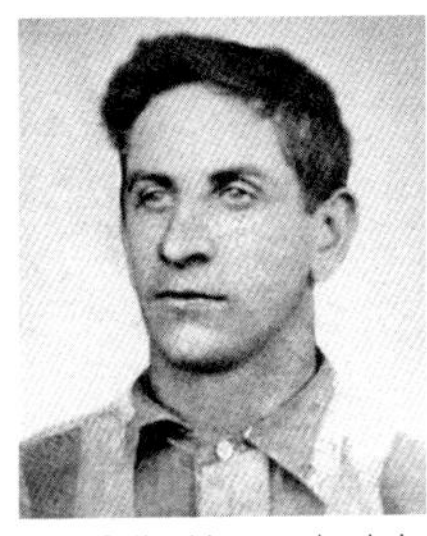

**A worker in a cloth factory before turning professional as a footballer, winger Galbraith hoped to provide made to measure crosses, but had desperately little opportunity to do so with Sunderland in the last season at Newcastle Road.**

As Sunderland moved to Roker Park, Galbraith moved to Leicester where he was top scorer with 17 goals, including one in the cup as they finished third in Division Two. However, despite his success in the midlands, Tom spent just one year there before returning to Scotland.

## GALLACHER, Patrick (Patsy)

**POSITION:** Inside-forward

**BIRTHPLACE:** Bridge of Weir, Renfrewshire

**DATE OF BIRTH:** 21/08/1909 - 04/01/1992

**HEIGHT:** 5' 7½" **WEIGHT:** 11st 4lbs

**SIGNED FROM:** Bridge of Weir, 14/09/1928

**DEBUT:** v Arsenal, H, 21/09/1929

**LAST MATCH:** v Preston North End, H, 19/11/1938

**MOVED TO:** Stoke City, 29/11/1938

**TEAMS:** Bridge of Weir, Sunderland, Stoke City, Newcastle United (WW2 Guest), Morton (WW2 Guest), Notts County, (WW2 Guest), Aldershot (WW2 Guest), Dundee United (WW2 Guest), Leicester City (WW2 Guest), Crewe Alexandra (WW2 Guest), Coleraine, Cork United, Cheltenham Town

**INTERNATIONAL:** Scotland

**SAFC TOTALS:** 308 appearances / 107 goals

**The scorer of the winning goal in the 1937 FA Cup semi-final, the season before, Gallacher had scored 19 league goals as he helped the Lads to the league title. A mesmeric dribbler who was a craftsman of an inside-forward, Patsy warranted far more than his solitary Scotland cap, especially as he scored in that 1934 international against Ireland in Belfast when he had clubmate Jimmy Connor on the wing.**

The scorer of exactly 100 league goals including six hat-tricks, Gallacher reached double figures in league goals alone in five successive seasons in the early thirties, his best league tally being 20 goals in 1934-35 as Sunderland were runners-up. For a man so small he was useful in the air, one of his hat-tricks all being headers, as was his semi-final winner which saw him chaired off the pitch.

Gallacher came to Sunderland having been spotted by the club's renowned Paisley-based scout Sammy Blyth. Patsy's first 'manager' was a 'Miss Mary' who got up a team in Bridge of Weir where Gallacher's skills were honed playing with a ball made from rags.

Perhaps those humble beginnings led to his wish to always be exceptionally smart off the pitch as well as on it. Away from the game he wore spats. These are an accessory worn above the shoes covering the instep and the ankle and covering the lower part of the trousers. This led to him being known as 'Sir Spatrick' by his teammates.

Gallacher served as a physical training instructor in the RAF during World War Two when he played extensively as a 'Guest' player. At the start of the war he played in one game asa 'Guest' for Newcastle at Hartlepool in October 1939, while

after the war, he also had brief spells playing in Ireland before joining Cheltenham Town in September 1948. later moving to the north west where in 1954, he found employment working in a restaurant in Preston, opponents in the 1937 final. Patsy passed away on the day Sunderland's run to the 1992 FA Cup final began.

Incidentally, many records you will read elsewhere on Gallacher are thrown into confusion due to Patrick 'Paddy' Gallacher who was born 9 January 1913. He was also an inside-forward who played for Third Lanark, Blackburn Rovers then Bournemouth, as well as guesting for many London teams in WW2 before becoming Weymouth manager in 1948.

## GALLOWAY, Brendan Joel Zibusiso

**POSITION:** Full-back

**BIRTHPLACE:** Harare, Zimbabwe

**DATE OF BIRTH:** 17/03/1996

**HEIGHT:** 6' 1" **WEIGHT:** 13st 10lbs

**SIGNED FROM:** Everton, 05/07/2017, on loan

**DEBUT:** v Derby County, H, 04/08/2017

**LAST MATCH:** v Wolverhampton Wanderers, A, 09/12/2017

**MOVED TO:** Everton, 07/05/2018, end of loan

**TEAMS:** MK Dons, Everton, Sunderland (L), WBA (L), Luton Town, Plymouth Argyle (to June 2022)

**INTERNATIONAL:** England Under 21 / Zimbabwe

**SAFC TOTALS:** 6+2 appearances / 0 goals

**Capped by England at Under 17, 18, 19 and 21 level, much was expected of Galloway, but he endured a torrid time in a struggling team at Sunderland. Having been selected to start six of Simon Grayson's first eight games at the start of the 2017-18 season, the defender was then consigned to the bench from where he was called upon only twice more.**

Galloway moved to England as a youngster and started out at MK Dons. Such was his promise, he became their youngest debutant, at just over 15 years and 6 months old, in a 6-0 win over Nantwich Town in the FA Cup first round in 2011. More than a dozen first-team appearances in 2013-14 persuaded Everton to offer the teenager a five-year contract.

He started 16 Premier League games for Everton, debuting against West Ham in May 2015 and came off the bench early in a 6-2 win over Sunderland the following November, coming on for future SAFC man Bryan Oviedo. Following his spell at Sunderland, Galloway played three more times in the Premier League on loan to West Brom for whom he also appeared in both domestic cups.

Released by the Toffees in 2019, he joined Luton Town, but was released in 2021 having played just six times, none of which were a league start. As he left Luton, he accepted a call up to represent Zimbabwe in World Cup qualifying games and joined Plymouth Argyle ahead of the 2021-22 campaign.

## GARDNER, Craig

**POSITION:** Midfielder

**BIRTHPLACE:** Solihull, West Midlands

**DATE OF BIRTH:** 25/11/1986

**HEIGHT:** 5' 11" **WEIGHT:** 12st 10lbs

**SIGNED FROM:** Birmingham City, 30/06/2011

**DEBUT:** v Newcastle United, H, 20/08/2011

**LAST MATCH:** v Cardiff City, H, 27/04/2014

**MOVED TO:** West Bromwich Albion, 20/05/2014

**TEAMS:** Aston Villa, Birmingham City, Sunderland, WBA

**INTERNATIONAL:** England Under 21

**SAFC TOTALS:** 77+23 appearances / 14 goals

**Gardner's spell on Wearside was his one venture away from his native second city where he played for three West Midlands clubs. The sort of character who lights up a dressing room as he was always in the thick of the banter and practical joking, Craig succeeded in remaining unaffected by the trappings of Premier League stardom.**

This was well illustrated on one occasion when he was suspended and went to support Sunderland at a derby match at St James' by travelling on the Metro and sitting with the fans. He also funded a boxing club in his home city to try and encourage local youngsters into competitive sport while another example of his spirit was the 2012 story revealed by a Stoke-on-Trent family who told a newspaper of a chance meeting with Craig who gave them £500 to help with their disabled toddler.

The possessor of an explosive shot and a set-piece specialist, Craig never lacked commitment in exactly 100 appearances for Sunderland. Able to play at right-back as well as in midfield, he numbered Kevin Phillips and Seb Larsson amongst his teammates at Birmingham City with whom he won the League Cup in 2011 after he scored the winning goal in the semi-final against West Ham. Reported to have cost Sunderland £6m during the reign of Steve Bruce, Gardner was later reunited with his old Villa boss Martin O'Neill at the Stadium of Light.

Returning to the midlands with West Brom, Craig's first goal for the Baggies was the winner against his first club Villa. It was one of six he netted in 59+26 outings. He also scored six times for Villa in 49+31 appearances while in four spells (including two loans) with Birmingham he scored 16 goals in 87+38 games.

The last of these came after he had taken up a coaching role at St Andrew's where he ended the 2019-20 season as joint caretaker-manager with Steve Spooner as they steered City away from relegation from the Championship. There was then a month-long spell as coach at Sheffield Wednesday under his old WBA boss Tony Pulis before a swift return to Birmingham in January 2021. In June of the same year, he was appointed Technical director with a brief to oversee the direction of the Club's football strategy, focusing on recruitment, squad development and performance.

At international level, Craig played in the 2009 European Championship final defeat to Germany when he came on as sub to be part of an England Under 21 team that included Lee Cattermole, Nedum Onuoha, Jack Rodwell and Adam Johnson. Gardner also played alongside Fraizer Campbell in the group stages in which he played against Spain and Germany.

Younger brother Gary also won England recognition at youth level and played for Villa and Birmingham in addition to a host of loans from Villa, most notably at Nottingham Forest.

## GATES, Eric Lazenby

**POSITION:** Forward

**BIRTHPLACE:** Ferryhill, Co Durham

**DATE OF BIRTH:** 28/06/1955

**HEIGHT:** 5' 6" **WEIGHT:** 10st 8lbs

**SIGNED FROM:** Ipswich Town, 09/08/1985

**DEBUT:** v Blackburn Rovers, H, 17/08/1985

**LAST MATCH:** v Swindon Town, N, 28/05/1990

**MOVED TO:** Carlisle United, 01/06/1990

**TEAMS:** Ipswich Town, Sunderland, Carlisle United, Newton Aycliffe, West Auckland

**INTERNATIONAL:** England

**SAFC TOTALS:** 199+21 appearances / 55 goals

**A top-class player with Ipswich with whom he had won the UEFA Cup and earned England caps, Eric Gates returned to his native County Durham having just turned 30. He was one of the big names brought in by Lawrie McMenemy and like most of that cohort, Eric initially struggled to show his undoubted talent.**

It was after the arrival of young striker Marco Gabbiadini that Gates blossomed. Under manager Denis Smith the striking duo became known as the 'G-Force' as they blew away the opposition, helping Sunderland rise from the third tier to the top-flight in three seasons before Eric moved on, recognising that a return to top-level was probably beyond him as a veteran.

It certainly had not been beyond Gates in his prime. With a low centre-of-gravity, a deft first touch, an astute football brain and the ability to create as well as finish, he shone in the Bobby Robson era at Ipswich. An FA Youth Cup winner in 1973, as an 18-year-old, he debuted for Ipswich as a sub at Derby in October 1975 and scored his first goal later that month in a UEFA Cup win over FC Bruges at Portman Road. European football would bring the best out of Gates.

He scored both goals in a 2-1 European Cup Winners' Cup quarter-final first leg against Barcelona in 1979 and started both legs of the UEFA Cup final as they beat AZ Alkmaar two years later. However, he was on the periphery of their 1978 FA Cup triumph, appearing in only the third round. By the time he ended his Suffolk sojourn, Eric had scored 96 times in 345+39 games. He was inducted into the Tractor Boys' Hall of Fame in 2012.

His two England caps came in World Cup qualifying games in the autumn of 1980, starting a 4-0 Wembley win over Norway and a 2-1 defeat against Romania in Bucharest. He was a teammate of Dave Watson on both occasions.

Part of the Sunderland side relegated to the third division for the first time in his second season - despite him scoring twice in the relegation Play-Off - Gates was Player of the Year as promotion was won at the first attempt. Two seasons later he scored one and made one for Gabbiadini in the dramatic Play-Off victory at Newcastle before signing off in the Play-Off final with Swindon at Wembley.

Moving to Carlisle, his first goal, on his eighth appearance was a winner against Hartlepool. It was one of eight he scored there

in 38+5 appearances, the last coming at Chesterfield in April 1991. A teammate of Barry Siddall and John Halpin at Brunton Park, he also played with Keith Walwyn who had partnered a young Marco Gabbiadini in attack at York.

Eric played out his career in non-league, playing occasionally for West Auckland in 1995 when his brother Bill - a former Middlesbrough player - was manager. He also worked as Youth team coach at Hartlepool in the mid-nineties before becoming Derby County's north-east scout. Most notably, Eric became a highly entertaining and opinionated radio summariser and pundit with Metro and Century radio stations while also being a regular on the talk-in circuit.

## GAUDEN, Allan

**POSITION:** Winger

**BIRTHPLACE:** Langley Park, Co Durham

**DATE OF BIRTH:** 20/11/1944 – 29/04/2020

**HEIGHT:** 5' 8" **WEIGHT:** 11st 0lbs

**SIGNED FROM:** Esh Winning Juniors, 01/07/1961

**DEBUT:** v Aston Villa, A, 06/09/1965

**LAST MATCH:** v Wolverhampton Wanderers, A, 09/03/1968

**MOVED TO:** Darlington, 15/10/1968

**TEAMS:** Esh Winning Juniors, Sunderland, Darlington, Grimsby Town, Hartlepool United, Gillingham, Blyth Spartans

**SAFC TOTALS:** 45+6 appearances / 7 goals

**The first substitute ever to be used by Sunderland in both the league and the FA Cup, Allan went on to have a career that spanned 329 league games and 75 goals, a cracking record for a winger. Goals were always part of Gauden's game. As a boy he once scored 105 times in a season for Esh Winning Juniors.**

In addition to the seven goals he scored for Sunderland, Gauden also scored twice in six games in the summer of 1967 as Sunderland played as the Royal Vancouver Canadians in the North American Soccer League.

After leaving Sunderland, Allan played for Darlington before being bought by Lawrie McMenemy for Grimsby with whom he won a Division Four Championship medal in 1972. Former Sunderland teammate Len Ashurst then signed him for Hartlepool and subsequently Gillingham.

Allan went on to play for Bishop Auckland and Blyth Spartans before managing Durham City for a short spell. Following his football career, he worked on building sites prior to joining the fire brigade having moved back to his native north east. His brother Joe played for Langley Park and Esh Winning in the 1950s and '60s.

## GAUGHRAN, Bernard Michael (Benny)

**POSITION:** Centre-forward

**BIRTHPLACE:** Dublin, Ireland

**DATE OF BIRTH:** 29/09/1915 - 20/09/1977

**HEIGHT:** 5' 9" **WEIGHT:** 11st 10lbs

**SIGNED FROM:** Southampton, 27/11/1937

**DEBUT:** v Leeds United, A, 04/12/1937

**LAST MATCH:** v Portsmouth, H, 11/12/1937

**MOVED TO:** Notts County, 29/07/1938

**TEAMS:** Bohemians, Celtic, Southampton, Sunderland, Notts County, Dundalk, Portadown, Distillery, Shamrock Rovers, Brideville

**SAFC TOTALS:** 2 appearances / 0 goals

**Benny Gaughran turned down Southampton, and interest from Arsenal and Manchester United, to move from Ireland to Celtic, but belatedly joined the Saints having not had a break at Celtic.**

Four goals in seven Second Division games early in the 1937-38 season persuaded cup-holders Sunderland to sign him, but after just two games, he was released at the end of the season. Following a single Division Three South game for Notts County he returned to Ireland, his spell in England totalling just ten games.

## GAYLE, Howard Anthony

**POSITION:** Forward

**BIRTHPLACE:** Toxteth, Liverpool, Lancashire

**DATE OF BIRTH:** 18/05/1958

**HEIGHT:** 5' 10" **WEIGHT:** 10st 9lbs

**SIGNED FROM:** Birmingham City, 08/08/1984

**DEBUT:** v Southampton, H, 25/08/1984

**LAST MATCH:** v Stoke City, H, 03/05/1986

**MOVED TO:** Released, 31/05/1986

**TEAMS:** Bedford, Liverpool, Fulham (L), Newcastle United (L), Birmingham City, Sunderland, Dallas Sidekicks, Stoke City, Blackburn Rovers, Halifax Town, Accrington Stanley

**INTERNATIONAL:** England Under 21

**SAFC TOTALS:** 48+13 appearances / 5 goals

**An exciting player full of pace, Howard could play wide or through the middle. His best moment was scoring a screamer that decided a League (Milk) Cup tie with Nottingham Forest in the run to the 1985 final, in which he came on as a substitute. Four years earlier he had been an unused sub in the European Cup final as his Liverpool side defeated Real Madrid with a goal from future Sunderland man Alan Kennedy.**

## GAYLE, Howard (Continued)

He was perhaps unfortunate not to play in that final after starring in the second leg of the semi-final away to Bayern Munich after coming on as an early sub for Kenny Dalglish - albeit wily manager Bob Paisley had subbed him late on for fear Howard might be sent off for retaliation. Gayle could certainly blow hot and cold and in his Sunderland days was sent off in a derby at Newcastle.

Liverpudlian Gayle had started on Merseyside with Bedford FC before becoming Liverpool's first-ever player of colour when he debuted on 4 October 1980 at Manchester City, but he was to be mainly a reserve for the hugely successful Reds who he played just five first-team games for, although he scored 62 times in 156 appearances for their reserves. As a pioneer he also became the first player of colour to play for Newcastle and Blackburn.

Prior to his Liverpool debut, Howard had 14 Second Division games on loan to Fulham beginning at Preston in January 1980, in the Cottagers first league fixture after playing Sunderland. Playing alongside Ron Guthrie's brother Chris, he was unable to stop Fulham going down.

Having stepped in for Dalglish for Liverpool in Munich, he was called upon to replace the injured Kevin Keegan at Newcastle during a second loan from Anfield. Debuting against Cambridge United at St James' in November 1982, he scored twice in eight games for the Magpies under Arthur Cox.

A third loan to Birmingham City evolved into a permanent transfer to the Blues. After eight goals in 23 games in his first season at St Andrew's, playing alongside Tony Coton and Mick Harford, three of his 44+1 games (8 goals) in 1983-84 were against Sunderland, including an FA Cup win at Roker.

Signed by his fellow Scouser Len Ashurst, Gayle struggled with injury towards the end of his first season and failed to impress Ashurst's successor Lawrie McMenemy who released him. Following a spell playing indoor soccer in America, next stop was Stoke where Howard scored twice in six league outings before a five-year spell at Blackburn. Debuting on the opening day of the 1987-88 season at Hull, he managed only 16 appearances in total in his first season, but a year later missed just one match as he netted 22 times towards his eventual Rovers total of 34 goals in 119+25 games.

Leaving Blackburn in 1992, he joined fourth-tier Halifax, playing the first five games of the campaign alongside fellow former Liverpool player Jimmy Case, but by a 12 September game at Lincoln, his time with the Shaymen was over in what was the season they dropped out of the Football League. Subsequently, he played in non-league for Accrington Stanley and had unsuccessful trials with Carlisle United and Wrexham.

In his post-playing career, Howard became a champion of the under-privileged, doing much invaluable work with social inclusion programmes in schools and prisons. As well as working as a coach at Tranmere Rovers, he had a spell as Stoke City's 'Special Inclusion Officer', but mainly devoted himself to the Stanley House Youth Project on Merseyside.

His autobiography, '61 minutes in Munich' was published in 2016. In the same year Howard turned down an MBE for his work with Show Racism the Red Card.

## GEMMELL, James (Jimmy)

**POSITION:** Inside-forward / centre-forward
**BIRTHPLACE:** Hutchesontown, Glasgow, Lanarkshire
**DATE OF BIRTH:** 08/08/1880 - Q3 1958
**HEIGHT:** 5' 9" **WEIGHT:** 12st 7lbs
**SIGNED FROM:** Clyde, 12/11/1900 and Leeds City, 30/05/1910
**DEBUT:** v Wednesday, H, 08/12/1900
**LAST MATCH:** v Woolwich Arsenal, H, 23/03/1912
**MOVED TO:** Stoke, 03/05/1907 and Third Lanark, 11/04/1912
**TEAMS:** Clyde, Sunderland, Stoke, Leeds City, Sunderland, Third Lanark, West Stanley
**SAFC TOTALS:** 227 appearances / 45 goals

**After breaking into the team the previous season Jimmy Gemmell was top-scorer as the title was won in 1901-02, scoring ten goals in 31 league games, the first of those goals being a winner away to Newcastle.**

Two seasons later he reached double-figures again, but only scored three goals in 37 games across two seasons in a second spell with the club. In between, he spent six months with Stoke before joining Leeds City where his 14 goals in 73 games began with a goalscoring debut at Oldham in November 1907 and included an appearance back at Sunderland in the English (FA) Cup in January 1910.

He became player/manager of West Stanley from July 1913 to 1915 and later worked in a factory in Birmingham. One of five brothers, his son James played for West Stanley, Bury, Leicester City (in World War Two) and particularly Southport before being trainer at Lincoln City in 1948-49.

## GEORGE, William Samuel (Billy)

**POSITION:** Right-half
**BIRTHPLACE:** Aston, Warwickshire
**DATE OF BIRTH:** 27/07/1895 - 29/09/1962
**HEIGHT:** 5' 8" **WEIGHT:** 11st 0lbs
**SIGNED FROM:** Merthyr Town, 01/08/1920
**DEBUT:** v Huddersfield Town, H, 02/10/1920
**LAST MATCH:** v Newcastle United, H, 16/10/1920
**MOVED TO:** Shildon, 01/08/1921
**TEAMS:** Aston Motor Works, Leicester Fosse (WW1 Guest), Merthyr Town, Sunderland, Shildon, Burton All Saints, Birmingham Corporation Trams
**SAFC TOTALS:** 2 appearances / 0 goals

**Billy played in two home games in October 1920, but otherwise had no other Football League appearances.**

A toolmaker before he played professionally George later drove both lorries and trams in Birmingham and endured chronic knee problems in later life. Reported to be a First World War veteran of Gallipoli, his two sons and daughter all later emigrated to Australia.

## GIACCHERINI, Emanuele

**POSITION:** Midfielder
**BIRTHPLACE:** Bibbiena, Italy
**DATE OF BIRTH:** 05/05/1985
**HEIGHT:** 5' 5½" **WEIGHT:** 9st 6lbs
**SIGNED FROM:** Juventus, 16/07/2013
**DEBUT:** v Fulham, H, 17/08/2013
**LAST MATCH:** v Chelsea, A, 24/05/2015
**MOVED TO:** Napoli, 16/07/2016
**TEAMS:** Cesena, Forli (L), Bellaria Igea (L), Pavia (L), Juventus, Sunderland, Bologna (L), Napoli, Chievo
**INTERNATIONAL:** Italy
**SAFC TOTALS:** 27+16 appearances / 5 goals

**One of the host of signings during the regime of Roberto De Fanti and Paolo Di Canio, Giaccherini was a good player, as you would expect from an Italy international. He had won back-to-back Serie A titles with Juventus in the two seasons before coming to Sunderland, as well as the Coppa Italia in 2012. Overseas players are known to usually take time to acclimatise to British football and in the circumstances, the diminutive left-sided midfielder did well, even scoring with a header at Southampton on his away debut.**

He went on to score against Liverpool and Arsenal amongst others and came on for the final 13 minutes of the 2014 League (Capital One) Cup final against Manchester City at Wembley. It was the following month's league game at City where the Italian was at his best. In the game where Sunderland began a miraculous fight-back to survive relegation, Giaccherini's creativity laid on both of Sunderland's goals in a 2-2 draw.

Although previously a regular Italy international in his trophy-laden days with Juve, Emanuele missed out on Italy's squad for the 2014 FIFA World Cup and then suffered the misfortune of sustaining an injury-hit second season at Sunderland after which he spent his third term as a Sunderland player on a season-long loan to Bologna. Debuting away to Sampdoria, he scored seven times in 27+1 Serie A appearances, at one point scoring in five games out of eight including a San Siro winner against Milan.

In contrast, after being sold to Napoli for approximately a third of the £6.5m Sunderland had paid for him, only one of the league

appearances Giaccherini made for Napoli was from the start, one of his appearances as sub being in a 7-1 win back at Bologna.

Loaned to Chievo in January 2018, the move became permanent the following summer. He played 33+6 Serie A games for the 'Flying Donkeys' and three cup ties, with his Coppa Italia appearance at Cagliari in August 2019 being the last of his career.

Giaccherini had begun with Cesena in 2008 who loaned him to Forli (22 games, 1 goal) Bellaria Igea (37/3) and Pavia (28/9). Having broken through at Cesena, he helped them to promotion to the top flight Serie A in 2010. After debuting at that level in a goalless draw at Roma, he scored in the next match as Milan were beaten and went onto claim seven goals and four assists from 36 appearances. This led to a move to Juventus, initially on loan. Debuting in a home win over Parma in September 2011 he made 23 appearances in his first season, playing his way into Italy's Euro 2012 draws with Spain and Croatia, playing as a left wing-back in a tournament where Italy reached the final after knocking out England.

A year later, he scored Italy's quickest-ever goal, netting after 19 seconds against Haiti in a match played in Rio de Janeiro. He went on to excel in the 2013 Confederations Cup and score against Belgium at Euro 2016 while still technically on Sunderland's books. In all, he won 29 caps for Italy, scoring four times.

## GIBB, Thomas (Tommy)

**POSITION:** Midfielder

**BIRTHPLACE:** Bathgate, Lothian

**DATE OF BIRTH:** 13/12/1944

**HEIGHT:** 5' 10½" **WEIGHT:** 11st 1lb

**SIGNED FROM:** Newcastle United, 01/07/1975

**DEBUT:** v Middlesbrough, H, 02/08/1975

**LAST MATCH:** v Liverpool, A, 01/01/1977

**MOVED TO:** v Liverpool, A, 01/01/1977

**TEAMS:** Wallhouse Rose, Armadale Thistle, Bathgate United, Bathgate Thistle, Partick Thistle, Newcastle United, Sunderland, Hartlepool United

**INTERNATIONAL:** Scotland Under 23

**SAFC TOTALS:** 9+4 appearances / 2 goals

**Tommy Gibb played briefly for Sunderland as a 30-year-old after coming from Newcastle where he had been a hero of their 1969 Inter-Cities Fairs Cup winning side when he scored in three ties during the cup-run.**

Having been signed from Partick where he played 153 games, he played 251+18 for Newcastle, at one point setting a club record of 171 consecutive appearances. He came on as a substitute as they lost the 1974 FA Cup final to Liverpool. Tommy scored 19 goals for the Magpies, including a 25-yarder against Chelsea on his home debut in 1968. Earlier that year he had won one Under 23 cap for Scotland, playing against England at Hampden Park in February when Harry Hood was Scotland's scorer in a 2-1 defeat.

For Sunderland, after scoring on his debut in the Anglo-Scottish Cup, he played in the opening six games of the 1975-76 promotion season, but then did not play again until four appearances in the winter of the following season. Moving to Hartlepool in the summer of 1977, he first appeared for Pools in a friendly against an Army XI and went on to play a total of 47+4 competitive games, all in the first of his two seasons at the club.

Following his retirement from football, Gibb returned to Scotland where he managed a pub in Armadale before moving into the haulage trade.

## GIBSON, Darron Thomas Daniel

**POSITION:** Midfielder

**BIRTHPLACE:** Derry, Northern Ireland

**DATE OF BIRTH:** 25/10/1987

**HEIGHT:** 6' 0" **WEIGHT:** 12st 4lbs

**SIGNED FROM:** Everton, 30/01/2017

**DEBUT:** v Crystal Palace, A, 04/02/2017

**LAST MATCH:** v Barnsley, H, 01/01/2018

**MOVED TO:** Contract terminated, 31/03/2018

**TEAMS:** Institute, Manchester United, Royal Antwerp (L), Wolves (L), Everton, Sunderland, Wigan Athletic, Salford City

**INTERNATIONAL:** Republic of Ireland

**SAFC TOTALS:** 22+8 appearances / 0 goals

**Signed by David Moyes who had signed him for Everton, Gibson was a quality player who had won the Premier League with Manchester United in 2011 when a dozen of his 20 appearances for the Red Devils came in the league.**

He had also won the League Cup in 2009 and 2010, starting alongside John O'Shea, Jonny Evans and Danny Welbeck and against Darren Bent (and unused sub Ben Alnwick) of Spurs in 2009, and coming on as a late sub in the following year's final against Martin O'Neill's Aston Villa side that included Carlos Cuellar and Stewart Downing. In total, he made 60 appearances for Manchester United, Liam Miller and Kieran Richardson scoring the first two goals on his debut against Barnet in the League Cup in October 2005.

Internationally, having won caps at Under 16 level with Northern Ireland, Gibson went on to win 27 caps for the Republic of Ireland, being an unused member of their 2012 Euro 2012 squad. In 2013, he suffered an ACL injury playing for Ireland against Kazakhstan.

He had had the chance to join Sunderland when choosing to leave Manchester United for Everton, but in an injury-hit six seasons at Goodison Park made just 51+18 appearances, scoring twice.

At Sunderland, Gibson caused controversy by being revealed to have been publicly disparaging about his teammates. He later had his contract terminated after driving into parked cars near the Academy of Light training ground. He was initially suspended by the club due to suspicion of driving over the alcohol limit. He later pleaded guilty in court and was given a two year community order. Gibson had previously been sentenced to a twelve month community order in 2015 after admitting drink driving and failing to stop at the scene of an accident.

Five months after leaving Sunderland, Gibson joined Wigan Athletic where he was released after 11+7 games in his sole season. The following February (2020), he signed for Salford City, but broke his leg in a game against Port Vale the following October on his tenth appearance. In 2021, he was reported to be fronting a consortium looking to take over his old club Wigan Athletic.

## GIBSON, George

**POSITION:** Outside-left

**BIRTHPLACE:** New Brancepeth, Co Durham

**DATE OF BIRTH:** 07/04/1890 - 03/06/1929

**SIGNED FROM:** Esh Winning Rangers, 23/03/1910

**DEBUT:** v Tottenham Hotspur, A, 25/03/1910

**LAST MATCH:** v Middlesbrough, H, 02/04/1910

**MOVED TO:** Left club, 01/06/1910

**TEAMS:** Esh Winning Rangers, Sunderland, New Brancepeth

**SAFC TOTALS:** 2 appearances / 0 goals

**Unearthed through research by Mike Gibson during the preparation of Sunderland AFC: The Absolute Record Volume One, this George Gibson had previously been thought to be a player called Fred Gibson. Both George and Fred Gibson were outside-lefts, Fred being South African while George was a local lad.**

George played twice in his few months at Sunderland, debuting in a 5-1 drubbing at struggling Spurs. A week later he got another game when England winger Arthur Bridgett was ruled out of a Wear-Tees derby with a heavy cold.

After leaving SAFC, George worked as an analytical chemist at the Weardale Steel Coal and Coal Company's colliery in Spennymoor up to his death at the age of 39. He also played cricket for Spennymoor who he joined from Durham, and also won county honours for Durham.

## GIBSON, George Eardley

**POSITION:** Centre-forward

**BIRTHPLACE:** Biddulph, Staffordshire

**DATE OF BIRTH:** 29/08/1912 - 30/12/1990

**HEIGHT:** 5'8½" **WEIGHT:** 10st 3lbs

**SIGNED FROM:** Frickley Colliery, 05/04/1932

**DEBUT:** v Bolton Wanderers, A, 11/03/1933

**LAST MATCH:** v Chelsea, A, 06/05/1933

**MOVED TO:** Leicester City, 08/11/1934

**TEAMS:** Kidderminster, Frickley Colliery, Sunderland, Leicester City, Valenciennes, Distillery, Racing Club De Roubaix, Shelbourne, Workington, Bradford City, Carlisle United (WW2 Guest)

**SAFC TOTALS:** 2 appearances / 1 goal

**A joiner by trade, Gibson came to Sunderland from non-league football, having earlier had an unsuccessful trial with Stoke. Although he scored to earn a point at Chelsea on the last day of the season, there was no future for George, who fared no better after joining Leicester for whom he also played just twice.**

He then played in France and Ireland, being popular at Valenciennes, but being suspended by the French FA for not completing a contract with Roubaix who he had signed to play for throughout the 1936-37 season. Instead, he left to join Shelbourne in December 1936 having begun the calendar year with Distillery.

He then had a spell with Workington before they entered the Football League before playing three consecutive league games with Bradford City in October 1938, losing them all, the last against Hartlepools. Finally, in the first season of war-time football during the World War Two, he played six times for Carlisle, scoring once.

After retiring from football, he followed his father's profession, as a proprietor of a hotel, in Accrington.

## GIBSON, John Rutherford (Jock)

**POSITION:** Right-back

**BIRTHPLACE:** Philadelphia, USA

**DATE OF BIRTH:** 23/03/1898 - July 1974

**HEIGHT:** 5' 11" **WEIGHT:** 11st 5lbs

**SIGNED FROM:** Blantyre Celtic, 01/11/1920

**DEBUT:** v Everton, A, 20/11/1920

**LAST MATCH:** Manchester City, H, 14/01/1922

**MOVED TO:** Hull City, 19/05/1922

**TEAMS:** Netherburn, Blantyre Thistle, Sunderland, Hull City, Sheffield United, Luton Town, Vauxhall Motors

**SAFC TOTALS:** 5 appearances / 0 goals

**Born in the USA of Scottish parents, Jock left America as a two-year-old and came to Sunderland when he was 22 after being brought up in Sheffield and Scotland. After a handful of games for the Lads, he enjoyed seven personally successful seasons with Hull City, missing only one game in 1927-28 and totalling 218 games for the Tigers.**

179 of his 210 league appearances saw him partner Matt Bell at full-back. In an era when the offside law was changed, the pair perfected their offside trap to the extent that 50 clean sheets were achieved when they were paired and only once were more than four goals conceded.

A fee of £5,000 took him to Sheffield United in March 1929. He added 77 appearances for the Blades before a summer 1933 move to Luton for whom he played only four times in his one season, after which he played for Vauxhall Motors where he worked and became an inspector.

## GIBSON, William

**POSITION:** Full-back / Half-back

**BIRTHPLACE:** London

**DATE OF BIRTH:** 16/02/1868 - 15/09/1911

**HEIGHT:** 5' 9" **WEIGHT:** 12st 8lbs

**SIGNED FROM:** Cambuslang, 01/08/1888 and Rangers, 07/05/1895

**DEBUT:** v Elswick Rangers, H, 27/10/1888

**LAST MATCH:** v Small Heath, A, 11/04/1896

**MOVED TO:** Rangers,18/05/1894 and Notts County, 27/05/1896

**TEAMS:** Flemington Thistle, Cambuslang, Sunderland, Rangers, Notts County, Bristol City, Lincoln City

**INTERNATIONAL:** Scottish League XI

**SAFC TOTALS:** 100 appearances / 6 goals

**A title winner in back-to back seasons with Sunderland, Will Gibson was ever-present in the second of those in 1892-93. In that campaign he scored half of his six goals as Sunderland became the first club to register 100 league goals in a season.**

With Sunderland for two years before they were admitted to the Football League, he made many more than his 100 official competitive appearances in an age when fiercely contested friendlies were staged throughout the season. When Sunderland did join the league he played in the first-ever league fixture against Burnley.

He had two spells with Sunderland. In between he played for Rangers with both of his transfers seeing him move in exchange for Scotland international Andrew McCreadie. During his time at Ibrox, Gibson played 17 games, his one goal being an early season winner at home to Dundee. During this season he also earned a representative honour for the Scottish League.

Returning to Sunderland, he played in what was Tom Watson's final season in charge of 1895-96 before moving on to Notts County who he helped to the Division Two title in his first season, before a further year on joining Lincoln where, after his playing days, he became a publican. In between, and reportedly overweight and out of condition, he played a few Southern League games for Bristol City at the end of 1897-98 season.

Will became related to a quartet of Sunderland players. He was brother-in-law to both James Millar and John 'Dowk' Oliver and father-in-law to Albert Milton and Ernest Hodkin.

## GIBSON, William Kennedy

**POSITION:** Right-back

**BIRTHPLACE:** Glasgow, Lanarkshire

**DATE OF BIRTH:** 01/10/1876 - 09/12/1949

**HEIGHT:** 5' 10" **WEIGHT:** 11st 7lbs

**SIGNED FROM:** Cliftonville, 23/03/1902

**DEBUT:** v Bury, H, 16/04/1902

**LAST MATCH:** v Bury, H, 16/04/1902

**MOVED TO:** Cliftonville, 30/04/1902

**TEAMS:** Cliftonville, Sunderland, Bishop Auckland, Sunderland Royal Rovers, Cliftonville

**INTERNATIONAL:** Ireland

**SAFC TOTALS:** 1 appearance / 0 goals

**W K Gibson played just once for Sunderland, but did so in the game that sealed the league title in 1902 - subsequently being awarded a medal. As an amateur he offered his services to play for Sunderland should they need him in the following couple of seasons, whilst also playing occasionally for Bishop Auckland.**

Eight years before his short spell at Sunderland, he had become Ireland's youngest-ever international when he was capped at the age of 17 years and 146 days against Wales on 24 February 1894. In the same month four years later, he captained Ireland against Wales in their first-ever victory outside of Belfast. He had been born in Glasgow, but had moved across the Irish Sea in the early 1880s when his father took up a position as a shipping agent.

With Cliftonville, he won the Irish Cup in 1897 and 1901 going on to become President of the club towards the close of the decade. His father Andrew had been President of Cliftonville and vice-President of the Irish FA in the early 1890s. William's fame continued after becoming vice-President of the Irish FA in 1907. He combined playing football with working as a solicitor and became legal advisor to the Irish FA. In January 1909, he was elected as a councillor in Belfast, a position he held until 1920. In 1921, he became the major shareholder in Belfast Distillery FC.

## GILBERT, Timothy Hew

**POSITION:** Defender / midfielder

**BIRTHPLACE:** South Shields, Co Durham

**DATE OF BIRTH:** 28/08/1958 - 29/05/1995

**HEIGHT:** 5' 9" **WEIGHT:** 11st 12lbs

**SIGNED FROM:** Tynemouth Schools, 01/09/1973

**DEBUT:** v Newcastle United, A 27/12/1976

**LAST MATCH:** v Swansea City, A, 10/11/1979

**MOVED TO:** Cardiff City, 11/02/1981

**TEAMS:** Sunderland, Cardiff City, Darlington

**SAFC TOTALS:** 42+2 appearances / 3 goals

**Tim Gilbert died suddenly at the age of 36 while he was coaching a schoolboys side in Cleadon. He had retired from football and was working as a sports centre manager.**

He had made 129+5 league appearances. The first 34+2 of these were for Sunderland. Initially a sub in a derby at Newcastle, he scored on his first start against Blackburn a year to the day later. It was one of three goals he scored for Sunderland after which he added one for Cardiff and three for Darlington.

Tim always did well for Sunderland, but was unable to permanently dislodge Joe Bolton from the number three shirt and in February 1981 moved on to Cardiff for regular football, only to be injury-hit during his time at Ninian Park.

Released after his first full season in Wales, Tim joined Darlington where he spent two seasons.

His son Peter had an extensive career of 234 league appearances with eight different clubs, mostly with Plymouth Argyle where he won the third tier title in 2004 and also won Under 21 caps for Wales.

## GILHESPY, Thomas William Cyril

**POSITION:** Outside-right

**BIRTHPLACE:** Fence Houses, Co Durham

**DATE OF BIRTH:** 18/02/1898 - March 1985

**HEIGHT:** 5' 8½" **WEIGHT:** 11st 2lbs

**SIGNED FROM:** Chester-le-Street, 01/09/1920

**DEBUT:** v Bradford City, H, 30/10/1920

**LAST MATCH:** v Tottenham Hotspur, A ,02/04/1921

**MOVED TO:** Liverpool, 10/08/1921

**TEAMS:** Chester-le-Street, Sunderland, Liverpool, Bristol City, Blackburn Rovers, Reading, Mansfield Town, Crewe Alexandra

**SAFC TOTALS:** 15 appearances / 1 goal

**Such a speed-merchant winger, he was nicknamed 'The Whippet'. Gilhespy made all of his appearances in 1920-21, enjoying a run of nine consecutive games in the spring during which he got on the scoresheet at Chelsea.**

A £250 fee took the right-winger to Liverpool where he played in 19 first-division games spread over four seasons including ten in 1921-22 when the Anfielders took the title. He went on to win promotion to the second division during four years with Bristol City after which he returned to the top-flight with Blackburn in 1929, where he spent a single season as he did with all of his remaining clubs.

With Rovers he played the opening three games of the season, but only twice more before dropping down the leagues. After retiring from football, he became a supervisor at a mail order store in Huyton, Merseyside. Before his football career, he served in the Royal Navy towards the end of World War One.

## GILHOOLEY, Michael

**POSITION:** Centre-half

**BIRTHPLACE:** Glencraig, Fife

**DATE OF BIRTH:** 26/11/1894 - 17/05/1969

**HEIGHT:** 6' 1" **WEIGHT:** 12st 0lbs

**SIGNED FROM:** Hull City, 02/03/1922

**DEBUT:** v Sheffield United, H, 04/03/1922

**LAST MATCH:** v WBA, A, 21/04/1924

**MOVED TO:** Bradford City, 04/05/1925

**TEAMS:** Glencraig Celtic, Celtic, Vale of Leven, St Bernards, Clydebank, Hull City, Sunderland, Bradford City, QPR, Nithsdale Wanderers, Troon Athletic

**INTERNATIONAL:** Scotland

**SAFC TOTALS:** 19 appearances / 0 goals

**Signed for a world record fee of £5,250, this player nicknamed 'Rubberneck', due to his outstanding heading ability, was never able to bounce back from breaking his leg on only his fourth appearance for Sunderland.**

According to contemporary reports, Gilhooley and Bradford City's record signing of the time, Willie Watson, clashed when challenging for the ball, with the City player landing heavily on top of Gilhooley who had to be stretchered off. Having won what proved to be his solitary international cap against Wales a month before his record transfer, Gilhooley - who was a mobile and ball-playing centre-half with a fine range of passing - appeared set to take his career to new levels.

Following his injury, he did not play again for almost a year. When he did return, he managed just a handful of games in each of his second and third seasons on Wearside before he was given a free transfer. Having seen what he was capable of, having been the opposition in two of his four games before his injury, Bradford were quick to snap him up.

Former club Hull City were the opposition for Gilhooley's Bradford debut in the third match of the 1925-26 season. The Bantams had been relegated since the fateful day he was injured, but playing at a lower level was easier to cope with for Michael who made 30 appearances in his first season and 23 the year after, but could not stop Bradford dismally propping up the table.

The former international would spend the next season in Division Three, but in the Southern section with QPR rather than the Northern section Bradford were headed to. A man who had once been on Celtic's books as a 16-year-old, now found himself playing for Rangers, albeit the Loftus Road variety.

Still dogged by injury, Michael managed the first four games of the season for his London club, but was then out until late in 1927-28. He returned for the final five of his nine matches for Queens Park Rangers.

Determined to keep playing, in February 1929 he made his final move, signing for Ayrshire side Troon Athletic. It was a far cry from being the world's most expensive player. Perhaps appropriately for a footballer whose top-class career was unluckily snatched from him, Gilhooley was the most expensive player on the planet for just 24 hours. A day after signing him, Sunderland smashed the world record fee again when paying £5,500 for full-back Warney Cresswell from South Shields.

Hull had paid £2,500 to sign Gilhooley from Vale of Leven and having debuted at West Ham on 28 August 1920, he had played 72 times for the Tigers, scoring once. Previously, he had been with Celtic without playing for their first-team. During World War One, he served in the Highland Light Infantry and also played for Clydebank and St Bernards. A noted golfer, after his football career he found employment as an Assurance Inspector.

## GILLESPIE, James

**POSITION:** Outside-right

**BIRTHPLACE:** Govan, Glasgow

**DATE OF BIRTH:** 22/03/1868 - 05/08/1932

**HEIGHT:** 5' 7" **WEIGHT:** 11st 7lbs

**SIGNED FROM:** Sunderland Albion, 05/05/1892

**DEBUT:** v Notts County, H, 10/09/1892

**LAST MATCH:** v Newton Heath, H,26/04/1897

**MOVED TO:** Third Lanark, 06/05/1897

**TEAMS:** Star Juniors, Third Lanark, Clyde, Sunderland Albion, Sunderland, Third Lanark, Ayr FC

**INTERNATIONAL:** Scotland

**SAFC TOTALS:** 144 appearances / 51 goals

**Twice a significant member of title-winning teams in the age of 'The Team of All The Talents', Gillespie's final game saw him score both goals in a crucial victory over Newton Heath, the team who became Manchester United. That game was in the play-offs of the era, known as Test Matches. Gillespie's goals kept an ageing Sunderland side in the top flight - a record they preserved for over 60 years.**

Signed from local rivals Sunderland Albion for whom he scored against Sunderland in a friendly in April 1892, Gillespie was an upholsterer by trade and arrived as Sunderland were reigning league champions. He proceeded to play in 23 of the 30 league games as the title was retained, James contributing eleven goals. Two years later, he was joint second-top scorer with 13 goals from 26 games, two of which came in the game immortalised in the Thomas M M Hemy painting which adorns the entrance hall of the Stadium of Light.

During the same season he also scored in the 11-1 cup win over Fairfield which remains the club's record score in a major competition, and he also played in the match at Hearts where Sunderland were proclaimed 'World Champions'.

Across his five seasons Gillespie gave fine service, finishing top-scorer in that last year of struggle thereby maintaining his personal consistency, regardless of the team's performance. He never missed more than the seven games he did not feature in during his first season.

In March 1898, after leaving Sunderland and returning to Third Lanark where he had played before coming to England, he won his solitary cap for Scotland. Although he scored a hat-trick against Wales, he was not picked again, but perhaps the fact he had done well against Wales contributed to him becoming known as 'Taffy.' He also won a representative honour for the Scottish Football League.

## GILLESPIE, John

**POSITION:** Left-back

**BIRTHPLACE:** Govan, Glasgow

**DATE OF BIRTH:** 26/09/1870 - 25/08/1943

**SIGNED FROM:** St Mirren, 09/09/1892

**DEBUT:** v Blackburn Rovers, A, 18/02/1893

**LAST MATCH:** v Derby County, A, 08/04/1893

**MOVED TO:** Bury, 15/08/1893

**TEAMS:** Elmwood, Denny, St Mirren, Sunderland, Bury, Stenhousemuir

**SAFC TOTALS:** 6 appearances / 0 goals

**John, also known as 'Jock', was described as a 'lanky' defender. All of his five league appearances came in the last eight games of the 1892-93 season in which Sunderland retained the league title.**

Shortly before his league debut in a 5-0 win at Newton Heath (Manchester United), he had made his bow in a cup defeat at Blackburn Rovers. He also made five Football League appearances for Bury. He did not retire from football until 1926 after over 30 years service as a player, referee and legislator.

Many of these years in his post-playing career were with Alva Albion Rangers while he also had a spell as the vice President of the Stirlingshire Junior FA. Gillespie had worked in a colliery prior to beginning his football career in Scotland, after which he became an iron moulder.

At Stenhousemuir, he played alongside his brother, Fulton, who had kept goal for Denny and Bury in the early 1890s.

## GILLESPIE, John Scott

**POSITION:** Inside-right

**BIRTHPLACE:** Greenock, Renfrewshire

**DATE OF BIRTH:** 06/11/1866 - 10/09/1947

**SIGNED FROM:** Greenock Morton, 04/04/1890

**DEBUT:** v Wolverhampton Wanderers, H, 15/09/1890

**LAST MATCH:** v Accrington, H, 18/10/1890

**MOVED TO:** Retired from playing in November 1890

**TEAMS:** Renton, Greenock Morton, Sunderland

**SAFC TOTALS:** 2 appearances / 1 goal

**J S Gillespie's two appearances came in Sunderland's second and third home games as a league club, the player marking his debut with a goal. He appears to have left the club in the autumn of 1890, but remained on Wearside and was listed as a marine draughtsman working in Sunderland when he was married in Greenock on 30 March 1893.**

Until the publication of the Absolute Record, Volume One, previous publications had attributed his two games for the Lads to James Gillespie with the belief being that the latter had had a short spell at Sunderland before playing for Sunderland Albion prior to his five-season stint with Sunderland in their Newcastle Road days.

It was research for The Absolute Record by Mike Gibson which established that this was not the case with the Athletic News reporting at the time of James Gillespie's signing for Albion that he had, 'No connection with a player of the same name who for some time was in the Sunderland team'.

## GIVEN, Seamus John James (Shay)

**POSITION:** Goalkeeper

**BIRTHPLACE:** Lifford, Co Donegal

**DATE OF BIRTH:** 20/04/1976

**HEIGHT:** 6' 2" **WEIGHT:** 13st 4lbs

**SIGNED FROM:** Blackburn Rovers, 19/01/1996, on loan

**DEBUT:** v Leicester City, A, 21/01/1996

**LAST MATCH:** v Barnsley, A, 06/04/1996

**MOVED TO:** Blackburn Rovers, 19/04/1996, end of loan

**TEAMS:** Lifford Celtic, Celtic, Blackburn Rovers, Swindon Town (L), Sunderland (L), Newcastle United, Manchester City, Aston Villa, Middlesbrough (L), Stoke City

**INTERNATIONAL:** Republic of Ireland

**SAFC TOTALS:** 17 appearances / 0 goals

**Shay Given was superb at Sunderland, but became a legend at Newcastle where his 463 appearances place him third on the Magpies all-time list and their most capped international as he won 82 caps while at St James'. Brought to Wearside as a youngster on loan by Peter Reid, Given was thrust into a promotion campaign and kept 12 clean sheets in his 17 games.**

His athleticism, agility and assurance marked him as a star of the future and indeed he won the first two of his 134 international caps while on loan to Sunderland. However, he turned down Sunderland's attempts to sign him permanently as he preferred to sign for Newcastle where his boyhood hero and former Blackburn boss Kenny Dalglish was in charge.

As a youngster, Shay had trials with Manchester United and Bradford City prior to a spell in the youth ranks at Celtic before signing for Blackburn where Bobby Mimms was one of the goalkeepers he worked with. Rovers gave him a debut as a sub for England international Tim Flowers in a League Cup tie at home to Brentford on 24 September 1996.

Having been on the bench throughout the season (often when future Sunderland manager Chris Coleman was in defence), Shay played in two away Premier League games the following December conceding just one goal. However, like Ted Doig over a century before, this goalkeeping Goliath went on to star in the north-east after a very brief opportunity at Blackburn.

After leaving Newcastle, Given added 69 appearances for Manchester City and 53 for Aston Villa where he doubled up as assistant manager. Shay went on to join the select group to have played for all three major north-east clubs with a 16-game loan at Middlesbrough and finished with eight games with Stoke, his final appearance on 18 September 2016, meaning he was the last player to end his career having also played for Sunderland at Roker Park, which closed almost 20 years earlier.

He featured in four FA Cup finals, losing to Arsenal with Newcastle in 1998, being an unused sub as Newcastle lost to Manchester United a year later and as Manchester City beat Stoke in 2011 (Thomas Sorensen being in goal for the Potters, who included Kenwyne Jones, Marc Wilson, Rory Delap, Dean Whitehead and Danny Collins in their matchday squad) and in 2015 when he played alongside Kieran Richardson and Alan Hutton as Villa were thrashed 4-0 by Arsenal.

In June 2018, he became goalkeeping coach under Frank Lampard at Derby County, later becoming first-team coach before the Ram's financial problems led to his departure. Shay was awarded the Freedom of County Donegal in 2006.

## GLADWIN, Charles Edward (Charlie)

**POSITION:** Right-back

**BIRTHPLACE:** Worksop, Notts

**DATE OF BIRTH:** 11/12/1887 - 21/06/1952

**HEIGHT:** 5' 10½" **WEIGHT:** 12st 6lbs

**SIGNED FROM:** Blackpool, 08/10/1912

**DEBUT:** v Middlesbrough, H, 12/10/1912

**LAST MATCH:** v Blackburn Rovers, H, 20/02/1915

**MOVED TO:** Watford, 20/08/1919

**TEAMS:** Dinnington Main Colliery, Blackpool, Sunderland, Watford, Treeton Reading Room

**SAFC TOTALS:** 63 appearances / 1 goal

**Charlie Gladwin can stake a claim to the right-back berth in an all-time Sunderland team. His game would not suit modern tastes for attacking cultured full-backs who become auxiliary wingers, but given the clue to the position is in the title of the position, Gladwin ruled supreme in his defensive capacity.**

In Sunderland's finest-ever season of 1912-13, the club were one off the bottom after five defeats and two draws when they signed Gladwin from Blackpool and goalkeeper Joe Butler from Glossop. Gladwin barely missed a game to the end of the season as Sunderland swept to the league title and reached the cup final. Yet another ex-miner who came into the game, Gladwin was a rugged, but effective defender. In an era when the game was extremely physical, not only did Charlie take no prisoners but no-one would want to be his prisoner.

At defensive corners, he was renowned to tell his fellow defenders to keep out of his way while he attacked the ball to thunderously head away. He was also known to make his pre-match routine pushing his finger down his own throat to make himself vomit as a way of conquering nerves.

Before coming to Sunderland, Gladwin had almost four years with Blackpool who he joined just before Christmas in 1908. He did not debut until a 2-0 home win over Wolves the following September, the Seasiders having propped up the second division the season before, in the days when there was no third division to be relegated to.

Sixteen appearances that season helped Blackpool to an improved mid-table position after which he more than doubled his appearances to 36 the following year as the club climbed five places to seventh.

Playing at left-back in 1911-12, he played 30 times, but missed the closing stages as his team finished 14th. Finally in the season he signed for Sunderland, Gladwin played the first ten games of the season for Blackpool who went on to once again prop up Division Two as their former full-back became a league champion with Sunderland. That must have been a feather in the cap of the red and white recruitment staff.

After the Great War, in which he served in the Royal Garrison Artillery, Gladwin joined Watford who had won the Southern League in the last season before the war brought normal league football to a halt.

He played a dozen games for the Hornets, the last at Portsmouth before taking over from the fatally-ill Tom Coulson as trainer until May 1920. The following season Charlie was back playing, turning out in the early stages of the English (FA) Cup for Treeton Reading Room.

## GLOAG, Robert (Bob)

**POSITION:** Forward

**BIRTHPLACE:** Edinburgh, Midlothian

**DATE OF BIRTH:** 28/08/1867 - 12/07/1937

**HEIGHT:** 5' 7" **WEIGHT:** 9st 8lbs

**SIGNED FROM:** Towerhill, 24/10/1887

**DEBUT:** v Middlesbrough, A, 26/11/1887

**LAST MATCH:** v Middlesbrough, H, 03/12/1887

**MOVED TO:** Sunderland Albion, 01/10/1888

**TEAMS:** Roseburn, Towerhill, Sunderland, Sunderland Albion

**SAFC TOTALS:** 2 appearances / 2 goals

**Bob Gloag scored both goals as Sunderland drew 2-2 at Middlesbrough in the English (FA) Cup in 1887. He also played in the replay which Sunderland won 4-2 only to be disqualified after Middlesbrough won an appeal claiming that the Wearsiders had illegally fielded three professionals.**

These were Gloag's only official appearances in senior professional games, but in his time, most matches were friendlies. He had signed for Sunderland after impressing in a reserve game against Morpeth Harriers on 22 October 1887 having previously played in Glasgow for Towerhill and Roseburn. Having left Sunderland for local rivals Albion. he played in their second-ever game against Newcastle West End on 12 May 1888.

He was the brother-in-law of George Drummond who won two league titles and the cup with Preston North End. After giving up football, Gloag became a house painter. He is then believed to have emigrated to Canada around 1908 and according to the 1911 census, was living in Toronto.

After serving in the Canadian forces during World War One, he moved to Hollywood to become a set painter. Unlike 1950s inside-forward Harry Clark who became a set designer on some well-known TV programmes, the films this Sunderland forward of the 1880s worked on, remain a mystery.

## GODBOLD, Harold (Harry)

**POSITION:** Outside-left

**BIRTHPLACE:** Springwell, Co Durham

**DATE OF BIRTH:** 31/01/1939

**HEIGHT:** 5' 8½" **WEIGHT:** 9st 13lbs

**SIGNED FROM:** Usworth Juniors, 12/05/1956

**DEBUT:** v Portsmouth, H, 14/12/1957

**LAST MATCH:** v Brighton & Hove Albion, A, 02/01/1960

**MOVED TO:** Hartlepools United, 13/01/1961

**TEAMS:** Usworth Juniors, Sunderland, Hartlepools United, Boston United, Boston FC, Lincoln City, Spalding United, Boston FC, Gateshead, Crawcrook

**SAFC TOTALS:** 13 appearances / 1 goal

**Godbold's appearances for Sunderland were spread over three seasons as he shadowed England winger Colin Grainger. His goal came on his third appearance, joining Don Revie on the scoresheet in a home win over Leeds United. Relegated after his first season, Harry got six games in the following campaign and one the year after before joining Hartlepools as a part-time player as he underwent his National Service at Bicester in the Ordnance Corps.**

Debuting for Hartlepools on 14 January 1961 in a fourth division fixture at home to Crystal Palace, Harry went on to score eight times in 70 games in what was a difficult time for the club who regularly had to apply for re-election while he was there. Leaving Pools in 1963, he played in non-league before returning to Football League ranks in 1966 with Lincoln, only to again be part of a side that had to apply for re-election in both of his seasons at Sincil Bank.

After completing his playing days back in non-league circles, he returned to Washington where he worked in a factory until retirement.

## GODDARD, George

**POSITION:** Inside-forward

**BIRTHPLACE:** Gomshall, Surrey

**DATE OF BIRTH:** 20/12/1903 - 23/04/1987

**HEIGHT:** 5' 11" **WEIGHT:** 12st 4lbs

**SIGNED FROM:** Wolverhampton Wanderers, 23/10/1934

**DEBUT:** v Birmingham, H, 08/12/1934

**LAST MATCH:** v Sheffield Wednesday, H, 26/10/1935

**MOVED TO:** Southend United, 14/03/1936

**TEAMS:** Redhill, QPR, Wolves, Sunderland, Southend United

**SAFC TOTALS:** 14 appearances / 5 goals

**QPR's record goalscorer, Goddard was a veteran when he joined Sunderland. He scored in a home win over Liverpool in one of three appearances in the 1935-36 title-winning season having netted in the final three games of the previous campaign.**

Such were Sunderland's attacking riches at the time (indeed on both his first and last appearances, Sunderland won 5-1 without him scoring) that his opportunities were very limited. Had substitutes been in use at the time, the chances are he would have been a regular option from the bench.

Having been capped by his county as an amateur, George joined Queen's Park Rangers in 1926, debuting with a goal at Brentford on 11 September that year. A butcher by trade, he had been working in a bus garage when he signed for QPR after reputedly scoring over 200 goals with Redhill. He topped the Rangers scoring charts for seven successive seasons being Division Three South's top-scorer in 1929-30 with 39 goals from 45 league and cup games

In December 1933, he stepped up to the top-flight with Wolves managed by Major Frank Buckley. Debuting in a home win over Newcastle United on 9 December 1933, he got his first goal in his second home game as Manchester City were hammered 8-0. Quickly transferring his prolific scoring rate to the top level, this began a run of scoring in five consecutive games, the last of these seeing him net twice in a 3-3 draw with Sunderland at Roker Park, a performance that probably influenced Sunderland's interest in signing him after he ended the season with a dozen goals in 17 games for the Molineux club.

After completing his goal-laden career with Southend United, he had a newsagents in Esher and then took over a butcher's shop in central London before successfully running a café.

## GÓMEZ, Jordi Garcia-Penche

**POSITION:** Midfielder

**BIRTHPLACE:** Barcelona, Spain

**DATE OF BIRTH:** 24/05/1985

**HEIGHT:** 5' 10" **WEIGHT:** 11st 9lbs

**SIGNED FROM:** Wigan Athletic, 01/07/2014

**DEBUT:** v WBA, A, 16/08/2014

**LAST MATCH:** v Manchester City, A, 26/12/2015

**MOVED TO:** Wigan Athletic,17/08/2016

**TEAMS:** Barcelona, Espanyol, Swansea City (L), Wigan Athletic, Sunderland, Blackburn Rovers (L), Wigan Athletic, Rayo Vallecano, Levski Sofia, AC Omonia (to June 2022)

**INTERNATIONAL:** Spain Under 17

**SAFC TOTALS:** 31+8 appearances / 6 goals

**Once a teammate of Lionel Messi in the youth ranks at Barcelona, at Sunderland, Gomez was vaguely reminiscent of Ian Porterfield in that when in possession he was unhurried and invariably composed as well as being a precise passer. He could be frustratingly slow at times, but undoubtedly had aspects of his game that were clear assets, not least his ability to confidently convert penalties.**

Beginning with his home city club Barcelona, Gómez came through the C and B teams, scoring six goals in 59 games for the latter. He made one appearance at first-team level, playing the last 22 minutes of a 6-0 Copa del Rey victory over Zamora CF on 11 January 2006. He later made three La Liga appearances as a substitute having moved to city rivals Espanyol before moving into British football when his countryman Roberto Martinez took him on loan to Swansea in June 2008.

Scoring the winner in a derby against Cardiff made Jordi a Jacks hero. It was one of twelve goals he scored in 44+7 games before Martinez bought him for £1.7m - but after taking

## GOMEZ, Jordi (Continued)

over at Wigan Athletic. In a first spell of five seasons with the Latics, he played 112+50 times scoring 28 times including a 2012 hat-trick against Reading. He also played in the 2013 FA Cup final as Wigan sensationally defeated Manchester City with an injury-time winner from Ben Watson who had come on for Gómez with nine minutes left. Accompanying Jordi in the Latics line-up was Callum McManaman while City brought Jack Rodwell off a bench that also included Costel Pantilimon and Joleon Lescott.

Co-incidentally, it was Rodwell who Gómez came on for when making his Sunderland debut after which he scored on his first start in a League (Capital One) Cup win at Birmingham City. Named in the matchday squad for all but the final three games of his first season, he played only five times the following term before being loaned to Blackburn Rovers as the January transfer window closed. A debut scorer for Rovers against Middlesbrough, Gomez scored three times in 17+2 appearances before a free transfer back to Wigan where he completed his British career with another three goals in 12+4 appearances.

January 2017 saw Gómez return to Spain with Rayo Vallecano, debuting in a second-tier game with Almeria on 5 February. It was one of a dozen games he played (including five as a sub) before a summer move to Levski Sofia. He made a bright start in Bulgaria with two goals in a 4-0 derby win over Slavia Sofia on 26 August 2017, but there were just two more goals in his season there before moving to Omonia Nicosia after a single season.

In 2020-21, he won the Cypriot league championship with Omonia in a season where he scored in both the Champions League (in a win at Legia Warsaw) and in Europa league meetings with PSV Eindhoven and PAOK Salonika, the strike against PSV being a free-kick from 61.2 yards - officially the longest-range goal in the competition's history. Gómez's club had been leading their league when Covid 19 curtailed the season and while they were not awarded the title, they were awarded a Champions League place before dropping into the Europa League.

## GOOCH, Lynden Jack

**POSITION:** Forward

**BIRTHPLACE:** Santa Cruz, California, USA

**DATE OF BIRTH:** 24/12/1995

**HEIGHT:** 5' 9" **WEIGHT:** 11st 6lbs

**SIGNED FROM:** As trainee, 01/07/2012

**DEBUT:** v Exeter City, H, 25/08/2015

**LAST MATCH:**

**MOVED TO:**

**TEAMS:** Santa Cruz County Breakers, Sunderland, Gateshead (L), Doncaster Rovers (L)

**INTERNATIONAL:** USA

**SAFC TOTALS:** 156+57 appearances / 25 goals (to June 2022)

**Californian-born, but Sunderland through and through having first come to the club as a ten-year-old, 'Goooooch' (as the fans referred to him) made the noteworthy contribution of scoring the Wembley winner as Sunderland won the Football League (Papa John's) Trophy in 2021. It was Lynden's third Wembley appearance for Sunderland having played in the 2019 Football League (Checkatrade) Trophy and Play-Off final. Another Wembley appearance came in the successful 2022 Play-Off final by which time he was the club's longest serving player.**

Loaned to Gateshead prior to his red and white debut, Lynden first appeared for the Tynesiders in a Conference game against Bristol Rovers in February 2015 and scored his only goal in seven games for 'The Heed' on his second outing against Wrexham. At the start of the following season, he made his Sunderland debut in a 6-3 League (Capital One) Cup game with Exeter. Five months later, Lynden made his Football League debut on loan to Doncaster (at Fleetwood). It was the first of ten league appearances for Rovers.

On the opening day of the following 2016-17 campaign, Gooch made a Premier League bow at Manchester City. That season and the following one saw Sunderland suffer back-to-back relegations as Gooch gradually became more of a regular and by the time the team had slid into League One, he had become more important, reaching double figures in terms of goals by the curtailed 2019-20 campaign. Sometimes accused of trying to do too much on the ball and holding on to possession for too long, Lynden's commitment and willingness to work for the team were never in question. In particular, under Lee Johnson in 2020-21, he increasingly became a utility player, playing in both full-back positions as well as across the midfield and up front.

The son of an Irish mother and English father, he was initially capped by the Republic of Ireland at Under 18 level before switching to the USA at Under 20 level - actually debuting for them against the Republic of Ireland. In October 2016, he became a full international, playing for the USA against Cuba and New Zealand in friendlies before appearing as a substitute for future Chelsea star Christian Pulisic in a World Cup qualifying game lost 4-0 away to Costa Rica, for whom Bryan Oviedo was an unused sub, while Jozy Altidore led the line for the States. A fourth cap came in May 2018 against Bolivia.

Coming from a sporting family, his brother Anthony worked in Major League Soccer for San Jose Earthquakes while another brother, Darshan, is a professional surfer.

## GOODCHILD, George

**POSITION:** Outside-right

**BIRTHPLACE:** Seaham Colliery, Co Durham

**DATE OF BIRTH:** 01/02/1875 - 23/12/1927

**HEIGHT:** 6' 0"

**SIGNED FROM:** Ryhope Colliery, 27/08/1894

**DEBUT:** v Sheffield United, A, 09/03/1895

**LAST MATCH:** v Sheffield United, A, 09/03/1895

**MOVED TO:** Derby County, 04/06/1896

**TEAMS:** Ryhope Colliery, Sunderland, Derby County, Nottingham Forest, Burton Swifts, Jarrow, Stanley, Whitburn, South Shields, Ashington

**SAFC TOTALS:** 1 appearance / 0 goals

**Goodchild's only appearance coincided with a 4-0 defeat which was the heaviest of the season and the only league reverse after the turn of the year as 'The Team Of All The Talents' won a third league title in four years and were declared world champions after beating Scottish champions Hearts.**

No doubt it was a tough ask to get a game in a side that good and for Goodchild, it was a one-off opportunity for a winger who throughout his football career was a professional race-walker.

After spending most of the 1896-97 season with Derby where he played twice, he transferred to their East Midlands neighbours Nottingham Forest for whom he debuted at Wednesday in April 1897 and went on to play four league games, the last a local derby against Notts County the following September. He also played in six friendlies and a Testimonial for Forest.A month after his last competitive outing for Forest, Goodchild was on the move again, this time to Burton Swifts where he stayed for almost two years, scoring once in nine league games before returning to spend the rest of his career back in the north-east.

He went on to work as a coal miner while also becoming the secretary of the Sherburn Hill Unionist Association after World War One.

## GOODCHILD, John

**POSITION:** Outside-left

**BIRTHPLACE:** Littletown, Co Durham

**DATE OF BIRTH:** 02/01/1939 - 25/08/2011

**HEIGHT:** 5' 7" **WEIGHT:** 10st 6lbs

**SIGNED FROM:** Ludworth Juniors, 20/09/1955

**DEBUT:** v Leicester City, H, 04/09/1957

**LAST MATCH:** v Leeds United, A, 25/02/1961

**MOVED TO:** Brighton & Hove Albion, 15/05/1961

**TEAMS:** Sunderland, Brighton & Hove Albion, York City, Darlington, Goole Town

**SAFC TOTALS:** 45 appearances / 21 goals

**Given his record of almost a goal per two games, it seems a surprise that manager Alan Brown let a young talent go, Goodchild being just 22 when he moved on. Goodchild's goals record is all the more impressive as a player who operated on both wings and sometimes in both inside-forward berths, but not as a number nine.**

A scorer on his debut in the top-flight, he added another two games later and played seven times in what was Sunderland's first relegation season. In the inaugural year in the second tier, he came into the side in the second half of the campaign and finished as second top-scorer with 16 goals including a hat-trick against Sheffield United. Although he failed to score in nine games the following season there was another hat-trick in a 4-2 win at Leeds in what astonishingly was his final appearance and only one of the season.

Known as Ralphy which was his father's name, he moved to Brighton who suffered back-to-back relegations from the second tier to the fourth in his first two seasons before he helped them to the Division Four title two years later. In total he played 162+1 league games for Brighton scoring 45 goals, being joint top scorer with ten goals in his first year at the club.

In the summer of 1966 he returned to the basement division with a transfer to York City. Debuting on the opening day of the season at home to Chesterfield, he scored six goals in 36 games in all competitions before moving to Darlington after a single season. After just two games for the Quakers he moved into non-league football and became a postman and later a rent collector.

John was also an accomplished cricketer and represented Durham City, Ushaw Moor and Esh Winning as well as playing for Durham County second XI.

## GOODMAN, Donald Ralph

**POSITION:** Forward

**BIRTHPLACE:** Leeds, West Yorkshire

**DATE OF BIRTH:** 09/05/1966

**HEIGHT:** 5' 10" **WEIGHT:** 11st 10lbs

**SIGNED FROM:** West Bromwich Albion, 05/12/1991

**DEBUT:** v Wolverhampton Wanderers, A, 07/12/1991

**LAST MATCH:** v Port Vale, A, 29/11/1994

**MOVED TO:** Wolverhampton Wanderers, 05/12/1994

**TEAMS:** Collingham, Bradford City, WBA, Sunderland, Wolves, Hiroshima, Barnsley (L), Motherwell, Walsall, Exeter City, Doncaster Rovers, Stafford Rangers

**SAFC TOTALS:** 128+4 appearances / 47 goals

**Sunderland doubled their transfer record when paying £900,000 for Goodman who on his debut at Wolves found himself quickly in a nine-man team as Sunderland had two men sent off in the first seven minutes. A hard working and powerful player with plenty of pace, he was brought in to replace the recently sold Marco Gabbiadini and did a good job of doing so.**

Unfortunately for Don, he was in and out of the side as the Lads went on to the FA Cup final, but with Goodman unavailable as he was cup-tied having played in the first round for West Brom against non-league Marlow.

He finished his first season as top-scorer with eleven goals including a hat-trick from 20+2 games (having also scored five for WBA). He was top scorer again the following year with 17 goals in a struggling side and reached double figures again in his third and last full season. Always a team player, Goodman would often drift into wide areas seeking to make space, but many felt he would be more effective if he stayed in or near the box, but nonetheless, Don always remained deservedly popular.

Goodman started his professional career with Bradford City who he was playing for on the day of the Bradford fire disaster on 11 May 1985 in which his ex-girlfriend was reportedly one of the 56 victims. He had debuted 13 months earlier as a 17-year-old in a home game with Newport in which John Hawley scored the winner. At this point, Goodman was still working as an electrician and after turning professional was allowed a weekly day-release to attend college.

In November 1984, he came off the bench to score a seven minute hat-trick in a 7-2 FA Cup win over Tow Law, part of an overall record of 20 goals in 72+9 games before a March 1987 move to West Brom for whom he made his home debut against Sunderland. Goodman grabbed 60 goals in 163+18 games, 21 of those goals coming in 1989-90 when he became the first Albion striker to net 20 or more league goals in a season since 1970-71.

Ambitious to play in the top-flight, he left Albion for Sunderland and subsequently Sunderland for Wolves who missed out on promotion to the Premier League in the Play-Offs shortly after he moved to Molineux and again in 1997. Don's time with Wolves came to an end after 142+12 games and 39 goals. His spell with Wolves had been hampered by injury, including a fractured skull sustained against Huddersfield in April 1996.

In 1998, he made the bold move to venture into Japanese soccer although his spell with Sanfrecce Hiroshima brought just two goals from ten appearances before an eight-game loan back close to home with Barnsley where he did not score. Another loan to Motherwell in March 1999 saw him debut against Dundee United at Tannadice and subsequently sign for the club who he went on to assist in wins against both Celtic and Rangers. Following 47+17 games and twelve goals in Scotland he returned to the West Midlands with Walsall where he doubled as fitness coach. Don only scored three times in 25 games for the Saddlers, but one of those was an equaliser in a Play-Off final at the Millennium Stadium. In that match, Darren Byfield got an extra-time winner against a Reading side which included Phil Parkinson.

At his next club, Exeter, Goodman scored just one league goal, against Carlisle, in a season where Exeter were relegated to the Conference. The Grecians loaned him to Doncaster Rovers before he joined Stafford Rangers on a free transfer in the summer of 2003, retiring a year later.

Don has remained in the game working as a much in demand summariser on BBC Radio and Sky TV. His biography, 'The Don' My Story, was published in 2011.

## GORDON, Craig Anthony

**POSITION:** Goalkeeper

**BIRTHPLACE:** Edinburgh, Midlothian

**DATE OF BIRTH:** 31/12/1982

**HEIGHT:** 6' 4" **WEIGHT:** 14st 0lbs

**SIGNED FROM:** Heart of Midlothian, 08/08/2007

**DEBUT:** v Tottenham Hotspur, H, 11/08/2007

**LAST MATCH:** v Bolton Wanderers, H, 28/04/2012

**MOVED TO:** Contract not renewed, 30/06/2012

**TEAMS:** Hearts, Cowdenbeath (L), Sunderland, Celtic, Hearts (to 2022)

**INTERNATIONAL:** Scotland

**SAFC TOTALS:** 95 appearances / 0 goals

**Bought for an initial £7m plus £2m based on appearances, Gordon cost a British record fee for a goalkeeper. He was an accomplished shot-stopper and made the save officially rated as the best in the first 20 years of the Premier League. That stop in December 2010 came from Zat Knight of Bolton, a club that would be the opposition for Gordon's only game of his final season at Sunderland, and also a 4-1 home defeat in November 2008 that was the final match of the man who signed him, Roy Keane.**

In that heavy 2008 defeat by Bolton, Gordon was brought back after eight weeks out with injury. Indeed, it was his only game in exactly six months, although he did sit on the bench during that period. Injuries restricted Craig's appearances on Wearside. After his first season where he played 34 league games, his subsequent seasons saw him play just 12, 26, 15 and one league games, ultimately resulting in him being released.

After leaving Sunderland, he had two years out of the game battling his knee injury. During this time he worked as a TV pundit, coached Dumbarton and trained with Rangers during 2013-14 before signing for Celtic in July 2014. His return went so well that after three games he was recalled by Scotland and he was showered with silverware being part of five successive SPL titles between 2015 and 2019. Additionally, he twice won the Scottish Cup plus five League Cups as well as winning a host of individual honours including the SFWA Footballer of the Year in 2014-15. Craig had won the same award in 2005-06 with Hearts with whom he won the Scottish Cup in 2006, six years after winning the Scottish Youth Cup. Returning to Hearts in 2020, he won promotion with them in 2021 as Championship winners. He had been inducted into the Hearts Hall of Fame in 2007.

A decade later, he was inducted into the Scotland national team roll of honour. His international debut in May 2004 had seen the first goal he conceded for Scotland scored by Stern John who was accompanied in the Trinidad & Tobago team by Kenwyne Jones and Carlos Edwards while James McFadden and substitute Steve Caldwell were amongst Craig's colleagues. In winning his 55th cap in November 2020, he broke a record set three days earlier by David Marshall - which had previously stretched back to 1903 and Sunderland legend Ted Doig - for the longest span of a Scottish international career. In 2021, he was a member of Scotland's squad at the delayed Euro 2020, but did not get to play.

## GORMAN, James Joseph (Jimmy)

**POSITION:** Right-back
**BIRTHPLACE:** Liverpool, Lancashire
**DATE OF BIRTH:** 03/03/1910 - 01/02/1991
**HEIGHT:** 5' 9" **WEIGHT:** 11st 9lbs
**SIGNED FROM:** Blackburn Rovers, 14/01/1937
**DEBUT:** v Brentford, A, 23/01/1937
**LAST MATCH:** v Everton, H, 07/04/1939
**MOVED TO:** Hartlepools United, 25/10/1945
**TEAMS:** Skelmersdale United, Burscough Rangers, Blackburn Rovers, Sunderland, North Shields (WW2 Guest), Carlisle United (WW2 Guest), Middlesbrough (WW2 Guest), Hartlepools United
**SAFC TOTALS:** 100 appearances / 1 goal

**A member of the 1937 FA Cup-winning team, Gorman played all but the first of the nine games it took to win the trophy, having joined the club after the third round. He proceeded to play 34 league games in each of the next two seasons and also all three from the expunged 1939-40 season (these three are not included in his official tally above). He had come to the fore with Blackburn playing 225 games for them without scoring. As early as the fifth of those games for Rovers, he had played at Roker Park in October 1931.**

Jimmy's only goal in his career was for Sunderland, in an FA Cup third round tie at home to Plymouth in 1939, a 40-yard direct free-kick that sailed in over the goalkeeper's head.

A cabinet maker before becoming a footballer, Jimmy later worked as a Bevin Boy at Hylton Colliery, a lorry driver for ship repairers during World War Two and became a pub licensee on Wearside shortly before signing for Hartlepools with whom he played three war-time games. He debuted against Newcastle United in October 1939 while 'Guesting' for the club. He also played 13 war-time games for Carlisle in 1939-40 and 27 for Middlesbrough the following season as well as assisting North Shields. Finally in 1945-46, he made two appearances in the FL3 North East Championship for Hartlepools. A noted sportsman, Gorman also played baseball and cricket.

## GOW, Donald Robertson

**POSITION:** Full-back
**BIRTHPLACE:** Blair Atholl, Perthshire
**DATE OF BIRTH:** 08/02/1868 - 10/10/1945
**HEIGHT:** 5' 10" **WEIGHT:** 12st 3lbs
**SIGNED FROM:** Rangers, 23/07/1891
and again from Rangers, 28/10/1893
**DEBUT:** v Bolton Wanderers, A, 19/09/1891
**LAST MATCH:** v Newton Heath, H, 26/04/1897
**MOVED TO:** Rangers, 24/05/1892
and New Brighton Tower, 23/06/1897
**TEAMS:** Cessnock Bank, Rangers, Sunderland, Rangers, Sunderland, New Brighton Tower, Millwall Athletic, Girvan
**INTERNATIONAL:** Scotland
**SAFC TOTALS:** 115 appearances / 1 goal

**Donald Gow had two spells with both Sunderland and Rangers, winning the league title with both. A versatile player, he mainly operated at full-back and being a noted amateur sprinter his pace was an asset to any side.**

He captained Scotland against England at Hampden in March 1888. At the age of 20 years and 38 days he was the second youngest member of the team, but it remained Gow's only cap. This was probably due more to the Scots' reluctance to choose people playing in England than the fact that his team lost 5-0 on the day. When this policy was changed he did play in an Anglo Scots v Home Scots trial match, but failed to gain selection. While with Sunderland he became one of the first Scottish players to be honoured with selection for a Football League representative game.

In 1890-91, he played in 16 of the 18 league games Rangers played (scoring at Cambuslang) as they were proclaimed joint champions in the inaugural season of the Scottish League with Dumbarton, although had goal average or goal difference been in play, Dumbarton would have pipped them. Moving to Sunderland, he again played 16 league games as Sunderland won the title for the first time, but he missed out on retaining the trophy as he returned to Rangers.

After a season back in Glasgow where he played ten times as Rangers were runners-up to Celtic he returned to Wearside and subsequently won a second championship with the club in 1894-95 although he was restricted to just seven games that term. Injured after the first match of the season, he returned for the final six games and also appeared in the English Cup semi-final as well as the game at Hearts in which Sunderland were proclaimed world champions. Ever-present the following season, in the year after that he barely missed a game and signed off in the 'Test Match' which succeeded in the club avoiding relegation.

After a season with New Brighton Tower, he spent 1898-99 with Millwall Athletic where he scored against Royal Artillery in one of his six Southern League games as the Lions finished third. He also scored a penalty against Wellingborough in the opening game of the United League which Millwall went on to win with Gow making five appearances.

Finishing his career back in Scotland he played for Girvan in South Ayrshire and became a prominent referee in the early 1900s before becoming a farmer in the Scottish Highlands, although from 1937 until his death, he was known to be living in Middlesbrough. His brother John was also a Scotland international and Rangers player who became president of the Ibrox club.

## GRABBAN, Lewis James

**POSITION:** Forward
**BIRTHPLACE:** Croydon, London
**DATE OF BIRTH:** 12/01/1988
**HEIGHT:** 6' 0" **WEIGHT:** 12st 4lbs
**SIGNED FROM:** AFC Bournemouth, 26/07/2017, on loan
**DEBUT:** v Derby County, H, 04/08/2017
**LAST MATCH:** v Birmingham City, H, 23/12/2017
**MOVED TO:** AFC Bournemouth, 05/01/2018, end of loan
**TEAMS:** Crystal Palace, Oldham Athletic (L), Motherwell (L), Millwall, Brentford, Rotherham United, AFC Bournemouth, Norwich City, AFC Bournemouth, Reading (L), Sunderland (L), Aston Villa (L), Nottingham Forest (to May 2022)
**SAFC TOTALS:** 19+1 appearances / 12 goals

**A lethal penalty box poacher, Grabban became the first Sunderland player to score a penalty on his debut and also set a (since broken) record as the club's highest scoring loan player, but terminated his Stadium of Light season-long loan early at his own request.**

Unsurprisingly he preferred to swap a relegation battle for Sunderland; who had changed manager from Simon Grayson to Chris Coleman since he signed, for a promotion campaign with Aston Villa who he swiftly moved to on loan. He took his tally to 20 for the season with eight in 15 games - including one back at Sunderland - only for Villa to lose the play-off final.

Grabban debuted with his local club Crystal Palace in August 2005, going on to become the Eagles Academy Player of the Year that season. After 13 games for Palace and 16 over two loans without scoring, Millwall had seen enough to pay £150,000 for him. The Lions won promotion to the Championship while he was there, although he was a peripheral figure in their 2009-10 promotion season, some of which he spent on loan to Brentford who he subsequently signed for. In the summer of 2011, Lewis left London to join Rotherham where he was signed by Andy Scott who had worked with him at Brentford.

A spectacular goal on his debut got him off to a good start with the League Two Millers where 21 goals in 47 games led to a move to Bournemouth who were a division higher after he had been named PFA Fans League Two Player of the Year.

Promoted in his first season with the Cherries, things got even better as he was the club's Player of the Year in his second term after netting 22 Championship goals. This led to a reported £3m move to Norwich City where he scored a dozen goals as they were promoted to the Premier League. At the start of his second season with the Canaries, the player was reportedly suspended by the club for failing to report for a League Cup game with his old club Rotherham in which he had been named as a substitute.

After six appearances and one goal in the Premier League, Grabban was sold back to AFC Bournemouth in the 2016 January transfer window, but failed to score in 18 Premier League games. He had a loan with Reading before coming to Sunderland.

In 2018 he joined Nottingham Forest who he went on to captain to promotion to the Premier League in 2022 before deciding to leave the club where he had scored 56 goals in 121+28 games. Eligible for Jamaica, Grabban was twice selected for the country, but as of 2022 was still to be capped.

## GRAHAM, Allan

**POSITION:** Right-back
**BIRTHPLACE:** Ryhope, Co Durham
**DATE OF BIRTH:** 23/10/1937
**HEIGHT:** 5' 9½" **WEIGHT:** 11st 5lbs
**SIGNED FROM:** Silksworth Juniors, 01/05/1955
**DEBUT:** v Wolverhampton Wanderers, A, 31/08/1957
**LAST MATCH:** v Burnley, A, 12/10/1957
**MOVED TO:** Horden CW, 01/06/1958
**TEAMS:** Silksworth Juniors, Sunderland, Horden CW
**SAFC TOTALS:** 3 appearances / 0 goals

**Allan Graham was still in his teens when he got the longed-for chance to play in the top-flight for Sunderland. It was away to the famed Wolves side of the era, a team who went on to be champions this season and included Billy Wright, the first man to play 100 times for England.**

It was a rude awakening for the 19-year-old as Sunderland fell behind in the fourth minute and were trounced 5-0. One of three teenagers brought into the team for manager Alan Brown's third game in charge, Graham was reported to have drawn 'many rounds of applause for neat interceptions and no nonsense tackling against Mullen' - Mullen being Wanderers' Newcastle-born England winger.

Graham did well enough to hold his place for the following weekend's home win over Leicester City, but got just one more outing five weeks later in a 6-0 hammering at Burnley - famous for being Charlie Hurley's second game and the one where the future Player of the Century declared Sunderland had already improved with him as they had been beaten 7-0 on his debut.

Four days later Graham did get a fourth game in the first team, playing in a floodlit friendly at Middlesbrough where Brian Clough scored in a 2-0 win for the Teessiders.

## GRAHAM, Daniel Anthony William (Danny)

**POSITION:** Centre-forward
**BIRTHPLACE:** Gateshead, Tyne & Wear
**DATE OF BIRTH:** 12/08/1985
**HEIGHT:** 5' 11" **WEIGHT:** 13st 10lbs
**SIGNED FROM:** Swansea City, 31/01/2013 and as a free agent, 07/09/2020
**DEBUT:** v Reading, A, 02/02/2013
**LAST MATCH:** v Hull City, H, 09/01/2021
**MOVED TO:** Blackburn Rovers, 23/06/2016 and retired, 01/02/2021
**TEAMS:** Chester-le-Street Town, Middlesbrough, Darlington (L), Derby County (L), Leeds United (L), Blackpool (L), Carlisle United, Watford, Swansea City, Sunderland, Hull City (L), Middlesbrough (L), Wolves (L), Blackburn Rovers, Sunderland
**INTERNATIONAL:** England Under 20
**SAFC TOTALS:** 25+17 appearances / 2 goals

**Danny Graham was one of those players who seemed to do well everywhere else but Sunderland - even though he had two spells at the club, the first one after commanding a £5m fee. Only two of his career total of 174 goals were for Sunderland while he won Player of the Year awards at Watford and Blackburn, twice was selected in the PFA Divisional Teams of the Year and in 2010-11 was the Championship's top scorer with 27 goals in total for Watford.**

At Sunderland he struggled to hit a barn door. One of his two goals was a scrappy effort he seemed to know little about while his second came on his second-spell debut as a sub against a pliant Aston Villa Under 21s defence who leaked eight goals. After just that goal at Everton in 42 attempts in his first spell, his second debut augured well, but in 16 further appearances, the name Graham steadfastly refused to appear on the scoresheet and mid-way through the season, Danny announced his retirement at the age of 35.

He did score 15 other goals whilst a Sunderland player - just not in a Sunderland shirt. Six of those goals came in 17+1 games on loan to his former club Middlesbrough while there was another goal in the same 2013-14 season on loan to Hull (14+6 games) in the Premier League, along with one for Wolves the following season and seven in 18 games on loan to Blackburn Rovers.

Goals in the Northern League persuaded Middlesbrough to take him on. Debuting at Doncaster on loan to Darlington in March 2004, three weeks after Boro won the Carling Cup, he scored twice in seven games for the Quakers and earned a Premier League debut at Manchester United the following October, scoring on his home debut against Coventry. That would be Danny's only goal in his initial spell with the Teessiders who loaned him to Derby County, Leeds United and Blackpool where he scored just one goal in total from a combined 13+8 games.

Success started to come in another loan to Carlisle where after seven goals in eleven games the move was made permanent with a further 33 goals in 91+11 games, before a move to Watford where he was top scorer with 14 goals in his first campaign. He equalled the Hornets record of scoring in seven successive games in his second season as he went on to be the Championship's top scorer in a mid-table team.

Swansea paid £3.5m for him and made a handsome profit in selling him to Sunderland after he netted 21 times in 47+15 games. One of those goals came in a League (Capital One) Cup semi-final victory at Chelsea only for Graham to forego the chance to play in the final by moving to Sunderland. In between his two spells with Sunderland, Graham rediscovered his goal touch with Blackburn who he initially joined on loan. Following his loan being made permanent, he managed 13 goals in a struggling team that were relegated to League One before hitting 17 as Rovers returned to the Championship at the first time of asking. In total Danny scored 57 goals for Blackburn in 129+52 games, but once back at Sunderland that goal touch once again deserted him.

## GRAINGER, Colin

**POSITION:** Outside-left
**BIRTHPLACE:** Havercroft, West Yorkshire
**DATE OF BIRTH:** 10/06/1933 - 20/06/2022
**HEIGHT:** 5' 8" **WEIGHT:** 10st 12lbs
**SIGNED FROM:** Sheffield United, 05/02/1957
**DEBUT:** v Tottenham Hotspur, A, 09/02/1957
**LAST MATCH:** v Liverpool, A, 30/04/1960
**MOVED TO:** Leeds United, 26/07/1960
**TEAMS:** South Elmsall, Wrexham, Sheffield United, Sunderland, Leeds United, Port Vale, Doncaster Rovers, Macclesfield Town, Newmillerdam, Woolley Miners' Welfare
**INTERNATIONAL:** England
**SAFC TOTALS:** 124 appearances / 14 goals

**The scorer of two goals on his England debut against Brazil on 9 May 1956 'the singing winger' also recorded 'This I Know' and 'Are You?' on the HMV label in the late fifties and appeared on the same bill as The Beatles on 13 June 1963 at the Southern Sporting Club in Manchester. The Beatles were at number one that week with 'From Me To You' which was appropriate for Grainger who set up many a goal with his wing play which was noted for his supreme balance and body swerve.**

At Sunderland, sadly, Colin was part of the club's first-ever relegation side in his second season, but he remained for two more years, missing just one game in his final season and six in his penultimate term. One of his goals for the club was Sunderland's first-ever second division goal at Lincoln. In April 1957, he won his seventh and final cap for England while with Sunderland in a Wembley win over a Scotland side that included future Sunderland manager Ian McColl. Grainger's forward line teammates included Stanley Matthews and Tom Finney. As well as scoring against the next (1958) world champions Brazil. Colin also scored against World Cup holders West Germany in Berlin in 1956. He also twice won representative honours for the Football League.

Grainger's first six caps had come with Sheffield United who he joined in 1953 after previously signing for 1930s Sunderland player Les McDowall at Wrexham. After McDowall left, Colin debuted against Hartlepools United on 24 February 1951. He did his National Service in the RAF before being transferred after just five league games. Grainger made three appearances for the newly-promoted Blades in his first season. In 1955-56 he played against Sunderland four times in league and cup, scoring in a league loss at Roker Park in a season where his side went down. Having dropped into Division Two, Grainger scored eight goals in his first five games including a hat-trick in a 6-1 win at Barnsley and had a dozen goals in 21 games at the time of his move to Sunderland for a fee of £17,000 plus reserve winger Sam Kemp going in the opposite direction.

## GRAINGER, Colin (Continued)

Later after leaving Sunderland, Grainger returned to Yorkshire with Leeds, in the summer of 1960. Debuting in a second division game at Liverpool, he lined up alongside Jack Charlton, Billy Bremner, who would captain Leeds against Sunderland in the 1973 FA Cup final, and Don Revie who Colin had once joined on the scoresheet in a Sunderland win over Newcastle. Revie would become player/manager the following March and moved Grainger on to Port Vale in October 1961 for £6,000 after six goals in 37 appearances. Four months after joining Vale, he helped the Burslem club knock Sunderland out of the FA Cup, starring as Sunderland lost a fourth-round replay 3-1 at Vale Park with Grainger having a hand in the first two goals.

After 39 league games and six goals, Grainger moved on to Doncaster Rovers in 1964, playing 40 league games and scoring three times in two seasons before completing a lengthy and eventful career in non-league until 1978, after which he scouted for Barnsley, Leeds, Huddersfield, Oldham, Bury, Plymouth and particularly Sheffield United. For many years he was a distinctive figure in his long maroon coat watching Sunderland Reserves at Eppleton CW.

Colin's brother Jack was capped by England at 'B' level and played for Rotherham, Lincoln and Burton. Cousins Jack, Dennis and Edwin played professionally while brother-in-law Jim Iley, an England U23 international, listed Newcastle United amongst his clubs. In later life, Colin became a regional manager for a cash register company and then a rep for a wine merchants. In 2019 he released his autobiography, 'The Singing Winger.'

## GRAY, Andrew David (Andy)

**POSITION:** Centre-forward

**BIRTHPLACE:** Harrogate, Yorkshire

**DATE OF BIRTH:** 15/11/1977

**HEIGHT:** 6' 2" **WEIGHT:** 13st 5lbs

**SIGNED FROM:** Sheffield United, 10/08/2005

**DEBUT:** v Charlton Athletic, H, 13/08/2005

**LAST MATCH:** v Brentford, A, 28/01/2006

**MOVED TO:** Burnley, 01/06/2006

**TEAMS:** Leeds United, Bury (L), Nottingham Forest, Preston North End (L), Oldham Athletic (L), Bradford City, Sheffield United, Sunderland, Burnley, Charlton Athletic, Barnsley, Leeds United, Bradford City

**INTERNATIONAL:** Scotland

**SAFC TOTALS:** 13+9 appearances / 1 goal

**The son of former Sunderland player Frank Gray, Andy scored on his debut, but failed to find the back of the net again as he struggled in a newly-promoted team and was loaned out in the second half of his solitary season.**

Given a senior debut by Howard Wilkinson at Leeds in a September 1995 League Cup tie with Notts County, his only other appearance in that competition that season was to start the final which was lost 4-0 to Aston Villa, although he scored in none of the 19 games he played that term. At Elland Road in his formative years, teammates included Brian Deane, Lee Chapman and Ian Harte. After a total of 27 games without scoring - other than a goal in six games on loan to Bury - Leeds let Gray go to Nottingham Forest where his only goal came in the 71st of his 40+36 appearances, in a 2-2 draw with Wolves in March 2002.

Loans to Preston and Oldham also failed to produce a league goal from a total of nine outings meaning that when he joined Bradford City in 2002, he had scored just twice in 101 league games. All that changed with his spells at Bradford and

Sheffield United when he began to play as a striker having previously mainly played as a winger and even sometimes as a full-back. Gray scored 20 in 77 games for the Bantams and an even better 25 in 56+2 for the Blades. Player of the Year at Bradford in 2003, he was capped by Scotland against Lithuania and New Zealand towards the end of that season and was subsequently signed by Neil Warnock at Bramall Lane where he was sent off along with Gary Breen when Sunderland visited in September 2004.

The goal touch having deserted him at Sunderland was rediscovered with three in nine games on loan to Burnley before the Black Cats accepted a fee of roughly three-quarters of the £1.1m he had cost. It proved good value for the Clarets where Andy added another 25 goals in 60 league games before a £1.5m sale to Charlton where, including an initial loan period, he netted nine times in 45 league games. Gray completed his career back in his native Yorkshire with Barnsley (21 goals in 96 league games) and one goal each for former clubs Leeds and Bradford in eight and 15 league games respectively, before a 2014 retirement with a total of 114 goals in 530 games in all competitions.

In addition to his footballing father, his uncle Eddie played against Sunderland in the 1973 FA Cup final as a Leeds and Scotland legend, while cousin Stuart listed Celtic amongst his playing CV. Son Archie made it into the Leeds squad for the first time in December 2021 when only 15.

## GRAY, Francis Tierney (Frank)

**POSITION:** Defender / Midfielder

**BIRTHPLACE:** Castlemilk, Glasgow, Lanarkshire

**DATE OF BIRTH:** 27/10/1954

**HEIGHT:** 5' 10" **WEIGHT:** 11st 10lbs

**SIGNED FROM:** Leeds United, 19/07/1985

**DEBUT:** v Blackburn Rovers, H, 17/08/1985

**LAST MATCH:** v Brighton & Hove Albion, H, 29/04/1989

**MOVED TO:** Darlington, 15/05/1989

**TEAMS:** Leeds United, Nottingham Forest, Leeds United, Sunderland, Darlington, Wetherby Athletic, Harrogate Town

**INTERNATIONAL:** Scotland

**SAFC TOTALS:** 137+32 appearances / 8 goals

**Frank Gray was one of the big name veterans recruited by Lawrie McMenemy. That policy had been successful for the manager at Southampton, but failed spectacularly at Sunderland where Gray was a regular in the side that slumped to a first-ever relegation to the third division.**

Used predominantly as a sub by Denis Smith in that division, when he was often utilised as a sweeper, Frank helped Sunderland to promotion and then to consolidate back in the second tier. In each his four seasons at Roker Park he appeared in a minimum of 39 games, and two years after leaving Sunderland won the Conference with Darlington.

A decade earlier he had won the European Cup with Brian Clough's Nottingham Forest alongside Ian Bowyer, Martin O'Neill and John O'Hare with Jim Montgomery on the bench. Gray had also played in the 1975 European Cup final as Leeds lost to Bayern Munich. The previous season, he had featured in six league games as Leeds won the League title while in 1972-73 he had played in the European Cup Winners' Cup final as Leeds lost to AC Milan eleven days after losing to Sunderland at Wembley, a game in which his brother Eddie played. Frank also played in both legs of the 1979 European Super Cup as Forest beat Barcelona. A year later, he played in the first leg of the same competition as Valencia were beaten, but missed the return leg as Forest lost on away goals. In the same year he played in the League Cup final lost to a Wolves side that included Peter Daniel.

It was quite a pedigree along with 32 full caps for Scotland which included appearances against New Zealand, Brazil and the USSR at the 1982 World Cup finals. In total, he made 644 league appearances, 332 of them in two spells with Leeds for whom he played 397+10 times in all competitions, scoring 35 goals.

He managed Darlington, Farnborough Town, Grays Athletic, Woking, Basingstoke Town and Bashley until 2013 after which he relocated to Australia where he assisted Manly United and covered the English Premier League as a TV pundit. In addition to his son Andy and brother Eddie being fellow Scottish internationals, Frank's nephew Stuart played for Celtic.

## GRAY, Martin David

**POSITION:** Midfielder / full-back

**BIRTHPLACE:** Sedgefield, Co Durham

**DATE OF BIRTH:** 17/08/1971

**HEIGHT:** 5' 9" **WEIGHT:** 10 st 11lbs

**SIGNED FROM:** Ferryhill Athletic, 01/03/1989

**DEBUT:** v Blackburn Rovers, A, 29/04/1992

**LAST MATCH:** v Tranmere Rovers, H, 30/01/1996

**MOVED TO:** Oxford United, 28/03/1996

**TEAMS:** Ferryhill Athletic, Sunderland, Aldershot (L), Fulham (L), Oxford United, Darlington

**SAFC TOTALS:** 55+24 appearances / 1 goal

**Martin was working in a window manufacturing factory when he secured a contract with Sunderland after a successful one month trial. A wholehearted player, he had first appeared in the league on loan to Aldershot as a sub in a 6-2 defeat at Scunthorpe on 12 January 1991.**

After another game as sub, Martin started three games for the Shots including one against Darlington who would go on to play a huge part in his career.

Martin's best moment at Sunderland came, when he finished off a flowing move with a cracking goal in a big win over promotion-chasing Portsmouth at the Fulwell End of Roker Park in 1993, but mainly his time was characterised by his ability to break play up. Late in 1995, he had a couple of months on loan at Fulham, starting six third division games for the Craven Cottage club.

Denis Smith had been in charge at Sunderland when Martin came to the club and he paid £100,000 to take him to Oxford where he played 121 league games, scoring four times before moving to Darlington three years later following the U's relegation to the third tier. Debuting for Darlo at Halifax on the opening day of the 1999-2000 season where Marco Gabbiadini got the visitors' winner, Gray was also joined at Feethams by Gary Bennett, Paul Heckingbottom, Brian Atkinson, Craig Russell, Phil Brumwell, Neil Wainwright and future Sunderland academy manager Craig Liddle in a side managed by David Hodgson.

Martin played 40+1 times as the Quakers qualified for the fourth tier Play-Offs. He then played in both legs of the semi-final as Hartlepool were beaten and the Wembley final where he suffered a narrow defeat to Peterborough. After one more season with Darlington, where he took his total to 66 league appearances and a career tally of 262 and five goals, he moved into coaching and had a spell as joint caretaker-manager of Darlington with Neil Maddison in October 2006.

Following later stints as caretaker-manager at both Darlington and Oldham Athletic in 2012, he took over at Darlington at a time when the club had suffered financial meltdown and with it a tumble down the leagues.

Gray led the newly-named Darlington 1883, formed after the original team had been expelled by the FA, from the Northern League, through the Northern Premier League Division One and Premier Division into the National League North in four seasons, with only ground grading difficulties halting potential further progress when they qualified for Play-Offs only to be unable to participate. Resigning in October 2017, he became manager of York City until August 2018. He subsequently set up the Martin Gray Football Academy coaching youngsters across the north east including in Sunderland.

## GRAY, Michael

**POSITION:** Left-back / midfielder

**BIRTHPLACE:** Castletown, Sunderland

**DATE OF BIRTH:** 03/08/1974

**HEIGHT:** 5' 8" **WEIGHT:** 10st 7lbs

**SIGNED FROM:** Castle View School, 01/07/1990

**DEBUT:** v Derby County, A, 21/11/1992

**LAST MATCH:** v Millwall, H, 16/08/2003

**MOVED TO:** Blackburn Rovers, 27/01/2004

**TEAMS:** Sunderland, Celtic (L), Blackburn Rovers, Leeds United (L), Wolves, Sheffield Wednesday

**INTERNATIONAL:** England

**SAFC TOTALS:** 383+27 appearances / 17 goals

**Ninth in the all-time appearances list, Michael Gray played for Sunderland across twelve seasons, being ever-present in the 1995-96 second tier title-winning season and a key member of the 105-point team three years later. In both seasons he was named in the PFA Divisional Team of the Season.**

In between, in 1998, he had infamously been the fall guy who missed the decisive spot-kick in the Play-Off final shoot-out with Charlton, but had bounced back in such spectacular style that he played for England the following campaign.

Michael marked his home debut against Barnsley with a goal after only 40 seconds on 5 December 1992, and in 1996, scored the club's first-ever Premiership goal in a 4-1 win at Nottingham Forest. Tremendously consistent he made a minimum of 36 appearances in each of his last eight full seasons, but after playing as a substitute in the opening home game of his final campaign, he joined Martin O'Neill's Celtic on loan for four months before a January move to Graeme Souness' Blackburn Rovers.

Debuting for The Bhoys at home to Motherwell on 20 September 2003 (the day Mart Poom scored for Sunderland at Derby), Gray was on the winning side in all of his domestic games for Celtic, including a 1-0 win over Rangers at Ibrox when he came on as an early sub. He did suffer Champions League defeat at Lyon and also played in a win over Anderlecht, but in total only played ten times, six of those as sub.

At Blackburn, he debuted in a home defeat to Chelsea on 1 February 2004. A week later, he was joined by debutant Jon Stead whilst future Sunderland men Dwight Yorke, Andy Cole and Derek Ferguson's brother Barry were amongst his teammates.

Michael went on to play 73 times for Blackburn, all but one of those as starts. 30 of those games were in the Premiership in 2005-06 as he helped a side, now led by Mark Hughes, to qualify for the UEFA Cup in which he played seven times. Before leaving Blackburn to join Wolves in 2007, Rovers twice loaned him to Leeds United for whom he totalled 16 games and played alongside Paul Butler, Matt Kilgallon, David Healy, Brian Deane and Robbie Elliott, with Leeds dropping into the third tier at the end of Michael's second loan in 2007.

In the summer of 2007, he was signed for Wolves by his old Sunderland manager Mick McCarthy. Gray debuted alongside Gary Breen, Neill Collins and Stephen Elliott on the opening day of the season against Watford who would edge Wolves out of the Play-Off places on goal difference after Michael played in 29+4 Championship games, Kevin Kyle coming into the side for another Sunderland connection. Eventually totalling 38+9 games with Wolves for whom he scored four times, Michael moved to Sheffield Wednesday in January 2009. Debuting at Ipswich, his final appearance for the Owls at Coventry in March of the following year was Michael's 44th for the club (40+4/2). At Hillsborough, Gray played alongside Tim Gilbert's son Peter.

In total, Gray started 496 league games including two in Scotland and appeared a further 39 times off the bench, including five north of the border. In all competitions, Michael made over 550 appearances. For England, he started a match away to Bulgaria in June 1999 having come on as a sub against Sweden at Wembley four days earlier. The first of his three international appearances came the previous April when he came on as a sub away to Hungary for fellow debutant Wes Brown in a game which also marked Kevin Phillips' England debut. It was the first occasion England had included two Sunderland players since Albert McInroy and Warney Cresswell played against Ireland in 1926. Gray was also selected for the England squad when Phillips played against Belgium at the Stadium of Light in October 1999, but did not earn a cap on that occasion.

After his playing days, Michael became a frequent pundit on TV and radio and was also involved in attempts to take over his home town club where he will be remembered for his high pedigree play, particularly when partnering Allan 'Magic' Johnston on the left flank during the 1998-99 season when both made their international debuts.

# G

## GRAY, Philip

**POSITION:** Striker

**BIRTHPLACE:** Belfast, Northern Ireland

**DATE OF BIRTH:** 02/10/1968

**HEIGHT:** 5' 10" **WEIGHT:** 12st 3lbs

**SIGNED FROM:** Luton Town, 19/07/1993

**DEBUT:** v Notts County, A, 28/08/1993

**LAST MATCH:** v Birmingham City, A, 17/03/1996

**MOVED TO:** Nancy, 01/08/1996

**TEAMS:** Ballyclare Comrades, Tottenham Hotspur, Barnsley (L), Fulham (L), Luton Town, Sunderland, Nancy, Fortuna Sittard, Luton Town, Burnley, Oxford United, Boston United (L), Aldershot Town, Chelmsford City, Stevenage Borough, Maidenhead, Stotfold

**INTERNATIONAL:** Northern Ireland

**SAFC TOTALS:** 127+7 appearances / 41 goals

**Nicknamed 'Tippy' due to his initials, Gray was a clever striker whose debut was delayed by a car crash which led to him having eye surgery, but he still succeeded in being top-scorer in his first two seasons at Sunderland.**

Starting with Spurs in English football, Gray was one of four debutants on the last day of the 1986-87 season at Everton, Tottenham being fined for fielding a weakened team as they rested their stars ahead of the FA Cup final. He did not play again until the last day of the following term when he came off the bench against Luton at White Hart Lane.

There was one more substitute appearance the following season before a two and a quarter year wait for a fourth appearance, but he played in the next four games, three of those being his first starts. In total, he only started four league games with six appearances as sub, including one in the FA Cup. Never a scorer for Tottenham, his greatest claim to fame as a Hotspur player was probably being alphabetically listed next to Jimmy Greaves in their all-time roll call.

Spurs loaned Gray to Barnsley and Luton Town. Playing alongside Steve Agnew, the Tykes scored only once in the three games he played beginning in January 1990, which was one more than Luton managed in his three starts the following December. Nonetheless, top-flight Luton signed him the following summer after his release from Tottenham. A first goal on 31 August 1991 against Chelsea came on what was his fifth appearance and 21st in total. Briefly partnering Mick Harford, he got six league and cup goals as Luton were relegated, but missed most of the season through injury. However, in the following 1992-93 season, he missed just one game as he top-scored with 19 goals in a struggling side that finished just two points above relegation to the third tier - and just one point ahead of Sunderland who paid a reported £775,000 for him.

Phil had become a full international with a debut as a sub for Northern Ireland at home to Denmark in November 1992, followed by a full debut away to Albania in February 1993. His first goal came in his first game as a Sunderland player, against Latvia in a World Cup qualifying game in September 1993. He went on to score six times in 26 internationals, 15 of which were starts. All but one of his goals were scored while with Sunderland with whom he won 13 caps, all but three in the starting line-up.

After leaving Sunderland, Gray played in France (four goals in 15+1 games for Nancy) and the Netherlands (1 goal in twelve games for Fortuna Sittard) before a brief spell (one goal in five) with Burnley and a season and a half with Oxford where he netted 13 times in 39+9 games. Phil ended his career in non-league football with his final club being Stotfold, a Bedfordshire club whose home ground was called Roker Park.

Gray's son James was capped by Northern Ireland at Under 21 level and played in the Football League for Accrington Stanley and Northampton Town as well as having an extensive career in non-league.

## GRAYSTON, John Thomas

**POSITION:** Forward / Goalkeeper

**BIRTHPLACE:** Halifax, West Riding of Yorkshire

**DATE OF BIRTH:** 27/03/1862 - 28/03/1944

**WEIGHT:** 12st 4lbs

**SIGNED FROM:** Helped start the club in 1879. Returned, 20/12/1883

**DEBUT:** v Redcar, A, 08/11/1884

**LAST MATCH:** v Redcar, A, 08/11/1884

**MOVED TO:** Middlesex, early 1880s, Retired, 1885

**TEAMS:** Sunderland, Middlesex, Sunderland

**SAFC TOTALS:** 1 appearance / 0 goals

**Grayston's one 'official' game was in the club's first FA Cup tie - or English Cup as it was then known. In that match, he played up front, but in the earliest stages of the club's history, he regularly appeared as goalkeeper in friendly matches. Grayston was an enthusiastic 'pupil-teacher' when he helped James Allan to introduce association football to Wearside.**

Notably, he also scored the first goal when Sunderland first appeared in red and white. This was on 13 December 1884 when red and white halved shirts replaced the club's original blue in an 8-1 win over Castle Eden. The Sunderland Echo of the time described the shirts as quartered, but this description seemingly took account of the back of the shirt too.

During the early 1880s, Grayston played for Middlesex while at college, but returned just before Christmas almost a year before his English Cup appearance. Whilst at college, he was a volunteer with the 2nd Battalion South Middlesex Rifles, after his retirement from playing football he often acted as an umpire and in 1888 became a committee member at SAFC. John gave great service to the teaching profession, becoming headmaster at Stansfield Road School, a stone's throw from Roker Park, and not retiring until Christmas 1924.

As secretary of the club in the 1880s, Grayston oversaw the move to professionalism and also was influential in the recruitment of Tom Watson, the region's most successful manager who led the 'Team of All The Talents' to three league titles in the 1890s. In 1900, Grayston was the Master of Williamson Freemason Lodge and in the 1930s, was Chairman of the Royal Liver Friendly Society. In Autumn 1931, he recorded the early history of the club that he was present at from the beginning and though the chronological order of some of his elderly recollections were questionable, nonetheless, his first hand memories are an invaluable aid to understanding how the club developed.

## GREENWOOD, Rees

**POSITION:** Winger

**BIRTHPLACE:** Winlaton, Tyne and Wear

**DATE OF BIRTH:** 10/12/1996

**HEIGHT:** 5' 8" **WEIGHT:** 10st 10lbs

**SIGNED FROM:** Academy product, 01/07/2013

**DEBUT:** v Watford, A, 16/5/2016

**LAST MATCH:** v Watford, A, 16/5/2016

**MOVED TO:** Left club by mutual consent, 25/01/2018

**TEAMS:** Sunderland, Gateshead. Falkirk, Spennymoor Town, West Auckland Town, Al Sahel, Iprottafelag Reykjavikur, Ryton & Crawcrook (to May 2022)

**INTERNATIONAL:** England Under 20

**SAFC TOTALS:** 1 appearance / 0 goals

**Highly rated as a home-grown winger, Greenwood was handed a Premier League debut at Watford on the final day of the 2015-16 season. He did well and was substituted a minute after Sunderland took a 51st-minute lead, but with manager Sam Allardyce leaving in the summer, Rees never got another first-team chance and was allowed to leave the club he had been with since he was eight.**

A day after his release from the red and whites, Gateshead became Greenwood's new club. After eight games to the end of the season, he moved north to Falkirk where he played five league and cup games scoring in a Championship defeat at Partick Thistle before being released in October 2018 after just four months.

Returning to the north east, he signed for Spennymoor Town but swiftly moved to West Auckland Town, initially on loan after not playing for Spennymoor. There were three goals in 16 appearances for West Auckland before a surprise July 2020 move to Al-Sahel in the second division of the United Arab Emirates league where he made a blistering start with two goals and two assists on his debut against FC Atletico Arabia.

Like many wingers, Greenwood blew hot and cold and emulated that in his choice of clubs as he swiftly moved on again, this time to IR of Reykjavik in Iceland before coming back to the north east in March 2022 to play local football.

## GREENWOOD, Roy Thornton

**POSITION:** Winger

**BIRTHPLACE:** Leeds, Yorkshire

**DATE OF BIRTH:** 26/09/1952

**HEIGHT:** 5' 10" **WEIGHT:** 11st 0lbs

**SIGNED FROM:** Hull City, 08/01/1976

**DEBUT:** v WBA, A, 10/01/1976

**LAST MATCH:** v Cambridge United, H, 16/12/1978

**MOVED TO:** Derby County, 08/01/1979

**TEAMS:** Pudsey Juniors, Hull City, Sunderland, Derby County, Swindon Town, Huddersfield Town, Tranmere Rovers (L), Scarborough

**SAFC TOTALS:** 50+11 appearances / 9 goals

**Infamously banned from a seasonal team photo by Bob Stokoe who did not like his beard, that beard at least contributed to the fans nickname for Roy of 'Catweazle.' Despite the whiskers, Stokoe paid just £5,000 short of the club record fee when investing a reported £140,000 for Greenwood who had not only recently impressed for Hull at Sunderland, but had scored nine goals for the Tigers which would see him remain their top scorer come the end of the campaign. He added two more in 13+3 games as he helped his new club to promotion, both coming in a home win over Southampton.**

Greenwood was a slim, willowy winger who liked to take his man on. He could be very effective, but when subjected to rough treatment, it was felt he could be marked out of a game. Once promoted, he played in the same number of games in the second season during which he missed the second half of as Sunderland were relegated. He again featured in fewer than half of the fixtures in his third season before moving on midway through his fourth.

The most successful spell of his career came with his first senior club Hull where he scored 30 goals in 147+8 games, the first of which came against Swindon in September 1971, three days after his 19th birthday. After leaving Sunderland, he helped Derby avoid relegation, but left after one goal in a year that brought 31 league games. He then bagged seven goals in 53 games over two years at Swindon before a move to Huddersfield where injury on his fourth league start kept him out for 14 months. He eventually totalled eight league games for the Terriers after which he added another three on loan to Tranmere before finishing his career in non-league with Scarborough.

After retiring from playing, Roy did some scouting work for Newcastle United and Celtic and now spends his time playing golf near his East Yorkshire home.

## GREGOIRE, Roland Barry (Roly)

**POSITION:** Forward

**BIRTHPLACE:** Toxteth, Liverpool

**DATE OF BIRTH:** 23/11/1958

**HEIGHT:** 5' 9" **WEIGHT:** 10st 7lbs

**SIGNED FROM:** Halifax Town, 04/11/1977

**DEBUT:** v Hull City, H, 02/01/1978

**LAST MATCH:** v Blackburn Rovers, H, 16/04/1979

**MOVED TO:** Retired, 02/02/1980

**TEAMS:** Halifax Town, Sunderland

**SAFC TOTALS:** 6+4 appearances / 1 goal

**It took Sunderland almost a century to field a player of colour, but Roly Gregoire should be remembered for being a promising young player whose career was ruined by injury, as well as for being the first black player to become a Black Cat.**

The sad reality is that when Gregoire came to Sunderland a few weeks before he left his teens, he would have to have been a budding Pele to be accepted by some people, such was the ignorance and prejudice that existed. It must have been very difficult for a young lad who came to Sunderland having previously lived in the relatively ethnically diverse cities of Liverpool and Bradford. The son of a couple who came to Britain from Dominica in the Caribbean as part of the Windrush generation in the 1950s, Gregoire played for Bradford Boys as well as representing Great Britain Catholic Schools at 100m, 200m, triple jump and long jump.

After an unsuccessful trial in his home city with Everton, Roly broke into the Halifax team debuting on 3 September 1977 at Reading after he was selected by Alan Ball Senior, father of the England World Cup winner. He kept his place for the next two games in Division Four, the second of these at Darlington. The following month he got two more first-team games for the Shaymen, but those five first-team appearances were all Gregoire had to his name when he came to Sunderland.

He first came to the Wearsiders' attention with a hat-trick against the Reserves in a cup-tie at Halifax before impressing again in the second leg at Roker Park and then scoring in a reserve league game at Roker on 26 September 1977. However, it was the addition of Syd Farrimond to the Sunderland coaching staff that was the key motivator for Roly's move. Farrimond had coached him at Halifax and persuaded manager Jimmy Adamson to spend £5,000 on a player noted for his balance and body swerve. Gregoire signed on the same day as Wayne Entwistle who he shared digs with as a pair of young new strikers.

First appearing for Sunderland in a reserve game at Scunthorpe on 15 November 1977, he picked up an injury, but scored a hat-trick away to Barnsley reserves on his second appearance a month later, and then netted in the next game against Bradford Reserves at Roker.

Having travelled with the first-team to Bristol Rovers a week before Christmas, Roly was given a first-team debut at the beginning of January. Shortly afterwards, he got another chance as a sub and then played in the final five games of the season, scoring in the first of those, at Luton and being part of the side that won at promotion-bound Tottenham.

Unfortunately, Gregoire was dogged by injuries and played just twice towards the end of his second season before he retired 25 months to the day after his debut. Gregoire was only 21 when he had to call time on his football career after which he became a postman.

## GREGORY, Clarence

**POSITION:** Inside-left

**BIRTHPLACE:** Aston, Warwickshire

**DATE OF BIRTH:** 27/10/1900 - 17/09/1975

**HEIGHT:** 5' 8½" **WEIGHT:** 12st 0lbs

**SIGNED FROM:** Wellington, 18/03/1920

**DEBUT:** v Tottenham Hotspur, A, 02/04/1921

**LAST MATCH:** v Tottenham Hotspur, A, 02/04/1921

**MOVED TO:** QPR, 03/06/1922

**TEAMS:** Wellington Town, Sunderland, QPR, Yeovil & Petters United, Wellington Town, Hereford United, Leamington Town, Rugby Town

**INTERNATIONAL:** England Schools

**SAFC TOTALS:** 1 appearance / 0 goals

**Capped by England Schoolboys against Wales in 1914, Clarence's one late-season game for Sunderland saw him help the Lads prevent Spurs scoring at home for the first time all season, but the inside-forward was shot-shy himself as the game finished goalless. Although he remained at Roker Park for another year, Gregory never got another game before joining QPR for whom he scored once in 24 games in his solitary season of 1922-23, debuting against Watford on 26 August 1922.**

At QPR, he was a teammate of his brother Jack who had also debuted against Watford, but ten years earlier. Brother Jack played over 300 games in total for Rangers including war-time games. A third brother, Howard, won the league title as a regular with West Brom in 1919-20 and in total played 176 games for the Baggies. After retiring from football, Clarence worked as a chargehand in his native Birmingham.

## GREY, Thomas

**POSITION:** Centre-half

**BIRTHPLACE:** Walker, Newcastle

**DATE OF BIRTH:** 05/03/1885 - 31/03/1957

**HEIGHT:** 5' 9" **WEIGHT:** 12st 0lbs

**SIGNED FROM:** Whitley Bay Athletic, 26/04/1907

**DEBUT:** v Preston North End, A, 18/01/1908

**LAST MATCH:** v Preston North End, A, 18/01/1908

**MOVED TO:** Not re-registered in May 1910

**TEAMS:** Whitley Bay, Morpeth WMC, Bedlington United, Whitley Bay, Sunderland, Bedlington United, Newcastle United, Morpeth Harriers, Morpeth Town, Knaresborough, Blyth Spartans, Newcastle United, Newcastle Bohemians

**INTERNATIONAL:** England Amateur

**SAFC TOTALS:** 1 appearance / 0 goals

**Thomas Grey was a much-travelled amateur in the north east and his only appearance for Sunderland saw him debut alongside legendary goalkeeper L R Roose in the game following an English (FA) Cup defeat at non-league New Brompton (Gillingham).**

## GREY, Thomas (Continued)

As an amateur, Grey could decide which clubs he made himself available for; choosing Sunderland for seasons 1907-08, 1908-09 and 1909-10. Unlike Roose, Grey's time in the Sunderland spotlight was short-lived, but he went on to have two spells with Newcastle United although he only played a single game for the Magpies, at Aston Villa in April 1914 when he stood in for Wilf Low, the brother of Sunderland's Harry.

That appearance for Newcastle came between the last two of his three England amateur caps. Two months earlier, he had played in a 9-1 win over Wales at Plymouth whilst two months afterwards, he played in a 5-0 win away to Sweden. Grey's England debut had come in February 1912 when he played at Bishop Auckland alongside former Sunderland goalkeeper Ronald Brebner as Wales were beaten 3-0. Unlike Brebner, Grey missed out on the 1912 Olympics as GB won gold in Sweden. During World War One, Grey served with the Royal Engineers and after retiring from football worked as a land surveyor.

## GRIGG, William Donald

**POSITION:** Centre-forward

**BIRTHPLACE:** Solihull, West Midlands

**DATE OF BIRTH:** 03/07/1991

**HEIGHT:** 5' 11" **WEIGHT:** 11st 0lbs

**SIGNED FROM:** Wigan Athletic, 31/01/2019

**DEBUT:** v Oxford United, A, 09/02/2019

**LAST MATCH:** v Port Vale, A, 10/08/21

**MOVED TO:** Released 30/06/2022

**TEAMS:** Birmingham City, Stratford Town, Walsall, Brentford, MK Dons (L), Wigan Athletic, Sunderland, MK Dons (L), Rotherham United (L), MK Dons (to July 2022)

**INTERNATIONAL:** Northern Ireland

**SAFC TOTALS:** 37+25 appearances / 8 goals

**Viewers of the Netflix, 'Sunderland 'til I Die' series witnessed a close-up view of the purchase of Will Grigg for something in the region of £3m, almost three times more than manager Jack Ross valued him at.**

That investment was never remotely repaid, Grigg scoring three more league goals in a loan to MK Dons in the spring of 2021 than he had netted in two years at Sunderland. Moving on loan to Rotherham in 2021-22, Grigg scored on his debut at Doncaster, soon scored in three successive games and by the November international break had six goals in 10+3 appearances.

Unlike Jon Stead for example, who experienced an even worse goal drought at the Stadium of Light, but could be seen to be working hard for the team, Grigg appeared to be waiting for service and the signals his body language sent out made him seem lethargic. This was no doubt more an interpretation of style rather than anything else, but combined with the player's apparent reluctance to relocate to the region made his commitment questionable in the eyes of supporters.

Sixty-five goals and 14 assists in 113+37 games for Wigan included 25 goals as League One's leading scorer in 2015-16 as the Latics won promotion. February 2018 saw him sensationally score the only goal of the game as Wigan knocked Manchester City out of the FA Cup. Accompanied by the chant 'Will Grigg's on Fire', the Northern Ireland international enjoyed a strong reputation when he came to Sunderland for that inflated fee.

Qualifying for Ireland through a grandparent, Grigg was part of Northern Ireland's squad for Euro 2016. Although he did not play in the tournament, he was a well-established international. Having scored twice in 17 Under 19 internationals and once in ten Under 21 appearances by the end of the 2020-21 season, he had 13 full caps - but none with Sunderland. Grigg had debuted in a 6-0 defeat away to the Netherlands in June 2012 scoring against Belarus in 2016 and Bosnia-Herzegovina in 2018.

As a boy he was part of the Birmingham City Academy before starting in senior football with Stratford Town in the Midland Alliance, debuting in an FA Cup qualifying game with Hednesford Town in September 2007. The following summer he joined Walsall, debuting just before Christmas 2008 against Cheltenham Town, but waited over a year and a half for a second game. A first goal came at Bristol Rovers in January 2011, the first of 28 he scored for The Saddlers in 71+38 games where he was Player of the Year in 2012-13, before a July 2013 move to Brentford for whom he netted four goals in 17+19 outings. Spending the second of his two years with the Bees on loan to MK Dons, Will plundered 22 goals in 34+16 games - including two in a League Cup win over Manchester United - before his summer 2015 transfer to Wigan after he had helped MK Dons to promotion to the Championship. A final loan from Sunderland saw him help Rotherham to promotion from League One in 2022 before he signed for MK Dons that summer.

## GRIMSHAW, William (Billy)

**POSITION:** Outside-right

**BIRTHPLACE:** Burnley, Lancashire

**DATE OF BIRTH:** 06/05/1890 - 10/10/1968
Date of death to be verified

**HEIGHT:** 5' 9" **WEIGHT:** 12st 0lbs

**SIGNED FROM:** Cardiff City, 06/12/1923

**DEBUT:** v Huddersfield Town, A, 08/12/1923

**LAST MATCH:** v Aston Villa, A, 05/03/1927

**MOVED TO:** Released, 31/12/1927

**TEAMS:** Livingstone United, Barnoldswick United, Burnley, Colne, Bradford City, Hull City (WW1 Guest), Cardiff City, Sunderland, J S Drivers FC

**INTERNATIONAL:** Football League

**SAFC TOTALS:** 74 appearances / 6 goals

**Billy Grimshaw scored in Cardiff City's first-ever league victory which came on 4 September 1920 against Stockport County. It was one of 31 goals he scored in 131 league games for the Bluebirds.**

Before World War One, Grimshaw had played briefly for Bradford City who had been cup finalists in the two seasons before he signed for the top-flight club in the summer of 1912. He waited until the last two games of the season for a debut, the second of those appearances coming at Roker Park against Sunderland who had already won the league. Billy played just once the following season and four times in 1914-15 to give him seven league appearances before his post-war exploits at Cardiff. Grimshaw had never got a game with his first senior club Burnley who like Bradford City were a decent side in this era.

During World War One, he served with the Royal Garrison Artillery and played football as a 'Guest' with Hull City. After the war, he played in an England v Wales inter-league match in 1922 before coming to Sunderland. Having joined the Wearsiders in December 1923, Billy played in virtually every game as he helped the Lads mount a title challenge, even leading the table for much of the closing stages.

The following season he again played regularly, but in 1925-26, started and ended the season in the side, but played just once between September and April. After featuring in only six games in 1926-27, he was placed on the transfer list with an asking price of £1,000. This was halved by the Football League for the 37-year-old who was subsequently given a free transfer in December 1927 after his application to the Football League.

He duly retired and became a publican in Bradford where he resurfaced in October 1933 playing for a local side. Billy's father William had played for Blackburn Olympic and Burnley Union Star.

## GUNSON, Joseph Gordon

**POSITION:** Outside-left

**BIRTHPLACE:** Chester, Cheshire

**DATE OF BIRTH:** 01/07/1904 - 13/09/1991

**HEIGHT:** 5' 10" **WEIGHT:** 11st 4lb

**SIGNED FROM:** Wrexham, 31/05/1929

**DEBUT:** v Portsmouth, A, 14/09/1929

**LAST MATCH:** v Nottingham Forest, A, 19/02/1930

**MOVED TO:** Liverpool, 12/03/1930

**TEAMS:** Brickfields FC, Nelson, Wrexham, Sunderland, Liverpool, Swindon Town, Wrexham. Bangor City

**SAFC TOTALS:** 23 appearance / 12 goals

**Gordon Gunson was in the Liverpool line-up on the day Sunderland won 6-0 at Anfield in April 1930. The left-winger had only left Sunderland for Liverpool the previous month. He had been in the Sunderland side against the Merseysiders at Roker before Christmas, one of 23 appearances he made for the Lads. Gunson's goal tally suggests he deserved more games, especially as his dozen strikes came from the flank - the first of them being a winner on his home debut against Newcastle. Nonetheless, the club accepted an offer of £4,800 for the double-transfer of him and inside-forward David Wright.**

At Liverpool from 1930 to '34, the Chester born player scored a highly creditable 26 goals in 87 games, at one point making 61 consecutive appearances for the Reds. Transferred to Swindon Town on 7 June 1934, he was restricted with the Robins, and in the rest of his career, due to a cartilage injury he had sustained in 1933 with Liverpool.

Nonetheless, in his one Swindon season of 1934-35, Gunson played the opening 19 Division Three South games and 31 times in all, scoring seven times, the first in a draw in a West Country derby at Bristol Rovers. He went on to have an extensive career in Welsh football where before coming to Sunderland he had 90 goals in 190 games for Wrexham. Following a second spell with Wrexham, he moved into management as player/manager of Bangor City in the summer of 1938.

After serving in WW2 as an army physical training instructor, he briefly became a grammar school games master before returning to football as manager of Holywell Town in 1952-53.

He later had a spell as trainer, and then chief scout, at Crewe Alexandra. However, Gordon returned to Wales in June 1959 to manage Flint Town and then Welshpool. He was still active in 1964 as manager of Dolgellau. In his later years, he worked as an electrical fitter in an aircraft factory and scouted for several clubs, most notably Coventry City.

Gunson could have been an international as he was called up to represent Wales v Ireland in 1928. However, his honesty prevailed and after informing his Wrexham manager that he was born in England, the Welsh FA withdrew the offer.

## GURNEY, Robert (Bobby)

**POSITION:** Inside-right / centre-forward

**BIRTHPLACE:** Silksworth, Co Durham

**DATE OF BIRTH:** 13/10/1907 - 21/04/1994

**HEIGHT:** 5' 9" **WEIGHT:** 11st 0lbs

**SIGNED FROM:** Bishop Auckland, 07/05/1925

**DEBUT:** v West Ham United, A, 03/04/1926

**LAST MATCH:** v Blackburn Rovers, N, 20/02/1939

**MOVED TO:** Retired, 30/05/1946

**TEAMS:** Hetton Juniors, Silksworth Colliery, Bishop Auckland, Sunderland, Aberdeen (WW2 Guest), Holiday Sports Club (WW2 Guest)

**INTERNATIONAL:** England

**SAFC TOTALS:** 390 appearances / 228 goals

**Centre-forwards are measured in goals. Bobby Gurney scored more than anyone for Sunderland with whom he won the league title and FA Cup in consecutive seasons - with the Charity Shield thrown in for good measure. He contributed 31 goals as the league was won in 1936 and scored Sunderland's first-ever Wembley goal a year later.**

Bobby typified what supporters want to see. He never gave up and always gave a hundred per cent. Like Bobby Kerr, Gurney recovered from twice breaking his leg - and on his final appearance in 1939 infamously played on despite a fractured ankle and torn ligaments. He was renowned for scoring what were thought to be 'impossible' goals, sometimes from extremely narrow angles.

Bobby was a very modest man. A son of Silksworth, he remained untouched by the trappings of stardom. Sunderland were the only senior team he played for, but it was in his days with Bishop Auckland that he was spotted by the man whose record he exceeded as Sunderland's top scorer - Charlie Buchan. Previously, he had been scouted by Newcastle United only for the prospect to be rejected by Gurney's father. Sunderland paid £10 as a transfer fee in addition to arranging a friendly match with Bishop Auckland on 30 August 1926. Sunderland won that match 7-3 with Gurney getting a hat-trick.

Gurney had started as he meant to go on - scoring nine goals at Roker Park on his first appearance for the reserves in a 14-0 win over Hartlepools Reserves on 5 September 1925. He went on to join Buchan as the only man to score five goals in a top flight game for Sunderland. Gurney also scored nine hat-tricks and four times netted four goals. On one of the occasions he scored four, he did so in a 7-2 away win at Birmingham that sealed the 1936 league title.

Inducted into the SAFC Hall of Fame at the inaugural dinner in 2019, a mural was created in his honour in Silksworth the following year. The local football ground in Silksworth is also named in Bobby's honour with a blue plaque signifying his achievements in place at the ground. Bobby worked at Silksworth Colliery prior to becoming a professional footballer.

For England he won one cap, but played twice. His official cap came in front of 129,693 as England lost 2-0 to Scotland at Hampden Park on 6 April 1935, but he also played and scored in a 4-2 defeat at Hampden the following August in a match in aid of the Jubilee Fund and attended by 56,316. This was an unofficial match for which Bobby was given a Loving Cup instead of a cap. This item along with his full cap, his England shirt and 14 assorted medals from his career, including his league and cup-winning medals, are on permanent display at the Stadium of Light.

Having broken his leg a few months before World War Two, he managed to twice play for Aberdeen as a war-time guest and also turned out in 1941 in the Northumberland and Durham League for Holiday Sports Club. After the war, he became third-team trainer at Sunderland on 30 May 1946

In June of the following year, Bobby became manager of Horden CW and in 1949, was interviewed for the job as Carlisle United manager only to lose out to Bill Shankly, an opponent in the 1937 FA Cup final. In February 1950, Gurney left Horden to manage Peterborough United, then of the Midland League.

Two years and a month later, he returned to the north east as manager of Darlington where he remained until resigning in October 1957. He then scouted for Leeds United before returning to Horden as manager in May 1961. Between 8 April 1963 and his sacking on 6 January 1964, Bobby then managed Hartlepools United. He then left football to work for a confectioners in Hartlepool before becoming a brewery representative.

An honorary vice-president of the Sunderland Supporters' Association, Bobby Gurney was a Sunderland supporter through and through - one who scored more goals for the club than anyone in history. In terms of legends of the club, Bobby Gurney sits at the top table.

## GUTHRIE, Ronald George

**POSITION:** Left-back

**BIRTHPLACE:** Burradon, Northumberland

**DATE OF BIRTH:** 19/04/1944

**HEIGHT:** 5' 10" **WEIGHT:** 13st 0lbs

**SIGNED FROM:** Newcastle United, 15/01/1973

**DEBUT:** v Swindon Town, A, 20/01/1973

**LAST MATCH:** v Aston Villa, A, 26/04/1975

**MOVED TO:** Gateshead United, 12/08/1975

**TEAMS:** New Hartley Welfare Juniors, Newcastle United, Sunderland, Gateshead United, Luistano, Blyth Spartans, North Shields

**SAFC TOTALS:** 80+1 appearances / 2 goals

**Ron Guthrie brought in by Bob Stokoe to add experience to a young Sunderland side. Always dependable, Ron was consistency personified. He went on to play his part in the 1973 FA Cup triumph, holding some of the country's best attackers at bay and scoring in the quarter-final against Luton. Indeed he seemed set on scoring in the final when he had several near misses, but his priority was to defend and he did a solid job holding off the challenge of youngsters Keith Coleman and Joe Bolton.**

It was Bolton's emergence that led to Guthrie leaving after the second post cup-winning season failed to bring promotion. That 1974-75 campaign had seen him make just over half of his 66 league starts for the red and whites. His final game at Villa Park was the scene of his league debut for Newcastle on 20 August 1966.

Although he was at Newcastle for over a decade, Ron actually appeared more in red and white than black and white. He totalled 60+6 games for the Magpies, scoring twice for them as he did for the Wearsiders.

Ron's much younger brother Chris was a centre-forward who played for Newcastle and Sheffield United amongst others, including four clubs in the Netherlands. Ron also started out as a centre-forward or outside-left, but it was a left-back that he starred, although he found his way to the Newcastle first-team barred by future Sunderland assistant-manager Frank Clark.

When Newcastle won the Inter-Cities Fairs Cup in 1969, Guthrie appeared once, as a sub in a home game with Real Zaragoza where United's goals came from future Roker men Tommy Gibb and Bryan Robson.

After his time with the north-east's big two was over, Ron was still only 31 when he joined Gateshead United after being released by Sunderland at the end of May 1975. He then went to South Africa as player/manager of Luistano in 1976, but by the following year, he was back in the north east with Blyth Spartans where again he was struck by the romance of the FA Cup. Ron achieved the feat of playing in every round of the FA Cup having played thorough the qualifying rounds and all the way up to a fifth-round replay against Wrexham with Spartans, including a sensational fourth-round victory at Stoke City.

After leaving football, Guthrie worked as a milkman on Tyneside and then for a delivery firm with his Sunderland cup final full-back partner Dick Malone. Thereafter, he worked as a delivery driver for Fenwick's Department Store in Newcastle. In 2021, he accepted the Freedom of the City of Sunderland as part of the 1973 FA Cup winning legends.

## GYAN, Asamoah

**POSITION:** Centre-forward

**BIRTHPLACE:** Accra, Ghana

**DATE OF BIRTH:** 22/11/1985

**HEIGHT:** 5' 11" **WEIGHT:** 12st 2lbs

**SIGNED FROM:** Rennes, 31/08/2010

**DEBUT:** v Wigan Athletic, A, 11/09/2010

**LAST MATCH:** v Swansea City, A, 27/08/2011

**MOVED TO:** Al- Ain, 06/07/2012

**TEAMS:** Liberty Professionals, Udinese, Modena (L), Rennes, Sunderland, Al-Ain, Shanghai SIPG, Al-Ahli (L), Kayserispor, NorthEast United, Legon Cities (to 2021)

**INTERNATIONAL:** Ghana

**SAFC TOTALS:** 25+12 appearances / 11 goals

**Gyan was obsessed with the number three. As Kieran Richardson had this squad number when he signed, Gyan took the 33 shirt. Given number three at the start of his second season, he played just three Premier League games before leaving on loan to Al-Ain in the United Arab Emirates after the UK and European transfer window had closed. His departure was rumoured to be for a world record loan fee of £6m for the season. This was almost half the £13m reportedly paid for the Ghana striker just over a year earlier.**

Asamoah had created a decent impression at Sunderland with a creditable goals return starting with a well taken debut strike. He went on to net in a home derby with Newcastle shortly after a goal in a famous win at Chelsea which he followed up by a dance which Bolo Zenden suffered ridicule for attempting to emulate. Dancing came naturally to Gyan who like fifties winger Colin Grainger was also a recording artist, in Gyan's case under the name 'Babyjet.'

Always a larger than life character, Asamoah also obtained an aviation licence under the name Babyjet Airlines in 2017 as well as becoming involved in boxing and tennis promotions. He also went on to own an entertainment hub called Infiniti as well as JetLink Events and Logistics which specialises in building stages and installing LED screens and PA systems at major events. Never one to stand still, Gyan also owns 30 buses in the Ghanaian capital Accra as well as owning real estate and petrol stations as well as companies that produce drinking water, rice and noodles.

A superstar in Africa, for all his extra-curricular activities, like David Beckham, Gyan never lost sight of his footballing priorities and was named BBC African Footballer of the Year in 2010 while he was with Sunderland. In the same year he was Ghana Player of the Year (as he was in 2014) and in March 2011 scored to earn Ghana a draw with England at Wembley. Wearing the number three shirt, he had on-loan Sunderland men John Mensah and Sulley Muntari as his teammates while England introduced on-loan Sunderland forward Danny Welbeck for his debut with future Sunderland players Joleon Lescott and Jermain Defoe also coming off the bench on a night when ex-SAFC loanee Stewart Downing was in England's starting line-up. Gyan had made his international debut three days before his 18th birthday, becoming his country's youngest scorer with a last-minute goal against Somalia in 2003.

In 2006, he scored the quickest goal of the FIFA World Cup, netting against the Czech Republic after just 68 seconds. However, the tournament also saw him miss a penalty and be sent off. The 2010 World Cup saw him score penalties against Serbia and Australia as well as scoring against the USA. In the quarter-final, he missed a penalty in the last minute of extra-time, but then showed the character to convert in the shoot-out. In 2014, Gyan played at the finals of the FIFA World Cup again, captaining his country and this time scoring against Germany and Portugal to become the highest African goalscorer in the history of the FIFA World Cup.

In the African Cup of Nations, Gyan played in the tournaments of 2008, 2010 and 2012, 2013, 2015, 2017 and 2019, missing a penalty in the semi-final in 2012. He also represented Ghana at the 2004 Olympics. In total he scored 51 goals in 109 internationals, being Ghana's record scorer.

At club level, ten goals in 16 games for his first club in Ghana quickly alerted scouts of Italian club Udinese where he scored eleven goals in 39 league games and 15 in 53 matches while on loan to Modena. After moving to France, 14 goals in 48 league games with Rennes preceded his transfer to Sunderland.

Regularly on the move, his loan to Al Ain eventually became a transfer. 24 goals in 27 games there made him the league's top scorer as they took the title which Gyan helped them retain with 28 goals in 32 appearances. The goals kept coming as he bagged 44 in 41 games in 2013-14 and 20 in 29 matches in his final season there in 2014-15.

Tempted by the Chinese Super League, he scored eight times in 26 games across two seasons before a return to the UAE with Shabab Al-Ahli in Dubai where he scored eleven times in 26 games in 2016-17. Next stop was to Turkey with Kayserispor where there were nine goals in 34 games across two seasons. India then became the eighth country Gyan had plied his trade in when he signed for NorthEast United in the Indian Premier League where he scored four goals in eight games in 2019-20 before returning to Ghana with Legon Cities where, as of 2021 he had played just once.

His brother Baffour was also a Ghana international who played in Russia, the Czech Republic, Greece and Libya as well as in Ghana.

# H

## HAAS, Bernt

**POSITION:** Right-back

**BIRTHPLACE:** Vienna, Austria

**DATE OF BIRTH:** 08/04/1978

**HEIGHT:** 6' 1" **WEIGHT:** 12st 8lbs

**SIGNED FROM:** Grasshopper Zurich, 03/08/2001

**DEBUT:** v Ipswich Town, H, 18/08/2001

**LAST MATCH:** v Chelsea, A, 16/03/2002

**MOVED TO:** West Bromwich Albion, 14/07/2003

**TEAMS:** Grasshopper Zurich, Sunderland, FC Basel (L), WBA, Bastia, FC Koln, St Gallen

**INTERNATIONAL:** Switzerland

**SAFC TOTALS:** 28+1 appearances / 0 goals

**Signed by Peter Reid, Haas had moved to Switzerland from his Austrian birthplace when he was just a year old. He gained 36 Swiss caps, 14 of them while with Sunderland, during which time he scored two of his three international goals against Slovenia and Albania - although they came while he was on loan from the Wearsiders.**

Having won four Swiss league titles with Grasshopper Zurich, being a regular in the side for the last three of those, he came to Sunderland with considerable experience under his belt, including Champions League games against Rangers and international caps. Three days before his Sunderland debut, he played for Switzerland as they won away to Austria while he went on to be part of the side that qualified for Euro 2004 - a tournament in which he was sent off against England.

In Bernt's first season on Wearside, he started 27 Premier League games and appeared in a couple of cup ties, but as Sunderland narrowly escaped relegation he was loaned out to FC Basle for his second year. During that loan, Haas played in eleven Champions League games including home and away draws with Liverpool and a home defeat to Manchester United. He enjoyed success in the domestic cup while on loan to Basel, playing in the cup final, as under former Spurs manager Christian Gross, his side thrashed Neuchatel Xamax 6-0 although in the league they were runners up to Bernt's old club Grasshopper.

In the summer of 2003, he joined West Bromwich Albion who he had scored against with a screamer from fully 30 yards in a friendly for Sunderland on 4 August 2001, ahead of his competitive debut. He also scored on his home debut for West Brom in a Carling Cup win over Brentford and added another in the same competition against Manchester United in a season where he helped Albion to promotion. Haas made nine Premiership appearances, the last in a 4-0 derby defeat at Birmingham City just before an ill-fated Christmas party which resulted in him leaving the club the following month after reportedly being hospitalised through intoxication whilst dressed as Robin Hood. Hardly the expected look of a player who once modelled for Armani.

He went on to spend a season in France with Bastia (12/1), and two in Germany with FC Koln (19/0) before returning to Switzerland with St Gallen where he made just a single senior appearance. In October 2015, Bernt started his managerial career as Director of Football for Vaduz. Five years later, he took the same role at Schaffhausen and in July 2022 took over as Sporting Director at his first club Grasshopper.

## HACKETT, Jake Willis

**POSITION:** Midfielder

**BIRTHPLACE:** Durham, Co Durham

**DATE OF BIRTH:** 10/01/2000

**HEIGHT:** 6' 0" **WEIGHT:** 12st 8lbs

**SIGNED FROM:** Academy trainee, 01/07/2016

**DEBUT:** v Morecambe, H, 13/11/2018

**LAST MATCH:** v Newcastle United Under 21s, H, 08/01/2019

**MOVED TO:** Released, 30/06/2021

**TEAMS:** Sunderland, Whitby Town

**SAFC TOTALS:** 1+2 appearances / 0 goals

**Jake started playing for Sunderland at the age of eight and successfully worked his way through the academy, developing into a stylish midfielder, at his best on the left.**

He made his way to the first-team with all three of his appearances coming in the Football League Trophy. Hackett had enjoyed two loans with Whitby Town from October to January in 2019-20 and again a couple of months later. In June 2021, he was not offered a new contract and signed for Whitby the following August.

## HAGGAN, John

**POSITION:** Half-back

**BIRTHPLACE:** Usworth, Co. Durham

**DATE OF BIRTH:** 16/12/1896 - June 1982

**HEIGHT:** 5' 10" **WEIGHT:** 12st 4lbs

**SIGNED FROM:** Usworth Colliery, 22/12/1919

**DEBUT:** v West Bromwich Albion, A, 26/12/1919

**LAST MATCH:** v Derby County, A, 03/01/1920

**MOVED TO:** Brentford, 18/05/1922

**TEAMS:** Pelaw, Usworth Colliery, Sunderland, Brentford, Preston Colliery, Hamilton United, Usworth Colliery, Washington Co-op Wednesday

**SAFC TOTALS:** 2 appearances / 0 goals

**John Haggan experienced 4-0 and 3-1 defeats on his two first-team appearances. A miner before becoming a footballer, four days after signing from local football he was thrust into a top-flight fixture and within ten days his flirtation with first-team football at Sunderland was over.**

Nonetheless, he stayed at Sunderland for another two seasons before spending 1922-23 in Division Three South with Brentford for whom he played 18 league games plus three in the FA Cup.

He then returned to the north east with Preston Colliery who became North Shields in 1928. The following year he went to Hamilton United, a club in Ontario, Canada as a player/coach. After two years, he returned to the north east England where he played in local football and became an insurance agent.

## HAINING, James

**POSITION:** Winger

**BIRTHPLACE:** Glasgow*

**DATE OF BIRTH:** 1875* - date of death unknown

**SIGNED FROM:** Dalziel Rovers, 08/01/1898

**DEBUT:** v Notts County, A, 05/02/1898

**LAST MATCH:** v Notts County, A, 05/02/1898

**MOVED TO:** Released, 06/05/1898

**TEAMS:** Dalziel Rovers, Sunderland, Hamilton Academical, Carfin Emmett

**SAFC TOTALS:** 1 appearance / 0 goals

*Birthplace and date of birth not certain

**Standing in for Jim Leslie who would score the first-ever goal at Roker Park later in the year, James Haining's only appearance came on the right wing in a 1-0 win at Notts County.**

Fellow debutant Arthur Saxton scored the only goal of the game and enjoyed a run in the side, but Haining never appeared again and moved back to Scotland after only four months on Wearside.

## HALFORD, Gregory

**POSITION:** Right-back

**BIRTHPLACE:** Chelmsford, Essex

**DATE OF BIRTH:** 08/12/1984

**HEIGHT:** 6' 4" **WEIGHT:** 12st 10lbs

**SIGNED FROM:** Reading, 11/06/2007

**DEBUT:** v Birmingham City, A, 15/08/2007

**LAST MATCH:** v, Chelsea, A, 08/12/2007

**MOVED TO:** Wolverhampton Wanderers, 03/07/2009

**TEAMS:** Colchester United, Aylesbury United (L), Braintree Town (L), Reading, Sunderland, Charlton Athletic (L), Sheffield United (L), Wolves, Portsmouth, Nottingham Forest, Brighton & Hove Albion (L), Rotherham United, Birmingham City (L), Cardiff City, Aberdeen, Southend United, Waterford, Billericay Town

**INTERNATIONAL:** England Under 20

**SAFC TOTALS:** 9 appearances / 0 goals

**Signed for a reported fee of £3m, Halford's nine appearances, which included one in the League Cup, cost Sunderland a third of a million pounds each. He was sent off in two of those games and struggled to cope on Wearside, at one point in an interview I did with him seeming to be on the verge of tears as the pressures of playing for Sunderland and Roy Keane appeared to weigh heavily upon him.**

The best game Greg had at the Stadium of Light had come in the November before Sunderland signed him when he was outstanding for Colchester United. Halford had come through the ranks with the U's, playing 163 games with his tally of

## HALFORD, Greg (Continued)

24 goals, explained by him often playing in midfield or even up-front before becoming a right-back. Capped at Under 20 level by England, he played up front internationally, scoring his only goal in four appearances against South Korea in the Toulon Tournament in June 2005.

A reported, though officially undisclosed, fee of £2.25m took Greg to Reading in January 2007. He played only 2+1 Premier League games, conceding a penalty on his full debut, before a swift switch to Sunderland. Quickly discarded from Sunderland's plans, he went on loan to Charlton in the first transfer window after joining and spent all of his second season on loan to Sheffield United. He scored eight times in 49 games for the Blades and twice in 16 appearances for the Addicks, both clubs being in the Championship.

Sunderland sold Halford to newly-promoted Wolves in the summer of 2009, but after just 20 appearances over two seasons, he moved on to Portsmouth following a loan to the Fratton Park club. After playing regularly for Pompey in 2011-12 he was on the move again, this time to Nottingham Forest where after twelve goals in 77 games for Portsmouth he scored eight times in 82 games over two seasons before a 20-game (0 goals) loan spell with Brighton.

Joining Rotherham United in 2015, Halford became captain, but after just six appearances was loaned to Birmingham City where he played three times. After a total of 38 games, and three goals, for the Millers, Greg was transferred to Cardiff City where he scored once in 33 games over two seasons before a two-game stint with Aberdeen. In 2020-21, he scored once in 16 League Two games as Southend United lost their place in the Football League.

## HALL, Alexander Webster

**POSITION:** Full-back

**BIRTHPLACE:** Kirknewton, West Lothian

**DATE OF BIRTH:** 06/11/1908 - 05/09/1991

**HEIGHT:** 5'9½" **WEIGHT:** 11st 6lbs

**SIGNED FROM:** Dunfermline Athletic, 23/04/1929

**DEBUT:** v Sheffield United, A, 04/05/1929

**LAST MATCH:** v Wolverhampton Wanderers, A, 06/05/1939

**MOVED TO:** Hibernian, 05/10/1945, after guesting for them during WW2

**TEAMS:** East Calder Swifts, Oakbank Amateurs, Wallyford Bluebell, Dunfermline, Sunderland, Hibernian

**SAFC TOTALS:** 235 appearances / 1 goal

**Alex Hall missed the opening game of the title-winning 1935-36 campaign but then played every match until the title was won. The following term he played all nine games as the FA Cup was won and was also in the side when the Charity Shield was secured.**

Spotted and signed after just four months with Dunfermline he was given a taste of first-team football on the final day of the 1928-29 season as a 20-year-old. Having been nurtured in the reserves he next appeared in the final game of 1930 after which he made another 30 league appearances spread over four seasons. He then played regularly in the five seasons leading up to World War Two. Hall also played in the three games of the expunged 1939-40 seasons, not included in official records.

During the war, he played as a 'Guest' for Hibs, becoming coach of their third team from 1946-50 before spending two years coaching Sliema Wanderers in Malta. A Scottish branch of the Supporters' Association was later named the Alex Hall branch in his honour.

## HALL, Frederick Wilkinson

**POSITION:** Centre-half

**BIRTHPLACE:** Stanley, Co Durham

**DATE OF BIRTH:** 28/11/1917 - 08/01/1989

**HEIGHT:** 5' 11" **WEIGHT:** 13st 12lbs

**SIGNED FROM:** Blackburn Rovers, 16/08/1946

**DEBUT:** v Derby County, H, 31/08/1946

**LAST MATCH:** v Wolverhampton Wanderers, H, 15/09/1954

**MOVED TO:** Barrow, 01/09/1955

**TEAMS:** Ouston, Blackburn Rovers, Bath City (WW2 Guest), Arsenal (WW2 Guest), Chelsea (WW2 Guest), Tottenham Hotspur (WW2 Guest), Swindon Town (WW2 Guest), Sunderland, Barrow, Ransome and Marles FC

**SAFC TOTALS:** 224 appearances / 1 goal

**Given he was approaching his 29th birthday when he finally came to his local club, Fred Hall did well to total well over a double century of games for the Lads. A resolute stopper centre-half, Fred proved to be an inspirational skipper and had his best season in 1951-52 when he was ever-present. He was described by the great Newcastle (and war-time Sunderland) centre-forward Jackie Milburn as the hardest defender he had ever played against.**

Hall had been with Blackburn before the war. Having joined Rovers in 1935, he had debuted in a Division Two game at Leicester on 2 January 1937. The following season was his best. A nine-game run at right-back at the turn of the year included an FA Cup appearance in a narrow defeat at Spurs and the final 13 games of the season in his preferred position of centre-half. Blackburn won Division Two in 1938-39, but after playing in the first four fixtures, Fred only appeared twice more.

During the war, Hall started as a miner in his home town of Stanley before serving in the RAF and 'Guesting' for several clubs including Arsenal (8/0), Chelsea (1/0), Spurs (6/0) and Swindon (4/0), all of these from 1944 onwards. Although not capped, Fred was twelfth man as England drew 2-2 with France at Wembley in May 1945 on a day when Raich Carter was on the scoresheet - the only time Carter and Hall were (almost) teammates. Fred's only goal for Sunderland came on Christmas Day 1953 to earn a home point with Huddersfield.

Reputedly one of the north-east's finest pigeon fanciers during his time with Sunderland, Fred effectively finished his career with Barrow (16/1) who he helped to avoid relegation on goal average in 1955-56, before playing non-league in the Newark area with Ransome and Marles.

## HALL, Gareth David

**POSITION:** Right-back / midfielder

**BIRTHPLACE:** Croydon, Surrey

**DATE OF BIRTH:** 20/03/1969

**HEIGHT:** 5' 8" **WEIGHT:** 12st 0lbs

**SIGNED FROM:** Chelsea, 19/01/1996, after loan since 18/12/1995

**DEBUT:** v Derby County, A, 23/12/1995

**LAST MATCH:** v Wolverhampton Wanderers, A, 07/02/1998

**MOVED TO:** Swindon Town, 13/05/1998

**TEAMS:** Woking SFA, Chelsea, Sunderland, Brentford (L), Swindon Town, Havant & Waterlooville

**INTERNATIONAL:** England schoolboys, Wales

**SAFC TOTALS:** 46+7 appearances / 0 goals

**Sent off on his full debut at Leicester on the day Shay Given debuted, Hall initially came to Sunderland on loan and played regularly, often as sub, up to the end of the season as Endsleigh Division One was won. Signed for a fee of £300,000 a month after he arrived, Gareth started all but six games the following term as Sunderland were relegated, after which he added just two further appearances, spending a month of his third season on loan to Brentford where he played six times.**

He had previously spent over a decade with Chelsea who he joined after trials with Spurs and Aston Villa. After developing as an apprentice, he debuted against Wimbledon on 5 May 1987 - having played for the reserves earlier in the day! In 1990, he was a Wembley winner in the Full Members Cup (then sponsored as the Zenith Data Systems Cup) beating Colin Todd's Middlesbrough side that included Peter Davenport, Colin Cooper and captain Mark Proctor. Numbering Ian Porterfield amongst his managers at Stamford Bridge, Hall totalled 138 league appearances for the Blues, scoring four times.

Capped by England schools, however, due to his mother being from Caerphilly, Gareth gained nine full caps for Wales between March 1988 and April 1992, the highlight being a 1-0 win away to an Italy side that included Paolo Maldini and Franco Baresi.

Ending his Football League career with 87 games and three goals for Swindon he ended his career in non-league, becoming assistant manager at Hayes & Yeading United in May 2007 followed by the same role at Farnborough.

From 2006, he coached at Gordon's School, reaching county finals and national semi-finals at Under 18 level and still being in post in 2022. In 2018, Hall was announced as Head of Football Operations at AiSCOUT which he likened to an app for players at grassroots level.

## HALL, John (Jack)

**POSITION:** Full-back

**BIRTHPLACE:** Darlington, Co Durham

**DATE OF BIRTH:** 23/05/1862 - 27/03/1905

**SIGNED FROM:** Not known, 1883

**DEBUT:** v Redcar, A, 08/11/1884

**LAST MATCH:** v Redcar, A, 08/11/1884

**MOVED TO:** Retired, April 1887

**TEAMS:** Durham County, Sunderland

**SAFC TOTALS:** 1 appearance / 0 goals

**Jack Hall was the captain of Durham County and made his one officially recorded competitive appearance for Sunderland in the club's first-ever game in national competition, a 3-1 defeat at Redcar in the English (FA) Cup.**

His career was ended by a broken ankle sustained against St Bernards on 9 April 1887. After retiring from playing he continued with his trade as an upholsterer in Sunderland until his early demise from pneumonia.

## HALL, Matthew

**POSITION:** Inside-left

**BIRTHPLACE:** Renfrew, Renfrewshire

**DATE OF BIRTH:** 23/08/1884 - 31/01/1957

**HEIGHT:** 5' 8" **WEIGHT:** 10st 7lbs

**SIGNED FROM:** St Mirren, 11/05/1906

**DEBUT:** v Newcastle United, A, 01/09/1906

**LAST MATCH:** v Derby County, 10/11/1906

**MOVED TO:** Clyde, 26/06/1907

**TEAMS:** St Mirren, Sunderland, Clyde, Alloa Athletic

**SAFC TOTALS:** 8 appearances / 1 goal

**A pacey inside-forward noted as being clever on the ball, Hall played in the opening seven games of 1906-07, scoring in a 2-1 win at Liverpool.**

Losing his place for three games, he returned for a home defeat to Derby County only to find his Sunderland sojourn brought to a swift end. He returned to Scottish football with Clyde and subsequently Alloa, both clubs for whom his brother William also played. After retiring from football, Matthew became a dock labour superintendent in Glasgow.

## HALL, Thomas (Tom)

**POSITION:** Centre-forward

**BIRTHPLACE:** Newburn, Northumberland

**DATE OF BIRTH:** 03/09/1891 - 17/09/1978

**HEIGHT:** 5' 9" **WEIGHT:** 11st 2lbs

**SIGNED FROM:** Newburn Alliance, 01/01/1909

**DEBUT:** v Everton, H, 09/04/1910

**LAST MATCH:** v Sheffield United, H, 24/03/1913

**MOVED TO:** Newcastle United, 05/05/1913

**TEAMS:** Newburn Grange, Newburn Alliance, Sunderland, Newcastle United, Leeds City (WW1 Guest), Hartlepools United (WW1 Guest), Gillingham

**SAFC TOTALS:** 30 appearances / 8 goals

**Tom Hall's league championship medal from 1912-13 is on permanent display at the Stadium of Light. That campaign was Hall's last and best as he played two thirds of his games for the club and scored all but one of his goals, including a spell of scoring in four consecutive home matches. However, it was tough for him to hold a place in an all international five-man forward line and so he moved on to Newcastle United for £425.**

He later scored another goal at Roker Park on his debut for the Magpies in September 1913 - a fine individual goal in which he dribbled past two defenders before netting - and after World War One, scored Gillingham's first-ever Football League hat-trick against Norwich City in February 1922.

Sunderland signed Tom as a 17-year-old on the strength of his reputation as a prolific scorer. Best at centre-forward, he was also used on the wing or at inside-forward.

Hall once scored six goals for Sunderland reserves in a 9-0 North Eastern League win over Wingate Albion on 20 September 1911 and later bagged five in a game for Newcastle in a friendly against Alnwick. In official games, he scored 16 goals in 58 league and cup games for the Tynesiders. During World War One, he 'Guested' for Leeds City and Hartlepools. Eight goals came in 22 games for Leeds before a solitary appearance in Hartlepools' colours in a friendly at home Middlesbrough on 18 April 1919, prior to the resumption of post-war league football. In 1920, he left Newcastle for Gillingham as they began their first season as a Football League club, scoring 47 times in 190 league games despite the Gills struggling at the wrong end of Division Three South.

Hall became trainer with the Gills in the mid-twenties before returning to the north east as a pub landlord and subsequently, a grocer with a shop in Bedlington. The third eldest of eleven children from a family of keel-row men and blacksmiths, much younger brother Bertie played for Hartlepools United, Norwich City and Bristol City.

## HALLIDAY, David

**POSITION:** Centre-forward

**BIRTHPLACE:** Dumfries, Dumfries & Galloway

**DATE OF BIRTH:** 11/12/1901 - 05/01/1970

**HEIGHT:** 6' 0" **WEIGHT:** 12st 4lbs

**SIGNED FROM:** Dundee, 29/4/1925

**DEBUT:** v Birmingham, H, 29/08/1925

**LAST MATCH:** v Sheffield United, A, 26/10/1929

**MOVED TO:** Arsenal, 08/11/1929

**TEAMS:** Arrol-Johnston Works, Tayleurians, Queen of the South, St Mirren, Dundee, Sunderland, Arsenal, Manchester City, Folkestone, Clapton Orient, Yeovil & Petters United

**SAFC TOTALS:** 175 appearances / 165 goals

## HALLIDAY, David (Continued)

**Take a close look at the appearance and goal figures. Dave Halliday has the best goals to games ratio of any Sunderland player, a strike rate of 0.943 goals per match. Brian Clough managed 0.851, but sustained over 100 fewer matches. In each of his four campaigns at Sunderland, Halliday scored more goals than any other player has ever managed in a single season. It took him only 103 games to register 100 top-flight goals. No-one at any club has ever equalled this feat.**

In his four full seasons at Sunderland, Halliday's haul consisted of 42 goals in his first season of 1925-26, a new club record, netted in 46 games. The following season he scored 37 times in 34 games. A year later, Halliday hit 39 goals (41 games) before breaking his own record in 1928-29 when he scored 43 times in the same number of appearances, making him the country's leading scorer. No other player at any club has ever scored 30 top-flight goals in four successive seasons - Halliday managed a minimum of 35 league goals in each of his four full seasons at Roker Park. These figures are all the more remarkable when you take into consideration that just one of his 165 goals for Sunderland was a penalty.

Ten goals in his first four games for the club was a sensational start and he went on to score four times in a match on three occasions in addition to twelve hat-tricks. No-one else has hit as many hat-tricks for Sunderland. Signed to replace Charlie Buchan, Halliday was 23 when he came to Sunderland for £4,000 from Dundee where he had set their record for most goals in a season with 38 in 1923-24. He was Scotland's top scorer that year, when he became the top scorer in England five years later, he became only the second player (after David McClean of Rangers and Wednesday) to have been outright top-scorer in both countries.

At Dundee, he scored 90 league goals in 126 games having scored twice in 13 appearances for St Mirren. After playing as a winger in schools football, Dave played for the works team at the Arrol-Johnston car factory on the edge of Dumfries before making his senior debut with Queen of the South. As a 17-year-old he had taken part in trial matches as the club was starting in 1919, but did not join until 17 January 1920 after a short stint with a club called Tayleurians. He scored 13 times in 19 games in his first season. This tally included two against Dalbeattie Star in the Dumfries Charity Cup final after which St Mirren moved in for him.

Halliday's time at Sunderland came to an end when - like Charlie Buchan before him - he moved to Arsenal. Dave scored only four times in his first 14 games for the Gunners before doubling that tally in a remarkable 6-6 draw at Leicester in April 1929.

Astonishingly, that was to be Halliday's farewell to the club as he moved on to Manchester City where he scored 14 times in 25 games in his first season and 32 in 45 in his second, a figure which included a hat-trick back at Sunderland in a 5-2 City win. However, there were just eight more appearances and five goals over two seasons before he moved on to Clapton Orient in December 1933.

After 36 goals in 56 games over 18 months, Dave became player/manager of Yeovil & Petters United, top scoring with 22 and 47 goals in his two seasons. Three of his goals for Yeovil came in 'proper' rounds of the FA Cup, including a brace against Gainsborough Trinity that set up a third-round tie at Manchester United in 1938.

Immediately after that tie, he left the club for a 556 mile switch to Aberdeen where he became manager and the first man to lead Aberdeen to a senior trophy - the Scottish Cup in 1947 where they beat Hibs in the final. He had also won a trophy the year before when his side defeated Rangers in the final of the Southern League Cup which the following season became renamed as the League Cup and accepted as a major competition. Having taken the Dons to successive Scottish cup finals in 1953 and 1954, in 1955 he took the Dons to the league title, an achievement only Sir Alex Ferguson has matched.

From 1955 to 1958, Halliday managed Leicester City, guiding them to promotion in 1957 and a year later kept the Foxes up at Sunderland's expense. Halliday's team's last-day win at Birmingham City helping to condemn the Wearsiders to the drop for the first time. He continued to scout for Leicester in the Aberdeen area after he moved back as a hotel proprietor. His brothers William and John both began their playing days at Queen of the South and went on to have extensive careers, William listing Newcastle United amongst his clubs.

In the list of major goalscorers at any club. Halliday's record stands comparison with the greats of the game. Dave's son Ian accepted his father's induction into the Sunderland AFC Hall of Fame in 2020.

## HALLIDAY, Thomas

**POSITION:** Half-back

**BIRTHPLACE:** Troqueer, Kirkcudbrightshire

**DATE OF BIRTH:** 06/08/1862 - date of death unknown

**HEIGHT:** 5' 11" **WEIGHT:** 11st 10lbs

**SIGNED FROM:** Queen of the South Wanderers, 24/10/1887

**DEBUT:** v Newcastle West End, H, 05/11/1887

**LAST MATCH:** v Middlesbrough, H, 03/12/1887

**MOVED TO:** Queen of the South Wanderers, 31/08/1888

**TEAMS:** Queen of the South Wanderers, Sunderland, Queen of the South Wanderers, Rotherham Town, Queen of the South Wanderers

**SAFC TOTALS:** 3 appearances / 2 goals

**Nicknamed 'Lang Tam', this player signed for Sunderland after impressing in a match for the reserves against Morpeth Harriers reserves on 22 October 1887. At this time, he had already played in Scotland for nine seasons. His only officially registered Sunderland appearances came in English (FA) Cup games.**

From November 1889 until the end of April 1890, he was suspended by the Scottish FA for receiving payments as a professional at Queen of the South Wanderers, but during this period he continued to appear for Rotherham Town.

## HALOM, Victor Lewis

**POSITION:** Centre-forward

**BIRTHPLACE:** Coton Park, Burton upon Trent, Staffordshire

**DATE OF BIRTH:** 03/10/1948

**HEIGHT:** 5' 10" **WEIGHT:** 12st 10lbs

**SIGNED FROM:** Luton Town, 07/02/1973

**DEBUT:** v Sheffield Wednesday, A, 10/02/1973

**LAST MATCH:** v Oldham Athletic, A, 20/03/1976

**MOVED TO:** Oldham Athletic, 10/07/1976

**TEAMS:** Charlton Athletic, Orient, Fulham, Luton Town, Sunderland, Oldham Athletic, Arcadia Shepherds, Rotherham United, Northwich Victoria

**INTERNATIONAL:** England Schoolboys

**SAFC TOTALS:** 134+5 appearances / 42 goals

**One of the biggest characters ever to play for Sunderland, Vic arrived during the 1973 FA Cup run, scored one of Roker Park's greatest goals in the fifth-round replay, voted the 'Match of the Century,' hit the winner in the semi-final and went on to stand for parliament in Sunderland.**

Halom became a cult hero. He was a centre-forward who would dish out as much rough treatment to defenders as they would him - and did this in an era when those sort of tough physical challenges met with instant red cards these days were par for the course. Vic did all this with the cheekiest of grins, played to the crowd but over and above all this he could score goals as well as make them for his teammates. An unselfish player, this was never better seen than in the cup-final when he ran himself ragged in helping the team defend from the front, barged Leeds' keeper David Harvey into the net and knocked the ball down for Ian Porterfield to score the only goal of the game. Halom would later become player/coach at Rotherham under the management of Porterfield. Within a few minutes of his debut he was booked - and while the referee was writing his name down Halom was gesticulating to the crowd at Millmoor indicating he doubted the official's sexual prowess! Typical Vic.

Although he had offers from Derby County, Sheffield Wednesday and numerous others, Halom became an apprentice with Charlton Athletic in 1964 having scored a first-half hat-trick in a trial game. He went on to play for the Addicks under Bob Stokoe, who was sacked while Vic was on loan to Orient who he subsequently signed for, having made 9+3 league appearances without scoring for Charlton, who he played for as a centre-half. Having moved up-front, there were a dozen goals in 53 league games for Orient which led to Bobby Robson signing him for Fulham, under the nose of Brian Clough who was trying to buy him for Derby County.

Debuting at Craven Cottage against Portsmouth on 9 November 1968, Vic scored his first goal on his next home appearance with his second coming back at his former club Charlton. There would be just one other strike in his ten games as the Cottagers were relegated from the second division. Two seasons later, Halom helped Fulham to promotion. Mainly operating in midfield, he scored eight times in 30+5 league games, but left after three games of the following term having scored 25 goals in 76+6 appearances in total.

In September 1971, Halom moved on to Luton Town where he was reunited with Malcolm MacDonald who he had played alongside at Fulham. Halom did well at Luton, scoring 17 in 57+2 league games, many of these from midfield. A bid from Everton led to Halom being omitted from Luton's cup win at Newcastle, but it was on that trip that Halom spoke to Bob Stokoe and as the Toffees interest cooled Stokoe signed him straight after Sunderland's fourth-round replay win at Charlie Hurley's Reading. Earlier that season, Vic had scored as Luton won at Roker Park where he would go on to thrive as he and the crowd fed off each other.

At Oldham Vic played mainly in midfield, but still scored 43 times in 123 appearances. He also had a short stint in South Africa, scoring four times in eight games for Arcadia Shepherds before injury finished his career at Rotherham where he played 19+1 league games, scoring his second and last goal in a 2-0 win at Walsall on his last appearance on 16 September 1980.

Moving to Norway, after a trial at Northwich Victoria, Halom had two years in amateur football coaching Frederikstad before coming to Barrow in 1983 and guiding them to the Northern Premier League title. He then moved on to Rochdale where his squad included Peter Reid's brother Shaun. After doing well, economic pressures led to Halom being forced to sell his good players at which point Vic chose to leave the professional game and after briefly working for Burton Albion came out of the game to work for Ferrodo, starting off on the factory floor. In 1990 Halom briefly returned to football as Commercial Manager and a Director at North Shields. He then spent 23 years working for New Earth Water Services, two of those years being spent in Mexico with another spell in Aden.

In 1992, as Sunderland reached the FA Cup final for the (to 2021) only time since 1973, Halom returned to Sunderland North to stand for Parliament for the Liberal Democrats. He finished third with just over 10% of the votes, but the thought of Vic in the House of Commons made the mind boggle. In later life, he spent much of his time living in Bulgaria, but frequently returned to Wearside, and in 2022, was accepted as part of the Team of '73 to receive the Freedom of the City of Sunderland.

## HAMILTON, Andrew

**POSITION:** Outside-left

**BIRTHPLACE:** Falkirk, Stirlingshire

**DATE OF BIRTH:** 18/12/1873 - 20/03/1939

**HEIGHT:** 5' 10" **WEIGHT:** 11st 4lbs

**SIGNED FROM:** Falkirk, 01/05/1896

**DEBUT:** v Bury, H, 01/09/1896

**LAST MATCH:** v Bury, A, 16/04/1897

**MOVED TO:** Released, 04/05/1897

**TEAMS:** Falkirk Thistle, East Stirling, Falkirk, Sunderland, New Brighton Tower, Warmley, Ryde, Watford

**SAFC TOTALS:** 7 appearances / 2 goals

**Both of Hamilton's Sunderland goals came in a 4-3 home win over Liverpool in October 1896 during the season which brought all seven of his first-team appearances. The victory over Liverpool was one of only two wins he played in during a campaign where the club found itself involved in end of season 'Test Matches', although after playing in the final scheduled league fixture, Hamilton was not selected for the Test games.**

Having been released by Sunderland, he initially returned to Scotland, but by September of the same year was south of the border again playing for New Brighton Tower in the Lancashire League with the Merseyside club being admitted to the Football League at the end of his first season. After retiring from the game, it is known Andrew became a builder's labourer.

## HAMILTON, James (Jimmy)

**POSITION:** Midfielder

**BIRTHPLACE:** Uddingston, South Lanarkshire

**DATE OF BIRTH:** 14/06/1955

**HEIGHT:** 5' 10" **WEIGHT:** 10st 7lbs

**SIGNED FROM:** Coatbridge Juniors, 01/06/1971

**DEBUT:** v Preston North End, H, 25/09/1971

**LAST MATCH:** v Aston Villa, A, 20/04/1974

**MOVED TO:** Plymouth Argyle, 12/01/1976 after loan from 04/11/1975

**TEAMS:** WBA, Sunderland, Plymouth Argyle, Bristol Rovers, Carlisle United, Morton(L), Newcastle KB United, Apiea, Hartlepool United, Gretna, Queen of the South, Canberra

**SAFC TOTALS:** 9+8 appearances / 2 goals

**"Four-three, Ritchie Pitt, Dennis Tueart got two, and me" 16-year-old Jimmy Hamilton told a bus driver who asked him the score and scorers from the match as he travelled home to his digs in Whitburn after becoming Sunderland's youngest-ever scorer in 1971.**

The bus driver did not believe him, but at the age of 16 years and 103 days, Hamilton had become Sunderland's youngest-ever outfield player and also scorer when he came off the bench with ten minutes to go and settled a thrilling meeting with Preston North End with a header. Previously, he had been an unused sub in both home games in the Anglo-Italian Cup in the summer.

Nicknamed 'Chico' after the Aston Villa player of the period (Ian Hamilton, who took the name Chico after the Jazz drummer), Jimmy had only recently arrived at Sunderland after a brief spell on the ground-staff at West Bromwich Albion, but having done well in the juniors, he was thrust into the spotlight by Alan Brown, always a manager ready to turn to youth.

## HAMILTON, Jimmy (Continued)

Four days after his winner against Preston North End, Hamilton was given a full debut in a 4-1 win over Middlesbrough and went on to feature in seven games out of eight, only being left out of a meeting with top of the table Norwich. Although he was very occasionally named as a substitute, after that initial run Hamilton did not play again until the following season when he started in the first game at Middlesbrough.

He featured regularly in the opening months under Alan Brown, once under caretaker-manager Billy Elliott, but was only called upon by new boss Bob Stokoe when the gaffer made several changes for a league game at Luton a week before the Hatters were due at Roker for the FA Cup quarter-final. Jimmy then waited over a year for his one further appearance which came in a victory at Aston Villa. At this point, his Sunderland experience was over. He was still only 18, an age when many have yet to debut.

In November 1975, he joined Micky Horswill and Bobby Saxton at Plymouth Argyle, but did not debut until September 1976 as a sub against Bolton Wanderers. After another game as sub there were to be six starts for Argyle before a December 1976 move to Bristol Rovers. Ten months later, after 21+5 games, he returned north to sign for Bobby Moncur at Carlisle United. His only goal for Rovers had come at Carlisle, helping the Pirates to victory after trailing 2-0. Debuting in a home loss to Lincoln, Hamilton played alongside John Lathan and Trevor Swinburne at Brunton Park.

By now 21, Jimmy at last began to enjoy regular football, making 158+4 appearances for the Cumbrians over four years, scoring twelve goals. During his time at Carlisle, he went on to play for Martin Harvey and then Bob Stokoe, but as at Sunderland, it was under Stokoe he moved on. Following a loan to Morton, Jimmy went to Australia to play for Newcastle KB United and a Sydney-based side called Apiea before returning to the UK.

In November 1982, he came to Hartlepool United, debuting at home to Mansfield Town, but only made two more starts plus one game as sub before moving on to Gretna, subsequently Queen of the South and finally, a return to Australia with Canberra. After retiring from football he ran The Old Bank restaurant and coffee house in Dumfries before spending many years working at the Roucan Loch crematorium in Dumfries.

## HANNAH, David

**POSITION:** Inside-forward

**BIRTHPLACE:** Raffrey, Co Down

**DATE OF BIRTH:** 28/04/1867 -12/01/1936

**HEIGHT:** 5' 6" **WEIGHT:** 11st 3lbs

**SIGNED FROM:** Renton, 14/08/1889

**DEBUT:** v Blackburn Rovers, A, 18/01/1890

**LAST MATCH:** v Bolton Wanderers, A, 29/09/1894

**MOVED TO:** Liverpool, 02/11/1894

**TEAMS:** Renton Thistle, Renton, Liverpool, Dundee, Woolwich Arsenal, Renton

**SAFC TOTALS:** 92 appearances / 21 goals

**David Hannah played in 18 of the 26 league games as Sunderland became champions for the first time in 1892, and 20 of the 30 matches as the title was retained a year later. He also played in all five cup games as the semi-final was reached in 1892. Although he was not related to fellow, 'Team of All The Talents' teammate Jimmy Hannah, David's brother John was on the club's books in 1891-92, but only played as high as the 'A' team (Reserves).**

A scorer of great goals, David Hannah was more of a schemer than a prolific goalscorer. Two-footed, he had an eye for a killer pass and was a terrific team player. He had been with Sunderland since the days before the club joined the Football League and including friendlies and challenge matches topped a century of appearances.

Before coming to Wearside, he had been with the successful Scottish outfit Renton where he had moved to as a boy and worked in a local dyeworks from the age of 13, David left Sunderland for Liverpool in November 1894. Nicknamed 'Chippy' on Merseyside, David marked his second game with an excellent goal in an Anfield draw with Everton and scored again in his third game - against Sunderland at Roker Park, though Sunderland won. Despite Hannah's six goals in 17 games, Liverpool were relegated, but were promoted immediately, Hannah making eleven appearances.

Reunited with his old Sunderland boss Tom Watson at Liverpool, in 1896-97 he scored twice against Sunderland in a November 1896 victory for the home side at Anfield. They were two of the twelve goals he scored in 33 games for Liverpool who he left in May 1897. After a brief spell with Dundee in October 1897, he returned to England with Woolwich Arsenal. A debut goal against Walsall on the anniversary of his brace against Sunderland was the first of twelve in 20 second division games as he played every match to the end of the season, plus three more appearances in the cup.

Hannah's one full season with the Gunners was his last in England, the last of his 27 appearances (5 goals) that term coming at home to Manchester City on Easter Monday 3 April 1899. Davy Hannah finished his playing days back at his first club Renton and remained in the town until his death in 1936.

## HANNAH, James

**POSITION:** Forward

**BIRTHPLACE:** Hutchesontown, Glasgow, Lanarkshire

**DATE OF BIRTH:** 17/03/1869 - 01/12/1917

**HEIGHT:** 5' 10½" **WEIGHT:** 10st 8lbs

**SIGNED FROM:** Sunderland Albion, 21/05/1891

**DEBUT:** v Everton, H, 03/10/1891

**LAST MATCH:** v Newton Heath, H, 26/04/1897

**MOVED TO:** Third Lanark, 04/05/1897

**TEAMS:** Elmwood, Third Lanark, Sunderland Albion, Sunderland, QPR, Dykehead, Sunderland Royal Rovers

**INTERNATIONAL:** Scotland

**SAFC TOTALS:** 171 appearances / 76 goals

**Nicknamed 'Blood', James Hannah was a tremendous member of 'The Team of All The Talents.' In his six seasons at the club he made between 20 and 28 league appearances (when 26 to 30 was the maximum) and registered double figures in goals in each of the three seasons Sunderland were champions during this golden era. He was second top scorer to Johnny Campbell in the back-to-back titles of 1892 and 1893, 19 goals in 28 league games in 1893 being his best haul.**

'Blood' Hannah could play all along the forward line, frequently appearing on the wings, which makes his goals to games ratio all the more impressive. The origination of the nickname is unknown, but it seems feasible that at some point early in his career he was hurt and played in a very bloodied shirt. Maybe not. Perhaps it stemmed from blood samples he had to give at the start of the 1891-92 season when he suffered from typhoid fever?

After playing junior football in Glasgow with Elmwood, with whom he won the Glasgow Juvenile Cup as a 14-year-old, in 1888 he joined Third Lanark with whom he won the Scottish Cup in 1889. After scoring in the semi-final against Renton, Jimmy actually scored in what was supposed to be the final. Thirds beat Celtic 3-0 at Hampden Park at the beginning of February, but because of the terrible state of the pitch and weather in a game known as the 'Snow Final' - where the snow was reportedly ankle deep - it had been agreed that the final would actually be a friendly. The real final was played a week later, this time Thirds winning 2-1. In both games a teammate of Hannah's was Johnny Auld who would become the first captain of Sunderland's 'Talents.' Two months after the cup final, Jimmy was alongside Auld again as Hannah won his only Scotland cap in a goalless draw against Wales at Wrexham on 14 April 1889.

Hannah first came to Wearside to play for Sunderland Albion before making the switch across the Wear to Sunderland who by now were Football League members and with whom he went on to such great success.

During his last couple of seasons at Sunderland, he combined playing with being the landlord of the Aquatic Arms public house in Monkwearmouth while later, after his playing days, he worked in the Mountain Daisy in Millfield.

Having signed off his Sunderland career with one last hurrah in the Test Matches of 1897 as the aging 'Talents' avoided relegation, Jimmy went to London to sign for Queen's Park Rangers. Debuting in a 3-1 Southern League defeat at Sheppey on 25 November 1899, he played 17 Southern League games plus three in the English (FA) Cup, scoring twice before moving to Dykehead in 1900 and returning to Sunderland with Royal Rovers in 1901.

His son John signed amateur forms for Sunderland in 1922, without making a first-team debut, but the Hannah name lives on at SAFC into the 21st century. Audrey Hannah, the widow of Blood Hannah's Great Great Grandson James, remains the Players' Lounge tea lady as of 2021, a role she has carried out since the club was at Roker Park. James Hannah's league championship medal from 1892 is on permanent display in the entrance hall of the Stadium of Light.

## HANNIGAN, John Leckie

**POSITION:** Winger

**BIRTHPLACE:** Barrhead, Glasgow, Lanarkshire

**DATE OF BIRTH:** 17/02/1933 - 11/12/2020

**HEIGHT:** 5' 10" **WEIGHT:** 10st 10lbs

**SIGNED FROM:** Morton, 20/06/1955

**DEBUT:** v Birmingham City, A, 08/10/1955

**LAST MATCH:** v Preston North End, A, 01/03/1958

**MOVED TO:** Derby County, 06/05/1958

**TEAMS:** Morton, Sunderland, Derby County, Bradford Park Avenue, Weymouth, Bath City

**SAFC TOTALS:** 35 appearances / 10 goals

**Hannigan weighed in with a hat-trick against Charlton in an 8-1 win at Roker Park in September 1956. Strangely, on another occasion, Johnny scored a hat-trick in a North Eastern League game at Annfield Plain for the reserves in a 7-2 win where Danny Brannigan scored four and the scoring went: Brannigan, Hannigan, Brannigan, Hannigan, Brannigan, Hannigan, Brannigan!**

Johnny Hannigan had debuted in a 2-1 win at Birmingham City in October 1955, and scored his first goal on his second appearance at Preston the following month. He made his final appearance for the club back at the same ground in March 1958.

Glasgow-born, Hannigan began with Morton and came to Sunderland while doing his National Service at Catterick. During the scandal that hit the club in 1957, he was suspended indefinitely by the Football League for receiving illegal payments. The suspension was lifted within a month however, and after leaving Sunderland he scored 19 times in 75 games for Derby County where he was converted to a centre-forward. He then added 122 appearances in the colours of Bradford Park Avenue before completing his career with Weymouth and Bath City, winning honours with both clubs.

## HARDWICK, Stephen (Steve)

**POSITION:** Goalkeeper

**BIRTHPLACE:** Mansfield, Nottinghamshire

**DATE OF BIRTH:** 06/09/1956

**HEIGHT:** 5' 11" **WEIGHT:** 13st 0lbs

**SIGNED FROM:** Oxford United, 14/08/1987, on loan

**DEBUT:** v Brentford, A, 15/08/1987

**LAST MATCH:** v Bury, H, 12/09/1987

**MOVED TO:** Oxford United, 14/09/1987, end of loan

**TEAMS:** Chesterfield, Newcastle United, Detroit Express (L), Oxford United, Crystal Palace (L), Sunderland (L), Huddersfield Town, Kettering Town, Emley, Kettering Town, Boston United

**INTERNATIONAL:** England Youth and Amateur

**SAFC TOTALS:** 8 appearances / 0 goals

**Brought in by Denis Smith, Hardwick kept goal in Sunderland's first six games at third-tier level. He did okay, conceding just five goals and being beaten only twice in a two-legged League Cup tie with a Middlesbrough side who would win promotion to the top-flight that season. However, at the end of his loan Hardwick reportedly rejected the opportunity to stay at Sunderland, apparently being reluctant due to the pressure he felt in a previous stint in the north east with Newcastle.**

After beginning with Chesterfield where the first of his 44 appearances on 12 October 1974 came against a Blackburn side whose keeper was Roger Jones, who would be on the coaching staff when Hardwick came to Sunderland. In December 1976, Gordon Lee (who had been Blackburn's manager on Hardwick's debut) paid Newcastle's record fee for a goalkeeper of £80,000 to take him to Tyneside. He went on to play 101 times for the Magpies, debuting at Liverpool in August 1977 and broke into an England Under 21 squad, but without being capped. He also had a brief 1978 loan in American soccer. According to Newcastle United's official historian Paul Joannou in his excellent 'Ultimate Who's Who of Newcastle United, "...a series of lapses made him, to some sections of the crowd, something of a villain".

Perhaps it was that experience that made Steve feel the hotbed of soccer was too hot to stay in and so he went back to Oxford who he had joined in 1983 for £15,000. Hardwick excelled at Oxford, at one point making 158 consecutive appearances during which he was ever-present as the U's won back-to-back promotions from the third tier to the first in 1984 and '85.

Sunderland was the second of his loans from Oxford. He had previously been loaned to Crystal Palace where he made three appearances in March 1986. After a total of 196 appearances for Oxford, Hardwick moved to Huddersfield in the summer after his Sunderland loan and went on to turn out 129 times for the Terriers before finishing his career in non-league, with an unsuccessful attempt to get back into the Football League with a trial at then fourth division Scarborough in 1991. After retiring from football, he became groundsman at Hoylandswaine Cricket Club in South Yorkshire where he was captain and kept wicket.

## HARDYMAN, Paul George Thomas

**POSITION:** Left-back / midfield

**BIRTHPLACE:** Portsmouth, Hampshire

**DATE OF BIRTH:** 11/03/1964

**HEIGHT:** 5' 8½" **WEIGHT:** 11st 4lbs

**SIGNED FROM:** Portsmouth, 16/06/1989

**DEBUT:** v Swindon Town, A, 19/08/1989

**LAST MATCH:** v Liverpool, N, 09/05/1992

**MOVED TO:** Bristol Rovers, 14/07/1992

**TEAMS:** Fareham, Waterlooville, Portsmouth, Sunderland, Bristol Rovers, Wycombe Wanderers, Barnet, Slough Town, Basingstoke, New Milton Town

**INTERNATIONAL:** England Under 21

**SAFC TOTALS:** 123+6 appearances / 12 goals

**The 1992 FA Cup final was Hardyman's last appearance. He came on a minute after Sunderland went 2-0 down to Liverpool mid-way through the second half. Having played in every game during the cup run, Paul was understandably mightily disappointed to miss out and left the club that summer - but was seen at Wembley as a supporter on Sunderland's next visit in the 1998 Play-Off final. Hardyman had missed the 1990 Play-Off final through suspension. A penalty-taking left-back, he had been sent off in the aftermath of having his last-minute spot kick saved in the first leg of the semi-final at home to Newcastle.**

Initially a carpenter and joiner before becoming a professional footballer, after retiring from football, Paul ran his own carpentry business. He returned to the game with his home-town, and first professional, club Portsmouth as Youth Development Officer, a post he held from April 2000 to October 2009 while also working as a radio summariser on BBC Solent.

## HARDYMAN, Paul (Continued)

Just over 18 months after leaving the club, he returned to Pompey as Assistant Academy Manager having managed New Milton Town from March 2010 to May 2011. Although in his late forties by this stage, he picked himself for a handful of games - and was sent off on his debut. Leaving Portsmouth again in May 2015, he then took up a post at Watford. Initially coaching the Hornets Under 12 and Under 14 teams, he coached their Under 18s in 2017-18 before becoming lead coach for the Under 16s at Southampton.

As a player, before coming to Sunderland, Paul came to prominence as a winger with Waterlooville in 1982-83, attracting interest from Pompey for whom he appeared at reserve level whilst still with Waterlooville. Signed by the Fratton Park club in 1983, he joined a staff that included Steve Berry and later had Rob Hindmarch on loan from Sunderland.

Hardyman waited until 24 March 1984 for his debut as a sub in a home defeat to Crystal Palace, but went on to impress and earned international recognition with an England Under 21 debut (alongside Bobby Mimms) at Fratton Park against the Republic of Ireland a year and a day. after his club debut.

Two years to the month later, Hardyman earned his second and last cap alongside Barry Venison and goalscorer Nick Pickering as England won 1-0 in a UEFA Under 21 Championship quarter-final against Denmark in Copenhagen.

## HARFORD, Michael Gordon (Mick)

**POSITION:** Centre-forward

**BIRTHPLACE:** Sunderland, Co Durham

**DATE OF BIRTH:** 12/02/1959

**HEIGHT:** 6' 2" **WEIGHT:** 12st 9lbs

**SIGNED FROM:** Chelsea, 18/03/1993

**DEBUT:** v Barnsley, A, 21/03/1993

**LAST MATCH:** v Notts County, A, 08/05/1993

**MOVED TO:** Coventry City, 07/07/1993

**TEAMS:** Lambton Star BC, Lincoln City, Newcastle United, Bristol City, Newcastle United, Birmingham City, Luton Town, Derby County, Luton Town, Chelsea, Sunderland, Coventry City, Wimbledon

**INTERNATIONAL:** England

**SAFC TOTALS:** 10+1 appearances / 2 goals

**Renowned as one of football's hardest men, Mick Harford's time with his hometown team was little more than a footnote in a long and eventful career. He played just a handful of games towards the end of the 1992-93 campaign when Sunderland only escaped relegation to the third tier thanks to fortuitous results on the final day of the season when Harford's last appearance came in a dismal defeat at Notts County. He did make another contribution to SAFC, giving Grant Leadbitter his league debut on loan from Sunderland when manager of Rotherham United in October 2005.**

Having played for Sunderland Schoolboys and Lambton Star Boys Club, Harford made his way in the professional game with Lincoln City. The Imps soon converted him from a midfielder to a target man. It was a position in which he excelled and after 45 goals in 126 games, he returned to the north-east in a £216,000 deal with Newcastle United where he was signed by Sunderland's 1973 FA Cup-winning coach Arthur Cox.

Debuting for the Magpies at Grimsby Town on Boxing Day 1980, Mick managed four goals in 18+1 appearances before being

sold to Bristol City the following August for £56,000 less than had been paid for him. There were eleven goals in 30 league games for the Robins, but eight months later, he was technically a Newcastle player again for an hour before a switch to Birmingham City. This complication was due to Bristol City's apparent inability to meet their payments to Newcastle and to enable United to accept a £100,000 fee from Birmingham City.

Debuting on the opening day of 1982-83 at Manchester United, Harford scored six goals in 31 games, half of those goals coming in the last four fixtures, starting with one in a win at Sunderland. The following season, he scored at Roker Park again, this time in the FA Cup. It was one of 15 goals (including a League Cup hat-trick against Derby) he netted in 51 matches as Birmingham were relegated. By December he was back in the top flight after a £250,000 transfer to Luton, the club with which he would become most synonymous, three more goals in 15 appearances having taken his Blues total to 33 goals in 109 matches.

It was at Luton that Harford blossomed to become the complete centre-forward. Not just excellent in the air, he was mobile, aggressive and good with his feet. 92 goals in 217 games came his way while at Kennilworth Road as did two full England caps and a 'B' cap. Debuting for England as a sub in a goalless draw in Israel in February 1988, alongside Chris Waddle and Chris Woods, he then sat on the bench for three internationals before being given a start the following September in a 1-0 Wembley win against Denmark, this time numbering Terry Butcher (who later signed him for Sunderland) amongst his teammates. Harford's B cap had come in October 1987 when he scored in a 2-0 win in Malta where his teammates included Steve Bruce, Adrian Heath and Ian Snodin.

In January 1990, a £480,000 fee took him to Derby County where he scored 15 goals in 58 league games. He was with the Rams for under two seasons before going back to Luton for £325,000, but in the meantime scored an own-goal at Luton on the last day of the 1990-91 season playing for bottom of the table Derby, who lost in a match that kept Luton up and condemned Sunderland, who lost to Peter Reid's Manchester City.

Regularly on the move, Harford's next stop was to Chelsea in the summer of 1992 where he signed for Ian Porterfield who paid £300,000 for the 33-year-old who scored on his debut against Oldham and totalled eleven goals in 34+1 games before moving to Sunderland after nine months at Stamford Bridge. After less than half that time on Wearside, Mick was on the move again, Coventry City paying £200,000 for the player who headed the winner against Newcastle having come off the bench for his debut, but never played again due to back problems. A year later, Mick made his final move as a player to Wimbledon for £75,000 going on to score nine goals in 60 league games to take his career league total to 186 goals in 582 games.

At Wimbledon, Harford moved into coaching, going on to coach, manage or be director of football at: Luton Town, Nottingham Forest, Swindon Town, Rotherham United, Colchester United, QPR, Luton again, QPR again, MK Dons, Millwall and back to Luton. In 2018-19, he was League One Manager of the Year after taking the Hatters to the title, a decade after he had led them to the Football League Trophy (against Scunthorpe United) at Wembley, this in turn being 21 years since he was a Wembley winner as a player with Luton. In that 1988 League Cup final, he played alongside Andy Dibble against an Arsenal side that included future Sunderland caretaker manager Kevin Richardson and had Niall Quinn on the bench. Along with Keith Bertschin, to June 2022 Harford jointly holds the record of most goals against Sunderland by someone who played for Sunderland: eight goals including a League Cup hat-trick for Derby.

## HARGREAVES, Leonard (Len)

**POSITION:** Outside-left

**BIRTHPLACE:** Kimberworth, Yorkshire

**DATE OF BIRTH:** 07/03/1906 - Q3 1980

**HEIGHT:** 5' 10½" **WEIGHT:** 11st 2lbs

**SIGNED FROM:** Doncaster Rovers, 20/04/1927

**DEBUT:** v West Ham United, A, 01/09/1927

**LAST MATCH:** v West Ham United, A, 12/01/1929

**MOVED TO:** Sheffield Wednesday, 15/03/1929

**TEAMS:** Doncaster Rovers, Sunderland, Sheffield Wednesday, Workington, Doncaster Rovers, Luton Town, Peterborough and Fletton United, Bourne Town

**SAFC TOTALS:** 39 appearances / 12 goals

**Having played for Sunderland in the top-flight, Hargreaves was a big-name signing for Peterborough who were newly-formed. He went on to score the club's first-ever competitive goal in a Midland League game against Gainsborough Trinity on 1 September 1934.**

Seven years to the day earlier, Len made his debut for Sunderland against West Ham. An outside-left, Hargreaves had joined Sunderland from Doncaster Rovers in April 1927 for £2,000, shortly after his fellow Doncaster winger Alwyne Wilks had moved to Sunderland for £500 less than the fee for Hargreaves.

Len did well in his first season. His nine goals from 31 games made him second top scorer behind the prolific Dave Halliday. The last of Len's dozen goals for the Lads came in a 5-2 thumping of Newcastle in October 1928 while the last of his 39 appearances came as the first one had, at West Ham. Hargreaves bowed out after a cup loss at the Boleyn Ground in January 1929 after which he moved on to Sheffield Wednesday a couple of months later, playing twice - and scoring at Manchester United - as they won Division One.

Wednesday retained the title with a divisional points record, while Hargreaves was there the following season, but without him getting a game and he moved on to play for Workington and Luton either side of a second spell with Doncaster before finally pitching up at Peterborough. Prior to becoming a professional footballer, Hargreaves had worked as a locomotive fitter. He continued these engineering skills in WW2 working on the manufacture of torpedoes whilst also playing for Bourne Town, for whom he became manager in October 1948. He married the sister of Arthur Housam.

## HARKER, John James*

**POSITION:** Inside-right

**BIRTHPLACE:** Witton-le-Wear

**DATE OF BIRTH:** 10/10/1876 - Q1 1962

**SIGNED FROM:** Thornaby Utopians, 28/03/1899

**DEBUT:** v Blackburn Rovers, H, 03/04/1899

**LAST MATCH:** v Blackburn Rovers, H, 03/04/1899

**MOVED TO:** Thornaby Utopians, 04/04/1899

**TEAMS:** Thornaby Utopians, Sunderland, Thornaby Utopians

**SAFC TOTALS:** 1 appearance / 0 goals

***One of the most difficult to research early players, this player previously recorded simply as J Harker is most likely John James Harker born 10/10/1876 in Witton-le-Wear and who died in West Hartlepool in Q1 1962. This person was a railway clerk living in Thornaby in 1901.**

**Harker spent just a handful of days at Roker Park playing one game as Sunderland took a look at this player, described by the Sunderland Echo at the time as a 'promising player', and who had starred in the 1898-99 season for Thornaby Utopians as they achieved promotion from the second division of the Northern League.**

It is unknown why Sunderland played him at inside-right in place of Jim Leslie in his only game when he usually played left-half back for Utopians. The late season loss by 1-0 in Harker's only game cost Sunderland a league position as opponents Blackburn finished above seventh-placed Sunderland on goal average.

## HARPER, George Spencer

**POSITION:** Inside-left

**BIRTHPLACE:** Edgbaston, Birmingham, Warwickshire

**DATE OF BIRTH:** 15/08/1877 - 14/07/1949

**HEIGHT:** 5' 6" **WEIGHT:** 12st 7lbs

**SIGNED FROM:** Grimsby Town, 28/11/1902

**DEBUT:** v West Bromwich Albion, H, 29/11/1902

**LAST MATCH:** v Middlesbrough, H, 18/04/1903

**MOVED TO:** Left club, 01/05/1904

**TEAMS:** Saltley Gas Company, Burton United, Aston Villa, Hereford Thistle, Wolverhampton Wanderers, Grimsby Town, Sunderland, Earlestown, Newton-le-Willows

**SAFC TOTALS:** 11 appearances / 1 goal

**Like Charlie Chaplin and Stan Laurel, George Harper was once a member of Fred Karno's Army - Karno being a music hall star famed for inventing the custard pie in the face routine. In Harper's case, he became a dancer with Fred Karno's Army after retiring from football, also working as a silversmith in his later years.**

At Sunderland, all of his appearances came in 1902-03, the last of them technically being a home game, but staged at St James' Park as Roker was closed as a punishment for crowd trouble.

As a youngster, he was on Villa's books without getting a game and made his league bow with Wolves, scoring on his first two appearances against Derby and Liverpool in December 1897. Despite these goals, they were his only appearances of that season as Wolves finished just behind runners-up Sunderland. He went on to score 21 goals in 66 games, ten of these goals making him Wolves' top-scorer in 1899-1900. This haul included their first goal of the 20th century in a New Year's Day win at Sunderland.

He moved to Grimsby to make a total of 25 appearances in the Mariners first-ever top-flight campaign of 1901-02 (three goals) before coming to Wearside in part exchange for Bobby Hogg.

Both players would be dogged by injury at their new clubs. In Harper's case, injury ending his first-class career when he was just 27. However, he still managed a few games in the Lancashire league as well as performing with Fred Karno's Army. George went on to serve with the 6th Battalion Worcestershire Regiment in World War One until discharged as no longer fit for war service in April 1917.

## HARPER, William George (Willie)

**POSITION:** Goalkeeper

**BIRTHPLACE:** Wishaw, Lanarkshire

**DATE OF BIRTH:** 15/11/1900 - date of death unknown

**HEIGHT:** 5' 10" **WEIGHT:** 11st 9lbs

**SIGNED FROM:** Wishaw YMCA, 12/09/1921

**DEBUT:** v Manchester City, H, 14/01/1922

**LAST MATCH:** v Sheffield United, H, 11/04/1923

**MOVED TO:** Manchester City, 17/05/1923

**TEAMS:** Wishaw YMCA Juniors, Sunderland, Manchester City, Crystal Palace, Luton Town, Weymouth, Callender Athletic

**SAFC TOTALS:** 28 appearances / 0 goals

**Willie Harper came to Sunderland on a one month trial and immediately after signing returned home to Scotland to get married. He kept goal for all but one of the last 19 games of his first season and ten out of a late season sequence in his second year as Sunderland finished runners' up in 1922-23. That summer he moved to Manchester City but was restricted to just four appearances in his year there before transferring to Crystal Palace.**

Relegated from Division Two in his first year at Palace, where he missed just one game in 1924-25, he played for most of the first half of the following campaign before losing his place. Following 59 games for Palace, where he was known as Bill, Harper joined Luton in October 1926, making 31 league appearances for the Hatters before moving into non-league.

## HARRIS, Gordon

**POSITION:** Midfielder

**BIRTHPLACE:** Langold, Nottinghamshire

**DATE OF BIRTH:** 02/06/1940 - 10/02/2014

**HEIGHT:** 5' 10" **WEIGHT:** 11st 10lbs

**SIGNED FROM:** Burnley, 08/01/1968

**DEBUT:** v Sheffield Wednesday, A, 03/02/1968

**LAST MATCH:** v Watford, A, 21/08/1971

**MOVED TO:** South Shields, 03/07/1972

**TEAMS:** Firbeck Colliery, Burnley, Sunderland, South Shields

**INTERNATIONAL:** England

**SAFC TOTALS:** 134+1 appearances / 16 goals

**Although only 27 when he came to Sunderland and just over 31 at the time of his last game, Gordon Harris always looked older at Roker. Harris did not need to be quick. He let the ball do the work. The season after Gordon left, cup-winning skipper Bobby Kerr was dubbed 'The Little General' by Bob Stokoe, but in his time at Roker, Harris had been known as 'The General' as he dictated play.**

Capped by England two years to the week before joining Sunderland, Gordon's only full cap came in a 1-1 draw with Poland at Goodison Park. Eight of the eleven, just over six months later, became England's World Cup-winning team.

Joe Baker was one of Harris' other teammates in a match where Harris started the move from which Bobby Moore scored one of his two international goals. Harris was named in England's original squad of 40 for the 1966 tournament, but was cut when it was initially reduced to 28, although he was asked to remain on standby in case he was needed.

Harris had also played alongside England's future World Cup winning captain Moore when Gordon scored for England Under 23s in a 7-1 win over Israel at Leeds in 1961. Two years later, he also played in a goalless draw with Yugoslavia at Old Trafford. He also twice played for the Football League, scoring in a 6-1 win over the Irish League in 1961, a week before his England Under 23 debut.

Initially Gordon was an outside-left at Burnley where he was known as 'Bomber' Harris due to his powerful left-foot shot combined with a shared surname of the RAF's wartime head of Bomber Command. He scored on his debut against Leeds in January 1959 and played twice the following season as Burnley became league champions, but he played more regularly as the Clarets were runners-up in 1962.

That season he played in the FA Cup final under the captaincy of future Sunderland manager Jimmy Adamson as his side lost to Spurs - though it was from Gordon's cross that Burnley scored through Jimmy Robson. During that same campaign, Harris scored in a European Cup quarter-final second leg against Hamburg

It was the following 1962-63 season when Burnley finished third that he switched from left wing to central midfield due to the emergence of Eppleton-born Ralph Coates. Now able to dictate play, Gordon went on to star in the club's foray into the Inter-Cities Fairs Cup in 1966-67 before becoming captain.

Known to be outspoken, Gordon lost his place at Burnley for what were said to be disciplinary reasons which led to his transfer to Sunderland for £68,000. There had been 81 goals in 313 games for Burnley. At Sunderland he came in to effectively replace the recently departed Jim Baxter as schemer in chief.

Although he played in central midfield for Sunderland, where he was powerless to stop relegation in 1970, sometimes his old left wing crossing ability came to the fore. One memorable move saw him collect a pass from Colin Todd, motor up the left wing and deliver an inch-perfect cross for Billy Hughes to head home at the Fulwell End against QPR in December 1970. Motoring became Harris' future as after finishing his playing days with South Shields, he returned to Nottinghamshire to end his working days as a driver in the coal industry.

# H

## HARRIS, William

**POSITION:** Striker

**BIRTHPLACE:** South Shields, Tyne and Wear

**DATE OF BIRTH:** 01/10/2000

**HEIGHT:** 6' 1" **WEIGHT:** 12st 11lbs

**SIGNED FROM:** Free agent, 01/09/2020

**DEBUT:** v Lincoln City, A, 05/10/2021

**LAST MATCH:** v Doncaster Rovers, A, 27/12/2021

**MOVED TO:** Released, 25/05/2022

**TEAMS:** Hebburn Town, Burnley, Colne (L), Warrington Town (L), Sunderland, Barrow (L), Gateshead (to July 2022)

**SAFC TOTALS:** 3+4 appearances / 0 goals

**A member of the Burnley youth team from 2017 to 2019, Harris spent most of his final season with the Clarets out on loan. Initially, he scored nine goals in twelve games for Northern Premier League North West Colne FC before moving up to the Northern Premier League Premier Division with Warrington Town where his loan was cut short to join Sunderland on trial.**

Will played for Sunderland in the semi-final of the Durham Challenge Cup in 2019-20 before signing for the club early the following season. Shortly after a hat-trick for Sunderland in a 3-1 Under 23 side win at Wolves, Will broke into the first team leading the line in two Football League Trophy games within the space of eight days, a league debut at Gillingham following three days later. Released following nine games without a goal on loan to League Two Barrow he started the following season back at Sunderland with the Under 23s having signed a medical extension allowing him to play and train at Sunderland while looking to get fit and find a new club.

## HARRISON, Gerald Randall (Gerry)

**POSITION:** Midfielder

**BIRTHPLACE:** Lambeth, London

**DATE OF BIRTH:** 15/04/1972

**HEIGHT:** 5' 10" **WEIGHT:** 12st 3lbs

**SIGNED FROM:** Burnley, 10/07/1998

**DEBUT:** v York City, H, 18/08/1998

**LAST MATCH:** v York City, H, 18/08/1998

**MOVED TO:** Released, 30/06/2000

**TEAMS:** Watford, Bristol City, Cardiff City (L), Bath City (L), Huddersfield Town, Hereford United (L), Burnley, Sunderland, Luton Town (L), Hull City (L), Burnley (L), Halifax Town, Leigh RMI, York City, Northwich Victoria, Hyde United, Prestwich Heys

**INTERNATIONAL:** England Schools

**SAFC TOTALS:** 1 appearance / 0 goals

**Gerry played 69 minutes on his only appearance in a League Cup tie. Failing to impress, he came in for a fair amount of criticism, only for it to later become apparent that he was suffering from hepatitis.**

With Sunderland flying at the time, he never got another chance and two days before Christmas was loaned to third tier Luton who he had been on the verge of joining when Sunderland stepped in to sign him.

Playing alongside future Sunderland goalkeeper Kelvin Davis, Harrison played 14 league games for the Hatters followed by eight on loan to basement strugglers Hull City as he demonstrated his fitness. There was to be no second chance at Sunderland however, just another loan to Hull and then one to Burnley who he had been signed from.

A Londoner, Gerry trained with Crystal Palace as a youngster, played for London Schools and as England Schools javelin champion at the age of 15 went on to represent Great Britain. It was at Watford that Harrison took his first steps in senior football, often playing in both full-back positions before playing in his best position in central midfield where his drive and industry made his name. Always a versatile player, he even went in goal in one match with Luton.

Gerry was 17 when he made his league debut alongside Tony Coton for Watford at Ipswich on 7 April 1990. After 7+3 games for the Hornets, a free transfer took him to Bristol City in the summer of 1991. There were 32+16 appearances and one goal for the Robins who loaned him to Cardiff (10/1) and Bath before freeing him to go to Huddersfield in March 1993.

Harrison never played for the Terriers who loaned him to Hereford (8/0) before he found his footballing home at Burnley. 134 starts and twelve games as sub (3 goals) preceded his move to Wearside. Gerry did not add to his Turf Moor total in his second spell at the club and completed his Football League career with Halifax Town where the last of his 9+2 games (1) goal came under Paul Bracewell on 17 October 2000, a game in which new floodlights were unveiled at the Shay.

There followed a three year spell at Leigh Genesis (74+5/1) who he left in September 2004 shortly after their relegation to Conference North. Back in the top tier of the Conference with York, he made three substitute appearances for the club just relegated from the Football League, but after just a month, moved on to Northwich Victoria. After six games in a couple of months, culminating in a 5-0 defeat at Accrington in November 2004, he continued his non-league journey with Hyde United and Prestwich Heys.

Despite those liver problems at Sunderland, Gerry just kept on playing, turning out for Burnley old boys 'Vintage Clarets' after becoming head of football development at Burnley College, a role that also led to him teaching PE in several local secondary schools in the Burnley area.

## HARTE, Ian Patrick

**POSITION:** Left-back

**BIRTHPLACE:** Drogheda, County Louth

**DATE OF BIRTH:** 31/08/1977

**HEIGHT:** 5' 11" **WEIGHT:** 12st 6lbs

**SIGNED FROM:** Levante UD, 29/08/2007

**DEBUT:** v Arsenal, A, 07/10/2007

**LAST MATCH:** v Newcastle United A, 20/04/2008

**MOVED TO:** Contract not renewed, 30/06/2008

**TEAMS:** Home Farm, Leeds United, Levante UD, Sunderland, Blackpool, Carlisle United, Reading, AFC Bournemouth

**SAFC TOTALS:** 3+5 appearances / 0 goals

**Capped 64 times by the Republic of Ireland, Harte started 199 league games for Leeds and in total played 270+18 times for the Elland Road club. An accomplished free-kick and penalty taker, he scored 39 goals for the Yorkshire side. Future Sunderland manager Howard Wilkinson handed Harte his debut at Aston Villa on 3 February 1996 when he lined up alongside Brian Deane.**

In 1999-2000, Harte was a regular as Leeds finished third in the Premiership. He played all twelve games as Leeds reached the semi-final of the UEFA Cup, netting a spot-kick in a second round 3-0 win at Lokomotiv Moscow where Michael Bridges scored the other goals. The following term, Harte's 17 Champions League appearances were more than any of his teammates as he scored four times in Leeds' run to the semi-finals, where they lost to Valencia.

In 2004, Harte moved to Spain himself, signing for Levante who were relegated in his first season, but promoted at the first attempt before he left early in his third term to sign for Sunderland after ten goals in 66 league games.

At Sunderland, he signed for his old international teammate Roy Keane, but only played eight times and was released at the end of his first season. Unsuccessful trials with Wolves, Sheffield United, Valerenga of Norway and Charlton Athletic preceded a brief spell with Blackpool who he played five times for in the winter of 2008 before agreeing a contract with St Mirren, only to have a change of heart and join Carlisle.

He helped the Cumbrians to avoid relegation and went on to play for them at Wembley in a 2010 Football League Trophy final defeat by Southampton. Numbering Paul Thirlwell and Graham Kavanagh amongst his teammates, Harte was Carlisle's top scorer in 2009-10 with 18 goals, including seven penalties - exceptional going for a defender and unsurprisingly, he was named in the PFA League One Team of the Year.

Early the following season he moved to Reading, scoring a debut penalty against Crystal Palace and going on to be selected in the PFA Championship Team of the Year, after again reaching double-figures in the goals charts. There was better to come the following season when he won promotion to the Premier League with the Royals and for the third successive season gaining recognition in the PFA divisional Team of the Year. After 99 games and 15 goals, he made a final move to AFC Bournemouth in 2013. He played 35 times for the Cherries, scoring once, although there were only four league appearances as he helped them to promotion to the Premier League in 2015.

At international level, Ian debuted on 2 June 1996 against Croatia and helped the Republic of Ireland qualify for the 2002 FIFA World Cup finals, his play-off penalty against Iran being crucial. At the time of the tournament, Harte was with Leeds and was one of ten members of the squad named by Mick McCarthy who either played for, managed or scouted for Sunderland. Harte started all four of Ireland's games, but was subbed in all four, having had a penalty saved in the game against Spain.

After retiring, Ian became a football agent.

## HARTLEY, James Milburn (Jimmy)

**POSITION:** Inside-forward

**BIRTHPLACE:** Dumbarton

**DATE OF BIRTH:** 29/10/1876 - 12/11/1913

**HEIGHT:** 5' 6" **WEIGHT:** 11st 4 lbs

**SIGNED FROM:** Dumbarton, 03/10/1895

**DEBUT:** v Wednesday, A, 19/10/1895

**LAST MATCH:** v Wolverhampton Wanderers, H, 03/10/1896

**MOVED TO:** Burnley, 25/11/1896

**TEAMS:** Dumbarton, Sunderland, Burnley, Lincoln City, Tottenham Hotspur, Lincoln City, Rangers, Port Glasgow Athletic, Brentford, New Brompton, Port Glasgow Athletic

**SAFC TOTALS:** 11 appearances / 1 goal

**James Hartley was one of three brothers who played for Dumbarton. One of them, Abraham Hartley, also played for Everton in the 1897 cup final and listed Liverpool, Arsenal, Burnley and Southampton as the other clubs he played for.**

Jimmy went on to also have a well-travelled career before completing his English playing days from 1906 to 1908 with New Brompton (who became Gillingham in 1912), playing in the team that sensationally knocked Sunderland out of the cup in 1907-08.

Playing in that cup upset was a belated revenge for Hartley who had played five times for Sunderland in 1895-96 and had another six outings early in the following season. However, a single goal - in a defeat to Preston - signalled a rapid departure for a player who was discarded a few days after his 20th birthday. Hartley, like his father, was a tailor by trade whilst he played football, and passed away due to pneumonia in his birthplace when he was only 37.

## HARTLEY, Peter

**POSITION:** Centre-back

**BIRTHPLACE:** Hartlepool

**DATE OF BIRTH:** 03/04/1988

**HEIGHT:** 6' 1" **WEIGHT:** 12st 6lbs

**SIGNED FROM:** Academy product, 01/07/2004

**DEBUT:** v Leicester City, A, 01/01/2007

**LAST MATCH:** v Leicester City, A, 01/01/2007

**MOVED TO:** Hartlepool United, 28/05/2009

**TEAMS:** Sunderland, Chesterfield (L), Hartlepool United, Stevenage, Plymouth Argyle, Bristol Rovers, Blackpool, Motherwell, Jamshedpur

**SAFC TOTALS:** 0+1 appearance / 0 goals

**Although his Sunderland senior career lasted a mere eight minutes after coming through the club's academy, Hartley went on to have a long career. He made a dozen appearances with Chesterfield while on loan from Sunderland before joining his hometown team Hartlepool where he signed for Chris Turner.**

Peter went on to captain the club for whom he played 181 times, scoring ten times. Notably, one of those goals in a 2-1 win over Notts County in 2013 saw him joined on the scoresheet by James Poole. Subsequently, the club framed their Hartley-Poole shirts and displayed them in the club foyer.

In August 2013, he moved on to Stevenage after Hartlepool were relegated, but after tasting relegation again in his only season (38/3), he signed for Plymouth where the last of his seven goals over two years was an injury-time 2016 League

Two Play-Off semi-final winner against Portsmouth. He subsequently made his 96th and final Argyle appearance in the Wembley final, only to suffer defeat to AFC Wimbledon.

At his next club Bristol Rovers, there were six goals in 25 games, one of his goals being against Chelsea at Stamford Bridge in the League Cup. This led to a transfer to Blackpool where he appeared in just two cup ties before joining Motherwell, initially on loan. He went on to captain the club for whom he scored four goals in 48 games, before a 2020 move to the Indian Super League when he joined Jamshedpur where as of June 2022 he was captain.

## HARTNESS, George

**POSITION:** Inside-right

**BIRTHPLACE:** Monkwearmouth, Sunderland, Co Durham

**DATE OF BIRTH:** 18/12/1872 - 05/02/1943

**SIGNED FROM:** Monkwearmouth, 18/04/1895

**DEBUT:** v Wednesday, H, 05/12/1896

**LAST MATCH:** v Everton, H, 12/12/1896

**MOVED TO:** Released, 01/05/1897

**TEAMS:** White Star, St Peter's, Monkwearmouth, Sunderland

**SAFC TOTALS:** 2 appearances / 0 goals

**A boilermaker and shipyard plater who lived in Southwick after leaving football, Hartness played in two top-flight draws on consecutive weekends, but was not able to hold on to a first-team place in a season when Sunderland struggled.**

George's only other first-team game seems to have been a friendly on New Year's Day 1896 in which Sunderland beat Third Lanark 5-1. However, his performances, and the odd goal or two, for the 'A' team that season led to rumours that he would be signed by Small Heath (later Birmingham City) in May 1896.

## HARVEY, Martin

**POSITION:** Half-back / full-back

**BIRTHPLACE:** Belfast, Northern Ireland

**DATE OF BIRTH:** 19/09/1941 - 25/11/2019

**HEIGHT:** 5' 10½" **WEIGHT:** 12st 5lbs

**SIGNED FROM:** Youth product, 01/09/1957 Professional, 19/09/1958

**DEBUT:** v Plymouth Argyle, A, 24/10/1959

**LAST MATCH:** v Norwich City, A, 11/03/1972

**MOVED TO:** Retired, 01/12/1972

**TEAMS:** Sunderland

**INTERNATIONAL:** Northern Ireland

**SAFC TOTALS:** 353+5 appearances / 5 goals

**A member of the much-loved 1964 promotion team, but for an injury that prematurely ended his career in 1972, Martin may well have been a member of the side that lifted the FA Cup the following year. Harvey holds the record as the player who won the most caps for any of the UK countries while with Sunderland.**

All of his 34 caps were won while with Sunderland who were his only senior club. At the 1982 World Cup, Harvey worked as assistant to the man whose record he took - Billy Bingham - as the pair led Northern Ireland to winning their group having sensationally beaten host-nation Spain.

Martin was such a good player, he replaced Stan Anderson at Sunderland and Danny Blanchflower in his national side. Whether at full-back or in midfield, Harvey was composed, crisp in his passing, the master of the well-timed tackle and also possessed the pace to deal with speed merchants.

Later reserve team coach at Sunderland from his retirement from playing in December 1972 to the end of May 1977 Martin shaped the careers of an up-and-coming generation, not least 1973 FA Cup winner Mick Horswill who idolised him. Senior players also had the utmost respect for him and he was always very popular with the crowd. A regular in the side from 1963 to 1972, knee and back injuries ended Martin's playing days when he was only 30. Three years later, the club staged a Testimonial against Newcastle for Martin.

He went on to coach Carlisle where he became manager between February and September 1980. Having been assistant to Bobby Moncur at Brunton Park, when Moncur took over at Plymouth Martin re-united with him, staying at Argyle from 1981 to 1990, other than a brief spell in the mid-eighties when he again worked with Moncur, this time in Saudi Arabia.

From 1991 to early 1996 he worked as assistant manager at Raith Rovers prior to a year in the same position at Millwall. In both roles Martin assisted former Sunderland full-back Jimmy Nicholl. With Raith they won the Scottish Coca Cola Cup in 1994 and the following year led at Bayern Munich before going down 2-1.

Martin only ever scored five goals in over 350 games. One of them came on his final appearance for the Lads, but he was always concerned with stopping goals rather than scoring them.

## HARVIE, John

**POSITION:** Inside / outside-right

**BIRTHPLACE:** Glasgow, Lanarkshire

**DATE OF BIRTH:** 22/01/1867 - 11/02/1940

**HEIGHT:** 5' 4" **WEIGHT:** 11st 0lbs

**SIGNED FROM:** Renton, 22/06/1889 and Clyde, 09/09/1892

**DEBUT:** v Blackburn Rovers, A, 18/01/1890

**LAST MATCH:** v Newton Heath, H, 26/04/1897

**MOVED TO:** Clyde 10/08/1891 and Newcastle United, 10/05/1897

**TEAMS:** Renton, Sunderland, Clyde, Sunderland, Newcastle United

**SAFC TOTALS:** 109 appearances / 14 goals

**Sunderland's first-ever professional player remains the joint smallest player ever to play for the club. He was nicknamed 'The Little Big'un.' Harvie, who preferred his name to be spelled Harvey, but was really Harvie, played in two title-winning seasons at Sunderland.**

Having played in the club's inaugural league campaign, he spent 1891-92 with Clyde as Sunderland became league champions for the first time, but returned to feature strongly as the title was retained in 1893 and played in six league games as it was won again in 1895. He also scored in that year's game against Hearts when Sunderland were proclaimed world champions.

Two years later, he was one of five members of the ageing 'Team of All The Talents' to sign off in the Test Match that staved off relegation. He then moved to Newcastle United along with Johnny Campbell for a joint fee of £80. The Magpies would be the third club the pair had played at together having both been at Renton before coming to Wearside.

At the end of his first season on Tyneside, he scored the winner in a Test Match against Stoke, though this last set of Test Matches were rendered redundant when the Football League decided to expand the first division, allowing Newcastle to be promoted although their play-off position had been insufficient.

Having used his guile and experience to help guide Newcastle to the top level, Harvie played in their inaugural first division fixture against Wolves, who he had made his league debut against for Sunderland (He had previously played against Blackburn Rovers in the cup).

Going on to become trainer for United's reserves in the Alliance from 1899, by the end of the following decade, Harvie, who as a fitter by trade, was back on Wearside working as an electrical engineer. He later moved to Teesside where he worked for ICI until he retired.

## HASTINGS, Alexander Cockburn

**POSITION:** Half-back

**BIRTHPLACE:** Falkirk, Stirlingshire

**DATE OF BIRTH:** 17/03/1912 - 26/12/1988

**HEIGHT:** 5' 10½" **WEIGHT:** 11st 5lbs

**SIGNED FROM:** Stenhousemuir, 05/08/1930

**DEBUT:** v Portsmouth, A, 06/09/1930

**LAST MATCH:** v Birmingham City, H, 09/02/1946

**MOVED TO:** Retired, 18/02/1946

**TEAMS:** Carron Welfare, Rosewell Rosedale, Stenhousemuir, Sunderland, Hartlepools United (WW2 Guest)

**INTERNATIONAL:** Scotland

**SAFC TOTALS:** 297 appearances / 6 goals

**Captain of the 1935-36 league champions, Alex Hastings missed most of the second half of the following cup-winning campaign, but did play in the semi-final. Like the rest of his generation, Hastings missed many of what should have been his best years due to war.**

He was 27 when World War Two began. Officially he fell three games short of 300 for Sunderland, but he also played in the three league games of 1939-40 before that season was abandoned and removed from official records. On top of that, he made a further 128 appearances for Sunderland in war-time games, giving him a total figure of 428 that would place him in the all-time top ten were they all peacetime matches. A model of consistency, from his debut in 1930 until the outbreak of war, Alex played 30 games or more in all bar two seasons when he managed 22 and 27. During the war he worked as a maintenance engineer in Sunderland.

Mostly he played at left or right-half, but could also play at centre-forward, a position in which he had been a prolific scorer as a boy. During his title-winning season at Sunderland, he debuted for Scotland against Ireland at Tynecastle. The second of his two caps came against the same opposition at Aberdeen in November 1937.

From March 1948 until April 1950, he managed Kilmarnock and also continued as a scout for Stoke City and Hearts. Following retirement as a player he owned a post office /general dealer in Seaburn and also ran a hotel in Monkton as well as becoming a licensee in his native Falkirk and sports editor of a Sunday newspaper.

While in Sunderland, he lived in Malvern Gardens next door to the family of 1890s Sunderland skipper Johnny Auld. In 1965, he emigrated to Australia where he worked as an insurance agent and founded a coaches association. To add to this, he spent twelve years as President of the South Australian Soccer Federation and received the British Empire Medal in June 1981.

## HASTINGS, Andrew Straiten

**POSITION:** Forward

**BIRTHPLACE:** Dumfries, Dumfries & Galloway

**DATE OF BIRTH:** 09/11/1865 - 10/09/1946

**HEIGHT:** 5' 7½" **WEIGHT:** 10st 7lbs

**SIGNED FROM:** Queen of the South Wanderers, 24/08/1887

**DEBUT:** v Morpeth Harriers, H, 22/10/1887

**LAST MATCH:** v Middlesbrough, A, 26/11/1887

**MOVED TO:** Sunderland Albion, 27/08/1888

**TEAMS:** Dumfries Courier & Herald, Vale of Nith, Queen of the South Wanderers, Sunderland, Sunderland Albion

**SAFC TOTALS:** 3 appearances / 0 goals

**Reported in the contemporary press as Sunderland's first 'imported player.' He certainly caused problems! Along with fellow Scots George Monaghan and Joe Richardson he was deemed to have been a non-local professional which was against the rules of the English Cup at the time.**

This led to Sunderland being disqualified from the competition despite beating Middlesbrough in a replay which Hastings missed, although he had played in an earlier 2-2 draw at Middlesbrough who protested. Playing in a different position in every game, Hastings had also played in earlier rounds against Morpeth Harriers and Newcastle West End. Sunderland were found guilty of paying the trio's train fares from Dumfries with the players punished by a three month ban in addition to club being kicked out of the cup.

Hastings had begun playing football with the Dumfries Courier and Herald where he worked as a printer compositor both before and after his playing days, going on to become the proprietor of the Waverley Hotel in Dumfries after his days in print. In December 1888 he played against Sunderland for Sunderland Albion.

## HASTINGS, John George

**POSITION:** Right-back

**BIRTHPLACE:** Thornaby, North Yorkshire

**DATE OF BIRTH:** 31/03/1887 - 01/04/1972

**HEIGHT:** 5' 8" **WEIGHT:** 11st 7lbs

**SIGNED FROM:** Darlington St Augustine,03/02/1909

**DEBUT:** v Preston North End, H, 24/04/1909

**LAST MATCH:** v Preston North End, H, 24/04/1909

**MOVED TO:** Retired, 31/05/1913

**TEAMS:** Thornaby St Mark's Darlington St. Augustine, Sunderland

**SAFC TOTALS:** 1 appearance / 0 goals

**Sunderland signed John on professional forms after an impressive display for Darlington St Augustine against the Northern Nomads in an FA Amateur Cup tie.**

A full-back at the club for over four years Hastings' solitary appearance came in an end of season game. Unable to break into the side after that injury forced his retirement at the end of Sunderland's near double season of 1912-13 after which he became a shipwright.

## HAUSER, Thomas

**POSITION:** Centre-forward

**BIRTHPLACE:** Schopfheim, Germany

**DATE OF BIRTH:** 10/04/1965

**HEIGHT:** 6' 3" **WEIGHT:** 12st 6lbs

**SIGNED FROM:** Basle Old Boys, 22/02/1989

**DEBUT:** v Hull City, H, 25/02/1989

**LAST MATCH:** v Tranmere Rovers, A, 26/12/1991

**MOVED TO:** SC Cambuur, 09/10/1992

**TEAMS:** Sportclub Schopfheim, FC Basle, Basle OB, Sunderland, FC Koln (L), SC Cambuur

**INTERNATIONAL:** West Germany Schools

**SAFC TOTALS:** 26+39 appearance / 11 goals

**Thomas Hauser became the first German-born player to score in the first division when he netted at Southampton on 13 April 1991. Previously he had scored Sunderland's first goal of the 1990s and the final one of the 1980s. A gangly, but willing centre-forward, he was brought in by Denis Smith with the aim of replacing the ageing Eric Gates as Marco Gabbiadini's striker partner, but Hauser was a totally different player to Gates, more like Keith Bertschin who originally Gabbiadini had been bought to play alongside.**

The 'G-Force' had such an understanding that it was very difficult for anyone to replicate and Thomas was destined to spend most of his time as a sub, even coming off the bench to replace Gates at Wembley in the 1990 Play-Off final against Swindon Town.

Hauser had begun his senior career on 23 April 1983 in Switzerland for Basle with whom he soon won the Uhren Cup after scoring against FC Grenchen in the semi-final. He went on to score 77 times in 155 games for Basle including four in a 9-1 Swiss Cup win over Concordia Basle in September 1985 and all six in a 6-3 'Test game' on 6 October 1983 against SC Ciba-Geigy Rosental.

When FC Basle were relegated in 1988, he moved to Basle Old Boys before joining Sunderland after under a season for a reported fee of £200,000. After leaving Sunderland he played twice in the Eredivisie for SC Cambuur in the Netherlands where he went on to work in sales. Later he scouted for Rangers and in 2012, coached back at Basle Old Boys while later in the decade he focussed on supporting his daughter's budding tennis career. Hauser always remained a keen Sunderland supporter often enquiring about how things are at the club.

## HAWES, Arthur Robert

**POSITION:** Inside-left

**BIRTHPLACE:** Swanton Morley, Norfolk

**DATE OF BIRTH:** 02/10/1895 - 11/10/1963

**HEIGHT:** 5' 8" **WEIGHT:** 10st 7lbs

**SIGNED FROM:** South Shields, 22/12/1921

**DEBUT:** v West Bromwich Albion, H, 24/12/1921

**LAST MATCH:** v Sheffield United, A, 16/04/1927

**MOVED TO:** Bradford Park Avenue, 22/08/1927

**TEAMS:** Junior Institute, Norwich CEYMS, Boulton & Paul's, Norwich City, South Shields, Sunderland, Bradford Park Avenue, Accrington Stanley, Nelson, Hyde United, Wombwell, Rochdale, Goole Town

**SAFC TOTALS:** 147 appearance / 39 goals

**'Tricky' Hawes always played with a handkerchief in his left hand, but there was never any sign of surrender from a player who appeared in 75 out of 84 games across 1922-23 and 1923-24 as Sunderland finished second and third in the top flight. He remained a regular in 1924-25 as the Lads dropped to seventh. In all Hawes appeared in six seasons of the roaring twenties during which he was often a vital player.**

Named after his father, who spent over two decades as assistant trainer at Norwich City, Hawes first played for Thorpe Hamlet School before working his way to Norwich City via local football where he gained County honours. He scored on his Canaries debut against Newport County on 30 August 1919 and added seven more in a further 35 Southern League outings.

He came to the north-east at the end of that season, signing for South Shields who were in the second division of the Football League at the time. Eighteen goals in 52 games for Shields persuaded Sunderland to spend £1,750 on him just before Christmas in 1921. Debuting on Christmas Eve, he scored twice in a 5-0 thrashing of WBA. At Sunderland, he formed an effective left-flank partnership with Billy Ellis and developed a penchant for doing well against Newcastle United, scoring three of his goals against them.

After moving on to Bradford Park Avenue for £650, he came close to replicating his South Shields statistics with 17 goals in 53 games, winning the Third Division North in his first season of 1927-28. At Accrington Stanley, he scored nine in 39 and added four games for Nelson in their last campaign as a league club with a last 13-game league stint with Rochdale in 1932, either side of several spells with non-league clubs.

In later life he returned to his native Norfolk where he became trainer and Vice-Chairman of Eastern Counties League side Gothic FC and worked for Laurence and Scott who manufactured electrical motors.

## HAWKE, Warren Robert

**POSITION:** Forward

**BIRTHPLACE:** Durham, Co Durham

**DATE OF BIRTH:** 20/09/1970

**HEIGHT:** 5' 10" **WEIGHT:** 10st 11lbs

**SIGNED FROM:** Gosforth St Nicholas, 09/09/1987

**DEBUT:** v Portsmouth, A, 08/04/1989

**LAST MATCH:** v Luton Town, A, 19/12/1992

**MOVED TO:** Released, 13/05/1993

**TEAMS:** Gosforth St Nicholas, Sunderland, Chesterfield (L), Carlisle United (L), Northampton Town (L), Raith Rovers, Scarborough, Berwick Rangers, Greenock Morton, Queen of the South, Greenock Morton

**SAFC TOTALS:** 10+19 appearance / 1 goal

**Warren signed associate schoolboy forms with Sunderland whilst still at Monkseaton High School. An elegant and intelligent player, Hawke never started more than three league games in the five seasons where he appeared for the first team at Sunderland but played in two famous matches.**

As well as coming off the bench in the FA Cup final in 1992, he started the second leg of the 1990 Play-Off semi-final second leg at Newcastle. Although he had a hand in Marco Gabbiadini's killer goal in that game and had scored what was his only first team goal at Swindon on the opening day of the season, he was not involved as Sunderland met Swindon in the Play-Off final.

On 28 October 1989, he scored six goals for the youth team in a 7-1 win over Grimsby Town and during his time at SAFC had three loans, scoring once in seven games for each of Chesterfield and Northampton, either side of an eight-game and two-goal spell with Carlisle. Following his release from Roker Park, Hawke signed for Raith Rovers where Jimmy Nicholl and Martin Harvey were in charge. He played in the first two games of the season, the second as a substitute before switching to Berwick Rangers.

Debuting for the Borderers on 4 December 1993, he then played once more back at Scarborough a fortnight later in a home defeat to Hereford a week before returning to Berwick. It was there that he found regular football, going on to play 20 times that season and registering a dozen goals as they finished second in Division Two. The following season he top-scored with 16 goals in 35 league games including a late season hat-trick against Morton who he would go on to join at the end of the campaign. In four years at Greenock, Warren played 145 league games scoring 34 times before two years at Queen of the South where he scored seven in 55. He then returned to Morton to add another nine goals in 64 games playing until 2005, with a final appearance against Berwick on the last day of the season.

Returning to Morton in 2012, he became a consultant before joining the board of directors in June 2015 and becoming Chief Executive two years later. In 2017, he became the Scottish Championship's director at the Scottish Professional Football League. Hawke stayed with Morton until 2019 when he set up his own company, Strenua Ltd, providing sports consultancy services. A fitness fanatic, Hawke also completed Iron Man triathlon challenges and swam the length of Loch Lomond - two miles longer than the English Channel. His son Lewis listed Morton, Annan Athletic, Queen's Park, Stirling Albion and Montrose among his clubs, to 2022.

## HAWKES, Joshua Stuart

**POSITION:** Forward

**BIRTHPLACE:** Stockton, County Durham

**DATE OF BIRTH:** 28/01/1999

**HEIGHT:** 6' 0" **WEIGHT:** 11st 9lbs

**SIGNED FROM:** Free agent, 15/09/2020

**DEBUT:** v Fleetwood Town, A, 10/11/2020

**LAST MATCH:** v Lincoln City, H, 11/01/2022

**MOVED TO:** Tranmere Rovers, 25/01/2022

**TEAMS:** Hartlepool United, Marske United (L), Dunston UTS (L), Sunderland, Tranmere Rovers (to June 2022)

**SAFC TOTALS:** 2+1 appearance / 1 goal

**Debuting for Hartlepool as a sub against Crewe Alexandra on 28 February 2017, Hawkes again came off the bench in the next game, but these were his only two appearances before Pools dropped out of the Football League.**

The following season he appeared in twelve of the last 15 games, grabbing his first goals against Bromley and Sutton United, and went on to total twelve goals in 30+29 National League games. Josh also played twice for Marske and four times for Dunston, scoring twice for the latter during loans from Hartlepool.

Hawkes was a free agent when he signed for the Lads after being released by Hartlepool United at the end of June 2020. Two months after joining Sunderland, he got his only first-team game of his first season as part of a young team in a Football League Trophy game at Fleetwood. During his first season he impressed at Under 23 level, scoring his first goal in a 4-0 win at Newcastle on 5 October 2020 and reaching double figures for the season including a goal in a Play-Off semi-final win at Stoke.

Shortly after scoring his first goal for Sunderland in a League (Carabao) Cup tie at Port Vale in 2021 he was allowed to go on loan to Tranmere Rovers where he was a success and signed permanently a couple of weeks after being recalled due to a spate of injuries at Sunderland and making his only league appearance for the club as an 80th-minute substitute.

## HAWLEY, John East

**POSITION:** Centre-forward

**BIRTHPLACE:** Patrington, East Yorkshire

**DATE OF BIRTH:** 08/05/1954

**HEIGHT:** 6' 0" **WEIGHT:** 13st 12lbs

**SIGNED FROM:** Leeds United, 01/10/1979

**DEBUT:** v Manchester City, H, 03/10/1979

**LAST MATCH:** v Leeds United, A, 21/02/1981

**MOVED TO:** Arsenal, 09/09/1981

**TEAMS:** Hull City, St Louis Stars (L), Leeds United, Sunderland, Arsenal, Orient (L), Hull City (L), Happy Valley, Bradford City, Scunthorpe United

**SAFC TOTALS:** 31 appearance / 11 goals

**John Hawley had some memorable days in his short time at Sunderland. In December 1980, he scored one of Roker Park's greatest goals at the Roker End. It was a shot from 40 yards that flew past Arsenal's renowned goalkeeper Pat Jennings.**

At the start of that season he had smashed a hat-trick at Manchester City that took newly-promoted Sunderland to the top of the embryonic table. Manchester City had also been the opposition for his debut in the League Cup after which he marked his league debut with a hat-trick against Charlton.

Unfortunately, injuries hindered Hawley's time at Sunderland who he joined after playing for former Sunderland manager Jimmy Adamson. John had spent 18 months at Elland Road where he was a teammate of Frank Gray. Hawley top-scored for Leeds with 17 goals in his first season of 1978-79, but there was just one more game before a £200,000 move to Sunderland.

That goal against Arsenal no doubt helped when he joined the Gunners from Sunderland who recouped forty per-cent of their outlay just before the second anniversary of Hawley's arrival. After playing for Arsenal reserves in a Football Combination game against Leicester City, he debuted at home to Manchester United on 26 September 1981. Hawley scored in his next game at Notts County, but spent more time in the reserves than the first team at Highbury where his final first-team game came in a home defeat to Sunderland in May 1983. In total Hawley played 15+6 first-team games, scoring three goals as well as 30+1 games, scoring ten times for the reserves. He also scored twice in 9+2 friendlies for Arsenal who loaned him to Orient (4/1) and Hull (3/1) in October and November 1982.

Hull had been where John had begun his career. Committed to the family antiques business, he played as an amateur until he was 22. He made 114 league appearances for the Tigers, scoring 22 times and added eleven goals in 20 NASL games when on loan to St Louis Stars in 1975-76. There was more globe-trotting, possibly inspired by that loan to Orient, when he moved to Happy Valley in Hong Kong after being released by Arsenal. He came back to England in 1983 to join Bradford City.

Playing alongside his old Leeds teammates Trevor Cherry and Terry Yorath, Hawley top-scored with 23 goals (including a hat-trick v Wigan) in 45 games as the Bantams won Division Three. Playing alongside a young Don Goodman, Hawley scored another nine in 23+6 games the following season (68+6/32 total), his final match being on the tragic occasion of the Bradford fire where 56 people were killed at a match with Lincoln City on 11 May 1985. John was reported to have pulled a supporter to safety on that fateful day.

That summer, Hawley made his final move, joining Scunthorpe United where a hat-trick against Halifax three days before Christmas was the highlight of his seven goal spell in 23 league games which ended against Northampton on 18 March 1986. Following his retirement, Hawley returned to work in his father's antiques business in Beverley and became an auctioneer. Not a footballer with an encyclopaedic recollection of his own career, like Peter Davenport or Jermain Defoe for instance, John Hawley was a laid-back character, and one who had lots of great days, but not many great seasons.

## HAY, Alan Browning

**POSITION:** Defender

**BIRTHPLACE:** Dunfermline, Fife

**DATE OF BIRTH:** 28/11/1958

**HEIGHT:** 6' 0" **WEIGHT:** 12st 6lbs

**SIGNED FROM:** York City, 04/02/1989

**DEBUT:** v Ipswich Town, H, 25/03/1989

**LAST MATCH:** v Ipswich Town, H, 25/03/1989

**MOVED TO:** Released, 15/05/1989

**TEAMS:** Riverside Boys' Club, Dundee, Bolton Wanderers, Bristol City, St Mirren (L), York City, Tranmere Rovers, Hill of Beath, York City, Sunderland, Torquay United

**INTERNATIONAL:** Scotland Under 18

**SAFC TOTALS:** 1 appearance / 0 goals

**Signed by Denis Smith who had managed him at York, Hay's Sunderland career lasted under half an hour as a calf strain resulted in his substitution after 28 minutes of his only appearance following almost 18 months out of the senior game.**

In 1983-84, Hay missed just four of York's 46 league games as a teammate of Ricky Sbragia, John MacPhail, Malcolm Crosby, John Byrne and occasionally Viv Busby as the Minstermen won Division Four with 101 points. The following year as Marco Gabbiadini came into the York picture, Hay was part of the side that famously knocked Arsenal out of the FA Cup and held Liverpool to a draw at Anfield, although they were thrashed 7-0 in the replay. In total, Alan played 179+4 times for York, chipping in with four goals.

Hailing from Ian Porterfield and Jim Baxter country, Hay was a tough tackler who, after winning a Scottish Under 16 cup with Riverside BC, joined Dundee and spent over a year with Bolton before making his league breakthrough with Bristol City in the top-flight. Debuting as a sub in a goalless draw at Everton on 29 September 1979, he played alongside Tom Ritchie and went on to make three starts as the Robins were relegated. He appeared in 74 league games for the club, scoring once, before his move to York and added 28 league appearances for Tranmere Rovers. Alan then had a short spell back home with Hill of Beath before a single further game at York.

After his ill-fated time at Sunderland, Hay completed his football career with ten league appearances for Torquay United in 1989-90. From June to September in 1994, he worked as assistant manager to John MacPhail at Hartlepool United and then linked up as MacPhail's assistant again at South Tyneside United in the Wearside League in 1995. In later life, Hay found employment as a driver for a security company.

## HEALEY, Richard (Dick)

**POSITION:** Inside-forward

**BIRTHPLACE:** Darlington, Co Durham

**DATE OF BIRTH:** 20/09/1889 - 04/11/1974

**HEIGHT:** 5' 11" **WEIGHT:** 12st 7lbs

**SIGNED FROM:** Darlington, 10/03/1910

**DEBUT:** v Manchester United, A, 16/04/1910

**LAST MATCH:** v Aston Villa, A, 07/10/1911

**MOVED TO:** Bishop Auckland, 01/01/1912

**TEAMS:** Darlington, Sunderland, Stockton, Bishop Auckland, Middlesbrough, Darlington

**INTERNATIONAL:** England amateur

**SAFC TOTALS:** 3 appearances / 2 goals

**Dick Healey scored twice on his only home appearance. His goals came in a 3-0 win over Bradford City a week after his debut. It was the last home fixture of 1909-10, but he had to wait 18 months for his one further game.**

In between those second and third Sunderland appearances, his amateur status allowed him to turn out for Stockton in August 1910, but he was still a Sunderland player when he scored the opening goal in a 3-0 win for England amateurs against France in Paris on 23 March 1911. Two months later he scored against Switzerland in Bern where he was a teammate of former Sunderland goalkeeper Ron Brebner.

He won two further caps after he left Sunderland. A month after he joined Bishop Auckland he scored at the ground of his new club against Wales, again with Brebner as a colleague. The following November, Healey maintained his hundred-per-cent record of scoring in all four of his internationals, all of which were won, the last by 4-0 against Belgium at Swindon.

At Sunderland, Healey had played alongside George Holley and came up against him again in October 1913 when Holley scored twice for the Professionals as Healey played for the Amateurs. This was in a Charity Shield match at Millwall where the Professionals were almost entirely the same line-up as had appeared in England's most recent match, Sunderland's Frank Cuggy amongst them. With Brebner again in goal, the amateurs lost 7-2 in a game where the proceeds were donated to support the families of the 440 people killed in a colliery disaster at Senghenydd in South Wales.

In 1908, he commenced a course in science at Armstrong College in Newcastle and later became a teacher as well as working as a Special Constable in Darlington during the Second World War. In April 1914, he made a scoring debut for Middlesbrough in a 4-1 first division win over Preston where he was joined on the scoresheet by former Sunderland forward Walter Tinsley. Always likely to get a goal, Healey also scored against Bradford Park Avenue in one of his three other appearances for the Teessiders, which all came in 1914-15.

A keen cricketer who represented Darlington and County Durham, after World War One he made 22 league appearances, scoring five times, in Darlington's first two seasons as a Football League Club in 1921-22 and 1922-23.

## HEALY, Colin

**POSITION:** Midfielder

**BIRTHPLACE:** Ballincollig, County Cork

**DATE OF BIRTH:** 14/03/1980

**HEIGHT:** 6' 1" **WEIGHT:** 12st 13lbs

**SIGNED FROM:** Celtic, 14/08/2003

**DEBUT:** v Preston North End, A, 23/08/2003

**LAST MATCH:** v Coventry City, A, 08/12/2003

**MOVED TO:** Contract not renewed, 16/01/2006

**TEAMS:** Ballincollig, Wilton United, Celtic, Coventry City (L), Sunderland, Livingston, Barnsley, Bradford City (L), Cork City, Ipswich Town, Falkirk (L)

**INTERNATIONAL:** Republic of Ireland

**SAFC TOTALS:** 16+4 appearances / 0 goals

**One of the quietest players ever to wear red and white stripes, Colin Healy would invariably decline requests to interview to him with a smile and a gentle, "I'm grand" delivered in a Cork lilt as delicate as one of his finely weighted passes.**

Ironically, the talented midfielder was anything but grand after suffering an horrendous injury playing in his final game for Sunderland, one that had nearby Coventry midfielder Gary McAllister ignoring the ball and screaming for Sunderland physio Pete Friar to rush on and attend to the stricken Healy.

Colin had been thrown into the cauldron of an Old Firm fixture for his debut for Celtic against Rangers on 2 May 1999. He did well enough to be given a run of games in the side by manager Dr Joseph Venglos, but when John Barnes took over, he was left out of the first-team picture. Restored to the line-up during the reign of Kenny Dalglish, Healy went on to play for Martin O'Neill under whom he won a League Cup medal and helped O'Neill's men to the title in 2001, although he never featured in their successful Scottish Cup side.

O'Neill would go on to manage Sunderland and the Republic of Ireland, but it was Healy's old Republic of Ireland boss Mick McCarthy who brought Colin to Wearside. Ironically, as Healy recovered from his bad leg-break against Coventry, reportedly it was in a training tackle with McCarthy in September 2004 that he broke his leg once more. Healy seemed fated to be a nearly man. McCarthy had attempted to call him up for the Republic's 2002 FIFA World Cup squad as a replacement for Roy Keane only for the deadline for replacements to have passed.

Later, as he recovered again after playing briefly for Livingston, Barnsley and Bradford, he went to his native Cork to play for Cork City only for FIFA to ban him until July 2007 under their 'Three club rule.' After eventually proving his fitness with Cork, Roy Keane took him to Ipswich.

Loaned to Falkirk, he re-signed for Cork City in January 2012 and went on to win the President's Cup with them in March 2016, and play in the same year's FAI Cup final. His statistics in Britain other than at Sunderland read: Celtic 27+21/3, Coventry 17/2, Livingston 6+3/2, Barnsley 2+8/0, Bradford 4/0, Ipswich 18+10/2 and Falkirk 17+2/1.

At international level, he played in the FIFA World Youth Championships in Nigeria in 1999 (scoring against Australia) and was a bronze medallist the same year in Sweden in the UEFA Under 19 Championship. His full international debut came on 13 February 2002 in a Dublin friendly against Russia. He went on to play in eight more friendlies and four qualifying games for Euro 2004, his 13th and final cap coming in a defeat against Switzerland in Basle in October 2003 shortly before that leg break at Coventry.

## HEALY, David Jonathan

**POSITION:** Forward

**BIRTHPLACE:** Killyleagh, County Down

**DATE OF BIRTH:** 05/08/1979

**HEIGHT:** 5' 8" **WEIGHT:** 11st 12lbs

**SIGNED FROM:** Fulham, 21/08/2008

**DEBUT:** v Nottingham Forest, A, 27/08/2008

**LAST MATCH:** v Portsmouth, A, 23/01/2010

**MOVED TO:** Rangers, 30/01/2011

**TEAMS:** Manchester United, Port Vale (L), Preston North End, Norwich City (L), Leeds United, Fulham, Sunderland, Ipswich Town (L), Doncaster Rovers (L), Rangers, Bury

**INTERNATIONAL:** Northern Ireland

**SAFC TOTALS:** 3+18 appearances / 3 goals

**Awarded an MBE in 2008, Northern Ireland's record goalscorer was never given a league start at Sunderland. Thirteen times he came off the bench in league games, but his only occasions in the starting line-ups were in cup ties.**

A goalscoring legend for Northern Ireland, his 13 goals in the 2008 European qualifying campaign is an all-time record shared with Robert Lewandowski as of 2022. Two goals on his international debut against Luxembourg on 23 February 2000 set the tone for his Northern Ireland career. Another brace as he won his 35th cap against Trinidad & Tobago (who included Carlos Edwards, Stern John and sub Dwight Yorke, whilst Jeff Whitley was in the Irish line-up) on 6 June 2004, took his tally to 14, thereby making Healy his country's record scorer.

In September of the following year, David added to his status with the winner in a World Cup qualifier that gave Northern Ireland their first win over England since 1972. A year almost to the day later, his hat-trick against Spain was the first by a Northern Irish player in Belfast since George Best against Cyprus in 1971. Healy promptly became the first man to score two international hat-tricks for Northern Ireland in Belfast when he did so against Liechtenstein next time out. In total, he scored 36 international goals in 95 appearances.

At club level, he began with Manchester United after playing for Crossgar, Lisburn Youth and Down Academy High School. Debuting for United in a League Cup tie at Aston Villa on 13 October 1999, he made his second appearance in the same competition at Sunderland the following month.

## HEALY, David (Continued)

He then went on loan to Port Vale where he scored three times in 16 games before getting his only 30 minutes as a Premiership player with United in a 2-0 home win over Ipswich two days before Christmas in 2000, when the woodwork denied him a goal. Six days later, he joined Preston on loan with that move swiftly completed for a £1.5m (plus add-ons) fee, after he took just four minutes to score for his new club at Sheffield Utd.

There were to be 45 goals in 156 outings for North End with two in 14 games during a loan to Norwich before an October 2004 transfer to Leeds who paid £650,000. A teammate of Paul Butler, Matt Kilgallon and Liam Miller at Elland Road, Healy played as a sub in the 2006 Championship Play-Off final lost to Watford, but was relegated to League One a year later despite being top-scorer with ten goals.

This took his Leeds tally to 31 in 121 games, many of which saw him utilised in a wide right position. As Leeds went down, David went up with a move to Premier League Fulham when his former Northern Ireland manager Lawrie Sanchez invested £1.5m. There was an immediate return with a goal against Arsenal in the first minute of his debut and another strike on his second appearance, but there were just four more club goals that season, one of them against Sunderland at Craven Cottage in April 2008 - four months before his transfer to the Black Cats for a reported £1.2m.

During his time with SAFC, Healy was loaned to Ipswich Town (5+7/1) and Doncaster Rovers (6+2/2) who he made a scoring debut for (v Millwall 06/11/2010), as he had for Sunderland, Leeds, Fulham and Northern Ireland. Healy added Rangers and Bury to that list with a goal for the Gers against Motherwell following his January 2011 transfer from Sunderland and one for Bury at Coventry. This came after 18 months at Ibrox which brought five goals in 11+13 games which included a couple of substitute appearances in the Europa League. That debut penalty goal for Bury was his solitary strike for the Shakers who were relegated to League Two. He played another 18 times for the club, eight of those as sub.

Healy retired in December 2013, but seven months later appeared for Glenavon in a pre-season friendly with Leeds United. In October 2015 David became manager of Linfield and sold Trai Hume to Sunderland in 2022. In 2020-21 as he led his team to their fourth Northern Ireland Premiership title under him in a year he was named Northern Ireland Manager of the Year for the third time. That season also saw Linfield win the League Cup under him for the second time. Such success brought regular European football, most notably a Champions League meeting with Celtic in 2017.

## HEATHCOTE, Michael (Mick)

**POSITION:** Centre-back

**BIRTHPLACE:** Kelloe, Co Durham

**DATE OF BIRTH:** 10/09/1965

**HEIGHT:** 6' 2" **WEIGHT:** 12st 5lbs

**SIGNED FROM:** Spennymoor United, 19/08/1987

**DEBUT:** v Southend United, H, 03/11/1987

**LAST MATCH:** v Oldham Athletic, H, 05/05/1990

**MOVED TO:** Shrewsbury Town, 06/07/1990

**TEAMS:** Middlesbrough, Spennymoor United, Sunderland, Halifax Town (L), York City (L), Shrewsbury Town, Cambridge United, Plymouth Argyle, Shrewsbury Town, Colwyn Bay, Leek Town, Hucknall Town

**SAFC TOTALS:** 6+4 appearances / 0 goals

**Debuting as a sub for fellow debutant Richard Ord in a 7-0 win, Heathcote was stretchered off after playing for only 18 minutes, but was fit to play again later the same month - when Sunderland again scored seven, this time in a cup-tie with Rotherham.**

Heathcote did not play for the first team again for almost exactly two years during which he had loans to Halifax (8/1) and York (4/0). After making his long-awaited third Sunderland appearance there was a further five-month gap until his full debut. That came in the famous 4-3 win over West Ham remembered for Kieron Brady's superlative display. Heathcote featured in seven of the last eleven fixtures of the regular league season, but did not appear in the Play-Offs when the club requested he was the cover star of the match programme v Newcastle in recognition of his battles with injury.

Sold to Shrewsbury for £55,000 that summer, he moved on to Cambridge United for £150,000 after just over a season in which he helped Shrewsbury to an FA Cup fifth-round tie with Arsenal and was joint top league scorer for the struggling Shrews with six goals, mainly headers from corners. One of those goals came in a late-season match between the Shrews and the U's who won the third tier and felt Mick could help them at a higher level. A teammate of Tommy Lynch at Shrewsbury, Mick made 54+1 appearances in his first spell with the club.

At Cambridge, there were 13 goals in 128 league games over four years before a £75,000 move to Neil Warnock's Plymouth. Heathcote captained Argyle to promotion via the fourth tier Play-Offs in what was Plymouth's only appearance at the original Wembley. The Pilgrims defeated a Darlington side that included old Roker reserves Steve Gaughan and Phil Brumwell. Twice Plymouth Player of the Year, Heathcote continued to be troubled by back problems at Home Park, but managed 231+5 games (17 goals), the last appearance coming against his old loan club Halifax two days before Christmas in 2000.

Returning to Shrewsbury, Heathcote added two goals and 40 league appearances to his tally before finishing his career in non-league, notably scoring a shoot-out penalty in the 2005 FA Trophy final which his Hucknall Town team lost to Grays Athletic at Villa Park. At the opposite end of his career before coming to Sunderland for £15,000 from Spennymoor, Mick had worked for three years as a van driver after leaving Middlesbrough when he was 19.

## HEDLEY, John Robert (Jack)

**POSITION:** Full-back

**BIRTHPLACE:** Willington Quay, Co Durham

**DATE OF BIRTH:** 11/12/1923 - 02/06/1985

**HEIGHT:** 5' 9" **WEIGHT:** 11st 7lbs

**SIGNED FROM:** Everton, 03/08/1950

**DEBUT:** v Liverpool, A, 26/08/1950

**LAST MATCH:** v Charlton Athletic, H, 18/10/1958

**MOVED TO:** Gateshead, 01/07/1959

**TEAMS:** Willington Quay, North Shields, Everton, Sunderland, Gateshead

**SAFC TOTALS:** 295 appearances / 0 goals

**A largely unheralded member of the 'Bank of England' team of the 1950s, Jack Hedley gave excellent value for the £10,375 Sunderland paid for a full-back, who from 1950 to 1958 never made fewer than 27 appearances, and was ever-present in 1954-55 and 1956-57.**

Although a native of County Durham, Hedley came to Sunderland from Everton where he had played 61 games having joined them from local north-east football in 1945. Debuting against Aston Villa at Goodison Park on 17 September 1947, his last away appearance was at Sunderland in April 1950, a month after playing in an FA Cup semi-final against Liverpool at Manchester City. Only five (including his first three) games for the Toffees were at right-back with the rest spent in the number three shirt, but the 50,080 who saw his Sunderland debut on the other side of Stanley Park at Anfield saw him in the right-back berth he would nail down at Roker Park for almost a decade.

Hedley almost did not come to Sunderland. During the summer of his signature, he travelled to South America around the time England's first venture to the World Cup ended in humiliation in Brazil when they lost to the USA. This was in the age of the maximum wage. England centre-half Neil Frankin and future Newcastle manager Charlie Mitten had signed for Sante Fe in Columbia and Everton's Hedley along with Swansea's Roy Paul travelled to Columbia hoping to sign on for much more than they could earn in Britain. Both however, returned after a few days without signing, Paul signing for Manchester City that summer and captaining City against Hedley's Sunderland in the FA Cup semi-final of 1956. Sunderland legend Charlie Buchan - then a journalist working for the News Chronicle - tried endlessly to track them down on their journey via New York.

Hedley's highlights included playing in the FA Cup semi-final of 1955 as well as 1956, but as with his previous experience they ended in disappointment. After retiring from the game he became a noted competitor in the racing pigeon world.

## HEGAN, Daniel (Danny)

**POSITION:** Midfielder

**BIRTHPLACE:** Coatbridge, North Lanarkshire

**DATE OF BIRTH:** 14/06/1943 - 06/08/2015

**HEIGHT:** 5' 8" **WEIGHT:** 10st 6lbs

**SIGNED FROM:** Albion Rovers, 23/09/1961 and Wolverhampton Wanderers, 17/11/1973

**DEBUT:** v Nottingham Forest, H, 24/11/1973

**LAST MATCH:** v Oxford United, H, 12/01/1974

**MOVED TO:** Ipswich Town, 01/07/1963 and released, 30/06/1974

**TEAMS:** Bellshill Athletic, Albion Rovers, Sunderland, Ipswich Town, WBA, Wolverhampton Wanderers, Sunderland, Highlands Park, Coleshill Town, Clacton Town

**INTERNATIONAL:** Northern Ireland

**SAFC TOTALS:** 3+5 appearances / 0 goals

**As waits for a debut go, Danny's delay lasted longer than players who endured World War Two between them joining the club and being able to make a competitive debut. Over twelve years passed between Hegan signing and finally playing. He had almost two years at Sunderland in the early sixties as a teenager, leaving shortly after turning 20 without having been able to break into the side under Alan Brown.**

'Bomber' Brown was noted for giving youth a chance, but also for being a disciplinarian and Hegan was renowned for a social life more hectic than the midfield area he patrolled with the swagger of a natural talent.

With a low centre of gravity, natural ball control and immense self-belief, Hegan hailed from Coatbridge, home to the Hughes brothers, John Hughes being born just a couple of months before Danny. Leaving Sunderland, he was bought by Newcastle legend (and Sunderland war-time player) Jackie Milburn for Ipswich Town, who were beaten 6-0 by Bolton on his debut. There were better times as Hegan scored 38 goals in 230 games for Ipswich with whom he was a regular as they won the second division title in 1967-68 under Bill McGarry, who subsequently signed him for Wolves after he spent a year with West Brom in 1969-70.

Colin Suggett scored both goals as both ex-Sunderland men debuted for Albion in a 2-0 win at Southampton on the opening day of the 1969-70 season. Suggett had cost Sunderland's first £100,000 fee, while Hegan cost £88,000 plus Ian Collard in part-exchange. Hegan played in ten of the first twelve league games, but only made four more league appearances (one as sub) plus four in the League Cup as Albion went on to reach the final, although by then he was out of the side. One of his two goals earned a point against Liverpool.

May 1970 saw Hegan sign for nearby Wolves for £27,000, but after debuting at Newcastle on the opening day of the season he made only half a dozen more appearances as Wanderers finished fourth. The following year Danny played against Spurs in both legs of the UEFA Cup final having scored with an extravagant chip against Juventus in Wolves' run to the final, which they lost 3-2 on aggregate. A season later Hegan played against Spurs in another big game, the League Cup semi-final and also helped his side reach the FA Cup semi-final in the season Sunderland won it. On 27 October 1973 he made the last of his 65+5 appearances (8 goals) for Wolves back at Ipswich before a modest £5,000 fee finally brought him back to Roker Park after being disciplined by Wolves following another drinking binge.

After his twelve-year wait to wear red and white stripes, Hegan never appeared on a winning side at Sunderland, appearing as sub in both FA Cup games against Carlisle as Sunderland relinquished their grip on the trophy, Danny making his final appearance in senior football three days after the Lads were knocked out. Next stop was South Africa with Highlands Park after which he briefly played non-league before becoming a football coach at Butlins Holiday Camps at Minehead and Clacton; where he worked alongside charismatic County Durham-born former England cricketer Colin Milburn, and captained Clacton Town.

Hegan experienced international sport himself, winning seven caps for Northern Ireland who he qualified for due to his Irish father. Debuting in a World Cup qualifying defeat away to the USSR, a game that effectively cost the Irish a place at the 1970 World Cup, Hegan wore the number seven shirt vacated by George Best who was retained by Manchester United for a League Cup game. In May 1972, it was from Hegan's corner that player-manager Terry Neill scored the winner at Wembley in Northern Ireland's first win over England since 1957.

In 1982, Hegan spoke publicly of Billy Bremner's alleged attempt to bribe him at Wolves as Leeds went for the league title in 1972. Bremner successfully sued him for £100,000 in damages. In later life Danny settled in Birmingham working as a taxi-driver, labourer and industrial cleaner. In terms of talent he had been one of the best players of a golden generation, but the football world only saw fleeting glimpses of his greatness. He passed away after a battle with cancer.

## HELLAWELL, Michael Stephen (Mike)

**POSITION:** Outside-right

**BIRTHPLACE:** Keighley, Yorkshire

**DATE OF BIRTH:** 30/06/1938

**HEIGHT:** 5' 11" **WEIGHT:** 11st 6lbs

**SIGNED FROM:** Birmingham City, 23/01/1965

**DEBUT:** v Blackpool, H, 06/02/1965

**LAST MATCH:** v Arsenal, H, 20/08/1966

**MOVED TO:** Huddersfield Town, 22/09/1966

**TEAMS:** Salts FC, Huddersfield Town, QPR, Birmingham City, Sunderland, Huddersfield Town, Peterborough United, Bromsgrove Rovers, Nuneaton Borough

**INTERNATIONAL:** England

**SAFC TOTALS:** 45+1 appearances / 3 goals

**An England international, Mike Hellawell was a speed merchant on the wing but a little slower on the cricket pitch where as a right-arm medium-pace bowler he took six for 114 across his one first-class match for Warwickshire against Oxford University in 1962. In 1959-60, he had played in the Minor Counties Championship for Yorkshire Second XI and later became a professional cricketer with Walsall CC.**

Hellawell reached higher levels in football, winning two England caps in October 1962. He was one of four debutants as France held England to a draw at Hillsborough and also played in a 3-1 win over Northern Ireland at Windsor Park. Hellawell's international appearances came in between his two cup final appearances with Birmingham City.

In 1961, he scored against Roma in the first leg of the Inter-Cities Fairs Cup final which Blues lost on aggregate. In the semi-final, Mike had helped Birmingham beat Inter Milan in both legs. In 1963, he played in all nine games as City won the League Cup, including both legs of the final against Sunderland's semi-final conquerors and local rivals Aston Villa. In total, he played 213 games for Birmingham, scoring 33 goals.

Having been an amateur with Huddersfield, Hellawell made his league debut as a teenager for QPR against Exeter City in a Division Three South fixture on 26 February 1956. Although that was his only appearance of the season, he made the number seven shirt his own in the following campaign, missing just two late-season games and playing in an FA Cup defeat at Sunderland before a summer move to Birmingham after eight goals in a total of 50 appearances. He also gained a representative honour when playing for Division Three South in April 1957 against their Northern counterparts who included ex-Sunderland men Ivor Broadis and Bill Holden.

Hellawell came north himself when he joined Sunderland where he became the first-ever man named as a substitute by the club in the league when subs were introduced on the opening day of the 1965-66 season. The following month he became the first player to actually be substituted when he was replaced by Allan Gauden at Aston Villa. After a year and a half on Wearside he returned to finally play for Huddersfield where he had been an amateur as a youngster before finishing his football career with Peterborough.

Retiring in 1972 Hellawell became a greengrocer in Keighley where he was still living in 2021 when he published his autobiography, 'The Impossible is Possible - Keep Right On til the End of the Road.' Brother John played for Bradford City, Rotherham United, Darlington and Bradford Park Avenue between 1962 and 1969.

## HELMER, Thomas

**POSITION:** Centre-back

**BIRTHPLACE:** Herford, Germany

**DATE OF BIRTH:** 21/04/1965

**HEIGHT:** 6' 0" **WEIGHT:** 12st 1lb

**SIGNED FROM:** Bayern Munich, 09/07/1999

**DEBUT:** v Arsenal, H, 14/08/1999

**LAST MATCH:** v Leeds United, A, 21/08/1999

**MOVED TO:** Released from contract, 23/11/2000

**TEAMS:** Post SG, Bad Salzuflen, Armenia Bielefeld, Borussia Dortmund, Bayern Munich, Sunderland, Hertha Berlin (L)

**INTERNATIONAL:** Germany

**SAFC TOTALS:** 1+1 appearances / 0 goals

**Three years after playing in Germany's successful Euro '96 team Thomas Helmer came to Sunderland only for manager Peter Reid - in an echo of what had happened with Sweden international Jan Erikssen - to apparently decide 'his legs had gone.' Consequently, 34-year-old Helmer's adventure into English football spanned just eight days before he was loaned to Hertha Berlin for whom he scored once in five games.**

Best known as a centre-back or sweeper, Helmer had been at the pinnacle of the game in Germany for over a decade. He made 68 appearances for Germany, playing in the final of Euro '92 as well as '96 and in the FIFA World Cups of 1994 and 1998. The first of his five international goals was a winner against Italy while at club level, he played 190 Bundesliga games for Borussia Dortmund and 191 for Bayern having started in senior football with 39 appearances for Armenia Bielefeld.

A UEFA Cup winner as part of a star-studded Bayern team in 1996 he was an unused sub in the Champions League final three years later on the occasion of Manchester United's famous late comeback. That season he won the third of his three Bundesliga titles with Bayern, often captaining the side in his 26 appearances (21 in the Bundesliga) that term. In 1998 he had captained Bayern as they won the German Cup, the DFB-Pokal, although he had been part of a first-half tactical

## HELMER, Thomas (Continued)

double substitution as Bayern trailed to MSV Duisburg. He had won the same trophy in 1989 being part of the Dortmund side that defeated SV Werder Bremen and went on to beat Bayern in the German Supercup.

A big name in German football, after his playing days Helmer moved into journalism and TV as well as becoming Germany's ambassador to the children's charity 'FIFA for SOS Children's Villages'.

## HENDERSON, George Brown

**POSITION:** Centre-half

**BIRTHPLACE:** Kelty, Fife

**DATE OF BIRTH:** 09/01/1902 - 18/03/1975

**HEIGHT:** 6' 0½" **WEIGHT:** 12st 4lbs

**SIGNED FROM:** Edinburgh St Bernards, 15/08/1924

**DEBUT:** v Liverpool, A, 31/10/1925

**LAST MATCH:** v Bolton Wanderers, A, 20/02/1929

**MOVED TO:** Barnsley, 07/03/1929

**TEAMS:** Kelty Athletic, Edinburgh St Bernards, Sunderland, Barnsley, Glenavon, Cowdenbeath, Ross County

**SAFC TOTALS:** 50 appearances / 1 goal

**Henderson came to Sunderland in August 1924, a transfer fee of £750 going to Edinburgh St Bernards, once the Scottish Cup winners. It was on Halloween of 1925 that he debuted at Anfield. It looked like being something of a nightmare for the league leaders - that was Sunderland, not Liverpool - as the home side led 2-0 at half-time, but the Lads came back to take a point.**

Henderson's chance came on a day when Sunderland were without all three of their regular half-back line, Charlie Parker and Arthur Andrews being injured while Billy Clunas was otherwise occupied on the same afternoon scoring in Scotland's 3-0 win over Wales at Cardiff. Henderson did well enough to be called upon four more times during the season although Bob Kyle's side were unable to hold on to top spot, eventually finishing third, well behind Huddersfield who took the title for the third year in a row.

Third place was the outcome again the following season as Henderson managed 19 league and cup appearances. During the autumn he managed ten consecutive games, scoring his only goal for the club with the help of a deflection during that sequence to earn a 1-1 Roker draw with Aston Villa. However two and a half years later, his time at Roker was up after he had made another 18 appearances in 1927-28, and eight in his final season of 1928-29.

George moved to Barnsley for a fee of £1,300. It was to be a good move for Henderson who played 262 league and cup games for the Oakwell outfit, scoring a dozen goals and being part of the team who became Division Three North Champions in 1934 - having captained the club from 1931-32. Henderson stayed with Barnsley until 1937 when at the age of 35 after a trial with Glenavon he played a single game for Cowdenbeath. There was then a final stint with Ross County where he had two months as player-coach from January 1938. His much older brother John made one of his six appearances for Manchester City in a home defeat by Sunderland in April 1902 before going on to play for Southend United, Gillingham and Dunfermline Athletic.

## HENDERSON, Jordan Brian

**POSITION:** Midfielder

**BIRTHPLACE:** East Herrington, Sunderland, Tyne & Wear

**DATE OF BIRTH:** 17/06/1990

**HEIGHT:** 6' 3" **WEIGHT:** 11st 0lbs

**SIGNED FROM:** Trainee, 01/07/2006

**DEBUT:** v Chelsea, A, 01/11/2007

**LAST MATCH:** v West Ham United, A, 22/05/2011

**MOVED TO:** Liverpool, 09/06/2011

**TEAMS:** Sunderland, Coventry City (L), Liverpool (to June 2022)

**INTERNATIONAL:** England

**SAFC TOTALS:** 67+12 appearances / 5 goals

**First pictured in the Sunderland programme against Arsenal in May 1991, a month before his first birthday, Jordan Henderson was destined to become a star in red and white. He was still with Sunderland when he won his first full England cap at the age of 20 years and five months, when Fabio Capello gave him a Wembley start against a France side that included Yann M'Vila.**

While with Sunderland Jordan also won the first seven of his 25 Under 21 caps, scoring against Romania a month before his full debut. The previous year he had also made a single appearance at each of Under 20 and Under 19 level, the first against the Czech Republic in March 2009.

His appearance in the final of the delayed Euro 2020 championships which took place in the summer of 2021 was his 64th cap, one of which came at the Stadium of Light in May 2016 against an Australia side that included Bailey Wright. He also played in Euro 2012 and 2016 as well as the FIFA World Cups of 2014 and 2018 when he played in the semi-final. He was England Player of the Year in 2019 and England Under 21 Player of the Year in 2012. To July 2022 he had captained England eight times and won 69 caps.

Coming through the ranks in Sunderland's academy there had been question marks over his future at one point but Jordan's impeccable attitude won over any doubts. He first appeared in the first team as a sub in a home friendly against Juventus on 4 August 2007 and also impressed in a November 2007 Testimonial for Alex Lawrie at Falkirk. Shortly after that Jordan added to his growing reputation with a 30-yard goal at the Stadium of Light in an FA Youth Cup tie with Norwich. He went on to score screamers in the quarter finals and semi-final second leg at Charlton and Manchester City.

Debuting as a sub in a heavy Premier League defeat at Chelsea he was given a start in a League Cup tie with Blackburn before going out on a highly-successful loan to Coventry City where his first senior goal at Norwich on 18 February 2009 was the highlight of his 12+1 appearances for the Sky Blues.

The following 2009-10 campaign saw him play 38 times for Sunderland, 28 of those as starts and by 2010-11 all but one of his 39 games were in the starting line-up. For this writer at least, his sale to Liverpool that summer ranked as the most disappointing departure since the transfers of Dennis Tueart and Colin Todd in the 1970s. Sunderland pocketed a reported fee of £16m rising to £20m for a player who was about to turn 21.

To Liverpool it proved a bargain. Between 2010 and 2020 no one at any club played in more Premier League matches than Hendo's 308. To begin with, many Liverpool supporters were far from convinced by him and neither was Brendan Rodgers who tried to sell him to Fulham having inherited Jordan as part of the squad when he took over from Kenny Dalglish. Henderson however won Rodgers around to the extent that he appointed Jordan as captain following the departure of Steven Gerrard, a player who has consistently been unstinting in his praise for the Wearsider.

Henderson's success at Liverpool reached new heights once Jurgen Klopp took over. By 2022 his collection of honours was astonishing. In 2020 he captained Liverpool to their first-ever Premier League title. A year earlier, he led them to success in the Champions League, European Super Cup and World Club Championship. This haul added to his runners-up medals from the Champions League in 2018, Europa League in 2016, FA Cup in 2012, League Cup in 2016 and League Cup winner's medal from 2012. In 2022 Liverpool won both domestic cups and were runners-up in the Premier and Champions Leagues.

Sunderland's Young Player of the Year in 2010 and 2011, Henderson was Liverpool's Young Player of the Year in 2012, FWA Footballer of the Year in 2020 and Liverpool fans' Player of the Season in 2020. The Ultimate team player - and one who learned so much from being coached by Kevin Ball at youth level - the individual accolades were of little consequence to a player who always put everyone else first. An unofficial biography, 'Hendo: The Jordan Henderson Story' was published in 2020, by which time early in the Covid 19 pandemic he had already brought together the captains of all Premier League clubs to form #PLAYERSTOGETHER to raise money for the National Health Service. In 2021 he was awarded the MBE.

## HENDERSON, Michael (Mick)

**POSITION:** Full-back / midfielder

**BIRTHPLACE:** Gosforth, Northumberland

**DATE OF BIRTH:** 31/03/1956

**HEIGHT:** 5' 9" **WEIGHT:** 11st 4lbs

**SIGNED FROM:** School, 11/07/1972

**DEBUT:** v York City, A, 01/11/1975

**LAST MATCH:** v Orient, H, 24/03/1979

**MOVED TO:** Watford, 05/11/ 1979

**TEAMS:** Sunderland, Watford, Cardiff City, Sheffield United, Chesterfield, Matlock Town

**SAFC TOTALS:** 90+5 appearances / 2 goals

**A versatile and willing performer who operated at full-back or in midfield, Mickey was a regular in his final two seasons at Sunderland. He played 32 and 30 league games in 1977-78 and 1978-79 having played 8+1 in the relegation term of 1976-77 and 11+2 as the Division Two title was taken in 1975-76, when he scored his first goal in a Boxing Day win over Hull at Roker Park.**

Sold to Watford for £120,000 he lived in a hostel with Wilf Rostron and spent some of his time captaining the reserves. He was kept out of the side by ex-Arsenal man Pat Rice, having lost his place at Sunderland to former England full-back Steve Whitworth. Nonetheless, he topped half a century of appearances for the Hornets, playing 51 league games, including four at left-back, as Graham Taylor's side won promotion in 1982. At the end of that season he signed for Len Ashurst at Cardiff City, but only made eleven appearances in the league before moving to Sheffield United when Ian Porterfield signed him.

Playing alongside John MacPhail and Kevin Arnott, Henderson debuted at Portsmouth in Division Three on the opening day of the 1982-83 season in which he made 42+1 appearances in all competitions, many of them alongside former Sunderland youth team keeper Keith Waugh. Promotion came in his second season but after being a regular, injury ruled Mick out from February onwards. He returned the following October back at Portsmouth but moved on to Chesterfield after 87+2 games.

There were to be 136 league games for the Spireites where he was again joined by Arnott in his third season at Saltergate. Henderson's twelve goals for Chesterfield were his first since his two in his Sunderland days. The sudden scoring spree was explained by a move into midfield from his more common right-back berth rather than being a penalty taker. Mick's brother Ken had been a youth teamer at Sunderland and in 1971 had won a televised penalty competition ahead of a cup final at Wembley. Another brother, Tony, played for Rotherham in 1973 and went on to captain Australia after emigrating.

Player-coach at Chesterfield from the summer of 1987, Mick briefly became caretaker manager of the club in October 1988. After leaving football, he became a dog-handler with South Yorkshire police and maintained his passion for music, particularly rock band Wishbone Ash.

## HEPWORTH, Maurice

**POSITION:** Left-back

**BIRTHPLACE:** Barrasford, Northumberland

**DATE OF BIRTH:** 06/09/1953

**HEIGHT:** 5' 9" **WEIGHT:** 11st 5lbs

**SIGNED FROM:** School, 01/07/1969

**DEBUT:** v Bolton Wanderers, A, 12/04/1971

**LAST MATCH:** v Sheffield Wednesday, A, 24/04/1971

**MOVED TO:** Arcadia Shepherds (South Africa), 19/2/1975

**TEAMS:** Sunderland, Darlington (L), Arcadia Shepherds

**SAFC TOTALS:** 2 appearances / 0 goals

**Maurice Hepworth was in the 1973 FA Cup final squad at Selsdon Hall, but did not even see the match. He was one of four players who came home in midweek to play in a reserve team cup final against Middlesborough. In the first minute of that final, he was so badly injured in a challenge with Tony McAndrew that he was hospitalized with a ruptured spleen, burst duodenum, ruptured bowel and ruptured intestine.**

Hepworth credits physio Johnny Watters with saving his life that night, but he was on the danger list in hospital for two and a half weeks. He was in hospital when his cup-winning colleagues brought the trophy in to show him.

His two first-team appearances had come in away wins a couple of years earlier. A former youth team skipper, Hepworth took six months to recover before four league appearances on loan to Darlington early in 1975. He was then sent to South Africa to gain experience. Hepworth was a great success there, winning the league and cup double with Arcadia Shepherds where he returned after being freed by Bob Stokoe. Proud to have been part of the first club in South Africa to embrace multi-racialism, Maurice combined playing with working as a sales rep for a soft drinks company. After five years of regular football, injury struck him again when he suffered a double compound fracture in the semi-final of the South African Cup.

Coming back to the UK, he found employment with Pepsi International in London. In five years there he worked his way to becoming national accounts director after which he had five years with KFC, setting up their north-east division. He then became area manager for Scottish & Newcastle Breweries and helped set up Bobby Kerr and Micky Horswill running pubs. Those two members of the 1973 cup-winning side followed Hepworth when he set up a new brand called Barrass and Co which he ran for a decade before having three years as a training manager prior to taking up a role running a national sales force for Scottish & Newcastle.

In 2013 he became secretary of the Sunderland Former Players' Association, going on to become Chairman and being exceptionally pro-active in both roles. One of his six children continued Maurice's association at the club by taking up a job at the Stadium of Light.

## HERD, George

**POSITION:** Inside-right

**BIRTHPLACE:** Gartcosh, Glasgow

**DATE OF BIRTH:** 06/05/1936

**HEIGHT:** 5' 8" **WEIGHT:** 11st 2lbs

**SIGNED FROM:** Clyde, 24/04/1961

**DEBUT:** v Liverpool, H, 29/04/1961

**LAST MATCH:** v, Chelsea, A, 22/02/1969

**MOVED TO:** Hartlepool United, 08/06/1970

**TEAMS:** Gartcosh Thistle, Inverness Thistle, Queen's Park, Clyde, Hartlepool United

**INTERNATIONAL:** Scotland

**SAFC TOTALS:** 315+3 appearances / 55 goals

**An integral part of the first-ever promotion team in 1964, Herd was Sunderland's record signing when bought for £42,500. A highly intelligent and skilful player, he had the knack of opening up defences. Often a winger himself, George played his best football on Wearside at inside right, demonstrating his understanding of the wing-man's art by the supply line he provided for Brian Usher as promotion was won in a season when George enjoyed his best SAFC goals return with 16, including one on the day promotion was secured against Charlton.**

A fitness fanatic, George dealt with man markers by running them into the ground and then striking in the latter stages of games when his opponent had run out of steam. Substitutes were yet to be introduced when promotion was first won, but after they became part of the game, Herd became the first Sunderland sub to score when he did so at Blackpool in January 1967.

Capped five times by Scotland, he also won a cap at amateur level in his Queen's Park days (where he scored six goals in 31 games while working as a railwayman) and also represented the Scottish League three times, scoring a hat-trick in an inter-league game against the Irish league at Celtic Park. On the day of his full international debut he was making his way home by service bus. Waiting in a Glasgow bus station, two drunks with bottles in brown paper bags asked the 21-year-old where he had been that afternoon. "I've been playing for Scotland against England at Hampden" answered George truthfully only to be told by the doubtful 'wino's' he was drunker than them.

## HERD, George (Continued)

Always a live-wire character, George used to like to win bets when other teams were staying in the same hotel by betting he could ascend or descend a staircase without his feet touching the floor. Bets made, he would promptly go up or down the stairs by walking on his hands. Nonetheless he kept most of his party pieces for on the pitch, but George was not a show-boater - his aim was always to make a goal or score one.

On 4 May 1957, he signed for Clyde, debuting for them that evening against Rangers at Ibrox in the Glasgow Charity Cup semi-final. He went on to score 32 goals in 171 games for the club, one of which came at Hampden in the Scottish Cup final against Hibs a week after his international debut, while another occasion at Hampden saw George score in his Under 21 debut against the Netherlands. He also scored at the national stadium in a 4-0 victory over Rangers in the Glasgow Charity Cup final on 12 May 1958. His only full international goal came in a 3-3 draw with Hungary in Budapest. He was inducted into the Clyde FC Hall of Fame in 2011.

While still playing at Sunderland, Herd became a coach of the youth team from January 1968 to June 1970 when he left to sign for Hartlepool, where he contributed more as a coach than a player, but made 10+3 league appearances plus one in the cup after first appearing in a friendly against Raith Rovers.

From July 1974 until October 1976, he coached the juniors at Newcastle United where he was appointed by Joe Harvey. George returned to Sunderland in the summer of 1977 working as a coach for three years before taking over as manager of Queen of the South in 1980-81 where Dick Malone came out of retirement to play for him as the Doonhamers won promotion to the top-flight.

At this point George came back to the north east to coach at Darlington under Billy Elliott. When Elliot's time at Feethams came to an end Herd returned to Sunderland for two seasons as Youth Development Officer before spending four years coaching in Kuwait prior to a fourth spell at Roker Park, this time as youth team coach in 1993-94.

From August 1994 until July 1996, George again worked in Kuwait before a brief stint coaching Seaham Red Star, and finally a lengthy spell coaching Ryhope CA where well into his seventies he would be on the opposite side of the pitch to his coaching colleagues with Herd constantly using one simple word to urge his players on, "Pass" he would constantly cajole his players - and few people even at top level could pass as well as George.

## HESFORD, Iain

**POSITION:** Goalkeeper

**BIRTHPLACE:** Ndola, Zambia

**DATE OF BIRTH:** 04/03/1960 - 19/11/2014

**HEIGHT:** 6' 2" **WEIGHT:** 13st 12lbs

**SIGNED FROM:** Sheffield Wednesday, 20/09/1986 On loan from 08/08/1986

**DEBUT:** v Huddersfield Town, A, 23/08/1986

**LAST MATCH:** v Leicester City, A, 10/12/1988

**MOVED TO:** Hull City, 29/12/1988

**TEAMS:** Blackpool, Sheffield Wednesday, Fulham (L), Notts County (L), Sunderland, Hull City, Maidstone United, Eastern, Sig-Tao, South China

**INTERNATIONAL:** England Under 21 / Hong Kong

**SAFC TOTALS:** 112 appearances / 0 goals

**Iain Hesford went from zero to hero at Sunderland. Like Barry Siddall, he was a goalie who would have a bit of banter with the crowd behind the goal when the ball was at the other end, but he became massively unpopular when he endured a really tough time as a first-ever relegation to the third division was suffered in 1987.**

At the start of that third tier campaign Iain was left out in favour of the on loan Steve Hardwick. When Hardwick decided not to stay Hesford was brought back for a game at Gillingham. They were the side who had condemned Sunderland to relegation in the Play-Offs and astonishingly had scored 18 goals in their previous two home games, but Hesford excelled in keeping a clean sheet and went on to redeem himself to such an extent that he was runner-up to Eric Gates as Player of the Year. It was a fine testament to mental resilience.

Hesford came to Sunderland with an international pedigree. He had played for Brian Clough (and Ken Burton) alongside Sunderland's Alan Weir when playing in a 3-1 win over France for England Youths at Crystal Palace on 8 February 1978 and had gone on to win seven Under 21 caps, teaming up with David Hodgson, Mark Proctor and Adrian Heath. Hesford kept a clean sheet at Hampden Park in April 1982 and in September of that year helped England to beat West Germany in a two-legged European Under 21 Championship final.

At club level Hesford began with 230 games for Blackpool, debuting against Oldham on the opening day of the 1977-78 season in which he played 14 league games as the Tangerines tumbled into the third tier. Bob Stokoe then took over at Bloomfield Road, bringing in Dick Malone and Bobby Kerr. Jack Ashurst added to the Sunderland old boys the following season, but by then Stan Ternent, and later Alan Ball, were in charge. In 1980-81 Hesford missed only four league games as Blackpool's decline saw them slide into division four. By the time of Iain's final game for the club in a defeat at Hartlepool on the last day of the 1982-83 campaign the club were left to apply for re-election.

To have won his international caps when his club were struggling was testament to Hesford's quality and that was highlighted in the summer of 1983 when newly-appointed Sheffield Wednesday manager Howard Wilkinson made Iain one of his first signings. However, as Wednesday won promotion to the top-flight Hesford was back-up to Martin Hodge and had not made a debut by the time he went on loan to Fulham in January 1985. After such a wait he conceded four goals on debut at Portsmouth in a remarkable game where the Cottagers came back to draw 4-4. Hesford conceded three next time out at Shrewsbury but signed off with a clean sheet in his one home game as Brighton were beaten.

With Hodge never missing a game in any competition at Hillsborough during Hesford's time in Sheffield he never got a game for the Owls, but had ten league appearances on loan to Notts County from November 1985 and initially came to Sunderland on loan. After over a century of games for Sunderland, Iain was a make-weight (along with Billy Whitehurst) in the deal that brought Tony Norman in from Hull City as Sunderland's record signing. Debuting for the Tigers against Ipswich on New Year's Eve at the end of 1988, Hesford played 103 games in three seasons before signing for Maidstone United. Not only was he ever-present as the Stones finished 18th in Division Four, but he scored the winner against Hereford United with a massive clearance in November 1991.

From 1992 to 1998, he played in Hong Kong where he did so well he played against England on 26 May 1996 as a teammate of future Sunderland coach Carlton Fairweather. This was the game where the infamous England's Dentist's Chair drinking escapade dominated the trip. During four years with Eastern, Hesford won five trophies including league and cup and was named the league's best foreign player and in the league's Team of the Year three times, once going 827 minutes without conceding.

After returning to England in 1998 he became a hotelier in the Rochdale area, but died at the age of 54 due to a suspected heart attack. Hesford's father Bob played 203 league games in goal for Huddersfield as well the 1938 FA Cup final where he was only beaten by a last-minute penalty as Preston took the trophy a year after losing in the final against Sunderland. Hesford senior was called into three pre-war full England squads but never got a cap.

## HESLOP, Brian

**POSITION:** Half-back / inside-forward

**BIRTHPLACE:** Carlisle, Cumbria

**DATE OF BIRTH:** 04/08/1947

**HEIGHT:** 5' 9½" **WEIGHT:** 11st 0lbs

**SIGNED FROM:** Carlisle United, 13/05/1967

**DEBUT:** v Leeds United, A, 19/08/1967

**LAST MATCH:** v Bristol City, A, 15/08/1970

**MOVED TO:** Northampton Town, 03/03/1971

**TEAMS:** Carlisle United, Sunderland, Northampton Town, Workington, Northwich Victoria

**SAFC TOTALS:** 66+1 appearances / 0 goals

**Brian Heslop played in 15 of the first 16 games of the 1967-68 campaign, debuting in the unfamiliar position of centre-forward at Leeds on the opening day. A versatile and mobile player, he was best at half-back but after that initial run played just one league game until being picked for the last 13 games of the following season. He then played in exactly two thirds of the 1969-70 relegation season before his only league game for the club outside the top-flight came in the opening game of the following campaign.**

The following March Heslop joined Northampton for whom the first of his 49+1 league appearances was against Hartlepool. In September 1972, Brian returned to the north west with Workington for whom he played 139+1 league games. He had started with five games for Carlisle of which only one was in the season before Alan Brown picked up the promising young player for £5,000.

## HETHERINGTON, Henry (Harry)

**POSITION:** Outside-right
**BIRTHPLACE:** Chester-le-Street, Co Durham
**DATE OF BIRTH:** 07/11/1928
**HEIGHT:** 5' 7½" **WEIGHT:** 10st 9lbs
**SIGNED FROM:** St Oswalds, 01/05/1944
**DEBUT:** v Chelsea, A, 10/09/1947
**LAST MATCH:** v Blackburn Rovers, H, 13/09/1947
**MOVED TO:** Gateshead, 06/01/1949
**TEAMS:** St Oswalds, Sunderland, Gateshead, Wingate Colliery
**SAFC TOTALS:** 2 appearances / 0 goals

**An amateur who scored in a defeat on his war-time debut at York in the Tyne-Wear-Tees Cup on 5 May 1945, Hetherington also played in a heavy defeat at Newcastle, but had better luck in League North in 1945-46. He marked his home debut with the only goal of a game with Barnsley and made three further appearances that season.**

Signing as a professional on 11 May 1946, his two 'official' league appearances came in the space of four days after which he added two Division Three North games for Gateshead for whom he managed to get on the score-sheet once.

## HETZKE, Stephen Edward Richard (Steve)

**POSITION:** Centre-half
**BIRTHPLACE:** Marlborough, Wiltshire
**DATE OF BIRTH:** 03/06/1955
**HEIGHT:** 6' 2" **WEIGHT:** 13st 4lbs
**SIGNED FROM:** Blackpool, 05/03/1986
**DEBUT:** v Charlton Athletic, H, 08/03/1986
**LAST MATCH:** v Gillingham, A, 14/05/1987
**MOVED TO:** Chester City, 20/05/1987
**TEAMS:** Hungerford Town, Reading, Vancouver Whitecaps (L), Blackpool, Sunderland, Chester City, Colchester United
**SAFC TOTALS:** 33 appearances / 0 goals

**Steve Hetzke was a head it, kick it and keep things simple centre-half signed by Lawrie McMenemy. There was only one win in Hetzke's initial run of eight games as Sunderland battled relegation to the third tier. In his second and last season, Steve played in half the league games, a Full Members Cup defeat at Bradford and signed off in the first leg Play-Off defeat at Gillingham.**

Hetzke had joined Reading as an apprentice in 1971, becoming their youngest player when debuting at the age of 16 years and 193 days against Darlington in December 1971. Hetzke came under the managership of Charlie Hurley when Reading played Sunderland in the FA Cup in 1973, although he only featured in the final match of that season. Steve did not appear in over half his club's league games until 1978-79 when playing as a striker he scored nine goals in 42 games as Reading won Division Four.

It was his second promotion having also gone up in 1976, only to be immediately relegated. Following that first success Steve spent the summer of 1976 playing 18 times for Vancouver Whitecaps. After his second promotion Hetzke reverted to centre-half and became captain in his last season of 1981-82 before being transferred to Blackpool for a tribunal set fee of £12,500 after 33 goals in 293+10 games.

Two years later on 14 May 1984, he belatedly had a testimonial back at Reading, but against Oxford United rather than Blackpool who he had been ever-present for that season. Hetzke became captain of the Seasiders with whom who he totalled 160 games, scored 19 goals and won another promotion from Division Four in 1984-85.

After his time at Sunderland, he played 14 times for Chester before completing his playing days in 1988-89 with Colchester where he netted twice in 29 league games. Steve stayed in the game setting out on his coaching career at Chesterfield and

then becoming youth coach at QPR before scouting for Newcastle United in the early nineties. From 1995 to 2004, he was Technical Monitor for Youth Development with the Football League and then continued in the same role with the Premier League before becoming Academy mentor at Swansea.

## HEWITT, Joseph

**POSITION:** Inside-left / outside-left
**BIRTHPLACE:** Chester
**DATE OF BIRTH:** 03/05/1881 - 30/11/1971
**HEIGHT:** 5' 8" **WEIGHT:** 11st 6lbs
**SIGNED FROM:** Chester Locos, 08/08/1901
**DEBUT:** v Blackburn Rovers, A, 01/03/1902
**LAST MATCH:** v West Bromwich Albion, 31/10/1903
**MOVED TO:** Liverpool, 09/02/1904
**TEAMS:** Newtown Rangers, Chester Locos, Newton Rangers, Sunderland, Liverpool, Bolton Wanderers, Reading
**SAFC TOTALS:** 37 appearances / 10 goals

**At Sunderland Hewitt played five games, scoring once, in the 1901-02 title-winning season. His best campaign came the following year when he contributed seven goals in 26 games as well as scoring as the Sheriff of London Shield (A forerunner of the Charity/Community Shield) was won.**

Other than the 1910-11 season, when he scored three times in the first eleven games of the season with Bolton Wanderers in the second division before switching to Southern League Reading, having left Sunderland for Liverpool in January 1904, he went on to become one of the Anfield club's greatest-ever servants, He spent over six decades with the club, staying there until 1964.

Having paid Sunderland £150 for him he went on to score 74 goals in 164 games for Liverpool, winning a league title medal in 1905-06 when he was top scorer with 24 goals in 37 games. He had won promotion a year earlier after being relegated with Liverpool in his first season. Hewitt lived in Finchley Road in Anfield and after retiring in 1911, stayed with the club as coach, steward and finally long-standing press box steward. He died in the city after spending his final years in an old people's home in Croxteth.

## HEYES, James

**POSITION:** Inside-right
**BIRTHPLACE:** Prescot
**DATE OF BIRTH:** c 1902
**HEIGHT:** 5' 8" **WEIGHT:** 11st 0lbs
**SIGNED FROM:** Northwich Victoria, 04/05/1925
**DEBUT:** v Tottenham Hotspur, H, 26/09/1925
**LAST MATCH:** v Birmingham, A, 11/09/1926
**MOVED TO:** West Ham United, 20/07/1927
**TEAMS:** Skelmersdale, Bolton Wanderers, Northwich Victoria, Sunderland, West Ham United, Connah's Quay, Ashton National, Mossley, Ashton
**SAFC TOTALS:** 4 appearances / 0 goals

**Heyes had been an amateur with Bolton Wanderers from December 1921 to the end of the following season when they won the first Wembley FA Cup final, at which point he moved on to Northwich Victoria where he spent two seasons.**

When the chance came to sign for Sunderland, he did not want to miss the opportunity and signed on the day after the 1924-25 season ended. There were just a handful of games for SAFC before joining West Ham United where he did not get a first-team game and subsequently spent the rest of his career in non-league football.

## HEYWOOD, Albert Edwards

**POSITION:** Goalkeeper
**BIRTHPLACE:** Hartlepool, Co Durham
**DATE OF BIRTH:** 12/05/1913 - 25/05/1989
**HEIGHT:** 6' 0" **WEIGHT:** 11st 3lbs
**SIGNED FROM:** Spennymoor United, 16/01/1937
**DEBUT:** v Charlton Athletic, H, 01/04/1939
**LAST MATCH:** v Everton, A, 10/04/1939
**MOVED TO:** Hartlepools United, 29/11/1945
**TEAMS:** Hartlepool Expansion, Hartlepools United, Trimdon Grange Colliery, Luton Town, Spennymoor United, Sunderland, Stockton (WW2 Guest), Hartlepools United (WW2 Guest), South Durham Steelworks (WW2 Guest), Middlesbrough (WW2 Guest), Hartlepools United, Horden CW
**SAFC TOTALS:** 4 appearances / 0 goals

**Heywood's quartet of appearances late in the last season before World War Two began with a draw followed by three losses, the last to the tune of 6-2 at Goodison Park. Having waited two years for a debut, it was a disappointing outcome for the keeper who nonetheless went on to play another 79 games for Sunderland in war-time games (therefore not included in official appearances).**

Heywood's best season was in 1941-42 when he played in 39 of Sunderland's 40 games including both legs of the League War Cup final against Wolves. After the war, he added 39 league appearances in Division Three North after a £75 transfer to Hartlepools who he had first joined in 1931 and where he was nicknamed 'Napper.' Including war-time appearances he played 106 times for Hartlepools. Despite also having a spell with Luton Town it was not until he was at Sunderland that he made a league debut. Prior to coming to Roker Park he also had trials with Manchester City and Wolves. His father Sammy had played locally as a full-back for Deaf Hill United.

## HIGGINBOTHAM, Daniel John (Danny)

**POSITION:** Defender

**BIRTHPLACE:** Manchester, Greater Manchester

**DATE OF BIRTH:** 29/12/1978

**HEIGHT:** 6' 1" **WEIGHT:** 12st 3lbs

**SIGNED FROM:** Stoke City, 29/08/2007

**DEBUT:** v Manchester United, A, 01/09/2007

**LAST MATCH:** v Tottenham Hotspur, A, 23/08/2008

**MOVED TO:** Stoke City, 01/09/2008

**TEAMS:** Manchester United, Royal Antwerp (L), Derby County, Southampton, Stoke City, Nottingham Forest (L), Ipswich Town (L), Sunderland, Sheffield United, Chester, Altrincham

**INTERNATIONAL:** Gibraltar

**SAFC TOTALS:** 22 appearances / 3 goals

**Defender Higginbotham managed to score against both Newcastle and Middlesbrough in his modest number of games for Sunderland, Brought in by Roy Keane for a reported fee of £2.5m, plus appearance-based add-ons, he moved on for an undisclosed fee a year to the day after his debut.**

Keane had known Higginbotham from Manchester United where Danny made seven appearances between May 1998 and May 2000. One of these was at the Maracana Stadium in Brazil in a Club World Cup game against South Melbourne, while he also played in the Champions League against Sturm Graz where Keane struck the winner. In between his first and last appearances for United, Higginbotham spent the 1998-99 season with Royal Antwerp, scoring three times in 29 games, but becoming embroiled in controversy after a post-match incident with a referee, which Higginbotham strenuously denied.

Looking to play regularly, he signed for Derby County in millennium year for a reported £2m. He was Player of the Year, missing just one game, as the Rams were relegated in 2002 when he played in their final match at the Stadium of Light.

Midway through the following season, Higginbotham returned to the Premier League with Southampton after leaving Derby where he had played with Mart Poom and for Colin Todd and appeared in 92+6 games. Although his home debut for the Saints came in the FA Cup, he was left on the bench later that season as they lost the final to Arsenal.

After 97+10 appearances, during which he listed George Burley amongst his bosses, Higginbotham moved to Stoke City where he would have two spells either side of his time at Sunderland. In total he turned out 125+3 times for the Potters who he captained in his first spell and became Player of the Year in 2007. He also became penalty taker, scoring exactly half of career tally of 28 goals for the club. Despite the arrival of Danny Collins as one of a plethora of ex-Sunderland players at Stoke, Higginbotham was doing well when a cruciate ligament injury resulted in him missing the FA Cup final in 2011, a season in which he had scored the winner at the quarter-final stage.

Following loans with Nottingham Forest (5+1/1) and Ipswich Town (11+1/0) after moving on a free, there were 15+3 games with Sheffield United in the second half of 2012-13, the last being a League One Play-Off semi-final defeat to Yeovil Town. His teammates at Bramall Lane had included Neill Collins. A final move saw him join Chester in the Conference, debuting in a derby win at Wrexham, scoring at Gateshead and playing the last of his 15+2 games four days before Christmas 2013.

Internationally, Higginbotham captained Gibraltar in their first ever game on 19 November 2013, against Slovakia under the management of his uncle Allen Bula. After ending his club days with Chester he appeared in two further internationals, against the Faroe Islands and Estonia, both in March 2014.

## HINDMARCH, Robert

**POSITION:** Centre-half

**BIRTHPLACE:** Stannington, Northumberland

**DATE OF BIRTH:** 27/04/1961 - 06/11/2002

**HEIGHT:** 6' 1½" **WEIGHT:** 13st 4lbs

**SIGNED FROM:** North Shields Juniors, 01/06/1977

**DEBUT:** v Orient, A, 14/01/1978

**LAST MATCH:** v Notts County, H, 07/05/1984

**MOVED TO:** Derby County, 05/07/1984

**TEAMS:** Wallsend Boys Club, Sunderland, Portsmouth (L), Derby County, Wolves, Telford United, Cork City

**INTERNATIONAL:** England Youth

**SAFC TOTALS:** 125+3 appearances / 3 goals

**Rob Hindmarch was a colossally commanding centre-half who became Sunderland's youngest-ever captain on 20 December 1980 at Nottingham Forest at the age of 19 years and 237 days - on a day when Steve Whitworth and Shaun Elliott were alternative skippers in the side. Cruelly Rob was only 41 when he lost his life to Motor Neurone Disease, the same illness that Mel Holden suffered from.**

Hindmarch had become the club's fourth youngest player when he made his debut at the age of 16 and 262 days. He made one more appearance in that 1977-78 debut season and then waited until the 1979-80 promotion campaign for another opportunity, playing in exactly half the 42 league fixtures that term, including the final 15 of the run-in.

The following term Hindmarch started 29 games in the top flight. He had his best Sunderland season in 1981-82 when he started all but six of the 42 first division games. In contrast he only played in a third of the games in his last two Wearside seasons, being loaned to Portsmouth for a month from 8 December 1983. He played twice for Pompey, the first against Derby County who he joined the following summer.

Rob became captain of the Rams, leading Derby to back-to-back promotions in 1986 and 1987, scoring nine goals in 164 league games before joining Wolves in 1990 where again he took over the captaincy. The highlight of his 44 games with the men from Molineux was an injury-time equaliser in their derby with West Brom in 1990. Although a regular in 1990-91 he did not play in the next two seasons before he signed for Telford United, after which he became player/manager of Cork City from the summer of 1995 to March 1996, before he took up a position coaching junior football in New Jersey USA.

First capped by England at Youth level alongside Mark Proctor in a 1-0 win over the USSR in Las Palmas in August 1978, the following November Hindmarch won four caps under Brian Clough in a tournament in Monaco in which he scored England's goal in a 1-1 draw with Yugoslavia.

## HINDMARSH, James Lyons

**POSITION:** Inside-left

**BIRTHPLACE:** South Shields, Co Durham

**DATE OF BIRTH:** 19/04/1885 - 16/03/1959

**HEIGHT:** 5' 11" **WEIGHT:** 11st 12lbs

**SIGNED FROM:** Whitburn, 09/03/1905

**DEBUT:** v Notts County, H, 30/09/1905

**LAST MATCH:** v Notts County, H, 30/09/1905

**MOVED TO:** Fulham, 02/05/1906

**TEAMS:** Whitburn Colliery, Sunderland, Fulham, Watford, Plymouth Argyle, Stockport County, Manchester City, Whitburn Colliery, Newport County

**SAFC TOTALS:** 1 appearance / 0 goals

**Hindmarsh's only appearance came when he was one of several team changes that failed to halt a run of defeats, the Lads going down 3-1 at home to Notts County who had only avoided relegation the previous season due to the league being expanded. Nonetheless the former bricklayer (who had played cricket as well as football for Whitburn) went on to have a distinguished career in the game despite a slow start.**

At Fulham, who paid £20 for him, his only first-team game was in a 5-1 home Southern League defeat to Tottenham a week short of a year after his Sunderland appearance. After a six-month spell at Watford, Hindmarsh's career took an upturn when he signed for Plymouth in May 1908. Debuting for Argyle at Millwall on the opening day of the 1908-09 season, he got five goals in 15 Southern League and one in two Western League games as well as scoring twice in three FA Cup appearances in his first season.

The following term he was top scorer with 15 in 40 SL games and played twice against Tottenham in the FA Cup. His form persuaded Stockport County to pay £100 for him with Stockport converting him from centre-forward to a wing-half, starting with a 1910 English (FA) Cup meeting with Rochdale. By the start of his second season, Hindmarsh was captaining Stockport and went on to miss just one game that season eventually totalling 74 games and two goals for the Hatters.

In December 1912, Hindmarsh stepped up to Manchester City, first playing for them in 1913-14 when his one league goal from 24 appearances came in a home win against Sunderland. He also scored against another old club when he netted against Fulham in the FA Cup. There were only five more City appearances until football stopped because of World War One during which he was awarded the Military Medal.

After the war Hindmarsh joined Newport County and stayed there for 16 years. Initially in charge of the reserves as player-coach he took charge of first team affairs in 1920. During his time as secretary-manager he oversaw the development of the ground, with a new stand built in 1923. His best season was in 1925-26 when Newport were sixth in Division Three South, but generally it was a time of financial struggle.

In 1928, the club came close to bankruptcy and after having to apply for re-election four times were finally voted out of the league in 1931 only to regain their place two years later with Hindmarsh still at the helm.

## HINNINGAN, Joseph Peter (Joe)

**POSITION:** Full-back

**BIRTHPLACE:** Liverpool

**DATE OF BIRTH:** 03/12/1955

**HEIGHT:** 6' 0½" **WEIGHT:** 12st 10lbs

**SIGNED FROM:** Wigan Athletic, 20/02/1980

**DEBUT:** v Luton Town, H, 23/02/1980

**LAST MATCH:** v West Bromwich Albion, A, 11/12/1982

**MOVED TO:** Preston North End, 24/12/1982

**TEAMS:** South Liverpool, Wigan Athletic, Sunderland, Preston North End, Gillingham, Wrexham, Chester City

**SAFC TOTALS:** 65 appearances / 4 goals

**Joe Hinnigan became Sunderland's lucky mascot as an unbeaten 14-game run to promotion in 1980 coincided with his debut. A record fee for a fourth division defender of £135,000 had been paid to Wigan for his signature. He had scored ten goals in 66 league games for the Latics.**

Five of these had come in the season he signed for Sunderland in which he also scored in the FA Cup and played in Wigan's shock cup win at Chelsea. Joe had played in Wigan's first-ever league game in 1978, scored their first goal as a Football League club (against Newport on 2 September 1978) and scored in their first-ever league victory, against Rochdale.

Once promoted with Sunderland Hinnigan only played four times before coming into the side for twelve of the final 13 games, including a last-day win at his native Liverpool. During this run Joe had a golden spell of scoring four times from full-back in a run of three games, goals that were crucial in helping Sunderland stay up.

After joining Preston, he had a similar impact as at Sunderland. Coming into the North End side with them one off the foot of Division Three in mid-March 1983 only one defeat was suffered in his 13 games. Joe scored three times as they climbed to the safety of 16th place. After 51+1/8 games and goals he moved on to Gillingham (99+4/7), Wrexham (28+1/1) and Chester City (52+2/2), playing his final league game at Bury in March 1991.

Having qualified as a physiotherapist while still playing he became physio at Chester in 1990, staying there until September 1994 when he moved to Wigan for five years before becoming assistant manager at Rochdale in May 1999 under David Hamilton, who had been a reserve at Sunderland during Hinnigan's time.

Hamilton was quickly succeeded by Steve Parkin who later came to Sunderland as Phil Parkinson's assistant manager. In June 2001 Hinnigan returned to Chester as physio, took up the same position at Bury in July 2004 and returned to Chester from February to October 2006 as assistant manager to former England international Mark Wright. At Chester, Wigan, Rochdale and Bury Joe worked alongside his former teammate Graham Barrow who was on the coaching staff.

From October 2006 to May 2008, Hinnigan worked as physio at Shrewsbury Town before becoming physio at Accrington Stanley the following month. In 2011 his quick thinking helped save the life of Blackburn Rugby Union FC's groundsman Phil Isherwood who was having a heart attack in offices the two clubs shared. In 2016 Hinnigan took up a final position with Bangor City where he retired as physio after a match against Bala Town in March 2018.

## HIRD, Robert Keith Brian

**POSITION:** Goalkeeper

**BIRTHPLACE:** South Moor, Co Durham

**DATE OF BIRTH:** 25/11/1939 - 01/09/1967

**HEIGHT:** 5' 11½" **WEIGHT:** 11st 12lbs

**SIGNED FROM:** Annfield Plain, 13/09/1957

**DEBUT:** v Liverpool, H, 29/04/1961

**LAST MATCH:** v Liverpool, H, 29/04/1961

**MOVED TO:** Darlington, 01/07/1963

**TEAMS:** Annfield Plain, Sunderland, Darlington, Annfield Plain

**SAFC TOTALS:** 1 appearance / 0 goals

**Keith Hird made his only appearance on the last day of the 1960-61 season, future World Cup winner Roger Hunt scoring the only goal Keith conceded in a 1-1 draw.**

Tragically, six years later Keith drowned in an accident, his body having been in the water for a week before it was discovered near the quayside on the River Tyne.

At the time Keith had been working for a company called Cumberland Fibres at Hare Law, near Stanley. As well as his league appearance for Sunderland, Hird had played 17 league games for Darlington in addition to starting and ending his career with his local club Annfield Plain.

## HOBSON, Herbert Bertie

**POSITION:** Right-back

**BIRTHPLACE:** Tow Law, Co Durham

**DATE OF BIRTH:** 26/02/1890 – 22/11/1963

**HEIGHT:** 5' 8" **WEIGHT:** 11st 5lbs

**SIGNED FROM:** Crook Town, 29/08/1912

**DEBUT:** v Sheffield United, A, 24/03/1913

**LAST MATCH:** v Middlesbrough, A, 25/02/1922

**MOVED TO:** Darlington, 28/02/1925

**TEAMS:** Stanley United, Crook Town, Jarrow, Sunderland, Stoke (WW1 Guest), Wolves (WW1 Guest), Rochdale (L), Darlington, Jarrow, Spennymoor United

**SAFC TOTALS:** 172 appearances / 0 goals

**Hobson came to Roker after catching the eye in local football. Having signed for Sunderland from Crook Town in August 1912 he got a chance to fill in three times for Charlie Gladwin late in the glorious season of 1912-13 when the league title was won and the cup final reached.**

Debuting in a 3-1 win at Sheffield United, Bert then played in a 3-1 home win over Everton and a 5-2 victory at Liverpool. The following season he got into the side in October and stayed there for the rest of the season. Showing his versatility in 1914-15, before football stopped for the war, he played as much at left-back as in his preferred position on the right, appearing in all but ten of the campaign's 39 games.

Hobson joined the army in May 1915 and gained the Military Medal. He also played as a 'Guest' player for Stoke and Wolves during the Great War. When football resumed with a Victory League in 1918-19, he played 21 times for Sunderland although these games are not counted in official records and so are in addition to his recorded 172 appearances. During this season, Bert also had the joy of scoring his only goal for Sunderland, converting a penalty in a home win over Middlesbrough in January 1919.

When the Football League resumed in 1919-20 Hobson was a major player, missing just two games as the Lads finished fifth in the first division. He was to appear 36 times the following year and 22 times in 1921-22 by which time he was 32 at the season's end. He was placed on the transfer list in the summer of 1922 with an asking price of £1,500. This was reduced by half in November and to a third of the original valuation by the end of 1923. Hobson's choice had been to accept the maximum wage during this period, but he had refused unless also granted a Benefit Match. Had it not been for this dispute and the lost war-time years, it is entirely possible that Bert Hobson would have joined the esteemed ranks of those to have topped 300 appearances for the club.

He was not entirely inactive during his final season at SAFC as he was able to play for West Stanley in January 1923 and go on loan to Division Three North Rochdale in March. Having left Sunderland for good in 1924 he became player-coach at Jarrow and subsequently extended his career with Darlington and Spennymoor United where he was still involved in 1928 while working in an iron foundry. In the late 1930s, his nephew William Hobson was on Sunderland's books, but never got a game in the first team.

# H

## HODGSON, David James

**POSITION:** Forward

**BIRTHPLACE:** Gateshead, Co Durham

**DATE OF BIRTH:** 06/08/1960

**HEIGHT:** 5' 9" **WEIGHT:** 12st 2lbs

**SIGNED FROM:** Liverpool, 24/08/1984

**DEBUT:** v Chelsea, A, 27/08/1984

**LAST MATCH:** v Stoke City, H, 03/05/1986

**MOVED TO:** Norwich City, 18/07/1986

**TEAMS:** Redheugh Boys Club, Middlesbrough, Liverpool, Sunderland, Norwich City, Middlesbrough (L), Xerex CD, Sheffield Wednesday, Sanfrecce Hiroshima, Metz, Swansea City, Mainz, Rochdale

**INTERNATIONAL:** England Under 21

**SAFC TOTALS:** 42+10 appearances / 7 goals

**A Wembley finalist with Len Ashurst's Sunderland in 1985 in the League (Milk) Cup, Hodgson played seven times during the cup run, scoring in a third round tie at Nottingham Forest. In what was his first season at Roker he also scored four times in just over half the league games as Sunderland were relegated.**

The following season his only league goal, having played in around a third of the fixtures, was a penalty before he was one of seven men to make their final appearance in the last match of the season. Hodgson was not a player to stay long at a club in a career that saw him play in Spain, Japan, France and Germany before three spells managing Darlington between 1995 and 2006 - something that resulted in him publishing a biography called 'Three Times a Quaker' in 2004. During Hodgson's spells with Darlington he guided the Quakers to two Play-Off finals, making Martin Gray one of his most noted signings.

Hodgson's contribution to north-east football had begun with Middlesbrough where he played 134+9 times, scoring 20 goals. Debuting as a sub at Nottingham Forest on 23 September 1978 as a teammate of Mark Proctor, he played alongside Proctor for England Under 21s in a February 1981 win over the Republic of Ireland at Anfield six months before signing for Liverpool in a £450,000 deal.

Lee Chapman and Iain Hesford also played in that Anfield international while Chris Woods and Adrian Heath would be other England teammates as Hodgson won seven Under 21 caps. Debuting against Norway at Southampton in September 1980, he also played in a heavy defeat in Romania before scoring in a big win over Switzerland at Ipswich. He also netted in a win over Poland in Warsaw and played in both legs of the 1982 UEFA Under 21 Championship final as West Germany were beaten 5-4 on aggregate.

By the time of that final Hodgson was a Liverpool player and had got off to a great start with four goals in his first six Liverpool games playing alongside Kenny Dalglish and Ian Rush. Nine goals in 37 games was a better return than he had managed at Boro, but was not good enough at Liverpool where the arrival of Michael Robinson pushed him down the pecking order. Nonetheless, Hodgson got a European Cup winner's medal from the 1984 final against Roma in Rome when Alan Kennedy and Bob Bolder were also in the squad as Liverpool won on penalties. After a total of ten goals in 49 appearances for Liverpool, but impatient for regular first-team football, Hodgson came to Sunderland who he had supported as a boy.

When the time came to leave Sunderland David chose to go to Norwich rather than IFK Gothenburg who went on to win the UEFA Cup, but it would not be long until he decided to play on the continent. At Norwich he scored four times in nine games, including a League Cup hat-trick against Millwall. A loan back to Boro was unsuccessful and cut short after a red card and just two league appearances.

In 1987, he spent a year in Spain playing 14 league games without scoring for Xerex CD before a return to England with Sheffield Wednesday. Between October and January in the 1988-89 season he started six top-flight games and came off the bench another five times, scoring against Charlton and also Torquay in his one FA Cup appearance. Re-united with Mark Proctor he also played alongside Colin West, Chris Turner and Wilf Rostron for the Owls who were managed by Howard Wilkinson with Peter Eustace as coach.

Having played for Wilkinson, Hodgson's next move was to Japan with Sanfrecce Hiroshima where he spent the 1989-90 season before two years in France with Metz where he played 38 league games without scoring. In March 1992, he briefly joined Swansea City, starting once and coming off the bench twice prior to a move to Mainz in Germany, before finally ending his career with a very short stint at Rochdale without playing a game.

Having played around the world, in November 2001, Hodgson took up a role as European scout for Preston North End. He then spent a decade working for Basesoccer where initially he looked to identify players in South America before broadening his role to include Africa and Japan.

## HODKIN, Ernest

**POSITION:** Right-half

**BIRTHPLACE:** Grassmoor, Chesterfield

**DATE OF BIRTH:** 14/05/1889 - 20/05/1954

**HEIGHT:** 5' 7" **WEIGHT:** 12st 0lbs

**SIGNED FROM:** Mansfield Mechanics, 30/06/1910

**DEBUT:** v Oldham Athletic, A, 21/01/1911

**LAST MATCH:** v Arsenal, H, 28/01/1911

**MOVED TO:** Stoke, 05/04/1912

**TEAMS:** Clay Cross Works, Mansfield Mechanics, Sunderland, Stoke, Billingham Shirebrook, Mansfield Mechanics

**SAFC TOTALS:** 2 appearances / 0 goals

**Hodkin had twice as many relatives who played for SAFC than the number of games he played for the club. He was the nephew of both the legendary Jamie Millar and William Worrall, the son-in-law of William Gibson and the brother-in-law of Albert Milton of the great 1912-13 side. Hodkin's two games saw him play alongside Milton.**

Having joined Stoke late in the 1911-12 season, Hodkin managed five Southern League appearances, scoring against Northampton. As his former teammates swept to glory he played 22 times as the Potters were relegated. He also played twice in the English (FA) Cup in the first round against Reading, three times in all as the first meeting was abandoned. After a spell back in the north east with Billingham he finished his career in the midlands, but was living in Durham at the time of his death.

## HOFFMANN, Ron-Thorben

**POSITION:** Goalkeeper

**BIRTHPLACE:** Rostock, Germany

**DATE OF BIRTH:** 04/04/1999

**HEIGHT:** 6' 4" **WEIGHT:** 13st 7lbs

**SIGNED FROM:** Bayern Munich, 31/08/2021, on loan

**DEBUT:** v Accrington Stanley, H, 11/09/2021

**LAST MATCH:** v Doncaster Rovers, H, 05/02/2022

**MOVED TO:** Bayern Munich, 25/05/2022, end of loan

**TEAMS:** Hansa Rostock, Hertha Berlin, RB Leipzig, Bayern Munich, Sunderland (L), Eintracht Braunschweig (to August 2022)

**SAFC TOTALS:** 24 appearances / 0 goals

**Signed on a season-long loan from Bayern Munich. Hoffmann has a Champions League medal from the Stadium of Light having been on the bench when Bayern beat Paris Saint-Germain in the 2020 final at Benfica's ground in Lisbon. He was also on the bench as Bayern won the World Club Cup in February 2021, beating UANL of Mexico in Qatar.**

Hoffman made over 50 appearances for Bayern II who operate in the German third tier which Hoffmann won as a teammate of Leon Dajuku in 2020, only to be relegated from the same division a year later. Towards the end of the 2020-21 season his side were managed by former Manchester City defender Martin Demichelis who played against Sunderland in the 2014 League Cup final.

In 2020-21 Hoffmann was on the bench for six Bundesliga games in the spring, including a key clash with Borussia Dortmund. He won the first of his two international Under 18 caps against the Republic of Ireland in November 2016 and was included in Stefan Kuntz's extended squad for the 2020/2021 Olympics in Tokyo. Hoffmann's appearances for Bayern at first-team level came in the International Champions Cup, the first in a 2-0 loss to Inter Milan in Singapore in 2017 when Carlo Ancelotti introduced him for the last 21 minutes with the score already 2-0. Two years later Hoffmann played in a 3-1 win over Real Madrid in Houston.

At Sunderland he played regularly in the first half of a promotion winning season before losing his place through illness. On the bench for the 2022 Play-off final win against Wycombe at Wembley he chronicled his time at Sunderland via a column in the German magazine Kicker.

## HOGG, James William (Jimmy)

**POSITION:** Centre-forward

**BIRTHPLACE:** Fulwell, Sunderland

**DATE OF BIRTH:** 26/07/1898 - 10/11/1963

**HEIGHT:** 5' 9" **WEIGHT:** 11st 0lbs

**SIGNED FROM:** Whitburn, 16/11/1923

**DEBUT:** v Sheffield United, H, 19/01/1924

**LAST MATCH:** v Sheffield United, H, 25/12/1924

**MOVED TO:** Contract not renewed, 02/05/1925

**TEAMS:** Whitburn, Sunderland, Newcastle United

**SAFC TOTALS:** 9 appearances / 8 goals

**James William Hogg rivals the club's greatest strikers in terms of goals to games ratio - but only played nine times. He scored in his first six games - netting twice in two of them and ended his first term with eight goals in as many games as Sunderland finished third.**

Indeed, including a friendly at Stockport when he scored after running from the half-way line, Hogg scored in his first seven Sunderland games. He took only three minutes of his debut to find the back of the net after rifling in 13 goals in eight games for the reserves having joined from local football. Had he not missed a penalty at Nottingham Forest in March 1924, he would have had a hat-trick and an exact goal per game average. As it was, his brace took Sunderland to the top of the table.

The following season he waited until Christmas Day for his solitary and valedictory appearance, again against the Blades, but left the club after a personal clash with fellow forward Bobby Marshall. A proposed move to Sheffield United at the end of the season failed to materialise after which he worked as a clerk in Sunderland Corporation Tramways Offices and later as a bricklayer during World War Two.

## HOGG, Robert (Bobby)

**POSITION:** Centre-forward / inside-forward

**BIRTHPLACE:** Windlestone, Co Durham

**DATE OF BIRTH:** 20/03/1878 - 14/03/1963

**HEIGHT:** 5' 8" **WEIGHT:** 12st 3lbs

**SIGNED FROM:** South Shields, 22/08/1899

**DEBUT:** v Sheffield United, A, 02/10/1899

**LAST MATCH:** v Blackburn Rovers, H, 25/10/1902

**MOVED TO:** Grimsby Town, 15/11/1902

**TEAMS:** Selbourne Rovers, Whitburn, South Shields, Sunderland, Grimsby Town, Whitburn, Blackpool, Luton Town

**SAFC TOTALS:** 73 appearances / 20 goals

**The first Sunderland player to score a hat-trick against Newcastle United, Bobby blasted three goals in a 4-2 win at St James' two days before the last Christmas of the 1800s. He scored there in another win on the first visit of the twentieth century when he was joined on the scoresheet by his namesake Billy Hogg. The two were not related.**

Although he was selected to represent the Football League against the Irish League in 1901, Bobby's best season was in the title-winning year of 1901-02, when he played in 29 of the 36 league games, scoring five goals. After leaving Sunderland six months after winning his championship medal, he played only three times for Grimsby, without scoring. He then returned to Whitburn where he had grown up after moving from Windlestone, near Ferryhill, as a very young child. While playing for Sunderland he maintained his sporting links with Whitburn by playing cricket for them.

In 1904 Hogg returned to the Football League with Blackpool with whom he got off the mark in his second game at Burslem Port Vale, but it was one of only four goals he scored in 27 second division appearances before going on to finish his career in the Southern League. A joiner by trade, by 1911 he was back in Whitburn as the publican at the Jolly Sailor. In 1939 he was known to be still in the pub trade, but in Richmond.

## HOGG, William (Billy)

**POSITION:** Winger/ forward

**BIRTHPLACE:** Hendon, Sunderland

**DATE OF BIRTH:** 29/05/1879 - 30/01/1937

**HEIGHT:** 5' 9½" **WEIGHT:** 11st 10lbs

**SIGNED FROM:** Willington Athletic, 05/10/1899

**DEBUT:** v Notts County, H, 02/12/1899

**LAST MATCH:** v Bristol City, A, 17/04/1909

**MOVED TO:** Rangers, 11/05/1909

**TEAMS:** Portland Juniors, Walker Gate Rangers, Rosehill, Willington Athletic, Sunderland, Rangers, Dundee, Raith Rovers, Newcastle United (WW1 Guest), Hartlepools United (WW1 Guest), Dundee, Hibs, Montrose

**INTERNATIONAL:** England

**SAFC TOTALS:** 303 appearances / 86 goals

**Billy Hogg was joint top scorer as the league title was won in 1902, a year in which he won his three England caps, one of which is on display at the Stadium of Light. Born in Sunderland, Hogg moved to Heaton in Newcastle. This was as a result of the family wanting to have new surroundings following the tragic death of Billy's older brother Robert, an eight-year-old who was one of 183 children killed in the Victoria Hall disaster in Sunderland on 16 June 1883. Billy had only just turned four.**

Tragedy dogged Hogg. His son William died of cancer at the age of 30 after winning the FA Amateur Cup with Bishop Auckland, having also played for Gateshead, Blyth Spartans and Bradford City. Sunderland's Billy Hogg was also in the England team on the day of a disaster at Ibrox when 25 supporters were killed and 500 injured when a newly-built stand collapsed on 5 April 1902. Seven years later, Ibrox became Billy's home ground when he signed for Rangers with whom he won three successive league titles between 1911 and 1913. After six goals in 29 games in his first season in Scotland, he went on to excel, his best campaign being the middle one of his hat-trick of titles as he scored 20 times in 30 games.

While Billy sometimes played at centre-forward where his physicality came to the fore, he was mainly a right-winger which makes his goals per game ratio even more impressive. A model of consistency, over ten years the fewest number of games he played was the 22 he made in his first season. Most famously, he was one of two hat-trick scorers in the legendary 9-1 win at Newcastle. He had also scored a hat-trick in the previous away game at Woolwich Arsenal.

Later, after leaving Rangers, where he played 107 times, he stayed in Scotland with Dundee and then Raith Rovers where he became player-manager in 1914 after a year on Tayside. However, upon the outbreak of World War One, he returned to England where he worked as a fitter in Heaton and appeared as a 'Guest' in charity matches for Newcastle in November 1915 and May 1918, scoring once. In between, he scored twice in his one game as a guest for Hartlepools against the Durham Light Infantry in February 1916.

Following the war, and by now very much a veteran, he returned to Scotland to play for Dundee, Hibs and Montrose as well as coming close to signing for St Mirren. Around this time he contributed regular columns for the Dundee Courier and Northern Daily Mail while between 1925 and 27 he wrote engaging columns in the Football Echo in Sunderland.

For England, Billy debuted against future Sunderland goalkeeper LR Roose in a goalless draw with Wales at Wrexham. He then played in a 1-0 win over Ireland in Belfast before the fateful match against the Scots where he came up against his Sunderland colleague Ted Doig. Despite the disaster, that match was completed after a 20-minute delay, but was declared void and does not count as an official international. Hogg's third cap - but fourth game for England - came the following month in a re-arranged game with Scotland. Staged at Villa Park, the match raised funds for the victims of the disaster at Ibrox. Billy also represented the Football League on four occasions, twice scoring hat-tricks! He also played in a North v South match.

In 1922, he became trainer of Wolverhampton Wanderers, but returned to Sunderland as coach between 1927 and 1934 after which he had a spell as trainer at Barnsley. Always a larger than life character, Billy also became a publican on Wearside, managing the Fountain Head Hotel in Sunderland prior to 1927 and a pub in Southwick after leaving his job at Roker Park.

Brother Jack was also on Sunderland's books without breaking into the first team, but did play for Morpeth Harriers, Sheffield United, Southampton, West Stanley and Hartlepools United. With the Saints still a Southern League club, Jack's only Football League appearances were the three he made for the Blades. Most notably he once scored nine goals for Hartlepools in a 12-0 thrashing of Workington in April 1909.

Notwithstanding Billy's hat-trick in the 9-1 win for Sunderland at Newcastle, perhaps his most amazing statistic came on the cricket pitch where he once took seven wickets for no runs playing for Backworth as a boy. Billy's descendant Pat Ware later captured much of his life story in a privately written biography distributed to family and friends.

## HOLDEN, Melville George

**POSITION:** Centre-forward

**BIRTHPLACE:** Dundee

**DATE OF BIRTH:** 25/08/1954 - 31/01/1981

**HEIGHT:** 6' 1½" **WEIGHT:** 10st 4lbs

**SIGNED FROM:** Preston North End, 15/05/1975

**DEBUT:** v Carlisle United, H, 09/08/1975

**LAST MATCH:** v Cardiff City, A, 28/01/1978

**MOVED TO:** Blackpool, 22/07/1978

**TEAMS:** Preston North End, Sunderland, Blackpool, PEC Zwolle

**SAFC TOTALS:** 77+7 appearances / 28 goals

**Mel Holden was often seen as a gangly, ungainly and at times clumsy centre-forward. It was only in later years when he passed away at the terribly young age of 26 that people wondered if his displays at Sunderland had demonstrated early signs of motor neurone disease that caused his retirement a couple of years before his death, and only a year or two after he left Sunderland.**

He had first come onto the Roker radar when he played superbly against Sunderland in September 1974 as part of a three-pronged attack with Third division Preston where he was flanked by player-manager Bobby Charlton and future England winger Tony Morley. Bob Stokoe bought him for £120,000 at the end of the season and later signed him from Sunderland for Blackpool.

In Holden's first season on Wearside he scored twelve goals to finish one behind top-scorer Pop Robson as the Division Two championship was won. That season he started 31 league fixtures, came on as sub five times and was an unused sub in all the remaining games as well as scoring three more times in the cups. Once promoted, after featuring in the opening month and scoring against Arsenal, he was absent until January but shortly after returning, ended Sunderland's record league drought of ten games without a goal (he preceded this strike with a cup goal at Wrexham) to prompt a resurgence where he contributed five goals in four games. Holden went on to end the campaign with a creditable nine goals from 24 top-flight appearances. Back in the second division, he scored twice in the first home game, quickly added another in the League Cup against Middlesbrough, but then did not score on his last eleven outings after which he joined Blackpool.

Although he led the line for the Tangerines on the first day of the 1978-79 season, within three weeks, Holden had played his last game for the club after one more start and an appearance as sub. Sold to Dutch outfit PEC Zwolle for £40,000 he played ten times, scoring once before returning to the UK.

## HOLDEN, William Bill

**POSITION:** Centre-forward

**BIRTHPLACE:** Bolton, Lancashire

**DATE OF BIRTH:** 01/04/1928 - 25/01/2011

**HEIGHT:** 6' 0" **WEIGHT:** 11st 7lbs

**SIGNED FROM:** Burnley, 26/12/1955

**DEBUT:** v Newcastle United, A, 27/12/1955

**LAST MATCH:** v Wolverhampton Wanderers, A, 28/04/1956

**MOVED TO:** Stockport County, 24/10/1956

**TEAMS:** Radcliffe Works, Lomax's Corinthians, Everton, Burnley, Sunderland, Stockport County, Bury, Halifax Town, Rugby Town, Hereford United

**INTERNATIONAL:** England B

**SAFC TOTALS:** 24 appearances / 7 goals

**Signed on Boxing Day 1956 on the day of Sunderland's record defeat against Newcastle when the Magpies won 6-1 at Roker Park, Holden debuted against them at St James' the following day and while Newcastle won that day 3-1, he at least marked his debut with a goal. After those scorelines United were hot favourites when the sides met again later in the season on Tyneside in an FA Cup quarter-final only for Holden to score both goals in a 2-0 win to depose the cup-holders.**

A week after the cup triumph Holden scored twice in a win at Everton (where he had played as an amateur). Before he had been at the club a year, he left to sign for Stockport for half the £12,000 Sunderland had paid for him, nonetheless, a Stockport club record. He had wanted to be allowed to train in Burnley where his wife had a hairdressing business, but Sunderland refused at which point the player dug his heels in and refused to stay. His brief time at Sunderland rebounded on him in in May 1957 when he was one of 14 Sunderland players punished by the authorities for receiving illegal payments. Fined six months benefit qualifications, this was refunded in 1962 when the High Court ruled the Football League's decision illegal.

At Stockport he debuted at Crewe on 27 October 1956, scored 37 times in 87 league games and represented Division Three North against their Southern counterparts. Stockport allowed him to stay in Burnley but on at least one occasion he is known to have missed duty with County owing to a Burnley bus strike.

He went on to add 33 goals in 100 league games for Bury with whom he won Division Three in 1961 and finally ten in 37 for Halifax, the last against Reading in May 1963 before dropping into non-league football having only played for one of the two planned seasons with the Shaymen, due to travelling difficulties.

A couple of seasons before Sunderland signed him Holden had scored four goals against Sunderland in a 5-0 defeat at Burnley on a day when future Sunderland manager Jimmy Adamson scored the other. He also scored both goals as Sunderland lost 2-0 in the cup at Turf Moor that season and also at Roker Park earlier in the campaign thereby giving him seven goals against the Lads in 1952-53. It was an even more impressive achievement when it is noted he had recovered from a broken leg sustained in March 1952. Holden was top-scorer three times at Burnley and in total scored 75 goals in 187 league games for the Clarets, leading to a career league tally of 160 league goals in 430 appearances.

During his time with Burnley Bill won a B cap for England when playing alongside Adamson he scored in a 2-2 draw against Scotland at Hibs. Prior to joining Burnley he had worked at Walker's Tannery and been a Military Policeman while on National Service. Once a pupil at Tommy Lawton's old school, Everton gave Bill and his brother Stan trials but he did not play a first-team game for the Toffees.

For a player who apparently did not like to travel, Holden was always on the move. This continued after his playing days as he found employment by running a driving school, working as a chauffeur and subsequently owning a coffee bar in Lancaster where he also ran the University's recreation centre. He then owned a newsagent, ran a restaurant, rented flats in Blackpool, worked for the DHSS and bought a guest house.

## HOLLEY, George

**POSITION:** Inside-forward

**BIRTHPLACE:** Dawdon, Seaham Harbour, Co Durham

**DATE OF BIRTH:** 20/11/1885 - 27/08/1942

**HEIGHT:** 5' 9" **WEIGHT:** 11st 7lbs

**SIGNED FROM:** Seaham White Star, 16/11/1904

**DEBUT:** v Wednesday, A, 27/12/1904

**LAST MATCH:** v Everton, H, 06/04/1915

**MOVED TO:** Brighton & Hove Albion, 16/07/1919

**TEAMS:** Seaham Young Villa, Seaham Athletic, Seaham Villa, Seaham White Star, Sunderland, Fulham (WW1 Guest), Brighton & Hove Albion

**INTERNATIONAL:** England

**SAFC TOTALS:** 315 appearances / 157 goals

**One of the great names in Sunderland's history, no one has scored more goals for England while on the club's books than Holley who remains Sunderland's fourth highest-ever scorer. His three goals in the record 9-1 win at Newcastle in 1908 was one of eleven hat-tricks George scored for the Lads.**

Top scorer in five seasons, Holley had a seven-season spell between 1907-08 and 1913-14 when he bagged a minimum of 14 goals. His best haul of 25 in 1911-12 made him the top-flight's leading marksman, while in 1912-13 when he helped Sunderland to the league title he scored five goals in helping the club to their first-ever English (FA) Cup final. Not fit for the final, a pre-match team photo shows the team in their suits and smart shoes except for Holley who has his football boots on having been testing his fitness. In the end he played the 90 minutes, his intended replacement Walter Tinsley having been overwhelmed with the prospect of playing. In these days before subs, vice-captain Holley had to stay on for the full 90 minutes.

For England, George scored against his clubmate LR Roose 15 minutes into his debut against Wales at Nottingham Forest on 15 March 1909 when he played inside-left with his SAFC colleague Arthur Bridgett on the left wing. On his fourth and fifth international appearances be bagged braces in 8-2 and 8-1 away wins over Hungary and Austria. In 1912, he scored in all three British Championship games including a 1-1 draw with Scotland at Hampden in front of 127,307 - then a world record

attendance. Having scored against Roose on his debut, this time Holley escaped the clutches of his Sunderland teammate and Scotland centre-half Charlie Thomson while clubmate Charlie Buchan was an England reserve, leaving the lads short of three key men as they beat Woolwich Arsenal on the same day.

Sunderland won without Holley again the following season when he was on duty against Scotland at Stamford Bridge for what was his tenth and final cap, during which he scored eight goals. In addition to this, he scored three goals in as many games against South Africa in the summer of 1910 as a member of an FA touring party. Additionally, Holley played in a further five representative games for the Football League.

Regardless of his goals, justice cannot be done to Holley's career by noting his goals and games alone. He was an immensely skilful footballer with tremendous ball control, and this in an age of primitive sporting equipment compared to the modern day, on pitches that were often mudheaps in the depths of winter.

After World War One - during which he had guested for Fulham and was an apprentice boilermaker - he signed for Brighton at the age of 33, but within a year was back at Sunderland as a coach after five goals in a dozen games. Two years later, he took up a position as trainer at Wolves, staying there for a decade before accepting a similar position at Barnsley. When he passed away ten years later at the age of 56 in 1942, he was still living in Wolverhampton. At this point, his son Tom was a full-back with Leeds United after beginning his career with Barnsley while George was trainer there.

## HOLLOWAY, Darren

**POSITION:** Defender

**BIRTHPLACE:** Bishop Auckland, Co Durham

**DATE OF BIRTH:** 03/10/1977

**HEIGHT:** 5' 10" **WEIGHT:** 12st 5lbs

**SIGNED FROM:** School, 01/04/1994

**DEBUT:** v Stoke City, A, 25/10/1997

**LAST MATCH:** v Luton Town, H, 19/09/2000

**MOVED TO:** Wimbledon, 29/09/2000

**TEAMS:** Manchester United, York City, Sunderland, Carlisle United (L), Bolton Wanderers (L), Wimbledon, Scunthorpe United (L), Bradford City, Darlington, Gateshead

**INTERNATIONAL:** England Under 21

**SAFC TOTALS:** 54+12 appearances / 0 goals

**A Wembley finalist in the 1998 Play-Offs, that season was Holloway's best as he started 32 league games and 37 in total, although he was substituted at half-time at Wembley as he struggled with a back problem. As a boy Darren spent three years with Manchester United's Centre of Excellence where he was coached by Pop Robson before having a year with York City prior to coming to Sunderland.**

Initially a midfielder as much as a defender, as he got older, Darren played more in the back four, either in central defence or as a right-back. He first came into the first-team picture at Sunderland in December 1995 when he was named as a sub against Crystal Palace at Roker Park, but the club had moved to the Stadium of Light by the time he made his Sunderland debut.

In between he had five matches on loan to Carlisle, his league debut coming against Wigan Athletic at Brunton Park in the month before his first game for Sunderland. Darren did so well in his first season in the first team that in March of that season he earned an England Under 21 cap coming on as a sub (as did Darren Williams) for Jamie Redknapp against Switzerland in Aarau, in a game that also featured former Sunderland loan man Dominic Matteo and future SAFC coach Steve Guppy. The following month Holloway earned a call up for England B along with Darren Williams and Kevin Phillips for a game against Russia at QPR, but had to withdraw through an ankle injury.

Injury problems then stymied his progress with just 14 league starts in his remaining three seasons at Sunderland who loaned him to Sam Allardyce's Bolton Wanderers in December 1999. He started three third tier games for the Trotters before a final appearance as a substitute at Loftus Road. By the following September he was back in the capital, signing for Wimbledon who at the time were playing at Selhurst Park. Proving his fitness, Holloway played 92 league games for the Dons who loaned him to Scunthorpe where he marked his debut with a first goal against Yeovil in March 2004.

There were another four games for Scunthorpe before a transfer later that year to Colin Todd's Bradford City. Holloway scored once (against Hull City) in 57 league games for the Bantams before he played for another Sunderland old boy in David Hodgson at Darlington where he got the third and last league goal of his career (against Lincoln City) in a spell of 21 league appearances before completing his playing days with ten games at Gateshead in 2008-09, having been out of the game since 2007.

He began coaching with Willington Under 18s while doing his coaching badges and then became number two to Alun Armstrong at Blyth Spartans who they took to the Northern Premier League and Northumberland Senior Cup in 2017 before the pair moved to Darlington in the summer of 2019. With the Quakers, they brought about an FA Cup win away to league outfit Swindon in November 2020, Darlington's first win over league opposition since falling out of the Football League themselves.

## HOLTON, James Allan (Jim)

**POSITION:** Centre-half

**BIRTHPLACE:** Lesmahagow, South Lanarkshire

**DATE OF BIRTH:** 11/04/1951 - 05/10/1993

**HEIGHT:** 6' 1½" **WEIGHT:** 13st 5lbs

**SIGNED FROM:** Manchester United, 28/10/1976, on loan from 23/09/1976

**DEBUT:** v West Ham United, A, 25/09/1976

**LAST MATCH:** v Wrexham, A, 12/01/1977

**MOVED TO:** Coventry City, 04/03/1977

**TEAMS:** Celtic, WBA, Shrewsbury Town, Manchester United, Miami Toros (L), Sunderland, Coventry City, Detroit Express (L), Sheffield Wednesday

**INTERNATIONAL:** Scotland

**SAFC TOTALS:** 19 appearances / 1 goal

**A colossal centre-half whose time at Sunderland was too short, Holton's best performance came alongside Jeff Clarke in a 2-0 defeat at Newcastle over Christmas 1976 that would have been much worse but for the superb central defensive duo. Stretchered off just before half-time after being elbowed by Paul Cannell (as admitted in Cannell's autobiography), Cannell was shaking when the teams came out for the second half and there was Big Jim, ready for the battle!**

Holton played under three managers (Bob Stokoe, caretaker Ian MacFarlane and Jimmy Adamson) in his brief spell at Sunderland before being offloaded far too early. In signing him, Bob Stokoe insisted on an initial loan, as after two broken legs Holton had not played for Manchester United for 18 months. After being with Celtic as a boy and with West Brom without playing for them (though he did play against Sunderland in the 1969 FA Youth Cup final), Holton had played 76 games for Shrewsbury and 73 games for Manchester United as well as making 16 appearances for Miami Toros.

Holton debuted against West Ham (the same side he had made his United bow against) before playing against Everton at Roker and then making his second home appearance in the replay of a League Cup tie with Manchester United - he had watched the original meeting as a United player. He swiftly found himself back at Old Trafford (where he was given a great reception) in a Sunderland shirt for a second replay that proved to be the final game of Jim Montgomery. Holton was back at Old Trafford again the following month as Sunderland battled to a point in a 3-3 draw.

However, with new boss Adamson bringing in his own men Holton was sold to relegation rivals Coventry City and indeed played (as did Ian Wallace and Tom Ritchie) in the infamously delayed Coventry v Bristol City game that resulted in Sunderland's controversial relegation in 1977. After exactly 100 games for Coventry, Holton returned to the USA with Detroit Express in whom Coventry's Jimmy Hill had invested, Holton being one of a handful of Coventry connected players to link up with Detroit.

## HOLTON, Jim (Continued)

Having played 21 games and scored three goals for Detroit, Holton was selected for an NASL side to face New York Cosmos at the Giants Stadium in a farewell match for Franz Beckenbauer. Returning from the USA, Holton signed for Jack Charlton at Sheffield Wednesday but never played a game for the Owls. He retired at the age of 31, becoming a publican and running the Town Wall Tavern and then the Rising Sun in Coventry.

At the age of 42, Jim Holton died suddenly at the wheel of his car, a post-mortem revealing the cause of death as Ischaemic heart disease and coronary atheroma. A Scotland international, he won 15 caps (2 goals) including three games at the 1974 FIFA World Cup in which the Scots were unbeaten, including a goalless draw against reigning champions Brazil. Wherever he went Jim Holton was accompanied by the chant (and title of his 2019 biography) 'Six foot two, Eyes of Blue' (Big Jim Holton's after you) - although he was 6'1½" and had brown eyes!

## HONEYMAN, George Christopher

**POSITION:** Midfielder

**BIRTHPLACE:** Prudhoe

**DATE OF BIRTH:** 08/09/1994

**HEIGHT:** 5' 8" **WEIGHT:** 11st 0lbs

**SIGNED FROM:** School, 01/07/2011

**DEBUT:** v Bradford City, A, 15/02/2015

**LAST MATCH:** v Charlton Athletic, N, 26/05/2019

**MOVED TO:** Hull City, 02/08/2019

**TEAMS:** Sunderland, Gateshead (L), Hull City, Millwall (to June 2022)

**SAFC TOTALS:** 83+14 appearances / 15 goal

**Twice a Wembley captain with Sunderland, Honeyman came to the club's academy as a ten-year old, progressing through the ranks where by the time he was at Under 18 level it was evident that he was a cultured creator of chances. As he started to play first-team football George developed another aspect to his game, becoming more industrious and showing more of the defensive side of his attributes.**

Given a debut by Gus Poyet as a late sub in an FA Cup tie on a mudheap of a pitch at Phil Parkinson's Bradford City, Honeyman looked to have been given the short straw in terms of an opportunity to impress. The following autumn he went on loan to National League Gateshead, scoring at Boreham Wood on the second of his nine outings. At the end of that season he made a Premier League debut as a sub at Watford under Sam Allardyce before a third first-team appearance the following January came under a third different manager/head coach in David Moyes.

Going on to establish himself he became captain in 2018-19, skippering the side to the 2019 Football League (Checkatrade) Trophy final against Portsmouth and the same season's Play-Off final with Charlton, although on both occasions he mounted the steps to the Royal Box as the losing skipper. Sold to Hull City that summer he suffered relegation from the Championship in 2020 (as he had with Sunderland two years earlier), but inspired them to immediate promotion as champions in 2021. After 103+24 games and 10 goals for Hull Honeyman signed for Millwall in June 2022.

## HOOD, Henry Anthony (Harry)

**POSITION:** Inside-right / centre-forward

**BIRTHPLACE:** Glasgow

**DATE OF BIRTH:** 03/10/1944 - 26/05/2019

**HEIGHT:** 5' 9" **WEIGHT:** 11st 0lbs

**SIGNED FROM:** Clyde, 09/11/1964

**DEBUT:** v Burnley, H, 14/11/1964

**LAST MATCH:** v Sheffield United, A, 20/09/1966

**MOVED TO:** Clyde, 07/10/1966

**TEAMS:** Brunswick, Clyde, Sunderland, Clyde, Celtic, San Antonio Thunder, Motherwell, Queen of the South

**INTERNATIONAL:** Scotland Under 23

**SAFC TOTALS:** 33+1 appearances / 10 goals

**Harry was a right-winger or centre-forward who did well at Sunderland - once scoring the winner against Manchester United - and won a stack of silverware with Celtic. Harry had turned down Celtic to sign for Sunderland before later joining the Celts.**

Interviewed in Sunderland's match programme in 2010, Harry remembered the interest in him following his 40 goals in 63 league games for Clyde, "I was absolutely stunned when I ran out at Roker Park for my debut. Remember in my career I would ultimately play in front of huge raucous crowds in Glasgow, but I've never forgotten what the noise and atmosphere was like inside Roker Park".

Having debuted in a win over Burnley shortly after turning 20, Harry soon got his first goal against Everton - a club where his brother Jackie was a pro. After a more than decent first season on Wearside injury struck Harry who would miss the entire 1965-66 campaign after suffering a double hernia doing weight training in pre-season. When he returned in 1966-67, he would play just a handful of games despite scoring in a big win over Blackpool on his last appearance at Roker.

The problem was Harry became one of a group of players effectively frozen out by Ian McColl, the ex-Rangers man who had become Sunderland boss at the end of Hood's first season. In October '66 Sunderland cut their losses on Harry, selling him back to Clyde for under half the £26,000 he had cost. Once again he excelled and two and a half years later finally did sign for Jock Stein's all-conquering Celtic, not long after scoring against England in winning his only international cap at Under 23 level. He did tour with Scotland in 1967, but did not win a full cap.

At Parkhead Hood won five league titles, three cups and played in four other finals - scoring in the 1971 and '74 Scottish Cup finals as well as scoring a hat-trick in the 1974 semi-final against Rangers. In May 1976 Harry crossed the Atlantic to briefly play for San Antonio Thunder before finishing his playing days with Motherwell and having short spells as manager of Albion Rovers and Queen of the South in the early eighties. After leaving the game behind Harry became a hotelier in Lanarkshire and ran a chain of pubs in Glasgow. A Biography, 'Harry Hood: Twice as Good' was published in 2021.

## HOOPER, Harold (Harry)

**POSITION:** Outside-right

**BIRTHPLACE:** Pittington, Co Durham

**DATE OF BIRTH:** 14/06/1933 - 26/08/2020

**HEIGHT:** 5' 8" **WEIGHT:** 10st 10lbs

**SIGNED FROM:** Birmingham City, 28/09/1960

**DEBUT:** v Plymouth Argyle, A, 01/10/1960

**LAST MATCH:** v Huddersfield Town, H, 27/4/1963

**MOVED TO:** Kettering Town, 19/07/1963

**TEAMS:** Southwick St Hilda's, Hylton Colliery Juniors, West Ham United, Wolves, Birmingham City, Sunderland, Kettering Town, Dunstable Town

**INTERNATIONAL:** England B

**SAFC TOTALS:** 80 appearances / 19 goals

**Before coming to Sunderland Hooper had become the first player to score for a British club in a European final - against Barcelona no less - and had been the costliest winger in England, as well as scoring against SAFC the last time that six goals were conceded at home (to 2022).**

An England 'B' and Under 23 international, Harry represented the Football League three times and was on standby for the 1954 World Cup, although he never won a full cap. Interviewed in the club magazine Legion of Light in 2004, he explained why, "England had a couple of good wingers who kept me out" - referring to the legendary Sir Stanley Matthews and Sir Tom Finney! Hooper scored in England colours at Roker Park, netting in a 1-1 'B' international with Scotland on 3 March 1954 when he played alongside future Sunderland centre-forward Don Revie.

Later the same season he won further B caps against West Germany, Yugoslavia and Switzerland before playing against West Germany again in 1955. In January of that year he scored two late goals on his England Under 23 debut against Italy at Stamford Bridge in a game where Stan Anderson was an unused substitute. The following month, in a 6-0 win over Scotland in Glasgow, Hooper played alongside Anderson who came on as an early sub.

Harry was an amateur at Sunderland in 1950 having started with Southwick St Hilda's and Hylton Colliery Juniors. However, his dad would not let him sign for Sunderland, who at the time were signing big-name players with youngsters rarely given an opportunity. Instead Hooper signed for West Ham where his father, Harry senior, was a coach. Hooper senior had captained Sheffield United in the FA Cup final in 1936. Harry junior also had a brother, Alf, who played for Halifax Town.

Hooper junior debuted for the second division Hammers in 1951. He did so well that after 44 goals in 130 games Wolves paid a club record £25,000 for him in 1956. It was also a British record fee for a winger. Wolves were one of the top teams in the country at the time. Hooper had the task of taking over from club hero Johnny Hancocks and responded by being top-scorer with 19 goals in what was his solitary season at Molineux.

Hooper moved across the Second City to Birmingham, one of his goals in his first season coming in a 6-1 win at Roker Park in April 1958. Having already scored in European football as part of a London X1 who won an Inter-Cities Fairs Cup match in Basel in 1955, Harry scored on his European debut for Birmingham in the same competition in 1958 going on to score in four games out of five, including both legs of the semi-final, before scoring in the second leg of the final away to Barcelona. Birmingham lost on aggregate having become the first British club to reach a European final.

After 42 goals in 119 games for the Blues Harry finally got to play for Sunderland when £18,000 was paid for him. At Sunderland he would promise Charlie Hurley that corners would be delivered with the lace of the ball away from the target, Hurley's head, while he also became the provider of many of Brian Clough's goals for Sunderland. Hooper scored almost a goal every four games himself from the wing. Two of his best came in December 1960 at Swansea as Sunderland earned a point after being 3-0 down. Having dragged the Lads back into the game with a 25-yard screamer, Hooper equalised five minutes into injury time after dribbling past three men to net from just inside the box. Following his football career (which ended at Dunstable Town and not Heanor Town as sometimes reported), he worked for an American electronics company in Bedford during the 1990s. Eighty-seven when he passed away, Harry fought Alzheimer's disease and had spent the final year of his life in a care home in Norfolk.

## HOPE, James William

**POSITION:** Inside-right

**BIRTHPLACE:** Kelloe, Co Durham

**DATE OF BIRTH:** 28/03/1885 - 28/04/1925

**HEIGHT:** 5' 8½" **WEIGHT:** 11st 10lbs

**SIGNED FROM:** Horden Athletic,15/01/1908

**DEBUT:** v Leicester Fosse, A, 20/03/1909

**LAST MATCH:** v Leicester Fosse, A, 20/03/1909

**MOVED TO:** Horden Athletic 01/05/1909

**TEAMS:** Kelloe, South Moors Violet (West Stanley), Birtley, West Stanley, Horden Colliery, Horden Athletic, Sunderland, Horden Athletic

**SAFC TOTALS:** 1 appearance / 0 goals

**During a season and a half at Sunderland, Hope's only first-team game came on a day four regulars were missing and the Lads went down 4-3.**

He had come to prominence having done well in local football, notably helping Birtley to win the Gateshead League. In August 1914, he emigrated to Johnson City in Illinois where he became a coal miner.

## HOPE (O'NEILL), Alan

**POSITION:** Inside-left

**BIRTHPLACE:** Deptford, Sunderland, Co Durham

**DATE OF BIRTH:** 13/11/1937

**HEIGHT:** 5' 8" **WEIGHT:** 10st 11lbs

**SIGNED FROM:** Deptford School, 01/06/1953

**DEBUT:** v Cardiff City, A, 17/11/1956

**LAST MATCH:** v Middlesbrough, A, 24/09/1960

**MOVED TO:** Aston Villa, 17/10/1960

**TEAMS:** Sunderland, Aston Villa, Plymouth Argyle, Bournemouth & Boscombe Athletic, Cambridge United, South Africa, Drumcondra

**SAFC TOTALS:** 76 appearances / 28 goals

**Had he played in the modern era where players' names are incorporated into fans chants, there would have been no use singing 'There's only one Alan Hope' as mid-way through his time at Sunderland - in April 1957 - he changed his surname by deed poll from Hope to his step-father's surname of O'Neill. As if two names were not enough, he also had the nickname 'The Cod Liver Oil Kid.'**

Making his first-team debut four days after turning 19, he played eight games as Alan Hope without scoring, but bagged a brace on the last day of the season in his first game as O'Neill. Talented as a creator as well as a finisher, the following season was his best on a personal level, but despite the 13 goals from 32 games that made him top scorer he could not stop Sunderland being relegated for the first time. In his remaining seasons, he never played in more than a third of the league games and asked for a transfer several times before being sold for £10,000 to top-flight Aston Villa.

He made a sensational debut, scoring after just 25 seconds and adding a second in a 6-2 derby victory over Birmingham City on 22 October 1960. Another goal the following week in a win at local rivals West Brom, cemented his place in Villa hearts. He then wrote his name into the record books with a goal in the League Cup final second leg against Rotherham, albeit, this first-ever League Cup final was held over to the start of 1961-62. However, having made only three league appearances that season, he was transferred to second division

Plymouth Argyle in November 1962, signing off for Villa as he started, with a final goal against Birmingham in a total of eleven goals in 34 appearances.

As at Villa, O'Neill got off to a blistering start with Argyle with a debut goal at Chelsea followed by a brace against Luton on his home debut. By the end of the season he was second top scorer with eleven goals in 18 games, including a goal back at Roker Park. There would be just 18 more games, and six goals, before he was on the move again, this time to Bournemouth in February 1964. There were eight goals in 37 games for the Cherries before a switch to Cambridge United who were then in the Southern League followed by a short spell with Chelmsford City as well as a couple of years playing in South African football. In August 1970 he moved to Ireland as player/manager of Drumcondra after which he stayed in Drumcondra to run a Guest House.

## HOPKINS, William (Bill)

**POSITION:** Right-half / centre-half

**BIRTHPLACE:** Esh Winning, Co Durham

**DATE OF BIRTH:** 11/11/1888 - 26/01/1938

**HEIGHT:** 5' 10" **WEIGHT:** 11st 7lbs

**SIGNED FROM:** Stanley United, 04/05/1912

**DEBUT:** v Liverpool, A, 13/09/1913

**LAST MATCH:** v West Bromwich Albion, A, 20/03/1915

**MOVED TO:** Leeds City, 30/07/1919

**TEAMS:** Esh Winning Rangers, Crook Town, Stanley United, Sunderland, Leeds City, South Shields, Hartlepools United, Durham City

**SAFC TOTALS:** 10 appearances / 0 goals

**Known as 'Pop' or 'Tot', Bill Hopkins had a long career playing in the Football League for Durham City, South Shields and Leeds City as well as Sunderland and Hartlepools. Having become player/coach at Durham City in 1924-25, he served Hartlepools as trainer from July 1926 until the following February when he became assistant trainer at Sheffield United.**

He went on to become trainer of Charlton Athletic, Grimsby Town, Port Vale and Barnsley in the 1930s. Hopkins had just taken up his post at Oakwell when he passed away suddenly while with the club staying in Blackpool as they prepared for an FA Cup replay at Manchester United.

## HOPKINS, Bill (Continued)

Coming from local football, Hopkins had an enormous task in forcing his way into the side at Sunderland who were reigning league champions when he made his first six appearances in 1913-14.

Having managed another four games the following term, league football then ceased due to World War One. After the war, he was sold to Leeds City for £50. Debuting at Blackpool on 30 August 1919, he played in the first seven of their eight league games (under Herbert Chapman) before Leeds were expelled from the Football League due to a scandal concerning illegal payments to war-time 'Guest' players.

Their next game should have been at South Shields and it was Shields who bought Hopkin for £600 when the Leeds players were auctioned off in October - a twelve-fold increase on what Sunderland had sold him for after a handful of games. After 61 games and two goals for Shields, Hopkin moved to Hartlepools where he scored once in 56 league and cup games, debuting at Wrexham in August 1921. Almost exactly two years later, he transferred to Durham City, becoming coach a year later for a club where he added 50 league appearances to his total.

## HORNBY, Cecil Frederick (Cyril)

**POSITION:** Centre-half / centre-forward

**BIRTHPLACE:** West Bromwich, Staffordshire

**DATE OF BIRTH:** 29/04/1907 - Q3 1964

**HEIGHT:** 5' 11" **WEIGHT:** 11st 4lbs

**SIGNED FROM:** Leeds United, 05/02/1936

**DEBUT:** v Grimsby Town, H, 19/02/1936

**LAST MATCH:** v Grimsby Town, A, 12/04/1937

**MOVED TO:** Okengates Town, 05/07/1937

**TEAMS:** Okengates Town, Leeds United, Sunderland, Okengates Town, Brierley Hill Alliance, Cradley Heath

**SAFC TOTALS:** 13 appearances / 3 goals

**Signing for Sunderland on the day goalkeeper Jimmy Thorpe tragically passed away, Hornby managed eight games in the run-in to the season, scoring one of his two goals on the day the title was sealed with a stunning 7-2 win at Birmingham.**

He left shortly after the FA Cup was won in 1937, having scored in the opening game of the cup run at Southampton. His final appearance was not such a joyful occasion, playing in a 6-0 loss at Grimsby on a day when Sunderland changed eight outfield players two days after qualifying for their first Wembley FA Cup final.

Signed from Leeds United, Hornby had played 89 league and cup games, scoring five times, his fifth appearance coming at Roker Park in February 1931 as Leeds slumped towards relegation. Promoted in his second season when he played eleven times, Hornby's versatility was always invaluable although he largely held down the left-half position in his best season of 1934-35 when he played 34 top-flight games.

He became player/manager of his first club Okengates Town of the Birmingham League when he left Sunderland and after retiring from football found employment as a welder.

## HORSWILL, Michael Frederick (Micky)

**POSITION:** Midfielder

**BIRTHPLACE:** Annfield Plain, Co Durham

**DATE OF BIRTH:** 06/03/1953

**HEIGHT:** 5' 10½" **WEIGHT:** 11st 0lbs

**SIGNED FROM:** Annfield Plain, 01/07/1968

**DEBUT:** v Preston North End, A, 04/04/1972

**LAST MATCH:** v Middlesbrough, H, 02/03/19747

**MOVED TO:** Manchester City, 11/03/1974

**TEAMS:** Stanley Boys, Annfield Plain, Sunderland, Manchester City, Plymouth Argyle, Hull City, Happy Valley, Barrow, Carlisle United

**SAFC TOTALS:** 91+1 appearances / 5 goals

**The youngest member of the 1973 FA Cup-winning team, Horswill turned 20 mid-way through the cup run in which he played every game. Playing at the centre of midfield, he was the destroyer who quietened the most effective players of the opposition.**

The great Colin Bell of Manchester City and World Cup-winner Alan Ball felt Horswill's aggression and energy in the biggest games before the final when the twin Leeds axis of Johnny Giles and Billy Bremner had little or no time on the ball thanks largely to Micky's determination to stop them playing. Horswill however, was more than a destroyer. He could pass well and although he only scored five times one of those was a terrific goal at Manchester City in the cup run, with another remaining in 2022 the last goal scored by Sunderland in senior European competition. That came against Sporting Lisbon in the European Cup Winners' Cup, whilst he went close to scoring in the FA Cup final itself.

First associated with SAFC as a twelve-year-old, Horswill came under the spell of Martin Harvey who he looked up to and learned from. While he has retained a life-long love of the club, becoming the organiser of the Former Players' Association's many golf days, Micky's time at Sunderland ended just five days after his 21st birthday when he was valued at £100,000 in a deal that took him and Dennis Tueart to Manchester City with Tony Towers coming in the opposite direction.

A friend of Mike Summerbee and United's George Best while in Manchester, Micky was thrust into a Manchester derby two days after arriving and made 12+3 appearances for City, ending in a home win over Everton in February 1975 that was one of only two victories he enjoyed, the other coming against Newcastle. Ron Saunders who had signed him, left the club a month after Micky arrived, being replaced by Tony Book.

In June 1975, he began a three-year stint with Plymouth. Making his fourth Argyle appearance at home to Sunderland he appeared at Roker Park later in the season, coming back from injury in the only one of his 36 games to be off the bench. He made 40 starts the following 1976-77 season as Plymouth were relegated and left a year later following the arrival of Malcolm Allison (who had not been at City when Horswill was there). Micky totalled 112+6 appearances for Plymouth, scoring three goals.

Always tigerish in midfield, not least due to his hair colour, Horswill went to Hull City where he scored six times in 82 league games before moving to Hong Kong to play for Happy Valley in March 1982 before joining Barrow who were managed by Vic Halom. There was a final 1973 connection with Horswill's last move which re-united him with Bob Stokoe at Carlisle United, but he played just once - alongside Jackie Ashurst - in a home defeat to Blackburn Rovers on 29 August 1983.

Horswill went on to become a publican, ran a sports and social club attached to the Nissan car factory, managed Thorney Close Variety club, worked as a sales rep for a worktop supplier in Shildon in the mid 1990s and became transport manager for a flooring and kitchen worktop company. He also became very involved in charity work raising money for good causes and worked in corporate hospitality for SAFC. Additionally he became a popular radio personality on Real Radio North East and later Star Radio North East alongside Middlesbrough and Newcastle legends Bernie Slaven and Malcolm MacDonald. In 2022 Mick received the Freedom of the City of Sunderland as a 1973 FA Cup winner.

## HOUSAM, Arthur

**POSITION:** Half-back

**BIRTHPLACE:** Sunderland, Co Durham

**DATE OF BIRTH:** 01/10/1917 - 31/12/1975

**HEIGHT:** 5' 9½" **WEIGHT:** 11st 7lbs

**SIGNED FROM:** Hylton Colliery, 28/08/1936

**DEBUT:** v Preston North End, H, 04/05/1938

**LAST MATCH:** v Aston Villa, H, 27/08/1947

**MOVED TO:** Horden CW, 01/08/1948

**TEAMS:** Hylton Colliery, Sunderland, Sheffield Wednesday (WW2 Guest), Chester (WW2 Guest), Horden Colliery Welfare

**SAFC TOTALS:** 67 appearances / 3 goals

**Twelve of Arthur Housam's 67 official appearances came in the FA Cup, half of those being in the 1945-46 campaign of two-legged cup games before the Football League resumed the following season.**

Known to have been a big admirer of twenties star Billy Clunas, Housam broke into the side late in the season after the 1937 cup win and played 23 times in the last full season before World War Two. Arthur lost his best years to the war, but was still around to play 34 times in the first post-war league campaign before mirroring his first season of 1937-38 with two games in 1947-48. He was released on 31 July 1947 after undergoing operations on both eyes.

In addition to his official appearances, he played an additional 117 times for Sunderland in war-time games (including the expunged 1939-40 and League North 1945-46 seasons), appearing in both legs of the 1942 League War Cup final against Wolves and the first leg of the West Riding Cup final against Huddersfield the following year.

During the war, in which he served in the Police Force, he also scored three times in six games as a Guest player for Sheffield Wednesday in 1941-42 and appeared twelve times as a Guest for Chester across 1943-44 and 1944-45. From 1945 to 1957 he managed the Aquatic Arms pub in Monkwearmouth with his wife.

## HOWEY, Lee Matthew

**POSITION:** Centre-forward

**BIRTHPLACE:** Sunderland, Co Durham

**DATE OF BIRTH:** 01/04/1969

**HEIGHT:** 6' 3" **WEIGHT:** 13st 9lbs

**SIGNED FROM:** Bishop Auckland, 25/03/1993 following trial from 08/02/1993

**DEBUT:** v Portsmouth, H, 01/05/1993

**LAST MATCH:** v Wimbledon, A, 11/05/1997

**MOVED TO:** Burnley, 11/08/1997

**TEAMS:** Ipswich Town, Gateshead, AC Hemptinee, Seaham Red Star, Bishop Auckland, Sunderland, Burnley, Northampton Town, Forest Green Rovers, Nuneaton Borough, Bedford Town, Buckingham Town

**SAFC TOTALS:** 42+39 appearances / 11 goals

**A member of the Sunderland Boys squad that shared the English Schools FA Trophy with Middlesbrough in 1983 when his teammates included Dale White, Howey was snapped up by Ipswich Town. A physically imposing target-man, Lee did not get a game for the Tractor Boys but did enough to be remembered by their England centre-half terry Butcher who brought him out of non-league football to Sunderland seven years after Lee had left Ipswich due to a bad knee injury.**

While Howey came to Sunderland from Bishop Auckland, a fee of £6,000 was paid to Belgian club Hemptinee who still held his registration papers at a time when the player was combining turning out for Bishops with working as a clerk for BT.

Almost half of Howey's appearances for Sunderland came as a sub and while he was a centre-forward he was occasionally employed in the central-defensive position in which his brother Steven won England caps as well as listing Newcastle United and Manchester City amongst his clubs.

Undoubtedly Lee's best season was in 1995-96 when he started 17 games and came off the bench ten times as the Championship was won. Two of his three league goals that term were winners, while he scored twice on his one League Cup appearance and twice came on as a sub in the FA Cup against Manchester United. Unquestionably his best goal was a towering header that decided a home game with Middlesbrough in January 1994.

Lee went on to serve Burnley where all but five of his 31+3 games came in 1997-98 after a £200,000 sale. Used mainly in defence in a team that included Chris Waddle, Gerry Harrison and Chris Woods, his solitary goal came in the League Cup against Lincoln City. Initially loaned to Northampton in November 1998, he completed a £50,000 move to the Cobblers the following February and scored six goals in 47+1 league outings. With Conference club Forest Green Rovers in 2001-02 he played twice in the FA Cup against Football League side Macclesfield, scoring his side's eighth spot-kick in an 11-10 penalty shoot-out defeat against a side that featured ex-Sunderland man Chris Byrne.

In October 2002 Lee moved into management as player/assistant manager with Bedford Town. In October of the following year, he became assistant manager at Aylesbury for four months before a 14 month spell in the same role at Kettering Town. Almost a year after leaving Kettering, at the age of 37, he pulled his boots back on when becoming player-assistant manager of Buckingham Town. After retiring from football Howey worked in banking as well as becoming a committee member of the Sunderland Former Players' Association. In 2018, he released his biography, 'Massively Violent and Decidedly Average.'

## HOYTE, Justin Raymond

**POSITION:** Full-back

**BIRTHPLACE:** Leytonstone, London

**DATE OF BIRTH:** 20/11/1984

**HEIGHT:** 5' 11" **WEIGHT:** 10st 7lbs

**SIGNED FROM:** Arsenal, 31/08/2005, on loan

**DEBUT:** v Chelsea, A, 10/09/2005

**LAST MATCH:** v Aston Villa, A, 07/05/2006

**MOVED TO:** Arsenal, 08/05/2006, end of loan

**TEAMS:** Redbridge United, Arsenal Sunderland, Middlesbrough, Millwall, Dagenham & Redbridge, FC Cincinnati, Miami Beach

**INTERNATIONAL:** England Under 21 / Trinidad & Tobago

**SAFC TOTALS:** 30 appearances / 1 goal

**Justin Hoyte did really well for SAFC in a season-long loan from Arsenal, albeit he was part of a side relegated with just 15 points. Just 20 when he arrived, Hoyte's time on Wearside was tough, but coming from a sporting family he dealt with it impressively. His mother Wendy (nee Clarke) was a Gold medallist in the 4x100m relay at the 1982 Commonwealth Games and a silver medallist at the same event the same year in the European Championships as well as running at the Olympics in 1976.**

Father Les was also an international sprinter who went on to become Sprint coach at Arsenal's academy from 1998 to 2008. Cousin Chris Clarke MBE was a 400m gold medallist at the 2007 World Youth Championships while brother Gavin played four times for Arsenal, the first of his ten clubs (including loans) and represented England up to Under 20 level before going on to play for Trinidad & Tobago.

Justin had a personal best of 11.01 seconds for the 100 metres and reached the final of the English schools championship in that event. As a footballer, he began as a striker, joining Arsenal as a nine-year-old after playing Sunday League football. He converted to right-back at Under 17 level and also played regularly at left-back once he got into the first team at Arsenal.

An unused sub in the 2001 FA Youth Cup final, he made a senior debut as a late sub in a 6-1 win over Southampton in May 2003, came off the bench at Wembley in the 2004 and 2005 Community Shield games and went on to make a total of 50+18 appearances for the Gunners, including ten in the Champions League. His one goal - against Charlton - made him the first Englishman to score for Arsenal at the Emirates Stadium.

Mart Poom went on loan to Arsenal from Sunderland as part of the arrangement for Justin's loan move to the Stadium of Light where his highlight was putting Sunderland ahead against Newcastle, although that match ended in defeat. Two years after leaving Wearside he returned to the north-east when Middlesbrough paid £3m for him. Making his fifth appearance for Boro in a defeat at Sunderland he went on to play 142+20 games for the Teessiders, scoring twice to add to his single goals for Arsenal and Sunderland.

After a spell on loan back in London with Millwall, he signed for the Lions but only played 6+2 times for them in total before joining League Two Dagenham & Redbridge in October 2015. After 24+3 games for the Daggers, who lost their Football league status while he was there, Justin moved to Cincinnati in March 2017, initially playing indoor football.

His international career took a similar path across the Atlantic. After playing 58 times for England at Under 16, 19, 20 and 21 levels, he went on to make a full international debut for Trinidad & Tobago having turned down the opportunity to play for the country of his heritage at the 2006 FIFA World Cup finals. Subsequently, Justin played for Miami Beach Club de Futbal and set up the Justin Hoyte Academy in Miami.

## HUDGELL, Arthur John

**POSITION:** Left-back

**BIRTHPLACE:** Hackney, London

**DATE OF BIRTH:** 28/12/1920 - 13/10/2000

**HEIGHT:** 5' 9" **WEIGHT:** 11st 13lbs

**SIGNED FROM:** Crystal Palace, 29/01/1947

**DEBUT:** v Blackburn Rovers, A, 01/02/1947

**LAST MATCH:** v Portsmouth, A, 01/05/1957

**MOVED TO:** Retired, 06/05/1957

**TEAMS:** Eton Manor, Crystal Palace, Fulham (WW2 Guest), Sunderland

**SAFC TOTALS:** 275 appearances / 0 goals

**Hudgell cost a record fee of £10,000 for a defender when bought from Crystal Palace. Post war at Palace in 1945-46, he had played in 33 of the 36 games it took to win Division Three South (South Region), and finish fourth in the League Cup qualifying competition, one of those league games being a 10-1 win over Swindon Town.**

In the same season he also played three times in the FA Cup, all against QPR. The third game brought the tie's only goal. Played at Craven Cottage, it was on familiar turf for Hudgell who had made a single appearance as a war-time 'Guest' for Fulham the

## HUDGELL, Arthur (Continued)

previous season. Between 1939-40 and 1944-45 he played 137 times for Palace, scoring six times. He managed these games in the face of being in the RAF and spending two years based in Iceland during which he played in representative games against the navy and the army. In 1946-47, he played in Palace's first 25 Division Three South games, scoring the only goal of his peace-time career with a penalty against Ipswich. However, it was in a 6-2 defeat that he caught the eye. That was under three weeks before he signed for Sunderland and came at St James' Park in the FA Cup.

Once on Wearside, Arthur played every game bar one for the rest of his first season and made a minimum of 40 league appearances (out of 42) in each of his first four seasons. The next three saw that number decrease to between 20 and 30 with the final three campaigns seeing him reduced to between one and four appearances. Following his retirement, he continued at the club as a coach and became involved in developing Silksworth CW juniors.

## HUGGINS, John Warwick (Jack)

**POSITION:** Outside-left

**BIRTHPLACE:** Crosby Ravensworth, Westmorland

**DATE OF BIRTH:** 02/06/1886 - 26/04/1915

**HEIGHT:** 5' 8" **WEIGHT:** 12st 0lbs

**SIGNED FROM:** Bede College, 01/07/1906

**DEBUT:** v Manchester United, H, 20/10/1906

**LAST MATCH:** v Birmingham, H, 04/04/1908

**MOVED TO:** Reading, 12/05/1908

**TEAMS:** Workington, Leadgate, Bede College, Sunderland, Reading, Wingate

**SAFC TOTALS:** 14 appearances / 2 goals

**Jack Huggins was the first former Sunderland player to be killed in action during the First World War. A Private in the 1st & 8th Battalions of the Durham Light Infantry, he died at Ypres just five days after arriving in France.**

He came to SAFC while doing teacher training at Bede College. His sporting talent saw him play cricket for Durham while his footballing ability was first spotted by trainer Billy Williams at Leadgate. Initially signed as an amateur, Huggins enjoyed a stunning debut by setting up two goals and scoring another in a 4-1 win over Manchester United.

Once he qualified as a teacher Huggins left Sunderland to sign for Reading where he had accepted a teaching post. He netted six goals in 34 Southern League games in his first season. He then returned to Sunderland in the summer of 1909 after getting a teaching job at Wheatley Hill, but did not add to his first-team appearances.

In December 2014 Sunderland's Under 12s team visited his grave near Roulers as part of the Premier League's 'Football Remembers' project. In the same month, he was named on a plaque sited in tribute at the Garden of Remembrance adjacent to the Fans' statue near the main entrance of the Stadium of Light.

## HUGGINS, Niall Joseph

**POSITION:** Full-back

**BIRTHPLACE:** York, Yorkshire

**DATE OF BIRTH:** 18/12/2000

**HEIGHT:** 5' 8" **WEIGHT:** 10st 6lbs

**SIGNED FROM:** Leeds United, 20/08/2021

**DEBUT:** v Blackpool, A, 21/08/2021

**LAST MATCH:**

**MOVED TO:**

**TEAMS:** Heworth, Leeds Unite., Sunderland

**INTERNATIONAL:** Wales Under 21

**SAFC TOTALS:** 3+1 appearances / 0 goals (to June 2022)

**Having come through the ranks at Leeds where he had made a Premier League debut at Arsenal in February 2021, Huggins joined the group of young hungry players brought in by Sunderland in the summer of 2021 despite having two years left on his contract at Elland Road.**

A pacey player, he had started out as an eight-year-old with Heworth in Yorkshire before joining Leeds' academy in 2009. Injuries hampered him in his early years: an ankle injury in the Under 14s, back injury at Under 16 level and stress fracture of the femur in his first year as a scholar.

He overcame these hurdles to score twelve goals in 29 games at Under 19 level in 2018-19 before he stepped up to the Under 23s where he claimed a couple of goals and three assists as his side won promotion from PL2. At Leeds he became primarily seen as a left-back, but was also used at right-back, in midfield and also as a forward.

Qualifying through his father, Huggins represented Wales, winning his first cap in an Under 21 international against Albania on 9 June 2019.

## HUGHES, Ian James

**POSITION:** Midfielder

**BIRTHPLACE:** Sunderland, Co Durham

**DATE OF BIRTH:** 24/08/1961

**HEIGHT:** 5' 9" **WEIGHT:** 11st 11lbs

**SIGNED FROM:** Youth product, 01/08/1977

**DEBUT:** v Swansea City, A, 10/11/1979

**LAST MATCH:** v Swansea City, A, 10/11/1979

**MOVED TO:** Barnsley, 01/07/1981

**TEAMS:** Sunderland, Barnsley, Seaham Red Star

**SAFC TOTALS:** 1 appearance / 0 goals

**A local lad who played in an away defeat during a promotion season, it proved to be his only senior game, as he did not play for Barnsley in his time there and failed to add to his first-team appearances after returning to Sunderland as a non-contract player in 1982.**

He did go on to play in local football, his promise in the professional game being ended by torn medial ligaments. He continued to work at Sunderland, initially with schoolboys and subsequently coaching the youth team before leaving in 1985 to spend a season coaching the juniors at Newcastle United before becoming a senior scout for West Ham United. After retiring from coaching, Hughes became a business manager for a pharmaceutical company.

## HUGHES, John

**POSITION:** Centre-forward

**BIRTHPLACE:** Coatbridge, North Lanarkshire

**DATE OF BIRTH:** 03/04/1943 - 01/08/2022

**HEIGHT:** 6' 2" **WEIGHT:** 14st 2lbs

**SIGNED FROM:** Crystal Palace, 23/01/1973

**DEBUT:** v Millwall, H, 27/01/1973

**LAST MATCH:** v Millwall, H, 27/01/1973

**MOVED TO:** Retired, 28/03/1973

**TEAMS:** Shotts Bon Accord, Celtic, Crystal Palace, Sunderland

**INTERNATIONAL:** Scotland

**SAFC TOTALS:** 1 appearance / 0 goals

**The brother of 1973 FA Cup winner Billy, John was injured on his debut for Sunderland and never played again - other than in a testimonial for his brother in 1977. To 2022 it was the last time two brothers played together for the club, although Ricardo Gabbiadini's only game saw him come on as a sub for brother Marco. The Hughes' had a third brother, Pat, who played for Darlington as well as St Mirren and Hamilton.**

To 2022 John Hughes remains the eighth highest goalscorer in Celtic's history. His tally of 189 goals in 416 games included five in a 1965 game against Aberdeen, two penalties in a 2-1 League Cup final win over Rangers in the same calendar year, one in the League Cup final of 1967, as Dundee were beaten, and a whole host of spectacular goals for which he was famed.

A physically powerful player, he was almost impossible to knock off the ball. Nicknamed 'Yogi' after the cartoon character Yogi bear, Celtic fans would urge their team to 'Feed the bear.'

He played in seven league title-winning seasons and participated in nine domestic cup wins (not including the Glasgow Cup), although injury sometimes prevented him playing in finals. One such occasion was in 1967 when he was ruled out of the European Cup final as Celtic became the first British team to win the trophy - although he had played in five of the eight games to get there. Three years later after scoring in the semi-final against Leeds at Hampden in front of a UEFA record crowd of 136,505, John played in the European Cup final against Feyenoord. On that occasion he missed a good chance in extra-time as Celtic lost. He felt strongly that manager Jock Stein never forgave him.

Little over a year later after a final appearance in another European Cup game against BK1903 Copenhagen, he was sold - against his wishes - to Crystal Palace. One of his four goals in 23 games there - against Sheffield United where he beat three men before scorching a trademark screamer home from well outside the box - was runner-up in the BBC's first-ever 'Goal of the Season' competition. Hughes felt it deserved to win, but for Jock Stein being on the judging panel and not wanting to give the award to someone he had released.

John scored four goals in six inter-league games for the Scottish League. He dropped out of many Scotland squads because he was unhappy with what he saw as the Rangers dominated Scotland set up, but won eight caps. His one goal was a towering header against Gordon Banks of England in front of another crowd in excess of 130,000 at Hampden in 1968.

## HUGHES, William (Billy)

**POSITION:** Forward

**BIRTHPLACE:** Coatbridge, North Lanarkshire

**DATE OF BIRTH:** 30/12/1948 - 20/12/2019

**HEIGHT:** 5' 9" **WEIGHT:** 10st 2lbs

**SIGNED FROM:** Coatbridge Juniors, 01/09/1964

**DEBUT:** v Liverpool, H, 04/02/1967

**LAST MATCH:** v Wrexham H 08/01/1977

**MOVED TO:** Derby County, 03/09/1977

**TEAMS:** Coatbridge Juniors, Sunderland, Derby County, Leicester City, Carlisle United (L), San Jose, Corby Town

**INTERNATIONAL:** Scotland

**SAFC TOTALS:** 307+28 appearance / 81 goals

**Top scorer in the FA Cup-winning season of 1972-73, three of Billy's goals came in the fifth round against Manchester City, including two in the replay, voted the greatest game in Roker Park's history when it closed after 99 years. He also headed the winner in the semi-final against Arsenal, scored a league hat-trick against Huddersfield three days later and took the corner that led to the only goal of the final. Billy Hughes was a special player in that very special side.**

He went on to score Sunderland's first goal in European competition against Vasas Budapest in the European Cup Winners' Cup, while in the calendar year after the cup final, Manchester United manager Tommy Docherty stated, "Billy Hughes is the most exciting forward in the country" after Billy scored twice at Old Trafford. Docherty was not the only opposition manager to rate Hughes. Don Revie, boss of the Leeds side vanquished in the cup final and manager of the most successful side of the era, tried to sign Billy, describing him as, "one of the most exciting players I've seen".

Fast, strong and determined, Hughes was the ultimate flair player. In today's football, his value would be astronomical. Joining the 'H-bombers' of Hughes and Halom up front for Stokoe's stars was Dennis Tueart. With Vic Halom the battering ram in the middle, Hughes and Tueart were speed merchants with a razor-sharp cutting edge. If they were war-time planes, Vic was the bomber while Dennis and Billy were the Spitfire and Hurricane of the cup-winning team and no-one - absolutely no-one - could handle them.

'Hughesy' was a swashbuckling stylist who always saw himself as a centre-forward, but did much of his best work on the right of the attack. With his flowing black hair, tanned legs and swagger, in full flight he was a sight to behold. Billy was a box of tricks on the pitch, but it was his legendary laughing box which he set off to interrupt interviews ahead of the cup final that highlighted the difference in attitude between relaxed Sunderland and stiff Leeds ahead of the greatest day in Sunderland's post-war history. Billy Hughes was a massive part of that greatest day.

For all the impression of him as a joker, Billy was someone who took his football very seriously and was noted as a very disciplined trainer. He came through the ranks at Sunderland, playing in the FA Youth Cup finals of 1966 and 1967. He also played in the second division winning side of 1976, scoring in the game that sealed the title against Portsmouth. Late in his career, Billy turned out for Derby (19/8) , Leicester (35/5), Carlisle (5/0), San Jose Earthquakes (1/0) and Corby Town, but he remained synonymous with Sunderland. In later life, Billy - who while at Sunderland had a shoe-shop in the town centre called 'Billy's Shughes' was a licensee in Derby and club house manager of Stressholme Golf Club in Darlington, as well as running Keddleston Park golf club in Derbyshire. Shortly before his death he was uplifted when Jim Montgomery broke the news to him that he was to be inducted at the club's second Hall of Fame dinner, an award collected by his widow Linda and daughter Louisa. He was also posthumously awarded the Freedom of the City of Sunderland.

He warranted much more than the single Scotland cap he won against Sweden in 1975, two years before a Testimonial in which his brother John and stars such as Bobby Charlton, Graeme Souness, Malcolm MacDonald and Francis Lee turned out in his honour.

## HUME, Denver Jay

**POSITION:** Left-back

**BIRTHPLACE:** Ashington, Northumberland

**DATE OF BIRTH:** 11/08/1998

**HEIGHT:** 5' 10" **WEIGHT:** 11st 11lbs

**SIGNED FROM:** Youth product, 01/07/2018

**DEBUT:** v Wolverhampton Wanderers, H, 06/05/2018

**LAST MATCH:** v Lincoln City, H, 11/01/2022

**MOVED TO:** Portsmouth, 26/01/2022

**TEAMS:** Sunderland, Portsmouth (to June 2022)

**SAFC TOTALS:** 68+16 appearance / 3 goals

**At Sunderland from Under 9 level, Hume debuted on the final day of the 2017-18 season as the club completed its plummet from Premier League to League One in barely a year.**

After a handful of appearances the following year, including one as a Wembley sub in the Football League (Checkatrade) Trophy final against Portsmouth, he locked down the left back position in the Covid curtailed 2019-20 campaign, playing in 30+2 of the 36 league games.

An injury hit 2020-21 reduced him to 22+4 games in all competitions after which he prevaricated over signing a new contract and once he did, struggled with injury niggles and competition from new signing Dennis Cirkin before moving on to Pompey.

## HUME, Trai

**POSITION:** Right-back / midfield

**BIRTHPLACE:** Ballymena, Northern Ireland

**DATE OF BIRTH:** 18/03/2002

**HEIGHT:** 5' 11" **WEIGHT:** 11st 11lbs

**SIGNED FROM:** Linfield, 04/01/2022

**DEBUT:** v Cheltenham Town, A, 08/02/2022

**LAST MATCH:**

**MOVED TO:**

**TEAMS:** Linfield, Ballymena United (L), Sunderland (to January 2022)

**INTERNATIONAL:** Northern Ireland

**SAFC TOTALS:** 3 appearance / 0 goals (to June 2022)

**Signed for an undisclosed fee reported to be in the region of £200,000, Trai was an unused sub alongside his namesake Denver Hume at Accrington in mid-January 2022, the only occasion both Humes were named on the same teamsheet.**

## HUME, Trai (Continued)

Trai had made his name with Linfield and had nine Under 21 caps at the time of his move. He joined the club as an eleven-year-old and from the age of 16 was guided by David Healy and coached by George McCartney. Hume totalled 31+6 games, debuting as a sub in a 5-1 home win over Cliftonville on 23 April 2019 having been captain of their Swifts Steel and Sons cup winning side the previous December.

From 11 September 2020, he moved on a season-long loan to Ballymena United where he scored six goals from 37 games and became their Young Player of the Year. Returning to Linfield, he played in Champions League and UEFA Conference League qualifying games, and scored the last of his three goals for Linfield three days before signing for Sunderland. That last goal came in a 6-1 win over Dungannon whose goalkeeper was Niall Quinn's son Michael. On 29 March 2022 Trai came on as a late sub against Hungary to win his first full cap.

## HUNTER, George

**POSITION:** Right-half

**BIRTHPLACE:** South Hetton, Co Durham

**DATE OF BIRTH:** 11/04/1899 - 13/03/1981

**HEIGHT:** 6 '0" **WEIGHT:** 12st 4lbs

**SIGNED FROM:** Hylton Colliery, 25//05/1921

**DEBUT:** v Liverpool, H, 07/01/1922

**LAST MATCH:** v Huddersfield Town, A, 27/01/1923

**MOVED TO:** Exeter City, 09/05/1923

**TEAMS:** Hylton Colliery, Sunderland, Exeter City, Stockport County, Southend United, Doncaster Rovers, Scunthorpe & Lindsay United, Loughborough Corinthian

**SAFC TOTALS:** 12 appearance / 0 goals

**The only player known to have been employed at Wearmouth Colliery, site of what is now the Stadium of Light, George Hunter was an apprentice engine fitter immediately after World War One when he left the RAF having represented the Forces at football.**

One of five footballing brothers, he debuted in an FA Cup tie against Liverpool, but only played a handful of games. Leaving for Exeter City after two seasons at Roker Park, he played twice as many times for the Grecians (18 league, 6 FA Cup) as he had with his hometown team, before having spells with Workington and Southend United prior to pitching up at Doncaster in October 1925.

However, as with the Shrimpers, Hunter did not get a league game with Rovers and soon left for Scunthorpe and Lindsay United with whom he won the Midland League Championship in 1926-27, before finishing his football career with Loughborough Corinthians. He passed away in Scunthorpe in 1981 having lived there since retiring from playing in 1939.

## HUNTER, James

**POSITION:** Full-back

**BIRTHPLACE:** Newton, Ayrshire

**DATE OF BIRTH:** 22/09/1862 - 01/01/1911

**SIGNED FROM:** Queen of the South Wanderers, 10/02/1885

**DEBUT:** v Redcar, A, 24/10/1885

**LAST MATCH:** v Redcar, A, 24/10/1885

**MOVED:** 1886

**TEAMS:** Queen of the South Wanderers, Sunderland, North Sands Rovers

**SAFC TOTALS:** 1 appearance / 0 goals

**Left-back in his only FA Cup appearance in the days before the Football League was formed, Hunter also played in five other positions both in defence and attack during his outings in the friendly and challenge matches that were the order of the day in his era. He is known to have played 18 times in total in 1885-86.**

Most notably he scored Sunderland's first-ever goal at the Newcastle Road ground that was home to the club immediately before they moved to Roker Park. That goal came against Darlington on 3 April 1886. After leaving Sunderland he occasionally played for shipyard team North Sands Rovers in 1887-88 and for 15 years leading up to his death at the age of 48, was clubmaster at the Ayr and Newton Unionist Club.

## HUNTER, Jordan Paul

**POSITION:** Midfielder

**BIRTHPLACE:** Lancaster

**DATE OF BIRTH:** 06/12/1999

**HEIGHT:** 5' 11" **WEIGHT:** 10st 12lbs

**SIGNED FROM:** Liverpool 02/07/2018

**DEBUT:** v Morecambe, A, 13/11/2018

**LAST MATCH:** v Morecambe, A, 13/11/2018

**MOVED TO:** South Shields, 27/07/2020

**TEAMS:** Liverpool, Sunderland, South Shields (to June 2022)

**SAFC TOTALS:** 1 appearance / 0 goals

**One of five youngsters who debuted in a Football League (Checkatrade) Trophy victory at Morecambe, Hunter had joined Sunderland the previous summer two days after being released by Liverpool where he had made 25 appearances at Under 18 level.**

Loaned to South Shields from 20 August 2019 to 16 March 2020, he subsequently signed for Shields where he had won the Young Player of the Year and Supporters Player of the Year having played 39 times and scored once during his loan.

## HUNTLEY, Richard Bernard

**POSITION:** Right-half

**BIRTHPLACE:** Sunderland

**DATE OF BIRTH:** 05/01/1949 - 10/12/2021

**HEIGHT:** 5' 10" **WEIGHT:** 10st 8lbs

**SIGNED FROM:** Eppleton Juniors, 01/04/1966

**DEBUT:** v Everton, A, 02/11/1968

**LAST MATCH:** v Everton, A, 02/11/1968

**MOVED TO:** Released, 30/06/1969

**TEAMS:** Eppleton Juniors, Sunderland, Cambridge City, Dunstable Town, Fruilli, Marinello, Scarborough Italia

**SAFC TOTALS:** 1 appearance / 0 goals

**An FA Youth Cup winner with Sunderland in 1967 when he marked future England centre-forward Bob Latchford as Sunderland won both legs against Birmingham City 1-0, Huntley sustained a groin injury three weeks after his first-team debut after which he struggled to get back to his previous standard.**

He later played alongside George Best and Jeff Astle for Dunstable Town, even scoring in a pre-season friendly against Manchester United. After becoming an accountant in London, Richard moved to Ontario and went on to play for a couple of clubs in the Toronto area. He returned in 1980, managed Eppleton CW and then and took up a Sunderland season ticket.

## HURDMAN, Arthur Stanley

**POSITION:** Outside-right

**BIRTHPLACE:** Sunderland, Co Durham

**DATE OF BIRTH:** 31/05/1882 - 20/05/1953

**HEIGHT:** 5' 6" **WEIGHT:** 9st 9lbs

**SIGNED FROM:** Black Watch, 01/05/1906

**DEBUT:** v Woolwich Arsenal, A, 01/12/1906

**LAST MATCH:** v Wednesday, H, 17/04/1908

**MOVED TO:** Darlington, 14/08/1908

**TEAMS:** Sunderland Black Watch, Sunderland, Darlington, South Shields Adelaide

**SAFC TOTALS:** 8 appearances / 3 goals

**Hurdman scored twice and won a penalty in a 5-5 draw with Liverpool on his home debut, having previously played in three away games. All but one of his appearances came in 1906-07 when he also scored in the final home game of the season against Notts County.**

Having played as an amateur while still a teacher, he signed professional in the summer of 1907 and resumed his teaching career following his time in football. During his teacher-training at Borough Road College in Isleworth he played student football. Originally a centre-forward in local football despite his lack of physical stature, he switched to the right-wing with Sunderland's reserve or 'A' team.

## HURLEY, Charles Joseph (Charlie)

**POSITION:** Centre-half

**BIRTHPLACE:** Cork, Ireland

**DATE OF BIRTH:** 04/10/1936

**HEIGHT:** 6' 1" **WEIGHT:** 13st 10lbs

**SIGNED FROM:** Millwall, 26/09/1957

**DEBUT:** v Blackpool, A, 05/10/1957

**LAST MATCH:** v Burnley, A, 23/04/1969

**MOVED TO:** Bolton Wanderers, 02/06/1969

**TEAMS:** Millwall, Sunderland, Bolton Wanderers

**INTERNATIONAL:** Republic of Ireland

**SAFC TOTALS:** 400+1 appearances / 26 goals

**Inducted into the Sunderland Hall of Fame at the inaugural dinner in 2019, Charlie Hurley had been voted by fans as the club's Player of the Century in 1979. A colossus of a centre-half, 'King Charlie' was ahead of his time, in that as a central defender he was a skilled operator who excelled at bringing the ball out of defence. Long before it became the norm, he also made a habit of going forward to cause havoc at corner kicks. In addition to the goals Charlie scored, he made many more, as others (notably Nicky Sharkey) were primed to pounce on rebounds after opposition goalkeepers parried Hurley's headers.**

Over and above all this, Charlie carried an aura about him. His charisma meant that not only did the fans idolise him, but players looked up to him too. Charlie lapped this up with a smile. On a pre-season tour of Ireland when acting as the club's ambassador in 2007 he got into a taxi in his native Cork with chairman Niall Quinn and manager Roy Keane. "I've got the king of Cork" beamed the taxi driver delighted to have Keane as a passenger. "I'm the King of Cork" Charlie instantly informed them.

In 2016, when the club re-sited the gates of the former training ground, 'The Charlie Hurley Centre' to the Stadium of Light, CEO Martin Bain attempted to give a speech to the assembled company in the boardroom. Barely had he begun when 'The King' took over, his booming voice informing everyone that when he went to heaven, he'd definitely be captain. All this with a cheeky glint in his eye. On that occasion, Charlie was accompanied by the surviving members of the first-ever Sunderland promotion team he captained in 1964. Hurley himself had delivered a heart-felt eulogy at the funeral of Jim McNab, the first member of that side to pass away.

Alan Brown had made Hurley the king-pin of the new Sunderland side he was building. A fee of £20,000 bought Charlie from Millwall. He had grown up in London having moved to Rainham in East London when just six months old, but he always remained a fiercely proud Irishman. He was discovered by Bill Voisey while playing for Rainham Youth Club and joined Millwall as a professional in October 1963 having had trials with West Ham and Arsenal.

Charlie made his debut in a 2-2 draw at Torquay United in a Division Three South game on 30 January 1954, the first of 16 appearances that season. The following term he played 34 times in league and cup, but only 17 in 1955-56 when he required an operation due to serious cartilage trouble, which had initially happened when playing for his army unit at Aldershot in November 1955 during his National Service. That injury cost Hurley an expected first cap for the Republic of Ireland who entertained Spain at the end of that month.

Hurley's first cap duly arrived on 19 May 1957 in a World Cup qualifying game with England in Dublin. The game finished 1-1, the Irish having lost 5-1 to England at Wembley earlier in the month without Charlie. Hurley had returned to the Lions line-up in September 1956, playing 27 games including a London Floodlit Cup tie at QPR. The season saw Charlie score his first two goals, the first back at Plainmoor, the scene of his league debut at Torquay. That goal on 8 September 1956 was followed two days later by a first goal at the Den, against Aldershot. However, those games would be lost 2-7 and 1-5, to some extent mirroring Hurley's opening appearances for Sunderland. Before coming to Wearside in September 1957, Charlie played in nine of Millwall's first ten games, the last at QPR on 23 September taking his Millwall total to 110 games and two goals.

Hurley also had experience of European football before he came to Sunderland. With European football in its embryonic stages, a London XI took part in the Inter-Cities Fairs Cup. On 26 October 1955, Hurley lined up alongside such stars as Danny Blanchflower and Bobby Robson (who scored the winner) for a 3-2 win over a Frankfurt XI. London went on to reach the final where they lost to a Barcelona XI, but by then, Hurley was at Sunderland.

His Sunderland career did not get off to a good start with 7-0 (with an own goal) and 6-0 defeats in his first two games. Undaunted, Charlie gave an early indication of his wit and supreme self-confidence by telling doubtful local pressmen that he had made an improvement already! In reality though, it took some time to see the improvement as at the end of Hurley's first season of 1957-58 Sunderland were relegated for the first time in the club's history. It was an unwelcome double as Millwall, where he had started the season, were also relegated, to Division Four. Charlie had made 24 appearances for Sunderland by this point, including two in the cup.

In his first two full seasons of 1958-59 and 1959-60, Hurley played 36 and 40 times as Sunderland struggled. There was an improvement in 1960-61 as he played 41 times and for the first time in his era the Lads finished in the top half of the table. They also reached the quarter-final of the FA Cup, Charlie having scored the winner in the quarter-final at Norwich with a thunderous effort that stuck in the stanchion. It was the only goal of an away win in which Sunderland had been under the cosh only for 'The King' to be truly majestic. His first-ever goal for Sunderland had come on Boxing Day against Sheffield United when Stan Anderson had encouraged him to start going forward for corners. A few days later, he scored again in a 7-1 New Year's Eve thrashing of Luton Town.

Having got a taste for scoring goals as well as stopping them, the following season Charlie scored six as promotion was missed by a point, In the next 1962-63 campaign in which the League Cup semi-final was reached, Charlie scored five, this time promotion being missed on goal average. There was no mistake in 1963-64. Charlie missed just one match and scored five goals as a first-ever promotion was secured. He added another two goals - including one against reigning league champions Everton - as the quarter-final of the FA Cup was reached once again. Images of Hurley leading the lap of honour at Roker Park are amongst the most iconic post-war images of SAFC. That season he was runner-up to West Ham's FA Cup winning captain Bobby Moore as Footballer of the Year, despite playing in the second division. In 1963, Charlie had topped a magazine poll for the North East Player of the Year.

SLIM JIM
BAXTER

Once promoted, Charlie effectively ran the team ahead of the coaching staff for almost half a season as the directors did not appoint a successor to the departed Alan Brown until the 20th game of the season. Starting with this 1964-65 season, only in the last of his final five seasons at the club did Charlie top 30 games. Part of this was due to him largely being overlooked as manager Ian McColl largely sidelined or overlooked catholic players. Hurley was the natural leader in the squad, but for a period under Ibrox man McColl there were two distinct sections in the camp: those who followed Hurley and those who followed the talented, but wayward Jim Baxter. McColl even signed Baxter's cousin George Kinnell in Charlie's position.

The King's farewell appearance was his 400th start after which he saw out his playing days with Bolton where he scored three goals in 45+1 appearances, the very last in a 4-0 loss at Birmingham City on 20 February 1971, with Bolton destined to finish bottom of Division Two. His teammates that term including future Sunderland coach Syd Farrimond.

By January 1972, Hurley had become manager of Reading, a position he held until February 1977. Paired with Sunderland in the FA Cup in 1973, Charlie received a rapturous welcome on his return to Roker Park. He later scouted for Southampton after leaving management and worked as a sales manager for a packaging company in Hertfordshire where he settled after retiring from football.

His brother Chris played five times for Millwall in the mid-sixties, scoring twice. Chris also played in non-league for Rainham Town, Dover, Wimbledon and Ashford Town. He was a centre-half who made three of his league appearances at centre-forward, scoring twice in one of those games. Likewise Charlie sometimes played as a centre-forward, even at international level. In total, Charlie won 40 full caps, the last with Bolton and 38 with Sunderland making him the club's most capped international until overtaken by Seb Larsson. Charlie's biography, 'The greatest centre-half the world has ever seen', was published in 2008.

## HUTCHISON, Donald Oliver

**POSITION:** Midfielder

**BIRTHPLACE:** Gateshead, Co Durham

**DATE OF BIRTH:** 09/05/1971

**HEIGHT:** 6' 1" **WEIGHT:** 11st 8lbs

**SIGNED FROM:** Everton, 14/07/2000

**DEBUT:** v Manchester City, A, 23/08/2000

**LAST MATCH:** v Newcastle United, A, 26/08/2001

**MOVED TO:** West Ham United, 30/08/2001

**TEAMS:** Redheugh Boys Club, Hartlepool United, Liverpool, West Ham United, Sheffield United, Everton, Sunderland, West Ham United, Millwall, Coventry City, Luton Town

**INTERNATIONAL:** Scotland

**SAFC TOTALS:** 37+2 appearances / 10 goals

**Don Hutchison was what Sunderland had craved for an age - a goalscoring midfielder. Unfortunately, others had the same desire and so Don's time on Wearside was far too short. While he was at the Stadium of Light though, he fitted the bill. In his only full season he scored ten times, his goal in a 2-1 derby win at Newcastle (on the day of Tommy Sorensen's famous penalty save from Alan Shearer) being his third in as many Premier League games.**

A goal from a quickly taken free-kick in a win at West Ham technically put Sunderland top of the Premier League for a few minutes, but also perhaps increased the Hammers interest in the player who they came in for later in the year with a club record bid that doubled SAFC's outlay of £2.5m.

In addition to his ability to get on the scoresheet, Hutchison was a good all-rounder. Not shy of a tackle, he was physically strong and a skilled technician, able to see and execute a penetrating pass. His departure was one SAFC struggled to recover from. Seventh in his full season and the one before, the club just missed relegation after letting him go and went down dismally a year later. Hutchison's departure was not the only reason for the decline, but it was definitely a contributory factor.

He went from fork-lift truck driver to Pool player, that is Liverpool via Hartlepool. First appearing for Hartlepool in a friendly at Newcastle Blue Star on 31 July 1989, he made his league debut the following October in a home win over Scunthorpe and was snapped up by Liverpool for £300,000 after 23+6 competitive appearances which had brought three goals.

Debuting at Anfield as a sub against Notts County in the Premier League on 31 March 1992 he was not involved in that season's FA Cup final against Sunderland although he had played in the league a week earlier. Mainly a reserve in his first two seasons at Anfield Hutchison came to prominence with regular appearances and ten goals in 1992-93.

Unfortunately it was not just Don's football which came to prominence, as a series of off-field incidents reportedly led to Liverpool looking to offload him which they did when selling him to West Ham for £1.5 in August 1994, after ten goals and nine assists in his 60 appearances for the Reds.

After scoring on his West Ham debut against Newcastle, Don played 39 times before moving to Sheffield United for £1.2m in January 1996. In his first full season there he played in the Division One (Championship) Play-Off final lost to Crystal Palace after barely missing a game. By the time the Blades lost to Sunderland in the following season's Play-Off semi-finals, he had moved on again after 80+11 appearances and six goals.

In February 1998 Don had returned to Merseyside, this time with Everton where he signed for Howard Kendall who had bought him for Sheffield United. Coached by Adrian Heath, Hutchison went on to play his best football for the Toffees under Walter Smith, even becoming captain, although he was later stripped of that honour as contract negotiations rumbled on. After eleven goals (including two in a 5-0 win over Sunderland on Boxing Day 1999) in 81+8 games, he moved to Sunderland who would have happily kept him for longer only for him to want a return to West Ham.

A cruciate ligament injury spoiled his second spell at the Boleyn Ground where his overall total for the Irons reached 74+36 appearances and 18 goals before he moved on again. With Millwall from August to November in 2005, he scored on debut in an opening-day defeat at Leeds and added one more goal in 8+6 games before signing for Coventry City. An ankle injury restricted him to 32 league appearances and a single goal in 18 months before a final move to Luton in July 2007 brought 21 league games and another goal bringing his league total to 55 goals in a total of 430 games.

At international level, having qualified for Scotland through his father Don won 26 caps scoring six goals including winners in 1-0 away wins over Germany and England. In his post-playing career, Hutchison has become a well-known and at times outspoken media pundit.

## HUTTON, Alan

**POSITION:** Right-back

**BIRTHPLACE:** Penilee, Glasgow

**DATE OF BIRTH:** 30/11/1984

**HEIGHT:** 6' 1" **WEIGHT:** 11st 3lbs

**SIGNED FROM:** Tottenham Hotspur, 01/02/2010, on loan

**DEBUT:** v Wigan Athletic, H, 06/02/2010

**LAST MATCH:** v Wolverhampton Wanderers, A, 09/05/2010

**MOVED TO:** Tottenham Hotspur, 10/05/2010, end of loan

**TEAMS:** Rangers, Spurs, Sunderland (L), Aston Villa, Nottingham Forest (L), Real Mallorca (L), Bolton Wanderers (L)

**INTERNATIONAL:** Scotland

**SAFC TOTALS:** 11 appearances / 0 goals

**Brought in on loan by Steve Bruce, Hutton played in eleven of the final 15 games of the 2009-10 season as Sunderland finished in a comfortable 13th position. He won exactly 50 caps for Scotland, retiring from international football after reaching that milestone in March 2016 against the Czech Republic.**

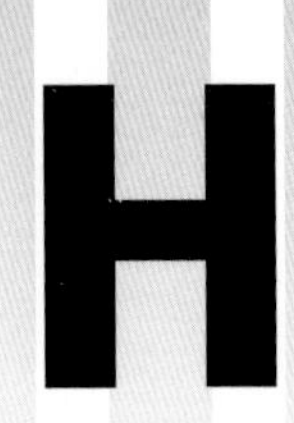

## HUTTON, Alan (Continued)

It was also against the Czech Republic that he won his only cap whilst on loan to Sunderland, albeit that officially counts as a cap won with his parent club Tottenham. Internationally, his highlight was being part of the Scotland side that beat France 1-0 in Paris in a Euro 2008 qualifying game.

Hutton had cost Spurs a reported £9m to sign him from Rangers where he was known as 'The Scottish Cafu'. The fee was a record sale for Rangers. Debuting in a home draw with Manchester United in February 2008, on only his third appearance he was part of the side who beat Chelsea in the League (Carling) Cup final.

Although he would play Champions League and UEFA Cup football for Spurs, that early highlight remained his peak before a move to Aston Villa just as the August transfer window was about to close in 2011. Villa were to loan Alan out to Nottingham Forest (7+0/0), Mallorca (17+0/0) and Bolton (9+0/0 ) before releasing him at the end of 2018-19 following 188+14 games and three goals. Having not found a club by February 2020, he announced his retirement.

He had begun with Rangers in September 2000 and debuted three days before Christmas in 2002, against Partick Thistle. He went on to play 115+7 games scoring four goals, including one in the UEFA Cup. He also played Champions League football while at Ibrox and made ten SPL appearances as they won the league in 2004-05.

## HYSEN, Glenn Tobias (Toby)

**POSITION:** Left-midfielder

**BIRTHPLACE:** Gothenburg, Sweden

**DATE OF BIRTH:** 09/03/1982

**HEIGHT:** 5' 10" **WEIGHT:** 12st 12lbs

**SIGNED FROM:** Djurgardens, 23/08/2006

**DEBUT:** v West Bromwich Albion, H, 28/08/2006

**LAST MATCH:** v Burnley, H, 27/04/2007

**MOVED TO:** IFK Gothenburg, 25/08/2007

**TEAMS:** Ubbhults IF, Lundby IF, BK Hacken, Djurgardens, Sunderland, IFK Gothenburg, Shanghai SIPG, IFK Gothenburg

**INTERNATIONAL:** Sweden

**SAFC TOTALS:** 16+11 appearances / 4 goals

**Signed by Niall Quinn, Hysen debuted in Quinn's last game as manager before scoring the first goal at the Stadium of Light under the management of Roy Keane. He then spent much of his time competing for a place on the left flank with Keane's signing Ross Wallace and spent just the one season in England.**

Having come through the ranks with Lundby IF he played in the Swedish top flight, the Allsvenskan, in 2001 when he was a teenager before progressing to Djurgarden in the capital Stockholm. He spent three seasons there, winning the title in the middle of those in 2005. After being part of a Championship winning side at Sunderland, once he returned to Sweden with Gothenburg he won the Allsvenskan in his first season meaning he had been part of a title-winning team with three clubs in four years.

He had seven seasons with Gothenburg before spending 2015 in China with Shanghai (22+4 /12) before three more seasons with Gothenburg took his total appearances for the club to 218+33 in which he scored 89 times to add to his 62+3 appearances for Djurgarden, for whom he scored 17 times.

At international level, Toby scored ten goals in 34 games for Sweden, the last two of those coming in a 5-3 defeat to Germany in Stockholm in October 2013.

Hysen was part of a footballing family. His step-brothers Alexander and Anton played for BK Hacken, his great Grandfather Erik, Grandfather Kurt and Great uncle Carl all played for IFK Gothenburg. Father, Glenn Hysen, was a major star, a former Sweden Footballer of the Year who twice won the UEFA Cup with IFK Gothenburg. He also played for PSV Eindhoven, Fiorentina, Liverpool (where he won the league title in 1990) and GAIS Gothenburg, as well as winning 68 caps for Sweden, captaining them at the FIFA World Cup at Italia 90.

## HYSLOP, Thomas (Tom)

**POSITION:** Inside-left

**BIRTHPLACE:** Auchinleck, Ayrshire

**DATE OF BIRTH:** 20/08/1871 - 21/04/1936

**HEIGHT:** 6' 1"

**SIGNED FROM:** Army, 25/01/1894

**DEBUT:** v Everton, H, 06/02/1894

**LAST MATCH:** v Wolverhampton Wanderers, A, 12/01/1895

**MOVED TO:** Stoke, 09/02/1895

**TEAMS:** Elderslie FC, Millwall Athletic, Army, Sunderland, Stoke, Rangers, Stoke, Rangers, Partick Thistle, Dundee Wanderers, Johnstone, Abercorn, Philadelphia Thistle

**INTERNATIONAL:** Scotland

**SAFC TOTALS:** 18 appearances / 10 goals

**Bought out of the 2nd Scots Guards by Sunderland for £18, Tom Hyslop proved worth the investment with an average of better than a goal per two games, although he only played one game for every pound he cost. He got the 1894-95 season (in which 'The Team of All The Talents' took a third title in four seasons) off to a brilliant start. Having scored twice in a famous opening day 8-0 win over Derby, he scored a hat-trick in the next match as Burnley were beaten 3-0. However, there were just two further appearances after November 1894.**

Hyslop had a double identity. Also known as Bryce Scouller, this was apparently his real name, with him reported to have taken his mother's maiden name Hyslop for his football career in which he called himself Thomas, Tommy or Tom.

He had first joined the Argyll and Sutherland Highlanders under the name of Bryce Scouller, but later enlisted with the Second Battalion of the Scots Guards at Windsor Castle.

Playing football for the Scots Guards, he won the Army Cup and Middlesex Cup twice each and once scored seven goals for Middlesex in a game with Sussex. Having applied for Home Leave in 1893, instead of going home he took part in a trial for Millwall Athletic and was subsequently arrested and had his time in the army extended. On 19 November 1892 he played in an FA (English) Cup defeat to Woolwich Arsenal and just under a month later played in a London Charity Cup win over Casuals.

After leaving Sunderland, where he could not hold down a place at the club who became 'World Champions' in his time on Wearside, Hyslop signed for Stoke where he scored 24 goals in a season and a half, including a spectacular hat-trick against West Brom. Having played alongside Ted Doig at Sunderland, Hyslop and Doig were teammates again when both were called up for an international against England at Celtic Park on 4 April 1896, an occasion when England were beaten for the first time in six years.

That summer, Rangers moved in for Hyslop who won the Scottish Cup, Glasgow Cup and Charity Cup in his first season, Hyslop being the Gers' joint top scorer in the league with eleven goals including four in a 7-2 win at Clyde on 5 December 1896. Additionally, one of his five Scottish Cup goals came in the final against Dumbarton. He also scored in a debut win over St Mirren where he was joined on the scoresheet by Sunderland great Jamie Millar. The pair were both on the mark together again on 3 April 1897 as Scotland beat England 2-1 at Crystal Palace. On that occasion they had Sunderland's Hugh Wilson as a teammate, but Sunderland had denied Doig permission to play (needing him for a key game at Stoke where he kept a clean sheet).

Hyslop's pace was confirmed later the same month when he won the 220 yards race for professional footballers. He stayed at Rangers for another year, winning the Scottish Cup again in 1898 when he played in the final against Kilmarnock. In the league he scored 13 goals, including hat-tricks against Clyde and St Bernards. However having moved to Stoke he failed to score. Returning to Rangers in 1899 things seemed back to normal when he scored three times in the first two games of the season, but there would be just three more games and one more goal (in a 12-0 cup win over Maybole) before he was allowed to leave for Partick Thistle in 1900.

It was shortly after his that the double life resumed. In March 1901 he signed up to fight the Boers in South Africa with the Scottish Yeomanry, once again as Bryce Scouller. Perhaps he simply did not want to be identified as a famous footballer? Returning to Scotland he played in Dundee before seeing out his Scottish career with clubs in Renfrewshire.

In 1906, he emigrated to Pennsylvania as Tom Hyslop, finding employment as a carpet weaver. Eleven years later he moved to Toronto to enlist with the Canadian Expeditionary Force, again calling himself Bryce Scouller and lying about his age to ensure he was under the maximum age for enlistment. He duly served in Europe, although apparently not on the front line. Although he returned to Canada, by 1922 he was back in Scotland, passing away 14 years later in Paisley.

# I

## INGHAM, Michael Gerard

**POSITION:** Goalkeeper

**BIRTHPLACE:** Preston, Lancashire

**DATE OF BIRTH:** 07/09/1980

**HEIGHT:** 6' 4" **WEIGHT:** 14st 7lbs

**SIGNED FROM:** Cliftonville, 19/05/1999

**DEBUT:** v Sheffield Wednesday, A, 12/09/2001

**LAST MATCH:** v Ipswich Town, A, 17/04/2005

**MOVED TO:** Wrexham, 01/07/2005

**TEAMS:** Newington Youth Club, Malachians, Cliftonville, Sunderland, Carlisle United (L), Lincoln City (L), Cliftonville (L), Stoke City (L), Stockport County (L), Darlington (L), York City (L), Doncaster Rovers (L), Wrexham, Hereford United, York City

**INTERNATIONAL:** Northern Ireland

**SAFC TOTALS:** 3+1 appearances / 0 goals

**Michael Ingham became known as 'Lord of the Gloves' due to his popularity at York, but things did not go well for him at Sunderland. It was harsh to judge him on conceding four goals on his debut at Sheffield Wednesday as the League Cup tie was 2-2 after 90 minutes.**

Two years later, he leaked four again in a home League Cup loss to Huddersfield, but had to wait three and a half years from his debut for a league bow. This came on 9 April 2005 when Thomas Myhre was injured in an important league game with Reading. With the Lads on the cusp of promotion, Ingham came on at half-time with the team in the lead, only for a 2-1 defeat to be suffered, the second goal from a penalty. A few days later, he was considered culpable for dropped points from a 2-2 draw at promotion rivals Ipswich in a match where Sunderland excelled and should have won. The following weekend Ingham was dropped in favour of untried teenager Ben Alnwick, thereby missing out on a day when Mick McCarthy's men clinched promotion. In total, Ingham warmed the bench 59 times, but only came off it once.

Like many young keepers he was regularly sent out on loan. He made 41 appearances as a player on loan from Sunderland, plus 20 back at Cliftonville who he had played 18 league games for before coming to Sunderland.

After his final Sunderland appearance he made an international debut for Northern Ireland as a sub against Germany in Belfast. He went on to win further caps against Uruguay and Wales, with one of his many games as an unused sub coming against England in a FIFA World Cup qualifying game in September 2005.

After leaving Sunderland, Michael signed for Wrexham in League Two where he played 71 times in the league, adding to the eleven he had made on loan there earlier in his career. Upon his release, he made a single appearance in a friendly on trial to Gretna, then of the Scottish Premier League. He then joined League Two Hereford United, but moved on to York without having played a league game, although he had appeared in the Football League Trophy.

Michael became a hero at York, playing 311 times, being Clubman of the Year in 2009-10 and helping the club back into the Football League half way through his eight season spell. Further success came in the same 2011-12 season when he kept a clean sheet at Wembley as Newport County were beaten in the final of the FA Trophy.

Ingham worked as a goalkeeping coach with Tadcaster Albion where he made the last 79 appearances of his career. He then coached at Scarborough before taking up a post as goalkeeping coach to Northern Ireland Under 19s in April 2022.

## INGLIS, J

**POSITION:** Full-back

**SIGNED:** 1885

**DEBUT:** v Redcar, A, 24/10/1885

**LAST MATCH:** v Redcar, A, 24/10/1885

**MOVED:** 1885

**TEAMS:** Sunderland

**SAFC TOTALS:** 1 appearance / 0 goals

**Known to have been at the club only briefly, Inglis's solitary competitive game came in a 3-0 English (FA) Cup loss at Redcar in what was Sunderland's second-ever came in the competition.**

It is possible that this player was Peter Inglis, born in Renfrew 25 April 1861 who moved down from Scotland to Sunderland in the early 1880s to be a blacksmith at Robert Thompson's Southwick shipyards. A keen footballer, he had played football for Renfrew Ramblers prior to moving south and is known to have played in both goal and defence for Monkwearmouth in 1884 and 1885. Peter later became Sunderland's first socialist alderman and was one of the oldest members of the town council when he passed away on 15 April 1936.

## IRWIN, Cecil

**POSITION:** Right-back

**BIRTHPLACE:** Ellington, Northumberland

**DATE OF BIRTH:** 08/04/1942

**HEIGHT:** 6' 1" **WEIGHT:** 13st 10lbs

**SIGNED FROM:** Youth product, 01/07/1958

**DEBUT:** v Ipswich Town, H, 20/09/1958

**LAST MATCH:** v Bristol Rovers, A, 07/09/1971

**MOVED TO:** Yeovil Town, 16/06/1972

**TEAMS:** Sunderland, Yeovil Town

**INTERNATIONAL:** England Youth

**SAFC TOTALS:** 349+3 appearances / 1 goal

**Irwin became Sunderland's youngest-ever player at the age of 16 years and 166 days, taking a record set by Jimmy Thorpe 28 years earlier. Sunderland had brought the young Northumbrian in after he had been on a month-long trial at Burnley.**

Cec did not play again during his debut season and appeared just nine times across the following two campaigns. He established himself in 1961-62 and remained a stalwart for the next decade. His best personal season came in 1966-67 when he missed just one of the 42 league games and made seven further cup appearances.

An integral part of the club's first-ever promotion team in 1964, Irwin missed just three league games that term. A long-striding, overlapping right-back at a time when it was becoming the

fashion for full-backs to tentatively venture forward, Irwin's self-admitted discipline would see him turn and sprint back into his defensive position as soon as the ball left his boot when he aimed a cross.

In representative football, Cec represented East Northumberland at schools level and was capped by England at youth level. Future World Cup-winners Nobby Stiles and Geoff Hurst were amongst Irwin's teammates on his international debut away to Wales five months after his Sunderland debut. Two months later, Irwin played against Greece during a tournament in Bulgaria.

Cec spent all of his Football League career with Sunderland who he supported as a boy and who he was still supporting as a regular at the match prior to Covid 19 striking in 2020. In 1972 he left Sunderland to become player-manager of Yeovil Town who staged a testimonial for him against Sunderland on May 1974. After three years in charge of Yeovil Irwin returned to the north east to run a newsagents in Ashington and returned to the game to manage Ashington between September 1996 and May 2002. Cec's brother Ray played as an amateur winger for Gateshead in the early 1960s.

## IVES, Albert Edward Bert

**POSITION:** Left-back

**BIRTHPLACE:** Newcastle, Northumberland

**DATE OF BIRTH:** 18/12/1908 - August 1980

**HEIGHT:** 5' 10½" **WEIGHT:** 11st 7lbs

**SIGNED FROM:** Spen Black & White,11/03/1930

**DEBUT:** v Aston Villa, H, 07/09/1932

**LAST MATCH:** v Arsenal, A, 21/04/1934

**MOVED TO:** Barnsley, 06/02/1936

**TEAMS:** Spen Black and White, Sunderland, Barnsley, Blyth Spartans

**SAFC TOTALS:** 12 appearances / 0 goals

**Four appearances in 1932-33 doubled to eight the season after, but in four of his six seasons at Roker, Ives was surplus to requirements.**

In February 1936 Barnsley were short of full-backs due to injuries and paid Sunderland a reported 'fairly substantial fee' for Bert's services, but he only appeared nine times for the Oakwell outfit. After his football career he became an engineering turner in a wireworks back in his native Tyneside.

## JACKSON, Archibald (Archie)

**POSITION:** Centre-half

**BIRTHPLACE:** Plumpstead, London

**DATE OF BIRTH:** 25/01/1901 - 11/11/1985

**HEIGHT:** 5' 9"" **WEIGHT:** 11st 0lbs

**SIGNED FROM:** Rutherglen Glencairn, 17/08/1922

**DEBUT:** v Middlesbrough, A, 18/04/1923

**LAST MATCH:** v Preston North End, A, 10/11/1923

**MOVED TO:** Southend United, 16/05/1924

**TEAMS:** Rutherglen Glencairn, Sunderland, Southend United, Third Lanark, Chester City, Tranmere Rovers, Accrington Stanley, Walsall, Southport, Northwich Victoria, Manchester NE, Rossendale United, Ellesmere Port Town

**SAFC TOTALS:** 6 appearances / 0 goals

**Archie Jackson came from a noted sporting family. His father James helped both Newcastle United and Arsenal to their first-ever promotions to the top-flight, indeed as skipper of the Gunners who he played over 200 times for.**

Woolwich Arsenal had been the side James had made the first of his 68 appearances for Newcastle against in September 1897. Archie's brother, also James, although in his case the Reverend James Jackson, captained Liverpool in the late twenties having earlier cost Aberdeen a club record fee to buy from Motherwell.

A Cambridge University student, he became ordained as a minister in the Presbyterian Church. Finally, Archie's namesake and cousin, Archibald Jackson played Test cricket for Australia, scoring 164 on his Test debut as a teenager against England in 1929, thereby becoming the youngest player to score a Test century. Sadly he died aged 23 of tuberculosis.

In contrast, the career of Sunderland's Archie Jackson was relatively modest. Although born in London he arrived on Wearside as a 21-year-old from Glaswegian club Rutherglen Glencairn. His debut came in a 2-0 defeat at Middlesbrough as a stand-in for Charlie Parker. The following season he played five times, but unable to hold down a place in the Sunderland side that finished second and third in the first division in his two seasons, he moved on in search of regular football in the summer of 1924.

That search continued, as in little over a year he moved between Southend United, Third Lanark and Chester, playing once in the Scottish top-flight before a successful three-year spell with non-league Chester. This led to a step up into Division Three North with Tranmere where he played 37 times before a five-month stint at Accrington Stanley in 1930 preceded three months with Walsall and two at Southport. A footballing nomad, he then made further moves to Northwich Victoria, Manchester North End and finally Rossendale United who he joined in July 1935. After retiring from football, he worked for an electricity company in Chester.

## JACKSON, Richard William (Dicky)

**POSITION:** Left-half

**BIRTHPLACE:** Middlesbrough

**DATE OF BIRTH:** 21/01/1877 - 11/11/1942

**HEIGHT:** 5' 8" **WEIGHT:** 11st 9lbs

**SIGNED FROM:** Middlesbrough, 26/05/1898

**DEBUT:** v Sheffield United, A, 17/12/1898

**LAST MATCH:** v Newcastle United, A, 22/04/1905

**MOVED TO:** Portsmouth, 02/05/1905

**TEAMS:** Ripley Athletic, Middlesbrough, Sunderland, Portsmouth, Crystal Palace, Darlington

**SAFC TOTALS:** 169 appearances / 11 goals

**Jackson played in all but two of the 34 league games of the 1901-02 league title-winning season. He had won an Amateur Cup medal with his home town Middlesbrough before coming to Wearside. His league-winning season saw him playing mainly on the left side of the midfield area from where he scored three goals. Only two men played more than Jackson as the title was won.**

Dicky had debuted in December 1898 adding a home debut on Christmas Eve against Newcastle. The following season he managed 13 games with 19 in the season before the title win. He was ever-present as Sunderland defended the title, missing out on retaining it, finishing a point off the top after a crucial final-day defeat at St James'.

Jackson remained a regular in 1903-04, being absent for just two games and then not missing a match until March in the following campaign, before signing off his Sunderland career by playing in a 3-1 win at Newcastle in April 1905. Earlier that season he had shared a 'Benefit' league game with Billy Hogg. A Benefit game meant a long-serving player received either a share of the gate receipts or a large payment.

Having moved to Southern League Portsmouth in May 1905, his time in the south was short. Despite helping Pompey to third and second-place finishes, after two years he left for Crystal Palace. However, Dicky soon returned to the north east, initially as a professional player for Darlington in 1908, as they relinquished their amateur status, then becoming their manager in May 1912.

He was frustrated when the Quakers failed to be admitted to the Football League after winning 31 out of 38 games and scoring 116 goals in winning the North Eastern League in his first season. Nonetheless, he stayed with Darlington until after the Great War, becoming assistant manager at Middlesbrough in 1919 until 1926 when he completed his career with a season in charge of Durham City who finished third bottom of Division Three North. A shipwright by profession before becoming a footballer, after retiring from football he managed an off license.

## JAMES, Craig Peter

**POSITION:** Left-back

**BIRTHPLACE:** Middlesbrough, Cleveland

**DATE OF BIRTH:** 15/11/1982

**HEIGHT:** 6' 2" **WEIGHT:** 12st 10lbs

**SIGNED FROM:** Youth product, 01/07/2000, trainee Professional, 30/08/2002

**DEBUT:** v Stoke City, A, 16/09/2003

**LAST MATCH:** v Huddersfield Town, A, 23/09/2003

**MOVED TO:** Port Vale, 02/04/2004

**TEAMS:** Sunderland, Hibernian (L), Darlington (L), Port Vale, Darlington, York City (L), Livingston, Barrow, Harrogate Town

**SAFC TOTALS:** 2 appearances / 0 goals

**Coming through the ranks Craig James seemed to have the physicality needed to do well at first-team level, but his time with the senior side was over in a flash. He had previously had almost a year on loan to Hibs.**

Debuting as a sub in a heavy home defeat to Dunfermline on 11 September 2002 he went on to start 20 SPL games along with one further sub appearance (plus three cup ties), scoring in away draws at Dundee United and Hearts. Shortly after his games for Sunderland he went on loan to David Hodgson's Darlington where the highlight of ten games was a goal in a 3-0 home win over York where he was joined on the scoresheet by Neil Wainwright on a day when another team mate was ex-SAFC youth-teamer Mark Convery. A third loan from Sunderland took him to Port Vale from 19 March 2004 with the move made permanent a couple of weeks later.

He found regular football at Port Vale making 83 appearances in just over two seasons, scoring once, before returning to Darlington where he played 29 games plus another ten on loan to York. 2007-08 was spent in Scotland with Livingston where he played 34 times. Released by Livingston, he had a month without playing at Barrow in the Conference before finishing his career in Conference North with Harrogate Town, scoring four goals in 52 games between his debut against Redditch United on 31 October 2009 and 2011.

## JAMES, Leighton

**POSITION:** Winger

**BIRTHPLACE:** Loughor, Glamorgan

**DATE OF BIRTH:** 16/02/1953

**HEIGHT:** 5' 9½" **WEIGHT:** 12st 5lbs

**SIGNED FROM:** Swansea City, 13/01/1983

**DEBUT:** v Aston Villa, H, 15/01/1983

**LAST MATCH:** v Notts County, 07/05/1984

**MOVED TO:** Bury, 13/07/1984

**TEAMS:** Burnley, Derby County, QPR, Burnley, Swansea City, Sunderland, Bury, Newport County, Burnley, Darwen

**INTERNATIONAL:** Wales

**SAFC TOTALS:** 55+2 appearances / 4 goals

**Leighton first came onto the Roker radar when he scored the only goal of the 1972 International Youth Festival final for Burnley against Sunderland at Roker Park. By then he was already making a name for himself as a star in the renowned Burnley youth system, but he was a month short of his 30th birthday by the time he signed for Sunderland.**

The pace had gone, but he was one of the finest crossers of a football imaginable. He still had the talent to beat his man with a trick rather than speed and added quality to a top-flight side. James also worked as youth team coach in the second of his two seasons at Sunderland. Predominantly left-footed, he was two-footed enough to sometimes take penalties with his right.

Ability led to apparent arrogance on the pitch as a youngster, one game for Derby against Sunderland at the Baseball Ground in particular standing out as an occasion when the travelling support really got at him and he responded in kind, which was not unusual for a footballer who played on the edge - and not just the touchline as a winger. Yet when Leighton came to Sunderland, he showed himself to be top drawer off the pitch as well as on it and while Burnley and Swansea were the clubs closest to his heart, he always speaks really well of his enjoyment of playing for the passionate fans of the north east.

In three spells at Burnley, James made 393+6 appearances between 21 November 1970 and 13 May 1989. He scored 81 times for the men from Turf Moor. Known as 'Taffy' at Burnley, he joined the club as an apprentice in October 1968, signing professional on his 17th birthday in 1970 and coming under the guidance of Jimmy Adamson. Relegated in his first season when he played in four league games, he was ever-present and scored ten goals as Burnley were promoted in the season Sunderland won the cup in 1973 and played in the FA Cup semi-final (alongside Colin Waldron and Doug Collins) against Newcastle the following year.

The first of 54 caps for Wales came as an 18-year-old against Czechoslovakia in Prague in October 1971. His teammates included Alan Durban who later signed him for Sunderland. The week after turning 30, he won his one cap as a Sunderland player as an 80th-minute sub against England at Wembley. Three years earlier, perhaps his best international performance saw him tear England apart and get on the scoresheet in a 4-1 win.

James was used to top-class football. When he left Burnley for the first time, it was to sign for reigning league champions Derby. After 88+1 games and 21 goals (including a hat-trick in a 12-0 UEFA Cup win over Finn Harps), and a change of manager, he moved to QPR (in part-exchange for Don Masson) scoring six times in 32+1 games before returning to Burnley in September 1978 as their record signing at a fee of £165,000.

A couple of years later, he went to play for Swansea near where he was born. Part of a golden era at Swansea under John Toshack, Leighton netted 27 goals in 88+10 league appearances before coming to Sunderland where his quality continued to shine.

A season and a half later, he linked up with a host of former Burnley players headed by Martin Dobson at Bury where he scored five goals in 46 league outings. Still not finished, he scored twice in 21+7 league games for Newport County before a final move back to Burnley where at the age of 33, he helped them survive having to apply for re-election as they struggled in Division Four. In 1988 he played at Wembley alongside Peter Daniel as a sub when Burnley lost the Associate Members (Sherpa Van) Trophy final to Wolves.

After becoming youth coach at Turf Moor Leighton continued to have the occasional first-team outing in a deeper role, and during summers showed himself to be a useful batsman in the Lancashire & Ribblesdale cricket leagues. Leighton left Burnley in May 1989 but by February the next year was appointed youth team coach at Bradford City as well as occasionally turning out for the reserve team. He went on to manage Gainsborough Trinity, Morecambe, Netherfield, Llanelli (twice),Garden Village and Aberdare Athletic plus a brief playing spell in 1995 with Darwen. In 2011, he also had a short spell as Director of Football at Haverfordwest County. Starting in Lancashire, Leighton also became a radio pundit, often an outspoken one. His dislike of Cardiff City resulted in a BBC ban and the recording of a song called, 'Leighton James Don't Like Us' by Leigh Bailey, a Cardiff musician.

Always good at crossing, in later life Leighton became a lollipop man at his nephew's school in Swansea and even won an award for that!

## JAMES, Reece

**POSITION:** Left-back

**BIRTHPLACE:** Bacup, Lancashire

**DATE OF BIRTH:** 07/11/1993

**HEIGHT:** 5' 6" **WEIGHT:** 11st 3lbs

**SIGNED FROM:** Wigan Athletic, 02/07/2018

**DEBUT:** v Sheffield Wednesday, A, 16/08/2018

**LAST MATCH:** v Portsmouth, N, 31/03/2019

**MOVED TO:** Doncaster Rovers, 19/06/2019

**TEAMS:** Rossendale United, Blackburn Rovers, Preston North End, Manchester United, Carlisle United (L), Rotherham United (L), Huddersfield Town (L), Wigan Athletic, Sunderland, Doncaster Rovers, Blackpool, Sheffield Wednesday (L) (to July 2022)

**SAFC TOTALS:** 30+4 appearances / 0 goals

**James spent the 2018-19 season at the Stadium of Light. After making his final appearance at Wembley in the Football League (Checkatrade) Trophy final, he then chose to leave in order to join Doncaster Rovers where over two seasons he played 78+2 games.**

He scored nine goals, seven of them in his second season having been moved into midfield. In 2021, he returned to the Championship when signing for newly-promoted Blackpool but in July 2022 moved on a season long loan to Sheffield Wednesday.

After playing youth football around the north west, he joined Manchester United in 2012 where he made one first-team appearance in a 2014 League Cup defeat at MK Dons. The previous season had seen him play twice on loan to Carlisle. Further loans followed at Rotherham (8/0) and Huddersfield (6/1) before a July 2015 transfer to Wigan where he scored once in 55+2 appearances.

His brother Matty played over 100 times for Leicester City in addition to loans with Preston, Barnsley and Coventry, having also started with Manchester United. An England Under 20 international, Matty signed for Bristol City in June 2021. Father Linton played non-league for Bacup Borough where he was also assistant manager.

## JANUZAJ, Adnan

**POSITION:** Winger

**BIRTHPLACE:** Brussels, Belgium

**DATE OF BIRTH:** 05/02/1995

**HEIGHT:** 6' 0" **WEIGHT:** 11st 11lbs

**SIGNED FROM:** Manchester United, 12/08/2016, on loan

**DEBUT:** v Manchester City, A, 13/08/2016

**LAST MATCH:** v Chelsea, A, 21/05/2017

**MOVED TO:** Manchester United, 22/05/2017, end of loan

**TEAMS:** FC Brussels, Anderlecht, Manchester United, Borussia Dortmund (L), Sunderland (L), Real Sociedad

**INTERNATIONAL:** Belgium

**SAFC TOTALS:** 21+7 appearances / 1 goal

**Good enough to start for Belgium as they beat England in the 2018 FIFA World Cup, Januzaj had been part of the Sunderland side lamely relegated from the Premier League a year earlier.**

Brought in on loan by David Moyes, who had given him his debut at Manchester United, Januzaj failed to make an impact at Sunderland where it seemed as if he was a player more suited to being in a team that dominated possession rather than having to scrap and fight, although he was sent off at Spurs for a tackle after a first yellow for dissent. His only goal came in the League Cup against Shrewsbury on his second home appearance.

He had scored twice against Sunderland at the SoL for United in October 2013, in a game where he was cautioned for diving. Not including a Community Shield appearance against Wigan at neutral Wembley, this was his first away game. They were two of five goals he scored for United in 31+32 appearances. Sunderland was Januzaj's second loan. The previous season he had played 3+9 games for Borussia Dortmund without scoring. Similarly, the 2018 World Cup was his second tournament. At the 2014 World Cup he played against Ki Sung-Yueng's South Korea.

Little was seen of it at Sunderland, but Adnan had the ability to warrant a £9m sale to Real Sociedad almost immediately after his loan to SAFC. Much of his time with Sociedad was spent as a substitute, 70 of his 169 appearances were as a sub while he was an unused sub as his club won the Copa Del Rey final in 2020. He was released in May 2022.

## JARVIE, Gavin

**POSITION:** Left-half

**BIRTHPLACE:** Newton, Lanarkshire

**DATE OF BIRTH:** 20/01/1879 - 25/07/1957

**HEIGHT:** 5' 8½" **WEIGHT:** 12st 0lbs

**SIGNED FROM:** Bristol Rovers, 02/05/1907

**DEBUT:** v Manchester City, H, 02/09/1907

**LAST MATCH:** v Middlesbrough, A, 30/12/1911

**MOVED TO:** Hamilton Academical, 11/05/1912

**TEAMS:** Cambuslang Rangers, Airdrieonians, Bristol Rovers, Sunderland, Hamilton Academical

**SAFC TOTALS:** 100 appearances / 2 goals

**Jarvie was a steel dresser before becoming a professional footballer. Gavin joined Airdrie in October 1901 and subsequently moved south to Bristol Rovers in May 1904; in both cases Thomas Tait followed him.**

He officially came to SAFC on 2 May 1907, one year after Thomas Tait, although some contemporary reports indicated he was signed earlier. His previous club Bristol Rovers were certainly were not happy and reported him to the FA for refusing to continue with them even though they had offered him what was then the maximum wage. He played 89 times for the Pirates, scoring once, and was part of their Southern League title team of 1904-05.

He had three good seasons at Roker Park playing 25, 27 and 33 games before twelve in his fourth campaign and just three in his final one. After being granted a free transfer he returned to Scotland and played 28 times in the first division for Hamilton as their team captain. As his former colleagues at Roker Park celebrated the League Championship and FA Cup runners-up spot, Gavin, or Guy as he was popularly known, retired from playing and took up farming in Uddingston, his wife Margaret being a former dairy maid.

## JI, Dong-won

**POSITION:** Forward

**BIRTHPLACE:** Chuja-Myeon, Jeju Island, South Korea

**DATE OF BIRTH:** 28/05/1991

**HEIGHT:** 6' 1½" **WEIGHT:** 12st 1lb

**SIGNED FROM:** Jeonnam Dragons, 30/06/2011

**DEBUT:** v Liverpool, A, 13/08/2011

**LAST MATCH:** v Carlisle United, H, 05/01/2014

**MOVED TO:** Augsburg, 16/01/2014

**TEAMS:** Jeonnam Dragons, Sunderland, Augsburg (L), Borussia Dortmund, Augsburg, Darmstadt 98 (L), Mainz 05, Eintracht Braunschweig (L), Seoul (to May 2022)

**INTERNATIONAL:** South Korea

**SAFC TOTALS:** 6+22 appearances / 2 goals

**Signed by Steve Bruce on the recommendation of a scout who he had known at Manchester United, Ji only ever started four Premier League games for Sunderland and scored just twice, but he was responsible for one of the great moments at the Stadium of Light.**

It was on New Year's Day 2012 that largely thanks to goalkeeper Simon Mignolet, champions-elect Manchester City had been kept at bay for 90 minutes. With the game scoreless in added time substitute Ji kept his balance as he rounded keeper Joe Hart to sensationally give Sunderland victory. It was without doubt Ji's finest moment in red and white.

The following summer he took Olympic Bronze in London while on Sunderland's books, but a year to the day on from his goal against City moved out on loan to Augsburg in Germany, debuting against Fortuna Dusseldorf. He went on to enjoy an extensive career in Germany. In total he played 76+49 times for Augsburg, scoring 15 times. While he did not get a first-team game for Borussia Dortmund he subsequently scored both goals against them as Augsburg beat the league leaders 2-1 in March 2019.

Ji also scored twice in 16 games for Darmstadt. At Mainz there was just one start plus ten games off the bench but no goals. At Braunschweig his only goal from 9+3 games came on his home debut against Hannover in February 2021, but he was sent off on his final appearance against Wurzburger Kickers before returning to South Korea.

Four years before coming to Sunderland Ji had a short spell in England as a youth player with Reading. He made his name with Jeonnam Dragons where a highlight was a hat-trick in a cup tie with Gyeongnam in July 2010 in a season where he was nominated for the Young Player of the Year in the K League.

At international level he debuted for South Korea on 30 December 2010 scoring the only goal of the game against Syria. The following month he scored four goals as his side took the bronze medal in the Asian Games. He gained more tournament experience in the 2014 FIFA World Cup, playing twice in Brazil against Algeria and Belgium.

## JOBLING, J

**POSITION:** Forward

**SIGNED:** 1887

**DEBUT:** v Newcastle East End, 17/11/1888

**LAST MATCH:** v Newcastle East End, 17/11/1888

**MOVED:** 1889

**TEAMS:** Sunderland, Monkwearmouth Workmen's Hall

**SAFC TOTALS:** 1 appearance / 0 goals

**Jobling's only competitive game was on the left wing in an English (FA) Cup win over Newcastle East End which was won 2-0. He is listed in second-team games from 1887-88 to 1889-90 after which he is known to have played for Monkwearmouth Workmen's Hall along with other former Sunderland players such as Reuben Smith and James Hunter.**

He was sometimes referred to, during this time, by the nickname of 'Boney'. It is very likely that Jobling was John Mitchell Jobling, a ship's caulker born in 1866 in Monkwearmouth. John was the brother-in-law of Reuben Smith and was known to have been a prize fighter before becoming verger at St Peter's Church, Monkwearmouth. He passed away on 7 December 1934.

## JOHN, Stern Christopher James

**POSITION:** Forward

**BIRTHPLACE:** Tunapuna, Trinidad

**DATE OF BIRTH:** 30/10/1976

**HEIGHT:** 6' 1" **WEIGHT:** 12st 13lbs

**SIGNED FROM:** Coventry City, 29/01/2007

**DEBUT:** v Coventry City, 03/02/2007

**LAST MATCH:** v Birmingham City, 15/08/2007

**MOVED TO:** Southampton, 29/08/2007

**TEAMS:** Mercer CC, Malta Carib Alcons, Carolina Dynamo, New Orleans Riverboat Gamblers, Columbus Crew, Nottingham Forest, Birmingham City, Coventry City, Derby County (L), Sunderland, Southampton, Bristol City (L), Crystal Palace, Ipswich Town (L), North East Stars, Solihull Moors, WASA FC, Central FC

**INTERNATIONAL:** Trinidad &Tobago

**SAFC TOTALS:** 10+6 appearances / 5 goals

**A powerfully built target-man who possessed a pleasantly deft touch, John was signed in the January transfer window of 2007 to bolster the team's successful charge for the second tier title. He had scored against Sunderland on the opening day of the season for Coventry who he debuted against under a week after leaving them.**

Stern did not take long to make an impact, scoring twice on his second home appearance with another couple of goals as he featured in all but one match to the end of the season. He then scored in a draw at one of his old clubs Birmingham when he came off the bench for his only appearance for Sunderland in the Premier League, after which he was swiftly moved out to Southampton as a makeweight in a deal that brought his fellow Trinidadian Kenwyne Jones to Wearside.

Including Mercer County Community College where he played his junior football, Stern had more clubs than he played games for Sunderland. Progressing in the USA, 44 goals in 55 games for Columbus Crew and selection for the MLS Best XI led to a £1.5m move to Nottingham Forest.

Debuting with a goal against Portsmouth in November 1999, he played 57+24 games scoring 20 goals. Despite that decent record - and a hat-trick at Millwall in October 2001, as well as seven goals in his last ten games - he was sold to Birmingham City in February 2002 for a tenth of what Forest paid.

After playing in the Gold Cup for Trinidad & Tobago John scored a debut winner against Barnsley and went on to help Blues to promotion. He scored the Play-Off semi-final winner at Millwall and in the final shoot-out against Norwich for Steve Bruce's team where his teammates included Darren Carter. During his Birmingham days, he played against Sunderland at St Andrew's on the day Sunderland's relegation was confirmed in 2003. Tempted to indulge in some show-boating, he was 'wiped out' by Marcus Stewart who was sent off.

After 21 goals in 48+33 games, in September 2004 John moved to Coventry where he added 29 goals in 74+14 appearances before his switch to Sunderland (having also had 6+1 games on loan to Derby without scoring). At Southampton, he notched nine goals in his first 15 games including a hat-trick against Hull. After two years with the Saints during which he totalled 20 goals in 40+12 games (and also scored twice in 14+12 games on loan to Bristol City) he wound down his English senior career with Crystal Palace (7+9/2) and Ipswich (7+2/1 on loan), his last goal being for George Burley's Crystal Palace at Derby in April 2010.

After a spell back in Trinidad with North East Stars, there was a return to England with Solihull Moors, but he did not play before joining WASA in Trinidad and Tobago. Finally, in 2016, he became player/coach of Central FC in Trinidad and Tobago where in 2022 he remains his national team's all-time top-scorer and second highest appearance maker with 70 goals in his 115 internationals, which included three games at the 2006 FIFA World Cup. Stern's cousin, Ansil Elcock, was also a Trinidad and Tobago international and played a big part in John's career by recommending him to Columbus Crew at the start of his journey. In November 2020, John became manager of the national side of Anguilla, a small island in the Caribbean.

## JOHNSON, Adam

**POSITION:** Winger

**BIRTHPLACE:** Easington, Co Durham

**DATE OF BIRTH:** 14/07/1987

**HEIGHT:** 5' 11" **WEIGHT:** 11st 5lbs

**SIGNED FROM:** Manchester City, 24/08/2012

**DEBUT:** v Morecambe, H, 28/08/2012

**LAST MATCH:** v Liverpool, A, 06/02/2016

**MOVED TO:** 12/02/2016, Contract terminated

**TEAMS:** Cleveland Juniors, Newcastle United, Middlesbrough, Leeds United (L), Watford (L), Manchester City, Sunderland

**INTERNATIONAL:** England

**SAFC TOTALS:** 112+29 appearances / 22 goals

**Johnson was jailed for six years for sexual activity with an under-age girl. He was also sacked by Sunderland and did not play again after serving half his sentence. He had been an excellent footballer.**

Capped twelve times by England, for whom he scored twice, he had cost Sunderland a reported £10m to sign him from Manchester City with whom he had won the FA Cup in 2011 and both the Premier League and Community Shield in 2012.

He had been an FA Youth Cup winner with his first club Middlesbrough in 2004 and played in the League (Capital One) Cup final for Sunderland against his old club City at Wembley in 2014 when he set up Sunderland's goal, scored by Fabio Borini.

Johnson also had a successful time in derbies, scoring in four games for Sunderland against Newcastle, but his misdemeanours ruined lives as well as his own career, as well as bringing shame upon the club.

His basic statistics for other clubs after being a youth player at Newcastle were: Boro 64+56/16, Leeds 4+1/0, Watford 11+1/5 and Manchester City 54+43/15. He was stripped of his England caps following his jail sentence which he served at HMP Moorland near Doncaster.

## JOHNSON, Joseph (Joe)

**POSITION:** Left-back

**BIRTHPLACE:** Felling, Co Durham

**DATE OF BIRTH:** 26/10/1894 - 19/10/1977

**HEIGHT:** 5' 8½" **WEIGHT:** 12st 0lbs

**SIGNED FROM:** Felling Colliery, 25/08/1919

**DEBUT:** v Preston North End, H, 10/04/1920

**LAST MATCH:** v Liverpool, H, 01/05/1920

**MOVED TO:** Ebbw Vale, 15/07/1921

**TEAMS:** Felling Colliery, Sunderland, Ebbw Vale

**SAFC TOTALS:** 3 appearances / 0 goals

**In April 1919, Joe played at South Shields in the Northern Victory League for Sunderland before signing for the Lads the following summer. After three first division games he left to move to Ebbw Vale in Wales, during which time he probably continued his profession as a coal miner.**

Local newspapers of the time state Johnson to be sound, reliable and a tower of strength in defence, however, he seems to have only played one season before leaving the Welsh Valleys, maybe due to the financial difficulties the Valians and local coal mines suffered during that season.

## JOHNSON, Simon Ainsley

**POSITION:** Forward

**BIRTHPLACE:** West Bromwich, West Midlands

**DATE OF BIRTH:** 09/03/1983

**HEIGHT:** 5' 9½" **WEIGHT:** 11st 9lbs

**SIGNED FROM:** Leeds United, 10/09/2004, on loan

**DEBUT:** v Gillingham, A, 11/09/2004

**LAST MATCH:** v Millwall, H, 16/10/2004

**MOVED TO:** Leeds United, 25/10/2004, recalled from loan

**TEAMS:** Leeds United, Hull City (L), Blackpool (L), Sunderland (L), Doncaster Rovers (L), Barnsley (L), Darlington, Hereford United, Bury, Halesowen Town, Solihull Moors, Guiseley, Hibernians (Malta), Hinckley United, Hinckley AFC

**INTERNATIONAL:** England Under 20

**SAFC TOTALS:** 1+4 appearances / 0 goals

**Simon was 21 when he came on loan to SAFC from Leeds United , a pacey, nimble attacker who could also operate in midfield. Sunderland was the third of five loans he had from Elland Road.**

The first had seen Simon mark his senior debut with a goal for Hull against Bristol Rovers in August 2002. He added another on his home debut against Bury eleven days later. However, games and goals were to be in short supply. He did not score again in a total of 4+9 games for Hull. There was one goal in 3+1 outings for Blackpool and after Sunderland, where he started just once, there were three goals in 8+3 games across two loans with Doncaster and two goals in a loan to Barnsley where he reached ten starts (plus one game as sub).

Interspersed with these loans came occasional appearances for his parent club. A debut for Leeds at Charlton in April 2003 came with his side already 5-1 up, finishing 6-1 after his twelve-minute cameo.

He would only ever start four games for Leeds, as well as eight games as sub, but never scored. Nonetheless, Johnson did well enough to earn a call up at international level although his debut came as a sub in an 8-0 hammering at Under 20 level by Argentina at the Toulon tournament in June 2003, where he later got starts against Turkey and Japan, Darren Carter being amongst his teammates.

Freed by Leeds in 2005, Simon got regular football with two years at Darlington (52+24/9) and Hereford (35+36/6) with whom he won promotion to League One in 2007-08. A final month-long spell at Bury in 2009 brought two starts and four substitute appearances but his last game in the Football League came when he was just 26. There followed a series of short-term non-league moves and a very brief stint in Malta before he finished playing in 2014. In February 2018, he emerged as a coach to WBA Under 13s after which he coached Evesham United alongside Shaun Cunnington and set up his own Simon Johnson Universal Soccer Academy.

## JOHNSON, Zak Robert

**POSITION:** Centre-back

**BIRTHPLACE:** Sunderland, Tyne and Wear

**DATE OF BIRTH:** 25/05/2005

**HEIGHT:** 6' 3" **WEIGHT:** 12st 5lbs

**SIGNED FROM:** Trainee, 01/07/2021

**DEBUT:** v Manchester United Under 21s, H, 13/10/2021

**LAST MATCH:**

**MOVED TO:**

**TEAMS:** Sunderland

**SAFC TOTALS:** 0+1 appearances / 0 goals (to June 2022)

**Zak became the club's fourth youngest player when given the last-minute of added time in a Football League Trophy game at the age of 16 years and 142 days.**

A student at Monkwearmouth Academy, Zak came to the Academy of Light as a seven-year-old and played in Fulwell Juniors under the guidance of the author's son! Zak's first professional deal was signed on 1 July 2022.

## JOHNSTON, Allan

**POSITION:** Winger

**BIRTHPLACE:** Glasgow, Lanarkshire

**DATE OF BIRTH:** 14/12/1973

**HEIGHT:** 5' 10" **WEIGHT:** 11st 0lbs

**SIGNED FROM:** Rennes, 26/03/1997

**DEBUT:** v Newcastle United, A, 05/04/1997

**LAST MATCH:** v Birmingham City, H, 09/05/1999

**MOVED TO:** Rangers, 01/07/2000

**TEAMS:** Hearts, Rennes, Sunderland, Birmingham City (L), Bolton Wanderers (L), Rangers, Middlesbrough, Sheffield Wednesday (L), Kilmarnock, St Mirren, Queen of the South

**INTERNATIONAL:** Scotland

**SAFC TOTALS:** 96+5 appearances / 20 goals

**Nicknamed 'Magic', Johnston was an outstanding winger best employed on the left-flank, although he was predominantly right-footed. His superb partnership with Mickey Gray during the 1998-99 promotion season was an integral part of the side who amassed an incredible 105 points.**

The epitome of the Scottish 'jinky' winger, Allan made his international debut during that season and went on to win the first nine of his 18 caps while with Sunderland, scoring his only two goals for Scotland in the summer promotion had been won. Fans were eager to see him unleashed on the Premier League because he undoubtedly had the quality to excel as shown by a trademark curler into the top corner in an end-of-season game with Liverpool staged to commemorate 100 years of the Football League.

Unfortunately, manager Peter Reid then froze Johnston - and Michael Bridges - out of the first-team picture. Having seen some other players at other clubs be poor in the final season of their contracts Reid was adamant that he would not play Johnston or Bridges unless they were signed on longer deals.

Reid was a very focussed and steely manager who after producing the 105-point side guided the team to successive seventh-placed finishes in the Premier League so can justify his actions, but there remains the lingering thought that could the Lads have done even better had they also had Johnston and Bridges to call upon?

Instead, Allan went on loan to Championship Birmingham making 7+2 appearances from mid-October 1999 and taking another loan to Sam Allardyce's Bolton from the following January. He played in all of the last 19 games of the season, scoring the first of his three league goals back at Birmingham. Having helped the Trotters to qualify for the Play-Offs, he scored against Ipswich Town only to lose to George Burley's Tractor Boys.

At the expiry of his contract at Sunderland in the summer of 2000, Johnston joined Rangers. He had scored a hat-trick at Ibrox with his first club Hearts who he had also played for against Rangers in the Scottish Cup final in 1996 when he was a teammate of former Sunderland winger John Colquhoun, although on that occasion they were beaten 5-1. After 54+41 games and 14 goals for Hearts (67+48 /21 including friendlies etc) he moved to France with Rennes in the summer of 1996, but after two goals in 23 games came to Sunderland after less than a season. As Sunderland vainly battled relegation Allan played in the final six games of that 1996-97 campaign, writing his name into the history books by scoring the last-ever league goal at Roker Park, against Everton.

He got off to a great start with Rangers, marking his debut with a goal in a home Champions League win against FBK Kaunas. Playing for Dick Advocaat and with Tore Andre-Flo and Claudio Reyna amongst his teammates Johnston played only 16+10 times, scoring three times before a £600,000 move to Middlesbrough after just over a season. Debuting in a Premiership home defeat to Newcastle he scored in his second Premiership appearance for Boro against West Ham but it was Allan's only goal for the Teessiders where he was limited to 18+5 appearances. There were also two goals in twelve games on loan to Sheffield Wednesday before a return to Scotland in August 2004 when he commenced a five-year spell with Kilmarnock linking up with his former Hearts manager Jim Jefferies.

Goals were few and far between, just five altogether, but the creative spark was still there as he totalled 107+23 appearances. He then spent 2009-10 with St Mirren where all but one of his ten league games were as sub (there were two cup starts, but no goals) before a final move to Queen of the South. In two and a half seasons in Dumfries Allan started 66 games in addition to six games as sub and scored eight times.

When he was a player at Sunderland, few thought of 'Magic' becoming a manager, but having begun coaching at Queen of the South he became player-manager in 2012 and enjoyed immediate success doing the double of being Second Division Champions and Challenge Cup winners in his first full season of 2012-13. Kilmarnock had to pay compensation to make Johnston (who at this point had a win percentage of over 74% and was Scotland Manager of the Year) their manager in June 2013. However, by February of his second season, he walked away from the club over transfer policy.

Appointed at Dunfermline in the summer of 2015 Johnston led his side to the Division One title in his first season. He spent three and a half seasons at the club enjoying a win percentage of 47% before returning to Queen of the South in May 2019, immediately guiding the side through relegation Play-Offs and staying with the club until February 2022.

Allan's brother Sammy played for St Johnstone, Ayr United and Partick Thistle amongst ten clubs in Scotland and Ireland while 'Magic's son Max made his debut for Motherwell as a 17-year-old in February 2021 having already represented Scotland at Under 16 level and played for his dad at Queen of the South in 2021-22. Allan Johnston's thoughts on his time at Sunderland and in particular his contract conundrum are included in the 2021 book, "Promotion Winning Black Cats.'

## JOHNSTON, Henry Wallace (Harry)

**POSITION:** Left-half / Left-back

**BIRTHPLACE:** Glasgow, Lanarkshire

**DATE OF BIRTH:** 18/09/1871 - 10/12/1936

**HEIGHT:** 5' 8½" **WEIGHT:** 12st 0lbs

**SIGNED FROM:** Clyde, 28/04/1894

**DEBUT:** v Derby County, H, 01/09/1894

**LAST MATCH:** v Wednesday, A, 10/10/1896

**MOVED TO:** Aston Villa, 26/02/1897

**TEAMS:** Airdrieonians, Cambuslang, Clyde, Sunderland, Aston Villa, Grimsby Town, Northfleet United, Third Lanark

**SAFC TOTALS:** 66 appearances / 4 goals

**Harry missed just one game as the league title was won in 1894-95, is one of the players pictured on the giant Hemy painting that dominates the foyer of the Stadium of Light and was married in Bishopwearmouth Church - quite a memorable first season on Wearside. He scored two of his four league goals that season and also scored (not included in totals) at Hearts in the famous game that saw Sunderland declared to be 'World Champions' in 1895.**

Again a regular the following season he was hampered early in his third and final Wearside campaign as he suffered from typhoid fever in the opening months of that season. Joining Aston Villa - the other great club of the period - late in that campaign, he could not get a game as Villa did the double and, probably still weakened by his illness moved on to Grimsby the following October, without ever wearing the claret and blue competitively.

Having started in a Testimonial against Newton Heath (Manchester United) for an old Grimsby stalwart Fletcher, he made his competitive debut for the Mariners against Newcastle at Abbey Park, 6 November 1897, when he was reported to have cordially shaken hands with his old Sunderland teammates Johnny Campbell and John Harvie before the game which Grimsby won 2-0 and in which he was described as having, 'lost none of his football since he left Sunderland, and it seems surprising that Aston Villa have so readily parted with him'.

By 18 December Johnston had played his last game for Grimsby (a 4-3 home defeat to Manchester City). It seems he failed to turn up for the festive fixtures and was suspended by the directors for misconduct. Moving on again, he spent the rest of 1897-98 with Northfleet United before returning to his native Scotland to play a season with Third Lanark. Having started with Airdrieonians in 1888, he soon became their captain, however, after a disagreement in April 1892, he played once for Cambuslang. This difference was not fully resolved and as a result he soon moved to Clyde to become their captain. Johnston scored once in 20 games for Clyde before joining Sunderland.

In the early 1920s, Airdrieonians granted Harry membership for life in gratitude for the valuable service rendered to the club. After retiring from the game he worked as a clerk for a soap manufacturing company in Glasgow.

## JOHNSTON, John B

**POSITION:** Left-back

**BIRTHPLACE:** Muirkirk, Ayrshire

**DATE OF BIRTH:** 11/10/1881 - 31/10/1954

**HEIGHT:** 5' 10" **WEIGHT:** 12st 0lbs

**SIGNED FROM:** Muirkirk, 05/01/1920

**DEBUT:** v Blackburn Rovers, A, 11/09/1920

**LAST MATCH:** v Derby County, A, 28/03/1921

**MOVED TO:** Bolton Wanderers, 20/05/1922

**TEAMS:** Muirkirk ,Sunderland, Bolton Wanderers

**SAFC TOTALS:** 2 appearances / 0 goals

**Not included in the excellent 'All the Lads' book which attributed John's two appearances to his near namesake Joseph Johnson, this player was a Scot whose only first-team appearance at Roker Park came after he left Sunderland.**

It was his solitary game for Bolton Wanderers for whom he played at right-back in September 1922 on a day Sunderland romped to a 5-1 victory. Charlie Buchan scored four times that day having scored all the goals in Johnston's only two appearances for Sunderland back in the 1920-21 season.

Johnston's first full season had started promisingly as he was included in two Public Practice Matches. On the first of these occasions, he was part of the Stripes team that hammered the Whites 10-1, but five days later he had been replaced in the stronger 'Stripes' team by Ernie England and so played for the Whites who were beaten 5-1.

Due to the donation of his SAFC contracts, we know that Johnston was initially paid £4 a week plus an extra ten shillings (50p) if in the first team when he signed. This had risen to £6 per week plus £1 if in the first team for the 1921-22 season.

## JOHNSTON, John Kerr

**POSITION:** Right-back

**BIRTHPLACE:** Dalmellington, East Ayrshire

**DATE OF BIRTH:** 11/10/1881 - 31/10/1954

**HEIGHT:** 5' 7" **WEIGHT:** 11st 7lbs

**SIGNED FROM:** Cambuslang Rangers, 29/08/1907

**DEBUT:** v Blackburn Rovers, A, 22/03/1909

**LAST MATCH:** v Blackburn Rovers, A, 22/03/1909

**MOVED TO:** Motherwell, 15/06/1909

**TEAMS:** Dalziel Rovers, Cambuslang Rangers, Sunderland, Motherwell

**INTERNATIONAL:** Scotland Junior

**SAFC TOTALS:** 1 appearance / 0 goals

**Johnston had played in the last two out of three pre-season practice games ahead of the 1907-08 campaign under the name of Johns and was subsequently given a contract.**

John became one of eight players to appear at right-back during the 1908-09 season. Unfortunately, eight was the key number, as on his solitary first-team appearance the side suffered a record 8-1 defeat. He moved to Motherwell three months later and played 13 times in 1909-10. After retiring from football he worked in a Coatbridge steelworks.

## JOHNSTON, Robert (Bert)

**POSITION:** Centre-half

**BIRTHPLACE:** Falkirk, Stirlingshire

**DATE OF BIRTH:** 02/06/1909 - 27/09/1968

**HEIGHT:** 5' 10½" **WEIGHT:** 11st 8lbs

**SIGNED FROM:** Alva Albion Rovers, 02/08/1929

**DEBUT:** v West Ham United, A, 25/04/1931

**LAST MATCH:** v Huddersfield Town, V, 29/04/1939

**MOVED TO:** Retired, 01/10/1945

**TEAMS:** Alva Albion Rovers, Sunderland, Hartlepools United (WW2 Guest), Lincoln City (WW2 Guest)

**INTERNATIONAL:** Scotland

**SAFC TOTALS:** 166 appearances / 0 goals

**A fine servant of SAFC, Bert Johnston's association with Sunderland stretched from 1929 to 1957. A regular player in the thirties, his best seasons were in 1934-35 (41 apps) and 1937-38 (36), but he also played ten league games as the league title was gained in 1935-36 and eight of the nine games - including the final - as the FA Cup was won a year later.**

He also played in two Charity Shield games for Sunderland. There was an additional appearance in the expunged 1939-40 season after which he served in the RAF as a physical training instructor during World War Two and appeared for Hartlepools United and Lincoln City.

From October 1945 until June 1951, Johnston served as assistant trainer at Sunderland before taking on the senior job from then until July 1957 when he left in the aftermath of the illegal payments scandal to become manager of Horden Colliery Welfare. After 18 months he moved from Horden to manage Consett and then later ran an off licence in Sunderland.

His son David played for Sunderland Boys and Bishop Auckland before joining Leicester City. He did not play for the Foxes but went on to play ten league games for Exeter City and 26 for Stockport County before a move to Tranmere Rovers where again he did not play.

Bert Johnston was good friends with the great Jimmy Connor and a small football in a glass case signed by all the big names of the thirties and belonging to Bert was donated to the club by David and is on display in Quinn's Bar.

## JOHNSTONE, Robert (Bob)

**POSITION:** Inside-left / Outside-left

**BIRTHPLACE:** Renton, West Dunbartonshire

**DATE OF BIRTH:** 1875/76

**HEIGHT:** 5' 6½" **WEIGHT:** 10st 3lbs

**SIGNED FROM:** Renton, 04/05/1896

**DEBUT:** v Wednesday, A, 10/10/1896

**LAST MATCH:** v Bury, A, 16/04/1897

**MOVED TO:** Third Lanark, 04/05/1897

**TEAMS:** Dumbarton West End, Dumbarton, Renton, Sunderland, Third Lanark, Dunfermline Athletic

**SAFC TOTALS:** 14 appearances / 1 goal

**Bob Johnstone came to prominence with 17 goals in 27 games for Dumbarton between 1892 to 1895. He then had a season with Renton, scoring five in 13 games before his season at Sunderland. His time on Wearside coincided with the year the aging 'Team of All The Talents' struggled and had to battle through the end of season Test Matches.**

Johnstone did not play for a few weeks after his debut due to inflammation of the kidneys and although he recovered and played in eleven of the last 20 league games, he was not selected for the important Test Matches.

Third Lanark signed Johnstone, James Hannah and James Gillespie within the same couple of days in May 1897. Within days they had helped their new side beat Queen's Park 3-1 in a Glasgow Charity Cup tie. Bob scored a dozen goals in 25 games for Third Lanark before finishing his career with Dunfermline.

## JONES, Billy

**POSITION:** Full-back

**BIRTHPLACE:** Shrewsbury, Shropshire

**DATE OF BIRTH:** 24/03/1987

**HEIGHT:** 5' 11" **WEIGHT:** 12st 6lbs

**SIGNED FROM:** West Bromwich Albion, 01/07/2014 Deal agreed 28/05/2014

**DEBUT:** v Birmingham City, A, 27/08/2014

**LAST MATCH:** v Fulham, A 27/04/2018

**MOVED TO:** Contract not renewed, 30/06/2018

**TEAMS:** Crewe Alexandra, Preston North End, WBA, Sunderland, Rotherham United, Crewe Alexandra (L) (to May 2022)

**INTERNATIONAL:** England Under 20

**SAFC TOTALS:** 89+7 appearances / 3 goals

**A hard working and determined defender who had the desire and energy to get forward as often as possible, Billy was a model professional but ultimately not quite good enough to succeed at the top level. His last two seasons saw him feature in consecutive relegations.**

Just 16 when he debuted for Crewe on 18 October 2003 as a sub against Derby County, he went on to become Alex's Young Player of the Year and added to his burgeoning reputation by also winning the club's Goal of the Year award for his first-ever goal (against Wigan on 20 December 2003) and gaining international recognition.

Twelve caps for England at Under 16 level, along with five and seven for the Under 17s and 19s preceded a single Under 20 cap won in a 4-0 defeat away to Russia in August 2005, when he played alongside future Sunderland caretaker manager Andrew Taylor.

As he developed Jones was frequently used in midfield by Crewe where he was ever-present, Player of the Year and top scorer (with seven goals) as they were relegated from the Championship in the season he had started by playing for England Under 20s.

## JONES, Billy (Continued)

Following 138+5 games and eight goals for Crewe, in August 2007 he was transferred to Preston. At Deepdale he became right-back and club captain, but again he would experience the bitter-sweet taste of being Player of the Year in a relegation season as North End went down in 2011, at which point he left for Premier League West Brom after 171+3 games and 13 goals. His one goal in three seasons with Albion came against Newcastle United. He made 70+4 appearances for the club before switching to Sunderland.

After his time in the north east, Jones joined Rotherham where in three seasons he was twice relegated from the Championship and promoted from League One. After only 34+7 games and no goals in those three seasons he had a three-game loan spell back at Crewe.

## JONES, John Edward (Jack)

**POSITION:** Left-back

**BIRTHPLACE:** Bromborough, Cheshire

**DATE OF BIRTH:** 03/07/1913 - 26/01/1995

**HEIGHT:** 5' 9" **WEIGHT:** 11st 10lbs

**SIGNED FROM:** Everton, 21/12/1945

**DEBUT:** v Grimsby Town, A, 05/01/1946

**LAST MATCH:** v Grimsby Town, A, 10/05/1947

**MOVED TO:** Retired, 01/05/1948

**TEAMS:** Bebington, Bromborough Pool, Port Sunlight, Ellesmere Port, Everton, Tranmere Rovers (WW2 Guest), Chester (WW2 Guest), Wrexham (WW2 Guest), Liverpool (WW2 Guest), Southport (WW2 Guest), Sunderland

**INTERNATIONAL:** England Touring XI

**SAFC TOTALS:** 31 appearances / 0 goals

**Jones played for Everton when they beat Sunderland 6-4 in the famous FA Cup tie of 1935, still thought by many to be the greatest game ever-played at Goodison Park. It was one of 108 games he played for the Toffees.**

Jack played a few games for an England Touring XI in South Africa a couple of months prior to the start of WW2; future colleague Johnny Mapson being another member of that touring squad. In war-time he is known to have played a couple of dozen times as a guest for several clubs, at least 13 of these with Wrexham, as well as around 50 times for The Toffees. He is also known to have played for Liverpool against Southport on 28 August 1944.

Coming to Sunderland after the war Jack made 23 League North appearances in 1945-46 in addition to his official tally of 31 league and cup games. While his official debut is the FA Cup tie at Grimsby listed here, he first played, initially as a guest, on 15 December 1945 in a League North game against Manchester United, staged at City's Maine Road.

Although his playing time at Sunderland was short-lived, Jack Jones remained at the club after hanging up his boots until May 1969 progressing from training the youths, to the reserves and finally the first team. After retiring from football, he became a hospital porter until 1976 after which he spent two more years as a technician in the operating theatre. Away from football, he was also a keen cricketer and a member at Ashbrooke in Sunderland.

## JONES, Kenneth

**POSITION:** Left-back

**BIRTHPLACE:** Easington Colliery, Co Durham

**DATE OF BIRTH:** 01/10/1936

**HEIGHT:** 5' 9" **WEIGHT:** 11st 0lbs

**SIGNED FROM:** Easington School, 01/07/1952

**DEBUT:** v Bristol Rovers, A, 23/01/1960

**LAST MATCH:** v Portsmouth, A, 18/04/1960

**MOVED TO:** Hartlepools United, 27/01/1961

**TEAMS:** Sunderland, Hartlepools United, King's Lynn

**INTERNATIONAL:** England Schools

**SAFC TOTALS:** 10 appearances / 0 goals

**An apprentice cabinet maker when he joined Sunderland, local lad Jones played for England schools three times in 1951-52. The first was a 1-0 win at Wembley in front of a crowd of over 80,000 in a team captained by Duncan Edwards.**

After a long wait for a Sunderland debut, all of his ten games came in the second half of 1959-60. The closest Ken got before then was a couple of Durham Senior Cup semi-finals appearances against Darlington in 1954 and 1956; during the second of which he scored from the penalty spot in a 5-0 win. At Hartlepools, he debuted against Bradford Park Avenue in April 1961 and went on to play 33 league games plus two cup ties before moving to Kings Lynn.

## JONES, Jordan Lewis

**POSITION:** Winger

**BIRTHPLACE:** Redcar, North Yorks

**DATE OF BIRTH:** 24/10/1994

**HEIGHT:** 5' 8½" **WEIGHT:** 11st 0lbs

**SIGNED FROM:** Rangers, 29/01/2021, on loan

**DEBUT:** v MK Dons, A, 02/02/2021

**LAST MATCH:** v Lincoln City, A ,19/05/2021

**MOVED TO:** Rangers, 24/05/2021, end of loan

**TEAMS:** Middlesbrough, Hartlepool United (L), Cambridge United (L), Kilmarnock, Rangers, Sunderland (L), Wigan Athletic, St Mirren (L), Kilmarnock (L)

**INTERNATIONAL:** Northern Ireland

**SAFC TOTALS:** 13+8 appearances / 3 goals

**Jordan Jones scored spectacularly at Crewe and added further well-taken goals at Portsmouth and Hull as he helped Sunderland to the League One Play-Offs in 2021, when his final appearance came in the first leg at Lincoln. Having returned to Rangers at the end of his loan, he duly signed for Sunderland's first-day opponents Wigan on the eve of the following season.**

He had started with his local club Middlesbrough, debuting on 5 January 2013 in an FA Cup tie with Hastings United. That substitute appearance would remain his only one for Boro. Over two years passed before his next first-team game which came on loan to Hartlepool for whom all but one of his eleven appearances were as a sub, the exception being a home defeat to Burton Albion on 7 March 2015 when the Brewers included Jon McLaughlin and ex-Sunderland reserve Robbie Weir, while another former Sunderland reserve Scott Harrison was amongst his teammates. November 2015 saw Jordan play his one game for Cambridge (at home to Notts County).

In the summer of 2016, he moved to Kilmarnock where he got regular football making 42 appearances in his first season, the first goal of his career being scored against Craig Gordon at Celtic. He repeated that feat the following season too, eventually netting eleven times in 99+19 games across three seasons before being signed by Rangers.

Fifteen of his 8+11 games for the Gers came in 2019-20 a season in which he was sent off in an Old Firm derby and played six times in the Europa League. His one goal for Rangers came in a 5-1 win at Motherwell, but just over a month later, he was suspended by the Ibrox giants after a high profile breach of Covid regulations. At Wigan Jones did not score in 6+11 games. He scored once in 12+1 games on loan to St. Mirren and re-joined Kilmarnock on loan in July 2022. Qualifying through an Irish father, to the start of 2022-23 Jones had a dozen Northern Ireland caps, his first goal being scored in Malta eleven days after his last Sunderland appearance.

## JONES, Kenwyne Joel

**POSITION:** Centre-forward

**BIRTHPLACE:** La Brea, Trinidad

**DATE OF BIRTH:** 05/10/1984

**HEIGHT:** 6' 2" **WEIGHT:** 13 st 5 lbs

**SIGNED FROM:** Southampton, 29/08/2007

**DEBUT:** v Manchester United, A, 01/09/2007

**LAST MATCH:** v Wolverhampton Wanderers, A, 09/05/2010

**MOVED TO:** Stoke City, 11/08/2010

**TEAMS:** Joe Public, West Connection, Southampton, Sheffield Wednesday (L), Stoke City (L), Sunderland, Stoke City, Cardiff City, AFC Bournemouth (L), Al Jazira (L), Atlanta United, Central (L)

**INTERNATIONAL:** Trinidad & Tobago

**SAFC TOTALS:** 88+13 appearances / 28 goals

**On his day, Kenwyne Jones was the complete centre-forward. Brilliant in the air, he was powerful, mobile and could finish - goals being accompanied by a flamboyant and spectacular somersault.**

Unfortunately, consistency was not amongst Kenwyne's attributes. At times games passed him by. Had he been able to produce his best on a more frequent basis Jones would have been a Champions League player. Nonetheless, overall he was a good centre-forward for Sunderland who made many goals in addition to a decent scoring record that saw him be top-scorer in 2007-08 and 2008-09.

Signed for a reported fee of £6m plus Stern John going to Southampton in part-exchange, the Saints had been Kenwyne's first European club (other than a trial at Manchester United) after starting in his home of Trinidad. Just over a month before coming to Southampton in July 2004, he had played against Scotland at Hampden when Craig Gordon, James McFadden and Steve Caldwell were amongst his opponents, and Carlos Edwards - who attended the same school as Kenwyne - was part of the Trinidad & Tobago team.

Kenwyne's first appearances came on loan to Sheffield Wednesday where he made a stunning start. Beginning with a goal in a 4-0 South Yorkshire derby win at Doncaster a week before Christmas in 2004, he scored in all of his first six games, bagging a brace in a 4-0 home win over Wrexham.

After one more game he made a Premiership debut as a late sub against Liverpool, but with Peter Crouch leading the line for Southampton he faced a challenge for a starting place. After two more appearances Kenwyne was quickly loaned out again to Stoke City in the Championship, a division higher than Sheffield Wednesday. Beginning with a debut winner at Millwall he scored twice more in 13 starts, the last of which came in front of a capacity crowd at the Stadium of Light as Mick McCarthy's side lifted the Championship trophy in 2005.

With Southampton having swapped places with Sunderland Jones established himself with the Saints in 2005-06, playing 38 times. Goals on his second and third appearances - including a winner back at Hillsborough - augured well, but there were just three more that term. Nonetheless, he had done well enough to play at the 2006 FIFA World Cup finals, the first of two appearances coming against England, with Stern John, Carlos Edwards and Dwight Yorke being amongst his teammates. In total Jones would go on to play 83 times for his country, scoring 23 goals. Trinidad & Tobago's Player of the year in 2007, he was appointed captain in 2011.

In the season after the World Cup he scored 16 goals in helping Saints reach the Play-Offs and scored on his final appearance for the club at Norwich at the start of 2007-08 prior to coming to SAFC. It was his 22nd goal in 51+29 games for Southampton.

After leaving Sunderland, he continued in red and white stripes, re-joining former loan-club Stoke for a Potters record fee of £8m. Jones scored 26 goals in 78+37 games for Stoke, scoring at Wembley in the 2011 FA Cup semi-final against Bolton and playing in the final which was lost 1-0 to Manchester City when his teammates included Tommy Sorensen, Marc Wilson and Rory Delap, while Dean Whitehead and Danny Collins were on the bench.

In January 2014 Jones moved to Cardiff City in exchange for Peter Odemwingie, a debut winner against Norwich being one of 19 goals he scored for the club in 47+20 games, but it was the only one he scored in his first season as the Bluebirds were relegated from the Premier League, his penultimate match of that season being in a 4-0 defeat at Sunderland.

Loaned to Bournemouth in his first full season at Cardiff, he again scored on debut, his only goal in six substitute appearances as they won promotion to the Premier League. Kenwyne's final game in British football came in December 2015 for Cardiff against Nottingham Forest after which he was loaned to Al Jazira in the United Arab Emirates a month later, before a summer switch to the MLS with Atlanta United.

Debuting against the New York Red Bulls in March 2017, his first goal came at Montreal Impact on his fifth appearance with his only other goal from 5+12 appearances coming against DC United with a final loan to Central back in Trinidad & Tobago where he scored four goals in five games.

Like most footballers, Kenwyne liked to have a moan. His skipper at Sunderland, Lorik Cana, used to pronounce his name 'Ken-whine.' No-one but Lorik ever knew if this was an innocent mispronunciation or a subtle dig.

# K

## KABOUL, Younes

**POSITION:** Centre-back

**BIRTHPLACE:** Saint-Julien-en-Genevois, France

**DATE OF BIRTH:** 04/01/1986

**HEIGHT:** 6' 3" **WEIGHT:** 13st 7lbs

**SIGNED FROM:** Tottenham Hotspur, 16/07/2015

**DEBUT:** v Leicester City, A, 08/08/2015

**LAST MATCH:** v Manchester City, A, 13/08/2016

**MOVED TO:** Watford, 19/08/2016

**TEAMS:** Auxerre, Tottenham Hotspur, Portsmouth, Tottenham Hotspur, Sunderland, Watford

**INTERNATIONAL:** France

**SAFC TOTALS:** 23+1 appearances / 0 goals

**Having rejected a move from Spurs to Sunderland in 2008, Kaboul made that switch in 2015 and went on to become a tremendous centre-back once Sam Allardyce had taken over. When Allardyce brought in French speakers Lamine Kone and Wahbi Khazri during the January 2016 transfer window Younes played a vital and effective role in helping them to settle in while on the pitch his partnership with Kone was immense.**

It was a blow at the beginning of the following season when after the departure of Big Sam, Kaboul announced he wanted to return south for family reasons and David Moyes allowed him to go. Sunderland crumbled to successive relegations with Kaboul much missed.

Younes was capped five times by France for whom he scored on his debut against Ukraine on 6 June 2011. Born on the French/Swiss border, he had played for Bellegarde (aged 5-7), Concordia (aged 7-13) and Plastics Vallee (aged 13-14) before beginning his professional career with Auxerre, debuting against Toulouse on 3 October 2004. A Coupe de France winner in his first season, he played alongside future Sunderland man Benjani Mwaruwari in the final against Sedan. After 59 games and three goals, a reported fee of £8m took him to Tottenham on 5 July 2007. He played his first game in English football at the Stadium of Light as Roy Keane's newly-promoted Sunderland beat his side 1-0.

As with Auxerre, Younes became a cup winner in his first season, coming on as an extra-time sub in the League Cup final against Chelsea. Alan Hutton, Pascal Chimbonda, Steed Malbranque, Teemu Tainio all played for Spurs who had Darren Bent as an unused sub, while Wayne Bridge was in the Chelsea line-up. Despite winning the second and last honour of his career with that trophy, at the end of the season Younes moved to Portsmouth for whom he scored against AC Milan in the UEFA Cup. This was one of five goals in 50 games over a season and a half before he re-signed for Spurs in January 2010, returning to the club to play for Harry Redknapp under whom he had thrived at Pompey.

Helping Spurs to qualify for the Champions League for the first time, he also scored the winner in a dramatic derby at Arsenal. He captained the club occasionally but was troubled by a number of injuries and when he did play found himself in midfield or at right-back as well as in his best position of centre-back. In total he played 129+11 times across both spells with Spurs, scoring eight times. Following his year in the north east he made 26 appearances for Watford scoring twice, two of those games being against Sunderland.

As of 2021 Younes was running a care home in Belgium for people with mental disabilities

## KACHOSA, Ethan Takudzwa

**POSITION:** Right-back

**BIRTHPLACE:** Leeds

**DATE OF BIRTH:** 23/01/2003

**HEIGHT:** 5' 6" **WEIGHT:** 10st 13lbs

**SIGNED FROM:** Leeds United, 01/07/2021

**DEBUT:** Manchester United Under 21s, H, 13/10/2021

**LAST MATCH:**

**MOVED TO:**

**TEAMS:** Leeds United, Sunderland

**SAFC TOTALS:** 0+2 appearances / 0 goals (to June 2022)

**Academy Player of the Year at Leeds in 2019, Kachosa played for the Whites Under 21s in a 7-0 Football League Trophy defeat at Accrington Stanley in September 2020 but was on the winning side when debuting for Sunderland as a sub in the same competition.**

The speed merchant initially came to Sunderland on trial and scored as well as winning a penalty on his first appearance for the under 18s at Everton. Of Zimbabwean heritage, Ethan is eligible for England or Zimbabwe.

## KASHER, Joseph William Robinson (Joe)

**POSITION:** Centre-half

**BIRTHPLACE:** Willington, Co Durham

**DATE OF BIRTH:** 14/01/1894 - 08/01/1992

**HEIGHT:** 5' 10½" **WEIGHT:** 11st 6lbs

**SIGNED FROM:** Crook Town, 17/05/1919

**DEBUT:** v Arsenal, A, 20/09/1919

**LAST MATCH:** v Liverpool, A, 06/09/1922

**MOVED TO:** Stoke, 18/10/1922

**TEAMS:** Hunwick Juniors, Willington Athletic, Crook Town, Sunderland, Stoke, Carlisle United, Accrington Stanley

**SAFC TOTALS:** 90 appearances / 0 goals

**Joe Kasher was Sunderland's oldest living player prior to his death in 1992, a week before what would have been his 98th birthday. He had always been a big pal of the legendary Charlie Buchan who was the scorer of both Sunderland's goals at Arsenal on Kasher's debut. Joe had left Crook Town for top-flight football after World War One, when he had been a prisoner of war having served in the naval division as a Petty Officer.**

At birth Joe had been registered as Joseph William Robinson. This was apparently a few months before his parents married, with the name Kasher being added once they tied the knot. Joe left school at the age of twelve and began working at Brancepeth pit as a 14-year-old. After a pre-World War One trial with Sunderland he eventually joined the club he was a lifelong supporter of after the war, becoming a professional at the age of 25.

Kasher made 27 appearances in each of his first two seasons and 32 in his third before moving on to Stoke after playing four times in the 1922-23 season. During the same campaign he turned out in 29 league games for his new club, but could not prevent them from being relegated. After taking his total number of the appearances for the Potters to 55 (1 goal) the following year he returned north, signing for Carlisle United as a part-time player in the North Eastern League. After helping the Cumbrians to sixth place Kasher returned to the Football League with Accrington Stanley playing 49 games (2 goals) across two seasons with the Third Division North outfit.

Following his retirement from football, Joe became a publican at the Three Tuns in Coundon and maintained a connection with football by serving on the committee at Bishop Auckland.

## KAVANAGH, Graham Anthony

**POSITION:** Midfield

**BIRTHPLACE:** Dublin, Ireland

**DATE OF BIRTH:** 04/01/1986

**HEIGHT:** 5' 10" **WEIGHT:** 13st 3lbs

**SIGNED FROM:** Wigan Athletic, 31/08/2006

**DEBUT:** v Derby County, A, 09/09/2006

**LAST MATCH:** v Wigan Athletic, H, 05/01/2008

**MOVED TO:** Carlisle United, 09/01/2009

**TEAMS:** Home Farm, Middlesbrough, Darlington (L), Stoke City, Cardiff City, Wigan Athletic, Sunderland, Sheffield Wednesday (L), Carlisle United

**INTERNATIONAL:** Republic of Ireland

**SAFC TOTALS:** 11+4 appearances / 1 goal

**One of Roy Keane's six deadline-day signings in 2006, 'Kav' was a player capable of dominating the centre of the park and driving the team on. He scored a cracking goal on his second appearance in a big win at Leeds but injury soon blighted his time at the Stadium of Light where he spent the bulk of his time in the treatment room or on loan.**

Having started in Ireland with Home Farm he began his English career with Middlesbrough. Debuting at home to Chelsea on 11 December 1992 he played 33+14 games for the Teessiders, scoring four times before joining Stoke City following a loan spell. One of his 45 goals in 239+10 games for the club, was the final one at their old Victoria Ground while he also scored the first at the Britannia Stadium, as well as in the 2000 Football League Trophy final at Wembley where Clive Clarke was amongst his teammates as Bristol City were beaten.

A club record £1m fee took him to Cardiff in July 2001 where he went on to win promotion from the third tier, beating QPR at Cardiff's Millennium Stadium while in the FAW Premier Cup final as captain he scored the winner against rivals Swansea. After 162+3 games and 31 goals in major competitions Graham moved to Wigan for less than half what Cardiff had paid. It was a fee explained more by Cardiff's financial desperation than Kav's performances.

There was also a cup final for Kav at Wigan. Playing alongside Pascal Chimbonda and one-time SAFC reserve keeper Mike Pollitt Wigan lost 4-0 in the League (Carling) Cup at Cardiff against a Manchester United side that included Wes Brown, John O'Shea, Louis Saha (who scored) and Kieran Richardson who came off the bench. That was one of 48+7 games Graham played for Wigan (0 goals) before he left the Premier League to join Sunderland's promotion chase.

Following his injury struggles at Sunderland he scored twice in 22+2 games in two loans to Sheffield Wednesday and four in 17 for Carlisle who he subsequently signed for in January 2009

as player/coach, going on to add 58+3 further games in which he netted seven times. From September 2013, he managed the Cumbrians for a year, but could not stop them going down. Graham went on to set up Clover Sports Management, an agency looking after young players, including his son Calum at Middlesbrough.

At international level, Kavanagh played 16 times for the Republic of Ireland, seven of those games being starts. His one international goal came in April 1999 in a 2-0 win over a Sweden team that included Stefan Schwarz and Joachim Bjorklund on a night when Mick McCarthy fielded nine men who at one time or another played for Sunderland.

## KAY, John

**POSITION:** Right-back

**BIRTHPLACE:** Sunderland, Co Durham

**DATE OF BIRTH:** 29/01/1964

**HEIGHT:** 5' 10" **WEIGHT:** 11 st 6lbs

**SIGNED FROM:** Wimbledon, 22/07/1987

**DEBUT:** v Brentford, A, 15/08/1987

**LAST MATCH:** v Birmingham City, H, 09/10/1993

**MOVED TO:** Released, 22/05/1996

**TEAMS:** Arsenal, Wimbledon, Middlesbrough (L), Sunderland, Shrewsbury Town (L), Preston NE, Scarborough, Workington

**SAFC TOTALS:** 236+3 appearances / 0 goals

**Featured in the book, Sunderland Cult Heroes, John Kay was an immensely popular right-back. Another example of a local lad arriving having previously played elsewhere. Kay had been born in Sunderland General Hospital, raised in Great Lumley, but began his career with Arsenal for whom he made his debut against WBA in February 1983.**

After 13+1 games for the Gunners, he joined Wimbledon where he appeared in 63 league games and scored the only two league goals of his career. John also played eight league games on loan to Middlesbrough before coming to Sunderland.

Signed for Sunderland's first-ever season in the third tier, Kay was ever-present as the league was won with his contribution being a telling one as Sunderland toughened up for the challenge. John played in an era when hard tackling was par for the course and he never needed a second chance to 'get stuck in.' Infamously, on one occasion at Elland Road, two days before Christmas in 1990, future Sunderland boss Howard Wilkinson grumbled that his player Peter Haddock looked like he had been 'run over by a tractor' having been tackled by Kay.

John did not just dish it out. On his 199th and last league game for Sunderland against Birmingham in 1993, he suffered a broken leg, but as he was stretched off 'Kaysie' sat up on the stretcher and pretended to row if off as if it was a boat.

Renowned by his teammates for always tutting when something did not suit him, for all his tough man demeanour, John was never far away from a laugh. He also always put the team first, not least when admitting he was not fit enough to take his place in the 1992 FA Cup final. He had however played for Sunderland at Wembley in the Play-Off final two years earlier.

Two and a half years after his last game for Sunderland John was still on the books - but had broken his leg again in a reserve game against Notts County on 22 November 1994 - and been loaned to Shrewsbury Town where he played seven league games before being released by SAFC. He then had seven league games as a non-contract player with Preston before a three-year stint with Scarborough alongside Gary Bennett and Stephen Brodie, even getting on the scoresheet in an FA Cup tie against his former loan club Shrewsbury.

After 98 league games for Scarborough, who were a Football League club at the time, he played and coached at Workington in 1999 and went on to find employment with Derwentside Council where he worked on a project called the New Leaf Project. This saw Kay work with drug addicts with chaotic lives, helping them to cope with life and even sometimes taking them to the match as his guest. John Kay was a great character in and around the club and a cult hero for a reason.

## KAY, Michael Joseph

**POSITION:** Right-back

**BIRTHPLACE:** Consett, Co Durham

**DATE OF BIRTH:** 12/09/1989

**HEIGHT:** 6' 1" **WEIGHT:** 11st 11lbs

**SIGNED FROM:** School, 01/07/2006

**DEBUT:** v Blackburn Rovers, A, 04/02/2009

**LAST MATCH:** v Blackburn Rovers, A, 04/02/2009

**MOVED TO:** Tranmere Rovers, 01/07/2011

**TEAMS:** Sunderland, Gateshead United (L), Tranmere Rovers, Chester

**INTERNATIONAL:** England Under 17

**SAFC TOTALS:** 1 appearance / 0 goals

**Highly rated as a youngster, Kay's solitary first-team appearance came in an FA Cup tie at Blackburn where he was substituted after under an hour having earlier picked up a caution. Eighteen months before Michael's debut, Roy Keane had named him as a sub for a Premier League game at Manchester United although he did not get on.**

Nonetheless, along with England Under 17 honours, that exposure propelled Michael into the spotlight, but it was never to shine on a player initially judged to have great potential. He debuted as a substitute for England U17 alongside Sunderland youth player Jamie Chandler in a 2-0 win over Sweden in the Nordic Cup in August 2005, making a first start in a 2-0 defeat to the Republic of Ireland in Iceland two days later.

After a loan to Gateshead in October and November 2010, he moved to Tranmere Rovers on loan on 6 January 2011, staying there for the rest of the season before completing a free transfer. A scorer against Mansfield in the Blue Square Premier League in the first of his eight games for Gateshead, Michael got a first league goal for Tranmere against Exeter later the same season, but after completing his move to Prenton Park only made 11+7 appearances having started 22 times while on loan.

In July 2013, he moved on a free transfer to Conference club Chester. Sent off on his home debut, he went on to play 67+2 games, scoring twice before announcing in December 2015, that at the age of 25, he wanted to take a break from football and by June 2016 had returned to his native north east to join the fire service.

# K

## KEETON, William Walter

**POSITION:** Inside-right

**BIRTHPLACE:** Shirebrook, Derbyshire

**DATE OF BIRTH:** 30/04/1905 - 10/10/1980

**HEIGHT:** 5' 10" **WEIGHT:** 10st 11lbs

**SIGNED FROM:** Grantham Town, 18/10/1930

**DEBUT:** v Arsenal, A, 17/01/1931

**LAST MATCH:** v Leicester City, A 21/11/1931

**MOVED TO:** Left by mutual agreement, 29/12/1931

**TEAMS:** Notts County, Grantham Town, Sunderland, Nottingham Forest, Loughborough Corinthians

**INTERNATIONAL:** England, at cricket

**SAFC TOTALS:** 12 appearances / 1 goal

**Keeton had made his debut as a cricketer for Nottinghamshire four years before he signed for Sunderland as a footballer, having caught the eye with Grantham Town. Playing in a forward line that included Bobby Gurney, Patsy Gallacher and Jimmy Connor, the £450 signing lined up for his debut against an equally star-studded Arsenal team as the Gunners included the legendary Eddie Hapgood, Alex James, David Jack and Cliff Bastin.**

Earning good reports, Keeton gave a good account of himself as Sunderland won 3-1 at Highbury. Having done himself no harm at all with his performance against the side who would go on to be champions that season Walter was picked a further five times before the end of the season. These included the last three games, during which he scored his only goal for the club in a 3-0 win at West Ham. Six more appearances early the following season did Keeton's prospects no harm at all, even though his final game was in a heavy loss at Leicester.

He asked for a transfer as his wife and new-born child were in ill health and he wanted to be with them in the Nottinghamshire family home. Sunderland retained his League registration and he subsequently transferred to Nottingham Forest on 17 September 1932. At Nottinghamshire County Cricket Club, a decision to give youngsters a chance, combined with the untimely death of batsman 'Dodger' Whysall, meant there was more chance of an opening for Keeton at the summer game.

In the calendar year of all twelve of his Sunderland appearances Keeton won his Nottinghamshire cap, when as an opening batsman, he scored his first centuries against Essex at Trent Bridge and Hampshire at Bournemouth. He had made his Notts first-team debut back in 1926.

Still on Sunderland's books in 1932 - although making no more first-team appearances - he scored seven centuries as he topped 2,000 runs averaging 42.60. In September 1932 Keeton got his wish of a transfer from Sunderland. Moving to Nottingham Forest, he debuted for them in a second division defeat at Bradford Park Avenue on 24 September 1932, but would play only five times, the last a week before Christmas. The following month he signed for Loughborough Corinthians, a Midland League club that former Sunderland winger Alwyne Wilks had played for a couple of years earlier.

Evidently, having quickly drifted from the top-flight to the second division and then to non-league Keeton was content to let his football take second place to cricket in which he was increasingly excelling. Having scored two double-centuries in 1934, Keeton was called up for his Test debut in an Ashes Test. It was a game in which Don Bradman scored 304 for the Aussies at Headingley. Keeton scored 25 and 12 as England scrambled to a weather assisted draw.

During the following winter, Walter was knocked down by a lorry and was seriously ill in hospital, but he eventually worked his way back to the peak of the game. He topped 2,000 runs again in 1937 and in 1938 scored what is still Notts record individual score of 312 not out against Middlesex at the Oval (an unusual venue as Middlesex's home ground of Lord's was staging the annual Eton v Harrow match).

Shortly afterwards he appeared again at the same ground on what was his second and last appearance for England against the West Indies in 1939. However a duck and a score of 20 in what was England's last Test Match before the war signalled the end of his international career.

Nonetheless, Keeton kept playing until 1952, retiring with the fine record that he had scored a century against every other county. When people think about Sunderland players who were cricketers thoughts automatically turn to Willie Watson who played for England at both sports, but in Walter Keeton, Sunderland had another player to become an England Test cricketer. He passed away in October 1980 in a place called Forest Town in Nottinghamshire, two days after Sunderland and Nottingham Forest had drawn 2-2 at Roker Park.

## KELLY, Caden Christopher

**POSITION:** Midfielder

**BIRTHPLACE:** Manchester, Greater Manchester

**DATE OF BIRTH:** 20/11/2003

**HEIGHT:** 5' 10½" **WEIGHT:** 10st 2lbs

**SIGNED FROM:** Trainee 01/07/2020

**DEBUT:** v Manchester United Under 21s, H, 13/10/2021

**LAST MATCH:**

**MOVED TO:**

**TEAMS:** Manchester City, Salford City, Sunderland

**SAFC TOTALS:** 0+1 appearance / 0 goals (to June 2022)

**An added-time debutant as a substitute against the Under 21s of his hometown team Manchester United in the Football League Trophy, Caden came to the SAFC Academy as a 16-year-old after previously attracting attention from Reading and West Bromwich Albion.**

An academy player as a youngster with Manchester City and Salford City, he joined the Football Flick Academy to aid his development before signing for where he signed a two year contract as a professional in July 2022.

## KELLY, David Thomas

**POSITION:** Centre-forward

**BIRTHPLACE:** Birmingham, Warwickshire

**DATE OF BIRTH:** 25/11/1965

**HEIGHT:** 5' 11" **WEIGHT:** 11st 3lbs

**SIGNED FROM:** Wolverhampton Wanderers, 19/09/1995

**DEBUT:** v Millwall, A, 23/09/1995

**LAST MATCH:** v Newcastle United, A, 05/04/1997

**MOVED TO:** Tranmere Rovers, 01/08/1997

**TEAMS:** Alvechurch, Walsall, West Ham United, Leicester City, Newcastle United, Wolves, Sunderland, Tranmere Rovers, Motherwell, Mansfield Town, Derry City

**INTERNATIONAL:** Republic of Ireland

**SAFC TOTALS:** 37+3 appearances / 2 goals

**A goalscoring success when firing Newcastle United to promotion under Kevin Keegan in 1993, Peter Reid made Kelly his major signing in his first season at Sunderland. Chairman and vice chairman Bob Murray and John Fickling footed much of the bill for a player who became Sunderland's first £1m player though the additional £100,000, dependent upon SAFC winning promotion.**

Kelly's former club Wolves duly collected the extra £100,000, but Kelly's contribution to promotion was minimal as injuries restricted him to 9+1 league games and just two goals in his first season. He would fail to score at all in the club's first Premiership season the following year, despite playing 28 games in all competitions, even failing from the spot when backing himself to score against Aston Villa.

Despite his unsuccessful time at Sunderland, Kelly virtually guaranteed goals everywhere else. At Newcastle he top-scored with 28 goals as they went up in 1993. Player of the Year that season and the scorer of a hat-trick against one of his old clubs, Leicester City, Kelly found how tough football can be when manager Keegan sold him to Wolves that summer.

Although he netted just twice for Sunderland, Kelly scored a career total of 250 goals. The first 80 came in 152+37 games for Walsall. Thereafter, his figures either side of his Sunderland sojourn were: West Ham 48+16/14, Leicester City 72+3/25, Newcastle 83/39, Wolves 96+7/36, Tranmere 91+21/35, Sheffield United 26+14/6, Motherwell 21/7 and Mansfield 11+6/4. He then won the Irish FA Cup with Derry City in 2002 in the final match of his career.

A Third Division Play-Off winner with Walsall in 1988, as well as a promotion winner with both of his north east clubs, David reached the League Cup final with Tranmere in millennium year. He scored his eighth goal in that season's competition in the final, lost 2-1 to Martin O'Neill's Leicester, on a day when Kelly's colleagues included future Sunderland reserve goalkeeper Joe Murphy.

The son of a Dubliner, David scored nine goals in 26 games for the Republic of Ireland, starting with a debut hat-trick against Israel in November 1987. He was part of the Irish squad at Italia 90 but did not play.

Known as Ned at many of his clubs, Kelly worked as assistant manager at Tranmere Rovers, Sheffield United, Preston North End, Derby County, Nottingham Forest, Walsall, Scunthorpe United and Port Vale having a brief spell as Vale's caretaker manager in the autumn of 2017. In June 2019, he took up a role as development coach of Northampton Town.

## KELLY, Peter White

**POSITION:** Left-back

**BIRTHPLACE:** Camelon, Falkirk, Stirlingshire

**DATE OF BIRTH:** 04/09/1886 - 23/08/1949

**HEIGHT:** 5' 11" **WEIGHT:** 11st 7lbs

**SIGNED FROM:** North Shields Athletic, 07/05/1908

**DEBUT:** v Liverpool, H, 01/01/1909

**LAST MATCH:** v Liverpool, H, 01/01/1909

**MOVED TO:** Merthyr Town, 01/08/1909

**TEAMS:** Laurieston Juniors, Berwick, Alnwick St James, North Shields Athletic, Sunderland, Merthyr Town, Wallsend Park Villa

**SAFC TOTALS:** 1 appearance / 0 goals

**Peter Kelly's only game was a 4-1 New Year's Day home defeat. It was to be his one foray into first-class football. In August 1909, Peter moved to become captain of Merthyr Town who had recently joined the Southern League.**

His spell in South Wales only lasted one season and he returned to Tyneside to join Wallsend Park Villa. After retiring from playing Kelly remained in Newcastle, except for a spell in the Royal Army Service Corps during WW1, working as a motor mechanic and then a car salesman until his death in Westgate Road General Hospital in 1949.

## KELLY, Robert (Bob)

**POSITION:** Inside-right / Outside-right

**BIRTHPLACE:** Ashton-in-Makerfield, Lancashire

**DATE OF BIRTH:** 16/11/1893 - 22/09/1969

**HEIGHT:** 5' 7" **WEIGHT:** 10st 1lb

**SIGNED FROM:** Burnley, 01/12/1925

**DEBUT:** v Manchester United, H, 05/12/1925

**LAST MATCH:** v Tottenham Hotspur, A, 05/02/1927

**MOVED TO:** Huddersfield Town, 10/02/1927

**TEAMS:** Ashton White Star, Ashton Central, Earleston Rovers, St Helens Town, Burnley, Sunderland, Huddersfield Town, Preston North End, Carlisle United

**INTERNATIONAL:** England

**SAFC TOTALS:** 53 appearances / 15 goals

**Signed for a British record fee of £6,550, Kelly never sustained his best form at Sunderland and only stayed at the club for 14 months. The son of Irish parents, he played 14 times for England scoring eight goals including one against Ireland at Roker Park in October 1920. Six months earlier he had scored twice on his debut in a 5-4 win over Scotland. One of his caps was won while with Sunderland, a home defeat to Wales in March 1926 by which time he was 32. He also represented the Football League seven times.**

Much of Kelly's career had been lost to World War One, during which his main sporting accolade was representing the Royal Field Artillery at water polo. Thought by many Burnley experts to be that club's greatest-ever player, he is the club's most capped England international and was renowned for his powerful shot, dribbling skills and body swerve. Kelly scored 88 goals in 275 games for the Clarets. Twenty of those goals came in 1920-21 as he helped fire Burnley to the league championship. This is astonishing, considering Bob did not play football until he left school.

Later, after his time with SAFC, he scored 39 times in 186 league games for Huddersfield for whom he played in the FA Cup finals of 1928 and 1930, losing to Blackburn Rovers and Arsenal.

Kelly went on to add 17 goals in 78 games for Preston and a single goal in a dozen appearances for Carlisle, where he became player/manager. From 13 November 1936 to 16 June 1938, he managed Stockport County, winning Division Three North in 1937, only to be relegated immediately. After World War Two, he moved to the continent becoming trainer of Sporting Lisbon before taking up coaching appointments in Switzerland with St Gallen, the Netherlands with Herenveen and Kooger as well as coaching in the Channel Islands.

Having started playing for Burnley before the World War One, Bob Kelly was still involved in the game in 1960-61, spending eight months as general manager of Southern League club Barry Town. He also became a publican, taking over The Woodman Inn in Stockport from 3 February 1939 and later running a pub in Blackpool.

## KELLY, Thomas (Tom)

**POSITION:** Right-half

**DATE OF BIRTH:** c 1884/1885

**HEIGHT:** 5' 8" **WEIGHT:** 11st 0lbs

**SIGNED FROM:** Seaham White Star, 05/04/1905

**DEBUT:** v Liverpool, H, 16/09/1905

**LAST MATCH:** v Liverpool, H, 16/09/1905

**MOVED TO:** Murton Colliery Red Star, 15/05/1906

**TEAMS:** Seaham White Star, Sunderland, Murton Colliery Red Star, Seaham Albion, Seaham Harbour

**SAFC TOTALS:** 1 appearance / 0 goals

**Like his namesake Peter Kelly, Tom Kelly's only game was in a home defeat by Liverpool - in his case, a little over three years before Peter's appearance, although by 2-1 rather than 4-1.**

Kelly was signed from Seaham White Star less than five months after future England forward George Holley moved in the same direction. Fellow defender Jack Tomlin also joined Sunderland from the same club a month earlier. Initially at Roker Park on an amateur basis, Tom soon returned to local non-league football and work in the coal mining industry.

## KELSALL, Josiah (Joe)

**POSITION:** Centre-forward

**BIRTHPLACE:** Maryport, Cumberland

**DATE OF BIRTH:** 20/05/1892 - 24/04/1974

**HEIGHT:** 5' 6" **WEIGHT:** 11st 0lbs

**SIGNED FROM:** Maryport, 05/11/1913, as an amateur

**DEBUT:** v Wednesday, H, 04/04/1914

**LAST MATCH:** v Wednesday, H, 04/04/1914

**MOVED TO:** Joined Army, 06/09/1914

**TEAMS:** Maryport, Sunderland, Houghton Rovers, Spennymoor United

**SAFC TOTALS:** 1 appearance / 0 goals

**A teacher by profession, Kelsall was assistant master at a school in Siddick near Workington when Sunderland signed him. After one game for the reserves against Darlington on 8 November 1913 he signed professional forms a fortnight later and relocated to Sunderland only to be confined to a single first-team game.**

An all-round sportsman, he played cricket for Whitburn for many years and also represented Durham County. In September 1914 Josiah joined the Territorial Force and went on to serve as a lance corporal in India during the Great War after which he returned to teaching. In 1939 he was a head teacher living in Thirsk.

## KEMP, Samuel Patrick (Sammy)

**POSITION:** Outside-right

**BIRTHPLACE:** Stockton, Co Durham

**DATE OF BIRTH:** 29/08/1932 - 02/08/1987

**HEIGHT:** 5' 10" **WEIGHT:** 11st 10lbs

**SIGNED FROM:** Whitby Town, 01/08/1951

**DEBUT:** v Tottenham Hotspur, H, 18/04/1953

**LAST MATCH:** v Manchester City, H, 12/01/1957

**MOVED TO:** Sheffield United, 05/02/1957

**TEAMS:** Portrack Shamrocks, Stillington St John's, Whitby Town, Sunderland, Sheffield United, Mansfield Town, Gateshead

**SAFC TOTALS:** 19 appearances / 2 goals

**Sammy was initially signed in the summer of 1951 on amateur forms. Eleven of Kemp's 19 appearances spread over five seasons came in 1955-56. Less than a year later Kemp was sold to Sheffield United as part of the deal that brought England winger Colin Grainger to Roker Park.**

In May 1957 he became one of 14 SAFC players disciplined for receiving illegal payments and was punished by the loss of six months benefit qualifications. This was refunded in 1962 when the Football League's decision was deemed illegal.

He went on to score one goal for each of Sheffield United, Mansfield Town and Gateshead in 16, three and seven games for those clubs. His Sunderland goals came at Chelsea in front of over 56,000 on his second appearance and at Manchester City.

## KENNEDY, Alan Phillip

**POSITION:** Left-back

**BIRTHPLACE:** Sunderland, Co Durham

**DATE OF BIRTH:** 31/08/1954

**HEIGHT:** 5' 9" **WEIGHT:** 10st 7lbs

**SIGNED FROM:** Liverpool, 20/09/1985

**DEBUT:** v Swindon Town, H, 24/09/1985

**LAST MATCH:** v Gillingham, H, 17/05/1987

**MOVED TO:** 31/05/1987, contract ended

**TEAMS:** Newcastle United, Liverpool, Sunderland, Husqvarna, Hartlepool United, Beerschot, Grantham Town, Sunderland, Wigan Athletic, Colne Dynamoes, Wrexham, Morecambe, Netherfield, Northwich Victoria, Racliffe Borough, Netherfield, Barrow

**INTERNATIONAL:** England

**SAFC TOTALS:** 66+1 appearances / 3 goals

**One of the big names brought in by Lawrie McMenemy, Alan Kennedy was 31 when he came to his hometown club having enjoyed a stellar career, mainly with Liverpool. Although a left-back he famously scored Liverpool's winner against Real Madrid in the 1981 European Cup final and the decisive shoot-out penalty in the final of the same competition three years later against Roma.**

He also scored in the 1983 League Cup final as Manchester United were beaten in one of three successful League Cup finals Kennedy played in for the Anfield club. He won five league titles with Liverpool and was twice capped by England in addition to eight 'B' caps and six at Under 23 level. One of his 'B' caps came at Roker Park against Spain in 1980. Finally recognised at full level, Kennedy's caps came in his 30th year in a narrow Wembley win over Northern Ireland (alongside Terry Butcher and against Martin O'Neill and Jimmy Nicholl) and a 1-0 defeat against Wales in Wrexham.

Almost exactly a decade before his two full caps Alan had been selected for a full squad against West Germany but had missed out through injury. It had been a long wait for a full cap. Liverpool's Hetton-born manager Bob Paisley had declared, "If this lad doesn't play for England, I'll throw myself in the Mersey - when the tide is out!".

Starting with Newcastle, Alan played in the 1974 FA Cup final, as a teenager, where he lost to his future club Liverpool. He also suffered defeat in the 1976 League Cup final through Dennis Tueart's spectacular bicycle-kick winning goal. Nicknamed after the Flintstones character Barney Rubble, Kennedy played 359 times in total for Liverpool, scoring 20 goals. At Newcastle he had scored ten times in 210+5 games before becoming Britain's costliest full-back when moving to Merseyside following the Magpies relegation in 1978. When the time came to leave Liverpool when Kenny Dalglish was building a new team, Kennedy had the chance to go back to St James' but chose to come to Sunderland.

Always famed for his determination and willingness to join the attack, in February 1986, he gave a glimpse of glories past with both goals in a home draw with Carlisle, one of those being a screamer at the Fulwell End. However, his Roker career was to end in ignominy, his final appearance being on the day Sunderland slumped into the third tier for the first time.

After Sunderland, he had an unsuccessful trial in Sweden with Husqvarna before a short spell at Hartlepool where he scored once in 5+2 games before joining Belgian side Beerschot and then Grantham Town. He then trained with Sunderland in December 1987, playing once for the reserves at Manchester United, before joining Wigan Athletic a couple of days before Christmas for whom he went on to play 22 times. Alan then extended his career with a host of non-league clubs, but also a 16 game spell with Wrexham in 1989-90.

In 1991-92 he combined playing for Netherfield with a venture into management but later found that being a Merseyside radio personality, after-dinner speaker and club ambassador for Liverpool was more his forte. With due respect to Ian Rush, it was at my request that Kennedy replaced Rush as Liverpool's representative to join yours truly and SAFC ambassador Jim Montgomery when a headstone was installed in Anfield cemetery to mark the grave of former Sunderland and Liverpool manager Tom Watson in 2015. Alan Kennedy's brother Keith played for Newcastle United, Bury and Mansfield Town.

## KERR, Andrew (Andy)

**POSITION:** Centre-forward

**BIRTHPLACE:** Ayr, Ayrshire

**DATE OF BIRTH:** 29/06/1931 - 24/12/1997

**HEIGHT:** 5' 10½" **WEIGHT:** 11st 6lbs

**SIGNED FROM:** Kilmarnock, 03/04/1963

**DEBUT:** v Preston North End, A, 06/04/1963

**LAST MATCH:** v Southampton, H, 30/11/1963

**MOVED TO:** Aberdeen, 21/04/1964

**TEAMS:** Lugar Boswell, Partick Thistle, Manchester City, Kilmarnock, Sunderland, Aberdeen, Glentoran, Inverness Caledonians

**INTERNATIONAL:** Scotland

**SAFC TOTALS:** 19 appearances / 5 goals

**No relation to Bobby Kerr, Andy played eleven times during the 1963-64 promotion season and all but one of his 19 games for Sunderland at centre -forward, with the other at centre-half, but his two Scotland caps were won as a full-back.**

His versatility also saw him play across the half-back line in a career that saw him play in six cup finals including a replay - although he was never on the winning side. His caps came while he was with Partick Thistle, playing in a 4-1 away victory over Austria and 3-1 defeat away to the great Hungary side of the era, both in May 1955.

He also represented the Scottish League four times. The following year, he played as a full-back at Hampden against Celtic in the goalless final of the Scottish League Cup and in the replay lost 3-0. He had also been on the losing side in the final in 1953 when future Sunderland forward Charlie Fleming was amongst East Fife's scorers as Partick went down 3-2 with Kerr at left-half.

Andy was also on the losing side in three cup finals with Kilmarnock. Playing at centre-forward in October 1960 he went down 2-0 to Rangers at Hampden, future Sunderland man Ralph Brand netting in a game in which Jim Baxter also played. It was a similar tale two years later when Kerr - again at number 9 - was part of a Killie side who lost 1-0 to Hearts in the League Cup final, while in his one Scottish Cup final appearance in 1960, he was at centre-forward in front of a crowd of 108,017 as Kilmarnock went down 2-0 to a Rangers side who included future Sunderland manager Ian McColl.

Although Andy did not manage to score in his cup finals, he did score a tremendous 119 goals in 137 matches for Kilmarnock. This included a five-goal haul in an 8-0 win against Airdrie in September 1962 and a total of 41 in 1960-61 and 28 from 32 games the following year. He then netted 35 goals in 1962-63 before joining Sunderland with eight games to go, for a fee of £22,250, after he signed off with a brace in a 6-0 hammering of Celtic. It bookended his time with Kilmarnock for whom he had scored on his debut in another win over Celtic. Killie's club record signing at £6,000, Kerr helped his new club to become runners-up in his first season - their highest-ever position to that point.

When Kerr came to Sunderland it was not his first venture south of the border. In between his stints with Partick (where he scored 44 times) and Killie, he had tried his luck in England with a six-month spell at Manchester City in 1959 where he played ten games without scoring under the management of former Sunderland player Les McDowall. Starting at Sunderland with two goals in eight games as promotion was missed by the whisker of goal average in 1963, Kerr scored the first goal of the 1963-64 promotion season. He netted twice more in the opening nine games before losing his place to Nick Sharkey and thereafter getting one more game as a stand-in at centre-half for Charlie Hurley.

None of Kerr's five goals for Sunderland came at home. A year after signing, he returned to Scotland with Aberdeen for little more than a third of what had been paid for him, debuting for the Dons at Dunfermline in April 1964. Despite eight goals in 16 games he was released by Aberdeen after a year. He then had a short spell with Glentoran before completing his career in the Highland League. Following his retirement Andy worked for a company manufacturing aeroplane parts and died in Aberdeen, aged 66.

## KERR, Robert (Bobby)

**POSITION:** Midfield

**BIRTHPLACE:** Balloch, Alexandria, Glasgow, Lanarkshire

**DATE OF BIRTH:** 16/11/1947

**HEIGHT:** 5' 4½" **WEIGHT:** 9st 3lbs

**SIGNED FROM:** Balloch Juniors, 01/07/1963

**DEBUT:** v Manchester City, H, 31/12/1966

**LAST MATCH:** v Stoke City, H, 30/08/1978

**MOVED TO:** Blackpool, 09/03/1979

**TEAMS:** Balloch Juniors, Sunderland, Blackpool, Hartlepool United, Whitby Town

**SAFC TOTALS:** 419+14 appearances / 69 goals

**The captain of the 1973 FA Cup winners, Bobby Kerr is sixth in the list of all-time appearance makers. 1973 was not the first time Kerr had captained Sunderland in a cup final. In 1966 he had skippered against Arsenal in the FA Youth Cup.**

Coming into the first team on New Year's Eve in 1966, he scored the winner against Manchester City and netted again in the next three home league games against Chelsea, Liverpool and Newcastle, where he scored twice in a 3-0 win. He also scored twice in a 7-1 FA Cup win at home to Peterborough which set up a tie with Leeds United. Going into that match the 19-year-old had seven goals in his first ten games when his leg was broken. It was subsequently broken again in Bobby's fourth reserve match of his comeback, against Ashington, but thankfully the redoubtable Scot made a full recovery.

Bobby was to go on to become consistency personified, missing just five league games between 1971-72 and 1975-76 when the Division Two title was won. He also played in all nine games as the cup was lifted in 1973 and all four European games the following season, indeed one of the league games he missed was due to being rested before such a tie. Minus the expletive, the chant fans honoured Kerr with summed him up, "He's here, he's there, he's every xxxxxxx where, Bobby Kerr, Bobby Kerr." At 5 '4½", Bobby was Wembley's smallest winning-captain, but that was an illusion as Kerr stood up to the biggest and fiercest opponents and gave as good as he got.

In the 1973 FA Cup semi-final Sunderland came up against Arsenal and Alan Ball, the diminutive 1966 World Cup-winner described as perpetual motion. Kerr was the same. He ran and ran - hence the chant. He always put the team first, notably in the cup final when he was detailed to help full-back Dick Malone on doubling up on Leeds dangerman Eddie Gray. Nonetheless, it was from Kerr's effort that Sunderland won the corner they scored from, just as it was Bobby's long throw that produced the winner in the semi-final.

Always a great character, Bobby even went in goal in Jim Montgomery's Testimonial and on the day Sunderland finally won at Wembley again, 48 years after Bobby lifted the FA Cup, a video emerged on twitter of Bobby with a replica FA Cup singing 'We've won the cup'. A publican (after a short spell selling insurance) in later life, Bobby remained a regular in the town's hostelries after giving up the trade, a section of his local, 'The Burton House' in the city centre, being devoted to photographs of his career.

The last of the cup winning-team to play a game for Sunderland, Bobby moved on to Blackpool where he was re-united with Dick Malone and signed by Bob Stokoe who had dubbed him 'The Little General' at Sunderland. Kerr played 22+4 games for the Seasiders where he also played for Stan Ternent and the aforementioned Alan Ball.

Bobby scored twice before a July 1980 return to the north east with Hartlepool United for whom he first appeared in a friendly at East Fife. He went on to play 56+1 competitive games, scoring twice before ending his playing days with Whitby Town.

Bobby's brother George played for Vale of Leven, Barnsley, Bury, Oxford United and Scunthorpe United between 1959 and 73. Bobby was inducted into the Sunderland AFC Hall of Fame in 2020 and produced, 'The Little General: Bobby Kerr's Football Scrapbook' in 2013. In 2022, along with the rest of his 1973 cup winners (except Jim Montgomery who already had the award) Bobby was given the Freedom of the City of Sunderland.

# K

## KHAZRI, Wahbi

**POSITION:** Midfielder

**BIRTHPLACE:** Ajaccio, Corsica, France

**DATE OF BIRTH:** 08/02/1991

**HEIGHT:** 5' 9" **WEIGHT:** 12st 0lbs

**SIGNED FROM:** Bordeaux, 30/01/2016

**DEBUT:** v Manchester City, H, 02/02/2016

**LAST MATCH:** v Barnsley A, 26/08/2017

**MOVED TO:** St Etienne, 17/07/2018

**TEAMS:** Bastia, Bordeaux, Sunderland, Rennes (L), St Etienne, Montpellier (to June 2022)

**INTERNATIONAL:** France Under 21 / Tunisia

**SAFC TOTALS:** 24+18 appearances / 3 goals

**Part of Sam Allardyce's successful transfer window of January 2016, Khazri was a flair player who was influential in a dramatic end-of-season run that saw relegation avoided.**

He scored within three minutes of his home debut to help beat Manchester United and added a spectacular strike in an exciting late-season win over Chelsea, but it was for his creativity rather than his goalscoring that Khazri's contribution was noteworthy.

After Allardyce departed to take over the England job, new manager David Moyes was unhappy at Wahbi's level of fitness and only gave him seven starts in the league, using him in twice as many games as sub as Sunderland struggled unsuccessfully against relegation. Not keen to play in the Championship, Khazri was quickly shipped out on loan back to French football with Rennes.

A scorer on his Rennes debut in a win at Marseille, he added another two games later at St Etienne which would be his next club after eleven goals in 27+1 games on loan to Rennes. Sold by Sunderland in July 2018 for a fee rumoured to be in the region of £6m, rising potentially to the £9m he had reportedly cost SAFC he scored in a debut win over Guingamp. Scoring 13 goals in his first season, five in his second and seven in his third - including a hat-trick against his old club Bordeaux - he suffered relegation with St Etienne in 2022, at which point he had played 92+15 times for them, scoring 36 goals. He moved on to Montpellier that summer.

Between the ages of five and 12, Wahbi had played for Juenesse Sportive Ajaccion before beginning his professional career with Bastia, debuting at Sochaux on 11 August 2002. He scored his first goal on his tenth appearance, against Bordeaux who bought him in August 2014 after 13 goals in 47+14 games helped the Corsican club to back-to-back promotions. At Bordeaux, Wahbi scored on his home debut against Monaco and totalled 14 goals in 52+6 games before his move to Sunderland.

At international level, Khazri played for France at Under 21 level against Italy in February 2012. He had previously represented Tunisia at the Under 20 age group and went on to make a full debut for Tunisia on 30 January 2013 against Togo in the African Cup of Nations. He also played at the 2015, 2017 and 2019 tournaments, scoring against Zimbabwe in January 2017 having left Sunderland in mid-season to take part. He was still technically a Sunderland player when he played against England at the 2018 FIFA World Cup and scored in the following two games against Belgium and Panama, thereby becoming the only Sunderland player to score twice at the finals.

## Ki, Sung-Yueng

**POSITION:** Midfielder

**BIRTHPLACE:** Gwangju, South Korea

**DATE OF BIRTH:** 24/01/1989

**HEIGHT:** 6' 2" **WEIGHT:** 11st 10lbs

**SIGNED FROM:** Swansea City, 31/08/2013, on loan

**DEBUT:** v Arsenal, H, 14/09/2013

**LAST MATCH:** v Everton, H, 12/04/2014

**MOVED TO:** Swansea City, 05/05/2014, end of loan

**TEAMS:** FC Seoul, Celtic, Swansea City, Sunderland (L), Newcastle United, Real Mallorca, FC Seoul

**INTERNATIONAL:** South Korea

**SAFC TOTALS:** 31+3 appearances / 4 goals

**An elegant high-class midfielder, Ki played for Sunderland in the 2014 League (Capital One) Cup final after being one of only two players (with Alonso) to convert in the semi-final penalty shoot-out. Earlier in the competition he had scored the winner against Chelsea. On loan from Swansea, Ki had played in the final the previous year as Swansea smashed Phil Parkinson's Bradford City (who brought on Jon McLaughlin as sub keeper) 5-0.**

The Swans had invested a club record fee of £6m to bring Ki from Celtic. He started 120 games for the Swans as well as coming off the bench a further 42 times and scored a dozen goals. At Celtic he hit eleven goals in 60+25 games as the Celts won the SPL in 2012, a year after lifting the Scottish Cup when he played alongside Glenn Loovens and sub Anthony Stokes in the final as Motherwell were beaten 3-0.

On 28 June 2018 Ki left Swansea to sign for Newcastle United initially playing for Rafa Benitez, but then coming under the management of Steve Bruce. Ki started only 16 games for the Magpies in addition to seven further games as sub but left without scoring. Surprisingly he played only one game for Mallorca in Spain, an eight-minute substitute appearance in a win at Eibar before returning to his native South Korea.

After playing youth football in Australia he started with FC Seoul, debuting on 4 March 2007 against Daegu and going on to impress sufficiently to be scouted by Celtic who he signed for after 64 games and seven goals. It was FC Seoul he returned to in August 2020, being appointed captain.

At international level Ki debuted in June 2008 against Jordan and played at the 2010, 2014 and 2018 FIFA World Cup finals, captaining his country in the third of those tournaments. He also played at the 2012 Olympics, scoring against hosts Great Britain, and against Australia in the final of the 2015 Asian Cup before retiring from international football in 2019, having played 110 internationals and scored ten times. Ki's father Ki Young-ok was general manager at K League side Gwangju from 2015-2019.

## KICHENBRAND, Donald Basil (Don)

**POSITION:** Centre-forward

**BIRTHPLACE:** Boksburg, South Africa

**DATE OF BIRTH:** 13/08/1933

**HEIGHT:** 5' 11½" **WEIGHT:** 12st 8lbs

**SIGNED FROM:** Rangers, 05/03/1958

**DEBUT:** v Sheffield Wednesday, H, 08/03/1958

**LAST MATCH:** Brighton & Hove Albion, H, 29/08/1959

**MOVED TO:** Johannesburg Ramblers, 01/07/1960

**TEAMS:** Boksburg, Delfos, Rangers, Sunderland, Johannesburg Ramblers, Vereeniging Athletic, Johannesburg Wanderers. Forfar Athletic, Keith

**INTERNATIONAL:** South Africa

**SAFC TOTALS:** 54 appearances / 28 goals

**A South African spearhead, Kichenbrand's nickname of Rhino explains his style of play. It was certainly effective as his goals to games tally illustrates. A goal on debut at Roker Park and another on his next home outing were part of six goals in his first ten games. This haul included four in the last three games of the season, including both goals in a final day 2-0 win at Portsmouth.**

Unfortunately results elsewhere meant that despite Don's goals Sunderland were relegated for the very first time. Had the Lads escaped, Rhino's goals would have written his name into Wearside footballing folklore. Certainly, the son of a miner from East Rand did all he could as a late-season signing to keep the Lads up.

In his one full season, he top-scored with 21 goals from 40 league games including a hat-trick at Rotherham in what was Don Revie's last game, but at the end of that season, despite being in his mid-twenties he elected to go part-time as he married and moved to Ireland to learn the hotel trade. After scoring on the first day of the 1959-60 season Don played just twice more. It was while watching former Rangers colleagues play in an exhibition golf tournament in Dublin that he fell for the daughter of the place he was staying. From then on he would travel to Ireland to see her at every opportunity. In 2019, the couple celebrated their diamond wedding anniversary but the courtship evidently contributed to the end of Kichenbrand's time at Sunderland.

He was to continue his career back in South Africa and subsequently in Scotland where he had made his name in Glasgow. Kichenbrand had signed for Rangers from Delfos in

South Africa on 26 September 1955 on the recommendation of former Rangers centre-half Charlie Watkins who made the South African promise he would keep the fact he was a Catholic a secret from those at Ibrox. He scored 30 times in 37 appearances for Rangers as they won the Scottish League title, a haul that included five in one match against Queen of the South in the first Scottish League fixture under floodlights on 7 March 1956.

Five days later he won his one representative honour. Lining up alongside Sunderland's Ted Purdon he was part of a South Africa team comprised of UK-based players who lost 2-1 to a Scotland XI at Ibrox in a game staged as part of a British Olympic Games appeal.

## KIERNAN, Cole David

**POSITION:** Forward

**BIRTHPLACE:** Hartlepool

**DATE OF BIRTH:** 03/01/2002

**HEIGHT:** 5' 11" **WEIGHT:** 11st 3lbs

**SIGNED FROM:** York City, 01/07/2018

**DEBUT:** v Grimsby Town, H, 08/10/2019

**LAST MATCH:** v Grimsby Town, H, 08/10/2019

**MOVED TO:** Middlesbrough, 03/07/2020

**TEAMS:** Sunderland, Middlesbrough, Bohemians

**INTERNATIONAL:** Republic of Ireland Under 18

**SAFC TOTALS:** 0+1 appearances / 0 goals

**Cole Kiernan joined Simon Ramsden in having the joint shortest-ever Sunderland career, his only appearance lasting just two minutes. Cole's cameo came in the only game James Fowler had as caretaker manager of SAFC, a Football League Trophy (Leasing.com Trophy) match.**

This came shortly after his international debut for the Republic of Ireland U18s, whom he qualifies for through his grandfather, in a friendly against Austria. He played 15 times for Sunderland at Under 18 level, scoring five goals and also played once at Under 23 level.

After being released by Sunderland Kiernan signed as a professional at Middlesbrough only to be released after a year following two goals in six Under 23 games. In the summer of 2021, he had trials with Colchester United, Darlington and Blyth Spartans before signing for Bohemians in Dublin.

## KIERNAN, Joseph (Joe)

**POSITION:** Left-half

**BIRTHPLACE:** Coatbridge, Lanarkshire

**DATE OF BIRTH:** 22/10/1942 - 01/08/2006

**HEIGHT:** 5' 10" **WEIGHT:** 11st 4lbs

**SIGNED FROM:** Coatbridge Juniors, 01/07/1958

**DEBUT:** v Southampton, A, 22/09/1962

**LAST MATCH:** v Oldham Athletic, H, 24/09/1962

**MOVED TO:** Northampton Town, 30/06/1963

**TEAMS:** Sunderland, Northampton Town, Kettering Town, Atherstone United, Wellingborough

**SAFC TOTALS:** 2 appearances / 2 goals

**Joe Kiernan was captain of Sunderland's junior team in the early sixties. He made his debut as a replacement for Jimmy McNab who had broken his nose a few days earlier in a floodlit friendly at home to Standard Liege.**

Brian Clough scored a hat-trick on Kiernan's debut in a 4-2 win at Southampton. Two days later Clough and Kiernan each got braces as Oldham were beaten 7-1 in the League Cup. Despite that fine record, Joe never got another game for Sunderland, but went on to play 352 games in a decade at Northampton (14 goals) who he was sold to for £2,000. During his spell with the Cobblers, they rose from Division Three to the top flight and then dropped back to Division Four where they had been shortly before Joe arrived. He was ever-present during their single top-flight season of 1965-66, appearing at Roker Park in October 1965.

Two cartilage operations the following season broke his run of being a regular, but it was not until July 1972 that he moved on to Kettering Town. Under Ron Atkinson, Kiernan captained the side that won the Southern League championship and later returned to the club as youth team coach after commencing his coaching career with Irthlingborough Diamonds.

He later became youth team coach and then assistant manager at Northampton Town (1986-1992) before reverting to his pre-football occupation of being a painter and decorator.

## KILBANE, Kevin Daniel

**POSITION:** Winger

**BIRTHPLACE:** Preston, Lancashire

**DATE OF BIRTH:** 01/02/1977

**HEIGHT:** 6' 0" **WEIGHT:** 12st 7lbs

**SIGNED FROM:** West Bromwich Albion, 15/12/1999

**DEBUT:** v Southampton, H, 18/12/1999

**LAST MATCH:** v Bradford City, A, 30/08/2003

**MOVED TO:** Everton, 01/09/2003

**TEAMS:** Sunderland, Middlesbrough, Bohemians

**INTERNATIONAL:** Republic of Ireland

**SAFC TOTALS:** 109+15 appearances / 9 goals

**Signed midway into the season when winger Allan Johnston had been frozen out of the first-team scene, Kevin Kilbane made an excellent start when within three minutes of coming on as a late sub on his debut he produced a terrific cross that created a goal for Kevin Phillips.**

However, Kilbane did not have the best of times at Sunderland where many fans did not take to him. This was harsh on Kevin who was a hard working player, full of commitment and with ability that should be unquestioned given his career as a whole. Add to that the fact that behind the scenes he was one of the nicest lads you could wish to meet and it was a tough experience. Even when he scored with a spectacular effort that inflicted Southampton's last-ever defeat at The Dell there were those that questioned whether Kilbane had meant it. Things came to a head in the summer of 2002 during a pre-season game in Belgium when Kevin's patience snapped and most uncharacteristically he flicked an offensive gesture at the travelling fans.

Having won 37 of his final total of 110 international caps while with Sunderland Kilbane is fourth on the list of players capped while with the club. He eventually left for Everton where his old Preston manager David Moyes invested a fee in the region of £1m for Kevin's signature. Kilbane went on to make 102+19 appearances for the Toffees, scoring five times.

Everton received double the fee they paid to Sunderland when selling Kilbane to Wigan as the summer 2006 transfer window closed. At Everton he had been used in a variety of roles rather than simply as a left-winger where he had been employed at Sunderland. At Wigan he increasingly found himself at left-back from where he won a Player of the Year award from the wiganer.net website. Debuting back at Goodison Park, 'Killa' played 70+14 games for the Latics scoring against Spurs and West Ham before a January 2009 switch to Hull City for a quarter of what Wigan had paid.

## KILBANE, Kevin (Continued)

There were to be 43+12 appearances in a three-and-a-half-year spell with the Tigers who loaned him to Huddersfield (30+1/3) and Derby County (8+2/1) before he moved to Coventry City on a free on July 2012. There were to be just 11+1 outings for the Sky Blues where both of his goals came in the League Cup, the curtain coming down on his career at Brentford in October 2012.

A grand total of 474+66 league games (37 goals) and 540+74 games (45 goals) in all competitions had commenced in August 1996 for Preston in a 2-1 defeat at Notts County. Such was Killa's impact that he played only one season as a first-teamer at Deepdale (46+8/3) before West Brom snapped him up for the Baggies first-ever £1m fee, Kilbane having helped North End to the Division Three title. A goal on his debut against Tranmere at the Hawthorns helped endear Kevin to the Throstles crowd who took to him as his long-striding direct wing play made him the hot property Sunderland eventually desired. He capped a fine performance against Sunderland with a goal in a 3-3 draw in his first season.

As a youngster Preston-born Kilbane's first international selection was to England's Under 18 squad, but he declined the offer; revealed to him by his Preston manager Sam Allardyce, as he wanted to play for the country of his parents. A Republic of Ireland debut arrived in September 1997. Five of his eight international goals came while with Sunderland. Only Billy Wright - the first man to play 100 times for England - surpasses Kilbane's record of 66 successive internationals (in Britain and Ireland). It was a run that ended with Kevin's final international appearance before injury caused his retirement from international football.

Having played at the 2002 FIFA World Cup finals while with Sunderland - when he missed in a penalty shoot-out as Spain eliminated the Republic - he worked at the 2010 World Cup for RTE and the 2014 World Cup as a BBC pundit having forged a career in the media. As with everything else Kilbane achieved, he worked for it, having attained a degree in Professional Sports Writing and Broadcasting.

Married to a figure skater, in 2020 Kevin competed on Dancing on Ice. Father-in-law Steve Harrison played for Blackpool, Vancouver Whitecaps, Watford and Charlton Athletic as well as managing Watford amongst a host of coaching and assistant manager roles. Kevin's brother Farrell played for Preston, Stafford Rangers, Barrow, Lancaster City, Southport, Stalybridge Celtic, Burscough Fleetwood Town, Hyde and Trafford.

## KILGALLON, Matthew Shaun

**POSITION:** Defender

**BIRTHPLACE:** York, Yorkshire

**DATE OF BIRTH:** 08/01/1984

**HEIGHT:** 6' 1½" **WEIGHT:** 12st 0lbs

**SIGNED FROM:** Sheffield United, 21/01/2010

**DEBUT:** v Everton, A, 27/01/2010

**LAST MATCH:** v Chelsea, A, 06/04/2013

**MOVED TO:** Contract not renewed, 30/06/2013

**TEAMS:** Leeds United, West Ham United (L), Sheffield United, Sunderland, Middlesbrough (L), Doncaster Rovers (L), Blackburn Rovers, Bradford City, Hamilton Academical, Hyderabad, Buxton

**INTERNATIONAL:** England Under 21

**SAFC TOTALS:** 24+2 appearances / 0 goals

**At one point nicknamed 'Skill-gallon' with just a slight touch of irony, Matt Kilgallon did show some flashes of terrific ability on the ball, but as his number of appearances and lack of contract renewal suggests he never quite established himself at SAFC. In four seasons, his best appearances return was in 2011-12 when he started nine league games and one cup game.**

Having begun as a centre-forward in the youth system of his home city club York where he played until he was twelve, Matt moved to Leeds. As a youngster, he acted as a ball boy at Champions League games and held the Champions League flag up while the anthem was played. A debut came on 14 November 2014 as a sub in the second leg of a UEFA Cup game against Hapoel Tel Aviv (played in Florence, Italy) when the tie was safe.

That was under Terry Venables as was his league debut the following February against West Ham, but by the last day of the season when Matt made his third appearance it was under Peter Reid. Kilgallon went on to play 86+9 times for Leeds, scoring three goals. Ian Harte, Dominic Matteo, Michael Bridges, Steve Caldwell, Simon Johnson, Paul Butler, Brian Deane, David Healy, John Oster, Michael Gray, Liam Miller, Danny Graham and Adam Johnson were amongst a vast number of Sunderland connections Kilgallon had in his time at Elland Road.

He also had a loan spell with West Ham, alongside Don Hutchison, playing four times including a League Cup derby with Spurs.

In January 2007 a fee of up to £2m saw him move to Sheffield United on his 23rd birthday and with it a rise from the Championship to Premier League. Player of the Year at Bramall Lane in 2008-09, he played 122+2 times for the Blades, scoring four goals before joining Sunderland in January 2010.

During his time on Wearside Matt was loaned to Middlesbrough and Doncaster where he made three and twelve appearances respectively. After leaving Sunderland Kilgallon signed for Blackburn on 8 July 2013 where he stayed for three seasons scoring twice in 64 appearances. He then totalled 58 games and four goals for Bradford City, the bulk of them in 2017-18 before a venture north of the border with Hamilton where he appeared 26 times in a season, before six months in the lucrative Indian Super League with Hyderabad and an August 2020 move to Northern Premier League Buxton.

At international level, 'Skill-gallon' was capped by England at Under 18, 19, 20 and 21 level. The first of his five Under 21 caps saw Michael Chopra score in a 2-2 draw away to Sweden in March 2004 when Justin Hoyte, Stewart Downing, Darren Bent and Jon Stead also played.

## KINNELL, George

**POSITION:** Centre-half

**BIRTHPLACE:** Cowdenbeath, Fife

**DATE OF BIRTH:** 22/12/1937 - 16/10/2021

**HEIGHT:** 5' 11" **WEIGHT:** 11st 11lbs

**SIGNED FROM:** Oldham Athletic, 17/10/1966

**DEBUT:** v Stoke City, H, 25/10/1966

**LAST MATCH:** v Southampton, H, 17/08/1968

**MOVED TO:** Middlesbrough, 15/10/1968

**TEAMS:** Crossgates Primrose, Aberdeen, Stoke City, Oldham Athletic, Sunderland, Middlesbrough, Juventus (Australia), Sydney Western Suburbs, Marconi-Fairfield, Olympic Kiev

**INTERNATIONAL:** Scottish League

**SAFC TOTALS:** 24+2 appearances / 0 goals

**An apprentice butcher at the Co-op in Kirkford before becoming a footballer, George Kinnell played as a defender in an era when butchery skills seemed relevant to some of the challenges that were allowed. Kinnell was capable of taking no prisoners. He was a tough, uncompromising stopper and not a bad player.**

The problem was he was not Charlie Hurley! Kinnell was the second cousin of Jim Baxter and was often played by manager Ian McColl ahead of Hurley much to the amazement of supporters. However, there was a spell in the autumn in 1967 when both Kinnell and Hurley were regularly selected in the same side, Kinnell also being able to operate in midfield where he had played elsewhere. Indeed, his versatility also saw him used at centre-forward at Stoke City especially in 1965-66. Once Alan Brown returned as manager in place of McColl, Kinnell was quickly moved on.

Nicknamed 'Kinks,' Kinnell played for Cowdenbeath Wednesday, Ballingry Rovers and Kirkford United in youth football before making his name with Aberdeen who he captained and scored for 25 times in a total of 164 appearances. Occasionally used up front, he twice scored hat-tricks for the Dons where he also took penalties. Although he never received a Scotland call up, Kinnell did earn a representative honour playing for the Scottish League against the Irish League in Belfast.

He went on to play 91 league games in three seasons with Stoke where he was a teammate of Stanley Matthews and scored in Stoke's 1964 League Cup final loss to Leicester when he was a teammate of Calvin Palmer (he also scored six league goals for the Potters).

After refusing to sell him to Sunderland, Stoke sold George to Oldham where he scored eight goals in a 13-game spell in the third tier with the Latics before Ian McColl succeeded in bringing him to Wearside. Later at Middlesbrough, where he played alongside Johnny Crossan, Kinnell made 13+1 appearances, scoring against Millwall before completing his playing days in Australia. In 1970, Kinnell won the State League with Juventus of Melbourne before enjoying Ampol Cup success with Western Suburbs of Sydney prior to a period with Marconi Fairfield and a final move to Olympic in Western Australia. He then returned to Scotland in 1978 and worked on and off shore in the oil industry.

Jim Baxter was not George's only footballing relation. Kinnell's brother Andy is a member of the Cowdenbeath Hall of Fame after over 200 games for 'the Blue Brazil' and 100 for St Johnstone where he became captain, while the brothers' mother Daisy, did the teas at Cowdenbeath. As a boy, he set up his own five-a-side team who were reputedly unbeaten for a decade before he left to do his National Service in Cyprus at the height of the EOKA crisis.

## KIRBY, Frederick

**POSITION:** Centre-forward

**BIRTHPLACE:** Bishop Auckland, Co Durham

**DATE OF BIRTH:** 10/06/1891 - 19/03/1982

**HEIGHT:** 5' 9" **WEIGHT:** 12st 0lbs

**SIGNED FROM:** Bishop Auckland, 16/11/1911, on trial

**DEBUT:** v Woolwich Arsenal, A, 18/11/1911

**LAST MATCH:** v Woolwich Arsenal, A, 18/11/1911

**MOVED TO:** Bishop Auckland, 20/11/1911, trial not extended

**TEAMS:** Bishop Auckland, Sunderland, Durham City, Middlesbrough, Halifax Town, Bradford Park Avenue, Halifax Town, Bishop Auckland, Halifax Town

**INTERNATIONAL:** England amateur

**SAFC TOTALS:** 1 appearance / 0 goals

**Fred Kirby's solitary appearance was while on trial from Bishop Auckland. According to contemporary press reports Kirby played well in difficult conditions, but was not given another opportunity.**

He was capped by England at amateur level in a 3-0 defeat by Denmark in Copenhagen on 5 June 1914, shortly after helping Bishop Auckland to victory in the FA Amateur Cup final against Northern Nomads at Elland Road. During that season Fred had experienced another chance in the first division playing for Middlesbrough at Everton on 4 October 1913 and in a 4-0 home win over Liverpool on the penultimate day of the season on a day when former SAFC man Walter Tinsley scored a hat-trick.

Always an amateur, after a brief spell with Halifax Town, Kirby again played in the top-flight with Bradford Park Avenue for whom he scored three times in ten games in 1914-15, one of his appearances coming in a 3-3 draw with Sunderland at Roker Park. Like many amateurs Kirby often cropped up playing for other teams.

Earlier that season he had scored against Bradford Reserves and Castleford Town in five Midland Counties League games for Halifax Town who he joined again for a short spell after the war.

He played the first two games of the 1919-20 season in the Midland Counties League, scoring a winner against Scunthorpe. During his time with Halifax and Bradford Park Avenue Fred worked as a surveyor in Brighouse, while he went on to serve in mechanical transport with the army service corps during the Great War.

By WW2 he had returned to the north east and served as an air raid shelter officer in Morpeth in addition to his role as a surveyor with the district council.

## KIRCHHOFF, Jan Tilman

**POSITION:** Midfielder

**BIRTHPLACE:** Frankfurt, Germany

**DATE OF BIRTH:** 01/10/1990

**HEIGHT:** 6' 5" **WEIGHT:** 12st 12lbs

**SIGNED FROM:** Bayern Munich, 07/01/2016

**DEBUT:** v Tottenham Hotspur, A, 16/01/2016

**LAST MATCH:** v Chelsea, H, 14/12/2016

**MOVED TO:** Contract not renewed, 30/06/2017

**TEAMS:** Eintracht Frankfurt, FSV Mainz 05, Bayern Munich, Schalke 04 (L), Sunderland, Bolton Wanderers, FC Magdeburg, Uerdingen 05

**INTERNATIONAL:** Germany Under 21

**SAFC TOTALS:** 20+3 appearance / 0 goals

**Signed from Bayern Munich in the 2016 January transfer window as Sunderland struggled, Kirchhoff looked anything but the answer to the Lads' problems as he marked his debut by coming off the bench at Spurs and deflecting a goal beyond fellow debutant Jordan Pickford and then giving away a needless penalty.**

However, the tall midfielder soon acclimatised and showed himself to be an outstanding footballer. The problem was he was injury prone but manager Sam Allardyce handled him highly effectively. As Sunderland mounted a dramatically successful escape from the drop, time after time Kirchhoff would be the outstanding performer on the pitch but with games on a knife-edge midway through the second half he would be substituted.

By so doing Big Sam ensured Kirchhoff would be available for the next game. In contrast, when David Moyes replaced Allardyce he appeared to push Kirchhoff too far and consequently, he started just five league games and played another two off the bench as Moyes' side finished bottom of the table.

While Kirchhoff played in midfield for Sunderland he often operated as a centre-back elsewhere. After playing youth football for clubs in his home city starting with SpVgg Kickers 16 where he played as an under 9, Jan made a senior debut for Mainz 05 against Rot Weiss Ahlen on 2 November 2008 in Bundesliga 2. After developing under future Chelsea manager Thomas Tuchel he moved to Bayern Munich in 2013 after 39+18 games for Mainz during which he won promotion in 2010.

Debuting for Bayern against Borussia Monchengladbach on 9 August 2013 he soon made a Champions League debut at Manchester City, but by the time he came to SAFC all ten of his appearances for star-studded Bayern were as a sub. He did however collect a winner's medal in the FIFA World Club Cup in 2013 when he was an unused sub in the final against Raja Casablanca. Munich twice loaned him to Schalke for whom he was allowed to play against his parent club Bayern in a 1-1 draw in August 2014, one of 14+6 appearances he made for Schalke.

After leaving Sunderland he stayed in England with Bolton where he made 2+2 appearances in March and April 2018 without being on the winning side. Returning to Germany with Bundesliga 2 outfit FC Magdeburg in January 2019, Jan debuted against Erzgebirge Aue and started ten games in the second half of the season before joining Uerdingen where he was appointed captain.

Debuting in a 1-0 win over Hallescher FC he went on to make 22 appearances, scoring against Carl Zeiss Jena and Waldhof Mannheim - his first goals in senior football. Unfortunately, Jan remained more au-fait with the treatment room than the dressing room in an injury-ravaged career.

It was such a pity for a talented player who was ultra-professional behind the scenes. If Jan's ability to stay fit was in question, his ability was not. Capped by Germany at Under 18 and 19 level - scoring against Lithuania Under 19s - he scored on his Under 21 debut in a 1-1 draw with the Czech Republic on 3 September 2009. It was one of three goals he netted in 18 Under 21 games.

Jan's father Theo played for VfL Germania Leer whilst younger brother Benjamin played for Stuttgart, Kickers Offenbach and TSV Steinbach to 2021.

## KIRKLEY, William (Bill)

**POSITION:** Goalkeeper

**BIRTHPLACE:** Monkwearmouth, Co Durham

**DATE OF BIRTH:** 16/01/1863 - 29/05/1941

**HEIGHT:** 5' 8½" **WEIGHT:** 10st 4lbs

**SIGNED FROM:** Monkwearmouth Workmen's Hall Club, 24/04/1885

**DEBUT:** v Redcar, A, 24/10/1885

**LAST MATCH:** Wolverhampton Wanderers, H, 15/09/1890

**MOVED TO:** Sunderland Albion, 02/09/1891

**TEAMS:** Monkwearmouth Workmen's Hall Club, Sunderland, Sunderland Albion

**SAFC TOTALS:** 11 appearances / 0 goals

**A stalwart of the early days of the club, Kirkley kept goal in all but the first of Sunderland's ten English (FA) Cup ties of the 1880s. Like most of the players at that time he was employed in the shipyards; Bill being a marine engine fitter.**

He also played in the club's first-ever two league games when the ruthlessness of football was quickly illustrated as he was blamed for defeats in those two fixtures during which seven goals were conceded.

Sunderland hurriedly replaced him with Teddy Doig for the next game and in doing so were docked two points and fined as Doig had not yet completed the 14-day registration period. Nicknamed 'Stonewall', Kirkley moved on to Sunderland Albion. In the mid-1930s, he was still associated with SAFC being in charge of the billiard table then situated at Roker Park Club House.

## KIRTLEY, John Henry M (Harry)

**POSITION:** Inside-right

**BIRTHPLACE:** Washington, Co Durham

**DATE OF BIRTH:** 23/05/1930 - 08/12/2007

**HEIGHT:** 5' 10" **WEIGHT:** 11st 2lbs

**SIGNED FROM:** Fatfield Juniors, 24/05/1948

**DEBUT:** v Manchester City, A, 16/04/1949

**LAST MATCH:** v Chelsea, A, 29/03/1955

**MOVED TO:** Cardiff City, 02/06/1955

**TEAMS:** Sunderland, Cardiff City, Gateshead, Rhyl, Sankeys FC, Holyhead

**SAFC TOTALS:** 101 appearance / 18 goals

**An apprentice colliery electrician before becoming a professional footballer, Kirtley initially signed amateur forms with Sunderland in 1946 only for his registration to not be renewed at the end of the season.**

Having signed again in May 1948, he appeared in seven seasons before moving to Cardiff in a deal that also involved John McSeveney and Howard Sheppeard. Harry's best seasons at Roker Park came in the early fifties when he made 74 of his 101 appearances and scored all but one of his goals.

Having moved to Cardiff Harry scored four goals in 38 games before a swift return to the north east with Gateshead who were still a Football League club. He scored 16 times in 95 league games before returning to Wales with Rhyl where he later settled and worked repairing bicycles.

## KIRTLEY, John Trotter (Jack)

**POSITION:** Goalkeeper

**BIRTHPLACE:** South Hylton, Co Durham

**DATE OF BIRTH:** 20/05/1863 - 22/11/1932

**SIGNED:** 1882

**DEBUT:** v Redcar, A, 08/11/1884

**LAST MATCH:** v Redcar, A, 08/11/1884

**MOVED:** 1885

**TEAMS:** Sunderland

**SAFC TOTALS:** 1 appearance / 0 goals

**Jack Kirtley's only official game for Sunderland was a notable one. He took part in the club's first-ever competitive game in a national competition. He also played in another notable match, being Sunderland's goalkeeper in the biggest win ever recorded by the club, a 23-0 friendly win over Castletown five days before Christmas in 1884.**

On that occasion, when club founder James Allan scored an incredible twelve goals, it is said that Kirtley kept score by notching the goals on his goal post! Perhaps he kept some chalk about his person as he was a chief draughtsman at Bartram's Shipyard.

Goalkeeping was not Kirtley's only sporting passion. He also captained Hendon Cricket Club where he kept wicket in the 1890s and 1900s. In 1901, he scored a club record 130 not out against Wearmouth Colliery.

## KNOTT, Billy Steven

**POSITION:** Midfielder

**BIRTHPLACE:** Canvey Island, Essex

**DATE OF BIRTH:** 01/10/1990

**HEIGHT:** 5' 8" **WEIGHT:** 10st 7lbs

**SIGNED FROM:** Chelsea, 01/01/2011

**DEBUT:** v Tottenham Hotspur, A, 19/05/2013

**LAST MATCH:** v Tottenham Hotspur, A, 19/05/2013

**MOVED TO:** Bradford City, 30/05/2014

**TEAMS:** West Ham United, Chelsea, Sunderland, AFC Wimbledon (L), Woking (L), Wycombe Wanderers (L), Port Vale (L), Bradford City, Gillingham, Lincoln City, Rochdale (L), Concord Rangers, Chelmsford City, Bowers & Pitsea, Billericay Town (L), Canvey Island, Great Wakering Rovers (to June 2022)

**INTERNATIONAL:** England Under 20

**SAFC TOTALS:** 0+1 appearance / 0 goals

**Only given 17 minutes in a Sunderland shirt on a last day of the season Premier League match at Tottenham, Knott was certainly not out of place and warranted more of an opportunity. He was later a key part of Phil Parkinson's Bradford City who knocked Sunderland out of the FA Cup in the fifth round in 2015 when Jon Stead was one of the scorers.**

Capped by England Under 20 against North Korea, Argentina, Mexico and Nigeria (alongside fellow Sunderland youngster Blair Adams and future Sunderland man Callum McManaman) as well as winning caps at Under 16 and Under 17 level, Knott had the ability to have spent his career at a much higher level.

Good on the ball, with an eye for a pass and a goal there always seemed to be a hint of potential trouble near Billy whose departure from Chelsea was clouded in mystery, but rumoured to have involved a smoke grenade. A youngster at West Ham, he was later schooled at Chelsea's academy after spending some of his childhood in Spain.

Sunderland loaned Knott to a quartet of clubs, his league debut coming in January 2012 for AFC Wimbledon at Port Vale after which he scored on his home debut. It was one of three goals for Billy in 14+6 games after which he scored eight in 20 games for Woking in the Blue Square Premier League, the last of those appearances at Tamworth coming a month before his Sunderland debut. There followed two goals in 20+3 games on loan to Wycombe and another two goals in 13+5 games for Port Vale in 2013-14.

At Bradford, Billy played in their sensational 4-2 FA Cup win at Chelsea in the round before playing Sunderland, and in the quarter-final lost to Reading in a replay. This was his best spell as over two seasons he made 62+17 appearances scoring eight times. He then played for Gillingham (20+4/1), Lincoln who he initially joined on loan (22+12/3), Rochdale on loan (1+3/0) before dropping into National League South where he represented Concord Rangers, Chelmsford City and Billericay.

In September 2020, he moved into the Isthmian League with Bowers & Pitsea for a couple of months before returning to National League South with Billericay Town after Covid curtained his season with Bowers & Pitsea.

## KNOWLES, Joseph (Joe)

**POSITION:** Left-back

**BIRTHPLACE:** Monkwearmouth, Co Durham

**DATE OF BIRTH:** 16/12/1871 - 14/01/1955

**HEIGHT:** 5' 6" **WEIGHT:** 11st 6lbs

**SIGNED FROM:** Monkwearmouth, 18/04/1895 and from QPR, 01/11/1901

**DEBUT:** v Bury, A, 16/04/1897

**LAST MATCH:** v Bury, A, 16/04/1897

**MOVED TO:** Tottenham Hotspur, 21/05/1897

**TEAMS:** Monkwearmouth, Sunderland, Tottenham Hotspur, South Shields, QPR, Sunderland

**SAFC TOTALS:** 1 appearance / 0 goals

**Knowles' only first-team game for Sunderland came in the final game of the League season. However, Sunderland had to then participate in four end-of-season Test Matches to maintain their top flight status, games in which Joe was not involved.**

After to-ing and fro-ing between the north east and London in his later career, he re-signed for Sunderland in 1901 and played for the reserves, known then as the 'A' team.

At Tottenham, he debuted on the opening day of the season on 4 September 1897 in a Southern League game at Sheppey United. He missed just three of the 22 league games playing in both full-back positions. He also played in an English (FA) Cup tie with Luton who also won the United League, a short lived midweek league for southern and central England teams, in which Spurs were second, Joe having played 14 of the 16 games in that competition.

It was to be Knowles' only season at Spurs after which he spent a year with South Shields in the Northern Alliance League. It was then back to the capital with QPR for their first season in the Southern League. Debuting away to his old club Tottenham, he played 22 of the 28 league games as well as appearing in seven of Rangers English Cup games as they negotiated the qualifying rounds and reached round two. After finishing his career with Sunderland, Knowles became a marine engine fitter.

## KONE, Lamine Gueye

**POSITION:** Centre-back

**BIRTHPLACE:** Paris, France

**DATE OF BIRTH:** 01/02/1988

**HEIGHT:** 6' 2½" **WEIGHT:** 14st 2lbs

**SIGNED FROM:** Lorient, 27/01/2016

**DEBUT:** v Manchester City, H, 02/02/2016

**LAST MATCH:** v Fulham A, 27/04/2018

**MOVED TO:** Strasbourg, 01/06/2019

**TEAMS:** Chateauroux, Lorient, Sunderland, Strasbourg, Lausanne (to June 2022)

**INTERNATIONAL:** France Under 20, Ivory Coast

**SAFC TOTALS:** 70+2 appearances / 3 goals

**Brought in by Sam Allardyce, Kone was a colossus of a centre-back as Sunderland successfully avoided relegation after his January capture. Two of Lamine's three goals came on the night safety was sealed against Everton, this making him the first central-defender to score twice in a top-flight game since Sandy McAllister against Bury in 1903.**

Partnered with Younes Kaboul, Kone was absolutely top class in that first season, and in the summer, was the subject of persistent interest from Everton who were reported to have offered £18m for him.

Given a lucrative new contract his decision to stay was warmly welcomed, but after Allardyce was replaced by David Moyes Kone was never as effective, particularly after the departure of fellow French-speaking Kaboul. After two seasons he moved on loan to Strasbourg with the move completed a year later. Ultimately, Lamine left the Lads with a feeling of what might have been if he had been able to continue the superb form he showed under Big Sam.

In his youth Kone made his senior debut for Chateauroux against Montpelier on 27 April 2007 after playing for SO Paris and US Alfortville as a boy. After 74 appearances and four goals he commanded a €1m fee when moving to Lorient where he debuted against Nice in Ligue 1 on 14 August 2010. He went on to play 119+9 games for the club scoring the first of his seven goals against Marseille in May 2011. Following his return to France he played 63+8 times for Strasbourg, scoring four times.

In 2019, he played in the Coupe de la Ligue final as Guingamp were beaten on penalties, his opponents having Papy Djilobodji as an unused sub. Having moved to Lausanne in November 2021, to June 2022 he had only made seven appearances. Capped at four levels up to Under 20 for France where he was born, Lamine later switched to Ivory Coast, the country of his parents, winning the first of his nine caps against Cameroon in 2014.

## KUBICKI, Dariusz Jan

**POSITION:** Right-back

**BIRTHPLACE:** Kozuchow, Poland

**DATE OF BIRTH:** 06/06/1963

**HEIGHT:** 5' 10" **WEIGHT:** 11st 7lbs

**SIGNED FROM:** Aston Villa, 13/07/1994, after loan from 03/03/1994

**DEBUT:** v Notts County, H, 05/03/1994

**LAST MATCH:** v Liverpool, H, 13/04/1997

**MOVED TO:** Wolverhampton Wanderers, 06/08/1997

**TEAMS:** Stal Mielec, Legia Warsaw Aston Villa, Sunderland, Wolves, Tranmere Rovers (L), Carlisle United, Darlington

**INTERNATIONAL:** Poland

**SAFC TOTALS:** 149+1 appearances / 0 goals

**A deservedly popular player at Sunderland, Kubicki was consistency personified and for some supporters the best right-back at the club in living memory. Composed and unflustered, Dariusz gained 46 caps for Poland who he captained.**

After playing for Meblarz Nowe Miasteczko and Lechia Zielona Gora whilst he was a youth, Kubicki debuted in senior football playing in the Polish Third Division for Stal Mielic where he played 24 league games and scored twice. This led to a 1983 move to Polish giants Legia Warsaw where Kubicki spent almost a decade, playing 190 league games.

In 1985 Kubicki helped Legia to qualify for the UEFA Cup after finishing runners-up while in 1986 he took part in the Great Wall Cup staged in Beijing and Tianjin, scoring the opening goal in a 3-0 win over Pyongyang of North Korea as Legia went on to win the six-team tournament by beating the national side of China at the Workers' Stadium in Beijing (future Sunderland player Tony Coton was part of the Watford side who won the tournament the following year).

After losing the Polish Cup final on penalties, Kubicki helped them to win the next two finals, beating Jagiellonia Bialystok and Widzew Lodz with a Polish Super Cup win over Ruch Chorzow in between.

Signed for £200,000 by the newly-appointed Ron Atkinson at Aston Villa, Dariusz debuted in a 1-1 draw at Southampton on 31 August 1991, future Sunderland coach Kevin Richardson getting the goal for a Villa side that also included Nigel Spink who later became goalkeeping coach at Sunderland. Beginning with a run of 23 consecutive starting top-flight appearances Kubicki also counted Dwight Yorke amongst his teammates. However, he would only total 32+2 games for the midlanders before he came to Sunderland on loan at a time when he had only played three times in two seasons, Southampton being his last opponents as they had been his first.

It was therefore all the more creditable that having arrived at Sunderland Dariusz did not miss a game for over two and a half years, during which time he was ever-present for two full seasons including the 1995-96 Championship-winning campaign. When he was finally left out he was just one game away from equalling George Mulhall's post-war record of 125 consecutive appearances.

Leaving Sunderland at the end of that 1996-97 season the Pole moved to Wolves where he only made twelve appearances, one of which was back at Sunderland in one of the early games at the Stadium of Light where he set up Wanderers' goal; albeit an own-goal by Andy Melville. Having played at left-back with Wolves he reverted to right-back as he ended the season with a dozen games on loan to Tranmere, one of which was in a home defeat by Sunderland.

In that summer of 1998 he joined Carlisle, making nine early season appearances including a couple of League Cup games against Tranmere. Within three months of moving to Brunton Park Dariusz returned to the north east with Darlington where the last of his 2+1 appearances for David Hodgson's side was as a sub at Chester in December 1998 where Marco Gabbiadini, Brian Atkinson and former Roker reserves David Preece and Phil Brumwell were amongst his teammates, with Gary Bennett also a colleague on his previous appearances.

For Poland, Dariusz debuted in a 4-0 defeat against Finland in an Olympic qualifying game in Helsinki on 4 May 1983. He went on to play in a goalless draw with Morocco at the 1986 FIFA World Cup (in England's group).

After his retirement from playing, Kubicki moved into management with Legia Warsaw in 1999, and as of 2018 had managed a dozen teams, most recently Olimpia Grudziadz and including a spell as caretaker manager of FC Sibir Novosibirsk in Russia. Although nothing was ever proved, Kubicki was suspended as manager of Lechia Gdansk having reportedly been arrested in 2007 as part of an alleged bribery scandal.

His son Patryk (born in Birmingham five months before Dariusz came to Sunderland and on Sunderland's books for a short time as a very young schoolboy) was a midfielder who in June 2022 was with his eighth club Mszczonowianka Mszczonów.

## KYLE, Kevin Alastair

**POSITION:** Centre-forward

**BIRTHPLACE:** Stranraer, Dumfries & Galloway

**DATE OF BIRTH:** 07/06/1981

**HEIGHT:** 6' 4" **WEIGHT:** 14st 8lbs

**SIGNED FROM:** Ayr Boswell, 25/09/1998

**DEBUT:** v Southampton, A 28/04/2001

**LAST MATCH:** v Southend United, A, 19/08/2006

**MOVED TO:** Coventry City, 25/08/2006

**TEAMS:** Ayr Boswell, Sunderland, Huddersfield Town (L), Darlington (L), Rochdale (L), Coventry City, Wolves (L), Hartlepool United (L), Kilmarnock, Hearts, Rangers, Ayr United, Newton Stewart

**INTERNATIONAL:** Scotland

**SAFC TOTALS:** 73+36 appearances / 19 goals

**In 1999-2000 as Kevin Phillips scored 30 Premier League goals as Europe's top scorer, Kevin Kyle scored 24 times in 23 Under 19 games and added a couple more in a handful of reserve appearances. 'Kyler' went on to make his first-team debut a year later and always gave absolutely everything he had.**

It was his misfortune to be a raw and gangly centre-forward coming through when fans were used to the deft touch of the brilliant Niall Quinn and the goalscoring prowess of the SuperKev of the Phillips variety. Kyle's ability was being recognised however, as on 20 May 2002, he made his full Scotland debut (v South Korea) before he had made his full debut for Sunderland. He went on to win ten full caps, getting a goal against a Hong Kong League XI.

It was not until the dismal relegation season of 2002-03 that Kyle made his first nine league starts with his first league goal not coming until the following season when he managed ten plus one in each leg of the unsuccessful Play-Offs against Crystal Palace. It was Kyle's best season as he scored 16 times in all competitions and appeared in 53 games. It was the only one of Kevin's seven seasons in which he played for the first team that he reached double figures in terms of league starts. In April 2005, 'Kyler', making a comeback from a hip injury, scored five times for Sunderland reserves as they beat Aston Villa reserves 7-5. Former Sunderland player Gavin McCann was also making a comeback in that game for Villa.

During his time on Wearside, Kyle was loaned to Huddersfield Town (0+4/0) Darlington (8/1) and Rochdale (3+3/0). The Terriers games - where he debuted at home to Bolton on 09/09/2000 came before he had played for Sunderland. Eventually sold to Coventry City for £600,000 in the same month he played against them for Sunderland in August 2006, he did not have the best of times with the Sky Blues despite scoring on his home debut against Norwich City. It was one of only five goals Kyle converted in 27+20 games for the club who loaned him to Wolves (4+9/1) and Hartlepool United (15/5).

In January 2009 Kevin decided to try his luck in his native Scotland, signing for Kilmarnock where he netted 18 goals in 45+3 matches. A goalscoring debut at St Mirren was marred by a red card at Inverness CT second time out, but he ended his first season on a high with seven goals in the final four fixtures of the season, starting with a hat-trick against Falkirk. After 18 months with Killie, 'Kyler' moved on a free to Hearts where he notched ten goals in 19+3 games before joining Rangers.

At the time, the Ibrox club were just beginning in the lowest tier of Scottish League football after their financial woes brought an end to their top-flight existence. After a League Cup debut at home to East Fife, Kevin made his league bow at Peterhead. He went on to play 4+9 appearances for Rangers, his three goals coming in his final four games.

After unsuccessful trials with Dunfermline and St Johnstone, in September 2013 Kyle moved to Ayr where he had begun his career, but this time with United rather than Ayr Boswell. He scored five goals in 25+4 games before signing off his career with an appearance for Newton Stewart in south-west Scotland. Kevin then retired because of injury when he was just 31. He went on to become a storeman on a ship in the Shetland Islands, work in the oil industry and become a baggage handler on ferries between Cairnryan, near his birthplace in Stranraer, and Northern Ireland.

In 2016 Kevin took part in the Scottish Open Darts tournament. Famed as one of the 'Wembley Wizards' who beat England 5-1 in 1928 was Kevin's great uncle Alan Morton. He played for Rangers between 1920 and 1933. Later a Rangers director, Morton is considered an all-time great of Scottish football. His brother and another uncle of Kevin Kyle's was Bob Morton who played alongside Alan at Queen's Park.

## KYRGIAKOS, Sotirios

**POSITION:** Defender

**BIRTHPLACE:** Megalochori, Greece

**DATE OF BIRTH:** 23/07/1979

**HEIGHT:** 6' 4" **WEIGHT:** 14st 6lbs

**SIGNED FROM:** VfL Wolfsburg, 31/01/2012, on loan

**DEBUT:** v Blackburn Rovers, A, 20/03/2012

**LAST MATCH:** v Manchester City, A, 31/03/2012

**MOVED TO:** VfL Wolfsburg, 14/05/2012 end of loan

**TEAMS:** Thyella Megalochoriou, Panathinaikos, Agios Nikolaos (L), Rangers, Eintracht Frankfurt, AEK Athens, Liverpool, VfL Wolfsburg, Sunderland (L), Sydney Olympic

**INTERNATIONAL:** Greece

**SAFC TOTALS:** 3+1 appearances / 0 goals

**Well known in British football before coming to SAFC on loan from German football, just six months before coming to Wearside Kyrgiakos had been on Liverpool's books. Strong in the air, but lacking pace, 'Soto,' as he was known at Liverpool, spent a lot of time on the bench at Anfield (he was named as a sub 25 times in 2009-10), but impressed when called upon, even winning the Reds Player of the Month award in January 2010.**

He had first come to prominence with former European Cup (now Champions League) finalists Panathinaikos where after breaking into the side in 2001-02 he played in twelve Champions League games the following term, but it would be in this competition in 2003-04 (in which Panathinaikos did their domestic double) that he suffered a knee ligament injury against Rangers who he would join in January 2005 after a loan with Agios Nikolaos (53/3). He had scored five goals in 60 games for Panathinaikos and scored twice for Rangers in a 5-1 League Cup final win over Motherwell, but trouble ensued at the end of the season when Rangers thought they could acquire the defender on a free transfer only for a furious Panathinaikos to demand the return of his registration.

The stand-off ended with Kyrgiakos moved to Eintracht Frankfurt (another club who had contested a European Cup final) where he spent two seasons in the Bundesliga finishing 14th and ninth before he moved back to Greece with AEK Athens after eight goals in 51 appearances. There were then 20 league outings (0 goals) and a cup final success against Olympiacos before his move to Liverpool.

Following nine games with VfL Wolfsburg, he signed for Martin O'Neill at Sunderland where he started just three times before ending his career on the other side of the world with Sydney Olympic for whom he played just twice.

At international level, Kyrgiakos won 61 caps, scoring four goals. Having missed Greece's success at Euro 2004 through injury he was the only player to play every minute of their qualifying campaign for Euro 2008 and played in all three of his country's games at the tournament - only for them all to end in defeat.

## LAFFERTY, Kyle Joseph George

**POSITION:** Centre-forward

**BIRTHPLACE:** Enniskillen, Northern Ireland

**DATE OF BIRTH:** 16/09/1987

**HEIGHT:** 6' 4" **WEIGHT:** 13st 12lbs

**SIGNED FROM:** Free agent, 10/01/2020

**DEBUT:** v MK Dons, A, 18/01/2020

**LAST MATCH:** v Bristol Rovers, A, 10/03/2020

**MOVED TO:** Released, 15/06/2020

**TEAMS:** NFC Kesh, Ballinamallard United, Burnley, Darlington (L), Rangers, Sion, Palermo, Norwich City, Caykur Rizespor (L), Birmingham City (L), Hearts, Rangers, Sarpsborg 08, Sunderland, Reggina, Kilmarnock, Anorthosis Famagusta, Kilmarnock (to June 2022)

**INTERNATIONAL:** Northern Ireland

**SAFC TOTALS:** 2+9 appearances / 2 goals

**On his only start at the Stadium of Light for Sunderland, Kyle Lafferty scored twice against Gillingham in what was the last home game before Covid 19 curtailed the season and with it Lafferty's time with the Black Cats.**

Most of Lafferty's appearances off the bench came late in games, but when he did play he generally did well leading the line as an old style centre-forward. The player certainly had a well-travelled, and at times chequered, career. Clubs in Northern Ireland, England, Switzerland, Italy, Turkey, Scotland, Norway and Cyprus all featured on the CV of the Northern Irishman.

At his best for his country when partnered with one-time Sunderland striker David Healy, Lafferty scored 20 goals in 85 full internationals (to June 2022). Northern Ireland International Personality of the Year in 2015, Kyle debuted for his country against Uruguay in the USA in May 2006. Ahead of the European Championships in 2016, Belfast City Airport was temporarily renamed the Kyle Lafferty Belfast City Airport. He played in three 1-0 defeats in the finals to Poland, Germany and Wales.

After playing in his home country, Lafferty came through the fabled Burnley youth system where he played his early football under Steve Cotterill and caused a divide of opinion between those who saw him as best through the middle and those who felt he was most effective wide on the left.

After five games with Burnley Lafferty was loaned to Darlington for whom he made a goalscoring debut at Notts County in January 2006. It was one of three goals Kyle scored in nine games for the Quakers and there were ten to come in 55+33 games for Burnley before a £3m move to Rangers in June 2008.

Celtic, Fulham (who wanted to partner him with Healy), Wolves and Ipswich all tried to take him but the 20-year-old player wanted to go to Ibrox having grown up a Rangers supporter. He enjoyed great success in Glasgow winning three SPL titles in his four years as well as the Scottish Cup and two League Cups, but when financial meltdown hit the club he was one of the players who refused to have his registration transferred to the new club.

Having debuted in the Champions League against FBK Kaunas in August 2008 he scored 38 times in 86+51 games, including a couple of hat-tricks, title-deciding goals and an Old Firm strike. He also was no stranger to a red card and was suspended for simulation and also by the club after a training ground bust-up during the reign of Ally McCoist. Lafferty also married a former Miss Scotland shortly before a transfer to Sion of Switzerland in June 2012, a move that required FIFA arbitration after objections from Rangers.

Five goals in 16+9 Swiss Super League appearances preceded a move to Palermo a year later. Signed by ex-Rangers man Gennaro Gattuso who had been player/coach with Lafferty in Sion, Kyle got eleven goals in 34 games as he helped Palermo to the Serie B title playing up front alongside future Juventus star Paulo Dybala. Despite this, Lafferty was sold one year into his three year contract as chairman Maurizio Zamperini described him as, "An out of control womaniser, an Irishman without rules".

Norwich City brought him back to England but there were three goals as a Norwich player for Northern Ireland before his first goal as a Canary on his 19th appearance for the club. There were only three others in 14+25 games during which time he was loaned to Rizespor in Turkey (4+10/2) and Birmingham City (4+2/1) before a free transfer to Hearts in July 2017.

A self-confessed gambler, during his time with Norwich Lafferty was fined and warned of his future conduct by the FA having broken FA betting rules. Four goals in his first three games got Kyle off to a good start with Hearts where there were goals against Rangers, in three games against Celtic and an Edinburgh derby with Hibs among a haul of 20 in 40+8 games in his one season of 2017-18. Such form led to a return to Rangers where he scored six times in 8+22 appearances during his second spell. Between then and coming to Sunderland Lafferty tried his luck in Norway with Sarpsborg where, after being sent off on his debut, the only goal in 8+1 appearances came against Billy Elliott's old club Brann.

Following his sojourn at Sunderland Kyle returned to Italy playing eleven times and scoring once for Reggina before a goal-laden spell of 13 goals in only 12+1 games for Kilmarnock in the spring of 2021. Sunshine once again beckoned with a move to Cyprus where he quickly scored for Famagusta in the Europa League against Rapid Vienna. Returning to Kilmarnock he helped them to promotion from the Championship in 2022 with a further eight goals in 13+2 appearances.

## LAING, Louis Mark

**POSITION:** Centre-back

**BIRTHPLACE:** Newcastle, Tyne and Wear

**DATE OF BIRTH:** 06/03/1993

**HEIGHT:** 6' 3" **WEIGHT:** 12st 12lbs

**SIGNED FROM:** Trainee, 01/07/2009

**DEBUT:** v Wolverhampton Wanderers, H, 14/05/2011

**LAST MATCH:** v Wolverhampton Wanderers, H, 14/05/2011

**MOVED TO:** Contract not renewed, 30/04/2014

**TEAMS:** Sunderland, Wycombe Wanderers (L), Nottingham Forest, Notts County (L), Motherwell, Notts County (L), Inverness Caledonian Thistle, Hartlepool United, Blyth Spartans, Darlington (to May 2022)

**INTERNATIONAL:** England Under 19

**SAFC TOTALS:** 0+1 appearance / 0 goals

**It remains a surprise that Louis Laing only played once for Sunderland and did not have a career at a much higher level. Having been associated with the Black Cats since the age of twelve, having already been with Montague Boys Club, Laing's solitary first-team appearance came as an 87th-minute sub on the final day of the 2010-11 season and was thought to herald a bright future.**

Possessed of what seemed to be the perfect physique for a footballer, Louis was not simply one of those young players who stands out at youth level because he is bigger and stronger than his contemporaries. He could play. Captain of England at Under 16 level, he made 18 international appearances from Under 16 to Under 19 and made his Under 18 debut for Sunderland against Barnsley in November 2008 when he was just 15 years and eight months old.

Loaned to Wycombe eight months after his very brief taste of the Premier League he made eleven League One appearances, all but one of them as starts, but after another couple of seasons signed for Nottingham Forest on a free transfer. However, his only games in Nottingham came during a loan to County on the other side of the Trent. Newcastle-born Laing played ten times for the 'other' Magpies before going to Motherwell initially on loan in a deal engineered by Gary Owers. Despite being sent off on his SPL debut against St Johnstone Louis did well and helped his side stay up, playing in both legs of the relegation/promotion Play-Off with Rangers who they handsomely defeated 6-1 on aggregate.

Having made his move to Motherwell permanent Louis barely doubled his 15 loan appearances, playing a further 14+2 games (2 goals in total) before returning to Notts County on loan in the summer of 2016. 25+2 games and two goals in the first half of the season persuaded Inverness CT to move in and sign him at the end of the January transfer window but after 14 appearances he moved to Hartlepool after six months. Playing in the National League at the age of 24 was not what was once envisaged for Louis but he has stayed in non-league ever since, dropping lower into National League North with Blyth and Darlington.

## LAIRD, William (Willie)

**POSITION:** Inside-left / centre-forward

**BIRTHPLACE:** Larkhall, Lanarkshire

**DATE OF BIRTH:** 21/02/1910 - 1978

**HEIGHT:** 5' 9½" **WEIGHT:** 11st 0lbs

**SIGNED FROM:** Blantyre Celtic, 07/12/1931

**DEBUT:** v West Ham United, A, 19/12/1931

**LAST MATCH:** v Derby County, H, 01/01/1932

**MOVED TO:** Gateshead, 08/07/1932

**TEAMS:** Kirkmuirhill, Blantyre Celtic, Sunderland, Gateshead, Excelsior Athletic Club de Roubaix, Airdrieonians, Notts County, East Stirlingshire

**SAFC TOTALS:** 2 appearances / 0 goals

# L

## LAIRD, Willie (Continued)

**A bus and tram conductor before signing for Sunderland, Willie Laird got no change out of the defences of West Ham and Derby on his two first-team appearances.**

He went on to score once in two Division Three North games for Gateshead before going to France in September 1933 to play for Roubaix Excelsior, a club who had just won the Coupe de France a year after turning professional. After a couple of months he returned to Britain with Airdrieonians and then Notts County.

After his registration was cancelled by the Magpies in March 1934, Willie returned to his native Scotland to briefly play for East Stirlingshire, but by 1938 when he got married, he had returned to working on the buses as a driver. Laird passed away aged 68 in the Motherwell area.

## LANE, James Charles (Joe)

**POSITION:** Centre-forward

**BIRTHPLACE:** Watford, Hertfordshire

**DATE OF BIRTH:** 11/07/1892 - 27/02/1959

**HEIGHT:** 5' 11½" **WEIGHT:** 11st 0lbs

**SIGNED FROM:** Watford, 10/07/1913

**DEBUT:** v Aston Villa, H, 20/09/1913

**LAST MATCH:** v Manchester City, H, 18/10/1913

**MOVED TO:** Blackpool, 20/11/1913

**TEAMS:** Watford, Ferencvaros, MTK Budapest, Watford, Sunderland, Blackpool, Birmingham, Millwall Athletic, Bourneville

**SAFC TOTALS:** 2 appearances / 0 goals

**Blackpool paid Sunderland £400 for the centre-forward in November 1913 after he had played just twice at SAFC. Lane had been signed only four months earlier, primarily due to scoring twice for MTK Budapest when SAFC beat them 4-2 as part of a seven-match post-season tour of Eastern Europe.**

Debuting for the Seasiders with a goal against Leeds City, Lane went on to be the club's top scorer scoring a third of their 33 goals as Blackpool became the lowest scorers in Division Two in 1913-14. The following season Joe netted 28 of his own - including a hat-trick at Hull - as he was ever-present in Blackpool's 38 games.

During the Great War Lane served with the Hertfordshire Yeomanry in Egypt but in the first season after the war he showed he had lost none of his ability in front of goal, scoring 28 league and cup goals in 42 games up to February 1920. This took his Blackpool total to 67 goals in 99 games - the last of which brought a 6-0 Second Division defeat to South Shields. However, with the club reeling financially, Lane was sold to Birmingham for a club record £3,300. Lane was rumoured to have received a third of the fee. Joe hit the ground running with Birmingham, scoring six times in his first three games. A debut goal against Lincoln was followed two games later with a hat-trick against the same club. The Imps must have been sick of the sight of him - he had scored another hat-trick against them earlier in the season for Blackpool. After 26 goals in 67 games for Birmingham Joe joined Millwall Athletic.

Having turned 30 Joe strangely found himself playing mainly on the wing for the Lions, scoring six goals in 19 games, four of those coming in successive late-season games. His second season brought just eleven appearances, the last in a November 1922 home defeat to Luton Town.

Next stop for Joe Lane was a move to Barcelona where he became their coach under Imre Pozsonyi, a former Hungary international who had played for MTK - as had Lane. Joe's father owned a printing company and before coming to Sunderland Joe had gone to Hungary on a two-year secondment due to that business. Watford-born, he had played for the Hornets as an amateur and began playing in Budapest with Ferencvaros before joining MTK. Oddly, when Pozsonyi left Barcelona in December 1924, he was replaced by Ralph Kirby - like Joe Lane, a former Blackpool and Birmingham player.

By 1929 Lane was back in England in the less glamorous company of Bourneville FC while in the mid-thirties he was coaching Watford Printing Works FC. He died in Hertfordshire at the age of 66.

## LARSSON, Bengt Ulf Sebastian (Seb)

**POSITION:** Midfielder

**BIRTHPLACE:** Eskilstuna, Sweden

**DATE OF BIRTH:** 06/06/1985

**HEIGHT:** 5' 10" **WEIGHT:** 11st 7lbs

**SIGNED FROM:** Birmingham City, 01/07/2011

**DEBUT:** v Liverpool, A, 13/08/2011

**LAST MATCH:** v Chelsea, A, 21/05/2017

**MOVED TO:** Rejected new contract, 30/06/2017

**TEAMS:** IFK Eskilstuna, Arsenal, Birmingham City, Sunderland, Hull City, AIK Solna

**INTERNATIONAL:** Sweden

**SAFC TOTALS:** 174+29 appearances / 14 goals

**Seb Larsson won more international caps while with Sunderland than any other player. Fifty-nine of Seb's magnificent total of 133 caps for Sweden were won while he was on Wearside with half of his ten international goals also coming while he was a Sunderland player.**

He debuted against Turkey in Istanbul in February 2008, played all three of his country's games at Euro 2012 - scoring against France - and all four of the Swedes games at the 2018 FIFA World Cup in Russia, as well as all four at the delayed Euro 2020 tournament in which he captained his country before retiring from international football.

Having come to England as a youngster Larsson debuted for Arsenal in a League (Carling) Cup win at Manchester City on 27 October 2004. Almost a year to the day later Larsson made his first appearance of the following season in a victory in the same competition at Sunderland. After 7+5 games for the Gunners Seb signed for Birmingham following a loan at St Andrew's. Over five years Larsson played 171+34 games for Blues, scoring 25 times. The highlight of his time with the club was winning the League Cup in 2011, playing in the Wembley final against his former club Arsenal when he was a teammate of Craig Gardner on a day when Kevin Phillips was amongst Birmingham's unused subs (Nicklas Bendtner coming off the bench for Arsenal).

Having claimed two assists for Birmingham at Sunderland on the opening day of the 2010-11 season, on the first day of the 2011-12 campaign - after being lured by his former Birmingham boss Steve Bruce - Larsson marked his Sunderland debut with a spectacular volley at Liverpool. That was from open play but six of the 14 goals Seb would score for Sunderland came from direct free kicks. That is more than any other player is known to have scored for the club and came in an era when his former Birmingham colleague Gardner also took a lot of the set-pieces. Stoke, Peterborough, Everton, Spurs, Arsenal and Blackburn were the teams he scored free-kicks against.

A League (Capital One) Cup finalist for Sunderland in 2014, he was Player of the Year in the following season. Larsson sometimes divided opinion but the telling thing was that even if he was not having a good time Seb never hid. He always wanted the ball and kept showing for it even at times when some of his teammates appeared not to want possession. He was a model professional.

After leaving the club following relegation in 2017 he joined Hull City where he played 37+3 games scoring twice before returning to Sweden with Stockholm-based AIK. A league title winner in his first season Seb scored in the Champions League the following season against Ararat-Armenia and Maribor and also in the Europa League against Celtic. To the end of May 2022, Seb had scored 23 goals in 107+8 games for AIK. His father Svante played for and managed IFK Eskilstuna.

## LASLANDES, Lilian

**POSITION:** Centre-forward

**BIRTHPLACE:** Pauillac, France

**DATE OF BIRTH:** 04/09/1971

**HEIGHT:** 6' 1" **WEIGHT:** 13st 5lbs

**SIGNED FROM:** Girondins Bordeaux, 27/06/2001

**DEBUT:** v Ipswich Town, H, 18/08/2001

**LAST MATCH:** v Southampton, A, 15/12/2001

**MOVED TO:** OGC Nice, 09/07/2003

**TEAMS:** Pauillac, Merijnac, Saint-Seurin, AJ Auxerre, Girondins Bordeaux, Sunderland, FC Koln (L), SC Bastia (L), OGC Nice, Girondins Bordeaux, OGC Nice

**INTERNATIONAL:** France

**SAFC TOTALS:** 5+8 appearances / 1 goal

**Lilian Laslandes was one of the forwards signed to try and replace Niall Quinn. In France he had been the scorer of spectacular goals and in his fourth game for Sunderland as well as scoring in a League Cup tie at Sheffield Wednesday he was unlucky to see a spectacular acrobatic shot crash back off the bar.**

Had that gone in, maybe history might have been different, people might have viewed him more favourably and perhaps his confidence would have boomed. Instead, Lilian quickly looked like a fish out of water in a Sunderland shirt. Reportedly, he did not fit into the dressing room with the rest of Peter Reid's squad and by the first transfer window after his arrival the striker

went out on the first of two loans, before permanently moving on two years later after only a handful of games for Sunderland.

Capped seven times by France, he scored three times for his country. He was also a league title-winner twice in his home country and played in three cup finals. As Sunderland won promotion titles under Peter Reid in 1996 and 1999, Laslandes won the French League in those years with Auxerre and Bordeaux, scoring twelve and 15 league goals in those seasons.

He scored the winner in the 1996 Coupe de France final as Auxerre did the double, beating Nimes Olympique 2-1. That goal came in the 88th minute - the same moment he had entered the final two years earlier as Auxerre beat Montpellier 3-0. In 1998 Laslandes played the full match for Bordeaux as they lost on penalties (he did not take one) to PSG in the final of the Coupe de la Ligue. He played extensively in European competition, notable moments including a Champions League winner against Rangers for Auxerre and a red card against Manchester United while with Bordeaux, as well as both goals in a 2-1 UEFA Cup win at Celtic for Bordeaux a few months before signing for Sunderland.

Laslandes scored 48 times in 97+29 games for Auxerre and 45 in 120+8 appearances in his first spell with Bordeaux. He had started with ten in 33 appearances for Saint-Seurin. Later loaned from Sunderland, he failed to score in five games with Koln but bagged eight in 30 back in French football with Bastia. Leaving Sunderland for Nice in 2003 he returned a decent ten goals on 33 games followed by another four in 23 games for the same club. This was after a three-season stint back at Bordeaux where he added nine goals in 53 games to his first spell with the club. He did return yet again to Bordeaux after his retirement from football in 2008, but this time as a handball player.

## LATHAN, John George

**POSITION:** Centre-forward / midfielder

**BIRTHPLACE:** Southwick, Co Durham

**DATE OF BIRTH:** 12/04/1952

**HEIGHT:** 5' 7" **WEIGHT:** 11st 0lbs

**SIGNED FROM:** Trainee, 01/07/1967

**DEBUT:** v Leeds United, A, 19/11/1969

**LAST MATCH:** v Nottingham Forest, H, 24/11/1973

**MOVED TO:** Mansfield Town, 21/02/1974

**TEAMS:** Sunderland, Mansfield Town, Carlisle United, Barnsley (L), Portsmouth, Mansfield Town, Wollongong, Arcadia Shepherds, Mamelodi Sundowns

**SAFC TOTALS:** 48+14 appearances / 18 goals

**An FA Youth Cup winner in 1969, John Lathan made first-team appearances across five seasons, his best being the cup-winning campaign of 1972-73. During that season John played in a couple of games early in the cup run - indeed he had a potential winner disallowed for offside in the fourth round at home to Reading.**

As well as playing in the League Cup that term he scored seven league goals in 20+2 appearances and was leading scorer at the time Bob Stokoe took over before finding himself largely side-lined. The previous season he had scored a hat-trick against Portsmouth who later signed him.

In his last season at Sunderland Lathan scored both of Sunderland's goals in a pulsating 2-2 League Cup draw against Brian Clough's Derby County at the Baseball Ground but otherwise hardly played that season. He left in February 1974 in part exchange for midfielder Dennis Longhorn from Mansfield Town.

Playing as an attacking midfielder Lathan became a huge hero at Field Mill. A debut goal at Newport three days after joining the Stags got him off to a good start, but it was in his first full season that he really excelled. The only game he missed was the first of the campaign due to a suspension carried over from the year before. He proceeded to score nine of the Stags 100 goals as they stormed the Division Four title, the pick of his strikes being a 25-yard volley against Lincoln City and a 35-yarder that was his second of the game as Scunthorpe were beaten 7-0 on the day Mansfield sealed the title.

In February 1976 John was sold to Carlisle for the same £11,000 he had been valued at in the Longhorn deal but come August 1979, Mansfield paid Portsmouth £20,000 to take him back. At second-tier Carlisle he made his second appearance in a 2-2 draw at home to Sunderland (Ray Train a scorer shortly before his move to Roker Park) and went on to score eight goals in 59+8 games for the Cumbrians where he came under the management of Bob Moncur. After a loan to Barnsley (7/0) Lathan moved to Portsmouth. As with John's transfer from Sunderland to Mansfield it was part of a player exchange move with Dave Kemp leaving Pompey for Cumbria. Veteran Portsmouth journalist Pat Symes claims Portsmouth boss Jimmy Dickinson signed Lathan by accident thinking he was actually signing Phil Bonnyman who he had apparently confused with Lathan when scouting!

Nonetheless, Lathan played 62 times for Portsmouth and even captained the Fratton Park club scoring four times before his second spell at Mansfield. Eventually totalling 115+2 games and 16 goals for the Stags, Lathan began globe-trotting.

In 1981 he moved to Wollongong near Sydney in Australia where he became player/coach. A year later he moved to South Africa in a similar role with Arcadia Shepherds before coaching Witbank Aces, coaching and being a sports administrator at Wits University, coaching at Dynamoes of Johannesburg and becoming assistant head coach of Ajax of Cape Town.

After 20 years in South Africa Lathan moved to the USA. Initially he coached at Oakland University in Michigan before moving to New York in 2003 as a High School Sports coach before becoming coach of Manhattan Ajax Soccer Club a year later. Settling in New York, John was still living there in 2021. Regardless of his worldwide adventures John remained a 'Suddicker' at heart and was delighted to receive a joint award as Freeman of the City as one of the players who took part in the early rounds of the 1973 cup run.

## LAVERY, John

**POSITION:** Outside-left

**BIRTHPLACE:** Gateshead, Co Durham

**DATE OF BIRTH:** 31/10/1872 - 07/05/1918

**HEIGHT:** 5' 8" **WEIGHT:** 12st 7lbs

**SIGNED FROM:** Gateshead NER, 01/12/1897

**DEBUT:** v Blackburn Rovers, A, 25/12/1897

**LAST MATCH:** v Blackburn Rovers, A, 25/12/1897

**MOVED TO:** Burton Swifts, 01/08/1898

**TEAMS:** Gateshead NER, Sunderland, Burton Swifts, Gateshead NER, Hebburn Argyle, Gateshead NER

**SAFC TOTALS:** 1 appearance / 0 goals

**Lavery had been on the list of Sunderland players for some time before his solitary first-team game on Christmas Day 1897, according to the Christmas Eve Sunderland Echo.**

In 1898-99 after leaving Sunderland he missed just four out of 34 second division games for Burton Swifts as they finished 13th out of 18 clubs.

A well-known local runner, he won many prizes as a sprinter. John was a pupil teacher who played football at Hammersmith Catholic Training College. He later became a brewer's clerk.

## LAW, John Forsyth

**POSITION:** Outside-left

**BIRTHPLACE:** Maxwelltown, Dumfries & Galloway

**DATE OF BIRTH:** 07/02/1887 - 1956

**HEIGHT:** 5' 10" **WEIGHT:** 11st 0lbs

**SIGNED FROM:** Maxwelltown Volunteers, 07/04/1906

**DEBUT:** v Bolton Wanderers, A, 13/10/1906

**LAST MATCH:** v Bolton Wanderers, A, 13/10/1906

**MOVED TO:** Maxwelltown Volunteers, 15/10/1906

**TEAMS:** Maxwelltown Volunteers, Sunderland, Maxwelltown Volunteers, Rangers, Lincoln City, Gainsborough Trinity, Carlisle United, Rangers, Kilmarnock, Falkirk, Abercorn, Queen of the South

**SAFC TOTALS:** 1 appearance / 0 goals

**John Law's brief stint with Sunderland came after he impressed against Sunderland's second team (Sunderland 'A') on 7 April 1906 for Maxwelltown Volunteers, at which point he was immediately signed as an amateur. In his only game for Sunderland he had the tough task of standing in for the brilliant Arthur Bridgett.**

Having played for the 5th Regiment of the King's Own Borderers prior to playing for Maxwelltown, Law did not quite have the pedigree required for being thrust into a first division fixture. Maxwelltown was merged into the town of Dumfries just over two decades later with Law finishing his playing days in that town's team, Queen of the South.

He is known to have had trial games at Heart of Midlothian and Rangers before he played 19 games for Lincoln City in 1907 and nine, with one goal, the following year for second division Gainsborough Trinity.

He was at Carlisle in 1909-10 long before they were a Football League club but in a season where they lost to West Ham in an English (FA) Cup first round replay. At Kilmarnock he played twice in September 1912 while at Rangers his four first-team appearances commenced with an Old Firm derby at Celtic in October 1916.

***This player is believed to be John Forsyth Law, born 07/02/1887 in Maxwelltown. This person took over his father's business as innkeeper of the Globe Inn, Maxwelltown after WW1 and kept it until ill health caused him to retire in 1939. He passed away in 1956 in Dumfries.**

## LAWLEY, George Harry

**POSITION:** Winger

**BIRTHPLACE:** Kinver, Staffordshire

**DATE OF BIRTH:** 10/04/1903 - 07/04/1987

**HEIGHT:** 5' 5" **WEIGHT:** 11st 0lbs

**SIGNED FROM:** Dundee, 18/05/1929

**DEBUT:** v Derby County, A, 31/08/1929

**LAST MATCH:** v Blackpool, H, 27/09/1930

**MOVED TO:** Swindon Town, 15/05/1931

**TEAMS:** Talbot Steelworks, Darlaston, Bloxwich Strollers, Walsall, Burton Town, Merthyr Town, Dundee, Sunderland, Swindon Town, Worcester City, Shrewsbury Town, Brierley Hill Alliance, Dudley Town, Hednesford Town, Cannock Town, Nuneaton Town

**SAFC TOTALS:** 10 appearances / 1 goal

**George Lawley was a winger who played ten games in his two seasons at Sunderland, between a 1929 £350 move from Dundee and a move to Swindon Town in May 1931. Debuting at Derby on the opening day of the 1929-30 season Lawley was unlucky to see what looked a good goal disallowed for a contentious offside given against a teammate after both teams had lined up for the game to re-start with a kick-off.**

While that ended in defeat and the Newcastle Journal reported that, 'Lawley does not appear to be of the standard required for first division football", he kept his place the following week and claimed an assist as Sunderland scored four in the first 17 minutes as Manchester City were thrashed 5-2. It was a splendid way to mark the opening of the new Grandstand at Roker Park.

However, after a third game - and defeat at Burnley - brought a third successive negative review of George in the local press, Lawley was dropped. He got another game the following month, but then had to wait until the end of the season when he played in five of the final six games. Now playing on the left-flank as opposed to the right-wing he had played on earlier, he came back with a bang, scoring in a 6-0 win away to Liverpool on a day Bobby Gurney got four. He kept his place for all but one of the five remaining fixtures but there would be just one more opportunity for him the following season.

Having moved to Swindon Lawley scored four times in 28 games for the Robins in his sole season there of 1931-32. He spent the rest of his career in non-league, mostly around his native west midlands, at the same time working as an electrical contractor. Shrewsbury were a Birmingham League side when he played for them in 1933-34.

## LAWRENCE, James Hubert (Jamie)

**POSITION:** Outside-right

**BIRTHPLACE:** Balham, London

**DATE OF BIRTH:** 08/03/1970

**HEIGHT:** 5' 10" **WEIGHT:** 12st 3lbs

**SIGNED FROM:** Free agent, 15/10/1993

**DEBUT:** v Middlesbrough, A, 17/10/1993

**LAST MATCH:** v Bristol City, H, 12/02/1994

**MOVED TO:** Doncaster Rovers, 17/03/1994

**TEAMS:** Cowes Sports, Sunderland, Doncaster Rovers, Leicester City, Bradford City, Walsall, Wigan Athletic (L), Grimsby Town, Brentford, Fisher Athletic, Woking, Dulwich Hamlet, Worthing, Harrow Borough, Margate Town, Croydon, Ashford Town, Banstead Athletic, Cobham, Lingfield

**INTERNATIONAL:** Jamaica

**SAFC TOTALS:** 2+3 appearances / 0 goals

**Signed by Terry Butcher for a £10,000 signing-on fee after a reserve team run-out against Leeds, Lawrence had been released from Camp Hill Prison on the Isle of Wight six months earlier since when he had been on trial with Southend United and Millwall. Lawrence had served over half of a four-year sentence for robbery and as he made his debut at Ayresome Park, Middlesbrough's DJ thought it was funny to play 'Jailhouse Rock'.**

A hard-running direct winger, Lawrence was more noted for his hair-style than his football at Sunderland and soon moved on after Butcher was replaced by Mick Buxton. A Londoner, Jamie's troubles with the law began after his parents moved back to Jamaica when he was 17. Staying to pursue a football career, Lawrence reportedly ended up with two prison sentences before he earned a football contract.

Debuting for Doncaster as a sub in a home defeat to Wycombe, seven of his nine games in his first season at Rovers were off the bench. However after three goals in a total of 25 appearances he had done enough to earn a transfer to Premier League Leicester City under Mark McGhee. Relegated under the former Newcastle forward, the Foxes were promoted and won the League Cup in 1997 under Martin O'Neill with Lawrence coming on as an extra-time sub in the final against Middlesbrough in which he was a teammate of future Sunderland boss Simon Grayson. That was one of 26 substitute appearances Lawrence made for Leicester where after just 21 starts and a single goal he moved on to Bradford in search of more game-time.

A promotion-winner with Bradford, Jamie enjoyed the best spell of his career, playing 155 times over six years and scoring six times before a move to Walsall (22/1), a loan to Wigan (4/0) and a final league season with Brentford in 2004-05 (14/0). Lawrence prolonged his late-starting career for as long as possible with a long list of non-league outfits.

By his own admission, he struggled with drink and depression as his playing days came to an end, but after coaching Sutton United in 2014 (he had been player/coach at Fisher Athletic and Ashford Town) he took up a post as fitness coach to the Ghana national team. Working alongside Avram Grant he helped Ghana to the final of the African Cup of Nations which was lost to Ivory Coast.

Always aware of his own background, Lawrence has since worked in a school for disadvantaged children and also set up his own academy in Tooting as well as working as a personal fitness coach - numbering Ruben Loftus-Cheek amongst his clients.

## LAWRENCE, Liam

**POSITION:** Midfielder

**BIRTHPLACE:** Worksop, Nottinghamshire

**DATE OF BIRTH:** 14/12/1981

**HEIGHT:** 5' 11" **WEIGHT:** 12st 6lbs

**SIGNED FROM:** Mansfield Town, 30/06/2004

**DEBUT:** v Coventry City, A, 07/08/2004

**LAST MATCH:** v Norwich City, A, 04/11/2006

**MOVED TO:** Stoke City, 02/01/2007

**TEAMS:** Mansfield Town, Sunderland, Stoke City, Portsmouth, Cardiff City (L), PAOK Salonika, Barnsley, Shrewsbury Town, Bristol Rovers, Rushall Olympic

**INTERNATIONAL:** Republic of Ireland

**SAFC TOTALS:** 54+26 appearances / 9 goals

**One of the players brought in from lower league clubs as Mick McCarthy tried to assemble a promotion-challenging side in 2004, 'Lennie' (nicknamed after well-travelled manager Lennie Lawrence) was a stylish attacking player who scored several spectacular goals and always brought a touch of flair, if not pace, to the side.**

Lawrence became the first Sunderland player to win BBC TV's Match of the Day, Goal of the Month competition courtesy of a stunning left-foot volley from the edge of the penalty area in a 2-1 defeat at Fulham on 2 January 2006. A promotion winner in his first season, he could not be faulted for effort and commitment as the team were immediately relegated with a record low points tally in 2006 and he featured in a dozen league games early in 2006-07 as promotion was won again.

By the time promotion was secured however, he was long gone having joined Stoke (initially on loan) in November 2006, although he was a promotion winner again with the Potters a year later. Lawrence also won promotion with three other clubs: Mansfield in 2002, Shrewsbury in 2015 and Bristol Rovers in 2016.

With his first club Mansfield, Liam scored 40 goals in 135+18 games. At Stoke, his figures were 108+17/24. For Portsmouth, he totalled 55+3/8 and at Cardiff 14+1/1. In Greece with PAOK, where he was sent off in back-to-back appearances early in his continental adventure, he scored three times in 22+9 games. Back home with Barnsley there was one goal in 10+4 games while with the Shrews his figures were 49+13/6 and finally at Bristol Rovers he played 10+7 games and scored once, his last game on 7 January 2017 seeing him part of a 5-0 win over Northampton.

Qualifying through a Kerry-born grandfather, Liam won 15 caps for the Republic of Ireland, scoring against South Africa and Paraguay.

## LAWTHER, William Ian

**POSITION:** Centre-forward

**BIRTHPLACE:** Belfast, Northern Ireland

**DATE OF BIRTH:** 20/10/1939 - 25/04/2010

**HEIGHT:** 5' 11" **WEIGHT:** 11st 4lbs

**SIGNED FROM:** Crusaders, 06/03/1958

**DEBUT:** v Aston Villa, A, 31/08/1959

**LAST MATCH:** v Ipswich Town, A, 22/04/1961

**MOVED TO:** Blackburn Rovers, 26/07/1961

**TEAMS:** Crusaders, Sunderland, Blackburn Rovers, Scunthorpe United, Brentford, Halifax Town, Stockport County, Bangor City

**INTERNATIONAL:** Northern Ireland

**SAFC TOTALS:** 83 appearances / 44 goals

**Forty Four goals in two seasons at better than a goal per two games illustrates how well Ian Lawther did at Sunderland. He came from footballing stock. His brother Derek played for Glenavon while an uncle, Fred Roberts, had played for Ireland, Glentoran and Distillery, entering the record books with 96 goals in a season for Glentoran in 1930-31.**

Lawther's goals at Sunderland were not a flash in the pan. In total he scored 178 league goals in 577+21 games while he also scored Sunderland's first-ever goal in the League Cup. That came at Brentford, a club he later signed for in the Committee Room at the House of Commons where Bees chairman Jack Dunnett was the Labour MP for Nottingham Central.

Lawther could have been one of the Busby Babes. As a 15-year-old apprentice book binder he was taken to Manchester United for a month's trial but quickly returned to Belfast due to homesickness and began playing for Crusaders. Sunderland picked up a lot of young lads from Ireland in the late fifties and early sixties and persuaded Ian, then known locally as Billy, to come to Roker Park. Top scorer in both of his seasons on Wearside with 18 and 26 goals, an £18,000 fee took him to top-flight Blackburn Rovers at a time when SAFC upgraded the number nine position even more with the purchase of Brian Clough.

Replacing his fellow Northern Irishman Derek Dougan, who had just been sold to Aston Villa, 20 goals in Lawther's first season at Ewood Park included five in the FA Cup as Rovers reached the semi-final. The following year (1962-63), he scored at Sunderland in the fifth round of the League Cup but had played his last game for the club by mid-March, moving to Scunthorpe United for £12,000 after 32 goals in 75 appearances, many of which were as an inside, rather than centre-forward. Three goals in his first five games for the Iron augured well but there were just nine in total as Scunthorpe were relegated from the second division. By November of the following term Lawther had hit the goals trail at which point he made that switch to Brentford via the Houses of Parliament having tallied 23 goals in 67 games for Scunthorpe. However, by 1966, he had tasted relegation again and in the summer of 1968 signed for Halifax after 44 goals in 151+1 games for the Bees.

Playing under Alan Ball senior, Lawther helped Halifax to promotion in his first season Lawther missing just one game and scoring 14 times plus another in the FA Cup. He stayed at the Shay for three seasons before moving on to Stockport County after 27 goals in 98+14 games for Halifax in all competitions. Used as a midfielder by Stockport he scored 34 goals in 177+6 games over five seasons before finishing his career with Bangor. After retiring from football Ian ran a tailor's shop in Halifax before settling in Swindon. For Northern Ireland he won four full caps, the first two while with Sunderland.

## LE TALLEC, Anthony

**POSITION:** Forward

**BIRTHPLACE:** Hennebont, France

**DATE OF BIRTH:** 03/10/1984

**HEIGHT:** 6' 0½" **WEIGHT:** 12st 1lb

**SIGNED FROM:** Liverpool, 02/08/2005, on loan

**DEBUT:** v Manchester City, H, 23/08/2005

**LAST MATCH:** v Aston Villa, A, 07/05/2006

**MOVED TO:** Liverpool, 08/05/2006, end of loan

**TEAMS:** Le Havre, Liverpool, Sunderland (L), Le Havre (L), St Etienne (L), Sochaux (L), Le Mans, Auxerre, Valenciennes, Atromitos, Astra Giurgiu, Orleans, Annecy

**INTERNATIONAL:** France Under 21

**SAFC TOTALS:** 15+16 appearances / 5 goals

**Le Tallec was a talented player on loan from Liverpool in a struggling side headed for a record low points relegation. Evidently he was more used to being part of a team that had the ball for the bulk of the time, rather than being part of a side who had to fight and scrap to try and stay in games. Consequently he started only 15 times, more often being introduced as a sub. He did however manage to be top-scorer with a meagre five goals, three of them in the Premier League.**

The cousin of France international Florent Sinama-Pongolle who played for Liverpool and Atletico Madrid amongst many others in a global career, and brother of Damien Le Tallec who listed Borussia Dortmund, Red Star Belgrade and AEK Athens on his CV, Anthony made 13+19 appearances for Liverpool. He scored his only goal for the Reds in the UEFA Cup against Olimpija Ljubljana.

Sunderland were one of several clubs Liverpool loaned him to. Initially he was sent back to Le Havre who they had signed him from. Eighteen of his 25 appearances there were as sub. He scored five goals for Le Havre but did not play at all when loaned to St Etienne before his Sunderland experience.

He then joined Sochaux where in 2007 he came off the bench to score and then net again in a penalty shoot-out in the final of the Coupe de France as a Marseille team including Lorik Cana and Djibril Cisse were beaten. Le Tallec also scored four times in a dozen Ligue One games during that loan.

A final loan at Le Mans became a permanent deal and brought regular football with 20 goals in 98 appearances across three seasons, but after relegation he was transferred again. Moves to Auxerre, Valenciennes and Greek side Atromitos continued to see Anthony shine as he tallied 21+27/4, 24+12/7 and 37+16/13 for those clubs. Le Tallec then moved to Romania with Astra Giurgiu where he scored once in 18 games before returning to France with Orleans where he scored twice in 21 league and cup games. Retiring in 2021 he had completed his career with Annecy where he managed two goals in 17 games. He won four caps for France at Under 21 level and six in the Under 17 age group.

## LEADBITTER, Grant

**POSITION:** Midfielder

**BIRTHPLACE:** Fence Houses, Co Durham

**DATE OF BIRTH:** 07/01/1986

**HEIGHT:** 5' 9" **WEIGHT:** 11st 11lbs

**SIGNED FROM:** Trainee, 01/10/2000 and Middlesbrough, 29/01/2019

**DEBUT:** v Huddersfield Town, H 23/09/2003

**LAST MATCH:** v Lincoln City, H, 22/05/2021

**MOVED TO:** Ipswich Town, 01/09/2009 Released, 30/06/2021

**TEAMS:** Sunderland, Rotherham United (L), Ipswich Town, Middlesbrough, Sunderland

**INTERNATIONAL:** England Under 21

**SAFC TOTALS:** 138+72 appearances / 18 goals

**Grant started and ended his career at Sunderland, starting 69 games in each of his two spells, but making all but 18 of his 72 substitute appearances during his first stint. That figure made him Sunderland's most used substitute at the time he announced his retirement in September 2021. Always focussed on his football, Leadbitter had a fine career giving lengthy service to all three of his clubs.**

## LEADBITTER, Grant (Continued)

After making his first two appearances across two seasons in the League Cup for Sunderland, Leadbitter's league debut was handed to him by Mick Harford on loan at Rotherham in October 2005. He made 5+2 appearances for the Millers, scoring the first of a career total of 65 goals against Swansea. He impressed sufficiently on loan to earn a Premiership debut with SAFC at Charlton a fortnight before Christmas in 2005, after which he stayed in and around the first team although it was a tough time as relegation was suffered.

The following 2006-07 season saw Grant play in all but two league games as promotion was won. Only in his final season of 2020-21 when he played a total of 40 league games did he start more league games: 30. In both of these campaigns he scored his highest number of goals: seven. In 2020-21 these were mainly penalties while in 2006-07 long-distance shots were his forte, something he reprised with a screamer at Doncaster in 2020-21.

Having been a leading light in England youth teams from Under 16 onwards, Leadbitter took his caps total to 34 with three Under 21 honours in 2007-08. His debut at this level came on 16 November 2007 at MK Dons in a 2-0 win over Bulgaria when along with Adam Johnson he came off the bench. Lee Cattermole was in the starting line-up. Throughout youth football, Leadbitter and Cattermole had many a feisty encounter in Sunderland v Middlesbrough games long before Leadbitter became a Boro stalwart and Cattermole showed just as much passion in the colours of Sunderland.

Leadbitter played alongside Fraizer Campbell (and Johnson) when he won his second Under 21 cap against Poland at Molineux, again as a substitute before he got a deserved start on his final international appearance in a 2-0 win against Wales in Wrexham when again he lined-up alongside Cattermole and Johnson.

Poignantly, in October 2008, Leadbitter scored a trademark screamer against Arsenal at the Stadium of Light. His celebration saw him sprint to the technical area where he sank to his knees at the spot where his father's ashes had been buried a few weeks earlier.

In years to come, Grant would regularly been seen touching that spot while on the night of his very last game for Sunderland - a Play-Off game with Lincoln - long after the final whistle he could be observed in that technical area surveying the empty stadium and seemingly running through a life-time of football memories. Reputedly, he took a sizeable wage cut when leaving Middlesbrough to finish his career at Sunderland. If ever an all-time team was picked based on commitment to the cause, surely Grant Leadbitter would have to be in it.

Someone who appreciated commitment and professionalism as much as anyone was Roy Keane. Having managed Leadbitter at Sunderland, Keane signed Grant for Ipswich for a reported £2.65m. Grant went on to play 120+6 games for Ipswich where he scored 14 times and became captain. After three seasons in Suffolk he returned to the north east with Middlesbrough in 2012. He made 224+20 appearances for Boro where he scored 32 goals failing to celebrate the last of them as it was against Sunderland in a 3-3 Stadium of Light draw in February 2018.

Grant played much of his best football for Middlesbrough where he was Player of the Year in his first season. Two years later he was named in the PFA Championship Team of the Year. That season he played in the Play-Off final lost to Norwich at Wembley but in the following 2015-16 season won promotion to the Premier League.

There were three more Wembley appearances after returning to Sunderland, the 2019 Play-Off final against Charlton and twice in the Football League Trophy final. In 2019 against Portsmouth he had been substituted in extra-time or would surely have taken a penalty in the unsuccessful shoot-out, but he earned a winner's medal two years later against Tranmere Rovers. In June 2022 Grant commenced his first coaching role with Middlesbrough.

## LEE, Robert Gordon **(Bob)**

**POSITION:** Centre-forward

**BIRTHPLACE:** Melton Mowbray, Leicestershire

**DATE OF BIRTH:** 02/02/1953

**HEIGHT:** 6' 1½" **WEIGHT:** 12st 5lbs

**SIGNED FROM:** Leicester City, 30/09/1976

**DEBUT:** v Everton, H, 02/10/1976

**LAST MATCH:** v West Ham United, H, 31/10/1979

**MOVED TO:** Bristol Rovers, 10/08/1980

**TEAMS:** Leicester City, Doncaster Rovers (L), Sunderland, Bristol Rovers, Carlisle United, Southampton, Darlington, Hong Kong, Boston United

**SAFC TOTALS:** 114+8 appearances / 33 goals

**Sunderland's first £200,000 signing, Bob Lee had an ideal physique for a centre-forward, but perhaps was not aggressive enough to make the most of it. Nonetheless, he succeeded in managing a decent goals to games record in what was a struggling side.**

Manager Bob Stokoe resigned after Lee had played just three games. Shortly afterwards Lee showed what he was capable of with four goals in four games including a brace in a fog-hit 3-3 draw at Manchester United. Later in the season after a club record ten-game goal drought, Lee hit another purple patch registering five in three games including a hat-trick in a 6-1 win over West Ham, but although he finished as top scorer with 13 in 32+1 league games he could not stop Sunderland from going down. He was still around when promotion was won three seasons later but made just seven league appearances in that successful campaign when his only and final goal came back at his old club Leicester.

At Leicester he had scored 19 goals in 62+9 appearances and had been top-scorer with 15 in total the season before he came to Sunderland when the Foxes finished seventh in the top flight. At Filbert Street he had been a teammate of Steve Whitworth and Frank Worthington with the rumour being that Sunderland had initially approached Leicester for Worthington only to be persuaded to turn their attention to the 23-year-old Lee who had also had a loan to Doncaster in which he scored four goals in 16 games under Stan Anderson.

At Bristol Rovers Lee scored just twice in 19+4 league games before being signed again by Bob Stokoe at Carlisle. Playing up-front alongside Pop Robson, Lee scored ten goals in 40+1 games (also netting in both cups) as he helped the Cumbrians to promotion with a side that also included Jackie Ashurst, Trevor Swinburne and (very briefly) Jimmy Hamilton.

In Division Two the following season Lee scored just twice in 7+7 games, one of those coming in a home win over Newcastle United. After a total of 15 goals in 55+10 games Lee went south to join Southampton but did not get a game and returned to the north east to complete his league career with five appearances for Darlington early in the 1983-84 season. After a short spell playing in Hong Kong, Bob then joined Boston United for whom he played at Wembley in the FA Trophy final lost to Wealdstone in 1985.

In December 1984, whilst playing part-time for Boston, Lee became a publican in Loughborough.

## LEE, Thomas

**POSITION:** Left-half

**BIRTHPLACE:** Choppington, Northumberland

**DATE OF BIRTH:** 22/09/1872 - Q1 1955

**HEIGHT:** 5' 8' **WEIGHT:** 11st 7lbs

**SIGNED FROM:** Alnwick Town, 27/03/1897

**DEBUT:** v Everton, A, 11/04/1898

**LAST MATCH:** v Nottingham Forest, H, 23/04/1898

**MOVED TO:** Bristol Rovers, 07/06/1899

**TEAMS:** Alnwick Town, Sunderland, Bristol Rovers, South Shields Athletic, Hebburn Argyle, Millwall Athletic, Ashington

**SAFC TOTALS:** 2 appearances / 0 goals

**Signed after playing in a trial game on 27 March 1897, Lee was given opportunities in the last two games of the season. While this was his sum total at Sunderland, he added 22 Southern League appearances for Bristol Rovers and five further Southern League games for Millwall Athletic in 1902-03.**

He also played once in the London League and four times in the Western League for the Lions during the same season but did not make their FA Cup side that reached the semi-final. After retiring from football Lee became a pit deputy in his native north east. By the start of WW2, in the late stages of his working life, he was working underground as a colliery wasteman.

## LEMON, Paul Andrew

**POSITION:** Midfielder / forward

**BIRTHPLACE:** Middlesbrough, Yorkshire

**DATE OF BIRTH:** 03/06/1966

**HEIGHT:** 5' 10" **WEIGHT:** 11st 7lbs

**SIGNED FROM:** Middlesbrough Schoolboys, 01/01/1982

**DEBUT:** v Aston Villa, A, 01/12/1984

**LAST MATCH:** Coventry City, A, 24/01/1990

**MOVED TO:** Chesterfield, 05/11/1990, after two-month loan

**TEAMS:** Sunderland, Carlisle United (L), Walsall (L), Reading (L), Chesterfield, Tromso, Derry City, Telford United

**SAFC TOTALS:** 107+20 appearances / 19 goals

**Known as Jack after the American actor Jack Lemmon, Paul always saw himself as a forward where he had played his youth and reserve team football, but spent most of his time at first-team level at Sunderland on the right of midfield.**

Unfairly sometimes the butt of the crowd's frustration, Lemon could never be faulted for application. His best season came when the third tier was won in 1987-88 when only penalty king John MacPhail and the celebrated front two 'G-Force' of Eric Gates and Marco Gabbiadini scored more than Paul's dozen goals. Nine of those came in the league with it being Lemon's misfortune that the two best goals he scored in his Sunderland career came in a Football League (Sherpa Van) Trophy game at Scarborough that only a small gate witnessed.

Prior to signing for Sunderland, Lemon first appeared in the youth team four days before Christmas in 1981 as a 15-year-old schoolboy. He scored in an FA Youth Cup semi-final against Manchester United at Roker Park in April 1982. Three weeks after his first-team debut for Sunderland 'Jack' was loaned to Bob Stokoe's Carlisle United where he stood in for John Cooke and played alongside Jackie Ashurst in home defeats to Blackburn and his native Middlesbrough a day or two either side of Christmas. Lemon's other loans came much later. In the winter of 1989-90 he had temporary moves to Walsall and Reading. Paul's pair of games for the Saddlers were alongside Keith Bertschin while with the Royals his three games came under the management of Ian Porterfield.

A final loan to Chesterfield in September 1990 led to a transfer to the Spireites where he went on to play 80+5 league games scoring ten times before continuing his career in Norway, Ireland and finally in non-league. Following his early retirement due to a cruciate ligament knee injury, Paul worked in insurance and scouted for Huddersfield Town, Sheffield United, Wigan Athletic, Scunthorpe United and from October 2020 returned to Chesterfield, again in a scouting capacity.

## LENS, Jeremain Marciano

**POSITION:** Winger

**BIRTHPLACE:** Amsterdam, Netherlands

**DATE OF BIRTH:** 24/11/1987

**HEIGHT:** 5' 10" **WEIGHT:** 12st 5lbs

**SIGNED FROM:** Dynamo Kiev, 15/07/2015

**DEBUT:** v Leicester City, A, 08/08/2015

**LAST MATCH:** v Southampton, A, 27/08/2016

**MOVED TO:** Besiktas, 01/06/2018

**TEAMS:** AZ Alkmaar, NEC Nijmegen (L), PSV Eindhoven, Dynamo Kiev, Sunderland, Fenerbahce (L), Besiktas, Fatih Karagumruk (L) (to May 2022)

**INTERNATIONAL:** Netherlands

**SAFC TOTALS:** 16+8 appearances / 4 goals

**A most frustrating footballer at Sunderland, Jeremain Lens was signed for a reported £8m by Dick Advocaat who had previously managed his fellow Dutchman at PSV Eindhoven. Advocaat's plan was to sign five top-class players of which Lens was intended to be the first, but when he was unable to sign further players of similar calibre Lens was to some extent like a fish out of water.**

He was used to being in teams that dominated. In the season before coming to Sunderland he had done the double in Ukraine with Dynamo Kiev, whilst he had also been a league winner with AZ and a cup winner with PSV. At Sunderland though he had to work without the ball and not simply wait to be given possession so he could unlock packed defences. The required increase in work-rate did not come easily to him. On one occasion in a behind closed doors friendly with Middlesbrough at the Stadium of Light, I watched the game with Grant Leadbitter - then of Boro - and Jonathan Woodgate the former Real Madrid and England defender. 'Who's that?' asked Woodgate of Lens after a few minutes. When told, his response is best unprinted, but suffice to say as a professional he was distinctly unimpressed with the Dutchman's lack of application. Lens was seemingly more animated when demonstrating his newly-acquired Rolls-Royce at the training ground.

Lens could certainly play. With almost his final kick in a Sunderland shirt he scored with a perfectly executed free-kick in a friendly at Hartlepool, while in perhaps his best game for Sunderland, he scored with an exquisitely flighted lob against West Ham only to then go on and be sent off in the same game.

A scorer on his international debut against Ukraine in August 2010, he starred at the 2014 FIFA World Cup playing as a sub in a 5-1 win over Spain who had beaten the Netherlands in the previous tournament's final. He then came off the bench as Australia were beaten and started as Chile were defeated. A fourth appearance followed as a sub when Costa Rica were beaten in the quarter-final, but he did not appear against Argentina or Brazil in the semi-final or third-place match. In total, Lens played 34 times for the Netherlands, scoring eight goals.

After moving around between VVA Spartaan, Ajax and Omnworld in his youth career, Lens made his senior debut for AZ in 2005-06, going on to score 13 times in 55 league games before joining PSV having also had a season-long loan to NEC in 2007-08 when he scored nine times in 31 appearances. At PSV he scored 13 times in 2010-11 including two in a sensational 10-0 win over rivals Feyenoord. He also netted the winner in a Europa League win at Rangers.

After 21 goals - including four at international level - in 2012-13, he moved to Dynamo Kiev where again he was in a successful side. His first two goals came in a 9-1 win over Metalurh Donetsk. Later that season it was another Donetsk side, Shaktar, who Lens played against in the Ukrainian cup final which his side won 2-1. He played against the same team in the following year's final which Kiev won on penalties, although Lens stepped up for none of their seven spot-kicks in a season where they also won the league.

While he was still contracted to Sunderland, he moved to Turkey on a season-long loan to Fenerbahce in 2016-17, scoring in a 2-1 Europa League win over Manchester United, one of five goals he scored in 30+1 appearances. A subsequent loan to Besiktas became a permanent move. After 61+29 games and eight goals including a Champions League appearance against Bayern Munich Lens moved to Fatih Karagumruk on loan in February 2021, debuting at Basaksehir where his teammates included Fabio Borini. Lens played 7+9 games scoring three goals.

## LEONARD, James (Jimmy)

**POSITION:** Inside-left

**BIRTHPLACE:** Inkerman, Paisley, Renfrewshire

**DATE OF BIRTH:** 07/10/1904 - 01/09/1959

**HEIGHT:** 5' 6" **WEIGHT:** 11st 0lbs

**SIGNED FROM:** Cowdenbeath, 01/10/1930

**DEBUT:** v Leeds United, A, 04/10/1930

**LAST MATCH:** v Portsmouth, H, 20/02/1932

**MOVED TO:** Released, 01/04/1932

**TEAMS:** Saltcoats Victoria, Cowdenbeath, Indiana Flooring, Cowdenbeath, New York Nationals, Cowdenbeath, Sunderland, Rhyl Athletic (L), Colwyn Bay United (L), Greenock Morton, Shelbourne, Dolphin FC (Dublin)

**SAFC TOTALS:** 42 appearances / 21 goals

**'Hookey' Leonard was so nicknamed because of his ability to hook the ball away from opponents. His goal per two games record was even better in his first season at Sunderland when he scored 17 times in 26 top-flight fixtures starting with a debut goal at Leeds and hat-tricks in 6-1 and 8-2 home wins over West Ham and Blackburn Rovers.**

He played far fewer games the following season, but despite scoring in a 5-1 win over Portsmouth it proved to be his final game as he left the club afterwards due to what was described as 'various breaches of discipline'.

Leonard was in his prime when he signed for Sunderland in the week of his 26th birthday. He came from the last of his three stints with Cowdenbeath having won promotion with them in his initial spell. He had also experienced football in the USA having played in New York with Indiana Flooring and New York Nationals. His family settled in the USA in later years.

After being put on the transfer list in May 1931 he failed to attract a league club so spent three months on loan at Rhyl Athletic followed by a week-long loan at Colwyn Bay in November 1931 before Sunderland recalled him as they desperately sought points to move out of a relegation position. When he later signed for Morton Sunderland received £500 as they still retained his registration. After retiring from football Leonard worked as a steel erector.

# L

## LESCOTT, Joleon Patrick

**POSITION:** Centre-back

**BIRTHPLACE:** Quinton, Birmingham,West Midlands

**DATE OF BIRTH:** 16/08/1982

**HEIGHT:** 6' 3" **WEIGHT:** 13st 0lbs

**SIGNED FROM:** Free agent, 24/01/2017

**DEBUT:** v Crystal Palace, A, 04/02/2017

**LAST MATCH:** v Chelsea, A, 21/05/2017

**MOVED TO:** Contract not renewed, 30/06/2017

**TEAMS:** Wolves, Everton, Manchester City, WBA, Aston Villa, AEK Athens, Sunderland

**INTERNATIONAL:** England

**SAFC TOTALS:** 1+1 appearances / 0 goals

**Signed by his former Everton manager David Moyes at a time when the club were making staff redundant, Lescott came on as a sub at Crystal Palace when Sunderland were already 4-0 up on a rare bright day in a dismal season. He made his only other appearance on the final day of the campaign in a 5-1 defeat at Chelsea after relegation had already been confirmed, after which he was released.**

Lescott had been a good player in his time, winning 26 England caps including playing against France on Jordan Henderson's debut and against Ghana when Danny Welbeck debuted while on loan to Sunderland, (when Ghana included three players with Sunderland connections in Sulley Muntari, John Mensah and goalscorer Asamoah Gyan). Lescott also played four times at the 2012 European Championships, scoring in a draw with France.

After playing for Grinham Giants as a boy Lescott joined Wolves where he was Player of the Year in 2005-06. Joleon scored 13 goals in 228+7 games for the Molineux club, winning promotion in 2003. At Everton, he won Player of the Year awards in 2006-07 and 2007-08 and scored 17 goals in 138+5 games, including the 2009 FA Cup final as David Moyes' side lost to Chelsea with Steven Pienaar, Louis Saha and James Vaughan appearing for the Toffees.

Moving on to Manchester City, Lescott won the Premier League in 2012 and 2014 playing a total of 142+18 times, netting nine goals. He was also an unused sub in the 2014 League (Capital One) Cup final against Sunderland.

At West Brom there were 39 appearances and one goal, followed by 31 games and again a single goal for Villa in a season (2015-16) where they finished rock bottom of the Premier League suffering the ignominy of the following description "...there is little question Lescott stands as Villa's worst-ever signing in 127 seasons of football" by the Villa website avfchistory.co.uk.

After this, a spell with AEK Athens brought just four appearances and a detached cartilage in his knee after which his contract was terminated in November 2016 following a dispute with the club. It was at this point that Moyes brought him to Sunderland. Lescott certainly does not qualify for the harsh assessment made of a talented player by that Villa website, but his contribution at Sunderland was negligible and a sad end to an excellent career.

Since retiring, Joleon has worked in the media as a pundit.

## LESLIE, James (Jimmy)

**POSITION:** Forward

**BIRTHPLACE:** Barrhead, Glasgow, Lanarkshire

**DATE OF BIRTH:** 21/08/1873 - 11/09/1920

**HEIGHT:** 5' 7" **WEIGHT:** 11st 7lbs

**SIGNED FROM:** Bolton Wanderers, 07/05/1897

**DEBUT:** v Wednesday, A, 04/09/1897

**LAST MATCH:** v Everton, A, 06/04/1901

**MOVED TO:** Middlesbrough, 01/05/1901

**TEAMS:** Clyde, Bolton Wanderers, Sunderland, Middlesbrough, Clyde, Arthurlie

**SAFC TOTALS:** 98 appearances / 29 goals

**The scorer of the first goal at Roker Park, against Liverpool on 10 September 1898, Leslie had signed league forms with Bolton Wanderers 18 months before joining Sunderland, but for domestic reasons never moved to Bolton. During this time he continued to play for Clyde, but technically Sunderland signed him from Bolton as they held his Football League registration.**

Leslie was the illegitimate son of an unmarried bleachfield worker. He went to work in the same industry (calico works) as his mother at a young age. Football then helped him to better himself as he joined Clyde in 1894.

He married back in Barrhead on 10 November 1898 (hence why he was missing for Sunderland's game 48 hours later), but his wife died less than 20 months later aged only 25. He moved in with a family a few doors down the street in Fulwell in Sunderland and remained as their lodger until he died aged only 47. Former colleagues Harry Low, Donald Gow and William Dunlop were three of the pall bearers at Mere Knolls Cemetery.

In his first three seasons at Sunderland Leslie played 30, 30 and 32 games, scoring 9, 11 and 7 goals before moving to Middlesbrough. His season on Teesside followed the same pattern as his fourth and final year on Wearside as he rarely played. Having debuted against West Brom in October 1901 he waited until February for a second appearance which he marked with a goal in a 7-2 thrashing of Barnsley.

Another goal next time out in a 5-0 win bought him a run of a further four consecutive appearances during which he scored one more, but that would be the sum total of his time in the second division before he returned to Clyde, only to soon return to live on Wearside. He was a barman after retiring from playing football and during the Great War, served in France.

## LEWIS, Albert Edward Talbot (Tal)

**POSITION:** Goalkeeper

**BIRTHPLACE:** Bedminster, Somerset

**DATE OF BIRTH:** 20/01/1877 - 22/02/1956

**HEIGHT:** 6' 1" **WEIGHT:** 13st 0lbs

**SIGNED FROM:** Sheffield United, 30/05/1904

**DEBUT:** v Preston North End, A, 03/09/1904

**LAST MATCH:** v Wolverhampton Wanderers, A, 17/09/1904

**MOVED TO:** Luton Town, 25/05/1905

**TEAMS:** Bedminster, Bristol City, Everton, Walsall, Sheffield United, Sunderland, Luton Town, Leicester Fosse, Bristol City

**SAFC TOTALS:** 4 appearances / 0 goals

**Sporting a fabulous moustache, 'Tal' Lewis was the epitome of the all-round sportsman of the early 20th century. Although he was a goalkeeper with Sunderland, he had played as a full-back with Bristol City and Everton (although he made no first-team appearances for the Toffees), while he was also a first class cricketer who played 208 games for Somerset between 1899 and 1914. For good measure he also developed into a billiards player of some repute becoming champion of Bristol in the mid 1920s.**

Lewis signed for Sunderland in a double deal from Sheffield United along with forward Alf Common, later to be the world's first £1,000 footballer. Clearly leading a busy life as he was simultaneously playing cricket in the summer for Somerset, 'Tal' was also a partner in, and manager of, Mettam and Lewis athlete outfitters shop in Taunton at the time of his transfer to Sunderland.

Unluckily for Lewis, in the month of his SAFC debut he suffered a knee cartilage injury which required an operation and ruled him out of the rest of the season. With Sheffield United he competed for a place in goal with the celebrated 24-stone Fatty Foulkes, making two of his 15 appearances for the Blades against Sunderland at Roker Park meaning that he played against Sunderland at Roker as many times as he played for them at home.

At cricket he scored nine first-class centuries with a best of 201 not out against Kent in 1909. An all-rounder, he also took over 500 wickets, once taking 14 in a match with Warwickshire which included a best of 8 for 103. In 1920 he went to India as a cricket coach.

## LIDDLE, Michael William

**POSITION:** Left-back

**BIRTHPLACE:** Hounslow, London

**DATE OF BIRTH:** 25/12/1989

**HEIGHT:** 5' 8" **WEIGHT:** 10st 10lbs

**SIGNED FROM:** Trainee, 01/07/2006

**DEBUT:** v Barrow, H, 02/01/2010

**LAST MATCH:** v Barrow, H, 02/01/2010

**MOVED TO:** Accrington Stanley, 18/07/2012 after a loan spell from 24/02/2012

**TEAMS:** Sunderland, Carlisle United (L), Leyton Orient (L), Gateshead (L), Accrington Stanley, Blyth Spartans, Darlington, Blyth Spartans

**INTERNATIONAL:** Republic of Ireland Under 21

**SAFC TOTALS:** 0+1 appearances / 0 goals

**Liddle's lone appearance came as a result of a very public pitch-side coin toss as manager Steve Bruce took this novel way of deciding whether a debut would go to Michael or fellow youngster Adam Reed in a cup tie with then non-league Barrow. Liddle called right and therefore got eight minutes of first-team action and inclusion in this book while Reed never got a first-team game for Sunderland.**

Liddle was a talented player who came through the Under 18 side who reached the FA Youth Cup semi-final in 2008. Qualifying via his Irish mother, he won Under 18 and Under 21 caps for the Republic. Prior to his Sunderland debut Liddle played 23 times on loan for Carlisle (all but one of those as starts). The season after his Sunderland appearance saw him make a single League One appearance for Leyton Orient at Yeovil before 23 Blue Square Premier starts for Gateshead, his only goal coming on his debut against Kidderminster almost exactly a year after his Sunderland bow.

He returned to the Football League when joining Accrington Stanley after an initial loan. Liddle went on to play 73+16 times for Stanley without scoring. Never the same player after injuries suffered early in his career, Michael spent the latter years of his career back in the north east in non-league football.

## LILLEY, Thomas (Tom)

**POSITION:** Left-back

**BIRTHPLACE:** Newbottle, Co Durham

**DATE OF BIRTH:** 13/12/1899 - Q4 1964

**HEIGHT:** 5' 10½" **WEIGHT:** 12st 0lbs

**SIGNED FROM:** Hartlepools United, 07/05/1926

**DEBUT:** v Portsmouth, H, 27/08/1927

**LAST MATCH:** v Portsmouth, H, 27/08/1927

**MOVED TO:** St. Mirren, 07/08/1928

**TEAMS:** Methley Perseverance, Huddersfield Town, Nelson, Hartlepools United, Sunderland, St. Mirren, Fulham, Annfield Plain, Herrington Colliery Welfare, Shiney Row Swifts, Sunderland District Omnibus Company

**SAFC TOTALS:** 1 appearance / 0 goals

**Lilley played three games for Huddersfield and twelve for Nelson who were then a Football League outfit. He then came to Hartlepools for whom he debuted against Rochdale in August 1924 only to break his collar bone twice. The first occasion came on only his seventh outing with the repeat coming against Bradford Park Avenue less than a month after his return.**

Thankfully he made a full recovery and in the next 1925-26 season became only the second player to be ever-present in a Football League campaign for Pools at which point Sunderland stepped in with a £750 fee after Lilley had made 63 appearances for the club. £350 of that investment was recouped when he moved on to St Mirren after just one first-team game in a year otherwise spent as a reserve. In Scotland, he scored seven times in 62 league games over two seasons before Fulham paid £350 for him. After playing in the opening six games of the Division Three South season Tom played just once more. He returned to the north east to captain Annfield Plain after which he remained in local football, becoming a colliery storeman after retiring from football.

## LINDSAY, Albert Fowler

**POSITION:** Goalkeeper

**BIRTHPLACE:** Stranton, Co Durham

**DATE OF BIRTH:** 26/09/1881 - 20/02/1961

**HEIGHT:** 5' 8" **WEIGHT:** 11st 0lbs

**SIGNED FROM:** West Hartlepool, 14/06/1902

**DEBUT:** v Notts County, H, 04/04/1903

**LAST MATCH:** v Bury, A, 26/09/1903

**MOVED TO:** Luton Town, 31/05/1904

**TEAMS:** Hartlepool Park Villa, Hartlepool St James's, West Hartlepool, Sunderland, Luton Town, Glossop North End, Sunderland Royal Rovers

**SAFC TOTALS:** 3 appearances / 0 goals

**Originally a centre-half with his first two clubs, Lindsay became a goalkeeper with West Hartlepool where he attracted Sunderland's attention. A shipyard labourer both before and after his time in football, he came into the side when Sunderland were defending league champions, but standing in for Teddy Doig was always going to be a tough challenge as the Scots keeper was so strongly established.**

Sunderland won two of Albert's three games, the keeper apparently making a tremendous save from John Carlin of Liverpool in his second match. A 3-1 defeat was suffered on his final outing away to Bury who had scored six in winning the previous season's English (FA) Cup final and other than a change of keeper, fielded their cup final side against the Lads.

Lindsay got his wish for regular first-team football after joining Luton where he made 33 Southern League appearances in 1904-05, but after losing his place, added two more Football league appearances in the second division for Glossop.

## LINDSAY, David

**POSITION:** Right-back

**BIRTHPLACE:** Cambuslang, Lanarkshire

**DATE OF BIRTH:** 29/06/1922 - 19/04/1987

**HEIGHT:** 5' 10" **WEIGHT:** 11st 9lbs

**SIGNED FROM:** Blantyre Victoria, 01/08/1946

**DEBUT:** v Preston North End, A, 05/04/1947

**LAST MATCH:** v Preston North End, A, 05/04/1947

**MOVED TO:** Southend United, 06/05/1948

**TEAMS:** Blantyre Victoria, Sunderland, Southend United, Yeovil Town

**SAFC TOTALS:** 1 appearance / 0 goals

**David Lindsay was unfortunate in that despite having what the local press described as, 'a first class debut' on a saturated pitch in a match played in torrential rain, he never got another opportunity.**

He moved on to Southend where he played in the FA Cup and made 52 appearances in Division Three South (scoring once) before joining Yeovil Town a couple of years after the Glovers had famously knocked Sunderland out of the FA Cup. In March 1952, only months after joining Yeovil, David suffered a badly broken right leg against Bedford Town and spent at least a week in hospital. This appears to have led to his retirement from football.

## LIVINGSTONE, George Turner

**POSITION:** Inside-left / outside-left

**BIRTHPLACE:** Dumbarton, Dunbartonshire

**DATE OF BIRTH:** 05/05/1876 - 15/01/1950

**HEIGHT:** 5' 9½" **WEIGHT:** 11st 7lbs

**SIGNED FROM:** Hearts, 30/06/1900

**DEBUT:** v Notts County, A, 01/09/1900

**LAST MATCH:** v Newcastle United, A 24/04/1901

**MOVED TO:** Celtic, 02/05/1901

**TEAMS:** Sinclair Swifts, Artizan Thistle, Parkhead FC, Dumbarton, Hearts, Sunderland, Celtic, Liverpool, Manchester City, Rangers, Manchester United

**INTERNATIONAL:** Scotland

**SAFC TOTALS:** 31 appearances / 12 goals

**The second man to play for both Celtic and Rangers, George Livingstone also played for both Manchester clubs, debuted for Scotland in the Ibrox disaster game of 1902, won the English (FA) Cup, played in the equivalent Scottish final, became a manager, and during World War One saw service in East Africa in the Royal Medical Corps. Combined with running a plumbing and gas fitting business during his football career, it was certainly a full life.**

Before coming to Sunderland he went to Everton but as he never played a game for the Toffees he was registered as a Sunderland player at the Football League meeting of 30 June 1900. A note in Everton's minute books reveals that on 23 May 1899 they resolved to bid £250 for the player but never actually did. He spent just one season at Sunderland, top-scoring as Sunderland were runners-up following his £175 transfer from Hearts. He had debuted for the Edinburgh club on 19 September 1896, going on to score 26 times in 50 appearances.

Having returned to Scotland from Sunderland when signing for Celtic, where he was known as Geordie, Livingstone debuted in a 1-0 win over Rangers in the Charity Cup a day after arriving at Parkhead. A Rangers supporter, he was to play two Old Firm games against them in the league and also played in an Inner-city League Match when he scored four times in a 5-1 victory. He scored hat-tricks against St Mirren in both league and cup. He also played for Celtic in the 1902 Scottish Cup final against Hibs when he hit the post as his side lost 1-0.

It was while he was with Celtic that Livingstone debuted for Scotland on 5 April 1902. It was a day of disaster as 26 people died and over 500 were injured when part of a newly-built stand collapsed at a game that featured Ted Doig as one of Livingstone's teammates and Billy Hogg amongst his opponents. He did subsequently win two official caps in 1906 and 1907 as well as representing the Scottish League.

The month after the Ibrox disaster he joined Liverpool for £600 and marked his debut with a goal against Blackburn Rovers on the first day of the following season. However, after just three more in 32 games he was transferred to Manchester City after one season at Anfield. 20 goals in 88 games for City over three seasons brought an English (FA) Cup winner's medal in 1904 when he set up the winning goal for Billy Meredith against Bolton.

Following a £100 fine and issuing of a lengthy suspension by the FA for receiving illegal payments, November 1906 brought a return to Glasgow, but this time with Rangers. He scored 23 goals in 53 games, but none of these came in nine appearances against Celtic in which the only victory he tasted came in a Glasgow Merchants Cup game. He did manage four in a game for the Gers against Partick Thistle but failed to win any silverware and having played for both sides of the Old Firm, played for Liverpool and almost played for Everton, the former Manchester City man returned to Manchester to end his playing career with United.

# L

## LIVINGSTONE, George (Continued)

Sensationally, he debuted with a double goal blast in a 3-1 win over City on 23 January 1909 but there were just two other goals in a total of 46 appearances over six seasons. He is the only player to score for both Manchester clubs as well as Celtic and Rangers.

Known as the dressing-room joker wherever he went, after World War One, Livingstone became manager of Dumbarton winning his first game in March 1919 against Hamilton and going on to take charge of 46 fixtures ending with a defeat by Greenock Morton 13 months later. There was then a brief spell managing Clydebank before, in the summer of 1920, he began a seven-year stint as trainer at Rangers followed by a further seven years as trainer at Bradford City.

Livingstone's elder brother Archie was also a footballer, playing over 100 games for Burnley (with whom he won promotion in 1898) and Norwich, as well as playing for numerous other clubs.

## LLOYD, Thomas

**POSITION:** Full-back

**BIRTHPLACE:** Wednesbury, Staffordshire

**DATE OF BIRTH:** 17/11/1903 - 20/01/1984

**HEIGHT:** 5' 9½" **WEIGHT:** 12st 0lbs

**SIGNED FROM:** Willenhall, 09/02/1925

**DEBUT:** v Leicester City, H, 27/03/1926

**LAST MATCH:** v Wednesday, A, 19/02/1927

**MOVED TO:** Bradford Park Avenue, 10/05/1927

**TEAMS:** Walsall, Willenhall, Sunderland, Bradford Park Avenue, Burton Town

**SAFC TOTALS:** 4 appearances / 0 goals

**Lloyd signed for Walsall in August 1922, made his Football League debut against Rochdale in February 1924 and, after a short spell with Birmingham League club Willenhall, joined SAFC in February 1925.**

After a year establishing himself on Wearside Tommy was called upon for the first time in March 1926 when he deputised for Ernie England. "His head and footwork was good and he is not shy of a tackle" reported the Newcastle Daily Chronicle as Lloyd impressed in a comfortable 3-0 home win over Leicester City.

Four days later he got another chance, but was swiftly replaced by England after a 3-1 home loss to Cardiff City. Lloyd had to wait until New Year's Day 1927 for a further opportunity, but playing in a 5-2 home defeat to lowly Blackburn Rovers failed to help his cause, especially as up to then Sunderland were undefeated at home having dropped only two points at Roker Park all season. Lloyd was to get just one more game in an unfamiliar right-back berth at (Sheffield) Wednesday in February, albeit all five of his league games for Walsall had been at right-back. Losing 4-1 at Hillsborough however meant that twelve goals had been conceded in the last three games he had played for Sunderland and consequently he did not play for the first-team again.

At the end of the season he left to join Bradford Park Avenue for whom he gave a decade's service playing 345 league and cup games, scoring a creditable 22 times. After helping Bradford PA to win Division Three North in 1928 he played the remainder of his league career in the second division, barely missing a game in 1929-30 or 1931-32 in an era when the Avenue only finished outside the top six once in the first six seasons after promotion.

At the age of 34 Lloyd became player-manager of Burton Town for the 1937-38 season but only lasted in the role until February 1938. He then became a silk packer with Courtaulds in Nuneaton as well as a qualified masseur.

## LLOYD, William Stanley

**POSITION:** Inside-forward

**BIRTHPLACE:** Thornley, West Auckland, Co Durham

**DATE OF BIRTH:** 01/10/1924 - 06/07/2011

**HEIGHT:** 5' 6" **WEIGHT:** 10st 6lbs

**SIGNED FROM:** Silksworth Juniors, 01/08/1941

**DEBUT:** v Derby County, H, 31/08/1946

**LAST MATCH:** v Manchester United, H, 18/10/1947

**MOVED TO:** Grimsby Town, 05/08/1948

**TEAMS:** Silksworth Juniors, Sunderland, Grimsby Town, Worksop Town, Scunthorpe & Lindsey United, Spalding United, Alford United

**INTERNATIONAL:** England schools

**SAFC TOTALS:** 24 appearances / 5 goals

**Signed initially as an amateur straight from school, Lloyd had been capped at schoolboy level against Scotland, Wales and Ireland shortly before World War Two, during which he served in the Royal Navy.**

He made his official debut in the first league game after the war having made eleven war-time appearances beginning with a game at Gateshead in March 1943, scoring in an 8-0 win over Middlesbrough on his home debut a week later, one of three he had netted in war-time. In peace-time, he also scored on his second appearance and played almost half the league fixtures in the first post war league campaign.

At Grimsby he scored 23 goals in 148 league games, often operating as a winger rather than as inside-forward as at Sunderland. He added a single further league appearance with Scunthorpe after a season with Worksop in 1953-54. In 1956, he became player/manager of Alford Town, remaining in charge of the club until 1962.

## LOCKIE, Alexander James (Alec)

**POSITION:** Centre-half

**BIRTHPLACE:** South Shields, Co Durham

**DATE OF BIRTH:** 11/04/1915 - 23/03/1974

**HEIGHT:** 5' 10" **WEIGHT:** 11st 7lbs

**SIGNED FROM:** South Shields St Andrews, 27/08/1935

**DEBUT:** v Manchester City, H, 14/04/1937

**LAST MATCH:** v Birmingham City, A, 13/02/1946

**MOVED TO:** Notts County, 12/09/1946

**TEAMS:** South Shields YMCA, South Shields, Reyrolles, St Andrew's, Sunderland, North Shields (WW2 Guest), Newcastle United (WW2 Guest), Notts County, Horden CW

**SAFC TOTALS:** 50 appearances / 1 goal

**Having broken into the team in the cup-winning season of 1936-37 and played nine games the following year, Lockie's career was interrupted by World War Two. In early September 1939 he returned to Reyrolles, where he had served his apprenticeship as an electrical engineering draughtsman. At the time Sunderland signed him from South Shields St Andrews he was working at Reyrolles and playing for them along with St Andrews.**

He signed professional forms with Sunderland, but continued to work to complete his apprenticeship until summer 1938.

Alec established himself in the final full post-war campaign playing 33 times and scoring his only official goal. When football resumed after the war he played in all six FA Cup games in 1945-46 but departed before the Football League resumed the following year. He had also played in two of the three games from the 1939-40 season that was expunged from official records as well as appearing in 170 war-time games in which he scored three times.

He also found time to play for North Shields during the war as well as making a single appearance for Newcastle United at York City on 23 November 1940 while he was working as an electrical engineering draughtsman on the Tyne. He also made 26 peace-time appearances for the Magpies - but those of the Notts County variety.

## LOGAN, Henry Morrison

**POSITION:** Inside-right

**BIRTHPLACE:** Shettleston, Glasgow, Lanarkshire

**DATE OF BIRTH:** 10/05/1886 - 04/02/1963

**HEIGHT:** 5' 7" **WEIGHT:** 10st 0lbs

**SIGNED FROM:** Shettleston, 30/06/1909

**DEBUT:** v Chelsea, H, 30/10/1909

**LAST MATCH:** v Bradford Park Avenue, H, 05/02/1910

**MOVED TO:** Arsenal, 28/06/1910

**TEAMS:** Cathcart Windsor, Myrtle XI, Glasgow Benburb, Shettleston, Sunderland, Arsenal

**INTERNATIONAL:** Scotland Junior

**SAFC TOTALS:** 2 appearances / 0 goals

**In addition to his pair of appearances for Sunderland, Logan played in eleven top-flight games for Woolwich Arsenal in 1910-11, dropping out of the team just before their home game with SAFC and returning in the first league match after their visit to Roker Park.**

A clerk in the Ministry of Labour, he died on a visit to two of his brothers in South Africa when he was 76. His brother William played for Vale of Leven and made seven Southern League appearances as a full-back for QPR in 1909 while another brother, James, played for Bury and Southend United between 1919 and 1921.

## LOGAN, James (Jimmy)

**POSITION:** Winger

**BIRTHPLACE:** Troon, Ayrshire

**DATE OF BIRTH:** 24/06/1870 - 25/05/1896

**HEIGHT:** 5' 8" **WEIGHT:** 11st 4lbs

**SIGNED FROM:** Ayr FC, 08/08/1891

**DEBUT:** v Preston North End, A, 12/09/1891

**LAST MATCH:** v West Bromwich Albion, A, 17/10/1891

**MOVED TO:** Ayr FC, 16/11/1891

**TEAMS:** Ayr FC, Sunderland, Ayr FC, Aston Villa, Notts County, Dundee, Newcastle United, Loughborough Town

**INTERNATIONAL:** Scotland

**SAFC TOTALS:** 2 appearances / 0 goals

**The scorer of a hat-trick in the 1894 English (FA) Cup final for Notts County against Bolton Wanderers at Goodison Park, Scotland international James Logan died just two years later of pneumonia while on the books of second division Loughborough Town. He played just twice for Sunderland, returning to Ayr FC after refusing to play in the second team.**

Logan had actually been paid by Sunderland for almost six months before he signed as a professional in August 1891 having agreed to sign in March, at which point Sunderland began to renumerate him. In that month of March 1891 he scored on his only full international appearance for Scotland against Wales at Wrexham. A confectioner by trade, he was used on the wing by Sunderland as Johnny Campbell was impossible to drop from the centre-forward spot Logan excelled in. Campbell hit 31 goals in 24 games as he was the country's top scorer as Sunderland won the league.

Returning to England with Aston Villa nine months after leaving Sunderland, the Wearsiders rather than Ayr were paid the £30 transfer fee as they still held the player's registration. Logan scored seven goals in ten games for Villa, but got no change out of Sunderland's defence when he played in a 3-0 defeat for Villa at Newcastle Road in January 1893 when Sunderland were en-route to retaining the title.

It was a similar story early the following season when he played in a 1-0 loss on Wearside. It was one of four games he played (adding one goal) before being sold to Notts County for £15. Villa went on to win the league that season, but Logan's medal came the following season with his cup exploits with second division Notts County. His hat-trick in the final took his tally in the cup run to six, part of a total of 37 in 56 games for the club.

He left Notts County in March 1895, but as when he left Sunderland, Logan's time north of the border was short-lived as he joined Newcastle United three months later. Logan scored in his first four games for Newcastle and altogether scored eight goals in nine games for them before joining Loughborough Town who he had made his United debut against.

The move proved to be a tragic one. In April 1896, Loughborough played Newton Heath (Who became Manchester United) in a game played in torrential rain. Worse was, the Loughborough kit did not arrive and so the team played in their own clothes, duly got soaked and had to travel home thoroughly drenched. Although he went on to play and score in a game against Crewe Alexandra, Logan - who had suffered from illness at Sunderland - developed a chill, which developed into pneumonia and caused his death desperately early. The road leading to Loughborough Town's ground is named the Jimmy Logan Way.

Jimmy's bother Peter played against Newcastle United in the 1911 cup final for Bradford City.

## LONGAIR, William (Bill)

**POSITION:** Centre-half

**BIRTHPLACE:** Dundee, Angus

**DATE OF BIRTH:** 19/07/1870 - 28/11/1926

**HEIGHT:** 5' 9½" **WEIGHT:** 11st 7lbs

**SIGNED FROM:** Dundee, 02/05/1896

**DEBUT:** v Bury, H, 01/09/1896

**LAST MATCH:** v Liverpool, A, 07/11/1896

**MOVED TO:** Burnley, 25/11/1896

**TEAMS:** Rockwell FC, Dundee East End, Dundee, Newton Heath, Dundee, Sunderland, Burnley, Dundee, Brighton United, Dundee

**INTERNATIONAL:** Scotland

**SAFC TOTALS:** 2 appearances / 0 goals

**Nicknamed 'Plum', Longair kept returning to his home town of Dundee having four spells as a player and being the club's trainer from August 1900 to 1924. He then became groundsman before his death two years later at the age of 56. An estimated 20,000 people lined the streets of Dundee as his coffin was taken from his home in Victoria Street to Eastern Cemetery.**

In 2009 he became the first person inducted into the Dundee Hall of Fame. Longair captained Dundee in their first-ever match against Rangers in 1893 and played a total of 114 league games (3 goals), 22 Scottish Cup matches (1 goal) and 89 friendlies (8 goals). He also never missed a match in his two decades plus as a trainer, a spell which included training the 1910 Scottish Cup winners.

Beginning his football career as a centre-forward he switched to centre-half in 1890, three years before first signing for Dundee. He won one cap for Scotland, becoming Dundee's first international (along with goalkeeper Bill March) when playing in a 2-1 win over Ireland at Cliftonville in Belfast on 31 March 1894. The following February, 'Plum' made his first venture into English football signing for Newton Heath, the forerunners of Manchester United.

His solitary appearance came on 20 April 1895 in a 3-3 draw with Notts County. This was followed by a return to Dundee two months later. He did not fare much better when he joined Sunderland, playing just twice, but he did return to Newcastle Road to play for Burnley on 2 March 1897. Burnley appear to have been attracted to Longair after he played against them in a friendly for Dundee on 25 April 1896 just over six months before joining them.

Longair's final English club were Brighton United with whom he played in their inaugural Southern League campaign of 1898-99. In 1905, whilst trainer at Dundee, Bill also acted in the same capacity for the Scottish national team against England at Crystal Palace. Three years later he was in charge of the Scottish team when they played Wales at Dens Park. His uncle and namesake was Lord Provost of the Burgh of Dundee from 1905 to 1908.

## LONGHORN, Dennis

**POSITION:** Midfielder

**BIRTHPLACE:** Hythe, Kent

**DATE OF BIRTH:** 12/09/1950

**HEIGHT:** 5' 11" **WEIGHT:** 11st 0lbs

**SIGNED FROM:** Mansfield Town, 21/02/1974

**DEBUT:** v Middlesbrough, H, 02/03/1974

**LAST MATCH:** v Aston Villa, H, 16/10/1976

**MOVED TO:** Sheffield United, 19/11/1976 made permanent after a one month loan

**TEAMS:** Bournemouth & Boscombe Athletic, Mansfield Town, Sunderland, Sheffield United, Aldershot, Colchester United, Chelmsford City

**SAFC TOTALS:** 41+5 appearances / 4 goals

**A long-striding midfielder who in one sense was a replacement for the departed and tenacious Micky Horswill, but was more like Ian Porterfield in style. Striker John Lathan went to Mansfield in part-exchange for Longhorn who never managed more than 15 league starts in his four seasons at the club, a loan to Sheffield United coming in his last term.**

Dennis began with 27+7 appearances for Bournemouth where he provided goals for goal-machine Ted MacDougall and scored twice himself, part of his time there seeing him help the Cherries to runners-up spot in the fourth division in 1970-71. He moved to Mansfield in December 1971, debuting against Plymouth and going on to score six times in 103+3 games.

At Sunderland he played just 6+2 league games in the 1975-76 promotion season scoring in an opening-day win over Chelsea, but rarely featured between then and a move to Sheffield United where he played 40+3 times, scoring once, before 51+9 games and three goals between 1978 and 1980 with Aldershot where he was a teammate of Malcolm Crosby.

# L

## LONGHORN, Dennis (Continued)

Shortly before his 30th birthday Longhorn signed for Colchester for whom he played 67+11 times (0 goals) ending his league career with a game at Stockport in April 1983. He subsequently played non-league for Chelmsford City and spent 1986 to 1989 as manager of Halstead, winning promotion in their first season as founder members of the Eastern Counties League during his time there. Following his retirement, Longhorn spent over two decades running a football school at Centre Parcs at Elveden.

## LOOVENS, Glenn

**POSITION:** Centre-back

**BIRTHPLACE:** Doetinchem, Netherlands

**DATE OF BIRTH:** 22/09/1983

**HEIGHT:** 6' 2" **WEIGHT:** 13st 1lb

**SIGNED FROM:** Free agent, 20/07/2018

**DEBUT:** v Charlton Athletic, H, 04/08/2018

**LAST MATCH:** v Portsmouth, A, 22/12/2018

**MOVED TO:** Contract terminated by mutual agreement 22/08/2019

**TEAMS:** Feyenoord, Excelsior (L), De Graafschap (L), Cardiff City, Celtic, Real Zaragoza, Sheffield Wednesday, Sunderland

**INTERNATIONAL:** Netherlands

**SAFC TOTALS:** 13 appearances / 0 goals

**A teammate of Edwin Zoetebier at Feyenoord, Loovens played 31 times for the Rotterdam giants and added 24 games on loan to Excelsior and eleven with De Graafschap, scoring twice for Excelsior. He came into British football with a loan to Cardiff City that was made permanent. Loovens went on to make exactly 100 league appearances with the Bluebirds and 113 in total.**

These included the 2008 FA Cup final where he had a goal disallowed in a defeat to Portsmouth, who he would be sent off against in his final career appearance for Sunderland. In the summer of his cup final appearance, Glenn went north to Celtic for a fee of over £2m.

Although he initially struggled to hold a place in the Celtic side, he won a League Cup winner's medal in his first season, playing in the final against Rangers who had wanted to sign him before Celtic stepped in. Following the replacement of Gordon Strachan by Tony Mowbray as Celtic manager, Loovens played

more regularly under the former Middlesbrough centre-half and earned the first of his two Netherlands caps against Japan in September 2009.

Unfortunately, niggling injuries and constantly changing central defensive partners symbolised Loovens' time at Parkhead. However, there were highlights, including playing alongside Ki Sung-Yueng and Anthony Stokes as Motherwell were beaten in the 2011 Scottish Cup final and scoring in a 6-0 win over Kilmarnock which sealed the 2011-12 title - although that was tempered when he was released that summer.

At this point he had a season in La Liga with Real Zaragoza, making 24 appearances before returning to the UK with Sheffield Wednesday where he became club captain. After 146+4 games for the Owls for whom his only goal was a winner at Newcastle (on Boxing Day 2016), he moved to Sunderland only to retire half way through a two-year contract having played his final game before Christmas. His father Hans played for FC Twente, SVV Schiedam, KSV Waregem and De Graafschap between 1978 and 1990.

## LORD, John Smith

**POSITION:** Forward

**BIRTHPLACE:** Parkgate, Rotherham, West Riding of Yorkshire

**DATE OF BIRTH:** 15/12/1864 - 11/08/1944

**SIGNED FROM:** Fulwell, Summer 1886

**DEBUT:** v Newcastle West End, H, 13/11/1886

**LAST MATCH:** v Newcastle West End, H, 13/11/1886

**MOVED TO:** Left, May 1889

**TEAMS:** Fulwell, Sunderland

**SAFC TOTALS:** 1 appearance / 0 goals

**Employed in an Ironworks in Sunderland during and after his football career, Lord only appeared in one competitive match for Sunderland in their pre-league days.**

It was only Sunderland's third-ever English (FA) Cup tie, but resulted in a 1-0 defeat. John's elder brother, Henry, played with him in some games for Fulwell and Sunderland reserves.

## LOVE, Donald Alistair

**POSITION:** Right-back

**BIRTHPLACE:** Rochdale, Greater Manchester

**DATE OF BIRTH:** 02/12/1994

**HEIGHT:** 5' 10" **WEIGHT:** 11st 5lbs

**SIGNED FROM:** Manchester United, 11/08/2016

**DEBUT:** v Manchester City, A, 13/08/2016

**LAST MATCH:** v Oxford United, H, 01/09/2018

**MOVED TO:** Shrewsbury Town, 12/07/2019

**TEAMS:** Northwich Town, Manchester United, Wigan Athletic (L), Sunderland, Shrewsbury Town, Salford City, Morecambe (to June 2022)

**INTERNATIONAL:** Scotland Under 21

**SAFC TOTALS:** 27+7 appearances / 1 goal

**One of two Manchester United reserves signed in a reported £5.5m package (along with Paddy McNair) by former Manchester United manager David Moyes, Love never established himself in a side relegated in both of his first two seasons at Sunderland.**

His only Premier League appearance for United had been in a defeat at the Stadium of Light on 13 February 2016. Five days later Love's second and last appearance for the Red Devils came in another loss, this time in the UEFA Cup at FC Midtjylland.

Manchester United had previously loaned Donald to Wigan Athletic where he played 5+3 games beginning as a sub for Will Grigg in a goalless draw with Walsall on 3 October 2015. Leaving Sunderland on a free, he played 50+6 games for Shrewsbury before being released by Steve Cotterill in 2021 at which point he joined Salford City. He totalled 22+7 appearances without scoring and left for Morecambe in the summer of 2022.. A Scottish Under 21 international, Donald qualified through his Stranraer-born grandmother.

## LOW, Henry Forbes (Harry)

**POSITION:** Half-back / centre-forward

**BIRTHPLACE:** Aberdeen, Aberdeenshire

**DATE OF BIRTH:** 15/08/1882 - 26/09/1920

**HEIGHT:** 5' 8" **WEIGHT:** 11st 6lbs

**SIGNED FROM:** Aberdeen, 04/05/1907

**DEBUT:** v Manchester City, H, 02/09/1907

**LAST MATCH:** v Tottenham Hotspur, H, 24/04/1915

**MOVED TO:** Did not agree contract, 31/05/1919

**TEAMS:** Orion, Aberdeen, Sunderland

**SAFC TOTALS:** 228 appearances / 38 goals

**There is no line in Harry Low's career details above listing him as an international, but that is because when selected to play for Scotland he chose to play for Sunderland. Offending the international selectors with such a choice meant he never got another chance to play for his country, for who his brother Wilf was capped.**

Wilf was in the opposition line-up Harry faced instead of making his international debut. The occasion was an English (FA) Cup quarter-final second replay with Newcastle, which Sunderland won and went on to their first final in a season when they also won the league title. Harry played in 46 of the 47 games that season. His shirt and medal from the cup final are on display at the Stadium of Light courtesy of his grandson Maurice.

Having started with Orion FC, who were one of the teams who merged to form Aberdeen for whom Harry played 103 times, he went on to play for Sunderland in seven seasons until football ceased due to World War One. During the hostilities Low served in the navy and then a munitions factory, but after the war, he left the club as he was unhappy with the terms offered to him for the 1919-20 season when league football resumed. Instead he played for the Sunderland Police team that season and became manager of the Fort Inn in Roker Avenue, but died suddenly at the age of 38. A benefit match in aid of his widow was organised by the club on 6 April 1921. The game featured past and present Sunderland players against a Mr Watt's XI. Watts being manager of Newcastle, his side for the Benefit game including five players from Newcastle, five from South Shields and one from Middlesbrough.

As mentioned, brother Wilf was a Scotland international who played for Newcastle and also Aberdeen. Two nephews were also footballers. William played for Aberdeen and South Shields and Norman was an amateur with Newcastle United and played for Liverpool, Newport County and Norwich City as well as managing Norwich, Workington Town and Port Vale.

## LOWREY, Patrick (Paddy)

**POSITION:** Forward

**BIRTHPLACE:** Newcastle, Northumberland

**DATE OF BIRTH:** 11/10/1950

**HEIGHT:** 5' 8" **WEIGHT:** 12st 3lbs

**SIGNED FROM:** Newcastle United, 12/12/1967

**DEBUT:** v Arsenal, H, 05/04/1969

**LAST MATCH:** v Preston North End, H, 25/09/1971

**MOVED TO:** RWD Molenbeek, 01/06/1972

**TEAMS:** Newcastle United, Sunderland, RWD Molenbeek, Royale Union, St-Gilloise, Darlington, Workington Town, Western Suburbs, Arcadia Shepherds

**INTERNATIONAL:** England Schools and Australia 'B'

**SAFC TOTALS:** 13+2 appearances / 3 goals

**The scorer of a hat-trick for Sunderland as they won the 1969 FA Youth Cup final, earlier in the season Lowrey had scored seven in a 14-2 Northern Intermediate League win for the youth team against Doncaster Rovers.**

Previously with Newcastle, where he played for their reserves as a 15-year-old, and although he was Tyneside-born, at the age of 17 he engineered a move to Sunderland who under Alan Brown were renowned for giving young players an opportunity. Paddy got into the first-team a couple of weeks after scoring twice in the FA Youth Cup semi-final and after three starts came off the bench to score a first-division winner at Burnley with a shot from outside the box.

However there would be just a handful of further appearances spread over the next three seasons before he moved into Belgian football, helping RWD Molenbeek to win their league title in 1974-75, before a brief stint with RU St-Gilloise. Returning to England, he played 14+6 league games for Darlington scoring twice, including on his debut, before adding three goals in 15 games for Workington in 1976-77.

Lowrey subsequently had spells in Australia with Western Suburbs in Sydney, doing well enough to be selected for the Australian second XI before going to South Africa with Maurice Hepworth at Arcadia Shepherds. Between 1985 and '95 he managed Ponteland United followed by over three years in charge of Whitley Bay and then two years with Gretna when they were a Northern League club. Paddy later became a landscape gardener, maintaining 17 houses in Darras Hall in Newcastle.

## LUALUA, Kazenga

**POSITION:** Forward

**BIRTHPLACE:** Kinshasa, Zaire

**DATE OF BIRTH:** 10/12/1990

**HEIGHT:** 5' 11" **WEIGHT:** 12st 0lbs

**SIGNED FROM:** Brighton & Hove Albion, 25/01/2018

**DEBUT:** v Birmingham City, A, 30/01/2018

**LAST MATCH:** v Norwich City, H, 10/04/2018

**MOVED TO:** Contract not renewed, 30/06/2018

**TEAMS:** Newcastle United, Doncaster Rovers (L), Brighton & Hove Albion, QPR (L), Sunderland, Luton Town, Genclerbirligi (to May 2022)

**SAFC TOTALS:** 0+6 appearances / 0 goals

**LuaLua failed to impress in half a dozen substitute appearances as Sunderland were relegated from the Championship having just dropped out of the Premier League. He had begun with Newcastle United where he was first named on the bench as a 16-year-old.**

He went on to play 15 times for the Magpies, all but three of these as sub. He also had loans to Doncaster (4/0) and Brighton where he excelled under Gus Poyet, scoring a 25-yarder on his debut. He was to have three loans with the Seagulls before signing for them in 2011, eventually totalling 76+101 games, the amount of sub appearances telling its own story. He scored 22 times for Brighton, four of these coming in the 2010-11 season under Poyet.

During his time at Brighton, LuaLua was twice loaned to QPR where all but four of his 19 games were as sub, his one goal coming at Preston. After Sunderland he had three seasons at Luton, scoring eight times in 37+50 appearances before moving into Turkish football in the summer of 2021.

Elder brother Lomana, won 31 caps for DR Congo and played for Colchester United, Newcastle United, Portsmouth, Olympiacos, Al-Arabi, Omonia, Blackpool and half a dozen clubs in Turkey before one game back in England with Peterborough Sports. Kazenga also had two footballing cousins: Yannick Bolasie who scored an eleven minute hat-trick at Sunderland for Crystal Palace in April 2015, who also played for Everton and Plymouth amongst others, and also Tresor Kandol, who played for Luton, Cambridge and Bournemouth.

## LUMSDON, Christopher (Chris)

**POSITION:** Midfielder
**BIRTHPLACE:** Killingworth, Tyne and Wear
**DATE OF BIRTH:** 15/12/1979
**HEIGHT:** 5' 7" **WEIGHT:** 10 st 3lbs
**SIGNED FROM:** As trainee, 30/09/1995
**DEBUT:** v Wolverhampton Wanderers, A, 07/02/1998
**LAST MATCH:** v Walsall, H, 14/09/1999
**MOVED TO:** Barnsley, 11/12/2001
**TEAMS:** Sunderland, Blackpool (L), Crewe Alexandra (L), Barnsley, Carlisle United, Darlington
**INTERNATIONAL:** England Under 18
**SAFC TOTALS:** 3+1 appearances / 0 goals

**Highly rated as a youngster when he was offered a five-year deal by Sunderland in the same week he was called up by England Under 18s, Lumsdon was loaned out three times by Sunderland with the third of those clubs - Barnsley - eventually paying £500,000 for his signature.**

After suffering relegation from the second tier with the Tykes where he played 70+15 league games, scoring 13 times, Chris signed for Carlisle who were then in the Conference. Reportedly, his contract with Barnsley involved payments to Sunderland which the cash-strapped Oakwell club struggled to meet, resulting in 'Lummy' being left out of some games.

Helping the Cumbrians back into the league, Lumsden played 115+9 league games, scoring nine times and helped them to a second successive promotion as well as playing against Swansea in the Football League Trophy final at the Millennium Stadium in Cardiff.

Despite a persistent back injury he signed for Colin Todd at Darlington but was only able to play two league games and retired age 30. At Blackpool and Crewe, his figures were 6/1 and 14+2/0. A popular player at Carlisle Lumsdon later worked as a radio summariser for the Cumbrians games and set up Lumsdon Elite Coaching in 2021. He won Player of the Year awards at both Barnsley and Carlisle.

## LUSCOMBE, Nathan John

**POSITION:** Midfield / left-back
**BIRTHPLACE:** New Hartley, Tyne & Wear
**DATE OF BIRTH:** 06/11/1989
**HEIGHT:** 5' 10" **WEIGHT:** 11st 7lbs
**SIGNED FROM:** School, 01/07/2006
**DEBUT:** v Blackburn Rovers, A, 04/02/2009
**LAST MATCH:** v Blackburn Rovers, A, 04/02/2009
**MOVED TO:** Hartlepool United, 01/07/2011
**TEAMS:** Sunderland, Hartlepool United, Celtic Nation
**SAFC TOTALS:** 0+1 appearances / 0 goals

**Top scorer for the Under 18s in the season the youth team reached the semi-final of the FA Youth Cup in 2007-08, with a side that included Jordan Henderson, Martyn Waghorn and Jack Colback, Nathan appeared to have the ability to go on to have a successful career.**

However his only first-team appearance at Sunderland consisted of playing the final 15 minutes of extra-time in an FA Cup tie at Blackburn. Able to play at left-back, Luscombe was at his best on the left of midfield where his direct running, willingness to whip over an early cross and his ability to cut in and shoot fiercely made him an eye-catching player to watch. Most unfortunately, there often seemed to be problems in Nathan's private life that ultimately impacted on his football career.

In 2010, he played in a reserve game for York against Middlesbrough as he sought pastures new and later, following a two-week trial, he agreed to join Hartlepool when his contract at Sunderland ended in 2011. His only league goal came in September 2011 for Hartlepool against Exeter, but even at this level, much below his capabilities, Nathan only managed 29 games with 23 of those being as a substitute, problems keeping his weight down hindering his progress. Luscombe's last league appearance at Oldham in March 2013 came when he was still only 23. He was last noted in action playing one game in the Northern League for Carlisle-based Celtic Nation.

## LYNAS, John

**POSITION:** Outside-right
**BIRTHPLACE:** Blantyre, South Lanarkshire
**DATE OF BIRTH:** 18/01/1907 - 18/12/1988
**HEIGHT:** 5' 4½" **WEIGHT:** 10st 0lbs
**SIGNED FROM:** Bo'ness, 26/05/1928
**DEBUT:** v Burnley, A, 25/08/1928
**LAST MATCH:** v West Ham United, H, 27/04/1929
**MOVED TO:** Third Lanark, 04/10/1929
**TEAMS:** Wishaw, Shettleston, Bo'ness, Sunderland, Third Lanark, Raith Rovers
**INTERNATIONAL:** Scotland Junior
**SAFC TOTALS:** 10 appearances / 1 goal

**All of Lynas' appearances for Sunderland came in 1928-29. He started the season by playing the first nine games, scoring in a 4-0 home win over Bolton. He was then out of the picture until the final home win at the end of April and added a further appearance 48 hours later in a benefit match for William McDonald at manager Johnny Cochrane's old club St. Mirren, on a day when Lynas was one of nine Scots in the Sunderland line up.**

Sunderland had paid £310 to bring Lynas from Bo'ness where he had been a teammate of former Sunderland goalkeeper Jimmy Dempster and scored four times in 27 appearances. Sunderland snapped up Lynas following Bo'ness' promotion which saw them become the first West Lothian club to reach the top flight. Returning to Scotland in October 1929 Lynas served Third Lanark for six years (it was the first time he had spent more than one season at a club) scoring 54 goals in 158 games after helping them to promotion in 1931 and 1935, after going down in between. He then finished his playing days with four games at Raith Rovers in 1935, but they all ended in defeats with an aggregate score of 5-19.

He then retired to become trainer at Blackpool in August 1936 under former England international Joe Smith. A qualified masseur, Lynas stayed at Blackpool as trainer until September 1956. He was an integral part of their FA Cup final defeats of 1948 and 1951 as well as the famous 'Matthews Final' of 1953 when the Tangerines beat Bolton 4-3. In 1958 he became a director of the club.

During World War Two, he had been captured in Singapore and forced to work in a Prisoner of War camp in Thailand for three and a half years.

## LYNCH, Craig Thomas

**POSITION:** Midfielder
**BIRTHPLACE:** Bowburn, Co Durham
**DATE OF BIRTH:** 25/03/1992
**HEIGHT:** 5' 9" **WEIGHT:** 10st 1lb
**SIGNED FROM:** Trainee, 01/07/2008
**DEBUT:** v Fulham, H, 30/04/2011
**LAST MATCH:** v Wolverhampton Wanderers, H, 14/05/2011
**MOVED TO:** Released from contract, 31/01/2014
**TEAMS:** Sunderland, Hartlepool United, Rochdale, Spennymoor, Blyth Spartans, Durham City, Seaham Red Star
**SAFC TOTALS:** 0+2 appearances / 0 goals

**A skilful, well-balanced, creative attacking midfielder, Lynch got just two first-team games, both times coming on for the final quarter of an hour. He was at Sunderland from the age of six and played in the Peace Cup In South Korea in 2012 and also in the Barclays Asia Cup in Hong Kong a year later.**

Sixteen months after his last game for Sunderland, he went on loan to Hartlepool where he was a teammate of Jack Baldwin and Peter Hartley, but was frustrated playing in a side who at the time were mainly playing long-ball football leaving a player like him virtually redundant. He played six League One games, scoring on one of his two starts although he was subbed in that game at Colchester before an hour was on the clock. He resurfaced in league football, having one game as a second-half sub for Rochdale at Newport County in May 2014 before returning to the north east to continue his career in non-league football.

In 2021 he became manager at Morpeth Town, alongside being UEFA B qualified coach and head of Football at Evolution Football Coaching Limited in the Durham and Gateshead area.

## LYNCH, Joel John

**POSITION:** Defender

**BIRTHPLACE:** Eastbourne, East Sussex

**DATE OF BIRTH:** 03/10/1987

**HEIGHT:** 6' 1" **WEIGHT:** 12st 11lbs

**SIGNED FROM:** Free agent, 26/08/2019

**DEBUT:** v Sheffield United, A, 25/09/2019

**LAST MATCH:** v Gillingham, H, 07/03/2020

**MOVED TO:** Contract not renewed, 30/06/2020

**TEAMS:** Brighton & Hove Albion, Nottingham Forest, Huddersfield Town, QPR, Sunderland, Crawley Town (to May 2022)

**INTERNATIONAL:** Wales

**SAFC TOTALS:** 19+2 appearances / 0 goals

**Brought in as a free agent by Jack Ross, Lynch was a physically strong, but at times seemingly cumbersome defender who played regularly in a season cut short due to the Covid pandemic in 2020. Subsequently released, he missed a season of his career but after advertising his availability on the internet resurfaced with Crawley Town in September 2021, debuting against Carlisle and scoring twice in 21+3 games to May 2022.**

He had begun his career in a south-coast Championship derby alongside Paul McShane for Brighton in a defeat at Southampton on 2 January 2006. It was the first of 81+14 appearances for the Seagulls which produced goals against Ipswich and Cheltenham, the second after his side were relegated to League One at the end of his first season.

A return to the Championship came in a £200,000 move to Nottingham Forest after a successful loan period with the former European champions. Joel played 80+15 times for Forest, scoring three times including one against his old club Brighton before a summer 2012 transfer to Huddersfield Town where he was signed by future Sunderland boss Simon Grayson. Again one of goals for the club came against former employers, in this case Forest.

In four years he scored nine times in 121+7 appearances. Next stop, after a reported £1.2m move, was QPR where he notched seven goals in 90+5 games, a steady return for a central-defender or left-back and indicating his prowess at set pieces.

Lynch won one international cap for Wales who he qualified for due to his Barry-born father. Joel's international career lasted for twelve minutes, having come off the bench in a friendly with Bosnia and Herzegovina in August 2012.

## LYNCH, Mark John

**POSITION:** Right-back

**BIRTHPLACE:** Manchester, Greater Manchester

**DATE OF BIRTH:** 02/09/1981

**HEIGHT:** 5' 11" **WEIGHT:** 11st 3lbs

**SIGNED FROM:** Manchester United, 15/07/2004

**DEBUT:** v QPR, H, 14/08/2004

**LAST MATCH:** v Cardiff City, H, 26/02/2005

**MOVED TO:** Hull City, 14/06/2005

**TEAMS:** Manchester United, St Johnstone (L), Sunderland, Hull City, Yeovil Town, Rotherham United, Stockport County, Altrincham

**SAFC TOTALS:** 7+6 appearances / 0 goals

**Mark Lynch played alongside John O'Shea and Kieran Richardson when he debuted for Manchester United in a European Cup game at Deportivo La Coruna in March 2003 when he was unfortunate to become the only Manchester United player to score an own-goal on his solitary first-team appearance.**

Despite that OG for United (where he had come through the youth system and been coached by Nobby Stiles), Alex Ferguson gave him a new contract, but he never played another first-team game for the Red Devils. Prior to his single game for United Mark had a lengthy loan with St Johnstone, making 20 SPL appearances, including games against both halves of the Old Firm.

All but two of his appearances for Sunderland came during the 2004-05 promotion season, but he was never successful in being able to hold down a first-team place. As Sunderland went up, he stayed in the Championship with Hull where he was injured on his debut and sent off in his second game, eventually making 15+2 appearances before dropping into League One with Yeovil after a year.

In his first season at Yeovil - as a teammate of Marcus Stewart - Lynch helped the Glovers to reach the Play-Offs, coming off the bench in a Wembley final defeat by Blackpool. A second season with Yeovil took Mark's tally with the club to 34+4 before he moved to Rotherham, where in two terms, he totalled 35+3 and scored the only two goals of his career. There were similar totals (39+2) in two seasons at Stockport County where Lynch was in the side relegated from the Football League at the end of his first season.

His final switch was to Altrincham where he was released after eight appearances, retiring at the age of 30. Post football, he set up his own fitness business MRK5 Business and completely stepped away from the game.

## LYNCH, Thomas Michael (Tommy)

**POSITION:** Left-back

**BIRTHPLACE:** Limerick, Ireland

**DATE OF BIRTH:** 10/10/1964

**HEIGHT:** 6' 0" **WEIGHT:** 12st 6lbs

**SIGNED FROM:** Limerick, 26/07/1988

**DEBUT:** v Charlton Athletic, A, 08/11/1988

**LAST MATCH:** v Reading, A, 06/01/1990

**MOVED TO:** Shrewsbury Town, 19/02/1990 after month-long loan

**TEAMS:** Wembley Rovers, Limerick, Sunderland, Shrewsbury Town, Waterford United, Limerick, Park Rangers

**INTERNATIONAL:** Republic of Ireland Olympic XI

**SAFC TOTALS:** 6 appearances / 0 goals

**A draughtsman before he was a footballer, Tommy was a flame-haired left-back who could raise a fair gallop once into his stride, but was never the quickest over the first five yards.**

Always a likeable lad, he enjoyed great success with Shrewsbury where he was inducted into the Shrews' Hall of Fame and voted into the club's greatest-ever XI, taking over half the fans vote as one of ten players nominated for the left-back slot. After 234 games and 14 goals for the Shrews, he was devastated to be left out of the line up at Wembley for a 1995-96 Play-Off final with Burnley.

That year he moved back to Ireland to become player manager of Waterford United taking his team to a Play-Off final in his first season before doing the double of league and cup in his second term. Born in Limerick, but raised in Shannon, Lynch played 178 games for Limerick between 1982 and 1988 and returned to the club as player-manager after he was replaced at Waterford by the former Charlton striker Micky Flanagan.

Lynch also managed Kilkenny City, returned to coach Limerick again in 2006 and three years later was managing Carew Park in Limerick. His nephew Lee was on West Bromwich Albion's books in 2008 before enjoying a decade-long career playing in Ireland.

## MACHO, Jurgen

**POSITION:** Goalkeeper

**BIRTHPLACE:** Vienna, Austria

**DATE OF BIRTH:** 24/08/1977

**HEIGHT:** 6' 4" **WEIGHT:** 13st 12lbs

**SIGNED FROM:** Bo'ness, 26/05/1928

**DEBUT:** v Arsenal, H, 19/08/2000

**LAST MATCH:** v Bolton Wanderers, A, 04/01/2003

**MOVED TO:** Chelsea, 05/06/2003

**TEAMS:** Casino Vienna, FC Vienna, Sunderland, Chelsea, Rapid Vienna (L), Kaiserslautern, AEK Athens, Lask Linz, Panionios, Admira Wacker

**INTERNATIONAL:** Austria

**SAFC TOTALS:** 24+3 appearances / 0 goals

**Having arrived from Austrian football, Macho came on as a half-time sub for the injured Thomas Sorensen on the opening day of the 2000-01 season. Impressing immediately Jurgen protected a clean sheet against Arsenal on the day the North Stand extension at the Stadium of Light was opened.**

Capped by Austria while with Sunderland, Macho became one of four full international goalkeepers at Sunderland along with Sorensen of Denmark, Thomas Myhre of Norway and Mart Poom of Estonia. In the face of such competition Jurgen was never able to establish himself as first choice keeper at Sunderland. His best season consisted of 16 appearances in his last year as the club were relegated with a measly 19 points. Undoubtedly Macho's most memorable game was a Man of the Match performance in a goalless draw away to Liverpool in November 2002. Evidently he had impressed, as when the relegation resulted in a 'fire-sale' of 23 players it was high-flying Chelsea who came in to sign Jurgen.

However he never got a game at Stamford Bridge where he suffered an injury and subsequently was released from his contract after an intended year-long loan to Rapid Vienna was cut short to allow him to join Kaiserslautern in Germany. He had played eleven games for Rapid (including three in the UEFA Cup) who won the league in that 2004-05 season. At Kaiserslautern he was initially a reserve yet again but went on to play 57 times, suffering relegation from the Bundesliga in 2005-06.

Jurgen continued his tour of the continent with a move to AEK Athens where he had 25 appearances before returning to his homeland with LASK Linz where there were 13 games before a switch back to Greece with Panionios. Following 28 games with a club Marco Gabbiadini once played for Macho made a final move back to Austria with Admira Wacker where the final match of his career - and twelfth for the club - saw him keep a clean sheet at Wolfsberger in May 2013.

Macho won 26 caps for Austria. He endured a terrifying moment against England in Vienna in November 2007 when he swallowed his tongue and was thankfully saved by excellent work from the Austrian medical team. A year later he played in all three of joint-hosts' Austria's three games at Euro 2008. After his retirement Jurgen stayed in the game, becoming goalkeeper coach at FC Vienna, SKN St Polten and then Rapid Vienna where he remained in position in June 2022.

## MAGUIRE, Christopher Patrick Joseph

**POSITION:** Midfielder

**BIRTHPLACE:** Bellshill, Glasgow, Lanarkshire

**DATE OF BIRTH:** 16/01/1989

**HEIGHT:** 5' 7" **WEIGHT:** 10st 8lbs

**SIGNED FROM:** Bury, 25/06/2018

**DEBUT:** v Charlton Athletic, H, 04/08/2018

**LAST MATCH:** v Lincoln City, H, 22/05/2021

**MOVED TO:** Lincoln City, 07/07/2021

**TEAMS:** Aberdeen, Kilmarnock (L), Derby County, Portsmouth (L), Sheffield Wednesday, Coventry City (L), Rotherham United, Oxford United, Bury, Sunderland, Lincoln City (to 2021)

**INTERNATIONAL:** Scotland

**SAFC TOTALS:** 84+41 appearances / 28 goals

**Nicknamed 'The King' for a while at Sunderland, in truth Maguire was no more the king than John MacPhail was Monty. Monty at Sunderland has to be Jim Montgomery while there is only one King on Wearside and that of course is Charlie Hurley.**

Nonetheless Maguire was a footballer who could excite. He scored some spectacular and important goals, not least a volley that was the only goal of a two-legged Play-Off semi-final with Portsmouth in 2019. He also became just the fourth player, after Jermain Defoe, Gordon Harris and Jim Baxter to finish their Sunderland career with a 100% record from the penalty spot having taken as many as six penalties.

Capped by Scotland against Northern Ireland in February 2011 - a game in which Phil Bardsley, Steve Caldwell, Alan Hutton, David Healy and Corry Evans also played - he won his second and last cap against the Republic of Ireland at the end of the same season, this time Bardsley, Shay Given, Paul McShane and Liam Lawrence were involved. Both of Maguire's international appearances were as a substitute, his playing time totalling 25 minutes.

Chris began with Aberdeen, debuting as a sub for the Dons against a Celtic side that included Stan Varga and Aiden McGeady in May 2006. The first of 24 goals in 86+72 games came the following Boxing Day against Kilmarnock, a club who he played 12+2 games for, netting four goals during a 2010 loan, a year before a £400,000 move to Derby County.

In a year with the Rams Maguire barely played. A debut goal against Shrewsbury was one of only two goals but he started only three games and played a further five games as a sub. A loan to Portsmouth (10+1/3) preceded a summer 2012 move to Sheffield Wednesday where there were 70+22 appearances and 19 goals in three seasons as well as a short loan to Coventry (1+2/ 2) before he moved across South Yorkshire with a free transfer to Rotherham United in 2015.

He lasted less than six months with the Millers where he did not score in 6+8 outings. His next move brought the most successful period of Maguire's career. In a season and a half with Oxford he twice reached the final of the Football League Trophy and won promotion from League Two in the first of those seasons. Former Sunderland youth player Conor Hourihane and Maguire's future SAFC teammate Josh Scowen were part of the Barnsley team who beat Oxford at Wembley in 2016, Lee Johnson having led the Tykes to Wembley, but moved on before the final. A year later Maguire lost in the final of the same competition to his former loan club Coventry who were captained by Jordan Willis and had Lee Burge in goal.

Despite doing well at Oxford Maguire moved on to Bury on a free in the summer of 2017. In his season at Gigg Lane Chris scored twice in 16+13 appearances before coming to Sunderland. After playing more games for the Black Cats than any of his English teams Maguire joined Lincoln City where for the third time he played for Michael Appleton, his manager at Portsmouth and Oxford.

Returning to the Stadium of Light in January 2022 Maguire etched his name into the history books alongside all-time greats Raich Carter and David Halliday in becoming the third man to score hat-tricks both for and against Sunderland. The first goal of his hat-trick for Lincoln was accompanied by a pointed celebration in front of Sunderland manager Lee Johnson who had released him the previous season. He scored only one other league goal (plus a cup goal) in that season in which he totalled 32+4 games.

## MAIN, David

**POSITION:** Centre-forward

**BIRTHPLACE:** Falkirk, Stirlingshire

**DATE OF BIRTH:** 19/08/1888 - 23/06/1961

**HEIGHT:** 5' 10" **WEIGHT:** 12st 0lbs

**SIGNED FROM:** Falkirk, 27/10/1910

**DEBUT:** v Notts County, A, 17/12/1910

**LAST MATCH:** v Manchester United, H, 24/12/1910

**MOVED TO:** Aberdeen, 08/05/1911

**TEAMS:** Bo'ness Our Boys, Falkirk, Sunderland, Aberdeen, Falkirk

**SAFC TOTALS:** 2 appearances / 0 goals

**Signed initially on a month-long trial in the reserves, David Main's two opportunities at first-team level took place in difficult circumstances: a very heavy pitch on his debut and strong winds on his second and last game a week later.**

On the latter occasion Main failed to impress as Sunderland's unbeaten home record ended on Christmas Eve with The Journal reporting, 'Main ran about aimlessly and had very little idea of what to do with the ball'.

Although he was not a success at Sunderland, David became the Main man at Aberdeen where he was top scorer in his first three seasons and scored 58 goals in 163 games in total. He first appeared for the Dons on 14 May 1911 in a friendly at Slavia Prague during the Scottish side's tour of Bohemia, Moravia and Galicia.

After four games on that tour and a Benefit match appearance at Dundee he turned 23 in between his first two league games against Raith Rovers and Third Lanark. David's final game for Aberdeen was at Morton in April 1917. He then finished his career back with the Bairns just after World War One.

## MAJA, Joshua Erowoli Orisunmihare Oluwaseun

**POSITION:** Striker

**BIRTHPLACE:** Lewisham, London

**DATE OF BIRTH:** 27/12/1998

**HEIGHT:** 5' 11" **WEIGHT:** 11st 9lbs

**SIGNED FROM:** Manchester City, 01/07/2015

**DEBUT:** v QPR, A, 21/09/2016

**LAST MATCH:** v Scunthorpe United, A, 19/01/2019

**MOVED TO:** Girondins de Bordeaux, 26/01/2019

**TEAMS:** Crystal Palace, Fulham, Manchester City, Sunderland, Girondins de Bordeaux, Fulham (L), Stoke City (L) (to June 2022)

**INTERNATIONAL:** Nigeria

**SAFC TOTALS:** 32+17 appearances / 17 goals

**Prodigiously talented, Maja once scored a goal in an Under 18 game against Manchester United - where Marcus Rashford was his opposite number 9 - that no matter how many replays were watched, no-one could fathom out how he had brought the ball under control and beat his man in an instant.**

Sam Allardyce recognised his talent, had him train with the first team and took Josh along to a last-day of the season game at Watford in 2016. He had to wait for a debut. Although David Moyes gave him a League Cup outing at QPR early the following season, the talented frontman was not called upon in the league until Simon Grayson brought him off the bench at Fulham in December 2017. Maja scored after five minutes against one of three clubs he had played for as a youngster. Known as Josh Ezenagu when he came to Sunderland, he changed his name to Maja before his first-team debut.

Josh had actually scored against league opposition before his official first goal, netting against Notts County's first team in the Football League (Checkatrade) Trophy for Sunderland Under 23s seven weeks after his cup debut at QPR. That goal is not included in his totals above as it was not scored for Sunderland's first team, although it was against an opposing first team - a statistical anomaly.

While his league debut goal v Fulham was the only one in 18 appearances that season, the following term he scored in his first four third tier league appearances under Jack Ross. The goals just kept coming and when he scored on what was his last appearance in January 2019 it was his 16th in half of a season. All but three of those had come before his 20th birthday shortly before his departure, making the player Sunderland's second highest teenage scorer behind Willie McPheat.

Many felt Maja's sale derailed Sunderland's promotion chances particularly as his replacement Will Grigg failed spectacularly in the scoring stakes. However, had Maja stayed who knows if the goals would have kept coming, especially if with his contract winding down he had been advised by his agent to make sure he did not get injured. It took him to the last game of the season to score his first goal for Bordeaux on what was his seventh appearance for his new club. In his first full season with Bordeaux, Josh scored on his first home appearance of the campaign and scored seven times in Ligue 1, including

a hat-trick in a 6-0 thrashing of Nimes. September of that season brought an international debut for Nigeria away to Ukraine, albeit as an 89th-minute substitute. There were two more goals for Bordeaux the following season before a return to England on loan to Fulham where he burst onto the scene with both goals in a 2-0 win at Everton on his second appearance on Valentine's Day 2021. However, just one more goal in 9+6 games could not stop the Cottagers going down after which he returned to Bordeaux.

Injury ruled him out of the first half of the 2021-22 season, squashing several rumoured moves back to British football. On the final day of the January 2022 transfer window, Josh joined Stoke City on loan. At this point, he had scored twelve times in 21+26 games for Bordeaux, the last two appearances having come in the two weeks before his move to the Potters.

## MAKIN, Christopher Gregory

**POSITION:** Full-back

**BIRTHPLACE:** Manchester, Lancashire

**DATE OF BIRTH:** 08/05/1973

**HEIGHT:** 5' 10" **WEIGHT:** 11st 2lbs

**SIGNED FROM:** Olympique Marseille, 05/08/1997

**DEBUT:** v Sheffield United, A, 10/08/1997

**LAST MATCH:** v Aston Villa, H, 05/03/2001

**MOVED TO:** Ipswich Town, 07/03/2001

**TEAMS:** Oldham Athletic, Wigan Athletic (L), Olympique Marseille, Sunderland, Ipswich Town, Leicester City, Derby County (L), Reading, Southampton, Radcliffe Borough

**INTERNATIONAL:** England Under 21

**SAFC TOTALS:** 136+7 appearances / 1 goal

**Born on the day the 1973 FA Cup winners brought the trophy back to Wearside, Chris Makin became a member of the record-breaking 105-point promotion team in 1998-99. In 2005-06 he made 11+1 league appearances for Reading as they became the only club (to 2022) to beat that points tally, the Royals registering 106.**

Makin missed the beginning of the 1998-99 campaign but played in the last 37 league games of the season. Behind winger - and close friend - Nicky Summerbee, the pair formed a formidably effective right-flank although Makin was not as dynamic going forward as his full-back partner Micky Gray. However after spectacularly scoring his solitary Sunderland goal at Spurs on the final day of the following season any time Makin got the ball anywhere in the final third of the pitch his gathering of possession would be accompanied by yells of 'Shoot' from the stands, so much so that 'Shoot' became his nickname.

Mancunian Makin was first spotted at Sunderland playing for England Under 15s at Roker Park in March 1988, on a night when Lee Clark and Marcus Stewart were also capped. Makin had attended the FA National School at Lilleshall while an associated schoolboy with Oldham Athletic who he joined after representing Manchester Schoolboys and Boundary Park Juniors.

As Oldham avoided relegation from the first-ever Premier League season on goal difference in 1992-93 Makin was loaned to third tier Wigan. Debuting in a home defeat to Swansea in August 1992, he played 14+1 games in a side that were relegated, though his involvement had ended in November. He had scored twice, against Hartlepool and WBA.

It was October of the following year before he made his bow for Oldham in a Premier League goalless draw at home to Arsenal. It was the first of 112+2 games he played for the Latics during which he scored four times before moving to Marseille who had been European champions three years earlier. He spent the 1996-97 season in France as a teammate of Tony Cascarino, the man whose goals for Gillingham relegated Sunderland to the third division for the first time in 1987, while another teammate was future Sunderland colleague Eric Roy. Makin debuted for Marseille in a 3-1 home win over Rennes in September 1996. He went on to make 29 appearances before swapping the Mediterranean for the North Sea.

After almost four seasons on Wearside Makin signed for Ipswich for almost three times the £500,000 he had cost. Five days after playing his final game for Sunderland against Aston Villa he lined up at Villa Park for Ipswich. There were 91+1 games for Ipswich - but no goals for 'Shoot.' Further moves saw Chris play for Leicester City (22/0), Derby, on loan, (13/0), Reading (17+2/0) and Southampton where he completed his senior career with 29+3 games (no goals), the last being a 1-1 home draw with Colchester in the Championship in September 2007.

Two years after officially retiring he briefly played for Radcliffe Borough and has since occupied himself with the management of properties he invested in when a Premier League footballer. Chris has also worked as a summariser for Al-Kass TV in Qatar alongside Nicky Summerbee. Although 'Shoot' only scored the one goal for Sunderland, it should be remembered he also scored at Wembley for Sunderland. Typical of his character he volunteered to take - and convert - in the 1997-98 Play-Off final shoot-out with Charlton Athletic.

## MALBRANQUE, Steed Claude

**BIRTHPLACE:** Mouscron, Belgium

**DATE OF BIRTH:** 06/01/1980

**HEIGHT:** 5' 8" **WEIGHT:** 11st 7lbs

**SIGNED FROM:** Tottenham Hotspur, 30/07/2008

**DEBUT:** v Liverpool, H, 16/08/2008

**LAST MATCH:** v West Ham United, A, 22/05/2011

**MOVED TO:** St Etienne, 03/08/2011

**TEAMS:** Olympique Lyonnais, Fulham, Tottenham Hotspur, Sunderland, St Etienne, Olympique Lyonnais, Caen, MDA Chasselay, FC Limonest

**INTERNATIONAL:** France Under 21

**SAFC TOTALS:** 95+17 appearances / 2 goals

**One of three players signed from Spurs - along with Pascal Chimbonda and Teemu Tainio - in the summer of 2008, Steed Malbranque was a top-class footballer. As a midfield creator who could both see and deliver exquisitely weighted passes he was the kind of high-calibre player signed during the reign of the Niall Quinn led Drumaville Consortium with the aim of taking Sunderland to the next level.**

Rather like Julio Arca, he combined high quality with high work-rate and consequently became deservedly popular with the crowd who as one would cry, 'Steeeeed' whenever he did something good. Undoubtedly Malbranque was a success on a personal level during his time at Sunderland although he disappointingly, scored only twice, once with a beautiful shot at Hull and once against then non-league Barrow in the FA Cup.

Off the field Steed would enjoy a crafty cigarette and was one of the most reluctant interviewees imaginable, although the one time I pinned him down for an in-depth interview he was forthcoming and engaging.

Malbranque came into British football when Fulham made him their record £4.5m signing in 2001. He had started with Lyon, debuting against Montpellier in February 1998 and going on to score six goals in 56+31 games. These included eight Champions League and seven UEFA Cup appearances, scoring in a Champions League victory at Herenveen in October 2000. He also won the French League Cup in 2001, although he was an unused sub in the final against AS Monaco shortly before his switch to England.

For Fulham - where he made his home debut against Sunderland - he showed himself to be a goalscoring midfielder, netting ten goals in his first season, including one at the Stadium of Light in January 2002. Highlighting the later shortage of goals when he came to Sunderland, Steed kept scoring in his second term at Craven Cottage where his 13 included a run where an FA Cup hat-trick against Charlton started a sequence of scoring in six successive games, with three of his seasonal tally coming in the UEFA Cup.

Five consistent years at Fulham produced 195+16 appearances and 44 goals before a £2m move to Tottenham where fans waited over three months between his transfer and debut in a League (Carling) Cup tie with Port Vale after Steed recovered from injury. Also a teammate of Younes Kaboul, Darren Bent and Alan Hutton at White Hart Lane, he played for Spurs as they beat Chelsea in the League Cup final in his second season, scoring in a 5-1 demolition of rivals Arsenal in the semi-final second leg. However, after twelve goals in 82+14 games over two seasons he was allowed to move to Sunderland.

Wearside would be his last destination in England as afterwards he returned to France where after just one game, as a sub at Marseille in August 2011, for St Etienne Steed's career was revitalised after a return to Lyon. In four seasons from August 2012 he added a further 78+36 games and six goals. A final move to Caen brought four starts and ten substitute appearances, his final professional game being at Toulouse in May 2017 before seeing out his playing days in amateur leagues.

Belgian-born and with an Italian mother and French father, Malbranque gained youth and Under 21 honours for France, playing in the 2002 European Under 21 Championships final lost to the Czech Republic. He was twice selected for full France squads, but never received a full cap.

## MALEY, Mark

**POSITION:** Right-back

**BIRTHPLACE:** Newcastle, Tyne & Wear

**DATE OF BIRTH:** 26/01/1981

**HEIGHT:** 5' 9" **WEIGHT:** 12st 3lbs

**SIGNED FROM:** Trainee, 01/08/1997

**DEBUT:** v York City, A, 18/08/1998

**LAST MATCH:** v Luton Town, H, 19/09/2000

**MOVED TO:** Contract not renewed, 31/05/2003

**TEAMS:** Sunderland, Blackpool (L), Northampton Town (L), York City (L)

**INTERNATIONAL:** England Youth

**SAFC TOTALS:** 3 appearances / 0 goals

**Mark Maley's career was ruined by an eye injury suffered in an incident with an air-gun pellet apparently involving teammate John Oster. Maley had captained England schools at Under 14, Under 15 and Under 16 levels and was still a teenager when he made the last of his Sunderland appearances, all of which came in the League Cup.**

Maley had a trio of loans in which he made 17 league appearances, two each in his first two loans and 13 in the final one with York City who his Sunderland debut had been against. Having seen his football career ended, Mark took a degree in corrosion engineering and went on to work in inspecting offshore oil rigs with the use of drones.

## MALONE, Richard Philip (Dick)

**POSITION:** Right-back

**BIRTHPLACE:** Carfin, Lanarkshire

**DATE OF BIRTH:** 22/08/1947

**HEIGHT:** 6' 0" **WEIGHT:** 12st 2lbs

**SIGNED FROM:** Ayr United, 13/10/1970

**DEBUT:** v Bristol City, H, 17/10/1970

**LAST MATCH:** v Newcastle United, A, 27/12/1976

**MOVED TO:** Hartlepool United, 06/06/1977

**TEAMS:** Shotts Bon Accord, Ayr United, Sunderland, Hartlepool United, Blackpool, Queen of the South, North Shields

**INTERNATIONAL:** Scotland Under 23

**SAFC TOTALS:** 281+1 appearances / 2 goals

**Dick Malone became one of the great characters of Sunderland AFC. He replaced long-serving right-back Cec Irwin and went on to win the FA Cup and the Division Two title, both under Bob Stokoe.**

A Scot, Malone settled in Sunderland and as of 2022 was still a regular face at the Stadium of Light, welcoming corporate guests after spending many years as an active member of the Former Players' Association. Malone has always been generous with his time and willingness to put something back into the community.

Signed by Alan Brown, Malone's marauding dribbles from right-back made him something of a cult hero at Roker Park where he was rewarded with the nickname and chant 'Super-Dick' in response to the 'Super-Mac' chants up the road at Newcastle when Malcolm MacDonald was in his prime.

Malone was a model of consistency. In his first four full seasons he missed just two league games with three missed in the 1975-76 campaign as promotion was won. The last nine of Dick's 236+1 league appearances for the club were his only ones in the top flight. He did not see eye to eye with Ian MacFarlane who had a spell as caretaker manager after Stokoe's resignation and then became one of the senior professionals sidelined by new boss Jimmy Adamson.

A shock move to Hartlepool saw Dick debut in a friendly against an Army XI on 22 July 1977 after which he went on to play 42+2 league and cup games in his season at the Victoria Ground before reuniting with Bob Stokoe at Blackpool. Debuting at Carlisle on 11 November 1978 he played in all the remaining league games, scoring in a big win over Swindon in the last home game of the season - being joined in seven of the games by Bobby Kerr, his right-flank partner in their glory years at Roker Park.

Malone took his total of Blackpool appearances to 50+1 with a second season at Bloomfield Road under Stan Ternent and Alan Ball, before playing for George Herd at Queen of the South where he won promotion in 1981 and made 43 appearances. Dick completed his career in non-league football back in the north east of England where he also managed Horden Colliery Welfare.

Capped by Scotland at Under23 level against France, he had played 235 games for Ayr United; scoring 30 goals including a hat-trick against Stenhousemuir in 1968, before coming into English football. At Ayr he played under future Scotland manager Ally MacLeod and in 2010 Dick was admitted into the Ayr United Hall of Fame. He received the Freedom of the City of Sunderland in 2022.

## MALTBY, John (Jack)

**POSITION:** Outside-right / centre-forward

**BIRTHPLACE:** Leadgate, Co Durham

**DATE OF BIRTH:** 31/07/1939

**HEIGHT:** 5' 8" **WEIGHT:** 11st 0lbs

**SIGNED FROM:** Crookhall Juniors, 01/06/1955

**DEBUT:** v Chelsea, H, 10/11/1956

**LAST MATCH:** v Huddersfield Town, H, 17/09/1960

**MOVED TO:** Darlington, 20/06/1961

**TEAMS:** Sunderland, Darlington, Bury, Southern Suburbs, Germiston Caledonians, South Shields

**SAFC TOTALS:** 23 appearances / 4 goals

**A top-flight debutant when he was just 17, Jack Maltby's 23 games were spread over five seasons, his best being the club's first second division campaign in 1958-59 when he scored twice in seven games and also played his only FA Cup tie for the Wearsiders.**

Serving in Germany as part of his National Service Maltby was sometimes flown over to play, as he did on the occasion of his first goal against Portsmouth. He went on to net 32 goals in 115 games for Darlington in the fourth tier before adding eight goals in 56+1 games in the second tier for Bury where he signed for Bob Stokoe.

Leaving the Shakers in 1967 Maltby played in South Africa, during which time he worked as a teacher, where he scored 61 goals for Southern Suburbs with whom he played in two UTC Bowls finals picking up both runners-up and winner's medals. He returned to play non-league football in the north east after which he became a secondary school teacher in Walbottle.

## MANDRON, Mikael Yann Mathieu

**POSITION:** Centre-forward

**BIRTHPLACE:** Boulogne-sur-Mer, France

**DATE OF BIRTH:** 11/10/1994

**HEIGHT:** 6' 3" **WEIGHT:** 13st 12lbs

**SIGNED FROM:** Boulogne, 09/07/2011

**DEBUT:** v Aston Villa, A, 29/04/2013

**LAST MATCH:** v Liverpool, H, 10/01/2015

**MOVED TO:** Contract not renewed, 31/05/2016

**TEAMS:** Boulogne, Sunderland, Fleetwood Town (L), Shrewsbury Town (L), Hartlepool United (L), Eastleigh, Wigan Athletic, Colchester United, Gillingham, Crewe Alexandra, Gillingham (to July 2022)

**SAFC TOTALS:** 0+3 appearances / 0 goals

**After impressing at youth and reserve level, Mandron hit the bar in a five-minute debut at Aston Villa, but is best remembered for scoring twice against Sunderland at the Stadium of Light - including an equaliser deep into injury time - for Gillingham in the last home match before the 2019-20 season was curtailed through Covid 19.**

As a youngster at Sunderland he had a trio of loans scoring for Fleetwood against York in February 2014. It was his only goal in 4+9 games for Fleetwood while he failed to score in 2+1 outings for Shrewsbury and got one goal in 4+3 games for Hartlepool. Two weeks after leaving Sunderland Mikael joined National League side Eastleigh where 15 goals in 28+5 games (including a hat-trick at Bromley) paved the way for a Football League return with Wigan where he got one start and a couple of appearances off the bench without scoring.

After six months with the Latics Mandron moved to Colchester where he bagged a dozen league goals in a total of 66+29 games before his move to Gillingham. For the Gills, he only scored six goals with his brace at the Stadium of Light being the last of his 17+11 appearances all of which were in 2019-20. For Crewe, he scored 24 times in 70+15 games to May 2022, suffering relegation to League Two that summer before returning to Gillingham that July.

## MANGANE, Abdou Kader

**POSITION:** Centre-back

**BIRTHPLACE:** Thies, Senegal

**DATE OF BIRTH:** 23/03/1983

**HEIGHT:** 6' 4" **WEIGHT:** 14st 2lbs

**SIGNED FROM:** Al-Hilal, 14/01/2013, on loan

**DEBUT:** v Newcastle United, A, 14/04/2013

**LAST MATCH:** v Everton, H, 20/04/2013

**MOVED TO:** Al-Hilal, 13/05/2013, end of loan

**TEAMS:** US Rail, Neuchatel Xamax, BSC Young Boys, Lens, Rennes, Al-Hilal Sunderland (L), Erciyesspor, GFC Ajaccio, Strasbourg

**INTERNATIONAL:** Senegal

**SAFC TOTALS:** 0+2 appearances / 0 goals

**Senegal international Mangane's SAFC career extended to just 19 minutes split between two substitute appearances. Those games against Newcastle and Everton were his only taste of English football - and came in the only two games won under Paolo Di Canio.**

Naturalised as a French citizen in 2011, much of Kader's career was spent in France. However he started in his home town of Thies in Senegal with US Rail for whom he played 17 times in 2000-01, scoring four times. Spotted by Neuchatel Xamax of Switzerland, he spent six years there, making 158 appearances and scoring 16 goals before a transfer to Young Boys of Bern where he played nine times, scoring twice. Mangane moved into French football with Lens where he played 18+5 games, again chipping in as a regular goalscorer with five goals. A summer 2009 move took him to Rennes where he started exactly 100 league games and totalled 103+2 appearances with ten goals, including one in the Europa League at Celtic in November 2011.

The winner of 23 caps with Senegal, Kader played in all three of his country's games at the 2012 African Cup of Nations, all of which were disappointingly lost when he was a teammate of Dame N'Doye who later came to Sunderland. After his brief stint on loan at Sunderland from Al-Hilal of Saudi Arabia, for whom he scored twice in 14 games, Mangane moved into the sixth country he had played in, this time to Turkey with Erciyesspor.

Debuting in a goalless draw at Antalyaspor in August 2013, he played regularly, getting his two goals in his first season against two of the biggest teams in Turkey, in a 3-2 defeat at Besiktas and then in a final-day game at Galatasaray. There was one more goal in his second season as he took his total of appearances for the club to 35+1 before a return to France with Corsican club GFC Ajaccio where he spent 2015-16 playing 32 times and scoring against Guingamp. A final move to Strasbourg brought one goal in 20 games, his final appearance coming at Nantes in May 2018.

## MANNONE, Vito

**POSITION:** Goalkeeper

**BIRTHPLACE:** Desio, Italy

**DATE OF BIRTH:** 02/03/1988

**HEIGHT:** 6' 2" **WEIGHT:** 12st 1lb

**SIGNED FROM:** Arsenal, 03/07/2013

**DEBUT:** v MK Dons, H, 27/08/2013

**LAST MATCH:** v Southampton, H, 11/02/2017

**MOVED TO:** Reading, 19/07/2017

**TEAMS:** Atalanta, Arsenal, Barnsley (L), Hull City (L), Sunderland, Reading, Minnesota United (L), Esbjerg (L), Monaco, Lorient (to September 2022)

**INTERNATIONAL:** Italy Under 21s

**SAFC TOTALS:** 79+1 appearances / 0 goals

**Mannone was an intensely focussed goalkeeper who was thrilled every time he was selected and immensely frustrated whenever he was left out. He loved being at Sunderland and deservedly enjoyed the chants of his teammates who sang, 'Oh Vito Mannone' over and over again in the dressing room after Vito had been the hero of a League (Capital One) Cup semi-final victory at Old Trafford against Manchester United. The Wembley final against Manchester City took place on Mannone's 26th birthday. Although Vito was on the losing side, he was faultless for any of the goals.**

When Sunderland were relegated in 2017 future England goalkeeper Jordan Pickford was sold for a huge fee. Mannone was happy to stay, but the club's new CEO Martin Bain sold him to Reading with the club bringing in Jason Steele and Robbin Ruiter with Lee Camp following later in the season. The trio of new keepers all endured disastrous times at Sunderland who plummeted to relegation for a second successive year.

Had Mannone stayed, the chances are that that second relegation would have been averted. Chatting to Vito in the Hilton Garden Inn adjacent to the Stadium of Light when he returned with Reading in December 2017, the Italian keeper made it abundantly clear that he had not wanted to leave, but that the club had been keen to sell him as they looked to raise money.

Arsene Wenger was the Arsenal manager when Mannone was recruited as a youngster having started at Atalanta. Loaned to Barnsley where future Sunderland reserve Nick Colgan was the goalkeeper, Mannone debuted with a preview of his later

## MANNONE, Vito (Continued)

heroics for Sunderland, saving a penalty in a successful League Cup shoot-out with Blackpool in August 2006. He had three further outings for the Tykes, including one as sub, and waited two years and eight months for another opportunity which came in an end of season debut for the Gunners in a Premier League win at home to Stoke. On that occasion his opposite number became Tommy Sorensen after the Dane came off the bench to join Liam Lawrence and Rory Delap in the Potters side.

The following season Mannone made eight appearances for Arsenal, including three in the Champions League, keeping clean sheets in three of his first four matches. There were then four clean sheets in his first five games of a loan to Hull where he played ten times. Returning to Arsenal the keeper had one more appearance in the Champions League before a second loan to Hull where he kept nine clean sheets in the first 13 of his 23 games. There would be back-to-back clean sheets - including one in a Premier League win at Liverpool - when he returned to Arsenal but the 13 games he played in the first half of the 2012-13 season would be his last as he took his Arsenal total to 25+1 before his transfer to Sunderland when Roberto De Fanti was in charge of recruitment.

Following his time in the north east Mannone made 47 appearances - all in the league - for Reading who loaned him to Minnesota where he played 34 times in the MLS and twelve for Esbjerg in Denmark before a summer 2020 move to Monaco, who he helped to a home win over Paris St Germain on his home debut. Vito made nine appearances in his first season, but as of May 2022, had not played for 16 months. In 2021, a rumoured return to Sunderland was mooted for the former Italy Under 21 international. This failed to materialise, but Vito would always be guaranteed a warm welcome whenever he came to Wearside.

## MANQUILLO GAITAN, Javier

**POSITION:** Right-back
**BIRTHPLACE:** Madrid, Spain
**DATE OF BIRTH:** 05/05/1994
**HEIGHT:** 5' 11" **WEIGHT:** 12st 0lbs
**SIGNED FROM:** Atletico Madrid, 25/08/2016, on loan
**DEBUT:** v Southampton, A, 27/08/2016
**LAST MATCH:** v Chelsea, A, 21/05/2017
**MOVED TO:** Atletico Madrid, 22/05/2017, end of loan
**TEAMS:** Real Madrid, Atletico Madrid, Liverpool (L), Olympique Marseille (L), Sunderland (L), Newcastle United (to June 2022)
**INTERNATIONAL:** Spain Under 21
**SAFC TOTALS:** 17+5 appearances / 1 goal

**Loaned to Sunderland from Atletico Madrid, where he made three La Liga appearances as they won the title in 2013-14, Manquillo had played youth football for Real Madrid alongside his twin brother Victor before both switched to Atletico after their release from Real.**

Capped by Spain at all six levels from Under 16 to Under 21, Javier debuted for Atletico in a Europa League defeat at Viktoria Pizen in the Czech Republic on 6 December 2012 and three days later was given a La Liga debut as a 74th-minute sub when his team were already 6-0 up against Deportivo (Radamel Falcao having scored five).

After nine appearances over two years - including one in the Champions League - Manquillo got his first experience of English football when he joined Liverpool on loan in August 2014. He made 18+1 appearances in his season at Anfield - one of four Champions League appearances being a return to Real Madrid. Loaned to Marseille in 2015-16, he doubled his playing time with 36+1 games, again tasting European football.

Arriving at Sunderland for a third season-long loan, it was a different experience as he played in a side that were relegated with a whimper, finishing in bottom place. Manquillo at least signed off with the first goal of his career in a final day 5-1 thrashing at champions Chelsea. Local rivals Newcastle had evidently been impressed with the performances of the on-loan defender on their doorstep as that summer they paid over £4m for his transfer. Debuting for the Magpies in a home defeat to Tottenham in August 2017, to May 2022 he had made 85+19 appearances for the black and whites, scoring once.

## MAPSON, John (Johnny)

**POSITION:** Goalkeeper
**BIRTHPLACE:** Birkenhead, Cheshire
**DATE OF BIRTH:** 02/05/1917 - 19/08/1999
**HEIGHT:** 5' 10½" **WEIGHT:** 12st 9lbs
**SIGNED FROM:** Reading, 10/03/1936
**DEBUT:** v Portsmouth, H, 04/04/1936
**LAST MATCH:** v Manchester City, H, 21/03/1953
**MOVED TO:** Retired, 31/05/1954
**TEAMS:** Highworth Town, Westrop Rovers, Swindon Town, Reading, Guildford City (L), Sunderland, Brentford (WW2 Guest), Reading (WW2 Guest)
**INTERNATIONAL:** FA Touring party, England wartime international
**SAFC TOTALS:** 383 appearances / 0 goals

**The only Sunderland goalkeeper to play in a side that won both the league and FA Cup, Johnny Mapson (or John as he called himself) lost six years of his career to the Second World War, but still managed almost 400 games for Sunderland.**

He was the last member of the 1937 FA Cup-winning side to play for the Lads and the last to pass away. Since Mapson's Wembley appearance (on the day before his 20th birthday) there has not been a younger FA Cup winning-goalkeeper. Not until Peter Shilton played for Leicester City in 1969 was there a younger FA Cup final goalkeeper, but unlike Mapson, Shilton finished on the losing side.

I interviewed Johnny for my first book 'Sunderland's Number Ones' shortly before he died. Mapson told me that when he signed for Sunderland and came to Wearside during the depression of the 1930s, it was the first time he had seen children without shoes. It was a tough time, but the efforts of Mapson and his teammates in winning the league, Charity Shield and FA Cup (the only three trophies available) in barely twelve months did all they could to lift the gloom.

Mapson had only played two league games before coming to Sunderland, saving a penalty on his debut for Reading at home to Newport County. Upon his return from his first away game at Exeter he was informed by Reading manager Billy Butler that Sunderland wanted to sign him for £1,500. Mapson had grown up in Wiltshire where his family moved when he was seven.

According to Johnny his Catholic School was the smallest in Swindon and at football they were well beaten every week. He considered it useful experience as he got into the Swindon Schools side. Perhaps that paid off as Johnny became renowned for his positional sense rather than his agility. Although he could be agile and make spectacular saves, he rarely needed to because he had the knack of being in the right place at the right time as he explained in 'Sunderland's Number Ones' when talking of one of his best games - a 1-0 cup win at Everton when Sunderland were the cup-holders.

Having come to Sunderland late in the title-winning season of 1935-36 when his seven games were not enough to warrant a medal, Mapson played in all nine games as the FA Cup was won in 1937. Three of those games were at the quarter-final stage against Wolves who tried to bribe the teenager before the second replay. "Although it was a lot of money I wasn't interested, so I just took it [a letter] to the manager and that was the last I heard of it." Johnny told me. Sunderland won the game without conceding.

A model of consistency, Mapson managed 40 or more of the 42 league games in no fewer than six seasons. In addition to his 383 official appearances for Sunderland, he played in the three games of the expunged 1939-40 season and a further 33 in the 1945-46 League North series.

During the war Johnny played one game for England against Wales at the City Ground in Nottingham in 1941. He was called up for a second appearance in the return with Wales, but chose to play for Reading in a London war-time cup final against Brentford (won 3-2) on the same day and was never selected again. In 1939, Johnny had played twice during an FA touring party to South Africa. In what were called Test Matches, he played in 8-2 and 2-1 wins over the Springboks in Durban and Johannesburg.

While with Reading one of his fellow Guest players was Matt Busby who subsequently tried to sign Johnny for Manchester United, although Sunderland refused to consider United's interest. After a persistent knee injury hastened the end of his career, Mapson was given a job as a manufacturer's agent in the furniture industry by Sunderland chairman Bill Ditchburn. He later returned to Swindon working part-time in a Garden Centre until he was in his seventies before returning to the north east to live with his daughter in Washington.

## MARANGONI, Claudio Oscar

**POSITION:** Midfielder

**BIRTHPLACE:** Rosario, Argentina

**DATE OF BIRTH:** 17/11/1954

**HEIGHT:** 6' 1" **WEIGHT:** 13st 0lbs

**SIGNED FROM:** San Lorenzo, 03/12/1979

**DEBUT:** v Cardiff City, H, 08/12/1979

**LAST MATCH:** v Manchester City, H, 12/11/1980

**MOVED TO:** Huracan, 05/01/1981

**TEAMS:** Rosario Central, Chacarita Juniors, San Lorenzo, Sunderland, Huracan, Independiente, Boca Juniors

**INTERNATIONAL:** Argentina

**SAFC TOTALS:** 21+1 appearances / 3 goals

**In the calendar year after Argentina had become world champions, Sunderland followed a trend of signing players from the South American country in making Marangoni their record signing. These days when a player arrives from abroad - even a European country - they are said to need a long period to acclimatise to UK conditions. Claudio was not afforded that luxury. He was expected to be brilliant straight away despite the different pace of the game, the climate and the language difference.**

He struggled. Instead of the silky South American touch and control fans expected, Marangoni was a gangly and awkward looking player seemingly on a different wavelength to his teammates. He did contribute three goals in his first eight games including a winner at Fulham, so he can be said to have helped in the promotion push although he did not play in the closing stages of the season. Used as a midfield creator in England, in Argentina he became much better known as a holding midfielder.

Once in the top-flight, Claudio started just three league games and came off the bench in another before returning to Argentina in a deal which meant that Sunderland ended up paying just £230,000 of the agreed £380,000 purchase price. At Brian Clough's request, in October 1980 Claudio played for Nottingham Forest as a Guest as the European champions beat Tampa Bay Rowdies 7-1 in a friendly.

In those pre-internet days, news occasionally filtered back as to how Claudio was doing back in Argentina. Given how disappointing he had been at Sunderland, eyes were increasingly raised as it was learned how well he did. Returning to Argentina he linked up with San Lorenzo's fiercest rivals Huracan, but moved on to Independiente in 1982 after 58 games and eleven goals.

At Independiente under Jose Pastoriza, Marangoni was part of a side that were twice runners-up before claiming the Metropolitano championship in 1983 when a final-day win over local rivals Racing Club saw them pip Claudio's old club San Lorenzo to the title. After going on to win the Copa Libertadores, Marangoni played in the Intercontinental Cup final as Liverpool (who included Alan Kennedy and had Bob Bolder on the bench) were beaten 1-0 in Tokyo in December 1984 - five years almost to the day since his Sunderland debut.

Following the win over Liverpool a rumoured return to England with Southampton failed to materialise. He stayed with Independiente until 1988 scoring 25 goals in 237 league appearances before joining Boca Juniors on 27 August that year. He helped the Buenos Aires giants to beat his old club Independiente on penalties in the 1989 Supercopa Sudamericana after scoring in the semi-final against Gremio of Brazil. This was followed up with the Recopa Sudamericana in 1990, shortly before his retirement after seven goals in 93 games for Boca.

Marangoni also won nine caps for Argentina and managed Banfield in 1998. Having qualified as a physiotherapist and a football coach, Marangoni established the Escuela Modelo de Futbol Deportes, a soccer school for children aged three to 13. This proved so successful that after expanding throughout Argentina it spread to Chile and Spain. In his own youth as a player, Claudio came to the fore with Chacarita Juniors for whom he played 62 times scoring seven goals before joining San Lorenzo where he played 135 league games before Ken Knighton took him to England.

## MARPLES, Emerson Arthur

**POSITION:** Right-back

**BIRTHPLACE:** Eckington, Chesterfield, Derbyshire

**DATE OF BIRTH:** 05/12/1878 - Q3 1964

**HEIGHT:** 5' 8" **WEIGHT:** 13st 0lbs

**SIGNED FROM:** Chesterfield Town, 26/02/1908

**DEBUT:** v Chelsea, A, 29/02/1908

**LAST MATCH:** v Bristol City, A, 20/04/1908

**MOVED TO:** Retired, 31/05/1910

**TEAMS:** Dronfield Town, Chesterfield Town, Sunderland, Chesterfield Town, Eckington Works

**SAFC TOTALS:** 10 appearances / 0 goals

**Nicknamed 'Emma', Marples was in his 30th year when he came into the top flight with Sunderland. He played in the final ten games of 1907-08, but did not feature in his remaining two seasons at the club.**

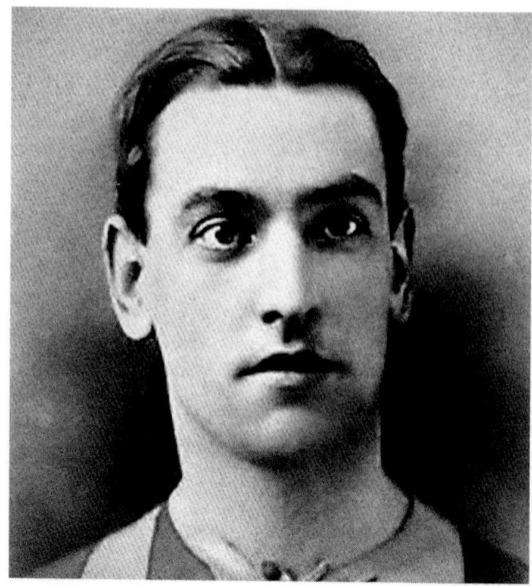

He underwent an operation in the summer of 1908 due to a cartilage problem and never really recovered, although having hung up his boots retired when leaving Sunderland he was persuaded to play for Chesterfield in the Midland League. After a handful of games he had to give up when his knee problem flared up again.

A native of Chesterfield, he became landlord of the Miners' Arms pub in the town. Before coming to Sunderland he had played 157 league and cup games for Chesterfield Town who dropped out of the Football League in the first season after he moved to Wearside. During World War One Marples worked as an engine fitter in Canada, but moved back home in 1919 and made his last appearances when in his early forties for Eckington Works FC.

## MARRIOTT, Andrew (Andy)

**POSITION:** Goalkeeper

**BIRTHPLACE:** Sutton-in-Ashfield, Nottinghamshire

**DATE OF BIRTH:** 11/10/1970

**HEIGHT:** 6' 0" **WEIGHT:** 12st 8lbs

**SIGNED FROM:** Wrexham, 28/09/1998 after loan spell from 17/08/1998

**DEBUT:** v Grimsby Town, A, 13/03/1999

**LAST MATCH:** v Wimbledon, A, 03/01/2000

**MOVED TO:** Barnsley, 13/03/2001

**TEAMS:** Arsenal, Nottingham Forest, WBA (L), Blackburn Rovers (L), Colchester United (L), Burnley (L), Wrexham, Sunderland, Wigan Athletic (L), Barnsley, Birmingham City, SC Beira Mar, Coventry City (L) Colchester United, Bury, Torquay United, Boston United, Exeter City

**INTERNATIONAL:** England Under 21 / Wales

**SAFC TOTALS:** 5 appearances / 0 goals

**Marriott was a reliable number 2 goalkeeper who kept a clean sheet on his debut in the 1998-99 promotion season and conceded just a single goal on his one appearance for Sunderland in the Premier League. Both of his first-team appearances were away from home, but he did play in between these games at the Stadium of Light in Jimmy McNab's Testimonial - as a forward alongside fellow goalkeeper Tommy Sorensen. He later scored the winning penalty in an FA Cup shoot-out for Torquay against Harrogate Town in 2005.**

Like many goalkeepers Marriott must have spent much of his time living out of a suitcase. He was constantly on the move. Even at international level he won five caps for Wales after being capped by England at Under 21 level, playing against Mexico in the Toulon tournament in France in May 1992 when he was with Nottingham Forest. Brian Clough played him in the League Cup final at Wembley in April 1992 when, as a teammate of Roy Keane, he was part of a Nottingham Forest team who went down 1-0 to a Manchester United side who included Steve Bruce.

It was one of 13 appearances Marriott made for Forest who had paid Andy's first club Arsenal £50,000 for a keeper who had never played for the Gunners.

Forest loaned him to WBA (3/0), Blackburn (2/0), Colchester (10/0) and Burnley (15/0) before quadrupling their investment when selling Andy to Wrexham in October 1993. Wrexham got their money's worth as Marriott made 278 appearances, winning the Welsh Cup in 1995 when they beat Cardiff City in the final.

From there he came to Sunderland for another reported £200,000 fee. Sunderland loaned him to Wigan (2/0) and Barnsley, a move which he made permanent, going on to make 56+1 appearances for the Tykes. There was then a single game for Birmingham in 2003 and a brief spell in Portugal where he played 24 times for Beira Mar before moves to Coventry and Colchester, although neither brought a league appearance. Next stop was Bury where after 21 games there followed 64 for Torquay and 49 for Boston, who were then a League Two outfit. A final move brought 56 games back in the south west with Exeter as his total career appearances topped 600.

He became General Manager at Exeter, then joined West Brom as assistant to the Sporting and Technical Director in January 2011 before moving into the world of motor racing with McLaren Formula One.

## MARSDEN, William (Billy)

**POSITION:** Inside-left

**BIRTHPLACE:** Silksworth, Sunderland

**DATE OF BIRTH:** 10/11/1901 - 19/09/1983

**HEIGHT:** 5' 8" **WEIGHT:** 10st 6lbs

**SIGNED FROM:** Silksworth CW, 01/10/1920

**DEBUT:** v Derby County, A, 28/03/1921

**LAST MATCH:** v Tottenham Hotspur, A, 27/10/1923

**MOVED TO:** Wednesday, 19/05/1924

**TEAMS:** Ryhope CW, Silksworth CW, Sunderland, Wednesday

**INTERNATIONAL:** England

**SAFC TOTALS:** 3 appearances / 2 goals

**Billy Marsden played for England and won two top-flight titles but barely got a chance at Sunderland despite scoring twice in his three games. He went on to manage Doncaster Rovers as well as becoming assistant coach to the Netherlands FA, but given his lack of opportunities at Roker Park perfectly fits the bill as one of SAFC's forgotten men.**

Having scored 45 goals in 1919-20, Billy joined Sunderland in October 1920 the month before his 19th birthday having already played for both Silksworth CW and Ryhope CW. Marsden debuted in a 1-0 win at Derby the following February but then did not get a second chance for two and a half years. He was to play twice in that 1923-24 season, scoring on both occasions, but in a season when Sunderland finished third, Billy could not get a regular game.

At the end of that season Marsden moved on to Wednesday (they were not yet officially called Sheffield Wednesday) with whom he would enjoy fabulous success after being converted from an inside-left to left-half, although he was right-footed. To begin with Billy remained as an attacker, scoring the winner on his debut at Crystal Palace on the opening day of the season. Having played in exactly a third of the Owls games in his first season, Billy was a revelation in his second having swapped position. He was ever-present as Wednesday won Division Two. Ever-present again in the following campaign he remained a regular in 1927-28 when after injury he returned to the team with Wednesday bottom with three games to play. His influence helped deliver a strong end to the season when they pulled up to 14th in the tightest of finishes.

That escape reaped immense rewards as in the next two seasons Wednesday were champions with Marsden ever-present in the first and missing just five of 42 in the second. One of those games saw him proudly back at Roker Park as the visitors won 4-2 at the end of the season having already retained their title.

It was during that season that the son of a miner from Stewart Street in Silksworth gained his three England caps. Having debuted in a 6-0 thrashing of Wales in November 1929, Billy had played in a 5-2 beating of Scotland at Wembley. Sadly, just a week after the final game of the season came an injury that ended his playing career. Playing in Berlin in the first Germany v England match since the Great War, Marsden was injured early in the game in a collision with teammate Roy Goodall of Huddersfield. Though he struggled on until half-time, he had to come off leaving England to earn a hard fought 3-3 draw with ten men. Taken to a local hospital Marsden had suffered a spinal injury and was lucky not to have lost his life as he had broken his neck. Only the skills of his surgeon saved Billy, who spent six weeks in hospital before being allowed home. Given £750 compensation by the FA and a benefit match by his club, he tried a comeback with Wednesday's reserves, but was hospitalised again after being knocked unconscious in a game against Stoke's second string two days after Christmas in 1930.

In December of the following year he became manager of Dutch side HBS Craeyenhout in Den Haag, staying with them until July 1934 when he returned to home turf to become trainer of Gateshead in Division Three North. Having been promised the manager's job which was not forthcoming, Billy resigned a week before Christmas. Returning to the Netherlands Marsden had a second spell at HBS Craeyenhout, swiftly moving to Be Quick 1887 and then on to Hermes DVS as well as working for the Netherlands FA.

Returning to England to escape the invading Germans in 1940, on 19 April 1944 he accepted a post as part-time manager of Doncaster Rovers. Having by now become a publican, Billy resigned from his post with Doncaster on 27 February 1946 as he did not want to accept Rovers proposal that they required a full-time manager, although he did stay on until the end of the season. A short spell as manager of Worksop Town in 1953 proved to be the swansong on Marsden's football career.

Amongst the pubs he ran were the Robin Hood Inn in Millhouses, the White Lion and The Crosspool Tavern - the latter one of my locals when I was a student in Sheffield in the late seventies and a pub known for being the singer Joe Cocker's watering hole of choice when at home in Sheffield. Whether Billy Marsden ever met up with the singer of 'With a Little Help from My Friends' is a matter for conjecture! Billy passed away in Sheffield on 19 September 1983.

## MARSHALL, Robert Samuel (Bobby)

**POSITION:** Inside / centre-forward

**BIRTHPLACE:** Hucknall, Nottinghamshire

**DATE OF BIRTH:** 03/04/1903 - 27/10/1966

**HEIGHT:** 5' 10" **WEIGHT:** 12st 7lbs

**SIGNED FROM:** Hucknall Olympic, 22/05/1920

**DEBUT:** v Bradford City, A, 23/10/1920

**LAST MATCH:** v Burnley, A, 04/02/1928

**MOVED TO:** Manchester City, 01/03/1928

**TEAMS:** Hucknall Olympic, Sunderland, Manchester City, Stockport County

**SAFC TOTALS:** 207 appearances / 73 goals

**Sunderland were attracted to Marshall after he had netted 74 goals in Hucknall Olympic's 1919-20 season. Renowned for his ball control Bobby scored a career total of 153 goals in 563 league and FA Cup games, winning the league, FA Cup and second division with Manchester City after leaving Sunderland.**

When in red and white he had been part of the Lads' attack for most of the 1920s. He was prominent from 1923-24 to 1926-27 when Sunderland finished third in three seasons out of four and had also made nine appearances in 1922-23 when Sunderland were runners-up.

A versatile player who occasionally played at centre-half, and became a regular in that position with Manchester City, Bobby even took over in goal once for Sunderland when Paddy Bell was injured with 40 minutes left to play against Leeds in March 1927.

At Manchester City he was signed to aid their promotion push, playing 14 late-season games as they took the divisional title. He went on to score six goals against Sunderland during his time as a City player and missed just four games as City succeeded Sunderland as league champions in 1936-37.

In 1934 he played at inside-right as Portsmouth were beaten in the FA Cup final. A year earlier he had played in the same position as an Everton team, including his old Sunderland teammate Warney Cresswell, beat City in the final. In November 1937 he was at centre-half as City beat cup-holders Sunderland in the Charity Shield at Maine Road - a season in which City were relegated a year after being champions. It was his last season for City for whom he scored 80 goals in 356 appearances.

Eleven months after his final game for City Marshall moved to nearby Stockport County, initially as a player but he soon took over as manager. He stayed in that post from March 1939 until February 1949, leading County to fourth place in Division Three North in the first post-war league campaign. He then managed Chesterfield until July 1952 taking the Spireites to sixth in the second division in 1949 only to be relegated two years later.

Marshall became a publican at the Glapwell Hotel, near Chesterfield, after leaving the game until passing away at the age of 64. His brother John signed for Sunderland on 23 August 1921, but never played for the first team. Another brother Harry played for Nottingham Forest, Southport, Wolves, Port Vale, Spurs, Kidderminster, Rochdale and Linfield between 1923 and 1938.

# M

## MARSHALL, Walter

**POSITION:** Half-back

**BIRTHPLACE:** Huddersfield, Yorkshire

**DATE OF BIRTH:** 18/01/1864 - 12/01/1950

**DEBUT:** v Redcar, A, 24/10/1885

**LAST MATCH:** v Redcar, A, 24/10/1885

**TEAMS:** Sunderland

**SAFC TOTALS:** 1 appearance / 0 goals

**An English (FA) Cup tie at Redcar is the only official appearance of Walter Marshall who is also known to have played in a series of friendlies in a wide variety of positions.**

Walter had moved from Yorkshire to Sunderland by the time he was seven years old, and like many of the playing staff in the 1880s worked in the shipyards as a boilermaker. After leaving Wearside he lived and worked in Wallsend before retiring to Whitley Bay.

## MARSTON, Maurice

**POSITION:** Right-back

**BIRTHPLACE:** Trimdon, Co Durham

**DATE OF BIRTH:** 24/03/1929 - 28/01/2002

**HEIGHT:** 5' 11" **WEIGHT:** 11st 11lbs

**SIGNED FROM:** Redby Juniors, Summer 1944
Exact date unknown

**DEBUT:** v Tottenham Hotspur, A, 15/03/1952

**LAST MATCH:** v Charlton Athletic, A, 20/12/1952

**MOVED TO:** Northampton Town, 10/07/1953

**TEAMS:** Redby Juniors, Silksworth Juniors, Sunderland, Rhyl (Guest) Northampton Town, Kettering Town

**SAFC TOTALS:** 9 appearances / 0 goals

**Maurice Marston initially joined Sunderland on amateur forms in 1944. He immediately started to play for Silksworth Juniors who were effectively a Sunderland AFC junior team at the time, until 1947 when National Service in the army was required until 1949, during which time he appeared as a guest player for Rhyl.**

In 1950 he was part of Sunderland's tour of Turkey and a couple of years later briefly broke into the first team. After his nine top-flight games for Sunderland he went on to play 149 games for Northampton Town between 1953 and 57. He scored twice for the Cobblers before completing his football career as captain of Kettering Town where he stayed until January 1983 having become both manager and later secretary.

## MARTIN, Henry (Harry)

**POSITION:** Outside-left

**BIRTHPLACE:** Selston, Nottinghamshire

**DATE OF BIRTH:** 05/12/1891 - 31/12/1974

**HEIGHT:** 5' 10" **WEIGHT:** 12st 0lbs

**SIGNED FROM:** Sutton Junction, 15/01/1912

**DEBUT:** v Liverpool, A, 05/04/1912

**LAST MATCH:** v Tottenham Hotspur, H, 05/04/1922

**MOVED TO:** Nottingham Forest, 20/05/1922

**TEAMS:** Selston, Sutton Junction, Sunderland, Hull City (WW1 Guest), Nottingham Forest, Rochdale

**INTERNATIONAL:** England

**SAFC TOTALS:** 230 appearances / 23 goals

**Harry Martin's final appearance came ten years to the day since his debut - World War One, in which he was hospitalised, coming in between. Despite losing time to the war Harry played 230 times for Sunderland, scoring exactly one goal per ten appearances. Taking over from the legendary Arthur Bridgett on the left-wing Martin's finest accolade must be that Bridgett was not missed. In the club's greatest season Martin was ever-present as the league title was won and the cup final reached in 1912-13.**

A tremendous winger, he is known to have set up at least 40 goals for Charlie Buchan alone, but it was Francis Cuggy who was his teammate on the occasion of Harry's one England cap, against Ireland at Middlesbrough on Valentine's Day 1914. He also played in two 'Victory' internationals and represented the Football League three times.

One of nine children - four of whom died as infants - Harry was the son of a coal miner and began working with his father at the pit. It was when playing in an English (FA) Cup tie against Swindon Town for Sutton Junction on 13 January 1912 that he convinced Sunderland to sign him for £75. (despite a 6-0 defeat). The following season Swindon would be one of the sides he helped Sunderland knock out on the way to the final. Swindon would go on to be a club Harry was connected to for even longer than his time at Sunderland.

During the war Harry played as a guest for Hull City and Nottingham Forest and, after recovering from a bullet wound in the shoulder in 1918, continued his Sunderland career until signing for his home county club in 1922, going on to score 13 times in 107 league games. In June 1925 Harry joined Rochdale where he added 18 goals in 93 league appearances before becoming their trainer in August 1928 and was pressed into a final league appearance during an injury crisis in the 1930-31 season by which time he was nearly 40.

Having become caretaker-manager of Rochdale in August 1930 following two years as trainer he moved on to become trainer at York City in August 1931. On 16 November 1933 Harry became trainer of Mansfield Town taking over as manager on 11 January 1934. Forced to resign by the Stags directors, 14 months later he joined Swindon Town as trainer in 1936, staying with them until the mid 1950s.

## MARTIN, Isaac George

**POSITION:** Half-back

**BIRTHPLACE:** Gateshead, Co Durham

**DATE OF BIRTH:** 25/05/1889 - 06/05/1962

**HEIGHT:** 5' 9" **WEIGHT:** 11st 7lbs

**SIGNED FROM:** Windy Nook, 19/02/1909

**DEBUT:** v Leicester Fosse, A, 20/03/1909

**LAST MATCH:** v Preston North End A, 20/04/1912

**MOVED TO:** Portsmouth, 07/06/1912

**TEAMS:** Gateshead Rodsley, Windy Nook, Sunderland, Portsmouth, Norwich City

**SAFC TOTALS:** 16 appearances / 0 goals

**George 'Pompey' Martin might more accurately have been nicknamed 'Canary' as he had captained Norwich during 14 years in Norfolk whereas he was injured for most of his single year with Portsmouth. It was at Norwich that he picked up the nickname 'Pompey' in order for him not to be confused with another George Martin who had played for the club.**

George had not yet become known as 'Pompey' when he joined Sunderland from Windy Nook as a teenager having previously played for Gateshead Rodsley. He had four years at Sunderland before a fee of £100 took him to Portsmouth.

Sunderland were a decent side who would finish third when he broke into the team in March 1909 but having conceded twelve goals in his two games he was quickly discarded. He got another chance the following Christmas playing in a double header with Bury and then waited until the end of the following campaign when he appeared in two of the last three fixtures.

Martin's best season at Sunderland was in 1911-12 when he held his place for the opening six games and ten in all, including a derby at Newcastle, although he was on the losing side on that occasion.

Had he stayed at Sunderland he might have got a game or two during the 1912-13 season when Sunderland won the league and reached the cup final, but he had gone south to Portsmouth before finding his footballing home in Norwich. Portsmouth made a £20 profit when they sold 'Pompey' to Norwich in July 1913 although he had played just 19 games for them in all competitions. In contrast, at Carrow Road he became a hero, captaining the Canaries in their first-ever Football League match at Plymouth. He went on to play 223 Football League games for Norwich in addition to his 83 Southern League games, 28 FA Cup appearances and three Southern Charity Cup outings. During World War One, he served in the Royal Engineers.

## MARTIN, Neil

**POSITION:** Centre-forward

**BIRTHPLACE:** Tranent, East Lothian

**DATE OF BIRTH:** 20/10/1940

**HEIGHT:** 6' 0" **WEIGHT:** 11st 3lbs

**SIGNED FROM:** Hibernian, 21/10/1965

**DEBUT:** v Sheffield Wednesday, A, 23/10/1965

**LAST MATCH:** v Norwich City, H, 31/01/1968

**MOVED TO:** Coventry City, 08/02/1968

**TEAMS:** Alloa Athletic, Queen of the South, Hibernian, Sunderland, Coventry City, Nottingham Forest, Brighton & Hove Albion, Crystal Palace, San Antonio Thunder (L), St. Patricks Athletic

**INTERNATIONAL:** Scotland

**SAFC TOTALS:** 99 appearances / 46 goals

**Neil Martin was an outstanding centre-forward who scored over 100 goals in both England and Scotland. He scored a hat-trick the first time I ever saw Sunderland, against Peterborough in the FA Cup in February 1967, a season in which he scored 26 times including 20 in the top-flight. Selling Martin to relegation rivals Coventry mid-way through the following season - a week after the return of Alan Brown as manager - seems to have been very short-sighted as Martin was a centre-forward who led the line well and scored at an excellent rate.**

He had first been seen at Roker Park playing alongside Jim Baxter for the Scottish League when Neil scored in a 2-2 draw against a Football League XI including Bobby Moore and Jimmy Greaves in March 1964. It was one of two times he represented the Scottish League. At the time Martin was playing for Hibs but he had started with Alloa Athletic while serving an apprenticeship as a mining engineer. 25 league and cup goals in 1960-61 - when minnows Alloa reached the quarter-final of the Scottish Cup - persuaded Queen of the South to invest £2,000 in the young striker.

Renowned for his cool temperament, both in front of goal and in refusing to be drawn into physical confrontations - although he could handle himself and was no pushover - Martin scored 30 goals in total in his first season at Palmerston Park as the Dumfries club won promotion from the second division. During his time with Queen of the South Neil again reached the Scottish Cup quarter-finals after he went in goal against Kilmarnock and kept a clean sheet. Thirty three goals in 61 league games led to a £7,500 move to his boyhood favourites Hibs where he netted 53 times in 65 league games in addition to his cup exploits, which included mercilessly scoring four in an 11-2 League Cup annihilation of his old club Alloa. He also smashed four against Queen of the South in a league game and played European football for Hibs against Valencia.

He was capped three times, just before and after his move to Sunderland. Debuting as Denis Law's partner in a World Cup qualifying draw in Poland he also played alongside Law in a win away to Finland. By his own admission the highlight of Martin's career was playing in front of over 100,000 at Hampden Park as Scotland beat Italy for the first time. He was joined by Sunderland teammate Jim Baxter for that 1-0 victory in November 1965.

Neil had debuted for Sunderland the previous month, marking his £45,000 transfer with a goal at Hillsborough. The same ground would be the scene of his final appearance on a Sunderland team-sheet, and also the only time he was named as a sub although he did not come on. Perhaps if he had, he might have persuaded Brown of the folly of selling him. Brown was managing the opposition days before returning to Roker.

Sunderland doubled their money when accepting £90,000 from Coventry where he teamed-up again with his former Queen of the South colleague Ernie Hannigan. Replacing Bobby Gould Martin got eight late-season goals to keep Coventry up by a point and finish as joint-top scorer - his eight goals for the Sky Blues taking his seasonal total to 20. Two seasons later, he was top scorer with 15 as Coventry finished sixth and Sunderland went down with top-scorer Gordon Harris' seven goals including three penalties.

Martin went on to score in Coventry's first-ever European game against Trakia Plovdiv of Bulgaria in the Inter-Cities Fairs Cup and also got on the scoresheet in the second round second leg against Bayern Munich - although the Sky Blues had been slaughtered 6-1 in Germany. After 45 goals in 120 games for Coventry a £66,000 move took him to Forest in February 1971, four years to the day since his hat-trick for Sunderland against Peterborough.

By now the wrong side of 30 and with injuries starting to affect him the goals dried up. Forest were relegated in his first full season but he was to provide an excellent foil to the emerging Duncan McKenzie. Martin also played for Forest in the infamous 1974 cup-tie at Newcastle where a pitch invasion with the Magpies trailing 1-3 led to an abandonment and eventually United reaching the final. Still at Forest when Brian Clough arrived as manager, Martin may have excelled, but was by now 34 and moved on to Brighton six months later, signing for Clough's former assistant Peter Taylor.

Scoring on his debut against Rotherham, he went on to net eight times in 17 league games before moving to Crystal Palace after three-quarters of a season. A final league goal against Halifax Town was Neil's only one for the Eagles in 8+1 appearances.

Having played in North America during Sunderland's 1967 summer as Vancouver Royal Canadians, Martin moved to the USA in 1976 with San Antonio Thunder where his teammates included former Sunderland man Harry Hood and Bobby Moore. After five goals in 19 games Martin completed his playing days in the Republic of Ireland with St Patrick's Athletic, scoring five goals in 14 games.

Neil started his coaching career in July 1977 with a season as Walsall's reserve team coach under manager Dave McKay. A lifetime in football continued with a decade in the Middle East, coaching alongside Dave Mackay in Kuwait and Dubai either side of a season-long spell as joint manager of Walsall alongside Alan Buckley in 1981-82. He also ran a couple of pubs in Birmingham before retiring to Tranent and becoming a regular at Hibs matches.

## MATETE, Jay

**POSITION:** Midfielder

**BIRTHPLACE:** Lambeth, Greater London

**DATE OF BIRTH:** 11/02/2001

**HEIGHT:** 5' 8" **WEIGHT:** 9st 6lbs

**SIGNED FROM:** Fleetwood Town, 31/01/2022

**DEBUT:** v Doncaster Rovers, H, 05/02/2022

**LAST MATCH:**

**MOVED TO:**

**TEAMS:** Reading, Fleetwood Town, Grimsby Town (L), Sunderland

**SAFC TOTALS:** 12+4 appearances / 0 goals (to May 2022)

**An energetic midfielder signed on a four and a half year contract shortly before his 21st birthday, Jay had made his name at Fleetwood Town. Given a debut by Joey Barton in September 2019, Matete went on to be guided by former Sunderland manager Simon Grayson.**

In 2020-21 Jay played 20 League Two games on loan to Grimsby, scoring his first three senior goals in his last four appearances. The last of these at Exeter was accompanied by his first senior red card curtailing his attempts to help the Mariners in their unsuccessful bid to avoid relegation from the Football League. A regular at Fleetwood - alongside Conor McLaughlin - in his last half-season before coming to Sunderland, Matete took his total of appearances for the Cod Army to 29+12 by the time of his move to Wearside.

## MATTEO, Dominic

**POSITION:** Defender

**BIRTHPLACE:** Dumfries, Dumfries & Galloway

**DATE OF BIRTH:** 28/04/1974

**HEIGHT:** 6' 1" **WEIGHT:** 11st 0lbs

**SIGNED FROM:** Liverpool, 22/03/1995, on loan

**DEBUT:** v Barnsley, A, 24/03/1995

**LAST MATCH:** v Barnsley, A, 24/03/1995

**MOVED TO:** Liverpool, 01/04/1995, end of loan

**TEAMS:** Liverpool, Sunderland (L), Leeds United, Blackburn Rovers, Stoke City

**INTERNATIONAL:** England B / Scotland

**SAFC TOTALS:** 1 appearance / 0 goals

## MATTEO, Dominic (Continued)

**Matteo played one game for Sunderland, but should not have. It was not his fault that he had not been properly registered in what was Mick Buxton's final game as manager. Sunderland were fined £2,500 at an FA Hearing in York a week later when the club were relieved not to receive a points deduction as they fought relegation.**

Matteo returned to Liverpool when the administrative discrepancy was discovered after the transfer deadline had passed. Matteo had been at Liverpool since as an eleven-year-old having been spotted while Kenny Dalglish watched Birkdale United. A first-team debut came in October 1993 under Graeme Souness but it was not until 1996-97 that he played regularly, appearing in two thirds of Liverpool's league programme. A summer 2000 £4.75m move to Leeds came days after signing a new five-year deal. There had been 115+12 games and three goals at Liverpool including exactly 100 league starts, while at Leeds he played 146 times, scoring four times, two of his goals coming in the Champions League. At Elland Road, Dominic was installed as club captain when Rio Ferdinand was transferred to Manchester United.

Of English parents and Italian grandparents, Matteo made four appearances for England Under 21s, one for England B and was twice called up for a full England squad by Glenn Hoddle before winning six full caps for his country of birth, Scotland, while he was with Leeds.

Leaving Leeds to re-unite with his former boss Souness at Blackburn, Matteo made 36+3 appearances (no goals) for Rovers who he captained before a free transfer to Stoke City (24+1/1) in January 2007. The Potters were promoted in Dominic's first full season, but he missed most of that campaign due to injury before retiring at the end of 2008-09. By this time he had apparently acquired a costly addiction to gambling. He was reported to be declared bankrupt in 2015. Four years later, emergency surgery was required for a brain tumour.

His autobiography, 'In My Defence' was published in 2011.

## MATTHEWS, Adam James

**POSITION:** Right-back

**BIRTHPLACE:** Swansea, Glamorgan

**DATE OF BIRTH:** 13/01/1992

**HEIGHT:** 5' 10" **WEIGHT:** 11st 2lbs

**SIGNED FROM:** Celtic, 03/07/2015

**DEBUT:** v Leicester City, A, 08/08/2015

**LAST MATCH:** v Southend United, A, 04/05/2019

**MOVED TO:** Contract not renewed, 30/06/2019

**TEAMS:** Cardiff City, Celtic, Sunderland, Bristol City (L), Charlton Athletic, Omonia (to July 2022)

**INTERNATIONAL:** Wales

**SAFC TOTALS:** 54+13 appearances / 2 goals

**Adam Matthews cost a reported £2m fee, but having been acquired by Director of Football Lee Congerton evidently, was not fancied by manager Dick Advocaat or his successors Sam Allardyce and David Moyes.**

After debuting as a sub on the opening day of his first season in 2015, he played once more soon afterwards in a League Cup tie and then not at all for Sunderland until 2017-18. From that point Adam played quite regularly during his last two seasons, being an unused sub at Wembley against Charlton after what proved to be his final appearance.

During his time at Sunderland Matthews twice had loans at Bristol City under Lee Johnson, totalling 22+1 games for the Robins. After ending his contract at the Stadium of Light he was snapped up by Sunderland's successful Play-Off opponents Charlton with whom he returned to the Championship, making 29 appearances as they were immediately relegated. He returned with the Addicks to inflict a first home defeat of the season on Johnson's Sunderland in October 2021, but was released at the end of the season after 83+6 games (no goals) for the club. In the summer of 2022 he moved to Cyprus, signing for Omonia.

His senior career had begun in August 2009 with a debut for Cardiff at Blackpool in the Championship, his first goal coming on his ninth appearance with a free kick from fully 50 yards at Watford when he was a teammate of Michael Chopra. It was his only goal in 31+17 outings for the Bluebirds before joining Celtic in July 2011. Matthews had exactly four years in Glasgow making 124 starts plus 24 substitute appearances and scoring five times. The title was won in all four of his seasons at Parkhead when his teammates included Craig Gordon, Jason Denayer and Anthony Stokes. During this time Champions and Europa League football were regular occurrences, with highlights including a Champions League win over a Barcelona side which included Messi, Iniesta and Xavi.

Capped 20 times at Junior levels with Wales he won 14 full caps between 2011 and 2018. His appearance against Uruguay as a sub in the China meant he made the 100th appearance for Wales by a Sunderland player.

## MATTHEWS, Remi Luke

**POSITION:** Goalkeeper

**BIRTHPLACE:** Swansea, Glamorgan

**DATE OF BIRTH:** 10/02/1994

**HEIGHT:** 6' 0½" **WEIGHT:** 12st 4lbs

**SIGNED FROM:** Bolton Wanderers, 21/08/2020

**DEBUT:** v Aston Villa Under 21, H, 08/09/2020

**LAST MATCH:** v Shrewsbury Town, A, 09/02/2021

**MOVED TO:** Contract not renewed, 30/06/2021

**TEAMS:** Norwich City, Burton Albion (L), Doncaster Rovers (L), Hamilton Academical (L), Plymouth Argyle (L), Bolton Wanderers, Sunderland, Crystal Palace, St Johnstone (L) (to July 2022)

**SAFC TOTALS:** 10+1 appearances / 0 goals

**Signed for Sunderland by Phil Parkinson who he had played for at Bolton, Matthews had a torrid time at the club, made just half a handful of appearances but walked away with a Wembley winner's medal. That medal came as an unused sub as Sunderland won the Football League (Papa John's) Trophy in 2021.**

Four of Matthews' games for Sunderland came in the competition. In the league he was at fault for a goal at home to Burton, generally failed to impress or inspire confidence and cost a goal again on his final appearance in a defeat at Shrewsbury. With Sunderland leading he came for a cross, failed to deal with it and saw the home side equalise.

Freed at the end of the season, he was surprisingly signed by Premier League Crystal Palace, but as of May 2022, his solitary first appearance for the Eagles had been in a 3-0 Football League Trophy defeat to league new boys Sutton United and in July 2022 he joined St Johnstone on loan.

Matthews had come through Norwich City's academy system, but never played a first-team game for the Canaries. Instead, he went on a series of loans, debuting in a 2-1 win for Burton Albion against Scunthorpe United in the Brewers first League One fixture in August 2015. That was his only league start for Albion for whom he played 5+1 times in total after which he had nine games for Doncaster, and 27 for each of Hamilton and Plymouth. A loan to Bolton became a permanent move with Remi eventually tallying 58 games for the Trotters.

## MAVRIAS, Charalampos (Charis)

**POSITION:** Winger

**BIRTHPLACE:** Zakynthos, Greece

**DATE OF BIRTH:** 21/02/1994

**HEIGHT:** 5' 9½" **WEIGHT:** 11st 9lbs

**SIGNED FROM:** Panathinaikos, 22/08/2013

**DEBUT:** v MK Dons, H, 27/08/2013

**LAST MATCH:** v Arsenal, A, 09/01/2016

**MOVED TO:** Left club by mutual consent, 31/08/2016

**TEAMS:** Panathinaikos, Sunderland, Panathinaikos (L), Fortuna Dusseldorf (L), Karlsruher SC, HNK Rijeka, Hibernian, Omonia Nicosia, Apollon Limassol (to June 2022)

**INTERNATIONAL:** Greece

**SAFC TOTALS:** 2+5 appearances / 1 goal

**'Charis' Mavrias is one of those players who can look back on their time at Sunderland and genuinely believe they deserved more opportunities that came their way, although by the time he was approaching his late twenties the fact was that he had never solidly established himself at any of his eight clubs in six countries.**

He had come to Sunderland as a teenager with the distinction of being the second youngest player to have appeared in the Champions League. At the time of his debut for former European Cup finalists Panathinaikos as a late sub at home to Rubin Kazan on 20 October 2010, only Celestine Babayaro (then of Chelsea) had played in Europe's top competition at a younger age. He also already had two full caps to his name for Greece when he became one of a host of signings brought in by Director of Football Roberto De Fanti while Paolo Di Canio was Head Coach.

Mavrias always seemed to be putting a shift in and had some speed and talent. On his debut, he came on with Sunderland trailing 2-0 to MK Dons in the first match of the run to the 2013-14 League (Capital One) Cup final and helped the Lads to fight back to a 4-2 win. He went on to make all but one of his Sunderland appearances during this season. Despite scoring a very good goal five minutes into his second and last start - in a 1-0 FA Cup win over non-league Kidderminster Harriers - Mavris waited almost exactly two years for his solitary remaining Sunderland appearance having been loaned back to Panathinaikos in between.

After impressing when playing in all but one of the eight pre-season games leading into 2014-15 it seemed as if Mavrias' time had come only for injuries to frustrate any possible progress. In October and November of that season he did win full caps for Greece against Finland and the Faroe Islands as a Sunderland player, but his next club football did not occur until that loan return to Panathinaikos the following February. During that spell he added 6+3 further appearances and one goal to the 24+34 he had made in his original time at the club, during which he scored five goals including home and away Champions League goals against Motherwell. Perhaps his most significant goal came in a high profile Greek Super League draw with rivals Olympiakos in December 2012, three days after he had played at Tottenham in the Europa League.

North London was also the scene of Mavrias' final appearance for Sunderland as a late sub in an FA Cup defeat at Arsenal in January 2016. Three months later Sunderland loaned him to Fortuna Dusseldorf where he played 3+1 games starting with a home draw with St Pauli. Released by Sunderland that summer, he was quickly snapped up by another Bundesliga 2 side, Karlsruher. This time playing in a home draw with St Pauli on his home debut, Charis made 16+6 appearances without scoring, sometimes playing at right-back rather than right-wing. After a season with Karlsruher he moved to Croatia with HNK Riejka for whom he debuted in a 7-0 home win over Cibalia and more significantly as a sub in a 2-0 Europa League win over Milan on his next home appearance. However there was only a total of 3+1 appearances in a year at the club before he was on the move again.

December 2018 brought a brief return to the UK where he played for Hibs against St Mirren (who included Anton Ferdinand) and Hamilton (who included Matt Kilgallon). He moved on to play more Champions League football in August 2020 in a total of 52 appearances (3 goals) for Cypriot side Omonia Nicosia, before joining their rivals Apollon Limassol in July 2021. There he linked up again with Valentin Roberge who had arrived in the same transfer window as him at Sunderland. To June 2022, Mavrias had 13 caps for Greece.

## MAXWELL, William Sturrock **(Willie)**

**POSITION:** Inside-forward

**BIRTHPLACE:** Arbroath, Angus

**DATE OF BIRTH:** 21/09/1876 - 14/07/1940

**HEIGHT:** 5' 10" **WEIGHT:** 11st 7lbs

**SIGNED FROM:** Third Lanark, 20/05/1902

**DEBUT:** v Nottingham Forest, H, 01/09/1902

**LAST MATCH:** v Wolverhampton Wanderers, H, 03/01/1903

**MOVED TO:** Millwall Athletic, 06/05/1903

**TEAMS:** Hearts Strollers, Arbroath, Dundee, Heart of Midlothian, Arbroath, Stoke, Third Lanark, Sunderland, Millwall Athletic, Bristol City

**INTERNATIONAL:** Scotland

**SAFC TOTALS:** 7 appearances / 3 goals

**Willie Maxwell was one of those pre-First World War characters who barely played for Sunderland, but had a fascinating career. He was a Scotland international who went on to coach Belgium to an Olympic Gold medal. In 1904, he also played once for Staffordshire in a Minor Counties cricket match against Dorset.**

He was with Stoke when he played alongside Jamie Millar for Scotland against England at Celtic Park in April 1898, Millar getting the Scots goal in a 1-3 defeat on a day when Sunderland refused to allow Ted Doig and Hugh Wilson to play for the Scots as Sunderland had a chance of overtaking league leaders Sheffield United, only to lose to them at Bramall Lane on the same day as the international. The cap was Maxwell's only full international appearance although he first played representative football when twice playing County matches for Angus as a 17-year-old. Two-weeks before his Scotland appearance he scored in one of four annual Home Scots v Anglo Scots trial matches he took part in. Later with Arbroath he also played for the Scottish League.

Maxwell had two spells with Arbroath and one with Dundee before coming south of the border for the first time with Stoke where he became a professional in August 1895 having given up his job as a solicitor's clerk. He had also played twice for Heart of Midlothian, a Benefit game against Fair City Athletic on 29 August 1894 and a league appearance against St Bernards in October of the same year, getting on the scoresheet in the process. At Stoke he scored 74 goals in 153 games between 1895 and 1901, scoring on his debut against Bolton Wanderers. He became the Potters top scorer for five successive seasons from 1896-97, 19 goals in 1898-99 being his best return. Known for his pace, many of Maxwell's goals came from him out-stripping the defence.

With Third Lanark he scored twelve in 19 games before coming to Sunderland where all of his goals came against Wolves, two on his away debut in a 3-3 draw and one in a 3-0 home win. Having arrived at Sunderland he caught the eye with a goal from 30 yards in a pre-season public practice match between the Whites and the Stripes at Roker Park and then went on to score twice against Ted Doig in another public practice fixture. However he failed to hold down a regular place at Sunderland who were reigning league champions and after a year he moved on to Millwall Athletic.

Hitting two goals on his Lions debut against West Ham on the opening day of the season in the Southern League, Maxwell scored 34 times in 43 games in his first season. A hat-trick in a 4-0 win away to Swindon in October 1903 saw him register Millwall's 1,000th goal in all competitions. Eleven of his goals came in eleven games as the Lions won the London League Premier Division while he netted 23 in 29 Southern League games. Additionally, he also played twice in the Southern Professional Charity Cup and also in the English (FA) Cup against Middlesbrough. In total over two seasons Maxwell scored 57 times in 88 games including four in a late-season win over Wellingborough in April 1905 as he finished his time in London with a flourish.

The goals kept coming at his last club Bristol City where he struck 27 times as they won the second division in 1905-06 and 19 the following year as they were runners-up in the top flight. He had two more seasons with Bristol City, totalling 61 goals in 125 games.

Having retired in 1909 Maxwell moved to Belgium and became coach to Leopold FC of Brussels from September 1909 going on to become coach of the Belgium national team in 1910 until April 1914. After the war he again coached the country's team from September 1919 to June 1928, winning Olympic gold in 1920 alongside coach Raoul Daufresne. After beating Spain and the Netherlands, Belgium were awarded gold when opponents Czechoslovakia walked off six minutes before half-time in protest at English referee John Lewis. Maxwell gave a lifetime to sport. Three years before his death in 1940, he took up another coaching role in Belgium with Cercle Brugge in 1937-38.

## MBOMA NDEM, Henri **Patrick**

**POSITION:** Centre-forward

**BIRTHPLACE:** Doula, Cameroon

**DATE OF BIRTH:** 15/11/1970

**HEIGHT:** 6' 2" **WEIGHT:** 13st 6lbs

**SIGNED FROM:** Parma, 13/02/2002, on loan

**DEBUT:** v Newcastle United, H, 24/02/2002

**LAST MATCH:** v Derby County, H, 11/05/2002

**MOVED TO:** Parma, 13/05/2002, end of loan

**TEAMS:** Stade De L'Est Pavillonnais, Paris Saint-Germain, Chateauroux (L), Metz (L), Gamba Osaka, Cagliari, Parma, Sunderland (L), Al-Ittihad, Tokyo Verdy, Vissel Kobe

**INTERNATIONAL:** Cameroon

**SAFC TOTALS:** 5+4 appearances / 1 goal

**A massive figure in African football, Mboma won 57 caps for Cameroon between 1995 and 2004, scoring 33 goals and playing at the FIFA World Cup finals in 1998 and 2002. At the finals Mboma scored against Chile in 1998 and in 2002 against Mick McCarthy's Republic of Ireland team which included Shay Given, Gary Breen, Ian Harte, Jason McAteer and Kevin Kilbane.**

Patrick was Africa Player of the Year in 2000 when he won Olympic Gold and also the African Cup of Nations, retaining the latter trophy two years later when he was the tournament's top-scorer. When winning the African Cup of Nations in 2000 he scored four times including one in the final against Nigeria before scoring again in a successful penalty shoot-out. At the 2000 Olympics, he scored against Kuwait, the USA and Brazil.

## MBOMA, Patrick (Continued)

After coming through youth football in Paris, scoring 29 goals in 36 B team games for PSG he scored 22 in 48 games on loan to Chateauroux. After a second loan spell in France with Metz, Patrick went to Japan where he scored 24 goals and claimed 15 assists in his first season with Gamba Osaka, ending up with 29 goals in 34 games. A return to Europe took Mboma to Cagliari where he scored 22 times in 46 games across two seasons, before a move to Parma where he scored six goals in 27 games prior to his loan to Sunderland.

For Sunderland, he scored at Tottenham on his full debut but that would remain his only goal as Peter Reid's side finished fourth from bottom after which he left his parent club to join Al-Ittihad in Libya. Patrick's globe-trotting continued with a return to Japan where he ended his playing career.

Having obtained a UEFA masters degree in coaching, Mboma became deputy coach of Paris FC and in 2019 tried to get the job of head coach for the Cameroon team before becoming a much sought after Media consultant.

## MBUNGA-KIMPIOKA, Benjamin (Benji)

**POSITION:** Striker

**BIRTHPLACE:** Knivsta, Sweden

**DATE OF BIRTH:** 21/02/2000

**HEIGHT:** 5' 11" **WEIGHT:** 11st 0lbs

**SIGNED FROM:** Sirius IK, 01/07/2016

**DEBUT:** v Stoke City Under 21s, H, 04/09/2018

**LAST MATCH:** v Sheffield Wednesday, H, 30/12/2021

**MOVED TO:** AIK Stockholm, 31/03/2022

**TEAMS:** Sirius IK, Sunderland, Torquay United (L), Southend United (L), AIK (to May 2022)

**INTERNATIONAL:** Sweden Under 21

**SAFC TOTALS:** 4+14 appearances / 4 goals

**The young Swedish forward signed as an academy player on the strength of a four-day trial in October 2015 and scored after 123 seconds of his first start in a Football League Trophy (Checkatrade Trophy) game against Carlisle United a month after his debut in the same competition.**

Technically, he was out of contract between his loans to Torquay - managed by his Sunderland manager Lee Johnson's father Gary - and Southend - whose Sunderland-supporting manager Phil Brown was sacked while he was there. Kimpioka had refused to sign a new contract until 1 October 2020 after his previous one expired at the end of June.

He did not score for either Torquay or Southend, all but three of his ten games for Torquay were as sub including the 2021 National League Play-Off final lost to Hartlepool who included ex-Sunderland men David Ferguson and Luke Molyneux. Shortly before his second spell at Plainmoor Benji received a Football League Trophy winners' medal as an unused substitute in the 2021 final. At Southend Benji began in both of his appearances, only for his side to lose both games without scoring. He returned to Sweden after never starting a league game, but had signed off with a goal on his final appearance.

## MEARNS, Frederick Charles

**POSITION:** Goalkeeper

**BIRTHPLACE:** Sunderland, Co Durham

**DATE OF BIRTH:** 31/03/1879 - 21/01/1931

**HEIGHT:** 5' 10" **WEIGHT:** 12st 6lbs

**SIGNED FROM:** Whitburn, 15/05/1900

**DEBUT:** v Aston Villa, H, 05/10/1901

**LAST MATCH:** v Derby County, A, 05/04/1902

**MOVED TO:** Kettering Town, 09/05/1902

**TEAMS:** Whitburn, Sunderland, Kettering Town, Tottenham Hotspur, Bradford City, Grays United, Barrow, Bury, Stockton, Hartlepools United, Barnsley, Leicester Fosse, Newcastle City, West Stanley, Sunderland West End

**SAFC TOTALS:** 2 appearances / 0 goals

**Like many goalkeepers, Fred Mearns was well travelled, serving all but the last of his clubs before World War One. In 1910, he kept goal in the FA Cup final for Barnsley against Newcastle United, drawing 1-1 at Crystal Palace before losing 2-0 in the replay at Goodison Park.**

Born in Deptford in Sunderland, he started playing for Whitburn and turned down Newcastle United in order to sign for his hometown team after both big clubs had been impressed by his display in a friendly match against Selbourne at Southwick. As back up to the legendary Ted Doig Mearns was limited to just two games for Sunderland, conceding just one goal over his two appearances in what was a title-winning season.

Realising he had to move on Mearns joined Southern League Kettering Town where his prowess from penalty kicks saw him nicknamed 'the Penalty King' after reputedly saving as many as 17 penalties in his first season - this in the days when the keeper could rush off his line at the kicker. This led to a £20 move to Tottenham three days after he had kept a clean sheet against them on the last day of the 1902-03 season.

Understudying Charlie Williams at Spurs, Mearns made 14 appearances in his season at the club: five in the Southern League in which they were runners-up, five in the Western League which they won and four in the London League where again Spurs were runners-up.

Wanting to be number one, Fred was on the move again in the summer of 1904, joining Bradford City for their second season as a Football League club. He played the first 23 games of the season including a 9-0 win over Sunderland West End in an English (FA) Cup qualifying game. However after losing his place, he did not play again and carried on his nomadic existence, including a spell in the Lancashire Combination with Barrow. Returning to the top-flight of the Football League with Bury he was once again an understudy, this time to James Raeside, but over two seasons played ten league games, beginning with a debut against Newcastle United.

He returned to the north east with Hartlepools in 1908 when again Newcastle were his debut opponents, albeit in a friendly. A joiner by trade, Mearns was initially employed by Hartlepools to help maintain the ground before the season started. Playing in the North Eastern League his form over 30 league games and three cup appearances persuaded second division Barnsley to step in for his signature. It was with the Tykes that Fred enjoyed his greatest days. He helped the club to the 1910 cup final by living up to his reputation as the 'Penalty King'. With the score goalless in the semi-final against Everton at Old Trafford, he saved from Bert Freeman before Barnsley went on to win. Lined up against him in the final was Newcastle's Wilf Low, brother of Sunderland's Harry, while alongside Mearns was Harry Ness who three years later would play in Sunderland's first English Cup final.

After 25 league appearances for Barnsley Mearns moved on again, this time to Leicester Fosse (later City) where there were 68 league appearances over three seasons, the last being in April 1913, the month of that first Sunderland cup final appearance. That summer he joined Newcastle City as trainer and after the war played a few games for Sunderland West End.

Fred became manager of the bar at the Sunderland Empire and later ran the Percy Arms in Deptford as well as the Pallion Inn, but returned to his first job as a carpenter. This ultimately led to his demise at the age of 51 when he died after falling off a ladder into the hold of a ship he was working on.

## MEDINA, Nicolas Ruben

**POSITION:** Midfielder

**BIRTHPLACE:** Buenos Aires, Argentina

**DATE OF BIRTH:** 17/02/1982

**HEIGHT:** 5' 9" **WEIGHT:** 10st 4lbs

**SIGNED FROM:** Argentinos Juniors, 18/05/2001

**DEBUT:** v Bolton Wanderers, H, 14/01/2003

**LAST MATCH:** v Bolton Wanderers, H, 14/01/2003

**MOVED TO:** Real Murcia, 30/08/2004

**TEAMS:** Argentinos Juniors, Sunderland, Leganes (L), Real Murcia, Rosario Sante Fe, Nueva Chicago, Tallares de Cordoba, Gimnasia Y Esgrima La Plata, O'Higgins, Tiro Federal, La Piedad, El Porvenir, Union Comercio, Sport Huancayo, Independiente Rivadavia

**INTERNATIONAL:** Argentina

**SAFC TOTALS:** 1 appearance / 0 goals

**Julio Arca was such a success that much was expected when his countryman Medina was bought from the same club Arca had been acquired from. The £3.5m purchase though waited over 18 months for his debut. This turned out to be his only game although he did not look out of his depth in a cup tie which was won in a season where wins were as rare as hen's teeth, but he still did not get another chance.**

In his first season Medina was allowed to report late for pre-season training having played in all seven games during the summer as Argentina won the World Youth Cup, the FIFA Under 20 Youth Championship, beating Ghana in the final. Medina had been with Argentinos Juniors since he was an eight-year-old. Debuting at first-team level in Argentina against Boca Juniors on 3 September 1999, he scored his first goal against the same opposition 17 months later - his only strike in 48 games for the club.

At Sunderland he was restricted to that solitary appearance, but in 2003-04,played 32 times during a loan to Leganes in Spain. Two days before his contract at Sunderland was brought to a premature end Nicholas won an Olympic Gold medal as an unused sub as Argentina beat Paraguay in the Olympic final under the management of Marcelo Bielsa.

2004-05 saw Medina score twice in 20 games for Real Murcia before returning to Argentina with Rosario Central but after three appearances was loaned to Gimnasia La Plata, having a couple of loans before making nine appearances for his parent club after one game for Nueva Chicago and nine (with one goal) for Talleres Cordoba. Nicolas finished his playing career in 2018 back in the Argentinian Primera B Nacional second league after spells in Chile, Mexico and Peru.

## MEECHAN, Peter

**POSITION:** Full-back

**BIRTHPLACE:** Uphall, Broxburn, Linlithgowshire

**DATE OF BIRTH:** 28/02/1872 - 26/06/1915

**HEIGHT:** 5' 9" **WEIGHT:** 12st 8lbs

**SIGNED FROM:** Hibernian, 03/07/1893

**DEBUT:** v Aston Villa, H, 09/09/1893

**LAST MATCH:** v Sheffield United, A, 09/03/1895

**MOVED TO:** Celtic, 20/05/1895

**TEAMS:** Broxburn Emmett, Broxburn Shamrock, Broxburn, Hibernian, Sunderland, Celtic, Everton, Southampton, Manchester City, Barrow, Celtic, Broxburn Athletic, Clyde, Broxburn Shamrock

**INTERNATIONAL:** Scotland

**SAFC TOTALS:** 46 appearances / 1 goal

**Peter Meechan (parents' surname was Meehan and he was sometimes referred to by this name in records of some clubs) joined Sunderland who had just been crowned league champions for the first time and debuted in the first home game of the new season. Able to operate in both full-back positions he played 25 games in his first season when the Lads were runners-up and 21 in his second as the title was re-gained, scoring his only Sunderland goal in a Boxing Day win at West Brom.**

Before coming to Sunderland, Meechan was a coal miner in Linlithgowshire and played for Broxburn Emmett, Broxburn Shamrock and Broxburn FC before joining Hibs. He returned to Scotland after his time on Wearside, debuting for Celtic in a Charity Cup game at Queen's Park on 14 May 1895 and went on to help the club to win the League title and Charity Cup in 1895-96 as well as the Glasgow Cup final against Queen's Park in November 1895.

Twelve months later, following press criticism of Celtic's defeat in the final of the same competition against Rangers, Meechan was one of several players who refused to play in the next match unless certain members of the press were banned. As a consequence, Celtic suspended several players and sold Meechan to Everton after 25 games and one goal. Sunderland received £200 for this deal in addition to the £150 paid to Celtic because Sunderland still held Meechan's English League registration. At the time this made him a record transfer for Everton. While he was with Celtic, Peter played for the Scottish League and Scotland, both times against Irish opposition.

Making his league and cup debuts against Bury, he went on to play in the 1897 English (FA) Cup final lost to Aston Villa at Crystal Palace. After a total of 28 games - including a goalless draw at Sunderland just before Christmas in 1897 - he joined Southern League Southampton in May 1898 for a fee of £200. Having won trophies at Celtic and Sunderland, and reached the cup final with Everton, Meechan won the Southern League in his first season on the south coast and reached the Cup final in his second, playing in a 4-0 defeat to Bury.

Later that year he made a December move to Manchester City where he played six games in the remainder of that season before completing his career with Barrow and back in Scotland. Once his career was over in 1906, he moved to Cape Breton, Nova Scotia in Canada and continued his profession as a coal miner, but died at the age of 43 with his death attributed to appendicitis and pneumonia after a night searching for a missing nephew. However, the Glasgow Daily Record on 23 June 1915 gave the cause as an attack of pleurisy and pneumonia that necessitated an operation which proved fatal.

## MELVILLE, Andrew Roger (Andy)

**POSITION:** Centre-half

**BIRTHPLACE:** Swansea, Glamorgan

**DATE OF BIRTH:** 29/11/1968

**HEIGHT:** 6' 0" **WEIGHT:** 12st 0lbs

**SIGNED FROM:** Oxford United, 06/08/1993

**DEBUT:** v Derby County, A, 14/08/1993

**LAST MATCH:** v Birmingham City, H, 09/05/1999

**MOVED TO:** Fulham, 03/06/1999

**TEAMS:** Bangor City, Swansea City, Oxford United, Sunderland, Bradford City (L), Fulham, West Ham United, Nottingham Forest (L)

**INTERNATIONAL:** Wales

**SAFC TOTALS:** 235+1 appearances / 14 goals

**A composed but tough central-defender, Melville missed just two league games in the 105-point season of 1998-99. It was the last of Andy's six seasons at Sunderland during which he made at least 40 appearances in four of them and 35 in another.**

Capped by Wales for the first time against West Germany as a 20-year-old, he won 17 of his 65 caps while with Sunderland, scoring all three of his international goals while contracted on Wearside. The last of these goals came in a 6-4 defeat against Turkey in Istanbul in August 1997 on the occasion of the final cap he won as a Sunderland player.

Andy had debuted for Swansea as a 16-year-old and played 202+11 times (scoring 29 times) for his hometown team. He won the Welsh Cup in 1989 - before a £275,000 move to Oxford in July 1993. There were 159 appearances and 15 goals for the U's before a move to Sunderland which saw Anton Rogan and £450,000 go to Oxford, plus a further £50,000 after 50 appearances. In the spring of 1998 he played six games on loan to Bradford City from Sunderland and after leaving SAFC, as

Peter Reid re-structured in preparation for the Premier League, he moved to Fulham on a free transfer. In four and a half seasons at Craven Cottage Melville played 187+6 games scoring four times, winning promotion in 2001 and the Intertoto Cup a year later. January 2004 brought a move from west to east London where he played 17+4 times for West Ham from where he also had a 15-game loan to Nottingham Forest the last of his 823+22 games (63 goals) coming in a Championship game for Forest against Gillingham in May 2005.

From the summer of 2009 Melville spent five years coaching back at Oxford and then scouted for Birmingham City, Blackpool, Portsmouth and Brighton before becoming Head of Player Recruitment at Northampton Town from May 2016 to October 2018. On leaving this last job, Andy became a football agent.

## MENSAH, John

**POSITION:** Defender

**BIRTHPLACE:** Obuasi, Ghana

**DATE OF BIRTH:** 29/11/1982

**HEIGHT:** 5' 10" **WEIGHT:** 12st 6lbs

**SIGNED FROM:** Olympique Lyonnais, 28/08/2009 and 11/08/2010, both times on loan

**DEBUT:** v Hull City, H, 12/09/2009

**LAST MATCH:** v Wolverhampton Wanderers, A, 14/05/2011

**MOVED TO:** Olympique Lyonnais, 10/05/2010 and 23/05/2011 end of loans

**TEAMS:** MBC Accra, Bologna, Bellinzona (L), Genoa (L), Chievo Verona, Modena (L), Cremonese, Rennes, Olympique Lyonnais, Sunderland (L), Olympique Lyonnais, Sunderland (L), Rennes, Asanta Kotoko, Nitra, Eskilstuna

**INTERNATIONAL:** Ghana

**SAFC TOTALS:** 30+5 appearances / 1 goal

**Mensah was an absolutely top-class defender but unfortunately was injury prone. Capped 86 times by his country Mensah was one of three players at Sunderland at the time who played for Ghana against England at Wembley in 2011.**

A decade earlier he had played against Julio Arca and Nicolas Medina in the 2001 FIFA World Youth Championship final lost to Argentina. In an earlier game in the tournament against France he had come up against Djibril Cisse. Mensah went on to make a full international debut in December of that year against Algeria, quickly going on to play four times in the following month's African Cup of Nations finals.

## MENSAH, John (Continued)

Three years later he played in the 2004 Olympics before being named in the Team of the Tournament in his second ACN finals in 2006. Later that year he played in all four of Ghana's games at the World Cup including playing against Claudio Reyna of the USA. By the time of the 2008 ACN Mensah was captain of Ghana but was sent off in the quarter-final for a professional foul. Without him Ghana lost the semi-final before he returned as his team won the match for third place. Although he did not play at the 2010 ACN when Ghana reached the final, at the 2010 FIFA World Cup Mensah continued as captain in between two loan spells at Sunderland. He played four times - including against Jozy Altidore in another meeting with the USA - but missed in the penalty shoot-out to Uruguay for a place in the semi-finals. His final international tournament was the 2012 ACN where he played three times as Ghana finished fourth. John bade farewell to international football in August 2012 in a draw with China. He had scored three times for his nation and been Ghana's Player of the Year in 2006.

In club football, after playing youth football for MBC Accra he moved to Italy with Bologna where he played twice in the Coppa Italia before signing for Swiss side Bellinzona where he played 34 times, scoring once, before returning to Italy with a loan to Genoa where he scored three times in 26 games in all competitions in 2001-02. This led to a four year stint with the Flying Donkeys of Chievo from where he had loans to Modena (6/0) and Cremonese (14/0) while playing 22 times for Chievo.

January 2006 brought a move into French football with Rennes where by November France Football were naming him the joint best player in France and by January 2008 he was captaining the side. Six months later an £8m fee took Mensah to Lyon after 60 games and two goals for Rennes where his reputation had rocketed despite a series of thigh and calf injuries. Regular injuries continued to hamper his time at Lyon where he played Champions League football and by the end of his first full season a loan to Sunderland was arranged.

When he played John was outstanding, evidently a defender of the highest calibre but injuries meant he played just 15+2 times in his first loan and 15+3 in his second. In 2011 he returned to Olympique Lyonnais but only made a single appearance in the season and moved back to Rennes in January 2013. An unused sub in the Coupe de Ligue final against St Etienne four months after joining, once again injuries blighted his time at the club where he played just six times in his second spell.

Mensah briefly linked up with Ghanaian club Asante Kotoko (who Sunderland once had a partnership with) before returning to Europe with Nitra in Slovakia where he played five times before finishing his career in Sweden, although he made no league appearances for the club of Seb Larsson's birthplace Eskilstuna.

John's father, John Attu Mensah, played a few games for Cambridge United, was on the books of Norwich City and represented Ghana in the 1960s. He also played for Ghana in the 1968 Olympic football tournament.

## METCALF, George Watson

**POSITION:** Centre-half

**BIRTHPLACE:** Hendon, Co Durham

**DATE OF BIRTH:** 26/05/1887 - 13/07/1941

**HEIGHT:** 5' 8" **WEIGHT:** 11st 0lbs

**SIGNED FROM:** Black Watch, 21/12/1905

**DEBUT:** v Bolton Wanderers, H, 16/02/1907

**LAST MATCH:** v Bolton Wanderers, H, 16/02/1907

**MOVED TO:** Huddersfield Town, 13/07/1910

**TEAMS:** Black Watch, Sunderland, North Shields Athletic, Huddersfield Town, Houghton Rovers, Merthyr Town, Portsmouth

**SAFC TOTALS:** 1 appearance / 0 goals

**A reserve in his three years at Sunderland, Metcalf's first-team opportunity came in a home defeat when manager Bob Kyle decided to see what Metcalf and Harry Foster had to offer, leaving more experienced half-backs out for the afternoon.**

It was to be Metcalf's only first-team game. He went on to play 17 times for Huddersfield who took his League registration from Sunderland after George had a brief dalliance with North Shields Athletic in 1908-09 season. George, (by this time he had added an 'e' to his surname), had a trial with the Terriers, whilst still a Sunderland player, against Gainsborough Trinity reserves in February 1910 and played his final match in November of the following year at home to Nottingham Forest in Division Two.

George returned to the north east and played a few games for Houghton Rovers before joining Merthyr Town in May 1913. However after only one season he was on the move again, signing for Portsmouth. World War One interrupted his career and although known to have signed for Portsmouth he did not play a first-team game for Pompey. George returned to the north east and at the time of his death aged 54 he was a special constable and the proprietor of the Ideal Café in Seaburn.

George's brother Arthur played for Newcastle United, Liverpool, Stockport County, Swindon Town, Accrington Stanley, Aberdare Athletic and Norwich City between 1909 and 1926. They had a brief spell together for North Shields Athletic prior to Arthur joining Newcastle.

## MEYLER, David John Martin

**POSITION:** Midfielder

**BIRTHPLACE:** Cork, Ireland

**DATE OF BIRTH:** 29/05/1989

**HEIGHT:** 6' 2" **WEIGHT:** 11st 9lbs

**SIGNED FROM:** Cork City, 25/07/2008

**DEBUT:** v Blackburn Rovers, A, 28/12/2009

**LAST MATCH:** v MK Dons, A, 25/09/2012

**MOVED TO:** Hull City, 08/01/2013

**TEAMS:** Cork City, Sunderland, Hull City, Reading, Coventry City (L)

**INTERNATIONAL:** Republic of Ireland

**SAFC TOTALS:** 17+14 appearances / 0 goals

**Roy Keane was tipped off about the potential of his fellow Corkman at the start of Sunderland's pre-season tour of Ireland in 2007 at a time when Meyler had played just three games for Cork.**

A mobile, physically commanding midfielder Meyler (pronounced Myler) often impressed, but his first-team appearances were limited through injuries, most significantly a cruciate ligament tear sustained in a game where he was playing tremendously against Manchester United in May 2010. It was not until Steve Bruce - who had managed him at Sunderland - signed David for Hull (after an initial loan spell) that he fully blossomed.

Meyler made 145+46 appearances for the Tigers, scoring 19 goals. He won promotion in his first season and played in the FA Cup final against Arsenal in his second - after scoring against Sunderland in the quarter-final. In the final season of his career David joined Reading in 2018-19, but played only five times for them before a 2+3 game loan with Coventry.

At international level Meyler debuted at Under 21 level in his home city against Germany in February 2009 and made a senior bow in September 2012 in a game against Oman at Fulham. He went on to win 26 full caps in addition to his five at Under 21 level, a highlight being selected for Martin O'Neill's squad for Euro 2016 as one of seven players who eventually had SAFC connections although David did not appear at the finals.

His father, John, was manager of Hurling clubs at Carlow, Wexford, Kerry, Cork and in 2021 was managing Kilmoyley. He had been a hugely decorated player in hurling as well as playing soccer for Cork Alberts.

## MIDDLETON, Matthew Young

**POSITION:** Goalkeeper

**BIRTHPLACE:** Boldon Colliery, Co Durham

**DATE OF BIRTH:** 24/10/1907 - 19/04/1979

**HEIGHT:** 5' 10" **WEIGHT:** 11st 12lbs

**SIGNED FROM:** Southport, 19/08/1933

**DEBUT:** v Middlesbrough, A, 17/01/1934

**LAST MATCH:** v Wolverhampton Wanderers, A, 06/05/1939

**MOVED TO:** Plymouth Argyle, 08/05/1939

**TEAMS:** Southwick, Boldon CW, Southport, Sunderland, Plymouth Argyle, Sunderland (WW2 Guest), Middlesbrough (WW2 Guest), Carlisle United (WW2 Guest), Darlington (WW2 Guest), Stockton (WW2 Guest), Horden CW, Bradford City, York City, Blyth Spartans, Murton CW

**SAFC TOTALS:** 59 appearances / 0 goals

**Matt Middleton played 20 games in 1933-34 and 21 the following season. In the league title-winning campaign of 1935-36 he was drafted in for a nine-game run after the tragic death of Jimmy Thorpe, but was then replaced by new teenage signing Johnny Mapson and only made nine more appearances over the next three seasons.**

Prior to joining Sunderland, he had amassed 71 league and cup appearances for Southport, then a league club and briefly, whilst at Boldon CW, had been signed on amateur forms by Newcastle United.

After joining Plymouth before the start of World War Two he returned north as a war-time 'Guest' player, appearing for Sunderland against Sunderland Police in August 1940. He also made 106 'Guest' appearances for Middlesbrough from 1941 to 1945 as well as eight for Carlisle in 1939-40, and one each for Darlington in 1944-45 and Stockton in 1945-46. Despite Matt's time in the south-west seeing him spend much of his time as a 'Guest' player, he did manage 31 appearances for Argyle before an August 1946 move to Bradford City where he was ever-present in his first season in Division Three North, missed just two the following season and played twelve of the opening 14 fixtures of 1948-49 before a switch to York after 97 appearances in all competitions.

For the Minstermen he debuted back at Bradford City in February 1949, by which time Matt was well into his forties. Nonetheless he went on to play 56 times, the last making him York's oldest-ever player at the age of 42 years and 194 days when he appeared at New Brighton on the final day of the 1949-50 season, when York had to apply for re-election for the first time.

Still keen to play he continued in north-east non-league circles until around 1953 when he became assistant trainer at Hartlepools United. Middleton's grandson Grant Brown gave great service to Lincoln City, playing against Sunderland in the FA Cup in 1999 and also playing for Leicester City, Telford United, Alfreton Town and Grantham Town.

## MIDDLETON, Robert Connan (Bob)

**POSITION:** Goalkeeper

**BIRTHPLACE:** Brechin, Angus

**DATE OF BIRTH:** 24/01/1904 - 19/05/1984

**HEIGHT:** 5' 11" **WEIGHT:** 12st 6lbs

**SIGNED FROM:** Cowdenbeath, 12/11/1930

**DEBUT:** v Bolton Wanderers, A, 15/11/1930

**LAST MATCH:** v Sheffield United, A, 25/03/1933

**MOVED TO:** Burton Town, 08/09/1933

**TEAMS:** Edzell, Brechin Victoria, Brechin City, Cowdenbeath, Sunderland, Burton Town, Chester City, Brechin City

**INTERNATIONAL:** Scotland

**SAFC TOTALS:** 66 appearances / 0 goals

**Capped by Scotland against Northern Ireland in a 3-1 win at Parkhead in February 1930, Bob Middleton signed for Sunderland nine months later and played the final 30 games of that season, seven of those were in the FA Cup as Sunderland reached the semi-final. The following season, he made 27 league appearances, but there were just nine more as he lost his place to Jimmy Thorpe.**

Middleton started his career with as a right-back in the Kincardineshire League before moving between the posts during the 1925-26 season with Brechin Victoria. By November 1930, Bob arrived in English football with 72 Scottish top-flight appearances under his belt, but after a similar number of English top-flight games left Sunderland for Birmingham & District League side Burton Town. Five months later, Sunderland received a fee of £750 when he moved to Chester City as the Wearsiders still held his Football League registration.

He added 56 further league appearances with Chester before retiring just before the war to become a licensee in the city. He did make one further appearance almost a decade later appearing for Brechin at the age of 42 in a cup-tie in September 1946 when the club faced a goalkeeping emergency, although a hand injury limited his appearance to the first half only. The following month he joined the committee of Brechin City and remained active in that role until November 1952.

## MIGNOLET, Simon Luc Hildebert

**POSITION:** Goalkeeper

**BIRTHPLACE:** Sint Truiden, Belgium

**DATE OF BIRTH:** 06/08/1988

**HEIGHT:** 6' 4" **WEIGHT:** 13st 12lbs

**SIGNED FROM:** St Truidense, 17/06/2010

**DEBUT:** v Birmingham City, H, 14/08/2010

**LAST MATCH:** v Tottenham Hotspur, 19/05/2013

**MOVED TO:** Liverpool, 25/06/2013

**TEAMS:** St Truidense, Sunderland, Liverpool, Bruges (to June 2022)

**INTERNATIONAL:** Belgium

**SAFC TOTALS:** 101 appearances / 0 goals

**Simon Mignolet was a very good goalkeeper for Sunderland. Commanding, agile when he needed to be, he was also brave, as seen when he returned from over two months out to keep a clean sheet in a dramatic New Year's Day win over Manchester City while wearing a mask to protect himself.**

Mignolet was sold for over four times the £2m he was bought for after a century of games. Ever-present in the last of his three seasons on Wearside, he moved on to Liverpool for whom he kept clean sheets in his first three Premier League games, saving an 89th-minute penalty in a 1-0 win over Stoke on his home debut. He had also saved a penalty in a Tyne-Wear derby at St James' to thwart Demba Ba in 2012.

Simon established himself as number one at Anfield making 53 consecutive Premier League starts before being left out in December 2014. Quickly restored, he kept a series of clean sheets including one against Sunderland and added to his penalty-saving reputation with a spot-kick stop from Wayne Rooney in a big game with rivals Manchester United, albeit his side still lost. He was then the shoot-out hero with two saves in a League Cup semi-final shoot-out with Stoke in 2016 and in September 2017 saved a club record eighth penalty in a narrow win over Leicester City. However, later in 2016, Liverpool manager Jurgen Klopp dropped Mignolet in place of Loris Karius. Nonetheless, the resilient and determined Belgian not only was soon restored to the Liverpool line-up, but captained the side. However, after Klopp paid over £66m to make the Brazilian stopper Alisson the world's most expensive goalkeeper it was obvious Mignolet would have to move on - even though he had previously contested a first-team place with Britain's most expensive goalkeeper in Craig Gordon.

In both 2018 and 2019 Mignolet was an unused sub in Champions League finals, Karius making two glaring errors as Liverpool lost to Real Madrid in the first of those with Alisson keeping a clean sheet in a tame final against Tottenham a year later. Simon had also received runners-up medals in the League Cup and Europa League in 2015-16, playing against Manchester City in the domestic final lost on penalties and in a 3-1 defeat to Sevilla in the continental competition.

After 203+1 games for Liverpool Simon returned to Belgium with Club Brugge who agreed a reported £6.4m move in August 2019. Debuting with a Champions League clean sheet against Dynamo Kiev, he was unbeaten again on his domestic league bow at Oostende and by May 2022 had played 129 times for Brugge. Prior to leaving Belgium, he had played 104 times for St Truiden winning promotion with them in 2009.

At international level Mignolet had a long battle for a place as part of a golden generation of Belgian players with Thibaut Courtois of Chelsea and Real Madrid. By the end of June 2022, Mignolet had 35 full caps having broken into the side during his Sunderland days with a clean sheet against Austria on his debut in March 2011. In 2018, he went to the World Cup in Russia, but even in the third place match with England he was unable to displace Courtois.

## MILLAR, James (Jimmy or Jamie)

**POSITION:** Forward

**BIRTHPLACE:** Annbank, Ayrshire

**DATE OF BIRTH:** 10/02/1871 - 05/02/1907

**HEIGHT:** 5' 9" **WEIGHT:** 11st 10lbs

**SIGNED FROM:** Annbank, 14/08/1890 and from Rangers 17/05/1900

**DEBUT:** v Burnley, H, 13/09/1890

**LAST MATCH:** v Derby County, H, 26/03/1904

**MOVED TO:** Rangers, 02/05/1896 and West Bromwich Albion, 21/07/1904

**TEAMS:** Annbank, Sunderland, Rangers, Sunderland, WBA

**INTERNATIONAL:** Scotland

**SAFC TOTALS:** 261 appearances / 127 goals

**One of the great names in the history of the club, Millar is the only outfield player to win four league championship medals with Sunderland. He was also the first of only four men (to July 2022) to score five goals in a league or senior cup game, something he did in the club's record 11-1 English (FA) Cup game against Fairfield in 1895.**

A Scotland international, in between his third and fourth title medals on Wearside he won two league titles and two Scottish Cup medals with Rangers. Such a successful life, and yet Jamie died a few days before what would have been his 36th birthday.

Having impressed in local football he played a few games for Rangers as a teenager in 1889 shortly before league football started in Scotland. Consequently his early appearances for Rangers were in friendlies and challenge matches but on 7 September 1889 he played in a major competitive game for the first time when he turned out in a 6-2 Scottish Cup win over United Abstainers.

## MILLAR, Jamie (Continued)

No record is known to exist of the scorers in that game so while he may well have scored that remains a mystery. His first recorded competitive goal came against Third Lanark in a 2-0 Glasgow Cup victory two months later. By December 1889 Millar had returned to play for Annbank which included his uncle, and later Sunderland teammate, William Dunlop.

Joining Sunderland to bolster the ranks of Scottish talent ahead of Sunderland entering the Football League in 1890, he debuted in Sunderland's first-ever league game but had first appeared in a 5-1 friendly win over Renton. The scorer of two goals in Sunderland's first-ever league victory (although the points were docked as goalkeeper Doig had not been properly registered), he scored 14 goals in 20 league and cup games in his first season. An opening-day hat-trick against Wolves set him on the path to 18 in 28 games in his second season as Sunderland won the league and reached the cup semi-final, another hat-trick coming against Darwen. During this season, he also returned to Ibrox, playing in a 1-0 friendly win in April 1892.

The goals kept coming as he hit 17 in 24 games (including two more hat-tricks) as the league was retained in 1892-93. Thus far, Millar had not managed to score more goals per season than the prolific Johnny Campbell, but he outscored his countryman by 19 to 18 in 1893-94 (with another hat-trick against Wolves) as Sunderland were runners-up. He also scored in another Ibrox friendly, a 2-2 New Year draw.

1894-95 saw Jamie become the first Sunderland player to score five in a national competition when he went nap against Fairfield in the cup to set the Lads on the path to the semi-final. He also scored 13 league goals as 'The Team of All The Talents' won the league for the third time in four years after which he played in the win over Hearts in Edinburgh that saw Sunderland proclaimed world champions. Contemporary reports on this game contain serious discrepancies regarding the scorers with some claiming Millar equalised to make it 3-3 in the Wearsiders 5-3 victory, although other reports list other scorers. Millar missed much of the first half of the 1895-96 campaign, but still scored eleven goals including a hat-trick against WBA.

The close season of 1896 saw him return to Rangers where he made his second debut alongside former Sunderland teammate Tom Hyslop against St Mirren on 15 August, both scoring as Rangers eased to a 5-1 win. It was one of 16 goals in 29 games for Millar as he won three cups in his first season back in Scotland. These included the first and last goals in the Scottish Cup final as Dumbarton were defeated 5-1 (Hyslop getting the second). Millar also played as Celtic were beaten in the Glasgow Cup final and against Third Lanark as the Charity Cup completed a treble.

On 3 April 1897, Millar lined up once again alongside SAFC's Hugh Wilson as he marked his international debut by scoring the winner for Scotland in a 2-1 win over England at Crystal Palace - Hyslop again joining Jamie on the scoresheet. Two weeks later Millar appeared in a 5-2 win over Wales at Motherwell on a day when former Sunderland man James Gillespie scored a hat-trick on his only full international appearance. Jamie went on to score again on his third and last international appearance. This was in another game against England, a defeat for the Scots at Celtic Park on 2 April 1898.

1897-98 saw Millar again win the Scottish and Glasgow Cups in a season where he scored ten times in 15 games. Eight of those goals came in four-goal hauls against Partick Thistle and Dundee. By now he had three league medals with Sunderland and five cup winners medals with Rangers. 1898-99 was to bring him a Scottish league medal as Rangers spectacularly won all 18 games. Millar missed just two and contributed eleven goals including one in a 4-0 Old Firm win at Celtic. Inevitably there was another hat-trick, this time against Clyde who he scored against again on the final day of the campaign as Rangers registered a 100% record. However, despite league invincibility, Jamie played in cup final defeats to Celtic in both the Scottish and Charity Cups.

The following season, as the century turned, saw Millar score in a 5-1 Charity Cup win over Celtic and also win the league again although this time he played just seven times scoring once, thereby taking his Rangers total to 114 games and 59 goals.

Returning to Sunderland who were now at Roker Park, Millar got off to a bright start with the first goal of the season in the opening game at Notts County. As Sunderland finished runners-up, Millar missed just four of the 34 league games, scoring nine goals including yet another hat-trick against Wolves. Both Nottingham Forest and Bury were on the receiving end of Millar hat-tricks as he scored nine league goals from 32 games in helping Sunderland to a fourth league title. He was to play for two more seasons, scoring twice as the Sheriff of London Shield was won by beating Corinthians at White Hart Lane in 1903.

In the summer of 1904 he moved to West Brom as trainer. Pressed into action for what was his only game for Albion against Burton Town on 8 October 1904, he was made captain and set up goals for Laurie Bell and George Dorsett who scored a hat-trick in a 4-0 win. However, later that month, Millar moved further south, taking up an offer to become trainer of Chelsea only to die on 5th February the following year of tuberculosis.

Millar was related to four Sunderland players. He was the nephew of William Dunlop, the brother-in-law of William Gibson and father-in-law of both Ernest Hodkin and Albert Milton.

Often referred to as Jimmy, James or Jamie, his family name was officially Miller, but he was mainly known as Millar. As if this was not confusing enough, at Rangers in the last five matches of 1898-99, one of his teammates was also called Jimmy Millar, this one an Elgin-born half-back who later played for Bradford.

## MILLER, Liam William Peter

**POSITION:** Midfielder

**BIRTHPLACE:** Ballincollig, Co Cork, Ireland

**DATE OF BIRTH:** 13/02/1981 - 09/02/2018

**HEIGHT:** 5' 7" **WEIGHT:** 11st 6lbs

**SIGNED FROM:** Manchester United, 31/08/2006

**DEBUT:** v Derby County, A, 09/09/2006

**LAST MATCH:** v Bolton Wanderers, H, 29/11/2008

**MOVED TO:** QPR, 15/01/2009

**TEAMS:** Celtic, Aarhus (L), Manchester United, Leeds United (L), Sunderland, QPR, Hibernian, Perth Glory, Brisbane Roar, Melbourne City, Cork City, Wilmington Hammerheads

**INTERNATIONAL:** Republic of Ireland

**SAFC TOTALS:** 43+17 appearances / 3 goals

**One of the half dozen players signed on a sensational transfer deadline day shortly after Roy Keane was appointed as manager, Keane knew Miller from his time with both Manchester United and the Republic of Ireland. Very popular in the dressing room where he was reputed to be quite a wit, Liam was one of the world's most reluctant interviewees.**

A softly spoken, "I'm grand" would be the regular pleasant, but negative, comment when declining a request to do a piece with him. It was a pity because he had a good story to tell of a far too short life, Liam passing away of pancreatic cancer a few days before what should have been his 37th birthday.

At Sunderland, he played a significant role in the promotion of 2006-07, starting 24 league games and coming off the bench in a further six. A scorer on his second appearance in Roy Keane's second game at Miller's former loan-club Leeds, Liam's other goal that season was a dramatic last-minute header to win a key game at home to Derby County.

Liam started at Celtic where he debuted in a win over Dundee United in May 2000 before going on an 18-game loan to Aarhus in Denmark who were managed by ex-Celtic player Marc Reiper. In 2003, Miller's most memorable moment for Celtic saw him apply the finishing touch to a 24-pass move in a Champions League game against Lyon during the management of Martin O'Neill, but there were just 19+25 appearances and five goals in an injury-hit spell before a transfer to Manchester United where he began with a winning performance against Dinamo Bucharest in a Champions League qualifying round game in August 2004. It was one of just 11+11 games. A teammate of Roy Keane, John O'Shea, Wes Brown and David Bellion during his time at Old Trafford, Miller's last Premier League appearance for United was at Sunderland in October 2005 after which he signed off with the last of his two goals for the club in a League Cup victory over Barnet.

Prior to coming to Sunderland Miller made 31+2 appearances for Leeds (scoring once) while afterwards he managed 11+2 games in a brief spell at QPR in 2008-09. In September 2009, he joined Hibs going on to score seven goals in 72+4 games during a spell which saw him named in the 2009-10 PFA Scotland Team of the Year.

He then went to Australia for four years playing for Perth Glory (49/2), Brisbane Roar (23/3) and Melbourne City (2/0). During his time down under Miller played in the 2012 A League Grand Final as Perth lost to Brisbane Roar who became his next club and with whom he won the A League Grand Final in 2014.

In January 2015 Miller returned to home territory with Cork City where he played 35 games as his home city finished second in league and cup before adding 27 appearances and one last goal in the USA with Wilmington Hammerheads. Before leaving the USA, as he was struck by cancer, Miller became assistant coach at Real Monarchs. At international level Liam's lone goal in 21 games for his country came in a 3-0 win over Sweden in March 2006. A UEFA European Under 16 championship winner in 1998, he made a senior debut as a substitute against the Czech Republic on March 2004.

Following Liam's untimely death, a Benefit Match in Cork was staged in his honour. Roy Keane managed a Manchester United legends team against a combined Celtic / Ireland team managed by Martin O'Neill.

## MILLER, Thomas William **(Tommy)**

**POSITION:** Midfielder

**BIRTHPLACE:** Shotton Colliery, Co Durham

**DATE OF BIRTH:** 08/01/1979

**HEIGHT:** 6' 0" **WEIGHT:** 11st 7lbs

**SIGNED FROM:** Ipswich Town, 22/06/2005

**DEBUT:** v Charlton Athletic, H, 13/08/2005

**LAST MATCH:** v Barnsley, A, 10/03/2007

**MOVED TO:** Ipswich Town, 19/07/2007

**TEAMS:** Hartlepool United, Ipswich Town, Sunderland, Preston North End (L), Ipswich Town, Sheffield Wednesday, Huddersfield Town, Swindon Town, Bury, Hartlepool United, Halifax Town

**SAFC TOTALS:** 32+3 appearances / 3 goals

**Miller was a goalscoring midfielder who came back to his native north east to sign for Sunderland along with his ex-Ipswich teammate goalkeeper Kelvin Davis, as Sunderland prepared for life back in the Premier League following promotion in 2005.**

Although the ex-Ipswich duo excelled in a notable pre-season friendly win at AZ Alkmaar, where Miller scored the game's only goal, their first season at Sunderland proved to be an enormous struggle as the team went down with an ugly 15 points. Tommy at least scored the opening goal in the first win of the season at Middlesbrough in the seventh fixture of the campaign. It was one of three he scored in 27+2 league games, amazingly enough to make him joint top league scorer for the season.

With the club sold by Bob Murray to the Niall Quinn led Drumaville Consortium at the end of Miller's first season, Tommy played in the first three games under Quinn but after Roy Keane took over Miller's only appearance (following a seven-game loan to Preston) was as a sub on the day Keane left three latecomers behind and travelled without them, although he was named as an unused sub on a handful of other occasions. Having begun as a youth player at Ipswich, Miller had made his senior bow with Hartlepool United where his father, Tommy senior, was a long-standing servant, most notably as Head of Scouting.

Debuting at Chester in October 1997, Tommy (junior) went on to net 44 goals in 154+7 games, being top-scorer in 1999-2000 and 2000-2001. He was named in the fourth tier PFA Team of the Season in both years. Having rejected him as a youngster, Ipswich's George Burley then paid a Hartlepool club record £750,000 for Tommy in July 2001. As would happen at Sunderland later that decade, his side were relegated, although in the case of the Tractor Boys this was combined with taking part in the UEFA Cup, something they did again after relegation due to qualification via Fair Play standings. After over 100 league starts in this spell at Portman Road, he came to Sunderland only to return two years later for a further two seasons in Suffolk, eventually totalling 179+35 appearances and 47 goals.

There was a further relegation in his first season at Sheffield Wednesday in 2009-10, this time from the Championship to League One. There were a dozen goals in 46+17 games for the Owls. This was followed by a single season each with Huddersfield (30+3/2), Swindon (32+7/1) where he signed for Paolo Di Canio (and later had one game as joint caretaker manager), and Bury (26+4/0), before a return to Hartlepool (under Colin Cooper) where he did not score in 16+1 appearances in 2014-15. Tommy then stepped down into the National League with Halifax where he played in a heavy FA Cup defeat to Wycombe Wanderers in November 2015. Returning to the north east as assistant manager at Spennymoor, he took over as manager on 20 April 2021, but was sacked on 5 December later the same year.

At international level, Miller was eligible to play for Scotland as his grandmother was born north of the border and was called up by Bertie Vogts for a game against Wales in 2004, only to be ruled out by injury.

## MILTON, Albert

**POSITION:** Full-back

**BIRTHPLACE:** High Green, Sheffield, Yorkshire

**DATE OF BIRTH:** 18/10/1885 - 11/10/1917

**HEIGHT:** 5' 7" **WEIGHT:** 12st 0lbs

**SIGNED FROM:** Barnsley, 30/04/1908

**DEBUT:** v Middlesbrough, A, 09/09/1908

**LAST MATCH:** v Bolton Wanderers, A, 11/04/1914

**MOVED TO:** Swindon Town, 06/05/1914

**TEAMS:** Rotherham County, South Kirkby, Barnsley, Sunderland, Swindon Town

**SAFC TOTALS:** 140 appearances / 0 goals

**Just three and a half years after his last match for Sunderland, 1913 title-winning full-back Albert Milton was killed in action during World War One in Belgium, a victim of the first day of the battle of Passchendaele. Had the bombardier of the Royal Field Artillery lived, his 32nd birthday would have come a week later.**

He was a first-team regular for five years at Sunderland, having been signed from Barnsley (15/0) for the then maximum transfer fee of £350, but injury ruled him out of the climax to the 1912-13 season which meant he missed the cup final. Brother Ernest did win the cup after Albert died, being part of the Sheffield United side who won at Wembley in 1925. Another brother, Arthur, also played professionally for Coventry City and Gillingham. All three were left-backs. Albert was also the brother-in-law of Ernest Hodkin and the son-in-law of William Gibson.

Before becoming a footballer Albert had been a coal miner while he later worked in the engine works of MacColl and Pollock (people influential in the foundation of Seville FC). While at Sunderland, Milton also managed Monkwearmouth's Colliery Tavern adjacent to where the Stadium of Light now is. At the Stadium of Light, Milton's name is included on a plaque commemorating players who died in the war. This is sited next to the Fans' statue.

## MIMMS, Robert Andrew (Bobby)

**POSITION:** Goalkeeper

**BIRTHPLACE:** York, North Yorkshire

**DATE OF BIRTH:** 12/10/1963

**HEIGHT:** 6' 2" **WEIGHT:** 12st 13lbs

**SIGNED FROM:** Everton, 11/12/1986, on loan

**DEBUT:** v Barnsley, A, 13/12/1986

**LAST MATCH:** v Grimsby Town, H, 27/12/1986

**MOVED TO:** Everton, 03/01/1987, end of loan

**TEAMS:** Halifax Town, Rotherham United, Everton, Notts County (L), Sunderland (L), Blackburn Rovers (L), Manchester City (L), Tottenham Hotspur, Aberdeen (L), Blackburn Rovers, Crystal Palace, Preston North End, Rotherham United, York City, Mansfield Town

**INTERNATIONAL:** England Under 21

**SAFC TOTALS:** 4 appearances / 0 goals

**During Lawrie McMenemy's time as manager he regularly changed goalkeepers. The four-game loan of Mimms in December 1986 was just one element of this. Mimms had a good career. Earlier in the same calendar year Bobby had played in the all Merseyside FA Cup final alongside Peter Reid, Paul Bracewell and Adrian Heath. He also played in the 1986 and 1987 Charity Shield games at Wembley. Almost a decade later he would play three times in Blackburn's 1994-95 Premier League winning season.**

Having started with Halifax, Mimms' league debut came after moving to Rotherham where over 83 league appearances he impressed to the extent that Everton bought him. In three years at Goodison Park, he played 29 league games for Everton and in addition to his loan at Sunderland, played twice for Notts County, six times for Blackburn and three games for Manchester City.

At Spurs he played a total of 64+5 times before becoming Blackburn's record buy when Rovers paid £250,000 in December 1990. In 1992 Bobby kept a Wembley clean sheet as a Leicester line-up including Simon Grayson were beaten in the Play-Off final and was ever-present as Blackburn finished fourth in the first season of the Premiership in 1992-93. He was on the team-sheet for all 42 games the following term too as Rovers were runners-up, but only played in the opening 13 matches before being replaced by Tim Flowers.

After 160+2 games Bobby moved on to Crystal Palace (1), Preston (27), Rotherham (43), York (63) and Mansfield (45), eventually totalling 477 league appearances. At international level he was capped at Under 21 level by England, Nick Pickering being a teammate when Mimms debuted against Italy at Swindon in September 1986.

Like many keepers, he became a goalkeeping coach after retiring from playing. From February to October 2014, he was goalkeeping coach for Bahrain while he also coached the keepers at Wolves, Blackburn, Oldham, West Ham, Blackpool, Bolton, Hull, Jamshedpur, ATK, Bangladesh and SC East Bengal before taking over as Senior Academy goalkeeping coach at Norwich City in October 2021, thereby linking up with his old Everton colleague Neil Adams, the Canaries Assistant Sporting Director. Bobby's son Josh, also a goalkeeper, played for York between 2007 and 2010.

## MITCHELL, Adam

**POSITION:** Forward

**BIRTHPLACE:** Middleton-in-Teesdale, Co Durham

**DATE OF BIRTH:** 18/10/1993

**HEIGHT:** 5' 8" **WEIGHT:** 11st 0lbs

**SIGNED FROM:** Schoolboy, 01/07/2010

**DEBUT:** v Tottenham Hotspur, A, 19/05/2013

**LAST MATCH:** v Tottenham Hotspur, A, 19/05/2013

**MOVED TO:** Darlington 21/03/2014

**TEAMS:** Sunderland, Harrogate Town (L), Darlington, Spennymoor Town, West Auckland, Consett (to June 2022)

**SAFC TOTALS:** 0+1 appearances / 0 goals

**Adam Mitchell's four-minute substitute appearance in his only first-team game was just enough for him to have a close-up view as Gareth Bale scored a stunning winner for Spurs in the last match before his £85m move to Real Madrid.**

While Bale became a star on the global stage, this brief first-team appearance proved to be the peak of Mitchell's career which otherwise was spent in non-league. His brother, David, played briefly for Darlington and then coached in the same town at Martin Gray's football academy.

## MITCHELL, Robert (Bobby)

**POSITION:** Midfielder

**BIRTHPLACE:** Hebburn, Co Durham

**DATE OF BIRTH:** 04/01/1955

**HEIGHT:** 5' 8" **WEIGHT:** 10st 12lbs

**SIGNED FROM:** Hebburn Youths, 02/05/1970

**DEBUT:** v Hull City, A, 03/11/1973

**LAST MATCH:** v Hull City, H, 26/12/1975

**MOVED TO:** Blackburn Rovers, 10/07/1976

**TEAMS:** Sunderland, Arcadia Shepherds (L), Blackburn Rovers, Grimsby Town, Carlisle United, Rotherham United, Hamrun Spartans, Lincoln City, Louth United, Spalding United, Boston United, Louth United

**SAFC TOTALS:** 1+2 appearances / 0 goals

**Bobby Mitchell was a skilful midfield creator who perhaps should have had more games for Sunderland. His only start came in a game at Hull when Bob Stokoe rested all of his front five ahead of a European game at Sporting Lisbon. Mitchell went on loan to South Africa with Jimmy Hamilton and eventually moved on to Blackburn in the search for first-team football.**

Debuting for Blackburn as a sub at Plymouth in August 1976 Mitchell marked his first start with the opening goal in a 6-1 win over Notts County the following October. Although he only made 13+8 league appearances in his first season he finished as joint second top scorer with six goals. He remained on the fringe of the side in his second season, ending his spell at Ewood Park having scored seven times in 19+12 outings.

He moved on to Grimsby where he was ever-present as the Mariners won Division Three in 1980 and after a total of 142 league appearances and six goals, signed for Bob Stokoe at Carlisle. At Brunton Park Mitchell played alongside Trevor Swinburne and Jackie Ashurst. Debuting at Burnley in September 1982, Bobby played just once more before joining Rotherham where he played 86+9 times in the league scoring twice before again going abroad, this time to Malta with Hamrun Spartans. He returned to complete his Football League career with Grimsby's rivals Lincoln for whom he scored twice in 41+3 league games and played alongside Peter Daniel. After winding down his playing days in non-league, Bobby returned to Grimsby as Football in the Community Officer before venturing to the USA to coach in Ohio.

Brother Kenny played for Newcastle United, Morton, Darlington and Workington between 1975 and 1982 while another brother, Stewart, played for Woking Town.

## MITCHINSON, Thomas William **(Tommy)**

**POSITION:** Inside-forward

**BIRTHPLACE:** Sunderland, Co Durham

**DATE OF BIRTH:** 24/02/1943 - 20/04/2006

**HEIGHT:** 5' 8" **WEIGHT:** 10st 7lbs

**SIGNED FROM:** School, 01/06/1958

**DEBUT:** v Swansea Town, H, 01/09/1962

**LAST MATCH:** v Burnley, H, 13/11/1965

**MOVED TO:** Mansfield Town, 03/01/1966

**TEAMS:** Sunderland, Mansfield Town, Aston Villa, Torquay United, Bournemouth & Boscombe Athletic

**SAFC TOTALS:** 20+1 appearances / 3 goals

**Tommy Mitchinson's greatest day came on his penultimate start, but it seems his fate was sealed before then. He scored twice as a 2-0 deficit at home to Nottingham Forest was turned into a 3-2 win on a day which ended with Martin Harvey in goal after Jim Montgomery had to go off with seven minutes remaining. They were Mitchinson's only league goals for Sunderland although he had scored in a League Cup win over West Ham the previous season.**

Two years almost to the day before his last game Tommy stood in for Brian Usher for his only game of the 1963-64 promotion year. It was the first season back in the top-flight that he enjoyed his most successful campaign, making two thirds of his Sunderland appearances which were spread over four seasons. He had come to the club's attention after starring for Sunderland Boys, notably in a local derby against Newcastle.

Mansfield paid £8,000 to take Tommy to Field Mill where he scored 15 goals in 76 league games in which he impressed sufficiently for Aston Villa to pay £18,000 to make him manager Tommy Cummings' first signing 18 months later. Playing alongside future Sunderland assistant manager Lew Chatterley, he debuted at Derby in September 1967. Playing as an inside-forward (having operated as a winger on Wearside) Tommy scored once for every four of his 36 league games in his first season for Villa who had just dropped out of the top-flight.

In his second season at Villa Park Tommy was trained by Sunderland's 1973 FA Cup-winning coach Arthur Cox and started the season playing regularly, but after the appointment of Tommy Docherty just before Christmas he made just one more appearance (taking his Villa total to 52/9) before being transferred to Torquay in May 1969 for a third of what Villa had paid for him.

A success at Torquay where he played 108 times, scoring nine goals in two seasons, he finished his career at Bournemouth where over two seasons he played 32+1 times with the return of one goal, his last game coming against Tranmere in October.

As Sunderland were winning the FA Cup in May 1973, the same month saw Mitchinson forced to retire through injury. He returned to Wearside and was known to be a milkman in Whitburn around 2001. His Uncle, Jack Scott was on Sunderland's books without playing a first-team game, but after a similarly fruitless spell at Crystal Palace and a stint at Kettering Town, made a Football League debut for Nottingham Forest and went on to play for Northampton Town, Exeter City and Hartlepools United as well as Blyth Spartans, all before World War Two.

## MITTON, John **(Jack)**

**POSITION:** Half-back

**BIRTHPLACE:** Todmorden, Yorkshire

**DATE OF BIRTH:** 07/11/1895 - 05/08/1983

**HEIGHT:** 5' 11½" **WEIGHT:** 12st 0lbs

**SIGNED FROM:** Exeter City, 20/10/1920

**DEBUT:** v Bradford City, A, 23/10/1920

**LAST MATCH:** v Blackburn Rovers, A, 24/11/1923

**MOVED TO:** Wolverhampton Wanderers, 18/07/1924

**TEAMS:** Burnley, Bury (WW1 Guest), Exeter City, Sunderland, Wolverhampton Wanderers, Southampton

**SAFC TOTALS:** 82 appearances / 7 goals

**Normally a centre or wing-half, perhaps Mitton should have played more at centre-forward. During the second of his four seasons as a first-teamer he was pressed into action for a five-game sequence up front. He scored all seven of his goals for the club in the first four games of that spell, a run that included a hat-trick against WBA.**

Prior to beginning his senior career as an amateur with Burnley in their English (FA) Cup-winning year of 1914, the Yorkshireman had previously appeared for Portsmouth Rovers, Padiham and Brierford (all Lancashire Combination league teams). During World War One, he had played as a 'Guest' for Bury and resumed after the war with Exeter City before coming to the north east. His transfer to Sunderland seems to have stymied his cricket career as he had made two appearances as a bowler for Somerset in 1920.

After what was a decent stint at Sunderland, Wolves paid £500 for him as they prepared for life in Division Two after winning Division Three North. He soon reminded those in the north east of his ability, scoring twice at South Shields on his fifth appearance. These would be his only goals from 38 league and cup games at right-half in his first season as Wolves finished fourth. Over the next two seasons, Mitton took his Molineux total to 107 games and six goals, both of the latter two seasons involving cup defeats against Arsenal, the second at the quarter-final stage.

A move to Southampton in 1927 added just eight more league appearances after which he remained in Hampshire playing in the local county league before he retired in 1930 to become a licensee in Wolverhampton. During the twenties his brother James played for Exeter City and Stockport County.

## MOBERG-KARLSSON, Jens **David** Joacim

**POSITION:** Winger

**BIRTHPLACE:** Mariestad, Sweden

**DATE OF BIRTH:** 20/03/1994

**HEIGHT:** 5' 10½" **WEIGHT:** 12st 0lbs

**SIGNED FROM:** IFK Gothenburg, 19/06/2013

**DEBUT:** v MK Dons, H, 27/08/2013

**LAST MATCH:** v MK Dons, H, 27/08/2013

**MOVED TO:** Nordsjaelland, 13/08/2014

**TEAMS:** IFK Mariestad, IFK Gothenburg, Sunderland, Kilmarnock (L), Nordsjaelland, Norrkoping, Sparta Prague, Urawa Red Diamonds (to June 2022)

**INTERNATIONAL:** Sweden

**SAFC TOTALS:** 1 appearance / 0 goals

**One of a raft of signings due to the recruitment of Director of Football Roberto De Fanti while Paolo Di Canio was head coach, Moberg-Karlsson was replaced after 64 minutes of his solitary Sunderland game. Trailing 2-0 when he went off, Sunderland came back to win 4-2.**

In the next January transfer window he moved on loan to Kilmarnock for the rest of the season under the guidance of manager Allan 'Magic' Johnston. Evidently the Swede did not over impress. He waited until March for a debut and then made two starts and two appearances as sub. Moberg-Karlsson cost a fee reported to be in the region of £1.7m from Gothenburg for whom 17 of his 28 league appearances had been as a sub. Debuting at Djurgaardens in September 2011, David scored twice in his time in Sweden and also played against Djurgardens when he came on as a late sub in the 2013 Swedish Cup final. His team - captained by Toby Hysen - won on penalties.

After his time in the UK Moberg-Karlsson returned to Scandinavia with Danish outfit Nordsjaelland debuting in a home defeat by Brondby in August 2014. He did not score in his first dozen outings but then hit a purple patch, scoring in four successive games, however this did not last and there were no more goals in his remaining 32 appearances ending his two-year stint with 30+18 appearances. In 2016 he returned to Sweden for a three-year spell with Norrkoping where he scored 18 goals in 58+16 games. Ten of those goals came in his last season, leading to a transfer to Sparta Prague for whom he scored his first goal against Banik Ostrava in February 2019 and went on to total 21 goals in 36+24 games, including Champions League strikes against Rapid Vienna and Monaco, and a domestic league hat-trick against MFK Karvina on Valentine's Day 2021, a week after netting a brace against Sigma Olomouc.

He also helped Sparta to win the Czech Cup in 2020, scoring in the final against Slovan Liberec before moving to Japanese football when signing for Urawa Red Diamonds at the end of 2021. By the end of May 2022, he had scored twice in 5+2 games in Japan. Capped three times for Sweden by the end of 2021, he scored against Slovakia in Abu Dhabi in January 2017.

## MOLYNEUX, Luke James

**POSITION:** Winger

**BIRTHPLACE:** Bishop Auckland, Co Durham

**DATE OF BIRTH:** 29/03/1998

**HEIGHT:** 5' 11" **WEIGHT:** 11st 0lbs

**SIGNED FROM:** School, 01/07/2016

**DEBUT:** v Wolverhampton Wanderers, H, 06/05/2018

**LAST MATCH:** v Newcastle United Under 21s, H, 08/01/2019

**MOVED TO:** Hartlepool United, 12/06/2019

**TEAMS:** Sunderland, Gateshead (L), Hartlepool United, Doncaster Rovers (to June 2022)

**SAFC TOTALS:** 1+5 appearances / 0 goals

**Luke Molyneux was a winger who as a youngster seemed to have the potential to do better at Sunderland than he did. Possessing plenty of pace and an eye for goal, he caught the eye in junior football - not least through a well-taken goal in a game against the youngsters of Benfica at Eppleton in November 2016.**

Luke's first-team breakthrough came on the last day of the 2017-18 season. Appropriately, it came against Wolves, albeit not at Molineux. Starting against Wanderers, his debut was overshadowed by the late debut of 16-year-old Bali Mumba in a match which also witnessed the debut of Denver Hume and the final appearance of seven players as a season which brought a second successive relegation came to a close.

Luke came off the bench in the first two league matches of the following season, but otherwise was restricted to cup appearances before signing for Hartlepool United who he had been on loan to after an initial loan with Gateshead in the final four months of 2018. With the Heed, he notched three goals in 11+5 appearances, the first coming in an FA Cup qualifying game against Dunston UTS. Having made two of his last three Gateshead appearances against Hartlepool, he joined them on loan under three weeks after his spell on Tyneside came to an end,

As Pools were promoted back to the Football League, Molyneux converted a penalty as Torquay United were beaten in a shoot-out at Ashton Gate where he had come off the bench. Luke scored 15 goals in 65+29 games for Hartlepool before joining Doncaster in June 2022.

## MONAGHAN, George

**POSITION:** Forward

**BIRTHPLACE:** Straiton, Ayrshire

**DATE OF BIRTH:** 25/09/1862 - 31/12/1894

**HEIGHT:** 5' 7" **WEIGHT:** 11st 11lbs

**SIGNED FROM:** Queen of the South Wanderers, 24/08/1887 (played as a guest in 1885-86 season)

**DEBUT:** v Redcar, A, 24/10/1885

**LAST MATCH:** v Middlesbrough, H, 03/12/1887

**MOVED TO:** Sunderland Albion, 05/05/1888

**TEAMS:** Ayr, Queen of the South Wanderers, Sunderland, Sunderland Albion, Ayr

**SAFC TOTALS:** 4 appearances / 3 goals

**An important figure in the pre-league history of the club. Monaghan scored a hat-trick on his competitive debut in an English Cup tie against Morpeth Harriers on 15 October 1887. These goals and appearance were expunged from the records and are therefore not included in the figures above.**

This was because Morpeth successfully argued that Peter Ford had not been satisfactorily registered for the game. Consequently, a replay was ordered with Monaghan scoring twice this time as Sunderland won 3-2 rather than 4-2 as they had done in the original tie.

Monaghan was one of a number of Scottish players who were enticed over the border to be paid to play football and at the same time gain full-time employment. In George's case, he worked on the construction of the new Town Hall during the week and donned Sunderland's kit at the weekend.

After playing in a win over Newcastle West End in the next round, Monaghan then appeared in a drawn game at Middlesbrough and then scored as Boro were beaten in a replay. However, having already had to replay a game they had won in that season's competition, Sunderland were then disqualified after beating Boro after the Teessiders complaints regarding Monaghan, Andrew Hastings and Joe Richardson were upheld. Sunderland were found guilty by an FA Council of paying the trio's train fares from Dumfries, an offence that in an age of amateurism was frowned upon, but led to Sunderland becoming a club who embraced professionalism.

It seems that this was not Monaghan's only controversial moment. As described in the preface to this book it is believed that George Monaghan also played for Sunderland in the English Cup two years earlier at Redcar on 24 October 1885, but under an assumed name of D Logan. Monaghan is known to have played for Sunderland in a 9-0 friendly win over Cathedral (Jesmond) a week earlier.

Later re-instated after being banned for professionalism, Monaghan went on to play in Sunderland Albion's first game against Shankhouse Black Watch on 5 May 1888. Whilst with Albion he worked at Bartram and Haswell's shipyard. George returned to Scotland to play for his first club Ayr in the early 1890s and by August 1894 had become trainer for another of the town clubs, Ayr Parkhouse. Unfortunately, this work was cut short as he passed away due to heart problems only four months later, aged only 32.

## MONCUR, Robert (Bobby)

**POSITION:** Half-back

**BIRTHPLACE:** Perth, Perthshire

**DATE OF BIRTH:** 19/01/1945

**HEIGHT:** 5' 10" **WEIGHT:** 10st 9lbs

**SIGNED FROM:** Newcastle United, 17/06/1974

**DEBUT:** v Newcastle United, H, 03/08/1974

**LAST MATCH:** v Middlesbrough, A, 11/09/1976

**MOVED TO:** Carlisle United, 18/11/1976

**TEAMS:** Newcastle United, Sunderland, Carlisle United

**INTERNATIONAL:** Scotland

**SAFC TOTALS:** 101 appearances / 2 goals

**A legendary figure at Newcastle United, Bob Moncur had a successful spell at Sunderland in his late career. Like Stan Anderson in the previous decade, Moncur left the club he was synonymous with to steer their local rivals to promotion. Like Anderson, Moncur also oozed class off the pitch as well as on it. They played alongside each other in United's promotion season of 1964-65, Moncur making eleven appearances alongside Stan who missed just two games.**

Famously defender Moncur scored three times over two legs of the 1969 Inter-Cities Fairs Cup final win by Newcastle against Ujpesti Dozsa. In 1962, playing as an inside-forward, he had also scored as Wolves were beaten 2-1 in the final of the FA Youth Cup. A debutant for the Magpies at Luton on 30 March 1963, Moncur went on to play 357+3 games for the club, a third of his goals coming in that European final. He also captained Newcastle in the 1974 FA Cup final when they were beaten 3-0 by Liverpool.

Born in Perth in Scotland, Moncur moved to Kirkliston near Edinburgh when he was nine. He began his football career with Perth Life Boys, Uphall Boys Club and Tynecastle Boys Club before he was signed by Newcastle in October 1960, becoming a pro in April 1962.

For Scotland, Bobby won 16 full caps, captaining his country in half of those appearances. Debuting in a goalless draw away to the Netherlands in May 1968, three of his international appearances were against England.

At Sunderland he made his first appearance in a friendly at Hamilton and a competitive debut in a Texaco Cup win against his former club Newcastle - Moncur having maintained his cup final scoring record by hitting the extra-time winner in the previous season's final against Burnley. I remember seeing Bobby chatting to Alan Price of the Animals before the game on his Sunderland league debut at Millwall on the opening day of the 1974-75 season, in which he would be ever-present and captain as Bob Stokoe's side narrowly missed out on promotion. The following year Moncur missed a mere three games as he helped Sunderland to the second tier title, but after just five league matches of the following season his time in red and white came to an end.

A week later he became player/manager of Carlisle United, debuting against Millwall in a side that included John Lathan. Relegated from Division Two in Moncur's first season the Cumbrians (with Jim Hamilton added to their squad) finished mid-table and improved to sixth a season later (this was pre-Play-Offs) when they equalled a record (held by Tranmere, Aldershot and Chester) of 22 draws. Moncur remained in charge until February 1980 when he resigned to take over at Hearts and was replaced by Martin Harvey having played just 13 times. Moncur played once for Hearts - scoring twice in friendly against a North East XI on 11 May 1980 as Hearts celebrated winning promotion to the SPL - but only lasted until June 1981 when he was sacked. Moncur's sole full season in charge at Tynecastle saw the club relegated.

He then succeeded Bobby Saxton as manager of Plymouth Argyle where his side scored just six goals in their first twelve league games, failing to win any, only to recover and finish tenth. After an eighth-place finish the following season, Moncur was dismissed following a slow start to the campaign. He returned to the north east, accepting a role as coach at Whitley Bay although he then did not take up the post. October 1988 brought a return to management with Hartlepool United where he spent 14 months before moving out of football - other than radio and ambassadorial roles with Newcastle.

A talented all-round sportsman who had won the footballers' golf championship in 1967, for a while Bobby became Director of Corporate Events at Aldwark Manor hotel and golf complex near York. He also became manager of Gateshead Squash and Fitness Centre and worked in insurance. However, his greatest post football passion became sailing. He established a sailing school on the Tyne and headed for sunnier climes with a company sailing a catamaran from St Vincent in the Caribbean. He also became a master and instructor with the Royal Yachting Association. Bobby took part in many races including Trans-Atlantic crossings and the 1995 Tall Ships race. A member of the Newcastle United Hall of Fame, he became a Freeman of Gateshead in 2009.

## MONTGOMERY, James (Jim)

**POSITION:** Goalkeeper

**BIRTHPLACE:** Hendon, Sunderland, Co Durham

**DATE OF BIRTH:** 09/10/1943

**HEIGHT:** 5' 11" **WEIGHT:** 11st 9lbs

**SIGNED FROM:** Sunderland Boys, 01/06/1958 and Nottingham Forest, 07/08/1980

**DEBUT:** v Walsall, H, 04/10/1961

**LAST MATCH:** v Manchester United, A, 06/10/1976

**MOVED TO:** Birmingham City, 18/03/1977 and left SAFC, 01/07/1982

**TEAMS:** Sunderland, Southampton (L), Birmingham City, Nottingham Forest, Sunderland

**INTERNATIONAL:** England Under 23

**SAFC TOTALS:** 627 appearances / 0 goals

**Sunderland's record appearance holder, Monty's 627 appearances is surely a record that will never be broken. Jim played 169 more matches than Len Ashurst who is the club's second-highest appearance maker. Monty's games consist of 537 in the league, 41 in the FA Cup, 33 in the League Cup (in which he played his first and last games for the club), eight in the Anglo-Italian Cup, four in the European Cup Winners' Cup, three in the Texaco Cup and one in the Anglo-Scottish Cup.**

Jim's worldwide fame arrived when he made the save officially rated as Wembley's greatest. His double-save from Trevor Cherry and Peter Lorimer in the 1973 FA Cup final is rightly the stuff of legend, but it came as no surprise to the massed ranks of Sunderland supporters behind the goal.

Spectacular saves of incredible agility were Monty's stock in trade. The cup-final double save was special because of the magnitude of the match but 'The Mighty Jim' had already done his bit to get Sunderland to Wembley - not least a tremendous late save from Les Bradd at Notts County in the third round. Without that the cup run would never have happened.

Many believe Monty's greatest game was at Huddersfield in 1962. On that occasion Sunderland went on to win 3-0 after Montgomery produced an unbelievable display, in particular thwarting former Newcastle forward Len White. That season and the one after - in which Sunderland won a first-ever promotion - were two of five seasons Monty was ever-present in the league. He kept goal in 40 or more league games nine times while in the second division championship-winning campaign of 1975-76, he played in 38 of the 42 games.

Remarkably after that season, Jim made just six further league appearances for Sunderland. Shortly before he resigned, manager Bob Stokoe paid out big money to bring in Barry Siddall from Bolton. Siddall was a very good goalkeeper, but not in Monty's class. Soon afterwards, new manager Jimmy Adamson allowed Monty to move on. Adamson had been a senior player at Burnley when Jim went to Turf Moor as a youngster for a one-month trial before joining his hometown club. At the time the Clarets had quality goalkeepers in England international Colin McDonald, future Scotland cap Adam Blacklaw and Jim Furnell who went on to play for Arsenal.

It was SAFC physio Johnny Watters and one of Jim's old teachers Alfie Lavender, who arranged a trial for Jim at Sunderland. After giving great service to the club, the last of Jim's games for his hometown team came four days before his 33rd birthday. That is no age for a goalkeeper and the mind boggles as to how many games Monty might have totalled had he not been released. He did later return to the club three and a half years after being sold, but without adding to his appearances in his role as player/coach.

Five games on loan to Lawrie McMenemy's Southampton preceded a transfer to Birmingham City. Initially he went to St Andrew's on loan. Always a terrific saver of penalties, Jim saved one from Derby's Charlie George on his Birmingham debut. Player of the Year at Birmingham in 1977-78, after 73 appearances for Birmingham - where he played for Sir Alf Ramsay and alongside future Sunderland manager Ricky Sbragia - Monty was signed by his old Sunderland teammate Brian Clough at Nottingham Forest.

Forest were European champions and veteran Monty went as back-up to England goalkeeper Peter Shilton. A European Cup-winner's medal came Jim's way as an unused substitute in the 1980 European Cup final against Hamburg. Jim's former Sunderland teammate John O'Hare was another of the subs, while the starting XI included Frank Gray, Ian Bowyer and Martin O'Neill. Monty's only first-team appearance for Forest did come in a cup final, albeit a minor one - a County Cup final where Notts County were beaten 2-1 seven years and a day after Monty's Wembley exploits.

After two years back at Sunderland, Jim spent seven years at Meadowfield Sports Centre in Durham working alongside future SAFC Academy manager Ged McNamee. During this time, Jim coached goalkeepers at Sunderland, Newcastle, Darlington and Ryhope CA, the latter alongside George Herd with whom he had played and coached at Sunderland.

Jim went on to become chairman of the Sunderland Former Players' Association and the club's ambassador. He was awarded the British Empire Medal in 2015, became a Freeman of Sunderland in 2016 and was inducted at the inaugural SAFC Hall of Fame in 2019. He also had the biggest suite at the Stadium of Light named in his honour.

Above all else Jim Montgomery is an absolute gentleman. There is a saying that you should never meet your heroes, but Jim is as good off the pitch as he was on it. Without a shadow of a doubt he has always been my favourite player.

Despite playing in the same era as Gordon Banks, it is shocking that Monty never won a full cap for England. The nearest he got was being an unused substitute at Wembley for a game against France in March 1969. Called up at Under 18 level, he found his team 3-0 down within 34 minutes of his debut against the Netherlands at Brighton in January 1962, before England came back to win 4-3. Two months to the day later, Jim kept a clean sheet as West Germany were beaten 1-0.

The following May he played in two away games in Israel, winning 3-1 and losing 2-1. Under 23 recognition followed with his first two caps both coming at St James' Park against Scotland. After a debut in a 3-2 win (in which clubmate Nick Sharkey scored against him) in February 1964, Jim made five consecutive appearances between March and June 1967. After losing 3-1 to the Scots, Jim conceded just one goal from a home game with Austria in Hull and trips to Greece, Bulgaria and Turkey.

MITROX
IMPROVED FORMULA

## MONTGOMERY, William (Willie)

**POSITION:** Inside / outside-left

**BIRTHPLACE:** Gourock, Refrewshire

**DATE OF BIRTH:** 02/06/1884 - 21/11/1953

**HEIGHT:** 5' 8" **WEIGHT:** 11st 7lbs

**SIGNED FROM:** Bradford City, 08/07/1907

**DEBUT:** v Liverpool, A, 12/10/1907

**LAST MATCH:** v Preston North End, H, 24/04/1909

**MOVED TO:** Oldham Athletic, 05/10/1909

**TEAMS:** Rutherglen, Bradford City, Sunderland, Oldham Athletic, Rangers, Dundee

**SAFC TOTALS:** 11 appearances / 2 goals

**Willie Montgomery started in English football with Bradford City becoming one of the first signings of Peter O'Rourke who had just taken over from former Sunderland manager Robert Campbell. He got a goal on his debut at Hull in November 1905, but it was not enough to prevent a heavy defeat.**

There were three goals in 15 games during that first season, but after playing in the opening two fixtures of 1906-07 he did not play again until moving to Sunderland a year later. After four away appearances spread over 15 months, he finally made a home debut over a year and a half after signing - and marked the occasion by scoring against his former club.

In October 1909 Montgomery moved on to Oldham Athletic for a fee of £350, helping them to promotion in his first season and going on to score ten times in 42 games before a June 1912 move to Rangers. After seven games for the Ibrox club, he added 38 for Dundee in 1913-14.

In October 1920 he emigrated to the USA and worked as a machinist in the National Tube Company in McKeesport, Pennsylvania. Willie subsequently moved to Oakland in California where he died in 1953.

## MOONEY, Brian John

**POSITION:** Midfielder

**BIRTHPLACE:** Dublin, Republic of Ireland

**DATE OF BIRTH:** 02/02/1966

**HEIGHT:** 5' 11" **WEIGHT:** 11st 2lbs

**SIGNED FROM:** Preston North End, 06/02/1991

**DEBUT:** v Nottingham Forest, H, 16/02/1991

**LAST MATCH:** v West Ham United, H, 27/02/1993

**MOVED TO:** Released on free transfer, 13/05/1993

**TEAMS:** Stella Maris, Home Farm, Liverpool, Wrexham (L), Preston North End, Sheffield Wednesday (L), Sunderland, Burnley (L), Shelbourne, Bohemians, UC Dublin, Monaghan United

**INTERNATIONAL:** Republic of Ireland B

**SAFC TOTALS:** 23+6 appearances / 1 goal

**Brian Mooney was a talented creative winger/schemer who came to SAFC in the midst of an ultimately gallant, but unsuccessful, relegation battle. Unfortunately, Mooney never found his best form at Sunderland and moved on after a couple of years having never nailed down a regular first-team place, and having been out on loan to Burnley for a month from 11 September 1992.**

A product of the Dublin club Home Farm, renowned for producing young players including Kenny Cunningham, Ian Harte and Graham Kavanagh who also played for Sunderland,

Liverpool took him in August 1983. His only appearance for the Merseysiders came on 7 October 1986 as a sub in a League Cup tie at Fulham.

Loaned to Wrexham in 1985-86 Mooney played alongside a young Shaun Cunnington, the first of nine appearances coming at Stockport shortly before Christmas in 1985. His first goal came in a heavy defeat at Burnley on New Year's Day 1986, but he added another with a winner at Exeter. In November 1987 he left Liverpool for Preston where Brian played his best football. Nicknamed 'The Moon Man' at Deepdale, Mooney was North End's Player of the Year in 1988-89 when he was a teammate of Sam Allardyce. He totalled 128 games and 20 goals for PNE in three and a quarter years, one of these goals coming against Sunderland in the Rokerites third division promotion campaign of 1987-88. During this time he had an injury-curtailed loan to Sheffield Wednesday early in the 1990-91 season without getting a game for the Owls.

After leaving Sunderland, Mooney returned to Ireland playing for a quartet of teams. He scored 13 goals in 60 outings for Shelbourne for whom he twice scored in the European Cup Winners' Cup. There were also 19 goals in 117 games for Bohemians, three in 39 appearances for University College Dublin (where he studied for a degree and played in the Champions League and UEFA Cup) and finally a dozen games for Monaghan United.

At international level, at his best he came close to a full cap and won honours at 'B', Under 21, Under 23 level and for the League of Ireland. Just before the Italia 90 FIFA World Cup he played in a 4-1 win over England B at Cork. His autobiography Mooney, Mooney: The Man, the Magic and Preston on the Plastic, was published in 2000.

## MOORE, Gary

**POSITION:** Centre-forward

**BIRTHPLACE:** South Hetton, Co Durham

**DATE OF BIRTH:** 04/11/1945 - 17/11/2021

**HEIGHT:** 6' 0: **WEIGHT:** 11st 0lbs

**SIGNED FROM:** Youth team, 01/05/1962

**DEBUT:** v Wolverhampton Wanderers, A, 20/04/1965

**LAST MATCH:** v Arsenal, A, 17/12/1966

**MOVED TO:** Grimsby Town, 23/02/1967

**TEAMS:** Sunderland, Grimsby Town, Southend United, Colchester United, Chester, Swansea City

**INTERNATIONAL:** England Youth

**SAFC TOTALS:** 14 appearances / 2 goals

**An England youth international, Gary came through the youth system at Sunderland and went on to play 14 times, scoring against West Bromwich Albion and Sheffield United.**

He subsequently played for Grimsby Town (59+1/15), Southend United (183+7/55), Colchester United (11/7), Chester (32+16/ 6) and Swansea City (38+4/11) in a career that totalled 337+36 appearances and 96 goals. Gary was particularly successful at Southend where he later ran a sports shop and did scouting work.

In 1968-69 he scored four goals for Southend in a 10-1 FA Cup second-round game against Brentwood after scoring a hat-trick in a 9-0 first-round victory over Kings Lynn. Gary later became a sales representative for a pharmaceutical company and coached Blyth Spartans in 1988. He retired to Sunderland, living in Ashbrooke.

## MOORE, John

**POSITION:** Centre-forward

**BIRTHPLACE:** Blackhill, Consett, Co Durham

**DATE OF BIRTH:** 01/10/1966

**HEIGHT:** 6' 0" **WEIGHT:** 11st 11lbs

**SIGNED FROM:** Blackhill Juniors, 01/07/1983

**DEBUT:** v Chelsea, H, 30/03/1985

**LAST MATCH:** v Notts County, H, 19/03/1988

**MOVED TO:** Hull City, 29/06/1988

**TEAMS:** Sunderland, S. Patrick's Athletic (L), Newport County (L), Darlington (L), Mansfield Town (L), Rochdale (L), Hull City, Sheffield United, Utrecht, Shrewsbury Town, Crewe Alexandra, Newcastle Blue Star, Scarborough, Bishop Auckland, Sing Tao, Happy Valley, Sun Hei, Durham City

**INTERNATIONAL:** Hong Kong

**SAFC TOTALS:** 6+14 appearances / 3 goals

**John Moore was a target-man who played a handful of games and has the distinction of being the first Sunderland player to appear as a second substitute in a league game. He did this in the club's first-ever third-tier fixture at Brentford on 15 August 1987. John's first game was as a 16-year-old substitute in a friendly at Bishop Auckland in August 1983.**

His first and most important goal secured a 1-0 top-flight win at Coventry in April 1985, although it could not prevent the Lads going down at the end of the season. After being very much on the fringe in the next two seasons, twelve of John's 20 appearances came in 1987-88, all but one of them as a sub, his two goals coming in the Sherpa Van Trophy. Almost all of these 1987-88 games came in the early part of the season before the signing of Marco Gabbiadini.

During his time at SAFC Moore had five loans. After starting in Ireland with St Patrick's Athletic, he played twice each for Newport and Darlington, scoring his first goal for Darlo on his debut in a 1-0 win over Wigan in November 1986. He went on to score once in five games for Mansfield and twice in ten appearances for Rochdale before moving to Hull. There he made 11+3 early-season appearances, once again his solitary goal providing a 1-0 win, this time against Swindon.

## MOORE, John (Continued)

He then had five games on loan to Sheffield United before a switch to the continent with FC Utrecht where he netted eight goals in 30 games in 1989-90. Returning to England John scored once in eight games for Shrewsbury. After a single game for Crewe Alexandra there were seven games and one goal for Scarborough in 1991-92 - against Crewe. Scarborough were still a Football League club at this time, but this was not the period where they had a host of ex-Sunderland players.

Moore then dropped into non-league before heading to Hong Kong from 1992 to 2002. Having gained permanent residential status, he then played for Hong Kong in qualification games for the 2002 FIFA World Cup, winning seven caps - being sent off in a game against Palestine. Returning to the north east, John completed his playing career with Durham City in 2002-03.

## MOORE, Malcolm

**POSITION:** Centre-forward

**BIRTHPLACE:** Silksworth, Co Durham

**DATE OF BIRTH:** 18/12/1948

**HEIGHT:** 5' 10" **WEIGHT:** 12st 0lbs

**SIGNED FROM:** Dawdon Juniors, 01/07/1965

**DEBUT:** v Coventry City, H, 23/03/1968

**LAST MATCH:** v Ipswich Town, A, 04/04/1969

**MOVED TO:** Tranmere Rovers, 30/06/1970

**TEAMS:** Sunderland, Crewe Alexandra (L), Tranmere Rovers, Hartlepool United, Workington, Gateshead, North Shields, Chester-le-Street

**SAFC TOTALS:** 10+2 appearances / 3 goals

**Malcolm Moore played in eight of the nine games it took Sunderland to win the FA Youth Cup for the first time in 1967, scoring against Preston and Scunthorpe. The previous season he scored in both legs of the final which was lost to Arsenal. During that run, he top scored with seven in eight games.**

At first-team level Malcolm marked his debut as a sub with a top-flight goal that earned a point against Coventry. It made him the first substitute to score for Sunderland at Roker Park. The following season he scored in successive games against Stoke and Coventry but then faded from the Sunderland scene.

He did though go on to have a solid career in the lower leagues totalling 57 other league goals: 21 in 83+10 games for Tranmere Rovers, 34 in 127+2 matches for Hartlepool and two in 22 games for Workington. He also had eight games without scoring while on loan to Crewe when still at Sunderland. At Hartlepool, where he was twice top scorer, he also added eight goals in 19+1 cup appearances. After being relegated with Workington Malcolm played non-league football in the north east before spending six years in charge of Chester-le-Street in the early 1980s - spending his first year of 1979-80 as player/manager - after which he became a milkman and then set up a nursing home.

## MOORE, William Grey Bruce (Billy)

**POSITION:** Inside-forward / centre-forward

**BIRTHPLACE:** Newcastle-upon-Tyne, Northumberland

**DATE OF BIRTH:** 06/10/1894 - 26/09/1968

**HEIGHT:** 5' 8½" **WEIGHT:** 10st 0lbs

**SIGNED FROM:** Seaton Delaval, 15/11/1912

**DEBUT:** v Sheffield United, A, 07/02/1914

**LAST MATCH:** v Everton, A, 02/01/1922

**MOVED TO:** West Ham United, 13/05/1922

**TEAMS:** Seaton Delaval, Sunderland, West Ham United

**INTERNATIONAL:** England

**SAFC TOTALS:** 47 appearances / 11 goals

**A year after leaving Sunderland, Billy returned to Roker Park to play in West Ham United's first-ever first division fixture. The previous season (his first with the Irons) he had been ever-present as they won promotion and reached the Cup final - playing in the famous White Horse final, the first at Wembley.**

He had scored 20 goals that season including two in the cup semi-final. In total, Billy scored 48 goals in 202 games for West Ham (including two against Sunderland in London in December 1924) with whom he played until 1929. After retiring, Moore spent three years as the club's assistant trainer before being head trainer from 1932 all the way until his retirement at the end of the 1959-60 season.

Billy scored twice on his only full England appearance. The goals coming in a 3-1 win against Sweden in Stockholm in the month after his cup final appearance. Moore also won four amateur caps for England scoring twice on that debut in an 8-1 win over Belgium in Brussels in February 1914 when he was with Sunderland. He also scored three goals in two games against Sweden in the same year, as well as playing against Denmark in Copenhagen, also in 1914.

Moore had made his Sunderland debut just a fortnight before his amateur international debut. After missing four seasons due to World War One - during which he worked in a munitions factory - he played in three post-war seasons before his move to London. Billy's best season at Sunderland was in 1920-21 when he played 20 times.

## MORDUE, John (Jackie)

**POSITION:** Inside-right / outside-right

**BIRTHPLACE:** Edmondsley, Co Durham

**DATE OF BIRTH:** 13/12/1886 - 06/03/1938

**HEIGHT:** 5' 7" **WEIGHT:** 10st 8lbs

**SIGNED FROM:** Arsenal, 07/05/1908

**DEBUT:** v Middlesbrough, A, 09/09/1908

**LAST MATCH:** v Middlesbrough, H, 13/03/1920

**MOVED TO:** Middlesbrough, 11/05/1920

**TEAMS:** Sacriston, Spennymoor United, Barnsley, Arsenal, Sunderland, Hartlepools United (WW1 guest), Middlesbrough, Durham City, Ryhope CW

**INTERNATIONAL:** England

**SAFC TOTALS:** 293 appearances / 83 goals

**Part of the famed 'Roker triangle' with inside-right Charlie Buchan and right-half Francis Cuggy, Mordue scored 20 goals in 44 games in Sunderland's greatest season of 1912-13 when the league was won and the cup final reached. Eight of these goals were penalties including ones in the cup quarter and semi-finals against Newcastle and Burnley. He was also on the scoresheet against Newcastle in the legendary 9-1 win of 1908.**

Jackie followed his father down the pit, although his dad died before Jackie was 15. In February 1913, Jackie won his second England cap on a day clubmates Buchan and Cuggy were two of seven debutants for England. It is the only time Sunderland had three men in an England starting line-up. Unfortunately, they lost to Ireland for the first time in 31 meetings, although Buchan did score. On the same day Sunderland won 2-0 away to Middlesbrough (Boro also having two men in the England team). The first of Mordue's two caps had also been against Ireland. This came almost exactly a year earlier when his Sunderland teammate George Holley was amongst the scorers in a 6-1 win. One of Mordue's caps is on display in the entrance hall at the Stadium of Light.

Mordue was a model of consistency for Sunderland and would be a contender for the right-wing berth if picking an all-time Sunderland XI. In a career split by World War One - during

which he served in the Royal Garrison Artillery - only in one of his eight seasons did he play fewer than 30 games - making 26 appearances in 1913-14. In addition to his 293 league and cup appearances Mordue played in the only game of 1915-16 and played 22 times in the 1918-19 Victory League. Top-scoring with 17 goals (including a hat-trick against Newcastle) effectively took his grand total of Sunderland goals to at least 100. Including two in the Victory League, 29 of Mordue's goals were penalties (he took 33 in peace-time). Only Billy Clunas has scored more, while only Clunas, Tony Towers and Gary Rowell have a better conversion rate (of those to take a minimum ten penalties).

On 3 January 1916 he made one appearance for Hartlepools in a friendly against Bob Pailor's XI. For Middlesbrough Mordue scored his only goal in 35 appearances in his third game at Arsenal, a fortnight after his debut in September 1920. On 4 March 1923 he became player-manager of Durham City and scored once in six league games before he was sacked on 19 January 1924 after a defeat at Darlington left Durham sixth bottom of Division Three North.

Multi-talented, Mordue was also England 'Fives' champion in 1912-13 and came from a sporting family. His brother Michael played for Horden Athletic, nephew James played for Hull, Newcastle, Sheffield United and Hartlepools during the 1920s and brother-in-law James Ashcroft played for Everton, Gravesend United, Arsenal, Blackburn Rovers and Tranmere Rovers between 1897 and 1915.

## MORGAN, Hugh

**POSITION:** Inside-forward / centre-forward

**BIRTHPLACE:** Kilbarchan, Lanarkshire

**DATE OF BIRTH:** 01/08/1876 - 06/05/1959

**HEIGHT:** 5' 7" **WEIGHT:** 10st 11lbs

**SIGNED FROM:** Airdrieonians, 16/12/1896

**DEBUT:** v Everton, A, 26/12/1896

**LAST MATCH:** v Nottingham Forest, H, 14/01/1899

**MOVED TO:** Bolton Wanderers, 07/02/1899

**TEAMS:** Harthill Thistle, Airdrieonians, Sunderland, Bolton Wanderers, Newton Heath, Manchester City, Accrington Stanley, Blackpool, Hamilton Academical

**SAFC TOTALS:** 60 appearances / 19 goals

**Hugh Morgan should not be forgotten as he played an important role in testing times for the club. He scored on his debut at Everton on Boxing Day in 1896, but it was in a heavy defeat. He did well, but his six goals in twelve games were not sufficient to stop Sunderland slipping into the relegation Play-offs of the time, known as Test Matches. Hugh scored to earn a draw in a crucial match with Newton Heath who later became Manchester United. He also scored a winner on his FA (English) Cup debut away to Burnley, ending the season as joint second top scorer despite only debuting at Christmas.**

There were six goals in his first dozen games of his first full season which was the last at Newcastle Road in 1897-98. However there were no more in his remaining 16 games but nonetheless, he helped revive the team who finished as runners-up. Morgan was in the side for the first-ever game at Roker Park and ended up with five goals from 13 games before a fee of £225 took him to Bolton Wanderers. As at Sunderland, Morgan began with six goals in twelve games, but it was not enough to stop the Trotters from going down.

Spending much of what was his only full season at Bolton on the right-wing, Hugh hit ten goals in 30 games as he helped the club to instant promotion at a time when he was combining playing with working as a railway clerk. He had been a miner before becoming a footballer. After playing in Bolton's first four games back in the top-flight Morgan moved on again, this time to Newton Heath. Debuting in a Division Two game with Lincoln City in December 1900, he marked the occasion with one of the four goals he scored in 23 games, before joining Manchester City at the end of the season.

Again he was involved in a relegation season, City propping the table up as Sunderland were champions in 1901-02, Hugh scoring once in a dozen league games. He then had two seasons with Accrington Stanley before spending 1904-05 with Blackpool where he got five goals in 26 games in league and cup, the final league game of his career coming with a goal at Manchester United, before he moved back to his native Lanarkshire to play one season for Hamilton while he operated as a School attendance officer.

## MORGAN, Lewis

**POSITION:** Winger

**BIRTHPLACE:** Greenock, Renfrewshire

**DATE OF BIRTH:** 30/09/1996

**HEIGHT:** 5' 10" **WEIGHT:** 11st 11lbs

**SIGNED FROM:** Celtic, 31/01/2019, on loan

**DEBUT:** v AFC Wimbledon, H, 02/02/2019

**LAST MATCH:** v Charlton Athletic, N, 26/05/2019

**MOVED TO:** Celtic, 31/05/2019, end of loan

**TEAMS:** Rangers, St Mirren, Celtic, St. Mirren (L), Sunderland (L), Inter Miami, New York Red Bulls (to June 2022)

**INTERNATIONAL:** Scotland

**SAFC TOTALS:** 15+7 appearances / 2 goals

**Morgan went close with a couple of well-hit shots on his final appearance in a Play-Off final at Wembley, but otherwise Lewis' loan to Sunderland was largely uneventful. Like many wingers, he promised more than he ultimately delivered, although he did score in the semi-final of the Checkatrade Trophy at Bristol Rovers.**

As well as playing twice for Sunderland at Wembley, Lewis also played at Hampden Park for Celtic against Rangers in the final of Scottish League Cup in 2019. Lewis was subbed a minute before his side scored the only goal of the game on the hour mark, thereby not playing against Jermain Defoe who came on ten minutes later.

He did better in November 2019 when opening the scoring in a Europa League win against Rennes. It was one of two goals he scored in 13 European games for Celtic, although he failed to score in 18 league or domestic cup outings.

After starting in the Rangers youth system, Lewis made his first-team debut against Celtic in September 2014 having moved to St Mirren for whom he eventually totalled 94 league games and 21 goals, 15 of those appearances and five of those goals coming after Celtic loaned him back to his former club.

Having moved to the USA, he played in Inter Miami's first-ever match, against Los Angeles in March 2020. After seven goals in 57 games he was transferred to New York Red Bulls in December 2021. Having played in all of Inter Miami's first 50 games, he had certainly helped to establish the new team. At international level he won nine Under 21 caps and made a full international debut for Scotland against Peru in May 2018, adding a second cap against Mexico a few days later.

## MORLEY, John Bell

**POSITION:** Outside-right

**BIRTHPLACE:** Carlisle, Cumberland

**DATE OF BIRTH:** 30/01/1884 - 26/10/1957

**HEIGHT:** 5' 9" **WEIGHT:** 10st 9lbs

**SIGNED FROM:** Workington, 07/05/1907

**DEBUT:** v Aston Villa, A, 09/09/1907

**LAST MATCH:** v Everton, H, 14/12/1907

**MOVED TO:** Burnley, 08/06/1908

**TEAMS:** Carlisle Red Rose, Workington, Sunderland, Burnley, Preston North End

**SAFC TOTALS:** 5 appearances / 1 goal

**A nimble, tricky winger known to have good footwork, John Bell had the surname Morley added when his mother remarried shortly after he was born, although throughout his life he used the surname Bell on all legal documents.**

Starting with Carlisle Red Rose, he soon moved to Workington during their first season in the Lancashire Combination second division. After signing in March 1905 he scored his first goal against Chorley during that month. In his first full season Morley was a major supply line for the other four members of a forward line who contributed 80 of his team's 102 goals. Such form inevitably attracted scouts and Sunderland picked up Morley, in spite of interest from Burnley. He made five appearances all in the 1907-08 season, scoring on his home debut against Preston, who he would later play for.

Before moving to Deepdale however, he had four and half years with Burnley from June 1908. There were 108 games and 17 goals for the Clarets before he moved to their local rivals Preston in December 1912. That season he had the distinction on spending half a season with each of the two clubs promoted to the top flight which Sunderland had just won. At Preston, he linked up with former Sunderland striker Alf Common and scored 15 goals in 75 league games up to the closing of the Football League due to World War One.

After the war Morley combined with his former Preston teammates Billy Greer, Jack Warner and Bob Holmes in coaching the pre-eminent women's team of the 1920s: Dick Kerr's Ladies, before becoming a general fitter and turner in the Preston area.

## MORRIS, Samuel Walker (Sammy)

**POSITION:** Half-back

**BIRTHPLACE:** Prescot, Liverpool, Lancashire

**DATE OF BIRTH:** 16/04/1907 - 10/08/1991

**HEIGHT:** 5' 10" **WEIGHT:** 11st 3lbs

**SIGNED FROM:** Prescot Cables, 16/11/1928

**DEBUT:** v Arsenal, H, 01/01/1929

**LAST MATCH:** v Everton, A, 16/01/1932

**MOVED TO:** Charlton Athletic, 22/09/1932

**TEAMS:** Prescot Cables, Sunderland, Charlton Athletic, Chester, Bath City, Weymouth.

**INTERNATIONAL:** Scotland

**SAFC TOTALS:** 65 appearances / 0 goals

**Standing in for the renowned Billy Clunas shortly after stepping up from Prescot Cables, Morris made a positive impression on his debut in 1929 being part of a team who defeated Arsenal 5-1 on New Year's Day. He made five appearances that season and eight in the next, before a best year of 1930-31 when he started 33 games, before signing off with 19 appearances in 1931-32.**

After just under four years at Roker Park Sammy declined to accept the new contract terms that the club offered and he moved south to Charlton where he played a dozen games before a final move to Chester where he played just five times before drifting out of senior football. By 1939 Sammy was a fitter's labourer living in Weymouth.

## MORRISON, Evelyn Sneddon

**POSITION:** Centre-forward

**BIRTHPLACE:** Natal Province, South Africa

**DATE OF BIRTH:** 01/08/1902 -15/11/1968

**HEIGHT:** 5' 10" **WEIGHT:** 11st 0lbs

**SIGNED FROM:** Falkirk, 20/11/1929

**DEBUT:** v Grimsby Town, A, 23/11/1929

**LAST MATCH:** v Liverpool, A, 11/04/1931

**MOVED TO:** Partick Thistle, 11/05/1931

**TEAMS:** Moorpark Amateurs, Stenhousemuir, Falkirk, Sunderland, Partick Thistle

**SAFC TOTALS:** 16 appearances / 7 goals

**Evelyn was born in South Africa to Scottish parents, but moved to Hamilton, Lanarkshire, in 1908. His father had been working in the mining industry in Natal. Before turning professional Morrison ran a coal briquette making business with his father. When he signed for Sunderland he insisted on maintaining his business interests and so trained in Falkirk and only met up with the team on matchdays.**

With a record of seven goals in 16 games, he may well have been worth more opportunities, but perhaps the difficulties of incorporating a player who did not train with the team proved insurmountable and he returned to Scottish football as Bobby Gurney was making a name for himself. Moving to Partick from SAFC, he made a scoring debut on 31 May 1931 in a friendly in Denmark against Copenhagen Boldklub and went on to score 19 goals for Thistle in 20 appearances, the last coming in a Scottish Cup defeat at Airdrieonians on 5 March 1932.

Upon his retirement from football, Morrison concentrated on his business, but later became a woodwork teacher at St Joseph's Primary School in Blantyre and subsequently Uddingston Grammar School in Glasgow.

A goalscorer on his home debut for Sunderland against Manchester United, Evelyn had come to prominence as a schoolboy. Playing alongside his brother with Hamilton Academy they fired their team to the Scottish Schools Under16 Shield. After joining Moorpark Amateurs he won the Scottish Amateur League and West of Scotland Amateur Cup when reputedly scoring 150 goals across two seasons. Due to his business interests Morrison turned down approaches from bigger clubs, until at the age of 26 he joined second division Stenhousemuir for whom he netted 30 goals in 23 outings.

From there he moved to top-flight Falkirk where at one point he scored 29 goals in 16 games from November 1928 to the following February. That season he hit a record 45 goals for Falkirk - two more than Dave Halliday did in his record-breaking season at Sunderland the same year. Referred to as 'Sir Evelyn' at Falkirk, Morrison totalled 75 goals in 58 league games before his move to Sunderland who paid £6,500 for his signature.

## MORRISON, John Stanton Fleming

**POSITION:** Left-back

**BIRTHPLACE:** West Jesmond, Northumberland

**DATE OF BIRTH:** 17/04/1892 - 28/01/1961

**HEIGHT:** 5' 10"

**SIGNED FROM:** Cambridge University, 18/12/1919

**DEBUT:** v Manchester City, H, 20/12/1919

**LAST MATCH:** v Manchester City, H, 20/12/1919

**MOVED TO:** Cambridge University, 22/12/1919

**TEAMS:** Jarrow, Cambridge University, Sunderland, Cambridge University, Corinthians, Old Carthusians

**INTERNATIONAL:** England amateur

**SAFC TOTALS:** 1 appearance / 0 goals

**Tynesider John Morrison played one game for Sunderland. It was his only game in the Football League, but what an interesting biography he has. Evidently from a well to do family, he played football and cricket for Charterhouse School, is known to have played for Jarrow in 1913 and then became a sporting phenomenon at Trinity College at Cambridge University where he studied history and law. A multi-talented sportsman he excelled at cricket and golf as well as football.**

During World War One he gained the Distinguished Flying Cross and bar from being a bomber pilot in early aircraft. Later in World War Two he was a Wing Commander in the RAF Volunteer Reserve and became one of the first pilots to land on an aircraft carrier. At Cambridge University he gained a 'Blue' in 1913, 1914 and 1920. Between 1912 and 1919, he played cricket for Cambridge University, registering a best score of 223 not out against the MCC in 1914 in an innings of only 165 minutes. At the time this was a record score for Cambridge and the Fenner's Ground. He later played for the MCC in 1921 and 1922. In the summer after his one football match for Sunderland, Morrison also made a single appearance at cricket for Somerset, two years before his final first-class game which was for the combined universities.

A right-handed batsman, occasional wicket-keeper and briefly a bowler, during his career he also represented Oxford University, 'Gentlemen' HDG Leveson-Gower's XI, Free Foresters, PF Warner's XI and 'Demobilised Officers'. He played 38 first-class matches averaging 30.49 runs, including four centuries.

Morrison also played golf for England. In 1928 he was a member of the Walker Cup selection committee and a year later won the Belgian amateur golf championship. A double international, he played football for England as an amateur. He won one cap in a 9-0 win over Wales at Merthyr Tydfil on 24 January 1920. A month earlier he had played for Sunderland against Manchester City. The Newcastle Journal reported, "Particular interest centred on the home defence with the appearance of Cambridge amateur Morrison who made an extremely favourable impression by his display at full-back. His style was a little odd for first division play and seemed a trifle slow, but was effective nonetheless. His weight and massive build was a considerable factor in beating opponents, though he was perhaps too sparing in its use."

In 1952 he became managing director of Colt, Alison and Morrison, the golf course designers he had helped set up in the 1920s. He remained managing director until his death in 1961 in Surrey.

## MORRISON, Thomas Kelly (Tom)

**POSITION:** Right-back

**BIRTHPLACE:** Crookedholm, Kilmarnock, Ayrshire

**DATE OF BIRTH:** 21/07/1904 - Q1 1980

**HEIGHT:** 5' 9" **WEIGHT:** 11st 6lbs

**SIGNED FROM:** Liverpool, 06/11/1935

**DEBUT:** v Preston North End, H, 09/11/1935

**LAST MATCH:** v Derby County, A, 25/04/1936

**MOVED TO:** Contract cancelled, 11/12/1936

**TEAMS:** Troon Athletic, St Mirren, Liverpool, Sunderland, Ayr United, Drumcondra

**INTERNATIONAL:** Scotland

**SAFC TOTALS:** 23 appearances / 0 goals

**All of Tom Morrison's Sunderland appearances came in the title-winning season of 1935-36, all but two of them in the league. At Roker, he was re-united with manager Johnny Cochrane who he had played for when winning the Scottish Cup with St Mirren in 1926.**

After beating Rangers in the semi-final, Cochrane's side defeated Celtic in front of over 98,000 at Hampden Park with Morrison then at right-half, which is the position he played for Liverpool.

After 132 league appearances for St Mirren, Liverpool paid £4,000 for him on 8 February 1928. The previous April he had won his solitary Scotland cap in a 2-1 Hampden defeat by England watched by over 111,000. He did play other games for Scotland during the SFA tour of North America in the summer of 1928, but these were not regarded as full internationals.

At Liverpool, he played 240 times and scored four goals. Ever-present in his first full season of 1928-29 he averaged 36 appearances over the next five campaigns and was part of the Liverpool team who suffered a 6-0 home defeat at the hands of Sunderland in April 1930. After his final first-team appearance for the Anfield club in November 1934 he failed to turn up for a (reserve) Central League game on 9 February 1935. Liverpool imposed two suspensions which expired on 12 March at which point they reported him missing as he had not been seen since.

It was not the only time he went AWOL. He disappeared during Sunderland's championship celebration dinner in 1936 leaving behind his wife, children and medal. He resurfaced on the border of Cambridgeshire and Bedfordshire at a place called Gamlingay. Calling himself Jock Anderson, he worked as a pea-picker, sleeping in the open as part of a gang of men.

He started playing for the local club as a centre-forward. Clearly miles better than other players in this league he helped Gamlingay to top their table, but by early December 1936, he disappeared again after which the team fell away.

On 11 December 1936, the Cambridge Independent Press reported, "Gamlingay Football Club have been playing an international footballer unawares. The man was known as Anderson, but it transpires that he is Tom Morrison, the Scottish international and former Sunderland full-back, who mysteriously vanished from his home seven months ago".

Four days earlier Morrison had been back in Sunderland appearing in court. Charged with leaving his wife and child 'chargeable to the Public Assistance Committee', Morrison escaped punishment after promising to repay the money paid to his family by the authorities. He then signed for Ayr United, but never played as he never turned up and had his contract terminated.

While on Ayr's books he was arrested for housebreaking having broken into an empty cottage with some drinking pals. Obviously, Morrison had gone right off the rails, but still had his football ability to try and get him back on those rails. He tried his luck in Ireland with Drumcondra only to suffer a badly broken leg that ended his career in March 1939. He received compensation for this and went on to work as a coach in Ireland before finding employment at the Greene King brewery in Biggleswade.

## MORRISON, William (Willie)

**POSITION:** Right-half

**BIRTHPLACE:** Edinburgh, Lothian

**DATE OF BIRTH:** 31/03/1934 - 26/12/2001

**HEIGHT:** 5' 8" **WEIGHT:** 10st 11lbs

**SIGNED FROM:** Merchiston Thistle, 01/05/1951

**DEBUT:** v Leicester City, H, 02/04/1955

**LAST MATCH:** v Preston North End, A, 03/11/1956

**MOVED TO:** Southend United, 21/01/1958

**TEAMS:** Merchiston Thistle, Sunderland, Southend United, Bedford Town

**SAFC TOTALS:** 19 appearances / 0 goals

**A 17-year-old when coming to the club, Morrison was given a debut two days after his 21st birthday. In the days before substitutes of course, he was unfortunate to be in competition for the number four shirt with Stan Anderson, but enjoyed a run of twelve consecutive appearances in the autumn of 1956.**

His last appearance came in a 6-0 defeat at Preston when Tom Finney got two of the goals. At Southend, Willie - sometimes known as Bill - made 60 league appearances in the third tier after his £3,000 transfer and played in his only FA Cup tie. At the end of October 1960, Morrison left Roots Hall by mutual consent and concluded his career with Bedford Town.

## MULHALL, George

**POSITION:** Outside-left

**BIRTHPLACE:** Standburn, Falkirk, Stirlingshire

**DATE OF BIRTH:** 08/05/1936 - 27/04/2018

**HEIGHT:** 5' 8" **WEIGHT:** 11st 7lbs

**SIGNED FROM:** Aberdeen, 09/09/1962

**DEBUT:** v Rotherham United, A, 11/09/1962

**LAST MATCH:** v Burnley, A, 23/04/1969

**MOVED TO:** Cape Town City, 23/06/1969

**TEAMS:** Kilsyth Rangers, Aberdeen, Sunderland, Cape Town City, Greenock Morton

**INTERNATIONAL:** Scotland

**SAFC TOTALS:** 284+5 appearances / 67 goals

**George Mulhall scored 67 goals from the wing, a couple of the best known being a winner at Manchester United in 1968 and a 20-yarder that completed a 3-0 home win over Newcastle in March 1967.**

Playing in an era when every team had a 'hatchet-man' in defence, you had to earn the right to play. Many a winger was known to switch wings if a full-back had hacked him down once too often. George was the kind of winger who made full-backs feel like switching flanks.

I once put it to George that I remembered him as a winger who liked to get his retaliation in first. He laughed and acknowledged, "I did, aye. I used to let the full-back get there first. I used to think, I'll leave that one to you, but just as they got there I'd get there with the studs. They knew I was there alright. As a winger, full-backs liked to give you a kick early on just to see what you were made of and I liked to let them know I was there as well".

Ever-present in the 1964 promotion team, those appearances were part of a run of 124 games without missing a game after joining Sunderland as a 26-year-old in September 1962. Previously, George had spent almost a decade with Aberdeen who he signed for on his 17th birthday when Sunderland legend Dave Halliday was manager. With club great Jackie Hather in his way, and National Service to do, Mulhall waited until 13 August 1955 for his Dons debut which came at Hibs, but it was not until Hather retired in 1959 that Mulhall became first choice. In total, Mulhall played 150 games and scored 42 goals for the Dons.

As a boy, George started out with Denny YMCA before joining Junior club Kilsyth Rangers. The youngest of eight children, George was the third brother to become a footballer, Martin playing for Falkirk, Albion Rovers and Cowdenbeath while Edward represented East Stirlingshire. George liked to tell the tale of how he once played for Real Madrid! That was not strictly true, but in Jackie Milburn's Testimonial at Newcastle, he was part of an International XI with Ferenc Puskas as his inside-left as they wore a Madrid like all-white. The fact that Bobby Charlton was centre-forward indicates the company George was good enough to keep.

Two of his three Scotland caps were won while with Sunderland. Mulhall joined Denis Law and Ian St John on the scoresheet in a 4-0 win over Northern Ireland on his debut in October 1969. One of his Scotland shirts is on display at the Academy of Light. He also represented the Scottish League on three occasions.

Mulhall's farewell in red and white came in the same game as Charlie Hurley's final appearance in an away win at Burnley in 1969. In May, he was given a free transfer and shortly afterwards moved to South Africa to join Cape Town City. He scored a hat-trick in one of his first games, but soon afterwards developed pneumonia which he kept him out for a few months. In October the following year, playing as centre-forward, he scored twice and captained Cape Town to a Castle Cup final victory in Johannesburg. In August 1971, George returned home and finished his playing career with a couple of games for Greenock Morton.

## MULHALL, George (Continued)

George left Morton to initially coach, then manage Halifax Town, keeping them in the league and in a second spell returning them to the Football League, his Conference win being the first time The Shaymen had ever won any league title. He also managed Bradford City and Bolton Wanderers, scouted for Ipswich and was assistant manager at Tranmere and Huddersfield. Initially assistant manager at Bolton, he worked alongside his old Roker teammate Stan Anderson and tutored a young Peter Reid who as Sunderland manager took a team to Halifax for a testimonial for Mulhall in 1999. Mulhall suffered from Alzheimer's in his latter years, but remains firmly in the memory of those lucky enough to have seen him play.

## MULLIN, John Michael

**POSITION:** Forward

**BIRTHPLACE:** Bury, Lancashire

**DATE OF BIRTH:** 11/08/1975

**HEIGHT:** 5' 10" **WEIGHT:** 11st 8lbs

**SIGNED FROM:** Burnley, 17/07/1995

**DEBUT:** v Wolverhampton Wanderers, H, 26/08/1995

**LAST MATCH:** v Crewe Alexandra, A, 03/11/1998

**MOVED TO:** Burnley, 15/07/1999

**TEAMS:** Burnley, Sunderland, Preston North End (L), Burnley, Rotherham United, Tranmere Rovers, Accrington Stanley

**SAFC TOTALS:** 30+14 appearances / 4 goals

**Famed for scoring the final goal at Roker Park in the Farewell to Roker game against Liverpool, John Mullin was one of those forwards who was not bad, but not quite good enough, as his goals record illustrates. Including substitute appearances he played ten league games in three of his four seasons and 1+5 in the other when he had two loans in the spring of 1998.**

The first of those brought 5+3 games for Preston North End. He then returned to Burnley. There were six appearances on loan to the Clarets with whom he had started his career. He had debuted for them as a sub at Brighton in September 1993 and had played 9+11 games, scoring twice, prior to his move to Sunderland. He returned to Turf Moor in July 1999 and took his overall tally for the club to 61+11/11 before being sold to Rotherham United for £150,000 in October 2001.

Mullin cost Sunderland an initial tribunal set fee of £40,000 with the potential to rise to over five times that, although only a further £25,000 was activated. His best - if not most famous moment - came when he scored in a 2-1 home Premiership win over Manchester United in March 1997.

It was at Rotherham that Mullin played some of his most consistent football. By now he had matured into a central midfielder - a role he began at Sunderland. He spent almost five years with the Millers playing 173+22 games with a dozen goals. Ronnie Moore, who signed him for Rotherham, then signed John for Tranmere where Mullin's figures were 45+9/5, before a final move to Accrington Stanley.

There he linked up with brother Paul who he had played alongside in junior football at Burnley. Paul became Stanley's record scorer and later saw his son - and John's nephew - Alex, go on to play for Burnley in an FA Youth Cup semi-final in 2012. The last of John's 30+6 games for Stanley (for whom he did not score) came at Cheltenham in May 2010. He later returned to Burnley as part of the youth coaching staff before working as an academy coach and then scout for Manchester City.

## MUMBA, Bali

**POSITION:** Midfielder / full-back

**BIRTHPLACE:** Kinshasa, DR Congo

**DATE OF BIRTH:** 08/10/2001

**HEIGHT:** 5' 8" **WEIGHT:** 11st 0lbs

**SIGNED FROM:** Trainee, 01/07/2017

**DEBUT:** v Wolverhampton Wanderers, H, 06/05/2018

**LAST MATCH:** v Grimsby Town, H, 08/10/2019

**MOVED TO:** Norwich City, 27/07/2020

**TEAMS:** Sunderland, South Shields (L), Norwich City, Peterborough United (L),Plymouth Argyle (L) (to July 2022)

**INTERNATIONAL:** England Under 18

**SAFC TOTALS:** 5+5 appearances / 0 goals

**Technically, Bali became Sunderland's youngest-ever captain as he took the armband when replacing John O'Shea on his debut on the last day of the 2017-18 season as the Lads suffered a second successive relegation. At the age of 16 years and 210 days, he was the club's fourth-youngest player. His debut had been long awaited as his burgeoning reputation in Academy and youth international football indicated that Sunderland had another potential top player coming through the ranks.**

Whenever he played Mumba showed he was comfortable on the ball, technically gifted and a good decision maker. Only two of his starts came in the league with the others in the Football League Trophy. Nonetheless, when he was sold to Norwich for an undisclosed - but widely reported as £350,000 - fee, it came during a period when Sunderland were selling off a host of very highly-rated youngsters much to the frustration of the fans and more than a few members of the Academy staff.

While Bali was born in Africa, he was raised in and around South Shields (and had a loan spell with them), spoke with a local accent and had the makings of a real homegrown hero. Coming through the Academy from the age of eight there was much debate about his best position. Good enough to play across midfield, there was a general feeling that he would come to settle at right-back.

Used sparingly in his first year at Carrow Road, he played just seven times. At the beginning of his second term, he played the second half of a heavy Premier League defeat at Manchester City and then only featured in a couple of cup defeats before being loaned to Peterborough. For Posh he played 8+5 times scoring once. In July 2022 he went on loan to Plymouth.

## MUNRO, Alexander Iain Fordyce

**POSITION:** Left-back

**BIRTHPLACE:** Uddingston, Lanarkshire

**DATE OF BIRTH:** 24/08/1951

**HEIGHT:** 5' 7½" **WEIGHT:** 10st 5lbs

**SIGNED FROM:** Stoke City, 30/07/1981

**DEBUT:** v Ipswich Town, A, 29/08/1981

**LAST MATCH:** v Watford, A, 20/03/1984

**MOVED TO:** Dundee United, 30/03/1984

**TEAMS:** St. Mirren, Hibernian, Rangers, St Mirren, Stoke City, Sunderland, Dundee United, Hibernian

**INTERNATIONAL:** Scotland

**SAFC TOTALS:** 88 appearances / 0 goals

**Mainly remembered for a scything 'tackle' in a game with Coventry that saw him sent off in October 1981, Iain Munro was brought to Sunderland by Alan Durban who he had played for at Stoke City. Munro was a regular in 1981-82 and 1982-83 before making just ten appearances the following season during which he moved on to Dundee United.**

He played 17 games for the Terrors, before finishing his playing days at Hibs where 44 appearances were added to the 96 he had played between 1973 and 1976. In his second spell at Easter Road he played alongside Gordon Chisholm in the 1985 League Cup final lost 3-0 to Aberdeen for whom future Sunderland caretaker-manager Eric Black scored two of the goals. Hibs had been Iain's second club after he had played 105 times for St Mirren who he joined as a schoolboy in 1968 and debuted for in January 1970.

A goalscoring midfielder in his younger days, Munro scored 16 goals for the Pars and eleven in that first spell at Hibs during which he played in a 6-3 League Cup final defeat to Celtic in October 1974. In April 1976 he joined Rangers, but only played five league games before returning to St Mirren where he signed for Alex Ferguson and added three goals in 89 further league appearances before crossing the border.

Iain scored his only goal in English football on his Stoke debut at Southampton in October 1981. Once in the side, he played all remaining 32 Division One matches, mostly on the left of midfield before slotting in at left-back late in the season. At Stoke under Durban, his teammates included a raft of people who went on to come to Sunderland: Kevin Richardson, Loek Ursem, Adrian Heath, Lee Chapman and Paul Bracewell as well as Denis Smith who was injured during Munro's time with the Potters.

A £180,000 move to Stoke came after Munro had broken onto the international scene. The last of his seven caps came against England at Hampden in May 1980. With Dave Watson in the England side, Munro was replaced by another future Sunderland player in George Burley. All of his caps had come since June 1979 when he debuted against Argentina. In 1980 he also gained a further representative honour when playing for the Scottish League.

From 1987 to 1990 Munro was assistant manager of Dunfermline (when Jimmy Nicholl was one of his players), who he became manager of from August 1990 to September 1991 - making David Moyes one of his signings. The following month he took charge of Dundee until February of the same season. After a four-month gap, Iain took over at Hamilton Academical where he stayed until September 1996. Given his two spells playing for St Mirren it seemed inevitable he would return there as manager, but when he did in September 1996 he lasted just one day before almost immediately becoming manager of Raith Rovers. He stayed there until April 1997 when he began a four-year spell coaching at Ayr United.

A qualified PE teacher, Iain had taught in Scotland in his early days as a player and returned to teaching after leaving Ayr. He then moved to the USA in 2005 coaching an Under 14 team in Tampa in Florida. In 2013, he became director of Youth Soccer with Philadelphia Union where for a while he worked alongside former SAFC Press Officer Lee Marshall. As of the beginning of 2022 at the age of 70, he was Youth Director at YSC Sports in Wayne Pennsylvania as well as being a pundit for Philadelphia Union's MLS games.

## MUNTARI, Sulleyman Ali

**POSITION:** Midfielder

**BIRTHPLACE:** Konongo, Ghana

**DATE OF BIRTH:** 27/08/1984

**HEIGHT:** 5' 10½" **WEIGHT:** 11st 9lbs

**SIGNED FROM:** Internazionale, 29/01/2011, on loan

**DEBUT:** v Stoke City, A, 05/02/2011

**LAST MATCH:** v Bolton Wanderers, A, 07/05/2011

**MOVED TO:** Internazionale, 13/05/2011, end of loan

**TEAMS:** Liberty Professionals, Udinese, Portsmouth, Internazionale, Sunderland (L), AC Milan, Ittihad, Pescara, Deportivo La Coruna, Albacete, Hearts of Oak

**INTERNATIONAL:** Ghana

**SAFC TOTALS:** 7+2 appearances / 0 goals

**Muntari never seemed happy at Sunderland despite being matched up with his international teammates Asamoah Gyan and John Mensah. This may have been my incorrect impression, but particularly on a staff and squad day out at the races, the on-loan Inter player looked like he would rather be anywhere else.**

It might not have been a problem for Sulley just at Sunderland. He chose to leave Portsmouth and Inter straight after winning trophies and had more than one well-documented disciplinary issue with his national side, even at World Cups where he ended his international career after being sent home from the 2014 finals.

A high-class player who could have enhanced Sunderland's quality, Sulley had played in England before coming to Sunderland, winning the FA Cup with Portsmouth in 2008. Pompey's record buy when he joined from Udinese in May 2007, he debuted on 11 August that year against Derby and scored the quarter-final winner with a penalty at Manchester United.

Despite winning the cup in the first season of his five year Fratton Park contract, Muntari immediately returned to Italy to join Inter on 28 July 2008 after five goals in 33 games for Portsmouth.

Playing alongside superstars such as Luis Figo and Zlatan Ibrahimovic at the San Siro, Muntari won Serie A in both of his first two seasons with Inter, but as at Pompey, silverware alone failed to satisfy him and he was loaned to Sunderland where his one goal at Bolton was later attributed as an own-goal by Zat Knight.

During his time with Sunderland Muntari played at Wembley against England. He was one of three Sunderland loanees to play in the game along with Mensah and Danny Welbeck. The latter was making his England debut on a night when Stewart Downing, Joleon Lescott and Jermain Defoe also played for England and Sunderland's Gyan scored Ghana's goal in a 1-1 draw. It was one of 84 appearances Muntari made for his country. During this time, he scored a very creditable 20 goals from midfield including one at the 2006 FIFA World Cup finals against the Czech Republic and another against Uruguay in the quarter-final of the 2010 tournament. Muntari also played at the World Cup finals of 2014. He netted three times - including a 25-yard free-kick in the third-place match against Guinea - in the 2008 African Cup of Nations, a tournament in which he was voted as an 'All-Star Player.'

His first notable connection with Sunderland came in the 2001 FIFA World Youth Championship when he played alongside John Mensah in the final against an Argentina side that included Julio Arca and Nicolas Medina. Following this tournament he had a trial with Manchester United before joining Italian outfit Udinese for whom he debuted on 6 November 2002 against Milan. After 153 games and nine goals across five seasons he was transferred to Portsmouth.

Muntari was clearly a good player at Sunderland, but manager Steve Bruce evidently did not think he was a long-term solution for what was undoubtedly a lucrative pay packet and chose not to extend the deal after the player's loan expired. Instead, Muntari returned to Milan where Inter loaned him to AC Milan. He eventually totalled eight goals from 97 games with Inter and 13 goals from 83 appearances with Milan after his loan was converted to a full deal when his Inter contract ran out in the summer of 2012.

Highlights in the red and black of Milan included a Champions League goal against Barcelona and a Serie A brace against Juventus. These additions to his CV helped him secure a 2015 move to Ittihad FC of Saudi Arabia where he scored three goals in 18 months before returning once again to Italy, this time with Pescara. It was to be an unhappy period as after one goal in nine games he moved to relegation-threatened Deportivo La Coruna in Spain following a deplorable incident where he was yellow carded after complaining of suffering racial abuse in a match with Sardinian side Cagliari.

Signed for Deportivo by his old Milan teammate Clarence Seedorf, he was given the number 21 shirt of club legend Juan Carlos Valeron. Muntari made his La Liga debut as a late sub in a goalless draw with Espanyol and went on to start six games before a January 2019 move to Spanish second division Albacete.

He made two appearances there, the last seeing him cautioned and substituted in a 1-0 win at Alcoron on 7 April 2019. In 2022 he returned to Ghana, signing for Hearts of Oak. Muntari had a good career, but like so many other players, there remained the lingering feeling that it could have been so much better, including at Sunderland.

## MURDOCH, Duncan Bell

**POSITION:** Forward

**BIRTHPLACE:** Croydon, Surrey

**DATE OF BIRTH:** 12/06/1860 - 01/06/1944

**SIGNED:** 1883

**DEBUT:** v Redcar, A, 24/10/1885

**LAST MATCH:** v Redcar, A, 24/10/1885

**MOVED:** 1885

**TEAMS:** Sunderland

**SAFC TOTALS:** 1 appearance / 0 goals

**According to the 1881 census Murdoch was a schoolmaster. He is known to have been a private tutor and occasional footballer between 1882 and 1890 during which he played for Sunderland in one of the club's earliest English (FA) Cup ties.**

Educated at Glasgow University, the same as club founder James Allan, and maybe the reason for him playing for Sunderland, he was a Licentiate of the College of Preceptors in London (a system for the formal examination and qualification of secondary school teachers). In 1891 he emigrated to Hawaii where he became head bookkeeper for the Ewa pineapple plantation on the island of Oahu until 1903 when he became an auditor.

From 1926 until 1938 Murdoch was a magistrate for Makawao District court and as of 1931 was reported as a tea planter in Honolulu. Despite being in an isolated part of the world on the opposite side of the planet, he evidently retained an interest in SAFC, sending a telegram of congratulations to the club after the 1937 FA Cup win.

## MURPHY, Daryl Michael

**POSITION:** Forward

**BIRTHPLACE:** Waterford, Republic of Ireland

**DATE OF BIRTH:** 15/03/1983

**HEIGHT:** 6' 1" **WEIGHT:** 13st 13lbs

**SIGNED FROM:** Waterford United, 03/06/2005

**DEBUT:** v West Ham United, H, 01/10/2005

**LAST MATCH:** v Chelsea, A, 16/01/2010

**MOVED TO:** Celtic, 16/07/2010

**TEAMS:** Waterford United, Southend United*, Luton Town, Harrow Borough (L), Waterford United, Sunderland, Sheffield Wednesday (L), Ipswich Town (L), Celtic, Ipswich Town, Newcastle United, Nottingham Forest, Bolton Wanderers, Waterford

**INTERNATIONAL:** Republic of Ireland

**SAFC TOTALS:** 69+55 appearances / 15 goals

***Southend United are the Waterford based Southend United, not the English side.**

## MURPHY, Daryl (Continued)

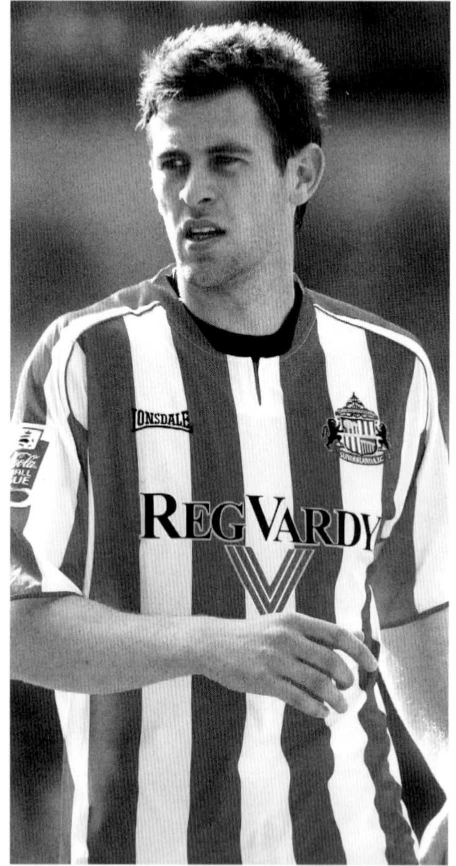

**For a forward, Daryl Murphy scored a low ratio of goals for the number of games he played, but those included some memorable strikes such as a dramatic late winner in an important game with Middlesbrough in April 2008 and two on the day the Championship title was secured at Luton in 2007.**

Daryl had tried his luck in England with Luton as a youngster but had returned home whilst still a teenager. Three years later former Republic of Ireland international manager Mick McCarthy saw potential in this 22-year-old and invested £100,000 of a modest transfer budget in taking Murphy from Waterford to Wearside as his newly-promoted squad prepared for the Premier League.

Murphy went on to win another Championship medal with Newcastle ten years later, two years after being the Championship's leading scorer when he bagged 27 goals for Ipswich in a season when he won the Tractor Boys' Player of the Year and Players' Player of the Year awards, as well as being named in the PFA Championship Team of the Year.

With Waterford, Murphy scored eight times as the club won the League of Ireland First Division in 2002-03 before winning the PFAI Young Player of the Year award the following season when he scored 14 goals in the Premier Division. For Sunderland Murphy debuted as an 87th-minute substitute against West Ham. After four appearances he joined Sheffield Wednesday on loan where he started four Championship games. The following February he scored his first goal to earn a point for Sunderland at home to Spurs. Relegated that term, Daryl scored the opening goal of the following campaign and two matches later scored the quickest goal seen at the Stadium of Light - as of June 2022 - when netting after only 28 seconds against Plymouth Argyle on 12 August 2006.

Murphy moved to Celtic in 2010 for a reported fee of £1 million but though he scored on his first appearance in a friendly against Lincoln City, he struggled to get a regular place - Anthony Stokes being one of his competitors. Although there were only three goals in 9+14 competitive games for Celtic, one against Dundee United on 1 May 2011 saw him win the ball, dribble past four defenders and score.

Twice loaned from Celtic to Ipswich, he made the move to Portman Road permanent and totalled 177+18 games and 67 goals for the Tractor Boys.

28 August 2016 brought a move to Newcastle United for an undisclosed fee thought to be in the region of £3m. Daryl was unable to debut until New Year's Day 2017 due to injury, he proved to be a back-up striker, scoring six times in 9+9 games as the Magpies won the Championship before signing for Nottingham Forest.

There he scored 13 goals in 43+17 games during a spell in which he was reported to have failed a drugs test, apparently after taking cocaine. Having had his contract terminated with Forest he joined Bolton Wanderers on 2 September 2019, playing for a team who were relegated from the third tier having suffered a points deduction as they struggled with severe financial difficulties.

Daryl played 25+1 times for the troubled Trotters, scoring eight goals - the last of his 105 Football or Premier League goals coming against Bristol Rovers in January 2020. In September of that year, his career went full circle when he returned to Waterford.

Murphy's record for Ireland (for whom he played for Martin O'Neill and Roy Keane amongst others) was similar to that at Sunderland and Celtic with relatively few goals, but some memorable ones. Having made his international debut in 2007 Daryl's first goal did not come until the 23rd of his 32 caps in August 2016, a year in which he played at the European Championships. Other than that first goal against Serbia, his only other international strikes came in a brace against Moldova in October 2017, all of his international goals coming in FIFA World Cup qualification matches.

## MURRAY, James Gerald (Jamie)

**POSITION:** Full-back

**BIRTHPLACE:** Cumnock, Ayrshire

**DATE OF BIRTH:** 27/12/1958

**HEIGHT:** 5' 9" **WEIGHT:** 10st 12lbs

**SIGNED FROM:** Cambridge United, 21/03/1984, on loan

**DEBUT:** v Tottenham Hotspur, H, 07/04/1984

**LAST MATCH:** v Tottenham Hotspur, H, 07/04/1984

**MOVED TO:** Cambridge United, 04/05/1984, end of loan

**TEAMS:** Rivet Sports, Cambridge United, Sunderland (L), Brentford, Cambridge United, Soham Town Rangers

**SAFC TOTALS:** 1 appearance / 0 goals

**Injured in what proved to be his only game for SAFC during a loan from Cambridge United, Jamie Murray's SAFC career lasted only 75 minutes. He became a major figure with Cambridge United where in two spells he played 242 league games. 147 of these were in consecutive games between 1980 and 1984.**

His loan to Sunderland that year was meant to be his big break, but although he played well against Spurs it remained his only appearance. Having helped Cambridge climb from the fourth tier to the second during his first spell at the club Murray moved to Brentford following his Sunderland loan. Ironically for a player whose brief spell at Sunderland was ruined by injury, he was once again a model of consistency with the Bees playing 166 times in a little over three years at the club.

Returning to Cambridge in September 1987 he stayed until the end of the season before dropping into the Eastern Counties League with Soham Town Rangers. He scored six league goals in his career, three with each of his permanent clubs. He went on to be assistant manager of Histon and a taxi driver in Cambridge. His son Antonio played for Histon as well as Ipswich, Hibs, Chelmsford City and Cambridge United before emigrating to play in Australia in 2011.

## MURRAY, John Winning

**POSITION:** Full back / half-back

**BIRTHPLACE:** Strathblane, Stirlingshire

**DATE OF BIRTH:** 24/04/1865 -16/09/1922

**HEIGHT:** 6' 0" **WEIGHT:** 13st 0lbs

**SIGNED FROM:** Vale of Leven, 15/09/1890

**DEBUT:** v Burnley, A, 27/09/1890

**LAST MATCH:** v Burnley, A, 30/04/1892

**MOVED TO:** Blackburn Rovers, 08/05/1892

**TEAMS:** Vale Wanderers, Vale of Leven, Sunderland, Blackburn Rovers

**INTERNATIONAL:** Scotland

**SAFC TOTALS:** 51 appearances / 0 goals

**A Scotland international, signed for a reported £220 and a two year contract, whose debut came in Sunderland's fourth-ever league game, Murray did not miss a match for over a year after joining and missed just four games in total from his debut to his departure at the end of the following season when he was part of the club's first-ever title-winning team.**

At Blackburn he was ever-present in his first season and missed just two games in his second when he played in the English (FA) Cup semi-final with Notts County. In total, he played 122 games for Rovers, without scoring. His son Bobby played ten games for Rovers, debuting against Bristol City in September 1909.

Throughout his working life Murray was employed in the Calico printing industry and was an engraver by trade. In December 1890 he opened a hosier's shop in Dundas Street, a street that for many years from the 1960s was the departure point for Supporters' Association buses leaving for away games. At the time of his death John was head of the engraving department of Broad Oak printworks in Accrington.

## MURRAY, William Brunton (Willie)

**POSITION:** Outside-left

**BIRTHPLACE:** Forres, Morayshire

**DATE OF BIRTH:** 15/11/1881 - 21/04/1929

**HEIGHT:** 5' 6" **WEIGHT:** 11st 7lbs

**SIGNED FROM:** Forres Mechanics, 12/06/1901

**DEBUT:** v Grimsby Town, H, 22/03/1902

**LAST MATCH:** v Derby County, A, 01/11/1902

**MOVED TO:** Northampton Town, 30/05/1903

**TEAMS:** Roysvale Juniors, Forres Mechanics, Sunderland, Northampton Town, Leeds City, Buckie Thistle, Forres Mechanics

**SAFC TOTALS:** 8 appearances / 2 goals

**Not to be confused with Bill Murray who played over 300 games and managed Sunderland from before World War Two to 1957, Willie Murray came to Sunderland from Forres Mechanics, a club that his brothers George and Alexander also played for, and played in seven of the last eight games as the league title was won in 1902.**

Getting games in a team that were winning the league brought Murray to prominence, so much so that he was selected for an international trial match, playing for the Anglo-Scots against the Home-Scots.

Although he scored on his one appearance the following season, the arrival of the legendary Arthur Bridgett meant there was no future for Murray at Roker Park at which point he moved to Northampton Town. After a short spell with the Cobblers Murray went further south to join Tottenham Hotspur in May 1904. At the time Spurs were playing in the Southern League. Debuting in a home defeat to his old club Northampton in October 1904, Willie went on to play 14 times in all competitions in his first season, one of which was against Newcastle United in the FA Cup, or English Cup as it was then known.

Murray made another 25 appearances for Tottenham in 1905-06 before spending 1906-07 with Leeds City. There were just eight appearances for Leeds between an early-season 5-0 defeat at West Brom and a final game against Port Vale in late February. His move from London to Leeds earned Sunderland £100, the Wearsiders having retained his Football League registration while he operated in the Southern League.

After retiring from the game Willie worked for a Glasgow-based shipbreaking company and it was whilst dismantling a yacht on Loch Linnhe that he was asphyxiated by fumes from a coal brazier, aged only 47.

## MURRAY, William Milne (Bill)

**POSITION:** Right-back

**BIRTHPLACE:** Aberdeen, Aberdeenshire

**DATE OF BIRTH:** 10/03/1900 - 15/12/1961

**HEIGHT:** 5' 9½" **WEIGHT:** 11st 7lbs

**SIGNED FROM:** Cowdenbeath, 30/04/1927

**DEBUT:** v West Ham United, A, 01/09/1927

**LAST MATCH:** v Bolton Wanderers, A, 11/04/1936

**MOVED TO:** St Mirren, 12/01/1937

**TEAMS:** Hall Russell FC, Aberdeen, Cowdenbeath, Sunderland, St Mirren

**SAFC TOTALS:** 328 appearances / 0 goals

**Bill Murray was involved in even more games for Sunderland than record appearance holder Jim Montgomery if his 510 games as manager are added to his 328 matches as a player. Murray's grand total of 838 surpasses even the club's longest-serving manager Bob Kyle who oversaw 817 competitive fixtures.**

Add a further 231 war-time games, Murray was in charge of, plus the three from the expunged 1939-40 season and Murray's total number of games as a Sunderland player or manager comes to an incredible 1,051 - even more than Ted Doig's total if all his challenge matches and friendlies are included.

Murray - no relation to future chairman Sir Bob - was at Sunderland from 1927 to 1957, bar a period from January 1937 to March 1939 when he returned to Roker Park as manager after finishing his playing days with St Mirren, the former club of Johnny Cochrane who Murray played almost a decade for.

During World War One Murray served in France having lied about his age in order to sign up for the Gordon Highlanders. An engineer before becoming a footballer, he turned down an offer to work for a shipping firm in Shanghai in China in order to become a footballer. Bill played for Aberdeen junior club Hall Russell before he joined Aberdeen as an amateur on 9 April 1920, debuting the following day for the reserves in an 8-2 win over Peterhead that sealed the reserve team their League title.

During the summer of 1921 clubs such as Aberdeen, Forfar and Chelsea were interested in signing Murray, however, he joined Cowdenbeath and later captained the team to promotion in 1924. Considered unlucky not to be capped, despite being named as reserve for Scotland for an international with Ireland, he made 217 league appearances before signing for Sunderland and is a member of the Cowdenbeath Hall of Fame.

Murray's move to Sunderland came in a double deal with David Wright that commanded a joint fee of £8,000. A mature player of 26 by the time he came to England Bill immediately became a regular missing just one game in his first season.

He played regularly during the first half of the thirties, the only time he played fewer than 30 league games was in his final season of 1935-36 when he played in half of the 42 league games as the league title was won.

A move to St Mirren four days before the successful 1937 FA Cup run got underway saw Murray make 75 league games for The Buddies before returning to Sunderland to succeed Johnny Cochrane as manager. Taking charge of his first match as manager in a 2-1 defeat at Preston on 29 March 1939, he oversaw the final nine games of the season - winning just one - and being in charge of many of his old teammates. World War Two saw Murray lead Sunderland to success in the West Riding Combined Counties Cup in 1943 and reach the final of the League War Cup in 1942. In May 1941 he was appointed Honorary Sports Welfare Officer for Durham County.

After the war he was in charge of what became known as 'The Bank of England Club.' The League title agonisingly was missed out on in 1950 and Murray took the team to successive FA Cup semi-finals in the mid-fifties before his enormously long career ended on a sour note. In May 1957 Murray was fined £200 for his involvement in the illegal payments scandal that rocked the club. In June of that year he left his job and the game of football. That fine was refunded in 1962 when the Football League's decision was declared illegal. This exoneration was too late for Murray who passed away the previous year in Aberdeen having moved back to his home town in 1960.

## M'VILA, Yann Gerard

**POSITION:** Midfielder

**BIRTHPLACE:** Amiens, France

**DATE OF BIRTH:** 29/06/1990

**HEIGHT:** 6' 0" **WEIGHT:** 12st 12lbs

**SIGNED FROM:** Rubin Kazan, 06/08/2015, on loan

**DEBUT:** v Norwich City, H, 15/08/2015

**LAST MATCH:** v Watford, A, 15/05/2016

**MOVED TO:** Rubin Kazan, 16/05/2016, end of loan

**TEAMS:** Rennes, Rubin Kazan, Internazionale (L), Sunderland (L), St Etienne, Olympiacos (to May 2022)

**INTERNATIONAL:** France

**SAFC TOTALS:** 38+2 appearances / 1 goal

**Yann M'Vila was a high-class powerful midfielder who excelled in his one season on loan to Sunderland. Brought in by Dick Advocaat, and later under the leadership of Sam Allardyce, M'Vila missed the first game of the season, but started every other Premier League fixture bar the last when he came on as a sub after safety had been assured.**

Sent off in his first game at any level for Sunderland, when he played as an over-age player in an Under 21 match against Norwich six days before his debut against the same club, M'Vila would often turn up as a spectator at Under 21 games and at the end of his loan was very keen to sign for the club. However, over the summer a change of senior personnel saw David Moyes installed as manager with a new CEO in Martin Bain. They had not seen M'Vila's impressive performances and baulked at the likely financial outlay to bring him in. Instead, they chose to pay a reported £13m for Didier Ndong, a player who proved to be not a patch on M'Vila .

M'Vila was a player of high calibre. He won one of his 22 full caps for France (there had already been 50 international appearances at junior levels) at Wembley on the day Jordan Henderson debuted for England. M'Vila is twelve days younger than Henderson and was winning his fifth cap on this occasion. At this time Yann was with his first club senior Rennes with whom he debuted against Nice in August 2009. He went on to play 126 league games in which he scored twice. M'Vila's first professional goal had come in a Coupe de France 7-0 win against Cannes in January 2011. He also played Europa League football for Rennes, scoring against Red Star Belgrade. Prior to his time with Rennes, between the ages of six and 14, Yann played for Sains-Saint-Fussien, Amiens and Mantes.

## M'VILA, Yann (Continued)

January 2013 brought a €12m move to Russian club Rubin Kazan. He was to stay with the club for five years, but during this time had a loan to Inter Milan as well as Sunderland. With Inter he played just eight Serie A games, five of these as a sub, including a late appearance in a Milan derby. He also made four Europa League appearances but returned to Kazan after a disagreement with Inter boss Roberto Mancini. Following his loan to Sunderland Yann took his total of league games for Rubin Kazan to 64 league games (3 goals) before a January 2018 return to France with St Etienne.

Debuting against Metz that month, he played 84+3 games (0 goals) before a move to Greece with Olympiacos. Having played Europa League football for St Etienne, Yann stepped up to the Champions League with Olympiacos, two of his eight appearances in that competition in 2020-21 coming against Manchester City. That season saw Yann voted Player of the Year in Greece after he helped Olympiacos to the league title and scored in the cup final which was lost 2-1 to PAOK. The following season M'Vila added a Champions League goal to his CV in a draw at Ludogorets of Bulgaria. As of June 2022 M'Vila had seven goals in 76+11 games for Olympiacos.

M'Vila comes from a footballing family. Father, Jean Elvis played for Amiens while brother Yohan appeared for Ajaccio, Dijon, Olympic Charleroi, FC Mantes and US Liffre. Yohan was selected for the national squad of the Democratic Republic of Congo, but as of June 2022 had not played.

## MWARUWARI, Mpenjani 'Mpe' (Benjani)

**POSITION:** Forward

**BIRTHPLACE:** Bulawayo, Zimbabwe

**DATE OF BIRTH:** 13/08/1978

**HEIGHT:** 6' 2" **WEIGHT:** 12st 3lbs

**SIGNED FROM:** Manchester City, 01/02/2010, on loan

**DEBUT:** v Wigan Athletic, H, 06/02/2010

**LAST MATCH:** v Wolverhampton Wanderers, A, 09/05/2010

**MOVED TO:** Manchester City, 10/05/2010, end of loan

**TEAMS:** Jono Cosmos, Grasshoppers (L), Auxerre, Portsmouth, Manchester City, Sunderland (L), Blackburn Rovers, Portsmouth, Chippa United, Bidvest Wits

**INTERNATIONAL:** Zimbabwe

**SAFC TOTALS:** 1+7 appearances / 0 goals

**Benjani's only start came in a 3-1 home win against Birmingham in the middle of his loan. It may have been simply a surface appearance, but at Sunderland he never seemed to be moving freely - although this may have been simply an unusual gait. Nonetheless, he rarely, if ever, showed glimpses of the quality that had impressed elsewhere.**

He came on loan from Manchester City. For City he had made a scoring debut in a Manchester derby at Old Trafford in February 2008 and scored seven goals in 25+7 games - being substituted in eleven of those.

As a youngster Benjani began with Lulu Rovers, Highlanders, FC Juniors, Zimba Africa Rivers, University of Zimbabwe and Air Zimbabwe Jets before coming to the fore with Jomo Cosmos where 20 goals in 45 games, along with impressive international appearances, led to a move to Europe after a stellar 2001 when he was Player of the Season and Players' Player of the Season in South Africa.

After unsuccessful trials in Norway, Turkey and China he was loaned to Grasshopper Club Zurich. Despite just one goal in 25 outings he was signed by Auxerre where he contested the striker's spot with Djibril Cisse and did so well he became top scorer in Ligue 1. He also scored in the 2005 Coupe de France final against PSG when he was a teammate of Younes Kaboul, with Teemu Tainio a substitute. Two years earlier, Benjani came off the bench in the final with under 20 minutes to go and helped his team (for whom Cisse scored) come from behind to beat PSG.

A first move to English football came in January 2006 when Portsmouth paid £4.1m. It was a transfer that the Stevens Inquiry of 2007 reportedly expressed concerns about. In 2007-08 hat-tricks against Reading and Derby contributed to Benjani being sold for £3.9m to Manchester City mid-way through the season - with his first home goal coming against his former club Pompey. Following his loan to Sunderland the Zimbabwean was given a free transfer to Blackburn where he scored three times in 8+12 games in 2010-11 before a return to Portsmouth where 6+11 appearances produced a single goal, after which he closed out his playing days in South Africa.

At international level Benjani captained his country and scored ten goals in 42 games. In 2020 he coached Evercreech Rovers in Somerset as part of his successful attempt to gain his UEFA A Licence.

## MYHRE, Thomas Harald

**POSITION:** Goalkeeper

**BIRTHPLACE:** Sarpsborg, Norway

**DATE OF BIRTH:** 16/10/1973

**HEIGHT:** 6' 4" **WEIGHT:** 14st 3lbs

**SIGNED FROM:** Besiktas, 10/07/2002

**DEBUT:** v Cambridge United, A, 01/10/2002

**LAST MATCH:** v Reading, H, 09/04/2005

**MOVED TO:** Fredrikstad, 21/07/2005

**TEAMS:** Moss, Viking Stavanager, Everton, Rangers (L), Birmingham City (L), Tranmere Rovers (L), Copenhagen (L), Besiktas, Sunderland, Crystal Palace (L), Fredrikstad, Charlton Athletic, Viking Stavanger, Kongsvinger

**INTERNATIONAL:** Norway

**SAFC TOTALS:** 40+2 appearances / 0 goals

**Stood behind a goal beside Peter Reid watching Thomas Myhre in pre-season training in Belgium in 2002, Reidy could not wipe the smile off his face. It was no surprise. Myhre was unbelievable, saving everything fired at him, no matter how fiercely.**

By the end of that season Sunderland would have a quartet of international keepers in Myhre of Norway, Sorensen of Denmark, Poom of Estonia and Macho of Austria. In a season when Sunderland went down dismally, it seemed as if all four of them could be played at the same time and the team would still lose and yet all four were good goalies. Myhre barely played in the first two of his three seasons but was a regular in the last. Unfortunately he was injured at the denouement of the season in which Mick McCarthy led the team to promotion.

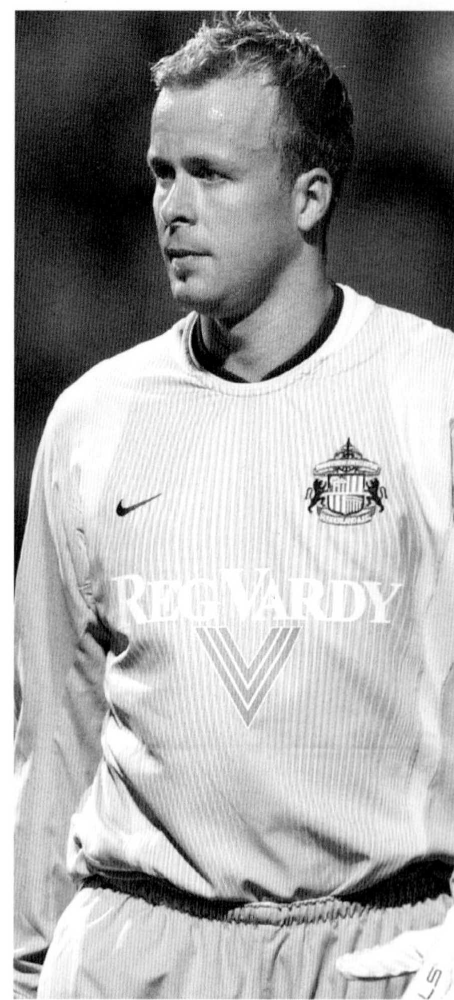


Capped 56 times, Myhre was part of Norway's squad at the 1998 FIFA World Cup without playing, but appeared in all three of his country's games at Euro 2000. Eight years later he again played at the Euros, although an uncharacteristically error strewn performance against Turkey proved to be a career low point and the end of Thomas' international career.

Early success in his home country with Viking, where he made 94 league appearances in the mid 1990s, led to an £800,000 move to Everton on 27 November 1997. Clean sheets in his first three games for the Toffees got Thomas off to a terrific start with his international debut coming before the end of his first season at Goodison Park.

Although he was to spend four years at Everton where he played 82 games in all competitions, Myhre was loaned out four times before a £375,000 switch to Turkish club Besiktas in November 2001. Six games for Rangers included two in the UEFA Cup while eleven for Birmingham in the same 1999-2000 campaign included two in the Championship Play-Offs. There were then four games at the same level for Everton's near neighbours Tranmere Rovers followed by a successful spell with FC Copenhagen whom he helped win the Danish Superliga.

There was one season in Turkey before Myhre's return to England with Sunderland after 17 appearances. During Thomas' second season on Wearside he played 15 games on loan to Crystal Palace where he returned to concede three goals for Sunderland later in the same season he was on loan at Selhurst Park. Following promotion with Sunderland in 2005 he chose to move back to Norway with Fredrikstad but after just three games in less than a month, he was soon back in England with Charlton. 21 of his 30 games for the Addicks were in the Premiership but after two seasons he was on the move again, this time back to Viking where he played 46 league games before finally adding 20 more with Kongsvinger in 2010-11. Three years later, he made one final appearance in a Sunderland shirt, playing in a Testimonial for Jody Craddock at Wolves.

In January 2021, Myhre became Director of Football at his first club, Moss FK, and after a year changed roles to become their manager following an eight-game caretaker manager role in the last three months of 2021.

## MacPHAIL, John

**POSITION:** Centre-half

**BIRTHPLACE:** Dundee, Angus

**DATE OF BIRTH:** 07/12/1955

**HEIGHT:** 6' 0" **WEIGHT:** 12st 3lbs

**SIGNED FROM:** Bristol City, 31/07/1987

**DEBUT:** v Brentford, A, 15/08/1987

**LAST MATCH:** v Norwich City, A, 25/08/1990

**MOVED TO:** Hartlepool United, 13/11/1990 on loan from 16/09/1990

**TEAMS:** St Columba's, Dundee, Sheffield United, York City, Bristol City, Sunderland, Hartlepool United

**SAFC TOTALS:** 153 appearances / 22 goals

**Brought in by his former York manager Denis Smith, John MacPhail was a major reason Sunderland won promotion at the first attempt having slumped into the third division for the first time in 1987. It was not just due to the 16 goals, including eleven from consecutive penalties, he scored that season, which made him the most prolific goalscoring defender in Sunderland's history but the solidity he brought to the back four.**

Previously a Division Four winner with Sheffield United in 1982 and with Smith's York two years later, MacPhail was a cut above most lower league central defenders. He could play but knew when to and when not to.

MacPhail was ever-present in his first promotion season at Sunderland, missed just one match in his second term and only a handful in his third season as promotion was won again, John playing in all three Play-Off games. Having reached the top flight he played at Norwich on the opening day of the season. It was to be his last match for Sunderland and the only top-level game he played in a long career.

As an eleven and twelve-year-old, he played for Dundee Boys as a goalkeeper, but became a centre-half and made his debut as a 19-year-old at Rangers in April 1976. Coming on after 20 minutes with his side 2-0 down they eventually lost 4-2 but MacPhail earned rave reviews and was on his way. In 2010, as Dundee were threatened by a £400,000 bill from the taxman, MacPhail auctioned off a collection of signed sporting photographs to help save the club.

After 84 games for Dundee John joined Sheffield United after a month's trial early in 1979 and later played there for Ian Porterfield, although reputedly the pair did not bring the best out of each other.

Relegated from the second tier in his first season under Harry Haslam, MacPhail suffered relegation again the following term during which World Cup-winner Martin Peters took over as manager. Four days after the final league game MacPhail went in goal for the second half of a County Cup semi-final with Rotherham United. He did not concede although his side went down having trailed at the break.

With former Sunderland youth goalkeeper Keith Waugh (who he later played alongside at Bristol City) between the sticks, the following year (1980-81) MacPhail was a regular as the Blades won Division Four but he played rarely the following season when he was part of a squad that included Kevin Arnott, Terry Curran and Mick Henderson. MacPhail moved on after nine goals in 169 games for the Bramall Lane club.

Initially joining Denis' Smith's York on loan in February 1983, MacPhail scored 29 goals in 172+1 games over three and a half seasons playing alongside John Byrne, Alan Hay Ricky Sbragia, Roger Jones, Malcolm Crosby, Marco Gabbiadini and Viv Busby before joining Bristol City for a tribunal set fee of £14,000. He had one season at Ashton Gate playing alongside David Moyes who he later attempted to install as his number two when managing Hartlepool. There were 26 appearances - and one goal from a penalty - for the Robins before John came to Sunderland.

After leaving Wearside he went to Hartlepool United, initially on loan. MacPhail became massively popular at the club who he helped to only a second-ever promotion in his first season. He went on to make 192+4 appearances during which he scored four times. Appointed player/manager in November 1993 he took charge at a financially challenged time and won just seven of 36 games before being sacked. Nonetheless, retained as a player, he felt that new manager David McCreery did not pick him and sued the club for unfair dismissal before settling out of court.

MacPhail took over as player-manager of South Tyneside United who had just changed their name from Brinkburn CA. He also set up a furniture business in South Tyneside before becoming a car salesman in Houghton in 1996 and later on Teesside. Nicknamed 'Monty' throughout his career, despite his early goalkeeping, of course Monty at Sunderland has to mean Jim. As of June 2022, John was in seriously ill health after a bad fall.

## McALLISTER, Alexander (Sandy)

**POSITION:** Centre-half

**BIRTHPLACE:** Kilmarnock, East Ayrshire

**DATE OF BIRTH:** 06/09/1876 - 31/01/1918

**HEIGHT:** 5' 7" **WEIGHT:** 12st 0lbs

**SIGNED FROM:** Kilmarnock, 06/12/1896

**DEBUT:** v Stoke, H, 20/02/1897

**LAST MATCH:** v Sheffield United, A, 16/04/1904

**MOVED TO:** Derby County, 30/05/1904

**TEAMS:** Dean Park, Carrington Vale, Kilmarnock, Sunderland, Derby County, Oldham Athletic, Spennymoor United

**SAFC TOTALS:** 222 appearances / 5 goals

**Sandy McAllister's daughters Eileen and Nancy were still living in Sunderland in 2009, Eileen passing away at the age of 102. They also had a brother called Leslie, named after Sandy's Sunderland teammate Jim Leslie. Father Sandy's time on earth was much shorter, but he packed a lot into his 41 years.**

He was the only ever-present as he won the league title with Sunderland in 1902 having played in the first-ever match at Roker Park four years earlier. He had come into the side late in 1896-97, making his third appearance in the crucial final 'Test Match' against Newton Heath.

A miner before and during his football career, Sandy - who had never played a senior game for Kilmarnock before coming to Sunderland - worked at Ryhope Colliery. When he finally scored his first goals with a brace in his sixth season he was presented with a piano as a token of appreciation, directors Mr Ferry and Mr Foster supplying the piano from their shop in Fawcett Street.

In the summer of 1904 McAllister moved on to Derby County where he played 24 league games before joining Lancashire Combination League outfit Oldham Athletic where he scored eight times in 38 games plus two more in five FA Cup qualifying ties. Finally, Sandy returned to the north east with Spennymoor Utd.

Often recorded as dying of food poisoning, daughter Nancy confirmed that in fact he passed away of Bright's Disease whilst serving as a private in Italy with the 10th Battalion of the Northumberland Fusiliers. He is buried in the Giavera British Cemetery, Veneto, Italy. Although her dad died in the First World War when she was only four, Nancy became friends with some of the Sunderland players of the thirties, Bert Johnston even giving her away at her wedding.

## McATEER, Jason Wynne

**POSITION:** Midfielder

**BIRTHPLACE:** Birkenhead, Cheshire

**DATE OF BIRTH:** 18/06/1971

**HEIGHT:** 5' 11" **WEIGHT:** 12st 4lbs

**SIGNED FROM:** Blackburn Rovers, 19/10/2001

**DEBUT:** v Middlesbrough, A, 22/10/2001

**LAST MATCH:** v Crystal Palace H, 17/05/2004

**MOVED TO:** Tranmere Rovers, 19/07/2004

**TEAMS:** Marine, Washington Stars, Marine, Bolton Wanderers, Liverpool, Blackburn Rovers, Sunderland, Tranmere Rovers

**INTERNATIONAL:** Republic of Ireland

**SAFC TOTALS:** 61 appearances / 5 goals

**A £1m buy from Blackburn, McAteer had been sold for £500 and a bag of balls as a non-contract player from Marine to Bolton. After starting in Sunday League football on the Wirral he had signed for Marine having been approached while working in a pub and studying graphic design.**

In 1991 Jason went to work for an uncle in America where he played a handful of games for Washington Stars and gained a scholarship in Ohio. However before he took that up he played for Marine reserves as visa issues were dealt with, at which point he accepted Bolton's timely offer having impressed for Marine's reserves in a game against Bolton's 'A' team in 1992.

In November of that year Bruce Rioch gave him a league debut against Burnley with McAteer going on to win promotion the following season. In 1995 alongside skipper Alan Stubbs he played in the League Cup final, lost to Liverpool and also in the Play-Off final as Bolton fought back from 2-0 down to Reading to win 4-3 in extra-time. On 7 September 1995 Bolton accepted a fee of £4.5m from Liverpool.

Coming into the side as right wing-back and being a Reds regular from 1995 to 1997, Jason played in the 1996 FA Cup final alongside Phil Babb, losing to a Manchester United line-up that included Roy Keane and Andy Cole. A broken leg suffered against Blackburn in January 1998 was the beginning of the end for Jason at Liverpool where he scored six times in 139 appearances.

Ironically it was Blackburn he signed for in January 1999 but he could not stop Rovers being relegated that season.

## McATEER, Jason (Continued)

McAteer helped them back into the Premier League in 2001 and scored four times in 72 games before moving on to Sunderland in October of that year, but as at Rovers, was part of a relegation side. In 2003-04 he captained Sunderland to the semi-finals of the play offs and the FA Cup, being sent off in the cup semi-final against Millwall before being released at the end of that season and joining Tranmere Rovers as club captain. There were to be four goals in 81 games for Tranmere with whom Jason lost a League One play off semi-final on penalties to Martin Scott's Hartlepool in 2005.

At international level McAteer won 52 caps for the Republic of Ireland and played at the FIFA World Cup finals in 1994 and 2002. He was in the squad again for the 2002 finals playing against Cameroon in the finals Roy Keane sensationally withdrew from. Early the following season, by which time McAteer had been made Ireland captain, he was the victim of a challenge by Roy Keane that saw the future Sunderland manager sent off at the Stadium of Light. As Keane departed, wind-up merchant McAteer was gesturing that Keane should write about it in his next book!

He had a spell as player/caretaker manager at Tranmere in May and June of 2006 and coached at the club for a further year as well as coaching at Chester before returning to Tranmere for a five-month spell as assistant manager to John Barnes in 2009. McAteer also worked as a TV pundit. Renowned for being dim-witted - a caricature he played up to - Jason was always a decent lad. In 2005 he organised a Liverpool legends and celebrities 'Tsunami Soccer Aid' match at Anfield that raised over £400,000 for the disaster fund after the Indian Ocean Tsunami that took place on Boxing Day 2004. Jason's autobiography, 'Blood, Sweat and McAteer' was published in 2016.

## McCALLUM, Donald

**POSITION:** Full-back

**BIRTHPLACE:** Anderston, Glasgow, Lanarkshire

**DATE OF BIRTH:** 21/01/1881 - 15/07/1936

**HEIGHT:** 5' 8½" **WEIGHT:** 12st 7lbs

**SIGNED FROM:** Greenock Morton, 14/05/1904

**DEBUT:** v Aston Villa, A, 01/10/1904

**LAST MATCH:** v Derby County, H, 12/11/1904

**MOVED TO:** Middlesbrough, 05/12/1904

**TEAMS:** Strathclyde Junior Club, Queens Strollers, Queens Park, Liverpool, Greenock Morton, Sunderland, Middlesbrough, Kilmarnock, Renton

**INTERNATIONAL:** Scotland triallist

**SAFC TOTALS:** 3 appearances / 0 goals

**In addition to his handful of games for Sunderland, McCallum played twice for Liverpool in 1902-03. He made 21 appearances for Middlesbrough in 1904-05 and six the following term, the last at Sunderland on New Year's Day 1906.**

In Scotland his best return was 25 games for Kilmarnock. Reputedly a cool and composed defender, he played in a trial for the Scotland team in 1904. Donald emigrated to Canada in 1910, initially as a farm clerk then later becoming a cattle farmer. He passed away whilst on holiday in the resort of Seaside, Oregon and was buried in Edmonton, Alberta.

## McCANN, Gavin Peter

**POSITION:** Midfielder

**BIRTHPLACE:** Blackpool, Lancashire

**DATE OF BIRTH:** 10/01/1978

**HEIGHT:** 5' 11" **WEIGHT:** 11st 0lbs

**SIGNED FROM:** Everton, 26/11/1998

**DEBUT:** v Sheffield United, A, 28/11/1998

**LAST MATCH:** v Arsenal, H, 11/05/2003

**MOVED TO:** Aston Villa, 24/07/2003

**TEAMS:** Everton, Sunderland, Aston Villa, Bolton Wanderers

**INTERNATIONAL:** England

**SAFC TOTALS:** 121+14 appearances / 13 goals

**An effective midfielder who earned one England cap in Sven-Goran Eriksson's first match as manager against Spain in 2001, coming on as a half-time sub for Paul Scholes. Although Gavin did not get a second cap, he was named in the squad for two further internationals the following month.**

McCann was a powerful driving force who enjoyed the physical side of the game and was also an able technician. Bought for £500,000 after 5+6 games for Everton he was undoubtedly one of Peter Reid's stellar signings alongside the likes of Kevin Phillips, Niall Quinn and Thomas Sorensen.

Following relegation in 2003, he was sold for £2.25m to Aston Villa, Villa Park being the ground where he had played for England. At Villa he would play a similar number of games to his SAFC total: 127+2, scoring five goals in four years before a £1m move to Bolton where he added 68+20 games and three goals, two of his goals coming in the UEFA Cup.

Restricted by injury throughout his career, Gavin moved into coaching at Bolton before becoming assistant manager at Hyde United. He returned to Bolton coaching Under 15 and Under 18 teams before leaving the club in January 2021. From 2008, he also ran his own football academy with former Blackpool player Jamie Milligan.

## McCARTNEY, George

**POSITION:** Left-back

**BIRTHPLACE:** Belfast, Northern Ireland

**DATE OF BIRTH:** 29/04/1981

**HEIGHT:** 5' 11" **WEIGHT:** 11st 2lbs

**SIGNED FROM:** Trainee, 01/07/1997 and from West Ham United, 01/09/2008

**DEBUT:** v Luton Town, H, 19/09/2000

**LAST MATCH:** v Fulham, H, 28/02/2010

**MOVED TO:** West Ham United, 08/08/2006 and West Ham again, 01/07/2012

**TEAMS:** Sunderland, West Ham United, Sunderland, Leeds United (L), West Ham United

**INTERNATIONAL:** Northern Ireland

**SAFC TOTALS:** 175+28 appearances / 0 goals

**Never a scorer in either of his spells with Sunderland, McCartney scored on his international debut while a Sunderland player, the goal coming against Iceland in September 2001. It was his only goal in 34 international appearances, 26 of which were while with Sunderland. His caps total could have been far higher but for him twice retiring from international football when selected for his country. He also became the first Sunderland player to be sent off in a full international when dismissed against Greece in October 2003.**

Player of the Season at Sunderland in the Championship winning year of 2004-05 when he was also included in the PFA divisional Team of the Year, George also was named Players' Player of the Year at West Ham in 2012, again in a promotion winning season, McCartney appearing as a sub in the Play-Off final as West Ham beat Kevin Phillips' Blackpool at Wembley.

An excellent attacking left-back, George frustrated fans by his slowness in recovering his defensive position having gone forward, and twice left Wearside for West Ham. Astonishingly, when he re-signed after his first stint in London the undisclosed fee was believed to be the most paid to that date for a product of the Sunderland academy - and it had been paid rather than received by Sunderland! During his second spell on Wearside McCartney twice went on loan to Leeds, totalling 32 appearances without scoring.

After retiring from playing, George worked alongside David Healy as a coach at Linfield where he helped to develop Trai Hume before his move to Sunderland.

## McCLEAN, James Joseph

**POSITION:** Outside-left

**BIRTHPLACE:** Derry, Northern Ireland

**DATE OF BIRTH:** 22/04/1989

**HEIGHT:** 6' 0" **WEIGHT:** 12st 6lbs

**SIGNED FROM:** Derry City, 09/08/2011

**DEBUT:** v Blackburn Rovers, H, 11/12/2011

**LAST MATCH:** v Tottenham Hotspur, A, 19/05/2013

**MOVED TO:** Wigan Athletic, 08/08/2013

**TEAMS:** Derry City, Sunderland, Wigan Athletic, WBA, Stoke City, Wigan Athletic (to June 2022)

**INTERNATIONAL:** Republic of Ireland

**SAFC TOTALS:** 54+16 appearances / 11 goals

**A winger in the push it past the full-back and run mould rather than the jinky type, McClean did not have a trick as such, but he could be highly effective due to his pace, strength and ability to hit a cross on the run. He also had a goal in him and after being at the club for four months having been recruited by Pop Robson, he was given his debut by fellow Irishman Martin O'Neill. O'Neill had been impressed with McClean in a reserve game and gave James an opportunity in the manager's first game whereupon he proved to be something of a revelation.**

After one full season though he was on his way for a fee believed to be in the region of £2m. McClean became strongly disliked by many Sunderland supporters and indeed those of other clubs due to his principled stand to refuse to wear a poppy to commemorate Remembrance Day. He also declared his international allegiance to the Republic of Ireland rather than Northern Ireland with whom he had won seven Under 21 caps.

In two spells at Wigan James made 95+28 appearances with 20 goals to the summer of 2022 when he helped them to the League One title. For WBA and Stoke his figures were 66+46/5 and 90+21/12.

## McCOIST, Alistair Murdoch (Ally)

**POSITION:** Striker

**BIRTHPLACE:** Bellshill, Glasgow, Lanarkshire

**DATE OF BIRTH:** 24/09/1962

**HEIGHT:** 5' 10" **WEIGHT:** 12st 0lbs

**SIGNED FROM:** St Johnstone, 26/08/1981

**DEBUT:** v Ipswich Town, A, 29/08/1981

**LAST MATCH:** v West Bromwich Albion, H, 14/05/1983

**MOVED TO:** Rangers, 08/06/1983

**TEAMS:** St Johnstone, Sunderland, Rangers, Kilmarnock

**INTERNATIONAL:** Scotland

**SAFC TOTALS:** 46+19 appearances / 9 goals

**A prolific scorer in part-time football in Scotland, Ally became Sunderland's record signing when arriving for £350,000 and the teenager became the darling of the crowd despite finding goals hard to come by, before returning to Scotland where he became Rangers' record scorer.**

An impish back-heel that set up a goal for Mick Buckley away to UEFA Cup holders Ipswich on his debut as a sub earmarked McCoist as a player fans warmed to. 'Ally, Ally' tumbled from the terraces whenever he did anything good, while his bouncy personality reinforced his popularity. That personality helped to make him a household name later in his career as McCoist became a team captain on the BBC Question of Sport TV programme between 1996 and 2007, as well as a regular TV pundit and summariser while in 2000 he starred in a film called A Shot At Glory.

Having scored 27 goals in 68 games as a youngster for St Johnstone whilst also working as a civil servant, at Rangers Ally hit 355 goals in 581 games. During McCoist's time at Ibrox he won ten league titles between 1987 and 1997 in addition to nine League Cup winners' medals between 1984 and 1997. He also won a Scottish Cup winner's medal in 1992, a year in which he was the Scottish Football Writers' Association's Player of the Year and Scottish PFA Player of the Year. Two years later he was awarded the MBE. In both 1991-92 and 1992-93, McCoist won the European Golden Shoe as the continent's top scorer.

Having ended his playing days with 14 goals in 63 appearances over three seasons with Kilmarnock ending in 2000-01, he went on to manage Rangers through the most turbulent times in its long history, being in charge from June 2011 to December 2014 before being placed on twelve months leave and having his contract terminated in September 2015. During this period Rangers won back-to-back promotions from the fourth and third tiers in 2013 and 2014.

For Scotland he scored 19 goals in 61 internationals, playing at Italia 90 and captaining his country against Australia in March 1996. From February 2005 he had two years as a member of the Scotland coaching staff and was inducted into the Scottish Sports Hall of Fame in 2007.

## McCOLL, Donald

**POSITION:** Forward

**BIRTHPLACE:** Lismore, Argyllshire

**DATE OF BIRTH:** 18/02/1866 - 27/12/1949

**SIGNED:** 1884

**DEBUT:** v Redcar, A, 08/11/1884

**LAST MATCH:** v Redcar, A, 08/11/1884

**MOVED:** 1885

**TEAMS:** Sunderland, Newcastle West End, Newcastle East End

**SAFC TOTALS:** 1 appearance / 1 goal

**The scorer of Sunderland's first competitive goal (in a national competition), McColl's moment came in Sunderland's first-ever English (FA) Cup tie, lost 3-1 at Redcar. Like others of his era, McColl's only recognised first-team appearance(s) came in cup ties, but he also played many times in the frequent friendlies of the time - on one occasion, conceding eleven as a goalkeeper in a January 1885 game with Port Glasgow.**

Listed as a machinesman in the 1891 census, he played for both Newcastle West End and East End, retiring through ill health before the formation of United. A benefit game was staged in February 1896 at St James' Park by some of his former West End teammates, as he was unable to work due to rheumatism. Towards the end of World War One Don worked on a project to construct Cramlington Aerodrome and remained in that area as a roadman for Seaton Valley Council until his retirement.

## McCOMBIE, Andrew (Andy)

**POSITION:** Right-back

**BIRTHPLACE:** Dingwall, Ross-shire

**DATE OF BIRTH:** 30/01/1877 - 28/03/1952

**HEIGHT:** 5' 9½" **WEIGHT:** 12st 6lbs

**SIGNED FROM:** Inverness Thistle, 20/12/1898

**DEBUT:** v Wednesday, A, 18/02/1899

**LAST MATCH:** v Bury, H, 23/01/1904

**MOVED TO:** Newcastle United, 04/02/1904

**TEAMS:** Inverness Thistle, Sunderland, Newcastle United

**INTERNATIONAL:** Scotland

**SAFC TOTALS:** 165 appearances / 5 goals

**A league title winner with both Sunderland and Newcastle United, Andy McCombie was a celebrated and controversial character from the era before World War One, but his allegiance to Tyneside stretched all the way to 1950. The 46 years, three months and 27 days he served the Magpies has never been surpassed and yet his departure from red and white to black and white was caused by a financial dispute with Sunderland's directors.**

The controversy led to an FA enquiry and ultimately to the suspension of Sunderland manager Alec Mackie along with six Sunderland directors. In the summer of 1903 Sunderland provided him with the sum of £100 with which to start a business. In those days it was common for players to receive 'Benefit Games' where some or all of the gate receipts would go to the player as a reward for his loyalty.

McCombie had such a game at Sunderland. The player took £500 from the game against Middlesbrough, but having incurred the costs of staging the match the directors asked McCombie for the return of the original £100. The dispute centred around the club arguing this was a loan while the player insisted it was a gift. The case went to the County Court which ruled in favour of the club, but a subsequent FA investigation not only sided with McCombie, but led to them punishing SAFC who were found guilty of financial irregularities.

Hailing from a Gaelic-speaking family McCombie had come to Sunderland from Scotland in December 1898 and made

## McCOMBIE, Andy (Continued)

26 of his appearances in the league-winning season of 1901-02, adding a second piece of silverware the following term when he was part of the side who won the Sheriff of London Shield, a forerunner of the Community Shield. In March 1903 McCombie made his Scotland debut as a teammate of Jimmy Watson in a 1-0 win over Wales in Cardiff. A month later alongside fellow full-back Watson and goalkeeper Ted Doig, he helped Scotland to beat England 2-1 at Bramall Lane. Without them, Sunderland managed to beat Notts County at Roker Park on the same day. McCombie would win two further caps, again versus Wales and England, while with Newcastle in March and April 1905.

Sold to Newcastle for a world record £700, the fee was all the more remarkable as it was for a defender. McCombie became part of the most successful team of the Magpies' history. He won the league title with them in 1904-05 and 1906-07 as well as appearing once in their title-winning side of 1908-09. He also played in the losing Cup finals of 1905 and 1906 and played 131 times for the club before he retired from playing in 1910.

To 2022 Newcastle have only been league champions four times and McCombie was part of all four. When they were champions in 1926-27 he was still at the club helping behind the scenes where he was assistant trainer from April 1908 to January 1928 after which he became head trainer until 1930. Andy continued as assistant trainer looking after the second-team players up to the end of World War Two. Having changed his allegiance from red and white to black and white, McCombie became a NUFC shareholder and stayed with Newcastle until his retirement in 1950, two years before his death.

He never scored for Newcastle, but netted the last of his six goals for Sunderland against Newcastle. Moreover, on his first return to Wearside in black and white at Christmas in 1904, he put through his own goal in the first minute. The biggest own goal though was Sunderland's for the way they handled his departure.

## McCONNELL, David James English

**POSITION:** Half-back

**BIRTHPLACE:** Larne, Ireland

**DATE OF BIRTH:** 14/05/1883 - 13/06/1928

**HEIGHT:** 5' 9" **WEIGHT:** 11st 3lbs

**SIGNED FROM:** Cliftonville, 01/05/1903

**DEBUT:** v Blackburn Rovers, H, 28/10/1905

**LAST MATCH:** v Chelsea, A, 29/02/1908

**MOVED TO:** Wednesday, 06/05/1908

**TEAMS:** Larne Red Star, Cliftonville, Glentoran, Sunderland, Wednesday, Chelsea, South Shields, Linfield

**INTERNATIONAL:** Northern Ireland

**SAFC TOTALS:** 45 appearances / 0 goals

**Two thirds of English McConnell's appearances came in 1906-07 as Sunderland finished in mid-table. He was an apprentice engineer when he signed amateur forms for the Lads, but could not play until he had completed his apprenticeship in Belfast He had played for Glentoran while waiting to join Sunderland.**

After leaving Sunderland he joined Wednesday where he played more at centre-half having mainly occupied the left-half berth on Wearside. In his first season in Sheffield English equalled his best year at Sunderland with 23 league appearances including a 4-2 defeat on his return to Roker Park on his sixth outing.

Strangely, McConnell was presented with a monkey before the 1909 cup tie at Portsmouth by a friend who had returned from India. Named Jacko, the monkey became Wednesday's mascot, but only for a few games as they lost the next cup tie against Glossop. After exactly 50 games for Wednesday McConnell moved to Chelsea in April 1910, but a year later, needed a cartilage operation that effectively ended his top class career. He had played 21 games for Chelsea. Nonetheless, in January 1913, he was called up by Northern Ireland when with non-league South Shields only for injury to prevent him from playing. He did win a dozen caps for his country, four of them with Sunderland.

McConnell's brother Victor played for Cliftonville and Belfast Celtic before World War One. After his football career, English moved into business in Belfast, but passed away at the age of 45, the same number as his appearance total for Sunderland.

## McCREADIE, Andrew

**POSITION:** Centre-half

**BIRTHPLACE:** Girvan, Ayrshire

**DATE OF BIRTH:** 19/11/1870 - 04/04/1916

**HEIGHT:** 5' 5" **WEIGHT:** 11st 2lbs

**SIGNED FROM:** Rangers, 03/05/1894

**DEBUT:** v Derby County, H, 01/09/1894

**LAST MATCH:** v Nottingham Forest, H, 08/02/1896

**MOVED TO:** Rangers, 09/03/1896

**TEAMS:** Cowlairs, Rangers, Sunderland, Rangers, Bristol St George, Wishaw Thistle

**INTERNATIONAL:** Scotland

**SAFC TOTALS:** 45 appearances / 10 goals

**One of the players on the Hemy painting that dominates the entrance to the Stadium of Light, Andrew McCreadie was a centre-half in the days when centre-halves were half-backs rather than central-defenders - hence him playing there when only 5' 5".**

On the first occasion when he was signed from Rangers, it was in exchange for William Gibson. Between two spells with Rangers, McCreadie won the title with Sunderland in 1895, four years after being with Rangers when they shared the inaugural Scottish championship with Dumbarton. Andrew also won the Scottish Cup with Rangers in 1894 and 1897, either side of his spell at Sunderland. During his title-winning season on Wearside McCreadie scored eight league goals plus one in the cup in the club's record 11-1 victory over Fairfield.

Both of McCreadie's Scotland caps were won while with Rangers, an 8-0 win over Wales at Wrexham in 1893 and a 2-2 draw with England at Parkhead in 1894. He also played in an unofficial 5-1 win over Canada at Ibrox in 1891. Both before and after his football career he worked as a weaver while during World War One he served with the Royal Scots Fusiliers and then the 10th Battalion Scottish Kings Liverpool Regiment. Andrew's brother Hugh played for Rangers, Third Lanark and Linthouse.

## McCULLOUGH, Robert (Bob)

**POSITION:** Inside-right

**BIRTHPLACE:** Gateshead, Co Durham

**DATE OF BIRTH:** 20/06/1892 - Q1 1972

**HEIGHT:** 5' 6½" **WEIGHT:** 9st 5lbs

**SIGNED FROM:** Radley, 29/09/1911

**DEBUT:** v Newcastle United, A, 17/02/1912

**LAST MATCH:** v Newcastle United, A, 17/02/1912

**MOVED TO:** South Shields, 15/08/1913

**TEAMS:** Radley, Sunderland, South Shields, Jarrow

**SAFC TOTALS:** 1 appearance / 0 goals

**Bob McCullough's one game was a derby defeat at Newcastle on a day when his opportunity arose when Charlie Buchan, George Holley and Jackie Mordue were absent as they were playing for the Football League in an inter-league game. A week earlier McCullough had scored four goals in a 13-2 win for the reserves at Wallsend Park Villa in a North Eastern League game.**

A teacher before and after playing football, he was possibly irritated by often seeing his name spelled as McCulloch. He had signed for Sunderland after trials in the reserves having previously played for Gateshead-based side Radley. Upon leaving Sunderland he signed for South Shields as an amateur, but became a professional in May 1914. During World War One he was a gunner in the Royal Garrison Artillery and then returned to his scholastic duties after being demobilised in January 1919.

## McDERMID, Robert (Bob)

**POSITION:** Full-back

**BIRTHPLACE:** Alexandria, West Dumbartonshire

**DATE OF BIRTH:** 15/08/1866 - 14/05/1941

**HEIGHT:** 5' 7"

**SIGNED FROM:** Newcastle West End, 01/08/1888

**DEBUT:** v Elswick Rangers, H, 27/10/1888

**LAST MATCH:** v Newcastle East End, H, 17/11/1888

**MOVED TO:** Sunderland Albion, 02/09/1889

**TEAMS:** Renton Thistle, Renton, Newcastle West End, Sunderland, Sunderland Albion, Accrington, Burton Swifts, Stockton, Lincoln City, Renton, Dundee Wanderers, Newcastle United, Hebburn Argyle, Warmley, South Shields

**SAFC TOTALS:** 2 appearances / 0 goals

**Fined £20 for joining rivals Sunderland Albion while contracted to SAFC in 1889 (The equivalent of £2,600 today), McDermid played for Albion in the Football Alliance before crossing the Pennines to play for Accrington.**

At Lincoln he played in the last two games of the Imps first-ever Football League season in 1892-93 before making 18 appearances for Renton in a relegation season the following year. There were then five games and one goal in 1894 for Dundee Wanderers before returning to the north east with Newcastle United.

Previously he had played at St James Park when winning the Northumberland Senior Cup in the colours of Newcastle West End in 1888. During his time with Sunderland McDermid continued to play as a 'Guest' for West End as well as run a pub in Barclay Street. Having joined the Magpies he scored twice in 64 league and FA Cup games, one of his goals coming on his debut against Burton Wanderers in November 1894. At county level, at various points he represented Durham, Dumbartonshire and Northumberland, and was probably one of the most travelled footballers of the 1890s. After retiring he became a boilermaker and plater by trade before running a pub in South Shields.

## McDONAGH, James Martin (Jim/Seamus)

**POSITION:** Goalkeeper

**BIRTHPLACE:** Rotherham, Yorkshire

**DATE OF BIRTH:** 06/10/1952

**HEIGHT:** 6' 0" **WEIGHT:** 13st 9lbs

**SIGNED FROM:** Notts County, 02/08/1985, on loan

**DEBUT:** v Blackburn Rovers, H, 17/08/1985

**LAST MATCH:** v Grimsby Town, A, 17/09/1985

**MOVED TO:** Notts County, 20/10/1985, end of loan

**TEAMS:** Rotherham, Manchester United (L), Bolton Wanderers, Everton, Bolton Wanderers Notts County, Birmingham City (L), Gillingham (L), Sunderland (L), Wichita Wings, Scarborough, Huddersfield Town (L), Charlton Athletic, Galway United, Spalding United, Grantham Town, Telford United, Grantham Town, Arnold Town

**INTERNATIONAL:** England youth / Republic of Ireland

**SAFC TOTALS:** 8 appearances / 0 goals

**Notorious for claiming the goals were the wrong size when Sunderland played at Grimsby, McDonagh played in the first eight games of Lawrie McMenemy's ill-fated reign, conceding 17 goals while on loan. A little over quarter of a century later he returned as goalkeeping coach under Martin O'Neill.**

A Yorkshireman by birth and first known as Jim, he demonstrated his allegiance to Ireland having been capped by the Republic due to his Mayo born father by becoming known as Seamus.

McDonagh was a much better goalkeeper than Sunderland supporters were led to believe on the basis of his handful of appearances in a struggling side under McMenemy. His 25 full caps are evidence of that. Winning the first four while with Everton, he added ten during his time at Bolton, seven while at Notts County, three with Gillingham and a final one on November 1985 with Wichita Wings.

McDonagh was 18 when he debuted for his home town Rotherham against Wrexham in April 1970. Within a year he won England youth honours coming on as a sub as England turned a 2-1 deficit into a 3-2 win over Spain in Pamplona in March 1971. There were 121 league appearances for the Millers for whom he was ever-present as they won the fourth division in 1974-75. During this time (1973), Manchester United took him on loan, although he never got a first-team game for the Red Devils. McDonagh's move away from Rotherham proved to be to Bolton after he failed to regain his place at Millmoor after a broken leg. Debuting for the Trotters at Partick Thistle in the Anglo-Scottish Cup in September 1976, it was Barry Siddall's move to Sunderland than paved the way for him to take over as number one.

Ever-present in his first three full seasons, he set a club record of conceding only 33 goals in 42 games as a Wanderers side including Peter Reid, Sam Allardyce and Frank Worthington won Division Two. Between 1976 and 1980 the keeper made a club record 161 consecutive appearances, but following relegation moved to Everton for £250,000.

Debuting in a 3-1 defeat at Roker Park against newly-promoted Sunderland, McDonagh missed only three matches in his first season at Goodison as the Toffees reached the quarter-finals of the FA Cup. However, after one season he returned to Bolton under George Mulhall and missed just three games in his first year and none in his second. During that ever-present season that took his Trotters total to 274 games he also became the first-ever Bolton goalkeeper to score a goal, doing so with a clearance in a derby with Burnley. Unable to stop Bolton dropping into Division Three he was transferred to Notts County, being promoted to the top flight in his first season and relegated in his second. After 35 league appearances with Notts who loaned him out three times - Birmingham City (1 app), Gillingham (10 apps) and Sunderland - he joined Neil Warnock's Scarborough in 1987 making nine Division Four appearances.

After a brief spell in the USA Indoor League in Wichita he returned to make a final six league appearances with Huddersfield before becoming player/manager of Galway United from December 1988 until the following May. Seamus then managed Derry City before playing for Spalding, Grantham and Telford, doubling up as reserve-team manager at the latter.

After finally playing for Arnold Town he became goalkeeping coach at Coventry, Mansfield, Nottingham Forest, Millwall, Rotherham, Leicester, Celtic, Aston Villa, Plymouth and Hull as well as Sunderland and the Republic of Ireland, working alongside Martin O'Neill in several of those posts. Like O'Neill, he is a man of varied interests, in his case being passionate about the artist LS Lowry and playing the ukulele!

## McDONALD, John (Jock)

**POSITION:** Forward

**BIRTHPLACE:** Stirling, Stirlingshire

**DATE OF BIRTH:** 12/02/1860 - 10/09/1907

**SIGNED:** 1881

**DEBUT:** v Redcar, A, 08/11/1884

**LAST MATCH:** v Redcar, A, 24/10/1885

**MOVED:** 1885

**TEAMS:** Sunderland, Elswick Rangers, Newcastle West End

**SAFC TOTALS:** 2 appearances / 0 goals

**One of the first players at the club not to be a schoolteacher, McDonald spent five years at SAFC, but because most games at the time were friendlies, his two English (FA) Cup appearances are the only officially recognised competitive games he is credited with. He was the scorer of the first-ever goal at Abbs Field in September 1884 against Birtley and the first Sunderland player to achieve a hat-trick (four goals v Stanley Star on 20 January 1883).**

Jock also scored against Darlington in the Durham FA Challenge Cup final replay in May 1884. In October 1886 he was reported to be playing for Elswick Rangers and then had a spell at Newcastle West End while after retiring from football he earned his living as a licensed victualler. McDonald was a keen sportsmen and played many years for Sunderland Licensed Victuallers' Cricket Club as well as once turning out for Gosforth in a rugby union game against Sunderland Rovers in 1881 when the visitors arrived three players short.

## McDONALD, Joseph (Joe)

**POSITION:** Left-back

**BIRTHPLACE:** Blantyre, South Lanarkshire

**DATE OF BIRTH:** 10/02/1929 - 08/09/2003

**HEIGHT:** 5' 8" **WEIGHT:** 10st 8lbs

**SIGNED FROM:** Falkirk, 15/03/1954

**DEBUT:** v Sheffield United, H, 16/04/1954

**LAST MATCH:** v Luton Town, A, 08/02/1958

**MOVED TO:** Nottingham Forest, 30/06/1958

**TEAMS:** Bellshill Athletic, Falkirk, Sunderland, Nottingham Forest, Wisbech Town, Ramsgate Athletic

**INTERNATIONAL:** Scotland and Great Britain

**SAFC TOTALS:** 155 appearances / 1 goal

**A regular in the 'Bank of England' team of the mid-fifties, McDonald missed just four games across 1954-55 and 1955-56, playing in back-to-back FA Cup semi-finals and in the team that finished fourth in the top flight in 1955.**

Sunderland have not finished as high since. Joe finally got an FA Cup winner's medal in 1959 with Nottingham Forest, having his former Sunderland teammate Billy Bingham as his direct opponent at Wembley as Luton were beaten. Both Bingham and McDonald were Sunderland players when Bingham scored for Northern Ireland against Scotland on McDonald's international debut in October 1955, but while Joe was on the losing side on that occasion he was a winner against Wales the following month at Hampden. They were his only full Scotland caps but he also gained a representative honour for Great Britain, playing against Northern Ireland in a game to mark the 75th anniversary of the Irish FA in 1955. Additionally, he played in a B international against the army.

Joe played 109 league games for Forest before a season in non-league with Wisbech Town in 1961-62 followed by

## McDONALD, Joe (Continued)

a two-year spell as player/manager of Ramsgate Athletic. Finally, from August 1965 to March 1967 he managed Yeovil Town before emigrating to Australia. McDonald had started out with 79 appearances for Falkirk after playing as a goalkeeper in schools football. He was never called upon to take over between the sticks for Sunderland where in May 195, he was one of 14 players punished by the Football League for receiving illegal payments. The financial penalty imposed was restored to him in 1962 when the league's ruling was declared illegal.

## McDOUGALL, John (Jock)

**POSITION:** Centre-half

**BIRTHPLACE:** Port Glasgow, Renfrewshire

**DATE OF BIRTH:** 21/09/1901 - 26/09/1973

**HEIGHT:** 5' 10½" **WEIGHT:** 11st 12lbs

**SIGNED FROM:** Airdrieonians, 09/05/1929

**DEBUT:** v Manchester City, H, 07/09/1929

**LAST MATCH:** v Aston Villa, A, 27/01/1934

**TEAMS:** Airdrieonians, Sunderland, Leeds United

**INTERNATIONAL:** Scotland

**SAFC TOTALS:** 187 appearances / 5 goals

**McDougall was at his peak when he arrived at SAFC after spending the 1920s with Airdrieonians with whom he won the Scottish Cup in 1924, after scoring in the third round at Motherwell and playing in the final against Hibs.**

The same season was the second in four successive years that Airdrieonians finished second in the Scottish League while they also lifted the Lanarkshire Cup three times during Jock's time.

At Sunderland he was the club captain and a regular in the early thirties after which he added 59 league and cup appearances with Leeds United. His brother Jim was a fellow Scotland international who captained Liverpool as well as playing for Partick Thistle. Jock's solitary cap came against Northern Ireland in 1926. After his retirement Jock worked as a greenkeeper at Port Glasgow Golf Club while before his senior football days he worked in marine engineering.

## McDOWALL, Leslie James (Les)

**POSITION:** Defender

**BIRTHPLACE:** Gunga Pur, British India

**DATE OF BIRTH:** 25/10/1912 - 18/08/1991

**HEIGHT:** 5' 11" **WEIGHT:** 11st 9lbs

**SIGNED FROM:** Glentyan Thistle, 19/12/1932

**DEBUT:** v West Bromwich Albion, H 24/11/1934

**LAST MATCH:** v Liverpool, A, 12/03/1938

**MOVED TO:** Manchester City, 14/03/1938

**TEAMS:** Glentyan Thistle, Sunderland, Manchester City, St Mirren (WW2 Guest), Wrexham

**INTERNATIONAL:** Scotland Junior

**SAFC TOTALS:** 14 appearances / 0 goals

**The son of a Scottish missionary, McDowall was born in India, but brought up in Scotland. Signed after impressing in two trial matches for the reserves, he did not play much for SAFC although his handful of games were spread over four seasons in which the League, FA Cup and Charity Shield were won.**

He went on to give great service to Manchester City as both player and manager, reaching the FA Cup final in successive years in 1955 and '56. In 1955, McDowall's City beat Sunderland in the semi-final before losing to Newcastle at Wembley. A year later it was their turn to lift the trophy on the famous occasion goalkeeper Bert Trautman played on with a broken neck. McDowall managed Manchester City from 1 June 1950 to 1 May 1963.

Initially, he moved to City from Wearside for a Sunderland record transfer of £8,000 before the Second World War. He went on to captain the club for whom he made 120 league appearances and scored eight goals while in total, including war-time, he turned out 244 times and netted 16 times. During the war he also 'Guested' for St Mirren. In 1949-50, McDowall had a season as player/manager of Wrexham before being appointed at Maine Road where City had just been relegated.

Promoted in their first year under the former Sunderland player, City's best league position under him was in 1956 when they were fourth in addition to winning the cup. However, they twice finished one above the drop zone and finally went down in his final season.

A tactical innovator, McDowall instigated wing-backs in the mid-fifties and deployed the 'Revie Plan' featuring future Sunderland player Don Revie as deep lying centre-forward. McDowall also tried something called the 'Marsden Plan' in 1957, only for that to be quickly abandoned after a 9-2 defeat at West Brom. In 1960 he broke the British transfer record when paying Huddersfield £55,000 for Denis Law while one of his earliest signings was City great Roy Paul and he also signed Ivor Broadis from Sunderland.

After leaving City McDowall managed nearby Oldham Athletic from June 1963 to March 1965 before retiring when sacked. His route into football had been self-propelled. After training as a draughtsman he became unemployed during the great depression and with time on his hands, formed a football team called Glentyan Thistle in Kilbarchan, west of Paisley, from where he was spotted by Sunderland.

With all due respect to Bill Murray, who managed Sunderland through the same era as McDowall was at City, and at a time when Sunderland spent massive amounts, perhaps if McDowall had been appointed at Sunderland, the 'Bank of England Club' might have had more success.

## McFADDEN, James Henry

**POSITION:** Forward

**BIRTHPLACE:** Glasgow, Lanarkshire

**DATE OF BIRTH:** 14/04/1983

**HEIGHT:** 5' 11" **WEIGHT:** 12st 6lbs

**SIGNED FROM:** Free agent, 26/10/2012

**DEBUT:** v Manchester United, A, 15/12/2012

**LAST MATCH:** v West Ham United, H, 12/01/2013

**MOVED TO:** End of contract, 29/01/2013

**TEAMS:** Motherwell, Everton, Birmingham City, Everton, Sunderland, Motherwell, St Johnstone, Motherwell, Queen of the South

**INTERNATIONAL:** Scotland

**SAFC TOTALS:** 0+3 appearances / 0 goals

**James McFadden had a good career for clubs and country, but his Sunderland game-time across three appearances totalled a mere 35 minutes. Indeed, my main memory of him is James leaping out of a kit basket he had hidden in and trying to scare myself and the rest of the party as we boarded a flight home from an away game. It's not much of a memory.**

McFadden had missed all of the 2010-11 season due to a damaged cruciate ligament and been released by Everton at the end of the 2011-12 season after having had a failed trial at Wolves the previous year. Given a chance in the form of a three-month contract by Martin O'Neill at Sunderland, McFadden was twice an unused sub before a five minute appearance on his debut. He was an unused sub a further four times in addition to his three cameo appearances which proved to be his last games in England.

At his best, McFadden was a tearaway sight, able to leave defenders in his wake and find the back of the net. He was the Scottish Football Writers' Association's international Player of the Year in 2007-08 having been their Young Player of the Year in 2001-02. In 2005-06, James was Everton's Young Player of the Year and claimed the Toffees Goal of the Season in 2006-07 for his strike against Charlton.

David Moyes signed him for Everton for £1.25m from Motherwell where he had debuted as a sub in a home defeat to Dundee on Boxing Day in 2000. At Motherwell, where he played much of his best football under future Sunderland caretaker-manager Eric Black, McFadden made his name with mazy runs, set-pieces and good ability in the air. Regularly played out wide by Moyes instead of his preferred position through the middle, eventually in January 2008 McFadden moved to Birmingham where he was signed by his former international manager Alec McLeish for £5m, after 18 goals in 79+60 games in his first spell at Goodison. In 2011-12 he would add a further 3+5 games without scoring in a second stint on the blue half of Merseyside

With Birmingham his figures were 14 goals from 72+16 league and cup games, several of his strikes being from the penalty spot. His time at St Andrew's was largely ruined by injury with Blues relegated during his time there. After the injury 'Faddy' never seemed to be the same player. Following those short spells with Everton and Sunderland he returned to Scotland having two further periods with Motherwell in addition to one goal in 16 games for St Johnstone and none in eleven for Queen of the South. In total at Motherwell he scored 44 goals in 95+28 appearances.

For Scotland, McFadden first broke into the full squad as a 20-year-old at Motherwell under Bertie Vogts, making his debut on a Far East tour, only to miss the flight home after playing as a sub on his debut against South Africa. Maybe he was busy hiding in a kit skip? Nonetheless, he did very well for Scotland, the most famous and important of his 15 goals in 48 games being a 30-yarder that settled a Euro 2008 qualifying match away to France and which was commemorated in a huge mural at Hampden Park. After retiring from playing, James had a year-long spell as assistant to Scotland manager Alex McLeish between 2018 and 2019 following a similar spell as assistant manager at Motherwell in 2016-17 season. In 2019 McFadden was inducted into the Motherwell Hall of Fame and subsequently became a TV pundit in Scotland.

## McFADZEAN, Callum Jeffrey

**POSITION:** Left-back

**BIRTHPLACE:** Waterthorpe, Sheffield, South Yorkshire

**DATE OF BIRTH:** 16/01/1994

**HEIGHT:** 5' 11" **WEIGHT:** 11st 11lbs

**SIGNED FROM:** Free agent, 21/10/2020

**DEBUT:** v Mansfield Town, H, 07/11/2020

**LAST MATCH:** v Lincoln City, H, 22/05/2021

**MOVED TO:** End of contract, 30/06/2021

**TEAMS:** Sheffield United, Chesterfield (L), Burton Albion (L), Stevenage (L), Kilmarnock, Alfreton Town, Guiseley, Bury, Plymouth Argyle, Sunderland, Crewe Alexandra, Wrexham (to June 2022)

**INTERNATIONAL:** England U16 / Scotland U21

**SAFC TOTALS:** 29+5 appearances / 2 goals

**Signed by Phil Parkinson as a wing-back rather than as a full-back, McFadzean ended up often playing in a flat back four. Too often his weaknesses were exposed with the concession of unnecessary penalties being one aspect of this. Equally his strong point of going forward was not seen as much as it might have been if he was playing in a more advanced position.**

There was no question of a poor attitude by the player who played with heart and determination, but he was often looked upon as a weak link in a team who reached the League One Play-Offs, but ultimately were not good enough to win promotion. He did however, collect a Wembley winner's medal with Sunderland as part of the team who won the Football League (Papa John's) Trophy in March 2021.

Callum came through the ranks at Sheffield United for whom he scored in the first leg of the 2011 FA Youth Cup final against Manchester United and debuted at first-team level against Burton in a League Cup tie in August 2012. His first senior goal came at the end of that season on a League One Play-Off with Yeovil Town. Callum then began a series of loans registering 5/0 for Chesterfield, 18+3/2 for Burton Albion (including

a Wembley appearance in a League Two Play-Off defeat to Fleetwood in 2014) and 6/0 for Stevenage.

In the summer of 2016 he signed for Kilmarnock, but played just one cup tie and four league games, three of those as a sub. Loaned to Alfreton, he played three conference North games in April 2017 before joining National League Guiseley. After 16+9 appearances and one goal, he returned to the Football League with Bury for the 2018-19 season playing 45+4 games (0 goals) as the Shakers won promotion from League Two. When Bury were then expelled from the league he followed manager Ryan Lowe to Plymouth Argyle.

Scoring twice on his debut at Crewe got Callum off to a great start as he enjoyed a second successive promotion. There were 29 starts plus five substitute appearances and five goals in his season at Home Park, after which he rejected a new contract and was a free agent until joining Sunderland. Next stop was Crewe for whom one of 11+3 appearances came in a 4-0 home defeat to Sunderland in October 2021 before he re-united with Phil Parkinson at Wrexham on 27 January 2022.

At international level Callum played five Under 16 games for England, being a teammate of Jordan Pickford on his debut against Wales at Yeovil in October 2009. He went on to play against Northern Ireland, Scotland, Japan and Gabon all in the 2009-10 season. Five years later, he was called up by Scotland at Under 21 level and played against Hungary and Northern Ireland.

Older brother Kyle also began at Sheffield United and went on to play for Alfreton Town, Crawley Town, MK Dons, Burton Albion and Coventry City, where he was at the end of 2021. Internationally, he was capped by England at C level.

## McGEADY, Aiden John

**POSITION:** Winger

**BIRTHPLACE:** Glasgow, Lanarkshire

**DATE OF BIRTH:** 04/04/1986

**HEIGHT:** 5' 11" **WEIGHT:** 11st 7lbs

**SIGNED FROM:** Everton, 13/07/2017

**DEBUT:** v Derby County, H, 04/08/2017

**LAST MATCH:** Shrewsbury Town, A, 23/11/2021

**MOVED TO:** Hibernian, 24/06/2022

**TEAMS:** Celtic, Spartak Moscow, Everton, Sheffield Wednesday (L), Preston North End (L), Sunderland, Charlton Athletic (L), Hibernian (to July 2022)

**INTERNATIONAL:** Republic of Ireland

**SAFC TOTALS:** 123+27 appearances / 36 goals

**One of the most skilful players to grace the red and white stripes in the modern era, Aiden McGeady had already enjoyed a long career at a high level when he was signed by his former Preston manager Simon Grayson.**

Following Grayson's short tenure, McGeady, by his own admission, was not overly impressed when Chris Coleman took over, but Jack Ross brought the best out of Aiden who scored both of Sunderland's goals at Wembley in the 2019 Checkatrade Trophy final and netted again in the ill-fated penalty shoot-out.

When Ross was replaced by Phil Parkinson the manager took the astonishing decision to totally freeze McGeady - who was Sunderland's reigning Player of the Year - out of the picture, with the Irish international going on loan to Charlton Athletic in the division above the level Sunderland were playing at. The replacement of Parkinson with Lee Johnson saw McGeady instantly brought back into the fold. The player responded with some stellar performances, at one point providing four assists in one game and also sliding through a killer-ball for Lynden Gooch to go on and score the only goal of the 2021 final of the former Checkatrade Trophy now renamed the Papa John's.

Better with both feet than many players are with one, McGeady was a joy to watch. Like world greats Johan Cruyff and Zinedine Zidane, he even conjured up a trick of his own. Labelled the 'McGeady Spin' this was so good it was incorporated into the EA Sports' FIFA video game series. In contrast, the common consensus was that he was a winger who did not track back and work for the team, but that was not what my eyes told me, nor Johnson's apparently, as under Johnson, McGeady was appointed part of a 'leadership group' and sometimes captained the side. Released by Sunderland in 2022 McGeady re-joined Johnson at Hibs.

As an 18-year-old Aiden scored in the 17th minute of his debut for Celtic in a 1-1 draw at Hearts on 24 April 2004. Right from the start he had the ability and attitude to torture defenders, but an alleged tendency to do too much or not produce quality final balls consistently enough split the Celtic support. By 2007-08 that support was no longer split, but united in belief that here was an outstanding player nurtured particularly by the coaching of Tommy Burns. In total at Celtic, McGeady played 197+54 games scoring 37 goals.

In August 2010 he became the most expensive Scottish export when Spartak Moscow paid a reported fee of between £9.5m and £11m for the signature of a player who had won three successive titles with Celtic from 2006 to 2008 in addition to two wins in each of the major domestic cup competitions. Player of the Year at Celtic as the third of those league titles was claimed, he also won the club's Young Player of the Year accolade in the previous three seasons as well as scooping a host of national Player of the Year awards in 2008.

## McGEADY, Aiden (Continued)

In Moscow, McGeady propelled Spartak to runners-up spot and played against Celtic in the Champions League. After 93 games and 13 goals over four seasons, he returned to the UK, signing for Everton in January 2014 for a fee reported to be around £1m. However, he never found his best form at Goodison where 20 of his 43 appearances were off the bench, scoring his only goal at Leicester on the opening day of the 2014-15 season.

A loan to Sheffield Wednesday brought another goal in 10+3 appearances before a season-long loan to Preston North End in 2016-17 where he was the club's Player of the Year after 32+2 games and eight goals.

Aiden won 93 caps for the Republic of Ireland for whom he scored five times and was Republic of Ireland Young Player of the Year in 2009. Born in Scotland, he had promised his Donegal-born grandfather he would play for Ireland if given the chance. During his days with Celtic this resulted in regular abuse at the hands of opposition supporters, something brought to a head when he played at Celtic for Ireland against Scotland in a Euro 2016 qualifier. Aiden's father John was a winger who played 16 times for Sheffield United and twice for Newport County with 20 games in between for Southern California Lazers. Injury caused him to retire at the age of 23 having suffered a serious knee injury at Sheffield United when only 19.

In February 2008, no less a figure than Lionel Messi was quoted as saying, "I really like the way McGeady plays football. He is a natural talent who can create a brilliant piece of play in the blink of an eye".

## McGEOUCH, Dylan

**POSITION:** Midfielder

**BIRTHPLACE:** Glasgow, Lanarkshire

**DATE OF BIRTH:** 15/01/1993

**HEIGHT:** 5' 8" **WEIGHT:** 10st 12lbs

**SIGNED FROM:** Hibernian, 02/07/2018

**DEBUT:** v Gillingham, A, 22/08/2018

**LAST MATCH:** v Gillingham, A, 19/11/2019

**MOVED TO:** Aberdeen, 07/01/2020

**TEAMS:** Celtic, Coventry City (L), Hibs, Sunderland, Aberdeen (to July 2022)

**INTERNATIONAL:** Scotland

**SAFC TOTALS:** 29+13 appearances / 0 goals

**A neat and tidy player who kept the ball moving and rarely sacrificed possession, McGeouch did not seem to have a direct impact on the game but probably did not get enough of a chance to show what he could do.**

He was certainly in demand as a youngster, being part of the youth set-ups at both Celtic and Rangers. A Celtic fan, and ball boy, he started in the green and white half of Glasgow, but left when his brother Darren left the club (Darren went on to play for Greenock Morton and Stranraer amongst others). Dylan switched to Rangers who were awarded £100,000 by a tribunal when the player was persuaded to return to Celtic. A first-team debut came as a sub alongside Anthony Stokes on 6 November 2011 against Motherwell with Dylan scoring a tremendous individual goal on his second appearance against St Mirren, this time alongside Glenn Loovens as well as Stokes.

In February 2014, he went on loan to Coventry making eight League One appearances, all as sub. A second loan to Hibs materialised into a transfer and produced a Scottish Cup winner's medal as Rangers were beaten in the 2016 final in

which Anthony Stokes scored twice for Hibs and Rangers included Martyn Waghorn. McGeouch also won promotion with Hibs under his old Celtic boss Neil Lennon.

First called up by Scotland in March 2018, only to be ruled out by injury, McGeouch subsequently made his first two international appearances in May and June 2018 against Peru and Mexico shortly before coming to Sunderland. To June 2022, they remained his only two caps. Moving to Aberdeen in January 2020 Dylan debuted in a home cup win against Dumbarton and played Europa League football in his first full season and the new Europa Conference League in his second campaign at Pittodrie.

## McGHIE, Joseph (Joe)

**POSITION:** Centre-half

**BIRTHPLACE:** Dalmellington, East Ayrshire

**DATE OF BIRTH:** 22/03/1884 - 08/09/1976

**HEIGHT:** 5' 9" **WEIGHT:** 11st 7lbs

**SIGNED FROM:** Vale of Garnock Strollers, 19/05/1906

**DEBUT:** v Aston Villa, H, 08/09/1906

**LAST MATCH:** v Bury, H, 25/01/1908

**MOVED TO:** Sheffield United, 03/04/1908

**TEAMS:** Vale of Garnock Strollers, Sunderland, Sheffield United, Brighton & Hove Albion, Stalybridge Celtic, Clyde

**INTERNATIONAL:** Scotland Junior

**SAFC TOTALS:** 46 appearances / 0 goals

**An ironstone miner by trade before becoming a footballer, Joe McGhie built a reputation as a ball-playing centre-half as he helped Vale of Garnock Juniors to win the Ayrshire Junior Cup in 1905-06. He then signed for Sunderland, making 30 appearances in his first season and 16 in his second before a sizeable fee for the time of £250 took him to Sheffield United, for whom he debuted back at Sunderland on 12 September 1908.**

It was one of only six outings he had for the Blades before joining Brighton in the summer of 1909. In his first season, he helped the Seagulls to win their league title enabling the Southern League champions to take on Football League champions Aston Villa in the Charity Shield. McGhie had an outstanding game as Albion beat Villa at Stamford Bridge to take the only national trophy in their history. He was to make 156 appearances for Brighton, scoring three times before refusing new contract terms and moving to Central League Stalybridge Celtic in May 1913. Joe returned to his native Scotland in August 1916 to join his final club, Clyde.

McGhie worked in Glengarnock steelworks after retiring from playing before moving to Largs where he became a railway porter at the local station. Despite starting work as a nine-year-old in a mine, Joe maintained his health, still using his bicycle as his only mode of transport right up to his passing aged 92.

## McGILL, Brendan

**POSITION:** Winger

**BIRTHPLACE:** Dublin, Ireland

**DATE OF BIRTH:** 22/03/1981

**HEIGHT:** 5' 8" **WEIGHT:** 11st 0lbs

**SIGNED FROM:** Rivervalley Rangers, 29/07/1998

**DEBUT:** v Luton Town, A, 26/09/2000

**LAST MATCH:** v Luton Town, A, 26/09/2000

**MOVED TO:** Carlisle United, 15/08/2002

**TEAMS:** Rivervalley Rangers, Sunderland, Carlisle United, Gretna, Bohemians, Barrow, Drogheda United, Shelbourne

**INTERNATIONAL:** Republic of Ireland Under 17

**SAFC TOTALS:** 0+1 appearances / 0 goals

**Brendan was signed by Peter Reid from Rivervalley Rangers, a team based just north of Dublin, a couple of months after playing in the Irish U17 team in a UEFA tournament in Spain and helping the U16 team win their first European Championship final.**

Andy Reid played alongside McGill in both teams. Speeding down the wing and crossing on the run for Kevin Kyle to convert on a frequent basis at Under 18 level, right-winger McGill looked like he would have a first-team career more substantial than the 45 minutes he got in a League Cup second leg tie where Sunderland were already 5-0 up on aggregate when he was introduced. Brendan had been an unused sub in the first leg, but that was as far as he got.

Loaned to Carlisle from September to April the following season, he made 27+1 third-tier appearances scoring against Leyton Orient and Lincoln City as a teammate of former Sunderland reserve keeper Luke Weaver. Making the move permanent at the end of the season, McGill made 101+16 appearances in total for the Cumbrians, scoring 14 times.

In 2006 he crossed the border to Gretna with whom he won the Scottish First Division in his first season when he scored twice on his debut in a 6-0 opening-day win over Hamilton, but added just a further 5+2 league appearances. In 2007-08 he made 15+5 SPL appearances scoring against Motherwell, but after Gretna finished bottom and over-stretched themselves financially he was one of 40 people released.

Returning to Ireland McGill joined Bohemians, debuting as a sub at Galway. Alongside former Sunderland defender Mark Rossiter, Brendan won the FAI Cup in 2008, coming on as a sub as Derry City were beaten on penalties but after two goals in just six league games he joined Conference National club Barrow where he played 17 times without scoring. Brendan went back to Ireland to play 33 and 36 games for Drogheda and Shelbourne, scoring three goals and one goal respectively.

## McGINLEY, John

**POSITION:** Outside-left

**BIRTHPLACE:** Rowlands Gill, Co Durham

**DATE OF BIRTH:** 11/06/1959

**HEIGHT:** 6' 2" **WEIGHT:** 13st 8lbs

**SIGNED FROM:** Gateshead, 05/01/1982

**DEBUT:** v Stoke City, H, 10/02/1982

**LAST MATCH:** v Notts County, H, 27/02/1982

**MOVED TO:** Gateshead, 20/05/1982

**TEAMS:** Ashington, Gateshead, Sunderland, Gateshead, Charleroi, Nairn County, Lincoln City, Rotherham United, Hartlepool United (L), Lincoln City, Doncaster Rovers, Boston United

**SAFC TOTALS:** 3 appearances / 0 goals

**There was quite a stir when tall, gangly winger John McGinley was plucked from Gateshead to play in the top-flight in 1982. Manager Alan Durban gave the 22-year-old a debut at home to Stoke. Sunderland lost that without scoring, as they did to Swansea on the second of McGinley's three first-team appearances, although a point was earned in his final game, another home match, this time with Notts County.**

After his brief flirtation with professional football, McGinley returned to the Heed, for an agreed buy-back fee of a third of the original £3,000 transfer, before moving to Belgium the following year with Charleroi. He then had a short stint in Scotland with Nairn County before Lincoln City offered him a chance in September 1984.

It was at Sincil Bank that McGinley enjoyed a notable Football League career. He went on to make 150 league appearances scoring 33 goals. These were across two spells separated by a stint with Rotherham (1+1 app) and a loan at Hartlepool where he played twice. After leaving Lincoln for the last time in 1989, having helped the Imps win the Conference, John ended his playing days with a brief stint at Doncaster Rovers followed by a successful spell at Boston United where he was top scorer in 1990.

## McGIVEN, Michael (Mick)

**POSITION:** Midfielder

**BIRTHPLACE:** Kenton, Newcastle, Northumberland

**DATE OF BIRTH:** 07/02/1951

**HEIGHT:** 5' 10½" **WEIGHT:** 11st 4lbs

**SIGNED FROM:** Newcastle Juniors, 01/07/1966

**DEBUT:** v Coventry City, H, 09/08/1969

**LAST MATCH:** v Hull City, A 03/11/1973

**MOVED TO:** West Ham United, 22/12/1973
Loaned from 29/11/1973

**TEAMS:** Sunderland, West Ham United

**SAFC TOTALS:** 119+8 appearances / 12 goals

**An excellent player who may well have been part of the 1973 FA Cup-winning side, but for an injury sustained in the third-round replay. He returned from injury late in the season but was unable to wrestle the shirt for the show-piece game from Micky Horswill who had done so well during the cup run. McGiven had won a cup with Sunderland, playing all nine games as the FA Youth Cup was lifted in 1969.**

Debuting on the opening day of the following season, Mick was the only ever-present as the club suffered its second-ever relegation, the first of his four goals that term equalising

a George Best effort at Old Trafford. He recovered from a broken leg sustained against Luton on Halloween in 1970, but having lost his place at Sunderland following that 1973 injury, he moved on to West Ham United at the end of the calendar year, modestly batting off suggestions that the Hammers signed him to replace Bobby Moore. Nonetheless, after four games alongside England's World Cup-winning captain. McGiven did take over Moore's number six shirt. Playing alongside his Sunderland youth cup-winning teammate Keith Coleman, McGiven made 21 appearances in his first season at Upton Park before injury ruled him out from April 1974 until February 1976 when he returned in a London derby with Tottenham. He went on to play 52+3 games for the Hammers. Two of these were in Europe against FC Den Haag as West Ham were en-route to the final of the European Cup-Winners' cup in 1975-76. Two seasons earlier, he had been an unused sub in three of Sunderland's four games in the same competition.

Having retired from playing, McGiven coached at West Ham until 1990. There was then a nine-month stint coaching at Chelsea before he linked up with his old West Ham boss John Lyall at Ipswich. After almost two years coaching at Portman Road Mick took over as manager from July 1992 until December 1994. There followed six months as assistant manager at Luton Town in 1995 before 25 years' worth of service at Chelsea where Mick held a variety of coaching and scouting roles during an era in which the club was transformed. His son Paul worked as a fitness coach at West Ham and then moved to assist with scouting duties at Chelsea.

McGiven's brother Ross was a junior at Newcastle United during the 1960s, but never played first-team football. Sunderland remained Mick's first love and he was proud to accept a joint award of Freedom of the City in January 2022 as part of the group of players who played in the early rounds of the 1973 FA Cup triumph.

## McGORIAN, Isaac Moore (Ike)

**POSITION:** Full-back

**BIRTHPLACE:** Silksworth, Co Durham

**DATE OF BIRTH:** 19/10/1901 - 14/10/1978

**HEIGHT:** 5' 11" **WEIGHT:** 11st 3lbs

**SIGNED FROM:** Silksworth Colliery, 01/04/1924

**DEBUT:** v Newcastle United, A, 17/10/1925

**LAST MATCH:** v Cardiff City, A, 21/04/1928

**MOVED TO:** Notts County, 15/02/1929

**TEAMS:** Silksworth Colliery, Sunderland, Notts County, Carlisle United, Coleraine, Shotton Colliery, Thurnscoe Victoria

**INTERNATIONAL:** North of England XI, Griqualand West

**SAFC TOTALS:** 23 appearances / 1 goal

**One of ten children, McGorian succeeded in breaking into the Sunderland side of the twenties after impressing in local football. The red and whites were top of the table when wing-half 'Ike' was given his debut in a goalless derby at Newcastle in 1925.**

In 1926 he was selected to play at right-half for a North of England XI to face an FA XI but after several years on the fringes of the side McGorian left Sunderland in 1929 to join the other Magpies of Notts County, the team he had scored his solitary Sunderland goal against. He was better in red and white than black and white and after just one game in a year returned north with Carlisle.

There would be just three appearances for the Brunton Park outfit before Ike had a month-long trial with Coleraine and then dropped into non-league football prior to emigrating to South Africa in 1937. By this time Sunderland were FA Cup holders having been league champions a year earlier and Isaac had been Best Man at the wedding of fellow Silksworth lad Bobby Gurney, hero of both triumphs.

Having worked down the pit as a youngster before becoming a footballer, after his professional career McGorian returned to mining, this time as a diamond miner with De Beers. Although he was in his late thirties Isaac continued to play football in Africa and even captained Griqualand West against an FA Touring team in 1939. The tourists included Sunderland 'keeper Johnny Mapson in their party, winning 10-1. Thirteen years later McGorian would enjoy another reunion when as FA Cup holders Newcastle toured South Africa and Isaac met up with Stan Seymour, now United's manager and a former opponent in Wear-Tyne derbies.

Having met his wife-to-be Mary Emma Engelsman in Kimberly, Isaac married on 31 August 1940, a momentous day in which he left by train to take up a job as a timberman and live in Northern Rhodesia at the Roan and Antelope copper mine in Luanshya. Isaac remained active in sport, winning many bowls competitions and as a skilled billiards and snooker player, once took on world champion Horace Lindrum in an exhibition match in Modderfontein, South Africa.

The McGorians started their family as they enjoyed a somewhat nomadic lifestyle, briefly moving back to Kimberly before heading back to Northern Rhodesia; where the ex-Sunderland player took up a job at a copper mine in Nchanga, and later moving to Salisbury, still in Rhodesia. There, Isaac became a security officer at the airport.

By now, Isaac's son Laurence was making a name for himself. Having become an army captain, it was during a visit to a remote village that Ike's son came under rebel attack. Hearing a baby screaming, he risked his life under gun-fire to enter a blazing hut to find the baby whose parents had been shot dead. Again risking his life as he ran clear with the screaming child, he not only took the baby back to camp, but made arrangements to adopt the orphan.

Hearing about the heroics of Laurence McGorian, President Kuanda, who had become the first President of Zambia (formerly part of Northern Rhodesia), went to visit him. Kuanda, invited the son of the one-time Sunderland half-back to serve as his personal bodyguard, in addition to awarding him a medal for his bravery. McGorian's conscientious and reliability, qualities stemming from his Silksworth-born father led to him also being detailed to be a bodyguard of Nelson Mandela. Another relative, Isaac's nephew Joseph McGorian became President of Solihull Borough FC.

## McGREGOR, George Wilson

**POSITION:** Inside-right

**BIRTHPLACE:** Glasgow, Lanarkshire

**DATE OF BIRTH:** 17/11/1910 - 31/01/1982

**HEIGHT:** 5' 8" **WEIGHT:** 10st 12lbs

**SIGNED FROM:** St Mirren, 14/05/1929

**DEBUT:** v Portsmouth, A, 14/09/1929

**LAST MATCH:** v Portsmouth, A, 14/09/1929

**MOVED TO:** Norwich City, 27/05/1931

**TEAMS:** Saltcoats Victoria, St Mirren, Sunderland, Norwich City, Glasgow Benburb, India of Inchinnan

**INTERNATIONAL:** North of England XI

**SAFC TOTALS:** 1 appearance / 0 goals

**Signed by Johnny Cochrane who he had played five games for at St Mirren in 1927-28 (scoring once), McGregor played just once for Sunderland. He then had a six-month spell with Norwich before closing out his career in Scottish Junior football.**

Note that in Scotland, junior football refers to a level below the senior game and not necessarily youth football. George ended his playing career at the grandly-titled India of Inchinnan club which was a works team for the India Tyre & Rubber company based in the small Renfrewshire village.

## McGUIGAN, James (Jimmy)

**POSITION:** Winger

**BIRTHPLACE:** Glasgow, Lanarkshire

**DATE OF BIRTH:** 01/03/1924 - 30/03/1988

**HEIGHT:** 5' 11" **WEIGHT:** 11st 4lbs

**SIGNED FROM:** Hamilton Academical, 05/06/1947

**DEBUT:** v Stoke City, A, 20/03/1948

**LAST MATCH:** v Charlton Athletic, A, 30/10/1948

**MOVED TO:** Stockport County, 12/05/1949

**TEAMS:** Hamilton Academical, Sunderland, Stockport County, Crewe Alexandra, Rochdale

**SAFC TOTALS:** 3 appearances / 1 goal

**James McGuigan played shortly after the Second World War, scoring with a left-foot shot from the edge of the box in a 5-2 win at Sheffield United in September 1948, the middle one of his three first-team games.**

McGuigan had come to Sunderland in 1947 after playing for Hamilton during the war. Although he managed just three appearances for Sunderland, he played 323 league games, 207 of which were for Crewe. McGuigan was a firm favourite at Gresty Road as a player between 1950 and '56.

After playing for Stockport and Rochdale, he went on to manage for over two decades. After a couple of years at Rochdale he returned to Crewe in June 1959, initially as trainer, before managing the club from June 1960 to November '64. In 1963, he steered Alexandra to their first-ever promotion, going up from Division Four. He went on to also manage Grimsby, Chesterfield - where he won promotion in 1970 - Rotherham and Stockport, before coaching Sheffield United from 1983 to 1987, spending much of that period working with manager Ian Porterfield.

## McGUIRE, Douglas John

**POSITION:** Winger

**BIRTHPLACE:** Bathgate, West Lothian

**DATE OF BIRTH:** 06/09/1967

**HEIGHT:** 5' 8" **WEIGHT:** 11st 0lbs

**SIGNED FROM:** Celtic, 07/03/1988, on loan

**DEBUT:** v York City, A, 26/03/1988

**LAST MATCH:** v York City, A, 26/03/1988

**MOVED TO:** Celtic, 08/04/1988, end of loan

**TEAMS:** Celtic, Dumbarton (L), Sunderland (L), Coventry City, Cumnock Juniors, Queen of the South, Stranraer, Albion Rovers, Irvine Meadow, Ardeer Thistle, Irvine Meadow, Ardrossan Winton Rovers, Dalry Thistle

**INTERNATIONAL:** Scotland Youth

**SAFC TOTALS:** 1+0 appearances / 0 goals

**Doug McGuire's only appearance as a loan player during the 1987-88 third-division promotion season was in a defeat at York when he was replaced by fellow debutant Colin Pascoe who scored and went on to become a Roker regular.**

On McGuire's only other venture into English football he had an equally unsuccessful time at Coventry. The Sky Blues paid Celtic £40,000 for him in August 1988 after a trial in which McGuire was outstanding in a friendly against Gloucester. It was only after joining Coventry that Doug discovered he had glandular fever, an illness that delayed his debut by a calendar year. When it came (as a sub at Arsenal) it was one of only 1+3 times he turned out for the midlands club before being released in November 1990 and returning to Scotland.

Considered a hot prospect as a youngster, McGuire joined Celtic while still at school, St Michael's Academy in Kilwinning, the school that had produced Bobby Lennox and Lou Macari. McGuire put pen to paper as a 13-year-old to the disappointment of Liverpool, Manchester United, Aberdeen and St Mirren. Debuting as a sub at home to Falkirk in November 1986, he came on with Celtic trailing 2-1 and set up two goals as they came back to win 4-2. The following September he had another notable game away to Borussia Dortmund, but made just four appearances for the club.

After returning to Scotland his most notable contribution was to score a hat-trick of penalties in a game for Albion Rovers against Arbroath in August 1996. That was the first such occurrence in Scotland and was not equalled until Paul Hartley did so for Aberdeen against Hamilton on the opening day of the 2010-11 season. After spending the latter part of his playing days with clubs in Dumfries and Galloway and on the Ayrshire Junior circuit, he became player/manager of Ardeer Thistle in February 2004 and had a second spell as manager there in November 2009.

## McINALLY, Bernard (Tommy)

**POSITION:** Inside-left

**BIRTHPLACE:** Barrhead, Renfrewshire

**DATE OF BIRTH:** 18/12/1899 - 29/12/1955

**HEIGHT:** 5' 8½" **WEIGHT:** 12st 0lbs

**SIGNED FROM:** Celtic, 25/05/1928

**DEBUT:** v Burnley, A, 25/08/1928

**LAST MATCH:** v Aston Villa A, 28/09/1929

**MOVED TO:** Bournemouth & Boscombe Athletic, 11/11/1929

**TEAMS:** St Mungo's Academy, Croy Celtic, St Anthony's, Barrhead, Celtic, Third Lanark, Celtic, Sunderland, Bournemouth & Boscombe Athletic, Morton, Derry City, Coleraine, Armadale, Nithsdale Wanderers

**INTERNATIONAL:** Scotland

**SAFC TOTALS:** 36 appearance / 3 goals

**Tommy McInally appears to have been something akin to a pre-war 'Shack'. He only played three dozen games for Sunderland but is revered at Celtic, albeit with the caveat that students of the Glasgow club feel he should have achieved much more. Willie Maley managed Celtic for 43 years as well as being a Scotland international himself. Famously when asked, he remarked, "Best player? Why that was Tom McInally!"**

McInally scored four hat-tricks in his first eight games for Celtic, including one on his debut against Clydebank on 16 August 1919. He scored 39 times in his first season and went on to score a total of 127 goals in 213 games across two spells at the club. Like Len Shackleton though, statistics barely begin to scratch the surface the story. In an age of heavy footballs and often heavier pitches, his ball control was apparently superb, he was fast (indeed a noted sprinter), and evidently could score prolifically. But above all this, he was a showman who loved to play to the crowd, regardless of the fact this was sometimes to the exasperation of his teammates and manager.

Equally, his fondness for booze gave him weight problems with his weight varying considerably throughout his career. It was when his weight caused him to be on the receiving end of a host of derogatory nicknames that Celtic agreed to sell him to Sunderland. Indeed, reporting on his debut for Sunderland the Journal noted that, "McInally needs some hard training to get his weight down". He was also known for his wit, once telling a centre-half who said he would eat him that, 'At least that will get some football into you", while he was renowned for hating anyone swearing. During his second spell with Celtic, McInally was twice capped by Scotland, playing in 4-0 and 3-0 wins over Northern Ireland and Wales in February and October 1926.

A year before coming to Sunderland, McNally had been virtually ever-present for Celtic, scoring in the Scottish Cup final as Celtic beat East Fife at Hampden in April 1927.

McInally moved to SAFC as had his Celtic left-wing partner Adam McLean, as Johnny Cochrane wasted no time in signing McInally after becoming Sunderland's manager. Tommy scored with a tremendous drive from a free-kick in his second home game, but there would be only two more goals with all but four of his appearances coming in his first season of 1928-29 as Sunderland finished fourth in the top flight.

Known as 'Tommy Mac' or 'Snally,' he had a brother called Arthur who also played for St Mirren and Dunfermline amongst others while another brother John, played for Abercorn.

As a boy with Croy Celtic Tom scored a debut goal with his hand on the blind side of the referee and continued to make a name for himself with his outrageous talent after joining 'The Ants' - St Anthony's in Govan. It was during this period that he turned down Manchester City amongst others before joining Celtic for the first time. A league title-winner in both of his spells with Celtic - in 1921-22 and 1925-26 - in between he had three years with Third Lanark from September 1922 after Celtic lost patience with his waywardness only to eventually bring him back.

Following his time at Sunderland, McInally spent a year with Bournemouth and Boscombe Athletic helping them to a mid-table finish in Division Three South. Returning to Scotland, he had seven games with Morton before playing in Ireland and then finishing his playing days with Armadale near his birthplace, and finally Nithsdale Wanderers in Sanquhar in south west Scotland. Tommy later scouted for Celtic, occasionally supplied pieces to newspapers, and frequented nightclubs - sometimes in employment as a professional singer.

He died at the age of 56 having never conquered his over fondness for alcohol. Tommy McInally is not a big name at Sunderland, but in terms of sheer footballing ability, he is one of the most naturally talented players to have ever worn the red and white stripes.

'Celtic Bad Bhoy' by David Potter, published in 2009, investigated McInally's birth and death and concluded he was born Bernard McInally to Francis McInally and Annie nee Slaven and that was the name on his death certificate. An early document had him as Thomas Bernard McInally with the Thomas crossed out and replaced with John. His death was reported by his brother, Arthur.

## McINROY, Albert

**POSITION:** Goalkeeper

**BIRTHPLACE:** Preston, Lancashire

**DATE OF BIRTH:** 23/04/1901 - 07/01/1985

**HEIGHT:** 5' 11" **WEIGHT:** 13st 2lbs

**SIGNED FROM:** Leyland, 07/05/1923
and Newcastle United, 25/06/1934

**DEBUT:** v Manchester City, H, 29/09/1923

**LAST MATCH:** v Aston Villa, A, 28/09/1929

**MOVED TO:** Newcastle United, 03/10/1929
and Leeds United, 02/05/1935

**TEAMS:** Upper Walton, Cupull Central, High Walton United, Preston North End, Great Harwood, Leyland, Sunderland, Newcastle United, Sunderland, Leeds United, Gateshead, Stockton (WW2)

**INTERNATIONAL:** England

**SAFC TOTALS:** 227 appearance / 0 goals

**Despite the great tradition of goalkeepers at Sunderland, Albert McInroy is the only goalkeeper to be capped by England while with Sunderland (to June 2022). Johnny Mapson gained recognition on an FA tour of South Africa, Jim Montgomery won Under 23 caps and sat on the bench for England while Jordan Pickford's full caps came after leaving the Lads.**

McInroy was at Sunderland during the 1920s being the regular goalkeeper as Sunderland finished third in three of his first four seasons. Known as 'Albert the Great,' during his third campaign on Wearside, he won his one England cap alongside Sunderland teammate Warney Cresswell in a 3-3 draw with Ireland at Anfield. (incidentally, the last occasion Sunderland had two players in the England side until 1999 when Kevin Phillips and Mickey Gray played against Hungary) The previous February McInroy had also played for England v 'The Rest' (alongside former Sunderland reserve Jimmy Seed). The game - which finished 2-2 - was abandoned after 63 minutes due to a waterlogged pitch at Manchester City's Maine Road.

A Lancastrian, Albert was born Albert Pye, his mother marrying Walter McInroy when Albert was seven. He played schoolboy football as an outside-left and after becoming a goalkeeper played in the Preston and District and West Lancashire Leagues before signing amateur forms for Preston North End in 1921-22. Around this time his employment was in the Leyland Rubber Works and the Co-op in Preston.

Barely a week after the first-ever Wembley cup final in 1923 Sunderland signed McInroy in the unusual circumstances of signing him in a toilet in Manchester. Sunderland's Manchester scout Harry Bedford knew McInroy's contract with Leyland was about to run out and approached Albert in New Brighton a day before. Aware that other clubs were looking to sign him, a plot was arranged that they would meet with Sunderland manager Bob Kyle in the toilets of the Grand Hotel in Manchester at midnight. McInroy duly signed at two minutes past, receiving a £10 signing on fee while his club were paid £100.

At Sunderland he was a top-class goalie. Forty-five years to the day before Jim Montgomery's legendary Wembley double save, McInroy brought off a famous double save of his own, again in a tremendously important game. Never relegated until 1958, Sunderland would have gone down if they had lost at Middlesbrough on 5 May 1928. Sunderland won 3-0, but only after McInroy at his brilliant best repelled Boro with one save from point blank range from Jackie Carr seeing him miraculously push the ball onto the post and then block Bobbie Bruce's follow-up. After six years on Wearside McInroy moved to Tyneside. He debuted at Sheffield United in 1929 and won the FA Cup in 1932, playing all nine games of the cup run. However in 1934 after a dispute with the directors over a Benefit payment he was handed a transfer and returned to Sunderland after 160 appearances. During that last season at St James', in which the Magpies were relegated for the first time, he was unable to play after December after breaking his collarbone and also suffering a poisoned finger. Talk of possible amputation thankfully failed to materialise. In his first spell at Sunderland he had been known to play with his fingers strapped in an eel-skin if his hand was injured.

With Matt Middleton and Jimmy Thorpe preferred, McInroy only played a couple of reserve games at Sunderland in his season-long second spell. Had he stayed, given that Thorpe tragically died part way through the following campaign, perhaps McInroy might have been part of the Sunderland team who won the League and FA Cup in 1936 and 37?

However, Albert spent those two seasons with Leeds United. In 1935-36 he missed just one top-flight game for mid-table Leeds and took his total appearances with them to 71 the following year before returning to the north east with Gateshead who were a Football League side and with whom he added 71 league appearances until the outbreak of war. Retiring from the full-time game at this point, he played for Stockton and other local clubs as a war-time guest.

'Albert the Great' passed away in Sunderland after spending his post football career running pubs including The Crown in Gateshead, The Bacchus in Newcastle and the Havelock Arms at the top of Newbottle bank and living in Houghton. During the nineteen fifties and sixties, his son Harry played for Washington CW, Herrington and Washington Glebe.

## McINTOSH, Angus Munro

**POSITION:** Inside-forward / Centre-forward

**BIRTHPLACE:** Birkenhead, Cheshire

**DATE OF BIRTH:** 01/07/1884 - 18/01/1945

**HEIGHT:** 5' 7½" **WEIGHT:** 11st 0lbs

**SIGNED FROM:** Inverness Thistle, 09/03/1905

**DEBUT:** v Preston North End, H, 16/04/1906

**LAST MATCH:** v Blackburn Rovers, H, 17/10/1908

**MOVED TO:** Bury, 19/11/1908

**TEAMS:** Inverness Thistle, Sunderland, Bury, Aberdeen, Buckie Thistle

**SAFC TOTALS:** 46 appearance / 12 goals

**First appearing in the final four matches of 1905-06 in which he scored once, McIntosh made 24 appearances in his first and best full season. Playing mostly in the second half of the campaign, he netted seven times, three of them in the cup and at one point in three consecutive league games. In 1907-08, he returned four goals from 17 games before a final appearance in 1908-09, after which he joined Bury who he had scored his last Sunderland goal against in a 6-2 January 1908 victory.**

Angus added 13 goals in 236 first division games before returning to north-eastern Scotland where he had moved to as a six-year-old. He had started playing for a couple of minor sides before becoming an amateur with Inverness Thistle. McIntosh combined this with being an apprentice fitter at the railway works with his wish to complete his apprenticeship delaying his arrival at Roker Park by a year.

Having left Bury for Aberdeen, he scored close to one in three, netting 22 times in 65 Scottish League games up to 1914 after which he came to Newcastle, not as a footballer, but as a locomotive fitter proving his wisdom in completing his apprenticeship as a young man.

## McINTOSH, John William

**POSITION:** Centre-forward

**BIRTHPLACE:** Tow Law, Co Durham

**DATE OF BIRTH:** 23/04/1875 - 12/05/1951

**SIGNED FROM:** Tow Law, 01/02/1897

**DEBUT:** v Burnley, H, 02/03/1897

**LAST MATCH:** v Wolverhampton Wanderers, A, 13/11/1897

**MOVED TO:** South Shields, 10/03/1899

**TEAMS:** Pallion Star, Tow Law, Sunderland, South Shields

**SAFC TOTALS:** 2 appearances / 0 goals

**McIntosh - whose surname was actually Mackintosh, but was always spelled as McIntosh during his football career, joined Sunderland initially as an amateur in order to enable him to still play for Tow Law when not required by Sunderland.**

John signed professional forms five weeks after he played what turned out to be his last game for Sunderland. After joining South Shields in 1899, in the 1901 census he was given as a Mechanical Engineer living in Norton near Stockton and by 1911 he was married to the headteacher at Wynyard Park Church of England School. His son-in-law was a master butcher and John appears to have helped in this business, as in 1939 he was listed as a retired butcher living in the same house in Durham.

## McIVER, Frederick

**POSITION:** Midfielder

**BIRTHPLACE:** Birtley, Co Durham

**DATE OF BIRTH:** 14/02/1952

**HEIGHT:** 5' 7" **WEIGHT:** 11st 0lbs

**SIGNED FROM:** School, 01/07/1968

**DEBUT:** v Sheffield Wednesday, A, 18/09/1971

**LAST MATCH:** v Sheffield Wednesday, A, 18/09/1971

**MOVED TO:** King's Park (South Africa), 01/05/1972

**TEAMS:** Sunderland, King's Park, Racing Jet de Bruxelles, Sheffield Wednesday, Gateshead United

**INTERNATIONAL:** England semi-professional

**SAFC TOTALS:** 1 appearance / 0 goals

**Fred McIver always looked good enough to have played more than one game. He was selected in the 17-strong party that took part in the Anglo-Italian Cup in 1970 and was an unused substitute in the two away games. His solitary appearance came in a disappointing 3-0 defeat at Hillsborough and the player who had appeared in the final and semi-final of the FA Youth Cup two years earlier never got another chance.**

Having moved to a club in South Africa at the end of the season, and a year before Sunderland won the FA Cup, he must have looked on from the other side of the world and wondered as his old colleagues reached the FA Cup final on the same ground he had made his one first-team appearance, alongside seven of what would be the cup final XI.

Ironically, Hillsborough became his home ground when Fred returned to England after playing in South Africa and Belgium. At Sheffield Wednesday, McIver would be a teammate of future Sunderland manager and assistant Ken Knighton and Peter Eustace as well as future Roker centre-forward Rodger Wylde. Fred started the first nine games of the 1974-75 season with the first one he missed being against Sunderland. He was in the side though for a 3-0 defeat on Wearside that mirrored his Sunderland debut.

Going on to play 21+2 times (plus a couple of cup ties) as Steve Burtenshaw's team were relegated from the second division in his second season at Wednesday. He also played for Len Ashurst, totalling 16+1 games in his second and last season. Returning to the north east with Gateshead in August 1976, McIver was a teammate of Ron Guthrie and represented England at semi-professional level in May 1977 before retiring to become a milkman.

## McKAY, Robert McIness (Bob)

**POSITION:** Inside-forward

**BIRTHPLACE:** Govan, Glasgow, Lanarkshire

**DATE OF BIRTH:** 02/09/1900 - 24/05/1977

**HEIGHT:** 5' 6½" **WEIGHT:** 11st 2lbs

**SIGNED FROM:** Newcastle United, 03/10/1928

**DEBUT:** v Manchester City, A, 06/10/1928

**LAST MATCH:** v Middlesbrough, A, 18/10/1930

**MOVED TO:** Charlton Athletic, 02/12/1930

**TEAMS:** Vale of Clyde, Parkhead, Neilston Victoria, Morton, Rangers, Newcastle United, Sunderland, Charlton Athletic, Bristol Rovers, Newport County

**INTERNATIONAL:** Scotland

**SAFC TOTALS:** 51 appearances / 17 goals

**Bobby McKay arrived in a swap deal for left-back Robert Thomson, who like McKay, won one cap for Scotland. McKay played against Wales in October 1927, two years after representing the Scottish League against the Irish League during his time with Rangers for whom he played 29 times, scoring eight goals. Previously a Scottish Cup winner with Morton, he helped to beat Rangers in the 1922 final. It remains the only major trophy of Morton for whom McKay played 142 times, scoring 28 times.**

McKay scored a hat-trick on his Newcastle debut in November 1926 as Newcastle went on to win what remains their most recent league title (to 2022). In December 1927, his second Magpie hat-trick came in a stunning five-minute spell against Derby. He started well at Sunderland, scoring six goals in his first six games, including a brace as his old Magpies team were thrashed 5-2 at Roker. Playing alongside Dave Halliday who set a club record 43 league goals in that 1928-29 season, McKay had a hand in many of them and ended his first season as second top scorer with 15 goals from 35 games.

It was to be by far McKay's best season on Wearside. There would be just two more goals in another 16 games before he moved on to Charlton in December 1930 (52/8) followed by a move to Bristol Rovers just under two years later for a quarter of the £1,220 the Addicks paid for him. It was good value as the veteran plundered 20 goals in 106 games for the Pirates. In June 1935, he made his final move as a player, joining Newport County where he scored three times in 18 appearances before taking up a post as manager of Dundee United.

The outbreak of World War Two meant he managed just four games for the Terrors before his contract was terminated. After the war, he returned to management with Ballymena United from June 1947 to June 1949, winning the County Antrim Shield in 1948. He returned to Charlton as a scout and following his retirement from football became the owner of a billiards hall in his native Glasgow. As a boy he had won the Scottish Juvenile Cup, the Glasgow Junior Cup and the Glasgow North Eastern Cup with Parkhead. He also became a Freemason during his time with Newcastle, being initiated into Lodge Shettleston Saint John No 128 on 25 May 1926.

## McKENZIE, Archibald (Archie)

**POSITION:** Inside-forward

**BIRTHPLACE:** Greenock, Renfrewshire

**DATE OF BIRTH:** 1875 - Unknown

**HEIGHT:** 5' 7" **WEIGHT:** 11st 0lbs

**SIGNED FROM:** Millwall Athletic, 13/05/1895

**DEBUT:** v Burnley, A, 09/09/1895

**LAST MATCH:** v Wolverhampton Wanderers, H, 21/09/1895

**MOVED TO:** Millwall Athletic, 27/06/1896

**TEAMS:** Woodvale, Clyde, Millwall Athletic, Sunderland, Millwall Athletic, WBA, Portsmouth, Dumbarton, Third Lanark

**SAFC TOTALS:** 2 appearances / 1 goal

**A scorer in a 2-2 draw with Wolves on his only home appearance for the reigning league (and World) champions, McKenzie may have actually signed from Everton rather than Millwall Athletic. The Toffees seem to have held his registration when the Football League approved his transfer to Sunderland.**

He had played for Millwall Athletic 23 days before signing for Sunderland, being ever-present and top-scorer with 17 goals in 16 games as they won the first-ever season of the Southern League in 1894-95. He had also played in all five of Millwall's English (FA) Cup games, scoring four in four qualifying games before playing in a first-round defeat to Sheffield United.

Millwall retained the Southern League in the season McKenzie was with Sunderland and they were pleased to welcome him back whereupon he found things harder going as his club finished second. He missed one of their 20 league games, but this time only scored seven to which he added six in 8+1 United League games (a league which his club won) and four in four Cup games, including strikes against Woolwich Arsenal and Wolves. That goal against Wolves may have helped attract Wanderers near-neighbours West Bromwich Albion who gave Archibald another shot at the Football League when signing him in July 1897.

In his first season he was ever-present playing all 33 league and cup games. He only scored three goals - but two of them were in a 2-2 draw at home to ...you've guessed it, Sunderland. After six goals in 22 games in his second season at Albion he was one of four players suspended sine die in late March 1899 by the club's directors for persistently breaking training regulations. In October Archie joined Portsmouth, where he failed to make a first-team appearance during his four months, before finishing his career back in Scotland, with Dumbarton and Third Lanark, where his senior career had begun with seven goals in 27 games for Clyde between 1892 and 1894, after he joined Clyde from Woodvale.

## McKENZIE, Thomas

**POSITION:** Inside / Centre-forward

**BIRTHPLACE:** Glasgow, Lanarkshire

**DATE OF BIRTH:** 1883 - Unknown

**HEIGHT:** 5' 8½" **WEIGHT:** 11st 8lbs

**SIGNED FROM:** Third Lanark, 18/10/1905

**DEBUT:** v Woolwich Arsenal, A 21/10/1905

**LAST MATCH:** v Wednesday, A, 07/04/1906

**MOVED TO:** Plymouth Argyle, 16/05/1906

**TEAMS:** Petershill, Third Lanark, Sunderland, Plymouth Argyle, Portsmouth, Glossop North End, QPR, West Stanley

**SAFC TOTALS:** 8 appearances / 1 goal

**An engineer by trade, McKenzie joined Sunderland from Scottish League champions Third Lanark for the considerable sum of £350 in October 1905. Playing alongside Hugh Wilson, a leading member of SAFC's 'Team of All The Talents' of the 1890s, McKenzie had been joint top scorer with eleven goals in 21 games for Third Lanark as the title was won in 1904 while in 1905 he had played in the final as Third Lanark beat Rangers in the Scottish Cup final at Hampden.**

Debuting for Sunderland in defeat at Woolwich Arsenal a few days after signing he suffered an early injury and had to go off after ten minutes. He returned to hit the winner against Everton on his second home appearance but it would be his only goal in eight appearances in a disappointing season where Sunderland finished 14th, a drop of nine places on the previous term.

After barely half a season he moved on to Plymouth. A goal on his home debut against New Brompton (who became Gillingham) in September 1906 got Thomas off to a good start as he went on to get a goal for every one of his 20 Southern League games, although he failed to find the net in seven Western League appearances or in an FA Cup defeat to Millwall.

After a single season with Argyle McKenzie moved to second division Glossop North End where he disappeared from football after scoring once in six games. It was a glorious season for Glossop who reached the FA Cup quarter-final where they went down in a replay to eventual finalists Bristol City. At QPR, he debuted in September 1908 at West Ham United and played nine Southern League games scoring once.

## McLAIN, Thomas (Tommy)

**POSITION:** Half-back

**BIRTHPLACE:** Linton, Northumberland

**DATE OF BIRTH:** 19/01/1922 - December 1995

**HEIGHT:** 5' 9" **WEIGHT:** 10st 8lbs

**SIGNED FROM:** Ashington, 15/08/1946

**DEBUT:** v Portsmouth, A, 05/10/1946

**LAST MATCH:** v Charlton Athletic, A, 17/11/1951

**MOVED TO:** Northampton Town, 03/07/1952

**TEAMS:** Netherton Juniors, Ashington, Sunderland, Northampton Town, Headington United, Wellingborough Town

**SAFC TOTALS:** 73 appearances / 1 goal

**McLain was an ex-RAF pilot who had served in Ceylon (now Sri Lanka) during World War Two during which time he played alongside Tommy Reynolds and Ken Oliver. Prior to joining up he had played a few games for Ashington in 1940 whilst working at Linton Colliery.**

A speed merchant who had been a noted sprinter in his youth, Tommy was on the fringe of the side in the later forties and

early fifties having been recommended to manager Bill Murray by his former RAF sergeant from Ceylon. Appearing in six seasons, his best campaigns were in 1947-48 and 1950-51 when he reached 20 appearances. His solitary goal came on the opening day of his last campaign in 1951-52 when he scored in an opening-day 4-3 win at Derby.

In October 1951 Tommy passed an FA coaching exam and accepted a couple of appointments through the Sunderland Education Committee for schools and community centre coaching. After six years on Wearside McLain joined third division south side Northampton Town then moved to Oxford to play for Headington United. He finished his career as player manager for Wellingborough Town in 1957-58.

## McLATCHIE, Colin Campbell

**POSITION:** Inside-left / Outside-left

**BIRTHPLACE:** New Cumnock, Ayrshire

**DATE OF BIRTH:** 02/11/1876 - 07/01/1952

**HEIGHT:** 5' 10" **WEIGHT:** 13st 7lbs

**SIGNED FROM:** Preston North End, 03/10/1898

**DEBUT:** v Wolverhampton Wanderers, A, 05/11/1898

**LAST MATCH:** v Blackburn Rovers, H, 25/10/1902

**MOVED TO:** Grimsby Town, 12/11/1902

**TEAMS:** Lanemark, Kilmarnock, New Cumnock United, Preston North End, Sunderland, Grimsby Town, Lanemark, Nithsdale Wanderers, Lanemark

**SAFC TOTALS:** 130 appearances / 33 goals

**A debutant during the opening season of Roker Park, McLatchie was a thick-set, physically strong winger who was a regular at the turn of the 20th century. He played 25 of the 34 league games in the title-winning season of 1901-02.**

Two years earlier he had been top scorer with ten goals and reached double figures again in 1900-01 when Sunderland narrowly missed out on the title. In a particular game at Bury in October 1900, Colin was so incensed with the referee giving a foul against him that he strongly argued and then deliberately kicked the ball away after the Bury player had placed it to take the free-kick.

On refusing to fetch the ball, the referee sent him off. However, Sunderland contrived to ensure that McLatchie avoided a ban from the FA by dropping him the following week and fining him, so instead of at least a two-week ban for the player, the FA actually praised the club for 'acting so promptly in such a vital matter pertaining to the welfare of the game'.

A coal-miner before and after his playing days, McLatchie started and finished his career with Lanemark, a junior club in his native Ayrshire named after the Lanemark Coal Company, that he had three spells with. Sunderland saw the best of Colin who played nine games each for Preston and Grimsby and just one for Kilmarnock.

## McLAUGHLAN, Alexander Donaldson (Sandy)

**POSITION:** Goalkeeper

**BIRTHPLACE:** Kilwinning, Ayrshire

**DATE OF BIRTH:** 17/07/1936 - 13/04/1990

**HEIGHT:** 5' 8" **WEIGHT:** 11st 8lbs

**SIGNED FROM:** Kilmarnock, 02/09/1964

**DEBUT:** v West Bromwich Albion, H, 02/09/1964

**LAST MATCH:** v West Bromwich Albion, H, 01/01/1966

**MOVED TO:** Kilmarnock, 27/06/1967

**TEAMS:** Ardeer Recreation, Kilmarnock, Sunderland, Kilmarnock, Troon Juniors

**INTERNATIONAL:** Scotland Under 23 and Scottish League

**SAFC TOTALS:** 46 appearances / 0 goals

**It was never proven, but always rumoured that Sandy McLaughlan never played for the Lads again after conceding five goals at home to WBA on New Year's Day 1966 because he was alleged to have celebrated Hogmanay more heartily than was strictly professional.**

WBA had also provided the opposition for Sandy's first game 16 months earlier, in the evening of the day that he signed. His first touch for Sunderland was to pick the ball out of the net, although on that occasion he was only beaten twice.

McLaughlan had been signed for £12,000 after 15-year-old Derek Forster had started the season in place of the injured Jim Montgomery in the first division campaign after SAFC's first-ever promotion. After conceding five goals in his tenth game at Nottingham Forest he was dropped for the fit-again Montgomery but returned later in the season and went on to make 33 league and cup appearances in his first season, but there were only 13 in his second campaign before moving on 18 months after his final appearance.

In October 1962 McLaughlan was a teammate of Andy Kerr as Kilmarnock lost 1-0 to Hearts at Hampden Park in the Scottish League Cup final. The following month he represented the Scottish League in a representative fixture with the Italian League which was lost 4-3. During his first spell with Killie, after joining from Ardeer Recreation who he had joined after playing army football for the Ayrshire Yeomanry, he played 77 times, but surpassed this with 103 games in his second spell at the club.

## McLAUGHLIN, Conor Gerard

**POSITION:** Right-back

**BIRTHPLACE:** Belfast, Northern Ireland

**DATE OF BIRTH:** 26/07/1991

**HEIGHT:** 6' 0" **WEIGHT:** 11st 2lbs

**SIGNED FROM:** Millwall, 01/07/2019

**DEBUT:** v Oxford United, H, 03/08/2019

**LAST MATCH:** v Northampton Town, H, 09/05/2021

**MOVED TO:** Contract ended, 30/06/2021

**TEAMS:** Preston North End, Shrewsbury Town (L), Fleetwood Town, Millwall, Sunderland, Fleetwood Town

**INTERNATIONAL:** Northern Ireland

**SAFC TOTALS:** 42+8 appearances / 0 goals

**In two seasons at the Stadium of Light, McLaughlin failed to impress in his first year when he often looked hesitant, but in his second season the player was much improved. Often asked to fill in at left-back or centre-back, he was never less than solid and it came as something of a surprise when he was one of seven senior players whose departure was announced on 25 May 2021. Conor never scored for Sunderland, but did hit the bar at Wembley after coming on as a sub in the Football League (Papa John's) Trophy in 2021.**

He began the following season as a free agent before returning to Fleetwood Town on 7 October 2021, returning to league action later that month but being forced to retire through injury the following April. McLaughlin made his league debut in November 2010 for Preston North End in a home Championship loss to Hull City. He went on to play 18+10 games for North End who also loaned him to Shrewsbury (4/0), before he was freed and signed for League Two Fleetwood.

Debuting in August 2012 in a League (Capital One) Cup home defeat by Nottingham Forest, he went on to win promotion with them via the Play-Offs in his second season. After beating a Burton team that included former Sunderland reserve Robbie Weir at Wembley, Conor made his international debut five days later for Northern Ireland against Uruguay who included future SAFC defender Sebastian Coates. He won the last six of his 43 full caps for Northern Ireland while with Sunderland.

Progress continued in his initial spell with Fleetwood where he played in the League One Play-Offs in 2017, lost 1-0 on aggregate to Bradford City. Despite that defeat Conor moved into the Championship that summer with a transfer to Millwall after 190+10 appearances and eight goals. As with Fleetwood, Nottingham Forest provided the opposition for his debut for the Lions for whom he made 34+3 appearances over two seasons, scoring his only goal in a London derby with QPR.

Younger brother Ryan was also capped by Northern Ireland and made over 50 appearances for each of Oldham and Rochdale while playing a handful of games for other clubs.

## McLAUGHLIN, Hugh

**POSITION:** Half-back

**BIRTHPLACE:** Castlederg, County Tyrone, Ireland

**DATE OF BIRTH:** 29/05/1868 - 01/04/1931

**SIGNED FROM:** North Sands Rovers, 06/10/1888

**DEBUT:** v Elswick Rangers, H, 27/10/1888

**LAST MATCH:** v Newcastle East End, 17/11/1888

**MOVED TO:** Newcastle East End, 14/11/1889

**TEAMS:** Whitefield, North Sands Rovers, Sunderland, Newcastle East End

**SAFC TOTALS:** 2 appearances / 0 goals

**Hugh McLaughlin (surname sometimes spelled McLauchlan or McLaughlan) is known to have played 24 games in 1888-89, but other than two English (FA) Cup ties listed above, the other game in these early years of the club were all friendlies/challenge matches.**

Prior to coming to Sunderland Hugh played for Whitefield, a Govan-based club in Glasgow, whilst working in a sawmill. After coming to Sunderland he worked in JL Thompson's shipyard and played for one of the shipyard teams; North Sands Rovers. Sunderland signed him after impressing in a trial game against (Sheffield) Wednesday on 6 October 1888. In 1889-90 he played representative football for County Durham.

After retiring from playing, Hugh moved to Belfast for a short time where he worked as a rivetter, but by the start of WW1 was back in Sunderland at JL Thompson's shipyard until his death aged 62.

## McLAUGHLIN, Jonathan Peter

**POSITION:** Goalkeeper

**BIRTHPLACE:** Edinburgh, Scotland

**DATE OF BIRTH:** 09/09/1987

**HEIGHT:** 6' 3" **WEIGHT:** 13st 11lbs

**SIGNED FROM:** Free agent, 25/06/2018

**DEBUT:** v Charlton Athletic, H, 04/08/2018

**LAST MATCH:** v Bristol Rovers, A, 10/03/2020

**MOVED TO:** Rangers, 01/07/2020

**TEAMS:** Harrogate Railway Athletic, Harrogate Town, Bradford City, Burton Albion, Hearts, Sunderland, Rangers (to July 2022)

**INTERNATIONAL:** Scotland

**SAFC TOTALS:** 89+1 appearances / 0 goals

**Goalkeeper having traditionally been a strong point of Sunderland, the club had struggled badly in that department in the season before McLaughlin's arrival when they had plummeted straight from the Premier League to League One. The general consensus of supporters was that had McLaughlin signed a year earlier, that second consecutive relegation may well have been avoided.**

Jon was not a spectacular goalkeeper able to hit the heights of a Montgomery or a Pickford, but he was a solid, reliable custodian not prone to regular mistakes. He gave the defence a new-found confidence in the man behind them as he was ever-present in the league in his first season when he became the second keeper (after Tony Norman) to play for Sunderland at Wembley twice, and the first to do so in the same season. This was in the final of the Football League (Checkatrade) Trophy and the League One Play-Off final. Defeats to Portsmouth on penalties and Charlton to a very late goal were not McLaughlin's fault.

He had made previous Wembley appearances. In 2013 he came on as a sub in the League Cup final for Bradford City after goalkeeper Matt Duke was sent off for Phil Parkinson's Bantams, who were beaten 5-0 by a Swansea side that included Ki-Sung-Yueng. McLaughlin conceded two of the goals, one a penalty the minute he went on. Later the same season he returned to keep a clean sheet as Bradford beat a Northampton team including Roy O'Donovan in the League Two Play-Off final.

Ever-present the following season for the Bantams (where he took his total to 137+1 appearances) McLaughlin moved on to Burton Albion where he missed just six league games in three years and won back-to-back promotions from League Two to the Championship in 2015 and 2016.

After 138 games for the Brewers, the Scot spent 2016-17 with Hearts, at one point keeping eight successive clean sheets including one against Celtic and two versus local rivals Hibs. Fifteen clean sheets in 37 games for Hearts led to an international debut (alongside Dylan McGeouch) in June 2018 where he played the first half as Scotland were beaten by a 13th-minute goal against Mexico.

McLaughlin came to Sunderland later that month and gained a second cap whilst at the club, keeping an untroubled clean sheet as San Marino were walloped 6-0 in October 2019. Five months later McLaughlin made his last appearance for SAFC in the season curtailed because of Covid, after which he moved to Rangers to compete for the number one shirt after rejecting a contract extension at the Stadium of Light. He did not concede a goal until his seventh game for Rangers and was unbeaten in twelve of his 14 games during his first season including a Europa League debut at Lech Poznan in a campaign in which Rangers were league champions.

## McLEAN, Adam

**POSITION:** Inside-forward / winger

**BIRTHPLACE:** Greenock, Renfrewshire

**DATE OF BIRTH:** 27/04/1898 - 29/06/1973

**HEIGHT:** 5' 6" **WEIGHT:** 11st 0lbs

**SIGNED FROM:** Celtic, 27/08/1928

**DEBUT:** v Blackburn Rovers, H 29/08/1928

**LAST MATCH:** v Blackburn Rovers, A, 20/09/1930

**MOVED TO:** Aberdeen, 16/10/1930

**TEAMS:** Broomhill YMCA, Anderston Benburb Juveniles, Anderston Thornbank, Celtic, Sunderland, Aberdeen, Partick Thistle

**INTERNATIONAL:** Scotland

**SAFC TOTALS:** 71 appearances / 16 goals

**One of the Scots signed by ex-St Mirren manager Johnny Cochrane when he came to Sunderland, at Roker Park McLean teamed up again with his former Celtic partner Tom McInally. McLean was not as gifted as McInally (few were), but was more reliable. Hailing from Greenock he was brought up in Belfast before returning to Scotland just before World War One and starting his senior football career with Celtic.**

A teenage debutant for Celtic in a draw at Dumbarton on 20 January 1917, McLean was a talented and tricky winger who had been converted from a centre-forward by Celtic who instead made him a major supply line to Jimmy McGrory - the all-time British top scorer. McLean was a major figure at Celtic throughout the 1920s with many supporters outraged when the Mcs of McLean and McInally were poached by Cochrane at Sunderland. McLean made 408 appearances and scored 138 goals (including the club's 2,000th) for Celtic with whom he won the league in 1918-19, 21-22 and 1925-26 as well as cup winner's medals in 1923, 1925 and 1927.

At Sunderland he scored on his debut and missed just two games in his first season of 1928-29 when Dave Halliday set Sunderland's seasonal scoring record (43) with McLean the provider of many as he had been for McGrory at Celtic. He remained a regular the following season but after just two games in 1930-31 returned to Scotland. After moving to Aberdeen McLean refused to participate in a match-fixing

scam, instead revealing the racket to manager Paddy Travis. He debuted at East Fife on 18 October 1930 and went on to score 26 goals in 84 league and cup games for the Dons.

A boyhood Partick Thistle supporter, Adam realised his dream to play for the club when he signed for the Jags on 25 July 1933, debuting on 12 August that year in a 7-3 win at Hamilton Academical where despite by now being 35, he still ran the show, scoring twice. However he only played eight times for the club, scoring one more goal. After a brief spell in 1936 coaching Brann in Norway, he did some scouting for Leicester City and then returned to Partick where he remained until well into the 1960s, serving as trainer and then assistant manager.

Considered by many to have been Celtic's finest-ever left-winger he was mainly kept out of the Scotland team by Rangers legend Alan Morton, but did win four caps. He made a scoring debut against Wales on Halloween in 1925 as a teammate of Billy Clunas. McLean also played in 4-0 and 3-0 wins over Northern Ireland and Wales in 1926 and was on the losing side for the only time in April 1927 when two Dixie Dean goals gave England a 2-1 win with McLean setting up the Scots goal for Morton. McLean also made three appearances for the Scottish League.

## McMAHON, Hugh

**POSITION:** Outside-left

**BIRTHPLACE:** Grangetown, Yorkshire

**DATE OF BIRTH:** 24/09/1909 - 30/10/1986

**HEIGHT:** 5' 7½" **WEIGHT:** 10st 8lbs

**SIGNED FROM:** QPR, 08/11/1937

**DEBUT:** v Grimsby Town, H, 13/11/1937

**LAST MATCH:** v Leeds United, H, 15/04/1939

**MOVED TO:** Hartlepools United, 02/11/1945

**TEAMS:** South Bank St Peter's, Sheffield Wednesday, Mexborough Athletic, Southend United, Reading, QPR, Sunderland, Consett (WW2 Guest), Hartlepools United (WW2 Guest), Darlington (WW2 Guest), Middlesbrough (WW2 Guest), York City (WW2 Guest), Hartlepools United, Rotherham United, Stockton

**SAFC TOTALS:** 8 appearances / 1 goal

**All but two of McMahon's first-team outings came in 1937-38 when he scored to earn a point at Bolton. An understudy to Eddie Burbanks following injury to the legendary Jimmy Connor, McMahon made a couple of further appearances the next season.**

Born on Teesside, Hugh worked his way through the teams of St Mary's School, Upton FC, South Bank St Peter's and had trials with Hartlepools (scoring four times in a reserve match in April 1932), Sheffield Wednesday and Derby County. He signed for the Owls but very quickly was sold to Mexborough Athletic for whom he scored 30 goals between joining in December 1932 and the end of the season. This caught the attention of Southend and he moved there in early June 1933.

Hugh's first league goals came as a hat-trick in late October at Swindon Town, but again after only one season he was on the move; this time to Reading. His next move was to QPR, in May 1936, and it was whilst there that Hugh attracted Sunderland's interest. Having debuted for QPR in a Division Three South fixture at Notts County on 12 September 1936 he went on to score five times in 45 games before the cash strapped club accepted a payment of £2,500 for him from the Wearsiders.

After playing for several teams during World War Two, McMahon joined Hartlepools on a free transfer in November 1945, by which time he was 36. He had first played for Hartlepools in a war-time game against Newcastle United in February 1940 and eventually totalled 63 games for the club, scoring 21 times. 31 of the games and eleven of the goals do not count in official records as they were war-time fixtures. Looking to prolong his war-interrupted career Hugh joined Rotherham when he was almost 38 and proceeded to score eight goals in 59 league games before retiring after a handful of games for Stockton in 1949-50, playing for his old Hartlepool teammate Billy Brown.

## McMANAMAN, Callum Henry

**POSITION:** Winger

**BIRTHPLACE:** Whiston, Liverpool

**DATE OF BIRTH:** 25/04/1991

**HEIGHT:** 5' 8½" **WEIGHT:** 11st 3lbs

**SIGNED FROM:** West Bromwich Albion, 31/08/2011

**DEBUT:** v Sheffield United, H, 09/09/2017

**LAST MATCH:** Fulham, A, 27/04/2018

**MOVED TO:** Wigan Athletic, 20/07/2018

**TEAMS:** Everton, Wigan Athletic, Blackpool (L), WBA, Sheffield Wednesday (L), Sunderland, Wigan Athletic, Luton Town, Melbourne Victory, Tranmere Rovers

**INTERNATIONAL:** England Under 20

**SAFC TOTALS:** 14+12 appearances / 1 goal

**Man of the Match in the FA Cup final in 2013 when Wigan Athletic sensationally beat Manchester City, Callum McManaman evidently had ability, but very little of it was seen at Sunderland. His one goal for the Black Cats in February 2018 was an injury time equaliser against Middlesbrough where his celebration focussed on taunting Boro boss Tony Pulis who McManaman felt should have played him more when the pair were at West Brom.**

McManaman could have had at least two goals in Sunderland colours but bizarrely handled the ball into goal when it seemed as easy to head it in a game against Reading in December 2017. Already cautioned, the offence saw him sent off. Almost half of his games for the Lads were as a sub and in what was a difficult time for the club, he failed to impress as Sunderland slipped to a second successive relegation.

Released by Everton as a teenager, Callum made his first-team bow with Wigan Athletic in 2009. In the winter of 2011-12, he scored twice in 9+5 games on loan to Blackpool and in Wigan's cup-winning, but relegation season of 2012-13, he scored six times in 30 appearances. Come January 2015, West Brom invested £4.75m in a player who had scored 17 times in 69+40 games for the Latics, but there would be only seven league starts for the Throstles where McManaman totalled 7+18 games without scoring.

Employment as a hoped-for impact-sub was also the name of his game during a loan at Sheffield Wednesday where ten of his twelve appearances were off the bench. This was even more the

## McMANAMAN, Callum (Continued)

case after his sojourn at Sunderland. Returning to Wigan, 21 of his 22 league appearances were as a sub, while at Luton he again made more appearances as a sub than a starter. In total his second spell at Wigan saw him play 3+21 games for one goal while at Luton his overall figures were 11+15/4.

From November 2020 until the following July, he played in Australia, scoring four goals in 18 games for Melbourne Victory before signing for Tranmere Rovers where he made a goalscoring debut against Walsall and went on to play alongside Sunderland loanee Josh Hawkes before being released in the summer of 2022.

## McMILLAN, James (Jim)

**POSITION:** Half-back

**BIRTHPLACE:** Alnwick, Northumberland

**DATE OF BIRTH:** 28/04/1863 - 02/09/1930

**SIGNED:** 1881

**DEBUT:** v Redcar, A, 08/11/1884

**LAST MATCH:** v Newcastle West End, A, 13/11/1886

**MOVED TO:** Retired in summer 1887

**TEAMS:** Sunderland

**SAFC TOTALS:** 3 appearances / 0 goals

**A significant figure in the early history of the club. A Northumbrian, McMillan had moved to Sunderland as a three-year-old and played for the club in the team's first three English (FA) Cup ties, all of which ended in defeat.**

James joined the club in 1881 as one of the first players not from the teaching profession and was captain from 1885 to his retirement in summer 1887. During the mid-1880s, he played a number of times for Durham County and later became a member of the Durham Football Association.

In 1888, he became a Sunderland AFC committee member and succeeded James Marr as the Chairman for the 1893-94 season. Throughout his playing career, and after he retired, James worked as a stone mason and ornamental sculptor, taking over the family business in Hudson Road from his father in 1888.

## McNAB, Alexander (Sandy)

**POSITION:** Half-back

**BIRTHPLACE:** Glasgow, Lanarkshire

**DATE OF BIRTH:** 27/12/1911 - 19/09/1962

**HEIGHT:** 5' 5½" **WEIGHT:** 10 st 6lbs

**SIGNED FROM:** Glasgow Pollok, 14/05/1932

**DEBUT:** v Aston Villa, 29/08/1932

**LAST MATCH:** v Bolton Wanderers, A, 19/02/1938

**MOVED TO:** West Bromwich Albion, 10/03/1938

**TEAMS:** Tuesday Waverley, Bridgeton Waverley, Glasgow Pollok, Sunderland, WBA, Nottingham Forest (WW2 Guest), Newport County (WW2 Guest), Northampton Town (WW2 Guest), Walsall (WW2 Guest), Newport County, Dudley Town, Northwich Victoria, Cradley Heath

**INTERNATIONAL:** Scotland

**SAFC TOTALS:** 113 appearances / 6 goals

**Despite competition for the left-half shirt from captain Alex Hastings, Sandy McNab managed to play in 13 of the 42 league games as the league title was won in 1936 and then played in every game, bar the semi-final, as the FA Cup was lifted a year later. McNab was a very good player, but such was the standard of Sunderland in the mid-thirties that in the six seasons Sandy played for Sunderland, it was only in 1933-34 that he played in over half the league games.**

As a boy, McNab was a grocer's assistant who played football in a the Glasgow Shopkeeper's league for Tuesday Waverley from whom he joined Pollok, where after four months he moved on to Sunderland, signing-off for Pollok with a hat-trick in a 3-2 win at St Anthony's on 6 May 1932.

Internationally, McNab made his debut for Scotland eight days after winning the FA Cup with Sunderland. The 1-1 draw in Austria saw Sandy play alongside two of the Preston team vanquished at Wembley. At this time, Scotland players only received caps for playing in Home Internationals, so it was for an appearance in a 2-1 defeat against England at Hampden in front of 149,269 in April 1939 that he earned his cap, his second and last appearance for his country.

By this time McNab was with West Brom who had paid £6,750 at a time when the transfer record was £10,890. Joining Albion in March, he played twelve games in his first season, but was unable to prevent the Baggies being relegated. Although not full internationals, Sandy gained further representative honours at the end of the season as part of a Scottish FA touring party, playing in eight of the 14-game tour and scoring once.

War soon followed with McNab playing over 130 war-time games for WBA in addition to his 49 peace-time games in which he scored twice. He also guested for four other clubs, notably playing in a Nottingham derby on Christmas Day 1940, his Forest side losing 4-2. In 1943-44, McNab captained West Brom as they beat Forest in the final of the Midland Cup.

After the war, McNab signed for Newport who he had 'guested' for, but only played three league games, the last at Tottenham after which he wound down his career in non-league before retiring in 1952 having had a spell as player/manager of Northwich Victoria between September 1948 and May 1949. After retiring he took over the running of 'Ye Olde Littleton Arms' in Halesowen and then the nearby 'Summer Sports and Social Club' before moving back to Scotland in 1955. McNab spent his latter years working for the Radio Times in East Kilbride before passing away of a heart attack, aged 50.

'The Black and White Cats: The Careers of Alexander McNab and Charles Morgan Thomson' was published in 2008. This tells the story of the pair of former Glasgow Pollok players who won the cup with Sunderland.

## McNAB, James (Jimmy)

**POSITION:** Half-back

**BIRTHPLACE:** Denny, Stirlingshire

**DATE OF BIRTH:** 13/04/1940 - 29/06/2006

**HEIGHT:** 5' 9" **WEIGHT:** 11st 7lbs

**SIGNED FROM:** Denny Rovers, 01/05/1956

**DEBUT:** v Ipswich Town, H, 20/09/1958

**LAST MATCH:** v Blackpool, A, 07/01/1967

**MOVED TO:** Preston North End, 16/03/1967

**TEAMS:** Kilsyth Rangers, Denny Rovers, Sunderland, Preston North End, Stockport County

**INTERNATIONAL:** Scotland Schools

**SAFC TOTALS:** 322+1 appearances / 18 goals

**'Mac the knife' was an integral part of the great 1963-64 team, missing just five of the 42 league games as promotion was won for the first time. A fierce competitor who could create as well as destroy, McNab was so consistent that from 1959-60 onwards he played a minimum of 36 league games for six successive seasons, being ever-present in 1961-62. However, Jim twice broke his leg playing for Sunderland, against Rotherham in November 1958 and Norwich in February 1964.**

Sadly, he was one of the players disposed of by ex-Rangers man Ian McColl. Jimmy went on to also give great service to Preston. He played 222+2 times for North End winning the Division Three title under Alan Ball senior in 1971, and going onto play for Bobby Charlton who released him in May 1974. McNab completed his playing days with 30 league games for Stockport County where he stayed until 1976 before retiring due to a persistent shoulder injury.

In his post football career Jim worked in insurance. As a boy he had twice appeared for Scotland at schools level and had been a Scottish Schools' cup-winner with Stirlingshire. An uncle, Bert McNab, gained 18 junior caps for Scotland and played briefly for Falkirk and then Petershill.

In 1999, almost a third of a century after he left Sunderland, the first-ever testimonial at the Stadium of Light was staged in Jim's honour on 11 May 1999. When Jim passed away seven years later, Charlie Hurley provided the eulogy at his funeral at St Mary's in Bridge Street, Sunderland. Jim's widow Sylvia remained a regular attendee at former players' events for many years.

## McNAIR, Patrick James Coleman (Paddy)

**POSITION:** Midfielder

**BIRTHPLACE:** Ballyclare, Northern Ireland

**DATE OF BIRTH:** 27/04/1995

**HEIGHT:** 6' 0" **WEIGHT:** 11st 5lbs

**SIGNED FROM:** Manchester United, 11/08/2016

**DEBUT:** v Manchester City, A, 13/08/2016

**LAST MATCH:** v Wolverhampton Wanderers, H, 06/05/2018

**MOVED TO:** Middlesbrough, 26/06/2018

**TEAMS:** Ballyclare Colts, Manchester United, Sunderland, Middlesbrough (to July 2022)

**INTERNATIONAL:** Northern Ireland

**SAFC TOTALS:** 20+8 appearances / 7 goals

**Probably the best of the many players David Moyes signed from his former clubs Manchester United and Everton, McNair came from Old Trafford in a joint deal with Donald Love for around £5.5m. With Sunderland drawing at Manchester City on the opening day of the season in 2016, the manager sent McNair on for his debut in an attempt to protect the point only for McNair to score an own-goal as the game was lost 2-1.**

Despite that disappointing start, McNair went on to impress when he played, although during his time on Wearside, Paddy was injury prone and made a total of a meagre 28 appearances in his two seasons, both of which resulted in relegation. Sixteen of those games were in his second term, at which point there were hopes that a potential promotion side might be built around him, but the player decided to move on and went to Middlesbrough.

McNair's number of games for Sunderland was one more than he managed for his first club Manchester United (18+9), who he had debuted for in the Premier League at home to West Ham United on 27 September 2014 under Louis Van Gaal. At Boro, he largely stayed clear of injuries, was Player of the Year in 2021, and by the end of 2021-22 had played 143+17 times, scoring 13 goals.

For Northern Ireland, he debuted at Hampden Park against Scotland in March 2015 and was appointed captain on the occasion of gaining his 50th cap against Switzerland in October 2021.

## McNEILL, Edward Vincent (Ted)

**POSITION:** Goalkeeper

**BIRTHPLACE:** Warrenpoint, Co Down, Northern Ireland

**DATE OF BIRTH:** 26/03/1929 - 25/04/1989

**HEIGHT:** 5' 9" **WEIGHT:** 10st 7lbs

**SIGNED FROM:** Portadown, 08/12/1951

**DEBUT:** v Portsmouth, A, 19/09/1953

**LAST MATCH:** v Burnley, A, 05/12/1953

**MOVED TO:** Portadown, 26/06/1954

**TEAMS:** Warrenpoint United, Newry, Portadown, Sunderland, Portadown, Dundalk

**SAFC TOTALS:** 7 appearances / 0 goals

**Ted McNeill's first-team games came in his third and last season at Sunderland. He had grown up playing Gaelic football until beginning to play for Warrenpoint United when he was 18. Prior to coming to Sunderland, he had an unsuccessful three-month trial at Tottenham Hotspur in 1950.**

His long-awaited debut saw two Irish international selectors at Fratton Park to see him, as regular Northern Ireland 'keeper Norman Uprichard (of Portsmouth) was injured, but McNeill was badly at fault for the last two of Portsmouth's four goals, with one of them given against him as an own-goal. With regular Sunderland goalkeeper Jimmy Cowan struggling with injury, McNeill got another opportunity at the end of the following month when he got six consecutive appearances, but after conceding at least twice in each of the first five of those he never played again after being beaten 5-1 at Burnley.

During his run in the first-team McNeill also played in a couple of extra matches, conceding three in a home defeat to Rapid Vienna and being beaten just once in a Durham Senior Professional Cup game with Darlington. In his last season on Wearside McNeill celebrated his wedding with fellow Northern Irishman Billy Bingham as his best man. The wedding cake was adorned with a four inch high footballer decked out in a full Sunderland kit.

After returning to Ireland McNeill's highlight was keeping a clean sheet as Dundalk beat Shamrock Rovers in the FAI Cup final in April 1958. This game saw McNeill become only the second keeper to win the cup without conceding a goal, although this was a close thing as Shamrock Rovers missed the target from the penalty spot during the final. Sadly, the Cup winner's medal is no longer in the possession of the family as during a holiday in Sunderland in 1969, Ted's wife, who had the item for safekeeping in her handbag, accidentally left the bag in a phone box and that was the last he saw of it. After retiring from playing Ted worked as a forklift truck driver in a factory close to his home in Warrenpoint until he passed away aged 60.

## McNEILL, Robert Jamieson (Bob)

**POSITION:** Full-back

**BIRTHPLACE:** Port Glasgow, Renfrewshire

**DATE OF BIRTH:** 21/11/1873 - 18/06/1947

**HEIGHT:** 5' 10½" **WEIGHT:** 12st 7lbs

**SIGNED FROM:** Clyde, 30/06/1894

**DEBUT:** v Burnley, H, 08/09/1894

**LAST MATCH:** v Notts County, A, 01/09/1900

**MOVED TO:** Greenock Morton, 12/11/1900

**TEAMS:** Port Glasgow, Vale of Leven, Clyde, Sunderland, Greenock Morton

**SAFC TOTALS:** 159 appearances / 0 goals

**Some match reports claim that Bob McNeill scored the last two goals in the 5-3 win over Hearts that saw Sunderland proclaimed world champions in 1895. This seems unlikely as McNeill never scored in his 157 competitive games for Sunderland.**

Maybe, just maybe, McNeill did score at Tynecastle, but as explained in Volume One of the Absolute Record, he is not considered as one of the scorers. As a full-back of course, his job - at least then if not now - was to stop goals rather than score them.

He was a consistent player who captained the club as they finished third in the league in 1899-1900, but made just one appearance the following campaign before moving to Morton after a disagreement with the directors over training methods. He had played 22 of the 30 league games as the title was won in his first season of 1894-95 and played in all four 'Test Matches' in 1896-97. Like many players of his era Bob worked in the shipyards before and after his professional career and continued as a boilermaker after his retirement on the banks of the Clyde. His brother Alexander, who also played for Clyde, had a trial at Sunderland towards the end of 1894-95.

Official records show his surname as McNeil however during his football career he always used the spelling with two 'L's at the end.

## McNESTRY, George

**POSITION:** Outside-right

**BIRTHPLACE:** Winlaton, Co Durham

**DATE OF BIRTH:** 07/01/1908 - 16/03/1998

**HEIGHT:** 5' 8½" **WEIGHT:** 10st 11lbs

**SIGNED FROM:** Leeds United, 13/11/1929

**DEBUT:** v Leicester City, H, 16/11/1929

**LAST MATCH:** v West Ham United, A, 07/12/1929

**MOVED TO:** Luton Town, 13/05/1930

**TEAMS:** Chopwell White Star, Bradford Park Avenue, Doncaster Rovers, Leeds United, Sunderland, Luton Town, Bristol Rovers, Coventry City

**SAFC TOTALS:** 4 appearances / 0 goals

## McNESTRY, George (Continued)

**McNestry cost £200 from Leeds United, but the four consecutive games he got were to prove to be his Roker total before he moved on to Luton at the end of the season. It was one more game than the three he played for Leeds. Earlier in McNestry's career he had scored once in 14 games for Bradford Park Avenue in 1926-27 and once in nine games at Doncaster the following season.**

At Luton he scored 26 goals in 69 games over two seasons before moving on to Bristol Rovers. He did well at Eastville, bagging 42 goals in 112 games before a move to Coventry where injury curtailed his career after he had helped them to win the Third Division South Cup in 1935 and the double of the same cup and Third Division South title in 1936.

Debuting for Coventry at Reading at the end of August in 1935, he scored 20 times in 39 league games in his first season becoming the club's penalty-taker, although he missed from the spot in the final league game of 1935-36 against Torquay. That could have been a costly miss, but his side went on to win, and gain promotion, although after just seven games at the higher level McNestry was forced to retire because of a serious ankle injury. After retiring from football, George returned to the north east and worked for the forestry commission hauling timber.

## McNULTY, Marc Graeme

**POSITION:** Forward

**BIRTHPLACE:** Edinburgh

**DATE OF BIRTH:** 14/09/1992

**HEIGHT:** 5' 10" **WEIGHT:** 11st 0lbs

**SIGNED FROM:** Reading, 24/07/2019, on loan

**DEBUT:** v Oxford United, H, 03/08/2019

**LAST MATCH:** v Wycombe Wanderers, H, 11/01/2020

**MOVED TO:** Reading, 31/01/2020, end of loan

**TEAMS:** Livingston, Sheffield United, Portsmouth (L), Bradford City (L), Coventry City, Reading, Hibernian (L), Sunderland (L), Hibernian (L), Dundee United (L)

**INTERNATIONAL:** Scotland

**SAFC TOTALS:** 12+9 appearances / 5 goals

**Top scoring with 28 goals when firing Coventry City to promotion from League Two via the Play-Offs in 2018 (his tally including a hat-trick against a Grimsby defence including Danny Collins) earned McNulty a move to the Championship with Reading after his sole season with the Sky Blues.**

He found the going tougher at the higher level and only scored once in 8+9 games for the Royals from whom he began a series of loans after only half a season. He came to Wearside in between two loans with Hibs, the second of which saw him play for Jack Ross who had brought him to the Stadium of Light. At Sunderland, one of his two league goals came after just 31 seconds of a home game with Rotherham in September 2019, but over half of his 15 league appearances were off the bench and while he always looked likely to score, he never got a run in the side to really show what he could do. Ross had been replaced by Phil Parkinson while McNulty was at Sunderland, but evidently, liked what he had seen as he took him to Hibs under a fortnight after McNulty's half-season loan at Sunderland ended.

A hat-trick in his third match back with the Easter Road club got Marc off to a great start, but there was just one more goal as he took his total in two spells at the club to twelve goals in 21+4 games. His first spell at Hibs also had a Sunderland connection as he played for former Sunderland reserve Paul Heckingbottom. During this spell a purple patch of six goals in four games earned a Scotland call-up and two caps in March 2019 away to Kazakhstan and San Marino, both times as a sub.

After a couple of League Cup games back at Reading where he was subbed both times, in October 2020 McNulty returned to Scotland on loan to Dundee United where his first goal did not come until his ninth game. Goals remained few and far between although the club took him on a second loan the following season after there had been a change of management. To the end of 2021-22, McNulty had scored eight goals in 42+12 games for the club at which point he was released by parent club Reading.

McNulty started his career with Livingston, making a scoring debut in a third tier win at Montrose on Halloween in 2009. It was one of only two goals in his first two seasons before he blossomed in 2011-12 with 13 goals including a first hat-trick against Raith Rovers when he was still a teenager. Beginning the following season with another hat-trick at Stranraer helped him to double-figures again and when the next term brought 19 goals (including another hat-trick at Morton) it persuaded Sheffield United to sign him after 45 goals in 88+29 games for Livi with whom he had won back-to-back promotions in his first two seasons.

A goal on his second appearance for the Blades in August 2014 augured well and by mid-October he had found his stride with a sequence of scoring in five out of seven League One games. Thirteen goals that season helped his club to the Play-Offs. The following season he reached the Play-Offs again, but this time in League Two on loan to Portsmouth. Overall, he again scored 13 times - this time including a hat-trick versus York for Pompey. 2016-17 brought another loan, this time to Bradford City, but despite just one goal for either Bradford or Sheffield United, Coventry had seen enough to take him and get the best out of him. In total, McNulty scored once in 6+10 games for Bradford and 14 times in 25+31 games for the Blades.

## McPHEAT, William (Willie)

**POSITION:** Forward

**BIRTHPLACE:** Caldercruix, Lanarkshire

**DATE OF BIRTH:** 04/09/1942 - 06/04/2019

**HEIGHT:** 6' 0" **WEIGHT:** 13st 0lbs

**SIGNED FROM:** Calder Youths, 01/09/1959

**DEBUT:** v Leeds United, H, 08/10/1960

**LAST MATCH:** v Leeds United, A, 5/08/1962

**MOVED TO:** Hartlepools United, 13/09/1965

**TEAMS:** Calder Youths, Sunderland, Hartlepools United, Airdrieonians

**SAFC TOTALS:** 72 appearances / 23 goals

**When Willie McPheat debuted against Leeds shortly after turning 18, little did he know that his burgeoning Sunderland career would crash to a halt against the same opposition under two years later. There was much bad blood between Sunderland and Leeds during the era and much of it stemmed from the horror challenge by Leeds' Bobby Collins which broke McPheat's thigh bone and ended his top-class career. McPheat was still in his teens and had set a record which still stands in 2022 as the highest-scoring teenager in Sunderland's history.**

Willie was a strong two-footed player with good pace for a big man. McPheat's haul of goals included one on his debut against Leeds and another in a big win over Newcastle. Willie also scored in Sunderland's first-ever League Cup tie against Brentford, but it was in an FA Cup quarter-final against Spurs that he netted his most famous goal. That goal triggered a pitch invasion at Roker Park as Spurs escaped with a draw in the season where they became the first-team of the century to do the double of winning league and FA Cup.

How many more goals Willie McPheat would have scored during his career, if it was not effectively finished a month before his 20th birthday, we will never know. Three years after his injury, having tried and failed to regain sufficient fitness to play again for Sunderland, who were by now back in the top flight, he moved to Hartlepool where after four goals in 17 games he returned to Scotland to play for Airdrie where he played 100 times and returned 19 goals.

After retiring from the game, Willie worked in a whisky distillery in Inverhouse. In his later years, he struggled with Alzheimers and lived in a Glasgow nursing home where he was regularly visited by his old teammate John Dillon.

## McPHEE, John (Johnny)

**POSITION:** Outside-right

**BIRTHPLACE:** Stirling, Stirlingshire

**DATE OF BIRTH:** 27/05/1911 - 30/11/1963

**HEIGHT:** 5' 8" **WEIGHT:** 10st 6lbs

**SIGNED FROM:** Cowie Juveniles, 24/06/1929

**DEBUT:** v Portsmouth, A, 14/09/1929

**LAST MATCH:** v Everton, H, 02/10/1929

**MOVED TO:** Brentford, 15/05/1931

**TEAMS:** Cowie Thistle, Sunderland, Brentford, St Mirren, Albion Rovers

**SAFC TOTALS:** 4 appearances / 0 goals

**An accomplished athlete and Scottish dancer who won many titles as a teenager, McPhee joined Sunderland after winning the Scottish Juvenile Cup with Cowie Thistle in 1929. His first team experience at Sunderland consisted of four consecutive games early in the 1929-30 season, but after never being on the winning side, he was sidelined and left the club at the end of the following term.**

He never got a game at first-team level in the year he spent with Brentford and by mutual consent returned to Scotland in October 1931 where a week later he was signed on what turned out to be an unsuccessful month-long trial by St Mirren.

Johnny; also sometimes referred to as Jackie, signed for Albion Rovers in July 1932 and enjoyed the most successful days of his career as he went on to be Rovers' top scorer with 15 league goals as they won the second division title in 1934 before he was released on a free transfer in May 1936. An outside-left once back in Scotland, McPhee later served as lieutenant in the North Staffordshire Regiment and Royal Indian Army Corps during World War Two.

## McSEVENEY, John Haddow

**POSITION:** Outside-left

**BIRTHPLACE:** Shotts, Lanarkshire

**DATE OF BIRTH:** 08/02/1931 - 12/12/2020

**HEIGHT:** 5' 8" **WEIGHT:** 10st 9lbs

**SIGNED FROM:** Hamilton Academical, 17/10/1951

**DEBUT:** v Manchester United, A, 20/10/1951

**LAST MATCH:** v Manchester City, H, 04/12/1954

**MOVED TO:** Cardiff City, 02/06/1955

**TEAMS:** Carluke Rovers, Hamilton Academical, Sunderland, Cardiff City, Newport County, Hull City

**SAFC TOTALS:** 38 appearances / 4 goals

**While playing for Sunderland in the 1950s, McSeveney also had a job at Wearmouth Colliery where the Stadium of Light now stands. Having debuted in a 1-0 win at Manchester United, John explained to Red and White in 2006 that after that match he travelled back to his native Scotland to collect his belongings and when met on his return by teammate Billy Bingham, he went to a dance at the Rink in Sunderland and on that very evening met Joyce who was to become his wife of over 50 years.**

After four years at Roker where he was mainly understudy to England international Billy Elliott, McSeveney moved to Cardiff City and promptly scored twice on his debut - against Sunderland. He also scored the winner in the 1956 Welsh Cup final against Swansea. He played 75 league games for Cardiff City, 172 for Newport County and finally 183 in all competitions

for Hull City, scoring 70 goals, 22 of them coming in the 1962-63 season, before he ended his playing days in 1964. He went on to manage Barnsley, Home Farm, the national team of Guyana, Oman SC (in the United Arab Emirates) and Waterford as well as being assistant manager to Ian Porterfield at Rotherham Utd and Sheffield Utd.

After leaving Sheffield in March 1986, McSeveney spent the best part of the next 20 years as chief coach at Nottingham Forest, chief scout at Bolton Wanderers and then Coventry City before finally scouting for Ipswich Town, Derby County and Manchester United. John's brother, Willie, played for Dunfermline Athletic and Motherwell between 1948 and 1963.

## McSHANE, Paul David

**POSITION:** Defender

**BIRTHPLACE:** Kilpedder, Wicklow, Ireland

**DATE OF BIRTH:** 06/01/1986

**HEIGHT:** 6' 0" **WEIGHT:** 11st 5lbs

**SIGNED FROM:** West Bromwich Albion, 26/07/2007

**DEBUT:** v Tottenham Hotspur, H, 11/08/2007

**LAST MATCH:** v Manchester United, H, 11/04/2009

**MOVED TO:** Hull City, 30/08/2009

**TEAMS:** Manchester United, Walsall (L), Brighton & Hove Albion (L), WBA, Sunderland, Hull City, Barnsley (L), Crystal Palace (L), Reading, Rochdale, Manchester United

**INTERNATIONAL:** Republic of Ireland

**SAFC TOTALS:** 21+4 appearances / 0 goals

**A fully committed player, Paul McShane was always in demand. So much so, that at the age of 35 when his career of over 400 senior games appeared to have ended in an April 2021 match where he was substituted by Rochdale at Crewe, he was re-signed by his first club Manchester United.**

They wanted him to nurture their Under 23s and play alongside them to guide them on the pitch. Subsequently, McShane made his second appearance after his return back at the Stadium of Light for United's Under 21s in the Football League (Papa John's) Trophy in October 2021.

He had begun at Old Trafford, but never got a first-team appearance for the club who loaned him to Walsall (3+1/1) and Brighton (40/4) before he joined West Brom on a free transfer. At United, he had been a teammate of Phil Bardsley and Kieran Richardson as the FA Youth Cup was won in 2003, a Middlesbrough side including future Sunderland first-team coach Andrew Taylor being beaten in the final

42+1 games and two goals in his only season at the Hawthorns in 2006-07 persuaded Sunderland to splash out £1.5m on Paul, with a further £1m payable depending upon appearances. By this time, he was a full international, debuting for the Republic of Ireland in October 2006 against the Czech Republic. He went on to win 33 caps without scoring. Twelve of Paul's caps were won while he was with Sunderland, on half of those occasions playing alongside clubmates Liam Miller and/or Daryl Murphy.

McShane's biggest success came at Hull City who signed him from Sunderland after taking him on loan a year after he arrived on Wearside. Recalled by the Black Cats a month after he scored for the Tigers in a draw at Liverpool he had three games back at Sunderland - the last against his old club Manchester United before completing a transfer to Humberside.

Following his permanent move, McShane debuted back at Sunderland in September 2009, but it was a tough season as the Tigers were relegated from the Premier League. Half way through the next (2010-11) campaign he was loaned out to Barnsley which brought ten starts, one goal and one red card before he returned to Hull City. In 2011-12 there would be another loan to Crystal Palace where he played 9+3 games without scoring.

2012-13 brought promotion with Hull, with the next season seeing him play in the FA Cup final. Steve Bruce's Hull were leading when McShane came on in the 67th minute to join Ahmed Elmohamady and David Meyler only for Arsenal to come back and take the trophy. Leaving Hull in the summer of 2015 after 119+17 games and five goals, he joined Reading where there were four goals in 96+7 games over four seasons, before 35+2 games and one goal for Rochdale prior to the commencement of his coaching career and his return to Manchester United as playing coach, working with players from Under 15s to Under 23s. He retired from playing in May 2022.

Paul's elder brother John played for Llangefni Town in 2003-04 whilst a student at Bangor University.

## NAISBY, Thomas Henry (Tom)

**POSITION:** Goalkeeper

**BIRTHPLACE:** Sunderland, Co Durham

**DATE OF BIRTH:** 12/03/1878 - 03/05/1927

**HEIGHT:** 5' 8" **WEIGHT:** 12st 0lbs

**SIGNED FROM:** Black Watch, 01/05/1898 and Reading, 03/05/1905

**DEBUT:** v Blackburn Rovers, H, 03/04/1899

**LAST MATCH:** v Stoke, H, 02/03/1907

**MOVED TO:** Sunderland West End, 01/06/02 and Leeds City, 25/10/1907

**TEAMS:** Roker Park Villa, Black Watch, Sunderland, Sunderland West End, Reading, Sunderland, Leeds City, Luton Town, South Shields, Darlington

**SAFC TOTALS:** 41 appearances / 0 goals

**An accomplished violin maker, Naisby had little opportunity for virtuoso performances when back-up to the legendary Ted Doig, being restricted to a couple of games in 1898-99 in his first spell at the club. This was in the first season at Roker Park, Naisby having begun with a team called Roker Park Villa.**

He moved on in the search for first-team football and earned a return to Roker after back-to-back seasons as an ever-present with Southern League Reading who finished second to Bristol Rovers in 1904-05 after Naisby was beaten just 38 times in his 34 games.

He was Sunderland's first choice keeper in 1905-06, and to date the shortest keeper at 5' 8", making a total of 36 appearances, the final one only four days after his two-year-old son had died from diphtheria. Tom moved on again the following season after losing his place to Bob Ward. At Leeds City, Tom debuted on 26 October 1907 against Lincoln City and went on to hardly miss a game until losing his place to former Derby custodian Harry Bromage in 1909-10.

He made the last of his 68 league and cup games against Grimsby shortly before Christmas in that campaign. Leaving Leeds for Luton, Naisby again became first choice and played in all but three of the Hatters 76 Southern League fixtures across 1910-11 and 1911-12, before finishing his playing days back in the north east.

At the outbreak of World War One, Tom enlisted with the Royal Garrison Artillery, while having retired from the game, he became a plasterer and for a while joined his brother in Cleveland Ohio.

## N'DIAYE, Alfred John Momar

**POSITION:** Midfielder

**BIRTHPLACE:** Paris, France

**DATE OF BIRTH:** 06/03/1990

**HEIGHT:** 6' 2" **WEIGHT:** 14st 6lbs

**SIGNED FROM:** Bursaspor, 09/01/2013

**DEBUT:** v West Ham United, H, 12/01/2013

**LAST MATCH:** v Tottenham Hotspur, A, 19/05/2013

**MOVED TO:** Real Betis, 22/08/2014

**TEAMS:** Nancy, Bursaspor, Sunderland, Eskisehirspor (L), Real Betis, Villarreal, Hull City (L), Wolves (L), Malaga (L), Al Shahab

**INTERNATIONAL:** France Under 21 / Senegal

**SAFC TOTALS:** 15+1 appearances / 0 goals

**Alfred N'Diaye appeared to be exactly the sort of midfielder Sunderland have often needed: big, powerful and mobile. Shortly before he signed, I was flattered when manager Martin O'Neill invited me to watch some video clips of potential transfer targets fitting the bill that N'Diaye met in terms of physicality. I had to admit to the manager that it was impossible to judge a player on the basis of TV excerpts without seeing him in the flesh so I'm taking none of the blame for Alfred's signing!**

He only played a handful of games in which he showed himself to fill the requirements of physicality, but unfortunately physicality was not enough and he did not seem to possess the required quality on the ball to provide what Sunderland were looking for in the Premier League.

Having arrived half way through the season, by his first summer - and with O'Neill having been replaced by Paolo Di Canio - N'Diaye was shipped out on a season-long loan to Eskisehirspor who he had played against in his 68th and final appearance for Bursaspor prior to coming to Sunderland. During his loan from Sunderland, Alfred added another four goals in 19 appearances to the eight he had scored in his earlier stay in Turkey.

At the end of January 2014 Sunderland recalled N'Diaye from loan in order to loan him to Real Betis. Debuting in La Liga against Espanyol, he was quickly involved in Europa League games, playing against future SAFC midfielder Yann M'Vila in a tie with Rubin Kazan. After 16 games on loan to Betis, N'Diaye signed for the Spanish club in the summer despite their relegation during his loan. He went on to play a further 59+6 games for them including 29 in his first full season as promotion was immediately won. After one more season in La Liga - and a Cope Del Rey red card in a derby defeat to Sevilla - he was on the move again, this time to Villarreal.

Like his switch to Sunderland, this did not work out for the player despite a Europa League goal against 1299 Osmanlispor of Turkey. While there were four cup outings, only two of his nine La Liga games for 'the Yellow Submarine' were starts, one of his games off the bench seeing him help his side to a point away to Cristiano Ronaldo's Real Madrid.

Two and a half years after cutting his ties with Sunderland Alfred returned to England with a loan to Hull, getting off to a great start by scoring in a debut win against Liverpool. It was to be his only goal in 15 starts as the Tigers went down, N'Diaye playing in a home defeat to doomed Sunderland and a final-day 7-1 home embarrassment by Spurs.

N'Diaye stayed in England with a loan to Wolves after a couple of appearances back in Spain with his parent club. Twenty of his 37 games for Wanderers were as a sub including one against Sunderland at Molineux when he was on the bench with Danny Batth. Despite three goals in a promotion-winning season with the Old Gold, N'Diaye still did not fit into Villarreal's plans as they sent him on a third loan, this time to Malaga where he scored five times in 34 games including a debut goal in a win at Lugo.

In March 2019 it emerged that the previous October the player had been declared bankrupt. August 2019 saw Alfred move to Al-Shabab of Saudi Arabia on a three-year contract. As of June 2022 he was still a regular starter for the club.

Internationally, he played against Poland and Japan for Senegal at the 2018 FIFA World Cup. He had debuted for Senegal in 2013 having previously represented France, the country of his birth, in 31 games at four levels up to Under 21. He played in 27 full internationals for Senegal for whom he was an unused sub as they lost the 2019 African Cup of Nations final to Algeria.

## NDONG, Didier Ibrahim

**POSITION:** Midfielder

**BIRTHPLACE:** Lambarene, Gabon

**DATE OF BIRTH:** 17/06/1994

**HEIGHT:** 5' 10½" **WEIGHT:** 11st 11lbs

**SIGNED FROM:** Lorient, 31/08/2016

**DEBUT:** v Everton, H, 12/09/2016

**LAST MATCH:** v Cardiff City, A, 13/01/2018

**MOVED TO:** Contract terminated, 08/10/2018

**TEAMS:** Cercle Mberi Sportif, CS Sfaxien. Lorient, Sunderland, Watford (L), Guingamp, Dijon, Yeni Malatyaspor (L), (to June 2022)

**INTERNATIONAL:** Gabon

**SAFC TOTALS:** 48+6 appearances / 1 goal

**Often reported as Sunderland's record signing, Ndong cost €13m. This was indeed a record based on an agreed initial fee, but it was not as high as what had been paid for Darren Bent once add-ons to Bent's initial £10m fee had been taken into account.**

The word within the club when Ndong arrived was that he would develop into a player who would be sold for £40m. He did not. Instead, after being part of a team who were relegated, Ndong reportedly refused to play in the third tier and after a dispute between him and the club which saw him sacked, eventually left for nothing, but the promise that at some point Sunderland would receive some €4m compensation. Whether this ever happened remained a mystery. Sunderland though held his registration and so he or his next club Guingamp would have had to come to an agreement with Sunderland.

Ndong was an energetic midfielder let down by his passing which was sometimes poor. Certainly, it was not in the same class as Yann M'Vila who had impressed on loan during the previous season, but whose wages were apparently too much for the club's new hierarchy of CEO Martin Bain and manager David Moyes to consider.

A Gabon international since a November 2012 debut against Portugal, at what should have been the peak of his career in 2022, Ndong was not part of his country's squad at the African Cup of Nations although he did make three appearances at the 2015 tournament and another three in 2017.

Didier had impressed as a young player, and made a senior debut in Tunisia for CS Sfaxien where he scored twice in 40 games between 2011 and 2015, playing part of the time under Dutch defender Rudi Krol and helping the club to the league title. This led to a move to France with Lorient in January 2015 although his debut was delayed by participation in the African Cup of Nations. A first appearance in a 3-1 win at Reims on 7 February 2015 was followed by a red card in his third game.

Never a stranger to a card there were 14 yellows in his 38 games the following term, prior to his switch to Sunderland after a total of 49+3 appearances and two goals. Sent off in his last game for Lorient, he would also be red carded on his final appearance for Sunderland, having also collected ten yellows with the Wearsiders. Loaned to Watford from January to the end of the season in 2018, he never got a game for the Hornets and following his no-show at the start of the following season eventually re-surfaced at Guingamp who he signed for on 2 January 2019, debuting for them ten days later against St Etienne.

Two months later he played in the final of the French League Cup, lost on penalties after a goalless draw with Lamine Kone's Strasbourg, another Sunderland connection being Papy Djilobodji (who had left Sunderland in similar circumstances to Ndong) being an unused sub for Ndong's side. After 11+3 appearances, Ndong left Guingamp after seven months to join Dijon where he had played 57 games over two years - the last ten of these were all defeats as Dijon finished bottom of the table. He then joined Turkish outfit Yeni Malatyaspor on a season-long loan from August 2021, but was on the losing side in 13 of his 18 appearances and the winning team just once.

## N'DOYE, Dame

**POSITION:** Forward

**BIRTHPLACE:** Thies, Senegal

**DATE OF BIRTH:** 21/08/1985

**HEIGHT:** 6' 1" **WEIGHT:** 12st 11lbs

**SIGNED FROM:** Trabzonspor, 14/01/2016, on loan

**DEBUT:** v Manchester City, H, 02/02/2016

**LAST MATCH:** v Watford, A, 15/05/2016

**MOVED TO:** Trabzonspor, 16/05/2016, end of loan

**TEAMS:** Jeanne d'Arc, Al Sadd, Academica, Panathinaikos, OFI Crete, Copenhagen, Lokomotiv Moscow, Hull City, Trabzonspor, Sunderland (L), Copenhagen

**INTERNATIONAL:** Senegal

**SAFC TOTALS:** 5+6 appearances / 1 goal

**The least heralded of Sam Allardyce's January 2016 signings, N'Doye did contribute to a great escape from relegation with a goal in a home draw with Crystal Palace. He played club football in eight countries and enjoyed huge success in Denmark with Copenhagen where he won four league titles and two domestic cups while twice being the Superliga's leading scorer. In two spells at the club, he totalled 56 goals in 103+2 games, his 20 goals in 2011-12 earning him a move to Lokomotiv Moscow.**

Goals in his second and third games in Moscow derbies against Dinamo and Spartak (Spartak including Aiden McGeady) got Dame off to a great start and he continued to do well. After 27 goals in 51+15 league games over two and a half seasons, Hull City bought N'Doye for £3m early in 2015, the third of his five goals for the Tigers coming against Sunderland. That goal tally was not a bad return for 13+2 games, but was not enough to keep Hull up, at which point they quickly cut their losses and traded him to Trabzonspor for £2.2m. Dame had not scored in twelve games when the Turkish club loaned him to Sunderland, but upon his return he netted ten times in taking his total games for the club to 40+23 before a summer 2018 return to Copenhagen.

N'Doye's early career had seen him progress with clubs in his own country Senegal, Qatar and Portugal, before coming to prominence in Greece with former European Cup finalists Panathinaikos with whom he played against both Rangers and Aberdeen in the UEFA Cup, as well as making 23 domestic league appearances. He scored three goals there and seven with OFI Crete in just 15 games prior to his first move to Denmark.

It was while he was with Copenhagen that N'Doye played the first of his 28 games for Senegal, debuting against Gabon in November 2010. He scored seven goals for his country including one against Zambia at the 2012 African Cup of Nations. Brother Ousmane N'Doye won one fewer cap in an extensive career that included a spell with Dinamo Bucharest.

## NEIL, Daniel James

**POSITION:** Midfielder

**BIRTHPLACE:** South Shields, Tyne & Wear

**DATE OF BIRTH:** 13/12/2001

**HEIGHT:** 5' 11" **WEIGHT:** 11st 5lbs

**SIGNED FROM:** Trainee, 01/07/2018

**DEBUT:** v Morecambe, A, 13/11/2018

**LAST MATCH:**

**MOVED TO:**

**TEAMS:** Sunderland

**INTERNATIONAL:** England Under 20

**SAFC TOTALS:** 42+12 appearances / 4 goals (to June 2022)

**After being on the fringe of the side for three seasons, Dan Neil's breakthrough year was in 2021-22 when he established himself as a regular and went on to be named North East FWA Young Player of the Year.**

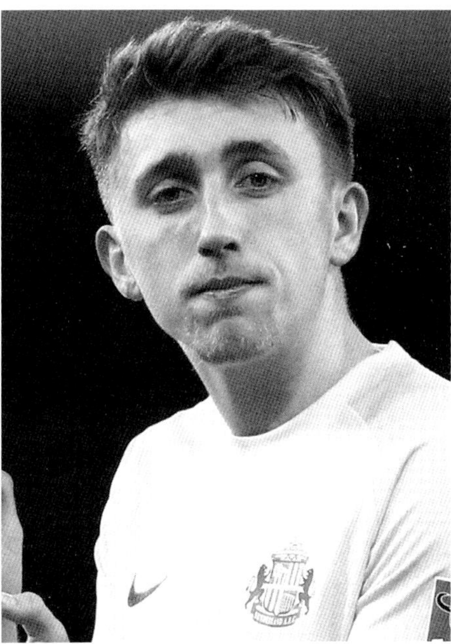

Having been at Sunderland since he was eight, Dan was capped at Under 16 level and earned a first England Under 20 call-up in November 2021 along with Dennis Cirkin and SAFC academy product Sam Greenwood for a game with Portugal. A debutant as a last-minute substitute at the age of 16 years and 335 days, at the time he became Sunderland's sixth youngest-ever player.

## NELSON, Colin Armstrong

**POSITION:** Full-back

**BIRTHPLACE:** East Boldon, Co Durham

**DATE OF BIRTH:** 13/03/1938

**HEIGHT:** 5' 9" **WEIGHT:** 11st 10lbs

**SIGNED FROM:** Usworth Juniors, 01/09/1957

**DEBUT:** v Bristol City, A, 25/10/1958

**LAST MATCH:** v Burnley, H, 14/11/1964

**MOVED TO:** Mansfield Town, 16/03/1965

**TEAMS:** Sunderland, Mansfield Town

**SAFC TOTALS:** 167 appearances / 2 goals

**Ever-present in 1960-61, Colin did not sign as a full-time professional until January 1964, a promotion season in which he only played three times due to the emergence of Cec Irwin. Sunderland signed Durham County Schoolboy wing-half Nelson from Chester-le-Street Junior League side Usworth and converted him to a full-back.**

After signing on a part-time professional basis in March 1958, Colin kept studying to be a pharmacist and would regularly travel on the bus from Newcastle to the Grange pub on Newcastle Road before walking to Roker Park to play in the second division after a morning's study. Colin had the unusual distinction of keeping goal for the Lads in a League Cup semi-final when he replaced the injured Jim Montgomery after 70 minutes in the first leg at Villa Park on 12 January 1963.

He almost kept a clean sheet, only to be beaten by a Derek Dougan tap in after failing to hold a long-range shot. After being part of the Sunderland 1964 promotion squad, Nelson only made one top-flight appearance before moving to Mansfield Town on transfer deadline day to help their Division Three promotion push. He added 38 league appearances with the Stags before retiring at the age of 28 to concentrate on his career in pharmacy. Colin was also an accomplished cricketer and played in the Durham Senior League for Boldon.

## NESS, Harry Marshall

**POSITION:** Full-back

**BIRTHPLACE:** Scarborough, Yorkshire

**DATE OF BIRTH:** 08/06/1885 - 26/06/1957

**HEIGHT:** 5' 10" **WEIGHT:** 13st 3lbs

**SIGNED FROM:** Barnsley, 30/06/1911

**DEBUT:** v Oldham Athletic, H, 28/10/1911

**LAST MATCH:** v Notts County, H, 08/11/1919

**MOVED TO:** Aberdeen, 22/05/1920

**TEAMS:** Parkgate, Rawmarsh Athletic, Barnsley, Sunderland, Aberdeen

**SAFC TOTALS:** 102 appearances / 0 goals

**Ness was an English (FA) Cup finalist with Sunderland in 1912-13 when he also helped win the league title. Three years earlier he had played in the cup final and replay alongside former SAFC goalkeeper Fred Mearns against Newcastle United.**

World War One saw Ness become a lance corporal in the Black Watch but he returned to play nine post-war games in 1919-20. At Aberdeen he linked up with former Sunderland goalkeeper George Anderson but after being injured in pre-season was used as a reserve at Pittodrie. In dispute with Aberdeen, he filed a claim against the club with the Scottish FA and left after the club settled with him. Returning to his native Scarborough, he became a publican and stayed in the town until his death. Harry's brother James played for Watford in 1911-12.

## NICHOLL, James Michael (Jimmy)

**POSITION:** Right-back

**BIRTHPLACE:** Hamilton, Ontario, Canada

**DATE OF BIRTH:** 28/02/1956

**HEIGHT:** 5' 9½" **WEIGHT:** 11st 8lbs

**SIGNED FROM:** Manchester United, 17/12/1981, on loan and Toronto Blizzard, 23/09/1982

**DEBUT:** v Rotherham United, H, 18/01/1982

**LAST MATCH:** v West Ham United, A, 09/04/1983

**MOVED TO:** Manchester United, 17/02/1982, end of loan and Toronto Blizzard, 12/04/1983

**TEAMS:** Manchester United, Sunderland (L), Toronto Blizzard, Sunderland, Toronto Blizzard, Rangers, West Bromwich Albion, Rangers, Dunfermline Athletic, Raith Rovers, Bath City

**INTERNATIONAL:** Northern Ireland

**SAFC TOTALS:** 40 appearances / 0 goals

**As of June 2022 Jimmy was his country's assistant manager, a role he had first held in 2015. Capped 73 times by Northern Ireland he played at two FIFA World Cups. In 1982, he played in all five games as the Irish reached the second stage after winning their group and famously defeating host nation Spain. In that tournament, he was in a side captained by Martin O'Neill and managed by Billy Bingham. Four years later in Mexico, he played in all three games for Bingham.**

Becoming a manager himself as player/manager of Raith Rovers, he led the club to the Scottish League Cup and First Division title before taking over at Millwall, after which he briefly played for Bath City. Returning to Raith Rovers as coach in March 1997, three months later he took over as manager for two more years. He later took caretaker charge of Dunfermline and had five years as assistant manager at Aberdeen followed by taking on the same role at Kilmarnock. After spending 2010-11 as manager of Cowdenbeath, he returned to his role at Kilmarnock and also served as assistant at Hibs before a second spell in charge at Cowdenbeath.

Fresh out of Belfast Central School, Jimmy joined Manchester United as a trainee in November 1971 becoming a professional in March 1974. Debuting for United in a second division match at Southampton in April of the following year Nicholl went on to play 248 times for United, including the FA Cup finals of 1977 and 1979. His six goals included one in European competition against Porto in November 1977.

A £250,000 fee took Canadian-born Jimmy to Toronto Blizzard in April 1982. At this point, he had already had a loan with Sunderland. He later returned to Sunderland in a permanent move from Toronto, his 'second debut' being an 8-0 defeat at Watford on 25 September 1982. Nicholl returned to his Canadian club seven months later with whom he became a Soccer Bowl finalist in 1983 and NASL Championship finalist a year later.

In his playing days Jimmy also played 67 times (1 goal) for West Brom and in two spells with Rangers made 73+2 league appearances winning a League title and the League Cup three times. At Dunfermline he made 24 appearances in 1989-90 before moving into management as a player/manager.

## NOBLE, Ryan Andrew

**POSITION:** Forward

**BIRTHPLACE:** Millfield, Sunderland, Tyne & Wear

**DATE OF BIRTH:** 06/11/1991

**HEIGHT:** 5' 11½" **WEIGHT:** 11st 0lbs

**SIGNED FROM:** As trainee, 01/07/2008

**DEBUT:** v Barrow, H, 02/01/2010

**LAST MATCH:** v Wolverhampton Wanderers, A, 04/12/2011

**MOVED TO:** Contract not renewed, 30/06/2013

**TEAMS:** Sunderland, Watford (L), Derby County (L), Hartlepool United (L), Burnley, Gateshead, Darlington 1883, Durham City, Sunderland Ryhope CA, South Shields, Seaham Red Star, Esh Winning, Whitley Bay, Easington Colliery, Bishop Auckland, Newton Aycliffe, Seaham Red Star, Jarrow, Billingham Synthonia

**INTERNATIONAL:** England Under 19

**SAFC TOTALS:** 0+6 appearances / 0 goals

**A prolific scorer at youth level, much was expected of Ryan Noble but it never quite happened for a local lad who won England youth honours. A loan to Watford, plus two loans each to Derby County and Hartlepool United failed to ignite Ryan's career.**

There were no appearances for Watford, just 1+2 for Derby and 18+3 at Hartlepool where he scored the only three goals of his league career in 2012. Released by Sunderland, Noble was given an opportunity in July 2013 by Burnley for whom he made a couple of substitute appearances, but after six months he moved on to Gateshead where all but one of his nine games were as a sub. He scored once in those games. His career continued in non-league football, but many were left to wonder why a natural goalscorer did not enjoy a more successful career.

## NORMAN, Anthony Joseph (Tony)

**POSITION:** Goalkeeper

**BIRTHPLACE:** Mancot, Flintshire

**DATE OF BIRTH:** 24/02/1958

**HEIGHT:** 6' 2" **WEIGHT:** 12st 8lbs

**SIGNED FROM:** Hull City, 29/12/1988

**DEBUT:** v Portsmouth, H, 31/12/1988

**LAST MATCH:** v West Bromwich Albion, H, 07/05/1995

**MOVED TO:** Huddersfield Town, 06/07/1995

**TEAMS:** Burnley, Hull City, Sunderland, Huddersfield Town

**INTERNATIONAL:** Wales

**SAFC TOTALS:** 227 appearances / 0 goals

**An excellent goalkeeper who played twice for Sunderland at Wembley. Two years before appearing in the 1992 FA Cup final Norman was only conquered by a deflection in a Play-Off final against Swindon when he had a blinder.**

Outstanding performances were not unusual for Tony who was nothing short of brilliant when playing against Sunderland for Hull City in a goalless draw at Humberside in 1988 on a day marked by thirties stars Raich Carter and Bobby Gurney appearing on the pitch. Given that performance it came as no surprise when Norman was soon made Sunderland's record signing in a deal that took goalkeeper Iain Hesford and Billy Whitehurst in the opposite direction.

Every goalkeeper makes mistakes, but Norman made very few, so it seemed harsh when a fanzine was named 'It's an easy one for Norman' following a piece of commentary relating to Tony dropping a last-minute cross that led to FA Cup elimination at Sheffield Wednesday in 1993.

During his time at Huddersfield, Tony came close to ending Sunderland's eight-game winning run in 1996 before he was beaten by two late Michael Bridges goals at Roker Park. It was one of just seven league appearances for the Terriers where he signed for his old Hull teammate Brian Horton. There had been 442 in all competitions for the Tigers (placing him fifth on the club's all-time appearances list), but none for Burnley where he came through the youth system, but did not play for the reserves or first team. At Hull, Tony signed for former Wales manager Mike Smith who knew Norman from Wales Under 21 squads. A model of consistency for Hull, as he later was at Sunderland, between August 1983 and September 1988, he made 226 consecutive league appearances for the Tigers.

Norman also won five caps for Wales, a total that would have been far higher but for him being a contemporary of Neville Southall. After retiring from goalkeeping Tony became a policeman and later worked as a goalkeeping coach at Darlington 1883, Gateshead and Blyth Spartans. He also had a spell back at Sunderland in the late 2000s working with young goalkeepers. Norman suffered from cardiomyopathy - a heart condition. As of 2022, Tony was working on producing a goalkeeping manual.

## NOSWORTHY, Nyron Paul Henry

**POSITION:** Defender

**BIRTHPLACE:** Brixton, London

**DATE OF BIRTH:** 11/10/1980

**HEIGHT:** 5' 11" **WEIGHT:** 13st 6lbs

**SIGNED FROM:** Gillingham, 10/06/2005

**DEBUT:** v Charlton Athletic, H, 13/08/2005

**LAST MATCH:** v Everton, A, 27/01/2010

**MOVED TO:** Watford, 10/01/2012

**TEAMS:** Gillingham, Sunderland, Sheffield United (L), Watford, Bristol City (L), Blackpool, Portsmouth (L), Dagenham & Redbridge

**INTERNATIONAL:** Jamaica

**SAFC TOTALS:** 113+12 appearances / 0 goals

**Signed on a free transfer from Gillingham who had just been relegated from the league Sunderland had just won, 'Nugsy' was intended as back-up to Stephen Wright, but when Wright was injured in the opening game of the season, Nosworthy came off the bench. His first two involvements saw him fail to do something simple and then succeed in doing something difficult.**

This became symbolic of Nosworthy's time at Sunderland where he became a cult-hero of supporters due to his whole-hearted commitment. If ever Nyron made a mistake, it rarely proved costly as he was always fast enough, strong enough and determined enough to rectify his error. Although he never scored a goal in competitive action, he did score against Sporting Lisbon on a pre-season game in Albufeira in 2008 that helped Sunderland to win a huge pre-season cup. This was Nyron's second piece of silverware at Sunderland. He had won the Championship in 2007 after being relegated in his opening campaign. During the Championship-winning season, manager Roy Keane converted Nugsy from his erstwhile right-back berth to centre-back where he was very successfully partnered with the young and talented Jonny Evans.

In his last three seasons at Sunderland Nyron had two loans to Sheffield United and another at Watford, not appearing at all for Sunderland in his final couple of years. He played 50+1 games for the Blades who were relegated in his second season there. At Watford, who he initially joined on loan on 28 October 2011, he went on to play 60+1 and scored his first two goals since his Gillingham days.

There was a further goal in a ten-game loan to Bristol City before a free transfer to Lee Clark's Blackpool where he played five first-team games and appeared back at the Academy of Light in a reserve team match. Blackpool loaned him to Portsmouth where he made 6+1 appearances before a final move to Dagenham & Redbridge brought a goal and 23+1 games, the final one in a 2-0 FA Cup defeat at Everton in January 2016 - the same venue and score-line as his final Sunderland appearance.

Qualifying for Jamaica through his father, Nyron won the first of his 14 caps against Guyana in May 2012 and scored an international goal against Antigua and Barbuda in a FIFA World Cup qualifying game. Fellow Jamaica international Ethan Pinnock who played for Barnsley and Brentford amongst others is a cousin.

## NUNEZ GARCIA, Milton Omar

**POSITION:** Forward

**BIRTHPLACE:** Tegucigalpa, Honduras

**DATE OF BIRTH:** 30/10/1972

**HEIGHT:** 5' 5" **WEIGHT:** 10st 7lbs

**SIGNED FROM:** PAOK Salonika, 23/03/2000

**DEBUT:** v Wimbledon, H, 08/04/2000

**LAST MATCH:** v Luton Town, A, 26/09/2000

**MOVED TO:** Released from contract, 01/06/2001

**TEAMS:** Deportivo Progreseno, Real Espana, Comunicaciones, Cuidad de Guatemala, Nacional, PAOK Salonika, Sunderland, Nacional, Comunicaciones, Pachuca, Necaxa, CD Marathon San Pedro Sula, Comunicaciones, Real Espana, Olimpia, CD Marathon, CD Jalapa, Universidad De San Carlos, Comunicaciones, Deportivo Ayutla, CD Victoria

**INTERNATIONAL:** Honduras

**SAFC TOTALS:** 0+2 appearances / 0 goals

**Officially listed as being 5' 5" tall, Milton Nunez seemed to be a couple of inches smaller than this, but did seem to have a jet-heeled spring when jumping for the ball. Controversy surrounded his signing when he reportedly cost £1.6m. When he was interviewed in the Honduran newspaper Diez in 2017 Nunez claimed that SAFC signed him by accident having mixed him up with another player.**

Apparently, Sunderland later reached an out of court settlement with Nunez's agent Pablo Betancourt. It was a murky story of complicated arrangements where reportedly the player's registration was held by Nacional in Uruguay. Having played in Honduras, Guatemala and Uruguay, Nunez came to Europe with PAOK in Greece where he had apparently played 4+6 games when Sunderland moved for him.

His first-team game-time with Sunderland comprised 44 minutes, two thirds of that time in a League Cup tie at Luton where he entered the fray with Sunderland leading 5-0 on aggregate. During his time with Sunderland, Nunez was capped by Honduras in FIFA World Cup qualifying games against Costa Rica, USA, Mexico, and Trinidad & Tobago who included Dwight Yorke, Carlos Edwards and Stern John, who scored. In total Nunez scored 33 goals in 88 games for his country.

Nunez played most games for Comunicaciones of Guatemala with whom he scored 18 goals in 88 games across three spells during a well-travelled post Sunderland career in Central and South America. Nicknamed 'Tyson', the player never lived up to a heavyweight reputation. Milton was still playing regularly into his 40s and played in the same side as his son, also called Milton, for his final club CD Victoria in the Honduran first division.

## NYATANGA, Lewin John

**POSITION:** Defender

**BIRTHPLACE:** Burton upon Trent, Staffordshire

**DATE OF BIRTH:** 18/08/1988

**HEIGHT:** 6' 2" **WEIGHT:** 12st 8lbs

**SIGNED FROM:** Derby County, 19/10/2006, on loan

**DEBUT:** v Barnsley, H, 21/10/2006

**LAST MATCH:** v Leicester City, A, 01/01/2007

**MOVED TO:** Derby County, 02/01/2007, end of loan

**TEAMS:** Derby County, Sunderland (L), Barnsley (L), Bristol City, Peterborough United (L), Barnsley, Northampton Town (L)

**INTERNATIONAL:** Wales

**SAFC TOTALS:** 9+2 appearances / 0 goals

**Borrowed from Derby, Nyatanga played a handful of games for Sunderland, joining in 2006 - a year when he was named Wales' Young Player of the Year and had been the Rams Young Player of the Year for 2005-06.**

Qualifying for Wales through his mother (his father was from Zimbabwe), Lewin won the Man of the Match award on his international debut against Paraguay (who included Paolo Da Silva and Cristian Riveros) on St David's Day 2006 when at 17 years and 195 days, he became his country's youngest full international. By the age of 21, Nyatanga had won the last of his 34 full caps.

Following his loan to Sunderland, Lewin had three loans with Barnsley totalling 51+2 games. He did not score for the Tykes, but got a first goal for parent club Derby at Portsmouth in January 2008, only for future Sunderland man Benjani to hit a hat-trick for the home side. Lewin eventually managed four goals in 69+7 games for the Rams before joining Bristol City in the summer of 2009 when the Robins were managed by Lee Johnson's father Gary.

In four years at Ashton Gate, Nyatanga played 102+8 times, contributing four goals. There were also three games on a loan to Peterborough during his second season as a Bristol player. Returning to Barnsley, who he joined on a free in July 2013, he made a further 87+4 games scoring eight goals. However, Paul Heckingbottom left him on the bench as a Barnsley side including Josh Scowen, Ashley Fletcher and captain Conor Hourihane beat a Millwall team including Carlos Edwards and sub Aiden O'Brien in the 2016 League One Play-Off final. A last loan to Northampton brought 39+3 games in Lewin's last season of 2016-17, the player still being in his 20s when he played his last game.

During his mid-twenties, Nyatanga began studying for a sports science degree and after giving up football early became a personal trainer with a Bedford-based company, the DVCC having turned down the offer of a new contract at Northampton.

Growing up as a fanatical Derby supporter, he played for the club from the age of seven, was released at eleven, re-signed at 14 and debuted for the first-team a few days after turning 17. He went on to play 69+7 games and score four goals for Derby in a club career of 361+25 games before walking away from the game he once loved.

# O

## OAKLEY, James Ernest (Jimmy)

**POSITION:** Full-back

**BIRTHPLACE:** Seghill, Northumberland

**DATE OF BIRTH:** 10/11/1901 - 23/09/1972

**HEIGHT:** 5' 7" **WEIGHT:** 11st 4lbs

**SIGNED FROM:** Blyth Spartans, 04/05/1922

**DEBUT:** v Bolton Wanderers, A, 09/09/1922

**LAST MATCH:** v Nottingham Forest, A, 19/02/1930

**MOVED TO:** Reading, 25/07/1930

**TEAMS:** Seaton Delaval, Blyth Spartans, Sunderland, Reading, Northampton Town, Kettering Town, Birtley

**SAFC TOTALS:** 90 appearances / 0 goals

**Having qualified as a mining engineer before becoming a footballer, Oakley played for SAFC in eight seasons throughout the 1920s. Bob Kyle was so keen to sign him that he waited for him, and signed him, outside the pit where he worked, which proved a good decision as there were representatives of three other clubs waiting for Oakley when he got home.**

After making a single appearance in his debut season the full-back, who could play on either side, managed between eight and 20 appearances in his other campaigns, reaching double figures five times. After spending his best years as a reliable reserve at Roker he went to Reading in search of regular football, being transferred in a double deal with Adam Allan for a joint fee of £2,500.

Oakley was to be disappointed, playing only nine league games in his year with the team, then known as the Biscuitmen, before a move to Northampton where he added 33 Division Three South appearances in two years before his return to the north east with Birtley via a short spell at non-league Kettering Town. After his playing days were over he worked as a coal miner before running a Durham hotel.

## O'BRIEN, Aiden Anthony

**POSITION:** Forward

**BIRTHPLACE:** Islington, London

**DATE OF BIRTH:** 04/10/1993

**HEIGHT:** 6' 0" **WEIGHT:** 11st 5lbs

**SIGNED FROM:** Millwall, 30/07/2020

**DEBUT:** v Hull City, H, 05/09/2020

**LAST MATCH:** v Portsmouth, H, 22/01/2022

**MOVED TO:** Portsmouth, 31/01/2022

**TEAMS:** Millwall, Staines Town (L), Hayes & Yeading (L), Crawley Town (L), Aldershot Town (L), Torquay United (L), Sunderland, Portsmouth, Shrewsbury Town (to August 2022)

**INTERNATIONAL:** Republic of Ireland

**SAFC TOTALS:** 39+27 appearances / 12 goals

**Half of O'Brien's goals came in cup competitions including a League Cup hat-trick at Blackpool, but despite that and scoring in his penultimate match for the club, he struggled to hold a regular place.**

This was particularly the case in his second season when he was transferred to Portsmouth in January after playing his final game against them.

His first season at Sunderland saw him play an unselfish role in helping Charlie Wyke notch 31 goals. O'Brien missed out on a Wembley final against Tranmere Rovers in the Football League (Papa John's) Trophy, but he did appear as a sub in a Play-Off game at home to Lincoln City. Sunderland signed O'Brien from his first club Millwall for whom he played 152+74 games and scored 44 goals including a hat-trick at Crewe in September 2015, but was unable to find the back of the net at Wembley in the League One Play-Off final with Barnsley.

On that occasion he came off the bench before half-time for a side that included Carlos Edwards against a Tykes team that featured Josh Scowen, Ashley Fletcher and Conor Hourihane. Skipper Hourihane had been a youth player at Sunderland as had Tykes manager Paul Heckingbottom. A year later, after 15 goals in his best season, O'Brien was in the winning side in the Play-Off final against a Bradford City side that included Charlie Wyke.

During his time with Millwall O'Brien had four loans, playing 6+1 games without scoring in the Blue Square Premier with Hayes & Yeading, none in nine League One substitute appearances for Crawley, three in five Conference games with Aldershot and none in three League Two games as a sub with Torquay United. At Portsmouth he scored five goals in 8+9 before switching to Shrewsbury in the summer 2022 by which time he had won five full caps with the Republic of Ireland, scoring against Poland.

## O'DONNELL, Dennis

**POSITION:** Inside-right

**BIRTHPLACE:** Willington Quay, Northumberland

**DATE OF BIRTH:** 24/12/1879 - 29/05/1939

**HEIGHT:** 5' 9½" **WEIGHT:** 11st 7lbs

**SIGNED FROM:** Lincoln City, 05/05/1905

**DEBUT:** v Blackburn Rovers, H, 28/10/1905

**LAST MATCH:** v Preston North End, H, 16/04/1906

**MOVED TO:** QPR, 02/05/1906

**TEAMS:** Willington Wednesday, Willington Athletic, Lincoln City, Sunderland, QPR, Notts County, Bradford Park Avenue

**SAFC TOTALS:** 22 appearances / 5 goals

**O'Donnell reputedly scored eight goals when SAFC reserves once scored 15 in a Northern Alliance game against South Shields Adelaide. He came to Sunderland from Lincoln City who received a club record of £350 after he had registered 31 goals in 118 Second Division games.**

The transfer also involved Peter Mackin going to Lincoln in part-exchange. Mackin was an 'A' team (Reserve) player who would be killed in action during World War One.

Dennis made a spectacular scoring debut for Sunderland, taking the ball from the half-way line, beating one defender and out-pacing another before firing home.

All of his games and goals came that season, all of the goals in home wins (including his final appearance) before he moved to QPR. Debuting at Luton in a Southern League game on 1 September 1906, he went on to score seven goals in 25 games in a struggling side in that competition, as well as appearing in two FA Cup games. His brother Magnus also played for the Imps as well as Barnsley.

## O'DONOVAN, Roy Simon

**POSITION:** Forward

**BIRTHPLACE:** Cork, Ireland

**DATE OF BIRTH:** 10/08/1985

**HEIGHT:** 5' 10" **WEIGHT:** 11st 9lbs

**SIGNED FROM:** Cork City, 07/08/2007

**DEBUT:** v Birmingham City, A, 15/08/2007

**LAST MATCH:** v Arsenal, H, 11/05/2008

**MOVED TO:** Coventry City, 25/06/2010

**TEAMS:** Blarney Street United, Coventry City, Cork City, Sunderland, Dundee United (L), Blackpool (L), Southend United (L), Hartlepool United (L), Coventry City, Hibernian (L), Northampton Town, Brunei DPMM, Mitra Kukar, Central Coast Mariners, Newcastle Jets, Brisbane Roar, Newcastle Jets, Sydney Olympic (to June 2022)

**INTERNATIONAL:** Republic of Ireland Under 21 and 'B'

**SAFC TOTALS:** 5+14 appearances / 0 goals

**Roy Keane's contacts in Ireland brought Roy O'Donovan to his attention with the manager impressed enough to commit a record League of Ireland transfer fee of €500,000 with the potential for that amount to double. It quickly became apparent that Cork City would not be receiving much more than the original fee because while O'Donovan was quick and had an excellent attitude, ultimately, he did not quite have the quality required for the Premier League which his fellow Corkman Keane had just guided the Lads into.**

Indeed, O'Donovan's most memorable moment in red and white came on his debut, but rather than being a flash of skill, it saw him fall on top of Birmingham goalkeeper Colin Doyle as Stern John scored a last-minute equaliser against his old club, much to the frustration of Blues future Sunderland boss Steve Bruce.

This is not to suggest O'Donovan was a bad player. He was not. He just was not Premier League quality either and never got a goal in red and white other than in pre-season games. From Sunderland he had a series of loans, the highlight being a hat-trick for Hartlepool against Southend who he had been loaned to earlier in the same 2009-10 season. Roy's quartet of loans from SAFC brought a total of 38+7 appearances, nine of his eleven loan goals coming in 15 of those games for Hartlepool.

Leaving Sunderland for Coventry, O'Donovan was joining a club he had been with as an untried youngster. He had left the Sky Blues without playing a senior match to join Cork where he scored 44 times in 100 games, including a UEFA Cup goal against Lithuanian outfit Ekranas and another in the Intertoto Cup against Hammerby of Sweden. He also tasted Champions League football, albeit in the qualifying rounds.

Returning to Coventry five years after leaving the club's academy, O'Donovan debuted against Morecambe in the League (Carling) Cup and got his solitary goal in 10+14 games against Bury. Troubled by injury, he was loaned to Hibs where he got a couple of goals in 6+10 games before leaving Coventry to sign for Aidy Boothroyd at Northampton after one game on trial for Cheltenham Town reserves, Boothroyd having signed him for Coventry from Sunderland.

Despite being troubled by a hernia injury, O'Donovan found the net eight times in 29+6 games for the Cobblers before leaving the UK to begin globe-trotting in 2015. From there to the time of writing in 2022, O'Donovan had plied his trade in the Singapore League with DPMM of Brunei scoring 26 goals in 35 games, had one game for Mitra Kukar in the short-lived Indonesian Super League and subsequently several clubs in Australia where he duly became an Australian citizen and had bagged 65 goals in 141 games up to May 2022.

## OGILVIE, Gary Francis

**POSITION:** Right-back

**BIRTHPLACE:** Dundee, Angus

**DATE OF BIRTH:** 16/11/1967

**HEIGHT:** 5' 10" **WEIGHT:** 12st 2lbs

**SIGNED FROM:** Dundee, 20/02/1988

**DEBUT:** v West Ham United, A, 12/10/1988

**LAST MATCH:** v Blackburn Rovers, A, 22/12/1988

**MOVED TO:** Airdrieonians, 09/02/1989

**TEAMS:** Dundee, Sunderland, Airdrieonians, Dundee St Joseph's, Carnoustie Panmure, Forfar West End

**INTERNATIONAL:** Scotland U-20

**SAFC TOTALS:** 0+3 appearances / 0 goals

**Each of Gary's three appearances for SAFC was in a different competition; a debut in the League Cup followed by a league game at Chelsea and then a final game in the Simod Cup.**

He went on to make eight appearances for Airdrieonians after leaving Sunderland before a contract dispute ultimately brought his professional career to an end. Defender Ogilvie changed career and became a policeman rising through the ranks to become Chief Inspector in the Dundee region. He also returned to the game he loved playing for a number of Scottish Junior teams into his early 40s.

## O'HARE, John

**POSITION:** Centre-forward

**BIRTHPLACE:** Renton, Dunbartonshire

**DATE OF BIRTH:** 24/09/1946

**HEIGHT:** 5' 9" **WEIGHT:** 11st 11lbs

**SIGNED FROM:** Drumchapel Amateurs, 01/07/1962

**DEBUT:** v Chelsea, A, 29/08/1964

**LAST MATCH:** v Everton, A, 16/05/1967

**MOVED TO:** Derby County, 14/08/1967

**TEAMS:** Drumchapel Amateurs, Sunderland, Derby County, Leeds United, Nottingham Forest, Dallas Tornado, Belper Town, Carriage and Wagon

**INTERNATIONAL:** Scotland

**SAFC TOTALS:** 59 appearances / 21 goals

**John O'Hare had a great career. He came through the Sunderland youth system a few years after his school friend Dominic Sharkey, and played under the watchful eye of Brian Clough who began his coaching career with the youth team at Sunderland and subsequently signed O'Hare for Derby, Leeds and Nottingham Forest winning medals with the Rams and Forest.**

Known as 'Solly' as a boy, O'Hare was only 17 when he debuted in the top division for Sunderland and only 20 by the time he was allowed to leave. He was even younger, when in November 1963, he played against Benfica in a Roker Park friendly as a sub. Derby got exceptional value for the £22,000 Clough paid for O'Hare who played 248 times for the Rams returning 65 goals and contributing to many more as he won the league title with them in 1972, having first won promotion in 1969. Capped 13 times by Scotland between 1970 and 72, he scored five international goals, including a debut winner away to Northern Ireland.

Like Clough, John's time at Leeds was short lived. He played just seven times in six months before going to Forest where he won promotion, the league title and ultimately the European Cup twice. An unused sub in the 1979 final, he came off the bench for the last of his 122+11 appearances for Forest as they retained the trophy against Hamburg in Madrid when Jim Montgomery was an unused sub to a team that included Martin O'Neill, Frank Gray and Ian Bowyer. O'Hare also won the League Cup with Forest in 1978, coming on as a substitute at Wembley against Liverpool and starting the replay at Old Trafford. O'Hare contributed 20 goals for Forest.

Following a spell in the USA, O'Hare ended up in the East Midlands League with Carriage and Wagon FC before managing local Derby sides Ockbrook and Stanton. He became a licensee in Derby before working for a combustion firm and a transport company as well as scouting for Leicester City and Aston Villa.

## OLIVER, James Henry Kenneth (Ken)

**POSITION:** Centre-forward / centre-half

**BIRTHPLACE:** Loughborough, Leicestershire

**DATE OF BIRTH:** 10/08/1924 - 13/05/1994

**HEIGHT:** 5' 11" **WEIGHT:** 10st 12lbs

**SIGNED FROM:** Brush Sports, 03/08/1946

**DEBUT:** v Preston North End, A, 25/10/1947

**LAST MATCH:** v Portsmouth, H, 12/03/1949

**MOVED TO:** Derby County, 16/09/1949

**TEAMS:** Brush Sports, Sunderland, Derby County, Exeter City

**SAFC TOTALS:** 8 appearances / 1 goal

**Having served with the RAF in Ceylon (now Sri Lanka) in World War Two, during which he played alongside Tommy Reynolds and Tommy McLain, Oliver signed from Loughborough side Brush Sports as soon as he was demobbed.**

Ken played four times in each of two seasons late in the forties, the first three games being at centre-forward, when he scored his only Sunderland goal. He went on to give Derby great service, helping them to win Division Three North in 1957 and playing in 184 league games (scoring once) before moving to Exeter where he added 92 further appearances after a £1,250 transfer in January 1958. An ever-present in his first full season as the Grecians narrowly missed out on promotion, he remained as a regular until April 1960 when his career ended when he dislocated his ankle playing against Darlington. Following his retirement from playing, he became director of a sports goods company in Derby.

## OLIVER, John Cook

**POSITION:** Left-back

**BIRTHPLACE:** Southwick, Co Durham

**DATE OF BIRTH:** 21/11/1868 - 12/09/1944

**HEIGHT:** 5' 6" **WEIGHT:** 11st 8lbs

**SIGNED FROM:** Southwick, 1886

**DEBUT:** v Newcastle West End, A, 13/11/1886

**LAST MATCH:** v Darwen, H, 12/12/1891

**MOVED TO:** Middlesbrough Ironopolis, 15/06/1892

**TEAMS:** Southwick, Sunderland, Sunderland Albion (L), Middlesbrough Ironopolis, Small Heath, Durham City

**SAFC TOTALS:** 34 appearances / 0 goals

**'Dowk' Oliver was a major figure in SAFC'S early history. His 34 games listed were just the officially competitive games he played, but he appeared in many more fiercely contested challenge matches of the era. Captain of the club in 1888-89, Oliver played in the club's first-ever league game in September 1890 and had played as a one-off appearance in Sunderland Albion's first-ever game on 5 May 1888.**

Having missed just three league games and played in every match of a cup run as the Lads reached the semi-final in Sunderland's first season as a Football League club, he was restricted to just three appearances during the following campaign when as a rare local player in a team of Scots, he lost his place to Donald Gow. As Sunderland were crowned champions in 1892, 'Dowk' departed for Teesside and the ambitious Middlesbrough Ironopolis. After two seasons with the club who were admitted to the Football League in his second season, Oliver joined Small Heath who later became Birmingham City.

# O

## OLIVER, John Cook (Continued)

In September 1894 he played in their first-ever top-flight game, a local derby with reigning champions Aston Villa. He missed only two games that season but had an unhappy return to Wearside as his team were hammered 7-1 by The Team of All The Talents. In his second season with Small Heath 'Dowk' missed just one game, but could not prevent the club going down, after which he returned to the north east with Durham City in 1896. The brother-in-law of William Gibson, 'Dowk' became a caulker and boilermaker after his football days were over. His death, aged almost 76, was caused by a pulmonary embolism sustained after a fall from staging whilst working in the shipyards.

## O'NEILL, Alan (See HOPE, Alan)

## O'NEILL, James (Jimmy)

**POSITION:** Centre-forward

**BIRTHPLACE:** Magheramorne, Co Antrim

**DATE OF BIRTH:** 24/11/1941

**HEIGHT:** 5' 10" **WEIGHT:** 10st 11lbs

**SIGNED FROM:** Magheramorne Juniors, 01/06/1958

**DEBUT:** v Bristol Rovers, H, 13/01/1962

**LAST MATCH:** v Preston North End, H, 21/03/1962

**MOVED TO:** Walsall, 14/12/1962

**TEAMS:** Sunderland, Walsall, Hakoah, Darlington, Coleraine, Hakoah

**INTERNATIONAL:** Northern Ireland

**SAFC TOTALS:** 7 appearances / 6 goals

**Two goals in a 6-1 debut win were understandably not sufficient for Jimmy O'Neill to keep his place as he was standing in for Brian Clough, but when Clough missed the next match, O'Neill came back in and scored again.**

The Irishman, who had been signed straight from school four years earlier, was dropped again immediately as Clough was fit to play the next game, but after two more matches on the sidelines, O'Neill was back in for a run of five games in which he scored another three goals. A month after what proved to be his final Sunderland appearance, Jimmy won his only full international cap in a 4-0 defeat to Wales.

Despite this outstanding record, he was sold to Walsall for £9,000 without being given another chance by Sunderland. In three years with the Saddlers, he scored a more modest 13 goals in 38 appearances before going to Australia in 1965 to play for Hakoah in Melbourne. Returning to England, Jimmy scored four times in 23 games for Darlington before a spell with Coleraine where he won domestic cups in 1968 and 1969 before once again returning to his team in Australia.

## O'NIEN, Luke Terry

**POSITION:** Midfielder / defender

**BIRTHPLACE:** Hemel Hempstead, Hertfordshire

**DATE OF BIRTH:** 21/11/1994

**HEIGHT:** 5' 9" **WEIGHT:** 11st 9lbs

**SIGNED FROM:** Wycombe Wanderers, 30/07/2018

**DEBUT:** v Charlton Athletic, H, 04/08/2018

**LAST MATCH:**

**MOVED TO:**

**TEAMS:** Watford, Wealdstone (L), Wycombe Wanderers, Sunderland (to June 2022)

**SAFC TOTALS:** 151+24 appearances / 15 goals (to June 2022)

**Deservedly immensely popular with fans, Luke O'Nien came to Sunderland and impressed with his commitment and willingness to always put the team first by playing in a wide variety of positions. Wherever he was asked to play, Luke's determination was always to the fore and when in an attacking area, he always possessed a goal threat.**

During 2021-22 he continued to play through the pain barrier due to a shoulder that had been dislocated, until having to give way to surgery after finding he was regularly targeted by the physical approach of opponents. He returned after three months out to help the Lads to promotion. A tremendously nice, polite and helpful person off the pitch, he left that persona at the touchline and morphed into a modern professional not afraid of using the tricks of the trade to try to gain whatever competitive edge he could.

O'Nien came through the ranks at Watford who he joined as a nine-year-old. Eventually, he got a few minutes first-team action in a Hornets shirt as a late sub against Barnsley at Vicarage Road in March 2014. He gained more experience with 31 games (and four goals) on loan to Wealdstone who progressed from the Isthmian League to Conference South during the timespan of Luke's two loans there. In his absence, Watford were promoted to the Premier League and released him in the summer of 2015 at which point he signed for Wycombe who were in League Two at the time.

A promotion winner in the last of his three seasons with the Chairboys, he made 111+8 appearances and scored 16 goals. A Community Player of the Year winner at Wycombe, O'Nien was Young Player of the Year in his first season at Sunderland. A great nephew of the Singapore politician Lim Kim San who received his country's highest honour, O'Nien is qualified to represent Singapore though his maternal grandfather.

## ONUOHA, Chinedum (Nedum)

**POSITION:** Defender

**BIRTHPLACE:** Warri, Nigeria

**DATE OF BIRTH:** 12/11/1986

**HEIGHT:** 6' 2" **WEIGHT:** 12st 4lbs

**SIGNED FROM:** Manchester City, 11/08/2010, on loan

**DEBUT:** v Birmingham City, H, 14/08/2010

**LAST MATCH:** v West Ham United, A, 22/05/2011

**MOVED TO:** Manchester City, 23/05/2011, end of loan

**TEAMS:** Manchester City, Sunderland (L), QPR, Real Salt Lake

**INTERNATIONAL:** England Under 21

**SAFC TOTALS:** 32 appearances / 1 goal

**Nedum Onuoha's only goal for Sunderland was brilliant. Channelling his inner Dick Malone, Onuoha danced his way through the rear-guard of defending champions Chelsea at Stamford Bridge to open the scoring in what became a famous 3-0 win as the Blues unbeaten home record was shattered.**

While Nedum's goal was a bonus, his bread and butter was solid defensive work and he showed himself to be a strong, intelligent and accomplished defender when playing 31 of the 38 Premier League games, as for the only time to date since the Peter Reid era, Sunderland succeeded in finishing in the top half of the top flight.

Raised in Manchester, Onuoha came through the ranks at Manchester City who he joined as ten-year-old, debuting in a Carling Cup clash with Arsenal in October 2004. He played 91+25 games for City, scoring five goals. Three of those games came after his loan to Sunderland, but despite City winning all three of those without conceding a goal, clearly the decision had already been taken to let him go and in the January following his Sunderland loan, Onuoha signed for QPR.

Nedum gave great service to the Londoners playing 210+14 times with eight goals, a highlight being playing in the 2014 Championship Play-Off alongside Danny Simpson as Derby County were defeated at Wembley. (Onuoha also had a spell as a teammate of Djibril Cisse at QPR). Shortly before his 32nd birthday, Nedum moved to Real Salt Lake and had three seasons in the USA. Debuting at Kansas City in September 2018, three of his five games straight after signing were in the MLS Play-Offs, Kansas City beating Onuoha's new club on aggregate. He took his total to 45+2 games (1 goal) playing in the 2019 MLS Play-Offs against Seattle Sounders before signing off in November 2020, once again against Kansas.

As a 14-year-old, he was runner-up in the English Schools Athletic Association Junior 100 metres, clocking 11.09 seconds, while he also excelled at triple jump. As an international, Nedum captained England at Under 21 level. He scored in the 2009 European Under 21 Championship semi-final against Sweden and played alongside Lee Cattermole and Adam Johnson in the final lost to Germany. Jack Rodwell and Craig Gardner also came on in that game, but after Onuoha was substituted. Following his retirement from playing, Onuoha moved into football punditry, released an autobiography called 'Kicking Back' and hosted his own podcast 'Kickback with Nedum'.

## ORD, Richard John (Dickie)

**POSITION:** Defender

**BIRTHPLACE:** Murton, County Durham

**DATE OF BIRTH:** 03/03/1970

**HEIGHT:** 6' 2" **WEIGHT:** 12st 8lbs

**SIGNED FROM:** Schoolboy, 01/07/1986

**DEBUT:** v Southend United, H, 03/11/1987

**LAST MATCH:** v Sheffield United, A, 10/05/1998

**MOVED TO:** Queen's Park Rangers, 24/07/1998

**TEAMS:** Sunderland, York City (L), QPR

**INTERNATIONAL:** England Under 21

**SAFC TOTALS:** 256+28 appearances / 8 goals

**Debuting as a 17-year-old in a 7-0 win, Dickie Ord went on to become a cult hero with fans even recording a CD of their terrace chant, 'Who Needs Cantona When We've Got Dickie Ord?' - these words were also used as the title of his highly entertaining biography. Ord grew up as a massive Sunderland supporter despite breaking his leg as a three-year-old when falling off the settee while watching TV as Ian Porterfield scored in the 1973 FA Cup final!**

He played for Sunderland in eleven seasons making 45 appearances in the 1995-96 second-tier title-winning season when he carried out a clean sweep of Player of the Year awards. It was the third time Richard had played in a promotion-winning season, the third tier being won in his first campaign and promotion to the top flight coming two years later, although he only played in a handful of games in those campaigns, indeed spending a month of the 1989-90 season playing three games on loan to York City. In between, he had won the Young Player of the Year award in 1988-89, but again in 1991-92 it was a season in which injuries restricted him to a smattering of games in a year when the FA Cup final was reached.

In December 1990, he played alongside Brian Atkinson for England Under 21s in a goalless draw with Wales at Tranmere while at the end of that season he also played with Atkinson in victories over Mexico and the CIS in the Toulon Tournament in France

Rather like Shaun Elliott who had left not long before Ord came on the first-team scene, Richard was a cultured central defender whose ability on the ball often meant he was used in other positions. In Ord's case, he had spells in midfield and particularly at left-back, but it was in his best role at centre-back that he was a key part of the defensively solid 1996 Championship champions when he partnered Andy Melville.

That summer saw Ord stage the last ever Testimonial match at Roker Park against Steaua Bucharest, but he was later allowed to move on to QPR for a reported fee of £675,000.

It was a disastrous move as after damaging ligaments in his right knee in pre-season, he was forced to retire in January 2000 without playing a competitive game for his new club.

A decade later 'Ordy' became Interim manager of Durham City. This was followed by a stint as assistant before becoming manager in September 2011. This period simultaneously saw him running the 'Soccerarena' adjacent to Durham City's New Ferens Park. A keen cricketer, Richard had played cricket for Murton and from 2015 took over the running of Eppleton Cricket Club's football team.

## O'SHEA, John Francis

**POSITION:** Defender

**BIRTHPLACE:** Waterford, Republic of Ireland

**DATE OF BIRTH:** 30/04/1981

**HEIGHT:** 6' 3" **WEIGHT:** 13st 11lbs

**SIGNED FROM:** Manchester United, 07/07/2011

**DEBUT:** v Swansea City, A, 27/08/2011

**LAST MATCH:** v Wolverhampton Wanderers, H, 06/05/2018

**MOVED TO:** Reading, 01/07/2018

**TEAMS:** Waterford Bohemians, Manchester United, Bournemouth (L), Royal Antwerp (L), Sunderland, Reading

**INTERNATIONAL:** Republic of Ireland

**SAFC TOTALS:** 245+11 appearances / 4 goals

**Negotiating his contract when moving from Manchester United, John O'Shea apparently showed his ambition and winning mentality by insisting there was a bonus for reaching a cup final. He did get to a cup final with Sunderland, playing his part in getting the club to the 2014 League (Capital One) Cup final.**

O'Shea had been in seven cup finals with Manchester United where he played 393 games and scored 15 times. A very versatile player, he played in every position for United, even going in goal once at Tottenham in February 2007.

While at Old Trafford, O'Shea won the Champions League, World Club Cup, five Premier League titles, the League Cup twice, the FA Cup and the Community Shield on four occasions. After becoming a professional at Old Trafford when he was 17, John was sent on loan to Bournemouth (10/1) and Antwerp (14/0) to gain experience

Sometimes criticised by supporters who had got the impression that behind the scenes he was disruptive, nothing could have been further from the truth. O'Shea only wanted the best for the club and the fans and was a genuine leader off the pitch as well as on it. Having captained Manchester United twice, O'Shea became Sunderland captain. Vocal on the pitch, he was a good organiser in addition to being a model professional.

Upon leaving Sunderland, John moved to Reading where he teamed up with David Meyler and added eleven appearances to take his career tally in senior club football to 684 games with 20 goals. It was at Reading that he moved into coaching having begun work on his coaching badges while at Sunderland. After leaving Reading he became first team coach at Stoke City in July 2022, combining this role with being assistant manager of the Republic of Ireland Under 21s, a position he took up in April 2020.

Internationally, O'Shea was capped 118 times by the Republic of Ireland with Mick McCarthy giving him his debut against Croatia in 2001. Qualifying for Euro 2012, O'Shea played in all of Ireland's games at the tournament while a Sunderland player and shortly afterwards took over as captain of his country. Named as Ireland's international Player of the Year in 2014, the last of his three international goals saw John commemorate his 100th cap with a last-minute equaliser away to Germany in October of that year. The goal earned a point in Euro 2016 qualifying in which he captained Ireland under Martin O'Neill for the first couple of games of the tournament.

On one occasion I saw John play for Ireland, he won the man of the match award for a masterclass of a defensive display against Sweden in Stockholm. This was shortly after Zlatan Ibrahimovic had scored four goals against England. O'Shea was detailed to do a man marking job on Ibrahimovic and completely nullified him. O'Shea never even attempted to make a tackle. He simply screened him and jockeyed him every time the superstar got the ball, forcing him to drop the ball off to a less talented teammate. It was an object lesson in experienced play. As usual, O'Shea's display was not headline making, but highly effective. He was underrated at Sunderland, but the facts of his career speak for themselves.

## OSTER, John Morgan

**POSITION:** Winger

**BIRTHPLACE:** Boston, Lincolnshire

**DATE OF BIRTH:** 08/12/1978

**HEIGHT:** 5' 9" **WEIGHT:** 11st 5lbs

**SIGNED FROM:** Everton, 06/08/1999

**DEBUT:** v Watford, H, 10/08/1999

**LAST MATCH:** v Sheffield United, A, 28/09/2004

**MOVED TO:** Contract terminated, 27/01/2005

**TEAMS:** Grimsby Town, Everton, Sunderland, Barnsley (L), Grimsby Town (L), Leeds United (L), Burnley, Reading, Crystal Palace, Doncaster Rovers, Barnet, Gateshead

**INTERNATIONAL:** Wales

**SAFC TOTALS:** 66+25 appearances / 6 goals

**John Oster had two distinct periods at Sunderland. Initially, following his £1m move, his form was largely disappointing and he was viewed as a weak link, but later after a series of loans, he came back rejuvenated and inspired a probably not printable, but slightly rude chant, which alluded to his improvement, the key line of the rhyme stating, 'but now he's alright.'**

In his first four seasons at Sunderland, Oster started just seven league games, but played twice on loan to Barnsley and 17 (with six goals) in two loans with Grimsby who had been his first club. A knee injury sustained in a reserve game with Manchester United also did not help his cause.

# O

## OSTER, John Morgan (Continued)

Forty-one of his 66 starts over six seasons came in 2003-04 as Sunderland reached the Play-Offs and the semi-final of the FA Cup. In that semi-final with Millwall at Old Trafford, he hit the underside of the bar with an early free-kick. Had that been an inch or two lower and Sunderland had reached the final (and guaranteed European qualification as cup final opponents Manchester United qualified for the Champions League), Oster would have had bona fide hero status. Such is the fine dividing line between success and failure in football.

Reportedly, at one point, Howard Wilkinson did not play Oster because one further appearance would trigger an additional £250,000 payment to Everton. In time, he did play further games for Sunderland with the additional payment apparently waived as part of the deal that took Kevin Kilbane from Sunderland to Everton.

Oster had missed a penalty against the Lads when a teammate of Thomas Myhre and Don Hutchison in a League Cup shoot-out at Goodison Park in the season before signing for Sunderland. Everton had paid £1.5m for Oster after he caught the eye with four goals in 18+2 games for Grimsby. Debuting for the Toffees against Crystal Palace in August 1997, he went on to score three times for Everton where 22 of his 50 appearances were as a substitute.

He later played for Leeds on loan from Sunderland after Mick McCarthy took over. After initially impressing, the loan was cut short when he was disciplined by Leeds and suspended due to an incident at a Christmas party. This was not the only unpleasant incident he was involved in. Shortly before his final departure from Sunderland he was arrested apparently for assault outside a night club in Durham, while in 2002 Sunderland teammate Mark Maley had to undergo an eye operation after Oster was reported to have accidentally shot him with an air-gun neither knew was loaded.

Subsequently released by Sunderland, he signed for Burnley two days later. There were 14+4 games and one goal for the Clarets followed by a successful spell at Reading where he played 43+47 times (3 goals) and featured in the 2005-06 team that broke Sunderland's record of 105 points in a season when winning promotion to the Premiership as a teammate of Chris Makin.

From Reading John moved to Crystal Palace where his figures were 29+4/4 in 2008-09. 108+12/2 followed in three years at Doncaster before a final Football League season with Barnet where he netted twice in 23+5 League Two games in 2012-13. He then had a final two seasons in the north east with Gateshead for whom he scored three times in 74+1 games, playing alongside Ben Clark and former Sunderland reserve Jamie Chandler.

Qualifying for Wales due to his mother's family, John won 13 full caps, ten of them while on Sunderland's books. During his time with Everton he was sent off in two consecutive internationals.

## OUTTERSIDE, Mark Jeremy

**POSITION:** Right-back

**BIRTHPLACE:** Hexham, Northumberland

**DATE OF BIRTH:** 13/01/1967

**HEIGHT:** 5' 11" **WEIGHT:** 11st 8lbs

**SIGNED FROM:** Schoolboy, 01/07/1983

**DEBUT:** v Oldham Athletic, H, 21/03/1987

**LAST MATCH:** v Oldham Athletic, H, 21/03/1987

**MOVED TO:** Released, 30/06/1987

**TEAMS:** Sunderland, Blackburn Rovers (L), Darlington, Blyth Spartans, Blue Star, Hebburn, Whitley Bay, Consett

**SAFC TOTALS:** 1 appearance / 0 goals

**Mark Outterside made just one appearance for Sunderland, appearing in a dismal home defeat in the penultimate home match of the troubled reign of Lawrie McMenemy. Since coming to the club from Ryton School Mark had worked his way up to the first team and had a loan to Bobby Saxton's Blackburn after turning professional in 1985, although he did not get a first-team game.**

After leaving Sunderland he returned to Roker Park to play in the FA Cup for Darlington in 1987-88. During that campaign he started the last 35 league games of the season as Darlo finished 13th in what was then Division four, finishing with 39+1 appearances in all competitions.

In the summer of 2002, after playing for a number of local non-league sides, Mark became manager of Ryton and later went into teaching and became headteacher at Westerhope and later Waverly Primary Schools on Tyneside.

## OVERFIELD, Jack

**POSITION:** Winger

**BIRTHPLACE:** Osmondthorpe, West Riding of Yorkshire

**DATE OF BIRTH:** 14/05/1932

**HEIGHT:** 5' 9" **WEIGHT:** 11st 0lbs

**SIGNED FROM:** Leeds United, 16/08/1960

**DEBUT:** v Swansea Town, H, 20/08/1960

**LAST MATCH:** v Charlton Athletic, A, 28/08/1962

**MOVED TO:** Peterborough United, 11/02/1963

**TEAMS:** Leeds United, Sunderland, Peterborough United, Bradford City

**SAFC TOTALS:** 74 appearances / 5 goals

**A speed-merchant winger, Overfield cost Sunderland £11,500 to secure him from his hometown team Leeds. He had been on trials with Sheffield United and Bolton before signing for the Elland Road outfit in May 1953 after spending his youth playing for Ashley Road Methodists and Yorkshire Amateurs. He also played in RAF representative matches during his National Service.**

Raich Carter gave him his debut against Nottingham Forest in a 3-0 home win on 8 October 1955 after which he went on to make 31 appearances as Leeds won promotion to the top flight, Overfield's six goals included one in a home win over Liverpool, while the great John Charles benefited from much of Overfield's wing play. Overfield scored Leeds' first goal back in the top flight two minutes into the season to spark a 5-1 thrashing of Everton and went on to be ever-present as Carter's Leeds finished eighth. After 20 goals in 163 games for Leeds, Overfield came to Sunderland where he scored five times in 74 outings, missing just two games in 1961-62.

February 1963 brought a £5,000 move to Peterborough United where he played just once before returning to Yorkshire the following year to finish his career with eleven appearances for Bradford, the last at Newport in March 1965.

## OVIEDO JIMENEZ, Bryan Josué

**POSITION:** Left-back

**BIRTHPLACE:** Quesada, Costa Rica

**DATE OF BIRTH:** 18/02/1990

**HEIGHT:** 5' 8" **WEIGHT:** 10st 13lbs

**SIGNED FROM:** Everton, 30/01/2017

**DEBUT:** v Crystal Palace, A, 04/02/2017

**LAST MATCH:** v Charlton Athletic, N, 26/05/2019

**MOVED TO:** Copenhagen, 29/07/2019

**TEAMS:** Saprissa, Copenhagen, Nordsjaelland (L), Everton, Sunderland, Copenhagen

**INTERNATIONAL:** Costa Rica

**SAFC TOTALS:** 66+11 appearances / 2 goals

**Oviedo was a good quality player, one of the best of the group brought in by David Moyes from his old clubs Everton and Manchester United. He joined at the same time as his fellow Evertonian Darron Gibson. A Costa Rica international who played at the 2018 FIFA World Cup while with Sunderland, he was part of the Black Cats team that was relegated in consecutive seasons before being allowed to leave as Sunderland were eager to get him off their wage bill.**

Oviedo's final appearance was at Wembley in the 2019 League One Play-Off final after which he not only played, but scored in the following month's CONCACAF Gold Cup. The previous summer he had played against Brazil and Switzerland at the World Cup and altogether played 14 times for his country while on Sunderland's books.

After leaving the red and whites, Bryan returned to FC Copenhagen who had been his first European club. Three months after signing off for Sunderland at Wembley, he was in Champions League action for his new club and a year later returned to England to play in the Europa League for Copenhagen at Manchester United.

Originally he had come to Copenhagen in August 2010 from Costa Rican club Saprissa. Following a loan to Nordsjaelland in Norway, he did so well at Copenhagen that after two years he earned a move to Everton where he made a debut as a late sub away to Swansea.

To start with he was a fringe player at Goodison, but a late winner against Manchester United in December 2013 raised his profile only for him to suffer a badly broken leg the following month. The injury kept him out for nine months before he returned to play for five months before suffering another injury. He went on to total 45+23 games for Everton with two goals before his move to Wearside. Remaining a regular international, Bryan had been capped 71 times up to June 2022.

## OWERS, Gary

**POSITION:** Midfielder / right-back

**BIRTHPLACE:** Newcastle, Northumberland

**DATE OF BIRTH:** 03/10/1968

**HEIGHT:** 5' 10" **WEIGHT:** 11st 10lbs

**SIGNED FROM:** Chester-le-Street Schoolboys, 17/06/1985

**DEBUT:** v Brentford, 15/08/1987

**LAST MATCH:** Bristol City, H, 17/12/1994

**MOVED TO:** Bristol City, 23/12/1994

**TEAMS:** Sunderland, Bristol City, Notts County, Forest Green Rovers, Bath City, Forest Green Rovers, Weston-super-Mare, Minehead, Yate Town

**SAFC TOTALS:** 307+13 appearances / 27 goals

**From his debut in Sunderland's first-ever third tier game until his departure seven and a half years later, Owers was a fixture in the Sunderland side, mainly in midfield, but on occasion at right-back - including the 1992 FA Cup final. A promotion winner in his first and third seasons, Gary was eventually sold to Bristol City in part exchange for Martin Scott.**

At Ashton Gate he scored nine goals in 130 league games, winning promotion in 1998 before joining Sam Allardyce's Notts County where he made 154 league appearances with a dozen goals before joining Forest Green Rovers in 2002 where he signed for future Sunderland goalkeeping coach Nigel Spink. After 50 games and one goal Gary became player/manager of Bath City for two years, combining that role with being a Somerset FA coach working in grassroots football.

He then became Forest Green Rovers first-ever full-time manager. During this time he welcomed Sunderland for their first match under Niall Quinn's Drumaville Consortium. Intending to bring himself on as a sub - which he did - he insisted on his team wearing their away kit because the club's kit at the time was black and white stripes and Gary said there was no way he was playing against 'his club' wearing black and white.

After two years Owers re-joined the FA as a coach before joining Portsmouth as Director and senior manager of Pompey in the Community as well as head of football development. After two years at Fratton Park Gary became assistant manager of Aldershot for another two years, after which he scouted for Leyton Orient prior to spending 2011-12 as first-team coach at Bristol City. Also employed as an OPTA analyst, he then moved to Plymouth Argyle where roles included assistant manager, head coach and coach to the Under 18s and Under 21s.

Continuing an extensive post-playing career, Owers then scouted for Gillingham before a geographical jump to become chief scout for Partick Thistle and subsequently Motherwell where as Head of Recruitment, Louis Laing was one of the players he brought to the club. Having played for Malcolm Crosby in the 1992 FA Cup final for Sunderland, he then took up a post as 'Crossa's' assistant manager at Gateshead where they took George Honeyman and Lynden Gooch on loan. Following that Gary once again scouted for Partick before managing Bath City in 2016-17 and Torquay United the following season. As of June 2022, Gary had been in a role as head of Player Development at the National League since 2019, while since 2017 he had been summarising Bristol City games on local BBC radio

Gary's son Josh came through the Bristol City academy and in 2021 went on loan to Bath City.

## OZTURK, Alim

**POSITION:** Centre-back

**BIRTHPLACE:** Alkmaar, Netherlands

**DATE OF BIRTH:** 17/11/1992

**HEIGHT:** 6' 3" **WEIGHT:** 13st 5lbs

**SIGNED FROM:** Boluspor, 01/07/2018

**DEBUT:** v Charlton Athletic, H, 04/08/2018

**LAST MATCH:** v Bristol Rovers, A, 10/03/2020

**MOVED TO:** Contract not renewed, 30/06/2020

**TEAMS:** SC Cambuur, Trabzonspor, 1461 Trabzon (L), Hearts, Boluspor, Sunderland, Ümraniyespor (to June 2022)

**INTERNATIONAL:** Turkey Under 21

**SAFC TOTALS:** 40+5 appearances / 0 goals

**Alim Ozturk's time at Sunderland came to a sudden end when the 2019-20 season was curtailed due to Covid 19. It was his second season on Wearside. In most of his early games he had looked awkward and gangly, but improved and had made more than twice as many league appearances in his second campaign than his first when the season was cut short.**

Born in the Netherlands to Turkish parents, Ozturk played in Turkey before and after his time at Sunderland. Playing regularly in a promotion campaign for Umraniyespor he was called up for the full national side in the autumn of 2021, but as of June 2022 awaited a full cap, although he had won Under 21 recognition before coming to Sunderland.

In the Netherlands Alim played youth football for AFC 34, Hellas Sport Combinatie and Groningen before making a senior debut for Cambuur in January 2012. After 13 games, Trabzonspor paid €125,000 for him, but his only appearances in Turkey were 18 on loan to 1461 Trabzon for whom he scored twice.

From 2014 to 2017 he made 62 league appearances in Scotland for Hearts where one of his five goals was a 40-yard shot in an Edinburgh derby against a Hibs side managed by Alan Stubbs. Unsurprisingly, this was named as the club's 2014-15 Goal of the Year. The same season saw him named in the Scottish Championship Team of the Year as promotion was achieved, after which he was appointed captain of the Tynecastle club before an 18-month stint back in Turkey where he played 40 times (scoring once) for Boluspor. To June 2022, he had made 33 league appearances and scored four goals for Ümraniyespor.

# P

## PAGE, John Abraham (Jack)

**POSITION:** Outside-right

**BIRTHPLACE:** Sunderland, Co Durham

**DATE OF BIRTH:** 14/02/1893 - 02/05/1964

**HEIGHT:** 5' 6" **WEIGHT:** 11st 0lbs

**SIGNED FROM:** Sunderland West End, 22/01/1920

**DEBUT:** v Preston North End. H, 10/04/1920

**LAST MATCH:** v Liverpool, H, 01/05/1920

**MOVED TO:** Sunderland West End, 01/05/1921

**TEAMS:** Sunderland West End, Sunderland, Sunderland West End

**SAFC TOTALS:** 3 appearances / 0 goals

**A brewer's clerk who got his opportunity with three appearances at Roker Park towards the end of his first season. Having not played at all in his second - and only full - campaign, he returned to his former club in local football.**

Two years later he emigrated to Australia, a year after getting married, along with his two brothers to become fruit growers in New South Wales. During World War One he had served with the 52nd Durham Light Infantry and 13th Yorkshire Regiment, seeing his last action as a corporal in northern Russia in the winter of 1918-19. In 1939, Jack enlisted at Wentworth, New South Wales, for the Australian Army Citizens Military Forces and remained a member until 1948.

## PALLISTER, William

**POSITION:** Right-half

**BIRTHPLACE:** Ryhope, Co Durham

**DATE OF BIRTH:** 09/09/1876 - 07/05/1930

**HEIGHT:** 5' 9" **WEIGHT:** 12st 2lbs

**SIGNED FROM:** Ryhope Colliery, 10/12/1897

**DEBUT:** v Bury, A, 31/03/1899

**LAST MATCH:** v Bury, A, 31/03/1899

**MOVED TO:** Lincoln City, 22/05/1902

**TEAMS:** Ryhope Colliery, Sunderland, Lincoln City

**SAFC TOTALS:** 1 appearance / 0 goals

**Pallister was one of the many players who left working in the coal mines to come and play for Sunderland and although he only managed a single first-team game in his four and a half years at the club he was at least on the winning side.**

During his time with SAFC he supplemented his income by working in the shipyards as a metal cleaner. At Lincoln City he took over from former Sunderland full-back Willie Gibson and played 61 times in Division Two as a full-back for the Imps, 58 of those appearances being as a left-back. After retiring from football he worked as a foundry casting cleaner.

## PALMER, Calvin Ian

**POSITION:** Midfield / full-back

**BIRTHPLACE:** Skegness, Lincolnshire

**DATE OF BIRTH:** 21/10/1940 - 12/03/2014

**HEIGHT:** 5' 10" **WEIGHT:** 11st 0lbs

**SIGNED FROM:** Stoke City, 22/02/1968

**DEBUT:** v Manchester City, A, 24/02/1968

**LAST MATCH:** v Liverpool, A, 09/09/1969

**MOVED TO:** Cape Town City, 09/08/1970

**TEAMS:** Skegness, Nottingham Forest, Stoke City, Sunderland, Cape Town City, Crewe Alexandra, Hereford United, Durban United, Berea Park

**SAFC TOTALS:** 37+6 appearances / 5 goals

**Calvin Palmer was a very versatile player who could be relied upon to give his best in any position. He even took over in goal from Jim Montgomery just ten minutes into a game back at Palmer's old team Stoke in April 1968, just a few weeks after Calvin had left the club where he had scored 27 goals in 196 games and had played alongside George Kinnell in both legs of the 1964 League Cup final against Leicester City.**

Palmer had arrived at Stoke from Nottingham Forest for £35,000 in 1963. He had signed for Forest in March 1958 and went on to play 91 league games for them, becoming captain. Returning to the City Ground a month after signing for Sunderland for a £70,000 fee, he scored in a 3-0 win.

After leaving Sunderland Calvin went on a free transfer to play in South Africa where he became player/manager of Cape Town City where his side included Denis Law and Ian St John. Palmer then became player/assistant manager at Hellenic FC before briefly returning to play a couple of games for Crewe under his old Stoke teammate Dennis Viollet, followed by non-league Hereford United.

Calvin returned to South Africa to play for a couple of clubs before retiring in 1975. Following retirement, he coached children at Butlins holiday camp back home in Skegness. Renowned as a club joker whose lack of discipline at times frustrated manager Alan Brown, Palmer had what was described as an infectious laugh.

Upon leaving Stoke, he addressed Stoke fans, good naturedly telling them they were the second best club in the division - after Sunderland. Known as a fiery character on the pitch it was believed by many that was the reason he was never called up by England. In the month following leaving Sunderland, he exposed his sometimes tempestuous relationship with SAFC manager Alan Brown in a series of articles in The People newspaper. He passed away at a hospice in Brighton after suffering from throat cancer for three years. No funeral was held for Calvin who donated his body to medical science.

## PANTILIMON, Costel Fane

**POSITION:** Goalkeeper

**BIRTHPLACE:** Bacau, Romania

**DATE OF BIRTH:** 01/02/1987

**HEIGHT:** 6' 8" **WEIGHT:** 15st 1lb

**SIGNED FROM:** Manchester City, 01/07/2014

**DEBUT:** v Birmingham City, A, 27/08/2014

**LAST MATCH:** v Chelsea, A, 19/12/2015

**MOVED TO:** Watford, 19/01/2016

**TEAMS:** Aerostar Bacau, Politehnica Timosoara, Manchester City, Sunderland, Watford, Deportivo La Coruna (L), Nottingham Forest, AC Omonia (L), Denizlispor

**INTERNATIONAL:** Romania

**SAFC TOTALS:** 49 appearances / 0 goals

**The tallest player to ever play for Sunderland, Pantilimon played against Sunderland at Wembley for Manchester City in the 2014 League (Capital One) Cup final. That same season he made 18 appearances for City including all seven of his Premier League appearances for them as they won the Premier League.**

Two years earlier Costel had played in another Wembley win as he helped City beat Chelsea in the Community Shield. After a total of 29 games for City, he joined Sunderland in the summer after playing against the Lads at the national stadium.

After two seasons on Wearside Pantilimon joined Watford where he only made two league appearances, both as a sub, although he did play in seven cup games. Watford loaned him to Deportivo La Coruna where he played seven times starting with a debut at Real Betis. A subsequent loan to Nottingham Forest became a permanent move with him totalling 57 games, all in the league before a six-game loan to Omonia Nicosia in Cyprus. From there Costel moved to Turkey with Denizlispor in the summer of 2020, conceding a goal to Fatih Karagumruk's Fabio Borini on the last if his 15 appearances - Borini being the man who scored against him at Wembley for Sunderland.

Capped 27 times by Romania, Pantilimon had started in his home country with 115 games for Politehnica after spending his time in youth football with Aerostar Bacau. As of June 2022 he was a free agent.

## PARK, Robert (Bobby)

**POSITION:** Midfielder

**BIRTHPLACE:** Coatbridge, North Lanarkshire

**DATE OF BIRTH:** 05/01/1952

**HEIGHT:** 5' 11" **WEIGHT:** 11 st 4lbs

**SIGNED FROM:** Coatbridge Juniors, 01/07/1967

**DEBUT:** v Crystal Palace, A, 13/08/1969

**LAST MATCH:** v Birmingham City, H, 14/08/1971

**MOVED TO:** Retired, 30/06/1975

**TEAMS:** Sunderland

**INTERNATIONAL:** Scotland Youth

**SAFC TOTALS:** 57+15 appearances / 5 goals

**Bobby Park signed professional forms with Sunderland two days after his 17th birthday. Four years later he may well have been part of the FA Cup winning team of 1973 but for a terrible broken leg he suffered in torrential rain on the opening day of the season before the cup triumph, as Park played what was his 72nd and ultimately last game, he was still a teenager.**

He tried to come back and stayed at the club for another four years, but never got beyond the reserve team, suffering two further leg breaks, one in training in December 1972 and another against Scunthorpe United reserves in February 1975.

His loss was a great one both to the player and the club. Bobby was a talented and creative player. His 'through the eye of a needle' pass for Gordon Harris to score what was the final home goal of the 1969-70 relegation season was the pass of a maestro.

Bobby staged a joint Testimonial with fellow injury victim Ritchie Pitt against AZ 67 in November 1975 and later became a member of the Former Players' Association while managing to still be playing local football at Brampton in Cumbria in the late 1990s when he was in his late forties. While he did not get to experience the 1973 FA Cup triumph on the pitch, he did play six games as the FA Youth Cup was won in 1969, scoring in the quarter-final, semi-final and final.

Bobby's father, also Robert, was a goalkeeper with Wishaw, Queen of the South, St Mirren, St Johnstone, Airdrie, Plymouth Argyle, Crewe Alexandra and Albion Rovers between 1947 and 1963. After retiring, Bobby junior worked as a journalist.

## PARKE, John

**POSITION:** Full-back

**BIRTHPLACE:** Bangor, Northern Ireland

**DATE OF BIRTH:** 06/08/1937 - 27/08/2011

**HEIGHT:** 5' 9½" **WEIGHT:** 11st 10lbs

**SIGNED FROM:** Hibernian, 09/11/1964

**DEBUT:** v Sheffield United, A, 21/11/1964

**LAST MATCH:** v Newcastle United, A, 26/12/1967

**MOVED TO:** KV Mechelen, 11/05/1968

**TEAMS:** Cliftonville, Linfield, Hibernian, Sunderland, KV Mechelen

**INTERNATIONAL:** Northern Ireland

**SAFC TOTALS:** 91+3 appearances / 0 goals

**Parke was a Northern Ireland international who won eleven of his 14 caps while with Sunderland. Noted for the accuracy of his passing, Parke played between 24 and 34 games in three of his four seasons. On one of his substitute appearances, he came on and went in goal at Manchester United after Jim Montgomery was injured and Charlie Hurley had initially taken over between the sticks.**

Having started playing for the 4th Bangor Boys Brigade, Parke signed for Cliftonville when he was 16 in 1953, winning five youth caps and a 'B' League medal with Cliftonville Olympic and then breaking into the first-team after impressing in a 1955 international youth tournament in Italy.

The following season - after rejecting a move to Burnley so he could stay at home and complete his qualifications as a mechanic - he joined Linfield as an amateur, not becoming a professional for a couple of seasons. At that time playing mainly as an inside-right Parke played in every outfield position and goalkeeper for Linfield where he was managed by Jackie Milburn. Parke played in the European Cup and won a total of 17 medals.

In 1958 - the year he played the first of his five inter-league games - he was on the losing side in the Northern Ireland cup final against Ballymena and was defeated again in 1961 against Glenavon. There was joy though in 1962 when he was left-half as Linfield thrashed Portadown 4-0 to lift the trophy, one of seven they won that season. A year later, Linfield sold John to Hibs for a club record £15,000 shortly after he had marked Rangers winger Willie Henderson out of the game on his full international debut against Scotland.

He did so well at Easter Road that by the following year Hibs more than doubled their money when manager Jock Stein sold him on to Sunderland for £33,000. Parke had made just 23 competitive appearances in Scotland, plus a stellar performance in a 2-0 prestige friendly win over Real Madrid a month before signing for Sunderland.

Leaving Wearside after being troubled by injury, he moved into Belgian football before retiring following a series of cartilage problems. In 1984, he returned to the sport as manager of 1st Bangor Old Boys, an Amateur League Club.

## PARKER, Charles William (Charlie)

**POSITION:** Half-back

**BIRTHPLACE:** Seaham Harbour, Co Durham

**DATE OF BIRTH:** 01/09/1891 - 27/12/1968

**HEIGHT:** 5' 9" **WEIGHT:** 10st 12lbs

**SIGNED FROM:** Stoke, 19/10/1920

**DEBUT:** v Bradford City, A, 23/10/1920

**LAST MATCH:** v Leeds United H, 13/04/1929

**MOVED TO:** Carlisle United, 03/05/1929

**TEAMS:** Seaham Harbour, Stoke, Sunderland, Carlisle United, Blyth Spartans, Chopwell Institute

**INTERNATIONAL:** England 'Victory' team

**SAFC TOTALS:** 256 appearances / 12 goals

**All of Parker's games for Sunderland came in the 1920s - the only decade between entering the league in 1890 and the start of the Second World War in which the club did not win anything. Despite this, Sunderland were a powerful team of the era. They finished in the top three in four years out of five in the middle of the decade.**

Renowned for his quality and consistency, Charlie was a major figure in the side playing a minimum of 32 games in five of his first six seasons at the club. In an era when the centre-half was a half-back, likely to get forward sometimes rather than being a centre-back in the modern sense, the sight of Charlie bursting forward became known as 'Parker's rush'.

Despite being a local lad he came to Sunderland from Stoke where he played before and after World War One. Debuting in the Southern League Division Two for the Potters against Brentford in February 1914, the following season he missed just two games as Stoke won their league in the last season before official football stopped due to the war, during which he continued to appear in war-time football for the club. With Stoke restored to the Football League in 1919, Parker excelled to the extent he was called up to play for England in a 'Victory' (unofficial) international which was played at his club ground in Stoke as Wales were beaten 2-0 in October 1919. He gained another representative honour when selected to play for the Football League against the Scottish League.

Emulating fellow centre-half Charlie Thomson of the previous decade, Parker was 29 when he signed for Sunderland and yet went on to become a long-serving stalwart of the club who he captained in 1923-24.

## PARKER, Charlie (Continued)

Leaving Sunderland for Carlisle as player/coach at the age of 38, Charlie debuted in a Division Three North opening-day win over Crewe Alexandra in August 1929 and went on to play nine games, scoring against South Shields. His final appearance came at Chesterfield in March 1930. Parker then returned briefly to his native north east as player/coach for Blyth Spartans until suffering fractured ribs during a game which effectively ended his playing days.

Charlie returned to Brunton Park in August 1933 as trainer until 1937. A coal miner before going into football, he worked for the air ministry warden during World War Two and up until his retirement in 1956. Brother Fred played for Manchester City, Nottingham Forest and Southport between 1914 and 1926 as well as turning out for Port Vale, Stoke and Chesterfield during World War One. Charlie was also a County-level bowls player after giving up his football career.

## PARKER, Richard (Dick)

**POSITION:** Centre-forward

**BIRTHPLACE:** Stockton, Co Durham

**DATE OF BIRTH:** 14/09/1894 - 01/02/1969

**HEIGHT:** 5' 8½" **WEIGHT:** 11st 3lbs

**SIGNED FROM:** Stockton, 21/04/1919

**DEBUT:** v Aston Villa, H, 30/08/1919

**LAST MATCH:** Bolton Wanderers, A, 01/11/1919

**MOVED TO:** Coventry City, 29/01/1920

**TEAMS:** South Bank, Stockton, Sunderland, Coventry City, South Shields, Wallsend, QPR, Millwall, Watford, Merthyr Town, Tunbridge Wells Rangers

**INTERNATIONAL:** 'Football League'

**SAFC TOTALS:** 6 appearances / 3 goals

**Parker scored in the first minute of his first game for SAFC as a guest player at Scotswood in a Victory League game on 22 February 1919. A speedy striker, who not surprisingly given his height, preferred the ball to be played to his feet rather than in the air, he was renowned for shooting on sight.**

He also scored on his official debut - the winner in the first post-war Football League match against Aston Villa. He proceeded to score in two of the next three matches before suffering an ankle injury and only got two matches later that season before being sold to Coventry for £1,500. Rather like Neil Martin, who saved Coventry after being sold to them by Sunderland in 1968, Parker became their hero, top-scoring with nine goals from 16 games in 1919-20 as he helped a team who had gone eleven games without scoring earlier in the season to finish one place above the line for re-election in what was the last season of just two divisions.

After just two more games for Coventry the following season, both against South Shields, he moved back to the north east to sign for Shields where he celebrated his league debut for them with a hat-trick. Once again, a player with evidently itchy feet did not stay long.

Eleven months later, he transferred to Wallsend and eleven months on from that, returned to the Football League with QPR, debuting on the first day of the 1922-23 season against Watford. Parker went on to be top scorer in both his years there with 34 goals in 66 games including 14 in a struggling side that had to apply for re-election in 1923-24 before crossing London to play for Millwall.

Continuing his record as a regular scorer with the Lions, on 28 August 1926, he became the first-ever player for any club to score five goals on the opening day of the season - Norwich City the victims as they were when Nick Sharkey scored five goals in a game for Sunderland. For Parker, it was the start of a season that saw him score a club record 37 league goals (in 40 games). For good measure, he also scored against Derby in the FA Cup and twice against Spurs in the London FA Challenge Cup.

After missing the start of the following campaign through injury, he returned with a hat-trick in a South London derby against Crystal Palace, but once he scored again next time out Millwall cashed in by selling the 33-year-old to Watford for £1,000. Parker totalled 74 goals in 107 games for the Lions. Over his career, Dick scored 128 Football League goals in 246 appearances, a fine record.

During World War One, he served in France with the Northumberland Fusiliers. Playing in an army international against Scotland, he scored a hat-trick. Clearly, he was a man with goals in his boots, although his time at the top level with Sunderland was short.

## PASCOE, Colin James

**POSITION:** Midfielder / winger

**BIRTHPLACE:** Bridgend, Glamorgan

**DATE OF BIRTH:** 09/04/1965

**HEIGHT:** 5' 9½" **WEIGHT:** 11st 10lbs

**SIGNED FROM:** Swansea City, 24/03/1988

**DEBUT:** v York City, A, 26/03/1988

**LAST MATCH:** v Blackburn Rovers, A, 29/04/1992

**MOVED TO:** Swansea City, 11/08/1993

**TEAMS:** Swansea City, Sunderland, Swansea City, Blackpool, Merthyr Tydfil, Carmarthen

**INTERNATIONAL:** Wales

**SAFC TOTALS:** 137+12 appearances / 25 goals

**Colin Pascoe was a good player at Sunderland, rarely outstanding, but generally consistent. Well balanced, he had quick feet and an eye for goal. 'Pasc' came in to bolster the third division promotion campaign of 1988 just before the old transfer deadline in March, debuting with a goal as sub for fellow debutant Doug McGuire.**

He chipped in with goals in two of his next three matches and four in total from 8+1 games as he helped Denis Smith's side to secure the divisional title. Colin ended the same season as Swansea's top scorer with 13 goals as a teammate of Andy Melville.

Swansea went on to win promotion via the Play-Offs making Pascoe a double promotion-winner in the same season. He did however, have a Wembley penalty saved for Sunderland a month after his debut, this coming in a Football League Centenary (Mercantile Credit) shoot-out with Wigan Athletic.

After scoring twelve times in 47 games in his first full season on Wearside, Colin's next campaign brought another promotion. Three seasons after playing in the basement division with The Swans, he completed his journey to the top flight. Although Sunderland were relegated, Colin performed creditably, scoring five goals in 25 league appearances, including a brace in a draw at Spurs and the winner at home to Chelsea.

In 1991-92 Pascoe remained as a regular under Smith, but once Malcolm Crosby took over he became a peripheral figure, although he did make two substitute appearances during the cup run as Sunderland reached the FA Cup final, playing his last game a fortnight before the final. During that summer he went back to Swansea on loan until November and re-signed for the Swans at the end of the season.

Eventually he took his totals for Swansea to 342 games and 73 goals, the highlight being an excellent performance as Huddersfield Town were beaten in the 1994 Autoglass Trophy win at Wembley. He had initially joined the club as a schoolboy player from Afan Nedd, going on to debut as a sub in March 1983 against Brighton and Hove Albion. That was a top-flight game but Swansea were in decline as he suffered further relegations in 1984 and 1986, although there was the bright spot of a Welsh Cup win over Wrexham in 1983.

1985-86 brought a twice broken leg, the first time in an FA Cup tie with Leyton Wingate, but he recovered to earn recognition with selection for the Division Four Team of the Season the following year. After leaving Swansea for the second time, in March 1996 Sam Allardyce signed him on a short-term contract for Blackpool but his only appearance came as a sub in a defeat to Walsall in the last home game of the season which contributed to the Tangerines missing out on promotion and Allardyce being sacked.

After seeing out his playing days in Welsh football, Pascoe became youth coach at Cardiff City before becoming a coach at Swansea and following manager Brendan Rodgers to Liverpool where he became assistant manager from May 2012 to June 2015. Twice during this period - against Arsenal and QPR - he took charge of Liverpool games when manager Rodgers was ill. After leaving Liverpool, he briefly assisted Barrow FC before working under Steve Cooper back at Swansea and moving into the pub business.

## PATERSON, John (Jock)

**POSITION:** Centre-forward

**BIRTHPLACE:** Dundee, Angus

**DATE OF BIRTH:** 14/12/1897 - 11/01/1973

**HEIGHT:** 5' 10" **WEIGHT:** 11st 7lbs

**SIGNED FROM:** Leicester City, 02/03/1922

**DEBUT:** v Sheffield United, H, 04/03/1922

**LAST MATCH:** v West Bromwich Albion, A, 13/09/1924

**MOVED TO:** Preston North End, 17/10/1924

**TEAMS:** Dundee, Leicester City, Sunderland, Preston North End, Mid Rhondda, QPR, Mansfield Town, Montrose

**INTERNATIONAL:** Scotland

**SAFC TOTALS:** 76 appearances / 40 goals

**The fee of £3,790 paid for Paterson was a club record but was overshadowed somewhat by the world record fee of £5,250 paid for Michael Gilhooley later the same day and a further world record one day later when it took £5,500 to prise Warney Cresswell from South Shields.**

Just under two years earlier, in April 1920 Jock had won his sole Scotland cap but had not scored in a 5-4 defeat to England at Hillsborough. At the time Paterson was with second division Leicester City where he top-scored in both of his full seasons and remained as joint top marksmen in the season he left midway through to join Sunderland. In total, he scored 34 times in 81 games, a highlight being a Christmas Day hat-trick against Stoke in 1920.

At Sunderland - where he scored in three successive wins over Newcastle - he scored an early hat-trick against Bolton as he netted five times in twelve games after his March arrival. Partnering Charlie Buchan, in his first full season he scored a cup hat-trick plus 21 league goals as Sunderland were runners-up in 1923. Restricted to 18 league games when Sunderland dropped to third a year later, he still managed one goal per two games as he did with just the first four games of the following season before moving on to Preston.

Things did not go well at North End who were relegated in his first year there when he did not score at all in 17 appearances, after which between September 1925 and January 1926 he played for Mid-Rhondda. He returned to Wales to debut for his next club QPR at Merthyr Town on 16 January 1926 in Division Three South, but as with Preston, he had joined a club in turmoil as they finished bottom of the table with Jock managing just three goals from his 19 games. The following season was replicated with three goals from 15 games as injury kept him out for five months. After finishing his career with Mansfield and Montrose he was reported to have emigrated to Canada in 1930.

As a boy Jock had played for Fort Hill and Dundee North End before World War One in which he served with the Black Watch and played in France for the 61st Division. Prior to going to Leicester, he played two games for Dundee in 1918-19.

## PATTERSON, Anthony William

**POSITION:** Goalkeeper

**BIRTHPLACE:** Newcastle, Tyne & Wear

**DATE OF BIRTH:** 10/05/2000

**HEIGHT:** 6' 2" **WEIGHT:** 12st 2lbs

**SIGNED FROM:** Sunderland Youths, 01/07/2016

**DEBUT:** v Fleetwood, A, 10/11/2020

**LAST MATCH:**

**MOVED TO:**

**TEAMS:** Sunderland, Sunderland RCA (L), Notts County (L)

**SAFC TOTALS:** 27 appearances / 0 goals (to May 2022)

**Having joined Sunderland as a nine-year-old, Patterson played a couple of games in the Football League (Papa John's) Trophy and one in the League (Carabao) Cup before keeping a clean sheet on his league debut against Wimbledon on what was also his home debut in August 2021.**

Having previously been on loan to Northern League Ryhope Community Association in March and April 2019, 'Patto' then joined National League Notts County on loan in September 2021. After eleven games, including two in the FA Cup against Rochdale, he was recalled by Sunderland due to illness to the senior goalkeepers at the club, but conceded six goals in his first two games. However, confidence soon blossomed under new manager Alex Neil as Anthony kept nine clean sheets in his last 15 games of the season including one at Wembley as Sunderland beat Wycombe to win promotion to the Championship.

## PAYNE, George Clark

**POSITION:** Inside-left

**BIRTHPLACE:** Hitchin, Hertfordshire

**DATE OF BIRTH:** 17/02/1887 - 21/08/1932

**HEIGHT:** 5' 9" **WEIGHT:** 12st 0lbs

**SIGNED FROM:** Crystal Palace, 01/04/1911

**DEBUT:** v Oldham Athletic, H, 28/10/1911

**LAST MATCH:** v Bolton Wanderers, A, 04/11/1911

**MOVED TO:** Leyton FC, 24/01/1912

**TEAMS:** Hitchin Town, Barnet Alston, Tottenham Hotspur, Crystal Palace, Sunderland, Leyton FC, Arsenal, Merthyr Town

**SAFC TOTALS:** 2 appearances / 0 goals

**George Payne played only a couple of games having come to Sunderland where he did not settle. He spent almost all of his career with London clubs. As a boy he played for Page Green Old Boys and Hitchin Union Jack before stepping up to Hitchin Town.**

At Spurs he signed as a professional in November 1906 but never got a game in their Southern League or English (FA) Cup teams, instead making a single appearance on 24 November 1906 in a Western League fixture against Portsmouth. A Southern League debut arrived on Christmas Day 1907 in a home win over Northampton. He went on to score three times in six Southern League games and totalled two goals in four Western League games before moving from north to south London with Crystal Palace in May 1909. This was after not getting a game in his last season at Tottenham which was their first as a Football League club (in 1908-09). During his time at the club he simultaneously worked as a clerk and a storeman.

At Palace Payne became a Southern League regular. He scored a debut winner on the opening day of the season against Brentford and finished as second top scorer with 20 goals from 42 games. George's haul included four goals in a game against New Brompton (later Gillingham) and back-to-back hat-tricks against Norwich City and Southampton while he also scored on his English Cup bow against Swindon Town. Five goals in eleven games the following season - including a hat-trick against Exeter - led to a transfer to Sunderland.

Once back in London with Leyton Orient, after half a season he signed for Arsenal - the middle one of his three appearances for the Gunners being back at Sunderland in a 4-1 New Year's Day defeat in a campaign where Sunderland finished top and Arsenal bottom. He also scored nine times in 16 South Eastern League games for Arsenal's reserves, but left the club at the end of the 1912-13 season.

A gunshot injury to his thigh while serving with the Bedford Regiment in World War One ended Payne's playing days with him becoming a turf accountant after retiring from football.

He married into a footballing family, his wife Miriam being the sister of George, Harry, Vic and Willie Furr who all played league football, while his wife's sister married William Grimes who played for Bradford City, Derby County and Glossop. Sadly, George drowned in August 1932 whilst saving three children, one of which was his seven-year-old son, when his motorboat overturned in rough sea off Clacton.

## PEACOCK, Andrew

**POSITION:** Forward

**BIRTHPLACE:** Kelvinhaugh, Glasgow, Lanarkshire

**DATE OF BIRTH:** 12/09/1864 - 24/04/1952

**SIGNED FROM:** Rangers, 01/08/1888

**DEBUT:** v Elswick Rangers, H, 27/10/1888

**LAST MATCH:** v Newcastle East End, H, 17/11/1888

**MOVED TO:** Returned to Scotland, 02/02/1889

**TEAMS:** Rangers, Sunderland, Cowlairs, Barrow

**SAFC TOTALS:** 2 appearances / 3 goals

**Peacock scored twice on his official debut in an English (FA) Cup tie and once in the second of his two cup games against Newcastle United's fore -runners in Sunderland's pre-league days. Andrew and his brother Wallie became the first siblings to play in the same Sunderland team when they turned out against Elswick.**

Notably, he scored the first-ever goal at Ibrox Stadium and thanks to the work of an organisation called The Founders Trail at Rangers the re-discovered grave of the brothers (in Glasgow) was being restored in the early 2020s. The Peacock brothers had left Wearside to return to Clydeside at the request of their parents. After returning to his native country, Andrew soon signed again for Rangers and also resumed his work in the shipyards.

The 1891 census listed him as a ship plater living in Govan. Peacock's football career at shipbuilding locations ended with a few games for Barrow in 1892-93. On 6 February 1909, he travelled to Santa Cruz in California where a relative had left him money, but he had returned to Glasgow within a couple of years.

## PEACOCK, William McIlraith (Wallie)

**POSITION:** Forward

**BIRTHPLACE:** Kelvinhaugh, Glasgow, Lanarkshire

**DATE OF BIRTH:** 23/02/1867 - 17/01/1948

**SIGNED:** 01/08/1888

**DEBUT:** v Elswick Rangers, H, 27/10/1888

**LAST MATCH:** v Elswick Rangers, H, 27/10/1888

**MOVED TO:** Returned to Scotland, 02/02/1889

**TEAMS:** Rangers, Sunderland, Rangers

**SAFC TOTALS:** 1 appearance / 0 goals

**As with his brother Andrew, Wallie's official debut came in the English (FA) Cup and identically, he left Sunderland at his parents' request, worked as a ship plater in Glasgow in 1891 and is buried alongside his brother - the grave being restored by The Founders Trail at Rangers.**

Like his brother, Wallie also quickly signed again for Rangers on returning to Glasgow and the two of them played in the Rangers side that lost at Newcastle Road to Sunderland in a friendly 3-0 on 23 March 1889.

## PEARCE, Reginald Stanley

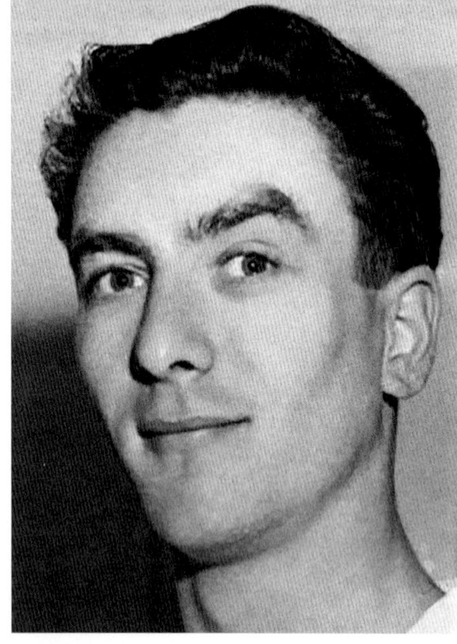

**POSITION:** Left-half

**BIRTHPLACE:** Liverpool, Lancashire

**DATE OF BIRTH:** 12/01/1930

**HEIGHT:** 5' 11" **WEIGHT:** 11st 5lbs

**SIGNED FROM:** Luton Town, 19/02/1958

**DEBUT:** v Burnley, H, 22/02/1958

**LAST MATCH:** v Norwich City, A, 03/04/1961

**MOVED TO:** Cambridge City, 19/07/1961

**TEAMS:** Liverpool, Marine, Winsford United, Luton Town, Sunderland, Cambridge City, Peterborough United, Cambridge City, Boston, Ely City, Newmarket Town, Haverhill Rovers

**INTERNATIONAL:** 'Football League'

**SAFC TOTALS:** 62 appearances / 4 goals

**As of June 2022, Reg was Sunderland's oldest living player and had been since the death of Ivor (Ivan) Broadis in April 2019. Reg arrived at Roker Park at a difficult time, playing the last dozen games of the season as SAFC suffered a first-ever relegation in 1958. Reg was part of the side who won the final game at Portsmouth.**

Liverpool-born and a lifelong Evertonian, Reg scored the first of his goals for Sunderland against Liverpool, a club he had been with as an amateur. During that 1958-59 season, Pearce was Sunderland's only ever-present in the first year out of the top-flight.

Twenty-eight when he joined Sunderland from Luton, Pearce had played for the Football League against the Scottish League at St James' Park and the Irish League at Windsor Park as well as in a game against the army. At Peterborough Pearce made 28 Third Division appearances scoring twice in 1963-64, his Posh debut coming in a 5-2 win against Wrexham in August 1963.

Earlier in his career Reg had been 25 when he stepped out of non-league football to sign for Luton Town, playing 75 league games and scoring five goals, almost all of his appearances coming in the top flight. Pearce finished his career in the 1960s playing for a number of non-league clubs in East Anglia. After retiring from football, Reg became a sports teacher at a school in Cambridge where he settled and later worked as a carpenter.

## PEETERS, Tom

**POSITION:** Midfielder

**BIRTHPLACE:** Bornem, Belgium

**DATE OF BIRTH:** 25/09/1978

**HEIGHT:** 5' 9" **WEIGHT:** 11st 0lbs

**SIGNED FROM:** KV Mechelen, 14/07/2000

**DEBUT:** v Luton Town, H, 19/09/2000

**LAST MATCH:** v Luton Town, H, 19/09/2000

**MOVED TO:** Released from contract, 16/10/2003

**TEAMS:** Meerhof, FC Boom, Ekeren, Beerschot AC, KV Mechelen, Sunderland, Royal Antwerp (L), KV Mechelen, KSV Roeselare, FCV Dender, Apollon Kalamarias, Pyrsos Grevena.

**INTERNATIONAL:** Belgium Under 18

**SAFC TOTALS:** 1 appearance / 0 goals

**Having played just one game for Sunderland, Tom Peeters' is best remembered on Wearside for his widely reported enthusiastic celebration when he heard Howard Wilkinson had been sacked. Peeters had been the Young Player of the Year in Belgium when he came to Sunderland on the same day as Don Hutchison and Jurgen Macho in the summer after Belgium played England at the Stadium of Light.**

Peeters made a first appearance back at his old club KV Mechelen in a pre-season friendly in July 2000. Bought for £250,000, Tom was to get just a single competitive first-team appearance in a League Cup tie with Luton Town under Peter Reid who signed him. From November 2001 to the end of that season Peeters returned to Belgium on loan to Royal Antwerp who Sunderland would visit shortly after Peeters' spell there, although Tom still did not get a game.

Once Howard Wilkinson replaced Reid, holding midfielder Peeters continued to get nowhere near the first team - not even being named on the bench in a season when 41 players were at least named as a substitute. Subsequently, when Wilkinson gathered the squad together to announce he had been dismissed, according to teammate Matt Piper, Peeters leapt to his feet shouting, 'Good! Good! Get in there! Good riddance! Great news!"

After over three years at Sunderland with just that solitary cup appearance to his name Peeters returned to the continent, continuing his career in lower league football in Belgium and Greece. After retiring from the game, Tom became a freelance IT consultant.

## PEGG, Frank Edward

**POSITION:** Outside-left

**BIRTHPLACE:** Beeston, Nottinghamshire

**DATE OF BIRTH:** 02/08/1902 - 09/08/1991

**HEIGHT:** 5' 8" **WEIGHT:** 11st 0lbs

**SIGNED FROM:** Loughborough Corinthians, 12/05/1925

**DEBUT:** v Bolton Wanderers, A, 07/04/1926

**LAST MATCH:** v Bolton Wanderers, A, 07/04/1926

**MOVED TO:** Lincoln City, 14/05/1926

**TEAMS:** Sawley United, Loughborough Corinthians, Sunderland, Lincoln City, Bradford City, Norwich City, New Brighton, Yarmouth Town

**SAFC TOTALS:** 1 appearance / 0 goals

**Despite being reported to have played 'quite well' on his only appearance by the Newcastle Journal, left-winger Pegg's only game for Sunderland came in a 3-2 defeat. He had had unsuccessful trials with Derby County, Blackpool and Nelson (then a Football League club) before coming to SAFC. He found success with Lincoln, scoring 51 times in 115 games before playing three times for Bradford City and six for Norwich.**

He added 41 league games for Division Three North New Brighton in 1933-34, scoring eight times. Following this, Pegg played for Yarmouth for whom he once scored four goals in a game. He was also a capable cricketer who played for West Park club in Long Eaton near Nottingham in the early 1930s. After retiring from football, Frank became an insurance agent.

## PEREZ, Lionel

**POSITION:** Goalkeeper

**BIRTHPLACE:** Bagnols-Sur-Ceze, France

**DATE OF BIRTH:** 24/04/1967

**HEIGHT:** 6' 0" **WEIGHT:** 14st 2lbs

**SIGNED FROM:** Bordeaux, 19/08/1996

**DEBUT:** v Southampton, A, 19/10/1996

**LAST MATCH:** v Charlton Athletic, N, 25/05/1998

**MOVED TO:** Newcastle United, 02/06/1998

**TEAMS:** Bagnols, Nimes Olympique, Bordeaux, Laval (L), Sunderland, Newcastle United, Olympique Lyonnais (L), Scunthorpe United (L), Cambridge United, Enfield, Chelmsford City, Stevenage Borough

**SAFC TOTALS:** 83+1 appearances / 0 goals

**Lionel Perez had more good games for Sunderland than bad ones, but his most notable mistake was extremely costly. Enormously colourful, after impressing in a friendly at Gateshead Perez signed for Sunderland as second choice goalkeeper to Tony Coton ready for SAFC's first season in the Premier League.**

An early season career-ending injury to Coton at Southampton saw Perez introduced as a substitute and thereafter as first choice. With long hair combined with rolled-up sleeves, the Frenchman cut a dashing figure - and he would often dash from his goal to take charge of dangerous situations.

After changing his image with short, dyed blonde hair ultimately this desire to come off his line would prove enormously costly as he got nowhere near a corner that he came for in the 1998 Play-Off final at Wembley, allowing Richard Rufus to head a late equaliser in a game Sunderland would ultimately lose on penalties. Almost certainly Sunderland would not have been at Wembley but for the best double save any SAFC stopper has made since Jim Montgomery in the 1973 FA Cup final. Perez's marvellous double save came on his last appearance at the Stadium of Light in the 1998 Play-Off semi-final with Sheffield United.

Released by Sunderland at the end of the season he joined Newcastle United but had an unhappy time there, never playing for the first team and not being warmly welcomed by supporters as an ex-Sunderland 'keeper.

In France he had been a teammate of Eric Cantona at Nimes and Zinedine Zidane at Bordeaux, winning promotion with Nimes in 1991. He returned to his homeland when the Magpies loaned him to Olympique Lyonnais whose goalkeeper Luc Borelli had been killed in a road accident. Newcastle later loaned him to Scunthorpe United for whom he played 13 times.

A later loan with Cambridge became a permanent and highly successful move. Debuting with a clean sheet against rival university town Oxford in March 2000, Perez played 102+2 games for the U's. In typical fashion he ended in eye-catching style. In his final match against Tranmere - one of two teams he had been sent off against that season - Perez stepped forward to take a penalty against one time Sunderland reserve Joe Murphy, then of Tranmere, who saved Lionel's kick, but in doing so was injured and stretchered off! Inducted into the Cambridge United Hall of Fame in 2021, Perez always maintained his time at Sunderland and Cambridge were the most enjoyable periods of his career.

Finishing his career with 33+1 appearances at Stevenage Borough in the Conference - his last game being a goalless draw at Barnet in March 2004 - Lionel stayed at Stevenage until April 2006 as goalkeeping coach before returning to France.

## PHILIP, George Gregory

**POSITION:** Centre-forward / inside-left

**BIRTHPLACE:** Newport-on-Tay, Fife

**DATE OF BIRTH:** 15/04/1890 - 10/11/1958

**HEIGHT:** 5' 9½" **WEIGHT:** 12st 0lbs

**SIGNED FROM:** Dundee, 22/04/1914

**DEBUT:** v Sheffield United, H, 02/09/1914

**LAST MATCH:** v Tottenham Hotspur, H, 24/04/1915

**MOVED TO:** Dundee, 26/06/1920

**TEAMS:** Dundee Wanderers, St Johnstone, Dundee, Sunderland, St Mirren (WW1 Guest), Rangers (WW1 Guest), Dundee (WW1 Guest), Sheffield United (WW1 Guest), Cupar Juniors (L), Dundee

**SAFC TOTALS:** 38 appearances / 22 goals

**George Philip's excellent goals-to-games record all came in the 1914-15 season. A hat-trick against Notts County combined with five braces contributed to George finishing just one goal behind top scorer Charlie Buchan in what was the last season before the Football League was suspended due to World War One.**

Philip enlisted in the RAF, later working in a Glasgow Munitions Factory from where he had a couple of games as a war-time guest for Rangers. George also played wartime football for Dundee and twice as a guest for Sheffield United in 1918-19 whilst serving locally as a corporal. Later that season he also played in two Christmas-time friendlies for Sunderland, scoring in both games. Sunderland continued to hold his registration during 1919-20 when he was allowed to play for Cupar Juniors as he had established a business there and had refused to move back to Wearside.

Before coming to Sunderland Philip had played at both centre-half and centre-forward for Dundee where he scored 16 goals in 70 Division One games before adding a further 27 appearances in 1920-21. After retiring from football Philip played bowls and curling, his brother David being president of the South African Bowling Association in the late twenties. Away from sport, George became a publican and hotelier before running a tobacconist shop.

## PHILLIPS, Kevin

**POSITION:** Striker

**BIRTHPLACE:** Hitchin, Hertfordshire

**DATE OF BIRTH:** 25/07/1973

**HEIGHT:** 5' 7" **WEIGHT:** 11st 0lbs

**SIGNED FROM:** Watford, 15/07/1997

**DEBUT:** v Manchester City, H, 15/08/1997

**LAST MATCH:** v Arsenal, H, 11/05/2003

**MOVED TO:** Southampton, 14/08/2003

**TEAMS:** Southampton, Baldock Town, Watford, Sunderland, Southampton, Aston Villa, WBA, Birmingham City, Blackpool, Crystal Palace, Leicester City

**INTERNATIONAL:** England

**SAFC TOTALS:** 233+2 appearances / 130 goals

**Sunderland's top post-war scorer, 35 goals in SuperKev's first season broke Brian Clough's post-war seasonal scoring record. Phillips oozed self-belief. If he missed a chance he would simply congratulate himself on being in the right place at the right time and make sure he was there again for the next opportunity.**

On a pre-season trip, I once light-heartedly suggested a golf shot over a lake might be difficult only to be met by a look of horror from SuperKev at the suggestion he might not be able to make it. Equally, a year or two after the last of his eight England appearances when it looked like he was not going to win any further caps - he did not - I suggested that as he had not played a competitive game for England, had he considered that he might still be eligible for Wales? He was not at all impressed with this suggestion. These examples might sound as if behind the scenes Phillips could be hard work, but nothing could be further from the truth. Kevin was always helpful and as his career became more and more successful he did not let it go to his head, but remained always willing to be accessible.

After 35 goals in his first campaign when injury forced him off at Wembley after he had scored in the 1998 Play-Off final, in his second season, Phillips rattled in 23 goals in 26 league games (having been injured early in the season) including four at Bury in the promotion-clinching game. Phillips took the Premier League by storm, scoring an incredible 30 goals in 36 Premiership games. That feat made him the first Englishman to become the winner of the Adidas Golden Shoe as Europe's top-scorer.

While teams tightened up on him, Kevin still reached double figures in each of the next two seasons, but by his final season when Sunderland went down with 19 points - only one of which was won after Christmas - only six Premier League goals came Kevin's way - although he added three more in four cup appearances. Overall, Phillips is the sixth highest scorer in the club's history, many of Kevin's goals stemming from his seemingly almost telepathic understanding with Niall Quinn.

Originally Phillips had been a full-back at Southampton who released him without giving him a first-team debut. Phillips went to non-league Baldock Town where he was converted into a striker by ex-Arsenal forward Ian Allinson. Attracting the attention of Watford, Kevin moved six days before Christmas in 1994 for £30,000. At Watford he scored 25 goals in 58+7 games before he came to Sunderland having been spotted by Alan Durban, the ex-Sunderland manager who had signed Ally McCoist and was doing some scouting for Peter Reid.

Having cost Sunderland an initial £325,000, he was sold for ten times as much when he went to Southampton, the Wearsiders having turned down much higher offers for him at his peak. He scored 27 goals in 57+16 outings for the Saints before a £1m move to Aston Villa in June 2005. There were just five goals in 22+5 appearances before Villa recouped £700,000 of their outlay in selling SuperKev to near neighbours West Brom after one season.

asics
REG VARDY

## PHILLIPS, Kevin (Continued)

Hat-tricks against Ipswich and Barnsley contributed to 22 goals in his first season which ended in Play-Off final defeat to Derby, but promotion was won a year later with Kevin contributing 24 goals including two in the FA Cup as the Baggies reached the semi-final. A year later he would be a promotion winner again having moved to newly-relegated Birmingham City on a free transfer. Playing alongside Seb Larsson and James McFadden Phillips's 14th goal of the campaign clinched promotion with a last-day winner at Reading. There were just five Premier League goals plus three in the cups over the next two seasons before Phillips moved on again having picked up a League Cup winner's medal as an unused sub in 2011.

Having signed for Blackpool, he scored twice on his home debut and went on to be their top scorer with 17 goals, helping them to reach the Play-Off final where he played in a defeat to West Ham. Two goals the following season took his tally to 19 in 34+30 appearances before a January move to Crystal Palace where he followed his Seasiders manager Ian Holloway. By now a veteran, Phillips only started two league games for the Eagles, but scored seven goals in a total of 2+19 games including a hat-trick against Hull and the only goal of the game in the 2013 Play-Off final against old club Watford at Wembley.

In the following 2013-14 season the 287th and final goal of his career came against Blackpool following a January transfer to Leicester for whom he scored twice in 2+10 games as Leicester won the second tier Championship. 250 of Phillips' 287 goal haul came in the league while in all competitions he played 518+147. It was a wonderful career of promotion with five clubs, plus that accolade as Europe's top scorer and Premier League Player of the Year award while with Sunderland.

At international level Phillips' eight England caps (all won with Sunderland) amounted to 371 minutes split between four starts and four appearances as sub with Kevin never given a full 90 minutes. On his debut in Hungary in April 1999, Michael Gray came off the bench, the pair being on the pitch together for 19 minutes - the first time two Sunderland players had appeared together for England since Warney Cresswell and Albert McInroy in 1926. Also debuting alongside the Sunderland pair was future Sunderland defender Wes Brown. All of Phillips' appearances came in friendlies, although he was a member of the squad for Euro 2000 without ever being given an opportunity.

After retiring from playing, Kevin coached at Derby County, Leicester City and Stoke City before making numerous attempts at getting into management and eventually taking up a post at South Shields in January 2022, after previously being turned down for the Sunderland job.

## PICKERING, Nicholas (Nick)

**POSITION:** Left-back / midfield

**BIRTHPLACE:** South Shields, Co Durham

**DATE OF BIRTH:** 04/08/1963

**HEIGHT:** 6' 0" **WEIGHT:** 11st 10lbs

**SIGNED FROM:** North Shields Schoolboys, 01/06/1979

**DEBUT:** v Ipswich Town, A, 29/08/1981

**LAST MATCH:** v Manchester United, H, 25/01/1986

**MOVED TO:** Coventry City, 29/01/1986

**TEAMS:** Sunderland, Coventry City, Derby County, Darlington, Burnley

**INTERNATIONAL:** England

**SAFC TOTALS:** 207+2 appearances / 18 goals

**Pickering was capped by England while at Sunderland, won the European Under 21 Championships in 1984, played at Wembley with the club in the League Cup final, scored a hat-trick and later, won the FA Cup with Coventry. With a distinctive long stride, Pickering ate up the yards when gambolling down the flank. Combined with his boundless energy Nick was a nightmare for opponents due to his sheer stamina and willingness to run and run.**

Coming into the team on the opening day of the 1981-82 season having just turned 18, he was one of those players who barely touched the reserves, moving almost directly from the youth team. Making 43 first-team appearances in his first season when he was Player of the Year, he upped that to 44 and 48 in the next two seasons. Nick then played 45 times in his fourth full season in 1984-85 as Sunderland were relegated having reached the League Cup final where Pickering played against Norwich. Norwich had been the opponents in April 1983 when after Chris Turner fractured his skull Pickering took over in goal.

Later that year Nick won his one full England cap on an end-of-season tour of Australia where he played in a back four alongside Terry Butcher. Pickering had broken into the England Under 21 team at the start of the season, coming on as a sub in a 4-1 win over Denmark in Copenhagen to partner his club colleague Barry Venison in the full-back berths - Paul Bracewell also being a member of that side managed by Howard Wilkinson. A first start followed in March at Portsmouth against Greece before he lined up at Newcastle against Hungary the following month. After receiving his full cap Pickering made twelve further Under 21 appearances up to April 1986 with Howard Gayle, Paul Hardyman, Bobby Mimms and Ian Snodin amongst his teammates.

In his penultimate appearance for Sunderland, Pickering plundered a hat-trick against Leeds with the aid of a penalty before he was sold by Lawrie McMenemy much to the frustration of supporters who as ever, did not like to see still youthful local talent sold off.

Debuting for Coventry at Newcastle, Nick played in all of the last 15 games of the season, scoring four times as he helped to keep Coventry up. He won the FA Cup in his first full season at Highfield Road playing in all six of their cup ties alongside Gary Bennett's brother Dave. Used predominantly in midfield by the Sky Blues until reverting to left-back after David Smith broke into the team, in total Pickering played 89+2 times for Coventry, scoring seven goals. In July 1988, he moved to Derby County for a £300,000 fee, but endured a torrid time through injury, making only 45 league appearances in three seasons (3 goals). He returned to the north east to score seven league goals in 57 games over two seasons with Darlington before finishing his career with four outings for Burnley in March and April 1993.

Nick went on to coach youngsters through the SAFC Football in the Community Scheme and his own soccer schools while he also had a spell as a summariser of Sunderland games on BBC local radio. Pickering appears to have taken his mother's maiden name of Burke when first born before becoming Pickering.

## PICKFORD, Jordan Lee

**POSITION:** Goalkeeper

**BIRTHPLACE:** Washington, Tyne & Wear

**DATE OF BIRTH:** 07/03/1994

**HEIGHT:** 6' 1" **WEIGHT:** 13st 0lbs

**SIGNED FROM:** School, 01/07/2010

**DEBUT:** v Arsenal, A, 09/01/2016

**LAST MATCH:** v Chelsea, A, 21/05/2017

**MOVED TO:** Everton, 01/07/2017

**TEAMS:** Sunderland, Darlington (L), Alfreton Town (L), Burton Albion (L), Carlisle United (L), Bradford City (L), Preston North End (L), Everton (to June 2022)

**INTERNATIONAL:** England

**SAFC TOTALS:** 35 appearances / 0 goals

**It was on a pre-season tour of Germany in 2011 that a then 17-year-old Pickford made a massive impression on the management and coaching staff. Although Jordan's debut did not come for over five years after that, it was always just a matter of time.**

During this period, the young keeper went on a series of loans culminating in him equalling Preston's record of six successive clean sheets in October and November 2015. That feat at such a historical club was part of a phenomenal record of twelve shut-outs in 24 league appearances with an additional one against Premier League Watford in one of his three League Cup games.

Recalled by Sunderland, Sam Allardyce threw Pickford in with a debut in the FA Cup at Arsenal followed by a Premier League debut at Tottenham a week later. He conceded seven goals in those two games, but unquestionably was a great talent playing behind what at the time was a leaky defence. The following season he made 32 appearances for Sunderland in a dismal relegation season under David Moyes. With Sunderland desperate for money as Ellis Short looked to offload the club, Pickford was sold for a club record £25m with the potential for that to climb to £30m. He had only made 35 appearances for Sunderland, but had become established as a future England international and that summer helped England Under 21s reach the semi-finals of the UEFA Under 21 Championship where they lost to Germany on penalties.

## PICKFORD, Jordan (Continued)

Albert McInroy remains the only goalkeeper to win a full cap while on Sunderland's books. Jimmy Montgomery was once an unused sub for England at Wembley. Pickford sat on the bench for the national side three times while still on Wearside in October and November 2016 before keeping a clean sheet against Germany on his full debut at Wembley in November 2017 following his move to Everton where he completed a hat-trick of Player of the Year, Players' Player of the Year and Young Player of the Year in his first season and was Player of the season again in 2021-22 when he also won the Premier League Save of the Season award.

As of May 2022, Jordan had amassed 43 full caps making him Everton's most capped England international. During this time he conceded just 31 goals at international level. Seven of his appearances came at the 2018 FIFA World Cup where he reached the semi-final. At the delayed 2020 Euros held in 2021, until conceding in the semi-final against Denmark he had been unbeaten in an England shirt for 726 minutes - an England record. He went on to play in the final against Italy where again his side lost on penalties despite Jordan saving two of Italy's five spot-kicks.

To May 2022, Pickford had played 199 times for Everton. His figures on loan from Sunderland were 17 for Darlington and 12 for Alfreton in non-league, 13 for Burton, 18 for Carlisle, 33 for Bradford plus those 27 for PNE. Jordan's brother, Richard Logan, played for Darlington, Workington (L), Gateshead (L) and Blyth Spartans between 2005 and 2007.

Born as Jordan Lee Logan, Logan being his mother's maiden name, Pickford remains a passionate Sunderland supporter and in 2022 should have many years left ahead of him in a game where he has already been at the peak for several seasons. A goalkeeper with incredible distribution ability and great agility, he has followed in a long line of exceptional goalkeepers at SAFC where it was a pity supporters saw so little of him.

## PIENAAR, Steven Jerome

**POSITION:** Midfielder

**BIRTHPLACE:** Johannesburg, South Africa

**DATE OF BIRTH:** 17/03/1982

**HEIGHT:** 5' 8" **WEIGHT:** 11st 3lbs

**SIGNED FROM:** Unattached, 19/08/2016

**DEBUT:** v Middlesbrough, H, 21/08/2016

**LAST MATCH:** v AFC Bournemouth, H, 29/04/2017

**MOVED TO:** Contract not renewed, 30/06/2017

**TEAMS:** Ajax Cape Town, Ajax, Borussia Dortmund, Everton, Tottenham Hotspur, Everton, Sunderland, Bidvest Wits

**INTERNATIONAL:** South Africa

**SAFC TOTALS:** 11+6 appearances / 0 goals

**Pienaar had been a very good player before coming to Sunderland, but was a slow veteran who failed to have any impact having been brought to the club as one of many old Evertonians by his former manager David Moyes. Pienaar's ability was not in question as a glance at the clubs he had previously played for illustrates. He had played at the 2002 and 2010 FIFA World Cup finals while winning 61 international caps and had gone double Dutch when winning both league and cup with Ajax in 2002, later adding a second Eredivisie title in 2004 and another domestic cup two years later.**

Having progressed via youth clubs West Ham Westbury, Westbury Arsenal, 'School of Excellence' and Ajax Cape Town he played senior football for the latter where after six goals in four times as many games he moved to parent club Ajax Amsterdam in 2001. At the home of the former European Champions he made 23+2 appearances in the Champions League scoring against Lyon and AC Milan. Additionally, he stroked home 15 Eredivisie goals in 83+11 games over five seasons and made one further appearance in the UEFA Cup.

After being an unused sub in the 2006 KNVB Cup final as Ajax beat PSV Eindhoven, Pienaar moved to Borussia Dortmund. After a single season in which he played 20+5 Bundesliga games without scoring he was signed by David Moyes at Everton. One of two goals in 39 games in his first season at Goodison came in a 7-1 rout over Sunderland in November 2007. After exactly 100 league starts for the Toffees Spurs gave Everton a £1m profit on the player but Pienaar only started five Premier League games out of his 12+6 appearances with his only goal coming against Shamrock Rovers in the Europa League.

Returning to Goodison, initially on loan, the Toffees decided to buy Pienaar back for £4.5m whereupon over four years he extended his total record for the club to 207+21 games and 23 goals before he joined Sunderland. Following his unhappy spell at Sunderland Pienaar returned to South Africa where he signed for a year with Bidvest Wits, but left six months later and retired in March 2018.

## PIPER, Matthew James

**POSITION:** Outside-right

**BIRTHPLACE:** Leicester, Leicestershire

**DATE OF BIRTH:** 29/09/1981

**HEIGHT:** 6' 1" **WEIGHT:** 12st 9lbs

**SIGNED FROM:** Leicester City, 21/08/2002

**DEBUT:** v Everton, H, 24/08/2002

**LAST MATCH:** v Cheltenham Town, H, 20/09/2005

**MOVED TO:** Contract terminated, 19/01/2006

**TEAMS:** Leicester City, Mansfield Town (L), Sunderland, Anstey Nomads, Oadby Town

**INTERNATIONAL:** England Under 21

**SAFC TOTALS:** 15+14 appearances / 0 goals

**As well as being a good - but injury-plagued - player, Matt Piper was one of the nicest lads you could wish to meet when he was at Sunderland, approachable and down to earth - so the revelations of his 2020 autobiography, 'Out of the Darkness: From Top to Rock Bottom' were even more shocking.**

'Pipes' explained how close he had come to suicide after suffering from reliance on alcohol and drugs. Thankfully he conquered his demons and re-found the kind, polite lad he was when he came to Sunderland. In 2022 Matt was working as a BBC summariser on local radio for his home town club Leicester City and concentrating his efforts on his FSD Academy trying to help inner city youngsters avoid the kind of problems Matt admitted the Sporting Chance clinic had helped him overcome.

Piper's popularity at Leicester was partly based on him having scored the final goal at their old Filbert Street ground. It was his only goal in 16 league games for the Foxes while there was another goal in an eight-game loan at Mansfield before coming to Sunderland. Pipe-cleaner thin, Piper was a speed merchant right-winger who the fans took to quickly as he was clearly a threat whenever he played, but the player was hard hit by injuries.

In particular he suffered from a condition called lax ligaments which meant that his ligaments were not tight enough to keep the capsule of his knee in place when twisting and turning at high speeds. Consequently despite a double figure number of operations Matt was forced to retire, although he later had unsuccessful trials at Coventry City (2006) and Mansfield Town (2007) and played very briefly for a couple of non-league clubs.

## PITT, Richard Ernest (Ritchie)

**POSITION:** Centre-half

**BIRTHPLACE:** Plains Farm, Sunderland, Co Durham

**DATE OF BIRTH:** 22/10/1951

**HEIGHT:** 6' 1" **WEIGHT:** 12st 0lbs

**SIGNED FROM:** Ryhope Juniors, 01/07/1967

**DEBUT:** v Coventry City, A, 04/03/1969

**LAST MATCH:** v Luton Town, H, 22/09/1973

**MOVED TO:** Retired, 30/06/1975

**TEAMS:** Sunderland, Arsenal (L)

**INTERNATIONAL:** England schools

**SAFC TOTALS:** 144+1 appearances / 7 goals

**Pitt was the only member of the 1973 FA Cup-winning team to have played at Wembley before the cup final. Ritchie had played there for England schoolboys in 1966. A few days later, he played in another international in Manchester at Old Trafford. Watching Manchester City scouts were so impressed they immediately offered Pitt and his parents £5,000 and a Ford Capri for his signature.**

That was serious money at the time but Ritchie made it clear that he wanted to sign for Sunderland. As soon as he could he joined on associated schoolboy forms leading to a reserve team debut at Middlesbrough two months after his 16th birthday.

Pitt left school in November 1968 and signed professional forms, debuting at the age of 17. He made 24 top-flight appearances - the first few of them when he was still a member of St Paul's Church Choir in Ryhope along with yours truly who would look forward to his Sunday morning assessments of the match.

Following relegation, as he matured Ritchie became a regular making 36 league appearances in 1970-71 and missing just one match the following year. The FA Cup-winning season of 1972-73 saw Pitt play in only half the league fixtures as new manager Bob Stokoe brought in the more experienced David Young in his position. After the fourth-round replay at Reading Stokoe sent him on loan to Arsenal who wanted to sign Ritchie after playing him in the reserves, however, due to an injury to Young, Sunderland recalled him.

However Pitt returned to reclaim his place through the sheer quality of his performances, complementing the majestic Dave Watson in central defence. Pitt's crunching first-minute tackle on England's Allan Clarke set the tone for the final, illustrating to Leeds that Sunderland would meet fire with fire and were there to win. Ritchie's role in helping Sunderland to keep a clean sheet was vital and his cup-winner's medal was something that helped to define his life.

Three days after helping Sunderland to another clean sheet in the club's first-ever European game away to Vasas Budapest, Ritchie was injured in a home game with Luton. Sadly, it was to be the final match of his career. He had not yet reached his 22nd birthday, but had amassed almost 150 appearances.

Finding a new career in teaching he went on to have a successful career in education, but remained proud of his time playing for the Lads. He became Chairman of the Former Players' Association, organised the 45th anniversary dinner of the cup-winning team and along with his teammates was awarded the Freedom of the City of Sunderland in 2022.

## POOLE, John Smith (Jack)

**POSITION:** Half-back

**BIRTHPLACE:** Codnor, Derbyshire

**DATE OF BIRTH:** 01/09/1892 - 21/03/1967

**HEIGHT:** 5' 10½" **WEIGHT:** 12st 4lbs

**SIGNED FROM:** Sutton Junction, 03/06/1919

**DEBUT:** v Aston Villa, H, 30/08/1919

**LAST MATCH:** v Arsenal, A, 12/04/1924

**MOVED TO:** Bradford City, 20/05/1924

**TEAMS:** Sutton Junction, Sherwood Foresters, Sheffield United (WW1 Guest), Nottingham Forest (WW1 Guest), Sunderland, Bradford City

**SAFC TOTALS:** 152 appearances / 2 goals

**Like Charlie Buchan, Jack Poole served with the Sherwood Foresters during the First World War. Stationed in Roker in June 1918 he was reputedly spotted by Sunderland manager Bob Kyle while playing on Roker beach with the Notts & Derbyshire Regiment.**

On 18 January 1919 he appeared as a guest player in a 2-0 Victory League win over Middlesbrough and after his signature was secured at the end of that season he came into the team for the first post-war Football League season, missing only the last match of the campaign. A reliable player, Poole remained a regular for the next four seasons, but made only eight league appearances in his last season of 1923-24 when he scored his only league goal in his penultimate game, against Middlesbrough who he had played his first match against.

Moving to Bradford City he was the Bantams only ever-present in his first two seasons as they finished 16th in Division Two in both terms. Injured for almost all of the 1926-27 season, his team finished bottom of the league. Retiring after 101 appearances (0 goals), he became City's reserve-team coach at the start of 1927-28, becoming first-team trainer three years later and staying until 1935 when he joined Mansfield Town.

After three years training the Stags, he became manager in May 1938, holding that role until August 1944 when he joined Notts County as trainer. During World War Two he had also served with the Police reserve. After the war Poole became trainer at Derby County from 1946 to 1956 before staying in the game back in Sutton Town in the Central Alliance having started with Sutton Junction. Jack's final football role, as Town's groundsman, ended in March 1959.

## POOM, Mart

**POSITION:** Goalkeeper

**BIRTHPLACE:** Tallin, Estonia

**DATE OF BIRTH:** 03/02/1972

**HEIGHT:** 6' 4½" **WEIGHT:** 13st 13lbs

**SIGNED FROM:** Derby County, 10/01/2003 after loan from 17/11/2002

**DEBUT:** v Birmingham City, A, 12/04/2003

**LAST MATCH:** v Watford, A, 19/10/2004

**MOVED TO:** Arsenal, 23/01/2006, after loan from 31/08/05

**TEAMS:** Lovid, Sport Tallin, Flora Tallin, Kuopio PS, Flora Tallin, FC Wil, Portsmouth, Flora Tallin (L), Derby County, Sunderland, Arsenal, Watford

**INTERNATIONAL:** Estonia

**SAFC TOTALS:** 67+1 appearances / 1 goal

**Mart Poom will forever be known as the goalkeeper who scored a goal, which is a bit unfair as Poom was a first-rate goalkeeper. Renowned for his exceptionally rigorous personal training regime, Mart was totally dedicated to making himself as good as he could be.**

Before coming to Sunderland he had become a huge hero at Derby County which was the scene of his sensational goal which saw radio commentator Simon Crabtree dub him 'The Poominator' with Wearside's Darwin Brewery later producing a beer with that name and featuring a photograph of Poom celebrating his last-minute equaliser in September 2003.

In typical fashion, Poom's celebration was understated. Despite scoring with as good a header as imaginable, Mart's first thought was to rush back to his goal and prepare to defend. It summed up his total professionalism. His goal was one of two firsts Poom managed at Sunderland. He also became the first goalkeeper to be sent off in a first-team game, his dismissal coming at Crystal Palace in April 2004.

Capped 120 times by Estonia, Poom was his country's Player of the Year in 1993, 1994, 1997, 1998, 2000 and 2003. Before first coming to England when joining Portsmouth in 1994, Poom had played in Finland and Switzerland as well as his homeland where after playing for Tallina Lovid, he played in Russia in the Soviet Second League with Estonian club Sport Tallin.

After 20 games for Lovid and 59 for Sport Tallin he had nine games with Finnish outfit KuPS, and 22 back in Tallin with FC Flora prior to FC Wil, a second-tier Swiss side where after a season he was sold to Portsmouth in August 1994.

Debuting for Pompey with a clean sheet in a League Cup win over Cambridge in August 1994, Poom would only make four league appearances and three cup games for the club despite him establishing a club record of 756 minutes without conceding a goal when loaned back to Flora in Estonia. In March 1997, Poom was purchased by Derby County with whom he became massively popular, becoming Player of the Year in 1999-2000. The first of his 163+3 appearances came in a win at Manchester United in April 1997 and featured a superb display at the Stadium of Light on the final day of the 2001-02 season as already relegated Derby hung on for a point.

Before Christmas of that year Poom joined Sunderland, initially on loan with the move confirmed in the January transfer window. His debut did not arrive until mid-April when he played at Birmingham in a game that confirmed Sunderland's long inevitable relegation.

Mart was given his debut by Mick McCarthy having never been selected by the manager who bought him, Howard Wilkinson. Poom went on to become Sunderland's first choice keeper, playing 52 of the 56 games the following season including the semi-finals of the FA Cup and Play-Offs. In the latter the Poominator saved two of Palace's last three penalties in a shoot-out, but it was not enough to help Sunderland through.

After leaving Sunderland for Arsenal, he got just two games for the Gunners, keeping a clean sheet at his old club Portsmouth in May 2007 having previously played as a sub in a League Cup tie with Everton. He did however pick up a Champions League runners-up medal against Barcelona in 2006 as a member of the squad, although he was not actually an unused sub.

In 2007 Mart joined Watford in a search of first-team football, but after 19 games dislocated his shoulder in what proved to be his final match against Reading five years to the day since he scored for Sunderland. After retiring Mart returned to Arsenal as a goalkeeping coach, served in the same role for his national team and became Director of Sport at Flora Tallinn as well as managing a soccer school in Estonia from where he would occasionally bring youngsters to train at Sunderland.

As of June 2022, his Derby-born son Markus, had won twelve caps as a midfielder for Estonia and was playing for Flora Tallinn with whom he had twice won the league in Estonia.

## PORTEOUS, Thomas Stoddart (Tom)

**POSITION:** Right-back

**BIRTHPLACE:** Elswick, Northumberland

**DATE OF BIRTH:** 21/09/1865 - 23/02/1919

**HEIGHT:** 5' 9" **WEIGHT:** 11st 10lbs

**SIGNED FROM:** Kilmarnock, 08/08/1889

**DEBUT:** v Blackburn Rovers, A, 18/01/1890

**LAST MATCH:** v Everton, A, 30/09/1893

**MOVED TO:** Rotherham Town, 15/08/1894

**TEAMS:** Springville Juniors, Kilmarnock, Sunderland, Rotherham Town, Manchester City, South Shore

**INTERNATIONAL:** England

**SAFC TOTALS:** 93 appearances / 0 goals

**Sunderland's first-ever international, Porteous' one England cap came against Wales at Sunderland's Newcastle Road ground on 7 March 1891. One of the club's early top players, Porteous played in many of the fierce friendlies of the era. He was ever-present in Sunderland's first season in the Football League and went on to win league title medals in 1892 and 1893, missing just one league game across those two seasons.**

Before coming to Sunderland the Tynesider had been captain of the Ayrshire County team during the 1888-89 season having already won the Ayrshire Cup in 1886 with Kilmarnock and later the Ayr Charity Cup. He had begun his career as a forward with Springville Juniors in 1878, going on to become captain of Kilmarnock where he had been brought up after moving to Scotland before he was aged six.

After his most successful years at Sunderland - during which he represented the Durham FA as well as England - Tom became player/coach at Rotherham Town for whom he made the first of 49 appearances on 1 September 1894 in a 3-1 home defeat to Burton Wanderers. After two years with the Millers, he moved to fellow second division club Manchester City where his five appearances all came in February 1896 as he helped City to runners-up spot.

Before his footballing career Porteous worked as a tinsmith and after retiring became a glazier then a house painter. He also took in boarders as he and his family lived in Blackpool where he had ended his career with South Shore, a Blackpool club who never succeeded in gaining election to the Football League.

## PORTERFIELD, John (Ian)

**POSITION:** Midfielder

**BIRTHPLACE:** Dunfermline, Fife

**DATE OF BIRTH:** 11/02/1946 - 11/09/2007

**HEIGHT:** 5' 11" **WEIGHT:** 11st 6lbs

**SIGNED FROM:** Raith Rovers, 29/12/1967

**DEBUT:** v Newcastle United, H, 30/12/1967

**LAST MATCH:** v Chelsea, A, 20/12/1975

**MOVED TO:** Sheffield Wednesday, 26/07/1977

**TEAMS:** Lochgelly Albion, Lochore Welfare, Raith Rovers, Sunderland, Reading (L), Sheffield Wednesday, Rotherham United

**SAFC TOTALS:** 256+12 appearances / 19 goals

**As the scorer of the only goal of the 1973 FA Cup final Ian Porterfield did not so much write his name into the record books, as cement it. The goal in such a fairy-tale final made Porterfield world famous and helped him to go on and enjoy a worldwide career in management.**

Porterfield was a quality midfielder who could kill a ball stone dead and pass it immaculately. While his legendary status rests on his goal at Wembley, 'Porter' was always more of a deliverer than a scorer, his passing being top class.

He had come to Sunderland's attention when playing and scoring against the Lads in a charity match at Dunfermline which raised funds for the Michael Colliery Disaster Fund. Michael Colliery was a pit in Fife where nine men had been killed in a pit disaster in September 1967. Other than in the nineteenth century when Fife played some games on a county basis, this was the first time the quartet of Fife clubs had united to play as a representative side.

So it was that an XI made up of players from Dunfermline, East Fife, Cowdenbeath and Porterfield's Raith Rovers came together under the management of George Farm, the former Scotland international 'keeper who had played against Newcastle in the 1951 FA Cup final for Blackpool. Farm was the boss of Dunfermline, having recently moved from Raith Rovers where he had overseen Porterfield's development. Former Scotland manager Ian McColl was in charge of Sunderland who included two Cowdenbeath locals in the legendary Jim Baxter and his cousin George Kinnell.

Porterfield came to Sunderland for a Raith record fee of £35,000 with a further £10,000 guaranteed after he had played 20 league games. Debuting in a Wear-Tyne derby, Porterfield looked a useful player before being entirely frozen out of the team in the relegation season of 1969-70, his only top-flight goal coming in a home win over Leicester in 1968. Once in the second division, Porterfield played 40 or more games in each of the next four seasons including the cup-winning campaign.

On 7 December 1974, Ian was involved in serious a car accident. He was on top form at the time. In his last appearance a few hours before the crash, Porterfield provided a majestic performance in a 4-1 home win over Portsmouth. The car crash fractured Ian's skull and almost cost him his life. Years later, the Gosforth-based surgeon who had operated on Ian and saved his life gave me a Sunday Mirror tankard commemorating 1973. Ian had given the surgeon this as a thank you when he recovered and the aging doctor wanted to return it to the club for display. It is now on show in the foyer of the Stadium of Light along with Ian's medal, Golden Boot for scoring the Wembley winner and the match-ball, all of which I once took receipt of from Ian's widow, a former Miss Trinidad.

When he was on the road to recovery - although sadly, Ian never got back to his pre-accident quality - he played in the first half of the 1975-76 promotion season. Almost a year later he a month on loan to Reading before his former Roker teammate Len Ashurst signed him for Sheffield Wednesday. As a student in Sheffield at the time, while still watching Sunderland, I would frequently go and watch Wednesday in midweek. Mams being mams, mine wrote to Ian telling him I was going to watch Wednesday because he was playing. Porterfield wrote back personally saying, in future to let him know when I was going and he would leave me a ticket whenever I wanted - which I did for the rest of my time there.

Meeting Ian on the train to Sheffield once, I introduced myself and thanked him for the tickets he had been leaving for me. I intended it to be a short thank you, but Ian insisted I sat with him and talked football while he bought my teas and coffees. This was Sunderland's cup hero with an impoverished raggy 70s student. Did it leave a positive impression? You bet it did.

Ian played 126+4 times for Wednesday, scoring six goals before stepping into the world of management a few miles away at Rotherham where he appointed Vic Halom as his assistant. After taking the Millers to promotion, Porterfield took over at Sheffield United where he won promotion in 1984 before succeeding Alex Ferguson at Aberdeen after which he managed Reading and Chelsea.

He became the first manager to lose his job in the Premier League when Chelsea dispensed with his services. Nonetheless, Porterfield's worldwide fame led to him taking charge of the national sides of: Zambia, Zimbabwe, Oman, Trinidad and Tobago and Armenia as well as managing Kumasi Asante Kotoko in Ghana, Al Ittihad in Saudi Arabia and Busan I'Park in South Korea. In 2001 Ian led Trinidad & Tobago to the Caribbean Cup, while in 2004, he was an FA Cup winner again with Busan I'Park in South Korea. In 1996, between spells in Saudi Arabia and Zimbabwe, he worked at Bolton Wanderers as first-team coach.

Ian's adventures in South Korea were documented in a 2020 book, 'Who ate all the Squid?' while his Sunderland cup story led to the 1973 book 'The Impossible Dream.' Inducted into the Raith Rovers Hall of Fame in 2018, he was due to be added to the Sunderland Hall of Fame in 2022, having been posthumously awarded the Freedom of the City earlier that year.

ITRE
PERMAWHITE
FINNEY

## POULTER, Henry (Harry)

**POSITION:** Centre-forward

**BIRTHPLACE:** Shiney Row, Co Durham

**DATE OF BIRTH:** 24/04/1910 - 25/02/1985

**HEIGHT:** 5' 10½" **WEIGHT:** 12st 7lbs

**SIGNED FROM:** Shiney Row Swifts, 01/09/1931

**DEBUT:** v Southampton, H, 09/01/1932

**LAST MATCH:** v Stoke City, H, 23/01/1932

**MOVED TO:** Exeter City, 15/07/1932

**TEAMS:** Shiney Row Swifts, Sunderland, Exeter City, Hartlepools United

**SAFC TOTALS:** 3 appearances / 2 goals

**Poulter played as an amateur under FA Rule 33, because he could not be registered as a professional as his Royal Navy discharge had been obtained by purchase. He served in the Navy's Atlantic fleet and played for Shiney Row Swifts when available.**

During his time with the navy Harry also signed North Eastern League forms with Middlesbrough, but was not retained by Boro at the end of the 1930-31 season, after which he joined Sunderland. Home supporters did not see him score in his two appearances at Roker Park, but he scored with a header and an angled hook shot in his one away game, a 4-2 FA Cup replay win at Southampton, all three of his games coming in the cup.

Unable to get into the first team, after his brief cup exploits Poulter swapped the red and white stripes of Sunderland for those of Exeter at the end of the season when he finally became a professional. A scoring debut against Bristol City in August 1932 got him off to a good start but it was not until 1934-35 that he played regularly, scoring 16 goals in 26 league games out of his total of 33 in 50 league games for the Grecians. In September 1935 he was taken ill, not returning until January, but never recapturing his previous form and was released at the end of the season. He joined Hartlepools for a month's trial, but never played for them, and by 1939 was still single, living in Horatio St, Sunderland with his parents, and working as a port maintenance fitter and serving in the Police War Reserve. During World War Two, he served in the Atlantic fleet of the Royal Navy.

## POWER, Lee Michael

**POSITION:** Forward

**BIRTHPLACE:** Lewisham, London

**DATE OF BIRTH:** 30/06/1972

**HEIGHT:** 5' 11" **WEIGHT:** 11st 2lbs

**SIGNED FROM:** Norwich City, 13/08/1993, on loan

**DEBUT:** v Derby County, A, 14/08/1993

**LAST MATCH:** v Crystal Palace, A, 11/09/1993

**MOVED TO:** Norwich City, 13/09/1993, end of loan

**TEAMS:** Norwich City, Charlton Athletic (L), Sunderland (L), Portsmouth (L), Bradford City, Millwall (L), Peterborough United, Dundee, Hibernian, Ayr United, Plymouth Argyle, Halifax Town, Boston United

**INTERNATIONAL:** Republic of Ireland

**SAFC TOTALS:** 3+2 appearances / 1 goal

**Signed on loan by Terry Butcher, the manager wanted to keep Lee after his loan, during which he had scored on his home and full debut in a League Cup tie with Chester. However, Butcher had already spent more that summer than any Sunderland manager in history and the funds for another signing were not available. At the time, Power was the Republic of Ireland's Young Player of the Year and had won a record 13 Under 21 caps.**

The striker went on to have a well-travelled career, but never settled at any club, never equalling the 44 league games he played for his first team Norwich or matching the ten goals he scored for the Canaries. Only at Peterborough (38/6), Bradford City - who paid £200,000 for him (30/5) and Halifax (25/5) did he play as many as 20 league games while there were only 25 league appearances and six goals in total divided between the trio of Scottish clubs he represented. In between spells at Ayr United and Plymouth, he also played one match on trial for Carlisle against Rangers.

Forced to retire through injury when only 28 he stayed in the game initially as an agent and then as a sports publisher. Several times he came to my office at the Stadium of Light asking me to give his company the contract for the Sunderland programme. After a failed bid as part of a consortium seeking to take over Luton Town, Power joined the board of Cambridge United, becoming chairman and eventually caretaker-manager. He later became a board member of Rushden and Diamonds, then at the same Conference level as Cambridge.

In 2013 he became part owner of Swindon Town, investing a reported £1.2m in the Robins. Again, he later became caretaker-manager and while still heavily involved with Swindon in 2016 also became owner and chairman of Waterford United in the Republic of Ireland, changing the club's name to its old name of Waterford FC. He sold Waterford in June 2021, the same month that he was reported to be selling Swindon where two months earlier he had reportedly been charged with breaching FA regulations. In 2009, Power emigrated to live in Switzerland.

## POWER, Max McAuley

**POSITION:** Midfielder

**BIRTHPLACE:** Birkenhead, Merseyside

**DATE OF BIRTH:** 27/07/1993

**HEIGHT:** 5' 11" **WEIGHT:** 12st 4lbs

**SIGNED FROM:** Wigan Athletic, 10/08/2018, on loan Permanent from 01/01/2019

**DEBUT:** v Luton Town, A, 11/08/2018

**LAST MATCH:** v Lincoln City, H, 22/05/2021

**MOVED TO:** Wigan Athletic, 16/06/2021

**TEAMS:** Tranmere Rovers, Colwyn Bay (L), Wigan Athletic, Sunderland, Wigan Athletic (to June 2022)

**SAFC TOTALS:** 122+15 appearances / 13 goals

**Max Power captained Sunderland to a Wembley win over his first club Tranmere Rovers in the final of the Football League (Papa John's) Trophy in 2021, thereby becoming the first Sunderland skipper to lift a trophy at the national stadium since Bobby Kerr in 1973 at the original, rather than re-built Wembley.**

A headline writer's dream, Power was a hard working player with a powerful shot, several of his goals being spectacular ones from outside the box. In his final season at Sunderland, he made 54 appearances, the highest total for an outfield player since Andy Melville made the same number in 1993-94.

After being released by Sunderland Max returned to his former club Wigan and made his first appearance back at the Stadium of Light on the opening day of the next season. Having won promotion from League One with Wigan in 2016 and 2018, he achieved the same feat with the Latics in his first season back, although at Sunderland - where he received three red cards in his first 13 games, he had been unable to do so. Max made three Wembley appearances for Sunderland, playing in the 2019 Football League (Checkatrade) Trophy final against Portsmouth - when he scored in the unsuccessful penalty shoot-out - and also in the same season's Play-Off final lost to Charlton. His final game for the Wearsiders came in a 2021 Play-Off semi-final with Lincoln City.

Max made 99 league starts out of a total of 111+16 games (19 goals) for his first club Tranmere who he had been with since the age of eight and for whom he debuted against Port Vale in August 2011, scoring in a penalty shoot-out of that Football League (Johnstone's Paints) Trophy tie. As of the summer of 2022, Power had played 180+17 games for Wigan scoring 16 times.

## POWER, Peter Jeffrey (Geoffrey)

**POSITION:** Inside-right

**BIRTHPLACE:** Grangetown, Middlesbrough, Yorkshire

**DATE OF BIRTH:** 07/04/1898 -17/01/1963

**HEIGHT:** 5' 6½" **WEIGHT:** 11st 12lbs

**SIGNED FROM:** Grangetown St Mary's, 25/08/1919

**DEBUT:** v Liverpool, A, 15/01/1921

**LAST MATCH:** v Burnley, A, 07/05/1921

**MOVED TO:** Blackpool, 15/12/1921

**TEAMS:** Grangetown St Mary's, Sunderland, Blackpool, Chester-le-Street, Fleetwood, Wheatley Hill Colliery, Scarborough, Eston United, Grangetown

**SAFC TOTALS:** 10 appearances / 0 goals

**Geoffrey Power served in the Great War, but only because he lied about his age and signed up as Geoffrey Power rather than admitting to his real name of Peter Jeffrey Power or his real birthdate. Power saw service with the Yorkshire Regiment and Lancashire Fusiliers and went on to have a lengthy football career after the war regardless of not being able to get going until he was in his early twenties.**

Having started with local Middlesbrough side Grangetown St Mary's, he signed for Sunderland in 1919 and got a first-team debut in a goalless draw at Liverpool. By the end of the season having played ten games including all of the last four he must have felt he had done well, but there were to be no further opportunities and in December, he moved on to second division Blackpool for a fee of £350.

Although the Seasiders were involved in a relegation battle they narrowly won, Power was not called upon until the following 1921-22 season when he made all 19 of his appearances for the club. A purple patch at the turn of the year saw him score in five games out of six with his sixth and final goal coming against South Shields in April. Following a short spell with Chester-le-Street, he then joined Fleetwood in 1923 before representing Wheatley Hill Colliery, Scarborough, Eston United and Grangetown.

## PRICA, Rade Stanislav

**POSITION:** Centre-forward

**BIRTHPLACE:** Ljungby, Sweden

**DATE OF BIRTH:** 30/06/1980

**HEIGHT:** 6' 0" **WEIGHT:** 12st 8lbs

**SIGNED FROM:** Aalborg BK, 24/01/2008

**DEBUT:** v Birmingham City, H, 29/01/2008

**LAST MATCH:** v Chelsea, H, 15/03/2008

**MOVED TO:** Rosenborg, 09/03/2009

**TEAMS:** Ljungby IF, Helsingborgs, Hansa Rostock, Aalborg BK, Sunderland, Rosenborg, Maccabi Tel Aviv, Helsingborgs, Maccabi Petah Tikva, Landskrona BoIS

**INTERNATIONAL:** Sweden

**SAFC TOTALS:** 0+6 appearances / 1 goal

**Swedish-born as the son of Serb and Croat parents, Prica told me in an interview before his debut that the strong point of his game was that he was tough, but he never seemed physically capable of excelling in the Premier League and justifying his reported £2m transfer fee. Not only did he fail to start a game, but on one occasion at Liverpool, he was substituted after coming on as a sub. The span of his first-team career at Sunderland lasted under three months although it was almost a year after his final appearance before he moved on.**

Other than at Sunderland, Rade enjoyed a good career, winning 14 full caps, scoring goals in a couple of friendlies against Ecuador and Montenegro as well as becoming the first player to win league titles in Sweden, Denmark and Norway. He lifted the Allsvenskan with Helsingborgs in 1999 when as a teenager he made four appearances including two as sub. Nine years later, he won the Danish Superliga with Aalborg before completing his hat-trick of Scandinavian titles in Norway with Rosenborg in 2009 when he was the Tippeligaen's top scorer.

A year later, he retained the title with Rosenborg before adding three further league title medals in successive years in the Israeli Premier League between 2013 and 2015. The final year of that run was a treble-winning year for Rade whose club also won the Israel State and Toto cups. After a brief spell back in Sweden with Helsingborgs, Prica won the Toto Cup again in 2016 having joined his old club's rivals Maccabi Petah Tivah.

His only goal for Sunderland came on his debut, a game in which he had another disallowed. He might feel he never got sufficient chance at Sunderland given what he achieved elsewhere, but Prica never looked the part at Sunderland, although overall enjoyed a career of 204 goals in 563 appearances. eleven of these goals and 59 appearances came in European competition, including two in the UEFA Cup against Ipswich in 2001-02.

## PRINCE, Thomas

**POSITION:** Inside-left / outside-left

**BIRTHPLACE:** Hetton-le-Hole, Co Durham

**DATE OF BIRTH:** 20/02/1879 - 10/03/1940

**SIGNED FROM:** Selbourne, 01/06/1897 and Bishop Auckland, 01/08/1903

**DEBUT:** v Nottingham Forest, H, 23/04/1898

**LAST MATCH:** v Blackburn Rovers, H, 16/03/1901

**MOVED TO:** Bishop Auckland, 12/08/1902 Retired, 06/05/1906

**TEAMS:** Selbourne, Sunderland, Hebburn Argyle (L), Bishop Auckland, Sunderland

**SAFC TOTALS:** 4 appearances / 0 goals

**'Tot' Prince signed from a local Sunderland club as an 18-year-old, debuted at the end of his first season and then did not play at all the following season before making a single appearance in his third campaign and two in his fourth.**

Although still on Sunderland's books in the following 1901-02 campaign - when the first-team were so good they won the league title - Prince was allowed to play a few games for Hebburn Argyle. At the end of that season he left to join Bishop Auckland but a year later returned to SAFC without adding to his first-team appearances. Prince is one of the few players to have played at three of Sunderland's home grounds; at Abbs Field with Sunderland third team in the late 1890s and with the first-team at Newcastle Road and then Roker Park.

A school-teacher whilst playing for Sunderland, in later life he became headmaster of Redby Junior School near the Roker Park ground, a job he was still doing at the time of his death. A talented cricketer, he played the summer sport for Wearmouth and Durham County.

## PRIOR, George

**POSITION:** Inside-right / centre-forward

**BIRTHPLACE:** Aberdeen, Aberdeenshire

**DATE OF BIRTH:** 06/01/1880 - 15/03/1952

**HEIGHT:** 5' 9" **WEIGHT:** 13st 0lbs

**SIGNED FROM:** St Bernards, 23/10/1901

**DEBUT:** v Stoke, A, 09/11/1901

**LAST MATCH:** v Notts County, A, 19/04/1902

**MOVED TO:** Third Lanark, 07/07/1902

**TEAMS:** Lochgelly United, St Bernard's, Sunderland, Third Lanark, Lochgelly United

**SAFC TOTALS:** 5 appearances / 0 goals

**A Scottish Division Two champion with Edinburgh side St Bernard's in 1901 while working as a plumber, George Prior was one of several players to leave the club that summer following their failure to secure promotion. This was despite winning their league at a time when promotion also hinged on votes at the Scottish League's AGM.**

After coming to Wearside George made all five of his Sunderland appearances in the title-winning season of 1901-02, but could not hold down a first-team place and returned to Scotland after under a year. Prior ended his playing career at his first club in Lochgelly after they agreed terms in October 1903 with Sunderland who still held his league registration papers. From Fife he emigrated to Ontario, Canada, in June 1913 where he remained working as a plumber with his family until his death.

## PRIOR, Jack

**POSITION:** Outside-right

**BIRTHPLACE:** Choppington, Northumberland

**DATE OF BIRTH:** 02/07/1904 - 29/08/1982

**HEIGHT:** 5' 9" **WEIGHT:** 11st 5lbs

**SIGNED FROM:** Blyth Spartans, 16/03/1923

**DEBUT:** v Manchester City, H, 30/03/1923

**LAST MATCH:** v Tottenham Hotspur, H, 18/09/1926

**MOVED TO:** Grimsby Town, 05/02/1927

**TEAMS:** Choppington Colliery, Blyth Spartans, Sunderland, Grimsby Town, Ashington, Mansfield Town, Stalybridge Celtic, Pressed Steel FC

**SAFC TOTALS:** 71 appearances / 11 goals

**Jack Prior was part of a footballing family. Brother George (known as Geordie) was a full-back who captained (Sheffield) Wednesday, Watford and Ashington between 1921 and 1933, while in the 1950s, nephew Kenneth George played for Newcastle United - alongside Bob Stokoe, Millwall - alongside Charlie Hurley, and Berwick Rangers.**

As a fourteen-year-old, Jack had signed for Sunderland as an amateur, but later signed for Newcastle having been invited to do so by Jackie Milburn. Further footballing family connections included Ken's sister marrying Newcastle legend Bobby Cowell, cousin Stuart Chapman signing for Sir Stanley Matthews at Port Vale and for good measure Chapman's niece marrying Durham and England cricketer Paul Collingwood. Four other brothers of Jack all played local football.

Jack Prior lined up as an 18-year-old on his Sunderland debut, playing alongside Charlie Buchan against Manchester City and got his first goal on City's next visit the following season. Sunderland finished in the top three in four of the five seasons Prior played, including his best year of 1925-26 when he scored a creditable nine goals in 32 games from the right-wing, including a brace in a 4-1 victory against a Huddersfield side en-route to their third successive title.

After leaving Sunderland Jack scored 34 goals in 160 league games for Grimsby and after a short spell at Ashington in 1932 scored seven goals in 32 1932-33 league appearances for Mansfield Town before winding down in non-league. In 1939, Jack was working as a slinger on cranes in Oxford and in later life spent his time living in Devon.

## PRITCHARD, Alex David

**POSITION:** Midfielder

**BIRTHPLACE:** Orsett, Essex

**DATE OF BIRTH:** 03/05/1993

**HEIGHT:** 5' 7" **WEIGHT:** 9st 8lbs

**SIGNED FROM:** Free agent, 09/07/2021

**DEBUT:** v Port Vale, A, 10/08/2021

**LAST MATCH:**

**MOVED TO:**

**TEAMS:** West Ham United, Tottenham Hotspur, Peterborough United (L), Swindon Town (L), Brentford (L), WBA (L), Norwich City, Huddersfield Town, Sunderland

**INTERNATIONAL:** England Under 21

**SAFC TOTALS:** 34+13 appearances / 4 goals (to June 2022)

**Alex Pritchard came to Sunderland as a 28-year-old looking to revive his fortunes in League One after an injury-hit period in a career that had seen him command reported fees of £8m and £11m when signing for his two previous clubs. After initially being kept out of the team by Elliott Embleton, by the middle of his first season Pritchard had not only nailed down a place, but had established himself as the team's creative force with his eye for a telling pass allied to superb set-piece delivery, making him an invaluable member of the side which won promotion from League One in his first season.**

Pritchard played youth football for West Ham United and Spurs, eventually making two Premier League appearances for Tottenham after gaining experience on loan with Peterborough (2+4/0) and Swindon (41+3/8). Further loans from White Hart Lane followed with Brentford (45+2/12) and WBA (0+2/0). At the age of 23, Pritchard left Spurs, turning down a transfer to Brighton in order to join Norwich where he played for Alex Neil who later became his manager at Sunderland. At Norwich, Pritchard blossomed under the leadership of Alan Irvine and Daniel Farke prior to a January 2018 transfer to Premier League Huddersfield following 29+14 appearances and eight goals for the Canaries.

Debuting for the Terriers in a 4-1 home defeat to West Ham Pritchard played his part in helping keep the club up but in his second season only 16 points were mustered as the Terriers went down. Injuries restricted him so that he only played in around half of the games in each of the next two seasons eventually tallying 55+28 games with four goals.

At international level, Alex won nine caps for England Under 21s having made two of his three Under 20 appearance at the 2013 FIFA Under 20 World Cup. He debuted for the Under 21s as a sub in a 1-0 win away to Lithuania in September 2014. After two further appearances off the bench, Alex got his first start against the Czech Republic the following March.

## PROCTOR, Mark Gerard

**POSITION:** Midfielder

**BIRTHPLACE:** Middlesbrough, North Riding of Yorkshire

**DATE OF BIRTH:** 30/01/1961

**HEIGHT:** 5' 9" **WEIGHT:** 11st 10lbs

**SIGNED FROM:** Nottingham Forest, 28/07/1983
After loan from 15/03/1983 - 15/04/1983

**DEBUT:** v Swansea City, H, 19/03/1983

**LAST MATCH:** v Mansfield Town, H, 31/08/1987

**MOVED TO:** Sheffield Wednesday, 03/09/1987

**TEAMS:** Nunthorpe Athletic, Middlesbrough, Nottingham Forest, Sunderland, Sheffield Wednesday, Middlesbrough, Tranmere Rovers, St Johnstone, Blyth Spartans, South Shields, Hartlepool United

**INTERNATIONAL:** England Under 21

**SAFC TOTALS:** 136+2 appearances / 23 goals

**Mark Proctor was a classy midfield schemer who was part of Alan Durban's promising side of the early eighties, but missed much of the 1984-85 relegation season under Len Ashurst. That injury also cost Mark a place in the League (Milk) Cup final side after he had helped the team into the quarter-finals.**

Having been out since New Year's Day 1985, Mark made his comeback just before Christmas by which time Lawrie McMenemy was in charge. Proctor scored in the last three games of that term to help keep Sunderland up, that contribution included a pressure penalty in a last-day win against Stoke to climax a season in which he was the club's Player of the Year.

Twelve months on from that with Sunderland 2-1 up in a last-day game with Barnsley, Proctor failed from the spot after which Sunderland lost and slipped into the relegation Play-Offs of the time. Proctor then scored twice, including a penalty, in a first-leg defeat at Gillingham, but in the second leg again failed from the spot with Sunderland 2-1 up. Subsequently, the side went down into the third tier for the first time. Such penalty problems would be unfair to pin on Proctor as the main memory of his time at the club is he was a quality and committed performer who at least had the bottle to take those spot-kicks.

After a trial with Leeds United, Mark had begun his professional career with Middlesbrough for whom he debuted in a win at Birmingham City in August 1978 as a 17-year-old. Nine goals during his first campaign established Proctor as a goalscoring midfielder. In 1981, he signed for fellow Teessider Brian Clough at Nottingham Forest. Debuting in a home win over Southampton in August 1981, his first competitive goal came against Sunderland the following month. It was one of nine goals he scored in 75 appearances before coming to Wearside.

Following his time at Sunderland, Proctor moved on to Sheffield Wednesday for whom he debuted in a 1-1 draw at Southampton in September 1987, Lee Chapman being Wednesday's goalscorer while Colin West also became one of his teammates in Howard Wilkinson's team with Chris Turner, David Hodgson and Wilf Rostron also going on to play alongside him at Hillsborough. Proctor would go on to score five times in 69 games for the Owls before a return to Middlesbrough. In his second spell at Boro Proctor took his total of appearances for the club to 246+27 games and 20 goals. This included captaining the side at Wembley when Peter Davenport and Colin Cooper were part of Colin Todd's side which lost to Chelsea in the Full Members' Cup final.

Proctor wound down his career with Tranmere Rovers (31/1) and St Johnstone (6/0) as well as in local football in the north east. From 1998 to June 2004 he was youth-team manager at Middlesbrough before becoming assistant manager at Darlington. In October 2006, he coached at Hibernian, briefly becoming caretaker-manager and subsequently, reserve team coach. From May 2007 until June 2008 he managed Livingston before returning to Middlesbrough where he managed the youth team before becoming joint caretaker manager in October 2010. He then set up his own football academy and was still running the Mark Proctor Academy in 2022.

## PROCTOR, Michael Anthony

**POSITION:** Forward

**BIRTHPLACE:** Monkwearmouth, Sunderland

**DATE OF BIRTH:** 03/10/1980

**HEIGHT:** 6' 0" **WEIGHT:** 11st 8lbs

**SIGNED FROM:** Trainee, 01/07/1996

**DEBUT:** v Everton, A, 11/11/1998

**LAST MATCH:** v Nottingham Forest, H, 10/01/2004

**MOVED TO:** Rotherham United, 06/02/2004

**TEAMS:** Sunderland, Hvidovre IF (L), Halifax Town (L), York City (L), Bradford City (L), Rotherham United, Swindon Town (L), Hartlepool United, Boston United (L), Wrexham

**SAFC TOTALS:** 22+26 appearances / 5 goals

**Proctor was a pacey homegrown forward who came on the scene at a time when Sunderland were flying under Peter Reid, but it was difficult for young lads to get into the team and stay there, especially for forwards. After debuting as a sub in a League Cup tie at Everton shortly after his 18th birthday, Michael did not get a second appearance for three and a half years having suffered a cruciate ligament injury.**

During this time, he had loans in Denmark from July to November in 2000 before marking his league debut with a goal at Cheltenham for Halifax Town under Paul Bracewell. Michael scored four goals in 11+1 games for a struggling side who finished second bottom of the Football League.

In the following season of 2001-02 on loan to York City he was the Minstermen's top-scorer with 14 goals from 40+1 games plus a further seven cup appearances. Early in the 2002-03 term he went on yet another loan, this time to Bradford City for a couple of months, scoring four times in twelve league games before being recalled to Sunderland by the recently installed Howard Wilkinson. In what became a harrowing season of relegation with a record low number of points, Michael made all but six of his starts for Sunderland in addition to a dozen of his appearances off the bench. In a season when everything that could go wrong, did go wrong, Michael was once responsible for two of the three own-goals Sunderland scored in a 3-1 home defeat by Charlton, both were unfortunate deflections. More positively, Michael at one point scored in successive home Premier League games including a well-taken late winner against Liverpool.

After leaving the Lads he joined Rotherham in a deal that brought Darren Byfield to Sunderland. There were seven goals in 36+13 games for the Millers who loaned him to Swindon (4/2) before freeing him to join Hartlepool. After seven goals in 25+7 games, Proctor joined Wrexham who Hartlepool had previously loaned him to. Despite Michael managing a dozen goals in 2007-08 the club slipped out of the Football League after which he spent a season in the Blue Square Premier,

a goal on his last appearance against Weymouth in April 2009 taking his total for Wrexham to 42+27/15.

After retiring from playing, Michael became a coach at East Durham College Football Performance Centre and from July 2015, commenced coaching at the SAFC Academy. As coach of the Under 23 team in February 2022 alongside Mike Dodds, he had two games as caretaker-manager of the first-team following the sacking of Lee Johnson and then continued alongside Alex Neil, helping the club to promotion via the Play-Offs.

## PRUDHOE, Mark

**POSITION:** Goalkeeper

**BIRTHPLACE:** Washington, Co Durham

**DATE OF BIRTH:** 11/11/1963

**HEIGHT:** 6' 0" **WEIGHT:** 12st 12lbs

**SIGNED FROM:** Washington Youths, 01/06/1980

**DEBUT:** v West Bromwich Albion, A, 11/12/1982

**LAST MATCH:** v West Bromwich Albion, H, 14/05/1983

**MOVED TO:** Birmingham City, 24/09/1984

**TEAMS:** Sunderland, Hartlepool United (L), Birmingham City, Walsall, Doncaster Rovers (L), Sheffield Wednesday (L), Grimsby Town (L), Hartlepool United (L), Bristol City (L), Carlisle United, Darlington, Stoke City, Peterborough United (L), Liverpool (L), York City (L), Bradford City, Darlington (L), Southend United, Bradford City, Macclesfield Town

**SAFC TOTALS:** 7 appearances / 0 goals

**Mark Prudhoe only played seven games for Sunderland, his high-spot being keeping a clean sheet in an important late season win at Arsenal in 1983. He went on to have a long and varied career, first as a goalkeeper and then as a highly-respected goalkeeping coach. After spending many years as a peripatetic coach and six seasons at Hull City, he came back to Sunderland as Academy goalkeeping coach in January 2011 and was still at the club in 2022, England number one Jordan Pickford attributing much of his development to 'Prud'.**

From his long list of clubs, Prudhoe reached double figures in league appearances with just five of them. 146 games for Darlington included winning the Conference and Division Four in successive seasons between 1989-1991. This led to a £120,000 transfer to Stoke for whom he made 82 league appearances (and was Player of the Year in 1996) while there were 26 for Walsall, 34 for Carlisle and 16 across two spells with Hartlepool. At Liverpool, during a 1994 loan, he did not play for the first team.

Coaching took Prudhoe to a host of clubs including Hartlepool, Stockport, Macclesfield, Huddersfield, Carlisle, Darlington and Grimsby before his long-term spells with Hull and Sunderland.

## PURDON, Edward John (Ted)

**POSITION:** Centre-forward / inside-forward

**BIRTHPLACE:** Johannesburg, South Africa

**DATE OF BIRTH:** 12/03/1931 - 29/04/2007

**HEIGHT:** 6' 0" **WEIGHT:** 13st 0lbs

**SIGNED FROM:** Birmingham City, 07/01/1954

**DEBUT:** v Cardiff City, H, 16/01/1954

**LAST MATCH:** v Aston Villa, H, 25/12/1956

**MOVED TO:** Workington, 14/03/1957

**TEAMS:** Maritz Brothers Club, Birmingham City, Sunderland, Workington, Barrow, Bath City, Bristol Rovers, Buffalo White Eagles, Toronto City, Toronto Roma, Toronto City, New York Ukrainians

**SAFC TOTALS:** 96 appearances / 42 goals

**Ten seconds into a game against Arsenal at Highbury on 23 January 1954, Ted Purdon scored the quickest goal in Sunderland's history. Without an away win in 15 months Sunderland went on to win 4-1 at the home of the reigning league champions with Purdon going on to complete a hat-trick. It was only Purdon's second game.**

A week earlier he had scored twice on his debut and scored again the following week in a home win over Portsmouth. In between his second and third games, he also scored in a friendly against a Leeds United team for whom their manager Raich Carter played again at Roker Park. While maintaining his superb scoring start would have placed Purdon in the Dave Halliday class of goals return, the South African succeeded in continuing to score at a healthy rate although his best seasonal return was a modest 18 in his first full season. In 1954, he collided with West Brom goalkeeper Norman Heath who never played again, an incident that some felt Purdon never really got over. In May 1957, he was one of the players punished when Sunderland were found guilty of making illegal payments in the age of the maximum wage. Purdon was fined six months benefit qualifications although this was refunded five years later when the decision was ruled illegal.

Signed from second division Birmingham City where he had scored 30 goals in 70 games, 15 of these came in 23 games in the season he moved to Sunderland, meaning he remained Blues top scorer at the end of the season. The South African had signed for Birmingham after touring England with the Maritz Brothers Club when he was 20, Blues snapping him up ahead of Arsenal and Manchester City who were also keen.

After leaving Sunderland, Ted went on to win the Southern League title in 1960 with Bath City before moving to Canada. After completing his playing days in the USA where he won the USA Open Cup in 1965 with New York Ukrainians, he returned to Canada. Ted became a proud president of the Black Cats of North America supporters group based in Toronto. Sadly, he suffered a stroke shortly after watching on television Sunderland's crucial last home game of the season against Burnley in 2007 and passed away a couple of days later.

Purdon was also a useful cricketer and was once named as twelfth man for a county championship match by Warwickshire against Lancashire in June 1952. During his time on Wearside, he regularly played as a medium-paced bowler and hard-hitting batsman for Philadelphia.

## QUINN, Alan

**POSITION:** Midfielder

**BIRTHPLACE:** Dublin, Republic of Ireland

**DATE OF BIRTH:** 13/06/1979

**HEIGHT:** 5' 9" **WEIGHT:** 11st 3lbs

**SIGNED FROM:** Sheffield Wednesday, 03/10/2003, on loan

**DEBUT:** v Walsall, H, 18/10/2003

**LAST MATCH:** v Coventry City, A, 08/12/2003

**MOVED TO:** Sheffield Wednesday, 01/01/2004, end of loan

**TEAMS:** Sheffield Wednesday, Sunderland (L), Sheffield United, Ipswich Town, Handsworth

**INTERNATIONAL:** Republic of Ireland

**SAFC TOTALS:** 5+1 appearances / 0 goals

**Dynamic midfielder Alan Quinn was on loan at Sunderland in the season after which he had won an Owls online poll as Sheffield Wednesday's Player of the Year, one of two seasons in which he won such an award at Hillsborough.**

To June 2022, he holds a place in football history by being the only player to score for both sides in the Sheffield derby. He also broke his leg in a Steel City derby playing for Wednesday in April 2001. In January 2003 he scored for the Owls in a defeat at Bramall Lane. Later in the season he also scored for an already relegated Wednesday in a 7-2 win at Burnley on the first occasion in history that the club had scored seven in a league away game. Freed by Wednesday in 2004 after 169+11 games and 17 goals, he returned to Hillsborough in December 2005 to score the only goal of the game for United during a season in which the Blades were promoted to the Premier League.

After eleven goals in 85+24 games for Sheffield United, he was released in January 2008, moving to Ipswich after an initial emergency loan. He scored against Sheffield Wednesday on the second of his 56+20 appearances and got another of his four goals in an East Anglican derby against Norwich in April 2009. In 2014, he played half a dozen games for Sheffield based non-league club Handsworth.

At international level, Alan scored in the final as the Republic of Ireland won the 1998 European Under 18 championships in 1998 and went on to win eight senior caps, the first in 2003. Alan's brothers Stephen and Keith also played for Sheffield United with Stephen also representing Hull and Reading in addition to loans at MK Dons and Rotherham. The Quinns were from a family of nine brothers with another of those, Gerry, playing in the League of Ireland for St Patrick's Athletic. Before coming to Sheffield, Alan had played youth football in Ireland for Old Church United, Manortown United and Cherry Orchard before impressing Wednesday after playing against them in a youth game.

## QUINN, Albert

**POSITION:** Inside-left

**BIRTHPLACE:** Lanchester, Co Durham

**DATE OF BIRTH:** 18/04/1920 - 26/06/2008

**HEIGHT:** 5' 9" **WEIGHT:** 11st 2lbs

**SIGNED FROM:** Esh Winning, 01/06/1946

**DEBUT:** v Grimsby Town, H, 30/08/1947

**LAST MATCH:** v Bolton Wanderers, H, 24/01/1948

**MOVED TO:** Darlington, 28/05/1948

**TEAMS:** Esh Winning, Sunderland, Darlington, West Stanley, Consett

**SAFC TOTALS:** 6 appearances / 2 goals

**A baker before becoming a professional player, Albert came to Sunderland from non-league local football. His most outstanding day came in November 1947 when he scored both of his first-team goals in a 5-1 demolition of Liverpool at Roker Park when he combined superbly with 1937 cup final goal-scorer Eddie Burbanks on the left flank.**

Six months earlier Albert had been in even more prolific form for Sunderland 'A' team, netting a hat trick followed a couple of weeks later by getting five goals against Stockton Reserves. Quinn had only a handful of other top-flight appearances but appeared to find his level in the third tier with the Quakers for whom he had a splendid record of scoring 43 times in 86 Division Three North outings. After leaving Darlington Albert saw out his playing days back in local football working in insurance and then as a colliery storeman.

## QUINN, Niall John

**POSITION:** Centre-forward

**BIRTHPLACE:** Dublin, Republic of Ireland

**DATE OF BIRTH:** 06/10/1966

**HEIGHT:** 6' 4" **WEIGHT:** 13st 10lbs

**SIGNED FROM:** Manchester City, 15/08/1996

**DEBUT:** v Leicester City, H, 17/08/1996

**LAST MATCH:** v West Ham United, H, 19/10/2002

**MOVED TO:** Retired, 10/11/2002

**TEAMS:** Manortown United, Arsenal, Manchester City, Sunderland, BEC Tero Sasana

**INTERNATIONAL:** Republic of Ireland

**SAFC TOTALS:** 183+37 appearances / 69 goals

**Niall's fellow Irishman Charlie Hurley was voted Sunderland's player of the club's first century in 1979. As we move towards Sunderland's 150th anniversary surely Niall Quinn is the man of the second century so far. Rather like Hugh Wilson was a man of firsts in the 1890s, Quinn registered more than his fair share of firsts.**

Sunderland's record buy when becoming the first man the club paid over £1m for, the £1.3m signing scored twice in Sunderland's first-ever Premier League victory (at Nottingham Forest). He went on to score the first-ever goal and the first-ever hat-trick at the Stadium of Light and later became the first man to serve the club as player, manager and chairman.

Quinn had scored twice against Sunderland for Manchester City on the day Sunderland were relegated in 1991. Brought to Sunderland by his ex-City manager Peter Reid, Quinn missed most of his first season through injury but returned when nowhere near fit in an unsuccessful attempt to help stave off the drop. In his second season Quinn scored against his old club Manchester City in the opening competitive game at the Stadium of Light and began what became a marvellous partnership with Kevin Phillips.

At the end of that season Quinn became the first man to score twice for Sunderland at Wembley. That 1998 Play-Off final with Charlton finished 4-4 after which Niall - not normally a penalty taker - stepped forward to convert his spot kick. After Sunderland lost on penalties Quinn was at the forefront of lifting the squad's spirits, urging them to stick together and win the league the following season. This the team did with a record 105 points, Niall scoring 18 league goals in 36+3 league games. In typical headline-grabbing fashion, having scored what proved to be the only goal of the game away to eventual runners-up Bradford City Niall went in goal when Thomas Sorensen was injured and duly kept his goal intact.

Back in the Premier League, Niall notched 14 league goals while helping SuperKev (Phillips) to becoming Europe's top-scorer. In what was an exciting attacking team, Quinn was the focal point, the player everything revolved around. As a target man, Quinn was as good as anyone. His ability to take a ball, hold it and bring other people into play was top drawer while he could give even the best centre-backs the toughest of times. In back-to-back 2-1 wins at Newcastle after promotion, Quinn headed goals in both famous victories and continued to give everything for the cause despite his veteran status.

Awarded a Benefit Match by chairman Sir Bob Murray, Quinn played part of the game for each team as Sunderland faced his international side the Republic of Ireland shortly before the Irish set off for the 2002 FIFA World Cup. The match raised £1m which Quinn donated in its entirety to children's hospitals in Sunderland and his birthplace Dublin, with money that would normally be paid to players in such circumstances donated to an Indian street children's charity.

In an echo of the retirement of Len Shackleton after one game under the management of Alan Brown in 1957, following the sacking of Peter Reid, Niall retired from playing after one game under the management of Howard Wilkinson in 2003. Having famously being quoted saying, "I learned my trade at Arsenal, became a footballer at Manchester City, but Sunderland got under my skin. I love Sunderland", Niall then came to me as programme editor and donated a brand new car to give away as a prize in the next match programme by way of a thank you to the supporters.

Sunderland struggled badly after Niall's retirement. Having contacted chairman Murray to see what help he could offer, Sir Bob suggested to Niall that he took over the club. Quinn duly pulled together a consortium of mainly Irish businessman called the Drumaville Consortium and bought SAFC. Initially unable to attract a suitably high-profile manager for the start of the season, Quinn began the 2006-07 campaign as both manager and chairman. After losing the first four games and going out of the League Cup to bottom of the Football League Bury, Quinn's consortium appointed Roy Keane as manager with Niall signing off with a victory over WBA.

As Keane was backed with a host of new signings and another group of newcomers in the January transfer window, Niall saw Keane lead the club to promotion at the first time of asking. With the eventual collapse of the Irish economy, Quinn's consortium sold up to Ellis Short with Niall stepping down as chairman and becoming director of International Development. Knowing when to step off the stage, he left the club in March 2012 at a point when Sunderland were in the top half of the Premier League and in the FA Cup quarter-final.

Granted the Honorary Freedom of Sunderland on 11 November 2013, Niall Quinn deservedly holds legendary status on Wearside. The only honour he would accept from the club was the renaming of the stadium sports bar as Quinn's - an appropriate honour from a person who always enjoyed a good time and made sure everyone else had one too.

Famously, one day when I was with him coming back from a match at Cardiff, he organised taxis home for a planeload of fans unfairly bumped off a flight from Bristol. Less famously, on a pre-season tour of Ireland he sent taxis to pick up myself and a handful of colleagues to bring us to a pub in Blarney to join him and Charlie Hurley for a very late night sing-song. Quinn and Hurley together, you couldn't go wrong!

Internationally, Niall won 31 of his 92 caps while with Sunderland, scoring seven of his 21 goals for Ireland while with the Wearsiders. At the time of his retirement Niall was Ireland's all-time top-scorer and had played at the 1990 and 2002 FIFA World Cups. Early in his career, he scored 20 goals in 93 games for Arsenal. In March 2006, to promote the club's link with Arsenal, Quinn played one league game in the Thai Premier League with Bangkok based BEC Tero Sasana.

Niall went on to score 76 times in 240 appearances for Manchester City where he was Player of the Year in 1991, a year after being Ireland's Young Player of the Year. In the 105-point season of 1998-99, Niall was Sunderland's Player of the Year, a member of the PFA First Division team of the Year and North East Football Writers' Player of the Year. He also has an honorary MBE while a recording of the fans' chant, 'Niall Quinn's Disco Pants' reached no 56 in the charts in 1999.

As a youngster Niall also played Gaelic football for Perrystown and captained a Dublin Colleges GAA tour of Australia. As a 16-year-old he played in the All-Ireland Minor Hurling Championship final and after retiring from playing association football played Gaelic football for Eadestown.

His 2002 eponymously titled autobiography was named Best Autobiography at the British Sports Book awards. Niall went on to become a TV soccer pundit, became chairman of a satellite broadband company in Ireland and from January to September 2020 served as interim deputy CEO of the FA of Ireland. Niall's father played hurling for Tipperary while his son Michael was in goal for Dungannon Swifts when Trai Hume scored on his last appearance before moving to Sunderland in 2022.

Niall also contributed a foreword for volume one of Sunderland: The Absolute Record and if in the second half of this century, the club have someone with a stronger claim to be the person of the second century, they will be some character and some player!

# R

## RAE, Alexander Scott

**POSITION:** Midfielder

**BIRTHPLACE:** Glasgow, Lanarkshire

**DATE OF BIRTH:** 30/09/1969

**HEIGHT:** 5' 9" **WEIGHT:** 11st 11lbs

**SIGNED FROM:** Millwall, 11/06/1996

**DEBUT:** v Newcastle United, H, 04/09/1996

**LAST MATCH:** v Blackburn Rovers, H, 08/09/2001

**MOVED TO:** Wolverhampton Wanderers, 19/09/2001

**TEAMS:** Bishopbriggs, Falkirk, Millwall, Sunderland, Wolverhampton Wanderers, Rangers, Dundee, MK Dons

**INTERNATIONAL:** Scotland B

**SAFC TOTALS:** 109+27 appearances / 15 goals

**A popular midfielder who combined incisive passing and fierce shooting with a wish to get stuck in! Alex was a fiery character who in later life did brilliantly to overcome problems with alcohol. He became as incisive with his punditry of Scottish football as he had been as a player.**

Rae's distinctive sharp whistle in the thick of midfield instantly let teammates know where he was and that he wanted the ball. He was a good man to give the ball to because he was invariably positive, but the problem was that through a mixture of injury and suspension, sequences of 18 and 13 successive league appearances were Alex's longest runs in the side and in five full seasons at Sunderland his league starting figures were just 13, 24,12, 22 and 18.

Rae was the first player Sunderland agreed a £1m fee for, previous million pound man David Kelly having been signed for £900,000 plus a further £100,000 depending upon promotion.

The Glaswegian came to prominence with Falkirk after a three-month trial with Rangers. Two excellent years with Falkirk led to a £125,000 move to Millwall for whom he debuted in August 1990 and moved into the Lions list of top ten all-time goalscorers with 71 before switching to Sunderland after 241+15 appearances for the Londoners, where in contrast to his time on Wearside, he started a minimum of 36 league games in five of his six seasons.

Sunderland made a profit on the player when he went to Wolves for £1.2m with the Wearsiders receiving an extra £50,000 when he helped the Molineux men to promotion in 2003. Alex top-scored for Wolves with eight goals in 2003-04, but despite the goalscoring midfielder the club went straight back down.

At this point Rae returned to his boyhood club at Ibrox where he won the league title in his first season, when he also came off the bench in the League Cup final against Motherwell in which future Sunderland defender Sotirios Kyrgiakos scored twice in a 5-1 win. By now 35, Rae was released after twelve games of the following season.

In May 2006 Alex became player-manager of Dundee taking them to the quarter-finals of the Scottish Cup in 2008 where they lost to Gordon Chisholm's Queen of the South. Sacked in October 2008, Rae took up a role as first-team coach at MK Dons, playing three games for the club under the management of his old Wolves teammate Paul Ince who he later worked alongside at Notts County, Blackpool and as of February 2022, Reading. Rae also teamed up with former Scotland manager Alex McLeish as assistant manager of KRC Genk in Belgium in 2014 and from December 2015 until the following September managed St Mirren.

Like Bobby Kerr and Ian Porterfield, Alex Rae was a Scottish midfielder who was unlucky not to be capped by his country. In Rae's case he won nine Under 21 caps, scoring three times. In November 2005, he committed to work with the '2nd chance' project in Glasgow helping people with drug and alcohol issues.

## RAINE, James Edmundson (Jimmy)

**POSITION:** Outside-right

**BIRTHPLACE:** Elswick, Newcastle

**DATE OF BIRTH:** 03/03/1886 - 04/09/1928

**HEIGHT:** 6' 0" **WEIGHT:** 12st 8lbs

**SIGNED FROM:** Newcastle United, 14/12/1906

**DEBUT:** v Manchester City, H, 22/12/1906

**LAST MATCH:** v Middlesbrough, A, 15/02/1908

**MOVED TO:** Bohemians, 08/04/1908

**TEAMS:** Scotswood, Sheffield United, Newcastle United, Sunderland, Reading (L), Bohemians, Glossop North End, South Shields

**INTERNATIONAL:** England amateur

**SAFC TOTALS:** 28 appearances / 7 goals

**James Raine scored six goals in 15 games in his first season at Sunderland, but just one in 13 in his second. He was a top amateur international who also represented the Football League against the Irish League in 1908. A month before joining Sunderland he scored in a 15-0 win for England against France in Paris.**

Shortly after coming to Sunderland he was part of the England Amateurs who lost 4-2 to the Professionals at Sheffield while he went on to play in 2-1 and 6-1 wins over Ireland in Dublin and London as well as scoring in a 12-2 win over the Netherlands at Darlington. After missing out on the 1908 Olympics, in which GB took gold, Raine returned to the England amateur XI in April 1909, playing in a 4-0 win over the Netherlands in Amsterdam, scoring in an 11-2 win over Belgium at Tottenham, twice in a 9-0 win over Switzerland in Berne and a hat-trick in Paris against France in 1909.

He was a teammate of Ronald Brebner in those last two games before being called up for an FA tour of South Africa in May 1910 in which he scored nine goals. In November 1910 he won a ninth and final England amateur cap in a 3-2 defeat to Ireland in Belfast.

He played four times for Newcastle, scoring once, played once for Sheffield United and scored three times in 51 games for Glossop, then of the second division. Jimmy moved from Sunderland to play for local Newcastle team Bohemians after a making solitary appearance for Reading in March 1908. Away from football he played cricket and rugby for Northumberland and served in World War One as a major in the 9th Battalion of the Durham Light Infantry.

Jimmy had been playing rugby as Percy Park captain for two years when in April 1913 he decided to come out of football retirement to play for South Shields. He later became managing director of an iron and steel company, having studied metallurgy at Sheffield University, and died in Davos, Switzerland, where he had gone to seek a cure for illness.

## RAISBECK, William

**POSITION:** Half-back

**BIRTHPLACE:** Wallacestone, Stirlingshire

**DATE OF BIRTH:** 22/12/1875 - 02/11/1946

**HEIGHT:** 5' 10½" **WEIGHT:** 12st 2lbs

**SIGNED FROM:** Clyde, 21/12/1896, re-signed, 06/05/1898

**DEBUT:** v Preston North End, A, 03/09/1898

**LAST MATCH:** v Blackburn Rovers, H, 16/03/1901

**MOVED TO:** Released, 04/05/1897 and 05/05/1901

**TEAMS:** Larkhall Thistle, Hibernian, Clyde, Sunderland, Royal Albert, Clyde, Sunderland, Derby County, New Brompton, Reading, Lethbridge Miners

**SAFC TOTALS:** 74 appearances / 7 goals

**Raisbeck made his debut for Sunderland on the opening day of the season that the club moved to Roker Park in 1898. Unfortunately, from the point of view of claiming a place in the record books, Raisbeck's bow came in an away game at Preston and he was not involved when the curtain came up on the new ground a week later against Liverpool. He did end up playing in 27 of the 36 league and cup games that season, scoring one of his two goals at home to Newcastle on Boxing Day.**

The following season Raisbeck was even more of a regular, missing a mere four of the 37 games in both competitions. Usually a wing-half, he scored three goals that season, being the scorer in 1-0 wins over Liverpool and Preston as well as opening the scoring in a 5-0 victory against Notts County, as he helped Sunderland to third place in the turn of century table. In his third and final season he again grabbed three goals, but this time in just 14 appearances. Sunderland were runners-up that season but that summer, Bill moved on to Derby County and therefore was not involved as the Lads took the title for the fourth time in 1901-02.

In 1903, Derby reached their third English (FA) Cup final in six years, but again Raisbeck missed out as by this time he was with Gillingham - or New Brompton as they were then known. He had moved to the Southern League club after being restricted to just three league games for Derby, but managed 56 appearances for the Kent club before moving on to Reading where he concluded his career with 14 appearances in 1904-05.

Raisbeck actually signed for Sunderland twice. He arrived for the first time on the day before his 21st birthday just before Christmas in 1896, but was released at the end of the season without playing due a leg injury but having a short spell with a team called Royal Albert. After a season impressing back at Clyde (who he had joined Sunderland from in the first place) Raisbeck returned to Wearside in May 1898. As a young player, he had also played for Hibernian and Larkhall Thistle.

Bill had two footballing brothers, Alex and Andrew who both played for Liverpool amongst other clubs, Alex also being an international with Scotland. Following his retirement from full-time football, Bill travelled to work for another brother, Luke, who was managing a coal mine in Canada. During this time he played for a team called Letheridge Miners. After leaving mining he remained in Canada, working as a policeman and coaching children's football. He died in Taber, Alberta, Canada.

## RAMSAY, Stanley Hunter

**POSITION:** Inside-forward

**BIRTHPLACE:** Ryton, Co Durham

**DATE OF BIRTH:** 10/08/1904 - 19/07/1989

**HEIGHT:** 5' 10" **WEIGHT:** 11st 6lbs

**SIGNED FROM:** Ryton, 28/03/1924

**DEBUT:** v Sheffield United, H, 12/09/1925

**LAST MATCH:** v Burnley, A, 04/02/1928

**MOVED TO:** Blackpool, 01/03/1928

**TEAMS:** Stargate Rovers, Ryton, Sunderland, Blackpool, Norwich City, Shrewsbury Town, Dereham Town

**SAFC TOTALS:** 25 appearances / 14 goals

**Stan started in senior football at Sunderland after making a name for himself by banging in the goals in local football with Ryton and Stargate Rovers. He came to Sunderland shortly before his 20th birthday and waited until a month after turning 21 before being given a debut against Sheffield United.**

Stan's opportunity at inside-left came at absolutely the right time. Goal machine centre-forward Dave Halliday had just arrived. Halliday added to his lightning goalscoring start by finding time to create Ramsay's debut goal against the cup-holders.

Stan's performance assisted him in being selected for the next three games and then after missing a couple of matches, he returned with another goal as Everton were slaughtered 7-3. Ramsay retained his place for two more fixtures including a goalless draw at Newcastle as Sunderland stayed top of the league. He got one more game in his first season - a 4-1 home win over West Ham - although the title challenge faded as the team finished third.

Sunderland finished third again in Stan's second season but he did all he could to help with eight goals from nine appearances. Not called upon until the spring, Ramsay returned with a brace in a 4-1 home win over Birmingham that took Sunderland to joint top of the league with Newcastle. The following month, Ramsay had his greatest day when both he and Halliday bagged hat-tricks as Leeds lost 6-2 at Roker Park.

Sunderland did not do so well in Stan's third season, but he always seemed to do well himself, contributing four goals in eight appearances, including a Christmas Eve winner against Middlesbrough. He also retained his knack of being part of big scorelines, helping the Lads to a handy 5-2 win away to Liverpool in his penultimate appearance.

Moving to Blackpool for what was described as a 'substantial fee' in March 1928, Ramsay could be proud of his Roker record of 14 goals in 25 games as an inside-forward. It was certainly in stark contrast to his time with Blackpool where he only scored twice in 107 games - not least because they converted him into a centre-half and then a left-back. Debuting for the second division Seasiders on the opening day of 1928-29 at Preston at his normal inside-left position, Stan played only five games in that role before being switched to defence late in the season. Despite conceding 13 goals in his first three away games in that role Blackpool persevered with him and in his first full season he played 37 times as Blackpool won their league.

A month into the season, Ramsay returned to Roker in his defensive role as his side won 4-2, but not all went to plan. Later in the campaign, he played in a 10-1 defeat at Huddersfield but remained a regular as Blackpool avoided the drop by a point. They did the same the following season but having only played half as many times, Stan was on the move again, this time joining Norwich.

It was at Carrow Road that Ramsay had perhaps his greatest days, captaining the Canaries to their first major honour, the Division Three South title in 1934 and going on to be inducted into the club's Hall of Fame. After 82 appearances for Norwich and by now 31-years-old, Ramsay took on the role of player-manager at Shrewsbury Town. Having started as a forward at Sunderland, but played as a defender elsewhere, it was evident where his natural inclinations lay as Stan encouraged attacking football. His team scored an astonishing 124 goals (and let in 70) in 38 Birmingham & District League fixtures as they finished third as well as reaching the semi-finals of the Welsh Cup.

## RAMSDEN, Bernard (Barney)

**POSITION:** Full-back

**BIRTHPLACE:** Sheffield, Yorkshire

**DATE OF BIRTH:** 08/11/1917 - 27/03/1976

**HEIGHT:** 5' 10" **WEIGHT:** 12st 0lbs

**SIGNED FROM:** Liverpool, 15/03/1948

**DEBUT:** v Stoke City, A, 20/03/1948

**LAST MATCH:** v Yeovil Town, A, 29/01/1949

**MOVED TO:** Hartlepools United, 21/02/1950

**TEAMS:** Hampton Sports, Sheffield Victoria, Liverpool, Brighton (WW2 Guest), Leeds United (WW2 Guest), York City (WW2 Guest), Sunderland, Hartlepools United

**SAFC TOTALS:** 13 appearances / 0 goals

**Ramsden had as many years with Liverpool as he made appearances for Sunderland, but lost much of his Anfield career to World War Two after debuting for the Merseysiders as a 19-year-old at Chelsea on the first day of the 1937-38 campaign. He had made 28 first-team appearances when the war caused the Football League to stop, three of those being expunged when the 1939-40 season was cancelled.**

During the war he served in the King's Liverpool Regiment and played eight games each for Brighton and Leeds plus one for York. Twenty-seven when the war ended, Barney added 33 more games for Liverpool who released him in March 1948 after he had won a league title medal in 1946-47 when he had played in the opening 18 games of the season.

At this point he joined Sunderland, playing twice that season and eleven games in 1948-49 before ending his career with Hartlepools, where 13 games began against Southport in January 1950. He combined his time with Hartlepools with being a Durham FA coach, and being something of a singer was also reported by the Daily Express in March 1948 of having the chance to go into music halls.

His time in the north-east with Sunderland and Hartlepools only delayed a move to America where he had intended to move to New York in 1947 to marry a girl called Audrey and set up a florists business. He had saved the life of one of her relatives and been told to call if ever he passed by. Fate decreed that Liverpool toured the USA in 1946 and he did just that with the couple falling in love. He emigrated to California in May 1952 and remained in America working as an office clerk and passed away in Los Angeles at the age of 59.

## RAMSDEN, Simon Paul

**POSITION:** Right-back

**BIRTHPLACE:** Bishop Auckland, Co Durham

**DATE OF BIRTH:** 17/12/1981

**HEIGHT:** 6' 0" **WEIGHT:** 12st 4lbs

**SIGNED FROM:** School, 01/07/1998

**DEBUT:** v Ipswich Town, A, 21/01/2004

**LAST MATCH:** v Ipswich Town, A, 21/01/2004

**MOVED TO:** Grimsby Town, 18/06/2004

**TEAMS:** Sunderland, Notts County (L), Grimsby Town, Rochdale, Bradford City, Motherwell, Gateshead, Whitby Town

**SAFC TOTALS:** 0+1 appearances / 0 goals

**Playing two minutes of injury time in his only appearance enabled Ramsden to enter the record books as the Sunderland player with the shortest first-team career, but Simon proved to be one of those home-produced players who went on to have a good career at a lower level elsewhere. Although he had just two minutes playing for the Lads in an FA Cup tie, 'Rammer' had 'Sunderland 'Til I Die' tattooed on his back - for some reason in Italian.**

Before coming to SAFC Simon played for Newton Aycliffe Youth Centre. Sunderland loaned him to Notts County where he made 23+11 appearances. After being released, he played 34+7 games for Grimsby, 119+5 for Rochdale (6 goals) and 54+3 for Bradford City (1 goal). In July 2012 he began three years with Motherwell where former Sunderland midfielder Gary Owers was Head of Recruitment. After 75+8 games and one goal in Scotland, Simon returned to England to play 24 times (1 goal) for Gateshead before finishing his career with Whitby and became a car salesman and fitness instructor in Sunderland.

## RAYBOULD, Samuel

**POSITION:** Centre / inside-forward

**BIRTHPLACE:** Staveley, Derbyshire

**DATE OF BIRTH:** 11/06/1875 - 17/12/1953

**HEIGHT:** 5' 10" **WEIGHT:** 13st 0lbs

**SIGNED FROM:** Liverpool, 10/05/1907

**DEBUT:** v Manchester City, H, 02/09/1907

**LAST MATCH:** v Bristol City, A, 20/04/1908

**MOVED TO:** Arsenal, 06/05/1908

**TEAMS:** Seymour Exchange, Poolsbrook United, Staveley Colliery, North Staveley, Ilkeston Town, Derby County, Ilkeston Town, Poolsbrook United, Ilkeston Town, Bolsover Colliery, New Brighton Tower, Liverpool, Sunderland, Woolwich Arsenal, Chesterfield Town, Sutton Town, Barlborough United

**INTERNATIONAL:** Football League XI

**SAFC TOTALS:** 28 appearances / 13 goals

**In his only season at Sunderland Raybould impressed, at one point scoring eight goals in a five-match spell. Converted from a right-winger to a centre-forward at New Brighton, he responded with ten goals in 13 games in half a season. At this point he was 24 but he went on to great things with Liverpool where he played for Tom Watson, became the first man to score 100 league goals for that club and was top scorer with 17 when Liverpool won their first top-flight title in 1901, pipping Sunderland to the trophy. Two years later he scored 32 in 34 games becoming the first Liverpool player to register 30 in a season.**

He was then suspended for seven months for accepting financial inducements to sign for Southern League Portsmouth along with two other Liverpool players. During his ban, he turned to running, winning four professional quarter-mile handicaps before returning to football eventually totalling 130 games in 226 games for Liverpool who he helped to promotion in 1905.

After his season on Wearside Raybould went to London where he had a season with Woolwich Arsenal, a hat-trick against Bury being part of his haul of seven goals in 27 league and FA Cup games, after which his career wound down at lower levels with him becoming a publican while with Chesterfield after which he scouted for Liverpool.

## READ, William Henry (Harry)

**POSITION:** Outside-right

**BIRTHPLACE:** Blackpool

**DATE OF BIRTH:** 01/10/1885 -18/04/1951

**HEIGHT:** 5' 8" **WEIGHT:** 11st 4lbs

**SIGNED FROM:** Colne, 23/04/1910

**DEBUT:** v Wednesday, A, 30/04/1910

**LAST MATCH:** v Manchester City, H, 25/02/1911

**MOVED TO:** Chelsea, 19/ 05/1911

**TEAMS:** Preston North End, Blackpool, Colne, Sunderland, Chelsea, Dundee, Swansea Town

**SAFC TOTALS:** 4 appearances / 2 goals

**As at Sunderland where despite scoring twice on his last appearance, he only got four games, Read barely played at several of his clubs. He also played four times for each of Chelsea and Dundee, but made 33 appearances for Blackpool where he scored three times.**

At Preston he never got a first-team game. During World War One, he was discharged from the navy in 1917 after suffering an injury playing football in Italy. After retiring from football, Read became a bookmaker, shellfish merchant and later a painter and decorator in Blackpool.

## REDDY, Michael Jason

**POSITION:** Centre-forward

**BIRTHPLACE:** Graignamanagh, Republic of Ireland

**DATE OF BIRTH:** 24/03/1980

**HEIGHT:** 6' 1" **WEIGHT:** 11st 7lbs

**SIGNED FROM:** Kilkenny City, 01/08/1999

**DEBUT:** v Wimbledon, A, 12/10/1999

**LAST MATCH:** v Bristol Rovers, A, 31/10/2000

**MOVED TO:** Grimsby Town, 20/07/2004

**TEAMS:** Kilkenny City, Sunderland, Swindon Town (L), Hull City (L), Barnsley (L), York City (L) Sheffield Wednesday (L), Grimsby Town

**INTERNATIONAL:** Republic of Ireland Under 21

**SAFC TOTALS:** 2+12 appearances / 2 goals

**A teenager when he came to Sunderland, many felt that Michael's first name should have been Not. He did however score a hat-trick on his debut for the reserves against Durham City and scored as many goals as he was given first-team starts. He did make 50 league starts during his numerous loans from Sunderland in a total of 56+12 games as a loan player in which he netted 16 goals.**

Freed in the summer of 2004 after a ruptured knee ligament injury took away much of his pace, he went on to be part of the PFA League Two team of the year after helping Grimsby to promotion. He scored a total of 23 goals in 78+28 games for the Mariners but had to retire through a persistent hip injury despite his former Grimsby manager Russell Slade giving him an extended trial at Yeovil Town. He tried to resurrect his career in Greenland before going on to work in the sports marketing industry after studying sports science at university in Manchester.

At international level Michael scored against Ghana, Portugal and Cyprus while winning eight Under 21 caps. While with Sunderland he was an unused sub for the senior side against Finland in November 2000 but remained uncapped.

## REED, Graham

**POSITION:** Half-back

**BIRTHPLACE:** King's Lynn, Norfolk

**DATE OF BIRTH:** 06/02/1938

**HEIGHT:** 5' 10" **WEIGHT:** 11st 3lbs

**SIGNED FROM:** King's Lynn, 19/08/1954

**DEBUT:** v West Bromwich Albion, A, 23/11/1957

**LAST MATCH:** v Aston Villa, A, 11/01/1958

**MOVED TO:** Wisbech Town, 12/05/1959

**TEAMS:** King's Lynn, Sunderland, Wisbech Town

**SAFC TOTALS:** 7 appearances / 0 goals

**Well into his eighties Graham remained an ever-helpful font of knowledge on the first team and reserve players of his era.**

Graham came to the club as a 16-year-old, signed professional forms on his 17th birthday and fought his way into the first team, all seven of his appearances coming in the first-ever relegation season of 1957-58. He remained as an engineering apprentice whilst on Sunderland's books and carried on this profession after retiring from football.

## REID, Andrew Matthew (Andy)

**POSITION:** Midfielder

**BIRTHPLACE:** Dublin, Republic of Ireland

**DATE OF BIRTH:** 29/07/1982

**HEIGHT:** 5' 7" **WEIGHT:** 12st 8lbs

**SIGNED FROM:** Charlton Athletic, 31/01/2008

**DEBUT:** v Wigan Athletic, H, 09/02/2008

**LAST MATCH:** v Notts County, H, 08/01/2011

**MOVED TO:** Blackpool, 31/01/2011

**TEAMS:** Lourdes Celtic, Cherry Orchard, Nottingham Forest, Tottenham Hotspur, Charlton Athletic, Sunderland, Sheffield United (L), Blackpool, Nottingham Forest

**INTERNATIONAL:** Republic of Ireland

**SAFC TOTALS:** 56+24 appearances / 6 goals

**Andy Reid was a wonderful footballer to watch. Blessed with a delicate touch and an innate ability to see the game a step or two ahead of most players, his passing was incisive. Never the quickest, he was often criticised for what appeared to be a weight issue which some felt prevented him from reaching even greater heights as a player.**

A product of the famous Irish Cherry Orchard club after starting with Lourdes Celtic, he came through the youth system at Nottingham Forest. He scored on his second league appearance on 29 November 2000 against Sheffield United who he later also netted against for Forest in a 2003 Division One Play-Off semi-final. He would later score twice in nine games for the Blades on loan from Sunderland. Although a midfielder Reid top-scored for Forest with 13 goals in 2003-04 when he

was Player of the Year and was chosen for the PFA Division One Team of the Year. That summer he left Forest for Spurs in a double deal with defender Michael Dawson for a combined fee of £8m.

At Spurs he scored just once from 20+6 games before moving across London to Charlton in August 2006 for £3m only for his club to be relegated from the Premier League at the end of his first season. Midway through his second season with the Addicks Reid was sold to Sunderland for £5m after nine goals in 40 appearances. At Sunderland Andy's highlights included a spectacular injury-time volleyed winner against West Ham and an exquisite brace in a League Cup win at Norwich.

Following a five match spell at Blackpool Reid returned to Nottingham Forest where ten years after his 2003-04 success he again achieved a personal double of being Forest's Player of the Year as well as being named in the PFA divisional Team of the Year. Due to injury, Andy retired in the summer of 2016 having totalled 241+49 games for Forest, scoring 42 times.

For the Republic of Ireland Reid won 29 full caps scoring against Bulgaria, Cyprus, Italy and San Marino. He also scored four times in 15 Under 21 internationals and in the final against England when Ireland won the Under 16 Nordic Cup in 1998.

An accomplished guitarist, Reid also has a love of literature, particularly Irish greats such as Joyce, Wilde and Yeats, even naming one of his children Oscar, after Wilde. Reid is also a socialist, proud of his tattoos of Che Guevara and James Connolly.

After taking charge of the Republic of Ireland Under 18 team in 2019, in 2020, Reid returned to Forest as a coach, combining that role with being an engaging radio pundit. Reid's father Bob played for St Patrick's Athletic and Fatima Rangers while an uncle Victor played for Shelbourne.

## RENNIE, Henry William

**POSITION:** Half-back

**BIRTHPLACE:** St Vigeans, Arbroath, Angus

**DATE OF BIRTH:** 25/03/1865 - 08/07/1909

**SIGNED FROM:** Arbroath, 01/08/1888

**DEBUT:** v Elswick Rangers, H, 27/10/1888

**LAST MATCH:** v Elswick Rangers, H, 27/10/1888

**MOVED TO:** Left club, 12/11/1888

**TEAMS:** Arbroath, Sunderland, Arbroath

**SAFC TOTALS:** 1 appearance / 0 goals

**Hen Rennie played just one competitive game for Sunderland, an English (FA) Cup tie, but he is famous for playing for Arbroath in the record breaking Scottish Cup tie when they beat Bon Accord 36-0 on 12 September 1885.**

An iron moulder during and after his footballing days he re-joined Arbroath the month after leaving Sunderland. His surname was sometimes recorded as Renny. Rennie's twin great nephews Gavin and Ralph Laing respectively played football for Preston, Forfar and in South Africa in the 1960s and cricket for Scotland from 1969 to 1979.

## REVEILLERE, Anthony Guy Marie

**POSITION:** Right-back

**BIRTHPLACE:** Doue-la-Fontaine, France

**DATE OF BIRTH:** 10/11/1979

**HEIGHT:** 5' 11" **WEIGHT:** 12st 2lbs

**SIGNED FROM:** After one week trial, 23/10/2014

**DEBUT:** v Crystal Palace, A, 03/11/2014

**LAST MATCH:** v Leicester City, H, 16/05/2015

**MOVED TO:** Contract not renewed, 30/06/2015

**TEAMS:** Rennes, Valencia (L), Olympique Lyonnais, Napoli, Sunderland

**INTERNATIONAL:** France

**SAFC TOTALS:** 16+1 appearances / 0 goals

**French international Reveillere was almost 35 when he came to Sunderland but he looked a class act worth more than his modest number of appearances. Anthony had won Ligue 1 with Lyon in five successive seasons between 2003-04 and 2007-08.**

The last of those campaigns had seen him do the double by adding the Coupe de France which he won again in 2011-12, a season in which he also reached the Coupe de la Ligue final. There were also six Trophee des Champions successes between 2003 and 2012, while after moving to Italy he won the Coppa Italia with Napoli in 2014, although he was an unused sub in the final when on opponents Fiorentina's bench was Modibo Diakite who was on loan from Sunderland.

In addition to 50 international appearances at Under 17, 18 and 21 level he went on to win 20 full caps, scoring against Albania in 2011. He went to the 2010 FIFA World Cup without getting a game but did play in the quarter-final against Spain at Euro 2012.

After playing junior football with SO Vihiers and Angers Anthony made his way into the first team with Rennes, debuting at Bastia on 3 February 1998. The full-back had 140 games, scoring twice, and also had 18 games (1 goal) on loan to Valencia in 2003. It was after joining Lyon that Reveillere found great success. 286 league appearances (3 goals) were added to by 77 Champions League games in which he scored twice. Released by Sunderland in the summer of 2015, he announced his retirement the following November.

## REVIE, Donald George

**POSITION:** Inside-forward / centre-forward

**BIRTHPLACE:** Middlesbrough, Yorkshire

**DATE OF BIRTH:** 10/07/1927 - 26/05/1989

**HEIGHT:** 5' 11" **WEIGHT:** 12st 9lbs

**SIGNED FROM:** Manchester City, 09/11/1956

**DEBUT:** v Cardiff City, A, 17/11/1956

**LAST MATCH:** v Rotherham United, A, 22/11/1958

**MOVED TO:** Leeds United, 28/11/1958

**TEAMS:** Leicester City, Hull City, Manchester City, Sunderland, Leeds United

**INTERNATIONAL:** England

**SAFC TOTALS:** 66 appearances / 15 goals

**Leeds United's manager against Sunderland in the 1973 FA Cup final, Revie had been the direct opponent to SAFC's '73 manager Bob Stokoe in the 1955 FA Cup final when Bob was playing for Newcastle and Revie for Manchester City. Revie could have been Sunderland's manager having publicly expressed interest in the vacancy when Alan Brown left after both Sunderland and Revie's Leeds had been promoted together in 1964.**

Revie's Leeds were reviled throughout the country for their gamesmanship and dirty play while Stokoe (referring to his time as manager of Bury) was one of numerous people to make unproven allegations that Revie offered bribes to win key games. There was also massive controversy when Revie walked out of his post as England manager to accept a lucrative job as manager of the United Arab Emirates.

In contrast with this seemingly darker side of Don, Revie offered much to the game. His Leeds side was very talented while as a player, a strategy he helped to devise at Manchester City became widely known as 'The Revie Plan' as it centred around Revie being used as a deep-lying centre-forward - something that pre-dated Pep Guardiola's 'False 9' at City by over half a century.

## REVIE, Don (Continued)

As a boy Revie started with Newport Boys Club on Teesside, followed by Middlesbrough Swifts during which time he worked as an apprentice bricklayer. Having signed for Leicester City, he was mentored by Whitburn-born England international Sep Smith. After 33 war-time games for Leicester Revie made his league debut on 31 August 1946 against future employers Manchester City. A stylish inside-forward, Revie established himself but missed the 1949 FA Cup final after sustaining a badly broken nose which caused a significant loss of blood which even threatened his life.

Don had scored twice in the semi-final against Portsmouth. After 29 goals in 110 peace-time games he left Leicester for Hull. Starting with a Division Two debut at home to Coventry on 12 November 1949, his Tigers career spanned 700 days until an 82nd and final appearance at home to Sheffield Wednesday in October 1951. He scored 13 goals including three when he was joined on the scoresheet by Raich Carter and netted another goal when Eddie Burbanks (like Carter, a 1937 FA Cup final scorer for Sunderland) also scored. All but the first eight of Revie's games for Hull came under the management of Carter.

Moving to Manchester City in October 1951 Revie came under the tutelage of another former Sunderland player in Les McDowall. It was while Revie was with City that he broke into the England team. His first representative honour came at Roker Park when he played in a 1-1 'B' international with Scotland. A first full cap followed the next October when he was one of seven England debutants, an occasion he marked with a goal in a 2-0 win over Northern Ireland in Belfast. Sunderland's Billy Bingham was in the Irish line-up. Revie scored again on his home debut - a 7-2 Wembley win over Scotland the following April and ended up with four goals from his six full international appearances. His last cap was won the month before he signed for Sunderland. Revie also twice represented the Football League.

At Manchester City Revie scored 41 goals in 178 games. In 1955 when he was Footballer of the Year, he was part of the City side that beat Sunderland in the FA Cup semi-final before losing to Stokoe's Magpies. A year later he achieved a cup winner's medal after beating Birmingham at Wembley.

Coming to Sunderland during the era of 'The Bank of England' team, Revie only scored twice in 16 games in his first season. 1957-58 would be Don's only full campaign at Roker Park. It was the infamous year that Sunderland were relegated for the first time. Revie's only goal for Sunderland in the second tier came on his final appearance. Having scored in a 4-1 win at Rotherham, he apparently came to blows in the dressing room with manager Alan Brown after being refused permission to travel home alone. Within a week he was transferred to Leeds United.

At Elland Road Revie became as important to Leeds as Bill Shankly was to Liverpool or Sir Matt Busby to Manchester United. He was the man who 'made' Leeds. Later as a manager he would be Manager of the Year in 1969, 1970 and 1972 as well as receiving the OBE in 1970. His side were league champions in 1969 and 74, FA Cup winners in 1972, League Cup winners in 1968 and reached a host of finals and semi-finals domestically and in Europe. As a player, Revie debuted for Leeds against Newcastle, briefly became captain and scored twelve goals in 81 appearances before retiring in May 1963.

He left Leeds to become England manager on 4 July 1974 taking charge of 29 matches, the last against Uruguay in Montevideo in June 1977. Selling his story to the Daily Mail before his letter of resignation had been received by the FA contributed to the bad feeling surrounding his departure. Revie was subsequently banned for a decade although several years later he won a court case to overturn this suspension. Having taken a job as coach of the United Arab Emirates, Revie kept that until July 1980 after which he managed club side Al-Nasr from 1980 to 84 before taking charge of Al-Ahly of Egypt. Revie returned to England following his court victory and briefly took up a consultancy role at Leeds United. A road near Elland Road is named in his honour and a stand at the ground was named after him in 1994. A statue to Revie was erected in Leeds, ironically 39 years to the day since his Leeds lost to Sunderland at Wembley.

In 1988 Revie revealed he was suffering from motor neurone disease. He died in Edinburgh the following year, aged 61. 'Don Revie: The Biography' written by MP Chris Evans was published in 2022. Amongst numerous portrayals of his time at Leeds there is also a biography, 'Don Revie: Portrait of a Footballing Enigma' published in 2003.

## REYNA, Claudio

**POSITION:** Midfielder

**BIRTHPLACE:** Livingston, New Jersey, USA

**DATE OF BIRTH:** 20/07/1973

**HEIGHT:** 5' 9" **WEIGHT:** 11st 9lbs

**SIGNED FROM:** Rangers, 07/12/2001

**DEBUT:** v Southampton, A, 15/12/2001

**LAST MATCH:** v Bolton Wanderers, A, 28/10/2002

**MOVED TO:** Manchester City, 29/08/2003

**TEAMS:** Bayer Leverkusen 04, VfL Wolfsburg, Rangers, Sunderland, Manchester City, New York Red Bulls

**INTERNATIONAL:** USA

**SAFC TOTALS:** 29 appearances / 4 goals

**It was a pity that largely through an anterior cruciate ligament injury Reyna did not play more for Sunderland. He was a class act who not only went to the 2002 FIFA World Cup as a Sunderland player, as USA captain, but was named in the FIFA 'Team of the Tournament'. Claudio won 13 of his 112 caps for the USA while with Sunderland. He also played at the 1998 and 2006 World Cups and was selected for the squad in 1994.**

He also played at the Olympics in 1992 and 1996 as well as captaining the country of his birth. Father Miguel was from Argentina and had played professionally while Claudio's mother is Portuguese. Claudio's wife Danielle Egan was also a USA international. Son Giovanni was born in Sunderland and as of 2022 was a USA international playing for Borussia Dortmund. He was named after Giovanni van Bronckhorst, Claudio's teammate at Rangers. Tragically another of the Reyna's four children, Jack, passed away aged 13 from cancer.

Germany was the professional starting point for Claudio. In the US he played for Saint Benedict's Preparatory School who were unbeaten in his three years. He then spent three years with the University of Virginia winning their championship in each of his seasons as well as winning a host of individual honours.

Selected for the host nation's squad at the 1994 USA FIFA World Cup he did not get a game through injury, but afterwards signed for Bayer 04 Leverkusen. After five games there he was loaned to VfL Wolfsburg where he became the first American to captain a major European club. In April 1999 Reyna signed for Rangers where he played under Dick Advocaat. While at Ibrox he played 89+7 games scoring eleven goals, the most famous one against Italy legend Gianluigi Buffon to knock UEFA Cup holders Parma out of the Champions League.

At Sunderland Reyna was excellent, not least in a key game against Leicester when in a 2-1 win he scored both of Sunderland's goals with a volley and a free-kick as well as twice hitting the woodwork. Having moved to Manchester City Claudio continued to have injury problems but eventually managed 77+10 appearances and four goals before a return to the USA. At New York Red Bulls he reconnected with former US head coach Bruce Arena who had been his coach at university. With injuries continuing to plague him Reyna played 27 times before retiring in July 2008.

After retiring from playing Claudio launched his own foundation aimed at developing sport in America as well as fighting poverty and childhood obesity. He became youth technical director for US Soccer before becoming Director of Football Operations at the newly-formed MLS franchise New York City FC in 2013. The Foreword to his 2004 autobiography 'More than Goals' was provided by Pele.

## REYNOLDS, Thomas (Tommy)

**POSITION:** Outside-left

**BIRTHPLACE:** Felling, Co.Durham

**DATE OF BIRTH:** 02/10/1922 - 13/03/1998

**HEIGHT:** 5' 5" **WEIGHT:** 9st 10lbs

**SIGNED FROM:** Felling, 01/08/1946

**DEBUT:** v Charlton Athletic, A, 11/09/1946

**LAST MATCH:** v Burnley, A, 11/04/1953

**MOVED TO:** King's Lynn, 03/10/1953

**TEAMS:** Felling, Sunderland, King's Lynn, Darlington

**SAFC TOTALS:** 172 appearances / 18 goals

**Ever-present in 1949-50 as Sunderland narrowly missed out on the league title, Reynolds played in the first seven post-war league seasons. He had signed for Sunderland straight after serving as a wireless operator in the RAF where he had been stationed in Ceylon (now Sri Lanka). During the war he had played football along with Tommy McLain and Ken Oliver.**

A maker rather than a taker of goals, all 18 of his goals came in his first 110 league games with none at all in his final three seasons. Before coming into football Reynolds had worked in a paint factory as a lab assistant. After leaving Sunderland he was player/manager at King's Lynn before returning to the north east to make 42 Division Three North appearances for Darlington after which he retired to run pubs in Hendon and Durham. He also bred and ran greyhounds at the dog track in Sunderland.

## RHODES, Ephraim

**POSITION:** Full-back
**BIRTHPLACE:** Middlesbrough, Yorkshire
**DATE OF BIRTH:** 16/08/1882 - 30/9/1960
**HEIGHT:** 5' 10" **WEIGHT:** 12st 5lbs
**SIGNED FROM:** Grangetown Athletic, 24/04/1902
**DEBUT:** v Bury, A, 18/10/1902
**LAST MATCH:** v Sheffield United, H, 22/02/1908
**MOVED TO:** Brentford, 08/07/1908
**TEAMS:** South Bank, Grangetown Athletic, Sunderland, Brentford
**SAFC TOTALS:** 120 appearances / 5 goals

**Signed the day after impressing in a trial game, this defender had worked in a Teesside Ironworks before coming to Sunderland. Known as 'Dusty', he made his debut against Bury and later had a Benefit match against the same opposition in January 1908. Unusually for the time, tickets for his Benefit game also bore his photograph.**

Dusty appeared in six seasons, all but 28 of his games coming in the third, fourth and fifth of those campaigns. He went on to become player/manager of Brentford until the cessation of the Football League for World War One. Altogether he totalled 206 Southern League games for the Bees, scoring twice and added another 103 appearances and three goals in war-time soccer.

After serving in the Royal Fusiliers army pay corps he continued to serve Brentford as trainer from July 1922 to 1925 and later became a park keeper in Hounslow after retiring from the game. His brother Ernest signed for Sunderland in 1907, but never got a first-team game although he did play for Grangetown, Gravesend United, Crystal Palace and Sheppey United in a two decade career commencing in 1905.

## RICHARDSON, James

**POSITION:** Centre-forward
**BIRTHPLACE:** Glasgow, Lanarkshire
**DATE OF BIRTH:** 28/03/1885 - 31/08/1951
**HEIGHT:** 5' 8½" **WEIGHT:** 11st 10lbs
**SIGNED FROM:** Huddersfield Town, 08/08/1912
**DEBUT:** v Newcastle United, A, 07/09/1912
**LAST MATCH:** Bradford City, H, 28/02/1914
**MOVED TO:** Ayr United, 10/03/1914
**TEAMS:** Glenitber, Blantyre Victoria, Kirkintilloch Rob Roy, Third Lanark, Huddersfield Town, Sunderland, Ayr United, Millwall Athletic
**INTERNATIONAL:** Scotland 'Victory', Scottish League
**SAFC TOTALS:** 45 appearances / 30 goals

**Eleven goals in 18 matches and six in nine cup games in Sunderland's greatest-ever single season of 1912-13 were followed by nine goals in 17 league games and one cup tie in which he scored four goals in his second and last season on Wearside before a return to Scotland with Ayr United.**

Richardson did not stay to plunder more goals as his wife wanted to be back in Glasgow for family support with their young children. By chance his granddaughter was living in East Rainton as of 2013 and still had his football boots. Those boots twice scored four goals in cup ties: against Clapton Orient and Chatham in first-round ties in 1913 and 1914. Richardson played in all nine cup games including the final in 1912-13. More importantly that season he scored two of the goals as the league title was clinched in a 3-1 victory at Bolton.

Sunderland had signed Richardson from second division Huddersfield who he joined after winning the 1909 Glasgow Cup with Third Lanark. At Huddersfield he scored 25 times in 44 games between November 1910 and April 1912. He took the step up to the top flight in his stride and on the other side of the Great War, seven years after leaving Sunderland, he moved to London in 1921 to try his luck with Millwall Athletic in their second season as a Football League club.

Debuting in a Division Three South fixture at home to Northampton on the opening day of 1921-22, he scored twice in his first four games but only managed four in total from 19 appearances. He did also net against Chelsea in the London FA Challenge Cup, one of three additional games he played that year. Jimmy was not re-signed by Millwall in May 1922 and after not playing at all in 1922-23, Richardson returned to Ayr in the summer of 1923 to take over as manager of Ayr United, leaving after a season to have a year in charge of Cowdenbeath.

Recognised twice by Scotland in Victory internationals in 1919 as well as in two inter-league matches, during the war Jimmy had been discharged due to stomach trouble after experiencing the trenches. In later life Richardson worked for Rolls Royce and for an electrical firm in Glasgow.

## RICHARDSON, Joseph Gregan

**POSITION:** Half-back
**BIRTHPLACE:** Dumfries, Dumfries & Galloway
**DATE OF BIRTH:** 15/06/1865 - 15/11/1935
**HEIGHT:** 5' 6½" **WEIGHT:** 10st 2lbs
**SIGNED FROM:** Queen of the South Wanderers, 24/08/1887
**DEBUT:** v Morpeth Harriers, A, 22/10/1887
**LAST MATCH:** v Middlesbrough, H, 03/12/1887
**MOVED TO:** Sunderland Albion, 05/05/1888
**TEAMS:** Queen of the South Wanderers, Sunderland, Sunderland Albion
**SAFC TOTALS:** 4 appearances / 0 goals

**All of Joseph Richardson's competitive appearances for Sunderland came in the English (FA) Cup in 1887-88, but after the last of these he was suspended by the English FA for playing as a professional.**

Later re-instated, he joined local rivals Sunderland Albion, playing for Albion in their first-ever game on 5 May 1888 against Shankhouse Black Watch. The following year he began working for Armstrong Addison on the North Dock in Sunderland and remained in their employment until his death.

## RICHARDSON, Kenton Terry

**POSITION:** Right-back
**BIRTHPLACE:** Durham, Co Durham
**DATE OF BIRTH:** 26/06/1999
**HEIGHT:** 6' 1" **WEIGHT:** 13st 2lbs
**SIGNED FROM:** Free agent, 28/08/2020
**DEBUT:** v Lincoln City, A, 05/10/2021
**LAST MATCH:** v Bradford City, H, 09/11/2021
**MOVED TO:** Released, 25/05/2022
**TEAMS:** Hartlepool United, Sunderland, Notts County (L), Spennymoor United (L), Gateshead
**SAFC TOTALS:** 3 appearances / 0 goals

**The grandson of Fred Richardson who played for Chelsea, Hartlepools, Barnsley, WBA, Chester and South Shields, Kenton made 50 appearances for Hartlepool including twelve as sub after debuting in League Two at Mansfield in February 2017.**

After eleven appearances that season he was part of the Pools side who lost their place in the Football League. Freed by Hartlepool in 2020, he signed for Sunderland and made a single National League appearance on loan to Notts County at home to Halifax in March 2021 before re-joining Sunderland where he had been part of the academy set-up before going to Hartlepool.

Three days after his third Football League Trophy appearance for Sunderland, on 12 November 2021, he moved to National League North side Spennymoor - then under the management of former Sunderland midfielder Tommy Miller - on a loan that was extended to the end of the season in which he made 27 appearances for the club.

## RICHARDSON, Kieran Edward

**POSITION:** Midfielder
**BIRTHPLACE:** Greenwich, Greater London
**DATE OF BIRTH:** 21/10/1984
**HEIGHT:** 5' 9" **WEIGHT:** 11st 13lbs
**SIGNED FROM:** Manchester United, 16/07/2007
**DEBUT:** v Tottenham Hotspur, H, 11/08/2007
**LAST MATCH:** v Arsenal, A, 18/08/2012
**MOVED TO:** Fulham, 31/08/2012
**TEAMS:** West Ham United, Manchester United, WBA (L), Sunderland, Fulham, Aston Villa, Cardiff City
**INTERNATIONAL:** England
**SAFC TOTALS:** 138+11 appearances / 15 goals

**Forever famed for 'Richardson's rocket' which screamed into Newcastle United's net to give Sunderland their first home derby win in 28 years in 2008, Kieran Richardson had scored twice on his debut for England, had played 81 games for Manchester United and was a player of versatility, pace and ability, although there was always the lingering doubt that he had it in him to reach even greater heights.**

After being at West Ham as a youth he moved to Manchester United and debuted in a European Cup game at Olympiakos two days after his 18th birthday in October 2002. He made a Premiership debut in a 5-3 win over Newcastle the following month having already registered his first goal in a League Cup win over Leicester.

In 2003 Kieran helped United win the FA Youth Cup, scoring in the final where he played alongside Phil Bardsley and Paul McShane against a Middlesbrough side managed by Mark Proctor and including future Sunderland caretaker-manager Andrew Taylor. In an era when United were as star-studded as the brightest galaxy, Kieran managed to amass 44+37 appearances including coming on as sub in the 2006 League Cup final as Wigan were beaten 4-0 and the 2004 Community Shield which was lost to Arsenal. As the Premier League title was won in 2006-07, Kieran started seven league games and came on in a further eight.

During his time at Old Trafford Richardson was loaned to West Brom in January 2005, scoring three goals in twelve games as he helped the Baggies achieve a remarkable escape from relegation.

## RICHARDSON, Kieran (Continued)

Having played for United legend Bryan Robson at the Hawthorns, he signed for former Old Trafford teammate Roy Keane when coming to Sunderland. Richardson's best moments included his unforgettable free-kick against Newcastle in the week of his 24th birthday and a stellar and unselfish performance in a 3-0 win at Chelsea in 2010, when utilised on the right of midfield he totally nullified England left-back Ashley Cole who earlier in the calendar year had been chief instigator when the Lads lost 7-2 on the same ground. On one occasion against Wolves after scoring he revealed a t-shirt that proclaimed 'I belong to Jesus' and in later life Kieran declared himself to be a born-again Christian.

At Fulham he scored six goals in 41+7 games over two years before a summer 2014 switch to Aston Villa where he never scored in 32+9 appearances. October 2016 brought a brief spell at Cardiff where he played just 2+4 games without scoring. Four months after leaving Fulham he had an unsuccessful trial in Spain with Granada CF before ending his playing days. For England he made a remarkable debut, scoring twice in a 2-1 win over the USA in Chicago. Despite those goals on his only start in which he was replaced after just under an hour, his other seven caps all came as substitute. He also won twelve caps at Under 21 level.

## RIERA, Arnau Caldentey

**POSITION:** Midfielder

**BIRTHPLACE:** Manacor, Spain

**DATE OF BIRTH:** 01/10/1981

**HEIGHT:** 5' 8½" **WEIGHT:** 11st 7lbs

**SIGNED FROM:** Barcelona, 10/08/2006

**DEBUT:** v Southend United, A, 19/08/2006

**LAST MATCH:** v Bury, A, 22/8/2006

**MOVED TO:** Contract not renewed, 30/06/2009

**TEAMS:** Real Mallorca, Ferriolense (L), Mataro (L), Barcelona C & B, Sunderland, Southend United (L), Falkirk (L), Atletico Baleares, CD Manacor

**SAFC TOTALS:** 1+1 appearances / 0 goals

**Having come off the bench to be the lone bright spark in a dismal 3-1 defeat at Southend during Niall Quinn's brief tenure as manager, Arnau was rewarded with a start a few days later in a League Cup tie at Bury only to be sent off after only three minutes and never play for Sunderland again.**

Southend at least were impressed and took him on loan three months later. After two games for the Shrimpers he went on to have two lengthy loan spells with Falkirk with an unsuccessful short trial at Blackpool in between. His only goal in 36 league appearances for Falkirk came against Rangers in a 7-2 defeat while he also netted in a League Cup tie with Aberdeen.

In 2009 Arnau returned to his native Spain with Atlético Baleares before finishing his career in his home town of Manacor in Majorca where he scored once in 18 games in 2011-12 before retiring to run a hotel in the town. At the other end of his career he had started with local club Mallorca, experiencing a couple of loans before signing for Barcelona where for two seasons he captained the B side that included Lionel Messi and made a handful of first-team appearances in friendlies for the Catalan giants. I last saw him at a Halloween party with Julio Arca where he came dressed as a prisoner from Guantanamo Bay!

## RITCHIE, Thomas Gibb (Tom)

**POSITION:** Centre-forward

**BIRTHPLACE:** Edinburgh, Midlothian

**DATE OF BIRTH:** 02/01/1952

**HEIGHT:** 6' 1" **WEIGHT:** 12st 8lbs

**SIGNED FROM:** Bristol City, 29/01/1981

**DEBUT:** v Southampton, A 31/01/1981

**LAST MATCH:** v Stoke City, H, 10/02/1982

**MOVED TO:** Bristol City, 10/06/1982

**TEAMS:** Bridgend Thistle, Bristol City, Sunderland, Carlisle United (L), Bristol City, Yeovil Town

**SAFC TOTALS:** 37+3 appearances / 11 goals

**Ken Knighton's reply when he was telephoned to be told Tom Ritchie had scored a hat-trick in the first match he played after Knighton - who had signed him for a big fee of £185,000 - had been sacked is unprintable. Ritchie had played ten games under Knighton without scoring, but netted all the goals in a 3-0 home win over Birmingham as Sunderland fought to stave off relegation.**

In his second season Tom scored in the opening two games of the season, but between then and December only scored a penalty other than three goals in a two-legged League Cup clash with Rotherham.

Having lost his place midway through the season, Ritchie was shipped out on loan to Bob Stokoe's Carlisle for the last couple of months of the campaign. Playing the final 15 games of the season (14 of them starts), Tom did not score but helped a team including Pop Robson, Jackie Ashurst and Trevor Swinburne to promotion from the third tier.

At this point Ritchie returned to Bristol City who had dropped from Division Two to Division Four in his absence. He had been part of the Robins side on the infamous evening when they manufactured a draw at Coventry in 1977 to send Sunderland down. Tom had helped City to promotion as runners-up to Sunderland the previous season when he was top scorer with 18 goals.

His second spell at Ashton Gate saw him become one of five players to amass over 500 appearances for the club (only Jim Montgomery has reached that figure for Sunderland in competitive games). Ritchie reached 504 games for Bristol City, scoring 132 goals. A member of the Bristol City Hall of Fame, Tom finished his career in the Southern League with Yeovil Town where he signed for his former Bristol City teammate Gerry Gow.

Tom became a postman after retiring from football - in Clevedon where Ken Knighton settled! He did not deliver for the former Sunderland manager - as he hadn't on the pitch! Tom's brother Steve played for Bristol City, Morton, Hereford United, Aberdeen and Torquay United.

## RIVEROS NUNEZ, Cristian Miguel

**POSITION:** Midfielder

**BIRTHPLACE:** Saldivar, Paraguay

**DATE OF BIRTH:** 16/10/1982

**HEIGHT:** 5' 11½" **WEIGHT:** 12st 0lbs

**SIGNED FROM:** Cruz Azul, 11/05/2010

**DEBUT:** v Birmingham City, H, 14/08/2010

**LAST MATCH:** v West Ham United, A, 22/05/2011

**MOVED TO:** Kayserispor, 01/05/2012

**TEAMS:** Tacuary, Sportivo San Lorenzo (L), Club Libertad, Cruz Azul, Sunderland, Kayserispor, Gremio, Olimpia Ascunción, Libertad, National Ascunción, Libertad (to June 2022)

**INTERNATIONAL:** Paraguay

**SAFC TOTALS:** 7+7 appearances / 1 goal

**Riveros became the first player to score at the FIFA World Cup finals while on Sunderland's books (with an assist from Sunderland's Paulo Da Silva), although when he scored for Paraguay against Slovakia in South Africa in 2010 he was yet to debut for Sunderland. He had put pen to paper on his Sunderland contract before the finals.**

Riveros played in every game as Paraguay reached the quarter-finals where they narrowly lost to eventual winners Spain. He scored in a penalty shoot-out with Japan as Paraguay progressed to the quarters. He had also played all three games at the 2006 World Cup, playing against Stewart Downing in a defeat to England, and Carlos Edwards, Dwight Yorke and Stern John in a victory over Trinidad and Tobago. Riveros also appeared in the 2007, 2011 and 2015 Copa Americas. A great servant to his county, Cristian finished one game short of 100 caps. He scored 16 goals for Paraguay, the goal against Slovakia being the only one against a European country.

Not given enough games to acclimatise to the speed and physicality of top-level English football, he was allowed to move on after scoring in a win at relegated West Ham on his final Sunderland appearance. Spending his second year at Sunderland on loan to Kayserispor, he subsequently joined the Turkish club.

At the start of his career, Riveros played youth football for Cristóbal Colón before playing 108 games - with 16 goals - for Tacuary between 2000 and 2005. He also had a 24-game loan at Sportivo San Lorenzo before a transfer to Club Libertad with whom he won the Primera Division in 2006 and 2007. In July 2007, he moved to Mexico with Cruz Azul for whom he bagged 17 goals in 111 games before coming to Sunderland.

After a total of 63 games and two goals with Kayserispor, Riveros returned to South America, this time to Brazil with Gremio. Five goals in 43 games over two years preceded a return to Paraguay. After eleven goals in 107 games for Olimpia Asunción, he returned to Libertad where he took his total figures for that club to nine goals in 103 games. From 2020 to 2022, he played 59 times for Nacional Ascunción, netting four times before a January 2022 move back to Libertad.

I last bumped into Riveros in a hotel ahead of a World Cup qualifier between Bolivia and Paraguay in 2012, a game in which he scored Paraguay's late consolation in a 3-1 defeat at altitude in La Paz. Typically Riveros never gave up. He was a good player that Sunderland supporters did not see enough of.

## ROBERGE, Valentin Sebastien Roger

**POSITION:** Centre-back

**BIRTHPLACE:** Montreuil, France

**DATE OF BIRTH:** 09/06/1987

**HEIGHT:** 6' 2" **WEIGHT:** 11st 10lbs

**SIGNED FROM:** Maritimo, 01/07/2013

**DEBUT:** v Fulham, H, 17/08/2013

**LAST MATCH:** v West Bromwich Albion, A, 16/08/2014

**MOVED TO:** Contract not renewed, 30/06/2016

**TEAMS:** Guingamp B, Paris Saint Germain B, Aris Thessaloniki, Maritimo, Sunderland, Reims (L), Apollon Limassol

**SAFC TOTALS:** 10+3 appearances / 1 goal

**One of the players brought in by Director of Football Roberto De Fanti, Roberge never seemed happy on or off the pitch. Possibly this was simply through frustration at not playing regularly. Undoubtedly, his best game was in a Boxing Day 1-0 win away to Everton when he partnered Modibo Diakité in central defence.**

After playing on the opening day of the following season he returned to his native France on a season-long loan to Reims where he played eleven times. Most of Roberge's career had been spent with Maritimo in the Portuguese League where his 79+3 games included a goal in a Europa League draw with Bordeaux, one of three he scored for the club.

He also played Europa League football for his final club (to 2022) Apollon Limassol in Cyprus. Prior to playing for Madeira-based Maritimo, Valentin had played 19+6 games in Greece for Aris Thessaloniki where he debuted against Panathinaikos, but eventually became financially stranded when the club collapsed economically. As a youngster he played for ESD Montreuil, Les Lilas and Paris FC before stepping up to B level with Guingamp and PSG, making 28 appearances (1 goal) for the for the former and 31 for the latter.

## ROBERTS, Patrick John Joseph

**POSITION:** Winger

**BIRTHPLACE:** Kingston upon Thames, Greater London

**DATE OF BIRTH:** 05/02/1997

**HEIGHT:** 5' 6" **WEIGHT:** 10st 6lbs

**SIGNED FROM:** Manchester City, 21/01/2022, and as free agent, 25/06/2022

**DEBUT:** v Bolton Wanderers, A, 29/01/2022

**LAST MATCH:**

**MOVED TO:**

**TEAMS:** AFC Wimbledon, Fulham, Manchester City, Celtic (L), Girona (L), Norwich City (L), Middlesbrough (L), Derby County (L), Troyes (L), Sunderland

**INTERNATIONAL:** England U-20

**SAFC TOTALS:** 9+8 appearances / 2 goals (to May 2022)

**Naturally gifted and with a low centre of gravity, when at his best such as in an early appearance at Lincoln and the 2022 Play-Off games against Sheffield Wednesday (in which he scored the decisive goal), Patrick looked to be an excellent player which made people wonder why he found himself in League One in his mid-twenties after a long series of loans from Manchester City. After succeeding on an initial short-term contract at Sunderland he signed a two-year deal in June 2022.**

He had debuted for Fulham as a sub in a heavy defeat at Manchester City in the month City had played Sunderland at Wembley in 2014. Sixteen months later City bought Patrick for a reported £12m after he had made just three senior starts with a further 19 games as a sub. Roberts' City debut came at Sunderland in a 4-1 League (Capital One Cup) win in September 2015. Four days later he made a Premier League debut, but his four minutes in a 4-1 loss at Spurs would be his only league outing for City.

After one more appearance as sub in another cup game, Patrick began the first of what would be three loans with Celtic where he totalled 51+28 games and scored 18 goals - including one that earned Celtic a Champions League draw at his parent club Manchester City. Each spell with Celtic was highly successful, winning the league in his first season and the domestic treble in each of his last two loans.

For 2018-19 Roberts moved to Spain on a season-long loan with Girona. All but six of his 21 games were as sub with him not scoring at all as Girona were relegated. This was followed by 1+3 games (0) goals on loan to Norwich and one goal in 14+7 appearances across two loans with Middlesbrough and another single goal in 7+8 games with Derby. A final loan in France with Troyes brought just a single game as a sub against an Olympique Lyonnais side that included former Sunderland loanee Jason Denayer.

As a boy, Roberts began with Molesey Juniors and AFC Wimbledon before switching to Fulham when he was 13. He went on to score for them in the 2014 FA Youth Cup final against Chelsea. At international level he has won 47 England caps across five age levels up to Under 20, scoring 19 goals in the process and being selected for the Team of the Tournament when helping England to win the UEFA European Under 17 Championship in 2014.

## ROBINSON, Carl Philip

**POSITION:** Midfielder

**BIRTHPLACE:** Llandrindod Wells, Powys

**DATE OF BIRTH:** 13/10/1976

**HEIGHT:** 5' 11" **WEIGHT:** 12st 9lbs

**SIGNED FROM:** Portsmouth, 10/06/2004 after loan from 25/03/2004

**DEBUT:** v Wimbledon, A, 06/04/2004

**LAST MATCH:** v Arsenal, A, 05/11/2005

**MOVED TO:** Norwich City, 17/01/2006 after loan from 24/11/2005

**TEAMS:** Wolverhampton Wanderers, Shrewsbury Town (L), Portsmouth, Sheffield Wednesday (L),Walsall (L), Rotherham United (L), Sheffield United (L), Sunderland, Norwich City, Toronto, New York Bulls

**INTERNATIONAL:** Wales

**SAFC TOTALS:** 55+4 appearances / 5 goals

**Carl completed his move to Sunderland after a loan spell that included playing in both legs of an ill-fated Play-Off with Crystal Palace. An industrious crisp-passing central midfielder, he went on to start 40 games as the Championship was won the following season, one of his four goals being the winner on the final day of the season in front of a capacity crowd against Stoke. However after signing a new two-year contract he made just three Premier League starts plus a couple as sub and played a couple of League Cup games before moving to Norwich.**

After a successful loan at Carrow Road, the £50,000 received by Sunderland was the first time a fee had been paid for him. He was to make 54 appearances for the Canaries, scoring twice before he was released in January 2007 in order to sign for MLS new boys Toronto. After three years and three goals in 74 games with the Canadian club Carl signed for New York Red Bulls in March 2010. He scored once in twelve appearances before returning to Canada as assistant coach of Vancouver Whitecaps in January 2012.

Robinson had a long held wish to move to British Columbia. On a pre-season tour there with Sunderland in July 2005, I sat with him in a hotel while he looked to invest in property in the area with a Real Estate salesman. After just under two years as assistant, Robinson became head coach of the Whitecaps nine days before Christmas in 2013. He remained until September 2018, having taken them to their best-ever position of third in the MLS in 2015, qualifying for the CONCACAF Champions League.

## ROBINSON, Carl (Continued)

Turning down the opportunity to manage Costa Rica in 2019, in February 2020 Robinson re-emerged in Australia as head coach of A-League outfit Newcastle Jets. Impressing with seven win and three draws from his first eleven games drew the attention of West Sydney Wanderers who he assumed control of after just eight months with the Jets. Thirteen months after taking over he signed former Sunderland and England midfielder Jack Rodwell.

Carl had begun his footballing journey with Wolves who he played more games for than anyone else. There were 153 starts and 36 games as sub for the team in old gold for whom he scored 23 times. Early in his career Carl had 2+3 games on loan to Shrewsbury, making his league debut against Hull in March 1996 and playing at Wembley (alongside John Kay and Tommy Lynch) against Rotherham just two weeks later in the final of the Football League Trophy which his side lost 2-1. In the summer of 2002 he joined Portsmouth who loaned him out five times. There were just 12+8 appearances for Pompey and four (1 goal) on loans to Sheffield Wednesday, 10/1/1 with Walsall, 16/0/0 with Rotherham, and 4/1/0 with Sheffield United before coming to Sunderland.

Carl won 52 caps for Wales as well as representing his country at Under 21 and 'B' level. His cousin Andy played for Tranmere Rovers, Swansea City, Leeds United, Shrewsbury Town and Stockport County from 2002 until 2015.

## ROBINSON, George Henry

**POSITION:** Outside-right
**BIRTHPLACE:** Ilkeston, Derbyshire
**DATE OF BIRTH:** 11/01/1908 - 14/01/1963
**HEIGHT:** 5' 8½" **WEIGHT:** 10st 9lbs
**SIGNED FROM:** Ilkeston Town, 23/04/1927
**DEBUT:** v Middlesbrough, A, 05/05/1928
**LAST MATCH:** v Sheffield United, H, 02/05/1931
**MOVED TO:** Charlton Athletic, 24/06/1931
**TEAMS:** Ilkeston Town, Sunderland, Charlton Athletic, Burton Town (L), Sunderland (WW2 Guest), Birmingham (WW2 Guest), Notts County (WW2 Guest), Crewe Alexandra (WW2 Guest), Fulham (WW2 Guest), West Ham United (WW2 Guest), Hartlepools United (WW2 Guest), Linfield (WW2 Guest)
**SAFC TOTALS:** 32 appearances / 8 goals

**At the age of 20, George Robinson's debut saw him thrust into the most important Tees-Wear derby ever played. A last-day-of-the-season shoot-out would see one of the clubs relegated. Robinson played his part in a Sunderland victory and went on to play 25 times the following season. Coming into the side in a 5-1 win over Manchester United in November these appearances were all consecutive as from the right-wing he was part of the supply line in a season when Dave Halliday's 43 goals set a seasonal scoring record that still stands in 2022.**

Robinson's run of games ended at home to Leeds where he went off with a knee injury. This kept him out for 18 months. At this point he returned for three games and then missed six more months before being brought back for the last three fixtures of the season. Despite scoring in two of these he was sold in the summer to Charlton who got great value for their £650.

Having completely recovered from his injury George was ever-present as the Addicks won Division Three South in 1934-35 and continued to play a major role as astonishingly, they won a second successive promotion and a year later were runners-up in the top-flight - making a return to Roker Park a week before Sunderland played in the FA Cup semi-final. In two spells with Charlton, punctuated by a spell with Burton Town, Robinson played 238 league games for Charlton scoring 42 times.

During World War Two he played as a guest for a host of clubs including Sunderland. In 1941-42 he played for Sunderland in both legs of the League War Cup final against Wolves, A year later he played for the Lads in the second leg of the West Riding Combined Counties Cup final and in total added 59 games and a dozen goals to his peace-time tally. In 1944 he was part of the Charlton side who beat Chelsea at Wembley in the Football League War Cup South final. There was another war-time cup final in 1945 when he helped Linfield beat Glentoran in Ireland.

After the war Robinson became assistant coach at Charlton from September 1947, becoming assistant manager in April 1949. Robinson's son-in-law Eddie Firmani became a well known manager of Charlton as well as managing in the USA. As a player between 1950 and 1975, Firmani played for Charlton, Sampdoria, Inter, Genoa, Southend United and Tampa Bay Rowdies.

## ROBINSON, John (Jackie)

**POSITION:** Inside-right
**BIRTHPLACE:** Shiremoor, Northumberland
**DATE OF BIRTH:** 10/08/1917 - 30/07/1972
**HEIGHT:** 5' 9½" **WEIGHT:** 10st 12lbs
**SIGNED FROM:** Sheffield Wednesday, 14/10/1946
**DEBUT:** v Grimsby Town, H, 19/10/1946
**LAST MATCH:** v Charlton Athletic, H, 23/04/1949
**MOVED TO:** Lincoln City, 15/10/1949
**TEAMS:** Shiremoor, Sheffield Wednesday, Hartlepools United (WW2 Guest), Newcastle United (WW2 Guest), Sunderland, Lincoln City
**INTERNATIONAL:** England
**SAFC TOTALS:** 85 appearances / 33 goals

**A Sunderland debut goal was a sign of things to come for a player who was 29 at the time having lost the peak years of his career to World War Two. Sixteen goals - including four in a 5-0 win at Blackpool - saw Jackie net 17 times in 31 league and cup games, making him joint top scorer.**

The Northumbrian had started his professional career with Sheffield Wednesday after playing for Newbiggin Juniors and West Wylam Colliery before Shiremoor. He scored the winner for the Owls on his debut at West Brom in April 1935 and scored 39 goals in 119 peace-time games plus 90 in 110 war-time appearances. In 1942-43, one of six hat-tricks came in a record 8-2 win over local rivals Sheffield United.

During the war he also played four games for Hartlepools and one for Newcastle. Robinson is considered to be one of Wednesday's all-time greats based not just on his goals to games ratio, but also on his pace, passing prowess and renowned body swerve.

At Lincoln, his goalscoring prowess showed no signs of abating as he rattled in five goals in eight games only to have his career ended on Christmas Eve 1949 when he broke his leg in a game against Wrexham.

Jackie's ability to score on his debut extended to international football with a goal in an 8-0 win away to Finland in the month Sunderland first won the FA Cup in 1937, when Robinson was still in his teens. Given a second cap almost exactly a year later, he scored twice in a 6-3 win over Germany in Berlin. This was on the infamous occasion the England team gave the Nazi salute before the match. Robinson was to win two more caps in defeats away to Switzerland and Wales.

After retiring from the game, Jackie became a builder and subsequently ran the Ship Inn in Gateshead, but passed away of cancer when only 54. At one point, he was believed to be younger, but he had knocked two years off his real age at the time of his transfer to Sunderland.

## ROBINSON, Raymond Wilson

**POSITION:** Outside-right
**BIRTHPLACE:** Blaydon, Co Durham
**DATE OF BIRTH:** 25/06/1895 - 06/01/1964
**HEIGHT:** 5' 6" **WEIGHT:** 10st 13lbs
**SIGNED FROM:** Newcastle United, 20/08/1920 and from Grimsby Town, 06/1922
**DEBUT:** v Sheffield United, A, 28/08/1920
**LAST MATCH:** v Preston North End, H, 23/04/1921
**MOVED TO:** Grimsby Town, 10/05/1921 and to Eden CW, 10/1922
**TEAMS:** Scotswood, Grimsby Town (WW1 Guest), Newcastle United, Sunderland, Grimsby Town, Sunderland, Eden CW, Lancaster Town, Liverpool Police, Shirebrook, Silverwood Colliery
**SAFC TOTALS:** 10 appearances / 2 goals

**This ex-Newcastle winger from Blaydon could get up a head of steam when in possession but was far from a speed merchant. He only played ten times for Sunderland, all of them in the 1920-21 season when he scored on his first two home performances.**

He had made the trip from St James' Park to Roker Park for a fee of £750. For the Magpies, he had scored four times in 29 games having come into the team in the first season after World War One. During the war Robinson had been with the Cyclists Corps before serving as a corporal in France with the Tanks Corps.

Having played for Grimsby as a war-time 'Guest', he later played nine Division Three North games for the Mariners. There was then a brief return to Sunderland although he moved on again without adding to his competitive first-team record. A coal miner prior to becoming a footballer, he returned to the mines once his career was at an end and also worked as a Life Assurance Rep.

## ROBINSON, Robert

**POSITION:** Goalkeeper
**BIRTHPLACE:** Rainton, Co Durham
**DATE OF BIRTH:** 27/03/1910 - 22/01/1989
**HEIGHT:** 5' 10" **WEIGHT:** 10st 12lbs
**SIGNED FROM:** Hetton Juniors, 14/05/1926
**DEBUT:** Aston Villa, A, 01/09/1947
**LAST MATCH:** v Leicester City, H, 25/12/1930
**MOVED TO:** Guildford City, 18/07/1931
**TEAMS:** Hetton Juniors, Sunderland, Guildford City, Norwich City, Barrow, Scarborough, Gainsborough Trinity
**SAFC TOTALS:** 38 appearances / 0 goals

**One of two goalkeepers called Robert Robinson to play for Sunderland, this one played for the Lads before World War Two with his namesake playing shortly after it.**

This former Durham County stopper was a young understudy to England international Albert McInroy and got his breakthrough in 1929-30 when he made 26 appearances with the rest coming the following season before he was transfer listed at the end of April 1931.

After a season with Guildford Robinson signed for Norwich City where he made 34 appearances followed by 32 with Barrow, in both cases these being in the different geographical sections of the third tier. His younger brother, Thomas, a centre-half, signed amateur forms for Newcastle United in August 1935.

## ROBINSON, Robert (Bobby)

**POSITION:** Goalkeeper
**BIRTHPLACE:** Newbiggin-by-the-sea, Northumberland
**DATE OF BIRTH:** 23/06/1921 - 28/03/1975
**HEIGHT:** 5' 11" **WEIGHT:** 13st 0lbs
**SIGNED FROM:** Newbiggin, 26/02/1947
**DEBUT:** v Aston Villa, A, 01/09/1947
**LAST MATCH:** v West Bromwich Albion, A, 26/04/1952
**MOVED TO:** Newcastle United, 25/08/1952
**TEAMS:** Coleraine, Burnley, Newbiggin, Sunderland, Newcastle United
**SAFC TOTALS:** 33 appearances / 0 goals

**Although a Northumbrian, Robinson began playing in the Irish League with Coleraine during WW2 before joining Burnley as an amateur, followed by a brief spell with his home town Newbiggin. He later became a professional with Sunderland after being demobbed from the army.**

Robert was to be a reliable back-up keeper at both Sunderland and Newcastle United. On Wearside he played 18 times in his final season of 1951-52 and ten games in 1948-49, his other three years seeing him confined largely to the reserves. Some of this absence was due to a broken hand sustained with the reserves at Middlesbrough on 19 November 1949 followed by a broken leg six weeks later.

Newcastle paid £2,500 for him in 1952 as cover whilst their senior goalkeeper was taking part in National Service, but in his two years there he only played five games, one of them against Sunderland, a 2-2 draw on Tyneside in September 1952. After finishing with the professional game he played local football and returned to his birthplace of Newbiggin to become landlord at the Queen's Head.

## ROBINSON, Robert Smith

**POSITION:** Inside-right / centre-forward
**BIRTHPLACE:** Sunderland, Co Durham
**DATE OF BIRTH:** 22/10/1879 - 11/10/1950
**HEIGHT:** 5' 9" **WEIGHT:** 12st 5lbs
**SIGNED FROM:** Royal Rovers, 06/11/1902
**DEBUT:** v Stoke, A, 08/11/1902
**LAST MATCH:** v Notts County, A, 12/12/1903
**MOVED TO:** Liverpool, 09/02/1904
**TEAMS:** South Hylton, Royal Rovers, Sunderland, Liverpool, Tranmere Rovers
**SAFC TOTALS:** 25 appearances / 7 goals

**'Whitey' was a regular with Liverpool when they won the second and first division championships in successive seasons in 1905 and 1906, being top-scorer with 24 goals in 1905, scoring all four goals in a win over Leicester Fosse that season.**

Known as Bobby on Merseyside, in total he scored 65 goals in 271 games for the Anfielders between 1904 and 1912, one of those goals coming against his hometown team Sunderland. A forward in his early years at Liverpool, as he aged he moved into the half-back line.

Liverpool signed him from Sunderland where he had worked in marine engine works before becoming a professional footballer. He had been a prolific schoolboy scorer with Thomas Street Board School in Sunderland. Despite playing at outside-right rather than centre-forward, he once scored 15 goals in a single game against Simpson Street School. In one remarkable season, he scored 132 goals in a spell where his school team won the Elementary Schools League for three years in a row.

At the age of 16 he played for Sunderland juniors who merged with Sunderland's third team before Robinson spent a season with South Hylton who he helped to the Wearside League title. Moving on to Sunderland Royal Rovers, 'Whitey' (he was also called Snowy because of the colour of his hair) again won the Wearside League and also the Shipowners' Cup where he scored a Roker Park hat-trick in the final as Black Watch were beaten 3-0.

Although he went on to do very well at Liverpool, Whitey struggled to hold down a regular place at Sunderland, playing 17 times in his first season and just eight in his second, despite scoring three times in those eight outings. He was to stay on Merseyside where after finishing his playing career with Tranmere Rovers in the Lancashire Combination he became trainer for Marine FC, a crane driver at the docks and ran a sweet and tobacconists shop in Anfield. In later life, he had to have a leg amputated due to gangrene.

## ROBINSON, William (Bill)

**POSITION:** Centre-forward
**BIRTHPLACE:** Whitburn, Co Durham
**DATE OF BIRTH:** 04/04/1919 - 07/10/1992
**HEIGHT:** 5' 10" **WEIGHT:** 12st 0lbs
**SIGNED FROM:** Hylton Juniors, 01/08/1934
**DEBUT:** v Leicester City, A, 30/08/1937
**LAST MATCH:** v Leeds United, H, 15/04/1939
**MOVED TO:** Charlton Athletic, 31/05/1946
**TEAMS:** Sunderland, Barnsley (WW2 Guest), Luton Town (WW2 Guest), Charlton Athletic (WW2 Guest), Aberdeen (WW2 Guest), Hamilton Academical (WW2 Guest), Stockport County (WW2 Guest), Charlton Athletic, West Ham United
**SAFC TOTALS:** 24 appearances / 14 goals

**Eleven goals in 14 games in the last completed pre-World War Two season augured well for a player who only left his teens behind in the last weeks of the season. Late in that season he scored a five-minute hat-trick against Manchester United and added another later in the match. He played in the three games of the expunged 1939-40 campaign and went on to score twice more in eight war-time games for SAFC. He also played extensively as a war-time guest elsewhere.**

Robinson turned out twice for Barnsley and seven times for Luton in 1939-40. As well as serving in the army, he played war-time football for Aberdeen and Hamilton in 1942-43, and also played twice for Stockport County. In 1943-44, he scored twelve goals in 20 games for Charlton. The Addicks paid Sunderland £1,000 for Robinson's signature after the war.

In 1947 he was on the winning side in the FA Cup final for Jimmy Seed's side, one of 60 league and cup appearances in which he netted 18 goals. In January 1947, he was sold to West Ham for £7,000. A debut goal at West Brom was soon followed by him being top scorer in his first two full seasons, only for the third to be curtailed after four games through injury. In total, he scored 61 goals in 105 games for the Irons including hat-tricks against Leicester City and Sheffield United.

After retiring from playing he stayed on the club's coaching staff until November 1959 being assistant manager to Ted Fenton as the Hammers won the second division before Robinson became manager of Hartlepool where the club had to apply for re-election in all of his three of his years in charge. It had been a long career in the game, 29 years earlier he had won the England Schools' Shield in 1933 with Durham Boys.

## ROBSON, Bryan Stanley

**POSITION:** Forward

**BIRTHPLACE:** Sunderland, Co Durham

**DATE OF BIRTH:** 11/11/1945

**HEIGHT:** 5' 7" **WEIGHT:** 11st 8lbs

**SIGNED FROM:** West Ham United, 18/06/1974 & 15/06/1979 and from Chelsea, 28/07/1983

**DEBUT:** v Newcastle United, H, 03/08/1974

**LAST MATCH:** v Leicester City, A, 12/05/1984

**MOVED TO:** West Ham United, 13/10/1976, Carlisle United, 03/03/1981 & 23/07/1984

**TEAMS:** Clara Vale Juniors, Newcastle United, West Ham United, Sunderland, West Ham United, Sunderland, Carlisle United, Chelsea, Carlisle United (L), Sunderland, Carlisle United, Gateshead

**INTERNATIONAL:** England Under 23

**SAFC TOTALS:** 172+10 appearances / 68 goals

**'Pop' Robson had a record six periods of employment at Sunderland, three as a player and three behind the scenes. After the sacking of manager Len Ashurst Robson had one game as caretaker-manager against Arsenal in March 1984. In November 1988 he became Community officer at Sunderland before a spell as a coach at Manchester United from 1991.**

Between June 1995 and May 2000 he was reserve team coach at Sunderland before a four-year spell as assistant academy director at Leeds United. After scouting for Birmingham, Blackburn and Chelsea he returned to SAFC to be chief scout between July 2011 and May 2013.

As a player Robson was top class. A great goalscorer, he was also a fine all-round footballer and a model professional. Married to England international table tennis player Maureen Heppell, Robson's father-in-law was balance and dance expert Len Heppell who worked with Pop and numerous other top sports stars right up to Robson's West Ham teammate and England World Cup winning captain Bobby Moore.

In the season Sunderland won the FA Cup in 1973, Robson was the top-flight's top scorer with 28 goals for West Ham, 16 of which came in braces with a hat-trick against Southampton. Outrageously Robson never won an England cap although he did represent the Football League as well as winning three Under 23 caps.

Pop had begun with Newcastle United after trials at Leicester City and Northampton Town. The scorer of the winning goal on his debut at Charlton in September 1964 it was not until 1968-69 that he began to flourish in black and white. After 97 goals in 243+1 games for the Magpies West Ham paid a club record £120,000 in February 1971 after Pop had gone on record complaining about Newcastle's lack of professionalism. Robson had played in both legs of the final as Newcastle won the Inter Cities Fairs Cup in 1969, having won promotion with the Tynesiders four years earlier.

As he had done with Newcastle Pop marked his West Ham debut with a goal (against Nottingham Forest) and went on to score 104 goals in 254 games for the Hammers either side of his first move to Sunderland. The Wearsiders paid £145,000 for him in the summer of 1974 and recouped £80,000 when selling him back in October 1976 shortly after Pop had top-scored for Sunderland as the second division title was won.

He returned to Roker to again be top-scorer as promotion was won in his first season back. Once again he was regretfully discarded part-way through a first season back at top level, this time to Carlisle where he re-united with Bob Stokoe who had first brought him to Sunderland. Once again he scored on debut (he had scored on his home league debut in red and white). In three spells with the Cumbrians Robson would rattle in 29 goals in 77+1 appearances.

Between the second and third of his Carlisle spells Pop went to Chelsea in 1982-83. Yet again scoring on debut - a winner at Cambridge - he scored five times in 12+5 games before being loaned back to Carlisle. Next stop was another return to Sunderland, for whom he marked his final appearance with a goal at Leicester that made him Sunderland's oldest goalscorer at the age of 38 years and 183 days. As of the summer of 2022, Pop's record still stood. Having spent the 1983-84 season at Sunderland, the next campaign would be Pop's last in the league. Playing for Carlisle his last goal came at Barnsley - the 266th league goal of his career.

There was still time to see out his career with Gateshead, after which he coached at Hartlepool Manchester United, Leeds United, Middlesbrough and Sunderland as well as scouting for Chelsea and Spurs. Rightly, hugely-respected throughout the game Robson was an excellent servant of Sunderland on and off the pitch. Despite his goalscoring prowess the nickname Pop was because as a child he and two of his friends were known as Snap, Crackle & Pop after a breakfast cereal advertisement rather than it having anything to do with his life-long penchant for popping goals in.

## ROBSON, Edward Riddell (Ned)

**POSITION:** Goalkeeper

**BIRTHPLACE:** Hexham, Northumberland

**DATE OF BIRTH:** 21/08/1890 - 02/02/1977

**HEIGHT:** 6' 0" **WEIGHT:** 12st 0lbs

**SIGNED FROM:** Portsmouth, 29/05/1922

**DEBUT:** v Nottingham Forest, A, 26/08/1922

**LAST MATCH:** v Manchester City, A, 22/09/1923

**MOVED TO:** Swansea Town, 19/05/1924

**TEAMS:** Hexham Northern Star, Hexham Athletic, Gateshead, Watford, Portsmouth, Sunderland, Swansea Town, Wrexham, Grimsby Town, Rochdale

**SAFC TOTALS:** 40 appearances / 0 goals

**Thirty-four of Robson's 40 appearances came in 1922-23 as Sunderland were runners-up to Liverpool. His remaining six games came the following year before he moved on to Swansea Town where he played 29 league games in two years before switching to Wrexham.**

Ned had two years there too, but played 70 games before spending 1928-29 with Grimsby prior to a final move to

Rochdale. He did not play at all for Grimsby, but made twelve appearances for Rochdale. In the earlier part of Robson's career, he played 112 times for Portsmouth, winning a Southern League Championship medal with them in 1920, leading to a transfer to Sunderland. After retiring from playing, Ned coached at Hexham and Hexham Hearts during the 1930s whilst also working as a foreman road maker in the town.

## ROBSON, Ethan

**POSITION:** Midfielder

**BIRTHPLACE:** Houghton le Spring, Tyne and Wear

**DATE OF BIRTH:** 25/10/1996

**HEIGHT:** 5' 8" **WEIGHT:** 10st 12lbs

**SIGNED FROM:** Trainee, 01/07/2013

**DEBUT:** v Everton, A, 20/09/2017

**LAST MATCH:** v Manchester City Under 21s, H, 22/01/2019

**MOVED TO:** Contract not renewed, 30/06/2020

**TEAMS:** Sunderland, Dundee (L), Grimsby Town (L), Blackpool, MK Dons (to June 2022)

**SAFC TOTALS:** 9+5 appearances / 1 goal

**Named Ethan apparently after the Ethan Hunt character played by Tom Cruise in the Mission Impossible series, Ethan Robson's mission impossible at Sunderland seemed to be staying fit. An accomplished footballer, good on set pieces and possessing a lethal long-range shot, allied to good vision and technical ability, Robson was rated highly internally at the club who he joined as an eight-year-old, but only managed a handful of games.**

Other than 2+1 games in the Football League Trophy all of these came in the 2017-18 season when Sunderland dropped through the Championship in what was a second successive relegation season, a difficult time for a youngster to come into the team.

He also suffered relegation on loan to Dundee in 2018-19 in a side that included former Sunderland midfielder Martin Woods and ex-SAFC reserves Andrew Nelson and Roarie Deacon. After 12+1 appearances and two goals in Scotland, Ethan had 14+5 games on loan at Grimsby where he scored three times and played alongside Sunderland old-boy Jordan Cook.

Released by Sunderland in the summer of 2020, he went to Blackpool playing alongside Sunderland loanee Elliott Embleton. Robson made a total of 36 appearances as Blackpool won promotion from League One via the Play-Offs in 2021. Loaned to MK Dons the following season, he contributed a winning goal against Portsmouth and made 19+3 appearances for the Dons before being recalled by the Tangerines who released him in May 2022at which point he was signed by MK Dons.

## ROBSON, Thomas (Tom)

**POSITION:** Centre-half
**BIRTHPLACE:** Sunderland, Co. Durham
**DATE OF BIRTH:** 01/02/1936 - Q2 1981
**HEIGHT:** 6' 0" **WEIGHT:** 12st 0lbs
**SIGNED FROM:** Sunderland Juniors, 01/06/1953
**DEBUT:** v Huddersfield Town, H, 28/02/1959
**LAST MATCH:** v Huddersfield Town, H, 26/09/1959
**MOVED TO:** Darlington, 09/08/1960
**TEAMS:** Sunderland, Darlington, Horden CW
**SAFC TOTALS:** 5 appearances / 0 goals

**Locally-born defender Robson signed professional forms in September 1957. His first-team career spanned seven months in 1959 beginning and ending against Huddersfield, his penultimate appearance being a 6-1 thrashing at Ipswich.**

He had just one league appearance for Darlington in 1960-61 before playing non-league football back in the north east.

## ROBSON, Thomas (Tommy)

**POSITION:** Left-back
**BIRTHPLACE:** Stanley, Co Durham
**DATE OF BIRTH:** 11/09/1995
**HEIGHT:** 5' 10" **WEIGHT:** 11st 11lbs
**SIGNED FROM:** Darlington Youths, 01/07/2012
**DEBUT:** v Watford, A, 16/05/2016
**LAST MATCH:** v Watford, A, 16/05/2016
**MOVED TO:** Falkirk, 19/12/2017
**TEAMS:** Darlington, Sunderland, Limerick (L), Falkirk, Partick Thistle, Queen's Park (to June 2022)
**SAFC TOTALS:** 1 appearance / 0 goals

**Tommy's one first-team appearance came on the last day of the 2015-16 season as Sam Allardyce gave youngsters a chance having dramatically staved off relegation. The appointment of a new manager in David Moyes led to Robson not getting another chance, despite having grown into the game and impressed on his debut and also in a 22-game loan with Limerick.**

A versatile player able to play anywhere on the left-hand side Robson - whose father was well known in non-league circles, particularly at Consett - started at Darlington. When the Quakers disbanded, Robson followed coach Craig Liddle to Sunderland. Robson attracted interest from Fulham who offered him a deal before he became a professional at SAFC.

Moving on to Scotland, Robson played 42+5 games for Falkirk, scoring twice. Between July 2019 and October 2020, he made 17+11 appearances for Partick Thistle without scoring and in October 2020, moved to Queen's Park where, as of the summer of 2022, he had played 61+3 games, scoring once and helping the club to back-to-back promotions, rising into the Championship in 2022 under John Potter who coached at Sunderland under Jack Ross.

## RODGERSON, Ian

**POSITION:** Outside-right
**BIRTHPLACE:** Hereford, Herefordshire
**DATE OF BIRTH:** 09/04/1966
**HEIGHT:** 5'10" **WEIGHT:** 10 st 7lbs
**SIGNED FROM:** Birmingham City, 07/07/1993
**DEBUT:** v Portsmouth, H, 06/11/1993
**LAST MATCH:** v Notts County, A, 05/11/1994
**MOVED TO:** Cardiff City, 26/07/1995
**TEAMS:** Hereford United, Cardiff City, Birmingham City, Sunderland, Cardiff City, Hereford United
**SAFC TOTALS:** 5+5 appearances / 0 goals

**The most badly injured of the new signings hurt in a pre-season car crash having been signed by Terry Butcher in 1993, Rodgerson's debut was delayed until November by a dislocated shoulder. When he did play, Ian struggled to make an impression, his final game of ten coming almost exactly a year after his first-team bow.**

After starting in the Hellenic League with Pegasus Juniors, Rodgerson was an apprentice plumber for three years having not been offered terms by Hereford United where he had played as a schoolboy, but Hereford later took him on in 1985. He was to make exactly 100 league appearances for the Bulls including five as sub (plus 18+1 cup games) before a £35,000 transfer to Cardiff in 1988.

With the Bluebirds he fell one game short of a league century, totalling 122+2 games and four goals over two and a half seasons before a £50,000 move to Birmingham City. There were 95 league appearances in a total of 107+9 games and 16 goals prior to his ill-fated move to Sunderland after which Ian's career contained a certain symmetry with returns to Cardiff and Hereford where he took his totals with those clubs to 174+15/5 and 199+12/14, his final game coming for Hereford in the Conference at Stevenage in April 2002

Five years later he qualified as a chartered physiotherapist, starting as physio at Birmingham City Academy then Forest Green Rovers before opening his own clinic in Hereford. His father Alan was a teammate of Brian Clough at Middlesbrough and went on to re-join his Boro manager Bob Dennison at Hereford after a spell at Cambridge United. Rodgerson senior also played for Gloucester City and Cheltenham. Only injury prevented him from being part of the non-league Hereford team who famously knocked Newcastle out of the FA Cup in 1972.

## RODGERSON, Ralph

**POSITION:** Left-back
**BIRTHPLACE:** Sunderland, Co Durham
**DATE OF BIRTH:** 25/12/1913 - 18/04/1972
**HEIGHT:** 5'10" **WEIGHT:** 11st 4lbs
**SIGNED FROM:** Shotton Colliery, 27/12/1935
**DEBUT:** v Huddersfield Town, H, 18/04/1936
**LAST MATCH:** v Manchester United, H, 04/03/1939
**MOVED TO:** Retired, 01/06/1943
**TEAMS:** Shotton Colliery, Sunderland, North Shields (WW2 Guest)
**SAFC TOTALS:** 5 appearances / 0 goals

**A keen cricketer who played for the Sunderland Police team into the 1950s, Ralph's father Ralph senior had played for Sunderland during World War One as a guest player. Ralph senior also played for Huddersfield Town and Leeds United.**

In the case of Ralph junior, his five first-team games were spread over four seasons with the title-winning campaign of 1935-36 being the only term in which he played more than once. During WW2, and after retiring from professional football, Ralph was a policeman in Sunderland.

## RODWELL, Jack Christian

**POSITION:** Midfielder
**BIRTHPLACE:** Southport, Merseyside
**DATE OF BIRTH:** 11/03/1991
**HEIGHT:** 6' 2" **WEIGHT:** 12st 8lbs
**SIGNED FROM:** Manchester City, 05/08/2014
**DEBUT:** v West Bromwich Albion, A, 16/08/2014
**LAST MATCH:** v Everton, A, 20/09/2017
**MOVED TO:** Released from contract, 30/06/2018
**TEAMS:** Everton, Manchester City, Sunderland, Blackburn Rovers, Sheffield United, Western Sydney Wanderers (to June 2022)
**INTERNATIONAL:** England
**SAFC TOTALS:** 53+23 appearances / 7 goals

**In the eyes of almost all supporters Jack Rodwell became one of the biggest wastes of space in the club's history, although the circumstances of his disappearance from view remain shrouded in mystery. An England international signed by sporting director Lee Congerton for an undisclosed fee believed to be in the region of £10m, Rodwell's acquisition was hailed as a marquee signing as he came from reigning league champions Manchester City shortly after City and Sunderland had met at Wembley in the League (Capital One) Cup final.**

## RODWELL, Jack (Continued)

Sunderland failed to win a Premier League game which Rodwell started until the February of his third season, an astonishing run of 39 appearances with Rodwell being substituted early in the second half of the game in which he did actually start in a winning league XI. Reputedly, he was the only player not to take a pay cut when the side were relegated from the Premier League in 2017 at a time when over 40 of the club's staff were made redundant. Manager Chris Coleman openly wondered about the reasons for Rodwell's apparent lack of commitment and there were worries about his mental state - if not his bank balance.

Shortly after it was agreed to terminate his contract with one year still remaining, Rodwell joined Blackburn Rovers where he played 17+5 games (scoring once) in 18 months before leaving on a free to join Sheffield United where he made one start and had one game off the bench in just under two years. In November 2021, he moved to Australia where he was signed by ex-Sunderland midfielder Carl Robinson. As of June 2022, he had scored three times in 10+4 A League games.

He had been only 20 when winning the first of his three full England caps against Spain at Wembley. He started one game and came on as a sub twice for England, totalling 97 minutes playing time. He also won 21 Under 21 caps (scoring twice) and made a total of 17 further international appearances at younger levels.

Highly rated from a young age, he was only seven when he joined Everton, played Under 18 football when just 14, debuted for the reserves aged 15 and when making his first-team bow at the age of 16 years and 284 days in the UEFA Cup at AZ Alkmaar became the youngest Everton player to appear in Europe. His Premier League debut followed, as a late sub in a win at Sunderland.

After 68+41 games and eight goals, Manchester City paid £12m for Rodwell in August 2012. He was to claim a Premier League winner's medal in 2013-14 after making five Premier League appearances that season, the last as a late sub in a home draw with Sunderland. In total he played 110 minutes of Premier League action that season, 90 of them in a goalless draw with Stoke. He made only ten starts for City, also coming on as a sub 15 times (often in the last few minutes) and scoring twice.

His father's cousin Tony Rodwell played for Blackpool, Scarborough and Wigan Athletic between 1990 and 1995.

## ROGAN, Anthony Gerard Patrick (Anton)

**POSITION:** Left-back / centre-back

**BIRTHPLACE:** Lenadoon, Belfast, Co Antrim

**DATE OF BIRTH:** 25/03/1966

**HEIGHT:** 5' 11" **WEIGHT:** 12st 6lbs

**SIGNED FROM:** Celtic, 01/10/1991

**DEBUT:** v Brighton & Hove Albion, H, 05/10/1991

**LAST MATCH:** v Grimsby Town, A, 12/04/1993

**MOVED TO:** Oxford United, 06/08/1993

**TEAMS:** Distillery, Celtic, Sunderland, Oxford United, Millwall, Blackpool

**INTERNATIONAL:** Northern Ireland

**SAFC TOTALS:** 56+1 appearances / 1 goal

**A member of Sunderland's 1992 FA Cup final team, Anton was always popular with the fans and his teammates with whom he was renowned as a dressing room joker. Rogan came from Celtic where he had been part of their centenary season double winners in 1988 (when he had set up a goal in the cup final against Dundee United), but two years later he had seen his decisive cup final shoot-out spot-kick saved as his side lost 9-8 to Aberdeen.**

Rogan had come to Celtic from Distillery who he had joined after representing Red Star and St Oliver Plunkett FC as a youngster when he also played Gaelic football. Celtic had maintained their interest in the player who twice broke his leg - the first time in a game against Crusaders - after they expressed an interest in signing him. Anton was to make 153+13 appearances for Celtic, one of his five goals coming in a win over Rangers.

Former Sunderland winger Billy Bingham capped him for Northern Ireland but as a Celtic player and Catholic he was subjected to sectarian abuse. He was to later reveal that growing up during the Troubles in Northern Ireland, eight or nine people from his street of 30 houses had been killed. Anton won 18 caps, starting with a debut against Yugoslavia in 1988 and ending ten years later as a substitute against Germany.

He left Sunderland to join Oxford United as part of the deal to bring Andy Melville to Wearside. It was to prove a move with a bonus for 'Rogie' who married a local girl while playing for Oxford where he later settled and set up a business dealing in asbestos removal before running a taxi and tour company with his wife. There were 58 league appearances and three goals for Oxford, 34+6 and eight goals for Millwall where he played for Jimmy Nicholl and finally 11+5 games for Blackpool.

## ROGERS, John (Jack)

**POSITION:** Inside-right / centre-forward

**BIRTHPLACE:** Helston, Cornwall

**DATE OF BIRTH:** 08/02/1893 - 16/07/1965

**HEIGHT:** 5' 9" **WEIGHT:** 11st 7lbs

**SIGNED FROM:** Aberdare Athletic, 07/05/1923

**DEBUT:** v Arsenal, A, 12/04/1924

**LAST MATCH:** v Newcastle United, A, 21/02/1925

**MOVED TO:** Norwich City, 15/10/1925

**TEAMS:** Crystal Palace, Aberdare Athletic, Sunderland, Norwich City, Newquay

**SAFC TOTALS:** 9 appearances / 3 goals

**All but one of Jack Rogers' appearances came in 1924-25, but his time in the north east was short lived. It was thought by Sunderland that Jack was lacking in speed and he left to play 13 games for Norwich for whom he maintained a decent scoring record with four goals, before returning to the south west where he went on to become Mayor of his birthplace between 1951 and 53.**

Rogers was a 21-year-old professional at Crystal Palace when he, along with many other footballers, signed up to fight in December 1914. A member of the 23rd Middlesex regiment during his army days he had scored nine goals in 59 games for Aberdare who he played for in their first season as a Football League club in Division Three South. Before and after playing professional football, Jack had followed in his father's footsteps by working as a boot maker.

## ROOKS, Richard (Dickie)

**POSITION:** Centre-half

**BIRTHPLACE:** Sunderland, Co Durham

**DATE OF BIRTH:** 29/05/1940

**HEIGHT:** 5' 10" **WEIGHT:** 12st 0lbs

**SIGNED FROM:** Sunderland boys, 30/05/1957

**DEBUT:** v Norwich City, A, 03/04/1961

**LAST MATCH:** v Wolverhampton Wanderers, A, 20/04/1965

**MOVED TO:** Middlesbrough, 27/08/1965

**TEAMS:** Sunderland, Middlesbrough, Bristol City, Willington

**SAFC TOTALS:** 40 appearances / 3 goals

**One of the most successful centre-halves to understudy Charlie Hurley, Dickie Rooks played in five different seasons for Sunderland, his best year being in the top flight in 1964-65 when he scored twice in 16 games and additionally played a couple of League Cup games.**

Recovering from a cartilage injury, he went on to play 150 games for Middlesbrough where he signed for Raich Carter. Sometimes appearing at centre-forward, Rooks registered 14 goals for the Teessiders including a hat-trick against Cardiff in May 1966, although that was not enough for the club to avoid going down to Division Three. Stan Anderson had recently taken over as manager and under his old Sunderland teammate Rooks immediately helped Boro to promotion.

In the summer of 1969 he began a three year association with Bristol City for whom he made 96 league appearances and scored four goals. Rooks returned to the north east to finish his career as player/manager of Willington. He then managed in the Ipswich league with Hadleigh United before taking over the hot-seat at Scunthorpe United in December 1974, but had to seek re-election in 1975. He went on to coach the island of Zanzibar in east Africa before returning to the north east of England and becoming an FA coach as well as a self-employed builder in East Herrington.

## ROONEY, Peter

**POSITION:** Forward

**BIRTHPLACE:** Monkwearmouth, Co Durham

**DATE OF BIRTH:** 04/11/1865 - 01/01/1906

**SIGNED FROM:** Sunderland Bede's
signed between 26/01/1886 and 10/04/1886

**DEBUT:** v Newcastle West End, A, 13/11/1886

**LAST MATCH:** v Morpeth Harriers, A, 22/10/1887

**MOVED TO:** North Sands Rovers, 01/11/1887

**TEAMS:** Sunderland Bede's, Sunderland, North Sands Rovers, Monkwearmouth Workmen's Hall

**SAFC TOTALS:** 2 appearances / 0 goals

**This pre-league player met an untimely end when he died of choking on New Year's Day 1906 when he was 40, leaving behind eight children. As well as his English (FA) Cup appearances in games that were replayed after protests, he is known to have played in at least17 friendlies starting with a 3-3 home draw with Birtley on 10 April 1886 and scoring against a team called Cramlington Union Jacks and also against Notts Mellors in September 1887.**

Rooney had Irish ancestry. His family had come to England during the Irish potato famine. Both during and after his time as a footballer he worked as a shipyard rivetter and played for his shipyard side North Sands Rovers, vice captaining them in 1888-89 season. One of Peter's sons, Bernard, married the granddaughter of Rooney's 1880s teammate Willie Potts. Bernard had opportunities to sign for Sunderland and Arsenal, but rejected approaches to maintain a well-paid job in the shipyards while playing local football. A great grandson of Peter, also called Peter Rooney, was still a regular supporter at the Stadium of Light as of 2010.

## ROOSE, Leigh Richmond (Dick)

**POSITION:** Goalkeeper

**BIRTHPLACE:** Holt, Denbighshire

**DATE OF BIRTH:** 26/11/1877 - 07/10/1916

**HEIGHT:** 6' 1" **WEIGHT:** 13st 6lbs

**SIGNED FROM:** Stoke, 14/01/1908

**DEBUT:** v Preston North End, A, 18/01/1908

**LAST MATCH:** v Newcastle United, A, 19/11/1910

**MOVED TO:** Huddersfield Town, 04/04/1911

**TEAMS:** Aberystwyth, Aberystwyth Town, Druids, London Welsh, Stoke, Port Vale, Everton, Stoke, Sunderland, Celtic, Huddersfield Town, Aston Villa, Woolwich Arsenal, Aberystwyth Town, Llandudno Town

**INTERNATIONAL:** Wales

**SAFC TOTALS:** 99 appearances / 0 goals

**L R Roose was one of the great figures of pre-World War One football, but sadly was killed in action on the Somme, his body never being found. Roose was a huge character and a gigantic joker. He would think nothing of climbing on the crossbar and entertaining fans with gymnastic displays while play was at the other end while on one occasion he turned up for a Wales international against Ireland with his hand badly strapped saying he was unfit, only to remove the strapping shortly before the game and reveal it had been a hoax.**

When Roose played, goalkeepers could handle the ball anywhere in their own half. Most did not stray far from their goal but Roose was adept at bouncing the ball basketball style almost to the half way line and then launching powerful throws into the opposition box. It was largely through this that the Laws were changed restricting the keeper's handling to the penalty area. Roose was also known to have an incredibly powerful punch. This did not just apply to the football. Before signing for Sunderland, after a game for Stoke at Roker Park he overheard a Sunderland supporter describing his side as 'ten cads and a goalkeeper' and promptly knocked them out. He was also once suspended by the FA for 14 days for assaulting a Sunderland director.

Playing as an amateur Roose jumped from team to team although only at Stoke where he had two spells and totalled 159 league games did he play more than at Sunderland. On one occasion in March 1910 instead of playing for Sunderland at Chelsea he turned out as a one-off for Celtic in a Scottish Cup semi-final against Clyde. A week earlier he had played against Scotland and when Celtic's keeper Davy Adams caught pneumonia Celtic persuaded Roose to play for them. However Clyde won 3-1 with Roose running beyond the half-way line to sportingly shake the hand of the Clyde player who had scored the third goal.

He also played very briefly for Druids, Huddersfield (5), Aston Villa (10) and Woolwich Arsenal (13) while also turning out once for Port Vale reserves against the reserves of his old club Stoke in a match that determined the winners of the North Staffordshire and District League. In typical fashion he insisted on playing against Stoke in his old Stoke shirt and wound up the Stoke supporters so much that according to contemporary reports, it needed police to protect him afterwards.

Always the showman, on the final game of an overseas tour with Sunderland in May 1909 Roose played as a defender rather than a goalkeeper in a game at Nuremberg. Earlier that season he had been Sunderland's goalkeeper in the legendary 9-1 win at Newcastle but a subsequent game at St James in 1910 was to be his last for the club as he suffered a broken wrist.

Roose started with Aberystwyth Town, the first of 85 games coming in October 1895 in a 6-0 win over Whitchurch. Five years later he was the hero of a 3-0 Welsh Cup final win over Druids that saw him chaired off the pitch. He reached the semi-final of the English (FA) Cup with Everton in 1905.

Although an amateur he made a lot of money from the game through expenses. Most notably on one occasion when playing for Stoke at Aston Villa he missed his train from his London residence and so hired his own train at the cost of £31 (a fortune at the time) and instructed the train company to send the bill to the club!

Although he never qualified as a doctor Roose worked in hospitals mainly in London. Renowned to be a stylish dresser in Saville Row suits and a top hat, he dated many glamorous women including the huge music hall star Marie Lloyd. He had also been taught by the eminent author H G Wells and after retiring from football commanded large fees as an after dinner speaker. His brother-in-law Jack Jenkins was an international at rugby for Wales and never one to miss out Roose once turned out as a winger for Jenkins' club side London Welsh.

At the outbreak of war Roose served in the Medical Corps and then the Royal Fusiliers where his throwing ability came to the fore as a designated thrower of grenades. He was awarded the Military Medal for his bravery in repelling an attack by a flame thrower.

An excellent biography, 'Lost in France The Remarkable Life and Death of Leigh Roose, Football's First Superstar' was published in 2007. Without doubt L R Roose was one of Sunderland's best-ever goalkeepers and arguably even more so than 'Tim' Coleman or Len Shackleton, the greatest character to represent the Lads!

## ROSE, Daniel Lee (Danny)

**POSITION:** Left-back

**BIRTHPLACE:** Doncaster, South Yorkshire

**DATE OF BIRTH:** 02/07/1990

**HEIGHT:** 5' 8" **WEIGHT:** 12st 1lbs

**SIGNED FROM:** Tottenham Hotspur, 31/08/2012, on loan

**DEBUT:** v Liverpool, H, 15/09/2012

**LAST MATCH:** v Southampton, H, 12/05/2013

**MOVED TO:** Tottenham Hotspur, 13/05/2013, end of loan

**TEAMS:** Leeds United, Tottenham Hotspur, Watford (L), Peterborough United (L), Bristol City (L), Sunderland (L), Newcastle United (L), Watford (to June 2022)

**INTERNATIONAL:** England and Great Britain Olympic XI

**SAFC TOTALS:** 27+2 appearances / 1 goal

**Rose was an excellent player who was a class act during his year-long loan in the Premier League at Sunderland when he was named the club's Young Player of the Season. He joined the Black Cats just after playing for a Great Britain XI in the 2012 London Olympics. The Yorkshireman began at Leeds but moved to Spurs for £100,000 before making a debut for the Elland Road outfit. Sunderland were one of five clubs Tottenham loaned Danny to before eventually releasing him on a free in the summer of 2021.**

Rose played 165+29 games for Spurs, scoring ten goals. One of those games was the 2019 Champions League final as his side lost to Liverpool in Madrid. He also collected a runners-up medal in the 2015 League Cup final when Spurs were beaten by Chelsea. Runners-up trinkets were also Danny's bitter-sweet reward at international level in the European Championships at Under 17 and Under 19 level in 2007 and 2009. A full international debut came in March 2016 as Rose blossomed in a 3-2 win over Germany in Berlin. As of the end of the 2021-22 season, he had 29 full caps, the most recent in October 2019. When England played at SAFC in 2016, he was an unused sub.

## ROSE, Danny (Continued)

Five of his caps came at the 2018 FIFA World Cup finals in Russia, including a substitute appearance in the semi-final against Croatia.

Named in the PFA Premier League Team of the year in back-to-back seasons in 2016 and 2017. In his pre-Sunderland loans he made 3+4 appearances for Watford, 4+2 for Peterborough, and 13+4 for Bristol City. Six and a half years after being on loan to Sunderland he returned to the north east on loan to Newcastle where he made 12+1 appearances. As of June 2022, his goal for Sunderland in a 6-1 defeat at Aston Villa was his only one other than for Tottenham.

Danny's brother Mitchell played for Rotherham United, Crawley Town, Mansfield Town, Grimsby Town, Notts County and as of 2022, for South Shields. Cousin Michael Rankine played for a long list of league and non-league clubs including Gateshead. An uncle, Mark Rankine listed Wolves and Sheffield United amongst his clubs.

## ROSSITER, Mark

**POSITION:** Right-back

**BIRTHPLACE:** Oranmore, Republic of Ireland

**DATE OF BIRTH:** 27/05/1983

**HEIGHT:** 5' 11" **WEIGHT:** 12st 6lbs

**SIGNED FROM:** Galway United, 01/07/1999

**DEBUT:** v Arsenal, A, 06/11/2002

**LAST MATCH:** v Bolton Wanderers, A, 04/01/2003

**MOVED TO:** Released, 30/06/2004

**TEAMS:** Galway United, Sunderland, Whitby Town (L), Finn Harps, Bohemians, St Patrick's Athletic, Dundalk, Longford Town

**INTERNATIONAL:** Republic of Ireland Under 21

**SAFC TOTALS:** 2+1 appearances / 0 goals

**A talented full-back whose career was ruined by injury, Mark was signed after impressing during a Republic of Ireland U15 game v Wales followed a couple of months later by a week-long trial on Wearside in April 1999.**

He was given a debut at Highbury in a League Cup tie. Although his direct opponent Robert Pires gave the Gunners an early lead, Rossiter had a solid game in helping Sunderland come from two down to win. Having been on loan at Whitby the previous season there would be just two more appearances before he resurrected his career after injury by playing extensively in Ireland. It was on international duty for the Republic's Under 21s against Albania in April 2003 that he suffered a cruciate ligament injury which was followed by the diagnosis of a non-malignant tumour on his right knee.

Mark was to enjoy success with Bohemians with whom he did the double of league and cup in 2008, despite him missing a penalty in the cup final shoot-out with Derry City. He retained the league a year later and won it again in 2014 with Dundalk. His side won the cup the following season, although Mark missed the final against a Cork City side who included Liam Miller, Colin Healy and former Sunderland reserve Billy Dennehy. Rossiter's brother Ian played for five clubs in Ireland.

## ROSTRON, John Wilfred

**POSITION:** Midfielder

**BIRTHPLACE:** Sunderland, Co Durham

**DATE OF BIRTH:** 29/09/1956

**HEIGHT:** 5' 7" **WEIGHT:** 11st 2lbs

**SIGNED FROM:** Arsenal, 08/07/1977

**DEBUT:** v Hull City, A, 20/08/1977

**LAST MATCH:** v Charlton Athletic, H, 06/10/1979

**MOVED TO:** Watford, 18/10/1979

**TEAMS:** Arsenal, Sunderland, Watford, Sheffield Wednesday, Sheffield United, Brentford, Ryhope CW

**INTERNATIONAL:** England schools

**SAFC TOTALS:** 85+4 appearances / 18 goals

**Having played in the same St Thomas Aquinas school and England boys teams as Peter Stronach, Rostron eventually came to his hometown team having started with Arsenal for whom he made a goalscoring debut against Newcastle. He bagged another goal in his next match against Burnley but did not net again in his 15 further games for the Gunners.**

At Sunderland Rostron arrived as a winger, but played in a wide variety of positions, mainly in midfield. He played regularly in his first two seasons and claimed a hat-trick, including two penalties, in a 6-2 win over Sheffield United in a match Sunderland needed to win by four goals to go top of Division Two in late April 1979. Sunderland missed out on promotion that season with Wilf moving on early the following term, a season the Lads went on to be promoted. Perhaps the only Sunderland-born Leeds supporter at the time of the 1973 FA Cup final, Rostron went to Watford where a member of manager Graham Taylor's staff was Bertie Mee the ex-Arsenal manager who Wilf knew from his days there.

At Vicarage Road he gradually became a left-back, not least with John Barnes taking the left-wing berth. He was part of the Hornets team that beat Sunderland 8-0 in September 1982 and went on to be top flight runners-up that season after winning promotion the previous year. A sending off in a local derby with Luton caused him to miss the 1984 FA Cup final. After 317 league games and 22 goals for Watford, where he was Player of the Year twice, he moved to Sheffield where he played seven league games for Wednesday followed by 36 (3 goals) with United where he re-joined Dave Bassett who he had played for at Watford.

A final move took Rostron south again where he scored twice in 42 league games for Brentford where he was also assistant manager before he returned to the north east to run a pine furniture import business. In the autumn of 1983, he had a two-month stint coaching at Gateshead becoming caretaker manager for 24 hours on 4 November. From December 1993, he became player-manager of Ryhope CW until the end of the season.

## ROUTLEDGE, Ronald Wright

**POSITION:** Goalkeeper

**BIRTHPLACE:** Ashington, Northumberland

**DATE OF BIRTH:** 14/10/1937

**HEIGHT:** 5' 8½" **WEIGHT:** 11st 0lbs

**SIGNED FROM:** Burnley, 29/10/1954

**DEBUT:** v Portsmouth, A, 01/05/1957

**LAST MATCH:** v Burnley, A, 12/10/1957

**MOVED TO:** Bradford Park Avenue, 21/05/1958

**TEAMS:** Burnley, Sunderland, Bradford Park Avenue, Ashington

**SAFC TOTALS:** 2 appearances / 0 goals

**A schoolboy friend and teammate of Bobby Charlton with East Northumberland, Routledge initially joined Burnley before coming to Sunderland as a 17-year-old. He debuted in what was Bill Murray's final match as manager and Len Shackleton's last away appearance. Ronnie's second and last game was back at Burnley in the week he turned 20, but on what was Charlie Hurley's second appearance, a youthful Sunderland were on the receiving end of a 6-0 thrashing.**

At the end of the season Routledge moved on to Bradford Park Avenue who were then still a league side. He played 41 times for Park Avenue before joining his hometown team Ashington in August 1962 where he spent nine years whilst also working as a bricklayer. With Ashington, he also became assistant manager, joined the board and spent three years as chairman before retiring from football in 1997 when he was 60.

## ROWELL, Gary

**POSITION:** Midfielder / forward

**BIRTHPLACE:** Seaham, Co Durham

**DATE OF BIRTH:** 06/06/1957

**HEIGHT:** 5' 10" **WEIGHT:** 11st 3lbs

**SIGNED FROM:** Seaham Juniors, 01/07/1972

**DEBUT:** v Oxford United, H, 13/12/1975

**LAST MATCH:** v West Bromwich Albion, 23/04/1984

**MOVED TO:** Norwich City, 24/08/1984

**TEAMS:** Sunderland, Norwich City, Middlesbrough, Brighton & Hove Albion, Dundee, Carlisle United, Burnley

**INTERNATIONAL:** England Under 21

**SAFC TOTALS:** 269+28 appearances / 103 goals

**Forever famed for his hat-trick in a 1979 4-1 win at Newcastle, Rowell was Sunderland's record post-war scorer before Kevin Phillips came along. That achievement was all the more impressive when remembered that Gary played many of his games in midfield rather than as an out-and-out striker.**

Adept at arriving late in the box and snapping up the sort of half-chances fans often regret not being taken, Rowell was coolness personified in front of goal. Rarely would he blast a ball home, precision and placement were his forte. This was also the case with his expert penalty taking. He scored 25 of his 26 competitive penalties taken for Sunderland, giving him the highest percentage completion rate (96%) and putting him third on the converted list behind Billy Clunas (30) and Jackie Mordue (27).

## ROWELL, Gary (Continued)

A keen Sunderland supporter who once rang in sick saying he was unavailable for the youth team because really he wanted to go and watch the first-team during the1973 FA Cup run, he later played alongside several of his cup heroes. A month to the day after his St James' hat-trick, Gary suffered a bad knee ligament injury in a home game with Orient. Earlier in that game he had scored his 24th goal of the season, but the injury was to be followed by a personally barren season (just one goal from a penalty in an Anglo-Scottish Cup game) in a sequence of six seasons where it was the only one in which he was not top scorer.

Released by Len Ashurst in 1984, he joined Norwich. He was on crutches when the sides met in the League (Milk) Cup final at Wembley in 1985. Taking the trophy from his victorious teammates he poignantly raised it aloft in front of the Sunderland supporters who decades later were still regularly chanting, 'We all Live in a Gary Rowell World.' Gary was inducted into the Sunderland Hall of Fame in 2020. In May 1977 he won his solitary England Under 21 cap, coming on as a sub for Laurie Cunningham in a 1-0 win over Finland in Helsinki where his teammates included Peter Daniel and Peter Reid. At Norwich he made just 2+4 appearances scoring once before returning to the north east with Middlesbrough for whom he scored ten times in 27 games. He moved south for twelve games with Brighton, beginning with a debut as a sub back at Roker Park. However, hamstring and toe injuries restricted Gary, although he also made 20 reserve team appearances, scoring once.

This was followed by a brief trial with Dundee for whom he played once as a sub against St Mirren on 1 March 1988 and penultimately seven outings with Carlisle. Finally, he had 19 games for Burnley where he scored once. He stayed in the Burnley area as a financial consultant in the insurance business and became a popular radio summariser to commentator Simon Crabtree covering Sunderland matches as well as having a column in the Sunderland Echo. Rowell's father Jack was on Sunderland's books for six years in the fifties without making a first-team appearance.

## ROWELL, John Frederick

**POSITION:** Outside-left / right-back

**BIRTHPLACE:** Seaham, Co Durham

**DATE OF BIRTH:** 31/12/1918 - 09/03/1988

**HEIGHT:** 5' 11" **WEIGHT:** 11st 7lbs

**SIGNED FROM:** Seaham CW, 08/10/1937

**DEBUT:** v Manchester City, A, 03/11/1937

**LAST MATCH:** v Manchester City, A, 03/11/1937

**MOVED TO:** Brentford, 06/07/1938

**TEAMS:** Seaham CW, Sunderland, Brentford, Horden CW, Bournemouth & Boscombe Athletic, Wrexham, Aldershot, Weymouth, Portland United

**SAFC TOTALS:** 1 appearance / 0 goals

**Fred Rowell's solitary first-team game was the 1937 Charity Shield game when he played on the left-wing in a 2-0 defeat at Manchester City. He had been an apprentice bricklayer when he joined the Lads initially as an amateur before signing professional forms a week before his first-team game.**

He did not get a league game during his war-afflicted time with Brentford, but made 31 league appearances for Bournemouth after the conflict. During this time he grabbed eleven goals in addition to the five he scored in eleven war-time games for the club in 1941-42. He added 41 league appearances for Wrexham (4 goals) and five for Aldershot, becoming a full-back as he got older. After retiring from football Fred returned to Bournemouth where he became trainer for a gasworks team. His uncle Harry played in the Wearside League and brother Alan was a goalkeeper on Sunderland's books from 1947 to 1951.

## ROWLANDSON, Thomas Sowerby (Tom)

**POSITION:** Goalkeeper

**BIRTHPLACE:** Newton Morrell, North Riding of Yorkshire

**DATE OF BIRTH:** 22/02/1880 - 15/09/1916

**HEIGHT:** 5' 11"

**SIGNED FROM:** Preston North End, 20/11/1903

**DEBUT:** v Wolverhampton Wanderers, H, 01/04/1904

**LAST MATCH:** v Manchester City, H, 01/04/1905

**MOVED TO:** Newcastle United, 27/09/1905

**TEAMS:** Darlington, Preston North End, Cambridge University, Old Carthusians, Corinthians, Sunderland, Newcastle United, Corinthians

**INTERNATIONAL:** England Amateur

**SAFC TOTALS:** 12 appearances / 0 goals

**One of the former players to be killed in France during World War One, Rowlandson's name is on the plaque commemorating the Fallen adjacent to the Fans' statue at the Stadium of Light.**

From a well-to-do family, Tom was an all-round sportsman excelling at cricket, cycling and billiards as well as football. In 1903 and 1904 he gained a Blue from Cambridge University for keeping goal against their Oxford counterparts. Having played for Charterhouse School he went on to make 75 appearances for the famous Corinthians. These included the 1904 Sheriff of London Shield game when Corinthians came from 2-0 down to defeat cup-holders Bury 10-3.

He had not played the previous season when league champions Sunderland beat Corinthians. Bury were also the opponents on his sole appearance for Newcastle United in October 1905. He continued to play for Corinthians while with Sunderland but he was signed by Sunderland from Preston who held his registration forms.

Capped by England at amateur level he led an amateur team to South Africa, Hungary, Norway, Sweden and Canada. His international debut had come in a 2-1 win over Ireland in Dublin ten days before Christmas in 1906.

He also played in England amateurs next match, an 8-1 win away to the Netherlands before giving way to another goalkeeper who played for Sunderland, Ron Brebner.

A Justice of the Peace in the North Riding of Yorkshire, he handed over his home to the Red Cross during the Great War so it could be used as an Auxiliary Home Hospital. He was to need help himself when having been appointed temporary captain in the 2/4th Battalion of the Yorkshire Regiment on 8 October 2015, just under a year later, he was hit by a German grenade at the Battle of the Somme. A Harrogate born Private was injured by shrapnel in getting Tom back into the trenches only for Rowlandson to die of his wounds. He is buried at Becourt Military Cemetery. In the New Year's Honours List of 1916, he had been awarded the Military Medal for gallantry.

## ROY, Eric Serge

**POSITION:** Midfielder

**BIRTHPLACE:** Nice, France

**DATE OF BIRTH:** 26/09/1967

**HEIGHT:** 6' 1" **WEIGHT:** 10st 10lbs

**SIGNED FROM:** Olympique Marseille, 24/08/1999

**DEBUT:** v Leicester City, H, 11/09/1999

**LAST MATCH:** v Luton Town, A, 26/09/2000

**MOVED TO:** Troyes, 31/01/2001

**TEAMS:** OGC Nice, SC Toulon, Olympique Lyonnais, Olympique Marseille, Sunderland, Troyes, Rayo Vallecano, Nice

**SAFC TOTALS:** 27+7 appearances / 1 goal

**A tall, stylish midfielder, Eric's finest game was in a 4-1 win over Chelsea in December 1999. Sunderland were to be the only English club he played for in a career spent mainly in his homeland of France. He went on to be a well-known pundit on TV in France, but revealed on a visit back to Sunderland that the Wearsiders held very fond memories for him.**

Eric's father Serge was capped by France against Spain in Madrid in 1961 and played for Beaune, Besancon, Monaco, Valenciennes, Marseille and Nice. Eric started with Nice, scoring four goals in 86 league games before a 1992 move to Toulon where he scored twice in 34 games before moving to Lyon a year later.

After 111 games and nine goals he moved to Marseille in 1996, scoring ten times in 77 appearances before coming to Sunderland. Returning to France he played six games for Troyes before a twelve-game stint in Spain with Rayo Vallecano in 2001-02 after which he took his career total to over 400 league games with 52 further appearances (and two goals) with Nice.

Eric stayed with the club as director of marketing and PR before becoming sporting director prior to taking over as manager in March 2010. Two years later he was controversially dismissed only for him later to receive a payment reported to be almost €300,000 for wrongful dismissal.

He then had 18 months as sporting director of RC Lens before taking up the same role at Watford in December 2019 only to leave at the end of the season. Also an accomplished tennis player, Sunderland saw precious little of Eric Roy, but he was undoubtedly one of the better French players to come to the club.

## RUITER, Robbin Floris Dirk

**POSITION:** Goalkeeper

**BIRTHPLACE:** Amsterdam, Netherlands

**DATE OF BIRTH:** 25/03/1987

**HEIGHT:** 6' 5" **WEIGHT:** 12 st 4lbs

**SIGNED FROM:** Unattached, 02/08/2017

**DEBUT:** v Carlisle United, A, 22/08/2017

**LAST MATCH:** v Manchester City Under 21s, H, 22/01/2019

**MOVED TO:** PSV Eindhoven, 27/06/2019

**TEAMS:** Volendam, Utrecht, Sunderland, PSV Eindhoven, Willem II, Cambuur (to July 2022)

**SAFC TOTALS:** 27+1 appearances / 0 goals

**One of three goalkeepers who each endured a torrid time as Sunderland suffered a second consecutive relegation in 2018, Ruiter was a keeper who at times was beaten far too easily on his near post. One home game in particular - a 2-2 draw with Millwall in which Lions goalkeeper Jordan Archer had an even worse time - seemed to illustrate that the Dutch keeper was not up to the standard Sunderland required, although he did have better days.**

There was no problem with his attitude. Robin always appeared to be determined to do his best and in 2022, after being released from Willem II, was quoted as saying of Sunderland, "I love that club. I will go back to watch the club one day because I can't speak highly enough of it".

He made 78 appearances for his first club Volendam, 157 in the Dutch top flight with Utrecht and played twice for PSV. These were both 4-1 wins, away to Rosenborg in the Europa League and at home to a VVV Venlo side that included Lee Cattermole. He also played in the Europa League for Willem II, keeping a clean sheet in a 5-0 win at Progres Niederkorn of Luxembourg. He made a dozen Eredivisie appearances for Willem who released him at the end of January 2022. A few weeks later, Robbin had an unsuccessful trial at Ajax as they looked for a temporary goalkeeper due to an injury crisis and signed for Cambuur in July 2022.

## RUSH, David

**POSITION:** Centre-forward

**BIRTHPLACE:** Sunderland, Co Durham

**DATE OF BIRTH:** 15/05/1971

**HEIGHT:** 5' 11" **WEIGHT:** 10st 10lbs

**SIGNED FROM:** Notts County, 29/12/1988

**DEBUT:** v Fulham, H, 19/09/1989

**LAST MATCH:** v Watford, H, 19/03/1994

**MOVED TO:** Oxford United, 21/09/1994

**TEAMS:** Notts County, Sunderland, Hartlepool United (L), Peterborough United (L), Cambridge United (L), Oxford United, York City, Morpeth, Hartlepool United, Barrow, Seaham Red Star

**SAFC TOTALS:** 51+21 appearances / 13 goals

**An FA Cup finalist in 1992, that season was speed merchant Rush's best in terms of appearances as he played in a total of 32 games. He played in five different seasons, but only twice reached double figures in terms of starts.**

David was loaned out three times by Sunderland totalling 14 league games and scoring three times before being sold to Oxford United for £100,000 in 1994 when he signed for his former Sunderland manager Denis Smith. After 24 goals in 78+32 games for the U's, David had 2+2 games for York and 5+7 for Hartlepool without scoring.

He then moved onto the non-league scene with 7+9 games and three goals in 1999-2000 for Barrow before joining Seaham Red Star when he was still in his late twenties. David managed Hebburn Town in the Northern League between May and September 2009. Four years later he became assistant manager to his old SAFC teammate Anthony Smith at Gateshead, serving as caretaker boss before briefly carrying on under Gary Mills. Within days of leaving Gateshead in 2013 Rush established his own football academy in Whickham. In September 2017 Rush became a director of a football academy in Malta after spells coaching in Croatia and Thailand. He has also worked as a scout for Tranmere Rovers.

## RUSSELL, Craig Stewart

**POSITION:** Centre-forward

**BIRTHPLACE:** Jarrow, Co Durham

**DATE OF BIRTH:** 04/02/1974

**HEIGHT:** 5' 10" **WEIGHT:** 12st 4lbs

**SIGNED FROM:** Hebburn Juniors, 01/07/1990

**DEBUT:** v Watford, H, 02/11/1991

**LAST MATCH:** v Stockport County, A, 01/11/1997

**MOVED TO:** Manchester City, 14/11/1997

**TEAMS:** Sunderland, Manchester City, Tranmere Rovers (L), Port Vale (L), Darlington (L), Oxford United (L), St Johnstone, Carlisle United, Darlington, South Shields

**SAFC TOTALS:** 118+56 appearances / 34 goals

**Top scorer in the 1996 second tier-winning team, Craig came from an ardent Sunderland supporting family and claims he was conceived on the night Sunderland won the cup in 1973! Mascot for the Lads on his tenth birthday, 'Russ' scored four goals in a December 1995 win that took Sunderland to the top of the table after a 6-0 win against a Millwall side managed by Mick McCarthy and including Anton Rogan and Alex Rae.**

## RUSSELL, Craig (Continued)

At the time of his departure Craig was the most used substitute in Sunderland's history. Frustrated at often being used in wide positions rather than in his most effective role through the middle, Russell ended up not only sometimes playing wide after his transfer, but even being utilised as a wing-back. He went to Manchester City in a £1m rated swap deal with Nicky Summerbee and scored four goals in 27+10 games. Relegated to the third tier in his first season, City won immediate promotion, Craig making eleven appearances in a side that included Jeff Whitley.

The last of Russell's City outings came at Blackpool in January 1999 at which point he was loaned to Port Vale (8/1) having already had a spell on loan to Tranmere (3+1/0). City proceeded to loan him to Darlington (11+1/2), Oxford (5+1/0) and finally St Johnstone who he signed for after scoring on his debut at Motherwell in April 2000.

There were just three more goals in a further 20+21 games for the club before a January 2003 move to Carlisle where in 16+10 games his only goal came in a win at Torquay. After a year in Cumbria, Craig re-joined Darlington, then of League Two. 23+19 games produced two goals bringing his career total to 48, almost three-quarters of which had come for Sunderland.

Craig carried on playing with South Shields and in 2005 became a part-time masseur with Newcastle Falcons rugby club and subsequently, a fitness coach at Newcastle United. In July 2009 he returned to Sunderland as a masseur and also became part-time masseur for the Republic of Ireland. After leaving Sunderland in 2021, he once again took up a post at Newcastle.

## RUSSELL, James Walker

**POSITION:** Inside/ outside-right
**BIRTHPLACE:** Edinburgh, Midlothian
**DATE OF BIRTH:** 14/09/1916 - 17/08/1994
**HEIGHT:** 5' 9" **WEIGHT:** 10st 4lbs
**SIGNED FROM:** Craigmer Juveniles, 08/06/1934
**DEBUT:** v Derby County, A, 25/04/1936
**LAST MATCH:** v Wolverhampton Wanderers, A, 15/09/1937
**MOVED TO:** Norwich City, 14/05/1938
**TEAMS:** Sunderland, Norwich City, North Shields (WW2 Guest), Sunderland (WW2 Guest), Carlisle United (WW2 Guest), Middlesbrough (WW2 Guest), Crystal Palace, New Brighton, Fleetwood
**INTERNATIONAL:** Scotland Schoolboy
**SAFC TOTALS:** 5 appearances / 0 goals

**Russell came to Wearside as a 17-year-old in 1934 after failed trials with Queens Park and Hearts. A Scottish Schoolboy international in 1929, 1930 and 1931, he had caught the eye of SAFC manager John Cochrane during Edinburgh side Craigmer Juveniles' 1-1 draw at South Shields St Andrews on 16 April 1934.**

Russell played once in the title-winning season of 1935-36, making his debut in a 4-0 defeat at Derby on the last day of the season - but the trophy had been secured three games earlier. He waited almost a year for another game, but when it came the match went even more badly as the Lads lost 6-0 at Grimsby - 48 hours after Sunderland had qualified for the FA Cup final.

A fee of £1,500 took him to Norwich City before World War Two in which he worked as an electrician and turned out for North Shields, Carlisle and Middlesbrough as a 'Guest' player. In August 1940, he also 'Guested' for Sunderland in a 3-3 draw with Sunderland Police.

After the war he spent a season with Crystal Palace in Division Three South. Debuting against Notts County in December 1946 James went on to play 21 times scoring five goals before moving to New Brighton for two years and then joining Fleetwood in July 1949. Following his retirement from the game Russell emigrated to North America, living in Montreal, Detroit and finally Florida where he passed away in August 1994.

## RYAN, Richard (Richie)

**POSITION:** Midfielder
**BIRTHPLACE:** Templetuohy, Republic of Ireland
**DATE OF BIRTH:** 06/01/1985
**HEIGHT:** 5' 10" **WEIGHT:** 11st 9lbs
**SIGNED FROM:** Belvedere, 01/07/2001
**DEBUT:** v Newcastle United, H, 26/04/2003
**LAST MATCH:** v Arsenal, H, 11/05/2003
**MOVED TO:** Scunthorpe United, 31/05/2005
**TEAMS:** Belvedere, Sunderland, Scunthorpe United, Boston, Royal Antwerp, Sligo Rovers, Dundee United, Shamrock Rovers, Ottowa Fury, Jacksonville Armada, Miami, Cincinnati, El Paso Locomotive
**INTERNATIONAL:** Republic of Ireland Under 19, League of Ireland XI
**SAFC TOTALS:** 0+2 appearances / 0 goals

**This fair haired midfielder was signed from Dublin based youth team Belvedere, for whom Thomas Butler and Stephen Elliott started their careers, and was given a couple of late-season games - including a derby - as a substitute by Mick McCarthy in the 2002-03 relegation season. Despite being highly rated in his teens Ryan did not progress at top level, but went on to have a widely travelled career winning three trophies in Ireland and playing on the continent as well as extensively on the other side of the Atlantic.**

After leaving Sunderland he made 10+7 appearances for Scunthorpe, scoring his only goal in the League (Carling) Cup against Tranmere Rovers when he was a teammate of Peter Beagrie and in opposition to Sam Aiston. In the summer of 2006 he moved to Boston United, debuting in a League Two game with MK Dons and going on to play 9+5 times.

After a season at Boston he moved to Belgium making the first of eight appearances for Royal Antwerp against Kortrijk. Returning to Ireland in 2008 with Sligo, Richie went on to be PFAI Player of the Year in 2010 and the following season captained the club to the FAI Cup after beating Shelbourne on penalties.

In November of 2011 he tried his luck in Scotland with Dundee United. Twenty-six of his 44 appearances were as sub but he did play the full 90 minutes of a 2-2 home draw with Dinamo Moscow in the Europa League. After nine games back in Ireland with Shamrock Rovers, where he won the League of Ireland Cup, he moved to the North America in December 2013. As in his European career Ryan was often on the move but was Ottowa Fury's Player of the Year in 2014 and won the NASL Fall Championship with them the following year, later commanding a $750,000 fee, at the time a league record transfer fee, when moving between Jacksonville Armada and Miami FC. As of May 2022, he was still playing in America for El Paso Locomotive.

## SADDINGTON, Nigel John

**POSITION:** Centre-half
**BIRTHPLACE:** Sunderland, Co Durham
**DATE OF BIRTH:** 09/12/1965 - 25/01/2019
**HEIGHT:** 6' 1" **WEIGHT:** 12st 6lbs
**SIGNED FROM:** Doncaster Rovers, 17/01/1986
**DEBUT:** v Barnsley, H, 16/09/1986
**LAST MATCH:** v Derby County, H, 14/02/1987
**MOVED TO:** Carlisle United, 18/02/1988
**TEAMS:** Doncaster Rovers, Sunderland, Carlisle United, Gateshead
**SAFC TOTALS:** 5 appearances / 0 goals

**Nigel played for Silksworth Juniors, Coles Cranes and Sporting Club Vaux before Leeds United's captain against Sunderland in the 1973 FA Cup final - Billy Bremner - signed him for Doncaster Rovers. In January 1986 Lawrie McMenemy took Saddington on loan, before signing him on a permanent basis. Six months later Nigel netted a penalty in a successful shoot-out on his debut and was part of a promotion winning Central League reserve team.**

Moving on to Carlisle for £12,500 Nigel became captain and as well as playing against Liverpool in the FA Cup went on to play 97 league games, once scoring ten goals in a season, half of them penalties. At the age of 25, Saddington was diagnosed with ME and released by the Cumbrians. He continued to play football, firstly with Gateshead (17 games) and then in local football with Nissan, earning a living outside the game as a car salesman. Nigel also was the only former player known to buy a house on the former site of Roker Park.

## SAHA, Louis Laurent

**POSITION:** Forward
**BIRTHPLACE:** Paris, France
**DATE OF BIRTH:** 08/08/1978
**HEIGHT:** 6' 0" **WEIGHT:** 13st 5lbs
**SIGNED FROM:** Unattached, 16/08/2012
**DEBUT:** v Arsenal, A, 18/08/2012
**LAST MATCH:** v Chelsea, H, 08/12/2012
**MOVED TO:** Contract expired, 31/01/2013
**TEAMS:** Metz, Newcastle United (L), Fulham, Manchester United, Everton, Tottenham Hotspur, Sunderland, Lazio
**INTERNATIONAL:** France
**SAFC TOTALS:** 2+12 appearances / 0 goals

**Saha's stint at Sunderland was little more than a footnote on a distinguished career. A free agent when coming to the club he only stayed half a season and never started a league game.**

He had been suspended for the 2006 FIFA World Cup final for France having been cautioned in a brief appearance in the semi-final, but altogether scored four times in 20 internationals. Two years later he missed another showpiece occasion when injury ruled him out of the Champions League final whilst he was with Manchester United.

He scored 42 times in 124 games for United across five seasons in which he twice won the Premier League. He also won the League Cup in 2006 when he scored in the final in which he was teammates with Wes Brown, John O'Shea and Kieran Richardson against a Wigan line-up that featured Pascal Chimbonda, Graham Kavanagh and one time Sunderland reserve keeper Mike Pollitt.

Newcastle United had been Saha's first English club when he joined the Magpies on loan from Metz in 1998-99. 6+6 outings brought two goals while with Metz Louis scored six goals in 22+27 games. He had joined the club having progressed through youth football with FC Soisy-Andilly-Margency and the famed Clairefontaine academy. In the summer of millennium year Fulham paid £2.1m for Saha who excelled with 53 goals in exactly 100 league starts and totalled 61 goals in 120+24 games, winning the Football League First Division in 2001 and the Intertoto Cup the following year.

Such form led to his move to Manchester United with Everton Saha's destination after his time at Old Trafford. There were 35 goals in 78+37 appearances for Everton, one of those goals being the quickest-ever in an FA Cup final when he scored after just 25 seconds in 2009 but David Moyes' team still lost to Chelsea despite Saha's early goal for a team that included future Sunderland men Joleon Lescott, Steven Pienaar, James Vaughan as well as having Jack Rodwell as an unused sub.

Saha's stint at Goodison Park was followed by four goals in 6+6 games for Spurs before coming to Sunderland. After leaving Wearside, Louis completed his career with a solitary start plus five appearances in Serie A with Lazio. In 2012 he published a self-penned book of reflections on the game entitled 'Thinking Inside the Box.'

## SAMPSON, Ian

**POSITION:** Centre-half
**BIRTHPLACE:** Wakefield, Yorkshire
**DATE OF BIRTH:** 14/11/1968
**HEIGHT:** 6' 2" **WEIGHT:** 12st 8lbs
**SIGNED FROM:** Goole Town, 12/11/1990
**DEBUT:** v Millwall, A, 24/08/1991
**LAST MATCH:** v Charlton Athletic, A, 22/02/1994
**MOVED TO:** Northampton Town, 04/08/1994
**TEAMS:** Driffield Town, Bridlington Town, Goole Town, Sunderland, Northampton Town, Tottenham Hotspur (L)
**SAFC TOTALS:** 14+7 appearances / 1 goal

**Ian Sampson was a decent no nonsense centre-half although he did not get many games, eleven in the season of his debut being his best return. He went on to give great service to Northampton Town where after an initial loan from Sunderland he became the Cobblers' second highest appearance maker, totalling 440+11 games and scoring 30 times.**

In 1997 and 1998, Ian made successive Wembley Play-Off appearances, winning the first against Swansea but losing the second to Grimsby. He later managed the club after two spells as caretaker-boss having coached at youth and first-team level. During his time in charge, Northampton knocked Liverpool out of the League Cup in a penalty shoot-out at Anfield in September 2010. He also managed Corby Town, but returned to Northampton as Academy Manager in October 2019 and was part of their first-team backroom staff as caretaker-assistant manager when Northampton played their final game before relegation from League One at Sunderland in 2021.

As a player, Sampson also had a quirkily brief loan to Tottenham Hotspur in the summer of 1995. Spurs produced a patchwork side to play in their Intertoto Cup campaign with Sampson playing three times and scoring against NK Rudar Velenje of Slovenia.

## SANDERSON, Dion Dannie Leonard

**POSITION:** Defender
**BIRTHPLACE:** Wednesfield, Wolverhampton, West Midlands
**DATE OF BIRTH:** 15/12/1999
**HEIGHT:** 6' 2" **WEIGHT:** 12st 4lbs
**SIGNED FROM:** Wolverhampton Wanderers, 16/10/2020 on loan
**DEBUT:** v Rochdale, A, 27/10/2020
**LAST MATCH:** v Wigan Athletic, A, 13/04/2021
**MOVED TO:** Wolverhampton Wanderers, 27/04/2021 end of loan due to injury
**TEAMS:** Wolverhampton Wanderers, Cardiff City (L), Sunderland (L), Birmingham City (L), QPR (L), Birmingham City (L) (to July 2022)
**SAFC TOTALS:** 20+7 appearances / 1 goal

## SANDERSON, Dion (Continued)

**The nephew of 1984 Olympic gold medallist javelin thrower Tessa Sanderson, Dion was an outstanding loanee who Sunderland reportedly attempted to buy at the end of his loan period having brought him in after a serious injury to new signing Arbenit Xhemajli.**

Quick and comfortable on the ball, Sanderson had to be patient when he arrived at Sunderland as despite doing well whenever he played, it took a few weeks for him to gain a regular starting spot having been utilised in a variety of defensive roles. In December 2020 he became the first player to be used as a fourth substitute by Sunderland in a league game when he came off the bench at Burton Albion when additional subs were temporarily allowed during the Covid pandemic.

Sunderland was Dion's second loan from Wolves who he joined when he was nine. The previous season he had made nine starts plus one game as sub in the Championship with Cardiff. He returned to the Championship the season after his Sunderland sojourn, firstly with Birmingham (15+1/0) and subsequently (QPR 11+1/0) before a summer 2022 return to St Andrews on a second loan to Birmingham. To this point his solitary appearance for his parent club Wolves was a start in a League (Carabao) Cup defeat at Aston Villa in October 2019, although he had won the pre-season Asia Cup with them in China that summer.

## SAUNDERS, Percy Kitchener

**POSITION:** Inside-forward
**BIRTHPLACE:** Newhaven
**DATE OF BIRTH:** 09/07/1916 - 02/03/1942
**HEIGHT:** 5' 8" **WEIGHT:** 10st 8lbs
**SIGNED FROM:** Newhaven Town, 09/10/1934
**DEBUT:** v Portsmouth, A, 13/03/1937
**LAST MATCH:** v Bolton Wanderers, A, 08/04/1939
**MOVED TO:** Brentford, 29/06/1939
**TEAMS:** Newhaven Town, Sunderland, Brentford, Portsmouth (WW2 Guest).
**SAFC TOTALS:** 26 appearances / 6 goals

**The only former Sunderland player to die in action during World War Two, Percy Saunders' name joins those who died during World War One on a memorial plaque at the Fans' statue at the Stadium of Light. His ship, the SS Rooseboom was torpedoed in the Indian Ocean as evacuations took place due to the advance of Japanese forces.**

A sergeant in the Royal Army Ordnance Corps, there is also a memorial naming Saunders in Singapore cemetery. Born during World War One, Percy had been given the name of Kitchener after the World War One Secretary of State for War who had been killed the month before Saunders was born.

Percy scored a hat-trick 25 days after joining Sunderland on his debut for the reserves in a 9-1 win over Throckley Welfare. He had to wait another two and a half years before his full debut as a 20-year-old at Portsmouth who he would make three 'Guest' appearances for during the 1941-42 war-time season, scoring once. His best season was in 1937-38.

He joined Bobby Gurney on the scoresheet in a first-day-of-the-season win at Middlesbrough and held his place for the first seven games, scoring twice more before ending the campaign with five goals from 15 appearances, including a goal in a 6-1 win at WBA where Raich Carter scored a hat-trick. As a young player with the world at his feet, playing top-level football, who was to know that Saunders would be one of the millions to cruelly lose his life in the forthcoming war, in his case at the age of 25. Saunders had left Sunderland just before the war, joining fellow top-flight side Brentford for whom he scored once in playing two of their three games of the 1939-40 season that was abandoned when war was declared.

## SAXTON, Arthur William

**POSITION:** Outside-left
**BIRTHPLACE:** Breaston, Derbyshire
**DATE OF BIRTH:** 28/08/1874 - 06/02/1911
**HEIGHT:** 5' 7½" **WEIGHT:** 11st 7lbs
**SIGNED FROM:** Stalybridge Rovers, 19/01/1898
**DEBUT:** v Notts County, A, 05/02/1898
**LAST MATCH:** v Preston North End, H, 31/12/1898
**MOVED TO:** Dispensed with services, 27/02/1899
**TEAMS:** Long Eaton Rovers, Mansfield Greenhalgh, Loughborough, Glossop North End, Stalybridge Rovers, Sunderland, Bedminster, Luton Town, Northampton Town, Long Eaton Rovers
**SAFC TOTALS:** 19 appearances / 2 goals

**An assistant timekeeper before becoming a professional footballer, Saxton scored the only goal on his debut and played regularly in the final few weeks at the Newcastle Road ground, although he did not appear in the last game there.**

He was in the side for the opening game at Roker Park and scored in a win in the fourth game there but left before the end of the season. Although having a reputation as one of the Lancashire League's best forwards, Saxton did not meet expectations on Wearside and the club dispensed with his services in late February 1899. After heading home to Loughborough Arthur later joined Bedminster on 10 May 1899, the year before that club amalgamated with Bristol City. His only Football League appearances were with Sunderland. Arthur became a gardener after retiring from playing football.

## SCHWARZ, Stefan Hans Jurgen

**POSITION:** Midfielder
**BIRTHPLACE:** Kulladal, Sweden
**DATE OF BIRTH:** 18/04/1969
**HEIGHT:** 5' 10" **WEIGHT:** 11st 9lbs
**SIGNED FROM:** Valencia, 29/07/1999
**DEBUT:** v Watford, H, 10/08/1999
**LAST MATCH:** v Sheffield United, A, 03/12/2002
**MOVED TO:** Contract not renewed, 30/06/2003
**TEAMS:** Kulladals FF, Bayer Leverkusen, Malmo, Benfica, Arsenal, Fiorentina, Valencia, Sunderland
**INTERNATIONAL:** Sweden
**SAFC TOTALS:** 70+6 appearances / 3 goals

**In the halcyon days of the Stadium of Light's first Premiership season, the arrival of Stefan Schwarz brought a touch of top class glamour to SAFC, but Schwarz was anything but a continental show pony, much rather a complete thoroughbred. Recently turned 30 when he signed, Stefan had played for top clubs around the continent as well as in the latter stages of the FIFA World Cup and Euros, and it showed.**

He was a pleasure to watch and off the pitch was just as good, a true gentleman who fell in love with Sunderland, kept in touch with the club and in 2022 flew from his home in Lisbon to be at Wembley for the League One Play-Off final.

Schwarz appeared to glide over the surface, almost weightless in preparation for the space travel he famously wanted to undertake. He could always find space on the pitch, not least with his football brain which was top class.

Stefan had barely missed a game in his first season at Sunderland when he ruptured his Achilles tendon playing for Sweden against Austria at the end of March. It was an injury that kept him out of action until December. Perhaps Sunderland would have finished higher than seventh in 1999-2000, and qualified for Europe had Schwarz not been hurt on international duty - an injury which kept him out of Euro 2000.

Seven of Stefan's 69 international caps were won while he was with Sunderland. He scored six goals for Sweden including one with his first touch on his debut having come on as a substitute against the United Arab Emirates on Valentine's Day 1990. He played all three of Sweden's games at Italia 90 and made three appearances as his country reached the semi-finals of Euro '92. At the 1994 World Cup after playing in every game Schwarz was sent off in the quarter final (by Philip Don who two years earlier had refereed Sunderland in the FA Cup final against Liverpool). Suspension ruled Schwarz out of the semi-final, but he returned for the third-place match in which he set up a goal for Kennet Andersson in a 4-0 win over Bulgaria.

At club level Stefan won league titles in Sweden and Portugal, domestic cups in those countries and Italy and reached the final of the European Cup Winners' Cup with Arsenal in 1995. Having played youth football in Sweden and Germany he began his senior career with former European Cup finalists Malmo. Schwarz made 32 league appearances as they won the Allsvenskan in back-to-back seasons in 1987 and '88, followed by the Swedish Cup a year later, playing for Roy Hodgson's side as they beat Djurgardens 3-0 in the final.

After the World Cup in 1990 Stefan moved to Benfica where he scored seven times in 77 league games, winning the league in 1991 and 1994 and playing in the 1993 domestic cup final as Boavista were thrashed 5-2. In the summer of 1994 he moved to Arsenal, helping the Gunners to the final of the Cup Winners' Cup, scoring in the second leg of the semi away to Sampdoria. It was Italy he moved to after a single season at Arsenal where he scored four goals in 50 starts. At Fiorentina, he played 78 league games, scoring twice and played in the first leg of the 1996 Coppa Italia final as Claudio Ranieri's side beat Atalanta. Schwarz was also part of the Viola side who beat a star-studded Milan at the San Siro to lift the Italian Supercup in the same year.

Before coming to Sunderland Schwarz had a season with Valencia where he scored four times in 23 La Liga outings in a year (1999) when he was voted Sweden's best footballer. Having begun coaching at Sunderland in 2002-03 he later coached Sweden Under 21s and was assistant manager of Helsingborgs when Sunderland played there in 2012. He became a players' agent and more than once was understood to be part of consortiums seeking to take over Sunderland.

## SCOCCO, Ignacio Martin

**POSITION:** Forward

**BIRTHPLACE:** Hughes, Sante Fe, Argentina

**DATE OF BIRTH:** 29/05/1985

**HEIGHT:** 5' 8" **WEIGHT:** 11st 2lbs

**SIGNED FROM:** Internacional, 30/01/2014

**DEBUT:** v Southampton, H, 15/02/2014

**LAST MATCH:** v Manchester City, A, 16/04/2014

**MOVED TO:** Newells Old Boys, 24/07/2014

**TEAMS:** Newells, Club Universidad Nacional, AEK Athens, Al Ain, Newells Old Boys (L), Internacional, Sunderland, Newells Old Boys, River Plate

**INTERNATIONAL:** Argentina

**SAFC TOTALS:** 2+6 appearances / 0 goals

**One of the South American players brought in by Uruguayan head coach Gus Poyet, Scocco left Sunderland with a League (Capital One) Cup runners-up medal as an unused substitute in the 2014 final. He never started a league game for Sunderland and seemed to be an expensive acquisition given rumours of a signing on fee in the region of £3m and a transfer fee thought to be £2.1m.**

Capped once by Argentina he scored twice against Brazil and again in a penalty shoot-out which was lost in Buenos Aires in November 2012. He was called up for other squads and played in an unofficial international, but the Brazil game was his only

full international. At Under 20 level he won twelve caps, scoring three goals as well as playing twice at the 2005 FIFA World Youth Championship.

In 2012-13 and 2013-14, he was top-scorer in the Argentinian top-flight winning the 'Apertura' league with Newells Old Boys. He went on to win the Greek Cup with AEK Athens in 2011, two years after being a finalist. He also won the Pro-League in the United Arab Emirates with Al-Ain in 2012. Back in Argentina with River Plate he twice won the Copa Argentina as well as the Supercopa Argentina, the Copa Libertadores and the Recopa Sudamerica in successive years from 2017. 'Nacho' notched 20 goals in 52 games for River, 68 in 202 league games in four spells with Newells Old Boys and 18 in 53 for Club Universidad Nacional. There were 27 in 89 games for AEK and nine in 19 for Al Ain.

## SCOTSON, Reginald

**POSITION:** Stockton, Co Durham

**BIRTHPLACE:** Stockton, Co Durham

**DATE OF BIRTH:** 23/09/1919 - 15/02/1999

**HEIGHT:** 5' 10" **WEIGHT:** 11st 13lbs

**SIGNED FROM:** Ouston United, 05/04/1939

**DEBUT:** v Blackpool, A, 18/01/1947

**LAST MATCH:** v Wolverhampton Wanderers, A, 06/09/1950

**MOVED TO:** Grimsby Town, 07/12/1950

**TEAMS:** Ouston United, Sunderland, Grimsby Town, Skegness Town

**SAFC TOTALS:** 61 appearances / 1 goal

**A whole-hearted and uncompromising half-back, Scotson made five appearances in his first and last seasons as a first-teamer and between eleven and 22 in the three terms in between.**

Like many of the youngsters Sunderland signed in the late 1930s his career total could have been much higher if World War Two had not intervened. Whilst serving in the Army Reg made occasional war-time appearances whilst on leave. Sold to Grimsby for £5,000 he made 176 appearances for the Mariners, scoring six goals. After retiring from football Reg managed the Empire Bingo Hall and amusement arcade in Cleethorpes.

## SCOTT, Henry (Harry)

**POSITION:** Inside-right

**BIRTHPLACE:** Newburn, Newcastle, Northumberland

**DATE OF BIRTH:** 04/08/1901 - 22/03/1988

**HEIGHT:** 6' 0" **WEIGHT:** 11st 5lbs

**SIGNED FROM:** Newburn Grange, 26/01/1922

**DEBUT:** v Nottingham Forest, A, 07/03/1925

**LAST MATCH:** v Bury, H, 14/03/1925

**MOVED TO:** Wolverhampton Wanderers, 18/06/1925

**TEAMS:** Bank Head Albion, Newburn Grange, Sunderland, Wolverhampton Wanderers, Hull City, Bradford Park Avenue, Swansea Town, Watford, Nuneaton, Vauxhall Motors

**SAFC TOTALS:** 2 appearances / 0 goals

**Harry was deemed to have potential when he signed but needed to become stronger, especially after it was reported that he collapsed after his first session in the Roker gymnasium. By the time of his debut three years later the six footer had filled out and contemporary reports say Scott did well in a debut draw at relegation-doomed Nottingham Forest in March 1925.**

Scott's biggest problem was he was standing in at inside-right for the legendary Charlie Buchan. As it happened Buchan left for Arsenal at the end of the season but Scott sought pastures new that summer too having played just once more. He signed for Wolves where he went on to score six goals in 35 games, debuting at Fulham in early October. Almost a year to the day later he signed off in a home draw with Southampton.

Swapping Wolves for the Tigers in November 1926 he went on to score eight goals in 29 games before joining Bradford Park Avenue in June 1928. Four years later he went to Swansea for the 1932-33 season before spending 1933-34 with Watford. Further spells with Nuneaton Town and Vauxhall Motors brought an end to the career of the player who had played for Newburn Grange and Bank Head Albion before joining Sunderland. After retiring Harry became a motor fitter at Vauxhall's Luton plant and remained in the town until passing away in 1988.

## SCOTT, John Hamilton (Jock)

**POSITION:** Inside-left / outside-left

**BIRTHPLACE:** Whifflet, Lanarkshire

**DATE OF BIRTH:** 09/06/1867 - 19/01/1932

**HEIGHT:** 5' 6½" **WEIGHT:** 11st 6lbs

**SIGNED FROM:** Albion Rovers, 21/10/1889

**DEBUT:** v Blackburn Rovers, A, 18/01/1890

**LAST MATCH:** v Nottingham Forest, A, 18/01/1896

**MOVED TO:** South Shields, 05/08/1897

**TEAMS:** Third Lanark, Albion Rovers, Sunderland, South Shields

**SAFC TOTALS:** 111 appearances / 29 goals

**A member of 'The Team of All The Talents', Scott played and scored in the English (FA) Cup before the club's first Football League season in which he was ever-present and scored in the club's first-ever league victory. He played in three league title-winning teams, missing just two games and being third top scorer in the first title-winning season of 1891-92.**

According to the 1891 Census he was boarding with teammate John Spence. Scott scored five times in ten league games as the title was retained in 1893 and played 16 league games in the 1894-95 title-winning season, scoring once. He also played in the cup semi-finals of 1891, 1892 and 1895, scoring in the 1892 semi against Aston Villa.

## SCOTT, Jock (Continued)

During that summer of 1892, he played cricket for Whitburn and went on to umpire in Durham Senior cricket leagues either side of World War One. After retiring from football he ran a sports outfitters shop in Sunderland. Two brothers were involved in football. Simon was one of the founders of Albion Rovers while between 1892 to 1899 Adam played 211 games and scored three times for Nottingham Forest having started with Albion Rovers. He won the Football Alliance with Forest in 1892, the English (FA) Cup with them in 1898, and in 1892 played in Forest's first Football League game just as Jock played in Sunderland's first. Adam was in the Forest side on the occasion of Jock's final game for Sunderland. Jock did not play at all in the following season due to a shoulder injury.

## SCOTT, Leslie

**POSITION:** Goalkeeper
**BIRTHPLACE:** Sunderland, Co Durham
**DATE OF BIRTH:** 06/05/1895 - Q3 1973
**HEIGHT:** 5' 10½" **WEIGHT:** 11st 7lbs
**SIGNED FROM:** Roker St Andrew's, 01/05/1911
**DEBUT:** v Wednesday, H, 04/04/1914
**LAST MATCH:** v Chelsea, H, 22/04/1922
**MOVED TO:** Stoke, 20/07/1922
**TEAMS:** Roker St Andrew's, Sunderland, Stoke, Preston North End
**SAFC TOTALS:** 95 appearances / 0 goals

**Despite being a teenager, Scott was first choice in the last season before football stopped for the First World War, missing just one game, but after the war, never made as many as half as many seasonal appearances.**

He had been an amateur with various local clubs before joining Sunderland and during the war served in the 3rd battalion of the Durham Light Infantry. He was given a free transfer and £350 in lieu of a Benefit game in 1922, after which he joined Stoke for whom he played 20 games before two for Preston North End. He reverted to being an amateur in September 1929 when working as a storekeeper for Sunderland Corporation.

## SCOTT, Martin

**POSITION:** Left-back
**BIRTHPLACE:** Sheffield, Yorkshire
**DATE OF BIRTH:** 07/01/1968
**HEIGHT:** 5' 8" **WEIGHT:** 10st 10lbs
**SIGNED FROM:** Bristol City, 23/12/1994
**DEBUT:** v Bolton Wanderers, H, 26/12/1994
**LAST MATCH:** v Lincoln City, A, 02/01/1999
**MOVED TO:** Released, 03/06/1999
**TEAMS:** Rotherham United, Nottingham Forest (L), Bristol City, Sunderland
**SAFC TOTALS:** 124+2 appearances / 11 goals

**A popular full-back who was an accomplished penalty taker, Scott came to Sunderland for a fee of £450,000 plus the transfer of Gary Owers. He barely missed a game in his first season and a half, but thereafter was troubled by injury with his place further threatened by the emergence of Michael Gray.**

Martin had started with Rotherham as a 14-year-old, winning Division Four with the Millers in 1989 and going on to move to Bristol City for £200,000 in December of the following year after 118+3 games and seven goals. He had also had a two-month loan to Nottingham Forest in the spring of 1998 without getting a game. At Bristol City, Scott played 199 times, scoring 16 goals.

After leaving Sunderland Scotty looked like joining Bradford City only for his injury to end those plans at which point he moved into coaching. He became youth coach at Hartlepool United in September 2000, becoming reserve-team coach in 2005 and first-team boss from May 2005 to February 2006.

Scott returned to youth and then reserve team coach with Middlesbrough from July 2007 to May 2010. In January 2013, he was appointed as first-team coach at Barnsley and later resurfaced as assistant manager of South Shields in October 2016 as well as establishing his own football academy. On Christmas Eve 2021, Martin's son Olly joined King's Lynn Town from Consett.

## SCOTT, Matthew

**POSITION:** Goalkeeper
**BIRTHPLACE:** Elswick, Northumberland
**DATE OF BIRTH:** 27/07/1867 - 27/12/1897
**HEIGHT:** 5' 9"
**SIGNED FROM:** Newcastle East End, 15/10/1892
**DEBUT:** v Wolverhampton Wanderers, A, 06/01/1894
**LAST MATCH:** v Wolverhampton Wanderers, A, 06/01/1894
**MOVED TO:** Willington Athletic, 01/03/1896
**TEAMS:** Boundary, Elswick Rangers, Newcastle East End, Sunderland, Willington Athletic, South Shields, Elswick Leather Works
**SAFC TOTALS:** 1 appearance / 0 goals

**A machineman in Elswick while with Newcastle East End, Scott played once in a 2-1 defeat at Wolves where he stood in for legendary keeper Ted Doig. Scott had been a prominent goalkeeper for Newcastle United's forerunners Newcastle East End and had a trial for Newcastle United in 1895 after his sole match for Sunderland.**

With East End, he totalled 51 competitive games beginning with an English (FA) Cup qualification match against Darlington St Augustine's on 26 October 1889. Scott gained representative honours for Northumberland and also played for the Newcastle and District Combination League. Matthew died in Newcastle Infirmary aged 30 after suffering for some time with an abscess.

## SCOTT, Thomas (Tom)

**POSITION:** Outside-right
**BIRTHPLACE:** Newcastle, Northumberland
**DATE OF BIRTH:** 06/04/1904 - 24/12/1979
**HEIGHT:** 5' 9½" **WEIGHT:** 10st 2lbs
**SIGNED FROM:** Pandon Temperance, 07/12/1922
**DEBUT:** v Chelsea, H, 17/10/1923
**LAST MATCH:** v Tottenham Hotspur, H, 20/10/1923
**MOVED TO:** Darlington, 12/07/1924
**TEAMS:** Swifts, Pandon Temperance, Sunderland, Darlington, Liverpool, Bristol City, Preston North End, Norwich City, Exeter City, Hartlepools United, Bangor City
**SAFC TOTALS:** 2 appearances / 0 goals

**Two games four days apart represented the span of Scott's first-team experience at Sunderland but he went on to win a Division Three South Championship medal in 1934 for Norwich where he scored 26 goals in 53 league games. A versatile forward, Tom also scored 23 times in 47 games for Preston, six in 35 for Bristol City and four in 18 for Liverpool.**

His February 1925 move to Liverpool from Darlington saw him snatched from under the noses of Everton, Darlington having to compensate the Toffees to the tune of £250 for a player who had scored three times in seven games for the Quakers. Later at Exeter he scored 16 goals in 56 games over three seasons after an October 1934 debut at home to Reading. He returned to the north east with Hartlepools but did not appear in the league for them. After retiring from football he became a hotel licensee in Wallesey and then after World War Two he ran a hotel in Seacombe on the Wirral. Tom came from a footballing family with his younger brother Joseph also playing for Darlington.

## **SCOTT,** Thomas William **(Tom)**

**POSITION:** Midfielder
**BIRTHPLACE:** Kettering, Northamptonshire
**DATE OF BIRTH:** 06/11/2002
**HEIGHT:** 5' 9" **WEIGHT:** 10st 9lbs
**SIGNED FROM:** Northampton Town, 01/07/2021
**DEBUT:** v Manchester United Under 21s, H, 13/10/2021
**LAST MATCH:**
**MOVED TO:**
**TEAMS:** Northampton Town, Sunderland
**SAFC TOTALS:** 1 appearance / 0 goals (to June 2022)

**Signed after impressing on trial when he scored an excellent goal against West Brom at Under 18 level and also appeared against Norwich City, Scott came to SAFC after impressing on his scholarship at Northampton Town where his prowess from dead balls was well known.**

## **SCOTT, Walter**

**POSITION:** Goalkeeper
**BIRTHPLACE:** Worksop, Nottinghamshire
**DATE OF BIRTH:** 21/01/1886 - 16/09/1955
**HEIGHT:** 5' 11" **WEIGHT:** 13st 0lbs
**SIGNED FROM:** Everton, 28/06/1911
**DEBUT:** v Middlesbrough, H, 02/09/1911
**LAST MATCH:** v Blackburn Rovers, H, 18/09/1912
**MOVED TO:** Shelbourne, 19/10/1912
**TEAMS:** Worksop West End, Worksop Central, Worksop Town, Grimsby Town, Everton, Sunderland, Shelbourne, Belfast United, Brentford (WW1 Guest), Millwall (WW1 Guest), Worksop Town, Grimsby Town, Gainsborough Trinity, Ashington
**INTERNATIONAL:** Irish League XI
**SAFC TOTALS:** 38 appearances / 0 goals

**First choice in 1911-12 when he played 34 games Scott was sacked after conceding eleven goals in the first four games of what proved to be the club's greatest single season of 1912-13. Walter's contract was terminated on grounds of 'Palpable inefficiency'. Officially, this was for missing training, but Scott disputed his sacking in the local press complaining that a group of supporters had put him off his game by making him downhearted.**

Walter went under the nicknames of 'Buns' and 'the penalty king' - the latter from saving a record of three penalties in one game for Grimsby against Burnley in February 1909 - a season in which incredibly he is reputed to have saved 14 of a remarkable 17 penalties. This was at a time when goalkeepers could come off their line at penalties. 'Buns' made 80 league appearances for Grimsby and 18 for Everton, his Toffees debut seeing him help them to a 1-0 win away to Liverpool in February 1909. His sixth game brought the same result at Roker Park against Sunderland who later paid Everton the same £750 fee they had paid Grimsby for Scott's signature, a club record for the Mariners.

From Sunderland he went to play in Ireland where he broke his leg playing for Belfast United in February 1916. While in Ireland he represented the Irish League five times debuting against the Southern League (of Ireland) in Dublin in October 1913 when he was with Shelbourne. Sunderland recouped £550 from Grimsby when he returned there in February 1920 as the Wearsiders still held his Football League registration. After retiring from football, 'Buns' became a baker in Worksop. His nephew Thomas Greathead played for Worksop Town and Sheffield United.

## **SCOWEN, Joshua** Charles

**POSITION:** Midfielder
**BIRTHPLACE:** Cheshunt, Hertfordshire
**DATE OF BIRTH:** 28/03/1993
**HEIGHT:** 5' 10" **WEIGHT:** 11st 9lbs
**SIGNED FROM:** Queens Park Rangers, 27/01/2020
**DEBUT:** v Tranmere Rovers, A, 29/01/2020
**LAST MATCH:** v Lincoln City, H, 22/05/2021
**MOVED TO:** Contract not renewed, 30/06/2021
**TEAMS:** Wycombe Wanderers, Hemel Hempstead Town (L), Eastbourne Borough (L), Barnsley, QPR, Sunderland, Wycombe Wanderers (to June 2022)
**SAFC TOTALS:** 44+11 appearances / 3 goals

**Few players could win the ball as often and give it away as regularly as Josh Scowen seemed to do. Admirable for his industry, Scowen could frustrate by sometimes kicking the ball out of play when under no pressure. Fifty one of his games for Sunderland came in 2020-21 ending with an unsuccessful Play-Off semi-final against Lincoln.**

Released, he joined Wycombe where he swept the board with the Chairboys' Player of the Year awards the following season which ended with him playing against Sunderland at Wembley in a League One Play-Off final.

Scowen had debuted for Wycombe in his first spell as a late sub at Morecambe in March 2011. After exactly 100 games he moved on a free transfer to Barnsley in January 2015 shortly before his future Sunderland manager Lee Johnson became manager of the Tykes. After 90+16 games and ten goals another free transfer took Scowen to QPR where he played 81+22 times scoring four times before his free transfer to Sunderland.

Josh twice won the Football League Trophy, coming on as a sub for Barnsley against Oxford in 2016 and playing the full game for Sunderland against Tranmere five years later. In 2016 he was also a League One promotion winner, playing for Barnsley in a Play-Off final win against Millwall in which future Sunderland loanee Ashley Fletcher opened the scoring, ex-SAFC youth Conor Hourihane partnered him in midfield and former Sunderland man Lewin Nyatanga was on the bench against a Lions line-up that included Carlos Edwards.

## **SEMENYO, Antoine** Serlom

**POSITION:** Forward
**BIRTHPLACE:** Kensington, Greater London
**DATE OF BIRTH:** 07/01/2000
**HEIGHT:** 5' 11" **WEIGHT:** 11st 0lbs
**SIGNED FROM:** Bristol City, 31/01/2020, on loan
**DEBUT:** v Portsmouth, A, 01/02/2020
**LAST MATCH:** v Bristol Rovers, A, 10/03/2020
**MOVED TO:** Bristol City, 09/06/2020, end of loan
**TEAMS:** Bristol City, Bath City (L), Newport County (L), Sunderland (L) (to June 2022)
**INTERNATIONAL:** Ghana
**SAFC TOTALS:** 1+6 appearances / 0 goals

**Speed-merchant Semenyo saw his loan curtailed when the season of his time at SAFC was cut short because of the Covid 19 pandemic. Antoine had only just turned 20 when he came to Wearside and often looked like he could cause problems with his pace.**

By the end of 2021-22 he had 13 goals to his name in 57+41 games for parent club Bristol City where he was Championship Player of the Month for January 2022. He got three goals in seven games and five in 19+13 on loans to Bath and Newport. In June 2022 Semenyo made his debut for Ghana against Madagascar after a good season with Bristol City.

## **SESSEGNON, Stephane**

**POSITION:** Forward
**BIRTHPLACE:** Allahe, Benin
**DATE OF BIRTH:** 01/06/1984
**HEIGHT:** 5' 6" **WEIGHT:** 11st 9lbs
**SIGNED FROM:** Paris St Germain, 29/01/2011
**DEBUT:** v Chelsea, H, 01/02/2011
**LAST MATCH:** v Southampton, A, 24/08/2013
**MOVED TO:** West Bromwich Albion, 02/09/2013
**TEAMS:** Requins de L'Atlantique, Creteil, Le Mans, Paris St Germain, Sunderland, WBA, Montpellier, Genclerbirligi
**INTERNATIONAL:** Benin
**SAFC TOTALS:** 95+2 appearances / 18 goals

**Some readers may note that Sessegnon alphabetically is next to 'Shack'. According to Stephane's chant, God had taken Messi and Pele, merged them into one and come up with Stephane Sessegnon. He was not that good! Sessegnon had a low centre of gravity and no little skill, but ultimately his end product was not good enough, often enough, particularly when it is considered that often the team was constructed around him.**

He was however Sunderland's Player of the Year in 2011-12 and was undoubtedly a popular and eye-catching footballer. In 2008-09 he was twice Player of the Month in France and was named in the Ligue 1 Team of the Year and nominated as the Player of the Year.

Sessegnon commanded a fee from Sunderland believed to be in the region of £6m having won the Coupe de France with PSG the previous season when he played in the final as Monaco were beaten. Monaco would also be the opposition for the last of Stephane's 105 games for PSG which brought eleven goals and experience of UEFA Cup and Europa League football.

Previously he had played for Le Mans (61/6) and Creteil (68/10) in France after starting in his home country of Benin with Requins de l'Atlantique. Sessegnon made his international bow shortly before moving into French football in 2004 with a debut against Cameroon. He played 83 times for Benin, captaining them as they reached the quarter-finals of the African Cup of

## SESSEGNON, Stephane (Continued)

Nations in 2019. The last of his 24 goals came against Nigeria in that tournament with three of them scored while he was with Sunderland.

Although born in Benin, Stephane lived in the Ivory Coast (where his parents were from) between the ages of three and twelve. In 2010, he was named as Benin's best-ever player by a Benin sports magazine.

He missed just five Premier League games in his two full seasons at the Stadium of Light, scoring seven league goals in each of those campaigns, one of his best being at Newcastle in the famous 3-0 win engineered by Paolo Di Canio. Leaving Sunderland early the next season he scored against SAFC on his debut for West Brom in what proved to be Di Canio's last game in charge of SAFC. It was one of only eight goals Sessegnon scored in 74+18 games for the Baggies before a September 2016 return to France with Montpellier.

After three goals in 38+7 appearances he again scored a debut goal having moved to Turkey with Genclerbirligi. That goal against Konyaspor in January 2018 was one of six he scored in 44+2 games for his final club. In total, exactly half of his career total of 34 league goals in Europe were scored for Sunderland. Stephane is a distant cousin of twins Ryan and Steven who as of June 2022, were on the books of Spurs and Fulham with Steven on loan to Charlton.

## SHACKLETON, Leonard Francis (Len)

**POSITION:** Inside-left
**BIRTHPLACE:** Bradford, Yorkshire
**DATE OF BIRTH:** 03/05/1922 - 27/11/2000
**HEIGHT:** 5' 8" **WEIGHT:** 11st 5lbs
**SIGNED FROM:** Newcastle United, 04/02/1948
**DEBUT:** v Derby County, A, 14/02/1948
**LAST MATCH:** v Arsenal, H, 24/08/1957
**MOVED TO:** Retired, 26/08/1957
**TEAMS:** Bradford Park Avenue, Kippax United, Horton Banktop, Arsenal, London Paper Mills (L), Enfield (L), Dartford (L), Bradford City, Huddersfield Town (WW2 Guest), Bradford City (WW2 Guest), Newcastle United, Sunderland
**INTERNATIONAL:** England
**SAFC TOTALS:** 348 appearances / 100 goals

**Perhaps the most popular player in Sunderland's history, 'Shack' was probably also the most skilful. Inducted into the inaugural SAFC Hall of Fame ceremony, Len Shackleton was known as the 'Clown Prince of Soccer'. Stories of his ability with the ball, the tricks he would play - such as performing a one-two off the corner flag and putting back-spin on the ball so it tempted to defenders to lunge forward before he swept past them are legendary. A marvellous creator of goals 'Shack' was also a goalscorer who was the club's post-war record holder until overtaken by Gary Rowell and Kevin Phillips. Shack is still Sunderland's record post-war top-flight scorer.**

Signed by Sunderland from Newcastle for a British record transfer fee of £20,050, the fee was arrived at due to Sunderland being tipped off by a Newcastle director that the highest bid received had been £20,000. Shack's popularity was enhanced by his statement, "I'm not biased when it comes to Newcastle. I'm not bothered who beats them." Later as a highly-entertaining and well-connected journalist he wrote of Newcastle, "I've heard of selling dummies, but this club keeps buying them". Len had been a hero with the Magpies. He had scored six goals on his debut for United in a 13-0 second division win over Newport County on 5 October 1946. He scored 29 goals in 64 games during 18 months on Tyneside where he had arrived after Newcastle invested a record fee to Bradford PA for whom Len had scored 171 goals in 217 games.

Shackleton had started with Bradford PA as an amateur in 1937 and had played for clubs in the Bradford area before joining Arsenal as an amateur in August 1938. The Gunners gave him experience on loan to small-time local clubs, but ultimately rejected him. Suitably stung, Shackleton saved many of his best performances for games against them (and Newcastle). Most notably in September 1953 he destroyed the Gunners at Roker Park, scoring one, making two and tormenting the Londoners who were thrashed 7-1. Arsenal were reigning champions and as of May 2022, no reigning league champions have suffered as heavy a defeat.

Shack played once as a war-time 'Guest' for Huddersfield in 1940-41 and three times for Bradford City. During the war Len worked as a Bevan Boy at Fryston Colliery near Castleford and later also worked at Gosforth Colliery following his October 1946 move to Newcastle. During the war Shackleton also worked at GEC in Bradford assembling radios for aircraft while in the early part of the war he worked at the London Paper Mills in Dartford.

A fine all-round sportsman, Shackleton was a keen golfer and as a cricketer played once for Durham and four times for Northumberland. He represented Wearmouth, Benwell and various clubs in Yorkshire. For England at football he won five full caps, a figure that would surely have been multiplied many times but for his maverick style and reluctance to bow to authority, an attitude which made him unpopular with the blazered dignitaries who ran the game. England won four and drew one of his games. On his final appearance he scored following a mazy dribble against reigning world champions West Germany. His cap from a 4-1 win away to Wales in 1949 is on display at the Stadium of Light courtesy of his nephew Nigel Simpson. Len also played once for the England B team, once for England at amateur level, twice for the Football League and also for the FA and England youths.

A half-size statue of Len was installed in the now defunct 'Shackleton House' tax office in Sunderland. The statue now resides in the city centre museum. Infamously, Len left a blank page entitled, 'The average director's knowledge of football in his autobiography. In 1976 he became a director of Fulham! Len's brother John signed for Sunderland in June 1949, but did not make a competitive debut.

## SHARKEY, Dominic (Nick)

**POSITION:** Centre-forward

**BIRTHPLACE:** Helensburgh, Dunbartonshire

**DATE OF BIRTH:** 04/05/1943 - 08/02/2015

**HEIGHT:** 5' 7" **WEIGHT:** 11st 0lbs

**SIGNED FROM:** School, 05/08/1958

**DEBUT:** v Scunthorpe United, H, 09/04/1960

**LAST MATCH:** v West Bromwich Albion, H, 08/10/1966

**MOVED TO:** Leicester City, 14/10/1966

**TEAMS:** Sunderland, Leicester City, Mansfield Town, Hartlepools United, South Shields

**INTERNATIONAL:** Scotland Under 23

**SAFC TOTALS:** 117 appearances / 62 goals

**To July 2022 Sharkey is the only man to score five goals in a game for Sunderland since World War Two - a feat only Bobby Gurney, Charlie Buchan and Jamie Millar have ever equalled in competitive peace-time games. A diminutive striker, Sharkey had an excellent goals to games record. By his own admission he poached many by following up at corners when keepers parried Charlie Hurley headers.**

A prolific schoolboy scorer, Sharkey was still a teenager when he scored five in a 7-1 win over Norwich City in March 1963. He had debuted as a 16-year-old. Playing for the fifth team when he first arrived, Nick notched an incredible 140 goals in his first season.

Appallingly, he was allowed to leave because of his religion! A Catholic, Sharkey told me himself that when former Rangers player Ian McColl took over at Sunderland the manager gave Nick a rail pass, told him four clubs were interested and to visit them all and not come back. This was a story I detailed in the book, 'Sunderland: Match of My Life." McColl had been managing Scotland when Sharkey was picked by a committee of selectors. McColl picked the team. Sharkey did not get a game although he twice played for Scotland at Under 23 level as well as for Scotland Schools.

Nick chose to sign for Leicester to partner target man Derek Dougan only for 'The Doog' to be sold shortly afterwards. Sharkey scored five goals in just six games for the Foxes but after being plagued by injury, moved on to Mansfield where he scored 17 times in 67+2 league games before coming to Hartlepool where he added 15 goals in 57+4 games. He then completed his career with South Shields.

Sharkey spent many years working as a sales rep and dealing with vending machines in the north east of England as far north as Berwick who he had a spell training with in the summer of 1972. Very proud to be later the chairman of the Sunderland Former Players' Association, Nick Sharkey was a great goalscorer and a genuinely lovely person.

## SHAW, Harold Victor

**POSITION:** Left-back

**BIRTHPLACE:** Hednesford, Staffordshire

**DATE OF BIRTH:** 22/05/1905 - 14/06/1984

**HEIGHT:** 5' 10½" **WEIGHT:** 12st 6lbs

**SIGNED FROM:** Wolverhampton Wanderers, 15/02/1930

**DEBUT:** v Newcastle United, A, 22/02/1930

**LAST MATCH:** v Arsenal, A, 31/08/1935

**MOVED TO:** Retired, 30/07/1937

**TEAMS:** Hednesford Town, Wolverhampton Wanderers, Sunderland

**SAFC TOTALS:** 217 appearances / 5 goals

**A stalwart of the early 1930s who was ever-present in 1931-32, Shaw played once at the beginning of the title-winning 1935-36 season only to be injured and had to retire after aggravating the injury when attempting a comeback in October 1936 following the removal of a cartilage. An accomplished full-back, he had signed for Sunderland the year after playing for 'The Rest' in a trial game against England at Tottenham.**

With Wolves from May 1923 Shaw played 249 games without scoring. He missed just five games in his first season as Wanderers won Division Three North. An engineering fitter before becoming a footballer, he later became a builders' labourer and a commissioning agent in Wolverhampton as well as working at Cannock Colliery. He joined the South Staffs and Penn golf club and became part of a team that won the Midland Counties Golf Association competition in 1938. In the early fifties Harold became a member of the committee at Eastbourne United and became their caretaker-manager in 1953.

## SHAW, John Frederick

**POSITION:** Inside-left

**BIRTHPLACE:** South Hylton, Co Durham

**DATE OF BIRTH:** 05/10/1886 - 03/06/1916

**HEIGHT:** 5' 8" **WEIGHT:** 11st 0lbs

**SIGNED FROM:** Darlington, 06/04/1906

**DEBUT:** v Middlesbrough, A, 13/04/1906

**LAST MATCH:** v Middlesbrough, A, 13/04/1906

**MOVED TO:** Wallsend Park Villa, 01/10/1906

**TEAMS:** Whitburn, Darlington, Sunderland, Wallsend Park Villa, Clapton Orient, Barrow

**SAFC TOTALS:** 1 appearance / 0 goals

**John played once in a 2-1 defeat at Middlesbrough in which his brother Joseph scored. Ten years later, John was killed in action in World War One when he lost his life while repairing a telephone line near Ypres.**

He served as a gunner in a Canadian Artillery Brigade having emigrated initially to the USA, and then to Canada, to work for Vickers in Montreal having at first become a ship's draughtsman after retiring from football. At Clapton Orient he made 19 appearances in Division Two in 1908-09.

## SHAW, Joseph (Joe)

**POSITION:** Centre-forward

**BIRTHPLACE:** South Hylton, Co Durham

**DATE OF BIRTH:** 19/02/1883 - 17/05/1968

**HEIGHT:** 5' 9" **WEIGHT:** 11st 7lbs

**SIGNED FROM:** Darlington, 09/12/1905

**DEBUT:** v Middlesbrough, H, 01/01/1906

**LAST MATCH:** v Everton, A, 30/03/1907

**MOVED TO:** Hull City, 02/05/1907

**TEAMS:** St Marks, Sunderland West End, Armstrong College, Durham University, Bishop Auckland, Tottenham Hotspur, Darlington, Sunderland, Hull City, Grimsby Town

**SAFC TOTALS:** 35 appearances / 15 goals

**The brother of John Shaw, Joe was a teacher who played a lot of local football as he moved around in his teaching career which commenced as a student at Armstrong College in Newcastle and University in Durham. Before coming to Sunderland he had played a single game for Tottenham Hotspur Reserves on Boxing Day in 1904. At Sunderland he scored in six of his first seven home games as he endeared himself to supporters with ten goals in the second half of the 1905-06 season.**

He started the following campaign as a regular choice but after a Christmas Day game against his debut opponents Middlesbrough played just once more before moving on at the end of the season when he accepted a teaching position in Hull. As an amateur Joe added 22 goals in 48 games for Hull where his goals included a hat-trick against Gainsborough Trinity.

On Boxing Day 1908 he suffered a broken collarbone in a match against Wolves. This caused him to miss the end of the season at which point he was released and joined Grimsby for whom he played six league games without scoring.

After serving in World War One he resumed teaching in Hull and was appointed President of the Hull branch of the National Association of Schoolmasters in January 1928. He was known to be still teaching in Scarborough in 1939.

## SHEPPEARD, Howard Thomas

**POSITION:** Inside-left
**BIRTHPLACE:** Ynysybwl, Glamorgan
**DATE OF BIRTH:** 31/01/1933
**HEIGHT:** 6' 0" **WEIGHT:** 12st 5lbs
**SIGNED FROM:** Ynysybwl, 15/12/1951
**DEBUT:** v Preston North End, A, 24/10/1953
**LAST MATCH:** v Preston North End, A, 24/10/1953
**MOVED TO:** Cardiff City, 02/06/1955
**TEAMS:** Ynysybwl, Sunderland, Cardiff City, Newport County, Abergavenny Thursday, Ton Petre, Brecon Corries
**SAFC TOTALS:** 1 appearance / 0 goals

**Sheppeard's one game for a club outside of Wales was his solitary appearance for Sunderland - a 6-2 defeat at Preston on a day he filled in for Len Shackleton. Having come north as an 18-year-old, he had waited two years for that opportunity and had worked at Wearmouth Colliery in order to avoid having his potential football career curtailed by being called up for national service.**

He returned to Wales in a triple transfer with John McSeveney and Harry Kirtley also heading to Cardiff City for a combined fee of £9,000. Sheppeard did not get a game for the Bluebirds but went on to score six times in 31 Division Three South games for Newport. After breaking his leg playing for Newport's reserves Howard became captain of Abergavenny Thursday. Howard was a keen cricketer and often opened the bowling for Wearmouth CC with Len Shackleton during his time at Sunderland. As of 2020, Sheppeard was living in Mid-Glamorgan.

## SHERWIN, Harry

**POSITION:** Centre-half / half-back
**BIRTHPLACE:** Walsall, Staffordshire
**DATE OF BIRTH:** 11/10/1893 - 08/01/1953
**HEIGHT:** 5' 8" **WEIGHT:** 11st 0lbs
**SIGNED FROM:** Darlaston, 16/12/1913
**DEBUT:** v Tottenham Hotspur, H, 14/03/1914
**LAST MATCH:** v Cardiff City, H, 08/01/1921
**MOVED TO:** Leeds United, 05/05/1921
**TEAMS:** Darlaston, Sunderland, Sunderland Rovers (WW1), Leeds City (WW1 Guest). Leeds United, Barnsley
**INTERNATIONAL:** England Schools
**SAFC TOTALS:** 29 appearances / 0 goals

**In a career spanning both sides of the Great War the 16 games Sherwin managed in 1919-20 was his best campaign. During the war after spending 1915-16 with Sunderland Rovers he played as a 'Guest' for Leeds City, scoring nine times in 91 games for the club who were disbanded in 1919 to be replaced by Leeds United.**

Upon leaving Sunderland Harry joined Leeds, his free transfer being in lieu of a Benefit Match. He made 107 appearances for Leeds United (without scoring) playing at right-half as they won Division Two in 1923-24. In March 1925 he moved to Barnsley in a double deal with United teammate Lawrie Baker but returned to Leeds as assistant trainer in June of the following year. After a decade in that role Harry took up the same role at Bradford City before again returning to Leeds to become a publican in Beeston just before World War Two.

He remained in Leeds until his death. Back in April 1907, he had been a member of the first-ever England Boys team (against Wales) while before becoming a professional footballer he had been employed in a lock works.

## SHORE, Albert Victor

**POSITION:** Inside-forward
**BIRTHPLACE:** Darlaston, Staffordshire
**DATE OF BIRTH:** 11/02/1897 - 13/12/1981
**HEIGHT:** 5' 9" **WEIGHT:** 11st 7lbs
**SIGNED FROM:** Bean Car Works, 29/03/1920
**DEBUT:** v Preston North End, H, 10/04/1920
**LAST MATCH:** v Oldham Athletic, A, 16/04/1921
**MOVED TO:** Stoke, 21/05/1921
**TEAMS:** Sunderland, Stoke, Brierley Hill, Whitburn
**SAFC TOTALS:** 5 appearances / 1 goal

**The scorer of the only goal of the game on his dream debut, Shore did not get another opportunity in the three remaining games of that season but got four sporadic appearances the following term, starting with a 6-1 defeat at Newcastle.**

He added three more league appearances for Stoke the following season as the Potters were second division runners-up but otherwise Victor's career was spent in non-league. He had come to Sunderland from the Dudley car manufacturer Harper, Sons & Bean while he had a brother who played for Nuneaton Town just after World War One.

After retiring from playing Victor returned to the car manufacturing business in the Birmingham area as an inspector.

## SHOULDER, James (Jimmy)

**POSITION:** Left-back
**BIRTHPLACE:** Esh Winning, Co Durham
**DATE OF BIRTH:** 11/09/1946
**HEIGHT:** 5' 8½" **WEIGHT:** 10st 7lbs
**SIGNED FROM:** School, 01/07/1962
**DEBUT:** v West Bromwich Albion, A, 25/02/1967
**LAST MATCH:** v Burnley, A, 15/04/1967
**MOVED TO:** York City, 19/08/1969
**TEAMS:** Sunderland, York City, Scarborough, Hartlepool United
**SAFC TOTALS:** 3 appearances / 0 goals

**Known as 'Esh' within Sunderland footballing circles, as understudy to record outfield appearance holder Len Ashurst, Shoulder was restricted to a modest three first-team appearances but remained solidly red and white throughout a fabulously varied global career.**

Jimmy started his coaching career whilst still a player at Sunderland as he recovered from knee ligament damage sustained during the 1967 tour of North America as Vancouver Royal Canadians, in which he had scored his only goal for Sunderland / Vancouver. He later returned to Roker Park as first-team coach in the late seventies under long-term caretaker manager Billy Elliott who he went on to assist at Darlington between 1979 and 1981. In later life Jimmy became an active member of the Sunderland Former Players' Association, still being on the committee in 2022.

Jimmy joined Sunderland straight from St Aidan's School which he had attended while playing youth and even reserve team football as well as representing the town, county and having England schools trials. Having left Sunderland he signed a monthly contract with York where he played reserve team football for three months before joining Scarborough. This was at a time when he was looking to combine playing with attending university.

Shoulder played over 200 times for Scarborough. Seven days before Bobby Kerr raised the FA Cup at Wembley in 1973, Shoulder stood in the same place and lifted the FA Trophy as skipper of Scarborough who defeated Wigan Athletic. Jimmy's teammates included former Sunderland youth-teamer Bernie Fagan and future SAFC fitness coach Gerry Donoghue. After four years with Scarborough Shoulder returned to the Football League with Hartlepool where he was signed by none other than Len Ashurst with whom he remained close life-long friends. Debuting at home to Gillingham in September 1973 Shoulder played 75+1 games for Pools, scoring three times before being released.

Moving into coaching, Jimmy went to Australia coaching Canberra outfit ANUFC before taking over as coach of the national side who he brought to Sunderland for a friendly in November 1976 as part of an extensive tour. The previous summer his Australia side had hosted Sunderland in Sydney and Melbourne during Sunderland's southern hemisphere tour. Jimmy played a hugely influential role in developing the sport in Australia and indeed when Australia played England at the Stadium of Light in 2016, at my request the FA invited Jimmy along as a guest of honour.

He also worked as technical director of the FA of Wales, for many years running the Wales Under 21 team under Mark Hughes who he later assisted at Blackburn Rovers. Shoulder also worked at Sheffield Wednesday as academy director and coached the Singapore Armed Forces FC team in the S league in Singapore. Also in the Far East he became academy director of Shenzhen Town in China. Continuing his globe-trotting Jimmy worked for FIFA as a coach educator, training coaches around the world in such places as Pakistan and the Cook Islands. In 2010, he moved to Uzbekistan as academy director of FC Pakhtakor.

The holder of a sociology degree from Durham University, Jimmy also played cricket for the university and later had a horse race as a professional jockey. Truly a life well lived. Over and above all of this. Jimmy has remained deservedly popular with everyone and a real deep thinker on the game whose opinions are understandably widely sought.

# S

## SIDDALL, Barry Alfred

**POSITION:** Goalkeeper

**BIRTHPLACE:** Bromborough, Cheshire

**DATE OF BIRTH:** 12/09/1954

**HEIGHT:** 6' 1" **WEIGHT:** 14st 3lbs

**SIGNED FROM:** Bolton Wanderers, 29/09/1976

**DEBUT:** v Aston Villa, H, 16/10/1976

**LAST MATCH:** v Notts County, H, 27/02/1982

**MOVED TO:** Port Vale, 22/08/1982

**TEAMS:** Bolton Wanderers, Sunderland, Darlington (L), Vancouver Whitecaps, Port Vale, Blackpool (L), Stoke City, Tranmere Rovers (L), Manchester City (L), Blackpool, Stockport County, Mossley, Hartlepool United, WBA, Carlisle United, Chester City, Preston North End, Northwich Victoria, Horwich RMI, Burnley

**INTERNATIONAL:** England Youth

**SAFC TOTALS:** 192 appearances / 0 goals

**An always popular character, Siddall was variously nicknamed, 'Basil' (because he looked like Basil Fawlty) and less than kindly, 'the flying pig' while when he made a good save, it would often be greeted with a chant of 'Seeeeedalllll' similar to the 'Gooooooch' that greeted good play by Lynden Gooch four decades later.**

Siddall had one of the hardest tasks of any incoming player in history as he was bought to replace Jim Montgomery. Monty was cast aside appallingly early, but Siddall proved a popular player. He was a good, brave goalkeeper who enjoyed a moment in the spotlight with a last-minute penalty save in a 6-2 win over Sheffield United on a night when a four-goal winning margin was needed to take Sunderland to the top of the league late in the season in 1979.

From his arrival Barry missed just one game in over two and a half seasons but following the signing of Chris Turner in the summer of 1979, faced a battle for the number one spot. Barry had a month's loan to Darlington in the autumn of 1980 - although in his last season of 1981-82, he managed 29 appearances after spending the summer of 1981 playing for Vancouver Whitecaps.

Siddall had been a teammate of Peter Reid and Sam Allardyce at Bolton and was in the Trotters team at Roker Park when Sunderland clinched promotion. Barry had debuted for Bolton against Walsall, eleven years almost to the day since Montgomery made his debut against the same club. It was one of four appearances Siddall made in a third division title-winning campaign in 1972-73. He went on to play 162 times for the Trotters.

After exceeding that total at Sunderland (during which time he played four games for Darlington and 24 for Vancouver Whitecaps), he had 93 games for Port Vale, seven for Blackpool, 20 for Stoke, 16 for Tranmere, six for Manchester City, 140 for Blackpool, 29 for Stockport, eleven for Hartlepool, four for Mossley in the Northern Premier League, 24 for Carlisle, twelve for Chester and finally one for Preston, amassing an impressive career total of 746 games - Sunderland being the club Barry played for more than anyone else.

In the early 1990 he took up a post as goalkeeping coach at Manchester City but it was the post more than the coaching that marked his future as he became a postman in Kirkham in Lancashire after retiring, although at one point he combined working as a postie with being a part-time goalkeeping coach at Blackpool.

## SIMPSON, Daniel Peter (Danny)

**POSITION:** Full-back

**BIRTHPLACE:** Salford, Greater Manchester

**DATE OF BIRTH:** 04/01/1987

**HEIGHT:** 5' 9" **WEIGHT:** 11st 5lbs

**SIGNED FROM:** Manchester United, 25/01/2007, on loan

**DEBUT:** v Coventry City, H, 03/02/2007

**LAST MATCH:** v Burnley, H, 27/04/2007

**MOVED TO:** Manchester United, 08/05/2007, end of loan

**TEAMS:** Manchester United, Royal Antwerp (L), Sunderland (L), Ipswich Town (L), Blackburn Rovers (L), Newcastle United, QPR, Leicester City, Huddersfield Town, Bristol City (to June 2022)

**SAFC TOTALS:** 13+1 appearances / 0 goals

**Playing in twelve wins and two draws made Danny a record setter for the most unbeaten games by a Sunderland player in his entire time at the club. His loan spell produced a Championship medal and he won another one three years later after a transfer to Newcastle United.**

Six years on from that he added a Premier League medal after playing 30 times as Leicester City astonishingly took the title. A modern day full-back with plenty of pace and a willingness to get forward, in total Simpson played 127+6 times for Leicester although he never scored. He did score once for Newcastle where including an initial loan period he played 136+1 times.

Danny came through the ranks at Manchester United, playing 4+4 times. United twice loaned him to Royal Antwerp (30/1). He also had loans with Ipswich (7+1/0) and Blackburn Rovers (18+2). Simpson later played for QPR where one of his 40+1/1 appearances came alongside Nedum Onuoha in the 2014 Championship Play-Off final as they won promotion by beating Derby County. After leaving Leicester Simpson turned out for Huddersfield (24+1) and Bristol City where the last of his 6+2 games to the end of the 2021-22 season came in October 2021.

## SIMPSON, William (Billy)

**POSITION:** Inside-right

**BIRTHPLACE:** Sunderland, Co Durham

**DATE OF BIRTH:** 24/10/1877 - 20/03/1962

**HEIGHT:** 5' 9" **WEIGHT:** 11st 10lbs

**SIGNED FROM:** Selbourne, 30/08/1897

**DEBUT:** v Stoke, A, 25/03/1899

**LAST MATCH:** v Burnley, A, 08/04/1899

**MOVED TO:** Lincoln City, 02/06/1902

**TEAMS:** Selbourne, Sunderland, Lincoln City

**SAFC TOTALS:** 3 appearances / 1 goal

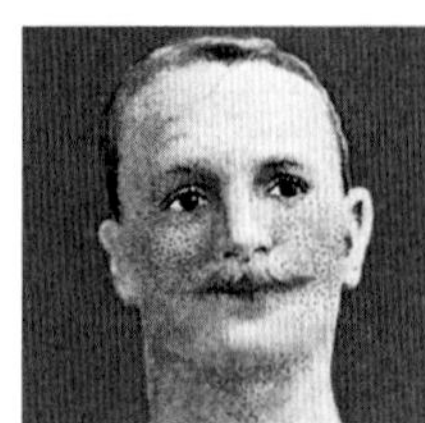

**After joining Sunderland from a local Wearside team, all of Simpson's first-team games were away from home, his goal coming in a victory at Bury.**

He was to have a much more successful time at Sincil Bank where he spent six seasons as a left-back, became skipper and topped 140 appearances before a knee injury ended his career. He stayed in Lincoln working in an engineering works and then becoming a pub landlord for 26 years until he retired on his 70th birthday. Sunderland-born, Bill Simpson passed away in Lincoln aged 84.

## SINCLAIR, Jerome Terence

**POSITION:** Centre-forward

**BIRTHPLACE:** Birmingham, West Midlands

**DATE OF BIRTH:** 20/09/1996

**HEIGHT:** 5' 11½" **WEIGHT:** 12st 6lbs

**SIGNED FROM:** Watford, 25/07/2018, on loan

**DEBUT:** v Charlton Athletic, H, 04/08/2018

**LAST MATCH:** v Newcastle United Under 21s, H, 08/01/2019

**MOVED TO:** Watford, 10/01/2019, end of loan

**TEAMS:** West Bromwich Albion, Liverpool, Wigan Athletic (L), Watford, Birmingham City (L), Sunderland (L), Oxford United (L), VVV Venlo (L), CSKA Sofia (L)

**INTERNATIONAL:** England Under 17

**SAFC TOTALS:** 11+8 appearances / 2 goals

**Having paid Liverpool £4m for Sinclair in 2016, he started just a single league match for the Hornets from a total of 5+9 games in which he did not score. Sunderland were one of five loans he had. Strong, and boasting a turn of pace, Sinclair looked like he had a goal in him at Sunderland, but rarely actually netted.**

After other domestic loans with Birmingham (3+2/0) and Oxford (10+6/4) he tried his luck abroad. He became a teammate of Lee Cattermole in the Netherlands at VVV Venlo but he was unable to score in 10+13 games in 2019-20. He then had a couple of League (Carabao) Cup opportunities for Watford before trying his luck in Bulgaria where a goal at Arda was his sole strike in 6+3 appearances, almost half of which were in the Europa League.

As of May 2022, he was without a club at the age of 25 and yet things had started spectacularly for a player capped at Under 16 and 17 level by England. Jerome had become Liverpool's youngest-ever player just six days after his 16th birthday when coming on as a League Cup sub in 2012 against WBA, whose academy he had left the previous year. Thirteen goals in 18 Under 18 games for Liverpool impressed before a loan to Wigan where he played just eight minutes - against Watford who would subsequently sign him after he had returned to Anfield to make two Premier League appearances for the Reds as a sub. Jerome's only goal in 1+4 outings for Liverpool came on his only start, an FA Cup tie with Exeter.

## SLACK, Melvyn

**POSITION:** Half-back

**BIRTHPLACE:** Coundon, Co Durham

**DATE OF BIRTH:** 07/03/1944 - 06/08/2016

**HEIGHT:** 5' 8" **WEIGHT:** 11st 8lbs

**SIGNED FROM:** Bishop Auckland Youths, 01/03/1961

**DEBUT:** v Stoke City, A, 24/04/1965

**LAST MATCH:** v Sheffield Wednesday, H, 28/04/1965

**MOVED TO:** Southend United, 27/08/1965

**TEAMS:** Sunderland, Southend United, Cambridge United, Cambridge City

**SAFC TOTALS:** 2 appearances / 1 goal

**Slack lived the dream as a County Durham lad who was signed by Sunderland after an unsuccessful trial at Burnley. He only played a couple of games, a belated 21st birthday present. He even scored on his debut in a defeat at Stoke, but played in a home win at Roker Park.**

Slack's games were in the final two fixtures of the 1964-65 season in the top flight, but evidently with a change of manager (Ian McColl) set to bring in one of the world's greatest half-backs in Jim Baxter, Mel could be cut no slack.

Having played at both left and right-half in his first-team appearances, the player who had played at both centre-half and right-back as a youngster was deemed surplus to requirements. Mel moved to Southend where he played 107+4 league games, scoring five goals. He then joined Cambridge United in 1969, helping them to win the Southern League in his first season and then playing in their first-ever Football League game in 1970. After 33+2 Football League games for United, he left to play for Cambridge City before he retired to run a pub and subsequently become a taxi driver.

## SMALL, John

**POSITION:** Right-half

**BIRTHPLACE:** South Bank, North Yorkshire

**DATE OF BIRTH:** 29/10/1889 - 09/12/1946

**HEIGHT:** 5' 10" **WEIGHT:** 12st 8lbs

**SIGNED FROM:** Craghead United, 12/07/1912

**DEBUT:** v Manchester United, A, 15/03/1913

**LAST MATCH:** v Manchester United, A, 15/03/1913

**MOVED TO:** Southampton, 13/08/1913

**TEAMS:** South Bank North End, Craghead United, Sunderland, Southampton, Thorneycrofts, Mid Rhondda, Harland & Wolff

**SAFC TOTALS:** 1 appearance / 0 goals

**One appearance for Sunderland in a 3-1 win at Manchester United in a season that Sunderland won the league was the pinnacle of a full and varied life. Having started at St Peter's School in his native South Bank, which lies between Middlesbrough and Redcar, he came through local football to Sunderland, signing as a professional after a series of practice matches.**

Small's opportunity to play a part in Sunderland's first-team history came when he was one of several fringe players used in a league game in between a fiercely fought English (FA) Cup replay and second replay with Newcastle. John did himself no harm with his performance, but Sunderland were so good at the time it was extremely difficult to get into the side.

At the end of the season, he moved on to Southern League Southampton for whom he scored twice in 51 league and cup games. With the outbreak of war he joined the Royal Army Medical Corps in 1915, going on to spend 16 months in Salonika in Greece before he was invalided back to Southampton having contracted malaria. John recovered well enough to play non-league football after the war, notably being part of the Thorneycrofts team who held the great Burnley side of the era to a draw in the cup in 1919-20. Some time after retiring totally from football he joined the merchant navy.

## SMART, Joseph (Joe)

**POSITION:** Half-back

**BIRTHPLACE:** Monkwearmouth, Co Durham

**DATE OF BIRTH:** 30/03/1864 - 11/08/1930

**SIGNED:** 1885

**DEBUT:** v Newcastle West End, A ,13/11/1886

**LAST MATCH:** v Newcastle West End, A ,13/11/1886

**MOVED TO:** Newcastle West End, September 1887

**TEAMS:** Sunderland, Newcastle West End

**SAFC TOTALS:** 1 appearance / 0 goals

**Joe Smart's contribution to Sunderland was massively more than playing in one official competitive game. For a start, that English (FA) Cup tie was actually three games. Only one counts in official records as the earlier two - both won by Sunderland - were expunged from records after the Tynesiders succeeded in protests and eventually won the tie. This was Sunderland's third-ever tie in the competition and the first against a team other than Redcar.**

Smart also played in friendlies for Sunderland and is known to have played occasional reserve matches around 1888-89 when he was noted as a veteran. From 1887 he was a long-term trainer of the 'A' team (Reserves). Into the 1890s he was also acting as a referee in some Sunderland reserve games.

He later became a steward at the Monkwearmouth Conservative Club from 1900 until 1914 after which he became the landlord of the Aquatic Arms in Monkwearmouth from 1914 to 1930. This was a pub that had earlier been run by Jimmy Hannah (1895-97) and would be run by Arthur Housam (1945-47). His earlier employment had been as a blacksmith and then a machinist in an engine works before, during and immediately after his football career. Joe's birth and baptism records give him as Joseph Smirk.

## SMEATON, John Raymond (Jock)

**POSITION:** Inside-left

**BIRTHPLACE:** Perth, Perthshire

**DATE OF BIRTH:** 05/08/1915 - 17/02/1984

**HEIGHT:** 5' 8½" **WEIGHT:** 11st 0lbs

**SIGNED FROM:** Blackburn Rovers, 20/06/1938

**DEBUT:** v Brentford, A 24/09/1938

**LAST MATCH:** v Wolverhampton Wanderers, A, 06/05/1939

**MOVED TO:** East Fife, 07/11/1945

**TEAMS:** Scone Thistle, St Johnstone, Blackburn Rovers, Sunderland, East Fife (WW2 Guest), Falkirk (WW2 Guest), Greenock Morton (WW2 Guest), Aldershot (WW2 Guest), Notts County (WW2 Guest), Watford (WW2 Guest), Swansea Town (WW2 Guest), East Fife, St Johnstone

**SAFC TOTALS:** 33 appearances / 5 goals

**Smeaton came to England after catching the eye with just eight appearances and a single goal for St Johnstone before he was snapped up by Blackburn Rovers. Debuting in a home second division win over Norwich City in September 1936, he scored four goals in 18 games in his first season but was injured after netting for a third successive late-season game and was forced to sit out a 9-1 win over Nottingham Forest.**

Injury again curtailed the second of Jock's two seasons at Ewood Park, the last of his 20 games (5 goals) coming in February, but Sunderland had seen enough and signed him that summer.

Taking over from Patsy Gallacher, Smeaton did well in his first season playing 33 games and returning five goals. He looked set to be a regular choice and started all three of the games in 1939-40 before the season was halted and expunged from records with the outbreak of the Second World War. But for that Smeaton may have become a much better known name in the annals of SAFC history.

He served as a lance corporal in the Black Watch and was wounded in Sicily in 1943 but also managed to play war-time football for several clubs including two appearances for Aldershot and one each for Notts County, Watford and Swansea. After the war he became player coach back at St Johnstone from 1948 to '51 and stayed in his home city of Perth as a joiner.

## SMELLIE, Robert (Bob)

**POSITION:** Left-back
**BIRTHPLACE:** Annbank, Ayrshire
**DATE OF BIRTH:** 09/11/1866 - 13/08/1941
**HEIGHT:** 5' 9" **WEIGHT:** 11st 10lbs
**SIGNED FROM:** Annbank, 27/07/1892
**DEBUT:** v Accrington, A, 03/09/1892
**LAST MATCH:** v Blackburn Rovers, A, 31/03/1893
**MOVED TO:** Walsall Town Swifts, 12/08/1893
**TEAMS:** Annbank, Sunderland, Walsall Town Swifts, Annbank
**SAFC TOTALS:** 25 appearances / 0 goals

**Originally a coal-miner in Scotland, Smellie came to Sunderland from Annbank, the same team that two years earlier had supplied Jimmy Millar, when the club were league champions and played the first 22 games of the 30-game season in which the title was retained.**

To make him feel at home the club arranged for him to lodge with Millar. He also played in two cup ties and made one further late-season appearance but despite his success, stayed just the one season before moving to Walsall Town Swifts and then back to Scotland to continue as a coal miner at Annbank Colliery.

This player is sometimes incorrectly confused with the more famous full-back of the same name who played for Queen's Park and Scotland, and to add to the confusion, the Sunderland player's birth and death certificate gave his surname as Smillie.

## SMITH, Anthony

**POSITION:** Left-back
**BIRTHPLACE:** Sunderland, Co Durham
**DATE OF BIRTH:** 21/09/1971
**HEIGHT:** 5' 10" **WEIGHT:** 11st 4lbs
**SIGNED FROM:** As trainee, 01/09/1988
**DEBUT:** v Aston Villa, A, 06/10/1990
**LAST MATCH:** v Swindon Town, H, 22/04/1995
**MOVED TO:** Released, 16/05/1995
**TEAMS:** Sunderland, Hartlepool United (L), Northampton Town
**INTERNATIONAL:** England Under 19
**SAFC TOTALS:** 24+1 appearances / 0 goals

**The elder of the Smith brothers who played for Sunderland after starting with Lambton & Hetton Boys. Anthony had a touch of class and was expected to go further in the game, especially after winning England youth honours although a series of injuries did not help his cause.**

Eleven of his appearances came in his initial season as a first-teamer (nine of them in the top-flight), but there were only 16 across the next four seasons, nine of those in 1992-93. In November 1993 Smith was released from his contract by Terry Butcher but following a trial at Peterborough was re-instated once Mick Buxton took over as manager.

A month's loan at Hartlepool in January 1992 brought 4+1 appearances. He then played twice on a non-contract basis for Northampton Town before an unsuccessful September 1995 trial at York City.

Anthony later joined up with David Rush to run a Football Academy in Boldon in 2010. He also managed Chester-le-Street, Gateshead and West Auckland between September 2011 and December 2014 at which point he became assistant manager of Spennymoor Town until January 2016. Anthony's grandmother was a cousin of Raich Carter.

## SMITH, Daniel

**POSITION:** Full-back
**BIRTHPLACE:** Sunderland, Tyne & Wear
**DATE OF BIRTH:** 05/10/1986
**HEIGHT:** 5' 9" **WEIGHT:** 10st 10lbs
**SIGNED FROM:** As trainee, 01/08/2003
**DEBUT:** v Cheltenham Town, H, 20/09/2005
**LAST MATCH:** v Arsenal, H, 01/05/2006
**MOVED TO:** Aberdeen, 18/08/2006
**TEAMS:** Sunderland, Huddersfield Town (L), Aberdeen, St Johnstone, Gateshead, Blyth Spartans, Chester-le-Street Town, Darlington 1883, Dunston UTS, Seaham Red Star, Gateshead, Holland Park Hawks, Peninsula Power
**SAFC TOTALS:** 2+3 appearances / 0 goals

**Brother to Anthony and therefore also grandson of a cousin of Raich Carter, Dan became the first-ever Sunderland player to be sent off on his debut.**

On the last of his handful of appearances Smith also upset Arsenal manager Arsene Wenger through a tackle which resulted in Gunner Abou Diaby being stretchered off. Despite these incidents Smith was not a notably dirty player, in fact like his elder brother, he always looked to try and play good football.

Early in 2006 he had 7+1 League One games on loan to Huddersfield, but after being released by Sunderland joined Aberdeen where he played 13 times over two seasons. Following trials at Port Vale and Darlington Dan played for St Johnstone in three league games as a triallist in 2008 before making 10+2 appearances for Gateshead. He then joined Blyth but got no further than being an unused sub.

After spending 2011-12 with Chester-le-Street he signed for Martin Gray at Darlington 1883 after which he continued playing locally, including a return to Gateshead when brother Anthony was manager. In 2014 he moved to Australia where he captained Holland Park Hawks to successive promotions, returning to England to establish a spray painting business after finishing his playing career with Peninsular Power in Queensland.

## SMITH, John (Jock)

**POSITION:** Inside-right / outside-right
**BIRTHPLACE:** Kilmarnock, East Ayrshire
**DATE OF BIRTH:** 19/12/1865 - 23/01/1911
**HEIGHT:** 5' 7" **WEIGHT:** 10st 3lbs
**SIGNED FROM:** Newcastle East End, 01/08/1889
**DEBUT:** v Blackburn Rovers, A, 18/01/1890
**LAST MATCH:** v Blackburn Rovers, H, 16/04/1892
**MOVED TO:** Liverpool, 09/05/1892
**TEAMS:** Kilmarnock, Newcastle East End, Kilmarnock, Newcastle East End, Sunderland, Newcastle East End (Guest), Liverpool, Wednesday, Newcastle United, Loughborough
**SAFC TOTALS:** 32 appearances / 6 goals

**The last fifty per cent of Jock Smith's appearances came in Sunderland's first league title-winning season of 1891-92. He had been with Sunderland before they entered the Football League in 1890 with him playing in the English (FA) Cup semi-final and replay in Sunderland's first season as a league club.**

Before coming to Wearside he had bounced between Kilmarnock and Newcastle United's forerunners East End, even captaining the Tyneside outfit. He later played for the latter as a guest while with Sunderland and re-joined them once they became Newcastle United. Jock played for East End in an English Cup tie against Port Clarence in October 1888 and went on to make 25 league and five cup appearances for United, scoring ten goals.

Although he did not play a first-team game for Liverpool he made 18 appearances for Wednesday. Smith gained representative honours in 1888-89 for Northumberland and also played for County Durham. While at Sunderland, he was employed as an iron turner. Later he became a publican in Byker but died suddenly aged 45 with his widow receiving the proceeds of a Benefit Match at St James'.

## SMITH, Kenneth

**POSITION:** Centre-forward
**BIRTHPLACE:** South Shields, Co Durham
**DATE OF BIRTH:** 21/05/1932 - 06/06/2011
**HEIGHT:** 5' 11" **WEIGHT:** 11st 12lbs
**SIGNED FROM:** Cleadon Juniors, 18/09/1948
**DEBUT:** v Fulham, H, 02/09/1950
**LAST MATCH:** v Stoke City, A, 28/03/1953
**MOVED TO:** Headington, 08/07/1953
**TEAMS:** Sunderland, Headington, Blackpool, Shrewsbury Town, Gateshead, Darlington, Carlisle United, Toronto Italia, South Shields, Halifax Town, Trowbridge Town
**SAFC TOTALS:** 5 appearances / 2 goals

**Ken was signed on amateur forms in September 1948 but continued to play for Cleadon Juniors for the rest of that season amassing over 100 goals for them to add to the 95 he scored in 1947-48. Given a debut as a teenager in 1950, a year after becoming a professional, Smith waited 30 months for a second opportunity when only a brilliant save by Portsmouth's Northern Ireland international goalkeeper Norman Uprichard prevented him completing a hat-trick.**

Sadly for Smith, his brace in a 5-2 defeat at Fratton Park cut little ice as manager Bill Murray was not there, but scouting at a match between Dundee and East Fife. Smith got three more games that season but was allowed to leave for Headington United a year later. After six months at the club who became Oxford United, a fee of £5,000 split equally between Headington

and Sunderland (who held his league registration) was received when he signed for Blackpool. Ken had had a difficult time at Sunderland in challenging Trevor Ford for the number nine shirt and it got no easier at Blackpool when he was asked to stand in for Stan Mortensen - although he did have Stanley Matthews providing his ammunition. Debuting for the Tangerines at Wolves in January 1955, he mirrored his Sunderland experience in waiting a long time for a second opportunity - over two years. With a point to prove, he emerged with a hat-trick at WBA in April 1957 and scored again at Newcastle three days later. It was not enough though as he was immediately left out when Jackie Mudie returned to fitness.

At this time Blackpool were a leading top-flight club. After one early season game in 1957-58 Smith switched to Shrewsbury in the search for regular football, scoring 20 goals in 44 games in his one season before returning to the north east with Gateshead who at this point were still in the Football League. There followed a season each with Darlington and Carlisle before a spell in Canada in Toronto. Smith came back to play for South Shields and have a final season in the league with Halifax Town in 1961-62 under former Sunderland winger Harry Hooper. After making his final league appearance against QPR in May 1962 Smith saw out his career in non-league with Trowbridge Town.

## SMITH, Martin Geoffrey

**POSITION:** Midfielder

**BIRTHPLACE:** Sunderland, Tyne & Wear

**DATE OF BIRTH:** 13/11/1974

**HEIGHT:** 5' 11" **WEIGHT:** 12st 6lbs

**SIGNED FROM:** As trainee, 01/11/1990

**DEBUT:** v Luton Town, H, 20/10/1993

**LAST MATCH:** v Sheffield United, H, 24/04/1999

**MOVED TO:** Sheffield United, 06/08/1999

**TEAMS:** Sunderland, Sheffield United, Huddersfield Town, Northampton Town, Darlington, Blyth Spartans, Kettering Town, Ryhope CA

**INTERNATIONAL:** England Under 21

**SAFC TOTALS:** 107+38 appearances / 28 goals

**Nicknamed 'The Son of Pele' at Sunderland such was his cult-hero status, Smith remained ever-popular on Wearside. Having attended Monkwearmouth School, adjacent to where the Academy of Light now stands, Martin shone for Grange Park Juniors before joining Sunderland where he became a professional in September 1992. A debut goal from a blistering free-kick enhanced the reputation he had built as a schoolboy and whenever he played, Martin's ability on the ball was a joy to watch.**

However, after 68 starts in his first two seasons from his debut, Smithy only once reached double figures in terms of league starts again, and that a meagre eleven starts (plus another in the League Cup) in 1997-98. In the tier-two title-winning season of 1995-96 his 20 league games included eleven as sub while the previous season, his late season goal against Swindon was crucial in keeping Sunderland up, and was rated the most important of his reign by then new manager Peter Reid.

Capped once by England Under 21 - as a sub at Newcastle in November 1994 against a Republic of Ireland team that included Gary Breen, Graham Kavanagh and Shay Given - Martin's only Under 18 international call up had seen him be an unused sub. He did play alongside Michael Gray for a Football League Under 21 team against Serie B from Italy at his future club Huddersfield in November 1995.

Martin moved on to play 30+3 times for Sheffield United, scoring 15 goals. In one well known moment after scoring at Newcastle in an FA Cup tie for the Blades, he was treated to a chorus of 'Mackem Mackem what's the score?' as Newcastle led 4-1. In response he signalled 2-1 with regard to Sunderland's win there earlier in the season.

Going on to Huddersfield he netted 29 goals in 80 league games, 17 of them as top-scorer for a struggling side which included Jon Stead and were relegated to the fourth tier in 2003. That summer, Smith signed for Northampton where he reached hero status again, helping the Cobblers to promotion to League One in 2006 as part of his record of 24 goals in 104 league appearances. Martin went on to add five further goals in 38 League Two games for Darlington before finishing his career in non-league. Following his retirement, Martin worked for a London-based football agency, became a radio summariser and a committee member of the Sunderland Former Players' Association.

## SMITH, Reuben

**POSITION:** Forward

**BIRTHPLACE:** Tipton, Staffordshire

**DATE OF BIRTH:** 20/03/1866 - 15/07/1939

**HEIGHT:** 5' 4" **WEIGHT:** 10st 0lbs

**SIGNED FROM:** Monkwearmouth Wanderers, 1885

**DEBUT:** v Newcastle West End, A, 13/11/1886

**LAST MATCH:** v Middlesbrough, H, 03/12/1887

**MOVED TO:** Monkwearmouth Workmen's Hall, 1888

**TEAMS:** Monkwearmouth Wanderers, Sunderland, Monkwearmouth Workmen's Hall

**SAFC TOTALS:** 4 appearances / 0 goals

**Having moved to Sunderland as a young boy, Sunderland were Smith's local club when he joined in the pre-Football League days, maintaining his employment as a boilermaker during and after his time with the club.**

Although he did not score in his officially recorded cup games, Reuben did score in other cup games that were expunged from the records after complaints from opposing clubs were upheld.

## SMITH, Thomas William (Tommy)

**POSITION:** Forward

**BIRTHPLACE:** Hemel Hempstead, Hertfordshire

**DATE OF BIRTH:** 22/05/1980

**HEIGHT:** 5' 9" **WEIGHT:** 10st 0lbs

**SIGNED FROM:** Watford, 25/09/2003

**DEBUT:** v Reading, H, 27/09/2003

**LAST MATCH:** v Crystal Palace, H, 17/05/2004

**MOVED TO:** Derby County, 25/06/2004

**TEAMS:** Watford, Sunderland, Derby County, Watford, Portsmouth, QPR, Cardiff City, Brentford

**INTERNATIONAL:** England Under 21

**SAFC TOTALS:** 25+16 appearances / 8 goals

**Tommy Smith was almost as big a cup hero as John Byrne had been when firing Sunderland to the FA Cup final under a decade earlier than Smith's exploits in guiding the Lads to the semi-final in 2004, when half of his tally of eight goals came in the cup. These included the only goal of a home quarter-final with Sheffield United and both goals in a fifth-round replay win at Birmingham City in the month 1973 Messiah Bob Stokoe passed away. The previous season, his goal for Watford had knocked Sunderland out in the fifth round.**

Smith was an intelligent player who joined Sunderland having been out of contract with his previous club Watford since when, he had been on trial with Perugia in Italy. His brother and father Jack and Dave also had Hornets connections. Jack played for Watford as well as Swindon Town and Millwall, while dad Dave had been a youth-teamer and academy coach at Vicarage Road.

Despite his exploits at Sunderland Smith was released at the end of his sole season and went on to cost Watford £500,000 to buy him back in 2006 after he scored 21 goals in 95+2 games for Derby where he won a Player of the Year award in 2005-06. Topping a century of games in each of his spells with Watford (where he was Player of the Year in 2007-08 and 2008-09), Tommy totalled 263+43 games for the club, scoring 64 times.

## SMITH, Tommy (Continued)

He was to subsequently cost Portsmouth and QPR £1.8m and £1.5m to buy him. In a year at Fratton Park, there was just one goal from 18+4 games. At QPR where he scored eight times, Smith was frequently used as a sub, 24 of his 53 games being off the bench. He won the Championship with QPR in 2011 and did so again two years later with Cardiff. There was again just one goal for Cardiff after an August 2012 move brought 20+7 games, while finally a debut goal for Brentford in 2014 was to be his only sting for the Bees where only one of his 28 league games was a start, although he did begin three of his four cup appearances for the club. After retiring, he joined with his brother to become an estate agent near Watford in Bushey Heath.

## SNELL, Albert Edward (Bert)

**POSITION:** Left-half

**BIRTHPLACE:** Dunscroft, West Yorkshire

**DATE OF BIRTH:** 07/02/1931 - 31/03/2007

**HEIGHT:** 6' 0" **WEIGHT:** 11st 2lbs

**SIGNED FROM:** Doncaster Youths, 01/08/1948

**DEBUT:** v Middlesbrough, A, 18/10/1952

**LAST MATCH:** v Leicester City, A, 13/11/1954

**MOVED TO:** Halifax Town, 28/11/1955

**TEAMS:** Sunderland, Halifax Town, Silksworth CW

**SAFC TOTALS:** 9 appearances / 1 goal

**A top-flight volleyed goal against Chelsea which kept Sunderland second in the table in 1954, and being part of the side who defeated reigning champions Arsenal 7-1 the previous season, were highlights for a player whose handful of games were spread over three seasons.**

Snell went on to sign for Willie Watson at Halifax Town. Debuting in a 5-1 Boxing Day win over Oldham in 1955 he went on to make 25 appearances for the Shaymen, all in Division Three North, only for his career to be ended by a knee injury.

He returned to the north east to become a teacher at Bede, deputy head at Monkwearmouth - where his children attended - and headmaster of Heworth Comprehensive. An accomplished photographer, he was recognised by the Royal Photographic Society and became President of local photographic organisations.

## SNODIN, Ian

**POSITION:** Midfielder

**BIRTHPLACE:** Rotherham, South Yorkshire

**DATE OF BIRTH:** 15/08/1963

**HEIGHT:** 5' 7" **WEIGHT:** 11st 0lbs

**SIGNED FROM:** Everton, 12/10/1994, on loan

**DEBUT:** v Burnley, H, 15/10/1994

**LAST MATCH:** v Watford, H, 19/11/1994

**MOVED TO:** Everton, 19/11/1994, end of loan

**TEAMS:** Doncaster Rovers, Leeds United, Everton, Sunderland (L), Oldham Athletic, Scarborough, Doncaster Rovers

**INTERNATIONAL:** England B

**SAFC TOTALS:** 6 appearances / 0 goals

**Excellent in his handful of matches on loan, Ian's brother Glynn later came to Sunderland as assistant manager to Simon Grayson who he also assisted at Leeds, Huddersfield, Preston and Bradford City. Like Ian, Glynn had an extensive playing career making over 500 league appearances for seven clubs, mainly Doncaster Rovers and Leeds United as well as managing Doncaster. Ian's family footballing connections continued with his son Jordan who was on Leeds United's books before continuing in non-league.**

After five youth caps Ian was capped at England Under 21 level, debuting as a sub away to Switzerland in September 1980 and making a first start away to Austria two days later. He was capped at 'B' level against Malta in October 1987 and as a sub against the Republic of Ireland in March 1990, while in February 1989 he was selected for a full England squad for a friendly with Greece only to have to withdraw through injury.

At this time Ian was with Everton, but injuries mounted to the extent that he missed all of the 1991-92 season. He came to Sunderland on loan late in 1994 and impressed in six successive appearances before returning. Later that season ex-Evertonian Peter Reid took over at Roker Park. Had that happened while Snodin was at Sunderland perhaps he might have stayed long-term. As it was, by the time Reid was installed Snodin had left Everton for Oldham who had recently been relegated from the Premier League.

For Everton Ian played exactly 200 times (190 starts) and scored seven goals. He joined the Goodison club for £840,000 from Leeds in January 1987 and after debuting as a sub at Nottingham Forest made 15 league starts in midfield, mostly alongside Peter Reid, as they went on to take the league title. At Leeds, Snodin played 57 times, scoring six goals. This followed a £200,000 May 1985 move from Doncaster where the highlight of 204+8 games and 27 goals was a hat-trick in a 7-5 win over Reading in September 1982. As well as playing alongside his brother for Rovers, Ian played for Leeds 1973 FA Cup final captain Billy Bremner, who later took over at Leeds and appointed Ian as skipper.

Later at Oldham Snodin played 57+2 games before adding 37+2 at Scarborough in 1997-98 where he played alongside John Kay, Gary Bennett and Stephen Brodie as well as former Sunderland reserves Paul Heckingbottom and Chris Tate. Finally at Doncaster as player/manager Snodin made 3+1 appearances. He did not score for any of the clubs he joined after Sunderland. After his time as manager of Doncaster concluded in April 2000 Ian worked for a company distributing football DVDs as well as undertaking TV and radio summarising roles in addition to producing a column for the Liverpool Echo.

## SOHNA, Harrison Sheriff

**POSITION:** Midfielder

**BIRTHPLACE:** Gloucester, Gloucestershire

**DATE OF BIRTH:** 01/07/2002

**HEIGHT:** 5' 10" **WEIGHT:** 11st 2lbs

**SIGNED FROM:** Aston Villa, 01/07/2021

**DEBUT:** v Lincoln City, A, 05/10/2021

**LAST MATCH:**

**MOVED TO:**

**TEAMS:** Aston Villa, Sunderland

**SAFC TOTALS:** 3 appearances / 0 goals (to June 2022)

**A neat passer of good balance, Sohna had been part of a youthful Aston Villa team who played Liverpool in the FA Cup on 8 January 2021. Forced to play a team entirely of youngsters due to a Covid 19 outbreak in their first-team squad, Sohna came on for the last 25 minutes after the scoring in a 4-1 defeat had been completed.**

Harrison's twin brother Myles was part of the Villa academy squad alongside him. Having played against Norwich City at development level on trial, Sohna signed for Sunderland following his release from Villa. At Sunderland to the end of 2021-22, he made three appearances, all in the Football League (Papa John's) Trophy and scored a 25-yarder for the reserves on his return to his former club Villa.

## SORENSEN, Thomas Lovendahl (Tommy)

**POSITION:** Goalkeeper

**BIRTHPLACE:** Fredericia, Denmark

**DATE OF BIRTH:** 12/07/1976

**HEIGHT:** 6' 4" **WEIGHT:** 13st 8lbs

**SIGNED FROM:** OB Odense, 02/07/1998

**DEBUT:** v QPR, H, 08/08/1998

**LAST MATCH:** v Arsenal, A, 11/05/2003

**MOVED TO:** Aston Villa, 08/08/2003

**TEAMS:** OB Odense, Vejle BK (L), Svendborg (L), Sunderland, Aston Villa, Stoke City, Melbourne City

**INTERNATIONAL:** Denmark

**SAFC TOTALS:** 197 appearances / 0 goals

**One of the goalkeeping greats of the Stadium of Light era, Sorensen wrote his name into red and white footballing folklore with a late penalty save from Alan Shearer to secure a derby win at Newcastle in November 2000. Even before then the great Dane had established himself as a favourite in the fine tradition of Sunderland goalkeepers.**

Tall, confident and agile, Sorensen kept a club record number of clean sheets in his first season as Sunderland were promoted with a record points haul in 1998-99. He went on to win the first 27 of 101 caps for Denmark while with Sunderland including four games at the 2002 FIFA World Cup finals where Denmark topped their group before being eliminated by England. In addition to his appearances at the 2002 FIFA World Cup Thomas helped his country to the quarter-finals of Euro 2004 and played in all three of Denmark's games at the 2010 World Cup.

Sorensen was one of the big names to depart Sunderland after relegation in 2003 - a season in which injury restricted Thomas to 21 league games. Aston Villa paid £2m for him. During his time at Villa he again thwarted a Magpie Shearer spot-kick. (he later saved a third penalty against Newcastle, taken by Loic Remy when with Stoke). After 158 games for Villa where he played under future Sunderland boss Martin O'Neill, Sorensen signed for Stoke City in the summer of 2008, becoming part of an extensive list of Sunderland old boys at the club.

In the 2011 FA Cup final, lost 1-0 to Manchester City, he was a teammate of Rory Delap and Kenwyne Jones along with subs Dean Whitehead and Danny Collins against a City side that featured Joleon Lescott and had Shay Given and Adam Johnson on the bench. The cup final was one of 126+1 appearances Thomas made for Stoke, 99 of them in the league.

Leaving Stoke in the summer of 2015, Sorensen cycled 4,000 miles across the USA in a charity exercise before moving to Australia to finish his football career with 36+1 games for Melbourne City. Thomas maintained his connection with Australia, working on TV on the English Premier League. Outside of football, he teamed up with ex-Sunderland players Phil Babb, Jason McAteer, Michael Gray and Steven Wright in saving Golf Punk magazine from closure.

## SPAIN, Jacob

**POSITION:** Half-back

**BIRTHPLACE:** Sunderland, Co Durham

**DATE OF BIRTH:** 16/04/1865 - 16/04/1940

**SIGNED:** 1885

**DEBUT:** v Newcastle East End, H, 17/11/1888

**LAST MATCH:** v Newcastle East End, H, 17/11/1888

**MOVED:** 1890

**TEAMS:** Sunderland

**SAFC TOTALS:** 1 appearance / 0 goals

**Spain's medal from the 1887 Durham Challenge Cup is the oldest medal on display at the Stadium of Light, courtesy of John Knox. Jacob's only official game in a national competition came in the English (FA) Cup when he played in a home win over Newcastle East End.**

Previously, Spain was thought to have played in other early English Cup ties, but research by Mike Gibson illustrated in Absolute Record Volume One, shows this not to be the case. Given as a builder in East Boldon in the 1901 census, he is reputed to have helped design Sunderland Empire Theatre.

Jacob was involved in setting up Durham Cycling Club and was a founder member of Boldon Cricket Club. During the Boer War he served with the 35th Battalion Imperial Yeomanry while in World War One he was with the 47th Battalion Canadian Expeditionary Forces.

## SPENCE, Alan Nicholson

**POSITION:** Centre-forward

**BIRTHPLACE:** Seaham, Co Durham

**DATE OF BIRTH:** 07/09/1940

**HEIGHT:** 5' 9" **WEIGHT:** 12st 2lbs

**SIGNED FROM:** Murton Juniors, 01/09/1955

**DEBUT:** v Blackpool, A, 05/10/1957

**LAST MATCH:** v Nottingham Forest, A, 07/12/1957

**MOVED TO:** Darlington, 02/06/1960

**TEAMS:** Sunderland, Darlington, Southport, Oldham Athletic, Chester City

**INTERNATIONAL:** England Youth

**SAFC TOTALS:** 5 appearances / 1 goal

**Spence made his debut in the same match as Charlie Hurley. Charlie went on to be the club's Player of the Century - but unfortunately for Alan, his SAFC career was over in a couple of months, although he did score a top-flight goal for the club in a 3-3 draw a Sheffield Wednesday. He always had the ability to score. Just a month before his first-team debut, Spence scored five on his reserve team bow in a 7-0 victory at Whitley Bay.**

A part-time player at Sunderland, Alan combined his football with training to be a teacher at Bede College in Durham. After joining Darlington he established a club record by scoring in seven successive games for the Quakers where he totalled ten goals in 24 league games before signing for Southport in 1962.

Still a Football League club then, at Southport Spence scored 98 league goals in 230 games, 27 of those goals coming in 1963-64. After six years with the club where he was playing part-time and working as an English teacher Alan signed for Oldham Athletic. He scored a dozen goals in 27 games for the Latics in 1968-69 before signing off with two goals in nine Division Four games for Chester in 1969-70 - a very healthy total of 123 league goals in a 295 game league career.

He continued in football as coach, then trainer, at Southport from 1970-72. Spence became manager of Skelmersdale United in August 1972 and managed Chorley from October 1974 until May 1979 when he became the club's General Manager until May 1982. He then went to coach in Saudi Arabia. In his youth, he twice represented England Grammar Schools and was capped by England at youth level, debuting alongside Bobby Moore against Belgium at Hillsborough a month after his Sunderland debut. Alan played alongside Moore again against France and Spain the following spring.

## SPENCE, John

**POSITION:** Outside-right / half-back

**BIRTHPLACE:** Airdrie

**DATE OF BIRTH:** 01/03/1867

**HEIGHT:** 5' 7"

**SIGNED FROM:** Airdrieonians, 21/10/1889

**DEBUT:** v Burnley, H, 13/09/1890

**LAST MATCH:** v Notts County, A, 15/12/1890

**MOVED TO:** Newcastle East End, 10/08/1891

**TEAMS:** Airdrieonians, Sunderland, Newcastle East End, Rendal

**SAFC TOTALS:** 5 appearances / 2 goals

**Only a handful of official appearances, but a significant contribution to the club's history as the scorer of Sunderland's first-ever Football League goal - in his and the club's opening league fixture as the first club to join the Football League after the twelve Founder Members.**

His second goal - in the return fixture and fourth game of the season - helped Sunderland to register their first-ever point as the previous week's win over West Bromwich Albion resulted in Sunderland having those points docked due to debutant Ted Doig not being correctly registered.

Spence's early years are shrouded in mystery, although it is known he worked in Glasgow and then during his time with Sunderland Spence worked at Dickinson's Engine Works and according to the 1891 Census, was boarding with teammate Jock Scot. Before coming to Sunderland Spence may have been with Scotland's second-oldest club Kilmarnock, but made no first-team appearances there. For Newcastle East End, he debuted in an English (FA) Cup tie at Tow Law Town on 3 October 1891 and went on to play five Cup games for one goal plus twelve Northern League appearances, scoring twice.

## SPUHLER, John Oswald (Johnny)

**POSITION:** Outside-right / centre-forward

**BIRTHPLACE:** Fulwell, Sunderland, Co Durham

**DATE OF BIRTH:** 18/09/1917 - 07/01/2007

**HEIGHT:** 5' 9" **WEIGHT:** 11st 4lbs

**SIGNED FROM:** Fulwell School, 01/05/1932

**DEBUT:** v Wolverhampton Wanderers, A 29/03/1937

**LAST MATCH:** v Aston Villa, H, 26/12/1938

**MOVED TO:** Middlesbrough, 25/10/ 1945

**TEAMS:** Sunderland, North Shields (WW2 Guest), Middlesbrough (WW2 Guest), Carlisle United (WW2 Guest), Hartlepools Utd. (WW2 Guest), Newcastle United (WW2 Guest), Middlesbrough, Darlington, Spennymoor United

**INTERNATIONAL:** England Schoolboys

**SAFC TOTALS:** 36 appearances / 4 goals

**At one time Sunderland's oldest living player, Spuhler undertook a grand tour of northern clubs including his appearances as a guest player during war-time. At Sunderland he signed professional forms on his 17th birthday and played in the three seasons leading up to World War Two (including the 1937 Charity Shield defeat to Manchester City).**

Additionally Johnny scored a further 81 goals in 161 war-time games for the Lads. These included three hat-tricks, two against Middlesbrough who signed him for £1,500 after the war.

## SPUHLER, Johnny (Continued)

It proved to be one of Boro's best-ever investments as he played 241 times for the Teessiders scoring 81 times. He had played once for Boro as a 'Guest' in 1941-42 before 27 games in the first post-war season before the Football League resumed. During the war, he also 'Guested' twice each for Newcastle, Carlisle and Hartlepools, scoring once for the Magpies.

Boro recouped half what they had paid for Spuhler when selling him as a 36-year old to Darlington in the summer of 1954. He was still fit enough to score 19 goals in 67 league games for the Quakers before finishing his playing days as player/manager of Spennymoor United. He went on to manage Stockton, Shrewsbury Town and coach Spennymoor and Stockton for a second time either side of a spell with West Auckland who he led to the FA Amateur Cup final at Wembley in 1961, where they lost to Walthamstow Avenue.

Completing his footballing CV with a stint coaching the British army in Germany, Spuhler went on to run a post office in Yarm for eight years and in later life lived in Bishop Auckland and Fishburn. In the year before his death Johnny attended a ceremony in Jarrow to unveil a plaque to his former Sunderland colleague, goalkeeper Jimmy Thorpe.

## STALEY, Clive Howard Victor

**POSITION:** Centre-forward

**BIRTHPLACE:** Newhall, Derbyshire

**DATE OF BIRTH:** 14/05/1899 - 18/03/1985

**HEIGHT:** 5' 8½" **WEIGHT:** 11st 7lbs

**SIGNED FROM:** Newhall Swifts, 04/03/1921

**DEBUT:** v Manchester City, H 14/01/1922

**LAST MATCH:** v Manchester City, H, 14/01/1922

**MOVED TO:** Stoke, 20/07/1922

**TEAMS:** Newhall, Newhall Swifts, Sunderland, Stoke, Burton All Saints

**SAFC TOTALS:** 1 appearance / 0 goals

**An estimated meagre crowd of 10,000 saw Staley's only Football League game for any of his clubs, but the chances are they saw precious little of the debutant as the game was played in very foggy conditions, with hailstones an added bonus in the days when most of the stands were uncovered.**

To add to Staley's woes, local press reports referred to him as Stanley rather than Staley. After retiring from football, Staley, who in the 1939 census gave his name as Clive, ran the Star Inn on Burton High Street and also worked as a packer in a local ordinance factory during WW2

## STANNARD, Paul

**POSITION:** Centre-forward

**BIRTHPLACE:** Warwick, Warwickshire

**DATE OF BIRTH:** 17/01/1895 - 24/11/1982

**HEIGHT:** 5' 10" **WEIGHT:** 11st 7lbs

**SIGNED FROM:** Tamworth Castle, 09/05/1921

**DEBUT:** v Liverpool, H, 27/08/1921

**LAST MATCH:** v Birmingham, H, 15/09/1923

**MOVED TO:** South Shields, 26/12/1923

**TEAMS:** Tamworth Castle, Sunderland, South Shields, Carlisle United, Workington, West Stanley, Jarrow

**SAFC TOTALS:** 14 appearances / 3 goals

**Eight of Stannard's 14 appearances came in the opening eight games of the 1921-22 season during which he scored both goals in a 2-1 win at Huddersfield.**

He went in to score once in three Second Division games for South Shields and later scored 17 North Eastern League goals for Workington after a short spell playing for Carlisle United in the same competition. After retiring from football, Paul became a coal merchant living in Tyseley, Birmingham.

## STEAD, Jonathan Graeme

**POSITION:** Centre-forward

**BIRTHPLACE:** Huddersfield, Yorkshire

**DATE OF BIRTH:** 07/04/1983

**HEIGHT:** 6' 3½" **WEIGHT:** 13st 3lbs

**SIGNED FROM:** Blackburn Rovers, 13/06/2005

**DEBUT:** v Charlton Athletic, H, 13/08/2005

**LAST MATCH:** v West Bromwich Albion, H, 28/08/2006

**MOVED TO:** Sheffield United, 11/01/2007

**TEAMS:** Huddersfield Town, Blackburn Rovers, Sunderland, Derby County (L), Sheffield United, Ipswich Town, Coventry City (L), Bristol City, Huddersfield Town, Oldham Athletic (L), Bradford City (L), Notts County, Harrogate Town

**INTERNATIONAL:** England Under 21

**SAFC TOTALS:** 26+14 appearances / 2 goals

**Going 1,706 minutes without scoring saw Stead wait longer than any Sunderland forward in history before scoring his first goal for the club. When he broke his duck it was from extremely close range at Everton. Stead's only other goal for SAFC was a last-minute strike in a dismal 3-1 defeat at Southend United shortly after Niall Quinn had taken over as manager.**

Regardless of this woeful goals return the crowd stuck with Stead as there was no doubting his willingness to graft and equally, he was not a bad player at all. He simply struggled to score in a struggling team.

Roy Keane did not fancy him. Stead's last game was the last before the appointment of Keane who never picked him, but sent him out on loan to Derby little more than a month after taking over. After six games without a goal for the Rams he suddenly scored in three successive matches, his only goals in 15+2 appearances for them before Sheffield United paid Sunderland just under £1m less than the £1.8m he had cost (with more promised depending upon performances). Stead scored eleven goals for the Blades in 32+15 games and went on to hit 20 in 42+25 games for Ipswich who he initially joined on loan. In turn, the Tractor Boys loaned him to Coventry where there were two goals in 9+1 outings.

Three years with Bristol City from August 2010 brought 20 goals in 64+19 games and a Player of the Year accolade in 2011-12. After this there were 10+13 games and two goals in a return to hometown Huddersfield where he had started his career with 24 goals in 62+14 games. Second-spell loans to Oldham and Bradford City brought figures of 4+1/0 and 43+5/6. Almost inevitably, one of those goals was against Sunderland as he helped Phil Parkinson's League One Bradford knock Premier League Sunderland out of the FA Cup in 2015. In the previous round, he had scored City's first goal as they sensationally came from two down to knock out Chelsea at Stamford Bridge.

June 2015 saw Stead start a four-year spell at Notts County where he scored 51 goals in 161+21 games. The final two years of his career were with Harrogate Town who he helped win promotion into the Football League in his first season via a Wembley Play-Off final against former club Notts County in which on-loan Sunderland forward Jack Diamond scored. A return to the Football League brought just two further goals as he finished with a total of nine goals in 26+28 games for the club and a career total of 165 goals for a man who found it really tough to score for Sunderland.

Upon retirement he moved to the USA as assistant coach of Hartford Athletic for a season before taking up a similar post at Tampa Bay Rowdies in 2022 under the management of his old Sunderland teammate Neill Collins. Perhaps his best time in the game came at his second club Blackburn Rovers where mid-way through the 2003-04 campaign he stepped up from the third tier to the Premier League and proceeded to score six goals in 13 games to help keep the club up.

However the goals dried up before his move to Sunderland with just two more added from an overall total of 33+14 games for Rovers and one in eleven games for England Under 21s between a February 2004 debut alongside Justin Hoyte and Darren Bent against the Netherlands and October 2005 v Poland. His one goal for England Under 21s against Wales came shortly after he had signed for Sunderland, but did not boost his chances of scoring for his club.

## **STEELE, Jason** Sean

**POSITION:** Goalkeeper

**BIRTHPLACE:** Newton Aycliffe, Co Durham

**DATE OF BIRTH:** 18/08/1990

**HEIGHT:** 6' 2" **WEIGHT:** 12st 8lbs

**SIGNED FROM:** Blackburn Rovers, 26/07/2017

**DEBUT:** v Derby County, H, 04/08/2017

**LAST MATCH:** v Wolverhampton Wanderers, H, 06/05/2018

**MOVED TO:** Brighton & Hove Albion, 21/06/2018

**TEAMS:** Middlesbrough, Northampton Town (L), Blackburn Rovers, Sunderland, Brighton & Hove Albion (to June 2022)

**INTERNATIONAL:** England Under 21 & Great Britain

**SAFC TOTALS:** 18 appearances / 0 goals

**Under CEO Martin Bain, the decision to sell Vito Mannone as well as Jordan Pickford after relegation from the Premier League resulted in a calamitous outcome. Bought for an undisclosed fee reported to be in the region of £500,000, Jason Steele conceded five goals on his Stadium of Light bow in a friendly with Celtic and went on to play fewer than 20 games in a season when further goalkeeper signings Robbin Ruiter and Lee Camp also endured torrid times.**

Steele's quality was underlined by his 34 appearances at various age levels for England including seven for the Under 21s. He was also selected for the Great Britain squad for the 2012 Olympics, although he did not appear at the tournament itself, but did play 45 minutes in a warm-up match against Brazil at his old club Middlesbrough. That ability was recognised when upon leaving Sunderland, he was signed by Premier League Brighton, albeit as a back-up keeper. To the end of 2021-22 after four seasons as a Seagull, he had played just once in the Premier League. In that time, Jason had played eight cup games. In one of those, he was at fault for a very late equaliser against Newport County only to go on and save four shoot-out spot-kicks.

Steele had made his league debut in February 2010 against Cheltenham on loan to Northampton from Middlesbrough. He played 13 games for the Cobblers before breaking into the team at his parent club. He did so well that in 2012-13 he was Boro's Player and Young Player of the Year as well as picking up the junior gong from the North East Football Writers'. After 142 games for the Teessiders Steele commanded a £1m fee when moving to Blackburn after an initial loan. For Rovers he came close to matching his Middlesbrough total with 137 games.

## **STEELS, Vinnie** Barry

**POSITION:** Winger

**BIRTHPLACE:** Hartlepool, Co Durham

**DATE OF BIRTH:** 09/08/2001

**HEIGHT:** 5' 10" **WEIGHT:** 11st 0lbs

**SIGNED FROM:** Burnley, 15/08/2020

**DEBUT:** v Fleetwood Town, A, 10/11/2020

**LAST MATCH:** v Fleetwood Town A, 10/11/2020

**MOVED TO:** Contract not renewed, 30/06/2022

**TEAMS:** Darlington, York City, Burnley, Sunderland Shildon (to August 2022)

**SAFC TOTALS:** 0+1 appearances / 0 goal

**Steels started with Sunderland, playing at Under 14 level before being released. After a short spell at Darlington he played for York between February and July 2018, making a National League debut when only 16 before joining the Development side at Premier League Burnley as an 18-year old.**

In November 2019 he had a trial with Doncaster Rovers reserves. After re-joining Sunderland he returned to Burnley in an August 2021 reserve game and scored twice in an inspired performance at his old club as he celebrated the renewal of a one-year contract. Introduced as a sub on his Sunderland debut, his 41 minutes as a sub for fellow sub Ciaran Dunne saw Sunderland fall to defeat in a Football League Trophy game after leading when he came on.

## **STELLING,** John Graeme Surtees **(Jack)**

**POSITION:** Right-back

**BIRTHPLACE:** Washington, Co Durham

**DATE OF BIRTH:** 23/05/1924 - 29/03/1993

**HEIGHT:** 5' 9" **WEIGHT:** 10st 8lbs

**SIGNED FROM:** Usworth Grange, 14/09/1944

**DEBUT:** v Grimsby Town, A, 05/01/1946

**LAST MATCH:** v Sheffield United, 21/04/1956

**MOVED TO:** Retired, 01/05/1958

**TEAMS:** Washington Home Guard, Usworth Grange, Sunderland

**SAFC TOTALS:** 272 appearances / 8 goals

**A fixture in the number two shirt for much of his decade in the team, no-nonsense defender Stelling was ever-present in 1949-50 when Sunderland came so close to the title. They might have won it, but for a crucial twice taken Stelling penalty failure in a late-season game with relegation bound Manchester City.**

It is harsh to flag that up as an overriding memory of a player who gave the club sterling service. He even played for Sunderland against Arsenal on the afternoon of 20 December 1947 having been married on the morning. Moreover, with eight penalty conversions Stelling remains Sunderland's fourth highest scoring full-back as of the summer of 2022. After retiring from playing Jack worked for a construction company until an accident forced retirement from that occupation.

A known joker in the squad, Fred Chilton told me that on one occasion in a league game goalkeeper Johnny Mapson could not keep still because Stelling had put itching powder in his shorts! Some of his time playing for Sunderland saw him combine playing with working as a plumber at Usworth Colliery. During the war, he had played for Washington Home Guard - therefore being the real-life equivalent of Pike from Dad's Army when joining Sunderland when the War was still ongoing. Whether he refused to give his name if cautioned is a matter for conjecture!

## **STEPHENSON,** James **(Jimmy)**

**POSITION:** Outside-right / inside-forward

**BIRTHPLACE:** New Delaval, Northumberland

**DATE OF BIRTH:** 10/02/1895 - 01/02/1958

**HEIGHT:** 5' 6" **WEIGHT:** 11st 2lbs

**SIGNED FROM:** Aston Villa, 09/05/1921

**DEBUT:** v Liverpool, H, 27/08/1921

**LAST MATCH:** v Tottenham Hotspur, A, 11/03/1922

**MOVED TO:** Watford, 07/09/1922

**TEAMS:** New Delaval Villa, Aston Villa, Leeds City (WW1 Guest), Sunderland, Watford, QPR, Boston Town, New Delaval Villa, Ashington, New Delaval Villa

**SAFC TOTALS:** 22 appearances / 2 goals

**Stephenson had two brothers who played for England. Clem played against Sunderland for Aston Villa in the 1913 English (FA) Cup final and famously correctly dreamt Villa would win 1-0 with a goal from Tommy Barber.**

Clem also played for Leeds City as a World War One guest as well as West Stanley and Huddersfield between 1909 and 1929 before managing Huddersfield from 1929 to 1942. He was a major player as Huddersfield won three successive league titles in the twenties. George, played for Leeds City, Villa, Derby, Sheffield Wednesday, Preston and Charlton between 1919 and 1937. The footballing family also includes Jimmy's nephew Bob who played for Derby, Shrewsbury and Rochdale in the 1960s as well as being an accomplished cricketer with Derbyshire and Hampshire.

Like his brothers, Jimmy played for Villa. He debuted alongside Clem at Everton in September 1914. He made 17 appearances for the club before the league stopped for World War One. He added 15 further games in the first post-war campaign, scoring once in each period. During the war in which he served in the Royal Field Artillery, Jimmy played 36 times as a 'Guest' for Leeds City, scoring four times.

Having joined Sunderland in May 1921, the fee of £300 was not determined by the FA until August 1922, but the following month Jimmy moved on to Watford. This was the most productive part of his career as he made 209 appearances for the Hornets, netting 20 goals. Moving on to QPR in the summer of 1927, he made the first of 18 appearances against Newport County. He never scored for QPR and after a year moved on to Boston before finishing his playing days in the north east. He returned to Watford to run the Nascot Arms pub, but spent his later life back in the north, passing away in Newcastle.

## STERLING, Kazaiah Roy Barrett (Kaz)

**POSITION:** Forward

**BIRTHPLACE:** Enfield, Middlesex

**DATE OF BIRTH:** 09/11/1998

**HEIGHT:** 5' 9" **WEIGHT:** 11st 3lbs

**SIGNED FROM:** Tottenham Hotspur, 31/01/2019, on loan

**DEBUT:** v AFC Wimbledon, H, 02/02/2019

**LAST MATCH:** v Southend United, A, 04/05/2019

**MOVED TO:** Tottenham Hotspur, 31/05/2019, end of loan

**TEAMS:** Tottenham Hotspur, Sunderland (L), Doncaster Rovers (L), Leyton Orient (L), Southend United (L), Greenock Morton (L), Potters Bar Town, South Georgia Tormenta (to June 2022)

**INTERNATIONAL:** England Under 18

**SAFC TOTALS:** 0+8 appearances / 1 goal

**Sterling's only league goal having played 10+24 games for six clubs (to the summer of 2022), was his strike for Sunderland at Accrington. He had also scored in the Football League Trophy for Doncaster and Southend.**

For Spurs, his only appearance consisted of three minutes against Apoel Nicosia in a Champions League game in December 2017. Leaving Tottenham in 2021, he played in the Isthmian League before moving to the USA to play in the third tier. Kaz was capped by England seven times at Under 17 level and twice for the Under 18s.

## STEVENSON, Adam (John)

**POSITION:** Right-half

**BIRTHPLACE:** Dublin, Ireland

**DATE OF BIRTH:** 20/04/1869 - 03/05/1926

**SIGNED FROM:** Kilbirnie, 31/07/1889

**DEBUT:** v Blackburn Rovers, A, 18/01/1890

**LAST MATCH:** v Blackburn Rovers, A, 18/01/1890

**MOVED TO:** Middlesbrough Ironopolis, 08/12/1890

**TEAMS:** Kilbirnie, Sunderland, Middlesbrough Ironopolis, Kilbirnie, St Mirren, Clyde, Dundee, Wigan County

**SAFC TOTALS:** 1 appearance / 0 goals

**Stevenson was born Adam John Conn. His family changed their surname after he moved to Scotland as a child. A glance at Stevenson's appearance total of one is misleading. His solitary officially recorded game in a national competition was in Sunderland's final English (FA) Cup tie before being admitted to the Football League.**

That season Blackburn Rovers went on to win the trophy by a record score of 6-1 in the final. Stevenson had helped Sunderland hold Rovers on their ground over 90 minutes before succumbing 4-2 after extra-time. That game was to prove influential in Sunderland being allowed into the League. Having played around 40 times in friendlies and challenge matches for Sunderland in 1889-90, Stevenson was a main player and was expected to be selected for Sunderland's first-ever Football League fixture, only for him to break his collar bone in a practice match on 21 August 1890. Hugh Wilson took his place and subsequently, Stevenson could not regain his position.

Stevenson started with Kilbirnie and represented Ayrshire. After leaving Wearside he went on to play as an amateur for Middlesbrough Ironopolis and extensively in Scotland before a final return to England with Wigan County. He worked in the shipyards whilst playing for Sunderland and was employed in linen mills before and after his football career.

Two sons became footballers: John for Ayr United, Beith, Bury, Nelson, St Johnstone and Falkirk between 1920 and 1932, while for a decade after World War Two George became a twelve times capped Scotland international and went on to manage Motherwell who he starred for in 510 league games, scoring 169 goals. A league title-winner with Motherwell in 1931-32, he helped them to three cup finals as a player and won both cups in reaching a total of four finals as a manager in the early fifties.

## STEWART, Duncan Smart

**POSITION:** Right-back

**BIRTHPLACE:** Dundee, Angus

**DATE OF BIRTH:** 08/09/1900 - 22/12/1956

**HEIGHT:** 5' 8" **WEIGHT:** 10st 6lbs

**SIGNED FROM:** Dundee Violet, 06/10/1922

**DEBUT:** v Aston Villa, H, 28/04/1923

**LAST MATCH:** v Aston Villa, H, 28/04/1923

**MOVED TO:** Southend United, 20/05/1924

**TEAMS:** Dundee Violet, Sunderland, Southend United, East Stirlingshire

**SAFC TOTALS:** 1 appearance / 0 goals

**Signed after a month-long trial, Stewart played just once for Sunderland and had just one game for Southend before returning to Scotland after three years south of the border.**

In December 1929 he rejected the chance to play in Ireland after a month's trial with Glentoran. Moving into refereeing he officiated in Stirlingshire and the Lothians going on to be elected as a member of the Scottish Referees' Association in 1936. He went on to become a shipyard engineer in Dundee.

## STEWART, Paul Andrew

**POSITION:** Forward

**BIRTHPLACE:** Wythenshawe, Manchester, Lancashire

**DATE OF BIRTH:** 07/10/1964

**HEIGHT:** 5' 11" **WEIGHT:** 12st 4lbs

**SIGNED FROM:** Liverpool, 04/03/1996
following loan from 29/08/1995 - 04/09/1995

**DEBUT:** v Port Vale, A, 30/08/1995

**LAST MATCH:** v Wimbledon, A, 11/05/1997

**MOVED TO:** Stoke City, 07/07/1997

**TEAMS:** Blackpool, Manchester City, Tottenham Hotspur, Liverpool, Crystal Palace (L), Wolverhampton Wanderers (L), Burnley (L), Sunderland, Stoke City, Workington

**INTERNATIONAL:** England

**SAFC TOTALS:** 34+5 appearances / 5 goals

**Man of the Match when scoring as Spurs beat Manchester City in the 1991 FA Cup final, Paul Stewart had an excellent career in terms of his football. In 2016, he bravely spoke out regarding his own appalling suffering of child sexual abuse.**

Beginning at Blackpool who he debuted for as a sub in February 1982, Stewart scored 61 goals in 205+13 games for the Tangerines where it was the silkiness of his touch allied to his strength that attracted bigger clubs to him. This was particularly the case as he blossomed alongside future Sunderland Performance Director Mark Taylor under the management of Peter Reid's old Manchester City assistant Sam Ellis. It was to his boyhood favourites Manchester City that the Seasiders sold Stewart for a club record £250,000 in March 1987. Initially, that meant a step up of two divisions, but City were relegated to Division Two at the end of his first season.

Stewart was soon back in the top flight. After top scoring with 28 goals in his one full season (in which he was one of three hat-trick scorers in a 10-1 humiliation of Huddersfield), City cashed in with a £1.7m sale to Spurs, the fee being a record for player from outside the top flight. Despite missing a late penalty on his debut against Manchester United, Stewart did well, going on to revert to the attacking midfield role he had originally played before Ellis converted him to a striker. At Tottenham Paul's figures were similar to those at Blackpool despite the step up in class: 57 goals in 209+7 games.

In the summer they had beaten Sunderland in the FA Cup final Liverpool signed Stewart for £2.3m, but he was to be troubled by injuries at Anfield after a debut goal against Sheffield United. Consequently, Liverpool sent him out on a series of loans.

There were three goals in 18 games for Palace, two in 7+3 for Wolves and none in six for Burnley. At Liverpool he was restricted to three goals in 38+4 matches. He did not play for the club at all in his last two years on their books and later revealed in his autobiography that during this period he had taken cocaine and drank heavily in an effort to wipe out memories of the abuse he had been subjected to.

It was around this period in Paul's life that he came to Sunderland. His full debut saw him substituted due to a leg injury that led to his loan being ended prematurely although six months to the day later, manager Peter Reid moved in to sign Stewart. During his short time at Roker, Stewart helped the Lads to promotion (winning a Division One medal as he had with Palace two years earlier), but could not prevent them going straight back down. Moving to Stoke, he played 24 times, scoring three goals - the last of his 147 senior strikes coming against Sunderland in October 1997. He added a further 15 goals in 55 games over two years with Workington, helping the Reds to promotion from the North West Counties League.

Capped three times, all as a sub, by England in 1991-92 whilst with Spurs, Stewart spent 81 minutes on the pitch for his country, but was never on the winning side. He also won five 'B' caps, scoring once as well as scoring on his only appearance for the Under 21s. Following his retirement from football, Stewart sold advertising space for a company he set up. An autobiography, entitled 'Damaged' was published in 2017.

## STEWART, Ross Cameron

**POSITION:** Centre-forward

**BIRTHPLACE:** Irvine, North Ayrshire

**DATE OF BIRTH:** 11/07/1996

**HEIGHT:** 6'3" **WEIGHT:** 13st 5lbs

**SIGNED FROM:** Ross County, 31/01/2021

**DEBUT:** v Accrington Stanley, A, 17/03/2021

**LAST MATCH:**

**MOVED TO:**

**TEAMS:** Ardeer Thistle, Kilwinning Rangers, Albion Rovers, St Mirren, Alloa Athletic (L), Ross County, Sunderland

**INTERNATIONAL:** Scotland

**SAFC TOTALS:** 54+12 appearances / 29 goals (to June 2022)

**Scoring his 26th goal of 2021-22 at Wembley to seal promotion to the Championship capped a wonderful first full season at Sunderland for the Scottish striker who had earned a first call up to the national squad in March of that term. A tall, mobile and hard-working all-round centre-forward, Stewart is good in the air and more than decent with his feet.**

His Wembley goal against Wycombe made him the first player to score five goals in a single season against the same club since Nicky Sharkey scored five in one game against Norwich in 1963. Stewart had scored twice in each league game against the Chairboys and gone so close to another when his header off the underside of the bar at Wycombe went in off the keeper and was adjudged an own goal. Had it been credited to Stewart it would have represented a second successive hat-trick as he had scored three against Sheffield Wednesday in his previous game. Wednesday would also concede to Stewart in the season's Play-Off semi-final.

Nicknamed 'The Loch Ness Drogba', due to signing from Ross County in the north of Scotland (and in comparison to the Chelsea legend Didier Drogba), Stewart is actually from that most productive of areas for Sunderland footballers, Ayrshire. Having started out in Scottish Junior football, his move into the senior game with Albion Rovers famously came about when his dad stepped in to pay Kilwinning Rangers a third of the required £1,500 fee.

Debuting as a sub on the opening day of the season at East Fife in August 2016, Stewart scored twice on his first start at Peterhead and ended the season as top scorer with twelve goals from 22+4 league appearances as well as coming up against Celtic in one of two Scottish Cup appearances. That one season was sufficient for St Mirren to move in for Stewart.

Under future Sunderland manager Jack Ross, Stewart scored a debut goal in a League Cup tie at Stranraer in July 2017.

Although he also scored in the separate Scottish League Challenge Cup, there were no goals in eight games as a sub and a single start in the league which led to him being shipped out to Ross' old club Alloa for the second half of a season in which St Mirren won the Championship. Again, there was a debut goal against Stranraer - this time in League One. A subsequent hat-trick against Arbroath helped Ross top-score for Alloa with seven goals as they qualified for the Play-Offs where he helped his team to promotion with three further goals, including one in the final against Dumbarton.

Returning to St Mirren as Ross left for Sunderland, Stewart played against the Wearsiders as a sub in a pre-season friendly under new manager, and Sunderland old boy, Alan Stubbs who allowed him to move to Ross County the following month. Eleven goals in his first season helped the Staggies to the double of the Championship and the Scottish Challenge Cup in which he played in the final against Connah's Quay Nomads.

Ross repeated his eleven-goal haul in 2019-20. The last of Stewart's 28 goals in 68+13 games for Ross County was in an away win at Celtic shortly before his switch to Sunderland. Once on Wearside a debut goal at Accrington augured well. Despite injuries and the goals of Charlie Wyke holding him up in his early months, Ross scored in the Play-Offs v Lincoln at the end of his first term, but that was just the appetiser for his first full season as he was Player of the Season as promotion to the Championship was secured.

Called up by Scotland in March he was selected again at the end of the season and won his first two caps as a substitute against Armenia and the Republic of Ireland.

## STEWART, Samuel (Sammy)

**POSITION:** Forward

**BIRTHPLACE:** Renfrew, Renfrewshire

**DATE OF BIRTH:** 02/05/1866 - 08/11/1950

**HEIGHT:** 5' 5" **WEIGHT:** 9st 6lbs

**SIGNED FROM:** Renfrew, 25/08/1887

**DEBUT:** v Morpeth Harriers, A, 22/10/1887

**LAST MATCH:** v Middlesbrough, H, 03/12/1887

**MOVED TO:** Sunderland Albion, 05/05/1888

**TEAMS:** Renfrew, Sunderland, Sunderland Albion

**SAFC TOTALS:** 4 appearances / 4 goals

**In the days before the Football League, all of Stewart's official games were in the English (FA) Cup. Before his official debut game in which he scored, Sammy had also played against the same opposition of Morpeth Harriers in a 4-2 home win, only for a replay to be ordered after Morpeth complained Sunderland's Ford had not been properly registered.**

Stewart scored twice in the next round against Newcastle West End and then after playing against Middlesbrough scored against them in the replay only for Sunderland to be disqualified after winning due to Boro successfully arguing Sunderland had illegally fielded a trio of professionals.

At the end of that season Stewart switched his allegiance to the rival club Sunderland Albion and played for them against Sunderland in a December 1888 friendly alongside his brother Jake who played for Albion in the period 1888-1890. The pair played again in another friendly between the clubs the following month. In fact, these games were anything but friendly, the January 1889 clash being the one where James Allan, the founder of both clubs, was assaulted - with Jake Stewart also injured.

Sammy Stewart became a boilersmith after finishing with football. He had gained county honours as a goalkeeper with Renfrew and despite his small stature, it is thought he may have been goalkeeper for Albion in their first game. The Stewart brothers had moved to Sunderland with their parents in July 1887.

## STEWART, Thomas Worley (Tom)

**POSITION:** Right-back

**BIRTHPLACE:** Sunderland, Co Durham

**DATE OF BIRTH:** 18/02/1881 - 03/11/1955

**HEIGHT:** 5' 9½" **WEIGHT:** 12st 0lbs

**SIGNED FROM:** Royal Rovers, 25/05/1904

**DEBUT:** v Nottingham Forest, H, 02/01/1905

**LAST MATCH:** v Wolverhampton Wanderers, H, 08/02/1905

**MOVED TO:** Portsmouth, 02/05/1905

**TEAMS:** Sunderland Nomads, Royal Rovers, Sunderland, Portsmouth, Clapton Orient, Brighton & Hove Albion, Brentford

**SAFC TOTALS:** 5 appearances / 0 goals

**A handful of games early in 1905 all came under caretaker-manager Fred Dale. Stewart had stepped up from local football where he had won the Wearside League four years in a row.**

Having been unable to hold down a first-team place after becoming a professional at Sunderland, he moved to the other end of the country with Portsmouth but only appeared in two Southern League games in his season there. From 1906-07 he fared better with Clapton Orient playing 54 times before joining Brighton. He captained the club in the Southern League and after 40 appearances over a season, joined Brentford in 1909-10 although he did not play at first team level.

## STEWART, Tom (Continued)

Becoming a publican, either side of World War One he ran the Railway Tavern in Wingate and then the Laburnum pub in Hendon before working as a haulage contractor. During World War One, he served with the Coldstream Guards.

## STEWART, William Marcus Paul

**POSITION:** Forward

**BIRTHPLACE:** Bristol, Gloucestershire

**DATE OF BIRTH:** 07/11/1972

**HEIGHT:** 5' 10½" **WEIGHT:** 12st 2lbs

**SIGNED FROM:** Ipswich Town, 30/08/2002

**DEBUT:** v Middlesbrough, A, 10/09/2002

**LAST MATCH:** v Stoke City, H, 08/05/2005

**MOVED TO:** Bristol City, 06/06/2005

**TEAMS:** Southampton, Bristol Rovers, Huddersfield Town, Ipswich Town, Sunderland, Bristol City, Preston North End (L), Yeovil Town, Exeter City

**INTERNATIONAL:** England Schools

**SAFC TOTALS:** 91+28 appearances / 39 goals

**Marcus Stewart was an accomplished and experienced striker with a touch of class and a steely attitude. He came to Sunderland at the same time as Tore Andre Flo, but was little used as Sunderland were dismally relegated in 2003.**

Sent off on the day demotion was confirmed at Birmingham, new manager Mick McCarthy declared that Stewart would be a main man for him as he liked his refusal to meekly accept some unnecessary show-boating from (future Sunderland man) Stern John. Stewart top-scored in the following two seasons as Sunderland reached the semi-finals of the Play-Offs and the FA Cup and followed that up by winning the Championship.

Marcus also won promotion to the Premier League via the Play-Offs with Ipswich in 2000 and a League Two promotion with Exeter in 2009. He was Bristol Rovers' Player of the Year in 1996 and took the Ipswich equivalent in 2001 while twice being selected for PFA Divisional Teams of the Year. In 2000-01 while at Ipswich, he was the Premier League's second-highest scorer with 19 goals. In total he scored 199 league goals and 254 overall.

Born with the surname Tubb, he changed it to Stewart by deed poll and was Stewart when he first played at Sunderland for England Under 15s at Roker Park against Brazil Under 15s alongside Chris Makin and Lee Clark in 1988, Stewart scoring in a 3-0 win.

Beginning his senior career with Bristol Rovers - after coming through the academy at Southampton - Stewart scored 79 in 171+36 games for the Gas. At Huddersfield from July 1996 to January 2000 he added 68 in 156+4 games before the Terriers more than doubled their £1.2m outlay when selling him to Ipswich where there were 40 goals in 84+12 outings. After Sunderland Stewart added five goals in 18+11 games for his boyhood favourites Bristol City as well as five games without scoring on loan to Preston. A further loan to Yeovil was made permanent and saw 14 goals in 73+1 games for the Glovers before a final swansong of nine goals in 78+15 games for Exeter - where he signed off in April 2011 with an away game back at his first club Bristol Rovers.

He duly returned to Rovers a year later as a Development coach having combined playing with coaching at his last two clubs. Marcus went on to coach at Walsall and covered Ipswich games for local radio before taking over as head coach of Maccabi GB in November 2021 before a June 2022 return to Yeovil as Head of Player Development. Sons Kian and Finlay took up rugby in Rochdale and Huddersfield.

## STOKES, Anthony

**POSITION:** Striker

**BIRTHPLACE:** Dublin, Ireland

**DATE OF BIRTH:** 25/07/1988

**HEIGHT:** 5' 11" **WEIGHT:** 12st 9lbs

**SIGNED FROM:** Arsenal, 08/01/2007

**DEBUT:** v Ipswich Town, H, 13/01/2007

**LAST MATCH:** v Aston Villa, A, 27/09/2008

**MOVED TO:** Hibernian, 21/08/2009

**TEAMS:** Shelbourne, Arsenal, Falkirk (L), Sunderland, Sheffield United (L), Crystal Palace (L), Hibernian, Celtic, Hibernian (L), Blackburn Rovers, Hibernian, Apollon Smyrni, Tractor, Adana Demirspor, Persepolis, Livingston, FC Nasaf

**INTERNATIONAL:** Republic of Ireland

**SAFC TOTALS:** 16+22 appearances / 5 goals

**Hailed as something of a scoop of a signing when bought from Arsenal, Stokes undoubtedly had talent but remained a case of largely unfulfilled potential. While he went on to win seven trophies with Celtic, he ended up plying his trade way off the beaten track having got himself into trouble more than once.**

Given a hefty fine and suspended prison sentence for assaulting an Elvis Presley impersonator, he was later reportedly convicted of stalking an ex-girlfriend and her mother. In the latter stages of his career, Stokes played in Greece, Iran, Turkey and Uzbekistan.

Adopted by his aunt and uncle when 18-months-old (having originally had the surname Byrne) Anthony had natural talent as a footballer and played for Kilnamanagh, Esker Celtic, Cherry Orchard and Shelbourne before being snapped up by Arsenal for whom he played at reserve level when only 15. In October 2005 he made his solitary Gunners' appearance as a late League Cup substitute at Sunderland on a night when his colleagues included Seb Larsson, Nicklas Bendtner, Mart Poom and Emmanuel Eboue, the latter once having a trial period at Sunderland.

Loaned to Falkirk, Antony's ability blazed with 16 goals in only 18 games, signing off with a third hat-trick. Within a fortnight Stokes was debuting for Sunderland with an international debut for Ireland coming under a month later in San Marino. It was to be the first of nine full caps. There was to be just one goal in his first full season at Sunderland. Loans to Sheffield United (5+7/0) and Palace (11+2/1) followed, and by the summer of 2009, he was allowed to leave on a free transfer. Stokes was signed by his old Falkirk boss John Hughes (not the one who played for Sunderland) at Hibs where he was to have three spells totalling 87+6 games and 44 goals, a more than decent return.

Upon his first departure from Hibs, Stokes signed for Celtic where his skill and goalscoring ability brought many sublime moments during his time with the club from August 2010 to June 2016. Seventy-six goals in 146+43 appearances included many in big glamour games but Celtic aficionados consider a brace as Celtic fought back against Kilmarnock in 2011 as being pivotal, especially for almost certainly saving manager Neil Lennon from the sack.

Less successfully, Stokes returned to England later with Blackburn (4+8/1) before playing in Greece for Apollon (4/0). Either side of six games and one goal in Turkey for Adana Demispor, Stokes played in the Persian Gulf League scoring eleven in 23 for Tractor and playing just once for Persepolis before a brief return to Scotland with Livingston. He left without making a debut before moving to Uzbekistan to play for Nasaf where he was as of the summer of 2022.

## STONEHAM, John

**POSITION:** Goalkeeper
**BIRTHPLACE:** Witham, Essex
**DATE OF BIRTH:** 15/06/1892 - 09/08/1950
**HEIGHT:** 6' 2" **WEIGHT:** 12st 0lbs
**SIGNED FROM:** Carlisle United, 03/05/1923
**DEBUT:** v Cardiff City, H, 05/09/1923
**LAST MATCH:** v Notts County, H, 24/04/1926
**MOVED TO:** Nelson, 08/06/1927
**TEAMS:** Witham, Carlisle United, Sunderland, Nelson
**SAFC TOTALS:** 15 appearances / 0 goals

**All but two of Stoneham's appearances came in 1925-26, a season in which Sunderland finished third in the league. He had played once in each of the two previous terms, but after not appearing at all in 1926-27 moved on to Division Three North strugglers Nelson but he was again unable to establish a first team place.**

He had come to Sunderland from Carlisle a year after helping them to win the North Eastern League in 1922. He was a flour mill dresser before becoming a footballer. After his career John worked as a gas stoker at Witham Gasworks.

## STRONACH, Peter

**POSITION:** Winger
**BIRTHPLACE:** Seaham, Co Durham
**DATE OF BIRTH:** 01/09/1956
**HEIGHT:** 5' 6" **WEIGHT:** 12st 0lbs
**SIGNED FROM:** Sunderland Boys, 01/07/1972
**DEBUT:** v Bolton Wanderers, H, 17/09/1977
**LAST MATCH:** v Bolton Wanderers, A, 07/03/1978
**MOVED TO:** York City, 06/06/1978
**TEAMS:** Sunderland, York City, Chester-le-Street
**INTERNATIONAL:** England Schoolboys
**SAFC TOTALS:** 2+1 appearances / 0 goals

**Gary Rowell always insists he was not the best player in his Sunderland youth team, giving that accolade to Peter Stronach. Peter was a very skilful and well-balanced winger who won eight caps for England boys, playing alongside his school teammate and future Sunderland player Wilf Rostron.**

But for a broken leg in November 1973, the expectation was that Stronach would go on to excel at the game's higher levels, but instead he briefly carried on his playing career with York City where he played 33+5 games scoring twice and playing alongside Leeds 1973 FA Cup finalist Peter Lorimer and John Byrne, a finalist with Sunderland in 1992.

Unable to carry on in the professional game through injury, 'Stron' commenced 37 years service with the Tyne & Wear Fire and Rescue Service while continuing to play football for Chester-le-Street. Never less than stylish on and off the pitch, Peter also played for West One clothes shop in the South Shields Business Houses League. He carried on playing locally until he was in his forties before becoming a referee in local leagues.

With the Fire Service, Peter was responsible for organising football and other sports activities on a national and sometimes international basis. He also became active in the Sunderland Former Players' Association, serving as chairman in 2021.

## STUBBS, Alan

**POSITION:** Centre-back
**BIRTHPLACE:** Kirkby, Lancashire
**DATE OF BIRTH:** 06/10/1971
**HEIGHT:** 6' 2" **WEIGHT:** 14st 2lbs
**SIGNED FROM:** Everton, 02/08/2005
**DEBUT:** v Liverpool, A, 20/08/2005
**LAST MATCH:** v Northwich Victoria, H, 08/01/2006
**MOVED TO:** Everton, 20/01/2006
**TEAMS:** Bolton Wanderers, Celtic, Everton, Sunderland, Everton, Derby County
**INTERNATIONAL:** England B
**SAFC TOTALS:** 9+2 appearances / 1 goal

**It was hoped when Stubbs was signed that he would have a similar impact on a newly-promoted side that Steve Bould had in 1999, but Stubbs was a major disappointment. He did not seem to be committed to the cause and returned to Everton six months after arriving.**

Shortly before his return to Goodison, he was allegedly seen celebrating the Toffees late winner at the Stadium of Light, despite still being on Sunderland's books. He went on to coach at Everton before becoming head coach at Hibs and managing Rotherham and St Mirren. At Rotherham, he took charge of the Millers in Sunderland's first game under his old Everton boss David Moyes, while at St Mirren, he managed against Sunderland when Jack Ross took the Wearsiders back to his old club.

Stubbs led Hibs to the Scottish Cup in 2016 but won just three of his combined 23 games in charge of Rotherham and St Mirren. As a player Stubbs won the League Cup in 1997 and SPL in 1998. Celtic's record signing when they paid Bolton £3.5m for him in 1996, in 1999 it was revealed that the player was suffering from testicular cancer so it was commendable that he played so much as a cameo role in his club's 2000-01 treble winning campaign. After eventually totalling 139+6 games for Celtic, where his six goals included one against Rangers, he joined Everton after his contract expired in the summer of 2001.

After four years at Everton he joined Sunderland after being unimpressed with Everton's offer of a one-year contract, but after swiftly returning took his Toffees total to 180+12 appearances and seven goals. A final January 2008 move to Derby brought the last nine of a 551+45 game (27 goals) career. The first 232+25 of those games and 13 of the goals had come with Bolton where he twice won promotion and reached the 1995 League Cup final. He captained a Trotters team that included Jason McAteer to Wembley defeat against a Liverpool line-up that featured Phil Babb, former SAFC triallist Stig Inge Bjornbye and had on-loan Sunderland keeper Alec Chamberlain on the bench. Stubbs was still with Bolton when he won his England B cap in 1994 as a substitute against Northern Ireland B.

## STUCKEY, Bruce George

**POSITION:** Forward
**BIRTHPLACE:** Torquay, Devon
**DATE OF BIRTH:** 19/02/1947
**HEIGHT:** 5' 8" **WEIGHT:** 11st 6lbs
**SIGNED FROM:** Exeter City, 31/10/1967
**DEBUT:** v Southampton, A, 25/11/1967
**LAST MATCH:** v Fiorentina, A, 23/05/1970
**MOVED TO:** Torquay United, 02/02/1971
**TEAMS:** Newton Abbot Spurs, Exeter City, Sunderland, Torquay United, Reading, Torquay United (L), AFC Bournemouth (L), Connecticut Centennials
**SAFC TOTALS:** 27+3 appearances / 2 goals

**Other than a late career spell in the USA, Stuckey's spell at Sunderland was the only time he ventured far from his Devonian roots. The Wearsiders paid £15,000 for the promising forward after he had scored six goals in 37+2 games for Exeter where he had been an apprentice since 1962 and a pro from 1965, his debut coming at Brentford in November of that year.**

At Sunderland Stuckey was in awe of the service supplied to him by Jim Baxter. Bruce only scored twice but one did come in a 3-3 derby draw at home to Newcastle. Returning to the south west he signed for Torquay - where his father was chairman of the Supporters' Club. After eight goals in 88 league games (and a famous League Cup goal against Tottenham in 1972) Stuckey joined Charlie Hurley's Reading in November 1973, scoring seven goals in the 97 league games in which he featured.

After loans back to Torquay (4/0) and Bournemouth (5/0) he was released by Reading in May 1977 and after his short stint Stateside settled in Torquay and became a child care officer in Dawlish, keeping up his sporting interest by playing cricket in the Devon County League for Barton in 1991. Bruce also became a Country & Western singer in local pubs before becoming a lorry driver.

## SUGGETT, Colin

**POSITION:** Inside-forward
**BIRTHPLACE:** Washington, Co Durham
**DATE OF BIRTH:** 30/12/1948
**HEIGHT:** 5' 9" **WEIGHT:** 10st 12lbs
**SIGNED FROM:** Chester-le-Street, 01/07/1964
**DEBUT:** v Stoke City, A, 18/03/1967
**LAST MATCH:** v Leicester City, A, 05/05/1969
**MOVED TO:** West Bromwich Albion, 25/06/1969
**TEAMS:** Sunderland, WBA, Norwich City, Newcastle United
**INTERNATIONAL:** England Youth
**SAFC TOTALS:** 90+3 appearances / 25 goals

**Colin Suggett had an excellent career in the game and in 2022 was still a regular at the Stadium of Light with his son. Captain of Sunderland's first-ever FA Youth Cup-winning team in 1967, Colin was ever-present and top scorer for the first-team in 1967-68.**

As well as scoring in a celebrated final-day-of-the-season win at Manchester United shortly before they became the first English European champions, Suggett scored three times in the two meetings against Newcastle. He had a happy knack of netting against the Magpies scoring five times against them in four games for Sunderland.

In the summer of 1969 Colin became West Brom's first £100,000 signing. In his first season he was ever-present and added to his dozen top-flight goals with three in the League Cup including one in the semi-final against Carlisle before playing in the final which was lost to Manchester City. Suggett went on to evolve into a midfielder rather than a striker but still scored a total of 30 goals for the Baggies in 165+5 games before a £75,000 February 1973 transfer to Norwich.

He was to spend five years at Carrow Road, tasting both relegation and promotion. Colin totalled 243 appearances and 29 goals, being the Canaries Player of the Year in 1974-75. He later returned to Norwich in 2012 as a scout with responsibility for the north east where he had returned to in 1978 when Newcastle United paid £65,000 for him following their relegation. Suggett never scored for Newcastle in 21+3 games before his playing career was curtailed by a ligament injury.

It was on Tyneside that Colin commenced his coaching career, staying at Gallowgate for a decade and having nine games as caretaker following the departure of Liam McFaul. Having captained Sunderland to the FA Youth Cup, Suggett won the trophy as youth team manager with Newcastle, his team including Paul Gascoigne and Lee Clark. Always in demand, after leaving Newcastle, Colin scouted for Norwich, Portsmouth, Rangers, Bolton and particularly at Ipswich and Carlisle where he was chief scout. Suggett's brother John played for Willington while by marriage Colin was related to Jack Bartley, the promising Sunderland player who died suddenly in the 1920s.

## SUMMERBEE, Nicholas John (Nicky)

**POSITION:** Right-winger
**BIRTHPLACE:** Altrincham, Cheshire
**DATE OF BIRTH:** 26/08/1971
**HEIGHT:** 5' 11" **WEIGHT:** 12st 8lbs
**SIGNED FROM:** Manchester City, 14/11/1997
**DEBUT:** v Portsmouth, A, 15/11/1997
**LAST MATCH:** v Tottenham Hotspur, A, 14/05/2000
**MOVED TO:** Bolton Wanderers, 04/01/2001
**TEAMS:** Swindon Town, Manchester City, Sunderland, Bolton Wanderers, Manchester City, Nottingham Forest, Leicester City, Bradford City, Swindon Town, Tranmere Rovers, Tamworth
**INTERNATIONAL:** England B
**SAFC TOTALS:** 100+8 appearances / 8 goals

**A key member of the 105-point promotion-winning side of 1998-99, Summerbee's quality of crossing was exceptionally good while his partnership with right-back Chris Makin carried on long after their playing careers. From a footballing family, Nicky's father Mike was an England international winger who played against the Lads for Manchester City in the 1973 FA cup run. Nicky also had a Great Uncle Gordon who played for Aldershot in the 1930s and a Grandad George who played for several clubs including Preston between 1934 and 1952.**

Nicky started at Swindon, joining Manchester City following Swindon's relegation from the Premier League for £1.5m in June 1994 after 107+28 games and ten goals. At City he made 143+14 appearances returning ten goals before arriving at Sunderland in a swap deal for Craig Russell valued at £1m.

Summerbee was a huge success at Sunderland and with a year left on his contract had amassed 100+8 games and had scored eight goals, one of them at Wembley in the 1998 Play-Off final with Charlton. He had maintained his standards back in the Premier League but a contractual dispute as he entered the last year of his deal led to him being frozen out of the first-team picture under Peter Reid. He went on Bolton for the second half of the season, scoring once in 12+3 games before re-joining Manchester City on a free.

This was short-lived as two months later he moved on to Nottingham Forest without having added to his City totals. After 18 games and two goals he moved on again at the end of that 2001-02 season, this time to Leicester City where all but ten of his 33 appearances were as a sub.

Nicky never scored for Leicester but there were four goals in 66+4 games for his next club Bradford City from where he was loaned to Swindon, where he made a single appearance, and Tranmere, where the last of 4+2 games came at Bristol City in October 2005. He went on to make four Conference appearances for Tamworth in the same season. Post playing career, Summerbee worked as a radio summariser and TV pundit.

## SWINBURNE, Trevor

**POSITION:** Goalkeeper

**BIRTHPLACE:** East Rainton, Co Durham

**DATE OF BIRTH:** 20/06/1953

**HEIGHT:** 6' 0" **WEIGHT:** 12st 12lbs

**SIGNED FROM:** East Rainton Youths, 01/07/1968

**DEBUT:** v Orient, A, 30/04/1973

**LAST MATCH:** v Middlesbrough, A, 11/09/1976

**MOVED TO:** Carlisle United, 25/05/1977

**TEAMS:** Sunderland, Arcadia Shepherds (L), Sheffield Utd (L), Carlisle United, Brentford, Leeds United, Doncaster Rovers (L), Lincoln City

**SAFC TOTALS:** 13 appearances / 0 goals

**An FA Youth Cup winner in 1969, Swinburne made his debut in the week of the 1973 FA Cup final but faced the insurmountable task of understudying the great Jim Montgomery. Having joined SAFC after he represented Lambton and Hetton Boys and East Rainton Youths, Trevor was from a line of goalkeepers. His dad Thomas kept goal for Hull and Newcastle whilst brother Alan was goalkeeper for Oldham.**

Trevor's appearances for Sunderland were spread over five seasons during which he had a month-long loan to Sheffield United from December 1976, but did not get a game. Two years earlier he had also had a short spell in South Africa playing alongside Maurice Hepworth, Jimmy Hamilton and Bobby Mitchell as Arcadia Shepherds did the treble.

It was at Carlisle where Trevor truly established himself after replacing club legend Alan Ross. Swinburne amassed 280 appearances for the Cumbrians including being ever-present in their Division Three promotion season in 1981-82 under Bob Stokoe. Leaving Carlisle for London Trevor played 45 league games for Brentford, returning north to play twice for Leeds and four times on a loan to Doncaster before finishing his career with 34 league outings for Lincoln in 1986-87.

He remained in Lincoln where he became chairman of the Imps Former Players' Association, hosted a radio sports programme and became governor of Lincoln prison. In 2022 he briefly returned to Wearside and became vice-chairman of the SAFC Former Players' Association before returning to Lincoln.

## SWINDLEHURST, David (Dave)

**POSITION:** Centre-forward

**BIRTHPLACE:** Edgware, London

**DATE OF BIRTH:** 06/01/1956

**HEIGHT:** 6' 2" **WEIGHT:** 13st 3lbs

**SIGNED FROM:** West Ham United, 07/08/1985

**DEBUT:** v Blackburn Rovers, H, 17/08/1985

**LAST MATCH:** v Gillingham, H, 17/05/1987

**MOVED TO:** Contract not renewed, 30/06/1987

**TEAMS:** Crystal Palace, Derby County, West Ham United, Sunderland, Anorthosis Famagusta, Wimbledon, Colchester United, Peterborough United (L)

**INTERNATIONAL:** England B

**SAFC TOTALS:** 72 appearances / 11 goals

**One of the big names brought in at the beginning of Lawrie McMenemy's ill-fated time at Sunderland, it was Swindlehurst who eventually scored the first goal of the season after none were forthcoming in the opening five fixtures. He ended the season with five - twice scoring twice - from 31 games. In his second season he had five goals by mid-November but there was just one more (in McMenemy's last match) as Sunderland were relegated to the third division for the first time.**

Swindlehurst started at Crystal Palace scoring 81 goals in 260+16 appearances and being top-scorer four times. Malcolm Allison gave Dave a debut against Notts County on the opening day of the 1973-74 season. Swindlehurst was part of the Palace side (along with future SAFC assistant manager Ian Evans) that beat Sunderland in a 1976 FA Cup quarter-final and won promotion from Division Three the following season. In 1979 he scored one of the goals that clinched the Division Two title and simultaneously denied Sunderland promotion.

Swindlehurst switched to Derby County, initially on loan before a £400,000 transfer. One hundred and twenty-five games and 33 goals later, he was back in London with West Ham, his value having fallen to £160,000. Eighteen goals in 61+10 appearances saw none in his last 27 games, the penultimate one at Sunderland which was his next stop. Following his ill-fated time at Roker Park, Dave went to Cyprus where after four goals in 13 games for Anorthosis he returned to play twice for Wimbledon, a dozen times for Colchester and four times on loan for Peterborough, scoring six times for Colchester and once for Posh.

In June 1989 he became manager of Bromley where he later became a director. He also managed Chipstead in Surrey before returning to Crystal Palace in the late nineties to work for the club's School of Excellence going on to become reserve team manager. From 2003 to 2005, he was assistant manager at Crawley Town before managing Whyteleafe from December 2006 to May 2008. He also worked as a PE teacher in London at the Harrodian School.

## SYMM, Colin

**POSITION:** Midfielder

**BIRTHPLACE:** Dunston, Co Durham

**DATE OF BIRTH:** 26/11/1946

**HEIGHT:** 5' 9" **WEIGHT:** 11st 4lbs

**SIGNED FROM:** Sheffield Wednesday, 14/06/1969

**DEBUT:** v Coventry City, H, 09/08/1969

**LAST MATCH:** v Swindon Town, H, 11/09/1971

**MOVED TO:** Lincoln City, 21/06/1972

**TEAMS:** Gateshead, Sheffield Wednesday, Sunderland, Lincoln City, Boston United

**SAFC TOTALS:** 12+5 appearances / 0 goals

**Brought from Sheffield Wednesday by Alan Brown who had managed him at Hillsborough, where he had played 19+4 games, Symm also made a modest number of appearances at Sunderland.**

A neat and tidy, get it and give it midfielder, Colin was a utility player at Sunderland, once even playing as a lone forward away to Fiorentina in the Anglo-Italian Cup. He found his level with Lincoln where he made 60+9 league appearances and scored seven goals to add to the one he got for Wednesday - with a delicate chip in a 5-0 win against Sunderland.

After finishing his career in non-league, Colin coached at Consett in 1978-79, gained a degree in Recreation Management and worked at a sports centre in north Nottinghamshire before becoming General Manager of Derwentside Leisure Operations. Having started out at Redheugh Boys Club, Symm remained a lifelong friend of Ian Branfoot for whom he scouted for Southampton.

## TAINIO, Teemu Mikael

**POSITION:** Midfielder

**BIRTHPLACE:** Tornio, Finland

**DATE OF BIRTH:** 27/11/1979

**HEIGHT:** 5' 9" **WEIGHT:** 11st 9lbs

**SIGNED FROM:** Tottenham Hotspur, 23/07/2008

**DEBUT:** v Liverpool, A, 16/08/2008

**LAST MATCH:** v Norwich City, A, 24/08/2009

**MOVED TO:** Contract terminated, 31/08/2010

**TEAMS:** TP 47, FC Haka, Auxerre, Tottenham Hotspur, Sunderland, Birmingham City (L), Ajax, New York Red Bulls, HJK Helsinki

**INTERNATIONAL:** Finland

**SAFC TOTALS:** 19+4 appearances / 1 goal

**Tainio was a decent player with a good pedigree but was badly hampered by injury at Sunderland. All but one of his appearances came in the first of his two seasons, the second of which saw him out on loan to Birmingham from 1st September to the end of the campaign. His first game, as one of three ex-Spurs debutants along with Steed Malbranque and Pascal Chimbonda, was at Anfield but Teemu never made more than four consecutive league starts.**

Teaming up with Seb Larsson, James McFadden and Craig Gardner when on loan at fellow Premier League side Birmingham, Teemu immediately played four successive games but thereafter made only one further start and a single substitute appearance all season. Prior to coming to Wearside he had played 61+8 times for Tottenham, scoring five goals, the first against Newcastle.

A defensive midfielder, thrash metal fan Tainio started in senior football with FC Haka where 14 goals in 46 games in his breakthrough season of 1996-97 culminated in a cup win as Haka beat TPS Turku after extra-time in the final. Immediately moving to France he spent eight years with Auxerre scoring 19 goals in his 204 appearances.

Auxerre twice won the Coupe de France in Teemu's time but he missed the 2003 final and was an unused sub in 2005 with Djibril Cisse and Benjani scoring for his side in those finals. He did get to play in the 2008 League Cup final for Spurs, coming on for the final 15 minutes as they defeated Chelsea.

After leaving Sunderland he signed for Ajax 24 hours later, re-joining his ex-Spurs coach Martin Jol. There were only five games for the Amsterdam club - including one in the Champions League against Real Madrid - before Tainio joined New York Red Bulls. He had 42 games there before returning to Finland where 36 games and three goals for HJK completed his playing career which had included 64 caps and six goals for his country.

Upon retiring, he worked for Spurs as a Scandinavian scout and on 1 November 2018 took up the post of manager of FC Haka, after being their assistant coach, where he won promotion in his first season. As of July 2022, he remains in the post.

## TAIT, Thomas Somerville (Tommy)

**POSITION:** Right-half

**BIRTHPLACE:** Carluke, South Lanarkshire

**DATE OF BIRTH:** 13/09/1879 - 02/10/1942

**HEIGHT:** 5' 9" **WEIGHT:** 11st 0lbs

**SIGNED FROM:** Bristol Rovers, 02/06/1906

**DEBUT:** v Newcastle United, A, 01/09/1906

**LAST MATCH:** v Liverpool, A, 05/04/1912

**MOVED TO:** Dundee, 17/05/1912

**TEAMS:** Cambuslang, Airdrieonians, Bristol Rovers, Sunderland, Dundee, Armadale, Jarrow

**INTERNATIONAL:** Scotland

**SAFC TOTALS:** 196 appearances / 2 goals

**Tait's only cap came in a 2-2 draw with Wales in Cardiff in March 1911 when he was 31. At the time he was a regular member of the Sunderland side who would finish third in that season's top flight. Tommy had been with Sunderland for almost five years at this point.**

He had signed from Bristol Rovers in 1906 having been part of their Southern League championship-winning team in 1905. He had also helped the Pirates to finish third and eighth in his other two seasons after joining them from Airdrieonians.

In total, Tait played 96 times for Bristol Rovers. He returned to Scotland to play for Dundee in 1912 and then joined Armadale, despite attempts in July 1913 by Hartlepools United to secure him as their player-manager, but two years later was back in the north-east of England turning out for Jarrow for a few months. During World War One Tommy worked in the shipyards.

## TAVARES VARELA, Adilson (Cabral)

**POSITION:** Midfielder

**BIRTHPLACE:** Praia, Cape Verde

**DATE OF BIRTH:** 22/10/1988

**HEIGHT:** 5' 10" **WEIGHT:** 10st 7lbs

**SIGNED FROM:** FC Basel, 01/07/2013

**DEBUT:** v Fulham, H, 17/08/2013

**LAST MATCH:** v MK Dons, H, 27/08/2013

**MOVED TO:** Left by mutual consent, 02/02/2015

**TEAMS:** Lausanne, FC Basel, Sevilla Atlético (L), Sunderland, Genoa (L), FC Zurich, Le Mont, Lausanne Sport (to July 2022)

**INTERNATIONAL:** Switzerland Under 21

**SAFC TOTALS:** 2 appearances / 0 goals

**One of a host of signings acquired under the recruitment policy of Roberto De Fanti, Cabral started the opening game of the season and a subsequent League (Capital One) Cup tie, but other than a further 14 times he was an unused sub, he had no further first-team involvement, although he had scored against Spurs in a pre-season Barclays Asia Trophy match in Hong Kong. He had been capped at four levels up to Under 21 by Switzerland and later was an unused sub in a full international for Cape Verde.**

Cabral possessed the pedigree of playing in five Swiss title winning seasons between 2008 and 2013 with Basel with whom he also won the Swiss Cup three times as well as the Uhrencup. Such success brought considerable European experience as a teammate of future Liverpool star Mo Salah. After a seven game loan from Sunderland to Genoa, Cabral signed for FC Zurich where he played 15 league games and came off the bench in the 2016 Swiss Cup final as his side beat FC Lugano. Subsequent moves brought a dozen league games for Le Mont and 15 for Lausanne Sport.

Cabral's cousins include Gelson Fernandes, who played for Manchester City and Leicester in addition to a host of continental clubs, Manuel Fernandes, who had loans with Portsmouth and Everton, and Edimilson Fernandes who numbered West Ham United amongst his clubs.

## TAYLOR, Brandon Lewis

**POSITION:** Defender

**BIRTHPLACE:** Gateshead, Tyne & Wear

**DATE OF BIRTH:** 10/05/1999

**HEIGHT:** 6' 0" **WEIGHT:** 11st 8lbs

**SIGNED FROM:** Trainee, 01/07/2015

**DEBUT:** v Morecambe, A, 13/11/2018

**LAST MATCH:** v Fleetwood Town, A, 10/11/2020

**MOVED TO:** Released, 30/06/2021

**TEAMS:** Sunderland, Darlington, South Shields (L), Bishop Auckland (L) (to June 2022)

**SAFC TOTALS:** 5+1 appearances / 0 goals

**Like so many players Brandon Taylor grew up at Sunderland, devoting much of his childhood to the dream of becoming a professional footballer. In the end he got four outings in the Football League Trophy and one appearance in the FA Cup - playing 120 minutes of a replay defeat at Gillingham.**

A handful of times he was named as an unused sub, including a couple in the league, but in the end Brandon did not quite manage to nail down a first-team place. He had begun attending SAFC as a nine-year-old and had continued whilst also playing for Birtley Town when at primary school. Upon joining Darlington in the sixth tier, he debuted against Alfreton Town and soon had short loans in the Northern Premier League and Northern League before being released by the Quakers in May 2022.

## TAYLOR, Ellis James

**POSITION:** Midfielder / winger
**BIRTHPLACE:** Hartlepool
**DATE OF BIRTH:** 14/04/2003
**HEIGHT:** 6' 0" **WEIGHT:** 11st 4lbs
**SIGNED FROM:** Trainee, 01/07/2019
**DEBUT:** v Port Vale, A, 10/08/2021
**LAST MATCH:**
**MOVED TO:**
**TEAMS:** Sunderland, Hartlepool United (L)
**INTERNATIONAL:** England Under 15
**SAFC TOTALS:** 3+1 appearances / 0 goals (to July 2022)

**No relation to Brandon Taylor who played as Ellis worked his way through the academy, Ellis came to Sunderland as an eight-year-old after attracting interest from Hartlepool United and Newcastle United as well as playing for Seaton FC.**

Capped twice by England Under 15s in December 2017 against the Netherlands at St George's Park, he signed a three-year contract with Sunderland in June 2021. A talented left-footed player who can operate on either wing, he debuted in a League (Carabao) Cup win at Port Vale and added three Football League Trophy (Papa John's) appearances the same season.In July 2022 he joined Hartlepool United on a season long loan.

## TAYLOR, Ernest (Ernie)

**POSITION:** Inside-forward
**BIRTHPLACE:** Sunderland, Co Durham
**DATE OF BIRTH:** 02/09/1925 - 09/04/1985
**HEIGHT:** 5' 5½" **WEIGHT:** 10st 4lbs
**SIGNED FROM:** Manchester United, 11/12/1958
**DEBUT:** v Cardiff City, H, 13/12/1958
**LAST MATCH:** v Rotherham United, H, 22/10/1960
**MOVED TO:** Altrincham, 31/05/1961
**TEAMS:** Hylton Colliery, Newcastle United, Distillery (WW2 Guest), Plymouth Argyle (WW2 Guest), Blackpool, Manchester United, Sunderland, Altrincham, Derry City
**INTERNATIONAL:** England
**SAFC TOTALS:** 71 appearances / 11 goals

**Ernie Taylor's sole full international cap came in the famous 1953 game when Hungary thrashed England 6-3 at Wembley. Earlier that year he had appeared at Wembley in 'The Matthews Final' as Blackpool beat Bolton 4-3. Two years earlier he had been in the Newcastle side who beat Blackpool in the FA Cup final, while in 1958 he was part of the post-Munich Manchester United side beaten in the final by Bolton. Brother Eddie beat him to being a Wembley winner, captaining Willington to the 1950 FA Amateur Cup against Bishop Auckland.**

The diminutive Ernie (so small he was known as Tom Thumb) was a suitable size for his war-time role as a submariner. It was during the war - in 1942 - that he signed for Newcastle having started with Hylton Colliery. He became the youngest player to score a hat-trick for Newcastle when he did so as a 17-year-old against Leeds. A skilful and finely-balanced player with a low centre of gravity, Taylor turned out in 117 peace-time and 26 war-time games for the Tynesiders, scoring a total of 28 goals including seven from war-time. As an inside-right he also made a lot, not least for Jackie Milburn one of which came in the 1951 cup final. Reputedly, after that final, Stanley Matthews told Blackpool manager Joe Smith he would love to dove-tail with Taylor and subsequently the Tangerines paid £25,000 for him six months later.

At Blackpool he played 242 games and scored 55 goals, not counting one netted after only 13 seconds in an abandoned 1956 FA Cup tie at Manchester City. In February 1958 he joined Manchester United debuting in the first match after the Munich air disaster. Two of the first eleven of his 30 games for United were against Sunderland, one of his four goals coming from the penalty spot in a European Cup semi-final against AC Milan.

After ten months at Old Trafford he was transferred to Sunderland where he had two and a half years but did not play in the last six months of his time at the club before returning to the north west with non-league Altrincham. He then played for Derry City and ran a pub in Hyde before emigrating to New Zealand. The journey was a dramatic one as having been taken ill en-route, the Australian RAF had to fly blood out to his ship. Consequently, he was late in starting his job of player/coach at New Brighton in Christchurch. He came back to the UK to work at Vauxhall's car plant at Ellesmere Port while retaining a connection with the game as an advisor to Heswall FC. A biography of Taylor was published in 2013.

## TAYLOR, Richard William (Richie)

**POSITION:** Outside-left
**BIRTHPLACE:** Silksworth, Sunderland, Co Durham
**DATE OF BIRTH:** 20/06/1951
**HEIGHT:** 5' 7½" **WEIGHT:** 11st 3lbs
**SIGNED FROM:** Trainee, 01/07/1967
**DEBUT:** v Blackpool, H, 13/11/1971
**LAST MATCH:** v Blackpool, H, 13/11/1971
**MOVED TO:** York City, 01/07/1972
**TEAMS:** Sunderland, York City
**SAFC TOTALS:** 0+1 appearances / 0 goals

**Richie played the first five games of the successful run to the FA Youth Cup in 1968-69, scoring twice. His first-team experience was limited to 45 minutes in a home goalless draw before he moved on to York where he debuted in another 0-0 on the opening day of the 1972-73 season at home to Grimsby.**

Richie scored after 30 seconds of his third game, against Notts County, and went on to make 27+2 appearances for the Minstermen that season scoring also at home to Scunthorpe before leaving the professional game.

## TEMPLE, James Leslie (Jimmy)

**POSITION:** Outside-right
**BIRTHPLACE:** Scarborough, North Riding of Yorkshire
**DATE OF BIRTH:** 16/09/1904 - 15/05/1960
**HEIGHT:** 5' 6" **WEIGHT:** 10st 4lbs
**SIGNED FROM:** Fulham, 04/05/1931
**DEBUT:** v Sheffield United, A, 26/09/1931
**LAST MATCH:** v Sheffield United, A, 25/03/1933
**MOVED TO:** Gateshead, 15/06/1933
**TEAMS:** Preston Colliery, Wallsend, Fulham, Sunderland, Gateshead, North Shields, Crook Town, Ashington Town, Murton CW
**SAFC TOTALS:** 34 appearances / 13 goals

**The nephew of Arthur Temple who scored 81 goals in 184 games for Hull City before the First World War, Jimmy notched 61 in 168 games for Division Three South Fulham between 1926 and his 1931 move to Sunderland when he was one of only three players sold by Fulham to a top-flight club in the inter-war years.**

## TEMPLE, Jimmy (Continued)

A speed-merchant of a winger, he had been an engineering fitter before joining Fulham having been turned down by Hull and Newcastle. For Sunderland, he made a goalscoring debut at Bramall Lane and bookended his time with the Wearsiders by signing off at the same ground the following season.

Moving on to Gateshead he played 18 Division Three North games, netting four times before winding down his career in local non-league football. During World War Two he served in the army and was still troubled by shrapnel wounds until his death in 1960. After retiring from football he worked as a bus conductor for Sunderland Corporation while in the Stadium of Light era a relation worked as a receptionist at SAFC.

## TERNENT, Francis Stanley

**POSITION:** Midfielder
**BIRTHPLACE:** Felling, Co Durham
**DATE OF BIRTH:** 16/06/1946
**HEIGHT:** 5' 8" **WEIGHT:** 11st 6lbs
**SIGNED FROM:** Carlisle United, 10/05/1974
**DEBUT:** v Newcastle United, H, 03/08/1974
**LAST MATCH:** v Middlesbrough, H, 06/08/1974
**MOVED TO:** Retired, 01/06/1976
**TEAMS:** Burnley, Carlisle United, Sunderland
**SAFC TOTALS:** 2 appearances / 0 goals

**Best known as manager of Burnley and Bury, but also Blackpool (where he paid a club record £130,000 to buy Jackie Ashurst from Sunderland), Hull, Gillingham and Huddersfield, Ternent's two first-team games for his boyhood favourites Sunderland were local derbies in the Texaco Cup.**

Brought in by his former Carlisle manager Bob Stokoe, after being released by the First Division newcomers, mainly to play alongside and guide youngsters in the reserves, Stan sat on the bench in a couple of league games, but never made a league appearance for the club and after tearing his medial ligaments in a reserve game at Rotherham in November 1974 had to retire.

He had begun as a player with Burnley as an apprentice in 1963. A debut came at Sheffield Wednesday in May 1967, but after five games he was transferred to Carlisle a year later for £4,000. He made 214+2 appearances for the Cumbrians scoring five times.

After retiring through injury Ternent worked his way up the coaching ladder at Roker Park, firstly under Bob Stokoe and then from December 1976 to June 1978 under Burnley legend Jimmy Adamson. Twelve days after his Sunderland contract expired he moved to Blackpool to reunite his partnership with Stokoe. Stan later returned to Wearside to take up a scouting brief with Sunderland in September 2009. Stan also worked as assistant manager at Bradford City, Crystal Palace and Chelsea (under Ian Porterfield) as well as coaching at Derby County and having a spell as European scout for Birmingham City.

Ternent's last footballing role was Chief Recruitment Officer at Hull City from September 2012 to January 2017. Renowned as a volatile character who Kevin Ball loved playing for at Burnley, a biography, 'Stan the Man' was published in 2004.

## THIRLWELL, Paul

**POSITION:** Midfielder
**BIRTHPLACE:** Springwell, Tyne & Wear
**DATE OF BIRTH:** 13/02/1979
**HEIGHT:** 5' 9" **WEIGHT:** 11st 4lbs
**SIGNED FROM:** Trainee, 01/03/1995
**DEBUT:** v York City, H, 18/08/1998
**LAST MATCH:** v Ipswich Town, A, 12/04/2004
**MOVED TO:** Sheffield United, 27/07/2004
**TEAMS:** Sunderland, Swindon Town (L), Sheffield United, Derby County, Carlisle United, Harrogate Town
**INTERNATIONAL:** England Under 21
**SAFC TOTALS:** 66+26 appearances / 1 goal

**Paul Thirlwell was always reminiscent of Paul Bracewell in that, for him, football was a game of give and take. Short passes were his stock in trade as he looked to keep the ball moving and establish midfield dominance. Bracewell was playing when Thirlwell was a mascot for a match against Brighton in February 1990 with the former England international at Roker Park, when Thirlwell was coming through the ranks as a young player.**

Sunderland had moved to the Stadium of Light by the time Thirlwell broke into the first team. In a successful period under Peter Reid it was hard for Thirlwell to nail down a first-team place. From his debut, there were 1, 7, 3, 11 and 12 league starts before his last and most productive season of 21 league starts in 2003-04, during which he also played in an FA Cup semi-final against Millwall. He had also had a dozen games on loan to Swindon in 1999.

Having been with Sheffield Wednesday's School of Excellence as a youngster when he played for Chester-le-Street and Durham schoolboys, Paul played 28+8 games for Sheffield United (1 goal) in 2004-05 before moving to Derby County where he played just 17+6 games in two and a half seasons before joining Carlisle following a loan spell with the Cumbrians.

He totalled 241+22 games for Carlisle, scoring seven times before finishing his career with three games and a goal for Harrogate Town in Conference North in 2015-16. Paul stayed with Harrogate and was still with them in the summer of 2022 by which time they had climbed into the EFL and established themselves with assistant manager Thirlwell influential in the development of on-loan Sunderland forward Jack Diamond.

A career highlight was captaining Carlisle to Wembley success in the 2011 Football League Trophy final against a Brentford line-up that included former Sunderland reserve Adam Reed and had Trevor Carson and Lewis Grabban on their bench with another ex-SAFC reserve Liam Noble coming on for United. At international level, Thirlwell won an Under 21 cap for England coming off the bench against Georgia at Middlesbrough in 2000 in a game in which Titus Bramble and future Sunderland caretaker manager Robbie Stockdale also played.

## THOME, Emerson Augusto

**POSITION:** Centre-back
**BIRTHPLACE:** Porto Alegre, Brazil
**DATE OF BIRTH:** 30/03/1972
**HEIGHT:** 6' 1" **WEIGHT:** 13st 12lbs
**SIGNED FROM:** Chelsea, 31/08/2000
**DEBUT:** v West Ham United, H, 05/09/2000
**LAST MATCH:** v Tottenham Hotspur, A, 08/02/2003
**MOVED TO:** Bolton Wanderers, 29/08/2003
**TEAMS:** SC International, Academia de Coimbra, Tirsense, Benfica, Alverca (L), Sheffield Wednesday, Chelsea, Sunderland, Bolton Wanderers, Wigan Athletic, Derby County (L), Vissel Kobe.
**SAFC TOTALS:** 52+1 appearances / 2 goals

**A Brazilian who Sunderland paid £4.5m for, Thome revelled in the nickname 'The Wall' or 'Paredão' in Portuguese, where it originated. Possessed of the most magnificent torso there was nothing Emerson liked better than parading around the old training ground at the Charlie Hurley Centre at Whitburn displaying his tanned six-pack!**

For all that, he was nothing other than a model professional who did so much to help his fellow South American, the much younger Julio Arca, settle in when he came to Wearside. Thome himself was 28 when he arrived at Sunderland at around the same time, debuting in the same game as Arca. Emerson already had the experience of playing in England and had been in Europe for several years having played in Portugal when he first came to the continent after starting in his own country. His Portuguese wife enabled Emerson to play in Europe without a work permit.

In Brazil, he helped Internacional win the Campeonato Gaúcho in 1992 and after coming to Portugal helped Tirsense to promotion two years later. After impressing in 55 games where he scored four goals, he made the big step to Benfica and their Stadium of Light. Emerson only played eight league games for Benfica, but when defender Ricardo Gomes was sent off seven minutes from the end of the 1996 cup final against Lisbon rivals Sporting he came off the bench to help Benfica see out their victory. After spending 1996-97 on loan to Alverca in the second tier (16/1), Thome moved to Sheffield Wednesday where he scored twice in 69+2 games in two years before a £2.7m transfer to Chelsea. Although he played in a Champions League win over Barcelona he found the established French defensive pair of Frank Leboeuf and Marcel Desailly impossible to dislodge and so after 20+2 games came to Sunderland.

Thome started 30 games in the Premiership in 2000-01 as Sunderland finished seventh, but only twelve the following year and there was just one in the relegation season of 2002-03 amidst rumours of further payment being due if he played any more. The summer of 2003 brought a ten-day trial at Rangers before he decided to stay in the English top-flight with Bolton under Sam Allardyce where he played 31+1 games including the 2004 League (Carling) Cup final which was lost to Middlesbrough for whom Bolo Zenden scored the winner.

After moving to Wigan that summer Emerson won promotion, but was sent out on loan to Derby in his second term, playing

3+1 games for the Rams and helping beat Newcastle 1-0 for Wigan in the last of his 16+4 games for the club. His only three games for Wigan in his last season there were in the League (Carling) Cup, but he was long since out of the picture when they lost to Manchester United in the final.

Emerson had one final hurrah in Japan in 2006-07 playing 39 times for Vissel Kobe before settling down in Portugal. After retiring, he worked as Everton's chief scout in Portugal and Northern Spain from 2008 to 2015 when he took up a similar role for West Ham for three years before beginning to scout for Bundesliga outfit PR Leipzig.

## THOMPSON, Andrew Pyle (Andy)

**POSITION:** Outside-right

**BIRTHPLACE:** Silksworth, Co Durham

**DATE OF BIRTH:** 23/06/1884 - 29/12/1923

**HEIGHT:** 5' 9½" **WEIGHT:** 11st 7lbs

**SIGNED FROM:** Sunderland West End, 14/03/1905

**DEBUT:** v Everton, H, 18/03/1905

**LAST MATCH:** v Small Heath, A, 25/03/1905

**MOVED TO:** QPR, 05/05/1905

**TEAMS:** Silksworth, Sunderland West End, Sunderland, QPR, Wingate Albion, QPR

**SAFC TOTALS:** 2 appearances / 0 goals

**A coal miner who signed for Sunderland after impressing for a Wearside League XI against Sunderland 'A' on Shrove Tuesday 1905, this winger had a couple of games before trying his luck in the capital with QPR.**

Thompson played 23 Southern League and one FA Cup game for the Londoners, debuting against Plymouth Argyle in October 1905. In May 1907 he returned to the north east with Wingate Albion but seven years later re-joined QPR. During World War One, he served in the 61st Battalion Gun Corps and became a radiator fitter in Harlesden, London until his death.

## THOMPSON, D

**POSITION:** Half-back

**DEBUT:** v Redcar, A, 08/11/1884

**LAST MATCH:** v Redcar, A, 08/11/1884

**TEAMS:** Sunderland

**SAFC TOTALS:** 1 appearance / 0 goals

**Known to have played in both full-back positions in the regular friendly and challenge matches of the era, Thompson's only official appearance in a national competitive match was in the club's first-ever such match in the English (FA) Cup.**

As is common of that era, this player could have been signed to play for the English Cup game and in fact was playing under the pseudonym of D. Thompson.

## THOMPSON, Frederick

**POSITION:** Goalkeeper

**BIRTHPLACE:** South Hetton, Co Durham

**DATE OF BIRTH:** 28/07/1873 - 13/01/1958

**HEIGHT:** 5' 8½" **WEIGHT:** 11st 4lbs

**SIGNED FROM:** Sunderland West End, 01/10/1892

**DEBUT:** v Burnley, A, 09/09/1895

**LAST MATCH:** v Bury, A, 03/04/1896

**MOVED TO:** Bury, 21/07/1896

**TEAMS:** Sunderland West End, Sunderland, Bury, Bolton Wanderers, Luton Town, Portsmouth, Fulham, Norwich City, Doncaster Rovers, Denaby United, Brodsworth

**SAFC TOTALS:** 2 appearances / 0 goals

**Another of the coal miners to play for Sunderland, Thompson did so while playing for Sunderland as well as later in his life, after an extensive football career. Although he played only twice for Sunderland (where he understudied Ted Doig), presumably he had a good game in the second of these as opponents Bury signed him later that year.**

He stayed with the Shakers for five years playing 65 league games and keeping a clean sheet in the English (FA) Cup final of 1900 as Bury beat Southampton. In March of that year, he kept goal for the North in a 4-4 trial match with The South.

Having moved to Bolton he played 20 top-flight games plus one in the Cup in 1902-03 as Wanderers finished bottom of the table. He returned to Roker Park for a 3-1 defeat shortly before Christmas but missed a late-season home win over the Wearsiders who would have retained the league title had they won.

Thompson went on to play for numerous other clubs regularly moving on as he was unable to nail down a regular first-team place, such as at Fulham where in 1905-06 as they won the Southern League, he played just four times plus an English (FA) Cup tie against QPR. Fred had more joy at Norwich where he played a total of 67 games, 53 in the Southern League, twelve in the United League and two in the FA Cup.

## THOMPSON, Harry

**POSITION:** Inside-forward / centre-forward

**BIRTHPLACE:** Mansfield, Nottinghamshire

**DATE OF BIRTH:** 29/04/1915 - 29/01/2000

**HEIGHT:** 5' 9½" **WEIGHT:** 10st 8lbs

**SIGNED FROM:** Wolverhampton Wanderers, 10/12/1938

**DEBUT:** v Liverpool, H, 17/12/1938

**LAST MATCH:** v Bolton Wanderers, A, 08/04/1939

**MOVED TO:** York City, 21/12/1945

**TEAMS:** Mansfield Town, Wolverhampton Wanderers, Sunderland, York City, Northampton Town, Headington United

**SAFC TOTALS:** 14 appearances / 1 goal

**Thompson joined Sunderland after 17 goals in 73 games for Wolves. He came into the Wanderers side in October 1935 and scored his second goal in his third game that month, a 4-3 home defeat to a Sunderland side en-route to the title.**

He also played in a defeat at Roker Park the following February. Having made Roker Park his home ground in December 1938 when Sunderland paid £7,500 for him, Harry played 14 times in the last full season before World War Two and added a further 15 appearances during the war when one of his two goals was a penalty against Newcastle.

During the war he worked in the police force and served in the RAF, but also scored ten goals in 35 games as a 'Guest' with York City who he signed for after the war. He was to make no peace-time appearances for the Minstermen and moved on to Northampton Town as player/coach in November 1946 before soon going to Norway to coach Ranheim for a season. Harry returned to Headington United (who became Oxford Utd) as player/manager in the summer of 1949. He signed Bobby Craig from Sunderland, won the Southern League in 1953 and remained as manager until November 1958. After leaving football, he worked for British Leyland until 1979.

## THOMPSON, John William (Billy)

**POSITION:** Inside-right / outside-right

**BIRTHPLACE:** Alnwick, Northumberland

**DATE OF BIRTH:** 28/04/1888 - 27/03/1938

**HEIGHT:** 5' 8" **WEIGHT:** 11st 7lbs

**SIGNED FROM:** North Shields Athletic, 03/05/1907

**DEBUT:** v Wednesday, A, 26/12/1907

**LAST MATCH:** v Woolwich Arsenal, A, 26/02/1910

**MOVED TO:** Preston North End, 07/05/1910

**TEAMS:** Alnwick St James, North Shields Athletic, Sunderland, Preston North End, Ashington

**SAFC TOTALS:** 34 appearances / 15 goals

**Two goals on his debut in a 3-2 win at Wednesday got Thompson off to a splendid start and he continued to score regularly, including a hat-trick against Aston Villa. However, even five goals in seven games in his middle season could not get him a regular spot in the team as he understudied the great Jackie Mordue on the right flank.**

A speedy winger with good ball control, he went on to score nine goals in 58 games for Preston. His son William played for Ashington Reserves shortly before World War Two and Gateshead immediately afterwards.

## THOMSON, Charles Bellany (Charlie)

**POSITION:** Centre-half

**BIRTHPLACE:** Prestonpans, Hoddingtonshire (now East Lothian)

**DATE OF BIRTH:** 12/06/1878 - 06/02/1936

**HEIGHT:** 5' 11" **WEIGHT:** 12st 8lbs

**SIGNED FROM:** Hearts, 25/04/1908

**DEBUT:** v Manchester City, A, 01/09/1908

**LAST MATCH:** v Tottenham Hotspur, H, 24/04/1915

**MOVED TO:** Retired, 10/07/1919

**TEAMS:** Prestonpans Athletic, Hearts, Sunderland, St Bernards (WW1 Guest)

**INTERNATIONAL:** Scotland

**SAFC TOTALS:** 264 appearances / 6 goals

**One of the true greats of Sunderland, Charlie Thomson captained the club in its greatest season of 1912-13 when the title was won and the cup final reached. In the cup final, he had such a battle royale with Aston Villa centre -forward Harry Hampton that they were both suspended until October of the following season. An uncompromising centre-half and a great leader, Thomson took no prisoners and deserves a place in the pantheon of truly great Sunderland centre-halves.**

The son of a fisherman, Charlie started his working life as a baker while playing juvenile football for a team called Pearl before catching the eye of Hearts when playing as a centre-forward for Prestonpans Athletic. On 16 April 1898, he scored against Kilmarnock in a trial for Hearts and immediately signed for them as a forward with an accompanying job at Forwell's Bakery. Thomson spent his first two seasons at Hearts at centre-forward becoming noted for his thunderous shots and headers - not least when he scored in the 1901 Scottish Cup final as Hearts beat Celtic 4-3.

It was in 1902-03 he preceded Dave Watson of 1972-73 vintage in moving from centre-forward to centre-half to great effect as he went from being a very good forward to an outstanding defender as Hearts again reached the cup final in 1903 where he played at right-back. The Edinburgh club rebuffed approaches from Middlesbrough and Liverpool as Thomson captained Hearts to league runners-up spots in 1904 and 1906 plus another cup triumph in 1906, this time defeating Third Lanark at Ibrox. Hearts lost the final to Celtic the following year when Charlie was absent through illness. In August 1905, he had a Benefit Match at Hearts against Rangers.

At the time of his move to Sunderland, a limit of £350 had been placed on transfers to try and prevent fees getting out of hand! Sunderland were culpable in undermining this as they paid £700 for the almost 30-year-old defender. They did this by also signing goalkeeper Tom Allan with both officially valued at £350. Allan was mainly a reserve at Roker and returned to Hearts on a free three years later. Thomson had played 218 competitive games for Hearts, scoring 47 goals. In total, he turned out almost 420 times for Hearts and including local competitions won no fewer than 23 winners medals with the club.

At Sunderland through his veteran years, Charlie was a consistent colossus, making between 34 and 44 appearances in each of his seven seasons until football ceased due to World War One. During his time on Wearside he lived next to the ground in Roker Baths Road. Following his career in England, Thomson became a licensee, running the Black Bull Pub in Prestonpans and spent 1915-16 playing for Edinburgh side St Bernards. Exempt from army service due to a strained heart and muscular rheumatism, he ended up being attached to the Italian army in 1917 where he was able to take up his trade of being a baker.

In 1919 he was back in Scotland running the Black Bull before returning to Wearside to run the Wheatsheaf pub between where Roker Park was and the Stadium of Light is. He stayed there until 1927 when he retired to Edinburgh having turned down the chance to manage Ashington (then a Football League club) in 1922. Only 57 when he passed away (in the same week as Jimmy Thorpe) - as Sunderland were on the cusp of winning the league title in 1936 for the first time since he captained the club to it in 1913 - after a private service at his home in Kingsknowe Gardens, the funeral cortege travelled to Sunderland where he was buried at Mere Knolls cemetery. Hundreds of supporters respectfully attended the interment as his grave was lined with red and white tulips with the chairman of Hearts attending along with SAFC dignitaries.

March 1904 brought the first of 21 caps for Scotland, nine of which would be won while with Sunderland. As well as captaining his country, Charlie also played for the Scottish League on five occasions, all but one against the Football League.

## THOMSON, Charles Morgan (Charlie)

**POSITION:** Right-half

**BIRTHPLACE:** Pollokshaws, Glasgow, Renfrewshire

**DATE OF BIRTH:** 11/12/1910 - 08/05/1984

**HEIGHT:** 5' 8" **WEIGHT:** 10st 4lbs

**SIGNED FROM:** Glasgow Pollok, 30/06/1931

**DEBUT:** v Blackburn Rovers, H, 03/10/1931

**LAST MATCH:** v Huddersfield Town, H, 29/04/1939

**MOVED TO:** Contract not renewed, 31/05/1946

**TEAMS:** Pollokshaws Hibs, Glasgow Pollok, Sunderland, Darlington (WW2 Guest), Chesterfield (WW2 Guest)

**INTERNATIONAL:** Scotland

**SAFC TOTALS:** 263 appearances / 8 goals

**No relation to his pre-World War One namesake the 'Thomson twins' had remarkable similarities, having almost exactly the same number of games and goals as well as both being Scotland internationals and half-backs who won the league title and played in FA Cup finals for Sunderland. There the similarity ends. While the earlier Thomson was a rugged, indomitable stopper, the Thomson of the great thirties side was a smaller, leaner schemer.**

Ever-present in the 1934-36 seasons as Sunderland won the league after being runners-up, he then missed a mere three games the following season when he played all nine in the cup as the trophy was won. He also appeared in both Charity Shield games in 1937 and 1938. Shortly after the cup final in 1937, he played his only international against Czechoslovakia. Sadly, Charlie never received a cap. At the time the SFA only awarded caps for games in Home Internationals and by the time a decision was made to award caps retrospectively in 1999, Thomson had long since passed away.

Growing up in the Rosendale area of Pollokshaws in Glasgow, he started with Pollokshaws Hibs in the City and District League before joining Pollok who he debuted for against Kirkintilloch Rob Roy on 28 April 1930. By 6 June he had won his first medal as Pollok won the Glasgow North Eastern Intermediate Cup. Three further local medals would follow before Johnny Cochrane signed him for Sunderland. Cochrane would return to Pollok to sign Sandy McNab. A book on the pair's time at Pollok, entitled 'The Black and White Cats' details their careers.

An engineer by trade, during World War Two Charlie worked as a painter and decorator and also played as a guest for South Shields, Carlisle United and Darlington in 1939-40 and three times for Chesterfield the following season. After being demobbed at the end of the war, he returned to Roker Park to assist the club between January and May 1946.

## THOMSON, Robert (Bob)

**POSITION:** Left-back

**BIRTHPLACE:** Falkirk

**DATE OF BIRTH:** 23/09/1903 - 28/12/1972

**HEIGHT:** 5' 9" **WEIGHT:** 11st 6lbs

**SIGNED FROM:** Falkirk, Stirlingshire, 08/04/1927

**DEBUT:** v West Ham United, A, 01/09/1927

**LAST MATCH:** v Manchester United, A, 25/04/1928

**MOVED TO:** Newcastle United, 03/10/1928

**TEAMS:** Falkirk, Sunderland, Newcastle United, Hull City, Olympique Marseille, Racing Club Paris, Olympique Marseille, Ipswich Town

**INTERNATIONAL:** Scotland

**SAFC TOTALS:** 22 appearances / 0 goals

**With competition from the renowned Ernie England, Thomson's time on Wearside was as short as the distance he travelled when transferred ...to Newcastle United. Thomson's transfers to and from Sunderland each involved another player. He arrived in a double deal from Falkirk with centre-half Adam Allan while when he went to Tyneside, Bobby McKay moved in the opposite direction.**

Sunderland signed Thomson in the same month he had won what would be his only full cap. It came against England at Hampden Park, but having led, the Scots lost at home to England for the first time in over two decades with Thomson outpaced by Dixie Dean for the equaliser before the future Sunderland man's attempted back-pass led to Dean grabbing the winner two minutes from time to the dismay of almost all of the vast attendance of 111,214.

Having a tough time in his international appearance did not put Sunderland off signing a player who had also recently represented the Scottish League. According to contemporary reports, Bob was not fully fit when making two early-season appearances in the space of three days at West Ham and Leicester. After these brief showings he waited until January for another chance when he was drafted in for a cup replay at Division Three South Northampton. In a game where the Cobblers hammered Sunderland in the first half, apparently, Thomson was excellent as was keeper Albert 'The Great' McInroy as the effervescent home side were kept at bay before Sunderland romped home with three second half goals. From then on Thomson played every game until missing the last two in a season where Sunderland famously had to win at Middlesbrough on the final day to stay up - something they did largely thanks to McInroy's heroics.

Come October 1928 Thomson joined Newcastle who he had played against in a Roker draw during his spell in the Sunderland side. At St James', Bob became a regular for a couple of seasons replacing Frank Hudspeth - still United's record outfield appearance maker. Thomson played 80 times for the Magpies before moving to Hull City for £340 in the summer of 1934. It was at this point that the career of a man who began with Laurieston Villa in Scotland took a distinctly exotic turn.

After a very short stint on Humberside, he went to France. First joining Olympique Marseille shortly before his 31st birthday, within a year he had joined Racing Club de Paris who were managed by former Southampton player and Coventry coach Sid Kimpton. During Thomson's time on Racing Club's books the club won their only league title and took the cup too. Thomson is not thought to have played at all however, and definitely did not play in the cup final.

It was after another spell with Marseille that he went to Ipswich Town, joining them in July 1936. It was not to be a successful move as a broken leg led to his retirement as a player a year later. However, Bob moved onto the club's staff staying with them until the end of the 1949-50 season having become head trainer, by which time the Portman Road club were a long established Division Three club, having been in the Southern League when Thomson arrived.

During World War Two Bob had served in the Middle East with the RAF, but after leaving Ipswich his football career still had one major chapter to be written. From December 1950 until 1953 he took up an appointment as coach to Ajax of Amsterdam. Football in the Netherlands was still amateur at this time but Ajax would rise to become one of Europe's biggest names and of course were the visitors for the Stadium of Light's first game in 1997. With former Sunderland man Bob Thomson coaching them, Ajax took their regional title in 1952.

## THORLEY, Ernest (Cliff)

**POSITION:** Outside-left

**BIRTHPLACE:** West Melton, West Riding of Yorkshire

**DATE OF BIRTH:** 12/11/1913 - 10/05/1968

**HEIGHT:** 5' 10" **WEIGHT:** 11st 7lbs

**SIGNED FROM:** Frickley Colliery, 27/09/1932

**DEBUT:** v Middlesbrough, H, 22/03/1933

**LAST MATCH:** v Blackburn Rovers, A, 20/10/1934

**MOVED TO:** Hull City, 28/11/1934

**TEAMS:** Dearne Valley, Sandymount United, Denaby, Frickley Colliery, Sunderland, Hull City, Kidderminster Harriers, Cheltenham Town, Bristol City

**INTERNATIONAL:** England

**SAFC TOTALS:** 4 appearances / 0 goals

**Rather like Jack Lemon of the 1987-88 promotion team - who was not called Jack at all, but Paul - Cliff Thorley was not called Cliff. Christened Ernest, Thorley nonetheless answered to Cliff.**

A Yorkshireman, Sunderland were his first league club after working his way through a footballing CV that read: Wath National School, Dearne Valley, Sandymount United, Denaby and Frickley Colliery where he was with that club for less than a week before signing for Sunderland.

Still a teenager when he joined Sunderland, 'Cliff' debuted in a goalless draw with Middlesbrough the following March. He did well enough to hold his place for the next match which was lost at Sheffield United, but Thorley's task was extremely difficult as Jimmy Connor normally occupied Thorley's left-wing position. There was another opportunity in an Easter Monday defeat at Birmingham, but it was a year and a half until 'Cliff's fourth and final Sunderland appearance, a goalless draw at Blackburn meaning Sunderland had not scored in any of his four games on the wing.

The following month - November 1934 - Thorley was allowed to join Hull City where he went on to play 36 times, scoring five goals before joining Kidderminster Harriers in the Birmingham League after a year and a half. A subsequent transfer to Cheltenham, who played in the Birmingham Combination, preceded a return to Football League action when Thorley joined Bristol City for whom he scored three times in 14 games before moving to Huddersfield in March 1939 to become a policeman. In 1949, Thorley emigrated to New Zealand where he became a grocer until his death in Upper Hutt, Wellington.

## THORNTON, Sean

**POSITION:** Midfielder

**BIRTHPLACE:** Drogheda, Republic of Ireland

**DATE OF BIRTH:** 18/05/1983

**HEIGHT:** 5' 10" **WEIGHT:** 13st 11lbs

**SIGNED FROM:** Tranmere Rovers, 08/07/2002

**DEBUT:** v Bolton Wanderers, H, 14/01/2003

**LAST MATCH:** v Ipswich Town, A, 17/04/2005

**MOVED TO:** Doncaster Rovers, 11/07/2005

**TEAMS:** Tranmere Rovers, Sunderland, Blackpool (L), Doncaster Rovers, Leyton Orient, Shrewsbury Town (L), Aberystwyth Town, Conwy Borough, Bala Town, Drogheda United, Rathmullen Celtic, Athboy Celtic, Newfoundwell, Moneymore

**INTERNATIONAL:** Republic of Ireland Under 21

**SAFC TOTALS:** 38+26 appearances / 9 goals

**A naturally gifted footballer, Sean sadly never fulfilled his potential having seemingly found it difficult to focus solely on his sport and experiencing difficulties with his weight and lifestyle, something that frustrated manager Mick McCarthy. Famously in one of his early appearances for Sunderland late in the dismal relegation season of 2002-03, the mercurial Italian international Gianfranco Zola knocked on the Sunderland dressing room door to give Sean his shirt in tribute to Thornton's performance in a game where both had scored, in Sean's case his first Sunderland goal with an exquisite free kick.**

Earlier that season Thornton had made 2+2 appearances on loan to Blackpool having previously played 9+4 times for Tranmere, scoring once while later in the same term he missed some of Sunderland's season due to playing for his country in the World Youth Championships. His move to Sunderland was valued via a tribunal with an initial fee of £225,000 potentially rising to £625,000 based on club and international appearances, with Sunderland reportedly fined £1,500 for having made an illegal approach to the player.

Doncaster Rovers paid a club record £175,000 to sign him. He was to make 49+28 appearances and net four times in two seasons with Rovers, producing an assist for the winner in the 2007 Football League Trophy final at the Millennium Stadium and scoring in a League Cup win over Aston Villa. The summer of 2007 brought a move to Leyton Orient and a debut goal from a free kick. It was one of twelve goals Sean scored in 83+19 games before being released after further weight problems, but his stature with the club's fans led to local singer Steve White recording a song in Sean's honour. In the second of his four seasons with the O's, Thornton had six games on loan to Shrewsbury, scoring once.

Dropping further down the footballing ladder Thornton's next move was to the Welsh Premier League where he spent two seasons with Aberystwyth Town, the first of eight goals in 24 games coming against Port Talbot Town. In 2013 he scored three goals in six games for Conwy Borough only to be released apparently for disciplinary reasons. He then played eleven times for Bala Town before returning to Ireland and scoring eleven times in 67 games for his hometown Drogheda United, before a series of short spells with various smaller Irish clubs.

At international level Sean had the talent to be a full international but never achieved that, contenting himself with nine Under 19 caps and twelve at Under 21 level. His brother Kevin played for a mixture of league, non-league and Irish clubs, but was mainly noted for his early spell at Coventry where over half of his 50 league appearances were as a sub.

## THORPE, James Horatio (Jimmy)

**POSITION:** Goalkeeper

**BIRTHPLACE:** Jarrow, Co Durham

**DATE OF BIRTH:** 16/09/1913 - 05/02/1936

**HEIGHT:** 5' 10" **WEIGHT:** 11st 10lbs

**SIGNED FROM:** Jarrow, 25/09/1930

**DEBUT:** v Huddersfield Town, H, 25/10/1930

**LAST MATCH:** v Chelsea, H, 01/02/1936

**MOVED TO:** Deceased, 05/02/1936

**TEAMS:** Jarrow, Sunderland

**SAFC TOTALS:** 139 appearances / 0 goals

**Jimmy Thorpe found playing sports very easy and could have been a cricketer or a footballer. He chose the latter and by the time he was 21, had amassed almost a century of appearances between the sticks for Sunderland.**

Tragically Jimmy died aged only 22. A diabetic, he passed away in hospital four days after sustaining - according to contemporary press reports - three kicks to the body and another to the head resulting in his left eye becoming swollen and closed in a goalmouth scramble against Chelsea.

According to Raich Carter's autobiography, Thorpe walked out of Roker Park after the game whereas nowadays he may well have gone straight to hospital for observation. Contemporary press reports quickly changed from initial post-match criticism of Jimmy letting Chelsea score their last two goals in the 3-3 draw to concern for his health as within 48 hours after the game he was reported as lying ill in bed at home.

He was only transferred to Monkwearmouth & Southwick Hospital for observation in the early hours of 4th February. At two o'clock the next afternoon, he sadly passed away. Sunderland went on to win the league that season, Thorpe's medal being presented to his widow. Son Ronnie, who was two when his dad died truly treasured that medal. Thorpe's case was influential in the Laws of the game being altered to outlaw players raising their foot to the goalkeeper. On the 70th anniversary of his death, plaques were unveiled in his honour in his birthplace of Jarrow and at the Stadium of Light. Previously an apprentice engineer in the shipyards in Jarrow where he had also played cricket, Jimmy Thorpe's young life ended horribly, but his place in Sunderland's history is assured.

## THREADGOLD, Joseph Henry (Harry)

**POSITION:** Goalkeeper

**BIRTHPLACE:** Tattenhall, Cheshire

**DATE OF BIRTH:** 06/11/1924 - 19/12/1996

**HEIGHT:** 5' 11" **WEIGHT:** 12st 3lbs

**SIGNED FROM:** Chester, 14/07/1952

**DEBUT:** v Charlton Athletic, H, 23/08/1952

**LAST MATCH:** v Cardiff City, H, 27/04/1953

**MOVED TO:** Southend United, 23/07/1953

**TEAMS:** Tarvin United, Chester, Sunderland, Southend United, Southchurch Rovers

**SAFC TOTALS:** 38 appearances / 0 goals

**The 'Bank of England Club' paid a modest £2,400 to buy Threadgold from third division Chester where he had played 83 league games. All of Harry's games for SAFC came in 1952-53 as the Lads finished ninth in the top-flight, but the signing of Scotland international Jimmy Cowan signalled Threadgold's transfer a month later.**

He went back to the third tier with Southend where he played 319 league games in a decade at the club. It was not just in goalkeeping that he was useful with his hands as he was also an accomplished boxer who had served with the Royal Marines during World War Two. Following his retirement, Threadgold stayed in Southend as a publican. His ashes were scattered on Southend's Roots Hall pitch after his cremation.

## TINSLEY, Walter Edward

**POSITION:** Inside-left

**BIRTHPLACE:** Ironville, Derbyshire

**DATE OF BIRTH:** 10/08/1891 - 07/03/1966

**HEIGHT:** 5' 9" **WEIGHT:** 11st 7lbs

**SIGNED FROM:** Sutton Town, 15/01/1912

**DEBUT:** v Woolwich Arsenal, H, 23/03/1912

**LAST MATCH:** v Derby County, A, 11/10/1913

**MOVED TO:** Middlesbrough, 02/12/1913

**TEAMS:** Alfreton Town, Sutton Town, Sunderland, Middlesbrough, Nottingham Forest, Reading, Heanor Town

**SAFC TOTALS:** 10 appearances / 3 goals

**Tinsley should have played eleven games rather than ten for SAFC. The one he missed was the 1913 English (FA) Cup final when overcome with nerves he was unable to play, necessitating an only partially fit George Holley to play the full 90 minutes in the days long before substitutes.**

Sunderland lost the final against Aston Villa a few days before Tinsley redeemed himself by scoring against the same opposition at Villa Park in a draw that almost guaranteed Sunderland would pip Villa to the league title. Walter went on to win the Division Two and Three South titles with Nottingham Forest and Reading in 1922 and 1926. With Forest, he scored 13 times in 64 games between August 1921 and March 1924 with the same number of goals from nine fewer appearances at the lower level with Reading who he stayed with until 1927. Between his time with Sunderland and Forest - with whom he first played as a war-time guest - Tinsley excelled for Middlesbrough where he scored 49 goals in 89 league and cup games. Starting with a hat-trick against Villa (in the same calendar year as his missed cup final) he scored 19 of those in 23 top-flight games in his first season on Teesside, another hat-trick coming against Liverpool with another three hat-tricks in the following campaign, including one against Goole in a 9-3 cup win. Walter was also a keen cricketer and continued to play for many years after retiring from football when he was a bricklayer back in his home county.

## TODD, Colin

**POSITION:** Half-back

**BIRTHPLACE:** Chester-le-Street, Co. Durham

**DATE OF BIRTH:** 12/12/1948

**HEIGHT:** 5' 9" **WEIGHT:** 11st 5lbs

**SIGNED FROM:** Chester-le-Street Boys, 14/05/1964

**DEBUT:** v Chelsea, A, 10/09/1966

**LAST MATCH:** v Cardiff City, H, 13/02/1971

**MOVED TO:** Derby County, 18/02/1971

**TEAMS:** Sunderland, Derby County, Everton, Birmingham City, Nottingham Forest, Oxford United, Vancouver Whitecaps, Luton Town, Whitley Bay

**INTERNATIONAL:** England

**SAFC TOTALS:** 188+3 appearances / 3 goals

**One of Sunderland's finest homegrown products, Colin Todd was still a visitor to the Stadium of Light in 2022 while scouting. He was capped 27 times by England and was PFA Footballer of the Year in 1975, a year in which he won the league title with Derby, as he had in 1972. Todd was taken for a record fee for a defender of £175,000 by Brian Clough who had coached Colin in the youth team at Sunderland.**

Todd had played at Roker Park on 9 May 1964 alongside Colin Suggett for Chester-le-Street Boys in the final of the English Schools FA Trophy final against Erdington and Saltley Boys, signing for Sunderland shortly afterwards.

In his first season, Todd played in every game as Sunderland reached the semi-final of the FA Youth Cup for the first time and played in both legs of the final against Arsenal the following year. Breaking into the first team during the next season, he quickly became a regular. Ever-present in his first full term of 1967-68, he missed just three league games in the next two seasons, but following relegation in 1970, it was inevitable that such a class player would move on.

Technically gifted, strong, fast and composed on the ball, my overriding memory of Toddo (he was known as Toddy elsewhere, but always Toddo at Sunderland - as per the graffiti in the background on the photo accompanying the contents page of 'All the Lads') was from one of his last games for Sunderland. QPR threatened to score at the Roker End I was in, in December 1970, only for Toddo to intercept, speed to the half-way line and sweep a beautiful ball to Gordon Harris on the left wing. Harris progressed to cross for Billy Hughes to score with a diving header - still one of my favourite Sunderland goals!

At Derby, Todd played 293 league games, scoring six times. There was one goal (his last in England) in 32 league games for Everton in 1978-79, 93 games for Birmingham City (winning promotion in 1980), 36 for Nottingham Forest (where he once again played for Clough) and twelve for Oxford United before a 1984 move to Vancouver. He played eight times for the Whitecaps in the west coast Canadian city where in the summer of 1967 he had played twelve times (scoring once) for the Sunderland side masquerading as Vancouver Royal Canadians. Todd returned to England to conclude his professional playing career with two appearances for Luton Town.

He had first been capped at Under 23 level against Hungary at Everton in May 1968 but would not gain a full cap until May 1972 against Northern Ireland at Wembley, by which time he was a league champion with Derby. His second cap came in Portugal in 1974 alongside Dave Watson on the latter's international debut. In their five appearances together for Sunderland, Watson was playing at centre-forward. Todd also played three times for the Football League and captained England Under 23s during his 14 appearances at that level.

Upon retiring Colin briefly became a brewery sales representative and played for Whitley Bay in 1985-86 before returning to the senior game in May 1986, initially as assistant manager/first-team coach at Middlesbrough.

From March 1990 to June of the following year he managed Boro before becoming assistant manager at Bradford City in January 1992 and Bolton five months later.

In June 1995 he began a seven-month spell as joint manager of Bolton and went on to manage Swindon from May to October 2000 before taking up a position back at Derby as assistant manager where he took over the hot-seat a year later. Lasting 98 days in that position preceded a return to Bradford City where after eight months as assistant he became manager from June 2004 to February 2007. Four months after losing that job Colin went to Denmark as manager of Randers FC, until January 2009.

Later that year he had five months managing Darlington before scouting for Birmingham City and a subsequent spell back at Randers as manager from 2012-16 despite heart by-pass surgery in February 2014. He then managed Esbjerg fB only to be sacked in December 2016 ending a phenomenal career in which he played in well over 700 games and managed in another 700 plus matches.

Colin's son Andy played for a dozen clubs including Middlesbrough, Derby County and Perth Glory in Australia. A biography of Colin, entitled 'Toddy' was published in 2008.

# T

## TOIVONEN, Nils Ola

**POSITION:** Forward

**BIRTHPLACE:** Degerfors, Sweden

**DATE OF BIRTH:** 03/07/1986

**HEIGHT:** 6' 2½" **WEIGHT:** 13st 0lbs

**SIGNED FROM:** Rennes, 28/08/2015, on loan

**DEBUT:** v Aston Villa, A, 29/08/2015

**LAST MATCH:** v Manchester United, H, 13/02/2016

**MOVED TO:** Rennes, 16/05/2016, end of loan

**TEAMS:** Degerfors, Orgryte IS, Malmo, PSV Eindhoven, Rennes, Sunderland (L), Toulouse, Melbourne Victory, Malmo (to August 2022)

**INTERNATIONAL:** Sweden

**SAFC TOTALS:** 11+3 appearances / 1 goal

**Brought in by Dick Advocaat who had managed him at PSV Eindhoven, Toivonen scored 14 goals in 64 internationals for Sweden including a goal against Germany at the 2018 FIFA World Cup finals. He also won two caps at Under 17 level, eleven for the Under 19s and 28 for the Under 21s where his goals included a hat-trick against Wales and a free-kick for the host nation against an England side including Nedum Onuoha, Lee Cattermole, Adam Johnson and Frazier Campbell (plus sub Jack Rodwell) in the semi-final of the 2009 European Championships.**

Toivonen started his career in his home town of Degerfors scoring eight goals in 41 games as an attacking midfielder before moving to top-flight Örgryte IS. Six goals in 25 games there for a relegated side earned him the Swedish 'Newcomer of the Year' award and a move to former European Cup finalists Malmö FF. After 17 goals in 51 games over two years he moved to PSV in 2009, spending five years in the Netherlands where he soon made a name for himself with four goals in a game against ADO Den Haag.

In 2012 he and Jeremain Lens scored as Toivonen captained PSV to the KNVB Cup as Heracles were beaten. Ola went on to play Europa League football before a 2013 switch to France with Rennes after 198 appearances and 79 goals. There were 14 goals in 46+4 matches for Rennes before his loan move to Sunderland where his only goal came in a League (Capital One) Cup tie with Manchester City.

Returning to France Ola scored nine goals in 31+32 games over two years with Toulouse before going to Australia where he bagged 25 goals in 37+3 games in a two-year spell with Melbourne Victory. A final move back to Malmo saw two Europa League goals against F91 Dudelange in August 2022 take Toivonen's total in his second spell at the club to 15 goals in 38+14 outings in which he won the league (Allsvenskan) in back-to-back seasons in 2020 and 2021. He also won the Svenska Cupen in May 2022 when he scored the decisive penalty in the final against Hammarby IF.

## TOMLIN, John (Jack)

**POSITION:** Centre-half

**BIRTHPLACE:** Dublin, Republic of Ireland

**DATE OF BIRTH:** 26/01/1882 - 14/05/1941

**HEIGHT:** 5' 10" **WEIGHT:** 12st 2lbs

**SIGNED FROM:** Seaham White Star, 09/03/1905

**DEBUT:** v Aston Villa, H, 28/02/1906

**LAST MATCH:** v Bury, H, 28/04/1906

**MOVED TO:** Middlesbrough, 20/09/1906

**TEAMS:** Seaham United, Seaham Albion, Seaham White Star, Sunderland, Middlesbrough, Murton Red Star

**SAFC TOTALS:** 13 appearances / 1 goal

**Having moved from Dublin to Seaham as a youngster, Tomlin signed as an amateur while continuing his joinery and undertaker's business.**

For Sunderland, he played in the last 13 games of 1905-06 and at Boro added four further league appearances the following September and October, the Teessiders taking just one point in that spell. After retiring from playing, Jack stayed in Seaham and was a foreman joiner in the building trade at the time of his death.

## TONES, John David

**POSITION:** Centre-half

**BIRTHPLACE:** Silksworth, Sunderland, Co Durham

**DATE OF BIRTH:** 03/12/1950

**HEIGHT:** 6' 2" **WEIGHT:** 13st 0lbs

**SIGNED FROM:** Sunderland Schoolboys, 01/06/1966

**DEBUT:** v Lazio, A, 17/05/1970

**LAST MATCH:** v Nottingham Forest, A, 24/04/1973

**MOVED TO:** Arsenal, 22/05/1973

**TEAMS:** Sunderland, Arsenal, Swansea City (L), Mansfield Town (L), Yeovil Town (L), Gateshead, Blyth Spartans, Whitby Town, Roker, Peterlee, Easington

**SAFC TOTALS:** 5+5 appearances / 1 goal

**Sunderland had just been relegated for the second time when Tones' debut came, two years after signing professional forms, in the Anglo-Italian Cup in Rome against Lazio when he scored Sunderland's first-ever competitive goal on foreign soil. From then he waited until the opening day of what would be the cup-winning season to play for the first-team again.**

Coming off the bench at Middlesbrough, he made another couple of substitute appearances before a full league debut in a goalless home draw with Preston in Bob Stokoe's third game as manager. John then played in the FA Cup third round with Notts County and the accompanying replay with his only other appearance coming back in Nottingham against Forest twelve days before the cup final. Arsenal signed Tones in the month of the final, but he never got a game for the Gunners who loaned him to Swansea and Mansfield who were both in the fourth tier, the Stags winning the division, although John played just three times for them.

Over the two seasons Tones was with the Gunners, he played 39 times for their reserves including four friendlies. All but three of these games were in his first season there during which he scored his two goals for the club. After playing under former Sunderland full-back Cec Irwin at Yeovil, Tones returned to the north-east in 1975 and between then and 1982 played in local football. John moved to Australia and as of 2022 was living in Melbourne. In 2022, having played in the early rounds of the 1973 cup triumph he was one of the players to receive a joint award of the Freedom of the City.

## TOSELAND, Geoffrey Vincent

**POSITION:** Outside-left

**BIRTHPLACE:** Kettering, Northamptonshire

**DATE OF BIRTH:** 31/01/1931 - 16/05/2019

**HEIGHT:** 6' 0" **WEIGHT:** 11st 6lbs

**SIGNED FROM:** Rothwell Town, 09/12/1948

**DEBUT:** v Derby County, H, 06/09/1952

**LAST MATCH:** v Tottenham Hotspur, A, 29/11/1952

**MOVED TO:** Kettering Town, 01/07/1953

**TEAMS:** Geddington, Rothwell Town, Sunderland, Kettering Town

**SAFC TOTALS:** 6 appearances / 1 goal

**Toseland was signed after scoring in a trial game for SAFC Reserves at Consett, but had to wait almost four years for his debut. All of Geoff's games came in the 1952-53 season. He scored on his debut in a 2-1 win over Derby and played in a 2-2 derby draw at Newcastle in his first away match.**

Toseland was a teammate to top stars such as Len Shackleton, Trevor Ford and Willie Watson and even served alongside Bob Stokoe in the army. A left-winger, he had been spotted playing for Rothwell Town and joined Sunderland as a 17-year-old at which point he was working in a shoe factory. Two of his six and a half years at Sunderland were spent in the army on National Service, before he was eventually released and signed for his hometown club Kettering Town.

Back on home turf he combined with the legendary ex-England international centre-forward Tommy Lawton who was player-manager. As well as creating many goals for Lawton, Geoff scored 93 goals in 144 games for the club with which he won the Southern League in 1957. After retiring from playing Geoff became a window cleaner and market trader.

## TOWERS, Mark Anthony (Tony)

**POSITION:** Midfielder

**BIRTHPLACE:** Manchester, Lancashire

**DATE OF BIRTH:** 13/04/1952

**HEIGHT:** 5' 9" **WEIGHT:** 11st 3lbs

**SIGNED FROM:** Manchester City, 11/03/1974

**DEBUT:** v Fulham, H, 16/03/1974

**LAST MATCH:** v Norwich City, A, 14/05/1977

**MOVED TO:** Birmingham City, 25/07/1977

**TEAMS:** Manchester City, Sunderland, Birmingham City, Montreal Manic, Tacoma Stars, Tampa Bay Rowdies, Vancouver Whitecaps, Rochdale

**INTERNATIONAL:** England

**SAFC TOTALS:** 124 appearances / 22 goals

**Towers was a class act who captained Sunderland to the second division title in 1976 and won his three England caps that summer having been selected for the PFA divisional Team of the Year. One of three debutants in an inexperienced England side who won against Wales in Wrexham two weeks after the end of Sunderland's season, he then played against Northern Ireland as a sub at Wembley before playing against Italy in New York having been in the squad for games against Scotland and Brazil.**

Tony had scored and been sent off against Sunderland for Manchester City during the 1973 FA Cup run before coming to Sunderland as part of the deal that took cup-winners Dennis Tueart and Micky Horswill to City nine days after Tony had played for City in the 1974 League Cup final. Four years earlier Towers had been part of the City side who won the European Cup Winners' Cup beating Górnik Zabrze in Vienna in front of a sub-8,000 crowd. Tony totalled 157+8 games for City for whom he scored a dozen times, the first goal coming in the ECWC in March 1970 against Academica Coimbra.

At Sunderland he showed himself to be an outstanding midfielder. A crisp passer of the ball, he was a fine tackler and an accomplished penalty taker, his conversion rate of twelve out of 13 spot-kicks giving him a percentage second only to Gary Rowell, of those to take more than ten penalties. Following a change of manager from Bob Stokoe to Jimmy Adamson it remains one of the mysteries of SAFC as to why Towers was dropped to the bench as an unused sub on the night Sunderland were relegated at Everton in 1977.

That summer he moved to Birmingham City having spoken to Jim Montgomery who was already at St Andrews. Playing alongside Keith Bertschin and Ricky Sbragia as well as Monty at Birmingham, where one of three managers in his first season was Sir Alf Ramsay, Towers went on to play 97+3 games scoring four goals. Relegated in his second season, Tony was promoted with the Blues alongside Sunderland in his third, but did not play at all in his fourth year before crossing the Atlantic to finish his career in the NASL and Major Indoor Soccer League. He returned to England for a two-game swansong at Rochdale as a favour to manager and former Sunderland colleague Vic Halom.

Towers ran a sawmill and then a pub after retiring before becoming a steward at a Manchester golf club and a wine and spirits salesman. In 2017, he attended a book launch at the Stadium of Light having been featured in a book called 'Tales from the Red & Whites, Volume 2'.

## TRAIN, Raymond

**POSITION:** Midfielder

**BIRTHPLACE:** Nuneaton, Warwickshire

**DATE OF BIRTH:** 10/02/1951

**HEIGHT:** 5' 7" **WEIGHT:** 10st 9lbs

**SIGNED FROM:** Carlisle United, 11/03/1976

**DEBUT:** v Orient, A, 13/03/1976

**LAST MATCH:** v Wrexham, H 08/01/1977

**MOVED TO:** Bolton Wanderers, 10/03/1977

**TEAMS:** Bedworth United, Walsall, Carlisle United, Sunderland, Bolton Wanderers, Watford, Oxford United, AFC Bournemouth (L), Northampton Town, Tranmere Rovers, Walsall

**SAFC TOTALS:** 36+1 appearances / 3 goals

**Having capped an impressive performance against Sunderland with a goal for Carlisle, Train was signed a fortnight later. Diminutive and industrious, he was reminiscent of Bobby Kerr who played alongside him in all but one of the last dozen games Train played in as the 1976 Division Two title was secured.**

He found the going tougher in the top-flight playing only 19+1 league games before moving on after a change of manager. He had been ever-present at the top level for Carlisle in 1974-75 in the Cumbrians only Division One campaign. Known as 'Puffer' at Carlisle he had helped them to promotion the previous season when he was part of the side that knocked holders Sunderland out of the FA Cup.

In total Train played 171+1 games and scored eight goals for Carlisle who he joined from Walsall in December 1971. There had been 75 appearances and eleven goals for the Saddlers who were Ray's first senior club. Leaving Sunderland for Bolton he partnered Peter Reid in midfield and as at Sunderland played the last dozen or so games, only this time to miss out on promotion by a point. However, with Sam Allardyce another of his colleagues, he played over 30 times in his only full season with the Trotters as he won his second Division Two Championship medal in three seasons.

By November of that year he was on the move again, this time to Watford after 55+2 games for Bolton in which he did not score, but he netted on debut for Watford who had just won Division Four under Graham Taylor and would win promotion again in Train's first season. A model of consistency, 86 of Ray's 109+3 appearances for the Hornets were consecutive. He scored four goals for the club he left in March 1982 when they were en-route to a promotion that completed their journey from fourth tier to first.

There were 49+1 league appearances in two third division seasons at Oxford, but only one in 1983-84 when they were promoted in a campaign where he had played seven games on loan to Bournemouth. 1984-85 saw him ever-present in 46 games (1 goal) with Northampton who finished one off the bottom of the Football League. He then spent 1985-86 with Tranmere, playing 36 league games as they finished 19th in division four before a 1986-87 swan-song back at Walsall where he made 16 third-tier appearances as he moved into coaching, combining playing with becoming youth team coach and later caretaker manager. In 1990, he worked for Port Vale as a community officer before taking up a coaching position with the reserves at Middlesbrough being there as they won promotion to the newly-formed Premier League. He stayed at Boro for 13 years, mainly as chief scout.

## TRAVERS, Bernard (Barney)

**POSITION:** Inside-left / centre-forward

**BIRTHPLACE:** Sunderland, Co Durham

**DATE OF BIRTH:** 29/08/1894 - 16/02/1955

**HEIGHT:** 5' 8" **WEIGHT:** 12st 4lbs

**SIGNED FROM:** Sunderland West End, 21/04/1919

**DEBUT:** v Aston Villa, H, 30/08/1919

**LAST MATCH:** v Cardiff City, H, 08/01/1921

**MOVED TO:** Fulham, 21/02/1921

**TEAMS:** Sunderland West End, Sunderland, Fulham, Vienna, Centre D'Esports Sabadell

**INTERNATIONAL:** England

**SAFC TOTALS:** 63 appearances / 27 goals

**Barney Travers had a more than decent goals-to-games ratio for Sunderland and once broke the net at Roker Park with his second goal against Sheffield United in September 1920.**

However, he was banned for life by the FA having been found guilty of trying to fix the result of a match against South Shields when playing for Fulham in March 1922. His Australian-based grandson explained to me that as a local lad he had been asked by the powers that be at Fulham to offer Shields £20 to lose the game as the Cottagers pushed for promotion. Instead Shields won 1-0 in what would prove to be Barney's last match. He had scored 18 in 33 league and cup games that season and 29 in 49 in total.

Travers emigrated to Australia to work for his brother's fruit growing business in Melbourne after a failed attempt to stay in football as player/coach at Vienna Club in Austria in May 1922. In 1924 he returned to Europe hoping to play in Spain with Sabadell under the name of Mr Barney, but again this was doomed to failure when his past was discovered. At this point, he returned to Sunderland to work in the family greengrocery business. His life ban was lifted in October 1945 as part of a post-war general amnesty. His nephew Charles Nicklas played for Hull, Darlington and Headington United (Oxford) between 1950 and 54.

## TROUGHEAR, William (Billy)

**POSITION:** Right-back
**BIRTHPLACE:** Workington, Cumberland
**DATE OF BIRTH:** 19/03/1885 - 15/10/1955
**HEIGHT:** 5' 8" **WEIGHT:** 11st 7lbs
**SIGNED FROM:** Workington 07/05/1909
**DEBUT:** v Blackburn Rovers, A, 06/11/1909
**LAST MATCH:** v Liverpool, H, 07/12/1912
**MOVED TO:** Leicester Fosse, 12/05/1914
**TEAMS:** Workington Marsh Mission, Workington, Sunderland, Leicester Fosse, Preston North End (WW1 Guest), Flimby Rangers, Workington, Whitehaven Recreation
**SAFC TOTALS:** 108 appearances / 0 goals

**Wonderfully nicknamed 'Toughlugs' Billy made exactly 100 league appearances and added another eight cup games. A regular in three seasons from 1909 to 1912, he dropped out of the side early in the successful 1912-13 season when he lost his place to new signing Charlie Gladwin.**

'Toughlugs' had been a labourer in an iron works before playing football and returned to the industry after his playing career. His former club Workington alleged that Sunderland had made illegal approaches for him, although an FA commission in September 1909 found no evidence of this. While with Workington, he had taken part in races as a professional athlete.

In May 1914 he joined Leicester Fosse where in the last season before the league ceased for World War One he made 16 league and cup appearances as the Foxes finished second bottom of Division Two. During the war, Troughear worked in a munitions factory and in the post-war years played in non-league football. By this time Billy had returned to his native Workington to work as a pneumatic gunner in the iron and steel industry.

## TUEART, Dennis

**POSITION:** Forward / winger
**BIRTHPLACE:** Walker, Newcastle, Northumberland
**DATE OF BIRTH:** 27/11/1949
**HEIGHT:** 5' 8" **WEIGHT:** 11st 0lbs
**SIGNED FROM:** Newcastle Schoolboys, 01/07/1966
**DEBUT:** v Sheffield Wednesday, H, 26/12/1968
**LAST MATCH:** v Portsmouth, H, 05/03/1974
**MOVED TO:** Manchester City, 11/03/1974
**TEAMS:** Sunderland, Manchester City, New York Cosmos, Manchester City, Stoke City, Burnley, Derry City
**INTERNATIONAL:** England
**SAFC TOTALS:** 208+6 appearances / 56 goals

**Without doubt, Dennis Tueart is the player I was always most excited about when he got the ball. Tueart was dynamite. Fast, direct and talented, he terrorised defences. It should come as no surprise that when New York Cosmos wanted to replace the world's greatest player Pele, it was Dennis they signed, from Manchester City who he joined from Sunderland in a package deal that involved Micky Horswill going to City with Tony Towers coming in the opposite direction.**

The scorer of a wide variety of spectacular goals, Tueart was not individualistic to the detriment of the team. How could he be when he was part of a side with the greatest team ethic imaginable, the 1973 FA Cup winners. In the following season's first European Cup Winners' Cup tie at Vasas Budapest he scored a goal George Best would have been proud of.

Picking up the ball from Ian Porterfield inside his own half, Dennis dribbled past five Hungarian defenders to leave himself one on one with the keeper who he beat with ease. Four days earlier he had scored with a sensational scissor-kick at Oxford. Famously he is remembered for the best goal ever seen in a League Cup final, a bicycle-kick for Manchester City against his hometown Newcastle in 1976.

Dennis deserved many more than the six caps he won for England under Don Revie - his first call-up coming the month after he left Sunderland. He scored four minutes into his first Wembley international start against Finland and got a late winner away to a Northern Ireland team that included Martin O'Neill and Jimmy Nicholl while a teammate was his former Sunderland colleague Colin Todd.

At Manchester City Tueart totalled 112 goals in 267+9 games in two spells. Top scorer with 24 goals in 1975-76, he was second top scorer in three other seasons including 1976-77 when City were league runners-up, a point behind Liverpool in a campaign when Dennis scored in both games against Sunderland. Tueart later became a director of Manchester City between December 1997 and July 2007.

Following his second spell with Manchester City, Tueart's career wound down with three league games in five months at Stoke in 1983 before a similar spell at Burnley where he scored five goals in 10+9 games. He then had nine games for Derry City who he was persuaded to play for by his old Sunderland youth team colleague Eamonn McLaughlin - the scorer of Sunderland's first-ever goal in an FA Youth Cup final in 1966.

After retiring from football, Dennis became a sales director for a sports promotions company and subsequently set up his own Premier Events Company specialising in live events, design and video. Fully involved still in 2022, Dennis remains as much a live-wire in business as he was on the pitch. His 2011 biography published in alternative Sunderland and Manchester City covers saw all of Dennis' royalties go to the teenage and young adult cancer unit at the Christie cancer centre in Manchester. In 2022, he received the Freedom of Sunderland as a member of the 1973 FA Cup winners.

## TURNBULL, Ronald William (Ronnie)

**POSITION:** Centre-forward
**BIRTHPLACE:** Newbiggin, Northumberland
**DATE OF BIRTH:** 18/07/1922 -17/11/1966
**HEIGHT:** 5' 9" **WEIGHT:** 11st 2lbs
**SIGNED FROM:** Dundee, 26/11/1947
**DEBUT:** v Portsmouth, H, 29/11/1947
**LAST MATCH:** v Birmingham City, H, 07/05/1949
**MOVED TO:** Manchester City, 09/09/1949
**TEAMS:** Dundee, Sunderland, Manchester City, Swansea Town, Dundee, Ashington Town
**SAFC TOTALS:** 43 appearances / 18 goals

**Four goals on his debut indelibly printed Turnbull's name into the record books. Supplied by 1937 FA Cup final wingers Len Duns and Eddie Burbanks, Ronnie pummelled Pompey who were beaten 4-1. It was Turnbull's golden day, but he continued to average a decent ratio of exactly a goal every three games in his remaining 42 matches before a £10,000 move to Manchester City in September 1949.**

Goals were hard to come by, one of just four in 30 games in his first season being a Maine Road winner against Sunderland in a season where City went down. There was just one further outing the following season as City were promoted, but by then Ronnie had moved on to Swansea where he fared better with 35 goals in 67 league games before he returned to Dundee. Sunderland had paid a Dee record of £9,000 for his signature at a point where he had scored 27 league goals in 26 games and 46 in 51 in total, including war-time games.

One of four league hat-tricks for Dee had included a four-goal haul against Albion Rovers a year and a day before his four-goal Sunderland debut. Turnbull returned to the north east of England to complete his career with Ashington. In the late fifties he was acting as Leicester City's north-east scout while working as a sales rep, having been a draper's assistant before becoming a professional footballer. He died in Sunderland nineteen years to the month after bursting onto the Wearside football scene.

## TURNER, Christopher Robert

**POSITION:** Goalkeeper

**BIRTHPLACE:** Sheffield, Yorkshire

**DATE OF BIRTH:** 15/09/1958

**HEIGHT:** 5' 10½" **WEIGHT:** 11st 11lbs

**SIGNED FROM:** Sheffield Wednesday, 02/07/1979

**DEBUT:** v Oldham Athletic, H, 11/08/1979

**LAST MATCH:** v Ipswich Town, H, 11/05/1985

**MOVED TO:** Manchester United, 01/07/ 1985

**TEAMS:** Sheffield Wednesday, Lincoln City (L), Sunderland, Manchester United, Sheffield Wednesday, Leeds United (L), Leyton Orient (L)

**INTERNATIONAL:** England Youth

**SAFC TOTALS:** 223+1 appearances / 0 goals

**One of the best goalkeepers to play for Sunderland, Chris Turner was not the biggest, but he was agile, brave and deservedly Player of the Season in 1984-85 when he captained the side on his last appearance before a record sale to Manchester United. Turner's last campaign had resulted in relegation, but also a first appearance in the League Cup final.**

At Wembley on that occasion, Turner was only beaten by a deflection after a string of superb displays that saw him be the single biggest reason the club reached the final. One of those came at Spurs in the cup run where his penalty save was one of four spot-kicks Chris saved that season, a feat only equalled by Robert Ward in 1906-07 and Lee Burge in 2020-21.

Turner had been signed from Sheffield Wednesday by Ken Knighton whose boots Chris had cleaned at Hillsborough. To start with Turner had to wrestle the goalkeeper's shirt off Barry Siddall but went on to top a double century of games, being ever-present in his last two seasons after recovering from a fractured skull sustained in a game at Norwich in April 1983. Notably, Chris was the first goalkeeper ever to come on as a sub in a competitive game for Sunderland, a pre-arranged takeover from Siddall on Turner's debut in an Anglo-Scottish Cup game with Oldham.

At Manchester United he vied with Gary Bailey, waiting until December 1985 for his debut at Aston Villa but quickly showing what he was about when conceding only twice in his first five matches. After those games he was left out for Bailey as United played Sunderland in the FA Cup, Sunderland supporters serenading Bailey with constant choruses of 'We all agree, Turner is better than Bailey' at Old Trafford. Nonetheless,

Turner made 20 appearances in his first season in Manchester, 29 in his second and 30 in his third, conceding under a goal a game before being sold to his first club Sheffield Wednesday for £100,000 less than United had paid Sunderland for him.

At Hillsborough where he had been Player of the Year in 1977, Chris went on to keep a clean sheet against United at Wembley in the 1991 League Cup final, a year in which he also helped the Owls to promotion. Len Ashurst had given Chris his league debut with Wednesday on the opening day of the 1976-77 season, like Jim Montgomery his first game coming against Walsall. A teammate of Ian Porterfield and Rodger Wylde at Hillsborough, he also had to contend with competition from Bob Bolder and in 1978-79 went on loan to Lincoln City where he played five games. Turner eventually totalled 205 games for Wednesday, slightly over half of them coming in his second spell. In the middle year of his three-season second period in Sheffield, he was loaned again, this time playing twice for Leeds.

In 1991-92 he transferred to Leyton Orient, being named in the PFA Division Three Team of the Year in his first season (he had made the same selection in 1978-79). There were 70 appearances for the O's, the last one at Hull in March 1995 being after he had been appointed as joint-manager with John Sitton. Turner went on to run the reserves at Leicester where in an emergency in September 1995 he put on the gloves again to play against Sunderland reserves. Chris went on to have two spells as manager of Hartlepool where he also worked as Director of Sport, as well as taking charge of Sheffield Wednesday and Stockport County in addition to a spell coaching at Wolves.

In 2010 Chris was part of a consortium who tried to buy Sheffield Wednesday and then spent just over five years with Chesterfield, mainly as chief executive before a seven-month spell as sales and marketing manager at Port Vale prior to becoming Director of Football at Wakefield in 2019.

Astonishingly, Turner did not play for England. He was called up for a shadow squad for the 1986 FIFA World Cup and was even measured up for a suit, but was overlooked in favour of Gary Bailey despite him keeping Bailey out of the Manchester United side.

## TURNER, Michael Thomas

**POSITION:** Centre-back

**BIRTHPLACE:** Lewisham, London

**DATE OF BIRTH:** 09/11/1983

**HEIGHT:** 6' 4" **WEIGHT:** 13st 5lbs

**SIGNED FROM:** Hull City, 31/08/2009

**DEBUT:** v Hull City, H, 12/09/2009

**LAST MATCH:** v Manchester United, H, 13/05/2012

**MOVED TO:** Norwich City, 27/07/2012

**TEAMS:** Charlton Athletic, Leyton Orient (L), Brentford, Hull City, Sunderland, Norwich City, Fulham (L), Southend United

**INTERNATIONAL:** England

**SAFC TOTALS:** 75+2 appearances / 2 goals

**Having been bullied by a physical Stoke team in August 2009, Steve Bruce brought in towering centre-half Michael Turner who debuted against the Hull side he had just left. Michael's first season would be his best as he played in 32 games before injuries restricted him, but when available Turner was a commanding aerial presence although not the quickest against speed-merchants.**

He had first come to Sunderland's attention in his Brentford days when he was part of the third tier team's line-up as they dumped Premier League Sunderland out of the FA Cup. He had initially joined the Bees on loan from Charlton Athletic where he never got a game. Michael's senior debut had come on loan to Leyton Orient where the first of seven appearances came in April 2003 with a first goal coming third time out.

After 110 games and three goals for Brentford, Hull paid £350,000 for him, garnering a handsome profit when selling him to Sunderland for £4m after three seasons in which he played 144+2 games with 13 goals. After his time on Wearside, Turner played 72+4 games for Norwich (4 goals) from where he had

nine and twelve-game loans to Fulham and Sheffield Wednesday, scoring once for each. A final move to Southend United in July 2017 brought 62+3 appearances and five goals, the very last appearance coming in a 2-1 win over Sunderland in May 2019 that kept Southend up.

## TURNER, Neil McDougall

**POSITION:** Outside-right

**BIRTHPLACE:** Hutchesontown, Glasgow, Lanarkshire

**DATE OF BIRTH:** 12/10/1891 - 28/01/1971

**HEIGHT:** 5' 11" **WEIGHT:** 10st 6lbs

**SIGNED FROM:** Kilmarnock, 25/08/1919

**DEBUT:** v Bradford Park Avenue, A, 17/04/1920

**LAST MATCH:** v Bradford Park Avenue, A, 17/04/1920

**MOVED TO:** Aberdare Athletic, 30/05/1920

**TEAMS:** Petershill, Leeds City, Raith Rovers, Glasgow Benburb (WW1 Guest), St Mirren, Kilmarnock, Vale of Leven (L), Sunderland, Aberdare Athletic, Dundee, Bethlehem Steel, New Bedford Whalers, Springfield Babes

**SAFC TOTALS:** 1 appearance / 0 goals

**Known as a speedy forward, Turner was well-travelled even before coming to Sunderland and went on to complete his career with three clubs in the USA where he finished playing in 1927 before becoming a sheet metalworker for General Electric in Massachusetts. He stayed in America and passed away in Florida.**

Hailing from Glasgow he had first come to England with Leeds City scoring on his debut at local rivals Huddersfield in November 1913. He only played a further three games for Herbert Chapman's second division team, netting again with a Good Friday winner against Bristol City. Between 1914 and 1916 he played 59 times for Raith Rovers, scoring a dozen goals. During the war he served with the Argyll & Sutherland Highlanders and then the Royal Medical Corps. He scored four goals in eleven games for St Mirren, five in nine for Kilmarnock and none in nine for Dundee, plus 22 (2 goals) for Aberdare Athletic when they finished eighth in Division Three South in 1921-22. In the US, his figures were 17 in 43 games for Bethlehem, 14 in 32 for New Bedford and six in 21 for Springfield.

## URSEM, Loek Aloysius Jacobus Maria

**POSITION:** Midfielder

**BIRTHPLACE:** Amsterdam, Netherlands

**DATE OF BIRTH:** 07/01/1958

**HEIGHT:** 5' 9" **WEIGHT:** 11st 4lbs

**SIGNED FROM:** Stoke City, 25/03/1982, on loan

**DEBUT:** v Middlesbrough, H, 03/04/1982

**LAST MATCH:** v Tottenham Hotspur, A, 14/04/1982

**MOVED TO:** Stoke City, 25/04/1982, end of loan

**TEAMS:** AZ 67, Stoke City, Sunderland (L), Haarlem, FC Wageningen, OSV Velsen

**INTERNATIONAL:** Netherlands U21

**SAFC TOTALS:** 0+4 appearances / 0 goals

**Loans were not as common in 1982 as they are in the modern day so Ursem was something of a novelty when Alan Durban returned to his old club Stoke to bring in the Dutchman on a temporary basis. Ursem never got a start and was an unused sub a couple of times in addition to his handful of appearances off the bench - one of his appearances being at his parent club Stoke where he obliged home fans singing' 'Ursem, Ursem give us a wave'.**

Capped nine times by the Netherlands at Under 21 level he had started with AZ 67 in the season they played at Roker Park in a Testimonial for Ritchie Pitt and Bobby Park. He did not play in that game but had played 35 games scoring eight goals when Durban - renowned as a spotter of young talent - brought him to Stoke after seeing him in a tournament in Haarlem.

25+4 of Ursem's 44 games for Stoke came in 1980-81 (including a home game with Sunderland) when his seven goals made him joint second top scorer to Lee Chapman in a team that also included Paul Bracewell and Adrian Heath.

In 1983 he returned to his homeland to play three games for FC Haarlem before finishing his career with FC Wageningen and OSV Velsen after which he became the owner of a TV repair shop in Purmerend in North Holland until October 2018.

## URWIN, Thomas (Tommy)

**POSITION:** Inside-right / outside-right

**BIRTHPLACE:** Haswell, Co Durham

**DATE OF BIRTH:** 05/02/1896 - 07/05/1968

**HEIGHT:** 5' 6" **WEIGHT:** 10st 0lbs

**SIGNED FROM:** Newcastle United, 06/02/1930

**DEBUT:** v Leeds United, A, 08/02/1930

**LAST MATCH:** v Preston North End, A, 22/04/1935

**MOVED TO:** Retired, 26/05/1936

**TEAMS:** Fulwell, Lambton Star, Shildon, Middlesbrough, Fulham (WW1), Scotswood (WW1), Newcastle United, Sunderland

**INTERNATIONAL:** England

**SAFC TOTALS:** 55 appearances / 6 goals

**Until the return of Jermain Defoe in 2022, Tommy Urwin had been Sunderland's oldest-ever player. The last of his appearances at the age of 39 years and 76 days came two years and four months after his penultimate game and came about as a result during a spate of injuries in the third fixture over four days at Easter in 1935 when Urwin was pressed into service whilst on the coaching staff - some 22 years after first playing in the Football League.**

A member of the select band of players to have played for Newcastle United and Middlesbrough as well as Sunderland, the diminutive and effective winger had made 32 of his Sunderland appearances in 1930-31, 13 the season before and seven the season afterwards before coming out of retirement as a one-off when by all accounts he did well in a fiercely contested match.

As far back as 1910 Urwin had been part of the Sunderland schoolboys team who won the England Schools Shield. A member of the Monkwearmouth Colliery School team Tommy played on the right-wing as Sunderland Schools won the national final in a replay against Walsall Schools at Roker Park on 21 May 1910. He also became an England schoolboy international. However, after playing in local football it was Middlesbrough with which Urwin set out in the senior game, debuting against Sunderland on New Year's Day 1915 as the Wearsiders won at Ayresome Park. Playing on the left-wing, his partner at inside-left was Walter Tinsley of 1913 cup final notoriety. Urwin was to play in another defeat at Roker Park on Good Friday, but scored his first goal 24 hours later in a game that was abandoned against Oldham.

Urwin played exactly 200 games for Boro, scoring 14 goals. Just seven of his appearances came before football stopped for World War One during which he appeared for Fulham and Scotswood as a 'Guest' and served in India and Turkey as a battery fitter with the Royal Artillery. He missed just three games in the first post-war Football League season for Middlesbrough and stayed with the club until August 1924 when after a dispute over benefits, a £3,200 fee took him from Teesside to Tyneside, apparently Newcastle managing to sign him at the Central Station when he was about to board a train to sign for Manchester United. By this time he was an England international having debuted as a 27-year-old against Sweden in Stockholm in May 1923 and playing against the same opposition on the same ground three days later. Three of his four caps were won with Boro, the last against Wales at Selhurst Park in March 1926 coming while with Newcastle.

For the St James' club he matched his Middlesbrough total of precisely 200 games, this time scoring 23 goals. Four of those came in the league in 1926-27 when he won a championship medal having missed just three games for the Magpies. Later at Sunderland who paid £525 for the veteran, he continued to give great service, including turning out long after thinking his playing days were over. After winning the title with Newcastle in 1927 he was part of the Sunderland set up when the Wearsiders were champions in 1935-36 as assistant trainer and was still on the coaching and scouting staff until 1958 having also become an accounts clerk at Sunderland Royal Infirmary.

## USHER, Brian

**POSITION:** Outside-right

**BIRTHPLACE:** Broomside, Co Durham

**DATE OF BIRTH:** 11/03/1944

**HEIGHT:** 5' 11" **WEIGHT:** 11st 5lbs

**SIGNED FROM:** Lambton & Hetton Boys Club, July 1959

**DEBUT:** v Huddersfield Town, A, 24/08/1963

**LAST MATCH:** v Wolverhampton Wanderers, H, 16/04/1965

**MOVED TO:** Sheffield Wednesday, 03/06/1965

**TEAMS:** Sunderland, Sheffield Wednesday, Doncaster Rovers, Yeovil Town

**INTERNATIONAL:** England Under 23

**SAFC TOTALS:** 71 appearances / 7 goals

**Still in his teens when he debuted on the opening day of Sunderland's first-ever promotion season in 1963-64, Usher missed just one game that term before re-uniting with his promotion-winning manager Alan Brown at Sheffield Wednesday a year later. At Hillsborough Brian vied with future Sunderland manager Howard Wilkinson for the number seven right-wing berth.**

As a left-winger Usher was kept out of the team by George Mulhall. Brian played on the right-wing instead of his preferred position for almost every game in his career until he signed for Doncaster under George Raynor who had managed Sweden to the FIFA World Cup final in 1958. Another World Cup connection was that future England World Cup winner Ray Wilson was Usher's direct opponent on his Sunderland debut.

With Wednesday, Brian made 66+2 appearances including one in a 5-0 win over Sunderland in his second season. He scored three goals for the Owls, one coming in a 1-1 draw with Manchester United when Wednesday were third in the league, with another being an FA Cup fifth-round winner against Huddersfield. Brown's Owls reached the final although Brian missed out having played up to the quarter-final.

With Doncaster between 1968 and '73 he made 164+4 league appearances and scored six goals, winning the Division Four title in 1969 under Lawrie McMenemy. Settling in Doncaster, Usher was good friends with another Doncaster resident, Stan Anderson, a former Sunderland teammate. It was another promotion-winning colleague in Cec Irwin who persuaded Brian to end his career with Yeovil Town after which he worked for an engineering company and then as an insurance agent.

At international level Brian was capped once at Under 23 level in his first season with Sunderland. He played in a 2-2 draw with France in Rouen in April 1964 supplying crosses for Geoff Hurst who two years later would score a hat-trick in the World Cup final.

## USTARI, Oscar Alfredo

**POSITION:** Goalkeeper

**BIRTHPLACE:** America, Argentina

**DATE OF BIRTH:** 03/07/1986

**HEIGHT:** 6' 0½" **WEIGHT:** 11st 12lbs

**SIGNED FROM:** UD Almeria, 21/01/2014

**DEBUT:** v Kidderminster Harriers, H, 25/01/2014

**LAST MATCH:** v Hull City, A, 09/03/2014

**MOVED TO:** Contract not renewed, 30/06/2014

**TEAMS:** Independiente, Getafe, Boca Juniors, UD Almeria, Sunderland, Newells Old Boys, Club Atlas, Liverpool Montevideo, Pachuca.

**INTERNATIONAL:** Argentina

**SAFC TOTALS:** 3 appearances / 0 goals

One of a group of South Americans brought in by Uruguayan head coach Gus Poyet, Ustari only played in the FA Cup where he became the first man to save a penalty in the competition for Sunderland, something he did in his final game at Hull. Oscar was also an unused sub in the League (Capital One) Cup final and semi-final second leg as well as in the last 16 games of the Premier League miracle escape from relegation as Poyet preferred his experience to that of the youthful Jordan Pickford.

Ustari played twice for Argentina, debuting against Norway in 2007. Two years earlier he played every game as his country won the 2005 FIFA Under 20 World Cup while in 2008 he missed the Olympic final having played three times earlier in the tournament only to be injured in the quarter-final. By then he was playing in Spain with Getafe having begun with 64 games for Independiente where he made his Primera Division debut against Newell's Old Boys in October 2005. Ustari also scored for Independiente with a penalty against the team of Julio Arca's birthplace Quilmes in 2007.

With Getafe he played in the final of the Copa Del Rey in 2008, losing to Valencia who he had made his debut against earlier in the season. After 41 La Liga games for Getafe, Oscar returned to Argentina with Boca Juniors where he played twelve league games and won the Copa Argentina final against Racing in August 2012. A subsequent return to Spain with Almeria did not work out as he did not play prior to his move to Sunderland after which he returned to South and Central America making 36 appearances for Newell's Old Boys in Argentina, 42 for Atlas in Mexico, 18 in Uruguay for Liverpool Montevideo and as of June 2022, 83 for Pachuca of Mexico.

Ustari's father-in-law Ricardo Giusti was a FIFA World Cup winner with Argentina in 1986 winning 53 caps. He also played for Newell's Old Boys, Argentinos Juniors, Independiente and Union de Santa Fé.

# V

## VAN AANHOLT, Patrick John Miguel

**POSITION:** Left-back

**BIRTHPLACE:** 's-Hertogenbosch, Netherlands

**DATE OF BIRTH:** 29/08/1990

**HEIGHT:** 5' 9" **WEIGHT:** 10st 7lbs

**SIGNED FROM:** Chelsea, 25/07/2014

**DEBUT:** v West Bromwich Albion, A, 16/08/2014

**LAST MATCH:** v West Bromwich Albion, A, 21/01/2017

**MOVED TO:** Crystal Palace, 30/01/2017

**TEAMS:** PSV, Chelsea, Coventry City (L), Newcastle United (L), Leicester City (L), Wigan Athletic (L) Vitese Arnhem (L), Sunderland, Crystal Palace, Galatasaray (to July 2022)

**INTERNATIONAL:** Netherlands

**SAFC TOTALS:** 91+4 appearances / 8 goals

**In an era where Sunderland usually lost money on players, they made a tidy profit on Patrick. Bought from Chelsea for a fee reported to be in the region of £1.5m to £2m in 2014, three years later he returned to London with Crystal Palace for a fee that apparently could rise to a maximum of £14m. That seven times plus increase in value came after just under 100 games for Sunderland.**

The Netherlands international was the epitome of the modern full-back or wing-back. Excellent going forward, Van Aanholt could frustrate by appearing to saunter back if the opposition launched a counter-attack. In contrast, sixties full-back Cec Irwin would deliver his cross and already be sprinting back to the half-way line before his centre reached its target.

Van Aanholt's attacking value was apparent from the day of his debut when he got around the back of the Throstles defence at West Brom to create an assist. He would go on to make many more and score eight of his own, including a free kick on the night a 3-0 win over Everton secured Sunderland's safety and confirmed Newcastle's relegation in 2016.

Despite signing a new four-year contract that summer, by the following January he was transferred to Palace as new manager David Moyes reshaped his side, bringing in Bryan Oviedo from one of his old clubs Everton.

Capped five times with the Netherlands during his time on Wearside, Van Aanholt had played only five Premier League games before coming to Sunderland, but made 82 appearances at that level with the Black Cats before topping a century with Palace. After playing four times at the delayed Euro 2020 Championships held in 2021, Van Aanholt signed for Galatasaray, debuting against St Johnstone in the Europa League, scoring his first goal in the same competition against Randers of Denmark. By the end of the 2021-22 season Patrick had scored three times in 45+2 games.

## VARGA, Stanislav

**POSITION:** Centre-half

**BIRTHPLACE:** Lipany, Czechoslovakia

**DATE OF BIRTH:** 08/10/1972

**HEIGHT:** 6' 4" **WEIGHT:** 14st 9lbs

**SIGNED FROM:** Slovan Bratislava, 27/07/2000 and from Celtic, 31/08/06

**DEBUT:** v Arsenal, H, 19/08/2000

**LAST MATCH:** v Coventry City, H, 03/02/2007

**MOVED TO:** Celtic, 12/02/2003 and contract not renewed 30/06/2008

**TEAMS:** Jas Bardejov, Tatran Presov, Slovan Bratislava, Sunderland, WBA (L), Celtic, Sunderland, Burnley (L)

**INTERNATIONAL:** Slovakia

**SAFC TOTALS:** 49+5 appearances / 2 goals

**'Stan' Varga made one of the all-time great debuts. Playing against Arsenal on the day the North Stand extension was opened, on the opening day of the 2000-01 season, Varga was phenomenal. Winning everything and spraying the ball around like Franz Beckenbauer he had supporters and scribes wondering where manager Peter Reid had unearthed him from.**

Varga appeared to be another golden find in the vein of Phillips, Sorensen, McCann and others Reid had recruited for bargain fees in recent seasons. Even losing goalkeeper Sorensen during that Arsenal game to be replaced by debutant keeper Jurgen Macho could not help the Gunners to find a chink in Varga's armour as Sunderland kept a clean sheet and won 1-0.

When he arrived Varga did not speak much English and was receiving lessons in his flat at Sunderland Marina from a Hungarian teacher with little knowledge of football, but this did not seem to hold him back. However, just as it looked as if Sunderland had signed a top class centre-half Stan got injured in his second game at Manchester City. He was able to start just one more game before Christmas and never recaptured the quality of performance he had shown on debut. His first goal came in January in a win at West Ham that took Sunderland to second in the Premier League, but he managed only a dozen league appearances in that first term.

## VARGA, Stanislav (Continued)

By the end of his second season Stan was on loan to West Brom, helping the Baggies to promotion. Released by SAFC the following January, he was snapped up by future Sunderland manager Martin O'Neill at Celtic where he played alongside another future Sunderland boss in Roy Keane. When Keane took over at the Stadium of Light, Varga was one of the six signings he sensationally made on the last day of the transfer window. Making his second debut in Keane's first game at Derby, he went on to play 20 times as promotion was won.

Capped 54 times with Slovakia he made 13 of those appearances while with Sunderland. Having won five pieces of silverware in Scotland with Celtic in addition to his 2006-07 Championship medal with Sunderland, 'Stan' went on to manage in his home country, taking Tatran Presov to promotion in 2016.

## VAUGHAN, David Owen

**POSITION:** Midfielder

**BIRTHPLACE:** Abergele, Conwy

**DATE OF BIRTH:** 18/02/1983

**HEIGHT:** 5' 7" **WEIGHT:** 11st 0lbs

**SIGNED FROM:** Blackpool, 08/07/2011

**DEBUT:** v Liverpool, A, 13/08/2011

**LAST MATCH:** v Arsenal, H, 14/09/2013

**MOVED TO:** Nottingham Forest, 01/07/2014 after being on loan from 31/10/2013

**TEAMS:** Crewe Alexandra, Real Sociedad, Blackpool, Sunderland, Nottingham Forest, Notts County, Nantwich Town (to July 2022)

**INTERNATIONAL:** Wales

**SAFC TOTALS:** 33+26 appearances / 3 goals

**Signed by Steve Bruce having been Blackpool's Player of the Year as the Tangerines were relegated from the Premier League, softly spoken David Vaughan was quietly efficient as a footballer. A good technician, Vaughan rarely grabbed the headlines, but even more rarely let anyone down.**

However, two of his three goals were spectacular strikes in first wins for new managers. He drilled home the first goal of Martin O'Neill's reign against Blackburn in December 2011 and also netted with a pile-driver at Newcastle in Paolo Di Canio's first victory in April 2013. Vaughan's only other goal was also a spectacular hit in a 4-1 win at Wigan early on O'Neill's reign.

Before coming to Sunderland he played over 100 games for Blackpool and almost 200 for Crewe with nine games and one goal in between for Real Sociedad in Spain where he signed for Chris Coleman.

## VAUGHAN, James Oliver

**POSITION:** Centre-forward

**BIRTHPLACE:** Birmingham, West Midlands

**DATE OF BIRTH:** 14/08/1988

**HEIGHT:** 5' 11" **WEIGHT:** 12st 8lbs

**SIGNED FROM:** Bury, 13/07/2017

**DEBUT:** v Derby County, H, 04/08/2017

**LAST MATCH:** v Middlesbrough, 06/01/2018

**MOVED TO:** Wigan Athletic, 12/01/2018

**TEAMS:** Everton, Derby County (L), Leicester City (L), Crystal Palace (L), Norwich City, Huddersfield Town, Birmingham City, Bury, Sunderland, Wigan Athletic, Portsmouth (L), Bradford City, Tranmere Rovers

**INTERNATIONAL:** England Under 21

**SAFC TOTALS:** 16+11 appearances / 2 goals

**Brought to Wearside by his former Huddersfield manager Simon Grayson, Vaughan's brief time at the club was not a happy one. Pre-season penalty failures against St Johnstone and Celtic set the tone for a player who initially played with energy and commitment but soon seemed to see those levels drop as success did not come his way.**

After just six months he moved on from the club having never established a rapport with supporters. Vaughan's career commenced with a bang as he became the Premier League's youngest goal-scorer at the age of just 16 years and 271 days when he netted for Everton against Crystal Palace but his career became one of a journeyman striker, Huddersfield, Bury and Tranmere being the only three of his 13 clubs (to 2022) that he managed to score as many as 20 goals for. 143 of his career 408 appearances were as a sub. He scored 120 goals.

## VENISON, Barry

**POSITION:** Right-back / midfielder

**BIRTHPLACE:** Stanley, Co Durham

**DATE OF BIRTH:** 16/08/1964

**HEIGHT:** 5' 9" **WEIGHT:** 11st 9lbs

**SIGNED FROM:** Stanley Boys, 17/05/1979 Professional, 04/01/1982

**DEBUT:** v Notts County, A, 10/10/81

**LAST MATCH:** v Stoke City, H, 03/05/1986

**MOVED TO:** Liverpool, 14/08/1986

**TEAMS:** Sunderland, Liverpool, Newcastle United, Galatasary, Southampton

**INTERNATIONAL:** England

**SAFC TOTALS:** 200+5 appearances / 3 goals

**Paired with Nick Pickering, Barry Venison was one of two England Under 21 full-backs who were part of the solid side Alan Durban was building in the early eighties but were sold during the reign of Lawrie McMenemy. In between those managers, Venison had become the youngest Wembley cup final captain when Len Ashurst installed him as stand-in skipper when regular captain Shaun Elliott was suspended for the 1985 League (Milk) Cup final against Norwich, when Venison was just 20 years and 220 days old.**

While he later developed into a midfielder earning England caps and winning two league titles and the FA Cup with Liverpool, 'Venners' scored just three times in his double century of games for Sunderland. The first of these came on his twelfth appearance, a late winner a week before Christmas in 1981 when he was just 17. The fair-haired Venison went on to become a flamboyantly dressed TV presenter, appeared in the movie 'Mike Bassett: England manager' and settled in America where he managed Orange County Blues.

For England he was capped twice in 1994-95 whilst with Newcastle United, but it was at Liverpool where he had most success despite injuries and an appendix operation restricting his second season in particular. Barry helped the Anfield club to win the league title in 1988 and 1990, appearing as a sub when the FA Cup final was won in 1989. He later played for former Liverpool manager Graeme Souness at Galatasaray and Southampton.

## VERGINI, Santiago

**POSITION:** Centre-back / Right-back

**BIRTHPLACE:** Rosario, Argentina

**DATE OF BIRTH:** 03/08/1988

**HEIGHT:** 6' 3" **WEIGHT:** 13st 0lbs

**SIGNED FROM:** Estudiantes, 20/01/2014, on loan signed, 07/08/2014

**DEBUT:** v Kidderminster Harriers, H, 25/01/2014

**LAST MATCH:** v Southampton, H, 02/05/2015

**MOVED TO:** Boca Juniors, 04/07/2016

**TEAMS:** Atletico Paz, Velez Sarsfield, Olimpia, Verona (L), Newell's Old Boys, Estudiantes, Sunderland, Getafe (loan), Boca Juniors, Bursaspor, San Lorenzo, Atletico Tucuman (L) (to July 2022)

**INTERNATIONAL:** Argentina

**SAFC TOTALS:** 46+5 appearances / 0 goals

**Part of the South American influence introduced by head coach Gus Poyet, the defining moment of Santiago Vergini's time at Sunderland sadly is the stunning own-goal he volleyed into his own net at Southampton in October 2014. It was the first of three own-goals Sunderland conceded in a record equalling 8-0 defeat.**

Capped three times by Argentina, two of those internationals were played while with Sunderland in October and November of 2014, a 7-0 win away to Hong Kong and a 2-1 win over Croatia at West Ham's Boleyn Ground. Vergini was an unused sub for Sunderland in the 2014 League (Capital One) Cup final. When signed from Estudiantes, Vergini's contract was held apparently held by Costa Rican club Sport Uruguay De Coronado.

## VINALL, Edward John (Jack)

**POSITION:** Forward

**BIRTHPLACE:** Witton, Birmingham, Warwickshire

**DATE OF BIRTH:** 16/12/1910 - 26/05/1997

**HEIGHT:** 5' 11" **WEIGHT:** 12st 0lbs

**SIGNED FROM:** Folkestone, 26/10/1931

**DEBUT:** v Middlesbrough, H, 31/10/1931

**LAST MATCH:** v Arsenal, A, 03/09/1932

**MOVED TO:** Norwich City, 24/06/1933

**TEAMS:** Allan & Everitt's FC, Birmingham, Folkestone, Sunderland, Norwich City, Luton Town, Walsall (WW2 Guest), Coventry City (WW2 Guest), Walsall, Worcester City

**SAFC TOTALS:** 21 appearances / 3 goals

**Jack Vinall belongs in the category of players who played a handful of games for Sunderland but excelled elsewhere. Signed when he was 20, Vinall scored on his second appearance at Bolton but managed just two more goals in 20 appearances in his first season, all of his goals coming away from home. Early the following season he got one more opportunity, but was cast aside after featuring in a 6-1 loss at Arsenal. Notably at Sunderland he had scored a hat-trick in the Durham Senior Cup final in November 1931 as Gateshead were beaten 4-0.**

Dropping two levels, Vinall found his groove with Norwich City where in his first season he was the Canaries joint top scorer with Billy Warnes, the pair scoring 21 each as they won the Division Three South title. Four of those goals came on Vinall's second appearance as Bristol City were thrashed 7-2 on 28 August 1933. Those goals were scored at the Canaries' old ground of the Nest. In May 1935 Vinall played at the final game at that ground and then scored twice in the first match at Carrow Road as West Ham were beaten 4-3 August 1935. Six months later Jack scored Carrow Road's first hat-trick in a 5-1 win over Southampton.

Younger brother Albert played for Norwich, Southampton, Aston Villa and Walsall while Jack went on to become player/coach of Walsall and player/manager at Worcester City from May 1947 to November 1950.

## VINCENT, Robert George

**POSITION:** Midfielder

**BIRTHPLACE:** Newcastle, Northumberland

**DATE OF BIRTH:** 23/11/1962

**HEIGHT:** 5' 11" **WEIGHT:** 12st 1lb

**SIGNED FROM:** Newcastle Juniors, 01/01/1979

**DEBUT:** v WBA, A, 20/04/1981

**LAST MATCH:** v Brighton & Hove Albion, H, 25/4/1981

**MOVED TO:** Leyton Orient, 15/05/1982

**TEAMS:** Sunderland, Leyton Orient, Heidelberg United, Brisbane Lions, Whitley Bay, Barrow, Whitley Bay

**INTERNATIONAL:** England Schoolboys

**SAFC TOTALS:** 1+1 appearances / 0 goals

**Rob Vincent made a couple of late-season league appearances at the age of 18 as Sunderland fought relegation under caretaker manager Mick Docherty. He also appeared as a substitute in the club's Centenary game against an England XI in 1979.**

Released a year after his first-team appearances, Vincent played a further eight league games for Leyton Orient before moving to Australia for a couple of years. In 2007, he was reported to be working at Nissan.

## VOKINS, Jake

**POSITION:** Left-back

**BIRTHPLACE:** Oxford, Oxfordshire

**DATE OF BIRTH:** 17/03/2000

**HEIGHT:** 5' 11" **WEIGHT:** 11st 2lbs

**SIGNED FROM:** 29/01/2021, Southampton, on loan

**DEBUT:** v MK Dons, A, 06/02/2021

**LAST MATCH:** v Accrington Stanley, A, 17/03/2021

**MOVED TO:** Southampton, 30/06/2021, end of loan

**TEAMS:** Southampton, Sunderland (L), Ross County (L), Woking (L) (to September 2022)

**INTERNATIONAL:** England Under 19

**SAFC TOTALS:** 4 appearances / 0 goals

**Cup-tied for a Wembley final in the Football League (Papa John's) Trophy while at Sunderland, Vokins time on Wearside was also hit by Covid and reportedly a slight heart problem. At this point he had already made all four of his Sunderland appearances, all of which were away from home.**

Loaned to Ross County the following season he played alongside former SAFC defender Jack Baldwin. At the end of January 2022, his twelfth appearance came in a dramatic 3-3 draw with Rangers. Capped at Under 17, 18 and 19 level, his highlight (to 2022) was as coming off the bench for Jadon Sancho as England lost to Spain on penalties in the 2017 UEFA European Under 17 final against Spain.

## WADDLE, Christopher Roland

**POSITION:** Outside-left

**BIRTHPLACE:** Heworth, Co Durham

**DATE OF BIRTH:** 14/12/1960

**HEIGHT:** 6' 0" **WEIGHT:** 13st 3lbs

**SIGNED FROM:** Bradford City, 17/03/1997

**DEBUT:** v Nottingham Forest, H, 22/03/1997

**LAST MATCH:** v Wimbledon, A, 11/05/1997

**MOVED TO:** Released from contract, 20/05/1997

**TEAMS:** Pelaw Juniors, Whitehouse SC, Mount Pleasant, HMH Printing Co, Leam Lane SC, Clarke Chapman, Tow Law Town, Newcastle United, Tottenham Hotspur, Olympique Marseille, Sheffield Wednesday, Falkirk, Bradford City, Sunderland, Burnley, Hollinshed Amateurs, Torquay United, Brunsmeer Athletic, Hill Top, Davy Sports, Brunsmeer, Worksop Town, Parkgate (L), Staveley Miners' Welfare, Glapwell, South Normanton Athletic, Stocksbridge Park Steels, Staveley MBNA, Greenhill White Hart, Belford, Tow Law Town, Worksop Parramore, Hallam

**INTERNATIONAL:** England

**SAFC TOTALS:** 7 appearances / 1 goal

**Chris Waddle had an outstanding career but was a veteran by the time he played for his boyhood favourites Sunderland where he had not been offered a contract after trials as a 16 and 18-year old. His blistering free-kick goal in the last-ever league game at Roker Park (against Everton) saw him score at the Fulwell End where he was once a regular.**

Tall and heavy for a winger, Waddle's idiosyncratic lolloping gait was deceptive as the best defenders in the world struggled to contain him in his prime. Like Frank Worthington, Waddle was a top class player who could have retired much earlier but was so in love with the game he kept playing until he was well into his forties and was well past 50 when he played for Worksop Parramore and Hallam.

Having come to prominence with 23 goals for Tow Law Town in 1979-80 while working for Cheviot Seasoning, a sausage and pie-makers, Chris signed for Newcastle. Along with Sunderland, Sheffield United and Coventry they had previously shown interest in him. At St James' Park Chris became a hero. He scored 52 goals and made many more in 190+1 appearances, starting with a debut against Shrewsbury Town in October 1980 and winning promotion in 1983-84 when he starred alongside Kevin Keegan and Peter Beardsley.

After winning his first cap for England in March 1985, that summer a tribunal set fee of £590,000 took him to Tottenham where he made 213+5 appearances. He found the back of the net 53 times, two of those goals coming on his debut against Watford with one of his many assists coming in the 1987 FA Cup final which was lost to Nick Pickering's Coventry.

After four years Spurs made a massive profit in selling Chris to Olympique Marseille, the fee of £4.5m making him the world's third most expensive player. Waddle won the league title with Marseille in three successive years from 1990 and played in the 1991 European Cup final. That was lost to Red Star Belgrade on penalties, Waddle not taking one after infamously missing in the previous year's FIFA World Cup semi-final for England against Germany. Six years after leaving France Chris was voted runner-up to Jean Pierre Papin as Marseille's Player of the Century.

Waddle came back to England for £1m in 1992 joining Sheffield Wednesday and becoming the first Wednesday player to win the Football Writers' Player of the Year award in his first season of 1992-93 - the first year of the Premier League. It was a season where he played in both domestic cup finals, scoring in the FA Cup final replay against Arsenal after a trademark spectacular goal in the all-Sheffield semi-final.

After 130+17 games and 15 goals for the Owls Chris rejected a player-coach role in preference for a free transfer. He signed a month-long contract with newly-relegated Falkirk to get fit. After just four games for the Bairns - including a brilliant debut goal against Clydebank - he returned to Yorkshire with Bradford City.

Six goals in 25 league games for the Bantams preceded his seven-game sojourn at Sunderland after which he scored once in 30+5 games with Burnley in 1997-98 as player-manager when his squad included Lee Howey, John Mullin and Chris Woods. Still refusing to call it a day, Waddle went to Torquay in September 1998, playing seven times before taking up a coaching appointment at Sheffield Wednesday. Unable to stop putting on his boots however, Chris simply kept playing for many years in non-league, often playing just one or two games for a club.

For England he scored six times in 62 internationals, playing at the 1986 and 1990 World Cups as well as Euro 88. In 1987 he reached number twelve in the pop charts along with Spurs and England teammate Glenn Hoddle with a song called, 'Diamond Lights'. A biography was produced in 1988 and updated in 1997.

In later years Waddle became a prominent radio and TV summariser. His son Jack played for Chesterfield and cousin Alan Waddle played for a long list of clubs ranging from Hartlepool to Liverpool.

## WAGHORN, Martyn Thomas

**POSITION:** Forward

**BIRTHPLACE:** South Shields, Tyne & Wear

**DATE OF BIRTH:** 23/01/1990

**HEIGHT:** 5' 9½" **WEIGHT:** 13st 0lbs

**SIGNED FROM:** Trainee, 01/07/2006

**DEBUT:** v Manchester United, H, 26/12/2007

**LAST MATCH:** v Colchester United, H, 24/08/2010

**MOVED TO:** Leicester City, 31/08/2010

**TEAMS:** Sunderland, Charlton Athletic (L), Leicester City, Hull City (L), Millwall (L), Wigan Athletic, Rangers, Ipswich Town, Derby County, Coventry City (to June 2022)

**INTERNATIONAL:** England Under 21

**SAFC TOTALS:** 3+5 appearances / 0 goals

**A member of the same youth team as Jordan Henderson, 'Waggy' played a prominent role in the side that reached the FA Youth Cup semi-final in 2008. He was the top scorer in that run with seven goals including a hat-trick against Norwich City. With Sunderland in the Premier League Martyn's opportunities were limited. In November 2008 he joined Charlton on loan in the Championship, scoring a first senior goal against one of his future clubs Derby while making 4+3 appearances for the Addicks.**

A further loan to Leicester was very successful with twelve goals and the club's Young Player of the Year award as they reached the Championship Play-Offs in 2009-10. After a brief spell back at Sunderland the Foxes paid £3m for him. Having found goals harder to come by Waghorn was loaned to Hull where his old Leicester manager Nigel Pearson had taken over. After one goal in five games for the Tigers Martyn moved to Millwall, again on loan, this time scoring three goals in 13+1 appearances.

Freed in January 2014 he signed for Wigan, scoring eight goals in 22+19 games before going north to Rangers. Twenty goals in 25 league games in his first season at Ibrox saw the Shields lad play a major role in returning Rangers to the top-flight as they were promoted from the Championship. Waghorn was the division's top scorer and Rangers Players' Player of the Year as they also won the Scottish Challenge Cup, although he missed the final against Peterhead. After 44 goals in 63+15 games for the Gers he traded their blue for the blue of Ipswich. There were 16 goals in 39+7 games in a season as a Tractor Boy before an August 2018 move to Derby. Martyn registered 30 goals for the Rams in 92+31 games over three seasons before a summer 2021 move to Coventry where in an injury-troubled first season he managed 11+18 appearances, his only goal coming in a home win against Middlesbrough.

For England he played twice at Under 19 level and scored on his first two Under 21 appearances against Azerbaijan and Israel in 2011 before winning a further three caps at that level.

## WAGSTAFFE, Thomas Daniel (Tom)

**POSITION:** Centre-forward

**BIRTHPLACE:** Dinapore, India

**DATE OF BIRTH:** 25/09/1896 - 21/11/1961

**HEIGHT:** 5' 7" **WEIGHT:** 10st 6lbs

**SIGNED FROM:** Fleetwood, 06/03/1923

**DEBUT:** v Manchester City, H, 30/03/1923

**LAST MATCH:** v Burnley, A, 21/04/1923

**MOVED TO:** Oldham Athletic, 28/08/1924

**TEAMS:** Fleetwood, Sunderland, Oldham Athletic, Fleetwood, Morecambe, Crewe Alexandra, Mossley

**SAFC TOTALS:** 2 appearances / 0 goals

**An incredible 28 goals in eleven games for Fleetwood persuaded Sunderland to take a chance on Wagstaffe in 1923 when a £550 fee represented 10% of the game's record transfer fee for a player from a club who finished the season sixth in the Lancashire Combination.**

It was a far-cry from what Wagstaffe had been used to compared to being immediately thrust into a top-flight debut, playing at centre-forward with the legendary Charlie Buchan as his inside-right. Evidently undaunted, contemporary reports record that the 35,000 crowd warmed to his display in a 2-0 victory over Manchester City with his 'clever play' creating a goal for Buchan. Three weeks later Wagstaffe got another chance, this time away to Burnley, but the 2-0 loss would be his last league game. Four days later however, he did play at inside-right in the semi-final of the Durham Senior Professional Cup as South Shields were beaten 2-0 at Roker Park - but he was not involved when Darlington were defeated in the final at the end of the season.

Having not done enough to warrant retention at Roker, Wagstaffe had a two-month trial at Oldham at the start of the following 1924-25 campaign before throwing his lot back in with Fleetwood. By 1926 he was back in the Football League with Division Three North Crewe Alexandra for whom he scored once in his three games before ending his career with Mossley.

A draughtsman by trade - after moving from India, where his father was stationed in the army, to England as a child - he served in the Manchester Rifle Brigade during World War One when he survived malaria. After hanging up his football boots, Tom found employment as a Rotary Press Assistant in Salford.

## WAINWRIGHT, Neil

**POSITION:** Midfielder

**BIRTHPLACE:** Warrington, Cheshire

**DATE OF BIRTH:** 04/11/1977

**HEIGHT:** 5' 11" **WEIGHT:** 10st 2lbs

**SIGNED FROM:** Wrexham, 17/06/1998

**DEBUT:** v York City, A, 11/08/1998

**LAST MATCH:** v Luton Town, H, 19/09/2000

**MOVED TO:** Darlington, 20/08/2001

**TEAMS:** Wrexham, Sunderland, Darlington (L), Halifax Town (L), Darlington, Shrewsbury Town (L), Mansfield Town (L), Morecambe, Barrow (L), Kendal Town, Darlington, Lancaster City

**SAFC TOTALS:** 5+3 appearances / 0 goals

**Sunderland took a chance on wide-man 'Wainy' after he had impressed as a youngster with Wrexham where he scored three times in 13 games in 1997-98. At Sunderland all of Neil's starts came in the League Cup. He was to spend the bulk of his career with Darlington where he made 213+79 appearances and scored 30 goals over three spells, all but the final dozen in 2012 coming when the Quakers were a Football League club.**

Throughout his career Neil had several loan spells, making 14 appearances for Halifax when they were still in the Football League and managed by Paul Bracewell in 2000-01. He made 2+1 appearances for Shrewsbury and 1+4 for Mansfield before joining Morecambe where a goal on his home debut against Rotherham in August 2008 was his only one in 43+24 games.

Morecambe twice loaned Neil to Barrow where he totalled eleven appearances before he returned to Darlington after a short spell at Kendal Town. He finished his playing days with Lancaster City, acting as joint-manager in his final five months before a February 2013 departure. As of August 2022 he was head of coaching at Morecambe academy, a position he took up in 2020.

## WAKEHAM, Peter Francis

**POSITION:** Goalkeeper

**BIRTHPLACE:** Kingsbridge, Devon

**DATE OF BIRTH:** 14/03/1936 - 25/02/2013

**HEIGHT:** 6' 0" **WEIGHT:** 12st 4lbs

**SIGNED FROM:** Torquay United, 23/09/1958

**DEBUT:** v Grimsby Town, H, 01/11/1958

**LAST MATCH:** v Middlesbrough, A, 31/03/1962

**MOVED TO:** Charlton Athletic, 28/06/1962

**TEAMS:** Torquay United, Sunderland, Charlton Athletic, Lincoln City, Poole Town

**SAFC TOTALS:** 151 appearances / 0 goals

**Having missed just one game in 1960-61 and been a regular for the best part of four seasons since signing for Sunderland, Wakeham may well have played many more times but for the emergence of the legendary Jim Montgomery. Having moved on to Charlton where he played 55 league games, he produced one of his finest performances at Roker Park in 1964 on the day Sunderland secured their first-ever promotion.**

Peter had been spotted impressing for Torquay where the first of 58 league appearances came in a 3-2 victory over Newport County in April 1954. He had done so well for the unfashionable club that in October 1957 he was a reserve for England Under 23s when they played at Wembley against Romania, Wakeham understudying Sheffield United's Alan Hodgkinson despite Torquay being bottom of Division Three South at the time. Later in his career Peter played 44 league games for Lincoln before finishing his career in non-league with Poole Town.

## WALDRON, Colin

**POSITION:** Centre-half

**BIRTHPLACE:** Bristol, Gloucestershire

**DATE OF BIRTH:** 22/06/1948

**HEIGHT:** 6' 0" **WEIGHT:** 13st 13lbs

**SIGNED FROM:** Manchester United, 19/07/1977 on loan from 28/02/1977

**DEBUT:** v West Ham United, H, 05/03/1977

**LAST MATCH:** v Brighton & Hove Albion, H, 01/10/1977

**MOVED TO:** Tulsa Toughnecks, 02/02/1978

**TEAMS:** Bury, Chelsea, Burnley, Manchester United, Sunderland, Tulsa Roughnecks, Philadelphia Fury, Mossley (L), Atlanta Chiefs, Rochdale

**SAFC TOTALS:** 22 appearances / 1 goal

**Bristol-born, but Oldham raised, Waldron was one of several former Burnley players brought in at Roker Park by former Clarets boss Jimmy Adamson. Waldron played a dozen games as Sunderland gallantly but unsuccessfully fought to stave off relegation in 1977. His debut coincided with a 6-0 win while his second home appearance saw him score the only goal of the game with a cracking shot on the turn that crashed in off the crossbar against Ipswich.**

Colin had started as an apprentice at Bury in May 1966, quickly catching the eye of Chelsea who he moved to for £25,000 after just 20 games and one goal. Still a teenager when he debuted for Chelsea in a 1-0 win at WBA in August 1967, he had a rough time in his fourth and fifth matches as Chelsea conceded eleven goals. After ten games the Blues cashed in, making a profit when Burnley paid a club record £30,000 to take him back to the north-west after less than five months in the capital.

Colin was to become a colossus at Turf Moor. Debuting at Southampton, he began at right-back but soon moved into his best position in central-defence and became captain in 1968-69. A fall-out with manager Harry Potts saw him lose his place until Jimmy Adamson took over as manager in February 1970 before relegation was suffered a year later, although the Second Division was won in Sunderland's cup-winning year of 1973, Waldron scoring the goal at local rivals Preston which secured the title. With Sunderland and league champions Liverpool declining places in the Charity Shield, Waldron then scored the only goal of that season's Shield game as Manchester City were defeated. Colin was re-appointed as captain of Burnley in 1974, eventually moving on in 1976 after 356 games and 18 goals.

The man who signed him for Manchester United was his old Chelsea manager Tommy Docherty, but he only played four times for United. The first and last of these were home games with Sunderland, both drawn, the first in the League Cup. The games came either side of Bob Stokoe's resignation with Waldron's move to Wearside coming after Adamson took over the reins at Roker. Following his time at Sunderland, Colin headed to America playing eleven games for Tulsa, 16 for Philadelphia and 14 for Atlanta, scoring once each for the first two of those clubs.

## WALDRON, Colin (Continued)

He returned to make a single appearance for Mossley in between his time with Philadelphia and Atlanta before a swan-song with Rochdale in 1979-80 where he signed for his old Sunderland and Burnley teammate Doug Collins. Bob Stokoe then took over, but in 22 league and cup games was unable to stop Dale finishing bottom of the fourth division, Waldron having partnered ex-Sunderland man Alan Weir in central-defence in front of on-loan Sunderland goalkeeper Ian Watson.

After retiring from the game, Waldron worked in the family bookmaker's business in Nelson while during the seventies he had been joint proprietor of a restaurant in Whitefield, Manchester with England international Colin Bell. Waldron's brother Alan played for Bolton, Blackpool, Bury and York from 1970 to '82.

## WALKER, Clive

**POSITION:** Outside-left
**BIRTHPLACE:** Oxford, Oxfordshire
**DATE OF BIRTH:** 26/05/1957
**HEIGHT:** 5' 8½" **WEIGHT:** 11st 4lbs
**SIGNED FROM:** Chelsea, 18/07/1984
**DEBUT:** v Southampton, H, 25/08/1984
**LAST MATCH:** v Stoke City, A, 30/11/1985
**MOVED TO:** QPR, 13/12/1985
**TEAMS:** Chelsea, Fort Lauderdale Strikers (L), Sunderland, QPR, Fulham, Brighton & Hove Albion, Woking Town, Cheltenham Town, Molesey
**INTERNATIONAL:** England Schoolboy
**SAFC TOTALS:** 61+3 appearances / 17 goals

**Infamously, Clive missed a penalty in the 1985 League Cup final. He had scored twice in the semi-final against his old club Chelsea and earlier in the same season had scored a first-half hat-trick including two penalties against Manchester United. A speedy flair player, Walker debuted for Chelsea as a sub at Oldham in April 1977 shortly before his 20th birthday. He went on to play 224+33 games for the club scoring 65 goals with a best of 17 in 1981-82 while there had been nine goals in 22 games during a 1979 loan with Fort Lauderdale Strikers.**

Clive returned to West London with QPR after leaving Sunderland, debuting at home to Aston Villa just before Christmas in 1985, but it was one of just 27 appearances in two years that brought just two goals. After moving to Fulham he scored 31 times in 113+8 games, two of those goals coming on his debut in the Cottagers first home game after the match in which Marco Gabbiadini scored his first goals for Sunderland. Clive again topped 100 games for his next club Brighton, netting eight goals in 106 league games. After unsuccessful trials with Swansea City and Slough Town, he moved into non-league with Woking where 91 goals in 203 Conference games saw him win four FA Trophy medals, be Conference Player of the Year in 1995 and play for a FA Representative XI against the Isthmian League.

In 1997-98 he had a spell as assistant manager at Brentford before signing as a player with Cheltenham, playing 56 times (13 goals) and helping them into the Football League in 1999. Walker continued his career with Molesey as player/coach in Ryman League Division Two having played until well into his forties after which he managed Dover.

After retiring from professional football, Clive became an auctioneer and worked as a summariser in BBC Radio London.

## WALKER, John (Jack)

**POSITION:** Full-back
**BIRTHPLACE:** Carluke, Lanarkshire
**DATE OF BIRTH:** 1868 - date of death unknown
**HEIGHT:** 5' 8" **WEIGHT:** 11st 0lbs
**SIGNED FROM:** Clyde, 14/06/1893
**DEBUT:** v Wednesday, A, 02/09/1893
**LAST MATCH:** v Sheffield United, A, 07/10/1893
**MOVED TO:** Nelson, 15/12/1893
**TEAMS:** Wishaw Thistle, Burnley, Ardwick, Burnley, Clyde, Sunderland, Nelson, Stoke, Manchester City, Wishaw Thistle
**SAFC TOTALS:** 6 appearances / 0 goals

**A brass moulder before becoming a footballer, Walker first played in England for Burnley, making his debut at Sunderland in the Wearsiders' first-ever league game. That was the first of 40 league games he played in two years for Burnley where he had two spells either side of a brief stint with Ardwick. He then returned to Scotland with Clyde for the 1892-93 season, playing in a 6-1 home Scottish Cup defeat to Dumbarton just before Christmas but helping them to win the Glasgow North Eastern Cup.**

Coming to Sunderland he joined the defending league champions and played the opening six games of the 1893-94 season, but lost his place after only one of those was won. Although signed from Clyde, the £50 transfer fee it cost to acquire him went to Burnley who held his Football League registration. Very short spells followed at Nelson and Stoke before he joined his old club Ardwick who had just changed their name to Manchester City. Debuting at Notts County in October 1894, the last of his 19 games came at Darwen the following April before returning to his first club Wishaw Thistle.

## WALKER, Nigel Stephen

**POSITION:** Midfielder
**BIRTHPLACE:** Gateshead, Co Durham
**DATE OF BIRTH:** 07/04/1959 - 02/02/2014
**HEIGHT:** 5' 10" **WEIGHT:** 11st 11lbs
**SIGNED FROM:** Crewe Alexandra, 07/07/1983
**DEBUT:** v Watford, H, 12/11/1983
**LAST MATCH:** v Watford, H, 12/11/1983
**MOVED TO:** Chester City, 01/06/1984
**TEAMS:** Whickham, Newcastle United, Plymouth Argyle (L), San Diego Sockers, Crewe Alexandra, Sunderland, Blackpool (L), Chester City, Hartlepool United, Blyth Spartans, Dunston Federation, RTM Newcastle
**SAFC TOTALS:** 0+1 appearances / 0 goals

**The eight minutes Nigel Walker was on the pitch for Sunderland made his career the shortest in the club's history at the time although to June 2022, six players have since appeared for a shorter time. He had initially had a month-long trial at Sunderland playing four reserve games eleven months before his solitary appearance and had played for Crewe in between.**

Having captained his County youth side at Rugby Union, Walker played local football before joining Newcastle where he made 69+5 appearances, scoring three goals having debuted on Guy Fawkes day in 1977 at home to Bristol City. A skilful and elegant footballer, Nigel was loaned to Plymouth in January 1982, but did not get a game for Argyle. In the USA, Nigel scored once in 19 games for San Diego as well as playing in indoor soccer.

There had been five goals in 20 league outings for Crewe. When Sunderland loaned him out to Blackpool he made his mark with a debut hat-trick against Northampton in a match where future Sunderland man Paul Stewart was also on the scoresheet, with Steve Hetzke also in the side. There were no further goals in Walker's 8+1 games for the Seasiders, but he was on the mark nine times in 41 league games for Chester in 1984-85 before signing for Hartlepool where his 87+5 appearances produced eight goals and a lot of impressive football as Pools' creator-in-chief.

Stepping into non-league Nigel played 216 games for Blyth where he became manager in January 1992 before stints with Dunston and RTM. While playing part-time, he took an Open University course in technology and design before gaining a first-class honours degree in computer sciences at Northumbria University and duly becoming a maths teacher.

## WALLACE, Ian Andrew

**POSITION:** Striker
**BIRTHPLACE:** Glasgow, Lanarkshire
**DATE OF BIRTH:** 23/05/1956
**HEIGHT:** 5' 8" **WEIGHT:** 11st 8lbs
**SIGNED FROM:** FC Brest, 16/01/1985
**DEBUT:** v Watford, A, 23/01/1985
**LAST MATCH:** v Stoke City, H, 03/05/1986
**MOVED TO:** Released, 31/05/1986
**TEAMS:** Yoker Athletic, Dumbarton, Coventry City, Nottingham Forest, Brest, Sunderland, Maritimo, Melbourne Croatia, Albion Turkagura
**INTERNATIONAL:** Scotland
**SAFC TOTALS:** 32+8 appearances / 6 goals

**One of the costliest players in the game when Brian Clough paid £1.25m to buy him for Nottingham Forest from Coventry in the summer of 1980, Wallace is best remembered at Sunderland for being preferred over semi-final hero Colin West for the 1985 League Cup final against Norwich. Ian had scored against the Canaries seven days earlier.**

A scorer on his debut for Scotland against Bulgaria in February 1978, and on his only Under 21 appearance, Ian surprisingly only won three caps, two of them as sub. Having started with Yoker Athletic near Clydebank in 1973-74, flame-haired Wallace attracted a £40,000 fee when moving to England with Coventry City after eleven goals in 34 games for Dumbarton. It was against Sunderland that he made his debut as a sub in October 1976, the same season in which he was part of the Sky Blues side on the night of the notorious draw with Bristol City as Sunderland were relegated. The following season Wallace became the first Coventry player to score 20 top-flight goals in a season and went on to total 59 goals in 138+2 games, despite being involved in a bad car-crash which for a time looked like threatening his sight.

At Forest in his first season Ian played in the European Super Cup with Valencia and an Inter-Continental Cup loss to Nacional Montevideo as well as playing for the defending champions in the European Cup. He was to score 46 goals in 154+11 competitive games for Forest. He notched a hat-trick against Birmingham City plus others in friendlies with Al-Hilal and Kettering Town as well as goals in two games against Sunderland.

Moving to France with Brest in May 1984, Ian scored three times in 16 games before coming to Sunderland, but after under a year and a half in the north-east; in which he was relegated, he returned to the continent with Maritimo of Madeira. There he played nine games without scoring in the Portuguese League after which the Scot continued his travels with a move to Australia where he scored once for every four of his 24 games for Melbourne Croatia where he became player-manager as he did with Albion Turkagura. Ian became manager of Dumbarton in November 1996 having scouted for them for a couple of years whilst running a newsagents in Glasgow and also scouting for Sheffield Wednesday. His time at Dumbarton ended acrimoniously after a period of suspension, as like so many former players he fell foul of a club's directors as they sold players and in Dumbarton's case even their ground.

## WALLACE, Robert

**POSITION:** Inside-right

**BIRTHPLACE:** Paisley, Renfrewshire

**DATE OF BIRTH:** c 1906/07 - date of death unknown

**HEIGHT:** 5' 7" **WEIGHT:** 10st 10lbs

**SIGNED FROM:** Cowdenbeath, 30/06/1928

**DEBUT:** v Blackburn Rovers, H, 29/08/1928

**LAST MATCH:** v Blackburn Rovers, A, 17/09/1928

**MOVED TO:** Third Lanark, 10/07/1929

**TEAMS:** St Mirren, Cambuslang Rangers, Cowdenbeath, Sunderland, Third Lanark, Bo'Ness, Hibernian, Alloa Athletic

**INTERNATIONAL:** Scotland Junior

**SAFC TOTALS:** 5 appearances / 0 goals

**Nicknamed 'Brick', Wallace arrived after six games and one goal for Cowdenbeath and after his short stay at Sunderland returned to Scotland to score eight goals in 28 games for Third Lanark between 1929 and 31. Twenty-eight goals in 35 Division Two games for Bo'ness in 1931-32 were only enough to help the club to 14th as they conceded 103 times in 38 fixtures.**

Debuting for Hibs at Dunfermline in September 1932 he scored his first goal later that month against Brechin City and went on to score 25 times in 60 games for the Edinburgh club. He was top scorer with 22 goals from 33 appearances as they won the second division in 1932-33.

## WALLACE, Ross

**POSITION:** Left-winger

**BIRTHPLACE:** Dundee, Angus

**DATE OF BIRTH:** 23/05/1985

**HEIGHT:** 5' 8" **WEIGHT:** 10st 0lbs

**SIGNED FROM:** Celtic, 31/08/2006

**DEBUT:** v Derby County, A, 09/09/2006

**LAST MATCH:** v Arsenal, H, 11/05/2008

**MOVED TO:** Preston North End, 12/01/2009

**TEAMS:** Celtic, Sunderland, Preston North End, Burnley, Sheffield Wednesday, Fleetwood Town, St Mirren

**INTERNATIONAL:** Scotland

**SAFC TOTALS:** 40+15 appearances / 8 goals

**An exciting player brought in immediately upon Roy Keane's appointment; along with the return of Stan Varga from Celtic where they had played with Keane, Wallace went straight into the side for Keane's first match at Derby and scored as Sunderland set off on a journey from one off the bottom to top of the league. Wallace scored his sixth of the season in a final-day 5-0 win at Luton that secured the Championship title after he had competed for the left-wing berth with Swedish international Toby Hysen.**

Wallace added two goals in the Premier League before going on loan to Preston who he subsequently signed for. After a total of 84+6 games and twelve goals for North End, Ross made the short move to Burnley where between the summers of 2010 and 2015 he scored 14 goals in 116+49 appearances, winning promotion to the Premier League in 2014. Following a free transfer he joined Sheffield Wednesday where he added another 105+19 games with 13 goals in three years prior to a 17-month spell at Fleetwood where he scored once in 36+6 games. A final move back to Scotland with St Mirren provided two substitute appearances and one start on his final outing in a home win over Hearts in March 2020 before Covid ended the season and with it Wallace's playing days.

As he got older Wallace moved back to left-back or left-wing-back, but never lost his attacking intent. While he was with Sunderland he broke into the Scotland B team for a game with the Republic of Ireland in November 2007, but it was not until he joined Preston that he won his solitary full cap against Japan in October 2009.

Before coming to Sunderland Ross had been given his league debut for Celtic by Martin O'Neill in October 2002. He was to play 24+28 games for Celtic, three of his four goals coming in an 8-1 League Cup win over Falkirk in September 2004. Always on the periphery at Celtic, he had been on trial with Birmingham City before coming to Sunderland although he helped the Celts to win the Scottish Cup in 2004, coming on as a sub for O'Neill's side as they defeated Dunfermline in the final. Two years later he started the League Cup final alongside Keane as once again Dunfermline were beaten at Hampden, this time in a season where Celtic also won the league. Following his retirement, Ross returned to Burnley as Youth Development Officer.

## WALLACE, Thomas Hall

**POSITION:** Centre-half

**BIRTHPLACE:** Jarrow, Co Durham

**DATE OF BIRTH:** 01/07/1906 - 12/04/1939

**HEIGHT:** 6' 2" **WEIGHT:** 11st 11lbs

**SIGNED FROM:** North Shields, 12/11/1931

**DEBUT:** v Southampton, H, 09/01/1932

**LAST MATCH:** v Southampton, H, 09/01/1932

**MOVED TO:** Burnley, 20/05/1933

**TEAMS:** Jarrow, North Shields, Sunderland, Burnley

**SAFC TOTALS:** 1 appearance / 0 goals

**Wallace's only game was a goalless FA Cup tie with Division Two Southampton when at the last minute he was drafted into the team when regular pivot Jock McDougall pulled out of the tie.**

Wallace went on to play another six cup-ties plus 61 league games for Burnley, but retired due to ill health when only 30.
He had been a miner before playing football and had continued to play cricket for Jarrow whilst on Sunderland's books. Sadly, he died prematurely aged just 32.

## WALSH, William (Bill)

**POSITION:** Centre-half / half-back

**BIRTHPLACE:** Horden, Co Durham

**DATE OF BIRTH:** 05/12/1923 - 31/07/2014

**HEIGHT:** 5' 11" **WEIGHT:** 11st 11lbs

**SIGNED FROM:** Horden Colliery, 04/12/1940

**DEBUT:** v Charlton Athletic, A, 11/09/1946

**LAST MATCH:** v Cardiff City, H, 27/04/1953

**MOVED TO:** Northampton Town, 10/07/1953

**TEAMS:** Horden Colliery, Sunderland, WBA, (WW2 Guest), Blackburn Rovers (WW2 Guest), Blackpool (WW2 Guest), Northampton Town, Darlington, Hakoah

**SAFC TOTALS:** 105 appearances / 1 goal

**Having signed for Sunderland in the early stages of World War Two, Walsh waited six years for a league debut. He was then with SAFC for seven seasons playing fewer than ten games in four of them and none at all in his penultimate season of 1951-52.**

However, in addition to 18 games in 1946-47 he played 68 times in 1949-50 and 1951-52 as the Lads went very close to being league champions in the former of those two campaigns. Serving in the Royal Artillery during the war he was not able to play at all for Sunderland, but did Guest for WBA and Blackburn

## WALSH, Bill (Continued)

(where he played one game for each) and Blackpool where he scored five goals in only four games. After leaving Wearside he made 19 and 28 appearances in Division Three South and North with Northampton and Darlington before emigrating to Australia in May 1955. There he played for Hakoah in Sydney and lived to the ripe old age of 90.

## WALSHAW, Kenneth

**POSITION:** Inside-left
**BIRTHPLACE:** Cullercoats, Northumberland
**DATE OF BIRTH:** 28/08/1918 - 16/05/1979
**HEIGHT:** 5' 9" **WEIGHT:** 11st 7lbs
**SIGNED FROM:** North Shields, 25/08/1944
**DEBUT:** v Bury, A, 29/01/1946
**LAST MATCH:** v Birmingham City, A, 13/02/1946
**MOVED TO:** Lincoln City, 23/07/1947
**TEAMS:** North Shields, Sunderland, Lincoln City, Carlisle United, Bradford City
**SAFC TOTALS:** 2 appearances / 1 goal

**Although he was only with Lincoln for four months in the second half of 1947, Walshaw's 17 appearances were sufficient to earn a medal as the Imps went on to win the Third Division North title. At Sunderland, the inside-left officially played just twice. These were in the FA Cup in the first season after World War Two. While not included in official records that season also saw him play nine times in League North, scoring the winner in a match against Bradford Park Avenue as well as netting in the semi-final of the Durham Senior Cup against Gateshead.**

Two seasons earlier he played in another semi-final, the war-time Tyne Wear Tees Cup first leg, lost to Newcastle. A couple of weeks later he scored in a League North draw with Boro having earlier played in the same competition against Gateshead. Walshaw's most productive Sunderland campaign was in 1944-45 when he grabbed eleven goals from 26 games most of which were on the left-wing. During the war he had been on the training staff of the Durham Light Infantry.

After his time with Lincoln, Walshaw went to Carlisle United for whom he scored on his debut on Boxing Day in 1947. This came at Tranmere in a 3-0 win where the other two goals came from player/manager and future Sunderland star Ivor Broadis. Kenneth's second goal came against his old club Lincoln, but in a heavy home defeat as the Imps moved towards that title and Walshaw's medal. In total he scored 15 goals in 50 games for the Cumbrians, playing for Bill Shankly after Broadis left for Roker. Walshaw completed his career with Bradford City, playing just the first four games of 1950-51 and in 1954 became manager of North Shields after which he scouted for WBA and Burnley whilst working as a joiner in Blyth.

## WARD, Darren

**POSITION:** Goalkeeper
**BIRTHPLACE:** Worksop, Nottinghamshire
**DATE OF BIRTH:** 11/05/1974
**HEIGHT:** 6' 0" **WEIGHT:** 13st 8lbs
**SIGNED FROM:** Norwich City, 04/08/2006
**DEBUT:** v Stoke City, A, 17/10/2006
**LAST MATCH:** v Aston Villa, H, 15/12/2007
**MOVED TO:** Retired, 31/05/2009
**TEAMS:** Mansfield Town, Notts County, Nottingham Forest, Norwich City, Sunderland, Wolverhampton Wanderers (L)
**INTERNATIONAL:** Wales
**SAFC TOTALS:** 35 appearances / 0 goals

**Thirty of Darren's games for Sunderland came in the promotion season of 2006-07 when he proved himself to be an entirely dependable goalkeeper - his save from the ambitiously-named Pele of Southampton in November 2006 being one of the best saves seen at the Stadium of Light. However, upon promotion Sunderland broke the British transfer record for a goalkeeper when signing Craig Gordon after which Ward played four games in the following season and none for Sunderland the year after. He also did not play during a loan to Wolverhampton Wanderers which was curtailed through injury after less than a month in March 2009.**

Five caps for Wales gave Ward the same number as Tony Norman and as goalkeepers and people they were not dissimilar, eminently reliable and, despite the reputation that goalkeepers are crazy, level-headed characters in the dressing room who both went on to be goalkeeping coaches. In Darren's case he coached at Derby, Peterborough and Preston before a long-term appointment at Sheffield United from June 2011 until March 2021. He then took up a role with the England women's team, being part of the Lionesses 2022 European Championship-winning team.

Ninety-seven appearances at his first club Mansfield preceded over 300 appearances at Notts County from 1995-2001 before a switch to the other side of the Trent with Forest. Darren made 50 appearances in each of his first two seasons there, reaching the First Division Play-Offs in 2003 where his side lost at the semi-final stage to Sheffield United. A clean sheet followed against Sunderland on the opening day of the following season when after 37 games his competitive Forest career was curtailed with an injury sustained against Gillingham.

After a couple of pre-season friendlies in the USA the following summer, he moved on to Norwich for a fee of £250,000. Signed as cover for England international Robert Green, Darren only played twice for Norwich where he was troubled by a back injury. Trials with Barnsley, Sheffield United and Leeds failed to procure a contract before he came to Sunderland, impressed, and won the only senior medal of his playing career.

## WARD, Robert (Bob)

**POSITION:** Goalkeeper
**BIRTHPLACE:** Greenock, Renfrewshire
**DATE OF BIRTH:** 17/04/1875 - date of death unknown
**HEIGHT:** 5' 8½" **WEIGHT:** 11st 0lbs
**SIGNED FROM:** Port Glasgow Athletic, 15/05/1906
**DEBUT:** v Liverpool, A, 15/09/1906
**LAST MATCH:** v Nottingham Forest, H, 07/03/1908
**MOVED TO:** Bradford Park Avenue, 14/08/1908
**TEAMS:** Port Glasgow Athletic, Abercorn, Port Glasgow Athletic, Sunderland, Bradford Park Avenue, Marsden Rescue
**SAFC TOTALS:** 54 appearances / 0 goals

**Robert Ward's record of four penalty saves in a season has only ever been equalled by Chris Turner (1984-85) and Lee Burge (2020-21). Ward made his four penalty saves from six faced in 1906-07 when he made 40 of his Sunderland appearances.**

He began his career at Greenock Overton Junior Club and came to Sunderland after a decade with Port Glasgow Athletic. Having debuted for them against Leith Athletic on 19 September 1896, he went on to play 191 games punctuated by an eleven-match period with Abercorn, the Paisley rivals of St Mirren. Nicknamed 'The Yawler' in Scotland, after leaving Sunderland he made seven further Football League appearances in 1908-09 in Division Two with Bradford Park Avenue.

## WARDLE, Henry (Harry)

**POSITION:** Inside-left
**BIRTHPLACE:** Monkwearmouth, Co Durham
**DATE OF BIRTH:** 09/11/1881 - 28/02/1918
**HEIGHT:** 5' 6"
**SIGNED FROM:** Sunderland Swifts, 21/04/1899
**DEBUT:** v Wolverhampton Wanderers, H, 01/04/1904
**LAST MATCH:** v Aston Villa, A, 01/10/1904
**MOVED TO:** North Shields Athletic, 29/09/1905
**TEAMS:** Sunderland Swifts, Sunderland, North Shields Athletic
**SAFC TOTALS:** 4 appearances / 1 goal

**The scorer of the winner on his debut against Wolves, Wardle did not score again and moved into local football during which time Sunderland continued to hold his Football League registration.**

He had scored on his first two games for Sunderland 'A' (Reserves), both of which ended in 10-0 victories against Birtley and St Peter's Albion within the same week of April 1899. Wardle met an untimely end. He died after he was hit on the head by a plank of wood that had been blown off a staging whilst working as a plumber in a shipyard on the Wear. Just over a couple of decades after his death, his nephew John Marsh was on Sunderland's books.

## WATKINS, Walter Martin (Mark)

**POSITION:** Centre-forward
**BIRTHPLACE:** Llanwnog, Montgomeryshire
**DATE OF BIRTH:** 21/03/1880 - 14/05/1942
**HEIGHT:** 5' 8" **WEIGHT:** 12st 8lbs
**SIGNED FROM:** Aston Villa, 20/10/1904
**DEBUT:** v Wednesday, H, 22/10/1904
**LAST MATCH:** v Derby County, A, 11/03/1905
**MOVED TO:** Crystal Palace, 03/05/1905
**TEAMS:** Caersws, Oswestry United, Stoke, Aston Villa, Sunderland, Crystal Palace, Northampton Town, Stoke, Crewe Alexandra, Stafford Rangers, Tunstall Park, Stoke
**INTERNATIONAL:** Wales
**SAFC TOTALS:** 16 appearances / 9 goals

**Watkins made a goalscoring bow with a brace against Sheffield Wednesday (or Wednesday as they were simply called then). A week later he repeated his two-goal haul against one of his old clubs Stoke. Four months later he scored another brace in the return match with Stoke having netted against another of his former clubs Aston Villa in his previous game. He had played six times for Villa, his only goal coming against Stoke on his home debut in January 1904.**

Later in his season at Roker Park Watkins became the first Sunderland player to win an international cap for Wales, playing in all three British Championship games, scoring against Scotland and Ireland. In two of his three internationals while with Sunderland Watkins was a teammate of legendary future Sunderland goalkeeper L R Roose, then with Everton. In total Watkins would win ten caps.

After leaving Stoke, having been with them for the first three seasons of the 20th century, including his year at Sunderland Watkins never stayed anywhere for more than a single season - eight clubs in eight years. He was a big signing for newly formed Palace who were about to start their first season in the Southern League Division Two. Indeed, Watkins played in their first three Southern League games although it was not until his fourth appearance that he found the back of the net.

Making up for lost time his two goals in a 5-0 win over Fulham Reserves helped Palace to their first-ever home league victory. He ended the campaign with seven goals in 15 games as the Londoners won their league. He also almost doubled his league tally with two FA Cup hat-tricks against Clapham and Chelsea.

Quickly on the move again, Watkins moved to Northampton for a season where he scored eleven times in 38 games. In 1907-08 he returned to Stoke but his five goals in 20 games were not enough for struggling Stoke as they resigned from the Football League having gone into liquidation despite finishing in mid-table. It was at this point that Watkins joined Crewe, then playing in the Birmingham and District League. Despite helping Alex to the runners-up spot the wandering Watkins was instantly on the move again seeing out his final two seasons with Stafford Rangers and Tunstall Park before a brief return to Stoke without getting a contract.

One of Watkins' five brothers, Ernie, also played for Wales. After starting with their home club of Caersws they both played for Oswestry United where Mark was scouted by Stoke. Scoring winning goals in the Potters last three games of 1900-01 helped the club to avoid relegation. Going on to score 16 and 13 in the next two seasons, he broke into his international team in March 1902 against an England team that included Sunderland's Billy Hogg. During World War One he served in the newly-formed RAF before becoming a railway fitter.

## WATMORE, Duncan Ian

**POSITION:** Forward
**BIRTHPLACE:** Wythenshawe, Greater Manchester
**DATE OF BIRTH:** 08/03/1994
**HEIGHT:** 5' 9" **WEIGHT:** 11st 4lbs
**SIGNED FROM:** Altrincham, 23/05/2013
**DEBUT:** v Carlisle United, H, 05/01/2014
**LAST MATCH:** v Fleetwood Town, H, 25/02/2020
**MOVED TO:** Contract not renewed, 30/06/2020
**TEAMS:** Altrincham, Clitheroe (L), Curzon Ashton (L), Sunderland, Hibernian (L), Middlesbrough (to July 2022)
**INTERNATIONAL:** England Under 21
**SAFC TOTALS:** 42+45 appearances / 8 goals

**Terribly unlucky with injuries at Sunderland, Watmore's potential was only partially realised on Wearside. Having been associated with Manchester United until the age of twelve, he was brought in from non-league when Sunderland were in the Premier League. He had scored 15 goals in 48 games with Altrincham.**

Duncan was direct. His desire to run at defenders caused all kinds of problems and while his control often would not be top class, goals came from his persistence at taking people on. After one FA Cup appearance for Sunderland he went on loan to Hibs where he made 5+5 appearances, scoring his first senior goal against Partick the week after his 20th birthday.

He won a host of individual awards with his ability to invariably catch the eye. Player of the Year at Altrincham in 2012-13, two years later he was Premier Under 21 League Player of the Year in 2014-15 and in the summer of 2015 was named as the Revelation of the Tournament as well as a member of the Team of the Tournament for England Under 21s at Toulon in France in which he scored against Morocco - one of three goals he scored in 13 Under 21 internationals. A season later he was Sunderland's Young Player of the Year.

After being released by Sunderland, he joined Middlesbrough where to the summer of 2022 he had netted 16 goals in 46+28 appearances and was top-scorer with nine goals in 2020-21. The son of former FA chief executive Ian Watmore, Duncan gained a first-class honours degree in economics and business management whilst playing for Sunderland.

## WATSON, David Vernon (Dave)

**POSITION:** Centre-half / centre-forward
**BIRTHPLACE:** Stapleford, Nottinghamshire
**DATE OF BIRTH:** 05/10/1946
**HEIGHT:** 5' 11½" **WEIGHT:** 11st 7lbs
**SIGNED FROM:** Rotherham United, 14/12/1970
**DEBUT:** v Watford, A, 19/12/1970
**LAST MATCH:** v Aston Villa, A, 26/04/1975
**MOVED TO:** Manchester City, 13/06/1975
**TEAMS:** Notts County, Rotherham United, Sunderland, Manchester City, Werder Bremen, Southampton, Stoke City, Vancouver Whitecaps, Derby County, Fort Lauderdale, Notts County, Kettering Town
**INTERNATIONAL:** England
**SAFC TOTALS:** 212 appearances / 33 goals

**Dave Watson won more caps for England than any other player while on Sunderland's books. He was also Man of the Match in the celebrated 1973 FA Cup final. Watson was Sunderland's first £100,000 purchase, a record from a third-tier team. He was signed as a centre-forward and was a very good one, but it was after being switched to centre-half that Dave showed himself to be international class.**

Centre-half had been Watson's original position. He had begun in that role at Notts County where he played 26 times in his first spell. Born nearby, Watson played youth football for Stapleford Old Boys and earned his living as a farm labourer and then as an electrician. It was after being made redundant that he turned to professional football, following in the footsteps of his older brother Peter, a centre-half with Nottingham Forest and Southend United.

## WATSON, Dave (Continued)

In January 1968 the father of future Sunderland player Mick Docherty - Tommy Docherty - signed Dave for Rotherham for a fee of £8,000 plus Millers man Keith Pring moving to Notts. Although Dave was not able to stop his new club being relegated in 1968, he established himself there, playing 141 times and bagging 21 goals.

Having come to Sunderland, a debut goal got Dave off to a good start in a 1-1 draw at Watford on a day when he was one of seven players who two and a half years later would sensationally win the FA Cup. Home supporters saw Dave score just one of a modest four goals he got in 17 games in his first season but it was immediately obvious that he was a good signing. Strong, determined, good on the ball and commanding in the air, Watson was ever-present and joint-top scorer (with Dennis Tueart) in the league in his first full-season. However, in 1972-73 Dave failed to score in his first 14 league and League Cup games at centre-forward.

Following the departure of manager Alan Brown, Billy Elliott took over as caretaker-manager. Elliott knew something about changing positions having moved from left-wing to left-half to left-back in his own career. Knowing Watson had started as a centre-half Elliott moved him there for a midweek match at Carlisle. It was carnage to begin with as Sunderland conceded twice in the first 15 minutes and eventually lost 4-3 to a Stan Ternent winner but long before the final whistle supporters could see that Watson's future was in the number five rather than number nine shirt.

Once Bob Stokoe came in - a centre-half himself, as was Brown - Dave stayed as a defender, but with occasional games up front to begin with. He was sometimes pushed forward late on if a goal was needed, such as when he scored an equaliser back at his old club Notts County in the opening game of the 1973 FA Cup run - that header being as good as any goal Watson scored for Sunderland.

At centre-half Watson went from strength to strength and was named in the PFA Division Two Team of the Year in his remaining two seasons with Sunderland before moving away when Sunderland failed to win promotion after losing at Aston Villa on the final day of the 1974-75 season. Watson was 29 and desperate to play in Division One for the first time. By this point he had won 14 England caps, not having debuted until he was 27. He would go on to win 65 full caps making him the player with the most caps not to play at a FIFA World Cup finals and the first player to be capped with five clubs.

He scored four times for England who he captained in three games. In June 1971 Watson had been selected as a centre-forward as part of a 16 player FA touring party who played nine games over five weeks in Australia, Dave scoring against New South Wales (in Newcastle) and the only goal in a Sydney meeting with Australia as the FA party won every match.

After leaving Sunderland Watson became a hero at Manchester City where he played 188 times (including twelve in European competition) and scored six goals, his last game coming against Villa as it had for Sunderland. A Wembley winner against Newcastle in the League Cup final in his first season with City, his second campaign saw Watson be ever-present and Player of the Year as City were league runners-up to Liverpool before he was made captain the following season.

A 1979 move to Werder Bremen was a disaster. Dave only played twice. Sent off in his second match for pushing an opponent, he was handed an eight-match man while there was also a dispute with the club regarding treatment for an injury. After five months he was back in England, signing for Lawrie McMenemy at Southampton and scoring eight goals in 83 games for the Saints. There were a further five goals in 59 league appearances for Stoke before a 1983 move to Vancouver Whitecaps where he was named in the NASL all-star team for 1983 after 26 games and three goals. 1983-84 brought 34 games and a goal back in England with Derby before a summer with Fort Lauderdale Sun where he won the USL Championship in 1984 before going full circle with 25 games and a goal for Notts County in 1984-85 and finally 14 games in non-league with Kettering Town.

After a career of well over 750 games in positions that require a lot of heading, in 2021 Watson won a landmark ruling to have injuries he suffered during his career to be ruled as 'industrial accidents'. His wife Penny became commendably active in campaigns to have such injuries recognised. She had also been the author of Dave's biography, 'My Dear Watson'. Dave played more games for Sunderland than for any of his other clubs and in 2020, attended his induction into the Sunderland Hall of Fame. Following his football career for many years, Dave ran a successful business arranging events and speaking engagements for former players. In 2022 he received the Freedom of the City of Sunderland.

## WATSON, Edward

**POSITION:** Right-back

**BIRTHPLACE:** Sunderland, Co Durham

**DATE OF BIRTH:** 06/10/1899 - 05/06/1956

**HEIGHT:** 5' 8½" **WEIGHT:** 11st 7lbs

**SIGNED FROM:** Sunderland West End, 27/09/1919

**DEBUT:** v Bradford City, H, 30/10/1920

**LAST MATCH:** v Bradford City, H, 30/10/1920

**MOVED TO:** Queen's Park Rangers, 21/05/1921

**TEAMS:** Sunderland West End, Sunderland, QPR, Rochdale, Sunderland West End, Carlisle United

**INTERNATIONAL:** England Schoolboys

**SAFC TOTALS:** 1 appearance / 0 goals

**Capped at schoolboy level against Scotland and Wales in 1914, local lad Watson lived the dream of playing for his hometown club just once, standing in for the injured Bert Hobson at right-back in a goalless home draw.**

Although he earned favourable reports in the press, Watson did not get another chance and moved on to QPR at the end of the season, but still finding himself a reserve did not debut until September 1922 when he was selected for a west London derby at Brentford in Division Three South. After only eight games for QPR he joined Rochdale for 1923-24 but played just once. Following a return to Wearside with West End he signed for Carlisle in the years before the Cumbrians joined the Football League.

Edward served as a gunner in the Royal Field Artillery during World War One and after retiring from football, worked as a locomotive guard then driver for the National Coal Board in Sunderland.

## WATSON, Ian

**POSITION:** Goalkeeper

**BIRTHPLACE:** North Shields, Northumberland

**DATE OF BIRTH:** 05/02/1960

**HEIGHT:** 5' 11" **WEIGHT:** 10st 11lbs

**SIGNED FROM:** North Shields Juniors, 01/07/1976

**DEBUT:** v Sheffield United, A, 12/08/1978

**LAST MATCH:** v Millwall, A, 03/03/1979

**MOVED TO:** Newport County, 01/10/1981

**TEAMS:** Sunderland, Rochdale (L), Newport County, Gloucester City (L), Berwick Rangers

**INTERNATIONAL:** England Under 21

**SAFC TOTALS:** 3 appearances / 0 goals

**Ian made his debut in the Anglo-Scottish Cup and kept a clean sheet at Millwall in his only league game but it is for the middle of his three appearances in the FA Cup he is most remembered. Brought in for an FA Cup fourth round replay with Burnley his only home game was marred by conceding a first-minute goal that he stopped just behind the line on a night when a 3-0 defeat was suffered when the prize was a trip to Liverpool the following weekend.**

Watson went on loan to Rochdale at the start of the following season and played the first 40 games of the season, some behind the former Sunderland defenders Colin Waldron and Alan Weir, but Dale were bottom of the entire league when Ian left there and stayed in that wooden spoon position. He then went to Newport County but without getting a game went on loan to Gloucester City in 1982-83. A brief switch to Carlisle brought no further senior appearances after which Ian joined Berwick Rangers where he played 87 times.

## **WATSON,** James **(Jimmy)**

**POSITION:** Left-back

**BIRTHPLACE:** Larkhall, South Lanarkshire

**DATE OF BIRTH:** 04/10/1877 - 12/06/1942

**HEIGHT:** 5' 10" **WEIGHT:** 12st 3lbs

**SIGNED FROM:** Clyde, 16/01/1900

**DEBUT:** v Glossop North End, H, 24/02/1900

**LAST MATCH:** v Manchester United, A, 25/03/1907

**MOVED TO:** Middlesbrough, 09/04/1907

**TEAMS:** Burnbank Athletic, Clyde, Sunderland, Middlesbrough, Shildon

**INTERNATIONAL:** Scotland

**SAFC TOTALS:** 227 appearances / 0 goals

**The 1901-02 title-winning season was one of six successive years that Scotland international Jimmy Watson topped 30 games for Sunderland. He emigrated to Canada in 1920 where he became a highly-regarded soccer coach.**

In 2005 when Sunderland played in Vancouver, eleven of Watson's descendants including his granddaughter met yours truly at the first-ever soccer game they had ever attended in order to see James' old club. Clearly seen on the few feet of the oldest film of Sunderland in action from 1904, my colleague Mike Gibson provided a videotape showing this for the Canadian relatives, demonstrating that no matter how far back in history someone played for Sunderland or where in the world they ended up, so often their families rightly remain proud of the connection.

The nickname of 'Daddy Long-legs' from his playing days gives a hint of Watson's attributes as a defender, apparently also stemming from his all-action running style. He was known to be strong, athletic and considered by many to be the best full-back of his era. At this time Scotland and England would often reserve the occasions they played their very strongest XIs for games against each other. The fact that four of Watson's six internationals were for games against the 'auld enemy' illustrates his stature. The first four of his caps were won with Sunderland. On the occasion of one of these in April 1903 his Sunderland full-back partner Andy McCombie and goalkeeper Ted Doig joined him in the Scotland line-up that defeated England at Bramall Lane. Without them on the same afternoon Sunderland won a league game against Notts County.

Having started with Burnbank Athletic in 1895, Watson moved to Clyde in 1897 playing 35 games and scoring once before coming to Sunderland in 1900 after trials with Hearts (who he turned down) and Sheffield United. A stalwart of Sunderland in the first decade of the 20th century, Watson added 107 games for Middlesbrough with whom he won his final two caps in 1909 and became assistant trainer before ending his playing days with Shildon and managing the Leviathan Hotel in Sussex Street Middlesbrough. Jimmy then managed the Mason's Arms in Shildon before emigrating to Canada in 1920.

## **WATSON, James**

**POSITION:** Right-half / right-back

**BIRTHPLACE:** Inverness, Inverness-shire

**DATE OF BIRTH:** 28/10/1879 - 09/06/1911

**HEIGHT:** 5' 10" **WEIGHT:** 12st 2lbs

**SIGNED FROM:** Inverness Thistle, 19/05/1903

**DEBUT:** v Wolverhampton Wanderers, A, 24/10/1903

**LAST MATCH:** v Preston North End, H, 31/12/1904

**MOVED TO:** Chelsea, 04/05/1905

**TEAMS:** Inverness Thistle, Sunderland, Chelsea, Brentford

**SAFC TOTALS:** 5 appearances / 0 goals

**No relation to the celebrated Scottish international James Watson, a fellow Scot who was already at Sunderland when James Junior signed from Inverness Thistle in May 1903, this James Watson was known to one and all as 'Dougal' James Junior.**

He played just five games before agreeing to join Portsmouth in January 1905 only to change his mind a week later. Nine months afterwards he transferred to Chelsea where he played 13 times in their first-ever Football League season of 1905-06 before returning to red and white stripes with Brentford, although he failed to make their first team.

## **WATSON,** William **(Willie)**

**POSITION:** Right-half / inside-forward

**BIRTHPLACE:** Bolton-on-Dearne, West Riding of Yorkshire

**DATE OF BIRTH:** 07/03/1920 - 24/04/2004

**HEIGHT:** 5' 8½" **WEIGHT:** 11st 4lbs

**SIGNED FROM:** Huddersfield Town, 01/05/1946

**DEBUT:** v Derby County, H, 31/08/1946

**LAST MATCH:** v West Bromwich Albion, A, 07/11/1953

**MOVED TO:** Halifax Town, 04/11/1954

**TEAMS:** Paddock, Huddersfield Town, Bournemouth (WW2 Guest) Wrexham (WW2 Guest), Sunderland, Halifax Town

**INTERNATIONAL:** England - at both football and cricket

**SAFC TOTALS:** 223 appearances / 17 goals

**The last of only twelve men to play for England at both football and cricket, Willie Watson won all four of his football caps whilst with Sunderland - one of them at Roker Park against Wales in 1950. It was also while Willie was with Sunderland that he made his Test Match debut at cricket against South Africa in 1951.**

The demands of the cricket season meant that Watson usually missed the beginning and end of the football season but nonetheless he made well over a double century of appearances for Sunderland. His versatility was not limited to being brilliant at two sports, as a footballer he was adept at half-back or inside-forward while he could also play on the wing or at centre-forward. Continuing the theme, if at half-back he would usually play on the right whereas if in the forward line he would normally play on the left. A good tackler and passer, Watson was simply an all-round class act.

At football - after playing in war-time internationals - Watson debuted for England at the age of 29 in a 9-2 win over Ireland in November 1949. He won another cap against Italy before being selected for England's first-ever FIFA World Cup finals squad for the 1950 tournament in Brazil. He did not get a game in the finals but played twice more later in the year. He also played in three away games for England at B level. Although all four of his caps were won in home games, none were at Wembley, although he did play for England at Lords.

Watson's cricket career lasted from 1951 to 1959. It took in 23 Test Matches, his best performance being a knock of 109 spread over six hours to help save an Ashes Test against Australia in 1953 when he was still a Sunderland player. He averaged 25.85 for England and 39.86 in County Cricket for Yorkshire and Leicestershire, while hitting a career high of 257 for the MCC against British Guiana. With Leicestershire he was assistant secretary as well as captain while he also became an England selector.

As a footballer he lost six of his early years to World War Two. Having started out in life sweeping up at an upholsterers while playing for local side Paddock, he joined Huddersfield Town and played eleven times in the last season before the war, following in the footsteps of his father Billy. Watson senior had been part of the Huddersfield team that won the league title in three successive seasons in the twenties as well as playing in the 1922 FA Cup final when Preston were beaten in a final incidentally refereed by Sunderland-born J W P Fowler. The family footballing connection was extended by Willie's brother Albert who played for Huddersfield, Oldham and Consett between 1937 and 1950.

During World War Two Willie 'Guested' for Wrexham (12/3) before coming to Sunderland to debut in the first post-war league match. He later added 37 league and cup appearances as player/manager of Halifax (2 goals), the last a 5-1 home win over Oldham on Boxing Day 1955. He resigned the following April, citing difficulty in devoting time to the job given his cricketing commitments.

However in August 1964 he once again became manager of Halifax, this time staying until April 1966 when he left to become manager of Bradford City where he built a team destined for promotion at the time he resigned in January 1968 to become manager of Wanderers in South Africa. Willie stayed in the country for 36 years until his death having become a poultry farmer in later life.

His memoir 'Double International' was written in 1956, a biography, 'Last of the Double Internationals' was published in 2011. No doubt many older supporters bought some of their sporting equipment at Willie Watson's Sports Shop in Sunderland.

## WAUGH, John

**POSITION:** Centre-forward

**BIRTHPLACE:** Bridgecastle, West Lothian

**DATE OF BIRTH:** 10/05/1892 - 10/03/1955

**HEIGHT:** 5' 11" **WEIGHT:** 12st 4lbs

**SIGNED FROM:** Bo'ness, 06/12/1913

**DEBUT:** v Newcastle United, A, 27/12/1913

**LAST MATCH:** v Newcastle United, A, 27/12/1913

**MOVED TO:** Released, 01/05/1914

**TEAMS:** Fern Thistle, Vale of Grange, Bo'ness United, Sunderland, (WW1 Guest for Hearts, Motherwell, Dunfermline, Dundee Hibs), Cowdenbeath, Gillingham, Guildford United

**SAFC TOTALS:** 1 appearance / 0 goals

**Waugh was marked out of his only game in which relegation-threatened Newcastle beat Sunderland who were looking to retain the title. Waugh was not considered again and certainly not after he was suspended by the club in April 1914 for refusing to play for the reserves against Blyth Spartans.**

He was then not retained for the following campaign. A Scot who had begun in Bo'ness, Waugh proceeded to represent numerous Scottish clubs during World War One before joining Gillingham in December 1920. By now playing at centre-half he played 60 Third division games and scored four times for the Kent club. John returned to his home town in West Lothian after retiring from football.

## WEARNE, Stephen Christopher

**POSITION:** Midfielder

**BIRTHPLACE:** Stockton-on-Tees, Co Durham

**DATE OF BIRTH:** 16/12/2000

**HEIGHT:** 5' 8½" **WEIGHT:** 11st 2lbs

**SIGNED FROM:** Middlesbrough, 09/09/2020

**DEBUT:** v Lincoln City, A, 05/10/2021

**LAST MATCH:** v Oldham Athletic, H, 01/12/2021

**MOVED TO:** Grimsby Town, 27/06/2022

**TEAMS:** Newcastle United, Middlesbrough, Sunderland, Torquay United (L), Grimsby Town (to July 2022)

**SAFC TOTALS:** 1+2 appearances / 2 goals

**Stephen burst onto the scene with the winners on his debut as a sub at Lincoln and his first full start eight days later at home to Manchester United Under 21s. All three of his Sunderland appearances came in the Football League (Papa John's) Trophy.**

A player with good control and an intelligent approach Wearne made a swift impression with his general play and not just his goals. After playing youth football on the Tyne and the Tees he completed his tour of the north-east's three major clubs by joining Sunderland before he left his teens. He then found the net three times in 14 National League games on loan to Torquay where he played for Sunderland manager Lee Johnson's father Gary. In June 2022, he signed a one-year deal with Grimsby.

## WEBB, Isaac (Ike)

**POSITION:** Goalkeeper

**BIRTHPLACE:** Worcester, Worcestershire

**DATE OF BIRTH:** 02/10/1874 - 15/03/1950

**HEIGHT:** 6' 1" **WEIGHT:** 12st 10lbs

**SIGNED FROM:** West Bromwich Albion, 15/12/1904

**DEBUT:** v Sheffield United, A, 17/12/1904

**LAST MATCH:** v Nottingham Forest, H, 14/04/1906

**MOVED TO:** QPR, 09/03/1907

**TEAMS:** Evesham Town, Wellington Town, Small Heath, WBA, Sunderland, QPR, WBA (WW1 Guest)

**SAFC TOTALS:** 24 appearances / 0 goals

**A spectacular and agile keeper Webb kept goal for 20 of the last 21 games of 1904-05. He kept four clean sheets as Sunderland finished fifth in the league, but following the appointment of Bob Kyle as manager, made just four appearances in his second and last term on Wearside.**

Webb had come into league football with Birmingham City when they were known as Small Heath. Debuting at Luton in Division Two in April 1898, he kept his first clean sheet later that month against Newcastle United, but after six appearances moved to West Brom in May 1901. There were 101 league and cup games for Albion but he did not get a debut for his first two seasons, getting a chance after the Baggies were relegated. Once in the side he missed just one game as WBA won Division Two. A November 1902 first visit to Roker Park brought a clean sheet against the reigning champions but after missing just two games all season he 'put his thumb out' in the March return with Sunderland and missed the rest of the season.

Ike recovered to play regularly the following season but a year to the week after his injury against Sunderland was knocked unconscious for four minutes in a match against Derby, again missing the end of the campaign as West Brom went down. Webb was in the team again by the start of the next 1904-05 season, playing the opening 13 games until his transfer to Sunderland. He later played one more game for West Brom as a 43-year-old 'Guest' in 1918. Before then Ike had continued his career with QPR where he played ten Southern League games debuting in a local derby with Brentford in March 1907 before returning to the Hawthorns and going on to serve in the Athletes' Volunteer Corps and the 14th Battalion West Yorkshire Regiment as a catering orderly. After retiring from football Webb became a bookmaker.

## WEDDLE, Derek Keith

**POSITION:** Centre-forward

**BIRTHPLACE:** Newcastle, Northumberland

**DATE OF BIRTH:** 27/12/1935

**HEIGHT:** 6' 0" **WEIGHT:** 12st 5lbs

**SIGNED FROM:** Walkergate Juniors, 01/07/1952

**DEBUT:** v Huddersfield Town, A, 24/12/1955

**LAST MATCH:** v Cardiff City, A, 17/11/1956

**MOVED TO:** Portsmouth, 05/12/1956

**TEAMS:** Sunderland, Portsmouth, Wisbech Town, Cambridge City, Middlesbrough, Darlington, York City, Gateshead

**SAFC TOTALS:** 2 appearances / 0 goals

**A debutant three days before his 20th birthday, Weddle made his first appearance while at home on leave from his National Service with the Northumberland Fusiliers and while on Sunderland's books was an apprentice motor mechanic. He was first picked as an 18-year-old, but his boss at Peartree Garage in Newcastle would not give him the time off to play at West Brom, leaving the teenager in tears.**

Derek was born too early. Had he come to the fore a little later when new manager Alan Brown was giving youngsters every chance, he may well have had much more of an opportunity. Weddle also missed out on international honours when having been called up along with young Sunderland goalkeeper Leslie Dodds for the England squad at the World Youth Championships, the FA then decided not to enter.

Derek did not score for Sunderland, but did score a winner against SAFC for Portsmouth on the last day of the 1956-57 season in the final game of Sunderland manager Bill Murray. Derek was still with Pompey when Sunderland were relegated for the first time on their return to Fratton Park on the final day of the following season, although he did not play on that occasion. After ten goals in 24 games for Pompey he left to join Wisbech Town where he played alongside Ted Purdon, Billy Elliott and Graham Reed. Weddle went on to play for Cambridge City, once scoring seven goals in an 8-0 hammering of Dartford on Guy Fawkes Day in 1960.

Returning to the north-east (where he had been on the books of Newcastle as a youngster) Derek scored once in three games in a year at Middlesbrough followed by ten in 36 games over two seasons with Darlington and another 14 in 49 league and cup games with York City before completing his playing days at Gateshead. At his last two league clubs he looked after the players' feet having qualified in chiropody and upon retiring set up his own practice in Wideopen. Later he linked up with Ron Guthrie and former Newcastle full-back David Craig in the dairy trade which he was employed in between 1966 and 1985 after which he bought a paper shop and finally became a lollipop man.

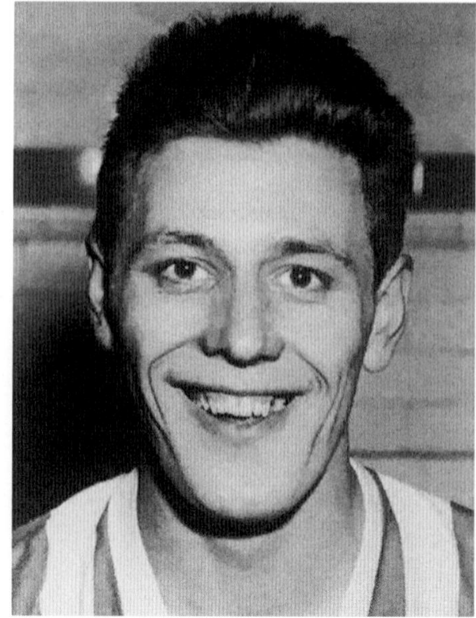

## WEIR, Alan

**POSITION:** Centre-half

**BIRTHPLACE:** South Shields, Co Durham

**DATE OF BIRTH:** 01/09/1959

**HEIGHT:** 5' 9" **WEIGHT:** 10st 0lbs

**SIGNED FROM:** Horsley Hill School, 01/05/1976

**DEBUT:** v Bolton Wanderers, A, 07/03/1978

**LAST MATCH:** v Bolton Wanderers, A, 07/03/1978

**MOVED TO:** Rochdale, 15/06/1979

**TEAMS:** Sunderland, Rochdale, Hartlepool United, Eppleton CW, Whitley Bay

**INTERNATIONAL:** England Youth

**SAFC TOTALS:** 1 appearance / 0 goals

**Having captained England at youth level much was expected of Alan Weir but he only played 64 minutes of his solitary appearance for Sunderland before moving on to Rochdale where he played alongside Colin Waldron and Ian Watson.**

Weir debuted for England Under 18s against Uruguay in a tournament in Gran Canaria in October 1977, five months after signing professional forms for Sunderland, playing alongside Chris Woods who later played for Sunderland in the Farewell to Roker Park match. A day later he played against Hungary as England won the Atlantic Cup before he played in an unofficial game, lost to Las Palmas. A third cap was won a month before his Sunderland debut in a win over France at Selhurst Park.

At Rochdale, who paid £12,000 for him, Alan made 96+1 league appearances and scored three goals. With Hartlepool there were just 10+1 appearances starting with a September 1983 debut at home to Chesterfield. He went on to play local non-league football and subsequently worked in the electronics industry.

## WELBECK, Daniel Nii Tackie Mensah (Danny)

**POSITION:** Forward

**BIRTHPLACE:** Longsight, Greater Manchester

**DATE OF BIRTH:** 26/11/1990

**HEIGHT:** 6' 1" **WEIGHT:** 11st 4lbs

**SIGNED FROM:** Manchester United, 12/08/2010, on loan

**DEBUT:** v Birmingham City, H, 14/08/2010

**LAST MATCH:** v Wigan Athletic, H, 23/04/2011

**MOVED TO:** Manchester United, 25/04/2011, end of loan

**TEAMS:** Manchester United, Preston North End (L), Sunderland (L), Arsenal, Watford, Brighton & Hove Albion (to June 2022)

**INTERNATIONAL:** England

**SAFC TOTALS:** 23+5 appearances / 6 goals

**A quality player, Welbeck won his first England cap while on loan to Sunderland from Manchester United. Playing against Ghana (the country of his parents) who included Asamoah Gyan, John Mensah and Sulley Muntari (who were all at Sunderland at the time) Welbeck came off a bench that included Jermain Defoe, Darren Bent and Joleon Lescott to link up with starter Stewart Downing. Welbeck's 42nd cap came in September 2018, but as of June 2022, he had fallen out of the England reckoning despite a decent record of 16 goals (one of his caps coming at the 2018 FIFA World Cup finals).**

A product of Manchester United's academy he made his Under 18 debut at Sunderland and went on to win the club's Jimmy Murphy Young Player of the Year award in 2008. He made his debut in September of that year in a League (Carling) Cup tie

with Middlesbrough. A goalscoring Premier League bow soon followed against Stoke. By March he was starting the League (Carling) Cup final as Spurs were beaten on penalties, although a return to Wembley a month later brought shoot-out defeat in the FA Cup semi-final to Everton.

Half-way through the next season Welbeck went out on loan to Preston, scoring twice in eight games. Returning to United he went on to total 29 goals in 90+52 appearances, along with his loan to Sunderland, before Arsenal invested £16m in him as the summer 2014 transfer window closed, his penultimate Premier League game for United having been back at the Stadium of Light.

Danny's first game as an Arsenal player saw him score both goals for England in a win in Switzerland. Within a month he netted a Champions League hat-trick against Galatasaray and soon scored on his Old Trafford return in an FA cup win. Exactly half of his 32 goals for the Gunners were in the Premier League, but after 78+48 games over five injury-hit seasons he was freed. Spending just over a year at Watford brought three goals in 10+10 games before an October 2020 free transfer to Brighton where as of June 2022 he had scored twelve times in 33+18 games.

## WELSBY, Arthur

**POSITION:** Forward

**BIRTHPLACE:** Ashton-in-Makerfield, Lancashire

**DATE OF BIRTH:** 17/11/1902 - 24/04/1980

**HEIGHT:** 5' 7" **WEIGHT:** 10st 5lbs

**SIGNED FROM:** Wigan Borough, 12/05/1931

**DEBUT:** v West Bromwich Albion, A, 07/09/1931

**LAST MATCH:** v Aston Villa, A, 28/03/1932

**MOVED TO:** Exeter City, 23/05/1932

**TEAMS:** Ashton St Mary's, Wigan Borough, Sunderland, Exeter City, Stockport County, Southport, Cardiff City, Wigan Athletic, Mossley

**SAFC TOTALS:** 3 appearances / 1 goal

**Having made a record 220 league appearances for Wigan Borough during their ten-year spell in league football, Welsby came to Wearside where he joined the greats of Patsy Gallacher and Bobby Gurney on the scoresheet in a big home win over Blackpool.**

Having moved to Exeter he made a goalscoring debut against Bristol City in August 1932 and went on to score eight times in 39 games over two seasons. At Stockport he was a reserve as he was with Cardiff having scored once in 21 appearances in between for Southport before dropping into non-league.

A coal-miner in his youth, after retiring from football Arthur worked for a company producing locks and hinges as well as joining North Ashton Pipe Band where he played the tenor horn.

## WELSH, Andrew Peter David (Andy)

**POSITION:** Outside-left

**BIRTHPLACE:** Manchester, Greater Manchester

**DATE OF BIRTH:** 24/11/1983

**HEIGHT:** 5' 8" **WEIGHT:** 10st 4lbs

**SIGNED FROM:** Stockport County, 23/11/2004

**DEBUT:** v Preston North End, A, 01/01/2005

**LAST MATCH:** v Aston Villa, A, 07/05/2006

**MOVED TO:** Toronto, 22/03/2007

**TEAMS:** Stockport County, Macclesfield (L), Sunderland, Leicester City (L), Toronto, Blackpool, Yeovil Town, Carlisle United, Scunthorpe United, FC United, Farsley, Ossett Albion

**INTERNATIONAL:** Scotland Under 19

**SAFC TOTALS:** 17+8 appearances / 2 goals

**Called Welsh, born in England and played for Scotland. Andy Welsh was a wiry winger who joined Sunderland after a three-day trial having played 85 times for Stockport where he scored three times. A goal on his home and full debut for Sunderland against Crystal Palace in the FA Cup helped Andy get off to a positive start and he added a league goal at QPR as he helped Sunderland to promotion in his first season.**

He was to be named on the team-sheet in all but one of the first 16 games of the next Premier League campaign, playing in twelve of them, but was then loaned to Leicester before returning for the last two games of the season. He was to go to Leicester again the following term, eventually turning out 17 times for the Foxes, scoring once.

In March 2007 Andy went to play in Canada for Toronto, but it was a brief six-month stay of 20 appearances and a single goal. Returning to England with Blackpool he made a further 20 league appearances. Only three of these were starts with another game as substitute against Spurs being one of three cup outings before he was released by Simon Grayson, having not scored for the Seasiders. Dropping down to League One

## WELSH, Andy (Continued)

with Yeovil Welsh played 82+31 times for the Glovers, scoring six times before a 2011 move to Carlisle. Once again Welsh found himself most often utilised from the bench, 24 of his 37 appearances (0 goals) coming as a sub for the Cumbrians where his teammates included Graham Kavanagh, Paul Thirlwell, Jordan Cook and ex-Sunderland reserve Liam Noble.

Moving to Scunthorpe in 2013-14 he became a teammate of one-time Sunderland reserve player and coach Cliff Byrne. Welsh played 2+6 times, but was severely restricted by knee surgery after which he moved into non-league football and studied for a degree in psychology. In September 2017 Andy became player/head coach at Ossett Albion where he stayed until becoming manager of Bury AFC who he led to their league title in his and the club's second season.

## WEST, Colin

**POSITION:** Centre-forward

**BIRTHPLACE:** Wallsend, Northumberland

**DATE OF BIRTH:** 13/11/1962

**HEIGHT:** 6' 2" **WEIGHT:** 13st 13lbs

**SIGNED FROM:** Wallsend Boys, 06/12/1978

**DEBUT:** v Tottenham Hotspur, H, 17/10/1981

**LAST MATCH:** v Watford, H, 12/03/1985

**MOVED TO:** Watford, 28/03/1985

**TEAMS:** Sunderland, Watford, Rangers, Sheffield Wednesday, WBA, Port Vale (L), Swansea City, Leyton Orient, Northampton Town (L), Rushden & Diamonds, Northwich Victoria, Hartlepool United

**SAFC TOTALS:** 103+19 appearances / 28 goals

**Four days after infamously not being selected for the 1985 League (Milk) Cup final Colin was transferred to Watford. He had scored three times in the two-legged semi-final having taken two penalties in the home leg, but had only scored three times in the league from 20+3 league games that term and had not been in the side seven days earlier when cup final opponents Norwich had been beaten. Colin's biggest impact at Sunderland had come three seasons earlier when he came into the team to supply a flurry of goals to help the club avoid relegation.**

At Vicarage Road a highly successful first full season saw him top-score in a team that included John Barnes and Luther Blissett as well as SAFC connections in Tony Coton and Wilf Rostron plus Sunderland-born Gary Porter, his 16 goals including a hat-trick against West Brom. After a total of 23 goals in 56 appearances Watford made a £65,000 profit when selling Colin for £180,000 to Rangers where he became new manager Graeme Souness' first signing.

Debuting alongside Ally McCoist, Terry Butcher, Derek Ferguson and (future Sunderland reserve) Chris Woods, West helped Rangers to win the title. His contribution was a modest 4+5 games due to a knee injury although he also scored in the League (Skol) Cup which Rangers went on to win. He also tasted the UEFA Cup, appearing as a sub in both legs of the quarter-final as Rangers were eliminated at the hands of Borussia Moenchengladbach on away goals.

Returning to England when signed by Howard Wilkinson for Sheffield Wednesday, he scored 13 goals in 55+5 games, one of which was the last goal scored against QPR on their artificial pitch. Teammates at Hillsborough included Lee Chapman, Mark Proctor, David Hodgson, Wilf Rostron and Gary Bennett's brother Dave. In February 1989 West went to West Brom in a swap deal for Carlton Palmer, but it was not a successful time as the Baggies were relegated to the third tier in the third of Colin's four seasons. During West's time at the Hawthorns he scored 23 goals in 72+9 games and played alongside Don Goodman, Tony Ford and Andy Marriott, although he was out injured when Sam Allardyce briefly played.

West Brom loaned Colin to Port Vale in November 1991 where he played five times and scored once, but there were two goals against Vale on debut for his next club Swansea where Colin signed for his former Sunderland coach Frank Burrows in August 1982. Twelve goals in 33 games helped the Swans to the Play-Off semi-finals only for Colin to be red-carded against his old club WBA. Linking up with his old Sheffield Wednesday (and Sunderland) coach Peter Eustace at Leyton Orient, Westie scored 42 goals in 142 games as well as having two games on loan to Ian Atkins' Northampton and five games and a goal for Rushden and Diamonds before single games for Northwich and Hartlepool.

Colin then went into coaching, spending much of his time assisting his old Sunderland teammate Chris Turner, Hartlepool, Sheffield Wednesday, Stockport, Millwall, Southend, Notts County, Carlisle and Northampton being the clubs he worked at, while as of June 2022, he was still in the game as assistant head coach at Oldham Athletic.

## WESTWOOD, Keiren

**POSITION:** Goalkeeper

**BIRTHPLACE:** Manchester, Greater Manchester

**DATE OF BIRTH:** 23/10/1984

**HEIGHT:** 6' 2" **WEIGHT:** 14st 3lbs

**SIGNED FROM:** Coventry City, 01/07/2011

**DEBUT:** v Brighton & Hove Albion, A, 23/08/2011

**LAST MATCH:** v Hull City, A, 02/11/2013

**MOVED TO:** Contract not renewed, 30/06/ 2014

**TEAMS:** Manchester City, Oldham Athletic (L), Carlisle United, Coventry City, Sunderland, Sheffield Wednesday, QPR (to June 2022)

**INTERNATIONAL:** Republic of Ireland

**SAFC TOTALS:** 23+1 appearances / 0 goals

**A confident and self-assured goalkeeper, Westwood did not play many games for Sunderland but was competent, could be commanding and had a long and varied career. He was second choice to Simon Mignolet in his first two seasons, being restricted to League (Capital One) Cup ties only in his second term. Following Mignolet's departure in 2013 he started 2013-14 as first choice but was soon replaced by newcomer Vito Mannone.**

In June 2022, Westwood left QPR who he joined in March 2022 after seven years at Sheffield Wednesday where he made two short of 200 appearances following his release from Sunderland. Manchester-born Keiren had joined City from local side Fletcher Moss Rangers, but despite a loan to nearby Oldham - where he broke his hand - never got a game until a second loan to Carlisle. He made 152+1 appearances for the Cumbrians, keeping clean sheets in three of his four Conference games as (alongside Chris Lumsdon and Brendan McGill) as he helped them back into the Football League in his first season. He went on play 35 times as they won League Two in 2006. Keiren did so well at Brunton Park that Coventry paid £500,000 for him in the summer of 2008 after which he made 138 appearances for the Sky Blues where he won a Player of the Year award as he did at Carlisle and Sheffield Wednesday in addition to three times being selected for a PFA divisional Team of the Year.

Qualifying for Ireland through his grandmother, he was capped 21 times and went to Euro 2012 and 2016 without playing in the tournaments.

## WHARTON, Sean Robert

**POSITION:** Midfielder

**BIRTHPLACE:** Newport, Monmouthshire

**DATE OF BIRTH:** 31/10/1968

**HEIGHT:** 5' 10" **WEIGHT:** 11st 4lbs

**SIGNED FROM:** Cardiff City, 01/07/1985

**DEBUT:** v Portsmouth, A, 08/04/1989

**LAST MATCH:** v Portsmouth, A, 08/04/1989

**MOVED TO:** Released from contract, 15/05/1989

**TEAMS:** Sunderland, Cwmbran Town, Inter Cable-Tel, Weston Super-Mare, Cwmbran Town

**INTERNATIONAL:** Wales Schoolboys

**SAFC TOTALS:** 1 appearance / 0 goals

**Released the month after his only appearance, Wharton had trials with the team he had played against - Portsmouth - as well as Hereford and Cardiff before retiring from professional football to play in his native South Wales where he became a social worker, councillor and co-owner of 'No Boundaries Anti Racism and consultancy'.**

He won the League of Wales with Cwmbran Town in 1993 being coach then assistant manager at the club from 2002 until becoming manager from October 2005 to April 2007. He later became manager of Port Talbot team Goytre in August 2010 and Abergavenny Town in 2021.

Sean's son Theo became an international with St Kitts and Nevis after representing Wales up to Under 21. He played for York amongst seven sides he had represented to 2022.

## WHELAN, William (Billy)

**POSITION:** Left-half / left-back

**BIRTHPLACE:** Airdrie, Lanarkshire

**DATE OF BIRTH:** 20/02/1906 -17/12/1982

**HEIGHT:** 5' 9" **WEIGHT:** 11st 0lbs

**SIGNED FROM:** Gartsherrie Athletic, 20/04/1927

**DEBUT:** v Birmingham, H, 07/09/1927

**LAST MATCH:** v Sheffield United, H, 02/05/1931

**MOVED TO:** Southend United, 25/04/1932

**TEAMS:** Gartsherrie Athletic, Sunderland, Southend United, Darlington

**SAFC TOTALS:** 19 appearances / 0 goals

**Having come to Wearside from Junior football in Scotland Whelan appeared in four seasons making seven, one, three and eight appearances respectively, but mainly played for the second team who he helped to a fourth successive North-Eastern League championship.**

He met his wife in Sunderland and then went on to make eight Third Division South appearances for Southend before adding ten for Darlington in Division Three North. Billy worked as a storekeeper in an aircraft factory near Sherbourne, Dorset, during World War Two and then settled in Somerset. In later life he returned to Sherbourne where he passed away.

## WHIPP, Percy Leonard

**POSITION:** Inside-right

**BIRTHPLACE:** Glasgow, Lanarkshire

**DATE OF BIRTH:** 28/06/1893 - 18/10/1962

**HEIGHT:** 5' 9½" **WEIGHT:** 11st 12lbs

**SIGNED FROM:** Clapton Orient, 02/06/1922

**DEBUT:** v Bolton Wanderers, A, 09/09/1922

**LAST MATCH:** v Bolton Wanderers, A, 09/09/1922

**MOVED TO:** Leeds United, 03/11/1922

**TEAMS:** Ton Pentre, Clapton Orient, Sunderland, Leeds United, Clapton Orient, Brentford, Swindon Town, Bath City

**SAFC TOTALS:** 1 appearance / 0 goals

**Although he played just once for Sunderland, Whipp did well elsewhere, in particular at Leeds where he scored a hat-trick against West Ham a day after signing for them (for £750) and going on to be top scorer with 16 goals in 32 games that season.**

Good in the air, he hit a further eleven the following term as they won Division Two and lined up against Sunderland on the opening day of 1924-25 in Leeds' first-ever top-flight game. After totalling 47 goals in 154 games for Leeds Percy returned to his first league club Clapton Orient where he ended up with 26 goals from 94 appearances.

He wound down his career in Division Three South with Brentford and Swindon, scoring one goal in seven for the Bees and five in nine for the Robins. A baker before becoming a footballer, during World War One he served with the Royal Field Artillery.

## WHITBOURN, John Giles

**POSITION:** Goalkeeper

**BIRTHPLACE:** Aldershot, Hampshire

**DATE OF BIRTH:** 29/12/1884 - 30/01/1936

**HEIGHT:** 5' 11" **WEIGHT:** 11st 8lbs

**SIGNED FROM:** South Bank, 01/06/1904

**DEBUT:** v Nottingham Forest, A, 15/10/1904

**LAST MATCH:** v Manchester City, A, 03/12/1904

**MOVED TO:** Tottenham Hotspur, 08/08/1905

**TEAMS:** South Bank, Sunderland, Tottenham Hotspur, Leyton, Darlington

**SAFC TOTALS:** 3 appearances / 0 goals

**A teammate of Charlie Buchan at Leyton 1910-11, Whitbourn had been an apprentice joiner before making his living as a footballer. John was signed by Sunderland from Middlesbrough team South Bank as SAFC looked to replace the great Ted Doig who left for Liverpool in summer 1904.**

This proved a tough task and he was one of four keepers used in his only season with the club. Spurs were still in the Southern League when he joined them from Sunderland. To start with he found himself third choice, playing just six of the second team's 20 Western League games in his first season, keeping a clean sheet on his debut against Brentford in November 1905.

A Southern League debut came against Fulham the following September with one more appearance before coming into the team for the final 14 fixtures - but after being selected for the opening three Southern and first two Western League matches of 1907-08 he lost his place through injury and moved on to Leyton at the end of the season.

## WHITE, Dale

**POSITION:** Forward

**BIRTHPLACE:** Sunderland, Co Durham

**DATE OF BIRTH:** 17/03/1968

**HEIGHT:** 5' 10" **WEIGHT:** 11st 4lbs

**SIGNED FROM:** Sunderland Schoolboys, 01/06/1983

**DEBUT:** v Sheffield United, A, 31/03/1986

**LAST MATCH:** v Scarborough, A, 29/10/1987

**MOVED TO:** Released from contract, 31/05/1988

**TEAMS:** Sunderland, Peterborough United (L), Preston Lions, Bulleen Lions, Bentleigh Greens, Gateshead

**INTERNATIONAL:** England Schools

**SAFC TOTALS:** 3+2 appearances / 0 goals

**Part of the Sunderland Boys team - with Lee Howey - who shared the English Schools Trophy with Middlesbrough after a draw at Roker Park in 1983, former Southmoor schoolboy White had a handful of first-team games, but was quickly discarded having not found the net.**

In December 1987 he went on loan to Peterborough, one of his four goals in 14 games coming at Carlisle. After leaving Sunderland Dale went down under, playing for three teams in Melbourne before returning to play for Gateshead. In 2009 he was coaching at Morwell Pegasus in Australia. At international level, he won five caps for England boys, scoring against Northern Ireland and Wales.

## WHITE, Thomas (Tommy)

**POSITION:** Inside-forward

**BIRTHPLACE:** High Handenhold, Co Durham

**DATE OF BIRTH:** 10/11/1924 - 19/06/1998

**HEIGHT:** 5' 7" **WEIGHT:** 10st 8lbs

**SIGNED FROM:** Chester Moor, 25/07/1945

**DEBUT:** v Grimsby Town, A, 05/01/1946

**LAST MATCH:** v Charlton Athletic, A, 11/09/1946

**MOVED TO:** Worcester City, 26/07/1947

**TEAMS:** Chester Moor, Sunderland, Worcester City, Blyth Spartans

**SAFC TOTALS:** 5 appearances / 2 goals

## WHITE, Tommy (Continued)

**Having debuted in the FA Cup White scored in the first minute of his league debut at Arsenal in September 1946, but was injured midway through the first half and spent the rest of the game as a 'passenger' on the wing, in the days before substitutes were allowed.**

His final game came in the next match. The previous season Tommy had scored in the FA Cup and also netted nine in 22 League North games including a Roker Park hat-trick against Blackpool, but games in this end-of-war competition are not credited in official records. White maintained a decent scoring record at Worcester where he scored 21 times in 33 games before returning to the north east.

## WHITEHEAD, Dean

**POSITION:** Midfielder

**BIRTHPLACE:** Abingdon, Oxfordshire

**DATE OF BIRTH:** 12/01/1982

**HEIGHT:** 5' 11" **WEIGHT:** 13st 4lbs

**SIGNED FROM:** Oxford United, 21/06/2004

**DEBUT:** v Coventry City, A, 07/08/2004

**LAST MATCH:** v Chelsea, H, 24/05/2009

**MOVED TO:** Stoke City, 24/07/2009

**TEAMS:** Abingdon Town, Oxford United, Sunderland, Stoke City, Middlesbrough, Huddersfield Town

**SAFC TOTALS:** 188+12 appearances / 14 goals

**An industrious midfielder, 'Deano' played in promotions in two of his first three seasons, the second, in 2006-07, being the first of three years where he skippered the side. Managing exactly 200 appearances in five years, Whitehead never played fewer than 28 games in a season, 98 of those matches being in the Premier League. He missed just one match in the record low 15 points season of 2005-06 when he was Player of the Year and a great example as one of the players in that side whose attitude was impeccable, as they never gave up, despite as a team simply lacking the required quality.**

Having graduated from Oxford's youth team, Dean debuted in December 1999. He went on to play 101+35 games, scoring nine goals for the club where he was Player of the Year in 2003-04 and for two and a half years was managed by Ian Atkins. Upon leaving Sunderland Whitehead did what several players did around that time and moved on to Stoke City where he spent five further seasons in the Premier League. There were 115+43 games (5 goals) for the Potters, including ten in the Europa League and the 2011 FA Cup final where he came on as a sub in a defeat to Manchester City.

2013 brought a return to the north east with Middlesbrough where he was a teammate of Grant Leadbitter. 50+10 games (1 goal) in two seasons with Boro ended at Wembley where he was substituted at half-time in a Play-Off final defeat to Alex Neil's Norwich. There was another Play-Off final in 2017, but as an unused sub as Huddersfield defeated Reading on penalties. This was the middle of three seasons with the Terriers where he played 47+16 times (0 goals) before taking up a coaching role initially with the Under 17s. In November 2019 he became a coach at Shrewsbury where after eight months he became assistant manager only for he and manager Sam Ricketts to be sacked just after the anniversary of Whitehead's arrival. July 2021 brought a coaching appointment at Port Vale who he helped to win the League Two Play-Off final in 2022, but he left the club in the summer to take up a coaching role at Turkish Super Lig club Besiktas.

## WHITEHURST, William (Billy)

**POSITION:** Centre-forward

**BIRTHPLACE:** Thurnscoe, West Riding of Yorkshire

**DATE OF BIRTH:** 10/06/1959

**HEIGHT:** 6' 0" **WEIGHT:** 13st 0lbs

**SIGNED FROM:** Reading, 15/09/1988

**DEBUT:** v Birmingham City, A, 17/09/1988

**LAST MATCH:** v Blackburn Rovers, A, 22/12/1988

**MOVED TO:** Hull City, 29/12/1988

**TEAMS:** Retford Town, Bridlington Trinity, Mexborough Town, Hull City, Newcastle United, Oxford United, Reading, Sunderland, Hull City, Sheffield United, Stoke City (L), Doncaster Rovers, Crewe Alexandra (L), St George Budapest, Hatfield Main, Kettering Town, Goole Town, Stafford Rangers, Mossley, Glentoran, South China, Voicelink, Frickley Athletic

**SAFC TOTALS:** 18 appearances / 3 goals

**A bricklayer with Doncaster Council before becoming a professional footballer, Whitehurst became renowned as one of the toughest men in the game. Never the most cultured of footballers, nonetheless his robust physical presence was constantly in demand, as indicated by his long list of clubs which included St George's Budapest, based in Sydney (1992) and South China and Voicelink in Hong Kong where he played in 1994.**

Billy was only at Sunderland for just over 100 days, being moved on to Hull as part of the player-package with Iain Hesford which brought Tony Norman to Sunderland. The move represented a return for Whitehurst to Hull who were the only team he made over 40 league appearances for, achieving 69 goals in 271 games for the Tigers.

It was playing against the RAF for a Midland League XI in October 1980 that first brought Billy to the attention of Hull where his raw power was honed by the club's record scorer Chris Chilton. Experiencing relegation and promotion with Hull in his formative years saw him grow as a player, scoring 24 times as a second promotion was won in 1985. A club record £232,000 was pocketed for Whitehurst when Newcastle brandished their cheque-book. Following seven goals in 31 games as a Magpie Billy moved on to Oxford where there were six goals in 49 appearances and eight in 19 matches for Reading before Denis Smith signed him for Sunderland.

Whitehurst's second spell at Hull ended when he clashed with manager Stan Ternent. Billy moved on to Sheffield United where 23 games produced just two goals as knee injuries began to take their toll. There were four goals from 26 games with Doncaster and eleven games without scoring for Crewe before his career wound down with clubs in non-league, Australia, Hong Kong and Ireland. After finishing with football he became landlord of the Cricketers Arms next to Bramall Lane in Sheffield and then worked at Drax Power Station and for BP chemicals in East Hull before taking over a pub in Ackworth, not far from his birthplace.

The toughest of characters physically, the more vulnerable side of Billy was seen once when I interviewed him shortly before he was due to go on stage for a football talk in at the Stadium of Light. The man who would make mincemeat of the game's supposedly other hard characters was genuinely extremely nervous about having to speak in public. It showed a different side to Billy as a human.

## WHITELAW, George

**POSITION:** Centre-forward / inside-forward

**BIRTHPLACE:** Glenburn, Paisley, Renfrewshire

**DATE OF BIRTH:** 01/01/1937 - 08/08/2004

**HEIGHT:** 5' 10" **WEIGHT:** 12st 8lbs

**SIGNED FROM:** St Johnstone, 26/02/1958

**DEBUT:** v Preston North End, A, 01/03/1958

**LAST MATCH:** v Charlton Athletic, H, 18/10/1958

**MOVED TO:** QPR, 12/03/1959

**TEAMS:** Renfrew Recreation, Newhill Amateurs, Petershill, St Johnstone, Sunderland, QPR, Halifax Town, Carlisle United, Stockport County, Barrow, St Johnstone, Stenhousemuir

**INTERNATIONAL:** Scotland amateur

**SAFC TOTALS:** 5 appearances / 0 goals

**While Billy Whitehurst was a notorious hard-man of relatively modern times, George Whitelaw was similarly rugged a generation or two earlier. Known to be a joker, George would sometimes entertain the crowd by pretending to tightrope walk along the touchline or pretending to trip over when taking a throw in.**

Stan Anderson once told me that Whitelaw went out shooting rabbits and that he once cut the whiskers off his landlady's cat when his dinner had cat hairs on - although he may well not have realised how cruel the latter was. Writing in his autobiography, Colin Grainger said of Whitelaw, "He was from a different century. He looked like a caveman, had little knowledge of how to use a knife and fork, and seemed permanently confused. When he smiled it was to reveal a set of teeth that had suffered from some frightful dentistry."

George came to Sunderland as a 21-year-old - having been a marine engineer by trade - despite not scoring he was sold to QPR for £500 more than the £4,500 that had been paid for him - £2,000 of the fee QPR paid coming from their supporters' club. Whitelaw repaid the fee with a series of performances that lifted the club away from relegation trouble in Division Three, starting with a goal on debut against Bradford City. At QPR he acquired the nicknames 'Garth' after the Daily Mirror comic strip character and 'Cheyenne' after a comic book character of the period. With ten goals in 27 games he had a decent goals ratio, but after just seven months moved on to sign for Harry Hooper at Halifax Town.

Whitelaw bagged 23 goals in 56 games before a February 1961 transfer to Carlisle where there were ten goals in 38 appearances, starting with a debut goal in a win over Crystal Palace. After eleven months in Cumbria he was on the move again, this time to Stockport where there were 18 goals in 52 matches followed by seven games without scoring for Barrow prior to a return to Scotland - his last two games for Barrow bringing 8-2 and 7-1 defeats.

In July 1988 George's son, Kieran, signed schoolboy forms as a 15-year-old for St Mirren, but after failing to make it professionally played for Gleniffer Thistle.

## WHITELUM, Clifford

**POSITION:** Centre-forward / inside-forward

**BIRTHPLACE:** Farnworth, Lancashire

**DATE OF BIRTH:** 02/12/1919 - 29/08/2000

**HEIGHT:** 5' 9" **WEIGHT:** 11st 4lbs

**SIGNED FROM:** Bentley CW, 16/12/1938

**DEBUT:** v Blackpool, A, 25/01/1939

**LAST MATCH:** v Blackburn Rovers, H, 13/09/1947

**MOVED TO:** Sheffield United, 24/10/1947

**TEAMS:** Bentley CW, Sunderland, Barnsley (WW2 Guest), Sheffield United, King's Lynn, Stowmarket Town

**SAFC TOTALS:** 50 appearances / 19 goals

**Jamie Millar, Charlie Buchan, Bobby Gurney and Nick Sharkey have all scored five goals in a game for Sunderland - Cliff Whitelum once scored six, and in a cup final! Whitelum's double hat-trick came against Huddersfield in the 1943 Combined Counties West Riding FA Cup final first leg.**

Five of these came before half-time and they were all needed as after winning 6-2, the second leg was lost 4-1. Whitelum scored 143 goals for Sunderland in wartime football in 177 games as he served in the Royal Artillery and gained representative honours for the AA Command XI. During the war he also played once as a guest for Barnsley.

At Sheffield United Cliff contributed 14 goals in 43 games before a drop from the top-flight to non-league with King's Lynn where he signed for his old Bramall Lane colleague Joe Cockroft just as the Blades were relegated. The goals kept coming as he scored 239 times in five years as he became player/coach and in 1951-52 played alongside his brother Alf. After retiring from the game Cliff worked as a clerk in an engineering company. He also joined the St John ambulance brigade in 1960 and in October of the following year was presented with the Order of St John.

## WHITFIELD, Michael (Mick)

**POSITION:** Right-back

**BIRTHPLACE:** Sunderland, Co Durham

**DATE OF BIRTH:** 17/10/1962

**HEIGHT:** 5' 8½" **WEIGHT:** 11st 0lbs

**SIGNED FROM:** As trainee, 01/07/1979

**DEBUT:** v Norwich City, A, 16/04/1983

**LAST MATCH:** v Birmingham City, H, 30/04/1983

**MOVED TO:** Hartlepool United, 30/07/1983

**TEAMS:** Sunderland, Hartlepool United, Bishop Auckland, Horden CW, Peterlee, Seaham Red Star

**SAFC TOTALS:** 3 appearances / 0 goals

**After coming through the youth system Whitfield made three appearances before following Mick Docherty to Hartlepool where after first playing in a friendly with Dumbarton he went on to play 19+1 games.**

After experiencing just a solitary victory in that time he moved to Horden CW after Docherty's dismissal and thereafter played in local non-league football as well as becoming a gas fitter.

## WHITLEY, Jeffrey

**POSITION:** Midfielder

**BIRTHPLACE:** Ndola, Zambia

**DATE OF BIRTH:** 28/01/1979

**HEIGHT:** 5' 8" **WEIGHT:** 11st 6lbs

**SIGNED FROM:** Free agent, 04/08/2003

**DEBUT:** v Mansfield Town, A, 13/08/2003

**LAST MATCH:** v Reading, H, 09/04/2005

**MOVED TO:** Cardiff City, 01/07/2005

**TEAMS:** Manchester City, Wrexham (L), Notts County (L), Sunderland, Cardiff City, Stoke City (L), Wrexham, Woodley Sports, Northwich Victoria, Droylsden

**INTERNATIONAL:** England Under 17 / Northern Ireland

**SAFC TOTALS:** 74+3 appearances / 2 goals

**The overriding memory of Whitley on Wearside was of his 'twinkle-toes' cartoon character run-up before failing to score in a 2004 Play-Off semi-final penalty shoot-out with Crystal Palace. For all Jeff missed, the fact that he stepped up to take one when not a natural goalscorer illustrates that he did not lack bottle.**

Reportedly, he was too familiar with bottles off the pitch too and to some extent that undermined his career. On one particular occasion on a pre-season tour in South Carolina in the USA, I found him and Marcus Stewart in a bar when they were not supposed to be drinking. Sworn to secrecy, we had a great time, but it was in some ways typical of Jeff. He later attended the Sporting Chance clinic after reportedly becoming addicted to alcohol and drugs. Having succeeded there Jeff went on to work for the Professional Footballers' Association having previously sold cars.

He was brought in by Mick McCarthy at a time when the manager had next to no money to turn the team around after a particularly dismal relegation. Whitley's desire and determination on the pitch were integral to Sunderland not sliding into further trouble as they did in 2017-18, but reaching the semi-finals of the FA Cup as well as the Play-Offs and then winning the league in Jeff's second season, in both of which he was a regular starter. Never the easiest on the eye in terms of style, he could not be faulted for effort.

Born in Zambia but raised in England he gained Under 17 caps for England before (qualifying through a Belfast-born father) winning 20 caps for Northern Ireland between 1997 and 2004, the last twelve of them while with Sunderland. One of those caps saw him score against Wales who included John Oster, while George McCartney was one of his teammates. His international breakthrough came while Whitley was with Manchester City. Debuting for City at home to Barnsley in September 1996 he made 111+30 appearances (8 goals) with a final game at Norwich in August 2001.

His best season was 1999-2000 when he played 44+3 times as City won promotion to the Premier League a year after promotion from the third tier. During his time at City he had loans to Wrexham (9/2) and Notts County (18/0), but after being released by Kevin Keegan in March 2003 he came to Sunderland where he won a medal before even signing for the club! Playing on a trial non-contract basis, Jeff won a Premier League Reserve League medal with Sunderland after playing eight times before signing for the club in the summer.

After leaving Sunderland Whitley went on to join Cardiff for whom he played 36+2 times scoring once. There were 1+3 games in a 2006 loan to Stoke before a further loan to Wrexham became a permanent transfer, although he only stayed at the club for five months after signing as his side were relegated from the Football League. There were 16+6 games and one goal for Wrexham before Jeff finished his playing days in non-league. His brother Jim was also a Northern Ireland international who played for Manchester City and Wrexham as well as having a host of loans.

## WHITWORTH, Stephen (Steve)

**POSITION:** Right-back

**BIRTHPLACE:** Ellistown, Leicestershire

**DATE OF BIRTH:** 20/03/1952

**HEIGHT:** 6' 0" **WEIGHT:** 12st 0lbs

**SIGNED FROM:** Leicester City, 24/03/1979

**DEBUT:** v Stoke City, A, 27/03/1979

**LAST MATCH:** v Tottenham Hotspur, H, 17/10/1981

**MOVED TO:** Bolton Wanderers, 22/10/1981

**TEAMS:** Leicester City, Sunderland, Bolton Wanderers, Mansfield Town, Barnet

**INTERNATIONAL:** England

**SAFC TOTALS:** 97 appearances / 0 goals

**The epitome of the consistent full-back Whitworth was solid, dependable and assured. Steve would rarely win you games as a marauding full-back in the modern day sense or as pioneered by Cec Irwin or Dick Malone, but he would not lose you games either. He did however, set up a goal for another ex-Leicester player Bob Lee at Leicester in 1979-80 in a season when both clubs were promoted.**

## WHITWORTH, Steve (Continued)

Whitworth was fast and he did get forward but quite rightly defending was always his priority. Wingers very rarely got the better of Steve who stuck to his task with terrific discipline. In his first full season at Sunderland in 1979-80 he was the only ever-present in a promotion-winning team, but despite this and his pedigree as an England international he was never a fans' favourite.

He did not get a medal as a runner-up in winning promotion with Sunderland, but he did get one in 1970-71 with Leicester. That season he missed just three games as the Foxes won Division Two and took double-winners Arsenal to a replay in the FA Cup quarter-final. This was Whitworth's first season. He had debuted on 2 September against Bristol City and from that moment went on to make a record 113 consecutive league and cup appearances - consistency from the word go. Between November 1972 and December 1977 Steve surpassed that with 198 consecutive league appearances in a total of 415 appearances for the club where he had a testimonial against Coventry City in November 1979, returning to Leicester to play in it after signing for Sunderland.

At Bolton Steve was signed by someone who knew a good right-back when he saw one, former Sunderland left-winger George Mulhall. Debuting in a second division fixture at Cambridge he made 73 appearances, playing alongside Jim (Seamus) McDonagh and Peter Reid, but suffering relegation in 1983. That summer Steve moved to Mansfield where he played 80 times before becoming player-assistant manager at Barnet for whom he played 27 games.

His only league goals were two penalties for Mansfield, but he did score a tap-in as Leicester beat Liverpool in the 1971 Charity Shield at Filbert Street as well as scoring for England Under 23s against Scotland Under 23s in 1975 - a 3-0 win at Aberdeen when Dennis Tueart got the other two goals. That was in one of six Under 23 internationals Whitworth played in in addition to schoolboy and youth honours. The first of seven full caps came in a win over reigning world champions West Germany in Wembley's 100th international in 1975 when he played alongside Dave Watson and Colin Todd. England were unbeaten with Steve in the side although at international level, he never played alongside his old Leicester colleague Frank Worthington.

## WICKHAM, Connor Neil Ralph Gibson

**POSITION:** Centre-forward

**BIRTHPLACE:** Hereford, Herefordshire

**DATE OF BIRTH:** 31/03/1993

**HEIGHT:** 6' 0" **WEIGHT:** 14st 1lb

**SIGNED FROM:** Ipswich Town, 29/06/2011

**DEBUT:** v Newcastle United, H, 20/08/2011

**LAST MATCH:** v Chelsea, A, 24/05/2015

**MOVED TO:** Crystal Palace, 03/08/2015

**TEAMS:** Reading, Ipswich Town, Sunderland, Sheffield Wednesday (L), Leeds United (L), Crystal Palace, Sheffield Wednesday (L), Preston North End, MK Dons, Forest Green Rovers (to August 2022)

**INTERNATIONAL:** England Under 21

**SAFC TOTALS:** 52+39 appearances / 15 goals

**The signing of 18-year-old Wickham for an undisclosed fee thought to be in the region of an initial £8m was seen as a big coup. He was a hot property having sensationally made his name with Ipswich where he became the club's youngest-ever player when debuting just eleven days after his 16th birthday.**

In just his fourth first-team game Connor scored twice and added a goal in a penalty shoot-out against Shrewsbury. Four months before being transferred to Sunderland he scored a Championship hat-trick in a 6-0 win at Doncaster as a highlight of 15 goals in 37+35 appearances as a Tractor Boy. He also excelled in international football as a young player. In 2008 he scored in the final as England won the Victory Shield at Under 16 level and scored the winner against Spain at the UEFA European Under 17 Championships when he was named the best player in the tournament. He went on to score six goals in 17 games at Under 21 level.

There was just one goal in 6+13 appearances in Connor's first campaign at Sunderland where there were some grumbles that a sizeable chunk of Steve Bruce's transfer budget had been spent on a player for the future when people were concerned about the here and now. There were two goals in Wickham's second season, but in 2013-14 Bruce's investment paid off although Bruce was long gone and it was Gus Poyet who benefited. Wickham hit form on a second loan at Sheffield Wednesday. Starting with a debut goal against Reading - where he had spent four years playing junior football - he scored seven times in eleven games.

After a brief return to Wearside he went on loan again to Leeds, but did not net in five games. However, shortly after returning again he came good in a run reminiscent of Colin West; another blond forward of similar stature, in 1981-82. After Poyet had proclaimed Sunderland needed a miracle, Wickham began with a brace to earn a point at Manchester City. A few days later he scored in a sensational win at Chelsea, followed that up with a brace in a big win against Cardiff and then provided the assist for Seb Larsson to score the winner at Manchester United as Poyet discovered that miracles do happen.

It was the highlight of Connor's time at Sunderland and brought him the Premier League Player of the Month award. After moving on to Crystal Palace he scored eleven goals in 26+24 games spread over six injury-hit seasons, one of which brought another loan to Sheffield Wednesday where he took his total for the Owls to eleven goals in 23+7 games.

A September 2021 move to Preston brought just 1+1 appearances in four months before a loan to MK Dons where his only goal in 2+13 games came at the Stadium of Light. After a trial with Reading Wickham joined Forest Green Rovers in August 2022.

## WILDING, Samual Jacob

**POSITION:** Midfielder

**BIRTHPLACE:** Walsall, West Midlands

**DATE OF BIRTH:** 31/01/2000

**HEIGHT:** 5' 8" **WEIGHT:** 11st 3lbs

**SIGNED FROM:** West Bromwich Albion, 15/08/2020

**DEBUT:** v Fleetwood Town, A, 10/11/2020

**LAST MATCH:** v Oldham Athetic, H, 11/12/2021

**MOVED TO:** Contract not renewed, 30/06/2022

**TEAMS:** WBA, Sunderland, Leamington (L), South Shields (L), Hednesford Town (to August 2022)

**INTERNATIONAL:** England Schools

**SAFC TOTALS:** 1+1 appearances / 0 goals

**Having been on trial at Sunderland in February 2020, Wilding twice appeared in the Football League (Papa Johns) Trophy. He had played twice in the same competition for West Brom, a club he spent twelve years with before being released and coming to Sunderland.**

He joined Kevin Phillips' South Shields on loan in 2021-22 before his release and also played 23 games in two loans to Leamington, the first from WBA in 2018-19 and the second in 2021-22 from Sunderland where he captained the Under 23s.

## WILKINS, Leslie

**POSITION:** Inside-right

**BIRTHPLACE:** Swansea, Glamorgan

**DATE OF BIRTH:** 21/07/1907 - 28/10/1979

**HEIGHT:** 5' 9" **WEIGHT:** 11st 7lbs

**SIGNED FROM:** Merthyr Town, 02/11/1929

**DEBUT:** v Grimsby Town, A, 23/11/1929

**LAST MATCH:** v Manchester United, H, 30/11/1929

**MOVED TO:** West Ham United, 21/05/1930

**TEAMS:** Swansea Town, Merthyr Town, Sunderland, West Ham United, Brentford, Swindon Town, Stockport County, Yeovil & Petters United

**SAFC TOTALS:** 2 appearances / 0 goals

**Having worked in the building trade before becoming a footballer Wilkins made his way to Wearside after starting in Welsh football. He did not get a game for Swansea Town who he signed for after impressing in youth football with Swansea Red Triangle, but after four goals in seven matches for Merthyr, Sunderland's scouts snapped him up.**

He was not a success however, but did at least play a couple of games whereas he failed to get an opportunity after joining West Ham. Across London at Brentford he scored once in 19 games and had a successful time with Swindon where he netted eight goals in 20 outings in 1932-33 - an achievement that was all the more impressive considering his club finished bottom of Division Three South. That summer he switched to Stockport, but after just three games and one goal moved to Yeovil. Les worked in an aircraft factory in Yeovil during World War Two and remained in the town until he passed away.

## WILKINSON, Reginald George

**POSITION:** Right-half

**BIRTHPLACE:** Norwich, Norfolk

**DATE OF BIRTH:** 26/03/1899 - 14/09/1946

**HEIGHT:** 5' 9" **WEIGHT:** 11st 0lbs

**SIGNED FROM:** Norwich City, 04/06/1923

**DEBUT:** v West Ham United, H, 25/08/1923

**LAST MATCH:** v Cardiff City, A, 27/08/1923

**MOVED TO:** Brighton & Hove Albion, 27/05/1924

**TEAMS:** Norwich City, Sunderland, Brighton & Hove Albion, Frost's Athletic, Norwich Electricity Works

**SAFC TOTALS:** 2 appearances / 0 goals

**Sadly, yet another player who died too young. Wilkinson was 47 when he collapsed while playing for the Norwich Electricity Works team against CEYMS and died on the way to hospital. He had played twice for SAFC, but managed 113 (9 goals) for Norwich and 361 (14 goals) for Brighton.**

At his hometown club Norwich he debuted in a Southern League match against Bristol Rovers on March 13, 1920. He also played in Norwich's very first Football League match the following season - a 1-1 Third Division draw away to Plymouth Argyle on the opening day of the 1920/21 season. A wing-half who had gained the reputation as something of a set piece specialist and ace penalty taker at Norwich, his move to First Division Sunderland was met with disfavour from City's supporters.

During World War One he served with the King's Royal Rifle Corps and in the Second War was a Local Government administrative clerk and Air Raid Precautions Warden with the electricity department.

## WILKS, Alwyne

**POSITION:** Outside-right

**BIRTHPLACE:** Eckington, Derbyshire

**DATE OF BIRTH:** 04/09/1906 - 27/08/1980

**HEIGHT:** 5' 7" **WEIGHT:** 11st 0lbs

**SIGNED FROM:** Doncaster Rovers, 19/02/1927

**DEBUT:** v Cardiff City, H, 12/03/1927

**LAST MATCH:** v Liverpool, A, 20/04/1929

**MOVED TO:** Reading, 18/05/1929

**TEAMS:** Brodsworth Main Colliery, Doncaster Rovers, Sunderland, Reading, Barrow, Loughborough Corinthians, Owston Park Rangers

**SAFC TOTALS:** 55 appearances / 2 goals

**Forty-three of pacey right-winger Wilks' 55 games came in his one full season of 1927-28 when he scored his two SAFC goals, one of them a screamer in a 5-1 home win over Arsenal. Nicknamed 'Pompa', Wilks went on to sign for Reading, but left without playing a league game.**

His next move to Barrow brought half a dozen appearances before he turned out for Loughborough Corinthians. He then had a spell with Owston Park Rangers - a local Doncaster side. He had scored three times in 14 games for Doncaster Rovers before coming to Sunderland. Following his retirement from playing he became a stores worker in a colliery near Doncaster.

## WILLIAMS, Darren

**POSITION:** Midfielder

**BIRTHPLACE:** Middlesbrough, Cleveland

**DATE OF BIRTH:** 28/04/1977

**HEIGHT:** 5' 10½" **WEIGHT:** 12st 6lbs

**SIGNED FROM:** York City, 15/10/1996

**DEBUT:** v Arsenal, A, 04/01/1997

**LAST MATCH:** v Crewe Alexandra, A, 21/09/2004

**MOVED TO:** Cardiff City, 10/12/2004

**TEAMS:** Middlesbrough, York City, Sunderland, Cardiff City, Hartlepool United, Bradford City, Dundee, Gateshead, Gainsborough Trinity, Whitby Town

**INTERNATIONAL:** England B

**SAFC TOTALS:** 190+49 appearances / 6 goals

**Darren Williams was excellent for Sunderland. He would not claim to be a world beater and he was not - regardless of his England B and Under 21 caps - but in a team game he was a real team player. Very versatile and with a model attitude he gave all he had to give in every appearance, was always genuinely appreciative of the supporters and generous with his time off the pitch.**

Famously, he was once selected to a man-marking job on the magical Brazilian Juninho back at Darren's hometown club. However, when Juninho did not play Williams found himself with more free-rein and headed the only goal of the game - something that brought him some grief on Teesside. His best season at Sunderland was in 1997-98 when he started 35 league games and played in all three of the Play-Offs that ended in penalty shoot-out defeat to Charlton at Wembley. He was on the fringes of the side that went up the following season and then had two seventh-place Premier League finishes, but nonetheless, played in 78 league games in those three campaigns, 50 of them starts.

Having gone on loan to Cardiff in September 2004 Darren signed for the Bluebirds a couple of months later. However, after 13 starts on loan he only added 4+3 appearances before returning to the north east the following summer with Hartlepool. In two years there he made 61+13 appearances, winning promotion in 2007 before spending 2007-08 with Bradford City where he played 31 times (all starts). 2008-09 brought a move to Dundee where he played 16+3 games. After leaving Sunderland Darren did not score at all. With York he had been part of the side that famously knocked Manchester United out of the League (Coca-Cola) Cup over two legs in 1995-96 having sensationally won 3-0 at Old Trafford.

At international level Darren played for England 'B' alongside Kevin Phillips in a 4-1 win over Russia at QPR in April 1998. A month earlier he debuted at Under 21 level alongside Darren Holloway as subs in a defeat away to Switzerland, future Sunderland coach Steve Guppy also being in that team. Williams also played against France Under 21s at Derby in February 1999, on that occasion alongside Wayne Bridge.

Williams became player/manager of Whitby Town between October 2011 and November 2015 and continued to occasionally pop up on local BBC radio as a pundit commenting on Sunderland.

## WILLIAMS, Henry Archibald (Harry)

**POSITION:** Inside-left

**BIRTHPLACE:** Hucknall Torkard, Nottinghamshire

**DATE OF BIRTH:** 29/07/1898 - 08/04/1980

**HEIGHT:** 5' 11" **WEIGHT:** 11st 10lbs

**SIGNED FROM:** Hucknall Olympic, 22/05/1920

**DEBUT:** v Chelsea, A, 12/03/1921

**LAST MATCH:** v Chelsea, A, 12/03/1921

**MOVED TO:** Chesterfield, 01/05/1921

**TEAMS:** Hucknall, Sunderland, Chesterfield, Manchester United, Brentford, Mansfield Town

**SAFC TOTALS:** 1 appearance / 0 goals

**Having originally signed for Sunderland as an amateur Harry became a professional in August 1920 and played his only game the following March. He got an opportunity at Chelsea on an occasion when Charlie Buchan was on duty in an international trial, but never featured again.**

He moved on to Chesterfield, scoring the Spireites first goal on their return to the Football League in the newly-formed Division Three North in 1921. Nine goals in 28 games led to a transfer to Manchester United and a Division Two debut at Wednesday on 28 August 1922. It was one of five games he played for United, in which he scored against Crystal Palace and Wolves, before moving on to Brentford in September 1923, going on to score seven times in 43 games.

Finally after an unsuccessful trial with Sittingbourne in August 1924 Harry finished off his career with Mansfield Town. After retiring from football Harry became a labourer in Sheerness, Kent, and remained in the county until his passing.

## WILLIAMS, Jonathan Peter (Jonny)

**POSITION:** Midfielder

**BIRTHPLACE:** Pembury, Kent

**DATE OF BIRTH:** 09/10/1993

**HEIGHT:** 5' 7" **WEIGHT:** 10st 0lbs

**SIGNED FROM:** Crystal Palace, 31/08/2017, on loan

**DEBUT:** v Sheffield United, H, 09/09/2017

**LAST MATCH:** v QPR, A, 10/03/2018

**MOVED TO:** Crystal Palace, 07/05/2018, end of loan

**TEAMS:** Crystal Palace, Ipswich Town (L), Nottingham Forest (L), MK Dons (L), Ipswich Town (L), Sunderland (L), Charlton Athletic, Cardiff City, Swindon Town (to August 2022)

**INTERNATIONAL:** Wales

**SAFC TOTALS:** 7+6 appearances / 1 goal

**At Sunderland during 2017-18 in a season of a second successive relegation and filming of a Netflix series on the club, Wales international Williams was talented on the ball and seemed to be blessed with a good attitude, but was afflicted by an apparent inability to stay fit for long periods.**

## WILLIAMS, Jonny (Continued)

By June 2022 - eleven years after his debut for Crystal Palace against Coventry - the player had only started a total of 136 league and cup games, with a further 118 appearances as a substitute. His spell at Sunderland was Jonny's seventh loan from Palace where he was Young Player of the Season in 2012-13. Four of those loans were at Ipswich with others to Nottingham Forest and MK Dons. A year and a half after leaving Sunderland he moved from Palace to Charlton for an undisclosed fee and at last played regularly.

In two years he made 66 appearances including 27 as sub - one of which was against Sunderland at Wembley in the 2019 League One Play-Off final. In February 2021 he moved to Cardiff, but only stayed half a season, making just a solitary start in addition to eight games off the bench. August 2021 brought a switch to Swindon with whom he reached the League Two Play-Offs in 2022 by which time he had made 28+17 appearances and scored five goals which took his career aggregate to eleven goals.

He went on to score for Wales against Poland in the Nations League in June 2022 - his second goal for his country as he won his 33rd cap, some of which were won under one-time Sunderland manager Chris Coleman.

## WILLIAMS, Paul Anthony

**POSITION:** Forward
**BIRTHPLACE:** Stratford, London
**DATE OF BIRTH:** 16/08/1965
**HEIGHT:** 5' 7" **WEIGHT:** 10st 3lbs
**SIGNED FROM:** Crystal Palace, 19/01/1995, on loan
**DEBUT:** v Notts County, H, 21/01/1995
**LAST MATCH:** v Charlton Athletic, A, 11/02/1995
**MOVED TO:** Crystal Palace, 17/02/1995, end of loan
**TEAMS:** Aveley, Clapton, Fulham, Woodford Town, Charlton Athletic, Brentford (L), Sheffield Wednesday, Crystal Palace, Sunderland (L), Birmingham City (L), Charlton Athletic, Torquay United (L), Southend United, Canvey Island, Bowers FC
**INTERNATIONAL:** England Under 21 & B
**SAFC TOTALS:** 3 appearances / 0 goals

**An accounts clerk before becoming a professional footballer, a keen eye was needed to keep track of Paul's frequent transfers. After coming to prominence in non-league he scored 23 times in 82 league appearances for Charlton from where he also had a loan to Brentford (7/3).**

In 1990 he signed for Sheffield Wednesday where he scored 28 in 94+20 games winning promotion and being a teammate of Chris Turner as Wednesday won the League Cup in 1991, beating Steve Bruce's Manchester United at Wembley. The following year he moved to Crystal Palace in an exchange deal for Mark Bright. Paul first played for Palace in their eighth Premiership game against Oldham in September 1992, playing alongside future Sunderland boss Chris Coleman (and future England manager Gareth Southgate). Although relegated in his first campaign, Paul's side immediately won the second tier with Williams scoring once for every three of his 21 starts. In total there were 44+9 appearances for the Selhurst Park club. During this time he scored nine goals amidst a loan to Birmingham (11/0) in addition to his three games for Sunderland.

Transferred to Charlton for 1995-96 there were nine games for the Addicks and as many on loan to Torquay before two years with Southend (40/7). Dropping into non-league, 14 goals in 25 games for Canvey Island helped towards two promotions and two cup wins before he became player/coach at Essex club Bowers in 2002. Subsequently, Williams coached in the academies of Charlton and Crystal Palace before a 2012 move to Florida where he became Director of Coaching at Florida Fire Juniors.

At international level Paul partnered Marco Gabbiadini for England Under 21s at the Toulon tournament in 1989, scoring against Bulgaria and twice against Senegal as well as playing against the Republic of Ireland and the USA. The following November he was capped at 'B' level coming on as a sub (as did Peter Beagrie) against Italy in Brighton.

## WILLIAMS, Paul Leslie

**POSITION:** Right-back
**BIRTHPLACE:** Liverpool, Lancashire
**DATE OF BIRTH:** 25/09/1970
**HEIGHT:** 6' 0" **WEIGHT:** 12st 2lbs
**SIGNED FROM:** Gateshead Youths, 01/07/1987
**DEBUT:** v Plymouth Argyle, H, 04/04/1989
**LAST MATCH:** v Birmingham City, H, 15/09/1992
**MOVED TO:** Released, 30/06/1993
**TEAMS:** Sunderland, Swansea City (L), Doncaster Rovers
**SAFC TOTALS:** 9+4 appearances / 0 goals

**Blessed with pace and a superb physique for a footballer, one of Paul Williams' few appearances was in the top flight when he was tortured by Lee Sharpe at Manchester United. Playing at right-back Williams was substituted at half-time with Sunderland 3-0 down.**

Paul had initially joined Sunderland on a Youth Training Scheme (YTS) before signing professional forms. He later ha a dozen games on loan to Swansea under former Sunderland coach Frank Burrows and won the Welsh Cup playing alongside Chris Coleman against Wrexham at Cardiff Arms Park. In July 1993 Paul signed for Doncaster a couple of months after being released from his contract at Sunderland. He played just eight times for Rovers before his contract was cancelled in November 1995 following a collision in a game that left him 90% blind in his left eye.

After leaving the game Williams worked as a warehouse clothes stock controller and then became a telephone engineer while developing a passion for West Brom due to a new group of friends. From 2002 onwards he started visiting Columbia before emigrating there having met his Columbian wife in London. In Bogota Paul became the Finance Director of a company producing biodiesel from palm oil.

## WILLIAMSON, John Robert

**POSITION:** Full-back
**BIRTHPLACE:** Gateshead, Co Durham
**DATE OF BIRTH:** 28/01/1887 - 02/10/1943
**HEIGHT:** 5' 10" **WEIGHT:** 12st 7lbs
**SIGNED FROM:** Gainsborough, 02/05/1914
**DEBUT:** v Notts County, H, 24/10/1914
**LAST MATCH:** v Manchester City, A, 06/03/1915
**MOVED TO:** Not offered a contract after WW1
**TEAMS:** Annfield Plain Celtic, Stourbridge, Aston Villa, Gainsborough Trinity, Sunderland
**SAFC TOTALS:** 5 appearances / 0 goals

**Before playing for Sunderland, Williamson's time at Villa was restricted to the reserves. Having left Villa he spent the 1913-14 season with Gainsborough Trinity who had dropped out of the Football League in 1912. Renowned as a penalty expert he helped the club to runners-up spot in the Midland League and was picked up by Sunderland who had to pay Villa £25 as they still held his Football League registration.**

Having debuted when standing in for Bert Hobson at left-back another opportunity came in his preferred right-back berth on New Year's Day in a win at Middlesbrough. There was better still 24 hours later when he was part of the side in a 4-0 win at home to his old club Villa. He returned to the side for two further games a couple of months later, although both were away defeats.

These games came in the last season before the Football League was suspended due to World War One. John played one game in May 1916 against Newcastle United and by December 1918, as thoughts started to focus on the resumption of football, he was given as still serving as a Private in the army in France. When league football resumed in summer 1919 Williamson, who was now 32, was no longer on Sunderland's books and he returned to mining which had been his occupation before becoming a footballer.

## WILLINGHAM, Charles Kenneth

**POSITION:** Right-half

**BIRTHPLACE:** Sheffield, West Riding of Yorkshire

**DATE OF BIRTH:** 01/12/1912 - 30/05/1975

**HEIGHT:** 5' 7½" **WEIGHT:** 10st 11lbs

**SIGNED FROM:** Huddersfield Town, 21/12/1945

**DEBUT:** v Grimsby Town, A, 05/01/1946

**LAST MATCH:** v Arsenal, H, 04/01/1947

**MOVED TO:** Leeds United, 03/03/1947

**TEAMS:** Ecclesfield, Worksop Town, Huddersfield Town, Barnsley (WW2 Guest), Bradford Park Avenue (WW2 Guest), Sunderland, Leeds United

**INTERNATIONAL:** England

**SAFC TOTALS:** 20 appearances / 0 goals

**The scorer of the quickest goal ever conceded by Sunderland, England international Willingham took only ten seconds to net against the Lads for Huddersfield eleven days before Christmas in 1935. Another ex-Huddersfield and Sunderland player Willie Watson played for England at football and cricket. Willingham was a triple international. As well as playing twelve times for England, six times for the Football League and in three war-time internationals, he also represented England at shinty and as the Yorkshire Schools half-mile champion ran for England at school level.**

He was a scorer on his international debut in an 8-0 win away to Finland in the month Sunderland won the FA Cup in 1937. A second cap almost a year later came at Wembley in a defeat by Scotland, but despite Sunderland's success in this era none of his twelve appearances saw him play alongside a Sunderland player, Ken's caps included games against the Rest of Europe and one against Norway at Newcastle.

Willingham was 33 by the time he came to Sunderland having lost many of his best years to the war. He had spent this time working as a turner in an aircraft factory as well as playing football whenever he could. In his first season he played in all six of the club's FA Cup games as well as 17 games in League North (not included in the totals above). His second and last season at Roker Park saw the resumption of the Football League. Ken played the first 13 post-war Football League games and then after a couple of months out of action returned for a final appearance in the first game of 1947.

Leaving for Leeds a further couple of months later he became player/coach and debuted against Arsenal in March 1947. He played ten times without being able to stop the Elland Road side propping up the division, one of those games being a loss on his return to Sunderland. In his one full season at Leeds, Ken played 24 times, the last at home to Spurs in April 1948 being the final game of his career. He stayed at Leeds until 1950 as a coach and a couple of years later took up a similar role at Halifax Town and after retiring became a publican in Hunslet, Leeds.

Willingham had begun in senior football with Huddersfield who he joined as an amateur in 1930, becoming a professional in November of the following year. His 270 appearances for the club included the 1938 FA Cup final when he was a teammate of Iain Hesford's father Bob as Town lost to Preston who had been losing finalists to Sunderland a year earlier.

## WILLIS, David Lalty (Dave)

**POSITION:** Half-back

**BIRTHPLACE:** Byker, Newcastle, Northumberland

**DATE OF BIRTH:** 16/07/1881 - 26/05/1949

**HEIGHT:** 5' 7" **WEIGHT:** 11st 7lbs

**SIGNED FROM:** Jarrow, 25/10/1901
Re-signed from Reading, 05/04/1904

**DEBUT:** v Derby County, A, 01/11/1902

**LAST MATCH:** v Notts County, H, 24/04/1907

**MOVED TO:** Reading, 07/05/1903
and Newcastle United, 07/05/1907

**TEAMS:** Jarrow, Sunderland, Reading, Sunderland, Newcastle United, Reading, Palmers, Jarrow

**SAFC TOTALS:** 52 appearances / 2 goals

**Willis had two spells with Sunderland, won the league title and played in a cup final with Newcastle, was trainer for England in a match against Scotland and for Raich Carter's Derby when they won the FA Cup in 1947. He was also a masseur for Derbyshire County Cricket Club and India as well as being the father-in-law of Arsenal and Scotland legend Alex James.**

First coming to Sunderland as a 20-year-old, after a trial game which ended in a 7-2 win against his former club Jarrow, Willis could not get into the team as the Lads won the league. After just one game the following season he moved on to Reading but returned after a season to make over 50 appearances for the red and whites, 33 of them in 1905-06. Following just 13 appearances the next season Newcastle paid £100 to take him to his native Tyneside.

He played 108 times for the Magpies, scoring four goals. A reserve for the 1908 English (FA) Cup final, he played in the final and final replay alongside Harry Low's brother Wilf as Newcastle lost to Bradford City in 1911. In 1908-09 he played in 20 of United's 38 league games as they became champions - including the record 1-9 home defeat to Sunderland.

A second spell with Reading preceded four years overseas during World War One after which he became manager of Jarrow in 1918. From June 1921 to June 1925 he was trainer at Tranmere Rovers before taking up a similar role at Nottingham Forest from July 1925 to June 1933. During this time he was chosen to be trainer for England when they beat a Scotland team, including his son-in-law Alex James, 5-2 at Wembley in April 1929. Upon leaving Forest Willis moved to Derby County where he stayed until June 1947 before taking up a post at Derbyshire CCC the following year as masseur, his services being utilised by India for a Test Match at Trent Bridge. In addition to being father-in-law of the great Alex James, Willis' son Robert played for Blyth Spartans, Dundee, Rochdale and Halifax Town during the 1920s.

## WILLIS, Jordan Kenneth

**POSITION:** Centre-back

**BIRTHPLACE:** Coventry, West Midlands

**DATE OF BIRTH:** 24/04/1994

**HEIGHT:** 5' 11" **WEIGHT:** 11st 0lbs

**SIGNED FROM:** Coventry City, 13/07/2019

**DEBUT:** v Oxford United, H, 03/08/2019

**LAST MATCH:** v Shrewsbury Town, A, 09/02/2021

**MOVED TO:** Released, 30/06/2022

**TEAMS:** Coventry City, Sunderland

**INTERNATIONAL:** England Under 19

**SAFC TOTALS:** 57+3 appearances / 2 goals

**A player very unlucky with injury, prior to being hurt he had looked an accomplished, strong and pacey defender in his two seasons at Sunderland. He had joined from his home club Coventry where he had played 194+14 games scoring seven goals, his debut against Southampton in November 2011 seeing him enter the list of the Sky Blues top ten youngest players at the age of 17 and 72 days.**

Playing alongside Lee Burge he captained Coventry at Wembley in 2017 as they defeated Oxford in the Football League (Checkatrade) Trophy final. A year later he scored at Wembley as City defeated Exeter in the League Two Play-Off final. Capped by England at Under 18 and 19 level he first played in March 2012 against Poland alongside Jordan Pickford.

Willis ruptured his patella tendon at Shrewsbury in February 2021 and suffered a second rupture during his recuperation. As he tried to work his way back to fitness he undertook scouting and analysis work, but eventually his departure from the club was announced in May 2022 having not played for 15 months.

## WILSON, Hugh

**POSITION:** Half-back

**BIRTHPLACE:** Mauchline, East Ayrshire

**DATE OF BIRTH:** 18/03/1869 - 07/04/1940

**HEIGHT:** 5' 10½" **WEIGHT:** 11st 7lbs

**SIGNED FROM:** Newmilns, 18/05/1890

**DEBUT:** v Burnley, H, 13/09/1890

**LAST MATCH:** v Newcastle United, A, 22/04/1899

**MOVED TO:** Bedminster, 12/05/1899

**TEAMS:** Newmilns, Sunderland, Bedminster, Bristol City, Third Lanark, Kilmarnock

**INTERNATIONAL:** Scotland

**SAFC TOTALS:** 256 appearances / 45 goals

## WILSON, Hugh (Continued)

**Captain of 'The Team of All The Talents' from 1894-95 Wilson remained as skipper for five seasons. The only player to play in both Sunderland's first league game (in1890) and the opening game at Roker Park (in 1898) he was one of the dominating figures of the era. At a time when throw-ins could be taken with one hand his prowess in launching the ball was one of the factors in the Laws of the game being changed to make throw-ins two-handed.**

Wilson was the first player to miss a penalty for Sunderland and also the first to be sent off, the latter for insulting referee Mr Kingscott in a match against Stoke on 14 March 1896. At Sunderland he won league title medals in 1892, 1893 and 1895 as well as playing in all four of the Test Matches of 1897 before being joint second top scorer the following year when Sunderland were runners-up.

Hugh left Sunderland for Bedminster who merged with Bristol City during Hugh's time there as he made a total of 88 appearances in which he scored 29 goals. In 1901 he signed for Third Lanark with whom he won the Scottish League in 1904 and scored twice in a 3-1 win over Rangers in the 1905 Scottish Cup final replay when he played at inside-left. A year later he again played in the final which this time was lost to Hearts. In total Wilson played 136 times for Third Lanark, scoring 37 times before a final season of 1907-08 with Kilmarnock where he scored three times in 22 games.

First capped against Wales in March 1890 when he scored in a 5-0 win while still with Newmilms, his only cap while with Sunderland came in a 2-1 win over England in April 1897 when Jamie Millar (then of Rangers) was one of the scorers. Further caps came against Wales and Ireland in 1902 and 1904 while with Third Lanark. He also played for both the Football League and the Scottish League.

Nicknamed 'Lalty', after retiring from the game Hugh returned to his occupation as a lace weaver. His Sunderland-born son John played over 400 league games in Scotland mainly for Hearts as well as Dunfermline, Hamilton, St Johnstone and a loan with Raith Rovers.

## WILSON, Joseph (Joe)

**POSITION:** Inside-right

**BIRTHPLACE:** Unknown, but most likely Sunderland

**DATE OF BIRTH:** Unknown

**SIGNED FROM:** Southwick, 01/05/1896 and South Shields, 26/05/1898

**DEBUT:** v Bolton Wanderers, A, 26/09/1896

**LAST MATCH:** v Wolverhampton Wanderers, H, 03/10/1896

**MOVED TO:** South Shields, 31/08/1897 and released, 1899

**TEAMS:** Southwick, Sunderland, South Shields, Sunderland, South Shields

**SAFC TOTALS:** 2 appearances / 0 goals

**Both of Wilson's games came in the first of his two spells at Sunderland. His debut probably prompted by scoring a late equaliser in a 1-1 home friendly against Newcastle three days earlier.**

At the time of his appearances Sunderland were bottom of the league and lost both games without scoring. Joe had a single season with South Shields, where he was reported as the former Southwick and Sunderland 'A' team flyer, before re-joining Sunderland. However, this second spell yielded no further first-team appearances and after being released in May 1899, he re-joined Shields.

## WILSON, Marc David

**POSITION:** Defender

**BIRTHPLACE:** Aghagallon, Northern Ireland

**DATE OF BIRTH:** 17/08/1987

**HEIGHT:** 6' 2" **WEIGHT:** 12st 5lbs

**SIGNED FROM:** Bournemouth, 31/08/2017

**DEBUT:** v Sheffield United, H, 09/09/2017

**LAST MATCH:** v Wolverhampton Wanderers, H, 06/05/2018

**MOVED TO:** Contract not renewed, 30/06/2018

**TEAMS:** Manchester United, Portsmouth, Yeovil Town (L), Bournemouth (L), Luton Town (L), Stoke City, Bournemouth, WBA (L), Sunderland, Bolton Wanderers, Próttur Vogum, ÍBV

**INTERNATIONAL:** Republic of Ireland

**SAFC TOTALS:** 21+1 appearances / 0 goals

**Supporters did not see the best of this player who played in just under half of the games in the dismal 2017-18 campaign when a second consecutive relegation was endured. Between 2011 and 2015 he won 25 caps for the Republic of Ireland, sometimes partnering John O'Shea in defence as he played for Martin O'Neill.**

Wilson had played Under15 games for Northern Ireland, but later chose to make himself available to play for the Republic. Three months after Marc's international debut he played in the 2011 FA Cup final as one of six Sunderland connected members of the Stoke squad which lost to Manchester City. A year earlier he had been with Portsmouth when they reached the cup final, but did not feature.

Pompey had given Wilson his senior chance after he played youth football for Lisburn and Manchester United. He made 27 appearances (3 goals) in two loans to Bournemouth as well as playing twice for Yeovil and four times for Luton before Pompey started to use him in 2007-08. After 46+3 appearances a £3.2m fee took him to Stoke where he turned out 157+19 times (1 goal). Bournemouth then invested £2m in Wilson in August 2016, but he only played three cup games (1 goal) and joined Sunderland a year later on a free transfer having had 3+1 games on loan to West Brom. After Sunderland he had 14+3 outings for Bolton before going to play in Icelandic football where he became player/coach at Próttur Vogum under his old Pompey colleague Hermann Hreidarsson.

## WINCHESTER, Carl

**POSITION:** Midfielder / defender

**BIRTHPLACE:** Belfast, Northern Ireland

**DATE OF BIRTH:** 12/04/1993

**HEIGHT:** 5' 10" **WEIGHT:** 11st 9lbs

**SIGNED FROM:** Forest Green Rovers, 10/01/2021

**DEBUT:** v AFC Wimbledon, A, 16/01/2020

**LAST MATCH:**

**MOVED TO:**

**TEAMS:** Linfield, Oldham Athletic, Cheltenham Town, Forest Green Rovers, Sunderland, Shrewsbury Town (L)

**INTERNATIONAL:** Northern Ireland

**SAFC TOTALS:** 54+12 appearances / 4 goals (to June 2022)

**Lee Johnson made Winchester his first signing having had Carl play for him at Oldham. When Winchester arrived from Forest Green, where he had been captain, a few eyebrows were raised as he was coming from that level as an almost 28-year-old rather than being an up and coming youngster. Carl proved himself to be an astute signing. As a midfielder he looked after the ball and covered a lot of ground without being spectacular while when pressed into service as a right-back he excelled and further demonstrated his versatility by also playing within a back three and even on the left side of defence.**

In the promotion season of 2021-22 he earned a recall to the Northern Ireland squad without being able to add a second cap to the one he had won as a substitute for the last 15 minutes v Wales at the Aviva Stadium in Dublin in May 2011, an international watched by an attendance of just 529. Additionally, he made 27 appearances at junior levels, scoring once for the Under 19s.

Sunderland-born scout Tony Philliskirk spotted Winchester playing for Linfield Swifts against Glentoran and brought him to England with Oldham in 2010. Debuting in an FA Cup tie at Accrington in November of that year Winchester played 101+39 times and scored eight goals for the Boundary Park club before a January 2017 move to Cheltenham on a free transfer. After 69+1 games in which he netted six goals Carl was on the move again. Joining Forest Green Rovers in the summer of 2018 he scored ten goals in 108+4 appearances before stepping into the big-time with Sunderland.

## WOOD, Albert

**POSITION:** Inside-forward

**BIRTHPLACE:** Seaham Harbour, Co Durham

**DATE OF BIRTH:** 20/04/1907 - Q1 1966

**HEIGHT:** 5' 10" **WEIGHT:** 11st 0lbs

**SIGNED FROM:** Seaham Harbour, 15/08/1927

**DEBUT:** v Tottenham Hotspur, A, 22/10/1927

**LAST MATCH:** v Manchester United, H, 04/04/1931

**MOVED TO:** Fulham, 04/05/1931

**TEAMS:** Seaham Harbour, Sunderland, Fulham, Crewe Alexandra, Tranmere Rovers, New Brighton, Hartlepools United

**SAFC TOTALS:** 32 appearances / 11 goals

**A two-week trial at Falkirk alerted Sunderland of the local 20-year-old and after a single trial game at Roker Park Wood was immediately signed on professional forms. Albert debuted at Spurs two months later in what became a sixth successive defeat for Bob Kyle's side.**

He would get two more opportunities later in the season and just one the following term, but in 1929-30 proved his worth with 21 appearances in which he scored eight times, at one point scoring in five consecutive appearances. The following season found him on the fringe again. Despite three goals in only six games he was surplus to requirements and was swapped for Jimmy Temple, a player who would eventually pass away in 1960 as a consequence of shrapnel wounds suffered during World War Two.

Upon moving to Fulham, Albert scored on his debut against Swindon in March 1932 but it was to be his only appearance of the season as Fulham became Division Three South champions. Having made his comeback from injury with a goal the unlucky Wood did not play for another year, again returning with a goal as he scored three in eight games as Fulham narrowly missed out on back-to-back promotions. After just five games in his third season Albert managed just three (again returning with a goal) in the last of his four injury-hit years in London.

Folk at Craven Cottage must have been amazed when after moving to Crewe in 1935 Wood was ever-present for Alex, playing in all 42 games and managing a scoring ratio of exactly one in three as an inside-forward. A fee of £400 took him to Tranmere after a year at Gresty Road.

Eleven goals in 27 games for Tranmere preceded eleven in 46 for New Brighton at which point he returned to the north-east with Hartlepools United, although he did not play at all for the club, even in war-time games. At the start of World War Two Albert was listed as a general labourer living with his wife and four children in Seaham.

## WOOD, Norman

**POSITION:** Left-half

**BIRTHPLACE:** Millfield, Sunderland, Co Durham

**DATE OF BIRTH:** 10/08/1932

**HEIGHT:** 6' 1" **WEIGHT:** 12st 1lbs

**SIGNED FROM:** Silksworth CW, 01/05/1954

**DEBUT:** v Charlton Athletic, H, 12/02/1955

**LAST MATCH:** v Charlton Athletic, H, 12/02/1955

**MOVED TO:** Retired through injury, 30/06/1957

**TEAMS:** Ryhope CW, Silksworth CW, Sunderland

**SAFC TOTALS:** 1 appearance / 0 goals

**"Do you recognise anyone?" Norman asked me when I spotted a 1950s team picture on his kitchen wall. It was the only football related item in the house I was looking at and later bought in Grangetown, Sunderland. "That's me" he pointed out after I'd picked out Shack, Stan Anderson and the other players I knew.**

Wood had played one game in a home defeat. It was Norman's solitary competitive outing for the first-team, but unlike so many other players who became pro's without ever getting as much as a single game, that appearance indelibly printed Norman Wood's name into the record books as a Sunderland player. He had originally signed for Sunderland on part-time forms and ended up retiring from the game due to a left knee injury sustained in the last reserve game of 1954-55.

Norman had worked for Vaux breweries before joining SAFC and returned to employment with Vaux before becoming a primary school teacher at South Hylton during the 1970s and 80s. Continuing complications from his left knee injury led to his early retirement and later an amputation. One of his grandsons joined Darlington's Under 10s team around 2010.

## WOOD, William (Billy)

**POSITION:** Left-back

**BIRTHPLACE:** Barnsley, West Riding of Yorkshire

**DATE OF BIRTH:** 28/12/1927 - 22/07/2010

**HEIGHT:** 5' 8" **WEIGHT:** 11st 4lbs

**SIGNED FROM:** Spen Juniors, 11/10/1948

**DEBUT:** v Aston Villa, H, 01/04/1950

**LAST MATCH:** v Aston Villa, H, 01/04/1950

**MOVED TO:** Hull City, 31/07/1951

**TEAMS:** Spen Juniors, Sunderland, Hull City, Sheffield United, Wisbech Town, North Shields

**SAFC TOTALS:** 1 appearance / 0 goals

**Wood's solitary game was a victory before Raich Carter paid £5,000 to take him to Hull in the summer of 1951. Billy never got a game, Carter leaving the club very early in the season.**

After a year at Hull Billy signed for Sheffield United. There he played in the first five games of a season where the Blades would become Division Two Champions, but the journey home from Wood's last game - a 5-2 defeat at Plymouth - was perhaps one where he might have realised his destiny was not in top class football and he duly moved on to Wisbech Town.

Wood, Yorkshire-born, but raised in Blaydon, had signed professional forms with Sunderland immediately after being demobbed from the Royal Navy having already been on amateur terms with Sunderland while serving in the Far East; manager Bill Murray had sent him amateur forms to sign prior to the 1948-49 season to prevent Portsmouth signing him.

## WOODS, Martin Paul

**POSITION:** Midfielder

**BIRTHPLACE:** Airdrie, North Lanarkshire

**DATE OF BIRTH:** 01/01/1986

**HEIGHT:** 5' 11" **WEIGHT:** 11st 13lbs

**SIGNED FROM:** Leeds United, 05/07/2005

**DEBUT:** v Liverpool, A, 20/08/2005

**LAST MATCH:** v Birmingham City, A, 25/02/2006

**MOVED TO:** Rotherham United, 01/08/2006

**TEAMS:** Celtic, Leeds United, Hartlepool United (L), Sunderland, Rotherham United, Doncaster Rovers, Yeovil Town (L), Barnsley, Ross County, Shrewsbury Town, Ross County, Partick Thistle, Dundee (L), FC Halifax Town, Doncaster City (to July 2022)

**INTERNATIONAL:** Scotland Under 21

**SAFC TOTALS:** 2+6 appearances / 0 goals

**All but one of Woods' games for Sunderland were in the Premier League, but his time at the club was short-lived. By far his most memorable moment on the pitch came in a pre-season friendly against a local select side at Victoria on Vancouver Island in 2005 when he scored with a tremendous shot from fully 35 yards.**

In a long career Martin's highlight was winning the Scottish League Cup in March 2016 when he was part of the Ross County line-up that beat Alan Stubb's Hibs who included Anthony Stokes. Woods had scored in the semi-final against his boyhood club Celtic who he left as a teenager to do his scholarship with Leeds. Loaned to Hartlepool, the first of 5+3 appearances was at Oldham in a League One game in September 2004 before a Boxing Day debut for Leeds at Sunderland where he came on as a late sub for David Healy in a line-up that included Matt Kilgallon and Paul Butler. That couple of minutes at the Stadium of Light was Woods only appearance for Leeds before he joined Sunderland the following summer.

After a season Martin was released and returned to Yorkshire where he would spend much of his career. There were 34+5 games and his first four senior goals in a year at Rotherham before a seven-year spell at Doncaster where he scored ten times in 113+23 games as well as making three appearances in a 2008 loan to Yeovil. Freed in January 2014 there were 6+2 games in half a season at Barnsley. Two spells with Ross County were punctuated by a very short stint of four games with Shrewsbury. After a total of 88+6 games and five goals for the Staggies Martin moved to Partick in October 2015. There were 19+2 games there along with 23+2 and two goals on loan to Dundee where he played alongside former Sunderland reserves Roarie Deacon and Andrew Nelson, as well as Ethan Robson who was on loan from SAFC as Dundee finished bottom of the top-flight.

Woods then had a year without a club before joining FC Halifax in September 2020, going on to play 50+20 times scoring six goals in reaching the National League Play-Offs in 2022. By this time he had also he returned to Doncaster as an academy coach working with the Under 11s. In July 2022 Martin signed for Terry Curran's newly formed Doncaster City.

## WORRALL, William Edward (Bill)

**POSITION:** Goalkeeper

**BIRTHPLACE:** Thornaby, North Riding of Yorkshire

**DATE OF BIRTH:** 18/07/1886 - 29/11/1947

**HEIGHT:** 6' 1" **WEIGHT:** 12st 0lbs

**SIGNED FROM:** Shildon Athletic, 06/05/1908

**DEBUT:** v Nottingham Forest, A, 18/02/1911

**LAST MATCH:** v Manchester United, A, 29/04/1911

**MOVED TO:** Sunderland West End, 05/09/1911

**TEAMS:** South Bank, Middlesbrough, Shildon Athletic, Sunderland, Sunderland West End, Wingate Albion

**SAFC TOTALS:** 12 appearances / 0 goals

**Worrall's games were the last dozen of 1910-11 before he left over an apparent dispute over wages. It was not the first time there had been a difficulty regarding Bill as SAFC had been fined £5 for signing him prior to agreeing his transfer with Shildon.**

Rather like goalkeeper Alex Stepney scoring two penalties for Manchester United in 1973-74, Worrall was something of a penalty-taking expert. In 1907-08 he had a 100% record for Shildon Athletic for whom he took nine penalties.

Perhaps more comforting for a goalkeeper he also notably saved the first one ever taken by a visiting goalkeeper at Roker Park. This was on 10 October 1908 for the 'A' team (reserves) against North Shields Athletic.

In February 1912 Worrall emigrated to Canada to become coach of Vancouver FC. Appropriately for a lover of clean sheets he was managing a laundry in Essondale, Vancouver at the time of his death. Bill had married the widow of Sunderland great Jamie Millar, making him the uncle of Ernest Hodkin.

## WORTHINGTON, Frank Stuart

**POSITION:** Centre-forward

**BIRTHPLACE:** Shelf, West Riding of Yorkshire

**DATE OF BIRTH:** 23/11/1948 - 23/03/2021

**HEIGHT:** 5' 11" **WEIGHT:** 11st 9lbs

**SIGNED FROM:** Leeds United, 01/12/1982

**DEBUT:** v Ipswich Town, H, 04/12/1982

**LAST MATCH:** v WBA, H, 14/05/1983

**MOVED TO:** Southampton, 17/06/1983

**TEAMS:** Ripponden United, Huddersfield Town, Leicester City, Dallas Tornado (L), Bolton Wanderers, Philadelpia Fury (L), Birmingham City, Mjällby AIF, Tampa Bay Rowdies (L), Leeds United, Sunderland, Southampton, Brighton & Hove Albion, Manchester United (Guest), Tranmere Rovers, Stockport County, Preston North End, Stockport County, Cape Town Spurs, Hinckley Town, Chorley, Stalybridge Celtic, Galway United, Weymouth, Radcliffe Borough, Guiseley, Preston North End, Cemaes Bay, Halifax Town

**INTERNATIONAL:** England

**SAFC TOTALS:** 19+1 appearances / 2 goals

**Frank Worthington was a truly great player and a wonderfully colourful character. He came to Sunderland as a veteran, but his skills and showmanship will not be forgotten by those who saw him. Under Alan Durban Sunderland were bottom of the top-flight when Frank arrived mid-way through 1982-83, but by the end of the season he had helped guide Sunderland to safety.**

He won promotions with Huddersfield, Bolton and Southampton in 1970, 1978 and 1984, the Bolton promotion as a teammate of Peter Reid and Sam Allardyce. In the summer of his promotion with the Saints he played as a 'Guest' for Manchester United on an end of season tour of Australia and almost a year later guested for United again in a Testimonial match at Oxford for Peter Foley.

Like so many footballing mavericks 'Worthy' warranted far more than the eight England caps he won. His finest international performance came in May 1974 when he capped an outstanding display with a goal in a 2-2 Wembley draw with Argentina.

In 1979 Worthington scored his most iconic goal. It came for Bolton against Ipswich as Frank left England centre-back and future Sunderland player/manager Terry Butcher wondering where the ball had gone as he juggled the ball on the edge of the box with his back to goal, before flicking it over both of their heads and swivelling to volley home as it dropped. It was BBC TV's 'Goal of the Season'. The goal encapsulated the unorthodox magic of a player who later lit up Roker Park. He was not just a scorer of great goals but a great goalscorer. In the same season Frank was the top-flight's top scorer.

A massive Elvis Presley fan, off the pitch Frank was as stylish as he was on it. He lived life to the full as his highly entertaining autobiography, 'One Hump or Two?' made crystal clear. He loved football and played in every year from 1966 to 1987 in the Football League scoring 266 goals in 882 games. He then carried on playing until 1992, spending his last season as player/manager of Halifax, by which time he was 44.

Being a big name and flamboyant character Frank's love of the game was illustrated by how long he continued playing and at such low levels compared to his peak when it would have been much easier to retire and not take the knocks that uncompromising defenders might want to dish out to a star name. Worthington had football in his blood.

He came from a family where two of his brothers played professionally, David for Halifax, Barrow, Grimsby and Southend and Bob for Halifax, Middlesbrough, Notts County, Southend and Hartlepool. Additionally, Frank's nephew Gary played for Darlington, Wrexham, Wigan, Exeter and Doncaster while father-in-law Noel Dwyer was a Republic of Ireland international goalkeeper who played for Wolves, West Ham, Swansea, Plymouth and Charlton.

Although he became a soccer nomad playing in the USA, Sweden, South Africa, Wales and Ireland in addition to clubs at all levels in England, Frank gave long service to his first two professional clubs. He played 166+5 league games (41 goals) for Huddersfield and 209+1 (72 goals) for Leicester. He had joined the Foxes after failing a medical at Liverpool, but won his England caps with Leicester. From July 1985 to February 1987 Frank was player/manager at Tranmere while he was player/coach at Halifax. 'Worthy' was also great crack as an after-dinner speaker and remained in demand throughout his life.

## WRIGHT, Arthur William Tempest

**POSITION:** Left-half

**BIRTHPLACE:** Burradon, Northumberland

**DATE OF BIRTH:** 23/09/1919 - 27/05/1985

**HEIGHT:** 5' 10" **WEIGHT:** 12st 6lbs

**SIGNED FROM:** Hylton Colliery Juniors, 23/09/1934

**DEBUT:** v Leeds United, H, 16/04/1938

**LAST MATCH:** v Sheffield United, A, 14/03/1955

**MOVED TO:** Retired, 01/05/1955, but remained at SAFC as trainer/coach until June 1969

**TEAMS:** Hylton Colliery Juniors, Sunderland, Linfield (WW2 Guest)

**INTERNATIONAL:** England Schools

**SAFC TOTALS:** 281 appearances / 14 goals

**An unsung, but major figure at the club, Arthur's son Billy continues in 2022 keeping his dad's memory alive with a series of excellent talks and exhibitions as well as the website arthurwright.org.uk. Arthur started at the club as a youngster. He had a clerical job at Roker Park before signing as a professional.**

He was around when the league and cup was won in the thirties prior to making his debut before the war. Thirteen of his 281 games were played before World War Two. During the war he managed to make six appearances across three seasons and also added another seven in League North in 1945-46, those games in war-time football taking his total to 294. Had it not been for the years he served with the Royal Engineers he may well have totalled more than the 458 games which makes Len Ashurst the record outfield appearance maker. Several of his goals came from thunderous shots.

Ever-present in 1948-49 Arthur remained a regular the following term when Sunderland came so close to the league title. Throughout this post-war period he was the left-half behind the mercurial inside-forward Len Shackleton, doing much hard work for the team which helped allow Shack to shine. By 1953-54 Wright played just under half the games with his final two coming the following season as Arthur became more important behind the scenes.

As he stopped playing he was retained as a trainer and coach. Following the departure of Alan Brown in 1964 he became first-team trainer and played a major role in team selection until the appointment of George Hardwick. Later after Brian Clough left his role as youth-team manager Wright became youth-team manager from January 1968 to June 1969 - having served the club for over a third of a century.

As well as playing for England at schoolboy level, Wright twice represented the Football League against the League of Ireland and was called up by England for a 1949 tour of Scandinavia only to have to withdraw as two of his children were ill and he put his family first. During the war he played as a 'Guest' for Linfield while stationed near Belfast. He scored on his debut against Distillery and totalled ten goals in 13 games. Two of these appearances were successful cup finals, winning the Irish Cup after beating Belfast Celtic in 1941 and Glentoran a year later. More importantly, he also met his future wife while in Ireland.

## WRIGHT, Bailey Colin

**POSITION:** Centre-back

**BIRTHPLACE:** Melbourne, Australia

**DATE OF BIRTH:** 28/07/1992

**HEIGHT:** 6' 0" **WEIGHT:** 12st 6lbs

**SIGNED FROM:** Bristol City, 02/08/2020, after loan from 21/01/2020

**DEBUT:** v Tranmere Rovers, A, 29/01/2020

**LAST MATCH:**

**MOVED TO:**

**TEAMS:** Dandenong Thunder, Victoria Institute of Sport, Preston North End, Bristol City, Sunderland

**INTERNATIONAL:** Australia

**SAFC TOTALS:** 82+9 appearances / 4 goals (to June 2022)

**A member of the Australia team that played England at the Stadium of Light in 2016, Wright's 25th cap came in the summer of 2022 as he helped his country to qualify for the FIFA World Cup by beating Peru on penalties in a Play-Off game in Qatar.**

It completed an outstanding season for the defender who had been a major influence in Sunderland winning promotion via a Play-Off final with Wycombe Wanderers. Wright had flown to that game by helicopter away from the rest of his team having been isolated through potential illness. Throughout the season his calmness, authority and experience had helped the club ride the rollercoaster of a campaign that ended in triumph. On the night of the promotion party at the team hotel in London it was Bailey who reached for the DJ's microphone to lead the chant of 'We are going up. Say we are going up".

It was the second time Wright had won a Play-Off final. He was part of Simon Grayson's Preston team who thumped Swindon 4-0 in 2015. That was one of 198+7 games for Preston (8 goals). He moved to Bristol City in January 2017 where he played for his future Sunderland manager Lee Johnson and made 81+2 appearances, his only goal coming against Norwich. During his time with Sunderland, Bailey studied for an MSc in Sports Directorship at the University of East London.

## WRIGHT, David (Dave)

**POSITION:** Inside-forward / centre-forward

**BIRTHPLACE:** Kirkcaldy, Fifeshire

**DATE OF BIRTH:** 05/10/1905 - 15/07/1953

**HEIGHT:** 5' 9" **WEIGHT:** 12st 4lbs

**SIGNED FROM:** Cowdenbeath, 30/04/1927

**DEBUT:** v Portsmouth, H, 27/08/1927

**LAST MATCH:** v Liverpool, H, 14/12/1929

**MOVED TO:** Liverpool, 12/03/1930

**TEAMS:** Raith Rovers, East Fife, Cowdenbeath, Sunderland, Liverpool, Hull City, Bradford Park Avenue

**SAFC TOTALS:** 53 appearances / 8 goals

**More of a maker than a taker of goals, Wright's modest ratio of goals to games at Sunderland was his undoing because as a footballer his creativity and industry could be sublime. As the Newcastle Daily Chronicle reported of his performance in a 4-2 September 1927 win over Birmingham, "By his speed, amazing footwork and true instinct for the game, Wright has proved himself to be the man Sunderland have wanted for so long. He was the best forward on the field".**

Reporting on the same game The Journal said, "Wright easily took the honours up front. With every game he is developing speed and in this game he swerved and feinted, headed and passed the ball with wonderful trickery and judgement ...he had the visitors' defence tied in knots". Ultimately though forwards need goals. Six in 33 during 1927-28, including the vital opening goal in the last-game relegation decider at Middlesbrough, was to be Wright's best return with one goal from ten games the identical record in his next two seasons before he moved on to Liverpool three months after his final match proved to be against the Merseysiders. His move in a double deal involving Gordon Gunson was valued at £4,800.

## WRIGHT, Dave (Continued)

At Liverpool he found the net more regularly, scoring 35 times in exactly 100 games, his best seasons bringing 14 and 13 goals with his best display being a hat-trick against Newcastle in 1931. A summer 1934 transfer to Hull brought eleven goals from 33 games before a move to Bradford Park Avenue where after just one goal in 20 games he retired to run a newsagents shop in Kirkcaldy before settling back on Humberside where he died after a lingering illness aged just 47.

As a boy Wright had come to the fore with Dunniker Juniors from whom he joined Raith Rovers, but his senior debut did not arrive until he moved to East Fife in September 1924 and proceeded to score 25 goals in a little over 50 games. The goals kept coming at Cowdenbeath where 17 goals in 35 games led to Sunderland flourishing their chequebook to the tune of £4,000.

## WRIGHT, Stephen John

**POSITION:** Right-back

**BIRTHPLACE:** Bootle, Merseyside

**DATE OF BIRTH:** 08/02/1980

**HEIGHT:** 6' 0" **WEIGHT:** 12st 8lbs

**SIGNED FROM:** Liverpool, 15/08/2002

**DEBUT:** v Blackburn Rovers, A, 17/08/2002

**LAST MATCH:** v Luton Town, A, 06/05/2007

**MOVED TO:** Coventry City, 08/08/2008

**TEAMS:** Liverpool, Crewe Alexandra (L), Sunderland, Stoke City (L), Coventry City, Brentford, Hartlepool United, Wrexham, Aberystwyth Town, Rhyl, Denbigh Town

**INTERNATIONAL:** England Under 21

**SAFC TOTALS:** 99+6 appearances / 2 goals

**Thirty-nine league starts in the 2004-05 promotion year was the best of Stephen's six seasons at Sunderland, the last three seeing him play just six times and go on loan to Stoke (16/0). A knee injury had ruined the first six months of 2005-06 after which he was sent off in his comeback game and then picked up an ankle injury.**

An Evertonian as a boy, Wright trained with the Blues before signing for Liverpool where his dad John was kit-man and where Stephen was first named on the bench in November 1998 against Celta Vigo. Almost exactly two years later he debuted as a sub in an 8-0 away win over Stoke in the League Cup. As part of his development there were 22 games on loan to Crewe. Stephen scored once in 21+1 games for Liverpool, a Kop End header in a Champions League game against Borussia Dortmund. He was an unused substitute against Alavés in the 2001 UEFA Cup final.

Upon leaving Sunderland he signed for Coventry City where after a year he became club captain. After 55 appearances for the Sky Blues, Wright joined Brentford (11/0), Hartlepool (11/0) and Wrexham (59/1) with whom he played twice at Wembley, losing to Newport in the 2013 Conference Play-Off final, but beating Grimsby on penalties in the FA Trophy.

Stephen stayed in Wales, playing 15 times in the Welsh Premiership for Aberystwyth in 2014-15 followed by 17 games for Rhyl and finally playing in the Cymru Alliance with Denbigh Town before retiring in March 2017 to become youth coach back at Wrexham.

For England he played at the FIFA World Youth Championships in 1999. The first of ten Under 21 caps came at Middlesbrough in August 2000 when he came on as a sub for Titus Bramble in a 6-1 win over Georgia. Other subs that night included Paul Thirlwell and future Sunderland coach and caretaker/manager Robbie Stockdale. Outside of the game Stephen was one of several Sunderland players to invest in the magazine Golf Punk in 2006.

## WRIGHT, Thomas (Tommy)

**POSITION:** Forward

**BIRTHPLACE:** Blairhall, Clackmannanshire

**DATE OF BIRTH:** 20/01/1928 - 05/05/2011

**HEIGHT:** 5' 9" **WEIGHT:** 11st 0lbs

**SIGNED FROM:** Partick Thistle, 10/03/1949

**DEBUT:** v Portsmouth, H, 12/03/1949

**LAST MATCH:** v Bolton Wanderers, H, 02/10/1954

**MOVED TO:** East Fife, 04/01/1955

**TEAMS:** Blairhall Star, Partick Thistle, Sunderland, East Fife, Oldham Athletic, North Shields, Horden CW, Spennymoor United

**INTERNATIONAL:** Scotland

**SAFC TOTALS:** 180 appearances / 54 goals

**Top-scorer at "The Bank of England Club' in 1953-54 when he scored 18 times, half-way through the following season Tommy was a make-weight in the deal that brought Charlie 'Cannonball' Fleming from East Fife. Tommy was no shrinking violet himself. In March 1951 he had crashed into a goalpost at the Roker End with such force in a match against Arsenal that he was out of action for a year.**

An outside or inside-right who could also play at centre-forward Tommy's memory had largely faded when I visited him in a care home in Ashbrooke shortly before his death, but constantly he would declare, 'Rock on Tommy!' with a beaming smile when prompted to remember his exploits in red and white.

Capped in all three of the Home Internationals in 1952-53 while with Sunderland, despite often playing wide he maintained a good goalscoring record at East Fife scoring once per two of his 36 games. He had done well with 23 in 71 at Partick, helping The Jags to their highest-ever place of third in 1947-48 before coming to Sunderland for £9,000 having signed off with a hat-trick in his final appearance against Dundee. At Partick he had debuted against Airdrieonians alongside Bill Shankly who was playing as a 'Guest' while stationed nearby. Wright would play again for Thistle as a 'Guest' himself, returning from Sunderland at the end of the season to play in two Charity Cup games. At the end of Tommy's career there were two goals from seven appearances at Oldham before he played in non-league back in the north-east.

His son of the same name played for Leeds, Oldham and Leicester while nephew Jackie Sinclair was a Scottish Cup finalist with Dunfermline and a Fairs Cup winner with Newcastle. Another nephew, Willie Sinclair, listed Falkirk and Huddersfield amongst his clubs.

## WYKE, Charles Thomas (Charlie)

**POSITION:** Centre-forward

**BIRTHPLACE:** Middlesbrough, Cleveland

**DATE OF BIRTH:** 06/12/1992

**HEIGHT:** 5' 10" **WEIGHT:** 11st 0lbs

**SIGNED FROM:** Bradford City, 01/08/2018

**DEBUT:** v Oxford United, H, 01/09/2018

**LAST MATCH:** v Lincoln City, H, 22/05/2021

**MOVED TO:** Wigan Athletic, 07/07/2021

**TEAMS:** Middlesbrough, Kettering Town, Hartlepool United (L), AFC Wimbledon (L), Carlisle United, Bradford City, Sunderland, Wigan Athletic (to June 2022)

**SAFC TOTALS:** 88+26 appearances / 42 goals

**Thirty-one goals in his final season at Sunderland included four headed goals in one game against Doncaster and a strike in his final appearance in a Play-Off semi-final with Lincoln. That record earned Charlie Sunderland's Player of the Year award and a place in the PFA League One Team of the Season.**

However, despite that success most supporters were not particularly devastated when he left at the end of his contract to throw in his lot with newly-monied Wigan. All but one of those 31 goals were one touch finishes, many of them having been 'put on a plate' by the mercurial Aiden McGeady - including all four of those headers v Doncaster. Fans knew that in the wings was recent signing Ross Stewart who was generally considered to be an all-round better footballer who was also capable of scoring regularly. This is in no way meant to belittle Wyke. Any forward who scores 30 or more goals at any level in a season of modern football has done well. That excellent 2020-21 season was by far Wyke's best on Wearside.

Despite a debut goal, after being on the pitch as a sub for seven minutes, there were only four others in his first season when he played at Wembley in both the Football League (Checkatrade) Trophy and League One Play-Off finals. His second term brought six goals, but generally too many of his performances in his first two seasons seemed sluggish - probably accounted for by his injury problems.

The Teessider came to Sunderland from Bradford City where he had netted 22 times in 60+2 games. Previously he had a good ratio of 39 goals in 72+17 games in two years with Carlisle. Charlie had not played at all for Middlesbrough who loaned him to Kettering (12/2), Hartlepool (36+4/6) and AFC Wimbledon (11+6/2).

At Wigan he scored five times in 17 games before collapsing in training in November 2021. He was hospitalised and missed the rest of the campaign. Thankfully, Charlie returned to training and was expected to resume his career with the Latics in 2022-23 after they were promoted along with Sunderland in his first season.

## WYLDE, Rodger James

**POSITION:** Centre-forward

**BIRTHPLACE:** Sheffield, West Riding of Yorkshire

**DATE OF BIRTH:** 08/03/1954

**HEIGHT:** 6' 1" **WEIGHT:** 12st 0lbs

**SIGNED FROM:** Sporting Lisbon, 17/06/1984

**DEBUT:** v Nottingham Forest, A, 01/09/1984

**LAST MATCH:** v Tottenham Hotspur, H, 21/11/1984

**MOVED TO:** Barnsley, 04/12/1984

**TEAMS:** Sheffield Wednesday, Burnley (L), Oldham Athletic, Sporting Lisbon, Sunderland, Barnsley, Rotherham United (L), Stockport County

**SAFC TOTALS:** 12+4 appearances / 5 goals

**It might be unkind to label Rodger Wylde a poor man's Frank Worthington, but he was reminiscent of 'Worthy' in style on and off the pitch - if not quite as flamboyant as Frank - albeit he was nicknamed Oscar at Wednesday. As a student, I often watched him alongside Ian Porterfield for Len Ashurst's Sheffield Wednesday. Rodger was a crowd favourite at Hillsborough and it was no surprise when Ashurst brought him to Sunderland.**

Nor was it unexpected when two of Wednesday's near neighbours brought him to their clubs to see if he could sprinkle some of the stardust and goals he liberally supplied in Sheffield. Rodger scored 66 goals in 182+12 games for the Owls for whom he debuted against Middlesbrough in November 1972 shortly after scoring a double hat-trick for the reserves. Wylde signed off against Chesterfield in February 1980 having also played alongside Chris Turner, Fred McIver and future Sunderland managerial team Ken Knighton and Peter Eustace in the meantime.

After suffering relegation from Division Two in 1975 Rodger blossomed after the appointment of Ashurst, top-scoring with 25 goals in 1976-77 and continuing to do well under Jack Charlton, although Big Jack's acquisition of Terry Curran saw a rival for the maverick in the team's line-up. Sold somewhat reluctantly shortly before the Owls won promotion in 1980 Rodger went to Oldham where he bagged 51 goals in 113 games, top-scoring in each of his three seasons before going to strut his stuff in Lisbon with Sporting.

Returning to play for Ashurst Rodger's time at Sunderland was his only spell in the English top-flight. After 19 goals in 52 games for Barnsley and one in six on a loan to Rotherham, Wylde went to Stockport where he combined playing with gaining a BSc (Hons) Degree in physiotherapy at Salford University. He took up a post as physio at Stockport, holding that job for over two decades before becoming Head of Sport Science and Medicine at Chesterfield in 2014, staying there until joining Peterborough as physio in February 2022.

Inducted into the Stockport County Hall of Fame in 2006, Rodger also fronted a rock band - called 'Fracture' and produced an unusual memoir, 'The Wylde Man of Football' which discussed his battle with cancer when he was 31.

## WYLIE, Thomas (Tom)

**POSITION:** Inside-left / centre-forward

**BIRTHPLACE:** Linwood, Renfrewshire

**DATE OF BIRTH:** 10/11/1907

**HEIGHT:** 5' 7" **WEIGHT:** 10st 7lbs

**SIGNED FROM:** Motherwell, 20/07/1936

**DEBUT:** v Preston North End, A, 02/01/1937

**LAST MATCH:** v Manchester City, H, 14/04/1937

**MOVED TO:** Queen of the South, 27/01/1938

**TEAMS:** Benburb, Motherwell, Sunderland, Queen of the South, Peebles Rovers

**SAFC TOTALS:** 7 appearances / 3 goals

**Nineteen goals in 30 games at Motherwell led to a move to Sunderland where Wylie's goals-to-games ratio was decent when he got the chance. However, if it had been tough to get a game at Motherwell who were doing so well at the time Wylie's appearances were spread over five years despite his goals, it was even harder to get into the Sunderland side who he joined just after they had become league champions.**

Indeed, after equalling Bobby Gurney's record of scoring nine goals in a reserve game (v West Stanley 12/09/1936) Tom still had to wait almost another three months for a first-team opportunity. All of his appearances came in the first of his two seasons, but he never got another game despite a goal on his final appearance.

A mechanic before becoming a footballer Wylie joined Queen of the South from Sunderland, but only scored once in seven outings in a season there before joining Peebles Rovers. Tom joined the Royal Armoured Corps in June 1942 and after training in northern England served out in the Middle East.

# X

## XHEMAJLI, Arbenit (Arby)

**POSITION:** Centre-back

**BIRTHPLACE:** Brugg, Switzerland

**DATE OF BIRTH:** 23/04/1998

**HEIGHT:** 6' 3" **WEIGHT:** 12st 11lbs

**SIGNED FROM:** Neuchatel Xamax, 04/09/2020

**DEBUT:** v Aston Villa Under 21s, H, 08/09/2020

**LAST MATCH:** v Fleetwood Town, H, 08/03/2022

**MOVED TO:** Contract not renewed, 30/06/2022

**TEAMS:** FC Zurich, Neuchâtel Xamax, Sunderland, Vaduz

**INTERNATIONAL:** Kosovo

**SAFC TOTALS:** 5 appearances / 0 goals

**Incredibly unlucky with injuries Xhemajli debuted in an 8-1 Football League (Papa John's) Trophy win over the Under 21s of Aston Villa, but soon afterwards suffered a knee injury in training on international duty with Kosovo who he had debuted for against Gibraltar in October 2019.**

The injury meant he did not play for the first-team again for 14 months, returning in the same competition. A league debut followed in February 2022 when after a slightly shaky start he did well in a 3-0 win at Wigan. However, after playing in the next two matches Arby found his time at the club was up when he was released at the end of the season. In August 2022 he joined Swiss side Vaduz.

Playing in an 8-1 win on his Sunderland debut paled into insignificance compared to his first game for Swiss side Neuchâtel Xamax. On that occasion in a Swiss Cup tie against Montfaucon on 12 August 2017 his side amazingly won 21-0! Arbenit went on to make 33+7 appearances in the Swiss league scoring against Thun and FC Sion.

# Y

## YEDLIN, DeAndre Roselle

**POSITION:** Full-back

**BIRTHPLACE:** Seattle, USA

**DATE OF BIRTH:** 09/07/1993

**HEIGHT:** 5' 9" **WEIGHT:** 11st 7lbs

**SIGNED FROM:** Tottenham Hotspur, 01/09/2015, on loan

**DEBUT:** v Manchester City, H, 22/09/2015

**LAST MATCH:** v Watford, A, 15/05/2016

**MOVED TO:** Tottenham Hotspur, 16/05/2016, end of loan

**TEAMS:** Seattle Sounders, Tottenham Hotspur, Sunderland (L), Newcastle United, Galatasaray, Inter Miami (to June 2022)

**INTERNATIONAL:** USA

**SAFC TOTALS:** 23+2 appearances / 0 goals

**Signed when Dick Advocaat was in charge, Yedlin became part of Sam Allardyce's side that steered clear of relegation with big end-of-season wins against Chelsea and Everton. A pacey full-back who was at his best going forward, the USA international was on loan from Tottenham and later returned to the north-east to win the Championship with Newcastle United in 2017.**

DeAndre stayed with the Magpies for four and a half years playing 105+20 games and scoring three times before transferring to Galatasaray. Debuting in a big win away to Fenerbahce he went on to play in the Champions and Europa Leagues, but was sent off in the only game he scored in against Rizespor.

After 31+4 games in a year in Turkey, Yedlin joined Inter Miami where, as of the end of June 2022, he had played 15+1 times and was yet to score. Yedlin had made 44+1 appearances (1 goal) for Seattle Sounders before joining Spurs in August 2014. The American's first-team experience at Tottenham was restricted to just eleven minutes of a Premier League defeat at home to Aston Villa. Before coming to prominence with Seattle, Yedlin played in youth football for Emerald City, Crossfire Premier, Northwest Nationals and college side. Akron Zips.

Capped 74 times by the USA (to June 2022), in 2014 Yedlin was a member of their FIFA World Cup squad alongside Jozy Altidore and played as a substitute against Portugal, Germany and Belgium.

## YORK, Andrew (Andy)

**POSITION:** Left-back

**BIRTHPLACE:** Newsham, Northumberland

**DATE OF BIRTH:** 14/06/1894 - Q4 1977

**HEIGHT:** 5' 10" **WEIGHT:** 12st 0lbs

**SIGNED FROM:** Bedlington United, 08/05/1921

**DEBUT:** v Arsenal, H, 08/10/1921

**LAST MATCH:** v Arsenal, H, 08/10/1921

**MOVED TO:** Coventry City, 06/05/1923

**TEAMS:** Blyth Spartans, Sleekburn Albion, Bedlington United, Sunderland, Coventry City, Northampton Town, Lincoln City, Newark Town, Scarborough

**SAFC TOTALS:** 1 appearance / 0 goals

**A coal miner from leaving school in his early teens before becoming a professional footballer, this defender played under the name Yorke although officially he was York.**

At Coventry he debuted in a home defeat by Barnsley in August 1923 and only played once more that season before getting 15 games the following year. A move to nearby Northampton saw him play 21 times before he found a home at Lincoln where he made 105 appearances and then dropped into non-league. While he was with Lincoln, Andy ran a sweet shop, but became a pub landlord after retiring from the game. During World War One he served for three years in the Royal Field Artillery.

## YORK, Charles Henry (Charlie)

**POSITION:** Inside-right / centre-forward

**BIRTHPLACE:** Edinburgh, Midlothian

**DATE OF BIRTH:** 27/03/1883 -20/03/1955

**HEIGHT:** 5' 8½" **WEIGHT:** 10st 6lbs

**SIGNED FROM:** Derby County, 11/01/1904

**DEBUT:** v Wednesday, A, 13/02/1904

**LAST MATCH:** v West Bromwich Albion, H, 27/02/1904

**MOVED TO:** Heart of Midlothian, 26/05/1904

**TEAMS:** Camberley, Reading, Derby County, Sunderland, Heart of Midlothian, Southampton, Sheppey United, South Farnborough

**SAFC TOTALS:** 2 appearances / 0 goals

**The season before coming to Sunderland York had played in the English (FA) Cup final for Derby. Deputising for the legendary, but injured, Steve Bloomer he became part of a side thrashed 6-0 by Bury, a score that remains a record only equalled by Manchester City's walloping of Watford in 2019.**

Rather like Andrew York who added an E onto his name while playing, Charlie did the same thing. He had been christened John Charles Henry York, but never used the name John in any official documents. Having played junior football for Reading he played 27 games for Derby scoring six times. After his brief stint at Sunderland, York returned to his home city of Edinburgh with Hearts, but only played in two league games and six in total including a friendly with Lochgelly United in which he scored.

He was still only 21 when in December 1904 he signed for Southampton who he had played for in a trial Hampshire League game for the reserves three years earlier. This was at a time when he worked as a barman at his father's pub, The Squirrel Tavern in Farnborough. In 1898 he had been known to be playing for Camberley. Having signed for the Saints he made just three Western League appearances before going into local non-league where he had two spells at South Farnborough. A forward who apparently liked to put himself about but was lacking in speed, he left the game early and followed his father into the trade of being a publican.

## YORKE, Dwight Eversley

**POSITION:** Midfielder

**BIRTHPLACE:** Canaan, Tobago

**DATE OF BIRTH:** 03/11/1971

**HEIGHT:** 5' 10" **WEIGHT:** 12st 12lbs

**SIGNED FROM:** Sydney, 31/08/2006

**DEBUT:** v Leicester City, H, 16/09/2006

**LAST MATCH:** v Manchester United, H, 11/04/2009

**MOVED TO:** Contract not renewed, 31/05/2009

**TEAMS:** St Clairs, Signal Hill, Aston Villa, Manchester United, Blackburn Rovers, Birmingham City, Sydney, Sunderland

**INTERNATIONAL:** Trinidad & Tobago

**SAFC TOTALS:** 49+13 appearances / 6 goals

**Dwight Yorke enjoyed a fabulous career in England mainly with Aston Villa and Manchester United. In his mid-thirties he had gone to sample life in the slower pace of football in Australia (winning the league in 2006) and enjoy the Sydney life-style when his phone rang. On the line was his old Manchester United teammate Roy Keane persuading him to swap the Down Under sunshine to come to Sunderland.**

For all Dwight's playboy image his love of the game was illustrated by the acceptance of the offer. Approaching his 35th birthday when he came to Wearside, Yorke was no longer the sprightly, nimble but strong attacker he had been in his heyday. Instead he was a deep-lying midfielder who used his experience and vision allied to his adhesive touch to still play an effective role despite his advancing years.

With Villa he scored in the 1996 League (Coca-Cola) Cup final as Howard Wilkinson's Leeds (who included Andy Gray) were beaten. With Manchester United he won the Premier League three times including in 1998-99 when the treble was completed with the FA Cup and Champions League - the Intercontinental Cup following later in the calendar year. In United's treble-winning season he was the Premier League's top scorer with 18 Premier League goals & 29 in total. The same season Yorke was also named in the PFA Team of the Year. His partnership with future Sunderland striker Andy Cole was a big factor in his success at Old Trafford where he also numbered John O'Shea and Wes Brown amongst his teammates. In four seasons in Manchester, Yorke scored 66 goals including three hat-tricks from 120+40 appearances in which his only red card came at Sunderland in November 2000.

July 2002 brought a transfer to Blackburn for £10m less than the £12.5m which had been paid to Aston Villa for his signature. Given Villa's stature as one of the game's great historical clubs the following description in the Aston Villa Complete Record is worth noting, "Dwight Yorke ranks among the greatest players in the club's history - and it is debatable if anyone has been more flamboyant". Sixty of his 98 goals for Villa came in the Premier League. In total he played 247+40 games for the club. In two years at Blackburn from 2002 to 2004 he scored 19 goals in 54+20 appearances before 6+10 games and two goals for Birmingham prior to his switch to Sydney.

Born in Tobago, Yorke played 72 times for his country in which he scored 19 goals. The final eight of these caps and four of the goals came while he was with Sunderland. He was captain at the 2006 FIFA World Cup when his teammates included Carlos Edwards, Kenwyne Jones and Stern John. Yorke later became assistant manager of the Trinidad and Tobago team and in July 2022 took over as manager of Macarthur FC in the Australian A League. He had made it public that he had applied for numerous managerial positions in England including at Sunderland and Villa.

A biography, 'Born to Score' was published in 2009 while his homeland has a stadium named after him in Bacolet. His brother Clint played for Trinidad &Tobago at cricket, a sport Dwight adores and has been seen carrying drinks out for the West Indies.

## YORSTON, Benjamin Collard (Benny)

**POSITION:** Centre-forward / Inside-forward

**BIRTHPLACE:** Nigg, Aberdeenshire

**DATE OF BIRTH:** 14/10/1905 - 19/11/1977

**HEIGHT:** 5' 5" **WEIGHT:** 9st 12lbs

**SIGNED FROM:** Aberdeen, 23/01/1932

**DEBUT:** v Blackpool, A, 30/01/1932

**LAST MATCH:** v Aston Villa, A, 27/01/1934

**MOVED TO:** Middlesbrough, 01/02/1934

**TEAMS:** Mugiemoss, Richmond, Montrose, Aberdeen, Sunderland, Middlesbrough, St Mirren (WW2 Guest), Aldershot (WW2 Guest), Brentford (WW2 Guest), Reading (WW2 Guest), Lincoln City, (WW2 Guest), West Ham United (WW2 Guest), Dundee United

**INTERNATIONAL:** Scotland

**SAFC TOTALS:** 52 appearances / 26 goals

**One of the smallest players to ever play for Sunderland, Benny was spring-heeled and surprisingly good in the air. Coming into the team in 1931-32 he scored seven goals in his first five games and continued to have an excellent goals record, registering a hat-trick against Stoke in September 1933.**

He had been even more prolific with Aberdeen. 125 goals in 156 appearances included a club record 38 from 38 league games (including three hat-tricks) in 1929-30, a season in which he added a further eight from just four cup matches. In February 1931 he won his only Scotland cap in a goalless draw away to Northern Ireland.

Benny had signed for the Dons on 27 March 1927 having originally come to Pittodrie to work in the office while playing for Mugiemoss Juniors and subsequently Richmond while he was also allowed to play for Montrose after a handful of third team appearances for Aberdeen. First given an opportunity on a 1927 tour of South Africa, a debut goal away to Raith Rovers on 20 August that year was the first of 17 in 28 games and the goals just kept coming for a natural goalscorer who was good with both feet.

Having paid £2000 for Yorston, Sunderland got excellent value and recouped the precise sum of £1,184 when selling him to Middlesbrough who were persuaded to take him instead of Raich Carter who the Teessiders had originally enquired about. At Boro Benny played alongside future Sunderland manager George Hardwick and bagged 54 goals in 159 games despite a broken leg at Blackpool in December 1937 checking his progress.

During World War Two when he was part of the Army Physical Corps he made a single appearance for Aldershot and Reading, played twice for West Ham, three times for Lincoln and scored five goals in eight games for Brentford, while after the war he played one official game for Dundee United, a 3-2 home defeat by Albion Rovers on 24 November 1945 the day after he signed for the club. He went on to become chief scout for Bury and also scouted for Barnsley before going into the flat-letting business in South Kensington in London. Benny's nephew Henry Yorston was a Scotland international who scored 141 goals in 277 games for Aberdeen between 1947 and 1957 before retiring at the age of 28 to become a fish-market porter.

## YOUNG, David

**POSITION:** Defender
**BIRTHPLACE:** Newcastle, Northumberland
**DATE OF BIRTH:** 12/11/1945
**HEIGHT:** 5' 10" **WEIGHT:** 10st 9lbs
**SIGNED FROM:** Newcastle United, 04/01/1973
**DEBUT:** v Brighton & Hove Albion, H, 06/01/1973
**LAST MATCH:** v Fulham, H, 16/03/1974
**MOVED TO:** Charlton Athletic, 30/07/1974
**TEAMS:** Newcastle United, Sunderland, Charlton Athletic, Southend United, Dartford
**SAFC TOTALS:** 34+7 appearances / 1 goal

**David Young is famed in Sunderland for a game he did not play in rather than one he did. In the days of a single substitute he was the unused twelfth man when the FA Cup was sensationally won in 1973. He played fewer than 50 times for the red and whites, but did play in all four of the games in the European Cup Winners' Cup in 1973-74. He had earlier played six European games amongst his total of 52+4/1 for his hometown team Newcastle.**

Upon leaving Sunderland, David played 89 games for Charlton and 67 for Southend captaining the Addicks to promotion in 1975 and winning promotion again with the Shrimpers three years later. David settled in the south, working in sports-centre management in Orpington, Bexleyheath and Gillingham.

Always delighted to return to the north-east for reunions, David regularly brought his FA Cup medal and generously allowed people to handle it. As part of the cup-winning squad he received the Freedom of the City of Sunderland in 2022.

## YOUNG, John (Jack)

**POSITION:** Centre-forward
**BIRTHPLACE:** Burnbank, Lanarkshire
**DATE OF BIRTH:** 01/10/1888 - Date of death unknown
**HEIGHT:** 5' 7" **WEIGHT:** 10st 9lbs
**SIGNED FROM:** Bradford City, 06/12/1911
**DEBUT:** v West Bromwich Albion, H, 09/12/1911
**LAST MATCH:** v Manchester City, A, 30/03/1912
**MOVED TO:** Port Vale, 14/08/1912
**TEAMS:** Burnbank Athletic, Bradford City, Sunderland, Port Vale, Hamilton Academical
**INTERNATIONAL:** Scotland Junior
**SAFC TOTALS:** 15 appearances / 1 goal

**Two goals against Sunderland in April 1911 took Young's total for Bradford City to eight in seven games since coming down from Scotland. Three days earlier he had scored a winner against Newcastle having hit a hat-trick against Wednesday the previous weekend.**

It was enough to persuade Sunderland to purchase him later that year after he had played three more games for the Bantams where his goals helped City finish level on points with third-placed Sunderland. Scoring the winning goal on his debut against WBA augured well but Young did not score again and was discarded the following year. He went on to score eleven goals in 20 Central League games for Port Vale in 1912-13 and one in four for Hamilton Academical the following season.

## YOUNG, Robert Thornton (Bob)

**POSITION:** Left-back
**BIRTHPLACE:** Brandon, Co Durham
**DATE OF BIRTH:** 18/02/1894 - 06/09/1960
**HEIGHT:** 5' 8" **WEIGHT:** 12st 4lbs
**SIGNED FROM:** Esh Winning Rangers, 25/03/1914
**DEBUT:** v Bradford City, H, 10/04/1915
**LAST MATCH:** v Everton, A, 04/02/1925
**MOVED TO:** Retired, 31/05/1926
**TEAMS:** Brancepeth Villa, Esh Winning Rangers, Sunderland
**SAFC TOTALS:** 56 appearances / 0 goals

**Having debuted in the third from last match before the Football League was suspended for World War One, Young went on the gain the Military Medal whilst serving in the Durham Light Infantry. This was for his bravery when severely wounded at Cambrin on the Western Front in France on 10 December 1916**.

In 1918-19 he played 18 times in what was called the Victory League, games in addition to those in the totals listed here. When the Football League resumed in 1919-20 Young had his best season, playing 28 times including four games in the FA Cup. Thereafter, he was a reserve player playing just 16 times in four seasons. During this period he captained the reserve team, winning the North Eastern League in 1924-25. Three times he gained representative honours for the league in games against the Central League.

After the removal of his left cartilage in 1925 Young learned to be a trainer at Sunderland under the highly-regarded Billy Williams. After being given a free transfer Bob became trainer at Norwich City in May 1927. He was to stay with the Canaries for almost two decades and later be inducted into their Hall of Fame. Having remained as trainer until February 1937 at that point he took over as manager and remained in post until the end of World War Two.

## YOUNGER, Oliver James (Ollie)

**POSITION:** Centre-back
**BIRTHPLACE:** Skipton, North Yorkshire
**DATE OF BIRTH:** 14/11/1999
**HEIGHT:** 6 0" **WEIGHT:** 12st 1lb
**SIGNED FROM:** Free agent, 16/09/2020
**DEBUT:** v Fleetwood Town, A, 10/11/2020
**LAST MATCH:** v Oldham Athletic, H, 01/12/2021
**MOVED TO:** Doncaster Rovers, 19/01/2022
**TEAMS:** Burnley, St Patricks Athletic (L), Sunderland, Doncaster Rovers (to June 2022)
**SAFC TOTALS:** 7+2 appearances / 0 goals

**On his only league appearance for Sunderland, Ollie did well in an unfamiliar right-back position and was replaced after 52 minutes of a home win over Rochdale. Other than another decent display in a League (Carabao) Cup win at Port Vale all of Younger's other appearances for the Black Cats came in the Football League (Papa John's) Trophy.**

Having moved to Doncaster his fourth game for Rovers was back at Sunderland where he helped his side to victory. By the end of that 2021-22 campaign Ollie had played 12+4 games, but was unable to stop Doncaster going down from League One.

He had started as a seven-year-old with Burnley at the Clarets Development Centre progressing on to his scholarship and being Player of the Year at Under 18 level before signing a professional contract. In February 2020 a loan move to Irish Premier League outfit St Patrick's Athletic was restricted to two games due to Covid 19.

# Z

## ZENDEN, Boudewijn (Bolo)

**POSITION:** Midfielder

**BIRTHPLACE:** Maastricht, Netherlands

**DATE OF BIRTH:** 15/08/1976

**HEIGHT:** 5' 8" **WEIGHT:** 11st 0lbs

**SIGNED FROM:** Free agent, 16/10/2009

**DEBUT:** v Liverpool, H, 17/10/2009

**LAST MATCH:** v West Ham United, A, 22/05/2011

**MOVED TO:** Contract not renewed, 30/06/2011

**TEAMS:** MVV Maastricht, PSV Eindhoven, Barcelona, Chelsea, Middlesbrough, Liverpool, Olympique Marseille, Sunderland

**INTERNATIONAL:** Netherlands

**SAFC TOTALS:** 13+37 appearances / 4 goals

**Bolo turned up at the Stadium of Light one day with a suit. It was a gift for Head of Media Louise Wanless. A life-long Middlesbrough supporter, Louise had talked to Zenden about how the greatest day for her and her dad was watching Bolo score with a penalty as Boro won their only major trophy when they beat Big Sam Allardyce's Bolton in the League (Carling) Cup final in Cardiff in 2004.**

The suit was Bolo's from the final and he had brought it in as a gift for Louise's father. That was typical of Bolo. He was thoughtful and an entirely decent chap with none of the stereotypical trappings of the superstar footballer regardless of a list of past clubs most players could only dream about. A La Liga winner with Barca in 1999, he played in the 2007 Champions League final for Liverpool who lost to AC Milan. Two years earlier he played alongside two-goal hero Djibril Cisse in the European Super Cup as Liverpool beat CSKA Moscow. Bolo also played in the 2006 Charity Shield as Liverpool defeated Chelsea in the same Cardiff Millennium Stadium that Boro had beaten Bolton two years earlier. With Chelsea, Zenden came on as a sub in the 2002 FA Cup final lost to Arsenal while with PSV he helped them to win the KNVB Cup in 1996, the Eredivisie a year later and the Johan Cruyff Shield in both years.

Altogether Bolo played 134 times for PSV scoring 35 goals. At Barcelona there were 95 appearances and three goals followed by four in 59 games for Chelsea, 15 in 88 for Boro, two in 49 at Liverpool and six in 76 at Marseille. At Sunderland his most memorable moment was a stunning acrobatic late volley that sealed victory in a pulsating game with Tottenham at the Stadium of Light in 2010 although almost as memorable was his attempt to join in with Asamoah Gyan's dancing the following season at Chelsea.

The year after leaving Sunderland, where as a veteran he was mainly utilised from the bench, Bolo returned to Chelsea as assistant manager. In the summer of 2013 he became reserve team coach at PSV before becoming coach to the first team in March 2016.

For the Netherlands he played in the 1998 FIFA World Cup semi-final against Brazil and went on to mark his fourth appearance in the tournament by scoring a terrific individual goal in the third-place Play-Off v Croatia. Two years later he excelled at Euro 2000 scoring against Denmark and playing all five of his country's games including the semi-final against Italy. He went on to also appear at Euro 2004 and totalled 54 internationals in which he scored seven times.

A strict vegetarian since his teens, Bolo was a three-time judo champion in his province of Limburg having been a black belt from the age of 14. His brother-in-law is Dutch International John Heitinga, who played for Ajax, Everton and Fulham.

## ZOETEBIER, Eduard Andraes Dominicus Hendrikus Jozef (Edwin)

**POSITION:** Goalkeeper

**BIRTHPLACE:** Purmerend, Netherlands

**DATE OF BIRTH:** 07/05/1970

**HEIGHT:** 6' 1" **WEIGHT:** 12st 9lbs

**SIGNED FROM:** FC Volendam, 12/06/1997

**DEBUT:** v Bury, A, 23/09/1997

**LAST MATCH:** v Middlesbrough, A, 15/10/1997

**MOVED TO:** Feyenoord, 06/01/1998

**TEAMS:** RKAV Volendam, FC Volendam, Sunderland, Feyenoord, Vitesse Arnhem, Feyenoord, PSV Eindhoven, NAC Breda

**INTERNATIONAL:** Netherlands Under 21

**SAFC TOTALS:** 2 appearances / 0 goals

**The face of new signing Edwin Zoetebier stared out from a big spread in the match programme for the opening match at the Stadium of Light against Ajax in 1997. Although Edwin came on as a half-time substitute he only played competitively twice, both times in the League Cup.**

Capped by the Netherlands at Under 21 level the rest of Zoetebier's career was spent in his home country. Having played 220 games for Volendam before coming to Sunderland in a deal thought to be worth around £225,000 he went on to play 59 times for Feyenoord, 37 for Vitesse, nine for PSV and 33 for NAC. In 2008 he returned to Volendam as goalkeeping coach. As of July 2022 he is goalkeeping coach at another of his former clubs Vitesse.

Edwin's career highlight came in 2002 when he played for Feyenoord as they beat Borussia Dortmund 3-2 in the UEFA Cup final. Later that year he also played in the UEFA Super Cup losing 2-1 to Real Madrid. His nephew, Stan, is following in his footsteps as a goalkeeper for RKAV Volendam and EVC Edam.

# Late Additions

## UP TO 1 SEPTEMBER 2022

**The players featured in this volume cover all those who played even a single game (even as a substitute) in a national or international competitive match for Sunderland up to the end of the 2021-22 season. Records of players who only appeared in war-time football are covered in Volume One of the Absolute Record.**

This late signings section adds players who arrived in the summer of 2022 up to 1 September when this volume went to print. Leon Dajaku, Patrick Roberts and Jack Clarke who signed in the summer of 2022, having already played for Sunderland the previous season, are included in the main sections of this volume.

### ALESE, Ajibola Joshua Odunayo Afolarin

**POSITION:** Centre-back / left-back
**BIRTHPLACE:** Islington, Greater London
**DATE OF BIRTH:** 17/01/2001
**HEIGHT:** 6' 4" **WEIGHT:** 12st 3lbs
**SIGNED FROM:** West Ham United, 15/7/2022
**DEBUT:** v Bristol City, A, 06/08/2022
**LAST MATCH:**
**MOVED TO:**
**TEAMS:** West Ham United, Sunderland (to August 2022)
**INTERNATIONAL:** England Under 20

**Coming through the academy system at West Ham United, Londoner Alese earned a total of 23 England caps at five age groups up to Under 20 before being transferred to Sunderland.**

A tall, strong, left-sided defender with the Irons, Alese's first-team opportunities had seen him play the full 90 minutes of a 5-1 home win over Hull in the League (Carabao) Cup in September 2020 and another full game 14 months later in a home Europa League loss to Dynamo Zagreb. Between his two outings for West Ham he had a start and an appearance as sub on loan to Cambridge United in League Two. Prior to his Hammers debut Aji made 11+4 appearances on loan to Accrington Stanley.

At international level Aji's most recent appearance before joining Sunderland had come in March 2022 when he came on as a sub for England Under 20s in a win over Germany at Colchester.

### BA, Abdoullah

**POSITION:** Midfielder
**BIRTHPLACE:** Saint-Aubin-lès-Elbeuf, France
**DATE OF BIRTH:** 31/07/2003
**HEIGHT:** 5' 9" **WEIGHT:** 11st 11lbs
**SIGNED FROM:** Le Havre, 31/08/2022
**DEBUT:**
**LAST MATCH:**
**MOVED TO:**
**TEAMS:** Le Havre, Sunderland (to August 2022)
**INTERNATIONAL:** France U19

**A debutant for Le Havre against Toulouse on 4 May 2021, Ba played in 19 senior games for Le Havre during 2021-22 and had appeared in five early season Ligue 2 fixtures before his switch to Sunderland.**

Abdoullah had been with CA Pitres in youth football and had made his international bow for France at Under 16 level. He went on to represent his country at Under 17 and Under 19 age groups prior to taking the step to Sunderland where he signed a five-year contract and linked up with fellow new recruit and youth international teammate Edouard Michut.

### BASS, Alex Michael

**POSITION:** Goalkeeper
**BIRTHPLACE:** Eastleigh, Hampshire
**DATE OF BIRTH:** 01/04/1998
**HEIGHT:** 6' 3" **WEIGHT:** 11st 0lbs
**SIGNED FROM:** Portsmouth, 26/07/2022
**DEBUT:** v Sheffield Wednesday, A, 10/08/2022
**LAST MATCH:**
**MOVED TO:**
**TEAMS:** Portsmouth, Salisbury (L), Torquay United (L), Southend United (L), Bradford City (L), Sunderland (to August 2022)

**An unused sub against Sunderland at Wembley for Portsmouth in the 2019 Football League (Checkatrade) Trophy final, Bass played 41 times for Pompey beginning at Coventry in August 2016.**

After 46 games on loan to non-league Salisbury Alex did not get an appearance on loan to Torquay. He played once on loan to Southend and had 21 League Two games for Bradford City in the second half of the season before he came to Sunderland.

### BENNETTE, Jewison Francisco Villegas

**POSITION:** Winger
**BIRTHPLACE:** Heredia, Costa Rica
**DATE OF BIRTH:** 15/06/2004
**HEIGHT:** 5' 9"
**SIGNED FROM:** Herediano, 25/08/2022
**DEBUT:**
**LAST MATCH:**
**MOVED TO:**
**TEAMS:** Herediano, Sunderland (to August 2022)
**INTERNATIONAL:** Costa Rica

**Just two months past his 17th birthday when becoming Costa Rica's youngest ever international when debuting against El Salvador in August 2021, Bennette went on to help his country qualify for the 2022 FIFA World Cup before signing for Sunderland.**

His international debut came under a month since he made a scoring debut at club level for Herediano against Jicarel. This was one of three goals he netted in 35 appearances. Jewison's father and namesake played for Costa Rica, as did uncle Try Bennett (not Bennette) who played against Liverpool in a 2005 World Club Championship semi-final for Deportivo Saprissa.

### BALLARD, Daniel George

**POSITION:** Centre-back

**BIRTHPLACE:** Stevenage, Hertfordshire

**DATE OF BIRTH:** 22/09/1999

**HEIGHT:** 6' 2" **WEIGHT:** 13st 5lbs

**SIGNED FROM:** Arsenal, 30/06/2022

**DEBUT:** v Coventry City, H, 31/07/2022

**LAST MATCH:**

**MOVED TO:**

**TEAMS:** Arsenal, Swindon Town (L), Blackpool (L), Millwall (L), Sunderland (to August 2022)

**INTERNATIONAL:** Northern Ireland

**English born to an Irish mother, Ballard had 15 full caps for Northern Ireland at the time of his transfer to Sunderland as a 22-year old. Schooled at Arsenal where he had been since he was an eight-year-old, the Gunners loaned him out three times.**

The first of these with Swindon was quickly curtailed after a knee injury following a two-minute appearance as a sub in League Two, a goal from a start against the Under 21s of Chelsea when he scored in a Football League Trophy game and a League Cup defeat at Colchester.

Having become a full international in September 2020 Ballard excelled on loan to Blackpool where he played alongside Sunderland loanee Elliott Embleton and Ellis Simms who was on loan from Everton. Ballard played a total of 29+1 games (2 goals) as he helped the Tangerines to promotion to the Championship via the Play-Offs, two of those appearances being in 1-0 wins over Sunderland. In 2021-22 he played against Blackpool in one of 31+2 games for Millwall (1 goal).

Ballard's signing was regarded as something of a coup by Sunderland. A strong, young defender already with international, championship and promotion experience Dan definitely got off to a good start with impressive displays in his first two appearances for Sunderland only for him to be injured on his third outing.

## DIALLO, Amad

**POSITION:** Winger

**BIRTHPLACE:** Abidjan, Ivory Coast

**DATE OF BIRTH:** 11/07/2002

**HEIGHT:** 5' 8" **WEIGHT:** 11st 5lbs

**SIGNED FROM:** West Ham United, 15/07/2022

**DEBUT:**

**LAST MATCH:**

**MOVED TO:**

**TEAMS:** Boca Barco, Atalanta, Manchester United, Rangers (L), Sunderland (L) (to August 2022)

**INTERNATIONAL:** Ivory Coast

**Raised in Italy, the Ivory Coast international cost Manchester United a reported fee of 25 million Euros, potentially rising to 40 million. Starting at Atalanta he showed immense promise in Serie A, the Champions League and Europa League, moving to Manchester after just five substitute appearances and one goal.**

He scored against Milan on only his third appearance for Manchester United in the Europa League but after just 3+6 games was loaned to Rangers. A debut goal at Ross County was one of three in 6+7 outings for the Ibrox club, the last of these coming in a victorious 2022 Scottish Cup final when he played against Ellis Simms and Craig Gordon as well as being a teammate of Jon McLaughlan. Diallo - formerly known as Amad Traoré - was also an unused sub in the 2022 Europa League final for Rangers.

## MICHUT, Edouard

**POSITION:** Midfielder

**BIRTHPLACE:** Aix-Les-Bains, France

**DATE OF BIRTH:** 04/03/2003

**HEIGHT:** 5' 10" **WEIGHT:** 10st 10lbs

**SIGNED FROM:** Paris St Germain, 31/08/2022, on loan

**DEBUT:**

**LAST MATCH:**

**MOVED TO:**

**TEAMS:** Paris St Germain, Sunderland (L) (to August 2022)

**INTERNATIONAL:** France Under 19

**Signed on a season-long loan with a view to a permanent transfer, Michut played youth football for FC Le Chesnay 78 and Versailles before joining PSG.**

Debuting on 27 February 2021 against Dijon he made a first start in the Coupe de France in January 2022 against Vannes and a week later became the youngest player to record a league assist for PSG since Kylian Mbappe. Capped at U16, U17 and U19 level by France his arrival at Sunderland was seen as a coup for the club.

## SIMMS, Ellis Reco

**POSITION:** Centre-forward

**BIRTHPLACE:** Oldham, Greater Manchester

**DATE OF BIRTH:** 05/01/2001

**HEIGHT:** 6' 2" **WEIGHT:** 11st 6lbs

**SIGNED FROM:** Everton, 29/07/2022, on loan

**DEBUT:** v Bristol City, A, 06/08/2022

**LAST MATCH:**

**MOVED TO:**

**TEAMS:** Blackburn Rovers, Manchester City, Everton, Blackpool (L), Hearts (L), Sunderland (L) (to August 2022)

**INTERNATIONAL:** England Under 20

**Two goals on his debut saw Simms become the first man to score twice on an away league debut for Sunderland in 94 years. Not since Robert McKay's brace at Manchester City in October 1928 had a Sunderland player scored twice on an away League debut.**

Chris Brown had scored twice on debut at Crewe in September 2004 although that was a League Cup game. Jimmy O'Neill had been the last man to score twice on his league debut, in his case in a home game with Bristol Rovers in January 1962. Simms took just four minutes to net his first goal, making him the quickest debut scorer since Gary Bennett's second-minute goal against Southampton in August 1985.

Borrowed from Everton, Simms had joined The Toffees as a 16-year-old having been part of the academy systems at Blackburn and Manchester City. In October 2018 he played away to his home town team Oldham in the Football League Trophy for the Under 21 team of Everton and scored in the same competition a year later at Burton. December 2021 brought a first-team debut for Everton. Playing alongside Jordan Pickford Simms started a Premier League draw at Chelsea. By then he had enjoyed a hugely successful loan at Blackpool in 2020-21. As a teammate of fellow loanees Elliott Embleton and Dan Ballard, Simms helped the Tangerines to win promotion from League One. Two of his ten goals from 19+5 games came in a semi-final Play-Off at Oxford although injury forced him to miss the Wembley final against Lincoln.

Mid-way through the following 2021-22 season, the month after his Premier League game against Chelsea Everton allowed Ellis out on loan again, this time to Hearts.

Starting with a debut goal against Motherwell, Simms scored seven times in 15+5 games. The pick of his goals was a screamer in a Scottish Cup semi-final at Hampden Park against Edinburgh rivals Hibs. As a teammate of Craig Gordon Simms returned to Hampden to also play in the final which was lost to Rangers.

Qualified to play for England, Jamaica and Poland, Simms was first involved with England at Under 18 level after being named as Everton's Under 18 Player of the Season after smashing 32 goals in 20+1 games in Premier League (North) - and a most impressive total of 46 goals in all competitions. In November 2020 Simms played as a sub in a training game at St George's Park for England Under 20s in a friendly with Aston Villa who included ex-Sunderland man Ahmed Elmohamady.

## SPELLMAN, Michael

**POSITION:** Outside-left

**BIRTHPLACE:** Durham, Co Durham

**DATE OF BIRTH:** 21/09/2002

**HEIGHT:** 6' 0" **WEIGHT:** 10st 12lbs

**SIGNED FROM:** Chester-le-Street United, 11/06/2022

**DEBUT:** v Sheffield Wednesday, A, 11/08/2022

**LAST MATCH:**

**MOVED TO:**

**TEAMS:** Chester-le Street United, Sunderland (to August 2022)

**Spellman signed a one-year contract at Sunderland where he was expected to become part of the Under 21 side having made ten appearances at Under 23 level the previous season when he had an extended trial period from local side Chester-le-Street United.**

During this time he played for Sunderland in ten PL2 games. He also won Chester-le-Street United's Goal of the Season competition for a magician's goal against Darlo Town, when after taking a throw-in, the ball was played back to Spellman who cut in, beat two men and curled a beautiful shot into the top corner. For good measure Michael also took third place in the same award for another excellent strike against Leam Rangers.

# In Charge

**People listed here are those who have been in charge of the team. In most cases this is the person who has been the manager. In modern times the person controlling team selection, tactics and training often has the title, head coach. In such cases usually they work with a director of football who amongst other things leads recruitment.**

In the early years of the game the manager was often primarily concerned with administration and secretarial work. This was especially true in the days when training was focussed firmly on fitness and players were allowed to play 'off the cuff' rather than to pre-determined tactical plans.

People who were appointed as manager/head coach after a period as caretaker manager are marked with an asterisk. People who were caretaker managers are indicated by (C). Teams listed here are teams these individuals have been in charge of. Teams where they have served in coaching or other capacities have not been listed, neither have the teams they played for.

## 1884 - 1889

Date of first competitive game in a national competition
English Cup v Redcar, A, 08/11/1884

| P | W | D | L |
|---|---|---|---|
| 9 | 5 | 1 | 3 |

## WATSON, Thomas (Tom)

**BIRTHPLACE:** Byker, Newcastle, Northumberland
**DATE OF BIRTH:** 08/04/1859 - 06/05/1915
**IN CHARGE AT SUNDERLAND:** 03/06/1889 - 17/08/1896

| P | W | D | L |
|---|---|---|---|
| 191 | 119 | 28 | 44 |

Won league title with Sunderland, 1892, 1893 & 1895
League runners-up, 1894
'World Champions' with Sunderland, 1895

**ALSO IN CHARGE OF:** Newcastle West End, Newcastle East End, Liverpool

## CAMPBELL, Robert

**BIRTHPLACE:** Cardross, Dunbartonshire
**DATE OF BIRTH:** 30/09/1864 - 22/09/1945
**IN CHARGE AT SUNDERLAND:** 17/08/1896 - 01/05/1899

| P | W | D | L |
|---|---|---|---|
| 103 | 41 | 22 | 40 |

League runners-up 1898

**ALSO IN CHARGE OF:** Bristol City, Bradford City

## WATSON, Alexander (Caretaker)

**BIRTHPLACE:** Patterdale, Westmorland
**DATE OF BIRTH:** 11/08/1864 - 12/07/1931
**IN CHARGE AT SUNDERLAND:** 01/05/1899 - 14/08/1899

| P | W | D | L |
|---|---|---|---|
| 0 | 0 | 0 | 0 |

**ALSO IN CHARGE OF:** Birmingham (Secretary)

## MACKIE, Alexander

**BIRTHPLACE:** Kirktown of Auchterless, Banffshire
**DATE OF BIRTH:** 24/12/1868 - 07/11/1944
**IN CHARGE AT SUNDERLAND:** 14/08/1899 - 16/06/1905

| P | W | D | L |
|---|---|---|---|
| 200 | 98 | 44 | 58 |

Won league title with Sunderland, 1902
League runners-up, 1901
Won Sheriff of London Shield with Sunderland, 1903

Was suspended by the FA for three months after financial irregularities were discovered in the club's books - hence the period with Fred Dale in charge.

**ALSO IN CHARGE OF:** Victoria United, Heatherley, Inverness Thistle, Middlesbrough

## DALE, Fred Hetherington (Caretaker)

**BIRTHPLACE:** Sunderland, Co Durham
**DATE OF BIRTH:** 14/09/1864 - 30/07/1927
**IN CHARGE AT SUNDERLAND:** 04/11/1904 - 31/01/1905
During suspension of Alex Mackie

| P | W | D | L |
|---|---|---|---|
| 15 | 7 | 2 | 6 |

Had played six (competitive) games for Sunderland

**ALSO IN CHARGE OF:** No-one

## KYLE, Robert Hugh

**BIRTHPLACE:** Belfast, Co Antrim
**DATE OF BIRTH:** 16/12/1870 - 17/02/1941
**IN CHARGE AT SUNDERLAND:** 02/08/1905 - 05/05/1928
Sunderland's longest serving manager

| P | W | D | L |
|---|---|---|---|
| 817 | 371 | 155 | 291 |

Won league title with Sunderland, 1913
League runners-up with Sunderland, 1923
Reached English (FA) Cup final with Sunderland, 1913

**ALSO IN CHARGE OF:** Distillery

Tom Watson

Alex Mackie

Robert Kyle

John Cochrane

Alan Brown

George Hardwick

Ian McColl

Bob Stokoe

## COCHRANE, John

**BIRTHPLACE:** Johnstone, Renfrewshire
**DATE OF BIRTH:** 27/01/1891 - 19/12/1961
**IN CHARGE AT SUNDERLAND:** 05/05/1928 - 03/03/1939

| P | W | D | L |
|---|---|---|---|
| 500 | 212 | 122 | 166 |

Won league title at Sunderland, 1936
Won FA Cup at Sunderland, 1937
Won Charity Shield at Sunderland, 1936-37
League runners-up with Sunderland, 1935

**ALSO IN CHARGE OF:** St Johnstone (Secretary), St Mirren, Reading

## CROW, George (Caretaker)

**BIRTHPLACE:** Monkwearmouth, Sunderland, Co Durham
**DATE OF BIRTH:** 22/09/1899 - 25/09/1972
**IN CHARGE AT SUNDERLAND:** 03/03/1939 - 24/03/1939

| P | W | D | L |
|---|---|---|---|
| 4 | 2 | 0 | 2 |

**ALSO IN CHARGE OF:** No-one

## MURRAY, William Milne (Bill)

**BIRTHPLACE:** Aberdeen, Aberdeenshire
**DATE OF BIRTH:** 10/03/1900 - 15/12/1961
**IN CHARGE AT SUNDERLAND:** 24/03/1939 - 26/06/1957

| P | W | D | L |
|---|---|---|---|
| 510 | 185 | 140 | 185 |

Also one win and two defeats from expunged 1939-40 season
Had played 328 games for Sunderland

**ALSO IN CHARGE OF:** No-one

## SCOTT, William (Bill/Will) (Caretaker)

**BIRTHPLACE:** Willington Quay, Northumberland
**DATE OF BIRTH:** 24/08/1894 - 29/03/1972
**IN CHARGE AT SUNDERLAND:** 26/06/1957 - 30/07/1957

| P | W | D | L |
|---|---|---|---|
| 0 | 0 | 0 | 0 |

**ALSO IN CHARGE OF:** Blackburn Rovers, Preston North End

## BROWN, Alan Winston

**BIRTHPLACE:** Corbridge, Northumberland
**DATE OF BIRTH:** 26/08/1914 - 08/03/1996
**IN CHARGE AT SUNDERLAND:** 30/07/1957 - 31/07/1964 and 09/02/1968 - 01/11/1972

| P | W | D | L | |
|---|---|---|---|---|
| 332 | 138 | 88 | 106 | First spell |
| 218 | 62 | 68 | 88 | Second spell |
| 550 | 200 | 156 | 194 | Total |

Won promotion to top flight, 1964

**ALSO IN CHARGE OF:** Burnley, Sheffield Wednesday

## CLUB DIRECTORS

**IN CHARGE AT SUNDERLAND:** 01/08/1964 - 13/11/1964

| P | W | D | L |
|---|---|---|---|
| 19 | 4 | 6 | 9 |

## HARDWICK, George Francis Moutrey

**BIRTHPLACE:** Saltburn, North Riding of Yorkshire
**DATE OF BIRTH:** 02/02/1920 - 19/04/2004
**IN CHARGE AT SUNDERLAND:** 14/11/1964 - 01/05/1965

| P | W | D | L |
|---|---|---|---|
| 28 | 13 | 3 | 12 |

**ALSO IN CHARGE OF:** Oldham Athletic, Gateshead

## McCOLL, John Miller (Ian)

**BIRTHPLACE:** Alexandria, Dunbartonshire
**DATE OF BIRTH:** 07/06/1928 - 25/10/2008
**IN CHARGE AT SUNDERLAND:** 21/05/1965 - 08/02/1968

| P | W | D | L |
|---|---|---|---|
| 125 | 40 | 27 | 58 |

**ALSO IN CHARGE OF:** Scotland

## ELLIOTT, William Henry (Billy) (Caretaker)

**BIRTHPLACE:** Bradford, Yorkshire
**DATE OF BIRTH:** 20/03/1925 - 21/01/2008
**IN CHARGE AT SUNDERLAND:** 01/11/1972 - 29/11/1972 and 13/12/1978 - 24/05/1979

| P | W | D | L | |
|---|---|---|---|---|
| 4 | 0 | 2 | 2 | First spell |
| 26 | 14 | 7 | 5 | Second spell |
| 30 | 14 | 9 | 7 | Total |

Had played 212 games for Sunderland

**ALSO IN CHARGE OF:** Libya (National team coach), Brann, Darlington

## STOKOE, Robert (Bob)

**BIRTHPLACE:** Mickley, Northumberland
**DATE OF BIRTH:** 21/09/1930 - 01/02/2004
**IN CHARGE AT SUNDERLAND:** 29/11/1972 - 18/10/1976 and 16/04/1987 - 30/05/1987

| P | W | D | L | |
|---|---|---|---|---|
| 197 | 92 | 49 | 56 | First spell |
| 9 | 3 | 2 | 4 | Second spell |
| 206 | 95 | 51 | 60 | Total |

Won FA Cup, 1973
Won promotion to top flight. 1976

**ALSO IN CHARGE OF:** Bury, Charlton Athletic, Rochdale, Carlisle United, Blackpool, Bury, Blackpool, Rochdale, Carlisle United

## MacFARLANE, Ian (Caretaker)

**BIRTHPLACE:** Lanark, Lanarkshire
**DATE OF BIRTH:** 26/01/1933 - 17/06/2019
**IN CHARGE AT SUNDERLAND:** 18/10/1976 - 30/11/1976

| P | W | D | L |
|---|---|---|---|
| 7 | 2 | 1 | 4 |

**ALSO IN CHARGE OF:** Carlisle United, Yeovil Town

## ADAMSON, James (Jimmy)

**BIRTHPLACE:** Ashington, Northumberland
**DATE OF BIRTH:** 04/04/1929 - 08/11/2011
**IN CHARGE AT SUNDERLAND:** 30/11/1976 - 25/10/1978

| P | W | D | L |
|---|---|---|---|
| 88 | 29 | 28 | 31 |

**ALSO IN CHARGE OF:** Burnley, Sparta Rotterdam, Leeds United

## MERRINGTON, David Robert (Dave) (Caretaker)

**BIRTHPLACE:** Barley Mow, Chester-le-Street, Co Durham
**DATE OF BIRTH:** 26/01/1945
**IN CHARGE AT SUNDERLAND:** 25/10/1978 - 11/12/1978

| P | W | D | L |
|---|---|---|---|
| 8 | 4 | 2 | 2 |

**ALSO IN CHARGE OF:** Southampton

## KNIGHTON, Kenneth

**BIRTHPLACE:** Barnsley, Yorkshire
**DATE OF BIRTH:** 20/02/1944
**IN CHARGE AT SUNDERLAND:** 07/06/1979 - 13/04/1981

| P | W | D | L |
|---|---|---|---|
| 94 | 35 | 24 | 35 |

Won promotion to top flight, 1980
**ALSO IN CHARGE OF:** Orient, Dagenham Town, Trowbridge Town

## DOCHERTY, Michael (Mick) (Caretaker)

**BIRTHPLACE:** Preston, Lancashire
**DATE OF BIRTH:** 29/10/1950
**IN CHARGE AT SUNDERLAND:** 13/04/1981 - 12/06/1981

| P | W | D | L |
|---|---|---|---|
| 4 | 2 | 0 | 2 |

Had played 79+1 games for Sunderland
**ALSO IN CHARGE OF:** Hartlepool United, Rochdale, Gillingham (C)

## DURBAN, William Alan

**BIRTHPLACE:** Port Talbot, Neath
**DATE OF BIRTH:** 07/07/1941
**IN CHARGE AT SUNDERLAND:** 12/06/1981 - 01/03/1984

| P | W | D | L |
|---|---|---|---|
| 130 | 37 | 40 | 53 |

**ALSO IN CHARGE OF:** Shrewsbury Town, Stoke City, Cardiff City

## ROBSON, Bryan Stanley (Pop) (Caretaker)

**BIRTHPLACE:** Sunderland, Co Durham
**DATE OF BIRTH:** 11/11/1945
**IN CHARGE AT SUNDERLAND:** 01/03/1984 - 05/03/1984

| P | W | D | L |
|---|---|---|---|
| 1 | 0 | 1 | 0 |

Had played 172+10 games for Sunderland
**ALSO IN CHARGE OF:** Carlisle United

## ASHURST, Leonard (Len)

**BIRTHPLACE:** Fazakerley, Liverpool
**DATE OF BIRTH:** 10/03/1939 - 25/09/2021
**IN CHARGE AT SUNDERLAND:** 05/03/1984 - 24/05/1985

| P | W | D | L |
|---|---|---|---|
| 66 | 21 | 16 | 29 |

Had played 452+6 games for Sunderland
Reached League (Milk) Cup final with Sunderland, 1985
**ALSO IN CHARGE OF:** Hartlepool United, Gillingham, Sheffield Wednesday, Newport County, Cardiff City, Kuwait (National team coach), Qatar (National team coach), Al-Wakrah, Cardiff City, Pahang, Weymouth, Weston-super-Mare

## BURROWS, Frank (Caretaker)

**BIRTHPLACE:** Larkhall, South Lanarkshire
**DATE OF BIRTH:** 30/01/1944 - 24/11/2021
**IN CHARGE AT SUNDERLAND:** 30/01/1944 - 24/11/2021

| P | W | D | L |
|---|---|---|---|
| 0 | 0 | 0 | 0 |

**ALSO IN CHARGE OF:** Portsmouth, Cardiff City, Portsmouth, Swansea City, Cardiff City, WBA (C), Leicester City (C)

## McMENEMY, Lawrence (Lawrie)

**BIRTHPLACE:** Saltwell Park, Gateshead, Co Durham
**DATE OF BIRTH:** 26/07/1936
**IN CHARGE AT SUNDERLAND:** 11/07/1985 - 16/04/1987

| P | W | D | L |
|---|---|---|---|
| 90 | 28 | 22 | 40 |

**ALSO IN CHARGE OF:** Bishop Auckland, Doncaster Rovers, Grimsby Town, Southampton, Northern Ireland

## SMITH, Denis

**BIRTHPLACE:** Stoke, Staffordshire
**DATE OF BIRTH:** 19/11/1947
**IN CHARGE AT SUNDERLAND:** 30/05/1987 - 30/12/1991

| P | W | D | L |
|---|---|---|---|
| 238 | 92 | 63 | 83 |

Won promotion to second tier with Sunderland, 1988
Won promotion to top flight with Sunderland, 1990
**ALSO IN CHARGE OF:** York City, Bristol City, Oxford United, West Bromwich Albion, Oxford United, Wrexham

## CROSBY, Malcolm*

**BIRTHPLACE:** South Shields, Co Durham
**DATE OF BIRTH:** 04/07/1954
**IN CHARGE AT SUNDERLAND:** 30/12/1991 - 01/02/1993 (caretaker until 29/04/1992)

| P | W | D | L |
|---|---|---|---|
| 60 | 21 | 15 | 24 |

Reached FA Cup final with Sunderland, 1992
**ALSO IN CHARGE OF:** Oxford United (C), Northampton Town (C), Birmingham City (C) Gateshead

Ken Knighton

Len Ashurst

Denis Smith

Malcolm Crosby

Mick Buxton

Peter Reid

Niall Quinn

Roy Keane

## FERGUSON, Robert Burnitt (Bobby) (Caretaker)

**BIRTHPLACE:** Dudley, Northumberland

**DATE OF BIRTH:** 08/01/1938 - 28/03/2018

**IN CHARGE AT SUNDERLAND:** 01/02/1993 - 05/02/1993

| P | W | D | L |
|---|---|---|---|
| 0 | 0 | 0 | 0 |

**ALSO IN CHARGE OF:** Barry Town, Newport County, Ipswich Town, Al-Arabi Sporting Club

## BUTCHER, Terence Ian (Terry)

**BIRTHPLACE:** Singapore

**DATE OF BIRTH:** 28/12/1958

**IN CHARGE AT SUNDERLAND:** 05/02/1993 - 26/11/1993

| P | W | D | L |
|---|---|---|---|
| 45 | 14 | 8 | 23 |

Had played 41+1 games for Sunderland

**ALSO IN CHARGE OF:** Coventry City, Motherwell, Sydney, Partick Thistle (C), Brentford, Inverness Caledonian Thistle, Hibernian, Newport County, Philippines

## BUXTON, Michael James (Mick)*

**BIRTHPLACE:** Corbridge, Northumberland

**DATE OF BIRTH:** 29/05/1943

**IN CHARGE AT SUNDERLAND:** 26/11/1993 - 29/03/1995

| P | W | D | L |
|---|---|---|---|
| 76 | 25 | 24 | 27 |

**ALSO IN CHARGE OF:** Huddersfield Town, Scunthorpe United

Appointed as manager of Zimbabwe in June 1995 only for deal to fall through before he took up the post

## REID, Peter*

**BIRTHPLACE:** Huyton, Liverpool, Lancashire

**DATE OF BIRTH:** 20/06/1956

**IN CHARGE AT SUNDERLAND:** 29/03/1995 - 07/10/2002

| P | W | D | L |
|---|---|---|---|
| 353 | 160 | 93 | 100 |

Won promotion to top-flight 1996 and 1999

**ALSO IN CHARGE OF:** Manchester City, Leeds United, Coventry City, Thailand, Plymouth Argyle, Kolkata, Mumbai City

## WILKINSON, Howard

**BIRTHPLACE:** Sheffield, Yorkshire

**DATE OF BIRTH:** 13/11/1943

**IN CHARGE AT SUNDERLAND:** 10/10/2002 - 10/03/2003

| P | W | D | L |
|---|---|---|---|
| 27 | 5 | 7 | 15 |

**ALSO IN CHARGE OF:** Boston United, England semi-professional team, Notts County, England (C) England Under 21s, Sheffield Wednesday, Leeds United, Shanghai Shenhua

## McCARTHY, Michael Joseph (Mick)

**BIRTHPLACE:** Barnsley, Yorkshire

**DATE OF BIRTH:** 07/02/1959

**IN CHARGE AT SUNDERLAND:** 12/03/2003 - 06/03/2006

| P | W | D | L |
|---|---|---|---|
| 147 | 63 | 25 | 59 |

Won promotion to top flight, 2005

**ALSO IN CHARGE OF:** Millwall, Republic of Ireland, Wolverhampton Wanderers, Ipswich Town, Republic of Ireland, Apoel Nicosia

## BALL, Kevin Anthony (Caretaker)

**BIRTHPLACE:** Hastings, Sussex

**DATE OF BIRTH:** 12/11/1964

**IN CHARGE AT SUNDERLAND:** 06/03/2006 - 09/05/2006 and 22/09/2013 - 07/10/2013

| P | W | D | L | |
|---|---|---|---|---|
| 10 | 1 | 2 | 7 | **First spell** |
| 3 | 1 | 0 | 2 | **Second spell** |
| 13 | 2 | 2 | 9 | **Total** |

Had played 375+13 games for Sunderland

**ALSO IN CHARGE OF:** No-one

## RICHARDSON, Kevin & CARTER, Tim

**BIRTHPLACE: Richardson -** Newcastle, Northumberland

**DATE OF BIRTH: Richardson -** 04/12/1962

**BIRTHPLACE: Carter -** Bristol, Avon

**DATE OF BIRTH: Carter -** 05/10/1967 - 19/06/2008

**IN CHARGE AT SUNDERLAND:** 09/05/2006 - 24/07/2006

| P | W | D | L |
|---|---|---|---|
| 0 | 0 | 0 | 0 |

The pair did have two pre-season games in charge
Carter had played 50 games for Sunderland

**ALSO IN CHARGE OF:** No-one

## QUINN, Niall John

**BIRTHPLACE:** Dublin, Republic of Ireland

**DATE OF BIRTH:** 06/10/1966

**IN CHARGE AT SUNDERLAND:** 25/07/2006 - 28/08/2006

| P | W | D | L |
|---|---|---|---|
| 6 | 1 | 0 | 5 |

Had played 183+37 games for Sunderland and also served the club as chairman

**ALSO IN CHARGE OF:** No-one

## KEANE, Roy Maurice

**BIRTHPLACE:** Cork, Republic of Ireland

**DATE OF BIRTH:** 10/08/1971

**IN CHARGE AT SUNDERLAND:** 28/08/2006 - 04/12/2008

| P | W | D | L |
|---|---|---|---|
| 100 | 43 | 16 | 41 |

Won promotion to top flight, 2007

**ALSO IN CHARGE OF:** Ipswich Town

## SBRAGIA, Richard (Ricky)*

**BIRTHPLACE:** Lennoxtown, Glasgow, Lanarkshire
**DATE OF BIRTH:** 26/05/1956
**IN CHARGE AT SUNDERLAND:** 04/12/2008 - 24/05/2009 (Caretaker from 04/12/2008 - 27/12/2008)

| P | W | D | L |
|---|---|---|---|
| 26 | 6 | 7 | 13 |

**ALSO IN CHARGE OF:** No-one

## BRUCE, Stephen Roger (Steve)

**BIRTHPLACE:** Corbridge, Northumberland
**DATE OF BIRTH:** 31/12/1960
**IN CHARGE AT SUNDERLAND:** 03/06/2009 - 30/11/2011

| P | W | D | L |
|---|---|---|---|
| 98 | 29 | 27 | 42 |

**ALSO IN CHARGE OF:** Sheffield United, Huddersfield Town, Wigan Athletic, Crystal Palace, Birmingham City, Hull City, Aston Villa, Sheffield Wednesday, Newcastle United, West Bromwich Albion

## BLACK, Eric (Caretaker)

**BIRTHPLACE:** Bellshill, Lanarkshire
**DATE OF BIRTH:** 01/10/1963
**IN CHARGE AT SUNDERLAND:** 30/11/2011 - 05/12/2011

| P | W | D | L |
|---|---|---|---|
| 1 | 0 | 0 | 1 |

**ALSO IN CHARGE OF:** Motherwell, Coventry City, Birmingham City (C), Blackburn Rovers (C), Aston Villa (C)

## O'NEILL, Martin Hugh Michael

**BIRTHPLACE:** Kilrea, Co Londonderry
**DATE OF BIRTH:** 01/03/1952
**IN CHARGE AT SUNDERLAND:** 03/12/2011 - 30/03/2013

| P | W | D | L |
|---|---|---|---|
| 66 | 21 | 20 | 25 |

**ALSO IN CHARGE OF:** Grantham Town, Shepshed Charterhouse, Wycombe Wanderers, Norwich City, Leicester City, Celtic, Aston Villa, Republic of Ireland, Nottingham Forest

## DI CANIO, Paolo

**BIRTHPLACE:** Rome, Italy
**DATE OF BIRTH:** 09/07/1968
**IN CHARGE AT SUNDERLAND:** 31/03/2013 - 22/09/2013

| P | W | D | L |
|---|---|---|---|
| 13 | 3 | 3 | 7 |

**ALSO IN CHARGE OF:** Swindon Town

## POYET DOMINGUEZ, Gustavo Augusto

**BIRTHPLACE:** Montevideo, Uruguay
**DATE OF BIRTH:** 15/11/1967
**IN CHARGE AT SUNDERLAND:** 07/10/2013 - 16/03/2015

| P | W | D | L |
|---|---|---|---|
| 75 | 23 | 22 | 30 |

Reached League (Capital One) Cup final with Sunderland, 2014
**ALSO IN CHARGE OF:** Brighton & HA, AEK Athens, Real Betis, Shanghai Shenhua, Bordeaux, Universidad Catolica, Greece

## ADVOCAAT, Dirk Nicolaas (Dick)

**BIRTHPLACE:** Den Hague, Netherlands
**DATE OF BIRTH:** 27/09/1947
**IN CHARGE AT SUNDERLAND:** 17/03/2015 - 04/10/2015

| P | W | D | L |
|---|---|---|---|
| 19 | 4 | 6 | 9 |

**ALSO IN CHARGE OF:** HFC Haarlem, SVV Schiedam, Dordrecht, Netherlands, PSV Eindhoven, Rangers, Netherlands, Borussia Moenchengladbach, United Arab Emirates, South Korea, Zenit St Petersburg, Belgium, AZ Alkmaar, Russia, PSV Eindhoven, AZ Alkmaar, Serbia, Fenerbahce, Netherlands, Sparta Rotterdam, FC Utrecht, Feyenoord, Iraq

## STOCKDALE, Robert Keith (Robbie) (Caretaker)

**BIRTHPLACE:** Redcar, Cleveland
**DATE OF BIRTH:** 30/11/1979
**IN CHARGE AT SUNDERLAND:** 05/10/2015 - 09/10/2015
22/07/2016 - 23/07/2016 (with Paul Bracewell)
01/11/2017 - 19/11/2017 (with Billy McKinlay)
30/04/2018 - 25/05/2018

| P | W | D | L | |
|---|---|---|---|---|
| 0 | 0 | 0 | 0 | First spell |
| 0 | 0 | 0 | 0 | Second spell |
| 2 | 0 | 1 | 1 | Third spell |
| 1 | 1 | 0 | 0 | Fourth spell |
| 3 | 1 | 1 | 1 | Total |

**ALSO IN CHARGE OF:** Grimsby Town (JC), Rochdale

## ALLARDYCE, Samuel

**BIRTHPLACE:** Dudley, Worcestershire
**DATE OF BIRTH:** 19/10/1954
**IN CHARGE AT SUNDERLAND:** 09/10/2015 - 22/07/2016

| P | W | D | L |
|---|---|---|---|
| 31 | 9 | 9 | 13 |

Had played 26+1 games for Sunderland
**ALSO IN CHARGE OF:** Limerick, Preston NE (C), Blackpool, Notts County, Bolton Wanderers, Newcastle United, Blackburn Rovers, West Ham United, England, Crystal Palace, Everton, WBA

## BRACEWELL, Paul William

**BIRTHPLACE:** Heswall, Cheshire
**DATE OF BIRTH:** 19/07/1962
**IN CHARGE AT SUNDERLAND:** 22/07/2016 - 23/07/2016 (jointly with Robbie Stockdale)

| P | W | D | L |
|---|---|---|---|
| 0 | 0 | 0 | 0 |

Had played 268+2 games for Sunderland. Bracewell and Stockdale did have one pre-season game in charge together
**ALSO IN CHARGE OF:** Fulham, Halifax Town, Walsall (C)

## MOYES, David

**BIRTHPLACE:** Glasgow, Lanarkshire
**DATE OF BIRTH:** 25/04/1963
**IN CHARGE AT SUNDERLAND:** 23/07/2016 - 22/05/2017

| P | W | D | L |
|---|---|---|---|
| 43 | 8 | 7 | 28 |

**ALSO IN CHARGE OF:** Preston North End, Everton, Manchester United, Real Sociedad, West Ham United

Martin O'Neill

Paolo Di Canio

Gus Poyet

Dick Advocaat

Paul Bracewell

Chris Coleman

Lee Johnson

Tony Mowbray

## GRAYSON, Simon Nicholas

**BIRTHPLACE:** Ripon, Yorkshire
**DATE OF BIRTH:** 16/12/1969
**IN CHARGE AT SUNDERLAND:** 29/06/2017 - 31/10/2017
(followed close-season spell with no named manager)

| P | W | D | L |
|---|---|---|---|
| 18 | 3 | 7 | 8 |

**ALSO IN CHARGE OF:** Blackpool, Leeds United, Huddersfield Town, Preston North End, Bradford City, Blackpool, Fleetwood Town, Bengaluru

## McKINLAY, William James Alexander (Billy)

**BIRTHPLACE:** Glasgow, Lanarkshire
**DATE OF BIRTH:** 22/04/1969
**IN CHARGE AT SUNDERLAND:** 01/11/2017 - 12/11/2017
(jointly with Robbie Stockdale)

| P | W | D | L |
|---|---|---|---|
| 1 | 0 | 0 | 1 |

**ALSO IN CHARGE OF:** Watford (C), Stabaek

## COLEMAN, Christopher Patrick

**BIRTHPLACE:** Swansea, West Glamorgan
**DATE OF BIRTH:** 10/06/1970
**IN CHARGE AT SUNDERLAND:** 19/11/2017 - 29/04/2018

| P | W | D | L |
|---|---|---|---|
| 29 | 5 | 8 | 16 |

**ALSO IN CHARGE OF:** Fulham, Real Sociedad, Coventry City, Athlitiki Enosi Larissa, Wales, Hebei China Fortune, Atromitos

## ROSS, John James (Jack)

**BIRTHPLACE:** Falkirk, Stirlingshire
**DATE OF BIRTH:** 05/06/1976
**IN CHARGE AT SUNDERLAND:** 25/05/2018 - 08/10/2019

| P | W | D | L |
|---|---|---|---|
| 75 | 39 | 25 | 11 |

**ALSO IN CHARGE OF:** Dumbarton (C), Alloa Athletic, St Mirren, Hibernian, Dundee United

## FOWLER, James (Caretaker)

**BIRTHPLACE:** Stirling, Stirlingshire
**DATE OF BIRTH:** 26/10/1980
**IN CHARGE AT SUNDERLAND:** 08/10/2019 - 17/10/2019

| P | W | D | L |
|---|---|---|---|
| 1 | 1 | 0 | 0 |

**ALSO IN CHARGE OF:** Queen of the South, Kilmarnock (C)

## PARKINSON, Philip John

**BIRTHPLACE:** Chorley, Lancashire
**DATE OF BIRTH:** 01/12/1967
**IN CHARGE AT SUNDERLAND:** 17/10/2019 - 29/11/2020

| P | W | D | L |
|---|---|---|---|
| 48 | 19 | 13 | 16 |

**ALSO IN CHARGE OF:** Colchester United, Hull City, Charlton Athletic, Bradford City, Bolton Wanderers, Wrexham

## TAYLOR, Andrew Derek (Caretaker)

**BIRTHPLACE:** Hartlepool, Co Durham
**DATE OF BIRTH:** 01/08/1986
**IN CHARGE AT SUNDERLAND:** 29/11/2020 - 05/12/2020

| P | W | D | L |
|---|---|---|---|
| 1 | 0 | 1 | 0 |

**ALSO IN CHARGE OF:** No-one

## JOHNSON, Lee David

**BIRTHPLACE:** Newmarket, Suffolk
**DATE OF BIRTH:** 07/06/1981
**IN CHARGE AT SUNDERLAND:** 05/12/2020 - 30/01/2022

| P | W | D | L |
|---|---|---|---|
| 78 | 42 | 17 | 19 |

Won Papa John's Trophy, 2021
**ALSO IN CHARGE OF:** Oldham Athletic, Barnsley, Bristol City, Hibernian

## DODDS, Michael James W (Mike) & PROCTOR, Michael (Caretakers)

**BIRTHPLACE: Dodds -** Leamington Spa, Warwickshire
**DATE OF BIRTH: Dodds -** 03/06/1986
**BIRTHPLACE: Proctor -** Monkwearmouth, Sunderland
**DATE OF BIRTH: Proctor -** 03/10/1980
**IN CHARGE AT SUNDERLAND:** 31/01/2022 - 11/02/2022

| P | W | D | L |
|---|---|---|---|
| 2 | 0 | 0 | 2 |

Michael Proctor had played 22+26 games for Sunderland
**ALSO IN CHARGE OF:** No-one

## NEIL, Alexander Francis

**BIRTHPLACE:** Bellshill, Glasgow, Lanarkshire
**DATE OF BIRTH:** 09/06/1981
**IN CHARGE AT SUNDERLAND:** 11/02/2022 - 26/08/2022

| P | W | D | L |
|---|---|---|---|
| 24 | 12 | 9 | 3 |

Won promotion to the Championship 2022
**ALSO IN CHARGE OF:** Hamilton Academical, Norwich City, Preston North End, Stoke City

## CANNING, Martin (Caretaker)

**BIRTHPLACE:** Glasgow, Lanarkshire
**DATE OF BIRTH:** 03/12/1981
**IN CHARGE AT SUNDERLAND:** 27/08/2022

| P | W | D | L |
|---|---|---|---|
| 1 | 0 | 0 | 1 |

**ALSO IN CHARGE OF:** Hamilton Academical

## MOWBRAY, Anthony Mark (Tony)

**BIRTHPLACE:** Saltburn, North Yorkshire
**DATE OF BIRTH:** 22/11/1963
**IN CHARGE AT SUNDERLAND:** 31/08/2022 -

| P | W | D | L | |
|---|---|---|---|---|
| 1 | 1 | 0 | 0 | to 31/08/2022 |

**ALSO IN CHARGE OF:** Ipswich Town (C), Hibernian, WBA, Celtic, Middlesbrough, Coventry City, Blackburn Rovers

# Updates

## TO SUNDERLAND AFC: THE ABSOLUTE RECORD

**Since the publication of Volume One of the Absolute Record some new information has come to light. Along with updates and corrections the following addendum should bring your copy of Volume One up to date.**

| PAGE | COMMENT |
|---|---|
| 15 | **1885-86.** Number 11 v Redcar should be G. Monaghan not D. Logan. See AR2 Preface. |
| 18 & 19 | **1891-92.** League competition should be 'The Football League' not 'Division One'. |
| 45 | **1904-05.** Match 11 - Attendance should be 36,300 not 30,000. |
| 51 | **1907-08.** The surname of goalkeeper Allen should be Allan. |
| 89 | **1929-30.** Match 31 - Attendance should be 31,016 not 31,106. |
| 99 | **1934-35.** Match 45 should be May 4 not May 5. |
| 109 | **1939-40.** Match 7 Attendance should be 5,018 not 5,000.<br>**1940-41.** For matches 2, 4, 5, 6, 7 & 10 starting at 'Connor' all appearance numbers should be moved one place to the right so that '1' is under Bircham, etc. All player totals are correct. |
| 111 | **1941-42.** Match 8 - Attendance 10,000.<br>**1941-42.** Match 11 - Attendance 8,000.<br>**1941-42.** Match 12 - Attendance should be 1,898 not 2,000.<br>**1941-42.** Match 13 - Attendance 1,500.<br>**1941-42.** Match 16 - Attendance 4,000.<br>**1941-42.** Match 20 - Attendance 6,000.<br>**1941-42.** Match 24 - Attendance 5,000.<br>**1941-42.** Match 25 - Attendance 2,101.<br>**1941-42.** Match 26 - Attendance 8,000.<br>**1941-42.** Match 27 - Attendance 5,000.<br>**1941-42.** Match 29 - Attendance 4,000. League position 13.<br>**1941-42.** Match 34 - Attendance 7,640.<br>**1941-42.** Match 36 - Attendance should be 20,500 not 19,500. |
| 113 | **1942-43.** Match 2 - Attendance 3,684.<br>**1942-43.** Match 7 - Attendance 3,490.<br>**1942-43.** Match 8 - Attendance 3,500.<br>**1942-43.** Match 10 - Attendance 2,500.<br>**1942-43.** Match 18 - Attendance 2,000.<br>**1942-43.** Match 19 - Half-time 0-0.<br>**1942-43.** Match 22 - Attendance 2,500.<br>**1942-43.** Match 24 - Attendance 4,000.<br>**1942-43.** Match 28 - Attendance 12,000.<br>**1942-43.** Match 29 - Attendance 6,915.<br>**1942-43.** Match 33 - Attendance 3,000.<br>**1942-43.** Match 36 - Attendance 4,030. |
| 115 | **1943-44.** Match 1 - Attendance 4,000.<br>**1943-44.** Match 2 - Attendance 4,000.<br>**1943-44.** Match 5 - Attendance 5,734.<br>**1943-44.** Match 10 - Attendance 6,816. |
| 117 | **1944-45.** Match 3 - Attendance 8,000.<br>**1944-45.** Match 4 - Attendance 8,000.<br>**1944-45.** Match 7 - Attendance 6,618.<br>**1944-45.** Match 8 - Attendance 8,500.<br>**1944-45.** Match 11 - Attendance 11,532.<br>**1944-45.** Match 13 - Attendance 8,197.<br>**1944-45.** Match 14 - Attendance 10,000.<br>**1944-45.** Match 30 - Attendance 9,000.<br>**1944-45.** Match 41 - Attendance 3,696. |
| 227 | The season title should be 1999-2000 not 1990-2000. |
| 259 | **2015-16.** Match 41 - M'Vila last game. |
| 261 | **2016-17.** Match 42 - remove Defoe last game. |
| 265 | **2018-19.** Match 36 - Hackett last game.<br>**2018-19.** Gooch, 8 League subs not 7. O'Nien, 13 League subs not 14. |
| 267 | **2019-20.** leasing.com Football League Trophy Winners: Salford City<br>**2019-20.** Match 24 - Connelly last game |
| 269 | **1955-56.** Top scorer Fleming - total should be 28 goals not 29 and 35.00% not 36.25% |
| 270 | **Draws.** Most in One Season section - highest total should read 19: 2018-19. |
| 272 | **Friendlies.** 14 January 1882 v Tyne was played as two 30-minute halves. |
| 289 | **Post War Lowest Home Attendances**<br>1st - 3,498 v Oldham Athletic (FLT), 1 December 2021.<br>5th - 3,960 v Manchester Utd U21 (FLT), 13 October 2021.<br>6th - 3,966 v Bradford City (FLT), 9 November 2021. |

George Monaghan

Yann M'Vila

Lynden Gooch

Charlie Fleming

Michael Kay

Sam Aiston

Aiden McGeady

James Chalmers

| PAGE | COMMENT |
|---|---|
| 295 | **Barnsley.** Played for Both - remove Len Shackleton (WW2).<br>**Barrow.** Played for Both - remove Vic Halom. |
| 297 | **Bournemouth.** Played for Both - remove Patrick Gallacher. |
| 298 | **Brentford.** Played for Both - remove WW1 from John Curtis as he also played in League games and remove Patsy Gallacher. |
| 299 | **Bristol City.** Played for Both - should include William Gibson. |
| 300 | **Cardiff City.** Played for Both - should include Greg Halford. |
| 301 | **Carlisle United.** Played for Both - remove Harry Thompson (WW2) and include Charlie Thomson (WW2).<br>**Charlton Athletic.** Played for Both - remove Patsy Gallacher. |
| 302 | **Cheltenham Town.** Played for Both - should include Patsy Gallacher.<br>**Chester City.** Played for Both - remove Joseph Hewitt and should include Michael Kay. |
| 303 | **Crewe Alexandra.** Played for Both - should include Patsy Gallacher (WW2).<br>**Crystal Palace.** Played for Both - should include Jack Rogers.<br>**Darlington.** Played for Both - should include Hugh McMahon (WW2). |
| 305 | **Fulham.** Played for Both - remove Patsy Gallacher.<br>**Fulham.** Played for Both - should include George Holley (WW1). |
| 306 | **Gainsborough Trinity.** Played for Both - should include Sam Aiston.<br>**Grimsby Town.** Played for Both - should include Jordan Cook and remove John Finlay (WW2).<br>**Hartlepool United.** Played for Both - should include John Finlay (WW2). |
| 307 | **Huddersfield Town.** Played for Both - should include Len Shackleton (WW2), Danny Simpson and Dean Whitehead.<br>**Hull City.** Played for Both - should include Harry Martin (WW1).<br>**Ipswich Town.** Played for Both - should include Stern John. |
| 308 | **Leicester City.** Played for Both - should include Patsy Gallacher (WW2). |
| 309 | **Leyton Orient.** Played for Both - remove Patsy Gallacher and George Payne.<br>**Lincoln City.** Played for Both - should include Bob McDermid. |
| 310 | **Luton Town.** Played for Both - remove Patsy Gallacher. |
| 311 | **Middlesbrough.** Played for Both - remove John Finlay (WW2). |
| 312 | **Millwall.** Played for Both - remove Patsy Gallacher.<br>**Newcastle United.** Played for Both - should include Billy Hogg (WW1). |
| 313 | **Northwich Victoria.** Played for Both - should include Vic Halom. |
| 314 | **Notts County.** Played for Both - should include Patsy Gallacher (WW2). |
| 315 | **Peterborough United.** Played for Both - should include Cyril Beach and remove Robert Ferguson.<br>**Portsmouth.** Played for Both - should include Archibald McKenzie. |
| 316 | **Preston North End.** Played for Both - remove Chris Makin. |
| 317 | **Reading.** Played for Both - should include Joseph Hewitt.<br>**Rochdale.** Played for Both - should include Jack Ashurst. |
| 318 | **Sheffield United.** Played for Both - should include George Philip (WW1). |
| 319 | **Southend United.** Played for Both - remove Daryl Murphy. |
| 323 | **Wigan Athletic.** Played for Both - remove Jack Jones (WW2).<br>**Wrexham.** Played for Both - should include Arthur Housam (WW2). |
| 324 | **York City.** Played for Both - should include Liam Agnew & Peter Boyle. |
| 346 | **WW1 Players.** Johnson was Richard Kemp (Dick) Johnson, born Gateshead, Q2 1895.<br>**WW1 Players.** Ralph Rodgerson, born 30/12/1892 not Q1 1893. |
| 348 | **WW2 Players.** N. Fraser should be Norman Fraser, born Broughty Ferry, 19/03/1916.<br>**WW2 Players.** Thomas Frederick Jenkins should be Thomas Frederick (Fred) Jenkins. |
| 354 | **Oldest Player.** 1st - Jermain Defoe, 39 years 163 days v Lincoln City (as sub), 19 March 2022.<br>**Youngest Player.** 3rd - Zak Johnson, 16 years 142 days v Manchester United U21 (as sub), 13 October 2021.<br>**Shortest Players.** John Lynas 5'4½". |
| 356 | **Youngest Goalscorers.**<br>10. Bobby Park, 17 years 336 days v Ipswich Town, 6 Dec 1969 (not Don McColl in 1884).<br>**Oldest Goalscorers.**<br>7. Aiden McGeady, 35 years 230 days v Ipswich Town, 20 November 2021.<br>10. Grant Leadbitter, 35 years 103 days v Hull City, 20 April 2021.<br>**Fastest to 50 Goals.**<br>1. John Campbell, 49 games not 48.<br>4. Jimmy Millar, 74 games not 70 (making Kevin Phillips 4th fastest). |
| 358 | **Record Transfers.** Arthur Hudgell from Crystal Palace, January 1947, £10,000, not Ron Turnbull November 1947, £9,000.<br>**Record Transfers.** John Murray from Vale of Leven, September 1890, £220, not Archibald McKenzie (£125) and George Livingston (£175).<br>**Record Sale.** David Hannah to Liverpool November 1894, £100. |
| 376 | **1960-61.** Sunderland v North Shields should be 24 December not 26 December. |
| 379 | **Quickest Goals.** James Chalmers, 1 minute, H, Nottingham Forest, 23 April 1898. |
| 384 | **Number of Wales caps.** 100 not 99. **Number of Wales players.** 12 not 11. |
| 387 | **Total number of England caps.** 100 not 99. |
| 390 | **Total number of Wales caps.** 100 not 99. |
| 391 | **4. Ian Lawther.** Second cap comment should state "with Harvey' (not debut). His first cap on 6 April 1960 should state 'Debut'. |

# 2020-21

## SKY BET LEAGUE ONE

# Wembley Winners

**Sunderland finished in a higher position than they did when they won promotion a year later. However, Play-Off failure at the semi-final stage against a Lincoln City line-up who had only finished beneath Sunderland on goal difference meant the season ended in huge disappointment despite a first Wembley win since 1973. Even the win at the National Stadium was tinged with a touch of sadness as after all the failed trips fans had experienced at Wembley, Covid restrictions meant supporters were not allowed into the arena to experience the joy of winning the Football League (Papa-John's) Trophy.**

Sunderland slipped quietly out of both major cups without scoring, despite home draws in both the Carabao and FA Cups. In the most important knock-out games, a first-leg Play-Off semi-final was lost 2-0 at Lincoln on the first occasion all season that supporters were allowed into a Sunderland fixture. Although the second leg at Wearside saw a Covid regulation restricted crowd of only 9,971, it still represented the biggest gate of the season at any EFL or Play-Off match. Regardless of the restricted numbers the atmosphere was cracking as goals from Ross Stewart and Charlie Wyke wiped out the first leg deficit with barely half an hour played. The Imps made life tough after the break though with Tom Hopper scoring the goal that ended Sunderland's season and condemned the Lads to a desperately unwanted fourth successive year in League One.

## FINAL LEAGUE TABLE

| | | HOME | | | | | | AWAY | | | | | TOTAL | | | |
|---|---|---|---|---|---|---|---|---|---|---|---|---|---|---|---|---|
| | | P | W | D | L | F | A | W | D | L | F | A | F | A | GD | P |
| 1 | Hull City | 46 | 14 | 4 | 5 | 32 | 14 | 13 | 4 | 6 | 48 | 24 | 80 | 38 | 42 | 89 |
| 2 | Peterborough United | 46 | 15 | 5 | 3 | 52 | 22 | 11 | 4 | 8 | 31 | 24 | 83 | 46 | 37 | 87 |
| 3 | Blackpool | 46 | 12 | 7 | 4 | 30 | 18 | 11 | 4 | 8 | 30 | 19 | 60 | 37 | 23 | 80 |
| **4** | **Sunderland** | **46** | **9** | **8** | **6** | **32** | **25** | **11** | **9** | **3** | **38** | **17** | **70** | **42** | **28** | **77** |
| 5 | Lincoln City | 46 | 9 | 5 | 9 | 35 | 30 | 13 | 6 | 4 | 34 | 20 | 69 | 50 | 19 | 77 |
| 6 | Oxford United | 46 | 13 | 4 | 6 | 39 | 21 | 9 | 4 | 10 | 38 | 35 | 77 | 56 | 21 | 74 |
| 7 | Charlton Athletic | 46 | 8 | 7 | 8 | 36 | 37 | 12 | 7 | 4 | 34 | 19 | 70 | 56 | 14 | 74 |
| 8 | Portsmouth | 46 | 9 | 5 | 9 | 29 | 24 | 12 | 4 | 7 | 36 | 27 | 65 | 51 | 14 | 72 |
| 9 | Ipswich Town | 46 | 12 | 5 | 6 | 25 | 18 | 7 | 7 | 9 | 21 | 28 | 46 | 46 | 0 | 69 |
| 10 | Gillingham | 46 | 10 | 5 | 8 | 31 | 30 | 9 | 5 | 9 | 32 | 30 | 63 | 60 | 3 | 67 |
| 11 | Accrington Stanley | 46 | 10 | 7 | 6 | 31 | 26 | 8 | 6 | 9 | 32 | 42 | 63 | 68 | -5 | 67 |
| 12 | Crewe Alexandra | 46 | 10 | 7 | 6 | 32 | 30 | 8 | 5 | 10 | 24 | 31 | 56 | 61 | -5 | 66 |
| 13 | Milton Keynes Dons | 46 | 10 | 7 | 6 | 36 | 28 | 8 | 4 | 11 | 28 | 34 | 64 | 62 | 2 | 65 |
| 14 | Doncaster Rovers | 46 | 11 | 4 | 8 | 34 | 32 | 8 | 3 | 12 | 29 | 35 | 63 | 67 | -4 | 64 |
| 15 | Fleetwood Town | 46 | 9 | 8 | 6 | 26 | 17 | 7 | 4 | 12 | 23 | 29 | 49 | 46 | 3 | 60 |
| 16 | Burton Albion | 46 | 7 | 4 | 12 | 32 | 42 | 8 | 8 | 7 | 29 | 31 | 61 | 73 | -12 | 57 |
| 17 | Shrewsbury Town | 46 | 5 | 8 | 10 | 28 | 31 | 8 | 7 | 8 | 22 | 26 | 50 | 57 | -7 | 54 |
| 18 | Plymouth Argyle | 46 | 11 | 4 | 8 | 31 | 39 | 3 | 7 | 13 | 22 | 41 | 53 | 80 | -27 | 53 |
| 19 | AFC Wimbledon | 46 | 7 | 5 | 11 | 32 | 39 | 5 | 10 | 8 | 22 | 31 | 54 | 70 | -16 | 51 |
| 20 | Wigan Athletic | 46 | 5 | 6 | 12 | 26 | 42 | 8 | 3 | 12 | 28 | 35 | 54 | 77 | -23 | 48 |
| 21 | Rochdale | 46 | 4 | 9 | 10 | 27 | 42 | 7 | 5 | 11 | 34 | 36 | 61 | 78 | -17 | 47 |
| 22 | Northampton Town | 46 | 8 | 5 | 10 | 20 | 26 | 3 | 7 | 13 | 21 | 41 | 41 | 67 | -26 | 45 |
| 23 | Swindon Town | 46 | 8 | 1 | 14 | 25 | 38 | 5 | 3 | 15 | 30 | 51 | 55 | 89 | -34 | 43 |
| 24 | Bristol Rovers | 46 | 7 | 2 | 14 | 23 | 32 | 3 | 6 | 14 | 17 | 38 | 40 | 70 | -30 | 38 |

It was a season of change. Following the departure of Phil Parkinson on 29 November, Lee Johnson took over on 5 December. Just over two months later control of the club passed from Stewart Donald to the youthful Kyril Louis-Dreyfus. What did not change is that once again Sunderland failed to win promotion despite spending much of the season looking like they had a good chance of going up.

## MATCH OF THE SEASON

### Sunderland 4-1 Doncaster Rovers

**SATURDAY 13 FEBRUARY 2021**

**While there was a Wembley win over the Rovers of Tranmere, this victory over Doncaster Rovers was the match of the season. While it was undeniably good to win a trophy at the National Stadium and the players and staff deserve credit for that, the blunt truth is that not only was the final played to an empty stadium due to Covid, but in reality it was a competition for clubs in the bottom two tiers - a trophy Sunderland's first team will hopefully never participate in again having secured promotion a year later.**

The Doncaster game was also played in front of just officials and press but it was a match worth three points. The mercurial Aiden McGeady produced his best performance for Sunderland. He laid on all four of the goals which were all scored with headers by Charlie Wyke. McGeady also superbly laid on an almost identical chance for Lynden Gooch as he did a month almost to the day later, when Gooch netted the only goal of the Wembley final against Tranmere.

In an action packed match Lee Burge saved two penalties from Jon Taylor and Jason Lokilo. In the history of the Stadium of Light, excluding shoot-outs there had only ever been one spot-kick save by a Sunderland 'keeper (Jon McLaughlin against Fleetwood's Paddy Madden in September 2018). Just to add to the eventful nature of the occasion Burge was also debited with an own-goal although he was powerless and unlucky to see a shot from Taylor Richards strike a post and then rebound in off him. After scoring a first half hat-trick, just a minute after Rovers reduced the deficit Wyke grabbed his fourth of the match. In doing so he became the first Sunderland player to score four in a match since Craig Russell against Millwall in 1995.

## MAJOR SIGNINGS

| | | |
|---|---|---|
| **Ross Stewart** | Ross County | **Undisclosed** |
| **Carl Winchester** | Forest Green Rovers | **Undisclosed** |
| **Aiden O'Brien** | Millwall | **Undisclosed** |
| **Bailey Wright** | Bristol City (after loan) | **Undisclosed** |
| **Danny Graham** | Blackburn Rovers | **Free** |
| **Dion Sanderson** | Wolves | **on loan** |

## DEBUTANTS FROM WITHIN

**Ciaran Dunne (Ex-Falkirk), Josh Hawkes (Ex-Hartlepool United), Anthony Patterson, Vinnie Steels (Ex-Burnley), Sam Wilding (Ex-WBA), Ollie Younger (Ex-Burnley)**

# 2020-21 SEASON

**GROUND:** Stadium of Light **SHIRT SPONSOR:** Great Annual Savings Group **HEAD COACHES:** Phil Parkinson, Andrew Taylor & Lee Johnson
**SKY BET LEAGUE ONE: Champions:** Hull City, 89 pts **Sunderland:** 4th, 77 pts

| MATCH | DATE | ROUND | VENUE | OPPONENTS | RESULT | HT | POSITION | SCORERS | ATT. |
|---|---|---|---|---|---|---|---|---|---|
| 3 | Sep 12 | | H | Bristol Rovers | D 1-1 | 0-1 | | Maguire | |
| 4 | 19 | | A | Oxford United | W 2-0 | 0-0 | 5 | O'Nien, Gooch | |
| 5 | 26 | | H | Peterborough United | W 1-0 | 0-0 | 4 | Leadbitter (pen) | |
| 6 | Oct 3 | | A | Charlton Athletic | D 0-0 | 0-0 | 4 | | |
| 8 | 17 | | A | Swindon Town | W 2-0 | 1-0 | 5 | Wyke, Maguire (pen) | |
| 9 | 20 | | H | Crewe Alexandra | W 1-0 | 1-0 | 5 | Offord o.g. | |
| 10 | 24 | | H | Portsmouth | L 1-3 | 1-2 | 6 | Wyke | |
| 11 | 27 | | A | Rochdale | D 2-2 | 2-2 | 7 | Wyke, Wright | |
| 12 | 31 | | A | Gillingham | W 2-0 | 0-0 | 6 | Maguire (pen), Gooch | |
| 13 | Nov 3 | | H | Ipswich Town | W 2-1 | 1-1 | 6 | Wyke, Leadbitter (pen) | |
| 16 | 14 | | H | MK Dons | L 1-2 | 1-1 | 6 | Power | |
| 17 | 21 | | A | Doncaster Rovers | D 1-1 | 1-0 | 8 | Leadbitter | |
| 18 | 27 | | A | Fleetwood Town | D 1-1 | 0-0 | 7 | Wyke | |
| 19 | Dec 1 | | H | Burton Albion | D 1-1 | 0-0 | 7 | Power | |
| 20 | 5 | | H | Wigan Athletic | L 0-1 | 0-1 | 9 | | |
| 22 | 12 | | A | Lincoln City | W 4-0 | 3-0 | 8 | Leadbitter (pen), Wyke (2), Diamond | |
| 23 | 15 | | H | AFC Wimbledon | D 1-1 | 0-1 | 9 | Wright | |
| 24 | Jan 2 | | A | Northampton Town | D 0-0 | 0-0 | 11 | | |
| 25 | 9 | | H | Hull City | D 1-1 | 1-1 | 10 | McGeady | |
| 27 | 16 | | A | AFC Wimbledon | W 3-0 | 1-0 | 8 | Wyke (3) | |
| 28 | 19 | | H | Plymouth Argyle | L 1-2 | 0-1 | 9 | O'Brien | |
| 29 | 23 | | H | Shrewsbury Town | W 1-0 | 1-0 | 7 | Wyke | |
| 30 | 26 | | A | Ipswich Town | W 1-0 | 1-0 | 7 | Wyke | |
| 31 | 30 | | H | Gillingham | D 2-2 | 2-1 | 6 | McGeady, Leadbitter | |
| 33 | Feb 6 | | A | MK Dons | D 2-2 | 1-2 | 7 | Wyke, O'Nien | |
| 34 | 9 | | A | Shrewsbury Town | L 1-2 | 1-0 | 7 | O'Brien | |
| 35 | 13 | | H | Doncaster Rovers | W 4-1 | 3-0 | 6 | Wyke (4) | |
| 37 | 20 | | A | Burton Albion | W 3-0 | 2-0 | 6 | Leadbitter, Gooch, Wyke | |
| 38 | 23 | | H | Fleetwood Town | W 2-0 | 0-0 | 5 | O'Brien, Power | |
| 39 | 27 | | A | Crewe Alexandra | D 2-2 | 0-2 | 5 | Jones, Maguire | |
| 40 | Mar 2 | | H | Swindon Town | W 1-0 | 0-0 | 4 | Wyke | |
| 41 | 6 | | H | Rochdale | W 2-0 | 2-0 | 4 | Sanderson, Wyke | |
| 42 | 9 | | A | Portsmouth | W 2-0 | 1-0 | 4 | Wyke, Jones | |
| 44 | 17 | | A | Accrington Stanley | W 2-0 | 0-0 | 3 | Stewart, Wyke | |
| 45 | 20 | | H | Lincoln City | D 1-1 | 1-0 | 3 | McFadzean | |
| 46 | 27 | | A | Bristol Rovers | W 1-0 | 1-0 | 3 | O'Brien | |
| 47 | Apr 2 | | H | Oxford United | W 3-1 | 1-1 | 3 | Gooch, McGeady, Power | |
| 48 | 5 | | A | Peterborough United | D 1-1 | 0-0 | 3 | McGeady | |
| 49 | 10 | | H | Charlton Athletic | L 1-2 | 0-1 | 3 | Scowen | |
| 50 | 13 | | A | Wigan Athletic | L 1-2 | 1-1 | 3 | Wyke | |
| 51 | 17 | | A | Blackpool | L 0-1 | 0-0 | 3 | | |
| 52 | 20 | | A | Hull City | D 2-2 | 2-1 | 3 | Jones, Leadbitter (pen) | |
| 53 | 24 | | H | Accrington Stanley | D 3-3 | 2-0 | 3 | Wyke (2), Power | |
| 54 | 27 | | H | Blackpool | L 0-1 | 0-0 | 4 | | |
| 55 | May 1 | | A | Plymouth Argyle | W 3-1 | 1-0 | 3 | Stewart, Maguire (pen), Hume | |
| 56 | 9 | | H | Northampton Town | D 1-1 | 0-0 | 4 | Winchester | |
| **PLAY-OFFS** | | | | **WINNERS: BLACKPOOL** | | | | | |
| 57 | May 19 | SF1 | A | Lincoln City | L 0-2 | 0-0 | | | 3,145 |
| 58 | 22 | SF2 | H | Lincoln City | W 2-1 | 2-0 | | Stewart, Wyke | 9,971 |
| **EMIRATES FA CUP** | | | | **WINNERS: LEICESTER CITY** | | | | | |
| 14 | Nov 7 | R1 | H | Mansfield Town | L 0-1 | 0-0 | | | |
| **CARABAO (LEAGUE) CUP** | | | | **WINNERS: MANCHESTER CITY** | | | | | |
| 1 | Sep 5 | R1 | H | Hull City | L 0-0 | 0-0 | 4-5 on pens | | |
| **PAPA JOHN'S EFL TROPHY** | | | | **WINNERS: SUNDERLAND** | | | | | |
| 2 | Sep 8 | Group | H | Aston Villa U-21 | W 8-1 | 2-0 | | Wyke (2), Feeney, Scowen, Power, Graham, Dobson, O'Brien | |
| 7 | Oct 6 | Group | H | Carlisle United | W 5-3 | 2-1 | | Maguire (2), Hume, Wyke, Diamond | |
| 15 | Nov 10 | Group | A | Fleetwood Town | L 1-2 | 1-0 | | McFadzean | |
| 21 | Dec 8 | R2 | A | Oldham Athletic | W 2-1 | 1-1 | | Maguire, Scowen | |
| 26 | Jan 12 | R3 | H | Port Vale | W 2-0 | 1-0 | | O'Brien, McGeady (pen) | |
| 32 | Feb 2 | R4 | A | MK Dons | W 3-0 | 1-0 | | Lewington o.g., McGeady, Wyke | |
| 36 | 17 | Semi | H | Lincoln City | W 1-1 | 1-1 | 5-4 on pens | Wyke | |
| 43 | Mar 14 | Final | Wembley | Tranmere Rovers | W 1-0 | 0-0 | | Gooch | |

| MATCH | Burge | O'Nien | Hume | Willis | Wright | Flanagan | Maguire | Dobson | Grigg | Power | O'Brien | Graham | Wyke | Gooch | Leadbitter | Scowen | McLaughlin | Diamond | Sanderson | Matthews | Embleton | McFadzean | McGeady | Curry | Winchester | Vokins | Jones | Neil | Younger | Stewart | Feeney | Taylor, B. | Xhemajli | Patterson | Hawkes | Dunne | Steels | Wilding | Almond | Richardson | Wearne | Mbunga-Kimpiok |
|---|---|---|---|---|---|---|---|---|---|---|---|---|---|---|---|---|---|---|---|---|---|---|---|---|---|---|---|---|---|---|---|---|---|---|---|---|---|---|---|---|---|---|
| 3 | 1 | 2 | 3 | 4 | $5^{3}$ | 6 | 7 | 8 | $9^{1}$ | 10 | $11^{2}$ | $12^{1}$ | $13^{2}$ | $14^{3}$ | U | U | | | | U | | | | | | | | | | | | | U | | | | | | | | | |
| 4 | 1 | 2 | 3 | 4 | 5 | 6 | 7 | | U | $10^{1}$ | $11^{3}$ | $9^{2}$ | $13^{2}$ | $14^{3}$ | 8 | $12^{1}$ | U | | | U | | | | | | | | | | | | | U | | | | | | | | | |
| 5 | 1 | 2 | 3 | 4 | 5 | 6 | $7^{1}$ | | U | | $12^{1}$ | $13^{2}$ | $9^{2}$ | $11^{3}$ | 8 | 10 | $14^{3}$ | U | | U | | | | | | | | | | | | | U | | | | | | | | | |
| 6 | 1 | 2 | 3 | 4 | 5 | 6 | | | $12^{1}$ | U | $7^{1}$ | $9^{2}$ | $13^{2}$ | 11 | 8 | 10 | U | U | | U | | | | | | | | | | | | | U | | | | | | | | | |
| 8 | 1 | 6 | | $4^{1}$ | 5 | | $7^{2}$ | U | U | 10 | $13^{2}$ | U | 9 | 3 | 8 | 11 | 2 | $12^{1}$ | | U | | | | | | | | | U | | | | | | | | | | | | | |
| 9 | 1 | 6 | 3 | | 5 | $14^{3}$ | $7^{1}$ | $13^{2}$ | U | 10 | $12^{1}$ | U | 9 | $2^{3}$ | 8 | $11^{2}$ | 4 | U | | U | | | | | | | | | | | | | | | | | | | | | | |
| 10 | 1 | 6 | 3 | 4 | 5 | U | 7 | U | $12^{1}$ | 10 | U | $13^{2}$ | 9 | 2 | $8^{2}$ | $11^{1}$ | U | | | U | | | | | | | | | | | | | | | | | | | | | | |
| 11 | 1 | | 3 | U | 5 | 6 | $7^{1}$ | 8 | U | 10 | U | $13^{2}$ | $9^{2}$ | 11 | U | $12^{1}$ | 2 | | 4 | U | | | | | | | | | | | | | | | | | | | | | | |
| 12 | 1 | 2 | 3 | | 5 | 6 | $13^{2}$ | | U | U | $10^{1}$ | $12^{1}$ | 9 | 11 | 8 | $7^{2}$ | 4 | U | U | U | | | | | | | | | | | | | | | | | | | | | | |
| 13 | 1 | 2 | 3 | | 5 | 6 | $7^{2}$ | | U | $12^{1}$ | U | $13^{2}$ | 9 | $11^{3}$ | 8 | $10^{1}$ | 4 | U | $14^{3}$ | U | | | | | | | | | | | | | | | | | | | | | | |
| 16 | U | 6 | 3 | $4^{3}$ | 5 | | $12^{1}$ | U | $11^{2}$ | $10^{1}$ | U | $13^{2}$ | 9 | 2 | 8 | 7 | | $14^{3}$ | U | 1 | | | | | | | | | | | | | | | | | | | | | | |
| 17 | U | 2 | 3 | | 5 | 6 | $7^{1}$ | | U | $13^{2}$ | | U | 9 | $11^{2}$ | 8 | 10 | 4 | U | U | 1 | $12^{1}$ | | | | | | | | | | | | | | | | | | | | | |
| 18 | U | 2 | $3^{3}$ | | 5 | 6 | $7^{2}$ | | $12^{1}$ | $13^{2}$ | | $11^{1}$ | 9 | | 8 | 10 | 4 | U | U | 1 | U | $14^{3}$ | | | | | | | | | | | | | | | | | | | | |
| 19 | U | $2^{4}$ | 3 | | 5 | $6^{3}$ | $13^{2}$ | U | $14^{3}$ | 10 | | $12^{1}$ | $9^{1}$ | | 8 | 11 | 4 | | $15^{4}$ | 1 | $7^{2}$ | U | | | | | | | | | | | | | | | | | | | | |
| 20 | 1 | | $3^{1}$ | | 5 | 6 | 7 | U | $9^{3}$ | $10^{2}$ | | $14^{3}$ | | | 4 | 8 | 2 | $15^{4}$ | U | U | $13^{2}$ | $12^{1}$ | $11^{4}$ | | | | | | | | | | | | | | | | | | | |
| 22 | 1 | | | | 5 | 6 | $12^{1}$ | $13^{2}$ | $16^{5}$ | 10 | | U | $9^{5}$ | | 4 | $8^{2}$ | $2^{4}$ | $7^{1}$ | $15^{4}$ | U | $14^{3}$ | 3 | $11^{3}$ | | | | | | | | | | | | | | | | | | | |
| 23 | 1 | | | $14^{3}$ | 5 | | | $8^{1}$ | $9^{2}$ | | 10 | | | $12^{1}$ | 4 | | 2 | 7 | 6 | | 11 | $3^{3}$ | | $13^{2}$ | | | | U | U | | | U | | U | | | | | | | | |
| 24 | 1 | | | U | 5 | 6 | $12^{1}$ | | | $10^{2}$ | $14^{3}$ | $15^{4}$ | $9^{4}$ | $13^{2}$ | 4 | 8 | 2 | $7^{1}$ | 3 | U | U | | $11^{3}$ | | | | | | | | | | | | | | | | | | | |
| 25 | $1^{1}$ | | | | 5 | | $15^{4}$ | | | 10 | U | $14^{3}$ | $9^{3}$ | $13^{2}$ | 4 | 8 | $2^{2}$ | $7^{4}$ | 6 | $12^{1}$ | $16^{5}$ | 3 | $11^{5}$ | | | | | | U | | | | | | | | | | | | | |
| 27 | 1 | U | | 6 | 5 | | $14^{3}$ | | | 2 | $10^{3}$ | | 9 | | 4 | 8 | | $13^{2}$ | U | U | $7^{1}$ | 3 | $11^{2}$ | | $12^{1}$ | | | | U | | | | | | | | | | | | | |
| 28 | 1 | U | | $6^{1}$ | 5 | | $14^{3}$ | | | $12^{1}$ | 10 | | 9 | | $15^{4}$ | 8 | | 7 | 2 | U | $13^{2}$ | $3^{2}$ | $11^{3}$ | | $4^{4}$ | | | | U | | | | | | | | | | | | | |
| 29 | 1 | $14^{3}$ | | 6 | 5 | | $12^{1}$ | | | 2 | 10 | U | 9 | | 4 | $8^{3}$ | | $7^{1}$ | U | U | U | 3 | $11^{2}$ | | $13^{2}$ | | | | | | | | | | | | | | | | | |
| 30 | 1 | $15^{4}$ | | 6 | $5^{2}$ | | U | | | 2 | $10^{4}$ | | 9 | $14^{3}$ | 4 | 8 | | U | $13^{2}$ | U | $12^{1}$ | 3 | $11^{3}$ | | $7^{1}$ | | | | | | | | | | | | | | | | | |
| 31 | 1 | $13^{2}$ | | 5 | | 6 | | | | 2 | 10 | | $9^{2}$ | $12^{1}$ | $4^{3}$ | 8 | | $7^{1}$ | $14^{3}$ | U | U | 3 | 11 | | U | U | | | | | | | | | | | | | | | | |
| 33 | 1 | $8^{2}$ | | 6 | 5 | | $15^{4}$ | | | 2 | $10^{4}$ | | 9 | $7^{1}$ | 4 | $13^{2}$ | | U | $14^{3}$ | U | | | 11 | | | $3^{3}$ | $12^{1}$ | U | | | | | | | | | | | | | | |
| 34 | U | $15^{4}$ | | $6^{1}$ | 5 | | U | | | $2^{3}$ | 10 | | 9 | $13^{2}$ | 4 | 8 | U | $14^{3}$ | $12^{1}$ | 1 | | | 11 | | | $3^{4}$ | $7^{2}$ | | | | | | | | | | | | | | | |
| 35 | 1 | $4^{2}$ | | | 5 | | | | | 10 | $14^{3}$ | | 9 | $7^{3}$ | $12^{1}$ | 8 | $2^{1}$ | $13^{2}$ | 6 | U | | 3 | $11^{4}$ | | | U | $15^{4}$ | U | | | | | | | | | | | | | | |
| 37 | 1 | 6 | | | | | $16^{5}$ | | | $10^{5}$ | 7 | | $9^{4}$ | 2 | $8^{1}$ | $14^{3}$ | 4 | $15^{4}$ | 5 | U | | | $11^{2}$ | | $12^{1}$ | $3^{3}$ | $13^{2}$ | U | | | | | | | | | | | | | | |
| 38 | 1 | 6 | | | | | $14^{3}$ | | | 10 | $7^{3}$ | | 9 | $2^{2}$ | 8 | | 4 | U | 5 | U | | 3 | $11^{1}$ | | $13^{2}$ | U | $12^{1}$ | | U | | | | | | | | | | | | | |
| 39 | 1 | 6 | | | | | $14^{3}$ | | | 10 | $7^{3}$ | | 9 | $2^{4}$ | $15^{4}$ | 8 | 4 | $12^{1}$ | 5 | U | | $3^{1}$ | $11^{2}$ | | $16^{5}$ | U | $13^{2}$ | | | | | | | | | | | | | | | |
| 40 | 1 | 6 | | | | | $12^{1}$ | | | 4 | $13^{2}$ | | 9 | $2^{2}$ | | $8^{4}$ | | $14^{3}$ | 5 | U | | 3 | $11^{3}$ | | 10 | U | $7^{1}$ | $15^{4}$ | U | | | | | | | | | | | | | |
| 41 | 1 | 6 | | | | | $12^{1}$ | | | 4 | 10 | | 9 | | | $13^{2}$ | | $14^{3}$ | 5 | U | | 3 | $11^{4}$ | | $8^{2}$ | U | $7^{3}$ | $15^{4}$ | $2^{1}$ | | | | | | U | | | | | | | |
| 42 | 1 | 6 | | | | $12^{1}$ | $13^{2}$ | | | 2 | $10^{1}$ | | 9 | $14^{3}$ | | 8 | | U | 5 | U | | 3 | $11^{3}$ | | 4 | U | $7^{2}$ | U | | | | | | | | | | | | | | |
| 44 | 1 | 6 | | | | | $15^{4}$ | | | 10 | | | $9^{4}$ | $2^{3}$ | $14^{3}$ | $13^{2}$ | 4 | $7^{1}$ | 5 | U | | $16^{5}$ | $11^{2}$ | | 8 | $3^{5}$ | | | U | $12^{1}$ | | | | | | | | | | | | |
| 45 | 1 | 6 | | | | | $14^{3}$ | | | 10 | | | 9 | $7^{3}$ | $4^{2}$ | $12^{1}$ | 2 | U | 5 | U | | 3 | 11 | | $8^{1}$ | | | U | U | $13^{2}$ | | | | | | | | | | | | |
| 46 | 1 | 6 | | | | | U | | | 2 | $10^{2}$ | | 9 | $7^{1}$ | $12^{1}$ | 8 | | U | 5 | U | | 3 | 11 | | 4 | | | U | U | $13^{2}$ | | | | | | | | | | | | |
| 47 | 1 | 6 | | | | | $13^{2}$ | | | 8 | U | | 9 | 10 | $14^{3}$ | 4 | $2^{1}$ | U | 5 | U | | 3 | $11^{3}$ | | U | | $7^{2}$ | | | $12^{1}$ | | | | | | | | | | | | |
| 48 | 1 | 6 | $15^{4}$ | | | | | | | 2 | $13^{2}$ | | 9 | $12^{1}$ | $4^{3}$ | $16^{5}$ | $14^{3}$ | U | 5 | U | | $3^{4}$ | 11 | | $8^{5}$ | | $7^{1}$ | | | $10^{2}$ | | | | | | | | | | | | |
| 49 | 1 | 6 | $15^{4}$ | | | | | | | 4 | $7^{1}$ | | 9 | $2^{4}$ | U | 8 | $12^{1}$ | U | 5 | U | | $3^{3}$ | 11 | | $10^{2}$ | | $13^{2}$ | | | $14^{3}$ | | | | | | | | | | | | |
| 50 | 1 | 2 | $3^{1}$ | | 5 | | | | | $8^{2}$ | U | | 9 | $15^{4}$ | $13^{2}$ | 4 | | $11^{4}$ | 6 | U | | $12^{1}$ | 10 | | U | | $7^{3}$ | | | $14^{3}$ | | | | | | | | | | | | |
| 51 | 1 | 6 | $12^{1}$ | | 5 | | U | | | 2 | $10^{2}$ | | 9 | $15^{4}$ | 4 | $8^{4}$ | | $14^{3}$ | | U | | $3^{1}$ | 11 | | U | | $7^{3}$ | | | $13^{2}$ | | | | | | | | | | | | |
| 52 | 1 | 6 | $14^{3}$ | | 5 | | $15^{4}$ | | | 2 | $12^{1}$ | | 9 | 11 | $4^{2}$ | 10 | | $13^{2}$ | | | | $3^{3}$ | | | $8^{1}$ | | $7^{4}$ | | U | U | | | | U | | | | | | | | |
| 53 | 1 | 6 | 3 | | 5 | | U | | | 2 | $10^{2}$ | | 9 | $7^{1}$ | $12^{1}$ | 8 | | $14^{3}$ | | U | | U | $11^{4}$ | | $4^{3}$ | | $13^{2}$ | | | $15^{4}$ | | | | | | | | | | | | |
| 54 | 1 | 6 | 3 | | 5 | | U | | | 2 | $10^{1}$ | | 9 | 7 | $4^{3}$ | $8^{2}$ | | U | | U | | U | 11 | | $14^{3}$ | | $13^{2}$ | | | $12^{1}$ | | | | | | | | | | | | |
| 55 | 1 | 6 | 3 | | 5 | | $13^{2}$ | | | 8 | $15^{4}$ | | | 10 | $14^{3}$ | $4^{3}$ | $2^{1}$ | $7^{2}$ | | U | | U | | | $12^{1}$ | | 11 | | U | $9^{4}$ | | | | | | | | | | | | |
| 56 | 1 | 6 | 3 | | 5 | | $13^{2}$ | | | $8^{3}$ | $15^{4}$ | | $9^{4}$ | 10 | $14^{3}$ | $4^{5}$ | $2^{2}$ | $7^{1}$ | | U | | U | $12^{1}$ | | $16^{5}$ | | 11 | | | | | | | | | | | | | | | |
| Appearances | 41 | 34 | 19 | 14 | 33 | 14 | 11 | 3 | 4 | 38 | 23 | 3 | 40 | 26 | 30 | 35 | 22 | 11 | 19 | 5 | 3 | 21 | 28 | | 12 | 4 | 11 | | 1 | 2 | | | | | | | | | | | | |
| Sub Appearances | | 4 | 4 | 1 | | 2 | 22 | 2 | 5 | 4 | 10 | 11 | 3 | 12 | 10 | 8 | 3 | 13 | 7 | 1 | 6 | 4 | 1 | 1 | 8 | | 8 | 2 | | 9 | | | | | | | | | | | | |
| Goals | | 2 | 1 | | 2 | | 5 | | | 5 | 4 | | 25 | 4 | 7 | 1 | | 1 | 1 | | | 1 | 4 | | 1 | | 3 | | | 2 | | | | | | | | | | | | |
| **PLAY-OFFS** | | | | | | | | | | | | | | | | | | | | | | | | | | | | | | | | | | | | | | | | | | |
| 57 | 1 | 2 | $3^{1}$ | | 5 | $6^{4}$ | U | | | $8^{2}$ | | | 9 | 10 | $13^{2}$ | 4 | | $15^{4}$ | | U | | $12^{1}$ | 11 | | U | | $7^{3}$ | | | $14^{3}$ | | | | | | | | | | | | |
| 58 | 1 | 6 | | | 5 | $16^{5}$ | $7^{1}$ | | | $13^{2}$ | $15^{4}$ | | 9 | $2^{5}$ | 4 | $8^{3}$ | | $12^{1}$ | | U | | $3^{2}$ | 11 | | $14^{3}$ | | U | | | $10^{4}$ | | | | | | | | | | | | |
| Appearances | 2 | 2 | 1 | | 2 | 1 | 1 | | | 1 | | | 2 | 2 | 1 | 2 | | | | | | 1 | 2 | | | | 1 | | | 1 | | | | | | | | | | | | |
| Sub Appearances | | | | | | 1 | | | | 1 | 1 | | | | 1 | | | 2 | | | | 1 | | | 1 | | | | | 1 | | | | | | | | | | | | |
| Goals | | | | | | | | | | | | | 1 | | | | | | | | | | | | | | | | | 1 | | | | | | | | | | | | |
| **EMIRATES FA CUP** | | | | | | | | | | | | | | | | | | | | | | | | | | | | | | | | | | | | | | | | | | |
| 14 | U | | | U | | 6 | $7^{1}$ | 8 | 11 | 10 | $14^{3}$ | $9^{2}$ | $13^{2}$ | | U | | 5 | 2 | 4 | 1 | $12^{1}$ | $3^{3}$ | | | | | | U | | | | | | | | | | | | | | |
| Appearances | | | | | | 1 | 1 | 1 | 1 | 1 | | 1 | | | | | 1 | 1 | 1 | 1 | | 1 | | | | | | | | | | | | | | | | | | | | |
| Sub Appearances | | | | | | | | | | | 1 | | 1 | | | | | | | | 1 | | | | | | | | | | | | | | | | | | | | | |
| Goals | | | | | | | | | | | | | | | | | | | | | | | | | | | | | | | | | | | | | | | | | | |
| **CARABAO (LEAGUE) CUP** | | | | | | | | | | | | | | | | | | | | | | | | | | | | | | | | | | | | | | | | | | |
| 1 | 1 | 2 | 3 | 4 | 5 | 6 | $7^{1}$ | 8 | 9 | 10 | $11^{2}$ | | $13^{2}$ | $12^{1}$ | U | U | | | | U | | | | | | | | U | | | U | | | | | | | | | | | |
| Appearances | 1 | 1 | 1 | 1 | 1 | 1 | 1 | 1 | 1 | 1 | 1 | | | | | | | | | | | | | | | | | | | | | | | | | | | | | | | |
| Sub Appearances | | | | | | | | | | | | | 1 | 1 | | | | | | | | | | | | | | | | | | | | | | | | | | | | |
| Goals | | | | | | | | | | | | | | | | | | | | | | | | | | | | | | | | | | | | | | | | | | |
| **PAPA JOHN'S EFL TROPHY** | | | | | | | | | | | | | | | | | | | | | | | | | | | | | | | | | | | | | | | | | | |
| 2 | U | | U | | | U | U | $14^{3}$ | | $8^{3}$ | $12^{1}$ | $13^{2}$ | $9^{2}$ | 3 | 7 | 11 | | 2 | | 1 | | | | | | | | $10^{1}$ | | | 4 | 5 | 6 | | | | | | | | | |
| 7 | U | 6 | 3 | $14^{3}$ | 5 | | 7 | 8 | | 10 | $13^{2}$ | $12^{1}$ | $9^{1}$ | U | U | | | 2 | | 1 | | | | | | | | $11^{2}$ | U | | | $4^{3}$ | | | | | | | | | | |
| 15 | | | | 5 | | | | 8 | | | 9 | | | | | | | 2 | | | 7 | $3^{3}$ | | U | | | | 11 | $6^{1}$ | | | 4 | | 1 | 10 | $12^{1}$ | $13^{2}$ | $14^{3}$ | U | U | U | |
| 21 | | | | | 5 | 6 | $11^{2}$ | $14^{3}$ | $9^{1}$ | 10 | | U | $12^{1}$ | | $4^{3}$ | 8 | 2 | 7 | | U | U | 3 | $13^{2}$ | | | | | U | | | | | | 1 | | | | | | | | |
| 26 | | | | $6^{3}$ | 5 | | $7^{2}$ | U | | 2 | 9 | | $15^{4}$ | $11^{4}$ | $12^{1}$ | 8 | | $16^{5}$ | | 1 | $10^{5}$ | 3 | $13^{2}$ | | | | | $4^{1}$ | $14^{3}$ | | | | | U | | | | | | | | |
| 32 | | 4 | | $5^{3}$ | | 6 | U | | | 2 | $9^{4}$ | | $15^{4}$ | 10 | $16^{5}$ | $8^{5}$ | | 7 | | 1 | | $3^{1}$ | $13^{2}$ | | | | $11^{2}$ | $12^{1}$ | $14^{3}$ | | | | | U | | | | | | | | |
| 36 | 1 | 6 | | | $5^{1}$ | | $14^{3}$ | | | 2 | $15^{4}$ | | 9 | $7^{4}$ | 4 | $10^{2}$ | $12^{1}$ | $13^{2}$ | | U | | 3 | 11 | | | | U | $8^{3}$ | | | | | | | | | | | U | | | |
| 43 | 1 | 6 | | | | $5^{1}$ | $10^{2}$ | | | 2 | | | 9 | 7 | 4 | 8 | $12^{1}$ | $13^{2}$ | | U | | 3 | 11 | | | | | U | U | U | | | | | | | | | | | | U |
| Appearances | 2 | 4 | 1 | 3 | 4 | 3 | 4 | 2 | 1 | 7 | 3 | | 4 | 5 | 4 | 6 | 1 | 5 | | 4 | 2 | 6 | 2 | | | | 1 | 5 | 1 | | 1 | 3 | 1 | 2 | 1 | | | | | | | |
| Sub Appearances | | | | 1 | | | 1 | 2 | | | 3 | 2 | 3 | | 2 | | 2 | 3 | | | | | 3 | | | | | 1 | 2 | | | | | | | 1 | 1 | 1 | | | | |
| Goals | | | 1 | | | | 3 | 1 | | 1 | 2 | 1 | 5 | 1 | | 2 | | 1 | | | | 1 | 2 | | | | | | | | 1 | | | | | | | | | | | |

**MATCH 1:** O'Brien debut. **MATCH 2:** Matthews and Xhemajli debuts & Feeney only game. **MATCH 11:** Sanderson debut. **MATCH 14:** McFadzean debut. **MATCH 15:** Patterson, Younger, Hawkes, Dunne and Wilding debuts; Steels only game; B.Taylor last game & substitute Dunne was substituted by Steels.
**MATCH 18:** Phil Parkinson last game as head coach. **MATCH 19:** Andrew Taylor only game as caretaker manager. **MATCH 20:** Lee Johnson first game as head coach. **MATCH 23:** Curry only game & Dobson last game. **MATCH 25:** Graham last game. **MATCH 27:** Winchester debut. **MATCH 32:** Jones debut. **MATCH 33:** Vokins debut.
**MATCH 34:** Matthews and Willis last games. **MATCH 39:** Substitute Leadbitter substituted by Winchester. **MATCH 44:** Stewart debut & Vokins last game. **MATCH 50:** Sanderson last game. **MATCH 56:** McLaughlin last game. **MATCH 57:** Jones last game. **MATCH 58:** Leadbitter, McFadzean, Maguire, Power, Scowen and Wyke last games.
**DID YOU KNOW THAT?** Games were played with no spectators due to Coronavirus regulations until 17 May 2021 when 25% or 10,000 spectators (which ever was lower) were allowed to attend.

# 2021-22

## SKY BET LEAGUE ONE

# Play-Off Success

**It had been nice to win at Wembley against Tranmere in 2021 but the Wembley win over Wycombe this time round was the stuff dreams are made of. It may have been a League One Play-Off final rather than an FA Cup final but for the first time since 1973 the red and white army were there to lap it up. The legions had gathered in Trafalgar Square and Covent Garden the night before with a sense of belief that it was finally Sunderland's time. They were right. Assured and controlled performances in all three Play-Off games against Sheffield Wednesday and Wycombe Wanderers saw Sunderland be full value for their promotion as they ended the season with a 16 match unbeaten record, the best since 1998-99.**

Under Lee Johnson the season had started brightly. A 4-0 win at Crewe in the 12th league fixture saw the Lads in an automatic promotion place, just two points behind leaders Plymouth with two games in hand. The following weekend a 100% home record was blemished with a controversial home defeat at the hands of Charlton. Although this was followed up with a penalty shoot-out win at QPR that took the team into the Carabao Cup quarter-final (which resulted in defeat at Arsenal) a run of losses that could have derailed the season followed.

January ended with a shock 6-0 hammering at Bolton, the sacking of Lee Johnson, the signing of Jermain Defoe and after two games with caretakers Mike Dodds and Michael Proctor in charge, the appointment of Alex Neil. The new head coach brought in a new defensive structure which provided a platform for a long unbeaten run. With just one loss from his first 18 games in charge Alex Neil registered the fewest defeats in that period of time of any Sunderland manager or head coach. 48 players used in first team games and 21 different goal-scorers were both records, although the number of players was inflated by the inclusion of 10 youngsters whose only appearances were in the Football League (Papa-John's) Trophy.

## FINAL LEAGUE TABLE

| | | | HOME | | | | | AWAY | | | | | TOTAL | | | |
|---|---|---|---|---|---|---|---|---|---|---|---|---|---|---|---|---|
| | | **P** | **W** | **D** | **L** | **F** | **A** | **W** | **D** | **L** | **F** | **A** | **F** | **A** | **GD** | **P** |
| 1 | Wigan Athletic | 46 | 13 | 5 | 5 | 36 | 22 | 14 | 6 | 3 | 46 | 22 | 82 | 44 | 38 | 92 |
| 2 | Rotherham United | 46 | 15 | 3 | 5 | 43 | 22 | 12 | 6 | 5 | 27 | 11 | 70 | 33 | 37 | 90 |
| 3 | Milton Keynes Dons | 46 | 13 | 5 | 5 | 34 | 21 | 13 | 6 | 4 | 44 | 23 | 78 | 44 | 34 | 89 |
| 4 | Sheffield Wednesday | 46 | 16 | 5 | 2 | 48 | 18 | 8 | 8 | 7 | 30 | 32 | 78 | 50 | 28 | 85 |
| **5** | **Sunderland** | **46** | **16** | **3** | **4** | **49** | **19** | **8** | **9** | **6** | **30** | **34** | **79** | **53** | **26** | **84** |
| 6 | Wycombe Wanderers | 46 | 14 | 5 | 4 | 39 | 26 | 9 | 9 | 5 | 36 | 25 | 75 | 51 | 24 | 83 |
| 7 | Plymouth Argyle | 46 | 14 | 4 | 5 | 32 | 19 | 9 | 7 | 7 | 36 | 29 | 68 | 48 | 20 | 80 |
| 8 | Oxford United | 46 | 13 | 6 | 4 | 47 | 27 | 9 | 4 | 10 | 35 | 32 | 82 | 59 | 23 | 76 |
| 9 | Bolton Wanderers | 46 | 12 | 7 | 4 | 45 | 26 | 9 | 3 | 11 | 29 | 31 | 74 | 57 | 17 | 73 |
| 10 | Portsmouth | 46 | 14 | 5 | 4 | 46 | 25 | 6 | 8 | 9 | 22 | 26 | 68 | 51 | 17 | 73 |
| 11 | Ipswich Town | 46 | 11 | 9 | 3 | 38 | 22 | 7 | 7 | 9 | 29 | 24 | 67 | 46 | 21 | 70 |
| 12 | Accrington Stanley | 46 | 12 | 6 | 5 | 41 | 33 | 5 | 4 | 14 | 20 | 47 | 61 | 80 | -19 | 61 |
| 13 | Charlton Athletic | 46 | 10 | 4 | 9 | 32 | 28 | 7 | 4 | 12 | 23 | 31 | 55 | 59 | -4 | 59 |
| 14 | Cambridge United | 46 | 8 | 8 | 7 | 28 | 29 | 7 | 5 | 11 | 28 | 45 | 56 | 74 | -18 | 58 |
| 15 | Cheltenham Town | 46 | 10 | 7 | 6 | 33 | 30 | 3 | 10 | 10 | 33 | 50 | 66 | 80 | -14 | 56 |
| 16 | Burton Albion | 46 | 10 | 6 | 7 | 34 | 26 | 4 | 5 | 14 | 17 | 41 | 51 | 67 | -16 | 53 |
| 17 | Lincoln City | 46 | 7 | 5 | 11 | 25 | 29 | 7 | 5 | 11 | 30 | 34 | 55 | 63 | -8 | 52 |
| 18 | Shrewsbury Town | 46 | 9 | 7 | 7 | 30 | 25 | 3 | 7 | 13 | 17 | 26 | 47 | 51 | -4 | 50 |
| 19 | Morecambe | 46 | 7 | 8 | 8 | 33 | 35 | 3 | 4 | 16 | 24 | 53 | 57 | 88 | -31 | 42 |
| 20 | Fleetwood Town | 46 | 5 | 8 | 10 | 33 | 37 | 3 | 8 | 12 | 29 | 45 | 62 | 82 | -20 | 40 |
| 21 | Gillingham | 46 | 4 | 8 | 11 | 13 | 36 | 4 | 8 | 11 | 22 | 33 | 35 | 69 | -34 | 40 |
| 22 | Doncaster Rovers | 46 | 7 | 3 | 13 | 20 | 32 | 3 | 5 | 15 | 17 | 50 | 37 | 82 | -45 | 38 |
| 23 | AFC Wimbledon | 46 | 2 | 14 | 7 | 27 | 34 | 4 | 5 | 14 | 22 | 41 | 49 | 75 | -26 | 37 |
| 24 | Crewe Alexandra | 46 | 5 | 5 | 13 | 22 | 40 | 2 | 3 | 18 | 15 | 43 | 37 | 83 | -46 | 29 |

## MATCH OF THE SEASON

### Sunderland 2-0 Wycombe Wanderers

**SATURDAY 21 MAY 2022**

**After four long years in League One this was a vitally important game for Sunderland. The three previous seasons had seen them lose in the Play-Off final in 2019, the semi-finals in 2021 and miss out altogether in the Covid curtailed points per game solution created in 2020. The prospect of yet another campaign in League One did not bear thinking about so this match was as important as any in recent decades. While there was an understanding that being the best team on the day might not necessarily translate into being the team who would win the game, due to Wycombe's ability to score from long throw-ins, corners and free-kicks, there was an inner belief that Sunderland would come out on top.**

Right from the kick-off Sunderland got on the front foot. Even before the opening goal in the 12th minute Alex Pritchard and Ross Stewart had gone close. The breakthrough came from local lad Elliot Embleton. He picked the ball up just inside his own half and drove directly through the heart of the Chairboys defence. Approaching the box Embleton leathered a shot that was just too hot to handle for goalkeeper David Stockdale. He had just won the 'Golden Gloves' award for the division and was criticised by some for not getting to the shot but Embleton's swerving effort was in the back of the net almost before he saw it.

Once in front, Sunderland continued to dominate. Sweeping the ball around the stadium they made Wycombe run and barely gave them a chance. When danger-man Sam Vokes did have an opening Anthony Patterson was off his line in a flash to smother the shot.

Eleven minutes from time Ross Stewart's 26th goal of the season doubled the lead and left Wycombe looking like a beaten team. Stewart was on the edge of the box when he was provided with possession by man of the match Pritchard. Soon to be capped by Scotland, Stewart got his head up, picked his spot and drilled home a low shot. In the closing minutes SAFC looked like adding a third as Patrick Roberts and Jack Clarke threatened but there was no need to ice the cake. Sunderland had secured promotion at last and as the final whistle went the chorus of 'Wise Men Say' from the 46,500 plus Sunderland supporters sent tingles down the spine.

## MAJOR SIGNINGS

| | | |
|---|---|---|
| **Ron-Thorben Hoffmann** | Bayern Munich | **on loan** |
| **Leon Dajaku** | Union Berlin | **initially on loan** |
| **Alex Pritchard** | Free agent | |
| **Corry Evans** | Blackburn Rovers | **Free** |
| **Dennis Cirkin** | Tottenham Hotspur | **Undisclosed** |
| **Nathan Broadhead** | Everton | **On loan** |
| **Callum Doyle** | Manchester City | **on loan** |
| **Patrick Roberts** | Manchester City | |
| **Jack Clarke** | Tottenham Hotspur | **on loan** |
| **Jermain Defoe** | Rangers | |
| **Danny Batth** | Stoke City | |

## DEBUTANTS FROM WITHIN

**Ellis Taylor, Jacob Carney (Ex-Manchester United), Tyrese Dyce (Ex-WBA), Will Harris (Ex-Burnley), Zak Johnson, Ethan Kachosa (Ex-Leeds United), Tom Scott (Ex-Northampton Town), Kenton Richardson (Ex-Hartlepool United), Harrison Sohna (Ex-Aston Villa), Stephen Wearne (Ex-Middlesbrough & Newcastle United).**

# 2021-22 SEASON

**GROUND:** Stadium of Light **SHIRT SPONSOR:** Great Annual Savings Group **HEAD COACHES:** Lee Johnson, Mike Dodds/Michael Proctor & Alex Neil

**SKY BET LEAGUE ONE: Champions:** Wigan Athletic, 92 pts **Sunderland:** 5th, 84 pts

| MATCH | DATE | ROUND | VENUE | OPPONENTS | RESULT | | HT | POSITION | SCORERS | ATT. |
|---|---|---|---|---|---|---|---|---|---|---|
| 1 | Aug 7 | | H | **Wigan Athletic** | W | 2-1 | 1-1 | | McGeady (pen), Stewart | 31,549 |
| 3 | 14 | | A | MK Dons | W | 2-1 | 1-0 | 3 | Stewart, Embleton | 9,830 |
| 4 | 17 | | A | Burton Albion | L | 0-1 | 0-0 | 8 | | 4,239 |
| 5 | 21 | | H | **AFC Wimbledon** | W | 1-0 | 0-0 | 5 | Winchester | 29,093 |
| 7 | 28 | | H | **Wycombe Wanderers** | W | 3-1 | 2-0 | 1 | Stewart (2), Embleton | 29,344 |
| 8 | Sep 11 | | H | **Accrington Stanley** | W | 2-1 | 1-1 | 1 | Neil, Winchester | 29,830 |
| 9 | 18 | | A | Fleetwood Town | D | 2-2 | 1-0 | 2 | Stewart, McGeady (pen) | 4,250 |
| 11 | 25 | | H | **Bolton Wanderers** | W | 1-0 | 1-0 | 2 | Winchester | 32,368 |
| 12 | 28 | | H | **Cheltenham Town** | W | 5-0 | 3-0 | 1 | Wright, Stewart (2), O'Nien, Dajaku | 28,313 |
| 13 | Oct 2 | | A | Portsmouth | L | 0-4 | 0-3 | 2 | | 17,418 |
| 16 | 16 | | A | Gillingham | W | 2-1 | 1-1 | 4 | O'Brien, Flanagan | 6,310 |
| 17 | 19 | | A | Crewe Alexandra | W | 4-0 | 2-0 | 2 | Thomas o.g., Stewart (2), Dajaku | 5,449 |
| 18 | 23 | | H | **Charlton Athletic** | L | 0-1 | 0-0 | 4 | | 31,833 |
| 20 | 30 | | A | Rotherham United | L | 1-5 | 1-2 | 5 | Stewart | 10,573 |
| 21 | Nov 2 | | A | Sheffield Wednesday | L | 0-3 | 0-2 | 5 | | 23,731 |
| 24 | 20 | | H | **Ipswich Town** | W | 2-0 | 0-0 | 6 | O'Nien, McGeady (pen) | 31,033 |
| 25 | 23 | | A | Shrewsbury Town | D | 1-1 | 1-0 | 6 | Pritchard | 6,253 |
| 26 | 27 | | A | Cambridge United | W | 2-1 | 2-1 | 5 | Mitov o.g., Broadhead | 7,974 |
| 28 | Dec 4 | | H | **Oxford United** | D | 1-1 | 1-1 | 5 | Dajaku | 26,634 |
| 29 | 7 | | H | **Morecambe** | W | 5-0 | 2-0 | 3 | Stewart, Broadhead (2), Pritchard, Dajaku | 26,516 |
| 30 | 11 | | H | **Plymouth Argyle** | W | 2-1 | 2-0 | 3 | Neil, Broadhead | 28,997 |
| 31 | 18 | | A | Ipswich Town | D | 1-1 | 0-1 | 3 | Broadhead | 29,005 |
| 33 | 27 | | A | Doncaster Rovers | W | 3-0 | 2-0 | 2 | Stewart (pen), Embleton, Blythe o.g. | 10,751 |
| 34 | 30 | | H | **Sheffield Wednesday** | W | 5-0 | 3-0 | 1 | Stewart (3), Doyle, Kimpioka | 34,562 |
| 35 | Jan 8 | | A | Wycombe Wanderers | D | 3-3 | 2-2 | 2 | Stockdale o.g., Stewart (2) | 7,229 |
| 36 | 11 | | H | **Lincoln City** | L | 1-3 | 0-1 | 2 | Stewart | 28,732 |
| 37 | 15 | | A | Accrington Stanley | D | 1-1 | 0-0 | 2 | O,Brien | 4,498 |
| 38 | 22 | | H | **Portsmouth** | W | 1-0 | 1-0 | 2 | Embleton | 32,220 |
| 39 | 29 | | A | Bolton Wanderers | L | 0-6 | 0-2 | 3 | | 20,059 |
| 40 | Feb 5 | | H | **Doncaster Rovers** | L | 1-2 | 0-2 | 4 | Evans | 38,395 |
| 41 | 8 | | A | Cheltenham Town | L | 1-2 | 1-0 | 4 | Pritchard | 5,744 |
| 42 | 12 | | A | AFC Wimbledon | D | 1-1 | 1-1 | 4 | Pritchard | 8,381 |
| 43 | 19 | | H | **MK Dons** | L | 1-2 | 0-0 | 7 | Stewart | 30,451 |
| 44 | 22 | | H | **Burton Albion** | D | 1-1 | 0-0 | 6 | Stewart | 30,237 |
| 45 | 26 | | A | Wigan Athletic | W | 3-0 | 2-0 | 5 | Wright, Stewart (2 pens) | 20,136 |
| 46 | Mar 5 | | A | Charlton Athletic | D | 0-0 | 0-0 | 7 | | 13,716 |
| 47 | 8 | | H | **Fleetwood Town** | W | 3-1 | 0-1 | 5 | Embleton, O'Nien, Clarke | 28,017 |
| 48 | 12 | | H | **Crewe Alexandra** | W | 2-0 | 0-0 | 5 | Neil, Roberts | 30,036 |
| 49 | 19 | | A | Lincoln City | D | 0-0 | 0-0 | 6 | | 10,346 |
| 50 | Apr 2 | | H | **Gillingham** | W | 1-0 | 0-0 | 6 | Broadhead | 31,619 |
| 51 | 9 | | A | Oxford United | W | 2-1 | 1-1 | 6 | Evans, Embleton | 11,690 |
| 52 | 15 | | H | **Shrewsbury Town** | W | 3-2 | 2-0 | 6 | Embleton, Broadhead (2) | 33,896 |
| 53 | 18 | | A | Plymouth Argyle | D | 0-0 | 0-0 | 6 | | 15,800 |
| 54 | 23 | | H | **Cambridge United** | W | 5-1 | 3-1 | 4 | Stewart (2, 1 pen), Embleton, Broadhead, Batth | 32,500 |
| 55 | 26 | | H | **Rotherham United** | D | 1-1 | 0-1 | 5 | Ihiekwe o.g. | 33,119 |
| 56 | 30 | | A | Morecambe | W | 1-0 | 1-0 | 5 | Broadhead | 5,831 |

| MATCH | Burge | Winchester | Neil | Evans | Flanagan | Doyle | Gooch | O'Nien | Stewart | Embleton | McGeady | O'Brien | Diamond | Wright | Cirkin | Pritchard | Broadhead | Patterson | Hoffmann | Alves | Dajaku | Huggins | Harris | Hume, D. | Mbunga-Kimpiok | Hawkes |
|---|---|---|---|---|---|---|---|---|---|---|---|---|---|---|---|---|---|---|---|---|---|---|---|---|---|---|
| | 1 | 15 | 24 | 4 | 3 | 6 | 11 | 13 | 14 | 8 | 28 | 10 | 23 | 26 | 17 | 21 | 9 | 20 | 39 | 5 | 7 | 2 | 37 | 33 | 48 | 27 |
| 1 | 1 | $2^{2}$ | 3 | 4 | 5 | 6 | 7 | 8 | 9 | $10^{3}$ | $11^{1}$ | $12^{1}$ | $13^{2}$ | $14^{3}$ | | U | | U | | | | | | | | U |
| 3 | 1 | 2 | 8 | $4^{1}$ | 5 | 6 | 7 | | 9 | 10 | $11^{2}$ | $13^{2}$ | U | $14^{3}$ | $3^{3}$ | $12^{1}$ | | U | | | | | | | | U |
| 4 | 1 | 2 | 8 | | 5 | 6 | 7 | 4 | 9 | $10^{2}$ | 11 | U | U | U | $3^{1}$ | $12^{1}$ | $13^{2}$ | U | | U | | | | | | |
| 5 | U | 2 | 3 | | 5 | 6 | 7 | 4 | 9 | $10^{3}$ | $11^{1}$ | U | | $14^{3}$ | $13^{2}$ | $8^{2}$ | $12^{1}$ | 1 | | U | | | | | | U |
| 7 | U | 2 | 8 | | 5 | 6 | 7 | 4 | 9 | $10^{2}$ | $11^{1}$ | $13^{2}$ | | $14^{3}$ | $3^{3}$ | $12^{1}$ | U | 1 | | U | | U | | | | |
| 8 | U | 2 | 8 | U | 5 | $6^{1}$ | 7 | 4 | 9 | $10^{2}$ | 11 | | | $13^{2}$ | 3 | $12^{1}$ | U | | 1 | U | | U | | | | |
| 9 | U | 2 | $8^{1}$ | $12^{1}$ | | 6 | 7 | 4 | 9 | $10^{2}$ | $11^{3}$ | | | 5 | 3 | U | $13^{2}$ | | 1 | $14^{3}$ | U | U | | | | |
| 11 | U | 2 | 8 | $13^{2}$ | 5 | $6^{4}$ | | 4 | 9 | $11^{2}$ | 7 | | | $15^{4}$ | $3^{3}$ | $10^{1}$ | U | | 1 | U | $12^{1}$ | $14^{3}$ | | | | |
| 12 | U | 2 | U | 8 | $5^{1}$ | | | 4 | $9^{3}$ | U | $11^{2}$ | 10 | | 6 | | $14^{3}$ | 7 | | 1 | $12^{1}$ | $13^{2}$ | 3 | | | | |
| 13 | U | 2 | $14^{3}$ | $8^{3}$ | 5 | $12^{1}$ | | 4 | 9 | $10^{1}$ | | 11 | | 6 | 3 | $13^{2}$ | | | 1 | U | $7^{2}$ | U | | | | |
| 16 | U | 2 | 8 | | 5 | 6 | | 4 | 9 | 7 | | $11^{2}$ | | $12^{1}$ | 3 | $10^{1}$ | | | 1 | | | | $13^{2}$ | U | | |
| 17 | U | 2 | 8 | | 5 | 6 | | 4 | 9 | | $11^{3}$ | 7 | | $14^{3}$ | $3^{2}$ | $10^{1}$ | | | 1 | | $12^{1}$ | | U | $13^{2}$ | | |
| 18 | U | 2 | $8^{3}$ | $14^{3}$ | 5 | 6 | $13^{2}$ | 4 | 9 | | 11 | $7^{2}$ | | U | 3 | $10^{1}$ | | | 1 | U | $12^{1}$ | | | U | | |
| 20 | U | 2 | 8 | $14^{3}$ | 5 | 6 | $12^{1}$ | $4^{2}$ | 9 | $10^{1}$ | 11 | U | | $13^{2}$ | 3 | | | | 1 | U | $7^{3}$ | | | | | |
| 21 | | 2 | $8^{1}$ | 10 | 5 | 6 | $7^{2}$ | 4 | 9 | $13^{2}$ | | $11^{3}$ | | U | 3 | $12^{1}$ | $14^{3}$ | | 1 | U | U | | | | | |
| 24 | | 2 | 8 | $4^{2}$ | U | 6 | 7 | 3 | 9 | $10^{1}$ | $12^{1}$ | U | | 5 | | $13^{2}$ | $11^{3}$ | U | 1 | U | $14^{3}$ | | | | | |
| 25 | | 4 | 8 | $12^{1}$ | U | 6 | $2^{2}$ | 3 | 9 | U | $14^{3}$ | $7^{1}$ | | 5 | | $10^{3}$ | 11 | U | 1 | U | $13^{2}$ | | | | | |
| 26 | | 8 | 10 | | 5 | 6 | 3 | | 9 | U | | U | | 4 | | $11^{1}$ | 7 | U | 1 | U | 2 | | $12^{1}$ | | | |
| 28 | | 8 | 10 | | 5 | 6 | 3 | | 9 | $12^{1}$ | | $13^{2}$ | | 4 | | $11^{2}$ | 7 | U | 1 | | $2^{1}$ | | | | U | |
| 29 | | $4^{1}$ | 8 | | 5 | 6 | 3 | | $9^{2}$ | $12^{1}$ | | $13^{2}$ | | 2 | | 10 | $11^{3}$ | U | 1 | U | 7 | | | | $14^{3}$ | |
| 30 | | 4 | 8 | | 5 | 6 | $3^{1}$ | | 9 | $12^{1}$ | | $13^{2}$ | | 2 | | $10^{2}$ | 11 | U | 1 | U | 7 | | | | U | |
| 31 | | 4 | 8 | | 5 | 6 | 3 | | 9 | $13^{2}$ | | $14^{3}$ | | 2 | | $10^{2}$ | $11^{3}$ | U | 1 | U | $7^{1}$ | | | $12^{1}$ | U | |
| 33 | U | | 8 | $4^{1}$ | 5 | 6 | 3 | | $9^{3}$ | 11 | | | | 2 | $12^{1}$ | $10^{2}$ | | | 1 | U | 7 | | $14^{3}$ | $13^{2}$ | U | |
| 34 | U | | $8^{2}$ | 4 | 5 | 6 | 3 | | 9 | 11 | | | | 2 | $12^{1}$ | $10^{1}$ | | | 1 | $14^{3}$ | $7^{3}$ | | U | U | $13^{2}$ | |
| 35 | | 2 | 8 | $4^{1}$ | 5 | 6 | 7 | | 9 | 11 | | | $12^{1}$ | | 3 | 10 | | 1 | | | | | | U | | U |
| 36 | | 4 | 8 | | 5 | 6 | 2 | | 9 | 11 | | $12^{1}$ | $7^{1}$ | | $3^{2}$ | $10^{3}$ | | 1 | | | | | | $13^{2}$ | | $14^{3}$ |
| 37 | | | 8 | | 5 | 6 | 11 | | 9 | 4 | | $12^{1}$ | U | 2 | 3 | $10^{1}$ | | U | 1 | | 7 | | | U | | U |
| 38 | | $12^{1}$ | 10 | 8 | 4 | 6 | 2 | | 9 | $11^{1}$ | | $13^{2}$ | U | | 3 | | | U | 1 | | $7^{2}$ | | | | U | |
| 39 | | 2 | $8^{2}$ | 4 | U | 6 | 11 | | 9 | 10 | | U | | | $3^{1}$ | $12^{1}$ | | U | 1 | | $7^{3}$ | | | | | |
| 40 | | $2^{1}$ | $8^{3}$ | 4 | | 6 | 7 | | 9 | $11^{2}$ | | | | | 3 | 10 | | U | 1 | | U | | | | | |
| 41 | | U | U | $4^{3}$ | | 6 | | | 9 | $14^{3}$ | | | | | 3 | 10 | | 1 | | | $7^{1}$ | | | | | |
| 42 | | $7^{1}$ | 8 | $12^{1}$ | | 6 | | | 9 | U | | | | 5 | 3 | 10 | | 1 | | | U | | | | | |
| 43 | | 2 | $10^{2}$ | $4^{3}$ | | 6 | | | 9 | $12^{1}$ | | | | 5 | 3 | 11 | | 1 | U | | $7^{1}$ | | | | | |
| 44 | | 2 | $14^{3}$ | $4^{1}$ | | 6 | $7^{3}$ | | 9 | $12^{1}$ | | | | 5 | 3 | 11 | | 1 | U | | U | | | | | |
| 45 | | 2 | $13^{2}$ | 4 | | | 7 | | 9 | $10^{1}$ | | | | 5 | 3 | $11^{2}$ | | 1 | U | | U | | | | | |
| 46 | | 4 | U | 8 | | U | $2^{3}$ | | 9 | $13^{2}$ | | | | 5 | 3 | $11^{2}$ | $7^{1}$ | 1 | U | | | | | | | |
| 47 | | 2 | U | $4^{2}$ | | U | $13^{2}$ | $14^{3}$ | 9 | 10 | | | | $5^{1}$ | 3 | | | 1 | U | | | | | | | |
| 48 | | 4 | $12^{1}$ | 8 | | U | $2^{2}$ | $7^{1}$ | 9 | U | | | | 5 | 6 | | | 1 | U | | $13^{2}$ | | | | | |
| 49 | | 4 | $11^{2}$ | 8 | | $14^{3}$ | $2^{3}$ | 7 | 9 | U | | | | 5 | 6 | | | 1 | U | | $12^{1}$ | | | | | |
| 50 | | $2^{1}$ | U | 4 | | | $12^{1}$ | $8^{2}$ | 9 | $13^{2}$ | | | | 5 | 3 | $10^{3}$ | $14^{3}$ | 1 | U | | | | | | | |
| 51 | | 4 | U | 8 | | U | 2 | $12^{1}$ | 9 | $14^{3}$ | | | | 5 | 6 | | $11^{2}$ | 1 | U | | | | | | | |
| 52 | U | 4 | $14^{3}$ | $12^{1}$ | | | $2^{2}$ | 11 | 9 | $8^{1}$ | | | | 5 | 6 | | 10 | 1 | | | | | | | | |
| 53 | U | 4 | $14^{3}$ | 8 | | | $12^{1}$ | $3^{1}$ | 9 | $11^{2}$ | | | | 5 | 6 | | 10 | 1 | | | | | | | | |
| 54 | | $4^{1}$ | $14^{3}$ | $8^{3}$ | | $12^{1}$ | 2 | 3 | 9 | 11 | | | | 5 | | $13^{2}$ | $10^{2}$ | 1 | U | | | | | | | |
| 55 | | | U | 8 | | 6 | 2 | 11 | 9 | $14^{3}$ | | | | 4 | | $12^{1}$ | $10^{1}$ | 1 | U | | | | | | | |
| 56 | | | $14^{3}$ | 7 | | | 2 | 6 | $9^{2}$ | 11 | U | | | 4 | | $8^{3}$ | $10^{1}$ | 1 | U | | | | | | | |
| Appearances | 3 | 39 | 31 | 26 | 25 | 33 | 33 | 24 | 46 | 26 | 12 | 7 | 1 | 28 | 31 | 25 | 15 | 20 | 23 | | 14 | 1 | | | | |
| Sub Appearances | | 1 | 8 | 7 | | 3 | 5 | 2 | | 12 | 2 | 10 | 2 | 9 | 3 | 11 | 5 | | | 3 | 8 | 1 | 3 | 4 | 2 | 1 |
| Goals | | 3 | 3 | 2 | 1 | 1 | | 3 | 24 | 8 | 3 | 2 | | 2 | | 4 | 10 | | | | 4 | | | | 1 | |

| MATCH | Batth | Clarke | Roberts | Defoe | Matete | Hume, T. | Xhemajli | Younger | Taylor | Grigg | Richardson | Sohna | Wearne | Carney | Almond | Scott | Dyce | Kachosa | Kelly | Johnson | Dunne | Wilding | Bond | Newall | Jessup | McIntyre | Middlemas | Ryder |
|---|---|---|---|---|---|---|---|---|---|---|---|---|---|---|---|---|---|---|---|---|---|---|---|---|---|---|---|---|
| | 5 | 25 | 77 | 10 | 27 | 32 | 19 | 21 | 18 | 22 | 41 | 43 | 45 | 31 | 30 | 51 | 34 | 42 | 60 | 58 | 36 | 46 | 35 | 40 | 38 | 47 | 53 | 52 |
| 1 | | | | | | | | | | U | | | | | | | | | | | | | | | | | | |
| 3 | | | | | | | | | U | | | | | | | | | | | | | | | | | | | |
| 12 | | | | | | | | | U | | | | | | | | | | | | | | | | | | | |
| 13 | | | | | | | | | U | | | | | | | | | | | | | | | | | | | |
| 16 | | | | | | | | U | | | | U | U | | | | | | | | | | | | | | | |
| 17 | | | | | | | | U | | | | | U | | | | | | | | | | | | | | | |
| 20 | | | | | | | | | | | | | U | | | | | | | | | | | | | | | |
| 28 | | | | | | | | U | | | | | | | | | U | | | U | | | | | | | | |
| 29 | | | | | | | | U | | | | | | | | | | | | | U | | | | | | | |
| 30 | | | | | | | | U | | | | | | | | | | | | | U | | | | | | | |
| 31 | | | | | | | | U | | | | | | | | | | | | | | | | | | | | |
| 33 | | | | | | | | U | | | | | | | | | | | | | | | | | | | | |
| 34 | | | | | | | | U | | | | | | | | | | | | | | | | | | | | |
| 35 | | | | | | | U | U | U | | | | | U | | | | | | | | | | | | | | |
| 36 | | | | | | | U | U | U | | | | | U | | | | | | | | | | | | | | |
| 37 | | | | | | U | U | | | | | | | | | | | | | | | | | | | | | |
| 38 | 5 | | | | | U | U | | | | | | | | | | | | | | | | | | | | | |
| 39 | 5 | $13^{2}$ | $14^{3}$ | | | U | | | | | | | | | | | | | | | | | | | | | | |
| 40 | 5 | $12^{1}$ | U | $13^{2}$ | $14^{3}$ | U | | | | | | | | | | | | | | | | | | | | | | |
| 41 | 5 | $11^{2}$ | $12^{1}$ | $13^{2}$ | 8 | $2^{D}$ | U | | | | | | | U | | | | | | | | | | | | | | |
| 42 | | $11^{2}$ | $14^{3}$ | $13^{2}$ | 4 | 2 | U | | | | | | | U | | | | | | | | | | | | | | |
| 43 | | $13^{2}$ | $14^{3}$ | U | 8 | U | U | | | | | | | | | | | | | | | | | | | | | |
| 44 | U | $13^{2}$ | U | $10^{2}$ | 8 | | | | | | | | | | | | | | | | | | | | | | | |
| 45 | | $12^{1}$ | U | U | 8 | U | 6 | | | | | | | | | | | | | | | | | | | | | |
| 46 | | $12^{1}$ | $14^{3}$ | | 10 | U | 6 | | | | | | | | | | | | | | | | | | | | | |
| 47 | | 11 | $7^{3}$ | $12^{1}$ | 8 | U | $6^{L}$ | | | | | | | | | | | | | | | | | | | | | |
| 48 | | 3 | $14^{3}$ | $10^{3}$ | 11 | U | | | | | | | | | | | | | | | | | | | | | | |
| 49 | | $3^{1}$ | 10 | $13^{2}$ | U | U | | | | | | | | | | | | | | | | | | | | | | |
| 50 | 6 | 11 | 7 | | U | | U | | | | | | | | | | | | | | | | | | | | | |
| 51 | $13^{2}$ | $3^{3}$ | $7^{1}$ | | 10 | U | | | | | | | | | | | | | | | | | | | | | | |
| 52 | U | 3 | $13^{2}$ | | $7^{3}$ | U | U | | | | | | | | | | | | | | | | | | | | | |
| 53 | U | 2 | $13^{2}$ | | $7^{3}$ | U | U | | | | | | | | | | | | | | | | | | | | | |
| 54 | 6 | U | 7 | | U | U | | | | | | | | | | | | | | | | | | | | | | |
| 55 | 5 | $13^{2}$ | U | | $7^{3}$ | $3^{2}$ | U | | | | | | | | | | | | | | | | | | | | | |
| 56 | 5 | $12^{1}$ | 3 | | $13^{2}$ | U | U | | | | | | | | | | | | | | | | | | | | | |
| Appearances | 8 | 9 | 6 | 2 | 12 | 3 | 3 | | | | | | | | | | | | | | | | | | | | | |
| Sub Appearances | 1 | 8 | 8 | 5 | 2 | | | | | | | | | | | | | | | | | | | | | | | |
| Goals | 1 | 1 | 1 | | | | | | | | | | | | | | | | | | | | | | | | | |

## PLAY-OFFS — WINNERS: SUNDERLAND

| MATCH | DATE | ROUND | VENUE | OPPONENTS | RESULT | | HT | SCORERS | ATT. |
|---|---|---|---|---|---|---|---|---|---|
| 57 | May 6 | SF1 | H | **Sheffield Wednesday** | W | 1-0 | 1-0 | Stewart | 44,742 |
| 58 | 9 | SF2 | A | Sheffield Wednesday | D | 1-1 | 0-0 | Roberts | 32,978 |
| 59 | 21 | Final | Wembley | Wycombe Wanderers | W | 2-0 | 1-0 | Embleton, Stewart | 72,332 |

| MATCH | Burge | Winchester | Neil | Evans | Flanagan | Doyle | Gooch | O'Nien | Stewart | Embleton | McGeady | O'Brien | Diamond | Wright | Cirkin | Pritchard | Broadhead | Patterson | Hoffmann | Alves | Dajaku | Huggins | Harris | Hume, D. | Mbunga-Kimpiok | Hawkes |
|---|---|---|---|---|---|---|---|---|---|---|---|---|---|---|---|---|---|---|---|---|---|---|---|---|---|---|
| 57 | | | U | 8 | | $14^{3}$ | 2 | 11 | 9 | $13^{2}$ | U | | | 4 | 6 | $10^{1}$ | | 1 | U | | | | | | | |
| 58 | | | U | 4 | | $14^{3}$ | 2 | 8 | 9 | U | | | | 5 | 3 | $10^{1}$ | $13^{2}$ | 1 | U | | | | | | | |
| 59 | | | U | 4 | | $13^{2}$ | 2 | 8 | $9^{3}$ | $11^{1}$ | U | | | 5 | 3 | $10^{2}$ | $14^{3}$ | 1 | U | | | | | | | |
| Appearances | | | | 3 | | | 3 | 3 | 3 | 1 | | | | 3 | 3 | 3 | | 3 | | | | | | | | |
| Sub Appearances | | | | | | 3 | | | | 1 | | | | | | | 2 | | | | | | | | | |
| Goals | | | | | | | | | 2 | 1 | | | | | | | | | | | | | | | | |

| MATCH | Batth | Clarke | Roberts | Defoe | Matete | Hume, T. | Xhemajli | Younger | Taylor | Grigg | Richardson | Sohna | Wearne | Carney | Almond | Scott | Dyce | Kachosa | Kelly | Johnson | Dunne | Wilding | Bond | Newall | Jessup | McIntyre | Middlemas | Ryder |
|---|---|---|---|---|---|---|---|---|---|---|---|---|---|---|---|---|---|---|---|---|---|---|---|---|---|---|---|---|
| 57 | 5 | $3^{3}$ | $7^{2}$ | | $12^{1}$ | U | | | | | | | | | | | | | | | | | | | | | | |
| 58 | 6 | $11^{1}$ | $7^{2}$ | | $12^{1}$ | U | | | | | | | | | | | | | | | | | | | | | | |
| 59 | 6 | $12^{1}$ | 7 | | U | | | | | | | | | | | | | | | | | | | | | | | |
| Appearances | 3 | 2 | 3 | | | | | | | | | | | | | | | | | | | | | | | | | |
| Sub Appearances | | 1 | | | 2 | | | | | | | | | | | | | | | | | | | | | | | |
| Goals | | | 1 | | | | | | | | | | | | | | | | | | | | | | | | | |

## EMIRATES FA CUP — WINNERS: LIVERPOOL

| MATCH | DATE | ROUND | VENUE | OPPONENTS | RESULT | | HT | SCORERS | ATT. |
|---|---|---|---|---|---|---|---|---|---|
| 22 | Nov 6 | R1 | H | **Mansfield Town** | L | 0-1 | 0-1 | | 8,620 |

| MATCH | Burge | Winchester | Neil | Evans | Flanagan | Doyle | Gooch | O'Nien | Stewart | Embleton | McGeady | O'Brien | Diamond | Wright | Cirkin | Pritchard | Broadhead | Patterson | Hoffmann | Alves | Dajaku | Huggins | Harris | Hume, D. | Mbunga-Kimpiok | Hawkes |
|---|---|---|---|---|---|---|---|---|---|---|---|---|---|---|---|---|---|---|---|---|---|---|---|---|---|---|
| 22 | 1 | $15^{4}$ | 8 | 4 | $5^{1}$ | $12^{1}$ | $13^{2}$ | $16^{5}$ | | 10 | | $11^{2}$ | | 6 | $3^{5}$ | $14^{3}$ | 9 | | U | $2^{4}$ | $7^{3}$ | | U | | | |
| Appearances | 1 | | 1 | 1 | 1 | | | | | 1 | | 1 | | 1 | 1 | | 1 | | | 1 | 1 | | | | | |
| Sub Appearances | | 1 | | | | 1 | 1 | 1 | | | | | | | | 1 | | | | | | | | | | |
| Goals | | | | | | | | | | | | | | | | | | | | | | | | | | |

| MATCH | Batth | Clarke | Roberts | Defoe | Matete | Hume, T. | Xhemajli | Younger | Taylor | Grigg | Richardson | Sohna | Wearne | Carney | Almond | Scott | Dyce | Kachosa | Kelly | Johnson | Dunne | Wilding | Bond | Newall | Jessup | McIntyre | Middlemas | Ryder |
|---|---|---|---|---|---|---|---|---|---|---|---|---|---|---|---|---|---|---|---|---|---|---|---|---|---|---|---|---|
| 22 | | | | | | | | U | U | | | | | | | | | | | | | | | | | | | |

## CARABAO (LEAGUE) CUP — WINNERS: LIVERPOOL

| MATCH | DATE | ROUND | VENUE | OPPONENTS | RESULT | | HT | | SCORERS | ATT. |
|---|---|---|---|---|---|---|---|---|---|---|
| 2 | Aug 10 | R1 | A | Port Vale | W | 2-1 | 1-0 | | Hawkes, O'Brien (pen) | 3,267 |
| 6 | 24 | R2 | A | Blackpool | W | 3-2 | 1-1 | | O'Brien (3) | 5,756 |
| 10 | Sep 21 | R3 | H | Wigan Athletic | W | 2-0 | 1-0 | | Broadhead, O'Nien | 6,511 |
| 19 | Oct 26 | R4 | A | Queens Park Rangers | W | 0-0 | 0-0 | 3-1 on pens | | 15,372 |
| 32 | Dec 21 | R5 | A | Arsenal | L | 1-5 | 1-2 | | Broadhead | 59,027 |

| MATCH | Burge | Winchester | Neil | Evans | Flanagan | Doyle | Gooch | O'Nien | Stewart | Embleton | McGeady | O'Brien | Diamond | Wright | Cirkin | Pritchard | Broadhead | Patterson | Hoffmann | Alves | Dajaku | Huggins | Harris | Hume, D. | Mbunga-Kimpiok | Hawkes |
|---|---|---|---|---|---|---|---|---|---|---|---|---|---|---|---|---|---|---|---|---|---|---|---|---|---|---|
| 2 | U | | 4 | U | 5 | $14^{3}$ | U | 8 | U | | $12^{1}$ | 9 | $7^{1}$ | 6 | | $10^{2}$ | | 1 | | | | | | | | 11 |
| 6 | | 4 | 8 | | | $14^{3}$ | U | | $13^{2}$ | $12^{1}$ | | 11 | 7 | 6 | 3 | $10^{1}$ | $9^{2}$ | 1 | | $5^{3}$ | | 2 | | | | U |
| 10 | 1 | | $14^{3}$ | 8 | U | U | | 4 | $12^{1}$ | $13^{2}$ | | 11 | | 6 | 3 | $10^{2}$ | 9 | | U | 5 | $7^{1}$ | $2^{3}$ | | | | |
| 19 | 1 | 2 | 10 | $8^{3}$ | U | $16^{5}$ | $11^{2}$ | 4 | 9 | | $13^{2}$ | $14^{3}$ | | 6 | $12^{1}$ | $15^{4}$ | | | U | $5^{5}$ | $7^{4}$ | | U | $3^{1}$ | | |
| 32 | 1 | 2 | 8 | $13^{2}$ | 5 | 6 | $3^{2}$ | | $9^{4}$ | $7^{3}$ | | $14^{3}$ | | 4 | U | 10 | $11^{1}$ | U | | | | | | $12^{1}$ | $15^{4}$ | |
| Appearances | 3 | 3 | 4 | 2 | 2 | 1 | 2 | 3 | 2 | 1 | | 3 | 2 | 5 | 2 | 4 | 3 | 2 | | 3 | 2 | 2 | | 1 | | 1 |
| Sub Appearances | | | 1 | 1 | | 3 | | | 2 | 2 | 2 | 2 | | | 1 | 1 | | | | | | | | 1 | 1 | |
| Goals | | | | | | | | 1 | | | | 4 | | | | | 2 | | | | | | | | | 1 |

| MATCH | Batth | Clarke | Roberts | Defoe | Matete | Hume, T. | Xhemajli | Younger | Taylor | Grigg | Richardson | Sohna | Wearne | Carney | Almond | Scott | Dyce | Kachosa | Kelly | Johnson | Dunne | Wilding | Bond | Newall | Jessup | McIntyre | Middlemas | Ryder |
|---|---|---|---|---|---|---|---|---|---|---|---|---|---|---|---|---|---|---|---|---|---|---|---|---|---|---|---|---|
| 2 | | | | | | | | 2 | $3^{3}$ | $13^{2}$ | | | | | | | | | | | | | | | | | | |
| 6 | | | | | | | | | U | | | | | | | | | | | | | | U | | | | | |
| 10 | | | | | | | | | U | | | | | | | | | | | | | | | | | | | |
| 19 | | | | | | | | | | | | | U | | | | | | | | | | | | | | | |
| 32 | | | | | | | U | U | | | | | | | | | | | | | U | | | | | | | |

## PAPA JOHN'S EFL TROPHY — WINNERS: ROTHERHAM UNITED

| MATCH | DATE | ROUND | VENUE | OPPONENTS | RESULT | | HT | | SCORERS | ATT. |
|---|---|---|---|---|---|---|---|---|---|---|
| 14 | Oct 5 | Group | A | Lincoln City | W | 2-1 | 1-0 | | Neil, Wearne | 3,060 |
| 15 | 13 | Group | H | **Manchester Utd U-21** | W | 2-1 | 0-0 | | Dyce, Wearne | 3,960 |
| 23 | Nov 9 | Group | H | **Bradford City** | L | 1-1 | 0-1 | 2-4 on pens | Broadhead | 3,966 |
| 27 | Dec 1 | R2 | H | **Oldham Athletic** | L | 0-1 | 0-0 | | | 3,498 |

| MATCH | Burge | Winchester | Neil | Evans | Flanagan | Doyle | Gooch | O'Nien | Stewart | Embleton | McGeady | O'Brien | Diamond | Wright | Cirkin | Pritchard | Broadhead | Patterson | Hoffmann | Alves | Dajaku | Huggins | Harris | Hume, D. | Mbunga-Kimpiok | Hawkes |
|---|---|---|---|---|---|---|---|---|---|---|---|---|---|---|---|---|---|---|---|---|---|---|---|---|---|---|
| 14 | 1 | | 8 | | | | | $13^{2}$ | | $14^{3}$ | | $11^{2}$ | | | | 10 | | | | 5 | | | 9 | 3 | | |
| 15 | | | | | | | | | | | | | | | | | | | | | | | 9 | $3^{1}$ | | |
| 23 | U | $13^{2}$ | | | | | 3 | 4 | | $11^{3}$ | | U | | U | | 10 | $9^{1}$ | | 1 | 5 | 7 | | $12^{1}$ | | | |
| 27 | 1 | | | | | | | | | $8^{1}$ | | 7 | | | | | | | | 4 | $2^{2}$ | | 10 | | 9 | |
| Appearances | 2 | | 1 | | | | 1 | 1 | | 2 | | 2 | | | | 2 | 1 | | 1 | 3 | 2 | | 3 | 2 | 1 | |
| Sub Appearances | | 1 | | | | | | 1 | | 1 | | | | | | | | | | | | | 1 | | | |
| Goals | | | 1 | | | | | | | | | | | | | | 1 | | | | | | | | | |

| MATCH | Batth | Clarke | Roberts | Defoe | Matete | Hume, T. | Xhemajli | Younger | Taylor | Grigg | Richardson | Sohna | Wearne | Carney | Almond | Scott | Dyce | Kachosa | Kelly | Johnson | Dunne | Wilding | Bond | Newall | Jessup | McIntyre | Middlemas | Ryder |
|---|---|---|---|---|---|---|---|---|---|---|---|---|---|---|---|---|---|---|---|---|---|---|---|---|---|---|---|---|
| 14 | | | | | | | | 6 | $7^{1}$ | | 2 | 4 | $12^{2}$ | U | U | | | U | | | | | | U | | | | |
| 15 | | | | | | | | 6 | $7^{2}$ | | 2 | 4 | $10^{3}$ | 1 | 5 | 8 | 11 | $12^{1}$ | $13^{2}$ | $14^{3}$ | | | | | U | U | U | U |
| 23 | | | | | | | | 6 | $14^{3}$ | | 2 | $8^{2}$ | | | | | U | | | | | | | | | | | |
| 27 | | | | | | | 5 | 6 | | | | | $12^{1}$ | U | U | U | $14^{3}$ | $13^{2}$ | | U | $3^{3}$ | 11 | | | | | | |
| Appearances | | | | | | | 1 | 4 | 2 | | 3 | 3 | 1 | 1 | 1 | 1 | 1 | | | | 1 | 1 | | | | | | |
| Sub Appearances | | | | | | | | | 1 | | | | 2 | | | | 1 | 2 | 1 | 1 | | | | | | | | |
| Goals | | | | | | | | | | | | | 2 | | | | 1 | | | | | | | | | | | |

**MATCH 1:** Evans and Doyle debuts. **MATCH 2:** Pritchard & Taylor debut & Grigg last game. **MATCH 3:** Cirkin debut. **MATCH 4:** Broadhead debut. **MATCH 6:** Alves and Huggins debuts. **MATCH 8:** Hoffmann debut. **MATCH 10:** Dajaku debut. **MATCH 11:** Sunderland allowed a 4th substitute as Cirkin had sustained a concussion injury. **MATCH 14:** Harris, Richardson, Sohna and Wearne debuts: Substitute O'Nien was substituted by Embleton. **MATCH 15:** Carney, Dyce, Scott, Kachosa, Kelly and Johnson debuts & Almond only game. **MATCH 23:** Richardson last game. **MATCH 25:** McGeady last game. **MATCH 26:** Only 6 substitutes named. **MATCH 27:** Dunne, Wilding, Younger, Wearne & Dyce last games. **MATCH 32:** Burge last game. **MATCH 33:** Harris last game. **MATCH 34:** Alves & Mbunga-Kimpioka last games. **MATCH 36:** Hawkes and D.Hume last games. **MATCH 38:** Batth debut & Flanagan & O'Brien last games. **MATCH 39:** Clarke & Roberts debuts & Lee Johnson last game as head coach. **MATCH 40:** Matete debut, Hoffmann last game & Mike Dodds / Michael Proctor first game as joint caretaker managers. **MATCH 41:** T.Hume debut & Mike Dodds / Michael Proctor last game as joint caretaker managers. **MATCH 42:** Alex Neil first game as head coach. **MATCH 47:** Xhemajli last game. **MATCH 49:** Defoe last game. **MATCH 59:** Broadhead & Doyle last games. **DID YOU KNOW THAT?** The 46,500 Sunderland supporters at the Play-Off final was more than any club have ever had at Wembley for any final between two English clubs.

# Absolute Record

THANK YOU TO THESE PEOPLE FOR PRE-ORDERING THE ABSOLUTE RECORD: THE PLAYERS

# Roll of Honour

Steve Airey
George Alderman
Harvey Amos
Tony Anderson
Darren Anderson
John C Anderson
Mark Norman Anderson
Stephen Armstrong
John P Ashbridge
David Atkin
Jack Barter
Ed Bartley
Colin Batey
Bob Beaney
Malcolm Beattie
Sharon Bell
Charles Thomas Bell
Cory Bellamy-Hibbert
Kevin Binney
Gavin Henry Bissett
Clive Bowman
Chris Boyle
George Bramfitt
Antony Briggs
Malcolm Briggs
Thomas Briggs
James Percy Brown
Paul Philip Brown

Fred Browne
Steve Burns
Richard William Butchart
Ian Charles Butchart
Nicholas James Butchart
Martin Cadwallader
Neil Cain
James Calderwood
Chris Callaghan
Carl Camilleri
Dennis Campbell
Phillip Adam Carr
Stephen Cartwright
Matthew James Casson
Colin Chapman
Jack Clark
Stephanie Clark
John Colbert
Mark Cole
Tony Collingwood
Sean Collins
Gary John Collinson
David Cook
Tony Cook
Kay Cook
Chris Cooper
Jack Cousin
Matthew Craggs

Robert Crosby
Elijah Crow
Niall Cusack
Brian Cuthbertson
Garry Cuthbertson
Raymond Cuthbertson
Nick Dagnall
Trevor Danby
Bob Darbyshire
John Davin
Kent Davinson
Chris Davis
Tom Davis
Michael Davison OBE
Mick Davison
Peter Davison
Ron Davison
Harry Days
Arthur Dinsdale
Bob Dixon
Elliot Dixon
Barry Dixon
Mick Dobson
John Douglas
Robert Douglas
Tim Dumble
Russell Dunbar
Gary Dunmore

Dave Dury

Ray Edwards

Les Faith

James Farrell

Martin Finlayson

Jay Foley

Ian Frank

Ken Gambles

Alan R Gibson

Bryan Gilliland

Charlie Michael Gilmore

Keith Goodwin

John Graham

Jude Graney

Bill Greaves

Kieron Green

Christopher Groves

David Hafferty

Norman Haggerston

Martin David Halcrow

Michael Hall

Ian Hall

Barry Hall

Benjamin Hardie

Rob Harding

David Harper 1947-1997

Ian Harrison

Dennis Heath

Neal Hendrie

Bill Hern

Jordan Herrington

Richard Hindmarch

John S Hodgson

Steven Holliday

Bob Hudson

John Hudson

Dave Hudson

Ian Humble

Jason R Huntley

Olga Huntley

Harry Hutchinson

William Hymers

Alan Irwin

Jeff Jameson

David Jensen

Trevor Johnson

Dominic Peter Johnson

Lewis & Paul Jones

Phil Keenlyside

Callum Keithley

Mark Kelly

Chris Kent

Leslie John Kidd

Paul Kingston

Jack R H Knight

Phillip Lamb

John Lane

Jonathan Laverick

Karel Lawson

Ken Lawson

David Lea

Steve Leach

William Andrew Leadbeater

Gary Lee

Malcolm Lindsey

Mike Love

Gavin Luke

Tom Lynn

Jim Macken

Robert Ernest Major

Kevin Mallam

The Marjoram Family

John Marshall

Terry Martin

Sebastian Masciandaro

Adam McCabe

George McCarthy

Adam Raymond McIlwraith

Caitlin Marie McIlwraith

Andrew McIntosh

Graeme McIntosh

James William McMurrough

E J Minto

Gary Moad

Roy Molloy

Barry Moon

Paul Morrison

Mike Muldoon

Andi Musk

Alex Mustard

Stephen Nary

Jake Dylan Newton

Richard Nichols

Clive Nichols

Michael O'Donnell

David Oliver

Ben Parker

Mal Patterson

Stuart Charlton Paul

Jerry Pearson
Derek Pemberton
John Pilkington
John Pilley
Dave Pockley
Tony Pottinger
Ian Powell
Jim Poxton
David Priestley
Stuart Puckrin
Fred Adam Quarmby
Lee Quinn
David Ratcliffe
Colin Reed
Stephen Campbell Renton
Kevin Richardson
Gary Riley
Margaret Rimonti
Shaun Roberts
Kirby Robinson
Phill Rodgers
Dennis Robert Rodgers
Eric Rogers
Brian Rose
Lakkara Grace Rotherham
Joseph Rowntree
Richard Rush
Tom Ruxton
Ronnie Scott
Robert Scott
Geoff Screeton
Stan Sharp
William Sherriff

John Sherriff
Jack Shimwell
Albert Short
Keith Shotton
Gary Robert Shovlin
Ralph Sidney
Geoffrey Anthony Simpson
George Simpson
Henry Smith
David Stanley Smith
David Soulsby
Richard Sowerby
Glenn Steel
Trevor Stephenson
J Mark Stephenson
Gary Stephenson
Liam Stevenson
Robin James Stewart
Ian Stewart
Bill Stobbs
James Max Alex Ellie Stokoe
George Storey
Neil Pearson Storey
Eddie Swinburn
David Tate
Craig Russell Taylor
Paul K Taylor
Alan Taylor
Stephen L Taylor
Raymond Taylor
Michael Teal
Michael John Thompson
Howard Thompson

Keith Thompson
Michael Thompson
Neil Phillip Thornton
Brian Thurlbeck
Sam Thurlbeck
James Edwin Turnbull
Peter Tyrrell
Jonathan Unsworth
Steven James Walker
Lee Walker
Martin Wanless
Anthony John Ward
Neil Wayman
Ian Webb
Patricia Wells
Philip West
Alan Westray
Mark Jonathan Wharrier
Jonny White
Sophia Grace White
Alan Wigham
Paul Wilkinson
Raymond Williamson
Katie Williamson
Paul Williamson
Tony Williamson
Dr Stephen Wilson
Paul Woodman
Michael Woodman
Jonathan Mitchell Wright
Keith Wright
Jeff Yellowley
Karen Young